FOUNDATIONS OF
ARTIFICIAL INTELLIGENCE

Foundations of Artificial Intelligence

Series Editors

J. Hendler
H. Kitano
B. Nebel

Cover picture by Helmut Simonis

ELSEVIER
AMSTERDAM–BOSTON–HEIDELBERG–LONDON–NEW YORK–OXFORD
PARIS–SAN DIEGO–SAN FRANCISCO–SINGAPORE–SYDNEY–TOKYO

Handbook of Constraint Programming

Edited by

Francesca Rossi
University of Padova
Italy

Peter van Beek
University of Waterloo
Canada

Toby Walsh
National ICTA Australia &
University of New South Wales
Australia

ELSEVIER
AMSTERDAM–BOSTON–HEIDELBERG–LONDON–NEW YORK–OXFORD
PARIS–SAN DIEGO–SAN FRANCISCO–SINGAPORE–SYDNEY–TOKYO

Elsevier
Radarweg 29, PO Box 211, 1000 AE Amsterdam, The Netherlands
The Boulevard, Langford Lane, Kidlington, Oxford OX5 1GB, UK

First edition 2006

Library of Congress Cataloging-in-Publication Data
A catalog record for this book is available from the Library of Congress

British Library Cataloguing in Publication Data
A catalogue record for this book is available from the British Library

ISBN-13: 978-0-444-52726-4
ISBN-10: 0-444-52726-5
ISSN: 1574-6525

For information on all Elsevier publications
visit our website at books.elsevier.com

Transferred to Digital Print 2007
Printed and bound by CPI Antony Rowe, Eastbourne

06 07 08 09 10   10 9 8 7 6 5 4 3 2 1

Foreword

Constraints are an ubiquitous concept, which in its broader sense pertains to every day experience: they represent the conditions which restrict our freedom of decision. In fact, how much our choices are constrained by the external world is a basic philosophical question. In the formalized reasoning of scientific disciplines, constraints have been employed extensively, from logic to numerical analysis, from mathematical programming to operations research. In computer science, constraints have been with us from the early days, for modeling, representing and reasoning (see the interesting historical remarks in Chapter 2 of this handbook, Constraint Satisfaction: An Emerging Paradigm).

I see several good reasons for this ubiquity: one is the conceptually clear separation between the perfectly declarative problem statements and the often cumbersome enumerative efforts for finding solutions. Another reason is the complexity challenge: the classical constraint satisfaction problem is NP-complete and in fact tautology checking in propositional calculus (a constraint problem on Boolean variables) has been the touchstone for this complexity class. A further reason is that large, complex constraint problems often occur in practice, they must be solved in one way or another, and fast, efficient, systematic solutions have an enormous economic value.

What I find surprising about constraints is that within artificial intelligence and computer science a relatively recent, relatively uniform body of knowledge has emerged which often yields decisive advantages over classical, extensively studied and well developed techniques. As for many success stories within computer science, success is largely due to a mixture of structures, algorithms, languages, programming techniques and system implementations. The aim of this handbook is to present this knowledge in all its facets. Different chapters are largely self contained and all contribute to put the subject into focus, similarly to the Hawaii Keck observatory, where the mirror is composed of 36 hexagonal segments.

From the conceptual point of view, the main characteristic features of constraint programming are constraint propagation, and the identification of various special cases which make complexity tractable. The former (see Chapter 3) is an inference technique which makes local constraints stronger without changing the global constraint. The latter issue concerns both the structure (see Chapter 7, Tractable Structures for Constraint Satisfaction Problems) and the kind of constraints (see Chapter 8, The Complexity of Constraint Languages). Less specific, but still very important issues are as follows: Backtracking Search Algorithms, in Chapter 4; Local Search, in Chapter 5; Global Constraints, in Chapter 6; Symmetry in Constraint Programming, in Chapter 10; and Modelling, in Chapter 11.

Another surprising fact about constraint theory is the incredibly close relationship with logic programming. In a rather precise sense logic programming is a way of expressing, and solving, certain classes of disjunctive, recursive constraints. Furthermore, logic programming can be very elegantly generalized to constraint logic programming (see Chapter

12), where the ordinary Herbrand constraint system, and its unification algorithm, are complemented with specific constraint solvers. The interaction with the committed choice languages studied in the Japanese projects of the eighties also yielded very interesting models of computation based on constraints. Amalgamation with more common (and efficiently implemented!) programming languages is also possible (see Chapter 13, Constraints in Procedural and Concurrent Languages).

Besides and beyond the beauty of its theoretical foundations, what contributes the most to the practical convenience of constraint programming are: (i) the development of specific results for important classes of constraints; (ii) the ability of extending the basic theory to various additional aspects which are very relevant in practice; and (iii) the flexibility and potential for integration with other modeling and solving methodologies.

About the development of specific results, this handbook includes chapters about constraints on finite (Chapter 14), structured (Chapter 17), temporal (Chapter 19), continuous and interval-based (Chapter 16) domains. The potential to extend the basic theory in evident in the case of soft constraints, considered in Chapter 9. Ordinary constraints are either satisfied or not, namely either true or false. Instead soft constraints return a more informative weight. Interestingly enough, the proposed extensions both accommodate several important cases (fuzzy, hierarchical, optimization, probabilistic constraints), and still often exhibit essentially the same solution algorithms. Extensions to random, changing and distributed/open constraints are treated in Chapters 18, 21 and 20 respectively.

About the last issue, in addition to the seamless integration with logic and imperative programming languages we mentioned already, quite remarkable are the paradigms resulting from the integration of constraint programming with operations research (see Chapter 15), with scheduling and planning (see Chapter 22), with vehicle routing (see Chapter 23), with component configuration (see Chapter 24), with (electricity, water, oil, data) networks (see Chapter 25), and with bioinformatics (see Chapter 26).

The global scenario based on service-oriented computing which is now under development offers additional theoretical and practical challenges to constraint programming. Conditions for service deployment and discovery, both functional and involving different aspects of quality of service, could be expressed in terms of hard and soft constraints, and the negotiation phases should involve substantial constraint solving abilities. Transactions among the various actors could also require partially backtrackable behavior or at least programmable compensations. Some level of real time, distributed, global constraint solving should be implemented in the middleware, since lots of higher level applications will be able to take advantage of, and pay for it.

I think that research and practical development in the area of constraint programming will be very active for quite a while in the future, establishing closer and closer connections with a variety of other design methodologies and even other disciplines. I consider this handbook not only a very nice piece of scientific work, but also a contribution quite instrumental at disseminating advanced knowledge about constraint programming both within the inner constraint community and across the much wider audience of potential users.

UGO MONTANARI
Dipartimento di Informatica
Università di Pisa, Italy

Editors

Francesca Rossi
University of Padova
Italy

Peter van Beek
University of Waterloo
Canada

Toby Walsh
National ICT Australia &
University of New South Wales
Australia

Contributors

Rolf Backofen
Albert-Ludwigs-Universität
Germany

Philippe Baptiste
CNRS LIX & École Polytechnique
France

Frédéric Benhamou
Université de Nantes
France

Christian Bessiere
LIRMM-CNRS
France

Kenneth N. Brown
Cork Constraint Computation Centre &
University College Cork, Ireland

Mats Carlsson
SICS AB
Sweden

David Cohen
Royal Holloway, University of London
United Kingdom

Rina Dechter
University of California, Irvine
USA

Boi Faltings
Swiss Federal Institute of Technology
Switzerland

Eugene C. Freuder
Cork Constraint Computation Centre &
University College Cork, Ireland

Thom Frühwirth
Universität Ulm
Germany

Ian P. Gent
University of St. Andrews
Scotland, United Kingdom

Carmen Gervet
Brown University
USA

David Gilbert
University of Glasgow
Scotland, United Kingdom

Carla Gomes
Cornell University
USA

Laurent Granvilliers
Université de Nantes
France

John N. Hooker
Carnegie Mellon University
USA

Holger H. Hoos
University of British Columbia
Canada

Peter Jeavons
University of Oxford
United Kingdom

Ulrich Junker
ILOG SA
France

Irit Katriel
University of Aarhus
Denmark

Philip Kilby
The Australian National University
Australia

Manolis Koubarakis
University of Athens
Greece

Philippe Laborie
ILOG SA
France

Claude Le Pape
ILOG SA
France

Alan K. Mackworth
University of British Columbia
Canada

Kim Marriott
Monash University
Australia

Pedro Meseguer
IIIA-CSIC
Spain

Laurent Michel
University of Connecticut
USA

Ian Miguel
The University of St. Andrews
Scotland, United Kingdom

Wim Nuijten
ILOG SA
France

Karen E. Petrie
University of St. Andrews
Scotland, United Kingdom

Jean-François Puget
ILOG SA
France

Francesca Rossi
University of Padova
Italy

Thomas Schiex
INRA Toulouse
France

Christian Schulte
KTH - Royal Institute of Technology
Sweden

Paul Shaw
ILOG SA
France

Helmut Simonis
CrossCore Optimization
United Kingdom

Barbara M. Smith
Cork Constraint Computation Centre &
University College Cork, Ireland

Peter J. Stuckey
University of Melbourne
Australia

Edward Tsang
University of Essex
United Kingdom

Peter van Beek
University of Waterloo
Canada

Willem-Jan van Hoeve
Cornell University
USA

Mark Wallace
Monash University
Australia

Toby Walsh
National ICT Australia &
University of New South Wales
Australia

Contents

Part I

Foundations

Handbook of Constraint Programming
Edited by F. Rossi, P. van Beek and T. Walsh

3

Chapter 1

Introduction

Francesca Rossi, Peter van Beek, Toby Walsh

Constraint programming is a powerful paradigm for solving combinatorial search problems that draws on a wide range of techniques from artificial intelligence, computer science, databases, programming languages, and operations research. Constraint programming is currently applied with success to many domains, such as scheduling, planning, vehicle routing, configuration, networks, and bioinformatics. The basic idea in constraint programming is that the user states the constraints and a general purpose constraint solver is used to solve them. Constraints are just relations, and a constraint satisfaction problem (CSP) states which relations should hold among the given decision variables. For example, in scheduling activities in a company, the decision variables might be the starting times and the durations of the activities and the resources needed to perform them, and the constraints might be on the availability of the resources and on their use for a limited number of activities at a time.

Constraint solvers take a real-world problem like this, represented in terms of decision variables and constraints, and find an assignment to all the variables that satisfies the constraints. Constraint solvers search the solution space either systematically, as with backtracking or branch and bound algorithms, or use forms of local search which may be incomplete. Systematic method often interleave search and inference, where inference consists of propagating the information contained in one constraint to the neighboring constraints. Such inference (usually called constraint propagation) is useful since it may reduce the parts of the search space that need to be visited.

While defining a set of constraints may seem a simple way to model a real-world problem, finding a good model that works well with a chosen solver is not always easy. A poorly chosen model may be very hard to solve. Thus much care must be devoted to choosing a good model and also to devising solvers that can exploit the features of the chosen model.

From this description it may seem that constraint programming is "programming" in the sense of "mathematical programming": the user declaratively states the constraints on the feasible solutions for a set of decision variables, and an underlying solver solves the constraints. However, constraint programming is also "programming" in the sense of "computer programming": the user needs to program a strategy to search for a solution.

Without this, the solving process would be very inefficient. This is very natural to do in logic-based programming languages, such as constraint logic programming, but it can also be done in other programming paradigms.

1.1 Purpose of the Handbook

The aim of this handbook is to capture the full breadth and depth of the constraint programming field and to be encyclopedic in its scope and coverage. While there are excellent books on constraint programming (see, for example, [1, 2, 3, 4, 5, 6, 7, 8]), such books necessarily focus on the main notions and techniques and cannot cover also extensions, applications, and languages. The handbook gives a reasonably complete coverage of all these lines of work, based on constraint programming, so that a reader can have a rather precise idea of the whole field and its potential. Of course each line of work is dealt with in a survey-like style, where some details may be neglected in favor of broader coverage. However, the extensive bibliography of each chapter will help the interested readers to find suitable sources for the missing details. Each chapter of the handbook is intended to be a self-contained survey of a topic, and is written by one or more authors who are leading researchers in the area.

The intended audience of the handbook is researchers, graduate students, upper-year undergraduates, and practitioners who wish to learn about the state-of-the-art in constraint programming. No prior knowledge about the field is necessary to be able to read the chapters and gather useful knowledge. Researchers from other fields should find in this handbook an effective way to learn about constraint programming and to possibly use some of the constraint programming concepts and techniques in their own work, thus providing a means for a fruitful cross-fertilization among different research areas.

1.2 Structure and Content

The handbook is organized in two parts. The first part covers the basic foundations of constraint programming, including the history, the notion of constraint propagation, basic search methods, global constraints, tractability and computational complexity, and important issues in modeling a problem as a constraint problem. The second part covers constraint languages and solver, several useful extensions to the basic framework (such as interval constraints, structured domains, and distributed CSPs), and successful application areas for constraint programming.

Part I: Foundations

In Chapter 2, Eugene C. Freuder and Alan K. Mackworth survey the emergence of constraint satisfaction as a new paradigm within artificial intelligence and computer science. Covering the two decades from 1965 to 1985, Freuder and Mackworth trace the development of two streams of work, which they call the language stream and the algorithm stream. The focus of the language stream was on declarative program languages and systems for developing applications of constraints. The language stream gave many special purpose declarative languages and also general programming languages such as constraint logic programming. The focus of the algorithm stream was on algorithms and heuristics for the constraint satisfaction framework. The algorithm stream gave constraint propagation algorithms such as algorithms for arc consistency and also heuristics and constraint propagation within backtracking search. Ultimately, the language stream and the algorithm stream merged to form the core of the new field of constraint programming.

In Chapter 3, Christian Bessiere surveys the extensive literature on constraint propagation. Constraint propagation is a central concept—perhaps *the* central concept—in the theory and practice of constraint programming. Constraint propagation is a form of reasoning in which, from a subset of the constraints and the domains, more restrictive constraints or more restrictive domains are inferred. The inferences are justified by local consistency properties that characterize necessary conditions on values or set of values to belong to a solution. Arc consistency is currently the most important local consistency property in practice and has received the most attention in the literature. The importance of constraint propagation is that it can greatly simplify a constraint problem and so improve the efficiency of a search for a solution.

The main algorithmic techniques for solving constraint satisfaction problems (CSPs) are backtracking search and local search. In Chapter 4, Peter van Beek surveys backtracking search algorithms. A backtracking search algorithm performs a depth-first traversal of a search tree, where the branches out of a node represent alternative choices that may have to be examined in order to find a solution, and the constraints are used to prune subtrees containing no solutions. Backtracking search algorithms come with a guarantee that a solution will be found if one exists, and can be used to show that a CSP does not have a solution or to find a provably optimal solution. Many techniques for improving the efficiency of a backtracking search algorithm have been suggested and evaluated including constraint propagation, nogood recording, backjumping, heuristics for variable and value ordering, and randomization and restart strategies.

In Chapter 5, Holger H. Hoos and Edward Tsang survey local search algorithms for solving constraint satisfaction problems. A local search algorithm performs a walk in a directed graph, where the nodes represent alternative assignments to the variables that may have to be examined and the number of violated constraints is used to guide the search for a solution. Local search algorithms cannot be used to show that a CSP does not have a solution or to find a provably optimal solution. However, such algorithms are often effective at finding a solution if one exists and can be used to find an approximation to an optimal solution. Many techniques and strategies for improving local search algorithms have been proposed and evaluated including randomized iterative improvement, tabu search, penalty-based approaches, and alternative neighborhood and move strategies.

In Chapter 6, Willem-Jan van Hoeve and Irit Katriel survey global constraints. A global constraint is a constraint that can be over arbitrary subsets of the variables. The canonical example of a global constraint is the `all-different` constraint which states that the variables in the constraint must be pairwise different. The power of global constraints is two-fold. First, global constraints ease the task of modeling an application using constraint programming. The `all-different` constraint, for example, is a pattern that reoccurs in many applications, including rostering, timetabling, sequencing, and scheduling applications. Second, special purpose constraint propagation algorithms can be designed which take advantage of the semantics of the constraint and are therefore much more efficient. Van Hoeve and Katriel show that designing constraint propagation algorithms for global constraints draws on a wide variety of disciplines including graph theory, flow theory, matching theory, linear programming, and finite automaton.

A fundamental challenge in constraint programming is to understand the computational complexity of problems involving constraints. In their most general form, constraint satisfaction problems (CSPs) are NP-Hard. To counter this pessimistic result, much work has been done on identifying restrictions on constraint satisfaction problems such that solving an instance can be done efficiently; that is, in polynomial time in the worst-case. Finding tractable classes of constraint problems is of theoretical interest of course, but also of practical interest in the design of constraint programming languages and effective constraint solvers. The restrictions on CSPs that lead to tractability fall into two classes: restricting the topology of the underlying graph of the CSP and restricting the type of the allowed constraints. In Chapter 7, Rina Dechter surveys how the complexity of solving CSPs varies with the topology of the underlying constraint graph. The results depend on properties of the constraint graph, such as the well-known graph parameter tree-width. In Chapter 8, David Cohen and Peter Jeavons survey how the complexity of solving CSPs varies with the type of allowed constraints. Here, the results depend on algebraic properties of the constraint relations.

The first part ends with three chapters concerned with modeling real world problems as CSPs. In many real world problems, not all constraints are hard. Some constraint may be "soft" and express preferences that we would like to satisfy but do not insist upon. Other real world problems may be over-constrained. In both cases, an extension of the basic framework of constraint satisfaction to soft constraints is useful. In Chapter 9, Pedro Meseguer, Francesca Rossi, and Thomas Schiex survey the different formalisms of soft constraints proposed in the literature. They describe the relationship between these different formalisms. In addition, they discuss how solving methods have been generalized to deal with soft constraints.

Symmetry occurs in many real world problems: machines in a factory might be identical, nurses might have the same skills, delivery trucks might have the same capacity, etc. Symmetry can also be introduced when we model a problem as a CSP. For example, if we introduce a decision variable for each machine, then we can permute those variables representing identical machines. Such symmetry enlarges the search space and must be dealt with if we are to solve problems of the size met in practice. In Chapter 10, Ian P. Gent, Karen E. Petrie, and Jean-François Puget survey the different forms of symmetry in constraint programming. They describe the three basic techniques used to deal with symmetry: reformulating the problem, adding symmetry breaking constraints, and modifying the search strategy to ignore symmetric states. Symmetry is one example of the sort of issues that need to be considered when modeling a problem as a CSP. In Chapter 11, Barbara M. Smith surveys a range of other issues in modeling a problem as a CSP. This includes deciding on an appropriate viewpoint (e.g. if we are scheduling exams, do the variables represent exams and their values the times, or do the variables represent the times and their values the exams?), adding implied constraints to help prune the search space, and introducing auxiliary variables to make it easier to state the constraints or to improve propagation.

Part II: Extensions, Languages, and Applications

To increase the uptake, ease of use, extensibility, and flexibility of constraint technology, constraints and search have been integrated into several programming languages and programming paradigms. In Chapter 12, Kim Marriott, Peter J. Stuckey, and Mark Wallace survey constraint logic programming (CLP), the integration of constraint solving into logic programming languages. Constraint solving and logic programming are both declarative paradigms, so their integration is quite natural. Further, the fact that constraints can be seen as relations or predicates, that a set of constraints can be viewed as the conjunction of the individual constraints, and that backtracking search is a basic methodology for solving a set of constraints, makes constraint solving very compatible with logic programming, which is based on predicates, logical conjunctions, and backtracking search. Marriott, Stuckey, and Wallace cover the elegant semantics of CLP, show the power of CLP in modeling constraint satisfaction problems, and describe how to define specific search routines in CLP for solving the modeled problem.

In Chapter 13, Thom Frühwirth, Laurent Michel, and Christian Schulte survey the integration of constraints into procedural and object-oriented languages, concurrent languages, and rule-based languages. Integrating constraint solving into these more traditional programming paradigms faces new challenges as these paradigms generally lack support for declarative programming. These challenges include (i) allowing the specification of new search routines, while maintaining declarativeness, (ii) the design of declarative modeling languages that are user-friendly and based on well-known programming metaphors, and (iii) the integration of constraint solving into *multi*-paradigm languages. Frühwirth, Michel, and Schulte include a discussion of the technical aspects of integrating constraints into each programming paradigm, as well as the advantages and disadvantages of each paradigm.

In Chapter 14, Christian Schulte and Mats Carlsson survey finite domain constraint programming systems. One of the key properties of constraint programming systems is the provision of widely reusable services—such as constraint propagation and backtracking search—for constructing constraint-based applications. Schulte and Carlsson discuss which services are provided by constraint programming systems and also the key principles and techniques in implementing and coordinating these services. For many applications, the constraint propagation, backtracking search, and other services provided by the constraint programming system are sufficient. However, some applications require more, and most constraint programming systems are extensible, allowing the user to define, for example, new constraint propagators or new search strategies. Schulte and Carlsson also provide an overview of several well-known finite domain constraint programming systems.

Operations research (OR) and constraint programming (CP) are complementary frameworks with similar goals. In Chapter 15, John N. Hooker surveys some of the schemes for incorporating OR methods into CP. In constraint programming, constraints are used to reduce the domains of the variables. One method for incorporating an OR method is to apply it to a constraint to reduce the domains. For example, if a subset of the constraints are linear inequalities, the domain of a variable in the subset can possibly be reduced by minimizing and maximizing the variable using linear programming on the subset of linear constraints. This example is an instance of a popular scheme for incorporating OR into CP: create a relaxation of the CP problem in the form of an OR model, such as a linear programming model. Other schemes for creating hybrid OR/CP combinations decompose a problem so that CP and OR are each used on the parts of the problem to which they are best suited. Hooker shows that OR/CP combinations using both relaxation and decomposition can bring substantial computational benefits.

Real-world problems often take us beyond finite domain variables. For example, to reason about power consumption, we might want a variable to range over the reals and to reason about communication networks we might want a variable to range over paths in a graph. Constraint programming has therefore been extended to deal with more than just finite (or enumerated) domains of values. In Chapter 16, Frédéric Benhamou and Laurent Granvilliers survey constraints over continuous and interval domains. The extension of backtracking search over finite domains to interval constraints is called branch-and-reduce: branching splits an interval and reduce narrows the intervals using a generalization of local consistency and interval arithmetic. Hybrid techniques combining symbolic reasoning and constraint propagation have also been designed. Benhamou and Granvilliers also discuss some of the applications of interval constraints and the available interval constraint software packages. In Chapter 17, Carmen Gervet surveys constraints over structured domains. Many combinatorial search problems—such as bin packing, set covering, and network design—can be naturally represented in the language of sets, multi-sets, strings, graphs and other structured objects. Constraint propagation has therefore been extended to deal with constraints over variables which range over such datatypes.

Early work in empirical comparisons of algorithms for solving constraint satisfaction problems was hampered by a lack of realistic or hard test problems. The situation improved with the discovery of hard random problems that arise at a phase transition and the investigation of alternative random models of constraint satisfaction, satisfiability, and optimization problems. Experiments could now be performed which compared the algorithms on the hardest problems and systematically explored the entire space of random problems to see where one algorithm bettered another. In Chapter 18, Carla Gomes and Toby Walsh survey these alternative random models. In addition to their interest as an experimental testbed, insight gained from the study of hard problems has also led to the design of better algorithms. As one example, Gomes and Walsh discuss the technique of randomization and restarts for improving the efficiency of backtracking search algorithms.

In Chapter 19, Manolis Koubarakis surveys temporal constraint satisfaction problems for representing and reasoning with temporal information. Temporal reasoning is important in many application areas—including natural language understanding, database systems, medical information systems, planning, and scheduling—and constraint satisfaction techniques play a large role in temporal reasoning. Constraint-based temporal reasoning formalisms for representing qualitative, metric, and combined qualitative-metric temporal information have been proposed in the literature and many efficient constraint satisfaction algorithms are known for these formalisms. Koubarakis also demonstrates the application-driven need for more expressive queries over temporal constraint satisfaction (especially queries combining temporal and non-temporal information) and surveys various proposals that address this need including the scheme of indefinite constraint databases.

In Chapter 20, Boi Faltings surveys distributed constraint satisfaction. In distributed constraint satisfaction, constraint solving happens under the control of different independent agents, where each agent controls a single variable. The canonical example of the usefulness of this formalism is meeting scheduling, where each person has their own constraints and there are privacy concerns that restrict the flow of information, but many applications have been identified. Backtracking search and its improvements have been extended to the distributed case. In synchronous backtracking, messages are passed from agent to agent with only one agent being active at any one time. A message consists of either a partial instantiation or a message that signals the need to backtrack. In asynchronous backtracking, all agents are active at once, and messages are sent to coordinate their the assignments that are made to their individual variables. Asynchronous backtracking has been the focus of most of the work in distributed constraint satisfaction. Faltings also surveys the literature on open constraint satisfaction, a form of distributed CSP where the domains of the variables and the constraints may be incomplete or not fully known.

The basic framework of constraint programming makes two assumptions that do not hold in many real world problems: that the problem being modeled is static and that the constraints are known with certainty. For example, factory scheduling is inherently dynamic and uncertain since the full set of jobs may not be known in advance, machines may break down, employees may be late or ill, and so on. In Chapter 21, Kenneth N. Brown and Ian Miguel survey the uses and extensions of constraint programming for handling problems subject to change and uncertainty. For dynamically changing problems, two of the alternatives are to record information about the problem structure during the solving process, such as explanation or nogood recording, so that re-solving can be done efficiently; and to search for robust or solutions that anticipate expected changes. For uncertain problems, different types of uncertainty can be identified including: the problem itself is intrinsically imprecise; there is a set of possible realizations of the problem, one of which will be the final version, and there are probability distributions over the full realizations. As well, many CSP formalisms have been proposed for handling uncertainty including fuzzy, mixed, uncertain, probabilistic, stochastic, and recurrent CSPs.

Constraint programming has proven useful—indeed, it is often the method of choice— in important applications from industry, business, manufacturing, and science. In the last five chapters of the handbook, some of these applications of constraint programming are highlighted. Each of the chapters emphasizes *why* constraint programming has been successful in the given application domain. As well, in the best traditions of application-driven research, the chapters describe how focusing on real-world applications has led to basic discoveries and improvements to existing constraint programming techniques. In a fruitful cycle, these discoveries and improvements then led to new and more successful applications.

In Chapter 22, Philippe Baptiste, Philippe Laborie, Claude Le Pape, and Wim Nuijten survey constraint programming approaches to scheduling and planning. Scheduling is the task of assigning resources to a set of activities to minimize a cost function. Scheduling arises in diverse settings including in the allocation of gates to incoming planes at an airport, crews to an assembly line, and processes to a CPU. Planning is a generalization of scheduling where the set of activities to be scheduled is not known in advance. Constraint programming approaches to scheduling and planning have aimed at generality, with the ability to seamlessly handle real-world side constraints. As well, much effort has gone into improved implied constraints such as global constraints, edge-finding constraints and timetabling constraints, which lead to powerful constraint propagation. Baptiste et al. show that one of the reasons for the success of a constraint programming approach is its ability to integrate efficient special purpose algorithms within a flexible and expressive paradigm. Additional advantages of a constraint propagation approach include the ability to form hybrids of backtracking search and local search and the ease with which domain specific scheduling and planning heuristics can be incorporated within the search routines.

In Chapter 23, Philip Kilby and Paul Shaw survey constraint programming approaches to vehicle routing. Vehicle Routing is the task of constructing routes for vehicles to visit customers at minimum cost. A vehicle has a maximum capacity which cannot be exceeded and the customers may specify time windows in which deliveries are permitted. Much work on constraint programming approaches to vehicle routing has focused on alternative constraint models and additional implied constraints to increase the amount of pruning performed by constraint propagation. Kilby and Shaw show that constraint programming is well-suited for vehicle routing because of its ability to handle real-world (or side) constraints. Vehicle routing problems that arise in practice often have unique constraints that are particular to a business entity. In non-constraint programming approaches, such side constraints often have to be handled in an ad hoc manner. In constraint programming a wide variety of side constraints can be handled simply by adding them to the core model.

In Chapter 24, Ulrich Junker surveys constraint programming approaches to configuration. Configuration is the task of assembling or configuring a customized system from a catalog of components. Configuration arises in diverse settings including in the assembly of home entertainment systems, cars and trucks, and travel packages. Junker shows that constraint programming is well-suited to configuration because of (i) its flexibility in modeling and the declarativeness of the constraint model, (ii) the ability to explain a failure to find a customized system when the configuration task is over-constrained and to subsequently relax the user's constraints, (iii) the ability to perform interactive configuration where the user makes a sequence of choices and after each choice constraint propagation is used to restrict future possible choices, and (iv) the ability to incorporate reasoning about the user's preferences.

In Chapter 25, Helmut Simonis surveys constraint programming approaches to applications that arise in electrical, water, oil, and data (such as the Internet) distribution networks. The applications include design, risk analysis, and operational control of the networks. Simonis discusses the best alternative formulations or constraint models for these problems. The constraint programming work on networks vividly illustrates the advantages of application-driven research. The limited success in this domain of classical constraint programming approaches, such as backtracking search, led to improvements in hybrid approaches which combine both backtracking and local search or combine both constraint programming and operations research methods. A research hurdle that must still be overcome, however, is the complexity and implementation effort that is required to construct a successful hybrid system for an application.

In Chapter 26, Rolf Backofen and David Gilbert survey constraint programming approaches to problems that arise in bioinformatics. Bioinformatics is the study of informatics and computational problems that arise in molecular biology, evolution, and genetics. Perhaps the first and most well-known example problem in bioinformatics is DNA sequence alignment. More recently, constraint programming approaches have made significant progress on the important problem of protein structure prediction. The ultimate goals and implications of bioinformatics are profound: better drug design, identification of genetic risk factors, gene therapy, and genetic modification of food crops and animals.

1.3 Future Research

The field of constraint programming is rapidly progressing. Many new research results are being published and new research areas are being opened in the field of constraint reasoning. We conclude this introduction with some speculation on lines of research that appear interesting and promising to us, and that in the future could be mature enough to constitute entire chapters in future revisions of this handbook.

Quantified constraint problems are a very interesting extension of classical CSPs where some variables may be universally quantified. This can help modeling scenarios where uncertainty does not allow us to decide the values for some variables. Many theoretical results on the complexity of such problems have already been developed. We envision a fast growth of this area and its applications.

When using a constraint solver, often it is not easy to understand what went wrong, or why a certain solution is returned rather than another one. *Explanation* tools could greatly help in making constraint technology easy to use in an interactive system. In general, *user interaction* in constraint systems deserves much attention and effort. Improvements in this respect could greatly widen the usability of constraint-based tools.

It is rare that all constraints are collected at the same time from the user of a constraint system. Usually such constraints, or preferences, are collected some at a time, but the system must be able to perform some amount of reasoning also with partial knowledge. Moreover, based on the partial knowledge it has, it should be able to ask the user only for those constraints or preferences that are useful to make the next inference. The issue of *preference elicitation* is crucial in such situations, and allows users to intelligently interact with a constraint system without being forced to state all their constraints, or preferences, at the beginning of the interaction. This can also be useful in scenarios where the users want to avoid revealing all their preferences, for example for privacy reasons.

Even when the user is willing to state all the information at the beginning of the interaction, sometimes it may be difficult for him to actually state it in terms of constraints. For example, it could be easier to state examples of desirable or unacceptable solutions. In this cases, machine *learning techniques* can be helpful to learn the constraints from the partial and possibly imprecise user statements. As for explanation and preference elicitation, this can greatly help in easing the interaction between users and constraint solvers.

Satisfiability is a mature research area with much interaction with constraint reasoning, since a satisfiability problem is just a constraint problem with Boolean variables. Thus, many theoretical results can be adapted from one field to the other one. We hope to see many such results in the future.

This handbook contains chapters on just some of the main application areas for constraint programming. Other application fields, which look very promising, are design, constraint databases, web services, global computing, and security. We hope to see constraint programming to be the base of many useful tools for such applications.

Acknowledgements

A project like this, which lasted almost two years and involved about sixty people, would not be possible without the support and encouragement of a great many people within the constraint programming community. First, we wish to thank the many authors of the chapters within this handbook. Many of them also helped us by reviewing other chapters. Additionally, we would like to thank Claire Bagley, Roman Bartak, Andrei Bulatov, Martin Henz, Andrea Lodi, Michela Milano, Luis Quesada, Francesco Scarcello, Peter Van Roy, and Roland Yap, who reviewed other chapters. Thanks also to Ugo Montanari, a pioneer of constraint programming, who wrote the foreword for the book.

We also wish to thank Zeger Karssen, originally at Elsevier and now at Atlantic Press, and Bernhard Nebel, one of the editors of the series where this book will appear. They have been very enthusiastic about this project since the very first time we described it to them in the Summer of 2004. Zeger and his assistants have helped us greatly to put the project together and to smoothly reach a satisfactory agreement on the format and style of the book.

Finally, we also would like to thank Helmut Simonis, who, besides being an author of the handbook, provided the very nice cover picture for this handbook. We think his beautiful rose can represent very well the spirit of this handbook: the petals are the many authors, who worked together in cooperation to produce what we hope is a book as beautiful as this rose.

Bibliography

[1] K. R. Apt. *Principles of Constraint Programming*. Cambridge University Press, 2003.

[2] R. Dechter. *Constraint Processing*. Morgan Kaufmann, 2003.

[3] F. Fages. *Programmation logique par contraintes*. Ellipses Marketing, 1998.

[4] T. Frühwirth and S. Abdennadher. *Essentials of Constraint Programming*. Springer, 2003.

[5] J. Hooker. *Logic-Based Methods for Optimization: Combining Optimization and Constraint Satisfaction*. Wiley-Interscience, 2000.

[6] K. Marriott and P. J. Stuckey. *Programming with Constraints*. The MIT Press, 1998.

[7] E. P. K. Tsang. *Foundations of Constraint Satisfaction*. Academic Press, 1993.

[8] P. Van Hentenryck. *Constraint Satisfaction in Logic Programming*. MIT Press, 1989.

Edited by F. Rossi, P. van Beek and T. Walsh

Chapter 2

Constraint Satisfaction: An Emerging Paradigm

Eugene C. Freuder and Alan K. Mackworth

This chapter focuses on the emergence of constraint satisfaction, with constraint languages, as a new paradigm within artificial intelligence and computer science during the period from 1965 (when Golomb and Baumert published "Backtrack programming" [34]) to 1985 (when Mackworth and Freuder published "The complexity of some polynomial network consistency algorithms for constraint satisfaction problems" [55]). The rest of this handbook will cover much of the material introduced here in more detail, as well as, of course, continuing on from 1986 into 2006.

2.1 The Early Days

Constraint satisfaction, in its basic form, involves finding a value for each one of a set of problem variables where constraints specify that some subsets of values cannot be used together. As a simple example of constraint satisfaction, consider the task of choosing component parts for the assembly of a bicycle, such as the frame, wheels, brakes, sprockets and chain, that are all mutually compatible.

Constraint satisfaction, like most fields of artificial intelligence, can be separated into (overlapping) concerns with representation and reasoning. The former can be divided into generic and application-specific concerns, the latter into search and inference. While constraint satisfaction has often been pigeon-holed as a form of search, its real importance lies in its broad representational scope: it can be used effectively to model many other forms of reasoning (e.g. temporal reasoning) and applied to many problem domains (e.g. scheduling). For this reason, constraint satisfaction problems are sometimes encountered in application domains that are unaware that an academic community has been studying the subject for years: one reason for the importance of a handbook such as this. Furthermore, while heuristic search methods are a major concern, the distinguishing feature of constraint satisfaction as a branch of artificial intelligence is arguably the emphasis on inference, in the form of constraint propagation, as opposed to search.

Constraint satisfaction problems have been tackled by a dizzying array of methods, from automata theory to ant algorithms, and are a topic of interest in many fields of computer science and beyond. These connections add immeasurably to the richness of the subject, but are largely beyond the scope of this chapter. Here we will focus on the basic methods involved in the establishment of constraint satisfaction as a branch of artificial intelligence. This new branch of artificial intelligence, together with related work on programming languages and systems that we can only touch upon here, laid the groundwork for the flourishing of interest in constraint programming languages after 1985.

Constraint satisfaction of course, predates 1965. The real world problems that we now identify as constraint satisfaction problems, like workforce scheduling, have naturally always been with us. The toy 8-queens problem, which preoccupied so many of the early constraint satisfaction researchers in artificial intelligence, is said to have been proposed in 1848 by the chess player Max Bazzel. Mythology claims that a form of backtrack search, a powerful search paradigm that has become a central tool for constraint satisfaction, was used by Theseus in the labyrinth in Crete. Backtrack search was used in recreational mathematics in the nineteenth century [51], and was an early subject of study as computer science and operations research emerged as academic disciplines after World War II. Bitner and Reingold [2] credit Lehmer with first using the term 'backtrack' in the 1950's [50]. Various forms of constraint satisfaction and propagation appeared in the computer science literature in the 1960's [16, 15, 34, 75].

In artificial intelligence interest in constraint satisfaction developed in two streams. In some sense a common ancestor of both streams is Ivan Sutherland's groundbreaking 1963 MIT Ph.D. thesis, "Sketchpad: A man-machine graphical communication system" [73].

In one stream, the versatility of constraints led to applications in a variety of domains, and associated programming languages and systems. This stream we can call the language stream. In 1964 Wilkes proposed that algebraic equations be allowed as constraint statements in procedural Algol-like programming languages, with relaxation used to satisfy the constraints [80]. Around 1967, Elcock developed a declarative language, Absys, based on the manipulation of equational constraints [22]. Burstall employed a form of constraint manipulation as early as 1969 in a program for solving cryptarithmetic puzzles [9]. In the very first issue of *Artificial Intelligence* in 1970, Fikes described REF-ARF, where the REF language formed part of a general problem-solving system employing constraint satisfaction and propagation as one of its methods [23]. Kowalski used a form of constraint propagation for theorem proving [48]. Sussman and others at MIT applied a form of constraint propagation to analysis, synthesis and fault localization for circuits [6, 17, 18, 67, 71], and Sussman with Steele developed the CONSTRAINTS language [72]. Borning used constraints in his ThingLab simulation laboratory [4, 5], whose kernel was an extension of the Smalltalk language; Lauriere used constraints in Alice, a language for solving combinatorial problems [49]. In the planning domain, Eastman did "constraint structured" space planning with GSP, the General Space Planner [21], Stefik used "constraint posting" in MOLGEN, which planned gene-cloning experiments in molecular genetics [68, 69], and Descotte and Latombe's GARI system, which generated the machining plans of mechanical parts, embedded a planner which made compromises among "antagonistic constraints" [20]. Fox, Allen and Strohm developed ISIS-II [25] a constraint-directed reasoning system for factory job-shop scheduling.

In the other stream, an interest in constraint solving algorithms grew out of the machine vision community; we cite some of the early work here. We refer to this stream as the algorithm stream. The landmark 'Waltz filtering' (arc consistency) constraint propagation algorithm appeared in a Ph.D. thesis on scene labeling [79], building upon work of Huffman [41] and Clowes [10]. Montanari developed path consistency and established a general framework for representing and reasoning about constraints in a seminal paper entitled "Networks of constraints: fundamental properties and applications to picture processing" [60]. Mackworth exploited constraints for machine vision [52], before providing a general framework for "Consistency in networks of relations" and new algorithms for arc and path consistency [53]. Freuder generalized arc and path consistency to k-consistency [26] shortly after completing a Ph.D. thesis on "active vision". Barrow and Tenenbaum, with MSYS [1] and IGS [74], were also early users of constraints for image interpretation. Rosenfeld, Hummel and Zucker, in "Scene labeling by relaxation operations", explored the "continuous labeling problem", where constraints are not 'hard', specifying that values can or cannot be used together, but 'soft' specifying degrees of compatibility [65]. Haralick, Davis, Rosenfeld and Milgram discussed "Reduction operations for constraint satisfaction" [38], and Haralick and Shapiro generalized those results in a two-part paper on "The consistent labeling problem" [36, 37]. Together with J. R. Ullman, they even discussed special hardware for constraint propagation and parallel search computation in [76].

The language and algorithm streams diverged, and both became more detached from specific application domains. While applications and commercial exploitation did proliferate, the academic communities focused more on general methods. While the generality and scientific rigor of constraint programming is one of its strengths, we face a continuing challenge to reconnect these streams more firmly with their semantic problem-solving roots.

The language stream became heavily influenced by logic programming, in the form of constraint logic programming, and focused on the development of programming languages and libraries. Hewitt's Planner language [40] and its partial implementation as Micro-Planner [70] can be seen as an early logic programming language [3]. The major early milestone, though, was the development of Prolog by Colmerauer and others around 1972 [14] and the logic as a programming language movement [39, 47]. Prolog can be framed as an early constraint programming language, solving equality constraints over terms (including variables) using the unification algorithm as the constraint solver. Colmerauer pushed this view much further in his introduction of Prolog II in 1982 [13, 12]. The integration of constraint propagation algorithms into interpreters for Planner-like languages was proposed by Mackworth [53]. Van Hentenryck developed and implemented CHIP (Constraint Handling in Prolog) as a fully-fledged constraint logic programming language [77]. In a parallel development Jaffar *et al.* developed the CLP(X) family of constraint logic programming languages [42] including CLP($\mathcal{R}$) [44]. For more on these developments in the language stream see the surveys in [11, 43] and other chapters in this handbook.

The algorithm stream, influenced by the paradigm of artificial intelligence as search, as exemplified in Nilsson's early textbook [61], and by the development of the science of algorithms, as exemplified by Knuth's *The Art of Computer Programming* [45], focused on algorithms and heuristics. The second stream remained more firmly within artificial intelligence, developing as one of the artificial intelligence communities built around reasoning paradigms: constraint-based reasoning [29], case-based reasoning, and the like. It also focused increasingly on the simple, but powerful and general, *constraint satisfaction problem* (CSP) formulation and its variants. We shall focus primarily on this stream, and the development of the CSP paradigm, in this chapter.

The challenge then became to reintegrate the language and algorithm streams, along with related disciplines, such as mathematical programming and constraint databases, into a single constraint programming community. This process began in earnest in the 1990's when Paris Kanellakis, Jean-Louis Lassez, and Vijay Saraswat chaired a workshop that soon led to the formation of an annual International Conference on Principles and Practice of Constraint Programming, and, at the instigation of Zsófia Ruttkay, Gene Freuder established the *Constraints* journal, which "provides a common forum for the many disciplines interested in constraint programming and constraint satisfaction and optimization, and the many application domains in which constraint technology is employed".

2.2 The Constraint Satisfaction Problem: Representation and Reasoning

Here we consider the representation of constraint satisfaction problems, the varieties of reasoning used by algorithms to solve them and the analysis of those solution methods.

2.2.1 Representation

The classic definition of a Constraint Satisfaction Problem (CSP) is as follows. A CSP $\mathcal{P}$ is a triple $\mathcal{P} = \langle X, D, C \rangle$ where X is an n-tuple of variables $X = \langle x_1, x_2, \ldots, x_n \rangle$ D is a corresponding n-tuple of domains $D = \langle D_1, D_2, \ldots, D_n \rangle$ such that $x_i \in D_i$, C is a t-tuple of constraints $C = \langle C_1, C_2, \ldots, C_t \rangle$. A constraint C_j is a pair $\langle R_{S_j}, S_j \rangle$ where R_{S_j} is a relation on the variables in $S_i = scope(C_i)$. In other words, R_i is a subset of the Cartesian product of the domains of the variables in S_i.[1]

A solution to the CSP $\mathcal{P}$ is an n-tuple $A = \langle a_1, a_2, \ldots, a_n \rangle$ where $a_i \in D_i$ and each C_j is satisfied in that R_{S_j} holds on the projection of A onto the scope S_j. In a given task one may be required to find the set of all solutions, $sol(\mathcal{P})$, to determine if that set is non-empty or just to find any solution, if one exists. If the set of solutions is empty the CSP is unsatisfiable.   This simple but powerful framework captures a wide range of significant applications in fields as diverse as artificial intelligence, operations research, scheduling, supply chain management, graph algorithms, computer vision and computational linguistics, to name but a few.

The classic CSP paradigm can be both specialized and generalized in a variety of important ways. One important specialization considers the extensionality/intensionality of the domains and constraints. If all the domains in D are finite sets, with extensional representations, then they, and the constraint relations, may be represented and manipulated extensionally. However, even if the domains and the relations are intensionally represented, many of the techniques described in this chapter and elsewhere in the handbook still apply. If the size of the scope of each constraint is limited to 1 or 2 then the constraints are unary and binary and the CSP can be directly represented as a constraint graph with variables as vertices and constraints as edges. If the arity of constraints is not so limited then a hypergraph is required with a hyperedge for each p-ary constraint ($p > 2$) connecting the p vertices involved. The satisfiability of propositional formulae, SAT, is another

---

[1] This is the conventional definition, which we will adhere to here. A more parsimonious definition of a CSP would dispense with D entirely leaving the role of D_i to be played by a unary constraint C_j with $scope(C_j) = \langle x_i \rangle$.

specialization of CSP, where the domains are restricted to be $\{T, F\}$ and the constraints are clauses. 3-SAT, the archetypal NP-complete decision problem, is a further restriction where the scope of each constraint (clause) is 3 or fewer variables.

The classic view of CSPs was initially developed by Montanari [60] and Mackworth [53]. It has strong roots in, and links with, SAT [16, 15, 54], relational algebra and database theory [58], computer vision [10, 41, 79] and graphics [73].

Various generalizations of the classic CSP model have been developed subsequently. One of the most significant is the Constraint Optimization Problem (COP) for which there are several significantly different formulations, and the nomenclature is not always consistent [19]. Perhaps the simplest COP formulation retains the CSP limitation of allowing only 'hard' Boolean-valued constraints but adds a cost function over the variables, that must be minimized. This arises often, for example, in scheduling applications.

2.2.2 Reasoning: Inference and Search

We will consider the algorithms for solving CSPs under two broad categories: inference and search, and various combinations of those two approaches. If the domains D_i are all finite then the finite search space for putative solutions is $\Omega = \bowtie_i D_i$ (where $\bowtie$ is the join operator of relational algebra [58]). Ω can, in theory, be enumerated and each n-tuple tested to determine if it is a solution. This blind enumeration technique can be improved upon using two distinct orthogonal strategies: inference and search. In inference techniques, local constraint propagation can eliminate large subspaces from Ω on the grounds that they must be devoid of solutions. Search systematically explores Ω, often eliminating subspaces with a single failure. The success of both strategies hinges on the simple fact that a CSP is conjunctive: to solve it, all of the constraints must be satisfied so that a local failure on a subset of variables rules out all putative solutions with the same projection onto those variables. These two basic strategies are usually combined in most applications.

2.2.3 Inference: Constraint Propagation Using Network Consistency

The major development in inference techniques for CSPs was the discovery and development, in the 1970's, of network consistency algorithms for constraint propagation. Here we will give an overview of that development.

Analysis of using backtracking to solve CSPs shows that it almost always displays pathological *thrashing* behaviors [3]. Thrashing is the repeated exploration of failing subtrees of the backtrack search tree that are essentially identical–differing only in assignments to variables irrelevant to the failure of the subtree. Because there is typically an exponential number of such irrelevant assignments, thrashing is often the most significant factor in the running time of backtracking.

The first key insight behind all the consistency algorithms is that much thrashing behavior can be identified and eliminated, once and for all, by tightening the constraints, making implicit constraints explicit, using tractable, efficient polynomial-time algorithms. The second insight is that the level, or scope, of consistency, the size of the set of variables involved in the local context, can be adjusted as a parameter from 1 up to n, each increase in level requiring correspondingly more work.

For simplicity, we will initially describe the development of the consistency algorithms for CSPs with finite domains and unary and binary constraints only, though neither restriction is necessary, as we shall see. We assume the reader is familiar with the basic elements of graph theory, set theory and relational algebra.

Consider a CSP $\mathcal{P} = \langle X, D, C \rangle$ as defined above. The unary constraints are $C = \langle R_{\langle x_i \rangle}, \langle x_i \rangle \rangle$. We use the shorthand notation R_i to stand for $R_{\langle x_i \rangle}$. Similarly, the binary constraints are of the form $C_s = \langle R_{\langle x_i, x_j \rangle}, \langle x_i, x_j \rangle \rangle$ where $i \neq j$. We use R_{ij} to stand for $R_{\langle x_i, x_j \rangle}$.

Node consistency is the simplest consistency algorithm. Node i comprised of vertex representing variable x_i with domain D_i is node consistent iff $D_i \subseteq R_i$. If node i is not node consistent it can be made so by computing:

$$D'_i = D_i \cap R_i$$
$$D_i \leftarrow D'_i$$

A single pass through the nodes makes the network node consistent. The resulting CSP is $\mathcal{P}' = \langle X, D', C \rangle$ where $D' = \langle D'_1, D'_2, \ldots, D'_n \rangle$. We say $\mathcal{P}' = NC(\mathcal{P})$. Clearly $sol(\mathcal{P}) = sol(\mathcal{P}')$. Let $\Omega' = \bowtie_i D'_i$ then $|\Omega'| \leq |\Omega|$.

Arc consistency is a technique for further tightening the domains using the binary constraints. Consider node i with domain D_i. Suppose there is a non-trivial relation R_{ij} between variables x_i and x_j. We consider the arcs $\langle i, j \rangle$ and $\langle j, i \rangle$ separately. Arc $\langle i, j \rangle$ is arc consistent iff:

$$D_i \subset \pi_i(R_{ij} \bowtie D_j)$$

where π is the projection operator. That is, for every member of D_i, there is a corresponding element in D_j that satisfies R_{ij}. Arc $\langle i, j \rangle$ can be tested for arc consistency and made consistent, if it is not so, by computing:

$$D'_i = D_i \cap \pi_i(R_{ij} \bowtie D_j)$$
$$D_i \leftarrow D'_i$$

(This is a semijoin [58]). In other words, delete all elements of D_i that have no corresponding element in D_j satisfying R_{ij}. A network is arc consistent iff all its arcs are consistent. If all the arcs are already consistent a single pass through them is all that is needed to verify this. If, however, at least one arc has to be made consistent (i.e. $D'_i \neq D_i$ – there is a deletion from D_i) then one must recheck some number of arcs. The basic arc consistency algorithm simply checks all the arcs repeatedly until a fixed point of no further domain reductions is reached. This algorithm is known as AC-1 [53].

Waltz [79] realized that a more intelligent arc consistency bookkeeping scheme would only recheck those arcs that could have become inconsistent as a direct result of deletions from D_i. Waltz's algorithm, now known as AC-2 [53], propagates the revisions of the domains through the arcs until, again, a fixed point is reached. AC-3, presented by Mackworth [53], is a generalization and simplification of AC-2. AC-3 is still the most widely used and effective consistency algorithm. For each of these algorithms let $\mathcal{P}' = AC(\mathcal{P}$ be the result of enforcing arc consistency on $\mathcal{P}$. Then clearly $sol(\mathcal{P}) = sol(\mathcal{P}')$ and $|\Omega'| \leq |\Omega|$.

The best framework for understanding all the network consistency algorithms is to see them as removing local inconsistencies from the network which can never be part of any global solution. When those inconsistencies are removed they may propagate to cause inconsistencies in neighboring arcs that were previously consistent. Those inconsistencies are in turn removed so the algorithm eventually arrives, monotonically, at a fixed point consistent network and halts. An inconsistent network has the same set of solutions as the consistent network that results from applying a consistency algorithm to it; however, if one subsequently applies, say, a backtrack search to the consistent network the resultant thrashing behavior can be no worse and almost always is much better, assuming the same variable and value ordering.

Path consistency [60] is the next level of consistency to consider. In arc consistency we tighten the unary constraints using local binary constraints. In path consistency we analogously tighten the binary constraints using the implicit induced constraints on triples of variables.

A path of length two from node i through node m to node j, $\langle i, m, j \rangle$, is path consistent iff:

$$R_{ij} \subset \pi_{ij}(R_{im} \bowtie D_m \bowtie R_{mj})$$

That is, for every pair of values $\langle a, b \rangle$ allowed by the explicit relation R_{ij} there is a value c for x_m such that $\langle a, c \rangle$ is allowed by R_{im} and $\langle c, b \rangle$ is allowed by R_{mj}.

Path $\langle i, m, j \rangle$ can be tested for path consistency and made consistent, if it is not, by computing:

$$R'_{ij} = R_{ij} \cap \pi_{ij}(R_{im} \bowtie D_m \bowtie R_{mj})$$
$$R_{ij} \leftarrow R'_{ij}$$

If the binary relations are represented as Boolean bit matrices then the combination of the join and projection operations (which is relational composition) becomes Boolean matrix multiplication and the $\cap$ operation becomes simply pairwise bit $\wedge$ operations. In other words, for all the values $\langle a, b \rangle$ allowed by R_{ij} if there is no value c for x_m allowed by R_{im} and R_{mj} the path is made consistent by changing that bit value in R_{ij} from 1 to 0. The way to think of this is that the implicit constraint on $\langle i, j \rangle$ imposed by node $\langle m \rangle$ through the relational composition $R_{im} \circ R_{mj}$ is made explicit in the new constraint R'_{ij} when path $\langle i, m, j \rangle$ is made consistent.

As with arc consistency the simplest algorithm for enforcing path consistency for the entire network is to check and ensure path consistency for each length 2 path $\langle i, m, j \rangle$. If any path has to be made consistent then the entire pass through the paths is repeated again. This is algorithm PC-1 [53, 60].

The algorithm PC-2 [53] determines, when any path is made consistent, the set of other paths could have become inconsistent because they use the arc between that pair of vertices and queues those paths, if necessary, for further checking. PC-2 realizes substantial savings over PC-1 just as AC-3 is more efficient than AC-1 [55].

Typically, after path consistency is established, there are non-trivial binary constraints between all pairs of nodes. As shown by Montanari [60], if all paths of length 2 are consistent then all paths of any length are consistent, so longer paths need not be considered. Once path consistency is established, there is a chain of values along any path satisfying the relations between any pair of values allowed at the start and the end of the path. This does *not* mean that there is necessarily a solution to the CSP. If a path traverses the entire network with a chain of compatible values, if that path self-intersects at a node the two values on the path at that node may be different. Indeed, it is a property of both arc consistency and path consistency that consistency may be established with non-empty domains and relations even though there may be no global solution. Low-level consistency, with no empty domains, is a necessary but not sufficient condition for the existence of a solution. So, if consistency does empty any domain or relation there is no global solution.

Parenthetically, we note that our abstract descriptions of these algorithms, in terms of relational algebra, are specifications not implementations. Implementations can often achieve efficiency savings by, for example, exploiting the semantics of a constraint such as the all different global constraint, *alldiff*, that requires each variable in its scope to assume a different value.

Briefly, let us establish that consistency algorithms do not require the finite domain or binary constraint restrictions on the CSP model. As long as we can perform $\bowtie$, π and $\bigcap$ operations on the domain and relational representations these algorithms are perfectly adequate.

Consider, for example, the trivial CSP $\mathcal{P} = \langle\langle x_1, x_2\rangle, \langle[0, 3], [2, 5]\rangle, \langle=, \langle x_1, x_2\rangle\rangle\rangle$ where x_1 and x_2 are reals. That is, $x_1 \in D_1 = [0, 3], x_2 \in D_2 = [2, 5]$. Arc consistency on arc $\langle 1, 2\rangle$ reduces D_1 to $[2, 3]$ and arc consistency on arc $\langle 2, 1\rangle$ reduces D_2 to $[2, 3]$.

If some of the constraints are p-ary $(p > 2)$ we can generalize arc consistency. In this case we can represent each p-ary constraint $C = \langle R_{S_j}, S_j\rangle$ as a hyperedge connecting the vertices representing the variables in S_j. Consider a vertex $x_i \in S_j$. We say we make the directional hyperarc $\langle x_i, S_j - \langle x_i\rangle\rangle$ generalized arc consistent by computing:

$$D'_i = D_i \bigcap \pi_i(R_{S_j} \bowtie (\bowtie_{m \in S_j - \langle x_i\rangle} D_m))$$
$$D_i \leftarrow D'_i$$

In other words the hyperarc is made generalized arc consistent, if necessary, by deleting from D_i any element that is not compatible with some tuple of its neighbors under the relation R_s. As with AC-3 any changes in D_i may propagate to any other hyperarcs directed at node i. This is the generalized arc consistency algorithm GAC [53]. One can also specialize arc consistency: Mackworth, Mulder and Havens exploited the properties of tree-structured variable domains in a hierarchical arc consistency algorithm HAC [57].

While there is no immediately obvious graph theoretic concept analogous to nodes, arcs and paths to motivate a higher form of consistency, the fact that consideration of paths of length two is, in fact, sufficient for path consistency, provides a natural motivation for the concept of *k-consistency* introduced by Freuder in 1978 [26]. *k*-consistency requires that given consistent values for any $k-1$ variables, there exists a value for any kth variable, such that all k values are consistent (i.e. the k values form a solution to the subproblem induced by the k variables). Thus 2-consistency is equivalent to arc consistency, and 3-consistency to path consistency. Freuder provided a synthesis algorithm for finding all the solutions to a CSP without search by achieving higher and higher levels of consistency.

Freuder went on in 1985 to generalize further to (i, j)-*consistency* [28]. A constraint network is (i, j)-consistent if, given consistent values for any i variables, there exist values for any other j variables, such that all $i + j$ values together are consistent. *k*-consistency is $(k - 1, 1)$-consistency. Special attention was paid to $(1, j)$-consistency, which is a generalization of what would now be termed 'singleton consistency'.

2.2.4   Search: Backtracking

Backtrack is the fundamental 'complete' search method for constraint satisfaction problems, in the sense that one is guaranteed to find a solution if one exists. Even in 1965, Golomb and Baumert, in a *JACM* paper simply entitled "Backtrack programming" [34], were able to observe that the method had already been independently 'discovered' many times. Golomb and Baumert believed their paper to be "the first attempt to formulate the scope and methods of backtrack programming in its full generality", while acknowledging the "fairly general exposition" given five years earlier by Walker [78].

Indeed, Golomb and Baumert's formulation is almost too general for our purposes here in that it is presented as an optimization problem, with the objective to maximize a function of the variables. Arguably Golomb and Baumert are presenting 'branch and bound programming', where upper and lower bounds on what is possible or desirable at any point in the search can provide additional pruning of the search. What we would now call a classic CSP, the 8-queens problem, they formulate by specifying a function whose value is 0 when the queens do not attack each other, and 1 otherwise. It is worth noting also that in this optimization context, again even in 1965, Golomb and Baumert acknowledge the existence of "learning programs and hill climbing programs" that converge on relative maxima. They observe dryly that while "the backtrack algorithm lacks such glamorous qualities as learning and progress, it has the more prosaic virtue of being exhaustive".

Basic backtrack search builds up a partial solution by choosing values for variables until it reaches a dead end, where the partial solution cannot be consistently extended. When it reaches a dead end it undoes the last choice it made and tries another. This is done in a systematic manner that guarantees that all possibilities will be tried. It improves on simply enumerating and testing of all candidate solutions by brute force in that it checks to see if the constraints are satisfied each time it makes a new choice, rather than waiting until a complete solution candidate containing values for all variables is generated. The backtrack search process is often represented as a search tree, where each node (below the root) represents a choice of a value for a variable, and each branch represents a candidate partial solution. Discovering that a partial solution cannot be extended then corresponds to pruning a subtree from consideration. Other noteworthy early papers on backtracking include Bitner and Reingold's "Backtrack programming techniques" [2] and Fillmore and Williamson's "On backtracking: a combinatorial description of the algorithm" [24], which used group theory to address symmetry issues.

Heuristic search methods to support general purpose problem solving paradigms were studied intensely from the early days of artificial intelligence, and backtracking played a role in the form of depth-first search of state spaces, problem reduction graphs, and game trees [61]. In the 1970's as constraint satisfaction emerged as a paradigm of its own, backtrack in the full sense we use the term here, for search involving constraint networks, gained prominence in the artificial intelligence literature, leading to the publication in the *Artificial Intelligence* journal at the beginning of the 1980's of Haralick and Elliott's "Increasing Tree Search Efficiency for Constraint Satisfaction Problems" [35]. This much-cited paper provided what was, for the time, an especially thorough statistical and experimental evaluation of the predominant approaches to refining backtrack search.

There are two major themes in the early work on improving backtracking: controlling search and interleaving inference (constraint propagation) with search. Both of these themes are again evident even in Golomb and Baumert. They observe that "all other things being equal, it is more efficient to make the next choice from the set [domain] with fewest elements", an instance of what Haralick and Elliott dubbed the "fail first principle", and they discuss "preclusion", where a choice for one variable rules out inconsistent choices for other variables, a form of what Haralick and Elliott called "lookahead" that they presented as "forward checking". Of course, preclusion and the smallest domain heuristic nicely complement one another.

In general, one can look for efficient ways to manage search both going 'forward' and 'backward'. When we move forward, extending partial solutions, we make choices about the order in which we consider variables, values and constraints. This order can make an enormous difference in the amount of work we have to do. When we move backwards after hitting a dead end, we do not have to do this chronologically by simply undoing the last choice we made. We can be smarter about it. In general, constraint propagation, most commonly in the form of partial or complete arc consistency, can be carried out before, and/or during, search, in an attempt to prune the search space.

Haralick and Elliott compared several forms of lookahead, carrying out different degrees of partial arc consistency propagation after choosing a value. Oddly their "full lookahead" still did not maintain full arc consistency. However, restoring full arc consistency after choosing values had been proposed as early as 1974 by Gaschnig [31], and McGregor had even experimented with interleaving path consistency with search [59]. Mackworth observed that one could generalize to the alternation of constraint manipulation and case analysis, and proposed an algorithm that decomposed problems by splitting a variable domain in half and then restoring arc consistency on the subproblems [53].

Basic backtrack search backtracks chronologically to undo the last choice and try something else. This can result in silly behavior, where the algorithm tries alternatives for choices that clearly had no bearing on the failure that induced the backtracking. Stallman and Sussman, in the context of circuit analysis, with "dependency-directed backtracking" [67], Gaschnig with "backjumping" [33], and Bruynooghe with "intelligent backtracking" [8] all addressed this problem. These methods in some sense remember the reasons for failure in order to backtrack over legitimate 'culprits'. Stallman and Sussman went further by "learning" new constraints ("nogoods") from failure, which could be used to prune further search. Gaschnig used another form of memory in his "backmarking" algorithm to avoid redundant checking for consistency when backtracking [32].

2.2.5 Analysis

While it was recognized early on that solving CSPs was in general NP-hard, a variety of analytical techniques were brought to bear to evaluate, predict or compare algorithm performance and relate problem complexity to problem structure. In particular, there are tradeoffs to evaluate between the effort required to avoid search, e.g. by exercising more intelligent control or carrying out more inference, and the reduction in search effort obtained.

Knuth [46] and Purdom [63] used probing techniques to estimate the efficiency of backtrack programs. Haralick and Elliott carried out a statistical analysis [35], which was refined by Nudel [62] to compute "expected complexities" for classes of problems defined by basic problem parameters. Brown and Purdom investigated average time behavior [7, 64]. Mackworth and Freuder carried out algorithmic complexity analyses of worst case behavior for various tractable propagation algorithms [55]. They showed the time complexity for arc consistency to be linear in the number of constraints, settling an unresolved issue. This result turned out to be important for constraint programming languages that used arc consistency as a primitive operation [56]. Of course, experimental evaluation was common, though in the early days there was perhaps too much reliance on the n-queens problem, and too little understanding of the potential pitfalls of experiments with random problems.

Problem complexity can be related to problem structure. Seidel [66] developed a dynamic programming synthesis algorithm, using a decomposition technique based on graph cutsets, that related problem complexity to a problem parameter that he called "front length". Freuder [27] proved that problems with tree-structured constraint graphs were tractable by introducing the structural concept of the "width" of a constraint graph, and demonstrating a connection between width and consistency level that ensured that tree-structured problems could be solved with backtrack-free search after arc consistency pre-processing. He subsequently related complexity to problem structure in terms of maximal biconnected components [28] and stable sets [30].

2.3 Conclusions

This chapter has not been a complete history, and certainly not an exhaustive survey. We have focused on the major themes of the early period, but it is worth noting that many very modern sounding topics were also already appearing at this early stage. For example, even in 1965 Golomb and Baumert were making allusions to symmetry and problem reformulation.

Golomb and Baumert concluded in 1965 [34]:

> Thus the success or failure of backtrack often depends on the skill and ingenuity of the programmer in his ability to adapt the basic methods to the problem at hand and in his ability to reformulate the problem so as to exploit the characteristics of his own computing device. That is, backtrack programming (as many other types of programming) is somewhat of an art.

As the rest of this handbook will demonstrate, much progress has been made in making even more powerful methods available to the constraint programmer. However, constraint programming is still "somewhat of an art". The challenge going forward will be to make constraint programming more of an engineering activity and constraint technology more transparently accessible to the non-programmer.

Acknowledgements

We are grateful to Peter van Beek for all his editorial comments, help and support during the preparation of this chapter. This material is based upon works supported by the Science Foundation Ireland under Grant No. Grant 00/PI.1/C075 and by the Natural Sciences and Engineering Research Council of Canada. Alan Mackworth is supported by a Canada Research Chair in Artificial Intelligence.

Bibliography

[1]   H. G. Barrow and J. M. Tenenbaum. MSYS: A system for reasoning about scenes. In *SRI AICenter*, 1975.

[2]   J. R. Bitner and E. M. Reingold. Backtrack programming techniques. *Comm. ACM* 18:651–656, 1975.

[3]   D. G. Bobrow and B. Raphael. New programming languages for artificial intelligence research. *ACM Computing Surveys*, 6(3):153–174, Sept. 1974.

[4]   A. Borning. ThingLab – an object-oriented system for building simulations using constraints. In R. Reddy, editor, *Proceedings of the 5th International Joint Conference on Artificial Intelligence*, pages 497–498, Cambridge, MA, Aug. 1977. William Kaufmann. ISBN 0-86576-057-8.

[5]   A. Borning. Thinglab: A constraint-oriented simulation laboratory. Report CS-79-746, Computer Science Dept., Stanford University, CA, 1979.

[6]   A. Brown. Qualitative knowledge, casual reasoning and the localization of failures. Technical Report AITR-362, MIT Artificial Intelligence Laboratory, Nov. 6 1976. URL http://dspace.mit.edu/handle/1721.1/6921.

[7]   C. A. Brown and P. W. Purdom Jr. An average time analysis of backtracking. *SIAM J. Comput.*, 10:583–593, 1981.

[8]   M. Bruynooghe. Solving combinatorial search problems by intelligent backtracking. *Information Processing Letters*, 12:36–39, 1981.

[9]   R. M. Burstall. A program for solving word sum puzzles. *Computer Journal*, 12(1): 48–51, Feb. 1969.

[10] M. B. Clowes. On seeing things. *Artificial Intelligence*, 2:79–116, 1971.

[11] J. Cohen. Constraint logic programming languages. *CACM*, 33(7):52–68, July 1990. ISSN 0001-0782. URL http://www.acm.org/pubs/toc/Abstracts/0001-0782/79209.html.

[12] A. Colmerauer. Prolog II reference manual and theoretical model. Technical report, Groupe d'Intelligence Arificielle, Univeristé d'Aix-Marseille II, Luminy, Oct. 1982.

[13] A. Colmerauer. Prolog and infinite trees. In K. L. Clark and S.-A. Tärnlund, editors, *Logic Programming*, pages 231–251. Academic Press, 1982.

[14] A. Colmerauer and P. Roussel. The birth of Prolog. In R. L. Wexelblat, editor, *Proceedings of the Conference on History of Programming Languages*, volume 28(3) of *ACM Sigplan Notices*, pages 37–52, New York, NY, USA, Apr. 1993. ACM Press. ISBN 0-89791-570-4.

[15] M. Davis and H. Putnam. A computing procedure for quantification theory. *J. ACM* 7:201–215, 1960.

[16] M. Davis, G. Logemann, and D. Loveland. A machine program for theorem-proving. *Comm. ACM*, 5:394–397, 1962.

[17] J. de Kleer. Local methods for localizing faults in electronic circuits. Technical Report AIM-394, MIT Artificial Intelligence Laboratory, Nov. 6 1976. URL http://dspace.mit.edu/handle/1721.1/6921.

[18] J. de Kleer and G. J. Sussman. Propagation of constraints applied to circuit synthesis. Technical Report AIM-485, MIT Artificial Intelligence Laboratory, Sept. 6 1978. URL http://hdl.handle.net/1721.1/5745.

[19] R. Dechter. *Constraint Processing*. Morgan Kaufmann, 2003.

[20] Y. Descotte and J.-C. Latombe. GARI : A problem solver that plans how to machine

mechanical parts. In *International Joint Conference on Artificial Intelligence (IJCAI '81)*, pages 766–772, 1981.

[21] C. M. Eastman. Automated space planning. *Artificial Intelligence*, 4(1):41–64, 1973.

[22] E. W. Elcock. Absys: the first logic programming language - A retrospective and a commentary. *Journal of Logic Programming*, 9(1):1–17, July 1990.

[23] R. E. Fikes. REF-ARF: A system for solving problems stated as procedures. *Artificial Intelligence*, 1:27–120, 1970.

[24] J. P. Fillmore and S. G. Williamson. On backtracking: A combinatorial description of the algorithm. *SIAM Journal on Computing*, 3(1):41–55, Mar. 1974.

[25] M. S. Fox, B. P. Allen, and G. Strohm. Job-shop scheduling: An investigation in constraint-directed reasoning. In *AAAI82, Proceedings*, pages 155–158, 1982.

[26] E. C. Freuder. Synthesizing constraint expressions. *Comm. ACM*, 21:958–966, 1978.

[27] E. C. Freuder. A sufficient condition for backtrack-free search. *J. ACM*, 29:24–32, 1982.

[28] E. C. Freuder. A sufficient condition for backtrack-bounded search. *J. ACM*, 32: 755–761, 1985.

[29] E. C. Freuder and A. K. Mackworth. Introduction to the special volume on constraint-based reasoning. *Artificial Intelligence*, 58:1–2, 1992.

[30] E. C. Freuder and M. J. Quinn. Taking advantage of stable sets of variables in constraint satisfaction problems. In *Proceedings of the Ninth International Joint Conference on Artificial Intelligence*, pages 1076–1078, Los Angeles, 1985.

[31] J. Gaschnig. A constraint satisfaction method for inference making. In *Proc. 12th Annual Allerton Conf. on Circuit System Theory*, pages 866–874, U. Illinois, 1974.

[32] J. Gaschnig. A general backtracking algorithm that eliminates most redundant tests. In *Proceedings of the Fifth International Joint Conference on Artificial Intelligence*, page 457, Cambridge, Mass., 1977.

[33] J. Gaschnig. Experimental case studies of backtrack vs. Waltz-type vs. new algorithms for satisficing assignment problems. In *Proceedings of the Second Canadian Conference on Artificial Intelligence*, pages 268–277, Toronto, 1978.

[34] S. Golomb and L. Baumert. Backtrack programming. *J. ACM*, 12:516–524, 1965.

[35] R. M. Haralick and G. L. Elliott. Increasing tree search efficiency for constraint satisfaction problems. *Artificial Intelligence*, 14:263–313, 1980.

[36] R. M. Haralick and L. G. Shapiro. The consistent labeling problem: Part I. *IEEE Trans. Pattern Analysis and Machine Intelligence*, 1(2):173–184, Apr. 1979.

[37] R. M. Haralick and L. G. Shapiro. The consistent labeling problem: Part II. *IEEE Trans. Pattern Analysis and Machine Intelligence*, 2(3):193–203, May 1980.

[38] R. M. Haralick, L. S. Davis, A. Rosenfeld, and D. L. Milgram. Reduction operations for constraint satisfaction. *Inf. Sci*, 14(3):199–219, 1978. URL http://dx.doi.org/10.1016/0020-0255(78)90043-9.

[39] P. J. Hayes. Computation and deduction. In *Proc. 2nd International Symposium on Mathematical Foundations of Computer Science*, pages 105–118. Czechoslovakian Academy of Sciences, 1973.

[40] C. Hewitt. PLANNER: A language for proving theorems in robots. In *Proceedings of the First International Joint Conference on Artificial Intelligence*, pages 295–301, Bedford, MA., 1969. Mitre Corporation.

[41] D. A. Huffman. Impossible objects as nonsense sentences. In B. Meltzer and D. Michie, editors, *Machine Intelligence 6*, pages 295–323. Edinburgh Univ. Press,

1971.

[42] J. Jaffar and J.-L. Lassez. Constraint logic programming. In *Fourteenth Annual ACM Symposium on Principles of Programming Languages (POPL)*, pages 111–119, München, 1987.

[43] J. Jaffar and M. J. Maher. Constraint logic programming: A survey. *Journal of Logic Programming*, 19(20):503–581, 1994.

[44] J. Jaffar, S. Michaylov, P. J. Stuckey, and R. H. C. Yap. The CLP($\mathcal{R}$) language and system. *TOPLAS*, 14(3):339–395, July 1992. ISSN 0164-0925. URL http://www.acm.org/pubs/toc/Abstracts/0164-0925/129398.html.

[45] D. E. Knuth. *Fundamental Algorithms*, volume 1 of *The Art of Computer Programming*. Addison-Wesley, 1973.

[46] D. E. Knuth. Estimating the efficiency of backtrack programs. *Mathematics of Computation*, 29:121–136, 1975.

[47] R. A. Kowalski. Predicate logic as a programming language. *Proc. IFIP '74*, pages 569–574, 1974.

[48] R. A. Kowalski. A proof procedure using connection graphs. *J. ACM*, 22(4):572–595, 1975.

[49] J.-L. Lauriere. A language and a program for stating and solving combinatorial problems. *Artificial Intelligence*, 10:29–127, 1978.

[50] D. H. Lehmer. Combinatorial problems with digital computers. In *Proc. of the Fourth Canadian Math. Congress*, pages 160–173, 1957.

[51] E. Lucas. *Récréations Mathématiques*. Gauthier-Villars, Paris, 1891.

[52] A. K. Mackworth. Interpreting pictures of polyhedral scenes. *Artificial Intelligence* 4:121–137, 1973.

[53] A. K. Mackworth. Consistency in networks of relations. *Artificial Intelligence*, 8: 99–118, 1977.

[54] A. K. Mackworth. The logic of constraint satisfaction. *Artificial Intelligence*, 58: 3–20, 1992.

[55] A. K. Mackworth and E. C. Freuder. The complexity of some polynomial network consistency algorithms for constraint satisfaction problems. *Artificial Intelligence* 25:65–74, 247, 1985.

[56] A. K. Mackworth and E. C. Freuder. The complexity of constraint satisfaction revisited. *Artificial Intelligence*, 59:57–62, 1993.

[57] A. K. Mackworth, J. A. Mulder, and W. S. Havens. Hierarchical arc consistency: Exploiting structured domains in constraint satisfaction problems. *Computational Intelligence*, 1:118–126, 1985.

[58] D. Maier. *The Theory of Relational Databases*. Computer Science Press, 1983.

[59] J. J. McGregor. Relational consistency algorithms and their application in finding subgraph and graph isomorphisms. *Inform. Sci.*, 19:229–250, 1979.

[60] U. Montanari. Networks of constraints: Fundamental properties and applications to picture processing. *Inform. Sci.*, 7:95–132, 1974.

[61] N. J. Nilsson. *Problem-Solving Methods in Artificial Intelligence*. McGraw-Hill, New York, 1971.

[62] B. Nudel. Consistent-labeling problems and their algorithms: Expected-complexities and theory-based heuristics. *Artificial Intelligence*, 21:135–178, 1983.

[63] P. W. Purdom Jr. Tree size by partial backtracking. *SIAM J. Comput.*, 7:481–491, 1978.

[64] P. W. Purdom Jr. Search rearrangement backtracking and polynomial average time. *Artificial Intelligence*, 21:117–133, 1983.

[65] A. Rosenfeld, R. A. Hummel, and S. W. Zucker. Scene labelling by relaxation operations. *IEEE Trans. on Systems, Man, and Cybernetics*, SMC-6:420–433, 1976.

[66] R. Seidel. A new method for solving constraint satisfaction problems. In *Proceedings of the Seventh International Joint Conference on Artificial Intelligence*, pages 338–342, Vancouver, 1981.

[67] R. M. Stallman and G. J. Sussman. Forward reasoning and dependency-directed backtracking in a system for computer-aided circuit analysis. *Artificial Intelligence*, 9:135–196, 1977.

[68] M. Stefik. Planning with constraints (MOLGEN: Part 1). *Artificial Intelligence*, 16: 111–140, 1981.

[69] M. J. Stefik. Planning and meta-planning (MOLGEN: Part 2). *Artificial Intelligence*, 16:141–169, 1981.

[70] G. Sussman and T. Winograd. Micro-planner reference manual. Technical Report AIM-203, MIT Artificial Intelligence Laboratory, July 1 1970. URL ftp: //publications.ai.mit.edu/ai-publications/0-499/AIM-203. ps;ftp://publications.ai.mit.edu/ai-publications/pdf/ AIM-203.pdf.

[71] G. J. Sussman and R. M. Stallman. Heuristic techniques in computer-aided circuit analysis. *IEEE Trans. on Circuits and Systems*, CAS-22(11), 1975.

[72] G. J. Sussman and G. L. Steele. CONSTRAINTS: a language for expressing almost-hierarchical descriptions. *Artificial Intelligence*, 14, 1980.

[73] I. E. Sutherland. SKETCHPAD: A man-machine graphical communications system. Technical Report 296, MIT, Lincoln Laboratory, Jan. 1963.

[74] J. M. Tenenbaum and H. G. Barrow. Experiments in interpretation-guided segmentation. *Artif. Intell*, 8(3):241–274, 1977.

[75] J. R. Ullmann. Associating parts of patterns. *Information and Control*, 9(6):583–601, 1966.

[76] J. R. Ullmann, R. M. Haralick, and L. G. Shapiro. Computer architecture for solving consistent labelling problems. *Comput. J*, 28(2):105–111, 1985.

[77] P. Van Hentenryck. *Constraint Satisfaction in Logic Programming*. MIT Press, 1989.

[78] R. L. Walker. An enumerative technique for a class of combinatorial problems. In *Combinatorial Analysis, Proceedings of Symposium in Applied Mathematics, Vol X, Amer. Math. Soc., Providence, RI, USA*, pages 91–94, 1960.

[79] D. Waltz. Understanding line drawings of scenes with shadows. In P. H. Winston, editor, *The Psychology of Computer Vision*, pages 19–91. McGraw-Hill, 1975.

[80] M. V. Wilkes. Constraint-type statements in programming languages. *CACM*, 7(10): 587–588, 1964. URL http://doi.acm.org/10.1145/364888.364967.

Chapter 3

Constraint Propagation

Christian Bessiere

> *Constraint propagation is a form of inference, not search, and as*
> *such is more "satisfying", both technically and aesthetically.*
> —*E.C. Freuder, 2005.*

Constraint reasoning involves various types of techniques to tackle the inherent intractability of the problem of satisfying a set of constraints. Constraint propagation is one of those types of techniques. Constraint propagation is central to the process of solving a constraint problem, and we could hardly think of constraint reasoning without it.

Constraint propagation is a very general concept that appears under different names depending on both periods and authors. Among these names, we can find constraint relaxation, filtering algorithms, narrowing algorithms, constraint inference, simplification algorithms, label inference, local consistency enforcing, rules iteration, chaotic iteration.

Constraint propagation embeds any reasoning which consists in explicitly forbidding values or combinations of values for some variables of a problem because a given subset of its constraints cannot be satisfied otherwise. For instance, in a crossword-puzzle, when you discard the words NORWAY and SWEDEN from the set of European countries that can fit a 6-digit slot because the second letter must be a 'R', you propagate a constraint. In a problem containing two variables x_1 and x_2 taking integer values in 1..10, and a constraint specifying that $|x_1 - x_2| > 5$, by propagating this constraint we can forbid values 5 and 6 for both x_1 and x_2. Explicating these 'nogoods' is a way to reduce the space of combinations that will be explored by a search mechanism.

The concept of constraint propagation can be found in other fields under different kinds and names. (See for instance the propagation of clauses by 'unit propagation' in propositional calculus [40].) Nevertheless, it is in constraint reasoning that this concept shows its most accomplished form. There is no other field in which the concept of constraint propagation appears in such a variety of forms, and in which its characteristics have been so deeply analyzed.

In the last 30 years, the scientific community has put a lot of effort in formalizing and characterizing this ubiquitous concept of constraint propagation and in proposing algorithms for propagating constraints. This formalization can be presented along two main lines: local consistencies and rules iteration. Local consistencies define properties that the constraint problem must satisfy *after* constraint propagation. This way, the operational behavior is left completely open, the only requirement being to achieve the given property on the output. The rules iteration approach, on the contrary, defines properties on the process of propagation itself, that is, properties on the kind/order of operations of reduction applied to the problem.

This chapter does not include *data-flow* constraints [76], even if this line of research has been the focus of quite a lot of work in interactive applications and if some of these papers speak about 'propagation' on these constraints [27]. They are indeed quite far from the techniques appearing in constraint programming.

The rest of this chapter is organized as follows. Section 3.1 contains basic definitions and notations used throughout the chapter. Section 3.2 formalizes all constraint propagation approaches within a unifying framework. Sections 3.3–3.8 contain the main existing types of constraint propagation. Each of these sections presents the basics on the type of propagation addressed and goes briefly into sharper or more recent advances on the subject.

3.1 Background

The notations used in this chapter have been chosen to support all notions presented. I tried to remain on the borderline between 'heavy abstruse notations' and 'ambiguous definitions', hoping I never fall too much on one side or the other of the edge.

A *constraint satisfaction problem (CSP)* involves finding solutions to a constraint network, that is, assignments of values to its variables that satisfy all its constraints. Constraints specify combinations of values that given subsets of variables are allowed to take. In this chapter, we are only concerned with constraint satisfaction problems where variables take their value in a *finite* domain. Without loss of generality, I assume these domains are mapped on the set $\mathbb{Z}$ of integers, and so, I consider only *integer* variables, that is, variables with a domain being a finite subset of $\mathbb{Z}$.

Definition 3.1 (Constraint). *A constraint c is a relation defined on a sequence of variables $X(c) = (x_{i_1}, \ldots, x_{i_{|X(c)|}})$, called the* scheme *of c. c is the subset of $\mathbb{Z}^{|X(c)|}$ that contains the combinations of values (or tuples) $\tau \in \mathbb{Z}^{|X(c)|}$ that satisfy c. $|X(c)|$ is called the* arity *of c. Testing whether a tuple τ satisfies a constraint c is called a* constraint check.

A constraint can be specified extensionally by the list of its satisfying tuples, or intensionally by a formula that is the characteristic function of the constraint. Definition 3.1 allows constraints with an *infinite* number of satisfying tuples. I sometimes write $c(x_1, \ldots, x_k)$ for a constraint c with scheme $X(c) = (x_1, \ldots, x_k)$. Constraints of arity 2 are called *binary* and constraints of arity greater than 2 are called *non-binary*. *Global* constraints are classes of constraints defined by a formula of arbitrary arity (see Section 3.8.2).

Example 3.2. The constraint $\texttt{alldifferent}(x_1, x_2, x_3) \equiv (v_i \neq v_j \wedge v_i \neq v_k \wedge v_j \neq v_k)$ allows the infinite set of 3-tuples in $\mathbb{Z}^3$ such that all values are different. The constraint

$c(x_1, x_2, x_3) = \{(2, 2, 3), (2, 3, 2), (2, 3, 3), (3, 2, 2), (3, 2, 3), (3, 3, 2)\}$ allows the finite set of 3-tuples containing both values 2 and 3 and only them.

Definition 3.3 (Constraint network). *A constraint network (or network) is composed of:*

- *a finite sequence of integer variables $X = (x_1, \ldots, x_n)$,*
- *a domain for X, that is, a set $D = D(x_1) \times \ldots \times D(x_n)$, where $D(x_i) \subset \mathbb{Z}$ is the finite set of values, given in extension,[1] that variable x_i can take, and*
- *a set of constraints $C = \{c_1, \ldots, c_e\}$, where variables in $X(c_j)$ are in X.*

Given a network N, I sometimes use X_N, D_N and C_N to denote its sequence of variables, its domain and its set of constraints. Given a variable x_i and its domain $D(x_i)$, $min_D(x_i)$ denotes the smallest value in $D(x_i)$ and $max_D(x_i)$ its greatest one. (Remember that we consider integer variables.)

In the whole chapter, I consider constraints involving at least two variables. This is not a restriction because domains of variables are semantically equivalent to unary constraints. They are separately specified in the definition of constraint network because the domains are given extensionally whereas a constraint c can be defined by any Boolean function on $\mathbb{Z}^{|X(c)|}$ (in extension or not). I also consider that no variable is repeated in the scheme of a constraint. This restriction could be relaxed in most cases, but it simplifies the notations. The vocabulary of graphs is often used to describe networks. A network can indeed be associated with a *(hyper)graph* where variables are nodes and where schemes of constraints are (hyper)edges.

According to Definitions 3.1 and 3.3, the variables X_N of a network N and the scheme $X(c)$ of a constraint $c \in C_N$ are sequences of variables, not sets. This is required because the order of the values matters for tuples in D_N or in c. Nevertheless, it simplifies a lot the notations to consider sequences as sets when no confusion is possible. For instance, given two constraints c and c', $X(c) \subseteq X(c')$ means that constraint c involves only variables that are in the scheme of c', whatever their ordering in the scheme. Given a tuple τ on a sequence Y of variables, and given a sequence $W \subseteq Y$, $\tau[W]$ denotes the restriction of τ to the variables in W, ordered according to W. Given $x_i \in Y$, $\tau[x_i]$ denotes the value of x_i in τ. If $X(c) = X(c')$, $c \subseteq c'$ means that for all $\tau \in c$ the reordering of τ according to $X(c')$ satisfies c'.

Example 3.4. Let $(1, 1, 2, 4, 5)$ be a tuple on $Y = (x_1, x_2, x_3, x_4, x_5)$ and $W = (x_3, x_2, x_4)$. $\tau[x_3]$ is the value 2 and $\tau[W]$ is the tuple $(2, 1, 4)$. Given $c(x_1, x_2, x_3)$ defined by $x_1 + x_2 = x_3$ and $c'(x_2, x_1, x_3)$ defined by $x_2 + x_1 \leq x_3$, we have $c \subseteq c'$.

We also need the concepts of projection, intersection, union and join. Given a constraint c and a sequence $Y \subseteq X(c)$, $\pi_Y(c)$ denotes the *projection* of c on Y, that is, the relation with scheme Y that contains the tuples that can be extended to a tuple on $X(c)$ satisfying c. Given two constraints c_1 and c_2 sharing the same scheme $X(c_1) = X(c_2)$, $c_1 \cap c_2$ (resp. $c_1 \cup c_2$) denotes the *intersection* (resp. the *union*) of c_1 and c_2, that is, the relation with scheme $X(c_1)$ that contains the tuples τ satisfying both c_1 and c_2 (resp. satisfying c_1 or c_2). Given a set of constraints $\{c_1, \ldots, c_k\}$, $\bowtie_{j=1}^{k} c_j$ (or $\bowtie \{c_1, \ldots, c_k\}$) denotes the *join*

---

[1]*The condition on the domains given in extension can be relaxed, especially in numerical problems where variables take values in a discretization of the reals. (See Chapter 16 in Part II.)*

of $c_1, \ldots, c_k$, that is, the relation with scheme $\cup_{j=1}^{k} X(c_j)$ that contains the tuples τ such that $\tau[X(c_j)] \in c_j$ for all j, $1 \le j \le k$.

Backtracking algorithms are based on the principle of assigning values to variables until all variables are *instantiated*.

Definition 3.5 (Instantiation). *Given a network $N = (X, D, C)$,*

- *An* instantiation I on $Y = (x_1, \ldots, x_k) \subseteq X$ *is an assignment of values* $v_1, \ldots v_k$ *to the variables* $x_1, \ldots, x_k$, *that is, I is a tuple on Y. I can be denoted by* $((x_1, v_1), \ldots, (x_k, v_k))$ *where* (x_i, v_i) *denotes the value* v_i *for* x_i.
- *An instantiation I on Y is* valid *if for all* $x_i \in Y$, $I[x_i] \in D(x_i)$.
- *An instantiation I on Y is* locally consistent *iff it is valid and for all* $c \in C$ *with* $X(c) \subseteq Y$, $I[X(c)]$ *satisfies c. If I is not locally consistent, it is* locally inconsistent
- *A* solution *to a network N is an instantiation I on X which is locally consistent. The set of solutions of N is denoted by* $sol(N)$.
- *An instantiation I on Y is* globally consistent *(or* consistent*) if it can be extended to a solution (i.e., there exists* $s \in sol(N)$ *with* $I = s[Y]$*).*

Example 3.6. Let $N = (X, D, C)$ be a network with $X = (x_1, x_2, x_3, x_4)$, $D(x_i) = \{1, 2, 3, 4, 5\}$ for all $i \in [1..4]$ and $C = \{c_1(x_1, x_2, x_3), c_2(x_1, x_2, x_3), c_3(x_2, x_4)\}$ with $c_1(x_1, x_2, x_3) = $ alldifferent(x_1, x_2, x_3), $c_2(x_1, x_2, x_3) \equiv (x_1 \le x_2 \le x_3)$, and $c_3(x_2, x_4) \equiv (x_4 \ge 2 \cdot x_2)$. We thus have $\pi_{\{x_1, x_2\}}(c_1) \equiv (x_1 \ne x_2)$ and $c_1 \cap c_2 \equiv (x_1 < x_2 < x_3)$. $I_1 = ((x_1, 1), (x_2, 2), (x_4, 7))$ is a non valid instantiation on $Y = (x_1, x_2, x_4)$ because $7 \notin D(x_4)$. $I_2 = ((x_1, 1), (x_2, 1), (x_4, 3))$ is a locally consistent instantiation on Y because c_3 is the only constraint with scheme included in Y and it is satisfied by $I_2[X(c_3)]$. However, I_2 is not globally consistent because it does not extend to a solution of N. $sol(N) = \{(1, 2, 3, 4), (1, 2, 3, 5)\}$.

There are many works in the constraint reasoning community that put some restrictions on the definition of a constraint network. These restrictions can have some consequences on the notions handled. I define the main restrictions appearing in the literature and that I will use later.

Definition 3.7 (Normalized and binary networks).

- *A network N is* normalized *iff two different constraints in C_N do not involve exactly the same variables.*
- *A network N is* binary *iff for all* $c_i \in C_N$, $|X(c_i)| = 2$.

When a network is both binary and normalized, a constraint $c(x_i, x_j) \in C$ is often denoted by c_{ij}. To simplify even further the notations, c_{ji} denotes its *transposition*, i.e., the constraint $c(x_j, x_i) = \{(v_j, v_i) \mid (v_i, v_j) \in c_{ij}\}$, and since there cannot be ambiguity with another constraint, I act as if c_{ji} was in C as well.

Given two normalized networks $N = (X, D, C)$ and $N' = (X, D', C')$, $N \sqcup_N N$ denotes the network $N'' = (X, D'', C'')$ with $D'' = D \cup D'$ and $C'' = \{c'' \mid \exists c \in C, \exists c' \in C', X(c) = X(c')$ and $c'' = c \cup c'\}$.

The constraint reasoning community often used constraints with a finite number of tuples, and even more, constraints that only allow valid tuples, that is, combinations of values from the domains of the variables involved. I call these constraints 'embedded'.

Definition 3.8 (Embedded network). *Given a network N and a constraint $c \in C_N$, the embedding of c in D_N is the constraint $\hat{c}$ with scheme $X(c)$ such that $\hat{c} = c \cap \pi_{X(c)}(D_N)$. A network N is embedded iff for all $c \in C_N, c = \hat{c}$.*

In complexity analysis, we sometimes need to refer to the size of a network. The *size* of a network N is equal to $|X_N| + \sum_{x_i \in X_N} |D_N(x_i)| + \sum_{c_j \in C_N} \|c_j\|$, where $\|c\|$ is equal to $|X(c)| \cdot |c|$ if c is given in extension, or equal to the size of its encoding if c is defined by a Boolean function.

3.2 Formal Viewpoint

This section formally characterizes the concept of constraint propagation. The aim is essentially to relate the different notions of constraint propagation.

The constraint satisfaction problem being NP-complete, it is usually solved by backtrack search procedures that try to extend a partial instantiation to a global one that is consistent. Exploring the whole space of instantiations is of course too expensive. The idea behind constraint propagation is to make the constraint network more explicit (or *tighter*) so that backtrack search commits into less inconsistent instantiations by detecting local inconsistency earlier. I first introduce the following preorder on constraint networks.

Definition 3.9 (Preorder $\preceq$ on networks). *Given two networks N and N', we say that $N' \preceq N$ iff $X_{N'} = X_N$ and any instantiation I on $Y \subseteq X_N$ locally inconsistent in N is locally inconsistent in N' as well.*

From the definition of local inconsistency of an instantiation (Definition 3.5) I derive the following property of constraint networks ordered according to $\preceq$.

Proposition 3.10. *Given two networks N and N', $N' \preceq N$ iff $X_{N'} = X_N$, $D_{N'} \subseteq D_N$,[2] and for any constraint $c \in C_N$, for any tuple τ on $X(c)$ that does not satisfy c, either τ is not valid in $D_{N'}$ or there exists a constraint c' in $C_{N'}$, $X(c') \subseteq X(c)$, such that $\tau[X(c')] \notin c'$.*

The relation $\preceq$ is not an order because there can be two different networks N and N' with $N \preceq N' \preceq N$.

Definition 3.11 (Nogood-equivalence). *Two networks N and N' such that $N \preceq N' \preceq N$ are said to be nogood-equivalent. (A nogood is a partial instantiation that does not lead to a solution.)*

Example 3.12. Let $N = (X, D, C)$ be the network with $X = \{x_1, x_2, x_3\}$, $D(x_1) = D(x_2) = D(x_3) = \{1, 2, 3, 4\}$ and $C = \{x_1 < x_2, x_2 < x_3, c(x_1, x_2, x_3)\}$ where $c(x_1, x_2, x_3) = \{(111), (123), (222), (333)\}$. Let $N' = (X, D, C')$ be the network with $C' = \{x_1 < x_2, x_2 < x_3, c'(x_1, x_2, x_3)\}$, where $c'(x_1, x_2, x_3) = \{(123), (231), (312)\}$. The only difference between N and N' is that the latter contains c' instead of c. For any tuple τ on $X(c)$ (resp. $X(c')$) that does not satisfy c (resp. c'), there exists a constraint in C' (resp. in C) that makes τ locally inconsistent. As a result, $N \preceq N' \preceq N$ and N and N' are nogood-equivalent.

---

[2]$D_{N'} \subseteq D_N$ *because we supposed that networks do not contain unary constraints, and so, instantiations of size 1 can be made locally inconsistent only because of the domains.*

Constraint propagation transforms a network N by tightening D_N, by tightening constraints from C_N, or by adding new constraints to C_N. Constraint propagation does not remove redundant constraints, which is more a reformulation task. I define the space of networks that can be obtained by constraint propagation on a network N.

Definition 3.13 (Tightenings of a network). *The space $\mathcal{P}_N$ of all possible* tightenings *of a network $N = (X, D, C)$ is the set of networks $N' = (X, D', C')$ such that $D' \subseteq D$ and for all $c \in C$ there exists $c' \in C'$ with $X(c') = X(c)$ and $c' \subseteq c$.*

Note that $\mathcal{P}_N$ does not contain all networks $N' \preceq N$. In Example 3.12, $N' \notin \mathcal{P}_N$ because $c' \not\subseteq c$. However, if $N'' = (X, D, C'')$ with $C'' = \{x_1 < x_2, x_2 < x_3, c'' = c \cup c'\}$, we have $N \in \mathcal{P}_{N''}$ and $N' \in \mathcal{P}_{N''}$. The set of networks $\mathcal{P}_N$ together with $\preceq$ forms a preordered set. The top element of $\mathcal{P}_N$ according to $\preceq$ is N itself and the bottom elements are the networks with empty domains.[3] In $\mathcal{P}_N$ we are particularly interested in networks that preserve the set of solutions of N. $\mathcal{P}_N^{sol}$ denotes the subset of $\mathcal{P}_N$ containing only the elements N' of $\mathcal{P}_N$ such that $sol(N') = sol(N)$. Among the networks in $\mathcal{P}_N^{sol}$ those that are the smallest according to $\preceq$ have interesting properties.

Proposition 3.14 (Global consistency). *Let $N = (X, D, C)$ be a network, and $G_N = (X, D_G, C_G)$ be a network in $\mathcal{P}_N^{sol}$. If G_N is such that for all $N' \in \mathcal{P}_N^{sol}, G_N \preceq N$ then any instantiation I on $Y \subseteq X$ which is locally consistent in G_N can be extended to a solution of N. G_N is called a* globally consistent *network.*

Proof. Suppose there exists an instantiation I on $Y \subseteq X$ locally consistent in G_N which does not extend to a solution. Build the network $N' = (X, D_G, C_G \cup \{c\})$ where $X(c) = Y$ and $c = \mathbb{Z}^{|Y|} \setminus \{I\}$. $N' \in \mathcal{P}_N^{sol}$ because $G_N \in \mathcal{P}_N^{sol}$ and I does not extend to a solution of N. In addition, I is locally inconsistent in N'. So, $G_N \not\preceq N'$. □

Thanks to Proposition 3.14 we see the advantage of having a globally consistent network of N. A simple brute-force backtrack search procedure applied on a globally consistent network is guaranteed to produce a solution in a backtrack-free manner. However, globally consistent networks have a number of disadvantages that make them impossible to use in practice. A globally consistent network is not only exponential in time to compute, but in addition, its size is in general exponential in the size of N. In fact, building a globally consistent network is similar to generating and storing all minimal nogoods of N. Building a globally consistent network is so hard that a long tradition in constraint programming is to try to transform N into an element of $\mathcal{P}_N^{sol}$ as close as possible to global consistency at reasonable cost (usually keeping polynomial time and space). This is constraint propagation.

Rules iteration and local consistencies are two ways of formalizing constraint propagation. *Rules iteration* consists in characterizing for each constraint (or set of constraints) a set of reduction rules that tighten the network. *Reduction rules* are sufficient conditions to rule out values (or instantiations) that have no chance to appear in a solution. The second —and most well-known— way of considering constraint propagation is via the notion of local consistency. A *local consistency* is a property that characterizes some necessary conditions on values (or instantiations) to belong to solutions. A local consistency property

---

[3]Remember that we consider that unary constraints are expressed in the domains.

(denoted by Φ) is defined regardless of the domains or constraints that will be present in the network. A network is Φ-consistent if and only if it satisfies the property Φ.

It is difficult to say more about constraint propagation in completely general terms. The preorder $(\mathcal{P}_N, \preceq)$ is indeed too weak to characterize the features of constraint propagation. Most of the constraint propagation techniques appearing in constraint programming (or at least those that are used in solvers) are limited to modifications of the domains. So, I first concentrate on this subcase, that I call *domain-based* constraint propagation. I will come back to the general case in Section 3.4.

Definition 3.15 (Domain-based tightenings). *The space $\mathcal{P}_{ND}$ of domain-based tightenings of a network $N = (X, D, C)$ is the set of networks in $\mathcal{P}_N$ with the same constraints as N, that is, $N' \in \mathcal{P}_{ND}$ iff $X_{N'} = X$, $D_{N'} \subseteq D$ and $C_{N'} = C$.*

Proposition 3.16 (Partial order on networks). *Given a network N, the relation $\preceq$ restricted to the set $\mathcal{P}_{ND}$ is a partial order (denoted by $\leq$).*

$(\mathcal{P}_{ND}, \leq)$ is a partially ordered set (*poset*) because given two networks $N_1 = (X_1, D_1, C_1)$ and $N_2 = (X_2, D_2, C_2)$, $N_1 \leq N_2 \leq N_1$ implies that $X_1 = X_2$, $C_1 = C_2$, and $D_1 \subseteq D_2 \subseteq D_1$, which means that $N_1 = N_2$. In fact, the poset $(\mathcal{P}_{ND}, \leq)$ is isomorphic to the partial order $\subseteq$ on D_N. We are interested in the subset $\mathcal{P}_{ND}^{sol}$ of $\mathcal{P}_{ND}$ containing all the networks that preserve the set of solutions of N. $\mathcal{P}_{ND}^{sol}$ has the same top element as $\mathcal{P}_{ND}$, namely N itself, and a *unique* bottom element $G_{ND} = (X_N, D_G, C_N)$, where for any $x_i \in X_N$, $D_G(x_i)$ only contains values belonging to a solution of N, i.e., $D_G(x_i) = \pi_{\{x_i\}}(sol(N))$. Such a network was named *variable-completable* by Freuder [56].

Domain-based constraint propagation looks for an element in $\mathcal{P}_{ND}^{sol}$ on which the search space to explore is smaller (that is, values have been pruned from the domains). Since finding G_{ND} is NP-hard (consistency of N reduces to checking non emptiness of domains in G_{ND}), domain-based constraint propagation usually consists of polynomial techniques that produce a network which is an approximation of G_{ND}. The network N' produced by a domain-based constraint propagation technique always verifies $G_{ND} \leq N' \leq N$, that is, $D_G \subseteq D_{N'} \subseteq D_N$.

Domain-based rules iteration consists in applying for each constraint $c \in C_N$ a set of reduction rules that rule out values of x_i that cannot appear in a tuple satisfying c. Domain-based reduction rules are also named *propagators*. For instance, if $c \equiv (|x_1 - x_2| = k)$, a propagator for c on x_1 can be $D_N(x_1) \leftarrow D_N(x_1) \cap [min_{D_N}(x_2) - k .. min_{D_N}(x_2) + k]$. Applying propagators iteratively tightens D_N while preserving the set of solutions of N. In other words, propagators slide down the poset $(\mathcal{P}_{ND}, \leq)$ without moving out of $\mathcal{P}_{ND}^{sol}$. Reduction rules will be presented in Section 3.7. From now on, we concentrate on domain-based local consistencies. Any property Φ that specifies a necessary condition on values to belong to solutions can be considered as a domain-based local consistency. Nevertheless, we usually consider only those properties that are stable under union.

Definition 3.17 (Stability under union). *A domain-based property Φ is stable under union iff for any Φ-consistent networks $N_1 = (X, D_1, C)$ and $N_2 = (X, D_2, C)$, the network $N' = (X, D_1 \cup D_2, C)$ is Φ-consistent.*

Example 3.18. Let Φ be the property that guarantees that for each constraint c and variable $x_i \in X(c)$, at least half of the values in $D(x_i)$ belong to a valid tuple satisfying c. Let $X = (x_1, x_2)$ and $C = \{x_1 = x_2\}$. Let D_1 be the domain with $D_1(x_1) = \{1, 2\}$

and $D_1(x_2) = \{2\}$. Let D_2 be the domain with $D_2(x_1) = \{2, 3\}$ and $D_2(x_2) = \{2\}$. (X, D_1, C) and (X, D_2, C) are both Φ-consistent but $(X, D_1 \cup D_2, C)$ is not Φ-consistent because among the three values for x_1, only value 2 can satisfy the constraint $x_1 = x_2$. Φ is not stable under union.

Stability under union brings very useful features for local consistencies. Among all networks in $\mathcal{P}_{ND}$ that verify a local consistency Φ, there is a particular one.

Theorem 3.19 (Φ-closure). *Let $N = (X, D, C)$ be a network and Φ be a domain-based local consistency. Let $\Phi(N)$ be the network (X, D_Φ, C) where $D_\Phi = \cup\{D' \subseteq D \mid (X, D', C)$ is Φ-consistent$\}$. If Φ is stable under union, $\Phi(N)$ is Φ-consistent and is the* unique *network in $\mathcal{P}_{ND}$ such that for any Φ-consistent network $N' \in \mathcal{P}_{ND}$, $N' \leq \Phi(N)$. $\Phi(N)$ is called the Φ-closure of N. (By convention, we suppose $(X, \emptyset, C)$ is Φ-consistent.)*

$\Phi(N)$ has some interesting properties. The first one I can point out is that it preserves the solutions: $sol(\Phi(N)) = sol(N)$. This is not the case for all Φ-consistent networks in $\mathcal{P}_{ND}$.

Example 3.20. Let Φ be the property that guarantees that all values for all variables can be extended consistently to a second variable. Consider the network $N = (X, D, C)$ with variables x_1, x_2, x_3, domains all equal to $\{1, 2\}$ and $C = \{x_1 \leq x_2, x_2 \leq x_3, x_1 \neq x_3\}$. Let D_1 be the domain with $D_1(x_1) = D_1(x_2) = \{1\}$ and $D_1(x_3) = \{2\}$. $(X, D_1, C$ is Φ-consistent but does not contain the solution $(x_1 = 1, x_2 = 2, x_3 = 2)$ which is in $sol(N)$. In fact, $\Phi(N) = (X, D_\Phi, C)$ with $D_\Phi(x_1) = \{1\}$, $D_\Phi(x_2) = \{1, 2\}$ and $D_\Phi(x_3) = \{2\}$.

Computing a particular Φ-consistent network of $\mathcal{P}_{ND}$ can be difficult. G_{ND} for instance, is obviously Φ-consistent for any domain-based local consistency Φ, but it is NP-hard to compute. The second interesting property of $\Phi(N)$ is that it can be computed by a greedy algorithm.

Proposition 3.21 (Fixpoint). *If a domain-based consistency property Φ is stable under union, then for any network $N = (X, D, C)$, the network $N' = (X, D', C)$, where D' is obtained by iteratively removing values that do not satisfy Φ until no such value exists, is the Φ-closure of N.*

Corollary 3.22. *If a domain-based consistency property Φ is polynomial to check, finding $\Phi(N)$ is polynomial as well.*

By *achieving* (or *enforcing*) Φ-consistency on a network N, I mean finding the Φ closure $\Phi(N)$.

I define a partial order on local consistencies to express how much they permit to go down the poset $(\mathcal{P}_{ND}, \leq)$. A domain-based local consistency Φ_1 is *at least as strong as* another local consistency Φ_2 if and only if for any network N, $\Phi_1(N) \leq \Phi_2(N)$. If in addition there exists a network N' such that $\Phi_1(N') < \Phi_2(N')$, then Φ_1 is *strictly stronger* than Φ_2. If there exist networks N' and N'' such that $\Phi_1(N') < \Phi_2(N')$ and $\Phi_2(N'') < \Phi_1(N'')$, Φ_1 and Φ_2 are *incomparable*.

When networks are both normalized and embedded, stability under union, Φ-closure, and the 'stronger' relation between local consistencies can be extended to local consistencies other than domain-based ones by simply replacing $\mathcal{P}_{ND}$ by $\mathcal{P}_N$, the union on domains $\cup$ by the union on networks $\sqcup_N$ (see Section 3.1), and the partial order $\leq$ on $\mathcal{P}_{ND}$ by the preorder $\preceq$ on $\mathcal{P}_N$ (see Section 3.4).

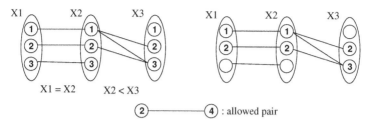

Figure 3.1: Network of Example 3.23 before arc consistency (left) and after (right).

3.3 Arc Consistency

Arc consistency is the oldest and most well-known way of propagating constraints. This is indeed a very simple and natural concept that guarantees every value in a domain to be consistent with every constraint.

Example 3.23. Let N be the network depicted in Fig. 3.1(left). It involves three variables x_1, x_2 and x_3, domains $D(x_1) = D(x_2) = D(x_3) = \{1, 2, 3\}$, and constraints $c_{12} \equiv (x_1 = x_2)$ and $c_{23} \equiv (x_2 < x_3)$. N is not arc consistent because there are some values inconsistent with some constraints. Checking constraint c_{12} does not permit to remove any value. But when checking constraint c_{23}, we see that $(x_2, 3)$ must be removed because there is no value greater than it in $D(x_3)$. We can also remove value 1 from $D(x_3)$ because of constraint c_{23}. Removing 3 from $D(x_2)$ causes in turn the removal of value 3 for x_1 because of constraint c_{12}. Now, all remaining values are compatible with all constraints.

REF-ARF [51], is probably one of the first systems incorporating a feature which looks similar to arc consistency (even if the informal description does not permit to be sure of the equivalence). In papers by Waltz [124] and Gaschnig [61], the correspondence is more evident since algorithms for achieving arc consistency were presented. But the seminal papers on the subject are due to Mackworth, who is the first who clearly defined the concept of arc consistency for binary constraints [86], who extended definitions and algorithms to non-binary constraints [88], and who analyzed the complexity [89].

I give a definition of arc consistency in its most general form, i.e., for arbitrary constraint networks (in which case it is often called generalized arc consistency). In its first formal presentation, Mackworth limited the definition to binary normalized networks.

Definition 3.24 ((Generalized) arc consistency ((G)AC)). *Given a network $N = (X, D, C)$, a constraint $c \in C$, and a variable $x_i \in X(c)$,*

- *A value $v_i \in D(x_i)$ is consistent with c in D iff there exists a valid tuple τ satisfying c such that $v_i = \tau[\{x_i\}]$. Such a tuple is called a* support *for (x_i, v_i) on c.*
- *The domain D is (generalized) arc consistent on c for x_i iff all the values in $D(x_i)$ are consistent with c in D (that is, $D(x_i) \subseteq \pi_{\{x_i\}}(c \cap \pi_{X(c)}(D))$).*
- *The network N is (generalized) arc consistent iff D is (generalized) arc consistent for all variables in X on all constraints in C.*
- *The network N is arc inconsistent iff $\emptyset$ is the only domain tighter than D which is (generalized) arc consistent for all variables on all constraints.*

By notation abuse, when there is no ambiguity on the domain D to consider, we often say 'constraint c is arc consistent' instead of 'D is arc consistent on c for all $x_i \in X(c)$' We also say 'variable x_i is arc consistent on constraint c' instead of 'all values in $D(x_i)$ are consistent with c in D'. When a constraint c_{ij} is binary and a tuple $\tau = (v_i, v_j)$ supports (x_i, v_i) on c_{ij}, we often refer to (x_j, v_j) (rather than to τ itself) when we speak about a 'support for (x_i, v_i)'.

Historically, many papers on constraint satisfaction made the simplifying assumption that networks are binary and normalized. This has the advantage that notations become much simpler (see Section 3.1) and new concepts are easier to present. But this had some strange effects that we must bear in mind.

First, the name 'arc consistency' is so strongly bound to binary networks that even if the definition is perfectly the same for both binary and non-binary constraints, a different name has often been used for arc consistency on non-binary constraints. Some papers use *hyper* arc consistency, or *domain* consistency, but the most common name is *generalized* arc consistency. In the following, I will use indifferently arc consistency (AC) or generalized arc consistency (GAC), though I will use GAC when the network is explicitly non-binary.

The second strange effect of associating AC with binary normalized networks is the confusion between the notions of arc consistency and 2-consistency. (As we will see in Section 3.4, 2-consistency guarantees that any instantiation of a value to a variable can be consistently extended to any second variable.) On binary networks, 2-consistency is at least as strong as AC. When the binary network is normalized, arc consistency and 2-consistency are equivalent. However, this is not true in general. The following examples show that 2-consistency is strictly stronger than AC on non normalized binary networks and that generalized arc consistency and 2-consistency are incomparable on arbitrary networks.

Example 3.25. Let N be a network involving two variables x_1 and x_2, with domains $\{1, 2, 3\}$, and the constraints $x_1 \leq x_2$ and $x_1 \neq x_2$. This network is arc consistent because every value has a support on every constraint. However, this network is not 2-consistent because the instantiation $x_1 = 3$ cannot be extended to x_2 and the instantiation $x_2 = 1$ cannot be extended to x_1.

Let N be a network involving three variables x_1, x_2, and x_3, with domains $D(x_1) = D(x_2) = \{2, 3\}$ and $D(x_3) = \{1, 2, 3, 4\}$, and the constraint $\texttt{alldifferent}(x_1, x_2, x_3$ N is 2-consistent because every value for any variable can be extended to a locally consistent instantiation on any second variable. However, this network is not GAC because the values 2 and 3 for x_3 do not have support on the $\texttt{alldifferent}$ constraint.

3.3.1 Complexity of Arc Consistency

There are a number of questions related to GAC reasoning. It is worth analyzing their complexity. Bessiere et al. have characterized five questions that can be asked about a constraint [21]. Some of the questions are more of an academic nature whereas others are at the heart of propagation algorithms. These questions can be asked in general, or on a particular class of constraints, such as a given global constraint (see Section 3.8.2). These questions can be adapted to other local consistencies that we will present in latter sections. In the following, I use the notation PROBLEM[data] to refer to the instance of PROBLEM with the input 'data'.

GACSUPPORT

Instance. A constraint c, a domain D on $X(c)$, and a value v for variable x_i in $X(c)$

Question. Does value v for x_i have a support on c in D?

GACSUPPORT is at the core of all generic arc consistency algorithms. GACSUPPORT is generally asked for all values one by one.

ISITGAC

Instance. A constraint c, a domain D on $X(c)$

Question. Does GACSUPPORT$[c, D, x_i, v]$ answer 'yes' for each variable $x_i \in X(c)$ and each value $v \in D(x_i)$?

ISITGAC has both practical and theoretical importance. If enforcing GAC on a particular constraint is expensive, we may first test whether it is necessary or not to launch the propagation algorithm (i.e., whether the constraint is already GAC). On the academic side, this question is commonly used to compare different levels of local consistency.

NOGACWIPEOUT

Instance. A constraint c, a domain D on $X(c)$

Question. Is there a non empty $D' \subseteq D$ on which ISITGAC$[c, D']$ answers 'yes'?

NOGACWIPEOUT occurs when GAC is maintained during search by a backtrack procedure. At each node in the search tree (i.e., after each instantiation of a value to a variable), we want to know if the remaining network can be made GAC without wiping out the domain. If not, we must unassign one of the variables already instantiated.

MAXGAC

Instance. A constraint c, a domain D_0 on $X(c)$, and a domain $D \subseteq D_0$

Question. Is $(X(c), D, \{c\})$ the arc consistent closure of $(X(c), D_0, \{c\})$?

Arc consistency algorithms (see next subsection) are asked to return the arc consistent closure of a network, that is, the subdomain that is GAC and any larger subdomain is not GAC. MAXGAC characterizes this 'maximality' problem.

GACDOMAIN

Instance. A constraint c, a domain D_0 on $X(c)$

Output. The domain D such that MAXGAC$[c, D_0, D]$ answers 'yes'

GACDOMAIN returns the arc consistent closure, that is, the domain that a GAC algorithm computes. GACDOMAIN is not a decision problem as it computes something other than 'yes' or 'no'.

In [20, 21], Bessiere et al. showed that all five questions are NP-hard in general. In addition, they showed that on any particular class of constraints, NP-hardness of a question implies NP-hardness of other questions.

Theorem 3.26 (Dependencies in the NP-hardness of GAC questions). *Given a class C of constraints,* GACSUPPORT *is NP-hard on C iff* NOGACWIPEOUT *is NP-hard on C.* GACSUPPORT *is NP-hard on C iff* GACDOMAIN *is NP-hard on C. If* MAXGAC *is NP-hard on C then* GACSUPPORT *is NP-hard on C. If* ISITGAC *is NP-hard on C then* MAXGAC *is NP-hard on C.*

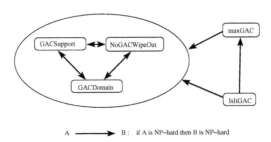

Figure 3.2: Dependencies between intractability of arc consistency questions

A summary of the dependencies in Theorem 3.26 is given in Fig. 3.2. Note that because each arrow from question A to question B in Fig. 3.2 means that A can be rewritten as a polynomial number of calls to B, we immediately derive that tractability of B implies tractability of A. Whereas the decision problems GACSUPPORT, ISITGAC, and NOGACWIPEOUT are in NP, MAXGAC may be outside NP. In fact, MAXGAC is D^P complete in general. The D^P complexity class contains problems which are the conjunction of a problem in NP and one in coNP [101].

Assuming P $\neq$ NP, GAC reasoning is thus not tractable in general. In fact, the best complexity that can be achieved for an algorithm enforcing GAC on a network with any kind of constraints is in $O(erd^r)$, where e is the number of constraints and r is the largest arity of a constraint.

Though not related to GAC, constraint *entailment* ([70]) is a sixth question that is used by constraint solvers to speed up propagation. An entailed constraint can safely be disconnected from the network.

ENTAILED
Instance. A constraint c, a domain D on $X(c)$
Question. Does ISITGAC$[c, D']$ answer 'yes' for all $D' \subseteq D$?

Entailment of c on D means that $D \subseteq c$. ENTAILED is coNP-complete in general. There is no dependency between intractability of entailment and intractability of the GAC questions. On a class C of constraints, ENTAILED can be tractable and the GAC questions intractable, or the reverse, or both tractable or intractable.

3.3.2 Arc Consistency Algorithms

Proposing efficient algorithms for enforcing arc consistency has always been considered as a central question in the constraint reasoning community. A first reason is that arc consistency is the basic propagation mechanism that is probably used in all solvers. A second reason is that the new ideas that permit to improve efficiency of arc consistency can usually be applied to algorithms achieving other local consistencies. This is why I spend some time presenting the main algorithms that have been introduced, knowing that the techniques involved can be used for other local consistencies presented in forthcoming sections. I follow a chronological presentation to emphasize the incremental process that led to the current algorithms.

Algorithm 3.1: AC3 / GAC3

function Revise3(**in** x_i: variable; c: constraint): **Boolean** ;
   begin
1   CHANGE ← **false**;
2   **foreach** $v_i \in D(x_i)$ **do**
3   **if** $\nexists \tau \in c \cap \pi_{X(c)}(D)$ *with* $\tau[x_i] = v_i$ **then**
4   remove v_i from $D(x_i)$;
5   CHANGE ← **true**;
6   return CHANGE ;
   end

function AC3/GAC3(**in** X: set): **Boolean** ;
   begin
       /* initalisation */;
7       $Q \leftarrow \{(x_i, c) \mid c \in C, x_i \in X(c)\}$;
       /* propagation */;
8   **while** $Q \neq \emptyset$ **do**
9   select and remove (x_i, c) from Q;
10   **if** $Revise(x_i, c)$ **then**
11   **if** $D(x_i) = \emptyset$ **then** return **false** ;
12   **else** $Q \leftarrow Q \cup \{(x_j, c') \mid c' \in C \wedge c' \neq c \wedge x_i, x_j \in X(c') \wedge j \neq i\}$;
13   return **true** ;
   end

AC3

The most well-known algorithm for arc consistency is the one proposed by Mackworth in [86] under the name AC3. It was proposed for binary normalized networks and actually achieves 2-consistency. It was extended to GAC in arbitrary networks in [88]. This algorithm is quite simple to understand. The burden of the general notations being not so high, I present it in its general version. (See Algorithm 3.1.)

The main component of GAC3 is the revision of an arc, that is, the update of a domain wrt a constraint.[4] Updating a domain $D(x_i)$ wrt a constraint c means removing every value in $D(x_i)$ that is not consistent with c. The function Revise(x_i, c) takes each value v_i in $D(x_i)$ in turn (line 2), and explores the space $\pi_{X(c) \setminus \{x_i\}}(D)$, looking for a support on c for v_i (line 3). If such a support is not found, v_i is removed from $D(x_i)$ and the fact that $D(x_i)$ has been changed is flagged (lines 4–5). The function returns true if the domain $D(x_i)$ has been reduced, false otherwise (line 6).

The main algorithm is a simple loop that revises the arcs until no change occurs, to ensure that all domains are consistent with all constraints. To avoid too many useless calls to Revise (as this is the case in the very basic AC algorithms such as AC1 or AC2), the algorithm maintains a list Q of all the pairs (x_i, c) for which we are not guaranteed that $D(x_i)$ is arc consistent on c. In line 7, Q is filled with all possible pairs (x_i, c) such that $x_i \in X(c)$. Then, the main loop (line 8) picks the pairs (x_i, c) in Q one by one (line 9) and calls Revise(x_i, c) (line 10). If $D(x_i)$ is wiped out, the algorithm returns false (line 11). Otherwise, if $D(x_i)$ is modified, it can be the case that a value for another variable

---

[4]The word 'arc' comes from the binary case but we also use it on non-binary constraints.

x_j has lost its support on a constraint c' involving both x_i and x_j. Hence, all pairs $(x_j, c'$ such that $x_i, x_j \in X(c')$ must be put again in Q (line 12). When Q is empty, the algorithm returns true (line 13) as we are guaranteed that all arcs have been revised and all remaining values of all variables are consistent with all constraints

Proposition 3.27 (GAC3). *GAC3 is a sound and complete algorithm for achieving arc consistency that runs in $O(er^3 d^{r+1})$ time and $O(er)$ space, where r is the greatest arity among constraints.*

McGregor proposed a different way of propagating constraints in AC3, that was later named *variable-oriented*, as opposed to the arc-oriented propagation policy of AC3 [91]. Instead of putting in Q all arcs that should be revised after a change in $D(x_i)$ (line 12), we simply put x_i. Q contains variables for which a change in their domain has not yet been propagated. When picking a variable x_j from Q, the algorithm revises all arcs (x_i, c) that could lead to further deletions because of x_j. The implementation of this version of AC3 is simpler because the elements in Q are just variables. But this less precise information has a drawback. An arc can be revised several times whereas the classical AC3 would revise it once. For instance, imagine a network containing a constraint c with scheme (x_1, x_2, x_3) If a modification occurs on x_2 because of a constraint c', AC3 puts (x_1, c) and (x_3, c) in Q. If a modification occurs on x_3 because of another constraint c'' while the previous arcs have not yet been revised, AC3 adds (x_2, c) to Q but not (x_1, c) which is already there. The same scenario with McGregor's version will put x_2 and x_3 in Q. Picking them from Q in sequence, it will revise (x_1, c) and (x_3, c) because of x_2, and (x_1, c) and (x_2, c) because of x_3. (x_1, c) has been revised twice. Boussemart et al. proposed a modified version of McGregor's algorithm that solves this problem by storing a counter for each arc [28].

From now on, I switch to binary normalized networks because most of the literature used this simplification, and I do not want to make assumptions on which extension the authors would have chosen. Nevertheless, the ideas always allow extensions to non normalized binary networks, and most of the time to networks with non-binary constraints.

Corollary 3.28 (AC3). *AC3 achieves arc consistency on binary networks in $O(ed^3)$ time and $O(e)$ space.*

The time complexity of AC3 is not optimal. The fact that function `Revise` does not remember anything about its computations to find supports for values leads AC3 to do and redo many times the same constraint checks.

Example 3.29. Let x, y and z be three variables linked by the constraints $c_1 \equiv x \leq$ and $c_2 \equiv y \neq z$, with $D(x) = D(y) = \{1, 2, 3, 4\}$ and $D(z) = \{3\}$. `Revise`(x, c_1) requires 1 constraint check for finding support for $(x, 1)$, 2 checks for $(x, 2)$, etc., so a total of 1+2+3+4=**10** constraint checks to prove that all values in $D(x)$ are consistent with c_1. All these constraint checks are depicted as arrows in Fig. 3.3.a. `Revise`(y, c_1) requires **4** additional constraint checks to prove that y values are all consistent with $(x, 1)$ `Revise`(y, c_2) requires **4** constraint checks to prove that all values are consistent with $(z, 3)$ except $(y, 3)$ which is removed. Hence, the arc (x, c_1) is put in Q. `Revise`(z, c_2) requires **1** single constraint check to prove that $(z, 3)$ is consistent with $(y, 1)$.

When (x, c_1) is picked from Q, a new call to `Revise`(x, c_1) is launched (Fig. 3.3.b). It requires 1+2+3+3=**9** checks, among which only $((x, 3), (y, 4))$ has not already been performed at the first call.

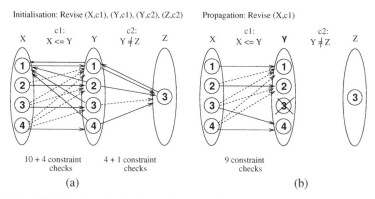

Figure 3.3: AC3 behavior depicted on Example 3.29. (Plain arrows represent positive constraint checks whereas dashed arrows represent negative ones.)

AC4

AC3 being non optimal, Mohr and Henderson proposed AC4 to improve the time complexity [92, 93]. The idea of AC4, as opposed to AC3, is to store a lot of information. AC3 performs the minimum amount of work inside a call to Revise, just ensuring that all remaining values of x_i are consistent with c and memorizing nothing. The price to pay is to redo much of the work if the same Revise is recalled. AC4 stores the maximum amount of information in a preprocessing step in order to avoid redoing several times the same constraint check during the propagation of deletions.

AC4 is presented in Algorithm 3.2. It computes a counter counter$[x_i, v_i, x_j]$ for each triple (x_i, v_i, x_j) where $c_{ij} \in C$ and $v_i \in D(x_i)$. This counter will finally say how many supports v_i has on c_{ij}. AC4 also builds lists $S[x_j, v_j]$ containing all values that are supported by (x_j, v_j) on c_{ij}. In the initialization phase, AC4 performs all possible constraint checks on all constraints. Each time a support $v_j \in D(x_j)$ is found for (x_i, v_i) on c_{ij}, counter$[x_i, v_i, x_j]$ is incremented, and (x_i, v_i) is added to $S[x_j, v_j]$ (lines 3 and 5). Each time a value is found without support on a constraint, it is removed from the domain and put in the list Q for future propagation (line 4). Once the initialization is finished, we enter the propagation loop (line 7), which consists in propagating the consequences of the removals of values in Q. For each value (x_j, v_j) picked from Q (line 8), we just need to decrement counter$[x_i, v_i, x_j]$ for each value $(x_i, v_i) \in S[x_j, v_j]$ to maintain the counters up to date (line 11). If counter$[x_i, v_i, x_j]$ reaches zero, this means that (x_j, v_j) was the last support for (x_i, v_i) on c_{ij}. (x_i, v_i) is removed and put in the list Q (lines 12 and 13). When Q is empty, we know that all values remaining in the domains have a non zero counter on all their constraints, and so are arc consistent.

AC4 is the first algorithm in a category later named 'fine-grained' algorithms [126] because they perform propagations (via list Q) at the level of values. 'Coarse-grained' algorithms, such as AC3, propagate at the level of constraints (or arcs), which is less precise and can involve unnecessary work.

Proposition 3.30 (AC4). *AC4 achieves arc consistency on binary normalized networks in $O(ed^2)$ time and $O(ed^2)$ space. Its time complexity is optimal.*

Algorithm 3.2: AC4

---

function AC4(**in** X: set): **Boolean** ;
  begin
     /* initialization */;
1     $Q \leftarrow \emptyset$; $S[x_j, v_j] = 0, \forall v_j \in D(x_j), \forall x_j \in X$;
2   **foreach** $x_i \in X, c_{ij} \in C, v_i \in D(x_i)$ **do**
3   initialize $\mathtt{counter}[x_i, v_i, x_j]$ to $|\{v_j \in D(x_j) \mid (v_i, v_j) \in c_{ij}\}|$;
4   **if** $\mathtt{counter}[x_i, v_i, x_j] = 0$ **then** remove v_i from $D(x_i)$ and add (x_i, v_i) to Q;
5   add (x_i, v_i) to each $S[x_j, v_j]$ s.t. $(v_i, v_j) \in c_{ij}$;
6   **if** $D(x_i) = \emptyset$ **then** return **false** ;
     /* propagation */;
7   **while** $Q \neq \emptyset$ **do**
8   select and remove (x_j, v_j) from Q;
9   **foreach** $(x_i, v_i) \in S[x_j, v_j]$ **do**
10   **if** $v_i \in D(x_i)$ **then**
11             $\mathtt{counter}[x_i, v_i, x_j] = \mathtt{counter}[x_i, v_i, x_j] - 1$;
12   **if** $\mathtt{counter}[x_i, v_i, x_j] = 0$ **then**
13   remove v_i from $D(x_i)$; add (x_i, v_i) to Q;
14   **if** $D(x_i) = \emptyset$ **then** return **false** ;
15   return **true** ;
  end

Example 3.31. Take again the network in Example 3.29 with constraints $c_1 \equiv x \leq y$ and $c_2 \equiv y \neq z$, and domains $D(x) = D(y) = \{1, 2, 3, 4\}$ and $D(z) = \{3\}$. In its initialization phase, AC4 first counts the number of supports of each value on each constraint and builds the lists of supported values. Thus, in its initialization, AC4 performs all possible constraint checks for every value in each domain, that is, $4 \cdot 4 = \mathbf{16}$ constraint checks on c_1 and $4 \cdot 1 = \mathbf{4}$ on c_2.[5] At the end of this phase, the data structures are the following:

$$
\begin{array}{lll}
\mathtt{counter}[x, 1, y] = 4 & \mathtt{counter}[y, 1, x] = 1 & \mathtt{counter}[y, 1, z] = 1 \\
\mathtt{counter}[x, 2, y] = 3 & \mathtt{counter}[y, 2, x] = 2 & \mathtt{counter}[y, 2, z] = 1 \\
\mathtt{counter}[x, 3, y] = 2 & \mathtt{counter}[y, 3, x] = 3 & \mathtt{counter}[y, 3, z] = 0 \\
\mathtt{counter}[x, 4, y] = 1 & \mathtt{counter}[y, 4, x] = 4 & \mathtt{counter}[y, 4, z] = 1 \\
& & \mathtt{counter}[z, 3, y] = 3
\end{array}
$$

$$
\begin{array}{ll}
S[x, 1] = \{(y, 1), (y, 2), (y, 3), (y, 4)\} & S[y, 1] = \{(x, 1), (z, 3)\} \\
S[x, 2] = \{(y, 2), (y, 3), (y, 4)\} & S[y, 2] = \{(x, 1), (x, 2), (z, 3)\} \\
S[x, 3] = \{(y, 3), (y, 4)\} & S[y, 3] = \{(x, 1), (x, 2), (x, 3)\} \\
S[x, 4] = \{(y, 4)\} & S[y, 4] = \{(x, 1), (x, 2), (x, 3), (x, 4), (z, 3)\} \\
& S[z, 3] = \{(y, 1), (y, 2), (y, 4)\}
\end{array}
$$

The only counter equal to zero is $\mathtt{counter}[y, 3, z]$. So, $(y, 3)$ is removed and AC4 enters the propagation loop with $(y, 3)$ in Q. When $(y, 3)$ is picked from Q, $S[y, 3]$ is traversed and $\mathtt{counter}[x, 1, y]$, $\mathtt{counter}[x, 2, y]$,$\mathtt{counter}[x, 3, y]$ are decremented (because $(x, 1), (x, 2), (x, 3)$ are in $S[y, 3]$). None of these counters are equal to zero and no

---

[5]In the original version of AC4 presented in [92], each constraint c_{ij} is processed twice (once for x_i and once for x_j), which gives 32 constraint checks on c_1 and 8 on c_2. The general version presented in [93] processes each constraint only once, updating all relevant counters and lists at the same time.

value is removed. We observe that the propagation of the deletion of $(y, 3)$ did not require any constraint check. It required traversals of $S[..]$ lists and updates of counters.

While being optimal in time, AC4 does not only suffer from its high space complexity. Its very expensive initialization phase can be by itself prohibitive in time. In fact, we can informally say that AC4 has optimal worst-case time complexity but it almost always reaches this worst-case. Wallace discussed this issue in [120]. In addition, even when the initialization phase has finished, AC4 maintains a so accurate view of the process that it spends a lot of effort updating its counters and traversing its lists. This is visible in Example 3.31, where the removal of $(y, 3)$ provoked traversal of $S[y, 3]$ and counter updates, whereas all remaining values had supports.

The non-binary version GAC4, proposed by Mohr and Masini in [93], is in the optimal $O(erd^r)$ time complexity given in Section 3.3.1, where r is the greatest arity among all constraints.

AC6

Bessiere and Cordier proposed AC6, a compromise between AC3 laziness and AC4 eagerness [15, 14]. The motivation behind AC6 is both to keep the optimal worst-case time complexity of AC4 and to stop the search for support for a value on a constraint as soon as the first support is found, as done in `Revise` of AC3. In addition, AC6 maintains a data structure lighter than AC4. In fact, the idea in AC6 is not to count all the supports a value has on a constraint, but just to ensure that it has *at least* one. AC6 only needs lists S, where $S[x_j, v_j]$ contains all values for which (x_j, v_j) is the *current* support. That is, $(x_i, v_i) \in S[x_j, v_j]$ if and only if v_j was the first support found for v_i on c_{ij}. [6]

In Algorithm 3.3, AC6 looks for one support (the *first* one or *smallest* one with respect to the ordering on integers) for each value (x_i, v_i) on each constraint c_{ij} (line 3). When (x_j, v_j) is found as the smallest support of (x_i, v_i) on c_{ij}, (x_i, v_i) is added to $S[x_j, v_j]$, the list of values currently having (x_j, v_j) as smallest support (line 4). If no support is found, (x_i, v_i) is removed and is put in the list Q for future propagation (line 5). The propagation loop (line 7) consists in propagating the consequences of the removal of values in Q. When (x_j, v_j) is picked from Q, AC6 looks for the *next* support on c_{ij} for each value (x_i, v_i) in $S[x_j, v_j]$. Instead of starting at $min_D(x_j)$ as AC3 would do, it starts at the value of $D(x_j)$ following v_j (line 11). If a new support v'_j is found, (x_i, v_i) is put in $S[x_j, v'_j]$ (line 12). Otherwise, (x_i, v_i) is removed and put in Q (line 14). When Q is empty, we know that all remaining values have a current support on every constraint.

Like AC4, AC6 is a fine-grained algorithm because it propagates along values. It does not reconsider constraint c_{ij} when the removed value (x_j, v_j) has no chance to provoke another removal in $D(x_i)$, that is, when $D(x_i) \cap S[x_j, v_j] = \emptyset$.

Proposition 3.32 (AC6). *AC6 achieves arc consistency on binary normalized networks in $O(ed^2)$ time and $O(ed)$ space.*

Example 3.33. I show what the data structures of AC6 are on the example used for AC3 (Example 3.29) and for AC4 (Example 3.31), i.e., constraints $c_1 \equiv x \leq y$ and $c_2 \equiv y \neq z$ and domains $D(x) = D(y) = \{1, 2, 3, 4\}$ and $D(z) = \{3\}$. In its initialization phase, AC6

---

[6]A similar technique, called 'watch literals', has independently been proposed by Moskewicz et al. for efficient unit propagation in their Chaff solver for SAT [97].

Algorithm 3.3: AC6

---

function AC6(**in** X: set): **Boolean** ;
   begin
      /* initialization */;
1      $Q \leftarrow \emptyset; S[x_j, v_j] = 0, \forall v_j \in D(x_j), \forall x_j \in X$;
2   **foreach** $x_i \in X, c_{ij} \in C, v_i \in D(x_i)$ **do**
3         $v_j \leftarrow$ smallest value in $D(x_j)$ s.t. $(v_i, v_j) \in c_{ij}$;
4   **if** v_j *exists* **then** add (x_i, v_i) to $S[x_j, v_j]$;
5   **else** remove v_i from $D(x_i)$ and add (x_i, v_i) to Q;
6   **if** $D(x_i) = \emptyset$ **then** return **false** ;
      /* propagation */;
7   **while** $Q \neq \emptyset$ **do**
8   select and remove (x_j, v_j) from Q;
9   **foreach** $(x_i, v_i) \in S[x_j, v_j]$ **do**
10   **if** $v_i \in D(x_i)$ **then**
11              $v'_j \leftarrow$ smallest value in $D(x_j)$ greater than v_j s.t. $(v_i, v_j) \in c_{ij}$;
12   **if** v'_j *exists* **then** add (x_i, v_i) to $S[x_j, v'_j]$;
13   **else**
14   remove v_i from $D(x_i)$; add (x_i, v_i) to Q;
15   **if** $D(x_i) = \emptyset$ **then** return **false** ;
16   return **true** ;
   end

---

looks for *one* support (the smallest) for each value on each constraint and stores the fact that a value (x_j, v_j) has been found as supporting (x_i, v_i) by adding (x_i, v_i) to $S[x_j, v_j$ Thus, in its initialization, AC6 performs the same number of constraint checks as AC3, namely 10+4 on c_1 and 4+1 on c_2. At the end of this phase, the data structures are the following,

$$S[x, 1] = \{(y, 1), (y, 2), (y, 3), (y, 4)\} \qquad S[y, 1] = \{(x, 1), (z, 3)$$
$$S[x, 2] = \{\} \qquad S[y, 2] = \{(x, 2)\}$$
$$S[x, 3] = \{\} \qquad S[y, 3] = \{(x, 3)\}$$
$$S[x, 4] = \{\} \qquad S[y, 4] = \{(x, 4)\}$$
$$S[z, 3] = \{(y, 1), (y, 2), (y, 4)\}$$

and the list Q contains $(y, 3)$ which has been removed. When AC6 enters the propagation loop it pops $(y, 3)$ from Q, $S[y, 3]$ is traversed and a new support *greater than* 3 is sought for $(x, 3)$. $(3, 4) \in c_1(x, y)$, so $(x, 3)$ is added to $S[y, 4]$, which supports now both $(x, 3)$ and $(x, 4)$. The deletion of $(y, 3)$ required a single constraint check and the traversal of list $S[y, 3]$. Note that $S[y, 3]$ contained less values than in AC4 because AC6 stores a single support per value.

AC2001

In fine-grained algorithms, such as AC4 or AC6, the propagation is value-oriented. The deletion of a value (x_j, v_j) is directly propagated through Q on values (x_i, v_i) that had

---

Algorithm 3.4: Function `Revise` for AC2001

---

function `Revise2001`(**in** x_i: variable; c_{ij}: constraint)**: Boolean** ;
   begin
1   CHANGE $\leftarrow$ **false**;
2   **foreach** $v_i \in D(x_i)$ *s.t.* `Last`$(x_i, v_i, x_j) \notin D(x_j)$ **do**
3          $v_j \leftarrow$ smallest value in $D(x_j)$ greater than `Last`(x_i, v_i, x_j) s.t. $(v_i, v_j) \in c_{ij}$;
4   **if** v_j *exists* **then** `Last`$(x_i, v_i, x_j) \leftarrow v_j$;
5   **else**
6   remove v_i from $D(x_i)$;
7   CHANGE $\leftarrow$ **true**;
8   return CHANGE ;
   end

(x_j, v_j) as support (that is, on values (x_i, v_i) that are in $S[x_j, v_j]$). Coarse-grained algorithms are arc-oriented. They do not propagate the consequences of value removals to other values. They propagate changes in the domain of a variable x_j on the other variables x_i sharing a constraint c with x_j: List Q contains pairs (x_i, c) for which some variable x_j in $X(c)$ has changed. Although coarse-grained algorithms are less precise in the way they propagate, they have a double advantage. First, the architecture of constraint solvers (see Section 3.8) usually supports an arc-oriented propagation and not a value-oriented one. Second, all fine-grained algorithms require lists $S[..]$ of supported values as data structure, which is more complex to implement and maintain. These were the motivations for AC2001, the first (and only) optimal coarse-grained algorithm [24, 126, 25].

AC2001 follows the same framework as AC3, but achieves optimality by storing the smallest support for each value on each constraint, like AC6. However, the way this information is stored and used differs from that in AC6. AC2001 does not use lists $S[x_j, v_j]$ to store those (x_i, v_i) that have v_j as smallest support on c_{ij}. It uses a pointer `Last`$[x_i, v_i, x_j]$ that contains v_j.

AC2001 differs from AC3 only by its `Revise` function and by its initialization phase which needs to initialize the pointers `Last`$[x_i, v_i, x_j]$ to some dummy value smaller than $min_D(x_j)$. In `Revise2001` (Algorithm 3.4), when a value v_j in $D(x_j)$ is found to support (x_i, v_i) on c_{ij}, AC2001 assigns v_j to `Last`$[x_i, v_i, x_j]$ (line 4). The next time (x_i, c_{ij}) will be revised, supports will be sought for (x_i, v_i) only if `Last`$[x_i, v_i, x_j]$ is no longer in $D(x_j)$ (line 2). More importantly, optimality is obtained because values in $D(x_j)$ that are smaller than `Last`$[x_i, v_i, x_j]$ are not checked again because they were already unsuccessfully checked in previous calls to `Revise2001` (line 3).

Proposition 3.34 (AC2001). *AC2001 achieves arc consistency on binary normalized networks in $O(ed^2)$ time and $O(ed)$ space.*

Example 3.35. Again I show the data structures of AC2001 on the example used for the other algorithms, i.e., constraints $c_1 \equiv x \leq y$ and $c_2 \equiv y \neq z$ and domains $D(x) = D(y) = \{1, 2, 3, 4\}$ and $D(z) = \{3\}$. In its initialization phase, AC2001 looks for the smallest support for each value on each constraint and stores it in the `Last` structure. It performs exactly the same constraint checks as AC3 or AC6. At the end of this phase, the data structures are the following,

$$
\begin{array}{lll}
\texttt{Last}[x,1,y] = 1 & \texttt{Last}[y,1,x] = 1 & \texttt{Last}[y,1,z] = 3 \\
\texttt{Last}[x,2,y] = 2 & \texttt{Last}[y,2,x] = 1 & \texttt{Last}[y,2,z] = 3 \\
\texttt{Last}[x,3,y] = 3 & \texttt{Last}[y,3,x] = 1 & \texttt{Last}[y,3,z] = nil \\
\texttt{Last}[x,4,y] = 4 & \texttt{Last}[y,4,x] = 1 & \texttt{Last}[y,4,z] = 3 \\
& & \texttt{Last}[z,3,y] = 1
\end{array}
$$

and the list Q contains (x, c_1) because $(y, 3)$ has been removed while revising c_2. When AC2001 enters the propagation loop it pops (x, c_1) from Q, and calls $\texttt{Revise}(x, c_1)$. It checks whether $\texttt{Last}[x, 1, y]$, $\texttt{Last}[x, 2, y]$, $\texttt{Last}[x, 3, y]$ and $\texttt{Last}[x, 4, y]$ are still in $D(y)$. $\texttt{Last}[x, 3, y]$ is no longer in $D(y)$, so a new support *greater than* 3 is sought for $(x, 3)$. $(3, 4)$ satisfies $c_1(x, y)$, so $\texttt{Last}[x, 3, y]$ receives value 4. The deletion of $(y, 3)$ required checking if the $\texttt{Last}$ pointers of values in $D(x)$ were still in $D(y)$, and a single constraint check to find a new support for $(x, 3)$.

AC2001 can easily be extended to a GAC2001 non-binary version [25].

3.3.3 Other Improvements

I have presented the main techniques to enforce arc consistency on a network. Other kinds of techniques exist to reduce the cost of arc consistency. They are usually added to one of the arc consistency algorithms presented above to improve its performance. I cannot be exhaustive, but here are two of those types of techniques.

Bidirectionality

Constraints are said to be *multidirectional* because when a tuple τ is found to support (x_i, v_i) on a constraint c, it is also a support for any $(x_j, v_j) \in \tau$ on the same constraint. The binary version of multidirectionality is called *bidirectionality*. This property, which can seem obvious, is not used as much as it could be by the algorithms presented so far.

In fact, AC3 partially uses it when it avoids putting (x_j, c) in Q after modifying x_i in $\texttt{Revise}(x_i, c)$ (line 12 in Algorithm 3.1): A value v_i removed from $D(x_i)$ had no support on c, so its removal cannot discard a support for a value in $D(x_j)$.

Gaschnig proposed to use bidirectionality more explicitly. The algorithm DEE [62] is an extension of AC3 that uses a 'Revise-both' procedure to process $\texttt{Revise}(x_i, c_{ij})$ and $\texttt{Revise}(x_j, c_{ij})$ in sequence. As a first step, Revise-both performs the same work as $\texttt{Revise}(x_i, c_{ij})$, but in addition, marks every value in $D(x_j)$ which has been found in a support for a value in $D(x_i)$. Once all values of x_i are checked, Revise-both revises x_j on c_{ij} by only looking for support for unmarked values of $D(x_j)$. Values marked during the first phase are guaranteed to have support. DEE does not store these marks from a call to Revise-both to another. Besides, in the propagation phase, arcs are often revised in only one direction at a time, which reduces the gain of DEE.

Van Dongen proposed a heuristic approach of using bidirectionality [114]. The algorithm AC_b uses the same idea as DEE, trying to avoid work when both arcs (x_i, c_{ij}) and (x_j, c_{ij}) are in Q. AC_b does not check supports in lexicographic ordering but tries to maximize the number of 'double-support' checks. A double-support check is a constraint check $c_{ij}(v_i, v_j)$ for which neither v_i nor v_j are known to be supported on c_{ij}. The motivation is that if $c_{ij}(v_i, v_j)$ is true, we deduce support for two values at the price of a single constraint check.

Bidirectionality was used even more extensively in AC7 [18, 19], an extension of AC6. Thanks to the lists of supported values of AC6, and additional pointers, AC7 fully exploits bidirectionality. This means that a constraint check $c_{ij}(v_i, v_j)$ is performed when looking for support for (x_i, v_i) on c_{ij} only if $c_{ji}(v_j, v_i)$ has never been checked while looking for supports for (x_j, v_j) on c_{ji} and there does not exist $v'_j \in D(x_j)$ such that $c_{ji}(v'_j, v_i)$ has already been successfully checked as support for (x_j, v'_j). The non-binary version of AC7 [23] is used in IlogSolver [71] to propagate general constraints. As for GAC4, it runs in the optimal $O(erd^r)$ time complexity.

Lecoutre et al. proposed several extensions of AC2001 that permit to adapt the techniques used in AC7 to coarse-grained algorithms [81]. AC3.2 is an algorithm that partially exploits bidirectionality on positive constraint checks. AC3.3 fully exploits bidirectionality on positive constraint checks. AC3.2* and AC3.3* are extensions of AC3.2 and AC3.3 that also exploit bidirectionality on negative constraint checks, like in AC7. An extensive experimentation suggests that AC3.3 is the best stand alone arc consistency algorithm, whereas AC3.2 is the best when maintained during search.

Ordering the propagation list

Another way of improving the time needed to enforce arc consistency is by revising first the arcs that will prune the most or that will be the cheapest to revise. In their seminal paper on the subject, Wallace and Freuder proposed several heuristics to reorder the propagation list in AC3 [121]. Among the different heuristics they analyzed, the best seemed to be the one selecting first the arcs (x_i, c_{ij}) such that the variable x_j against which to revise has the smallest domain.

Gent et al. applied to arc consistency the general criterion of 'constrainedness' defined in [65]. They proposed to select first the arc that minimizes the constrainedness κ_{ac} of arc consistency [64]. They show that this heuristic is a good way to reduce the number of constraint checks but is heavy to compute. Interestingly, approximations of their criterion give some of the good heuristics proposed by Wallace and Freuder.

The most comprehensive study on ordering heuristics for coarse-grained arc consistency algorithms was recently proposed by Boussemart et al. in [28]. They not only studied heuristics to reorder the propagation list Q, but also the type of information we put in it. Q can be a list of arcs to revise, as in regular AC3 (arc-oriented revision), a list of variables whose domain has been modified as in McGregor's version (variable-oriented revision), or a list of constraints which had a variable of their scheme modified. Lists of variables being much shorter than lists of arcs, they showed that heuristics handling Q are less time consuming when incorporated in variable-oriented implementations. Since McGregor's algorithm suffers from redundant revisions (see Subsection 3.3.2), Boussemart et al. proposed a modified version that avoids these redundant revisions while keeping the advantage of variable-oriented revision. As for saving constraint checks, they found that several heuristics close to that already proposed by Wallace and Freuder or by van Dongen [121, 113] show good performance. Among all, they recommend a variable-oriented implementation of coarse-grained algorithms (they experimented with AC3.2) in which the variable with the smallest domain is picked first from Q.

3.4   Higher Order Consistencies

In Section 3.3, we have seen that arc consistency, which is the most natural technique for tightening a network, has received great attention from the community. Nevertheless, this is not the only way to tighten a network, and as early as in the 70's, several authors proposed techniques that discover more inconsistencies than arc consistency.

3.4.1   Path Consistency

Path consistency was proposed by Montanari as a necessary condition for the consistency of pairs of values in binary normalized networks [95]. Roughly speaking, it says that if for a given pair of values (v_i, v_j) on a pair of variables (x_i, x_j) there exists a sequence of variables from x_i to x_j such that we cannot find a sequence of values for these variables starting at v_i and finishing at v_j, and satisfying all binary constraints along the sequence, then (v_i, v_j) is inconsistent.

Definition 3.36 (Path consistency). *Let $N = (X, D, C)$ be a normalized network.*

- *Given two variables x_i and x_j in X, the pair of values $(v_i, v_j) \in D(x_i) \times D(x_j)$ is path consistent iff for any sequence of variables $Y = (x_i = x_{k_1}, x_{k_2}, \ldots, x_{k_p} = x_j)$ such that for all $q \in [1..p-1], c_{k_q, k_{q+1}} \in C$, there exists a tuple of values $(v_i = v_{k_1}, v_{k_2}, \ldots, v_{k_p} = v_j) \in \pi_Y(D)$ such that for all $q \in [1..p-1], (v_{k_q}, v_{k_{q+1}}) \in c_{k_q, k_{q+1}}.$*

- *The network N is* path consistent (PC) *iff for any pair of variables $(x_i, x_j), i \neq j$ any locally consistent pair of values on (x_i, x_j) is path consistent.*

Example 3.37. Consider the network N with variables x_1, x_2, x_3, domains $D(x_1) = D(x_2) = D(x_3) = \{1, 2\}$, and $C = \{x_1 \neq x_2, x_2 \neq x_3\}$. N is not path consistent because neither $((x_1, 1), (x_3, 2))$ nor $((x_1, 2), (x_3, 1))$ can be extended to a value of x satisfying both c_{12} and c_{23}. The network $N' = (X, D, C \cup \{x_1 = x_3\})$ is path consistent.

Montanari observed that it is sufficient to enforce path consistency only on paths of length 2 to obtain the same level of local consistency as path consistency.

Definition 3.38 (2-path consistency). *Let $N = (X, D, C)$ be a normalized network.*

- *Given two variables x_i and x_j in X, the pair of values $(v_i, v_j) \in D(x_i) \times D(x_j)$ is 2-path consistent iff for any third variable $x_k \in X$ with $c_{ik} \in C$ and $c_{kj} \in C$, there exists a value $v_k \in D(x_k)$ such that $(v_i, v_k) \in c_{ik}$ and $(v_j, v_k) \in c_{kj}.$*

- *The network N is* 2-path consistent *iff for any pair of variables $(x_i, x_j), i \neq j$, any locally consistent pair of values on (x_i, x_j) is 2-path consistent.*

Proposition 3.39. *Path consistency and 2-path consistency are equivalent.*

Path consistency does not reduce domains of variables but removes pairs of values. As a result, the path consistent closure of a normalized network N is not in $\mathcal{P}_{ND}^{sol}$. I define $\mathcal{P}_{N2}$ as the subset of $\mathcal{P}_N$ where networks are normalized and differ from N only by adding or tightening binary constraints. The path consistent closure $PC(N)$ of N is the union (according to $\sqcup_N$) of all path consistent networks in $\mathcal{P}_{N2}$. In $\mathcal{P}_{N2}$, there can be several networks nogood-equivalent to $PC(N)$ because constraints with the same scheme can differ on non valid tuples, which does not change the set of locally inconsistent instantiations. Nevertheless, PC algorithms represent modified constraints extensionally, generating only embedded constraints. So, if we consider networks where all binary constraints are embedded, the relation $\preceq$ is a partial order on $\mathcal{P}_{N2}$ and PC algorithms are guaranteed to converge on $PC(N)$.

Several algorithms achieving PC were proposed in the literature. Each time a new technique was proposed for arc consistency, it was soon applied to path consistency. PC1 [95, 87] can be seen as the path consistency counterpart of the brute-force AC1. PC2 is the extension of AC3 to path consistency [87]. PC3 [92] and PC4 [68] use lists of support, like AC4, to reach optimality. PC5 [111] and PC6 [32] extend AC6. PC7 [31] and PC8 [33] are simplifications of PC6 that perform well in practice. PC5++ [111] applies bidirectionality of AC7. Finally, PC2001 [126, 25] extends AC2001.

A drawback of path consistency is that enforcing it can produce additional constraints that were not in C_N (see Example 3.37). Furthermore, even when a constraint $c(x_i, x_j)$ is already in C_N, its refinement by PC can impose to change its semantics and to represent this new constraint extensionally whereas it was given as a function.

Example 3.40. Consider the network with variables x_1, x_2, x_3, domains $D(x_1) = D(x_2) = D(x_3) = \{1, 2, 3, 4\}$, and $C = \{|x_1 - x_2| \geq 2, x_2 \neq x_3, x_1 \neq x_3\}$. These three constraints can be given by their arithmetic expression if the constraint toolkit in use permits them. However, enforcing PC will discard the tuples $(2, 4)$, and $(3, 1)$ from c_{13}, which probably requires a storage in extension of this constraint. If c_{13} had a specific propagation algorithm for enforcing AC on it (see Section 3.8), it no longer works on this new constraint.

The last thing we can notice is that even if path consistency is usually considered in binary normalized networks, nothing in Definition 3.36 prevents its use on non-binary normalized networks. Non-binary constraints are just ignored.

3.4.2 k-Consistencies

A few years after Montanari's paper, Freuder extended the notion of local consistencies stronger than AC to a whole class of consistencies, called k-consistencies [53, 54].

Definition 3.41 (k-consistency). *Let $N = (X, D, C)$ be a network.*

- *Given a set of variables $Y \subseteq X$ with $|Y| = k - 1$, a locally consistent instantiation I on Y is k-consistent iff for any kth variable $x_{i_k} \in X \setminus Y$ there exists a value $v_{i_k} \in D(x_{i_k})$ such that $I \cup \{(x_{i_k}, v_{i_k})\}$ is locally consistent.*

- *The network N is k-consistent iff for any set Y of $k - 1$ variables, any locally consistent instantiation on Y is k-consistent.*

Given a normalized network N, $\mathcal{P}_{Nk}$ denotes the subset of $\mathcal{P}_N$ containing all normalized networks N' in which only constraints of arity k can differ from N. More formally, $N' \in \mathcal{P}_{Nk}$ if and only if $N' \in \mathcal{P}_N$, $D_{N'} = D_N$, and any constraint in $C_{N'} \setminus C_N$ has arity k. The k-consistent closure of N is the union (according to $\sqcup_N$) of all k-consistent networks in $\mathcal{P}_{N(k-1)}$. (Enforcing k-consistency makes explicit nogoods of size $k-1$.) I restrict to normalized networks because $\sqcup_N$ is not defined on arbitrary networks (see Section 3.2). $\preceq$ is a partial order on $\mathcal{P}_{N(k-1)}$ only if all constraints of arity $k-1$ are embedded.

As observed by Dechter [46], even if 3-consistency has strong similarities with (2-)path consistency, it is not equivalent. Indeed, 3-consistency ensures that any instantiation of length 2 can be extended to an instantiation involving any third variable without violating *any* constraint, whereas (2-)path consistency only guarantees that *binary* constraints are not violated.

Example 3.42. Suppose a network involving variables x_1, x_2, x_3 with domains $D(x_1) = D(x_1) = D(x_1) = \{1, 2\}$, and a single constraint $c(x_1, x_2, x_3) = \{(1, 1, 1), (2, 2, 2)\}$ This network is path consistent because it does not contain any binary constraint. It is *not* 3-consistent because the instantiation ($x_1 = 1, x_2 = 2$), which is locally consistent, cannot be extended consistently to x_3. 3-consistency produces the three binary constraints $c_{12} = \{(1, 1), (2, 2)\}$, $c_{23} = \{(1, 1), (2, 2)\}$ and $c_{13} = \{(1, 1), (2, 2)\}$.

k-consistency ensures that each time we have a locally consistent instantiation of size $k-1$, we can consistently extend it to any kth variable. So, the question is 'how to build locally consistent instantiations of size $k-1$?'. Strong k-consistencies are properties that guarantee that the network is j-consistent for $1 \leq j \leq k$. Thus, we can build from scratch a locally consistent instantiation of size k without any backtrack.

Definition 3.43 (Strong k-consistency). *A network is* strongly k-consistent *iff it is j-consistent for all $j \leq k$.*

Given a normalized network N, $\mathcal{P}^*_{Nk}$ denotes the subset of $\mathcal{P}_N$ containing all normalized networks N' in which only the domains and constraints of arity at most k can differ from N. More formally, $N' \in \mathcal{P}^*_{Nk}$ if and only if $N' \in \mathcal{P}_N$, $D_{N'} \subseteq D_N$, and any constraint in $C_{N'} \setminus C_N$ has arity at most k. The strong k-consistent closure of N is the union of all strongly k-consistent networks in $\mathcal{P}^*_{N(k-1)}$. The relation $\preceq$ is not a partial order in $\mathcal{P}^*_{N(k-1)}$ even if we restrict to embedded constraints. As a consequence, an algorithm achieving strong k-consistency by iteratively enforcing j-consistency, $1 \leq j \leq k$, is not guaranteed to terminate on the strong k-consistent closure of N. It may terminate on a network of $\mathcal{P}^*_{N(k-1)}$ nogood-equivalent to the closure.

Example 3.44. Consider the network with variables $x_1, \ldots, x_6$, domains equal to $\{1, 2$ and $C = \{c_1(x_1, x_2, x_3, x_4), \ c_2(x_2, x_3, x_4, x_5), \ x_2 = x_6, \ x_6 \neq x_3\}$, with $c_1 = \{(1112)$ $(1121), (1211), (2122), (2212), (2221)\}$ and $c_2 = \{(1112), (1211), (1222), (2112)$ $(2122), (2222)\}$. If we apply 4-consistency on x_2, x_3, x_4 wrt x_1 and x_5, we derive the constraint $c_3(x_2, x_3, x_4) = \{(121), (122), (211), (212)\}$. 3-consistency on x_2, x_3 wrt x produces the constraint $c_4(x_2, x_3) = \{(12), (21)\}$. By applying first 3-consistency to x_2, x_3 wrt x_6, the constraint c_4 would have been produced before c_3. So c_3 would have never been generated because all its tuples are already inconsistent with c_4.

The algorithms proposed by Freuder and Cooper in [53, 37] both reach a fixpoint which is not the strong k-consistent closure. They make all constraints (up to arity $k-1$) as explicit as possible. For instance, if a pair of values $((x_i, v_i), (x_j, v_j))$ is path inconsistent, they create a constraint on every superset Y of $\{x_i, x_j\}$ with $|Y| < k$, and this constraint forbids all tuples τ on Y where $\tau[(x_i, x_j)] = (v_i, v_j)$. Cooper showed that his algorithm runs in $O(n^k d^k)$, which is the optimal time complexity for strong k-consistency. The algorithm proposed by Cooper requires $O(n^k d^k)$ space. The optimal space complexity for strong k-consistency is $O(n^{k-1} d^{k-1})$ because we must store all the constraints of arity $k-1$ that k-consistency creates each time an instantiation of size $k-1$ does not extend to a kth variable. .

I said in Section 3.2 that the maximal amount of simplification we can perform on a network is to reach a globally consistent network, that is, a network on which *all* locally consistent instantiations can be extended to solutions. Strong n-consistency guarantees that.

Proposition 3.45. *If a network is strongly n-consistent then it is globally consistent.*

Enforcing global consistency on an arbitrary network is far too space consuming (in $O(n^{n-1} d^{n-1})$). Freuder gave conditions on the associated hypergraph for which strong k-consistency ($k < n$) is sufficient to allow a backtrack-free search [54]. In [47], Dechter and Pearl developed *adaptive consistency (AdC)*, a technique inspired from dynamic programming. Given a total ordering on the variables, AdC adapts the level of k-consistency enforced on each variable x_i depending on the number of variables that share a constraint with x_i and that precede it in the ordering. The obtained network guarantees backtrack-free search. (See Chapter 7.)

In [55], Freuder proposed (i, j)-consistency, a generalization of k-consistency where we do not guarantee that instantiations of size $k-1$ can be extended to instantiations of size k, but instantiations of size i can be extended to j additional variables. k-consistency is $(k-1, 1)$-consistency. Since the main drawback of k-consistencies is the huge space they require to store all forbidden instantiations of size $k-1$, we can design local consistencies requiring less space by setting i to a small value in (i, j)-consistency.

3.4.3 Montanari's Decomposability and Minimality

Montanari characterized networks that can be made globally consistent in polynomial space. These are networks for which the set of solutions is a decomposable relation [95], also named binary decomposable relation in [46].

Definition 3.46 (Decomposable in the sense of Montanari).

- *A relation ρ with scheme X is binary-representable iff there exists a binary network N, $X_N = X$, such that $sol(N) = \rho$.*

- *A relation ρ with scheme X is decomposable in the sense of Montanari iff for all $Y \subseteq X$, $\pi_Y(\rho)$ is binary-representable.*

- *A network N is decomposable in the sense of Montanari iff $sol(N)$ is a decomposable relation.*

Example 3.47. ([95]) Consider the network N in Fig. 3.4, with variables x_1, x_2, x_3, x_4, domains $D(x_1) = \{1, 2, 3, 4\}$, $D(x_2) = D(x_3) = D(x_4) = \{0, 1\}$, and constraints as shown in the boxes on the figure. $sol(N)$ is equal to the relation R on the top right-hand corner of the figure, which is thus representable by a binary network. However, R is not decomposable in the sense of Montanari because $\pi_{\{x_2, x_3, x_4\}}(R) = \{(000), (101), (110), (111)\} = \{x_2 = x_3 \lor x_4\}$ cannot be represented by a binary network. (Any binary network on x_2, x_3, x_4 that accepts all tuples in the relation also accepts the tuple (100).)

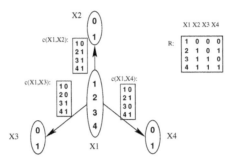

Figure 3.4: A relation R that can be represented by a binary network but which is non decomposable in the sense of Montanari.

Proposition 3.48. *If a network $N = (X, D, C)$ is decomposable in the sense of Montanari then there exists a binary network $G_N = (X, D, C_G)$, which is globally consistent and $sol(N) = sol(G_N)$.*

Decomposability of Montanari is stronger than what is commonly called 'decomposable constraint'. (See [63] or Section 3.8.2 for more details.)

Example 3.47 shows that it is not because a network is binary that it is decomposable in the sense of Montanari. For binary networks, Montanari proposed the concept of *minimal network*, which is the best approximating binary network for global consistency. This is thus another technique for tightening binary networks.

Definition 3.49 (Minimal network). *Given a binary network $N = (X, D, C)$, the minimal network of N is the binary normalized and embedded in D network $M_N = (X, D, C_M)$ such that any locally consistent instantiation of length 2 is globally consistent and $sol(M_N) = sol(N)$.*

Corollary 3.50. *Given a binary network N, if $sol(N)$ is decomposable in the sense of Montanari, the minimal network M_N is globally consistent.*

Minimality on a binary network could be considered as a kind of local consistency. But local consistencies usually refer to properties which are polynomial to enforce. Building the minimal network is obviously intractable because once we have the minimal network, it is constant time to decide consistency of the original network (by checking non emptiness of any constraint).

The question of building the minimal network was called the 'central problem' by Montanari. This led to some confusion as it was sometimes believed that generating a solution is polynomial if the network is minimal. Dechter partially fixed the ambiguity by saying that:

> "it is still not clear, however, whether or not generating a single solution of a minimal network is hard, even though empirical experience shows that it is normally easy. Nevertheless, we do speculate that generating a single solution from the minimal network is hard..."

We can say a little more about this.

Proposition 3.51 (Generating solutions of a minimal network). *Generating a solution of a minimal network M_N is not backtrack-free (unless $\Pi_2^P = \Sigma_2^P$).*

Proof. The clause entailment problem is known to be non compilable[7] unless $\Pi_2^P = \Sigma_2^P$ [29]. In [38], Cros reduced the clause entailment problem to the compilability of the problem of the global consistency of a partial instantiation in a binary network N. If building solutions in a minimal network was backtrack-free, it would be polynomial to answer whether a partial instantiation is globally consistent or not. Furthermore, a minimal network has a size in $O(n^2 d^2)$, which is polynomial in the size of N. Hence, the problem of the consistency of partial instantiations would be compilable, and clause entailment as well. □

3.4.4 Consistencies Based on Constraints

All consistencies I studied until now (except arc consistency) are properties of partial instantiations of variables wrt other variables. They do not take into account the network topology, i.e., which sets of variables are linked by a constraint and which are not. This is a limitation for constraint propagation, which creates new constraints everywhere in the network. This is also a limitation on non-binary networks if we want to link the level of consistency and the hypergraph structure in backtrack-free conditions. In this section, I restrict my attention to embedded networks because all the works I present used this restriction.

Janssen et al. proposed a first local consistency based on constraints instead of variables [72]. It was applied from works on relational databases [7].

Definition 3.52 (Pairwise consistency). *Given an embedded network N, a pair of constraints c_1 and c_2 in C_N is pairwise consistent iff any tuple on $X(c_1)$ (resp. on $X(c_2)$) satisfying c_1 (resp. c_2) can be extended to an instantiation on $X(c_1) \cup X(c_2)$ satisfying c_2 (resp. c_1), that is, iff $\pi_{X(c_1) \cap X(c_2)}(c_1) = \pi_{X(c_1) \cap X(c_2)}(c_2)$. N is pairwise consistent iff any pair of constraints in C_N is pairwise consistent.*

Example 3.53. Consider the network with variables x_1, x_2, x_3, x_4, domains $D(x_1) = D(x_2) = D(x_3) = D(x_4) = \{1, 2\}$ and constraints $c_1(x_1, x_2, x_3) = \{(121), (211), (222)\}$ and $c_2(x_2, x_3, x_4) = \{(111), (222)\}$. This network is generalized arc consistent. However, it is not pairwise consistent because the tuple (121) from c_1 is not compatible with any tuple in c_2.

Janssen et al. showed in [72] that pairwise consistency is equivalent to 2-consistency on the dual encoding of the network, where dual variables represent constraints of the original network [48].

In a database context, Gyssens proposed k-wise consistency, a direct extension of pairwise consistency where we consider k constraints at a time instead of two [67]. Jégou applied this notion to constraint networks [73].

---

[7]The problem of asking queries of a class Q to instances of a class P is said to be *compilable* if there exists a polynomial space transformation p' of any instance p of P (the time for the transformation should just be finite) such that any query q from Q asked on p can be answered in polynomial time by using p' [29].

Definition 3.54 (k-wise consistency). *Given an embedded network N, a set of constraints $\{c_1 \ldots, c_k\}$ in C_N is k-wise consistent iff for any $c_i, i \in [1..k]$, any tuple on $X(c_i)$ satisfying c_i can be extended to an instantiation on $\bigcup_{j=1}^{k} X(c_j)$ satisfying c_j for all $j \in [1..k$ that is, iff $c_i = \pi_{X(c_i)}(\bowtie_{j=1}^{k} c_j)$. N is k-wise consistent iff for all $\{c_1 \ldots, c_k\}$ in C_N $\{c_1 \ldots, c_k\}$ is k-wise consistent.*

k-wise consistency is the constraint-based counterpart of k-inverse consistency (see Section 3.5). Enforcing k-wise consistency does not alter the associated hypergraph. It just alters existing constraints.

In [74], Jégou proposed another duality between variables and constraints. He presents hyper k-consistency. This is the constraint-based counterpart of k-consistency.

Definition 3.55 (Hyper k-consistency). *Let N be an embedded network. A set $\{c_1, \ldots, c_{k-1}\}$ of $k - 1$ constraints in C_N is hyper k-consistent relative to a kth constraint c_k iff any instantiation on $\bigcup_{i=1}^{k-1} X(c_i)$ satisfying $c_1, \ldots, c_{k-1}$ has an extension on the variables in $X(c_k)$ that satisfies c_k, that is, iff $\pi_Y(\bowtie_{i=1}^{k-1} c_i) \subseteq \pi_Y(c_k)$, where $Y = (\bigcup_{i=1}^{k-1} X(c_i))$ $X(c_k)$. N is hyper k-consistent iff for all $\{c_1, \ldots, c_{k-1}\} \subseteq C_N$, for all $c_k \in C_N$ $\{c_1, \ldots, c_{k-1}\}$ is hyper k-consistent relative to c_k.*

Pairwise consistency is both 2-wise consistency and hyper 2-consistency.

Based on definition 3.55, Jégou characterized some sufficient conditions for a network to be consistent. These conditions link the level of hyper k-consistency of the network to the width of its hypergraph. Nevertheless, hyper k-consistency inherits one of the drawbacks of k-consistencies because enforcing hyper k-consistency creates new constraints on sets of variables that were not linked in the original network.

Dechter and van Beek proposed a new form of local consistency which is more bound to schemes of constraints already in the network than hyper k-consistency is. They refer to those new types of consistencies as *relational* consistencies [49].

Definition 3.56 (Relational arc consistency). *Let N be an embedded network. A constraint c in C_N is relationally arc consistent relative to a subset of variables $Y \subseteq X(c)$ iff any locally consistent instantiation on Y has an extension to a tuple on $X(c)$ that satisfies c is relationally arc consistent iff it is relationally arc consistent relative to every subset Y of $X(c)$. N is relationally arc consistent iff every constraint in C_N is relationally arc consistent.*

An advantage of relational arc consistency is that enforcing it does not create constraints between variables not linked in the original network. However, it creates subconstraints on subsets of the schemes of the original constraints, which can be prohibitive on large arity constraints because it can create up to $2^{|X(c)|}$ subconstraints for a constraint c

Definition 3.57 (Relational m-consistency). *Let N be an embedded network. A set $\{c_1, \ldots, c_m\}$ of m constraints in C_N is relationally m-consistent relative to a subset of variables $Y \subseteq \bigcup_{i=1}^{m} X(c_i)$ iff any locally consistent instantiation on Y has an extension to $\bigcup_{i=1}^{m} X(c_i)$ that satisfies $c_1, \ldots, c_m$ simultaneously. A set $\{c_1, \ldots, c_m\}$ of m constraints in C_N is relationally m-consistent iff it is relationally m-consistent relative to every subset Y of $\bigcup_{i=1}^{m} X(c_i)$. N is relationally m-consistent iff every set of m constraints in C_N relationally m-consistent.*

Relational m-consistency has the same drawbacks as hyper k-consistency because it can create new constraints on any subset of variables involved in one of m constraints. Dechter and van Beek proposed a *bounded* version of relational m-consistency that permits to tackle the space and time explosion.

Definition 3.58 (Relational (i, m)-consistency). *Let N be an embedded network. A set of constraints $\{c_1, \ldots, c_m\} \subseteq C_N$ is relationally (i, m)-consistent iff it is relationally m-consistent relative to every subset of variables $Y \subseteq \bigcup_{i=1}^{m} X(c_i), |Y| = i$. N is relationally (i, m)-consistent iff every subset of m constraints in C_N is relationally (i, m)-consistent. N is strong relational (i, m)-consistent iff it is relationally (j, m)-consistent for every $j \leq i$.*

Relational arc consistency corresponds to strong relational $(n, 1)$-consistency and relational m-consistency corresponds to strong relational (n, m)-consistency. Generalized arc consistency is relational $(1, 1)$-consistency. Relational $(1, m)$-consistencies are domain-based consistencies, and so, do not modify the set of constraints.

As in the case of strong k-consistencies, algorithms enforcing strong relational (i, m)-consistencies can converge to different networks depending on the order in which they generate new constraints.

Dechter and van Beek proposed an algorithm enforcing relational (i, m)-consistency. Its complexity is exponential in $i \cdot m$. They also proposed an algorithm for adaptive relational consistency. It is inspired from adaptive consistency (see Chapter 7) and applies the right level of relational consistency to guarantee a backtrack-free search for solutions wrt a given ordering of the variables.

Walsh performed an extensive theoretical comparison of relational consistencies with k-consistencies, k-inverse consistencies and generalized arc consistency [123].

3.5 Domain-Based Consistencies Stronger than AC

There exist local consistencies that permit to prune more values than arc consistency while keeping the set of constraints unchanged (as opposed to what is done by k-consistencies and consistencies based on constraints —see Section 3.4). The first ones I present are different kinds of reasoning we can apply on triples of variables. The others involve the whole neighborhood of a variable or check local consistency of the whole network after a single assignment of a variable.

3.5.1 Triangle-Based Local Consistencies

The local consistencies defined here are limited to binary normalized networks. They all deal with 'triangles' of constraints, namely triples of variables connected two-by-two by binary constraints.

The first local consistency following this line of research is *Restricted Path Consistency (RPC)*, proposed by Berlandier [13]. The motivation for RPC is to remove more inconsistent values than arc consistency whereas avoiding the cost of path consistency. Path consistency removes all pairs of values that cannot be extended to a third variable. The idea of RPC is to try to extend only those pairs of values that if removed, would lead to arc inconsistency of a value. So, in addition to arc consistency, RPC guarantees path

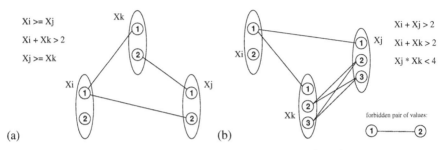

Figure 3.5: (a) Network on which RPC prunes more than AC: $(x_i, 1)$ is not RPC whereas the whole network is AC. (b) Network on which PIC prunes more than RPC: $(x_i, 1)$ is not PIC whereas the whole network is RPC.

consistency of the pairs of values $((x_i, v_i), (x_j, v_j))$ that are the only support for $(x_i, v_i$ on c_{ij}. If such a pair is path inconsistent, its deletion would lead to the arc inconsistency of (x_i, v_i). Thus (x_i, v_i) can be removed. These few additional path consistency checks allow the detection of more inconsistent values than arc consistency without having to delete any pair of values, and so leaving the structure of the network unchanged.

Definition 3.59 (Restricted path consistency). *A binary normalized network* $N = (X, D, C)$ *is restricted path consistent (RPC) iff it is arc consistent and for all* $x_i \in X$, *for all* $v_i \in D(x_i)$, *for all* $c_{ij} \in C$ *such that* (x_i, v_i) *has a unique support* $((x_i, v_i), (x_j, v_j))$ *on* c_{ij}, *for all* $x_k \in X$ *linked to both* x_i *and* x_j *by a constraint, there exists* $v_k \in D(x_k)$ *such that* $(v_i, v_k) \in c_{ik}$ *and* $(v_j, v_k) \in c_{jk}$.

RPC is strictly stronger than AC. An example of a network on which RPC prunes more values than AC is shown in Figure 3.5. Berlandier proposed an algorithm in $O(end^3)$. The optimal complexity of achieving RPC on a binary normalized network is in $O(en + ed^2 + td^2)$, where t is the number of triples of variables $(x_, x_j, x_k)$ with c_{ij}, c_{jk} and c_{ik} all in C An algorithm with this optimal time complexity was presented by Debruyne and Bessiere [42].

In [57], Freuder and Elfe proposed other alternatives to enforce local consistencies stronger than AC whereas modifying only the domains. The idea is to take the inverse of what is done by k-consistency. k-consistency (or $(k - 1, 1)$-consistency) ensures that any locally consistent instantiation of size $k - 1$ can be extended to any kth variable in a consistent way. This implies the explicit removing of all instantiations of size $k - 1$ that cannot fit this property. k-inverse consistency ensures that any locally consistent instantiation of size 1 can be consistently extended to any $k - 1$ additional variables. This is $(1, k - 1)$ consistency. Since 2-inverse consistency is the same as 2-consistency, the simplest non trivial such inverse consistency is 3-inverse consistency, or path-inverse consistency (PIC), as called in [57].

Definition 3.60 (Path inverse consistency). *A binary normalized network* $N = (X, D, C$ *is path-inverse consistent (PIC) iff for all* $x_i \in X$, *for all* $v_i \in D(x_i)$, *for all* $x_j, x_k \in X$ *there exists* $v_j \in D(x_j)$ *and* $v_k \in D(x_k)$ *such that* $((x_i, v_i), (x_j, v_j), (x_k, v_k))$ *is locally consistent.*

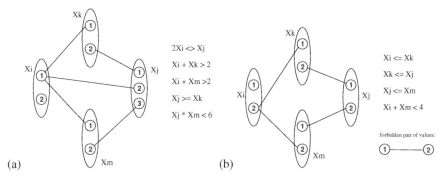

Figure 3.6: (a) Network on which maxRPC prunes more than PIC: $(x_i, 1)$ is not maxRPC whereas the whole network is PIC. (b) Network on which SAC prunes more than maxRPC: $(x_i, 2)$ is not SAC whereas the whole network is maxRPC.

PIC is strictly stronger than RPC. An example of a network on which PIC prunes more values than RPC is shown in Figure 3.5. Freuder and Elfe proposed an algorithm in $O(en^2d^4)$. In [41], Debruyne proposed some sufficient conditions for the path-inverse consistency of a network. They permit to avoid some constraint checks. Debruyne presented an optimal algorithm for PIC that runs in $O(en + ed^2 + td^3)$.

Following RPC and PIC, Debruyne and Bessiere proposed max-restricted path consistency (maxRPC) [42]. maxRPC still increases the amount of local consistency on triangles of variables. Given a value (x_i, v_i) and a constraint c_{ij}, maxRPC ensures that (x_i, v_i) has a support on c_{ij} path consistent on any third variable.

Definition 3.61 (Max-restricted path consistency). *A binary normalized network $N = (X, D, C)$ is max-restricted-path consistent (maxRPC) iff for all $x_i \in X$, for all $v_i \in D(x_i)$, for all $c_{ij} \in C$, there exists $v_j \in D(x_j)$ such that $(v_i, v_j) \in c_{ij}$ and for all $x_k \in X$ there exists $v_k \in D(x_k)$ with $((x_i, v_i), (x_j, v_j), (x_k, v_k))$ locally consistent.*

maxRPC is strictly stronger than PIC. An example of a network on which maxRPC prunes more values than PIC is shown in Figure 3.6. An optimal algorithm for maxRPC was proposed in [42]. It runs in $O(en + ed^2 + td^3)$.

3.5.2 Consistency According to the Neighborhood

Since k-inverse consistency is polynomial with the exponent depending on k, checking k-inverse consistency is prohibitive if k is large. However, if variables are not uniformly constrained, it can be worthwhile to adapt the level of k-inverse consistency to the size of their neighborhood, focusing filtering effort on the most constrained variables (as it is done in Adaptive consistency —see Section 3.4.2). This is the basis of neighborhood inverse consistency (NIC, [57]), which ensures that every value v_i in a domain $D(x_i)$ can be extended consistently to all the neighbors of x_i.

Definition 3.62 (Neighborhood inverse consistency). *A network $N = (X, D, C)$ is neighborhood-inverse consistent (NIC) iff for all $x_i \in X$, for all $v_i \in D(x_i)$, the instantiation*

(x_i, v_i) can be extended to a locally consistent instantiation on the set of all variables involved in a constraint with x_i.

An algorithm for NIC was proposed in [57]. It runs in $O(g^2(n + ed)d^{g+1})$, where g is the maximum degree of a variable in the associated hypergraph. It is not proved optimal. Anyway, it seems difficult to go below the exponential factor $nd \cdot d^g$ because every value of every variable must be proved consistent with its neighborhood (possibly of size g). NIC is strictly stronger than maxRPC.

NIC networks do not have the good property of backtrack-free search that adaptive consistent networks have. Although achieving NIC is exponential in the size of the largest neighborhood, it guarantees neither backtrack-free search nor consistency of the network. In addition, the behavior of NIC is dependent on the structure of the network. If two variables x_i and x_j are not neighbors, the network obtained by adding a universal constraint allowing all the pairs of values $(v_i, v_j) \in D(x_i) \times D(x_j)$ between x_i and x_j is equivalent to the initial one. However, as opposed to the other local consistencies, NIC is affected by this change because the neighborhood of x_i has changed. NIC can detect more inconsistent values. Obviously, this process increases time complexity because the sizes of neighborhoods increase.

3.5.3   Singleton Consistencies

A general technique, which has been used in several areas of automated reasoning consists in trying in turn different assignments of a value to a variable, and performing constraint propagation on the subproblem obtained by this assignment. If the problem is found to be inconsistent, this means that this value does not belong to any solution and thus can be pruned. This kind of technique was used on the bounds of interval domains in scheduling ('shaving' in [90]) or on continuous CSPs (3B-consistency in [83]). This technique was also used on literals as a way to derive better variable ordering heuristics in DPLL for SAT formulas (by counting the size of the remaining clauses after instantiation of a literal and unit propagation) in [52, 85]. Finally, it was formalized as a class of local consistencies in [43, 102, 44] under the name 'singleton consistencies'. I give the definition in the case where the amount of propagation applied to each subproblem is arc consistency. Any other local consistency can be used in a similar way. In the following, the subnetwork obtained from a network N by reducing the domain of a variable x_i to the singleton $\{v_i\}$ is denoted by $N|_{x_i = v_i}$.

Definition 3.63 (Singleton arc consistency). *A network $N = (X, D, C)$ is singleton arc consistent (SAC) iff for all $x_i \in X$, for all $v_i \in D(x_i)$, the subproblem $N|_{x_i = v_i}$ is not arc inconsistent.*

SAC is strictly stronger that maxRPC. An example of a network on which SAC prunes more values than maxRPC is given in Fig. 3.6. The first algorithm for SAC was proposed by Debruyne and Bessiere in [43], and was later named SAC1. It is a brute-force algorithm that checks SAC of each value by performing AC on each subproblem $N|_{x_i = v_i}$. It removes v_i from $D(x_i)$ if $N|_{x_i = v_i}$ is arc inconsistent. After each change in a domain, it rechecks SAC of every remaining value. It can then perform AC nd times on each subproblem, and because there are nd subproblems, it runs in $O(en^2d^4)$ on binary normalized networks, where AC is in $O(ed^2)$. In [6], Bartàk and Erben proposed SAC2, a smarter algorithm

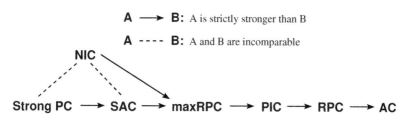

Figure 3.7: Summary of the comparison between domain-based consistencies lying between AC and Strong PC. $A \to B$ means that local consistency A is strictly stronger than local consistency B. (The stronger relation is transitive.)

that avoids unnecessary work by storing lists of supports, a bit like AC4. Unfortunately, its worst-case time complexity is still $O(en^2d^4)$. Recently, Bessiere and Debruyne showed that the complexity of SAC on binary normalized networks is in $O(end^3)$, and they proposed SAC-Opt, an algorithm with this optimal time complexity [16, 17]. To achieve optimal time, SAC-Opt stores a lot of information in large data structures that require $O(end^2)$ space. SAC-SDS (*Sharing Data Structures*) is a lighter version in which less structures are stored. Its $O(end^4)$ time complexity is a compromise between former SAC algorithms and SAC-Opt, whereas its space complexity is the same as SAC2, namely, $O(n^2d^2)$. Lecoutre and Cardon proposed SAC3, a different technique to enforce SAC [82]. SAC3 incrementally assigns values to variables in the network until arc consistency wipes out a domain. If the current sequence of assignments is $I = ((x_1, v_1), \ldots, (x_k, v_k))$, it deduces that the values $(x_1, v_1), (x_2, v_2), \ldots, (x_{k-1}, v_{k-1})$ are currently SAC. This technique permits to prove SAC of several values in a single arc consistency pass. SAC3 does not have optimal worst-case time complexity but it works well in practice.

Several extensions of SAC have been proposed. Prosser et al. proposed restricted-SAC, a weakened version of SAC that checks SAC of each value in one pass, without propagating removals to values already processed [102]. Some subtle extensions that are stronger than SAC itself have been proposed in [12, 34, 16]. Their effectiveness and efficiency in practice have not yet been assessed.

Many other singleton consistencies can be constructed because any local consistency can be used to detect the possible inconsistency of the network $N|_{x_i = v_i}$. If a local consistency can be enforced in polynomial time, the corresponding singleton consistency also has a polynomial worst-case time complexity. Prosser et al. analyzed this wider picture. In [102, 122], they theoretically compared the pruning capabilities of (i, j)-consistencies and singleton (i, j)-consistencies:

Theorem 3.64. *Strong $(i + 1, j)$-consistency is strictly stronger than singleton (i, j)-consistency. Singleton $(1, j)$-consistency is strictly stronger than $(1, j + 1)$-consistency.*

Fig. 3.7 summarizes the qualitative comparison between the local consistencies presented in this section. Complete proofs can be found in [44]. Verfaillie et al. proposed a generic algorithm schema that can enforce most of the local consistencies presented in this section, plus new ones that are combinations of existing ones [119].

3.6   Domain-Based Consistencies Weaker than AC

Arc consistency is not the weakest level of consistency we can define on a network. The 80's and first half of 90's have seen quite a lot of works trying to find the amount of filtering that should be performed by a backtrack search procedure. At that time, even if the studies were mostly interested in binary constraints, it was the conventional wisdom that AC was too expensive to be maintained. As a result, several other properties weaker than AC were proposed. The idea behind these properties is to reduce the number of times arc consistency of variables must be checked against constraints. In other words, these properties reduce the number of calls to function `Revise` in a coarse-grained algorithm. They are presented in Section 3.6.1.

More recently, and essentially because of the cost of arc consistency on non-binary constraints, other forms of consistency were introduced. These techniques do not try to reduce the number of calls to the `Revise` procedure, but instead, they try to reduce the amount of work such a `Revise` procedure performs. Section 3.6.2 describes them.

3.6.1   Reducing the Number of Times Constraints are Revised

The filtering techniques that try to reduce the number of times constraints are revised are based on properties a network must verify according to some additional parameter such as an ordering on the variables, or a partial instantiation. This extra parameter permits to specify which variables must be arc consistent with which constraints.

Directional arc consistency

Dechter and Pearl proposed directional arc consistency in [47]. The idea is to associate an ordering to the variables in the network and to impose that constraints are arc consistent in the direction of this ordering.

Definition 3.65 (Directional arc consistency). *A binary network* $N = (X, D, C)$ *is directional arc consistent (DAC) according to ordering* $o = (x_{k_1}, \dots, x_{k_n})$ *on* X, *where* $(k_1, \dots, k_n)$ *is a permutation of* $(1, \dots, n)$, *iff for all* $c(x_i, x_j) \in C$, *if* $x_i <_o x_j$ *then* x_i *is arc consistent on* $c(x_i, x_j)$.

Directional arc consistency is simpler to enforce than arc consistency. Removing a value v_i in $D(x_i)$ for some variable x_i cannot make a variable x_j directional arc inconsistent on c_{ij} if $x_i <_o x_j$. As a result, there is no need to use a propagation queue for an algorithm achieving DAC. It is sufficient to process the variables from the last in the ordering to the first, revising each variable preceding the current one on the constraint they share, if any (see Algorithm 3.5).

Algorithm 3.5: Algorithm for DAC

---

procedure $DAC(N, o)$;

1   **for** $j \leftarrow n$ ***downto*** 2 **do**

2   **foreach** $c_{ik_j} \in C_N \mid x_i <_o x_{k_j}$ **do**

3   **if** ***not*** $Revise(x_i, c_{ik_j})$ **then** return false

---

Example 3.66. Consider the network with variables $X = \{x_1, x_2, x_3\}$, domains $D(x_1) = D(x_2) = \{1..5\}$, $D(x_3) = \{1..3\}$, constraints $C = \{x_1 < x_2, x_2 = x_3, x_1 > x_3\}$, and ordering $o = (x_1, x_2, x_3)$. Revising x_1 on c_{13} and x_2 on c_{23} (in whatever order) prunes value 1 from $D(x_1)$ and values 4 and 5 from $D(x_2)$. Revising x_1 on c_{12} prunes values 3,4,5 from $D(x_1)$. Therefore, $N' = (X, D', C)$ with $D'(x_1) = \{2\}$, $D'(x_2) = D'(x_3) = \{1, 2, 3\}$ is the DAC closure of N. Note that arc consistency proves inconsistency.

Proposition 3.67. *The algorithm DAC enforces directional arc consistency according to ordering o in $O(ed^2)$ time.*

Forward checking

Even if they are often presented as stand alone preprocessing of a network, local consistencies are usually intended to be maintained during a backtrack search. It is thus natural to include in our analysis the filtering techniques that were only defined as associated with backtrack search. The amount of filtering performed by the famous *forward checking (FC)* [66, 69] can be defined as a local consistency. The FC search procedure guarantees that at each step of the search, all the constraints between already assigned variables and not yet assigned variables are arc consistent.

Definition 3.68 (Forward checking). *Let $N = (X, D, C)$ be a binary network and $Y \subseteq X$ such that $|D(x_i)| = 1$ for all $x_i \in Y$. N is* forward checking consistent (FC) *according to the instantiation I on Y iff I is locally consistent and for all $x_i \in Y$, for all $x_j \in X \setminus Y$, for all $c(x_i, x_j) \in C$, x_j is arc consistent on $c(x_i, x_j)$.*

Algorithm 3.6 presents a procedure that applies FC on a network N according to a subset of instantiated variables $Y \cup \{x_i\}$ if N is already FC according to Y.

Algorithm 3.6: Algorithm for FC

---

procedure $FC(N, Y, x_i)$;
1 **foreach** $c_{ij} \in C_N \mid x_j \in X \setminus Y$ **do**
2   **if *not*** $\mathtt{Revise}(x_j, c_{ij})$ **then** return false

---

Example 3.69. On the network of Example 3.66, where $X = \{x_1, x_2, x_3\}$, domains $D(x_1) = D(x_2) = \{1..5\}$, $D(x_3) = \{1..3\}$, and $C = \{x_1 < x_2, x_2 = x_3, x_1 > x_3\}$, applying FC according to $\{x_1\}$ after an instantiation $x_1 = 3$ (i.e., $D(x_1) = \{3\}$) prunes values 1,2,3 from $D(x_2)$ and 3 from $D(x_3)$.

FC has the property that once a variable x_j is made arc consistent on c_{ij} ($|D(x_i)| = 1$), it remains AC on c_{ij} in spite of any future domain reduction, because x_i is singleton. This means that each constraint needs to be revised only once along a branch of instantiations. As opposed to chronological backtracking, a procedure maintaining FC does not need to check consistency of values of the current variable against already instantiated ones. FC is the weakest level of local consistency with this property.

The complexity of a call to $\mathtt{Revise}$ in FC is in $O(d)$ because one of the domains involved is a singleton. Hence, enforcing FC on a binary network according to a partial instantiation of arbitrary length is in $O(ed)$.

Algorithm 3.7: Algorithms for PL and FL

---

procedure *PL*(N, Y, x_i);

1   $FC(N, Y, x_i)$;

2   **foreach** $j \leftarrow i + 1$ *to* n **do**

3   **foreach** $k \leftarrow j + 1$ *to* $n \mid c_{jk} \in C_N$ **do**

4   **if** *not* Revise(x_j, c_{jk}) **then** return false

procedure *FL*(N, Y, x_i);

5   $FC(N, Y, x_i)$;

6   **foreach** $j \leftarrow i + 1$ *to* n **do**

7   **foreach** $k \leftarrow i + 1$ *to* $n, k \neq j \mid c_{jk} \in C_N$ **do**

8   **if** *not* Revise(x_j, c_{jk}) **then** return false

The definition of FC can be extended to non-binary constraints in several different ways. Van Hentenryck proposed a basic one in [115]: A network is FC according to a partial instantiation I on a subset Y of X if and only if I is locally consistent and for all $x_j \in X \setminus Y$, for all $c \in C$ such that $X(c) \setminus Y = \{x_j\}$, x_j is arc consistent on c. Bessiere et al. presented five additional extensions of FC to non-binary constraints [22].

Other lookahead filterings

The idea of reducing the amount of filtering of arc consistency to avoid complex algorithms led to other forms of propagation. In [69], Haralick and Elliott proposed *partial lookahead (PL)* and *full lookahead (FL)*, two levels of propagation, stronger that FC. Haralick and Elliott gave operational definitions of PL and FL in terms of algorithms performing a given amount of filtering. As opposed to DAC and FC, no clear property on the output of PL or FL can be specified and thus, no clear fixpoint can be defined.

PL and FL are presented in Algorithm 3.7. Given a network N, an ordering $o = (x_1, \ldots, x_n)$, and a current variable x_i, PL first performs FC and then takes the variables x_j from x_{i+1} to x_n and calls Revise for x_j on each $c_{jk}, j < k \leq n$. FL performs a stronger level of filtering than PL. Given a network N, an ordering o, and a current variable x_i, FL takes the variables x_j from x_{i+1} to x_n and calls Revise for x_j on each $c_{jk}, i < k \leq n, k \neq j$.

PL and FL cannot guarantee any property on the arc consistency of arcs at the end of the process. After x_j has been made arc consistent on $c_{jk}, j < k$, values of x_k can be removed when making x_k arc consistency on arcs leaving x_k. Thus, it is no longer guaranteed that the arc (x_j, c_{jk}) is arc consistent at the end of the process because each arc is revised only once.

The complexity of function Revise is in $O(d^2)$ because it is called on constraints involving non singleton variables for both PL and FL. Thus, PL and FL are in $O(ed^2)$, like DAC.

In [98, 99], Nadel encapsulated these forms of consistency in a general schema, going from the consistency maintained by simple backtracking, i.e., local consistency of the instantiated variables (noted $AC_{1/5}$), to arc consistency. FC is denoted by $AC_{1/4}$ while PL and FL are denoted by $AC_{1/3}$ and $AC_{1/2}$ respectively.

In [112], Tsang gave a comparison of the pruning capabilities of these different levels of filtering. He proved that DAC and FL are strictly stronger than PL, which itself is strictly stronger than FC. FL and DAC are incomparable: There are cases where DAC prunes values FL does not prune and vice versa. AC is strictly stronger than all of them.

Selective revision

As a last technique to reduce the number of calls to function `Revise` in arc consistency, there is the work by Freuder and Wallace. They proposed to use criteria to discard arc revisions when they are not likely to be effective [58].

Given a coarse-grained arc consistency algorithm, *distance-bounded* propagation confines constraint propagation to a fixed distance δ from the variables at which it began. This is implemented by attaching a *stamp* to each arc in Q. Arcs put in Q in the initialization of the arc consistency call are stamped with zero. Forthcoming arcs are stamped with $t + 1$ if t is the stamp of the revised arc that provoked their addition to Q. When an arc is to be stamped with a value greater than the maximal distance δ, it is not put in Q.

Response-bounded propagation stops subsequent propagations when the amount of change in a domain falls below a given threshold r. This is implemented by testing if the ratio of values removed by a revision is greater than r before adding relevant arcs in Q.

3.6.2 Using the Order on the Domains to Relax `Revise`

The second form of local consistencies weaker than arc consistency do not try to reduce the number of arc revisions, but instead, they try to reduce the cost of revisions to overcome the prohibitive cost of generalized arc consistency on some constraints. The idea behind these local consistencies is to use the fact that domains are composed of integers. Integer domains inherit the total ordering on $\mathbb{Z}$ and by consequence they inherit the two particular values $min_D(x_i)$ and $max_D(x_i)$, called the *bounds* of $D(x_i)$. I present two ways of relaxing generalized arc consistency on a constraint c. The first option is to ensure support on c only for the bounds of the domain of each variable in $X(c)$. The second option is to look for supports not in $\pi_{X(c)}(D)$ but in $\pi_{X(c)}(D^I)$, where D^I is the domain such that for all x_i, $D^I(x_i) = \{v \in \mathbb{Z} \mid min_D(x_i) \leq v \leq max_D(x_i)\}$. Using the first option or the second, or combining both, give rise to three relaxed forms of local consistency.

Definition 3.70 (Consistencies on bounds). *Given a network $N = (X, D, C)$, given a constraint c, a bound support τ on c is a tuple that satisfies c and such that for all $x_i \in X(c), min_D(x_i) \leq \tau[x_i] \leq max_D(x_i)$, that is, $\tau \in c \cap \pi_{X(c)}(D^I)$. (A bound support in which each variable is assigned a value in its domain is a support.)*

- *A constraint c is* bound(Z) *consistent (BC(Z)) iff for all $x_i \in X(c)$, $(x_i, min_D(x_i))$ and $(x_i, max_D(x_i))$ belong to a bound support on c.*

- *A constraint c is* range *consistent (RC) iff for all $x_i \in X(c)$, for all $v_i \in D(x_i)$, (x_i, v_i) belongs to a bound support on c.*

- *A constraint c is* bound(D) *consistent (BC(D)) iff for all $x_i \in X(c)$, $(x_i, min_D(x_i))$ and $(x_i, max_D(x_i))$ belong to a support on c.*

The network N is bound(Z) / range / bound(D) consistent iff all its constraints are bound(Z) / range / bound(D) consistent.

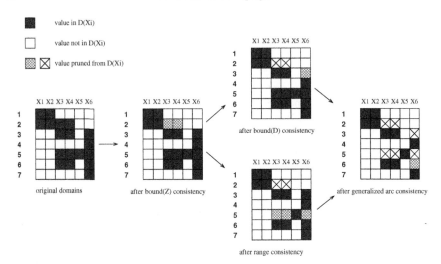

Figure 3.8: Amount of propagation performed by BC(Z), BC(D), RC and GAC on the constraint alldifferent($x_1 \ldots, x_6$) of Example 3.71.

Example 3.71. Consider the network with variables $x_1, \ldots, x_6$, domains $D(x_1) = D(x_2) = \{1, 2\}$, $D(x_3) = D(x_4) = \{2, 3, 5, 6\}$, $D(x_5) = \{5\}$, $D(x_6) = [3..7]$ and $C = \{$alldifferent($x_1 \ldots, x_6$)$\}$. These domains are depicted in Fig. 3.8 after BC(Z), BC(D), RC, and GAC are applied to the constraint.

The notion of local consistency on bounds comes from works on arithmetic constraints over real variables (variables taking values in intervals of reals). The move to integer is not so direct, and the names chosen in Definition 3.70 are not unanimously used in the literature.[8] Collavizza et al. presented a review of several local consistency notions for continuous domains [36]. One of these local consistencies is named bound consistency but has no link at all with those named bound(Z) or bound(D) consistencies in Definition 3.70. In [109, 2], Schulte and Stuckey, and Apt gave a definition for bound consistency on integer variables that is the direct application of the definition on reals. Choi et al. called it *bound(R) consistency* [35]. Bound(R) consistency differs from bound(Z) consistency in that it looks for bound supports composed of *real* values (instead of integer values). For instance, in Fig. 3.8 the bound $(x_3, 2)$, removed by BC(Z), is bound(R) consistent because it belongs to the tuple $(1, \frac{3}{2}, 2, 4, 5, 3)$ which satisfies the alldifferent constraint and where each variable takes a real value between its bounds. In [109], Schulte and Stuckey showed that there exist constraints on which BC(R) is polynomial to enforce whereas BC(Z) is NP-hard. The bound consistency of Dechter in [46] corresponds to bound(D) consistency in Definition 3.70. The local consistency named interval consistency by Van Hentenryck et al. and by Apt in [118, 2] corresponds to bound(Z) consistency in Definition 3.70. In recent papers dealing with integer variables, it seems that the name bound consistency is uniformly used to refer to BC(Z) [103, 105]. As seen in Fig. 3.8, these local consistencies do not all prune the same amount of values.

---

[8]We took the names bound(Z) consistency and bound(D) consistency in [35] and range consistency in [80].

Theorem 3.72. *Generalized arc consistency is strictly stronger than range and bound(D) consistencies, which are themselves strictly stronger than bound(Z) consistency, which itself is strictly stronger than bound(R) consistency. Bound(D) consistency and range consistency are incomparable.*

These local consistencies being all strictly weaker than GAC, the only reason to use one of them instead of GAC is to have a faster algorithm. BC(D) requires finding supports, as in GAC. Hence, it only decreases the cost by a factor d because it seeks supports for 2 values per domain (the bounds) instead of d values. RC, BC(Z) and BC(R) look for bound supports (on integers or on reals). Now, looking for bound supports is not necessarily simpler than looking for supports. To keep things simple, let us focus on BC(Z) but the same reasoning applies to BC(R) or RC.

Proposition 3.73 (Complexity of bound(Z) consistency). *Deciding bound(Z) consistency of a constraint can take exponential time, even if the constraint is binary, where arc consistency is in $O(d^2)$ time, d being the size of the largest domain.*

Proof. Let c be any binary constraint with no particular semantics that could be used by a propagation algorithm. It is well-known that deciding AC on such a constraint is in $O(d^2)$ time [92]. If $X(c) = (x_i, x_j)$, deciding BC(Z) is done by looking for a bound support for the four values $min_D(x_i)$, $min_D(x_j)$, $max_D(x_i)$, $max_D(x_j)$. Finding a bound support for $min_D(x_i)$ is done by exploring $D^I(x_j)$. Suppose c is characterized by a Boolean function requiring constant space (this is often the case), and suppose $D(x_i) = \{min_D(x_i), max_D(x_i)\}$, $D(x_j) = \{min_D(x_j), max_D(x_j)\}$, with $max_D(x_i) < max_D(x_j)$. The size of the input is in $O(log_2(max_D(x_j)))$. The cost of exploring the whole set $D^I(x_j)$ is thus exponential in the size of the input. $\square$

A direct consequence of Proposition 3.73 is that deciding BC(Z) is NP-hard. Suppose φ is a set of clauses on the Boolean variables $x_1, \ldots, x_n$ and $c(y, z)$ is the constraint satisfied by all tuples on (y, z) where $y \neq 0$ if and only if the bit vector of size n representing $z \bmod 2^n$ in base 2 is a tuple of 0/1 values for $x_1, \ldots, x_n$ that satisfies φ. If $max_D(z) - min_D(z) \geq 2^n$, deciding BC(Z) for a bound of $D(y)$ other than 0 is equivalent to deciding the satisfiability of φ.

This shows that bound(Z) consistency is useful only if the constraint we want to propagate has inherent properties that permit a computation of bound supports faster than supports. Take for example the constraint $\text{sum}_k(x_1, \ldots, x_n)$ that holds if and only if $\sum_{i=1}^n x_i = k$. Deciding generalized arc consistency on this constraint is NP-complete because we can easily transform the decision problem SUBSETSUM [60] into the problem of deciding whether a sum_k constraint has support.[9] On the contrary, testing bound(Z) consistency on the sum_k constraint is polynomial because it is sufficient to verify that $min_D(x_i)$ is at least $k - \sum_{j \neq i} max_D(x_j)$ and $max_D(x_i)$ is at most $k - \sum_{j \neq i} min_D(x_j)$, for all $i, 1 \leq i \leq n$.

Zhang and Yap showed that bound(R) consistency is equivalent to generalized arc consistency when constraints are linear [125]. For example, the constraint $\sum_{i=1}^n x_i \leq k$ is bound(R) consistent if and only if it is generalized arc consistent. Schulte and Stuckey

---

[9]The constraint $\text{sum}_k(x_1, \ldots, x_n)$ where $D(x_i) = \{0, j_i\}$ has support if and only if there exists a subset of $\{j_1, \ldots, j_n\}$ of sum k, which is exactly the SUBSETSUM problem.

gave other sufficient conditions on constraints that permit to guarantee that bound(R) consistency is equivalent to generalized arc consistency [109]. Even when a constraint does not fit the required conditions, there are cases where additional properties on the input domains guarantee that the output of enforcing BC(R) will be GAC. For instance, if all variables have interval domains, BC(R) on the sum_k constraint is equivalent to GAC. This is a polynomial case for GAC on sum_k, which is NP-hard in general. Interestingly, Schulte and Stuckey showed how to analyze a constraint model to discover on which constraints generalized arc consistency enforcing can be replaced by bound(R) consistency whereas preserving the amount of pruning.

3.7 Constraint Propagation as Iteration of Reduction Rules

Local consistency is a way to formally define which amount of consistency we want a network to guarantee, and as a consequence, which network will be produced by an algorithm enforcing this level of consistency. But nothing is said about the way the algorithm enforces it. Rules iteration takes the question on the other side. A reduction rule specifies under which conditions and on which constraints operations of filtering are performed. The network produced guarantees a formal property such as a given level of local consistency only if the reduction rules and the way they are applied have some good properties. The rules iteration approach was first formalized by Montanari and Rossi under the name *relaxation rules* [96]. Benhamou et al. studied rules iteration *via* interval arithmetics (that is, reducing only bounds) [10, 11]. Constraint Handling Rules (CHR) is a programming language based on reduction rules (see [59] and Chapter 13 in Part II). In [1, 2], Apt gave a comprehensive presentation of the rules iteration approach. I essentially follow Apt's presentation of the concept of reduction rule.

A reduction rule is simply a function that maps a network to another, where the image is a tightening of the input.

Definition 3.74 (Reduction rule). *Given a network N, a reduction rule is a function f from $\mathcal{P}_N$ to $\mathcal{P}_N$ such that for all $N' \in \mathcal{P}_N, f(N') \in \mathcal{P}_{N'}$.*

We should bear in mind that $\mathcal{P}_N$ contains all the networks that are tightenings of N (see Definition 3.13). In most cases, reduction rules are reduction steps that reduce a single variable domain according to a single constraint. I name them propagators.

Definition 3.75 (Propagator). *Given a constraint c in a network $N_c = (X, D, \{c\})$, a propagator f for c is a reduction rule from $\mathcal{P}_{N_c}$ to $\mathcal{P}_{N_c}$ that tightens only domains independently of the constraints other than c. That is, for all $N' = (X, D', C') \in \mathcal{P}_{N_c}$ $f(N') = (X, D'', C')$, with $D'' \subseteq D'$ and $D'' = D_{f(X, D', \{c\})}$.*

Propagators can verify some properties.

Definition 3.76 (Properties of propagators). *Given a network $N = (X, D, C)$ and two propagators f and g on $\mathcal{P}_{ND}$:*

- *f is called* monotonic *if $N_1 \leq N_2$ implies $f(N_1) \leq f(N_2)$ for all $N_1, N_2 \in \mathcal{P}_{ND}$,*
- *f is called* idempotent *if $ff(N_1) = f(N_1)$ for all $N_1 \in \mathcal{P}_{ND}$,*
- *we say that f and g* commute *if $fg(N_1) = gf(N_1)$ for all $N_1 \in \mathcal{P}_{ND}$,*

I give examples of propagators that do not verify these properties.

Example 3.77. Consider two networks $N_1 = (X, D_1, C)$ and $N_2 = (X, D_2, C)$ with $C = \{c \equiv (x_1 = x_2)\}$, $D_1(x_1) = \{1, 2\}$, $D_1(x_2) = \{2\}$, $D_2(x_1) = \{1, 2, 3\}$ and $D_2(x_2) = \{2\}$. Consider the propagator f that prunes all values from x_1 that have no support on c if less than half of them have support. f is *not* monotonic because $D_{f(N_1)} \not\subseteq D_{f(N_2)}$ whereas $D_{N_1} \subseteq D_{N_2}$ (f reduces $D_2(x_1)$ to $\{2\}$). Consider the propagator g that prunes *one of* the values from x_1 that have no support on c if such a value exists. g is *not* idempotent because $D_{gg(N_2)} \neq D_{g(N_2)}$ (g reduces $D_2(x_1)$ to $\{1, 2\}$ or $\{2, 3\}$ whereas gg reduces it to $\{2\}$). f and g do *not* commute because $D_{fg(N_2)} \neq D_{gf(N_2)}$ (fg reduces $D_2(x_1)$ to $\{1, 2\}$ or $\{2, 3\}$ whereas gf reduces it to $\{2\}$).

Most of the propagators used in practice satisfy the properties of Definition 3.76. Among them, monotonicity is particularly interesting. I first need to define what I mean by iteration and by stability of a propagator.

Definition 3.78 (Iteration). *Let $N = (X, D, C)$ be a network and $F = \{f_1, \ldots, f_k\}$ be a finite set of propagators on $\mathcal{P}_{ND}$. An iteration of F on N is a sequence $\langle N_0, N_1, \ldots \rangle$ of elements of $\mathcal{P}_{ND}$ defined by*

$$N_0 = N,$$

$$N_j = f_{n_j}(N_{j-1}),$$

where $j > 0$ and $n_j \in [1..k]$. We say that f_{n_j} is activated at step j.

Definition 3.79 (Stability). *Let $N = (X, D, C)$ be a network and F be a set of propagators on $\mathcal{P}_{ND}$. A network $N' \in \mathcal{P}_{ND}$ is stable for F iff for all $f \in F$, $f(N') = N'$.*

There can be many networks in $\mathcal{P}_{ND}$ that are stable for a given set of propagators. But monotonicity of propagators implies that only one of them will be produced.

Proposition 3.80 (Least fixpoint). *Let $N = (X, D, C)$ be a network and F be a set of propagators on $\mathcal{P}_{ND}$. If $S = \langle N_0, N_1, \ldots \rangle$ is an infinite iteration of F where each $f \in F$ is activated infinitely often, then there exists $j \geq 0$ such that N_j is stable for F. If all f in F are monotonic, N_j is unique and is called the* least fixpoint *of F on N.*

Algorithm 3.8 is a procedure that takes as input a network N and a set F of propagators on $\mathcal{P}_{ND}$. Thanks to Proposition 3.80, we are guaranteed that it terminates. If all f in F are monotonic, the output of Algorithm 3.8 is the least fixpoint of F on N.

Algorithm 3.8: Generic Iteration Algorithm

---

procedure *Generic-Iteration*(N, F);

    $G \leftarrow F$;

    while $G \neq \emptyset$ **do**

        select and remove g from G;

        if $N \neq g(N)$ **then**

            update(G);

            $N \leftarrow g(N)$;

    /* *update*(G) adds to G at least all functions f in $F \setminus G$ for which $g(N) \neq f(g(N))$ */

Sometimes, in addition to monotonicity, propagators can have some other properties. In those cases, Algorithm 3.8 can be simplified, while still ensuring to produce the same result.

Proposition 3.81 (Direct iteration). *Let $N = (X, D, C)$ be a network and $F = \{f_1, \ldots, f_k\}$ be a set of monotonic and idempotent propagators on $\mathcal{P}_{ND}$ that commute with each other. If an iteration $S = \langle N_0, N_1, \ldots, N_k \rangle$ is such that $N = N_0$ and for all $f_i \in F$ there exists $N_j \in S$ such that $N_j = f_i(N_{j-1})$, then N_k is stable for F and is the least fixpoint of F on N.*

Proposition 3.81 guarantees that Algorithm 3.9 produces the least fixpoint of F.

Algorithm 3.9: Direct Iteration Algorithm

---
procedure *Direct-Iteration*(N, F);
   $G \leftarrow F$;
   while $G \neq \emptyset$ **do**
      select and remove g from G;
      $N \leftarrow g(N)$;

By defining the appropriate set of propagators, we can obtain most of the local consistencies presented in previous sections. For instance, we can enforce arc consistency on a network $N = (X, D, C)$. I first define the propagators $f_{i,j}$ such that:

$$\forall N_1 = (X, D_1, C) \in \mathcal{P}_{ND}, \forall x_i \in X, \forall c_j \in C,\ f_{i,j}(N_1) = (X, D_1', C)\ \text{with}$$

$$D_1'(x_i) = \pi_{\{x_i\}}(c_j \cap \pi_{X(c_j)}(D_1))\ \text{and}\ D_1'(x_k) = D_1(x_k), \forall k \neq i.$$

I consider the set of propagators $F_{AC} = \{f_{i,j} \mid x_i \in X, c_j \in C\}$. They are all monotonic. Then, *Generic-Iteration*(N, F_{AC}) terminates on the least fixpoint for F_{AC}, which is the arc consistent closure of N.

It is shown in [2] that we can also enforce higher-order consistencies, such as path consistency, by defining sets of monotonic propagators that involve several constraints at a time and that alter the set of constraints.

3.8 Specific Constraints

In previous sections, I presented constraint propagation and local consistencies in a generic way without saying what should be done when we have some specific information on the semantics of a constraint. In this section, I develop some of the available techniques to take into account constraint semantics.

3.8.1 Specific Propagators in Solvers

All constraint solvers attach a specific propagation algorithm to the specific types of constraints they contain. In addition, most of them allow the user to design her own propagators for the new constraints she incorporates. The fact that arithmetic constraints are at the core of most constraint solvers influences the way these solvers are implemented. Not only all basic arithmetic constraints are present, but the programming possibilities they provide

---

Algorithm 3.10: AC3-like constraint propagation schema

---

function `Constraint-Propag`(**in** X: set): **Boolean** ;
   begin
1   **foreach** $c \in C$ **do** perform `init-propag` on c and update Q with relevant events;
2   **while** $Q \neq \emptyset$ **do**
3   select and remove $(x_i, c, x_j, Mtype)$ from Q;
4   **if** $Revise(x_i, c, (x_j, Mtype), Changes)$ **then**
5   **if** $D(x_i) = \emptyset$ **then** return **false** ;
6   **foreach** $c' \in \Gamma^C(x_i), Mtype \in Changes$ **do**
7   **foreach** $x_j \in X(c'), j \neq i$ **do** $Q \leftarrow Q \cup \{(x_j, c', x_i, Mtype)\}$;
8   return **true** ;
   end
   /* $\Gamma^C(x_i)$ is the set of constraints with x_i in their scheme */

---

for building new propagators is arithmetic-oriented. I give a brief overview of what is the common point to most solvers. The art of designing constraint propagators is not a mature science yet, and things can differ from one solver to another, and will most probably evolve in the next years. This topic has been addressed in some academic publications [79, 94, 117, 118, 78, 110] and in manuals of constraint solvers. See also Chapter 14 in Part II.

In most arithmetic constraints, it appears that a reduction of a domain does not produce the same effect on the other variables of the constraint, depending on if it is the removal of a value in the middle of the domain, if it is the increase of its minimum value, if it is the decrease of its maximum value, or if it is an instantiation to a single value. Then, it is worth differentiating these different types of *events* to be able to propagate exactly as necessary. The events usually recognized by constraint solvers are:

- `RemValue`: when a value v is removed from $D(x_i)$
- `IncMin`: when the minimum value of $D(x_i)$ increases
- `DecMax`: when the maximum value of $D(x_i)$ decreases
- `Instantiate`: when $D(x_i)$ becomes a singleton

The way these events are used in a constraint solver is usually bound to the type of propagation architecture handled by the solver. The description I give here is just an illustrative example of how to use those events. If we follow an AC3 like schema of propagation, the use of event types leads to a modified version of Algorithm 3.1 that takes into account the type $Mtype$ of reduction performed on a domain (see Algorithm 3.10). The modified function `Revise` has parameters $(x_i, c, (x_j, Mtype), Changes)$ where (x_i, c) is the arc to revise because of an $Mtype$ change in $D(x_j)$. In addition to a Boolean indicating if a domain has been changed, function `Revise` returns the set $Changes$ of the types of changes it performed on $D(x_i)$ (line 4). Each modification of type $Mtype$ on domain $D(x_i)$ requires the addition of 4-tuples $(x_j, c', x_i, Mtype)$ to the list Q of pending events (lines 6–7). The presence of $(x_j, c, x_i, Mtype)$ in Q means that x_j should be revised on c because of an $Mtype$ change in $D(x_i)$. I suppose that each constraint is associated with a function `init-propag` that performs the very first pass of propagation on the constraint and appends to list Q all 4-tuples relevant to events performed on some domains (line 1).

The benefit of this differentiation between types of events is twofold. First, it permits to process constraint propagation differently according to the type of event (line 4). As shown in the following example, this can have a dramatic effect on the cost of revision.

Example 3.82. Let $x_1 \leq x_2$, with $D(x_1) = D(x_2) = \{1..100\}$. If value 100 is removed from $D(x_2)$, the regular `Revise` procedure of AC3 takes each of the 100 values in $D(x_1)$ one by one, and looks for a support by traversing $D(x_2)$. This requires $1 + 2 + \ldots + 99 + 99 = \frac{100 \cdot 101}{2} - 1$ constraint checks to discover that $(x_1, 100)$ must be removed. An adapted `Revise` procedure knowing that 100 is a `DecMax` event simply decreases $max_D(x_1)$ to the same value as $max_D(x_2)$, i.e., 99. If the value removed from $D(x_2)$ is 50, again regular `Revise` performs around 5,000 constraint checks whereas a specific `Revise` knows that removing 50 is a `RemValue` event for which nothing should be done because the only events that can alter $D(x_1)$ are `DecMax` and `Instantiate`. Algorithm 3.11 is a specific function `Revise` for constraints $x_{k_1} \leq x_{k_2}$ (k_l is the index of the lth variable in the scheme of the constraint).

Algorithm 3.11: Function `Revise` for the constraint of Example 3.82

---

function `revise`(**inout** x_i; **in** $c \equiv x_{k_1} \leq x_{k_2}$; **in** $(x_j, Mtype)$; **out** $Changes$): **Boolean** ;
    $Changes \leftarrow \emptyset$;
  switch $Mtype$ **do**
      case `RemValue`
        nothing;
      case `IncMin`
        if $j = k_1$ **then** remove all $v < min_D(x_j)$ from $D(x_i)$;
      case `DecMax`
        if $j = k_2$ **then** remove all $v > max_D(x_j)$ from $D(x_i)$;
      case `Instantiate`
        if $j = k_1$ **then** remove all $v < min_D(x_j)$ from $D(x_i)$;
        else remove all $v > max_D(x_j)$ from $D(x_i)$;
    $Changes \leftarrow$ the types of changes performed on $D(x_i)$;

The second advantage of the information on events is that in some cases, we know that it is useless to propagate a constraint because a given event cannot alter the other variables of the constraint. For instance, in the constraint $x_1 \leq x_2$ of the example above, `RemValue` has no effect. Instead of having a set $\Gamma^C(x_i)$ of all constraints involving x_i, we can build such a set for each type of event. $\Gamma^C_{Mtype}(x_i)$ only contains constraints involving x_i for which an $Mtype$ event on x_i requires propagation. Line 6 in Algorithm 3.10 becomes:

6   **foreach** $c' \in \Gamma^C_{Mtype}(x_i), Mtype \in Changes$ **do** ...

Example 3.83. Let $c \equiv x_1 \leq x_2$. The only events that require propagation are `IncMin` and `Instantiate` on x_1, and `DecMax` and `Instantiate` on x_2. Thus, c is only put in $\Gamma^C_{IncMin}(x_1)$, $\Gamma^C_{Instantiate}(x_1)$, $\Gamma^C_{DecMax}(x_2)$, and $\Gamma^C_{Instantiate}(x_2)$. It avoids not only useless calls to `Revise` but also insertions and deletions of useless events in Q.

In the extreme case, the domains have been reduced in such a way that a constraint c is entailed. That is, c is satisfied for any valid combination of values on $X(c)$. (See [118, 110] or Section 3.3.1.) c can then be removed from the set of constraints of the network as long as the domains are not relaxed.

Example 3.84. Let $c \equiv x_1 \leq x_2$, $D(x_1) = \{1, 2, 4\}$ and $D(x_2) = \{5, 6, 7\}$. Any valid instantiation of x_1 and x_2 satisfies c. So, c can safely be removed from the network.

There is a third way of saving work during the propagation of changes in domains. It consists in storing not only the type of change performed on a domain $D(x_i)$ during a call to Revise, but also the set Δ_i of values removed. Function Revise has the extra parameter Δ_j of the values removed from $D(x_j)$ that led to this revision. In addition to *Changes*, Revise returns the set Δ_i of values it removes from $D(x_i)$. Δ_i is put in Q with the other information. Lines 3–7 in Algorithm 3.10 become:

3   select and remove $(x_i, c, x_j, Mtype, \Delta_j)$ from Q;
4   **if** Revise$(x_i, c, (x_j, Mtype, \Delta_j), Changes, \Delta_i)$ **then**
5   **if** $D(x_i) = \emptyset$ **then** return **false**;
6   **foreach** $c' \in \Gamma^C_{Mtype}(x_i), Mtype \in Changes$ **do**
7   **foreach** $x_j \in X(c'), j \neq i$ **do** $Q \leftarrow Q \cup \{(x_j, c', x_i, Mtype, \Delta_i)\}$

Such a facility was already proposed by Van Hentenryck et al. in the AC5 propagation schema [117]. This notably permits to decrease the complexity of arc consistency on functional or anti-functional constraints.

Example 3.85. The functional constraint $x_{k_1} = x_{k_2} + m$ can be propagated by the function Revise in Algorithm 3.12.

Algorithm 3.12: Function Revise for the constraint of Example 3.85

---

function revise(**inout** x_i; **in** $c \equiv x_{k_1} = x_{k_2} + m$; **in** $(x_j, Mtype, \Delta_j)$;
                                        out *Changes*; **out** Δ_i): **Boolean** ;

   Changes $\leftarrow \emptyset$;
   switch *Mtype* **do**
       case *RemValue*
           if $j = k_1$ **then**   **foreach** $v \in \Delta_j$ **do** remove $(v - m)$ from $D(x_i)$;
           else   **foreach** $v \in \Delta_j$ **do** remove $(v + m)$ from $D(x_i)$;
       case *IncMin*
           if $j = k_1$ **then** remove all $v < min_D(x_j) - m$ from $D(x_i)$;
           else remove all $v < min_D(x_j) + m$ from $D(x_i)$;
       case *DecMax*
           if $j = k_1$ **then** remove all $v > max_D(x_j) - m$ from $D(x_i)$;
           else remove all $v > max_D(x_j) + m$ from $D(x_i)$;
       case *Instantiate*
           if $j = k_1$ **then** assign $min_D(x_j) - m$ to x_i;
           else assign $min_D(x_j) + m$ to x_i;
   Changes $\leftarrow$ the types of changes performed;
   $\Delta_i \leftarrow$ all values removed from $D(x_i)$;

These four types of events permit to build efficient propagators for elementary constraints. But as soon as constraints are not arithmetic or do not have properties such as being functional, antifunctional or others, it is difficult to implement propagators with this kind of architecture.

3.8.2   Classes of Specific Constraints: Global Constraints

There are 'constraint patterns' that are ubiquitous when trying to express real problems as constraint networks. For example, we often need to say that a set of variables must all take different values. The size of the pattern is not fixed, that is, there can be any number of variables in the set. The `alldifferent` constraint, as introduced in CHIP [50], is not a single constraint but a whole class of constraints. Any constraint specifying that its variables must all take different values is an `alldifferent` constraint. The conventional wisdom is to name 'global constraints' these classes of constraints defined by a Boolean function whose domain contains tuples of values of any length. An instance c of a given global constraint is a constraint with a fixed scheme of variables which contains all tuples of length $|X(c)|$ accepted by the function defining the global constraint.[10] In the last years, the literature became quite verbose on this subject. Beldiceanu et al. proposed an extensive list of global constraints [9].

Example 3.86. The $\text{alldifferent}(x_1, \ldots, x_n)$ global constraint is the class of constraints that are defined on any sequence of n variables, $n \geq 2$, such that $x_i \neq x_j$ for all $i, j, 1 \leq i, j \leq n, i \neq j$. The $\text{NValue}(y, [x_1, \ldots, x_n])$ global constraint is the class of constraints that are defined on any sequence of $n + 1$ variables, $n \geq 1$, such that $|\{x_i \mid 1 \leq i \leq n\}| = y$ [100, 8].

It is interesting to incorporate global constraints in constraint solvers so that users can use them to express the corresponding constraint pattern easily. Because these global constraints can be used with a scheme of any size, it is important to have a way to propagate them without using generic arc consistency algorithms. (Remember that optimal generic arc consistency algorithms are in $O(erd^r)$ for constraints involving r variables —see Section 3.3.1.)

The first alternative to the combinatorial explosion of generic algorithms for GAC on a global constraint is to decompose it with 'simpler' constraints. A *decomposition* of a global constraint G is a polynomial time transformation δ_k (k being an integer) that, given any network $N = (X(c), D, \{c\})$ where c is an instance of G, returns a network $\delta_k(N$ such that $X(c) \subseteq X_{\delta_k(N)}$, for all $x_i \in X(c), D(x_i) = D_{\delta_k(N)}(x_i)$, for all $c_j \in C_{\delta_k(N)}$ $|X(c_j)| \leq k$, and $sol(N) = \pi_{X(c)}(sol(\delta_k(N)))$. That is, transforming N in $\delta_k(N)$ means replacing c by some new bounded arity constraints (and possibly new variables) whereas preserving the set of tuples allowed on $X(c)$. Note that by definition, the domains of the additional variables in the decomposition are necessarily of polynomial size.[11]

Example 3.87. The global constraint $\text{atmost}_{p,v}(x_1, \ldots, x_n)$ holds if and only if at most p variables in $x_1, \ldots, x_n$ take value v [116]. This constraint can be decomposed with $n+1$ additional variables $y_0, \ldots, y_n$. The transformation involves the constraint $(x_i = v \wedge y_i = y_{i-1} + 1) \vee (x_i \neq v \wedge y_i = y_{i-1})$ for all $i, 1 \leq i \leq n$, and the domains $D(y_0) = \{0\}$ and $D(y_i) = \{0, \ldots, p\}$ for all $i, 1 \leq i \leq n$.

---

[10]This definition does not allow constraints defined on several sequences of variables, such as the $\text{disjoint}([x_1 \ldots, x_n], [y_1 \ldots, y_m])$ constraint [9]. In such a case, we need to extend to Boolean functions with parameters giving the length of each sequence. This is essentially the same.

[11]Some decompositions depend only on the instance c of the global constraint and not on the domain. However, in other decompositions, the domain of the new variables depends on the domain of the variables in $X(c)$

Some global constraints G admit a decomposition δ_k that *preserves* GAC. That is, given any instance c of G and any domain D on $X(c)$, given any subdomain $D' \subseteq D$, GAC on $(X(c), D', \{c\})$ prunes the same values as GAC on the network obtained from $\delta_k((X(c), D, \{c\}))$ by reducing $D(x_i)$ to $D'(x_i)$ for all $x_i \in X(c)$. $\texttt{atmost}_{p,v}$ is a global constraint that admits a decomposition preserving GAC (see Example 3.87). But there are some constraints, such as the $\texttt{alldifferent}$, for which we do not know any such decomposition.[12] For those constraints, it is sometimes possible to build a specialized algorithm that enforces GAC in polynomial time on all instances of the global constraint. For instance, Knuth and Raghunathan, and Régin, made the link between GAC on the $\texttt{alldifferent}$ constraint and the problem of finding maximal matchings in a bipartite graph [77, 106], which is polynomial.

In [20], Bessiere et al. relaxed the definition of decomposition. They allow decompositions using constraints with unbounded arity as long as enforcing GAC on them is polynomial. The decomposition of a global constraint G is *GAC-polytime* if for any instance c of G and any domain on $X(c)$, enforcing GAC on the decomposition is polynomial. This enlarges the set of global constraints that can be decomposed. Nevertheless, there are global constraints for which we do not know any GAC-polytime decomposition that preserves GAC. Tools of computational complexity help us decide when a given global constraint has no chance to allow a GAC-polytime decomposition preserving GAC. In fact, if enforcing GAC on a global constraint G is NP-hard, there does not exist any GAC-polytime decomposition that preserves GAC (assuming P$\neq$ NP). For instance, enforcing GAC on $\texttt{NValue}$ is NP-hard. This tells us that there is no way to find a GAC-polytime decomposition on which GAC always removes all GAC inconsistent values of the original $\texttt{NValue}$ constraint.

Decompositions were limited to transformations in polynomial time, and so polynomial space. If we remove these restrictions, any global constraint allows a transformation into a binary network via the hidden variable encoding, where the unique additional variable has a domain of exponential size [45, 108]. GAC on this transformation is equivalent to GAC on the original constraint, even if enforcing GAC on it is NP-hard.

It is sometimes possible to express a global constraint as a combination of simpler constraints which is not a conjunction. Disjunctions are not naturally handled by constraint solvers. Van Hentenryck et al. proposed constructive disjunction as a way to partially propagate disjunctions of constraints [70]. Given a constraint $c = c_1 \vee c_2 \vee \ldots \vee c_k$, constructive disjunction propagates constraints c_i one by one independently of the others, and finally prunes values that were inconsistent with all c_i. This technique has been refined by Lhomme [84]. Bacchus and Walsh proposed a constraint algebra in which we can define meta-constraints as logical expressions composed of simpler constraints [4]. They give ways to propagate them and conditions under which GAC is guaranteed.

When enforcing GAC is too expensive on a global constraint, another possibility is to enforce a weaker level of consistency, such as BC(Z) or RC. BC(Z) and RC are significantly cheaper than GAC on constraints composed of arithmetic expressions (especially linear constraints). BC(Z) and RC are also used on other classes of constraints for which GAC is too expensive. In [80], Leconte showed that RC can be enforced on the

---

[12]In [26], Bessiere and Van Hentenryck characterized three types of globality for global constraints, depending on the non existence of decompositions preserving the solutions, preserving GAC or preserving the complexity of enforcing GAC.

alldifferent constraint at a cost asymptotically lower than that of Régin's GAC algorithm ([106]). Puget proposed a BC(Z) algorithm for alldifferent with an even lower complexity [103]. On the global cardinality constraint (gcc) defined by Régin [107], Quimper et al. showed that GAC is NP-hard if cardinalities are variables instead of fixed intervals [104]. Katriel and Thiel proposed a BC(Z) algorithm for gcc that runs in polynomial time even if cardinalities are variables [75]. In this case, BC(Z) is a means to propagate the constraint polynomially.

3.8.3   Creating Propagators Automatically

As an alternative to specialized algorithms for propagating a specific constraint, Apt and Montfroy proposed to generate sets of reduction rules [3]. A rule is of the form "if x_i takes value in S_{i_1}, ..., x_{i_k} takes value in S_{i_k} then y cannot take value v", where x_{i_j}'s and y belong to the scheme of the constraint and S_{i_j}'s are subsets of given domains $D(x_{i_j})$ For any constraint, there exists a set of rules that simulates arc consistency. However, its size can be exponential in the number of variables in the scheme of the constraint.

To avoid this combinatorial explosion, Dao et al. proposed to restrict their attention to rules in which variables x_{i_j} take values in intervals I_{i_j} instead of arbitrary subsets of the domains S_{i_j} [39]. This reduces the space of possibilities and permits to express the task of generating rules as a linear program to be solved by a simplex.

Another way to avoid combinatorial explosion when building propagators for a constraint c_{adhoc} is to take into account the internal structure of the constraint to factorize many satisfying tuples under the same rule. Barták proposed to decompose ad hoc binary constraints $c_{adhoc}(x_i, x_j)$ into *rectangles* [5]. The Cartesian product $r = S_i \times S_j$ of two sets of integers S_i and S_j is a rectangle for c_{adhoc} if $(v_i, v_j) \in S_i \times S_j \Rightarrow (v_i, v_j) \in c_{adhoc}$ Given a collection R of rectangles such that $\bigcup_{r \in R} r = c_{adhoc}$, Barták gives a propagation algorithm that revises c_{adhoc} more efficiently than a generic algorithm. Cheng et al. extended this technique by proposing to decompose (possibly non-binary) constraints into 'triangles' instead of rectangles [30]. More precisely, they decompose a constraint $c_{adhoc}(x_1, \ldots, x_k)$ into a disjunction of 'box constraints'. A box is a k-dimensional hypercube $[l_1..u_1] \times \cdots \times [l_k..u_k]$ where $[l_i..u_i]$ is an interval of integers for x_i. A box constraint is the conjunction of a box B and a *simple* constraint c_b, that is, a constraint of the form $\sum_1^k a_i x_i \leq a_0$ (the set of allowed tuples looks like a triangle when the constraint is binary). Cheng et al. proposed an algorithm that generates a representation of the constraint c_{adhoc} as a disjunction of box constraints. Applying constructive disjunction on this representation is equivalent to arc consistency on c_{adhoc}.

3.8.4   Priorities in the Propagation List

A simple way to improve the efficiency of propagation in constraint solvers is to put priorities on the different propagation events of the different constraints. We saw in Section 3.3.3 that the propagation list of arc consistency algorithms can be heuristically ordered. The main criterion in the case of generic AC algorithms for binary constraints was to put first the constraints that are expected to prune more. Constraint solvers contain various types of constraints and various types of propagation events for these constraints which can have different complexities. Laburthe et al. in [78] and Schulte and Stuckey in [110] proposed to maintain a propagation list with several levels of priority. The idea is to put a propagation event in a different level of the list depending on its time complexity. An event in the ith level is not popped while the $(i-1)$th level is not empty. The instantiation event on a simple arithmetic constraint is the kind of event that is put at the first level. Propagating GAC on an expensive global constraint is put at the last level. Propagating BC(Z) on the same constraint will be put in some intermediate level. The CHOCO solver uses a propagation list with 7 levels of priority [78].

Acknowledgements

I would like to thank especially Charlotte Truchet and Peter van Beek for their careful reading of this chapter and their many valuable comments. Thanks also to Eric Bourreau for having checked the section on specific constraints, to Peter Stuckey for his advice for choosing the names of the different consistencies on bounds, to Roland Yap for some pointers in the literature, and to Toby Walsh for interesting discussions on global constraints. Finally, I am very grateful to E.C. Freuder for the epigraph he kindly gave me for introducing this chapter.

Bibliography

[1]   K.R. Apt. The essence of constraint propagation. *Theoretical Computer Science*, 221(1-2):179–210, 1999.

[2]   K.R. Apt. *Principles of Constraint Programming*. Cambridge University Press, 2003.

[3]   K.R. Apt and E. Montfroy. Automatic generation of constraint propagation algorithms for small finite domains. In *Proceedings CP'99*, pages 58–72, Alexandria VA, 1999.

[4]   F. Bacchus and T. Walsh. Propagating logical combinations of constraints. In *Proceedings IJCAI'05*, pages 35–40, Edinburgh, Scotland, 2005.

[5]   R. Barták. A general relation constraint: An implementation. In *Proceedings of CP'00 Workshop on Techniques for Implementing Constraint Programming Systems (TRICS)*, pages 30–40, Singapore, 2000.

[6]   R. Barták and R. Erben. A new algorithm for singleton arc consistency. In *Proceedings FLAIRS'04*, Miami Beach FL, 2004. AAAI Press.

[7]   C. Beeri, R. Fagin, D. Maier, and M. Yannakakis. On the desirability of acyclic database schemes. *Journal of the ACM*, 30:479–513, 1983.

[8]   N. Beldiceanu. Pruning for the minimum constraint family and for the number of distinct values constraint family. In *Proceedings CP'01*, pages 211–224, Paphos, Cyprus, 2001.

[9]   N. Beldiceanu, M. Carlsson, and J.X. Rampon. Global constraint catalog. Technical Report T2005:08, Swedish Institute of Computer Science, Kista, Sweden, May 2005.

[10] F. Benhamou, D.A. McAllester, and P. Van Hentenryck. Clp(intervals) revisited. In *Proceedings of the International Symposium on Logic Programming (ILPS'94)*, pages 124–138, Ithaca, New York, 1994.

[11] F. Benhamou and W. Older. Applying interval arithmetic to real, integer and boolean constraints. *Journal of Logic Programming*, 32:1–24, 1997.

[12]   H. Bennaceur and M.S. Affane. Partition-k-ac: an efficient filtering technique com-
       bining domain partition and arc consistency. In *Proceedings CP'01*, pages 560–564,
       Paphos, Cyprus, 2001. Short paper.

[13]   P. Berlandier. Improving domain filtering using restricted path consistency. In *Pro-
       ceedings IEEE Conference on Artificial Intelligence and Applications (CAIA'95)*
       1995.

[14]   C. Bessiere. Arc-consistency and arc-consistency again. *Artificial Intelligence*, 65:
       179–190, 1994.

[15]   C. Bessiere and M.O. Cordier. Arc-consistency and arc-consistency again. In *Pro-
       ceedings AAAI'93*, pages 108–113, Washington D.C., 1993.

[16]   C. Bessiere and R. Debruyne. Theoretical analysis of singleton arc consistency. In
       B. Hnich, editor, *Proceedings ECAI'04 Workshop on Modelling and solving prob-
       lems with constraints*, pages 20–29, Valencia, Spain, 2004.

[17]   C. Bessiere and R. Debruyne. Optimal and suboptimal singleton arc consistency
       algorithms. In *Proceedings IJCAI'05*, pages 54–59, Edinburgh, Scotland, 2005.

[18]   C. Bessiere, E. C. Freuder, and J. C. Régin. Using inference to reduce arc consis-
       tency computation. In *Proceedings IJCAI'95*, pages 592–598, Montréal, Canada,
       1995.

[19]   C. Bessiere, E.C. Freuder, and J.C. Régin. Using constraint metaknowledge to re-
       duce arc consistency computation. *Artificial Intelligence*, 107:125–148, 1999.

[20]   C. Bessiere, E. Hebrard, B. Hnich, and T. Walsh. The complexity of global con-
       straints. In *Proceedings AAAI'04*, pages 112–117, San Jose CA, 2004. to appear.

[21]   C. Bessiere, E. Hebrard, B. Hnich, and T. Walsh. The tractability of global con-
       straints. In *Proceedings CP'04*, pages 716–720, Toronto, Canada, 2004. Short
       paper.

[22]   C. Bessiere, P. Meseguer, E.C. Freuder, and J. Larrosa. On forward checking for
       non-binary constraint satisfaction. *Artificial Intelligence*, 141:205–224, 2002.

[23]   C. Bessiere and J.C. Régin. Arc consistency for general constraint networks: pre-
       liminary results. In *Proceedings IJCAI'97*, pages 398–404, Nagoya, Japan, 1997.

[24]   C. Bessiere and J.C. Régin. Refining the basic constraint propagation algorithm. In
       Proceedings IJCAI'01, pages 309–315, Seattle WA, 2001.

[25]   C. Bessiere, J.C. Régin, R.H.C. Yap, and Y. Zhang. An optimal coarse-grained arc
       consistency algorithm. *Artificial Intelligence*, 165:165–185, 2005.

[26]   C. Bessiere and P. Van Hentenryck. To be or not to be ... a global constraint. In
       Proceedings CP'03, pages 789–794, Kinsale, Ireland, 2003. Short paper.

[27]   A. Borning. The programming language aspects of thinglab, a constraint-oriented
       simulation laboratory. *ACM Trans. Program. Lang. Syst.*, 3(4):353–387, 1981.

[28]   F. Boussemart, F. Hemery, and C. Lecoutre. Revision ordering heuristics for the con-
       straint satisfaction problem. In *Proceedings of the CP'04 Workshop on Constraint
       Propagation and Implementation*, pages 29–43, Toronto, Canada, 2004.

[29]   M. Cadoli and F.M. Donini. A survey on knowledge compilation. *AI Communica-
       tions*, 10(3-4):137–150, 1997.

[30]   K.C.K. Cheng, J.H.M. Lee, and P.J. Stuckey. Box constraint collections for adhoc
       constraints. In *Proceedings CP'03*, pages 214–228, Kinsale, Ireland, 2003.

[31]   A. Chmeiss and P. Jégou. Path-consistency: when space misses time. In *Proceedings
       AAAI'96*, pages 196–201, Portland OR, 1996.

[32]   A. Chmeiss and P. Jégou. Sur la consistance de chemin et ses formes partielles. In

Proceedings RFIA'96, pages 212–219, Rennes, France, 1996. (in French).

[33] A. Chmeiss and P. Jégou. Efficient path-consistency propagation. *International Journal on Artificial Intelligence Tools*, 7(2):121–142, 1998.

[34] A. Chmeiss and L. Saïs. About the use of local consistency in solving CSPs. In *Proceedings IEEE-ICTAI'00*, pages 104–107, Vancouver, Canada, 2000.

[35] C.W. Choi, W. Harvey, J.H.M. Lee, and P.J. Stuckey. Finite domain bounds consistency revisited. http://arxiv.org/abs/cs.AI/0412021, December 2004.

[36] H. Collavizza, F. Delobel, and M. Rueher. A note on partial consistencies over continuous domains. In *Proceedings CP'98*, pages 147–161, Pisa, Italy, 1998.

[37] M.C. Cooper. An optimal k-consistency algorithm. *Artificial Intelligence*, 41:89–95, 1989/90.

[38] H. Cros. *Compilation et apprentissage dans les réseaux de contraintes*. PhD thesis, University Montpellier II, France, 2003. in French.

[39] T.B.H. Dao, A. Lallouet, A. Legtchenko, and L. Martin. Indexical-based solver learning. In *Proceedings CP'02*, pages 541–555, Ithaca NY, 2002.

[40] M. Davis and H. Putnam. A computing procedure for quantification theory. *Journal of the ACM*, 7:201–215, 1960.

[41] R. Debruyne. A property of path inverse consistency leading to an optimal pic algorithm. In *Proceedings ECAI'00*, pages 88–92, Berlin, Germany, 2000.

[42] R. Debruyne and C. Bessiere. From restricted path consistency to max-restricted path consistency. In *Proceedings CP'97*, pages 312–326, Linz, Austria, 1997.

[43] R. Debruyne and C. Bessiere. Some practicable filtering techniques for the constraint satisfaction problem. In *Proceedings IJCAI'97*, pages 412–417, Nagoya, Japan, 1997.

[44] R. Debruyne and C. Bessiere. Domain filtering consistencies. *Journal of Artificial Intelligence Research*, 14:205–230, 2001.

[45] R. Dechter. On the expressiveness of networks with hidden variables. In *Proceedings AAAI'90*, pages 556–562, Boston MA, 1990.

[46] R. Dechter. *Constraint Processing*. Morgan Kaufmann, 2003.

[47] R. Dechter and J. Pearl. Network-based heuristics for constraint-satisfaction problems. *Artificial Intelligence*, 34:1–38, 1988.

[48] R. Dechter and J. Pearl. Tree clustering for constraint networks. *Artificial Intelligence*, 38:353–366, 1989.

[49] R. Dechter and P. van Beek. Local and global relational consistency. *Theoretical Computer Science*, 173(1):283–308, 1997.

[50] M. Dincbas, P. Van Hentenryck, H. Simonis, and A. Aggoun. The constraint logic programming language chip. In *Proceedings of the International Conference on Fifth Generation Computer Systems*, pages 693–702, Tokyo, Japan, 1988.

[51] R.E. Fikes. REF-ARF: A system for solving problems stated as procedures. *Artificial Intelligence*, 1:27–120, 1970.

[52] J.W. Freeman. *Improvements to propositional satisfiability search algorithms*. PhD thesis, University of Pennsylvania, Philadelphia PA, 1995.

[53] E.C. Freuder. Synthesizing constraint expressions. *Communications of the ACM*, 21 (11):958–966, Nov 1978.

[54] E.C. Freuder. A sufficient condition for backtrack-free search. *Journal of the ACM*, 29(1):24–32, Jan. 1982.

[55] E.C. Freuder. A sufficient condition for backtrack-bounded search. *Journal of the*

ACM, 32(4):755–761, Oct. 1985.

[56]   E.C. Freuder. Completable representations of constraint satisfaction problems. In *Proceedings KR'91*, pages 186–195, Cambridge MA, 1991.

[57]   E.C. Freuder and C.D. Elfe. Neighborhood inverse consistency preprocessing. In *Proceedings AAAI'96*, pages 202–208, Portland OR, 1996.

[58]   E.C. Freuder and R.J. Wallace. Selective relaxation for constraint satisfaction problems. In *IEEE-ICTAI'91*, pages 332–339, San Jose CA, 1991.

[59]   T.W. Frühwirth. Theory and practice of constraint handling rules. *Journal of Logic Programming*, 37(1-3):95–138, 1998.

[60]   M.R. Garey and D.S. Johnson. *Computers and Intractability: A Guide to NP-Completeness*. Freeman, San Francisco CA, 1979.

[61]   J. Gaschnig. A constraint satisfaction method for inference making. In *Proceedings Twelfth Annual Allerton Conference on Circuit and System Theory*, pages 866–874, 1974.

[62]   J. Gaschnig. Experimental case studies of backtrack vs waltz-type vs new algorithms for satisficing assignment problems. In *Proceedings CCSCSI'78*, pages 268–277, 1978.

[63]   I. Gent, K. Stergiou, and T. Walsh. Decomposable constraints. *Artificial Intelligence*, 123:133–156, 2000.

[64]   I.P. Gent, E. MacIntyre, P. Prosser, P. Shaw, and T. Walsh. The constrainedness of arc consistency. In *Proceedings CP'97*, pages 327–340, Linz, Austria, 1997.

[65]   I.P. Gent, E. MacIntyre, P. Prosser, and T. Walsh. The constrainedness of search. In *Proceedings AAAI'96*, pages 246–252, Portland OR, 1996.

[66]   S.W. Golomb and L.D. Baumert. Backtrack programming. *Journal of the ACM*, 12 (4):516–524, October 1965.

[67]   M. Gyssens. On the complexity of join dependencies. *ACM Trans. Database Syst.* 11(1):81–108, 1986.

[68]   C.C. Han and C.H. Lee. Comments on Mohr and Henderson's path consistency algorithm. *Artificial Intelligence*, 36:125–130, 1988.

[69]   R.M. Haralick and G.L. Elliott. Increasing tree search efficiency for constraint satisfaction problems. *Artificial Intelligence*, 14:263–313, 1980.

[70]   P. Van Hentenryck, V. Saraswat, and Y. Deville. The design, implementation, and evaluation of the constraint language cc(FD). In *Constraint Programming: Basics and Trends*. Springer Verlag, 1995.

[71]   ILOG. *User's manual*. ILOG Solver 4.4, ILOG S.A., 1999.

[72]   P. Janssen, P. Jégou, B. Nouguier, and M. C. Vilarem. A filtering process for general constraint-satisfaction problems: Achieving pairwise-consistency using an associated binary representation. In *Proceedings of the IEEE Workshop on Tools for Artificial Intelligence*, pages 420–427, Fairfax VA, 1989.

[73]   P. Jégou. *Contribution á l'étude des problèmes de satisfaction de contraintes: algorithmes de propagation et de résolution; propagation de contraintes dans les réseaux dynamiques*. PhD thesis, CRIM, University Montpellier II, 1991. in French.

[74]   P. Jégou. On the consistency of general constraint-satisfaction problems. In *Proceedings AAAI'93*, pages 114–119, Washington D.C., 1993.

[75]   I. Katriel and S. Thiel. Fast bound consistency for the global cardinality constraint. In *Proceedings CP'03*, pages 437–451, Kinsale, Ireland, 2003.

[76]   D.E. Knuth. Semantics of context-free languages. *Mathematical Systems Theory*, 2

(2):127–145, 1968.

[77] D.E. Knuth and A. Raghunathan. The problem of compatible representatives. *SIAM Journal of Discrete Mathematics*, 5(3):422–427, 1992.

[78] F. Laburthe and Ocre. Choco : implémentation du noyau d'un système de contraintes. In *Proceedings JNPC'00*, pages 151–165, Marseilles, France, 2000.

[79] J.L. Laurière. A language and a program for stating and solving combinatorial problems. *Artificial Intelligence*, 10:29–127, 1978.

[80] M. Leconte. A bounds-based reduction scheme for difference constraints. In *Proceedings of the FLAIRS'96 workshop on Constraint-based Reasoning (Constraint'96)*, Key West FL, 1996.

[81] C. Lecoutre, F. Boussemart, and F. Hemery. Exploiting multidirectionality in coarse-grained arc consistency algorithms. In *Proceedings CP'03*, pages 480–494, Kinsale, Ireland, 2003.

[82] C. Lecoutre and S. Cardon. A greedy approach to establish singleton arc consistency. In *Proceedings IJCAI'05*, pages 199–204, Edinburgh, Scotland, 2005.

[83] O. Lhomme. Consistency techniques for numeric CSPs. In *Proceedings IJCAI'93*, pages 232–238, Chambéry, France, 1993.

[84] O. Lhomme. Efficient filtering algorithm for disjunction of constraints. In *Proceedings CP'03*, pages 904–908, Kinsale, Ireland, 2003.

[85] C.M. Li and Anbulagan. Heuristics based on unit propagation for satisfiability problems. In *Proceedings IJCAI'97*, pages 366–371, Nagoya, Japan, 1997.

[86] A.K. Mackworth. Consistency in networks of relations. Technical Report 75-3, Dept. of Computer Science, Univ. of B.C. Vancouver, 1975. (also in Artificial Intelligence 8, 99-118, 1977).

[87] A.K. Mackworth. Consistency in networks of relations. *Artificial Intelligence*, 8: 99–118, 1977.

[88] A.K. Mackworth. On reading sketch maps. In *Proceedings IJCAI'77*, pages 598–606, Cambridge MA, 1977.

[89] A.K. Mackworth and E.C. Freuder. The complexity of some polynomial network consistency algorithms for constraint satisfaction problems. *Artificial Intelligence*, 25:65–74, 1985.

[90] P. Martin and D.B. Shmoys. A new approach to computing optimal schedules for the job-shop scheduling problem. In *Proceedings 5th International Conference on Integer Programming and Combinatorial Optimization (IPCO'96)*, volume 1084 of *LNCS*, pages 389–403, Vancouver, BC, 1996. Springer–Verlag.

[91] J.J. McGregor. Relational consistency algorithms and their application in finding subgraph and graph isomorphism. *Information Science*, 19:229–250, 1979.

[92] R. Mohr and T.C. Henderson. Arc and path consistency revisited. *Artificial Intelligence*, 28:225–233, 1986.

[93] R. Mohr and G. Masini. Good old discrete relaxation. In *Proceedings ECAI'88*, pages 651–656, Munchen, FRG, 1988.

[94] R. Mohr and G. Masini. Running efficiently arc consistency. In G. Ferraté et al., editor, *Syntactic and Structural Pattern Recognition*, pages 217–231. Springer–Verlag, Berlin, 1988.

[95] U. Montanari. Networks of constraints: Fundamental properties and applications to picture processing. *Information Science*, 7:95–132, 1974.

[96] U. Montanari and F. Rossi. Constraint relaxation may be perfect. *Artificial Intelli-*

gence, 48:143–170, 1991.

[97] M. Moskewicz, C. Madigan, Y. Zhao, L. Zhang, and S. Malik. Chaff: Engineering an efficient sat solver. In *Proceedings International Design Automation Conference (DAC-01)*, pages 530–535, Las Vegas NV, 2001.

[98] B.A. Nadel. Tree search and arc consistency in constraint satisfaction algorithms. In L.Kanal and V.Kumar, editors, *Search in Artificial Intelligence*, pages 287–342. Springer-Verlag, 1988.

[99] B.A. Nadel. Constraint satisfaction algorithms. *Computational Intelligence*, 5:188–224, 1989.

[100] F. Pachet and P. Roy. Automatic generation of music programs. In *Proceedings CP'99*, pages 331–345, Alexandria VA, 1999.

[101] C.H. Papadimitriou and M. Yannakakis. The complexity of facets (and some facets of complexity). *J. Comput. System Sci.*, 28:244–259, 1984.

[102] P. Prosser, K. Stergiou, and T Walsh. Singleton consistencies. In *Proceedings CP'00*, pages 353–368, Singapore, 2000.

[103] J.F. Puget. A fast algorithm for the bound consistency of alldiff constraints. In *Proceedings AAAI'98*, pages 359–366, Madison WI, 1998.

[104] C.G. Quimper, A. López-Ortiz, P. van Beek, and A. Golynski. Improved algorithms for the global cardinality constraint. In *Proceedings CP'04*, pages 542–556, Toronto, Canada, 2004.

[105] C.G. Quimper, P. van Beek, A. López-Ortiz, A. Golynski, and S.B. Sadjad. An efficient bounds consistency algorithm for the global cardinality constraint. In *Proceedings CP'03*, pages 600–614, Kinsale, Ireland, 2003.

[106] J.C. Régin. A filtering algorithm for constraints of difference in CSPs. In *Proceedings AAAI'94*, pages 362–367, Seattle WA, 1994.

[107] J.C. Régin. Generalized arc consistency for global cardinality constraint. In *Proceedings AAAI'96*, pages 209–215, Portland OR, 1996.

[108] F. Rossi, C. Petrie, and V. Dhar. On the equivalence of constraint satisfaction problems. In *Proceedings ECAI'90*, pages 550–556, Stockholm, Sweden, 1990.

[109] C. Schulte and P.J. Stuckey. When do bounds and domain propagation lead to the same search space. In *Proceedings of the Third International Conference on Principles and Practice of Declarative Programming*, pages 115–126, Florence, Italy, September 2001. ACM Press.

[110] C. Schulte and P.J. Stuckey. Speeding up constraint propagation. In *Proceedings CP'04*, pages 619–633, Toronto, Canada, 2004.

[111] M. Singh. Path consistency revisited. *International Journal on Artificial Intelligence Tools*, 5(1-2):127–141, 1996.

[112] E. Tsang. No more 'partial' and 'full' looking ahead. *Artificial Intelligence*, 98: 351–361, 1998.

[113] M.R.C. van Dongen. Lightweight arc-consistency algorithms. Technical Report TR-01-2003, Cork Constraint Computation Center, 2003.

[114] M.R.C. van Dongen and J.A. Bowen. Improving arc-consistency algorithms with double-support checks. In *Proceedings of the Eleventh Irish Conference on Artificial Intelligence and Cognitive Science*, pages 140–149, 2000.

[115] P. Van Hentenryck. *Constraint Satisfaction in Logic Programming*. MIT Press, Cambridge, MA, 1989. ISBN 0-262-08181-4.

[116] P. Van Hentenryck and Y. Deville. The cardinality operator: A new logical connec-

tive for constraint logic programming. In *Proceedings ICLP'91*, pages 745–759, Paris, France, 1991.

[117] P. Van Hentenryck, Y. Deville, and C.M. Teng. A generic arc-consistency algorithm and its specializations. *Artificial Intelligence*, 57:291–321, 1992.

[118] P. Van Hentenryck, V.A. Saraswat, and Y. Deville. Design, implementation, and evaluation of the constraint language cc(FD). *Journal of Logic Programming*, 37 (1-3):139–164, 1998.

[119] G. Verfaillie, D. Martinez, and C. Bessiere. A generic customizable framework for inverse local consistency. In *Proceedings AAAI'99*, pages 169–174, Orlando FL, 1999.

[120] R.J. Wallace. Why AC-3 is almost always better than AC-4 for establishing arc consistency in CSPs. In *Proceedings IJCAI'93*, pages 239–245, Chambéry, France, 1993.

[121] R.J. Wallace and E.C. Freuder. Ordering heuristics for arc consistency algorithms. In *Proceedings Ninth Canadian Conference on Artificial Intelligence*, pages 163–169, Vancouver, Canada, 1992.

[122] T. Walsh. Errata on singleton consistencies. Private communication, September 2000.

[123] T. Walsh. Relational consistencies. Technical Report APES report 28-2001, University of York, 2001.

[124] D.L. Waltz. Generating semantic descriptions from drawings of scenes with shadows. Tech.Rep. MAC AI-271, MIT, 1972.

[125] Y. Zhang and R.H.C. Yap. Arc consistency on n-ary monotonic and linear constraints. In *Proceedings CP'00*, pages 470–483, Singapore, 2000.

[126] Y. Zhang and R.H.C. Yap. Making AC-3 an optimal algorithm. In *Proceedings IJCAI'01*, pages 316–321, Seattle WA, 2001.

Chapter 4

Backtracking Search Algorithms

Peter van Beek

There are three main algorithmic techniques for solving constraint satisfaction problems: backtracking search, local search, and dynamic programming. In this chapter, I survey backtracking search algorithms. Algorithms based on dynamic programming [15]—sometimes referred to in the literature as variable elimination, synthesis, or inference algorithms—are the topic of Chapter 7. Local or stochastic search algorithms are the topic of Chapter 5.

An algorithm for solving a constraint satisfaction problem (CSP) can be either complete or incomplete. Complete, or systematic algorithms, come with a guarantee that a solution will be found if one exists, and can be used to show that a CSP does not have a solution and to find a provably optimal solution. Backtracking search algorithms and dynamic programming algorithms are, in general, examples of complete algorithms. Incomplete, or non-systematic algorithms, cannot be used to show a CSP does not have a solution or to find a provably optimal solution. However, such algorithms are often effective at finding a solution if one exists and can be used to find an approximation to an optimal solution. Local or stochastic search algorithms are examples of incomplete algorithms.

Of the two classes of algorithms that are complete—backtracking search and dynamic programming—backtracking search algorithms are currently the most important in practice. The drawbacks of dynamic programming approaches are that they often require an exponential amount of time and space, and they do unnecessary work by finding, or making it possible to easily generate, all solutions to a CSP. However, one rarely wishes to find all solutions to a CSP in practice. In contrast, backtracking search algorithms work on only one solution at a time and thus need only a polynomial amount of space.

Since the first formal statements of backtracking algorithms over 40 years ago [30, 57], many techniques for improving the efficiency of a backtracking search algorithm have been suggested and evaluated. In this chapter, I survey some of the most important techniques including branching strategies, constraint propagation, nogood recording, backjumping, heuristics for variable and value ordering, randomization and restart strategies, and alternatives to depth-first search. The techniques are not always orthogonal and sometimes combining two or more techniques into one algorithm has a multiplicative effect (such as combining restarts with nogood recording) and sometimes it has a degradation effect (such as increased constraint propagation versus backjumping). Given the many possible ways that these techniques can be combined together into one algorithm, I also survey work on comparing backtracking algorithms. The best combinations of these techniques result in robust backtracking algorithms that can now routinely solve large, hard instances that are of practical importance.

4.1 Preliminaries

In this section, I first define the constraint satisfaction problem followed by a brief review of the needed background on backtracking search.

Definition 4.1 (CSP). *A constraint satisfaction problem (CSP) consists of a set of variables* $X = \{x_1, \ldots, x_n\}$; *a set of values,* $D = \{a_1, \ldots, a_d\}$, *where each variable* $x_i \in X$ *has an associated finite domain* $dom(x_i) \subseteq D$ *of possible values; and a collection of constraints*

Each constraint C is a relation—a set of tuples—over some set of variables, denoted by $vars(C)$. The size of the set $vars(C)$ is called the *arity* of the constraint. A *unary* constraint is a constraint of arity one, a *binary* constraint is a constraint of arity two, a *non-binary* constraint is a constraint of arity greater than two, and a *global* constraint is a constraint that can be over arbitrary subsets of the variables. A constraint can be specified *intensionally* by specifying a formula that tuples in the constraint must satisfy, or *extensionally* by explicitly listing the tuples in the constraint. A *solution* to a CSP is an assignment of a value to each variable that satisfies all the constraints. If no solution exists, the CSP is said to be inconsistent or unsatisfiable.

As a running example in this survey, I will use the 6-queens problem: how can we place 6 queens on a 6×6 chess board so that no two queens attack each other. As one possible CSP model, let there be a variable for each column of the board $\{x_1, \ldots, x_6\}$, each with domain $dom(x_i) = \{1, \ldots, 6\}$. Assigning a value j to a variable x_i means placing a queen in row j, column i. Between each pair of variables x_i and x_j, $1 \le i < j \le 6$, there is a constraint $C(x_i, x_j)$, given by $(x_i \neq x_j) \wedge (|i - j| \neq |x_i - x_j|)$. One possible solution is given by $\{x_1 = 4, x_2 = 1, x_3 = 5, x_4 = 2, x_5 = 6, x_6 = 3\}$.

The satisfiability problem (SAT) is a CSP where the domains of the variables are the Boolean values and the constraints are Boolean formulas. I will assume that the constraints are in conjunctive normal form and are thus written as clauses. A literal is a Boolean variable or its negation and a clause is a disjunction of literals. For example, the formula $\neg x_1 \vee x_2 \vee x_3$ is a clause. A clause with one literal is called a unit clause; a clause with no literals is called the empty clause. The empty clause is unsatisfiable.

A backtracking search for a solution to a CSP can be seen as performing a depth-first traversal of a *search tree*. The search tree is generated as the search progresses and represents alternative choices that may have to be examined in order to find a solution. The method of extending a node in the search tree is often called a *branching strategy*, and several alternatives have been proposed and examined in the literature (see Section 4.2). A backtracking algorithm *visits* a node if, at some point in the algorithm's execution, the node is generated. Constraints are used to check whether a node may possibly lead to a solution of the CSP and to prune subtrees containing no solutions. A node in the search tree is a *deadend* if it does not lead to a solution.

The naive backtracking algorithm (BT) is the starting point for all of the more sophisticated backtracking algorithms (see Table 4.1). In the BT search tree, the root node at level 0 is the empty set of assignments and a node at level j is a set of assignments $\{x_1 = a_1, \ldots, x_j = a_j\}$. At each node in the search tree, an uninstantiated variable is selected and the branches out of this node consist of all possible ways of extending the node by instantiating the variable with a value from its domain. The branches represent the different choices that can be made for that variable. In BT, only constraints with no uninstantiated variables are checked at a node. If a constraint check fails—a constraint is not satisfied—the next domain value of the current variable is tried. If there are no more domain values left, BT backtracks to the most recently instantiated variable. A solution is found if all constraint checks succeed after the last variable has been instantiated.

Figure 4.1 shows a fragment of the backtrack tree generated by the naive backtracking algorithm (BT) for the 6-queens problem. The labels on the nodes are shorthands for the set of assignments at that node. For example, the node labeled 25 consists of the set of assignments $\{x_1 = 2, x_2 = 5\}$. White dots denote nodes where all the constraints with no uninstantiated variables are satisfied (no pair of queens attacks each other). Black dots denote nodes where one or more constraint checks fail. (The reasons for the shading and dashed arrows are explained in Section 4.5.) For simplicity, I have assumed a static order of instantiation in which variable x_i is always chosen at level i in the search tree and values are assigned to variables in the order $1, \ldots, 6$.

4.2 Branching Strategies

In the naive backtracking algorithm (BT), a node $p = \{x_1 = a_1, \ldots, x_j = a_j\}$ in the search tree is a set of assignments and p is extended by selecting a variable x and adding a branch to a new node $p \cup \{x = a\}$, for each $a \in dom(x)$. The assignment $x = a$ is said to be *posted* along a branch. As the search progresses deeper in the tree, additional assignments are posted and upon backtracking the assignments are retracted. However, this is just one possible branching strategy, and several alternatives have been proposed and examined in the literature.

More generally, a node $p = \{b_1, \ldots, b_j\}$ in the search tree of a backtracking algorithm is a set of *branching constraints*, where b_i, $1 \leq i \leq j$, is the branching constraint posted at level i in the search tree. A node p is extended by adding the branches $p \cup \{b_{j+1}^1\}, \ldots, p \cup \{b_{j+1}^k\}$, for some branching constraints b_{j+1}^i, $1 \leq i \leq k$. The branches are often ordered using a heuristic, with the left-most branch being the most promising. To ensure completeness, the constraints posted on all the branches from a node must be mutually exclusive and exhaustive.

Usually, branching strategies consist of posting unary constraints. In this case, a variable ordering heuristic is used to select the next variable to branch on and the ordering of the branches is determined by a value ordering heuristic (see Section 4.6). As a running example, let x be the variable to be branched on, let $dom(x) = \{1, \ldots, 6\}$, and assume that the value ordering heuristic is lexicographic ordering. Three popular branching strategies involving unary constraints are the following.

1. *Enumeration.* The variable x is instantiated in turn to each value in its domain. A branch is generated for each value in the domain of the variable and the constraint $x = 1$ is posted along the first branch, $x = 2$ along the second branch, and so

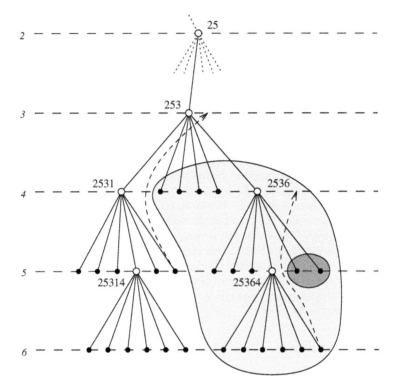

Figure 4.1: A fragment of the BT backtrack tree for the 6-queens problem (from [79]).

on. The enumeration branching strategy is assumed in many textbook presentations of backtracking and in much work on backtracking algorithms for solving CSPs. An alternative name for this branching strategy in the literature is d-way branching, where d is the size of the domain.

2. *Binary choice points.* The variable x is instantiated to some value in its domain. Assuming the value 1 is chosen in our example, two branches are generated and the constraints $x = 1$ and $x \neq 1$ are posted, respectively. This branching strategy is often used in constraint programming languages for solving CSPs (see, e.g., [72, 123]) and is used by Sabin and Freuder [116] in their backtracking algorithm which maintains arc consistency during the search. An alternative name for this branching strategy in the literature is 2-way branching.

3. *Domain splitting.* Here the variable is not necessarily instantiated, but rather the choices for the variable are reduced in each subproblem. For ordered domains such as in our example, this could consist of posting a constraint of the form $x \leq 3$ on one branch and posting $x > 3$ on the other branch.

The three schemes are, of course, identical if the domains are binary (such as, for example, in SAT).

Table 4.1: Some named backtracking algorithms. Hybrid algorithms which combine techniques are denoted by hyphenated names. For example, MAC-CBJ is an algorithm that maintains arc consistency and performs conflict-directed backjumping.

BT	Naive backtracking: checks constraints with no uninstantiated variables; chronologically backtracks.
MAC	Maintains arc consistency on constraints with *at least* one uninstantiated variable; chronologically backtracks.
FC	Forward checking algorithm: maintains arc consistency on constraints with *exactly* one uninstantiated variable; chronologically backtracks.
DPLL	Forward checking algorithm specialized to SAT problems: uses unit propagation; chronologically backtracks.
MC_k	Maintains strong k-consistency; chronologically backtracks.
CBJ	Conflict-directed backjumping; no constraint propagation.
BJ	Limited backjumping; no constraint propagation.
DBT	Dynamic backtracking: backjumping with 0-order relevance-bounded nogood recording; no constraint propagation.

Branching strategies that consist of posting non-unary constraints have also been proposed, as have branching strategies that are specific to a class of problems. As an example of both, consider job shop scheduling where we must schedule a set of tasks $t_1, \ldots, t_k$ on a set of resources. Let x_i be a finite domain variable representing the starting time of t_i and let d_i be the fixed duration of t_i. A popular branching strategy is to order or serialize the tasks that share a resource. Consider two tasks t_1 and t_2 that share the same resource. The branching strategy is to post the constraint $x_1 + d_1 \leq x_2$ along one branch and to post the constraint $x_2 + d_2 \leq x_1$ along the other branch (see, e.g., [23] and references therein). This continues until either a deadend is detected or all tasks have been ordered. Once all tasks are ordered, one can easily construct a solution to the problem; i.e., an assignment of a value to each x_i. It is interesting to note that, conceptually, the above branching strategy is equivalent to adding auxiliary variables to the CSP model which are then branched on. For the two tasks t_1 and t_2 that share the same resource, we would add the auxiliary variable O_{12} with $dom(O_{12}) = \{0, 1\}$ and the constraints $O_{12} = 1 \iff x_1 + d_1 \leq x_2$ and $O_{12} = 0 \iff x_2 + d_2 \leq x_1$. In general, if the underlying backtracking algorithm has a fixed branching strategy, one can simulate a different branching strategy by adding auxiliary variables. Thus, the choice of branching strategy and the design of the CSP model are interdependent decisions.

There has been further work on branching strategies that has examined the relative power of the strategies and proposed new strategies. Van Hentenryck [128, pp.90–92] examines tradeoffs between the enumeration and domain splitting strategies. Milano and van Hoeve [97] show that branching strategies can be viewed as the combination of a value ordering heuristic and a domain splitting strategy. The value ordering is used to rank the domain values and the domain splitting strategy is used to partition the domain into two or more sets. Of course, the set with the most highly ranked values will be branched into first. The technique is shown to work well on optimization problems.

Smith and Sturdy [121] show that when using chronological backtracking with 2-way branching to find all solutions, the value ordering can have an effect on the efficiency of the backtracking search. This is a surprise, since it is known that value ordering has no effect under these circumstances when using d-way branching. Hwang and Mitchell [71] show that backtracking with 2-way branching is exponentially more powerful than backtracking with d-way branching. It is clear that d-way branching can be simulated by 2-way branching with no loss of efficiency. Hwang and Mitchell show that the converse does not hold. They give a class of problems where a d-way branching algorithm with an optimal variable and value ordering takes exponentially more steps than a 2-way branching algorithm with a simple variable and value ordering. However, note that the result holds only if the CSP model is assumed to be fixed. It does not hold if we are permitted to add auxiliary variables to the CSP model.

4.3   Constraint Propagation

A fundamental insight in improving the performance of backtracking algorithms on CSPs is that local inconsistencies can lead to much thrashing or unproductive search [47, 89]. A *local inconsistency* is an instantiation of some of the variables that satisfies the relevant constraints but cannot be extended to one or more additional variables and so cannot be part of any solution. (Local inconsistencies are nogoods; see Section 4.4.) If we are using a backtracking search to find a solution, such an inconsistency can be the reason for many deadends in the search and cause much futile search effort. This insight has led to:

(a) the definition of conditions that characterize the level of local consistency of a CSP (e.g., [39, 89, 102]),

(b) the development of constraint propagation algorithms—algorithms which enforce these levels of local consistency by removing inconsistencies from a CSP (e.g., [89, 102]), and

(c) effective backtracking algorithms for finding solutions to CSPs that maintain a level of local consistency during the search (e.g., [31, 47, 48, 63, 93]).

A generic scheme to maintain a level of local consistency in a backtracking search is to perform constraint propagation at each node in the search tree. Constraint propagation algorithms remove local inconsistencies by posting additional constraints that rule out or remove the inconsistencies. When used during search, constraints are posted at nodes as the search progresses deeper in the tree. But upon backtracking over a node, the constraints that were posted at that node must be retracted. When used at the root node of the search tree—before any instantiations or branching decisions have been made—constraint propagation is sometimes referred to as a preprocessing stage.

Backtracking search integrated with constraint propagation has two important benefits. First, removing inconsistencies during search can dramatically prune the search tree by removing many deadends and by simplify the remaining subproblem. In some cases, a variable will have an empty domain after constraint propagation; i.e., no value satisfies the unary constraints over that variable. In this case, backtracking can be initiated as there is no solution along this branch of the search tree. In other cases, the variables will have their domains reduced. If a domain is reduced to a single value, the value of the variable is forced and it does not need to be branched on in the future. Thus, it can be much easier to find a solution to a CSP after constraint propagation or to show that the CSP does not have a solution. Second, some of the most important variable ordering heuristics make use of the information gathered by constraint propagation to make effective variable ordering decisions (this is discussed further in Section 4.6). As a result of these benefits, it is now standard for a backtracking algorithm to incorporate some form of constraint propagation.

Definitions of local consistency can be categorized in at least two ways. First, the definitions can be categorized into those that are constraint-based and those that are variable-based, depending on what are the primitive entities in the definition. Second, definitions of local consistency can be categorized by whether *only* unary constraints need to be posted during constraint propagation, or whether posting constraints of higher arity is sometimes necessary. In implementations of backtracking, the domains of the variables are represented extensionally, and posting and retracting unary constraints can be done very efficiently by updating the representation of the domain. Posting and retracting constraints of higher arity is less well understood and more costly. If only unary constraints are necessary, constraint propagation is sometimes referred to as domain filtering or domain pruning.

The idea of incorporating some form of constraint propagation into a backtracking algorithm arose from several directions. Davis and Putnam [31] propose unit propagation, a form of constraint propagation specialized to SAT. Golomb and Baumert [57] may have been the first to informally describe the idea of improving a general backtracking algorithm by incorporating some form of domain pruning during the search. Constraint propagation techniques were used in Fikes' REF-ARF [37] and Lauriere's Alice [82], both languages for stating and solving CSPs. Gaschnig [47] was the first to propose a backtracking algorithm that enforces a precisely defined level of local consistency at each node. Gaschnig's algorithm used d-way branching. Mackworth [89] generalizes Gaschnig's proposal to backtracking algorithms that interleave case-analysis with constraint propagation (see also [89] for additional historical references).

Since this early work, a vast literature on constraint propagation and local consistency has arisen; more than I can reasonably discuss in the space available. Thus, I have chosen two representative examples: arc consistency and strong k-consistency. These local consistencies illustrate the different categorizations given above. As well, arc consistency is currently the most important local consistency in practice and has received the most attention so far, while strong k-consistency has played an important role on the theoretical side of CSPs. For each of these examples, I present the definition of the local consistency, followed by a discussion of backtracking algorithms that maintain this level of local consistency during the search. I do not discuss any specific constraint propagation algorithms. Two separate chapters in this Handbook have been devoted to this topic (see Chapters 3 & 6). Note that many presentations of constraint propagation algorithms are for the case where the algorithm will be used in the preprocessing stage. However, when used during search to maintain a level of local consistency, usually only small changes occur between successive calls to the constraint propagation algorithm. As a result, much effort has also gone into making such algorithms incremental and thus much more efficient when used during search.

When presenting backtracking algorithms integrated with constraint propagation, I present the "pure" forms of the backtracking algorithms where a uniform level of local consistency is maintained at each node in the search tree. This is simply for ease of presentation. In practice, the level of local consistency enforced and the algorithm for enforcing it is specific to each constraint and varies between constraints. An example is the widely used all-different global constraint, where fast algorithms are designed for enforcing many different levels of local consistency including arc consistency, range consistency, bounds consistency, and simple value removal. The choice of which level of local consistency to enforce is then up to the modeler.

4.3.1   Backtracking and Maintaining Arc Consistency

Mackworth [89, 90] defines a level of local consistency called arc consistency[1]. Given a constraint C, the notation $t \in C$ denotes a tuple t—an assignment of a value to each of the variables in $vars(C)$—that satisfies the constraint C. The notation $t[x]$ denotes the value assigned to variable x by the tuple t.

Definition 4.2 (arc consistency). *Given a constraint C, a value $a \in dom(x)$ for a variable $x \in vars(C)$ is said to have a support in C if there exists a tuple $t \in C$ such that $a = t[x$ and $t[y] \in dom(y)$, for every $y \in vars(C)$. A constraint C is said to be* arc consistent *for each $x \in vars(C)$, each value $a \in dom(x)$ has a support in C.*

A constraint can be made arc consistent by repeatedly removing unsupported values from the domains of its variables. Note that this definition of local consistency is constraint-based and enforcing arc consistency on a CSP means iterating over the constraints until no more changes are made to the domains. Algorithms for enforcing arc consistency have been extensively studied (see Chapters 3 & 6). An optimal algorithm for an arbitrary constraint has $O(rd^r)$ worst case time complexity, where r is the arity of the constraint and d is the size of the domains of the variables [101]. Fortunately, it is almost always possible to do much better for classes of constraints that occur in practice. For example, the all-different constraint can be made arc consistent in $O(r^2d)$ time in the worst case.

Gaschnig [47] suggests maintaining arc consistency during backtracking search and gives the first explicit algorithm containing this idea. Following Sabin and Freuder [116], I will denote such an algorithm as MAC[2]. The MAC algorithm maintains arc consistency on constraints with *at least* one uninstantiated variable (see Table 4.1). At each node of the search tree, an algorithm for enforcing arc consistency is applied to the CSP. Since arc consistency was enforced on the parent of a node, initially constraint propagation only needs to be enforced on the constraint that was posted by the branching strategy. In turn, this may lead to other constraints becoming arc inconsistent and constraint propagation continues until no more changes are made to the domains. If, as a result of constraint propagation, a domain becomes empty, the branch is a deadend and is rejected. If no domain is empty, the branch is accepted and the search continues to the next level.

---

[1]Arc consistency is also called domain consistency, generalized arc consistency, and hyper arc consistency in the literature. The latter two names are used when an author wishes to reserve the name arc consistency for the case where the definition is restricted to binary constraints.

[2]Gaschnig's DEEB (Domain Element Elimination with Backtracking) algorithm uses d-way branching. Sabin and Freuder's [116] MAC (Maintaining Arc Consistency) algorithm uses 2-way branching. However, I will follow the practice of much of the literature and use the term MAC to denote an algorithm that maintains arc consistency during the search, regardless of the branching strategy used.

As an example of applying MAC, consider the backtracking tree for the 6-queens problem shown in Figure 4.1. MAC visits only node 25, as it is discovered that this node is a deadend. The board in Figure 4.2a shows the result of constraint propagation. The shaded numbered squares correspond to the values removed from the domains of the variables by constraint propagation. A value i is placed in a shaded square if the value was removed because of the assignment at level i in the tree. It can been seen that after constraint propagation, the domains of some of the variables are empty. Thus, the set of assignments $\{x_1 = 2, x_2 = 5\}$ cannot be part of a solution to the CSP.

When maintaining arc consistency during search, any value that is pruned from the domain of a variable does not participate in any solution to the CSP. However, not all values that remain in the domains necessarily are part of some solution. Hence, while arc consistency propagation can reduce the search space, it does not remove all possible deadends. Let us say that the domains of a CSP are *minimal* if each value in the domain of a variable is part of some solution to the CSP. Clearly, if constraint propagation would leave only the minimal domains at each node in the search tree, the search would be backtrack-free as any value that was chosen would lead to a solution. Unfortunately, finding the *minimal domains* is at least as hard as solving the CSP. After enforcing arc consistency on individual constraints, each value in the domain of a variable is part of some solution to the constraint considered in isolation. Finding the minimal domains would be equivalent to enforcing arc consistency on the *conjunction* of the constraints in a CSP, a process that is worst-case exponential in n, the number of variables in the CSP. Thus, arc consistency can be viewed as approximating the minimal domains.

In general, there is a tradeoff between the cost of the constraint propagation performed at each node in the search tree, and the quality of the approximation of the minimal domains. One way to *improve* the approximation, but with an increase in the cost of constraint propagation, is to use a stronger level of local consistency such as a singleton consistency (see Chapter 3). One way to *reduce* the cost of constraint propagation, at the risk of a poorer approximation to the minimal domains and an increase in the overall search cost, is to restrict the application of arc consistency. One such algorithm is called forward checking. The forward checking algorithm (FC) maintains arc consistency on constraints with *exactly* one uninstantiated variable (see Table 4.1). On such constraints, arc consistency can be enforced in $O(d)$ time, where d is the size of the domain of the uninstantiated variable. Golomb and Baumert [57] may have been the first to informally describe forward checking (called preclusion in [57]). The first explicit algorithms are given by McGregor [93] and Haralick and Elliott [63]. Forward checking was originally proposed for binary constraints. The generalization to non-binary constraints used here is due to Van Hentenryck [128].

As an example of applying FC, consider the backtracking tree shown in Figure 4.1. FC visits only nodes 25, 253, 2531, 25314 and 2536. The board in Figure 4.2b shows the result of constraint propagation. The squares that are left empty as the search progresses correspond to the nodes visited by FC.

Early experimental work in the field found that FC was much superior to MAC [63, 93]. However, this superiority turned out to be partially an artifact of the easiness of the benchmarks. As well, many practical improvements have been made to arc consistency propagation algorithms over the intervening years, particularly with regard to incrementality. The result is that backtracking algorithms that maintain full arc consistency during the search are now considered much more important in practice. An exception is the widely

used DPLL algorithm [30, 31], a backtracking algorithm specialized to SAT problems in
CNF form (see Table 4.1). The DPLL algorithm uses unit propagation, sometimes called
Boolean constraint propagation, as its constraint propagation mechanism. It can be shown
that unit propagation is equivalent to forward checking on a SAT problem. Further, it
can be shown that the amount of pruning performed by arc consistency on these problems
is equivalent to that of forward checking. Hence, forward checking is the right level of
constraint propagation on SAT problems.

Forward checking is just one way to restrict arc consistency propagation; many variations are possible. For example, one can maintain arc consistency on constraints with
various numbers of uninstantiated variables. Bessière et al. [16] consider the possibilities.
One could also take into account the size of the domains of uninstantiated variables when
specify which constraints should be propagated. As a third alternative, one could place *ad
hoc* restrictions on the constraint propagation algorithm itself and how it iterates through
the constraints [63, 104, 117].

An alternative to restricting the *application* of arc consistency—either by restricting
which constraints are propagated or by restricting the propagation itself—is to restrict the
definition of arc consistency. One important example is bounds consistency. Suppose
that the domains of the variables are large and ordered and that the domains of the variables are represented by intervals (the minimum and the maximum value in the domain).
With bounds consistency, instead of asking that each value $a \in dom(x)$ has a support in
the constraint, we only ask that the minimum value and the maximum value each have a
support in the constraint. Although in general weaker than arc consistency, bounds consistency has been shown to be useful for arithmetic constraints and global constraints as it
can sometimes be enforced more efficiently (see Chapters 3 & 6 for details). For example, the all-different constraint can be made bounds consistent in $O(r)$ time in the worst
case, in contrast to $O(r^2d)$ for arc consistency, where r is the arity of the constraint and
d is the size of the domains of the variables. Further, for some problems it can be shown
that the amount of pruning performed by arc consistency is equivalent to that of bounds
consistency, and thus the extra cost of arc consistency is not repaid.

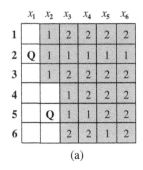
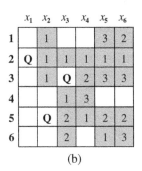

(a)   (b)

Figure 4.2: Constraint propagation on the 6-queens problem; (a) maintaining arc consistency; (b) forward checking.

4.3.2 Backtracking and Maintaining Strong k-Consistency

Freuder [39, 40] defines a level of local consistency called strong k-consistency. A set of assignments is *consistent* if each constraint that has *all* of its variables instantiated by the set of assignments is satisfied.

Definition 4.3 (strong k-consistency). *A CSP is k-consistent if, for any set of assignments $\{x_1 = a_1, \ldots, x_{k-1} = a_{k-1}\}$ to $k - 1$ distinct variables that is consistent, and any additional variable x_k, there exists a value $a_k \in dom(x_k)$ such that the set of assignments $\{x_1 = a_1, \ldots, x_{k-1} = a_{k-1}, x_k = a_k\}$ is consistent. A CSP is strongly k-consistent if it is j-consistent for all $j \leq k$.*

For the special case of binary CSPs, strong 2-consistency is the same as arc consistency and strong 3-consistency is also known as path consistency. A CSP can be made strongly k-consistent by repeatedly detecting and removing all those inconsistencies $t = \{x_1 = a_1, \ldots, x_{j-1} = a_{j-1}\}$ where $1 \leq j < k$ and t is consistent but cannot be extended to some j^{th} variable x_j. To remove an inconsistency or nogood t, a constraint is posted to the CSP which rules out the tuple t. Enforcing strong k-consistency may dramatically increase the number of constraints in a CSP, as the number of new constraints posted can be exponential in k. Once a CSP has been made strongly k-consistent any value that remains in the domain of a variable can be extended to a consistent set of assignments over k variables in a backtrack-free manner. However, unless $k = n$, there is no guarantee that a value can be extended to a solution over all n variables. An optimal algorithm for enforcing strong k-consistency on a CSP containing arbitrary constraints has $O(n^k d^k)$ worst case time complexity, where n is the number of variables in the CSP and d is the size of the domains of the variables [29].

Let MC_k be an algorithm that maintains strong k-consistency during the search (see Table 4.1). For the purposes of specifying MC_k, I will assume that the branching strategy is enumeration and that, therefore, each node in the search tree corresponds to a set of assignments. During search, we want to maintain the property that any value that remains in the domain of a variable can be extended to a consistent set of assignments over k variables. To do this, we must account for the current set of assignments by, conceptually, modifying the constraints. Given a set of assignments t, only those tuples in a constraint that agree with the assignments in t are selected and those tuples are then projected onto the set of uninstantiated variables of the constraint to give the new constraint (see [25] for details). Under such an architecture, FC can be viewed as maintaining one-consistency, and, for binary CSPs, MAC can be viewed as maintaining strong two-consistency.

Can such an architecture be practical for $k > 2$? There is some evidence that the answer is yes. Van Gelder and Tsuji [127] propose an algorithm that maintains the closure of resolution on binary clauses (clauses with two literals) and gives experimental evidence that the algorithm can be much faster than DPLL on larger SAT instances. The algorithm can be viewed as MC_3 specialized to SAT. Bacchus [2] builds on this work and shows that the resulting SAT solver is robust and competitive with state-of-the-art DPLL solvers. This is remarkable given the amount of engineering that has gone into DPLL solvers. So far, however, there has been no convincing demonstration of a corresponding result for general CSPs, although efforts have been made.

4.4   Nogood Recording

One of the most effective techniques known for improving the performance of backtracking search on a CSP is to add implied constraints. A constraint is *implied* if the set of
solutions to the CSP is the same with and without the constraint. Adding the "right" implied constraints to a CSP can mean that many deadends are removed from the search tree
and other deadends are discovered after much less search effort.

Three main techniques for adding implied constraints have been investigated. One
technique is to add implied constraints by hand during the modeling phase (see Chapter
11). A second technique is to automatically add implied constraints by applying a constraint propagation algorithm (see Section 4.3). Both of the above techniques rule out local
inconsistencies or deadends *before* they are encountered during the search. A third technique, and the topic of this section, is to automatically add implied constraints *after* a local
inconsistency or deadend is encountered in the search. The basis of this technique is the
concept of a nogood, due to Stallman and Sussman [124][3].

Definition 4.4 (nogood). *A nogood is a set of assignments and branching constraints that
is not consistent with any solution.*

In other words, there does not exist a solution—an assignment of a value to each variable that satisfies all the constraints of the CSP—that also satisfies all the assignments and
branching constraints in the nogood. If we are using a backtracking search to find a solution, each deadend corresponds to a nogood. Thus nogoods are the cause of all futile
search effort. Once a nogood for a deadend is discovered, it can be ruled out by adding
a constraint. Of course, it is too late for this deadend—the backtracking algorithm has
already refuted this node, perhaps at great cost—but the hope is that the constraint will
prune the search space in the future. The technique, first informally described by Stallman
and Sussman [124], is often referred to as nogood or constraint recording.

As an example of a nogood, consider the 6-queens problem. The set of assignments
$\{x_1 = 2, x_2 = 5, x_3 = 3\}$ is a nogood since it is not contained in any solution (see the
backtracking tree shown in Figure 4.1 where the node 253 is the root of a failed subtree).
To rule out the nogood, the implied constraint $\neg(x_1 = 2 \wedge x_2 = 5 \wedge x_3 = 3)$ could be
recorded, which is just $x_1 \neq 2 \vee x_2 \neq 5 \vee x_3 \neq 3$ in clause form.

The recorded constraints can be checked and propagated just like the original constraints. In particular, since nogoods correspond to constraints which are clauses, forward
checking is an appropriate form of constraint propagation. As well, nogoods can be used
for backjumping (see Section 4.5). Nogood recording—or discovering and recording implied constraints during the search—can be viewed as an adaptation of the well-known
technique of adding caching (sometimes called memoization) to backtracking search. The
idea is to cache solutions to subproblems and reuse the solutions instead of recomputing
them.

The constraints that are added through nogood recording could, in theory, have been
ruled out *a priori* using a constraint propagation algorithm. However, while constraint
propagation algorithms which add implied unary constraints are especially important, the

---

[3]Most previous work on nogood recording implicitly assumes that the backtracking algorithm is performing
d-way branching (only adding branching constraints which are assignments) and drops the phrase "*and branching
constraints*" from the definition. The generalized definition and descriptions used in this section are inspired by
the work of Rochart, Jussien, and Laburthe [113].

algorithms which add higher arity constraints often add too many implied constraints that are not useful and the computational cost is not repaid by a faster search.

4.4.1 Discovering Nogoods

Stallman and Sussman's [124] original account of discovering nogoods is embedded in a rule-based programming language and is descriptive and informal. Bruynooghe [22] informally adapts the idea to backtracking search on CSPs. Dechter [33] provides the first formal account of discovering and recording nogoods. Dechter [34] shows how to discover nogoods using the static structure of the CSP.

Prosser [108], Ginsberg [54], and Schiex and Verfaillie [118] all independently give accounts of how to discover nogoods dynamically during the search. The following definition captures the essence of these proposals. The definition is for the case where the backtracking algorithm does not perform any constraint propagation. (The reason for the adjective "jumpback" is explained in Section 4.5.) Recall that associated with each node in the search tree is the set of branching constraints posted along the path to the node. For d-way branching, the branching constraints are of the form $x = a$, for some variable x and value a; for 2-way branching, the branching constraints are of the form $x = a$ and $x \neq a$; and for domain splitting, the branching constraints are of the form $x \leq a$ and $x > a$.

Definition 4.5 (jumpback nogood). *Let* $p = \{b_1, \ldots, b_j\}$ *be a deadend node in the search tree, where* b_i, $1 \leq i \leq j$, *is the branching constraint posted at level* i *in the search tree. The* jumpback nogood *for* p, *denoted* $J(p)$, *is defined recursively as follows.*

1. p is a leaf node. Let C be a constraint that is not consistent with p (one must exist);

$$J(p) = \{b_i \mid vars(b_i) \cap vars(C) \neq \emptyset, 1 \leq i \leq j\}.$$

2. p is not a leaf node. Let $\{b_{j+1}^1, \ldots, b_{j+1}^k\}$ be all the possible extensions of p attempted by the branching strategy, each of which has failed;

$$J(p) = \bigcup_{i=1}^{k} (J(p \cup \{b_{j+1}^i\}) - \{b_{j+1}^i\}).$$

As an example of applying the definition, consider the jumpback nogood for the node 25314 shown in Figure 4.1. The set of branching constraints associated with this node is $p = \{x_1 = 2, x_2 = 5, x_3 = 3, x_4 = 1, x_5 = 4\}$. The backtracking algorithm branches on x_6, but all attempts to extend p fail. The jumpback nogood is given by,

$$
\begin{aligned}
J(p) &= (J(p \cup \{x_6 = 1\}) - \{x_6 = 1\}) \cup \cdots \cup (J(p \cup \{x_6 = 6\}) - \{x_6 = 6\}), \\
&= \{x_2 = 5\} \cup \cdots \cup \{x_3 = 3\}, \\
&= \{x_1 = 2, x_2 = 5, x_3 = 3, x_5 = 4\}.
\end{aligned}
$$

Notice that the order in which the constraints are checked or propagated directly influences which nogood is discovered. In applying the above definition, I have chosen to check the constraints in increasing lexicographic order. For example, for the leaf node $p \cup \{x_6 = 1\}$, both $C(x_2, x_6)$ and $C(x_4, x_6)$ fail—i.e., both the queen at x_2 and the queen at x_4 attack the queen at x_6—and I have chosen $C(x_2, x_6)$.

The discussion so far has focused on the simpler case where the backtracking algorithm does not perform any constraint propagation. Several authors have contributed to our understanding of how to discover nogoods when the backtracking algorithm does use constraint propagation. Rosiers and Bruynooghe [114] give an informal description of combining forward checking and nogood recording. Schiex and Verfaillie [118] provide the first formal account of nogood recording within an algorithm that performs forward checking. Prosser's FC-CBJ [108] and MAC-CBJ [109] can be viewed as discovering jumpback nogoods (see Section 4.5.1). Jussien, Debruyne, and Boizumault [75] give an algorithm that combines nogood recording with arc consistency propagation on non-binary constraints. The following discussion captures the essence of these proposals. The key idea is to modify the constraint propagation algorithms so that, for each value that is removed from the domain of some variable, an eliminating explanation is recorded.

Definition 4.6 (eliminating explanation). *Let $p = \{b_1, \ldots, b_j\}$ be a node in the search tree and let $a \in dom(x)$ be a value that is removed from the domain of a variable x by constraint propagation at node p. An* eliminating explanation *for a, denoted $\mathsf{expl}(x \neq a)$ is a subset (not necessarily proper) of p such that $\mathsf{expl}(x \neq a) \cup \{x = a\}$ is a nogood.*

The intention behind the definition is that $\mathsf{expl}(x \neq a)$ is sufficient to account for the removal of a. As an example, consider the board in Figure 4.2a which shows the result of arc consistency propagation. At the node $p = \{x_1 = 2, x_2 = 5\}$, the value 1 is removed from $dom(x_6)$. An eliminating explanation for this value is $\mathsf{expl}(x_6 \neq 1) = \{x_2 = 5\}$ since $\{x_2 = 5, x_6 = 1\}$ is a nogood. An eliminating explanation can be viewed as the left-hand side of an implication which rules out the stated value. For example, the implied constraint to rule out the nogood $\{x_2 = 5, x_6 = 1\}$ is $\neg(x_2 = 5 \wedge x_6 = 1)$, which can be rewritten as $(x_2 = 5) \Rightarrow (x_6 \neq 1)$. Similarly, $\mathsf{expl}(x_6 \neq 3) = \{x_1 = 2, x_2 = 5\}$ and the corresponding implied constraint can be written as $(x_1 = 2 \wedge x_2 = 5) \Rightarrow (x_6 \neq 3)$.

One possible method for constructing eliminating explanations for arc consistency propagation is as follows. Initially at a node, a branching constraint b_j is posted and arc consistency is enforced on b_j. For each value a removed from the domain of a variable $x \in vars(b_j)$, $\mathsf{expl}(x \neq a)$ is set to $\{b_j\}$. Next constraint propagation iterates through the constraints re-establishing arc consistency. Consider a value a removed from the domain of a variable x during this phase of constraint propagation. We must record an explanation that accounts for the removal of a; i.e., the reason that a does not have a support in some constraint C. For each value b of a variable $y \in vars(C)$ which could have been used to form a support for $a \in dom(x)$ in C but has been removed from its domain, add the eliminating explanation for $y \neq b$ to the eliminating explanation for $x \neq a$; i.e. $\mathsf{expl}(x \neq a) \leftarrow \mathsf{expl}(x \neq a) \cup \mathsf{expl}(y \neq b)$. In the special case of arc consistency propagation called forward checking, it can be seen that the eliminating explanation is just the variable assignments of the instantiated variables in C.

The jumpback nogood in the case where the backtracking algorithm performs constraint propagation can now be defined as follows.

Definition 4.7 (jumpback nogood with constraint propagation). *Let $p = \{b_1, \ldots, b_j\}$ be a deadend node in the search tree. The* jumpback nogood *for p, denoted $J(p)$, is defined recursively as follows.*

1. *p is a leaf node. Let x be a variable whose domain has become empty (one must exist), where $dom(x)$ is the original domain of x;*

$$J(p) = \bigcup_{a \in dom(x)} \textit{expl}(x \neq a).$$

2. *p is not a leaf node. Same as Definition 4.5.*

Note that the jumpback nogoods are not guaranteed to be the minimal nogood or the "best" nogood that could be discovered, even if the nogoods are locally minimal at leaf nodes. For example, Bacchus [1] shows that the jumpback nogood for forward checking may not give the best backjump point and provides a method for improving the nogood. Katsirelos and Bacchus [77] show how to discover *generalized* nogoods during search using either FC-CBJ or MAC-CBJ. Standard nogoods are of the form $\{x_1 = a_1 \wedge \cdots \wedge x_k = a_k\}$; i.e., each element is of the form $x_i = a_i$. Generalized nogoods also allow conjuncts of the form $x_i \neq a_i$. When standard nogoods are propagated, a variable can only have a value pruned from its domain. For example, consider the standard nogood clause $x_1 \neq 2 \vee x_2 \neq 5 \vee x_3 \neq 3$. If the backtracking algorithm at some point makes the assignments $x_1 = 2$ and $x_2 = 5$, the value 3 can be removed from the domain of variable x_3. Only indirectly, in the case where all but one of the values have been pruned from the domain of a variable, can propagating nogoods cause the value of a variable to be forced; i.e., cause an assignment of a value to a variable. With generalized nogoods, the value of a variable can also be forced directly which may lead to additional propagation.

Marques-Silva and Sakallah [92] show that in SAT, the effects of Boolean constraint propagation (BCP or unit propagation) can be captured by an implication graph. An implication graph is a directed acyclic graph where the vertices represent variable assignments and directed edges give the reasons for an assignment. A vertex is either positive (the variable is assigned true) or negative (the variable is assigned false). Decision variables and variables which appear as unit clauses in the original formula have no incoming edges; other vertices that are assigned as a result of BCP have incoming edges from vertices that caused the assignment. A contradiction occurs if a variable occurs both positively and negatively. Zhang et al. [139] show that in this scheme, the different cuts in the implication graph which separate all the decision vertices from the contradiction correspond to the different nogoods that can be learned from a contradiction. Zhang et al. show that some types of cuts lead to much smaller and more powerful nogoods than others. As well, the nogoods do not have to include just branching constraints, but can also include assignments that are forced by BCP. Katsirelos and Bacchus [77] generalize the scheme to CSPs and present the results of experimentation with some of the different clause learning schemes.

So far, the discussion on discovering nogoods has focused on methods that are tightly integrated with the search process. Other methods for discovering nogoods have also been proposed. For example, many CSPs contain symmetry and taking into account the symmetry can improve the search for a solution. Freuder and Wallace [43] observe that a symmetry mapping applied to a nogood gives another nogood which may prune additional parts of the search space. For example, the 6-queens problem is symmetric about the horizontal axis and applying this symmetry mapping to the nogood $\{x_1 = 2, x_2 = 5, x_3 = 3\}$ gives the new nogood $\{x_1 = 5, x_2 = 2, x_3 = 4\}$.

Junker [74] shows how nogood discovery can be treated as a separate module, independent of the search algorithm. Given a set of constraints that are known to be inconsistent,

Junker gives an algorithm for finding a small subset of the constraints that is sufficient to explain the inconsistency. The algorithm can make use of constraint propagation techniques, independently of those enforced in the backtracking algorithm, but does not require modifications to the constraint propagation algorithms. As an example, consider the backtracking tree shown in Figure 4.1. Suppose that the backtracking algorithm discovers that node 253 is a deadend. The set of branching constraints associated with this node is $\{x_1 = 2, x_2 = 5, x_3 = 3\}$ and this set is therefore a nogood. Recording this nogood would not be useful. However, the subsets $\{x_1 = 2, x_2 = 5\}$, $\{x_1 = 2, x_3 = 3\}$, and $\{x_2 = 5, x_3 = 3\}$ are also nogoods. All can be discovered using arc consistency propagation. Further, the subsets $\{x_2 = 5\}$ and $\{x_3 = 3\}$ are also nogoods. These are not discoverable using just arc consistency propagation, but are discoverable using a higher level of local consistency. Clearly, everything else being equal, smaller nogoods will lead to more pruning. On CSPs that are more difficult to solve, the extra work involved in discovering these smaller nogoods may result in an overall reduction in search time.

While nogood recording is now standard in SAT solvers, it is currently not widely used for solving general CSPs. Perhaps the main reason is the presence of global constraints in many CSP models and the fact that some form of arc consistency is often maintained on these constraints. If global constraints are treated as a black box, standard methods for determining nogoods quickly lead to saturated nogoods where all or almost all the variables are in the nogood. Saturated nogoods are of little use for either recording or for backjumping. The solution is to more carefully construct eliminating explanations based on the semantics of each global constraint. Katsirelos and Bacchus [77] present preliminary work on learning small generalized nogoods from arc consistency propagation on global constraints. Rochart, Jussien, and Laburthe [113] show how to construct explanations for two important global constraints: the all-different and stretch constraints.

4.4.2 Nogood Database Management

An important problem that arises in nogood recording is the cost of updating and querying the database of nogoods. Stallman and Sussman [124] propose recording a nogood at each deadend in the search. However, if the database becomes too large and too expensive to query, the search reduction that it entails may not be beneficial overall. One method for reducing the cost is to restrict the size of the database by including only those nogoods that are most likely to be useful. Two schemes have been proposed: one restricts the nogoods that are recorded in the first place and the other restricts the nogoods that are kept over time.

Dechter [33, 34] proposes i^{th}-order size-bounded nogood recording. In this scheme a nogood is recorded only if it contains at most i variables. Important special cases are 0-order, where the nogoods are used to determine the backjump point (see Section 4.5) but are not recorded; and 1-order and 2-order, where the nogoods recorded are a subset of those that would be enforced by arc consistency and path consistency propagation, respectively. Early experiments on size-bounded nogood recording were limited to 0-, 1-, and 2-order, since these could be accommodated without moving beyond binary constraints. Dechter [33, 34] shows that 2-order was the best choice and significantly improves BJ on the Zebra problem. Schiex and Verfaillie [118] show that 2-order was the best choice and significantly improves CBJ and FC-CBJ on the Zebra and random binary problems. Frost and Dechter [44] describe the first non-binary implementation of nogood recording and compare CBJ with and without unrestricted nogood recording and 2-, 3-, and 4-order size-bounded nogood recording. In experiments on random binary problems, they found that neither unrestricted nor size-bounded dominated, but adding either method of nogood recording led to significant improvements overall.

In contrast to restricting the nogoods that are recorded, Ginsberg [54] proposes to record all nogoods but then delete nogoods that are deemed to be no longer relevant. Assume a d-way branching strategy, where all branching constraints are an assignment of a value to a variable, and recall that nogoods can be written in the form,

$$((x_1 = a_1) \wedge \cdots \wedge (x_{k-1} = a_{k-1})) \Rightarrow (x_k \neq a_k).$$

Ginsberg's dynamic backtracking algorithm (DBT) always puts the variable that has most recently been assigned a value on the right-hand side of the implication and only keeps nogoods whose left-hand sides are currently true (see Table 4.1). A nogood is considered irrelevant and deleted once the left-hand side of the implication contains more than one variable-value pair that does not appear in the current set of assignments. When all branching constraints are of the form $x = a$, for some variable x and value a, DBT can be implemented using $O(n^2d)$ space, where n is the number of variables and d is the size of the domains. The data structure maintains a nogood for each variable and value pair and each nogood is $O(n)$ in length.

Bayardo and Miranker [10] generalize Ginsberg's proposal to i^{th}-order relevance-bounded nogood recording. In their scheme a nogood is deleted once it contains more than i variable-value pairs that do not appear in the current set of assignments. Subsequent experiments compared unrestricted, size-bounded, and relevance-bounded nogood recording. All came to the conclusion that unrestricted nogood recording was too expensive, but differed on whether size-bounded or relevance-bounded was better. Baker [7], in experiments on random binary problems, concludes that CBJ with 2-order size-bounded nogood recording is the best tradeoff. Bayardo and Schrag [11, 12], in experiments on a variety of real-world and random SAT instances, conclude that DPLL-CBJ with 4-order relevance-bounded nogood recording is best overall. Marques-Silva and Sakallah [92], in experiments on real-world SAT instances, conclude that DPLL-CBJ with 20-order size-bounded nogood recording is the winner.

Beyond restricting the size of the database, additional techniques have been proposed for reducing the cost of updating and querying the database. One of the most important of these is "watch" literals [103]. Given a set of assignments, the nogood database must tell the backtracking search algorithm whether any nogood is contradicted and whether any value can be pruned from the domain of a variable. Watch literals are a data structure for greatly reducing the number of nogoods that must be examined to answer these queries and reducing the cost of examining large nogoods.

With the discovery of the watch literals data structure, it was found that recording very large nogoods could lead to remarkable reductions in search time. Moskewicz et al. [103] show that 100- and 200-order relevance-bounded nogood recording with watch literals, along with restarts and a variable ordering based on the recorded nogoods, was significantly faster than DPLL-CBJ alone on large real-world SAT instances. Katsirelos and Bacchus [77] show that unrestricted generalized nogood recording with watch literals was significantly faster than MAC and MAC-CBJ alone on a variety of CSP instances from planning, crossword puzzles, and scheduling.

4.5   Non-Chronological Backtracking

Upon discovering a deadend, a backtracking algorithm must retract some previously posted branching constraint. In the standard form of backtracking, called chronological backtracking, only the most recently posted branching constraint is retracted. However, backtracking chronologically may not address the reason for the deadend. In non-chronological backtracking, the algorithm backtracks to and retracts the closest branching constraint which bears some responsibility for the deadend. Following Gaschnig [48], I refer to this process as *backjumping*[4].

Non-chronological backtracking algorithms can be described as a combination of (i) a strategy for discovering and using nogoods for backjumping, and (ii) a strategy for deleting nogoods from the nogood database.

4.5.1   Backjumping

Stallman and Sussman [124] were the first to informally propose a non-chronological backtracking algorithm—called dependency-directed backtracking—that discovered and maintained nogoods in order to backjump. Informal descriptions of backjumping are also given by Bruynooghe [22] and Rosiers and Bruynooghe [114]. The first explicit backjumping algorithm was given by Gaschnig [48]. Gaschnig's backjumping algorithm (BJ) [48] is similar to BT, except that it backjumps from deadends. However, BJ only backjumps from a deadend node when all the branches out of the node are leaves; otherwise it chronologically backtracks. Dechter [34] proposes a graph-based backjumping algorithm which computes the backjump points based on the static structure of the CSP. The idea is to jump back to the most recent variable that shares a constraint with the deadend variable. The algorithm was the first to also jump back at internal deadends.

Prosser [108] proposes the conflict-directed backjumping algorithm (CBJ), a generalization of Gaschnig's BJ to also backjump from internal deadends. Equivalent algorithms were independently proposed and formalized by Schiex and Verfaillie [118] and Ginsberg [54]. Each of these algorithms uses a variation of the jumpback nogood (Definition 4.5) to decide where to safely backjump to in the search tree from a deadend. Suppose that the backtracking algorithm has discovered a non-leaf deadend $p = \{b_1, \ldots, b_j\}$ in the search tree. The algorithm must backtrack by retracting some branching constraint from p Chronological backtracking would choose b_j. Let $J(p) \subseteq p$ be the jumpback nogood for p. Backjumping chooses the largest i, $1 \leq i \leq j$, such that $b_i \in J(p)$. This is the backjump point. The algorithm jumps back in the search tree and retracts b_i, at the same time retracting any branching constraints that were posted after b_i and deleting any nogoods that were recorded after b_i.

As examples of applying CBJ and BJ, consider the backtracking tree shown in Figure 4.1. The light-shaded part of the tree contains nodes that are skipped by Conflict-Directed Backjumping (CBJ). The algorithm discovers a deadend after failing to extend node 25314. As shown earlier, the jumpback nogood associated with this node is $\{x_1 = 2, x_2 = 5, x_3 = 3, x_5 = 4\}$. CBJ backtracks to and retracts the most recently posted branching constraint, which is $x_5 = 4$. No nodes are skipped at this point. The remaining

---

[4]Backjumping is also referred to as intelligent backtracking and dependency-directed backtracking in the literature.

two values for x_5 also fail. The algorithm has now discovered that 2531 is a deadend node and, because a jumpback nogood has been determined for each branch, the jumpback nogood of 2531 is easily found to be $\{x_1 = 2, x_2 = 5, x_3 = 3\}$. CBJ backjumps to retract $x_3 = 3$ skipping the rest of the subtree. The backjump is represented by a dashed arrow. In contrast to CBJ, BJ only backjumps from deadends when all branches out of the dead-end are leaves. The dark-shaded part of the tree contains two nodes that are skipped by Backjumping (BJ). Again, the backjump is represented by a dashed arrow.

In the same way as for dynamic backtracking (DBT), when all branching constraints are of the form $x = a$, for some variable x and value a, CBJ can be implemented using $O(n^2d)$ space, where n is the number of variables and d is the size of the domains. The data structure maintains a nogood for each variable and value pair and each nogood is $O(n)$ in length. However, since CBJ only uses the recorded nogoods for backjumping and constraints corresponding to the nogoods are never checked or propagated, it is not necessary to actually store a nogood for each value. A simpler $O(n^2)$ data structure, sometimes called a conflict set, suffices. The conflict set stores, for each variable, the union of the nogoods for each value of the variable.

CBJ has also been combined with constraint propagation. The basic backjumping mechanism is the same for all algorithms that perform non-chronological backtracking, no matter what level of constraint propagation is performed. The main difference lies in how the jumpback nogood is constructed (see Section 4.4.1 and Definition 4.7). Prosser [108] proposes FC-CBJ, an algorithm that combines forward checking constraint propagation and conflict-directed backjumping. An equivalent algorithm as independently proposed and formalized by Schiex and Verfaillie [118]. An informal description of an algorithm that combines forward checking and backjumping is also given by Rosiers and Bruynooghe [114]. Prosser [109] proposes MAC-CBJ, an algorithm that combines maintaining arc consistency and conflict-directed backjumping. As specified, the algorithm only handles binary constraints. Chen [25] generalizes the algorithm to non-binary constraints.

Many experiments studies on conflict-directed backjumping have been reported in the literature. Many of these are summarized in Section 4.10.1.

4.5.2 Partial Order Backtracking

In chronological backtracking and conflict-directed backjumping, it is assumed that the branching constraints at a node $p = \{b_1, \ldots, b_j\}$ in the search tree are totally ordered. The total ordering is the order in which the branching constraints were posted by the algorithm. Chronological backtracking then always retracts b_j, the last branching constraint in the ordering, and backjumping chooses the largest i, $1 \le i \le j$, such that b_i is in the jumpback nogood.

Bruynooghe [22] notes that this is not a necessary assumption and proposes partial order backtracking. In partial ordering backtracking the branching constraints are considered initially unordered and a partial order is induced upon jumping back from deadends. Assume a d-way branching strategy, where all branching constraints are an assignment of a value to a variable. When jumping back from a deadend, an assignment $x = a$ must be chosen from the jumpback nogood and retracted. Bruynooghe notes that backjumping must respect the current partial order, and proposes choosing *any* assignment that is maximal in the partial order. Upon making this choice and backjumping, the partial order must now be further restricted. Recall that a nogood $\{x_1 = a_1, \ldots, x_k = a_k\}$ can be written in the form $((x_1 = a_1) \wedge \cdots \wedge (x_{k-1} = a_{k-1})) \Rightarrow (x_k \neq a_k)$. The assignment $x = a$ chosen to be retracted must now appear on the right-hand side of any nogoods in which it appears. Adding an implication restricts the partial order as the assignments on the left-hand side of the implication must come before the assignment on the right-hand side. And if the retracted assignment $x = a$ appears on the left-hand side in any implication, that implication is deleted and the value on the right-hand side is restored to its domain. Deleting an implication relaxes the partial order. Rosiers and Bruynooghe [114] show, in experiments on hard (non-binary) word sum problems, that their partial order backtracking algorithm was the best choice over algorithms that did forward checking, backjumping, or a combination of forward checking and backjumping. However, Baker [7] gives an example (the example is credited to Ginsberg) showing that, because in Bruynooghe's scheme *any* assignment that is maximal in the partial order can be chosen, it is possible for the algorithm to cycle and never terminate.

Ginsberg proposes [54] the dynamic backtracking algorithm (DBT, see Table 4.1). DBT can be viewed as a formalization and correction of Bruynooghe's scheme for partial order backtracking. To guarantee termination, DBT always chooses from the jumpback nogood the most recently posted assignment and puts this assignment on the right-hand side of the implication. Thus, DBT maintains a total order over the assignments in the jumpback nogood and a partial order over the assignments not in the jumpback nogood. As a result, given the same jumpback nogood, the backjump point for DBT would be the same as for CBJ. However, in contrast to CBJ which upon backjumping retracts any nogoods that were posted after the backjump point, DBT retains these nogoods (see Section 4.4.2 for further discussion of the nogood retention strategy used in DBT). Ginsberg [54] shows, in experiments which used crossword puzzles as a test bed, that DBT can solve more problems within a fixed time limit than a backjumping algorithm. However, Baker [7] shows that relevance-bounded nogood recording, as used in DBT, can interact negatively with a dynamic variable ordering heuristic. As a result, DBT can also degrade performance—by an exponential amount—over an algorithm that does not retain nogoods such as CBJ.

Dynamic backtracking (DBT) has also been combined with constraint propagation. Jussien, Debruyne, and Boizumault [75] show how to integrate DBT with forward checking and maintaining arc consistency, to give FC-DBT and MAC-DBT, respectively. As with adding constraint propagation to CBJ, the main difference lies in how the jumpback nogood is constructed (see Section 4.4.1 and Definition 4.7). However, because of the retention of nogoods, there is an additional complexity when adding constraint propagation to DBT that is not present in CBJ. Consider a value in the domain of a variable that has been removed but its eliminating explanation is now irrelevant. The value cannot just be restored, as there may exist another relevant explanation for the deleted value; i.e., there may exist several ways of removing a value through constraint propagation.

Ginsberg and McAllester [56] propose an algorithm called partial order dynamic backtracking (PBT). PBT offers more freedom than DBT in the selection of the assignment from the jumpback nogood to put on the right-hand side of the implication, while still giving a guarantee of correctness and termination. In Ginsberg's DBT and Bruynooghe's partial order algorithm, deleting an implication relaxes the partial order. In PBT, the idea is to retain some of the partial ordering information from these deleted implications. Now, choosing any assignment that is maximal in the partial order is correct. Bliek [18] shows that PBT is not a generalization of DBT and gives an algorithm that does generalize both PBT and DBT. To date, no systematic evaluation of either PBT or Bliek's generalization have been reported, and no integration with constraint propagation has been reported.

4.6 Heuristics for Backtracking Algorithms

When solving a CSP using backtracking search, a sequence of decisions must be made as to which variable to branch on or instantiate next and which value to give to the variable. These decisions are referred to as the variable and the value ordering. It has been shown that for many problems, the choice of variable and value ordering can be crucial to effectively solving the problem (e.g., [5, 50, 55, 63]).

A variable or value ordering can be either static, where the ordering is fixed and determined prior to search, or dynamic, where the ordering is determined as the search progresses. Dynamic variable orderings have received much attention in the literature. They were proposed as early as 1965 [57] and it is now well-understood how to incorporate a dynamic ordering into an arbitrary tree-search algorithm [5].

Given a CSP and a backtracking search algorithm, a variable or value ordering is said to be *optimal* if the ordering results in a search that visits the fewest number of nodes over all possible orderings when finding one solution or showing that there does not exist a solution. (Note that I could as well have used some other abstract measure such as the amount of work done at each node, rather than nodes visited, but this would not change the fundamental results.) Not surprisingly, finding optimal orderings is a computationally difficult task. Liberatore [87] shows that simply deciding whether a variable is the first variable in an optimal variable ordering is at least as hard as deciding whether the CSP has a solution. Finding an optimal value ordering is also clearly at least as hard since, if a solution exists, an optimal value ordering could be used to efficiently find a solution. Little is known about how to find optimal orderings or how to construct polynomial-time approximation algorithms—algorithms which return an ordering which is guaranteed to be near-optimal (but see [70, 85]). The field of constraint programming has so far mainly focused on heuristics which have no formal guarantees.

Heuristics can be either application-independent, where only generic features common to all CSPs are used, or application-dependent. In this survey, I focus on application-independent heuristics. Such heuristics have been quite successful and can provide a good starting point when designing heuristics for a new application. The heuristics I present leave unspecified which variable or value to choose in the case of ties and the result is implementation dependent. These heuristics can often be dramatically improved by adding additional features for breaking ties. However, there is no one best variable or value ordering heuristic and there will remain problems where these application-independent heuristics do not work well enough and a new heuristic must be designed.

Given that a new heuristic is to be designed, several alternatives present themselves. The heuristic can, of course, be hand-crafted either using application-independent features (see [36] for a summary of many features from which to construct heuristics) or using application-dependent features. As one example of the latter, Smith and Cheng [122] show how an effective heuristic can be designed for job shop scheduling given deep knowledge of job shop scheduling, the CSP model, and the search algorithm. However, such a combination of expertise can be scarce.

An alternative to hand-crafting a heuristic is to automatically adapt or learn a heuristic. Minton [98] presents a system which automatically specializes generic variable and value ordering heuristics from a library to an application. Epstein et al. [36] present a system which learns variable and value ordering heuristics from previous search experience on problems from an application. The heuristics are combinations from a rich set of primitive features. Bain, Thornton, and Sattar [6] show how to learn variable ordering heuristics for optimization problems using evolutionary algorithms.

As a final alternative, if only relatively weak heuristics can be discovered for a problem, it has been shown that the technique of randomization and restarts can boost the performance of problem solving (see Section 4.7). Cicirello and Smith [27] discuss alternative methods for adding randomization to heuristics and the effect on search efficiency. Hulubei and O'Sullivan [70] study the relationship between the strength of the variable and value ordering heuristics and the need for restarts.

4.6.1 Variable Ordering Heuristics

Suppose that the backtracking search is attempting to extend a node p. The task of the variable ordering heuristic is to choose the next variable x to be branched on.

Many variable ordering heuristics have been proposed and evaluated in the literature. These heuristics can, with some omissions, be classified into two categories: heuristics that are based primarily on the domain sizes of the variables and heuristics that are based on the structure of the CSP.

Variable ordering heuristics based on domain size

When solving a CSP using backtracking search interleaved with constraint propagation, the domains of the unassigned variables are pruned using the constraints and the current set of branching constraints. Many of the most important variable ordering heuristics are based on the current domain sizes of the unassigned variables.

Definition 4.8 (remaining values). *Let $rem(x \mid p)$ be the number of values that remain in the domain of variable x after constraint propagation, given a set of branching constraints p.*

Golomb and Baumert [57] were the first to propose a dynamic ordering heuristic based on choosing the variable with the smallest number of values remaining in its domain. The heuristic, hereafter denoted dom, is to choose the variable x that minimizes,

$$rem(x \mid p),$$

where x ranges over all unassigned variables. Of course, the heuristic makes sense no matter what level of constraint propagation is being performed during the search. In the case of algorithms that do not perform constraint propagation but only check constraints which have all their variables instantiated, define $rem(x \mid p)$ to contain only the values which satisfy all the relevant constraints. Given that our backtracking search algorithm is performing constraint propagation, which in practice it will be, the dom heuristic can be computed very efficiently. The dom heuristic was popularized by Haralick and Elliott [63], who showed that dom with the forward checking algorithm was an effective combination.

Much effort has gone into understanding this simple but effective heuristic. Intriguingly, Golomb and Baumert [57], when first proposing dom, state that from an information-theoretic point of view, it can be shown that on average choosing the variable with the smallest domain size is more efficient, but no further elaboration is provided. Haralick and Elliott [63] show analytically that dom minimizes the depth of the search tree, assuming a simplistic probabilistic model of a CSP and assuming that we are searching for all solutions using a forward checking algorithm. Nudel [105], shows that dom is optimal (it minimizes the number of nodes in the search tree) again assuming forward checking but using a slightly more refined probabilistic model. Gent et al. [52] propose a measure called kappa whose intent is to capture "constrainedness" and what it means to choose the most constrained variable first. They show that dom (and dom+deg, see below) can be viewed as an approximation of this measure.

Hooker [66], in an influential paper, argues for the scientific testing of heuristics—as opposed to competitive testing—through the construction of empirical models designed to support or refute the intuition behind a heuristic. Hooker and Vinay [67] apply the methodology to the study of the Jeroslow-Wang heuristic, a variable ordering heuristic for SAT. Surprisingly, they find that the standard intuition, that "a [heuristic] performs better when it creates subproblems that are more likely to be satisfiable," is refuted whereas a newly developed intuition, that "a [heuristic] works better when it creates simpler subproblems," is confirmed. Smith and Grant [120] apply the methodology to the study of dom. Haralick and Elliott [63] proposed an intuition behind the heuristic called the fail-first principle: "to succeed, try first where you are most likely to fail". Surprisingly, Smith and Grant find that if one equates the fail-first principle with minimizing the depth of the search tree, as Haralick and Elliott did, the principle is refuted. In follow on work, Beck et al. [14] find that if one equates the fail-first principle with minimizing the number of nodes in the search tree, as Nadel did, the principle is confirmed. Wallace [132], using a factor analysis, finds two basic factors behind the variation in search efficiency due to variable ordering heuristics: immediate failure and future failure.

In addition to the effort that has gone into understanding dom, much effort has gone into improving it. Brélaz [20], in the context of graph coloring, proposes a now widely used generalization of dom. Let the degree of an unassigned variable x be the number of constraints which involve x and at least one other unassigned variable. The heuristic, hereafter denoted dom+deg, is to choose the variable with the smallest number of values remaining in its domain and to break any ties by choosing the variable with the highest degree. Note that the degree information is dynamic and is updated as variables are instantiated. A static version, where the degree information is only computed prior to search, is also used in practice.

Bessière and Régin [17] propose another generalization of dom. The heuristic, hereafter denoted dom/deg, is to divide the domain size of a variable by the degree of the variable and to choose the variable which has the minimal value. The heuristic is shown to work well on random problems. Boussemart et al. [19] propose to divide by the weighted degree, hereafter denoted dom/wdeg. A weight, initially set to one, is associated with each constraint. Every time a constraint is responsible for a deadend, the associated weight is incremented. The weighted degree is the sum of the weights of the constraints which involve x and at least one other unassigned variable. The dom/wdeg heuristic is shown to work well on a variety of problems. As an interesting aside, it has also been shown empirically that arc consistency propagation plus the dom/deg or the dom/wdeg heuristic can reduce or remove the need for backjumping on some problems [17, 84].

Gent et al. [50] propose choosing the variable x that minimizes,

$$rem(x \mid p) \prod_C (1 - t_C),$$

where C ranges over all constraints which involve x and at least one other unassigned variable and t_C is the fraction of assignments which do not satisfy the constraint C. They also propose other heuristics which contain the product term in the above equation. A limitation of all these heuristics is the requirement of an updated estimate of t_C for each constraint C as the search progresses. This is clearly costly, but also problematic for intensionally represented constraints and non-binary constraints. As well, the product term implicitly assumes that the probability a constraint fails is independent, an assumption that may not hold in practice.

Brown and Purdom [21] propose choosing the variable x that minimizes,

$$rem(x \mid p) + \min_{y \neq x} \left\{ \sum_{a \in rem(x \mid p)} rem(y \mid p \cup \{x = a\}) \right\},$$

where y ranges over all unassigned variables. The principle behind the heuristic is to pick the variable x that is the root of the smallest 2-level subtree. Brown and Purdom show that the heuristic works better than dom on random SAT problems as the problems get larger. However, the heuristic has yet to be thoroughly evaluated on hard SAT problems or general CSPs.

Geelen [49] proposes choosing the variable x that minimizes,

$$\sum_{a \in dom(x)} \prod_y rem(y \mid p \cup \{x = a\}),$$

where y ranges over all unassigned variables. The product term can be viewed as an upper bound on the number of solutions given a value a for x, and the principle behind the heuristic is said to be to choose the most "constrained" variable. Geelen shows that the heuristic works well on the n-queens problem when the level of constraint propagation used is forward checking. Refalo [111] proposes a similar heuristic and shows that it is much better than dom-based heuristics on multi-knapsack and magic square problems. Although the heuristic is costly to compute, Refalo's work shows that it can be particularly useful in choosing the first, or first few variables, in the ordering. Interestingly, Wallace [132] reports that on random and quasigroup problems, the heuristic does not perform well.

Freeman [38], in the context of SAT, proposes choosing the variable x that minimizes,

$$\sum_{a \in dom(x)} \sum_y rem(y \mid p \cup \{x = a\}),$$

where y ranges over all unassigned variables. Since this is an expensive heuristic, Freeman proposes using it primarily when choosing the first few variables in the search. The principle behind the heuristic is to maximize the amount of propagation and the number of variables which become instantiated if the variable is chosen, and thus simplify the remaining problem. Although costly to compute, Freeman shows that the heuristic works well on hard SAT problems when the level of constraint propagation used is unit propagation, the equivalent of forward checking. Malik et al. [91] show that a truncated version (using just the first element in $dom(x)$) is very effective in instruction scheduling problems.

Structure-guided variable ordering heuristics

A CSP can be represented as a graph. Such graphical representations form the basis of structure-guided variable ordering heuristics. Real problems often do contain much structure and on these problems the advantages of structure-guided heuristics include that structural parameters can be used to bound the worst-case of a backtracking algorithm and structural goods and nogoods can be recorded and used to prune large parts of the search space. Unfortunately, a current limitation of these heuristics is that they can break down in the presence of global constraints, which are common in practice. A further disadvantage is that some structure-guided heuristics are either static or nearly static.

Freuder [40] may have been the first to propose a structure-guided variable ordering heuristic. Consider the constraint graph where there is a vertex for each variable in the CSP and there is an edge between two vertices x and y if there exists a constraint C such that both $x \in vars(C)$ and $y \in vars(C)$.

Definition 4.9 (width). *Let the vertices in a constraint graph be ordered. The width of an ordering is the maximum number of edges from any vertex v to vertices prior to v in the ordering. The width of a constraint graph is the minimum width over all orderings of that graph.*

Consider the static variable ordering corresponding to an ordering of the vertices in the graph. Freuder [40] shows that the static variable ordering is backtrack-free if the level of strong k-consistency is greater than the width of the ordering. Clearly, such a variable ordering is within an $O(d)$ factor of an optimal ordering, where d is the size of the domain. Freuder [40] also shows that there exists a backtrack-free static variable ordering if the level of strong consistency is greater than the width of the constraint graph. Freuder [41] generalizes these results to static variable orderings which guarantee that the number of nodes visited in the search can be bounded *a priori*.

Dechter and Pearl [35] propose a variable ordering which first instantiates variables which cut cycles in the constraint graph. Once all cycles have been cut, the constraint graph is a tree and can be solved quickly using arc consistency [40]. Sabin and Freuder [117] refine and test this proposal within an algorithm that maintains arc consistency. They show that, on random binary problems, a variable ordering that cuts cycles can out perform dom+deg.

Zabih [136] proposes choosing a static variable ordering with small bandwidth. Let the n vertices in a constraint graph be ordered 1, ..., n. The bandwidth of an ordering is the maximum distance between any two vertices in the ordering that are connected by an edge. The bandwidth of a constraint graph is the minimum bandwidth over all orderings of that graph. Intuitively, a small bandwidth ordering will ensure that variables that caused the failure will be close by and thus reduce the need for backjumping. However, there is currently little empirical evidence that this is an effective heuristic.

A well-known technique in algorithm design on graphs is divide-and-conquer using graph separators.

Definition 4.10 (separator). *A separator of a graph is a subset of the vertices or the edges which, when removed, separates the graph into disjoint subgraphs.*

A graph can be recursively decomposed by successively finding separators of the resulting disjoint subgraphs. Freuder and Quinn [42] propose a variable ordering heuristic based on a such a recursive decomposition. The idea is that the separators (called cutsets in [42]) give groups of variables which, once instantiated, decompose the CSP. Freuder and Quinn also propose a special-purpose backtracking algorithm to correctly use the variable ordering to get additive behavior rather than multiplicative behavior when solving the independent problems. Huang and Darwiche [69] show that the special-purpose backtracking algorithm is not needed; one can just use CBJ. Because the separators are found prior to search, the pre-established variable groupings never change during the execution of the backtracking search. However, Huang and Darwiche note that within these groupings the variable ordering can be dynamic and any one of the existing variable ordering heuristics can used. Li and van Beek [86] present several improvements to this divide-and-conquer approach. So far the divide-and-conquer approach has been shown to be effective on hard SAT problems [69, 86], but there has as yet been no systematic evaluation of the approach on general CSP problems.

As two final structure-guided heuristics, Moskewicz et al. [103], in their Chaff solver for SAT, propose that the choice of variable should be biased towards variables that occur in recently recorded nogoods. Jégou and Terrioux [73] use a tree-decomposition of the constraint graph to guide the variable ordering.

4.6.2   Value Ordering Heuristics

Suppose that the backtracking search is attempting to extend a node p and the variable ordering heuristic has chosen variable x to be branched on next. The task of the value ordering heuristic is to choose the next value a for x. The principle being followed in the design of many value ordering heuristics is to choose next the value that is most likely to succeed or be a part of a solution. Value ordering heuristics have been proposed which are based on either estimating the number of solutions or estimating the probability of a solution, for each choice of value a for x. Clearly, if we knew either of these properties *exactly*, then a perfect value ordering would also be known—simply select a value that leads to a solution and avoid a value that does not lead to a solution.

Dechter and Pearl [35] propose a static value ordering heuristic based on approximating the number of solutions to each subproblem. An approximation of the number of solutions is found by forming a tree relaxation of the problem, where constraints are dropped until the constraint graph of the CSP can be represented as a tree. Counting all solutions to a tree-structured CSP is polynomial and thus can be computed exactly. The values are then ordered by decreasing estimates of the solution counts. Followup work [76, 94, 131] has focused on generalizing the approach to dynamic value orderings and on improving the approximation of the number of solutions (the tree relaxation can provide a poor estimate of the true solution count) by using recent ideas from Bayesian networks. A limitation of this body of work is that, while it compares the number of solutions, it does not take into account the size of the subtree that is being branched into or the difficultly or cost of searching the subtree.

Ginsberg et al. [55], in experiments which used crossword puzzles as a test bed, propose the following dynamic value ordering heuristic. To instantiate x, choose the value $a \in dom(x)$ that maximizes the *product* of the remaining domain sizes,

$$\prod_{y} rem(y \mid p \cup \{x = a\}),$$

where y ranges over all unassigned variables. Ginsberg et al. show that the heuristic works well on crossword puzzles when the level of constraint propagation used is forward checking. Further empirical evidence for the usefulness of this heuristic was provided by Geelen [49]. Geelen notes that the product gives the number of possible completions of the node p and these completions can be viewed in two ways. First, assuming that every completion is equally likely to be a solution, choosing the value that maximizes the product also maximizes the probability that we are branching into a subproblem that contains a solution. Second, the completions can be viewed as an upper bound on the number of solutions to the subproblem. Frost and Dechter [46] propose choosing the value that maximizes the *sum* of the remaining domain sizes. However, Geelen [49] notes that the product differentiates much better than summation. In the literature, the product heuristic is sometimes called the "promise" heuristic and the summation heuristic is sometimes called the "min-conflicts" heuristic—as it was inspired by a local search heuristic of the same name proposed by Minton et al. [99].

4.7 Randomization and Restart Strategies

It has been widely observed that backtracking algorithms can be brittle on some instances. Seemingly small changes to a variable or value ordering heuristic, such as a change in the ordering of tie-breaking schemes, can lead to great differences in running time. An explanation for this phenomenon is that ordering heuristics make mistakes. Depending on the number of mistakes and how early in the search the mistakes are made (and therefore how costly they may be to correct), there can be a large variability in performance between different heuristics. A technique called randomization and restarts has been proposed for taking advantage of this variability.

The technique of randomization and restarts within backtracking search algorithms goes back at least to the PhD work of Harvey [64]. Harvey found that periodically restarting a backtracking search with different variable orderings could eliminate the problem of "early mistakes". This observation led Harvey to propose randomized backtracking algorithms where on each run of the backtracking algorithm the variable or the value orderings are randomized. The backtracking algorithm terminates when either a solution has been found or the distance that the algorithm has backtracked from a deadend exceeds some fixed cutoff. In the latter case, the backtracking algorithm is restarted and the search begins anew with different orderings. Harvey shows that this randomize and restart technique gives improved performance over a deterministic backtracking algorithm on job shop scheduling problems. Gomes et al. [60, 61, 62] have done much to popularize and advance the technique through demonstrations of its wide applicability, drawing connections to closely related work on Las Vegas algorithms, and contributions to our understanding of when and why restarts help.

In the rest of this section, I first survey work on the technique itself and then survey work that addresses the question of when do restarts help. For more on the topic of randomization and restart strategies see, for example, the survey by Gomes [58].

4.7.1   Algorithmic Techniques

The technique of randomization and restarts requires a method of adding randomization to a deterministic backtracking algorithm and a restart strategy, a schedule or method for deciding when to restart.

Randomization

Several possible methods of adding randomization to backtracking algorithms have been proposed in the literature. Harvey [64] proposes randomizing the *variable* ordering. Gomes et al. [61, 62] propose randomizing the variable ordering heuristic either by randomized tie breaking or by ranking the variables using an existing heuristic and then randomly choosing a variable from the set of variables that are within some small factor of the best variable. They show that restart strategies with randomized variable orderings lead to orders of magnitude improvement on a wide variety of problems including both SAT and CSP versions of scheduling, planning, and quasigroup completion problems. Cicirello and Smith [27] discuss alternative methods for adding randomization to heuristics and the effect on search efficiency. Other alternatives are to choose a variable with a probability that is proportional to the heuristic weight of the variable or to randomly pick from among a suite of heuristics. One pitfall to be aware of is that the method of adding randomization to the heuristic must give enough different decisions near the top of the search tree. Harvey [64] proposes randomizing the *value* ordering so that each possible ordering is equally likely. As well, all the options listed above for randomizing variable orderings are also options for value orderings. Zhang [138] argues that randomizing a heuristic can weaken it, an undesirable effect. Prestwich [106] and Zhang [138] propose a random backwards jump in the search space upon backtracking. Although effective, this has the consequence that the backtracking algorithm is no longer complete.

Restart strategies

A restart strategy $S = (t_1, t_2, t_3, ...)$ is an infinite sequence where each t_i is either a positive integer or infinity. The idea is that the randomized backtracking algorithm is run for t_1 steps. If no solution is found within that cutoff, the algorithm is run for t_2 steps, and so on. A *fixed cutoff* strategy is a strategy where all the t_i are equal. Various restart strategies have been proposed.

Luby, Sinclair, and Zuckerman [88] (hereafter just Luby) examine restart strategies in the more general setting of Las Vegas algorithms. A Las Vegas algorithm is a randomized algorithm that always gives the correct answer when it terminates, however the running time of the algorithm varies from one run to another and can be modeled as a random variable. Let $f(t)$ be the probability that a backtracking algorithm $\mathcal{A}$ applied to instance x stops after taking exactly t steps. Let $F(t)$ be the cumulative distribution function of f i.e., the probability that $\mathcal{A}$ stops after taking t or fewer steps. $F(t)$ is sometimes referred to as the runtime distribution of algorithm $\mathcal{A}$ on instance x. The tail probability is the probability that $\mathcal{A}$ stops after taking more than t steps; i.e., $1 - F(t)$, which is sometimes referred to as the survival function. Luby shows that, given full knowledge of the runtime distribution, the optimal strategy is given by $S_{t^*} = (t^*, t^*, t^*, \ldots)$, for some fixed cutoff t^*. Of course, the runtime distribution is not known in practice. For the case where there is no knowledge of the runtime distribution, Luby shows that a universal strategy given by $S_u = (1, 1, 2, 1, 1, 2, 4, 1, 1, 2, 1, 1, 2, 4, 8, 1, \ldots)$ is within a log factor of the optimal strategy S_{t^*} and that this is the best performance that can be achieved up to a constant factor by any universal strategy. Further, Luby proves that, no matter what the runtime distribution of the original algorithm $\mathcal{A}$, if we apply $\mathcal{A}$ using restart strategy S_{t^*} or S_u, the tail probability of the restart strategy is small as it decays exponentially.

To use a restart strategy in practice, one must decide what counts as a primitive operation or step in the computation. Several methods have been used in the literature. Harvey [64] uses a fixed cutoff strategy which restarts the backtracking algorithm when the distance that the algorithm has backtracked from a deadend exceeds some fixed cutoff. Richards [112] restarts at every deadend, but maintains completeness by first recording a nogood so the deadend is not revisited. Gomes et al. [61] use a fixed cutoff strategy that restarts the backtracking algorithm when the number of backtracks exceeds some fixed cutoff. Kautz et al. [78, 115] use the number of nodes visited by the backtracking algorithm. For a fixed cutoff strategy, one must also decide what cutoff to use. So far it appears that good cutoffs are specific to an instance. Thus one must perform some sort of trial-and-error search for a good cutoff value. However, van Moorsel and Wolter [130] observe that for some runtime distributions a wide range of cutoffs perform well. They further observe that it is often safer to make the cutoff too large rather than too small. For the universal strategy, one does not need to decide the cutoff. However, it has been reported that the universal strategy is slow in practice as the sequence increases too slowly (e.g., [61, 78, 115]). Note that this does not contradict the fact that the universal strategy is within a log factor of optimal, since this is an asymptotic result and ignores constant factors. However, it may also be noted that one can scale the universal strategy $S_u = (s, s, 2s, \ldots)$, for some scale factor s, and possibly improve performance while retaining the optimality guarantee.

Walsh [134] proposes a universal strategy $S_g = (1, r, r^2, \ldots)$, where the restart values are geometrically increasing, and shows that values of r in the range $1 < r < 2$ work well on the problems examined. The strategy has the advantage that it increases more quickly than the universal strategy but avoids the search for a cutoff necessary for a fixed cutoff strategy. Although it appears to work well in practice, unfortunately the geometric strategy comes with no formal guarantees for its worst-case performance. It can be shown that the expected runtime of the geometric strategy can be arbitrarily worse than that of the optimal strategy.

Kautz et al. [78, 115] (hereafter just Kautz) observe that Luby makes two assumptions when proving the optimality of S_{t^*} that may not hold in practice. The assumptions are (i) that successive runs of the randomized algorithm are statistically independent and identically distributed, and (ii) that the only feasible observation or feature is the length of a run. As an example of where the first assumption may be false, consider the case where the current instance is drawn from one of two distributions but we do not know which. The failure to find a solution in previous runs can change our belief about the runtime distribution of the current instance. To show that the second assumption may be false, Kautz shows that a Bayesian model based on a rich set of features can with sufficient accuracy predict the runtime of the algorithm on the current instance. Kautz removes these assumptions and proposes context-sensitive or dynamic restart strategies. In one set of experiments, Kautz shows that a dynamic strategy can do *better* than the static optimal strategy S_{t^*}. The strategy uses a Bayesian model to predict whether a current run of the algorithm will be either "long" or "short", and restarts if the prediction is "long".

Van Moorsel and Wolter [130] consider a case that often arises in practice where a solution is useful only if it is found within some deadline; i.e., we are given a deadline c and we may run the restart strategy until a total of c steps of the algorithm have been executed. Van Moorsel and Wolter consider restart strategies that maximize the probability the deadline is met.

4.7.2   When Do Restarts Help?

The question of when and why the technique of randomization and restarts is useful has been addressed from two angles: For what kinds of runtime distributions are restarts helpful and what are the underlying causes for these runtime distributions.

Runtime distributions for which restarts are useful

In the case where restarts are helpful on satisfiable instances, Gomes et al. [61, 62] show that probability distributions with heavy-tails can be a good fit to the runtime distributions of backtracking algorithms with randomized heuristics. A heavy-tailed distribution is one where the tail probability or survival function (see above) decays polynomially; i.e., there is a significant probability that the backtracking algorithm will run for a long time. For unsatisfiable instances, Gomes et al. [61] report that in their experiments on random quasigroup completion problems, heavy-tailed behavior was not found and that restarts were consequently not helpful on these problems. As an interesting aside, Baptista and Marques-Silva [8] show experimentally that—because of synergy between the techniques—a backtracking algorithm that incorporates nogood recording can benefit from randomization and restarts when solving unsatisfiable instances.

Hoos [68] notes that restarts will not only be effective for heavy tails, but that its effectiveness depends *solely* on there existing some point where the cumulative runtime distribution is increasing slower than the exponential distribution. It is at this point, where the search is stagnating, that a restart would be helpful.

Van Moorsel and Wolter [129] provide necessary and sufficient conditions for restarts to be helpful. Their work can be seen as a formalization of Hoos' insight and its extension from one restart to multiple restarts. Let T be a random variable which models the runtime of a randomized backtracking algorithm on an instance and let $E[T]$ be the expected value of T. Under the assumption that successive runs of the randomized algorithm are statistically independent and identically distributed, Van Moorsel and Wolter show that *any* number of restarts using a fixed cutoff of t steps is better than just letting the algorithm run to completion if and only if,

$$E[T] < E[T - t \mid T > t]$$

holds; i.e., if and only if the expected runtime of the algorithm is less than the expected remaining time to completion given that the algorithm has run for t steps. Van Moorsel and Wolter also show that if a single restart improves the expected runtime, multiple restarts perform even better, and unbounded restarts performs best. For what kinds of distributions does the above condition hold? Restarts will be most effective (the inequality will be greatest) for heavy-tailed distributions, where the tail decays polynomially, but Van Moorsel and Wolter observe that the condition also hold for some distributions where the tail decays exponentially. For other exponentially decaying distributions, restarting will be strictly worse than running the algorithm to completion. Zhan [137] shows that this is not an isolated case and for many problems restarts can be harmful. For pure exponential distributions, the condition is an equality and restarts will be neither helpful or harmful.

Underlying causes for these runtime distributions

Various theories have been postulated for explaining why restarts are helpful; i.e., why do runtime distributions arise where restarts are helpful. It is superficially agreed that an explanation for this phenomenon is that ordering heuristics make mistakes which require the backtracking algorithm to explore large subtrees with no solutions. However, the theories differ in what it means for an ordering heuristic to make a mistake.

Harvey [64] defines a mistake as follows.

Definition 4.11 (value mistake). *A mistake is a node in the search tree that is a nogood but the parent of the node is not a nogood.*

When a mistake is made, the search has branched into a subproblem that does not have a solution. The result is that the node has to be refuted and doing this may require a large subtree to be explored, especially if the mistake is made early in the tree. In this definition, value ordering heuristics make mistakes, variable ordering heuristics do not. However, changing the variable ordering can mean either that a mistake is not made, since the value ordering is correct for the newly chosen variable, or that any mistake is less costly to correct. Harvey constructs a probabilistic model to predict when a restart algorithm will perform better than its deterministic counterpart. With simplifying assumptions about the probability of a mistake, it is shown that restarts are beneficial when the mistake probability is small. Clearly, the definition, and thus the probabilistic model on which it depends, only applies if a CSP has a solution. Therefore, the theory does not explain when restarts would be beneficial for unsatisfiable problems.

As evidence in support of this theory, Hulubei and O'Sullivan [70] consider the distribution of refutation sizes to correct mistakes (the size of the subtrees that are rooted at mistakes). They show that when using a poor value ordering in experiments on quasigroup completion problems, heavy-tailed behavior was observed for every one of four different high-quality variable ordering heuristics. However, the heavy-tailed behavior disappeared when the same experiments were performed but this time with a high-quality value ordering heuristic in place of the random value ordering.

Williams, Gomes, and Selman [135] (hereafter just Williams) define a mistake as follows.

Definition 4.12 (backdoor mistake). *A mistake is a selection of a variable that is not in a minimal backdoor, when such a variable is available to be chosen.*

A backdoor is a set of variables for which there exists value assignments such that the simplified problem (such as after constraint propagation) can be solved in polynomial time. Backdoors capture the intuition that good variable and value ordering heuristics simplify the problem as quickly as possible. When a mistake is made, the search has branched into a subproblem that has not been as effectively simplified as it would have been had it chosen a backdoor variable. The result is that the subproblem is more costly to search, especially if the mistake is made early in the tree. In this definition, variable ordering heuristics make mistakes, value ordering heuristics do not.   Williams constructs a probabilistic model to predict when heavy-tailed behavior will occur but there will exist a restart strategy that will have polynomial expected running time. With simplifying assumptions about the probability of a mistake, it is shown that both of these occur when the probability of a mistake is sufficiently small and the size of the minimal backdoor is sufficiently small. The theory can also explain when restarts would be beneficial for unsatisfiable problems, through the notion of a strong backdoor. However, the theory does not entirely account for the fact that a random value ordering together with a restart strategy can remove heavy-tail behavior. In this case the variable ordering remains fixed and so the probability of a mistake also remains unchanged.

Finally, some work contributes to our understanding of why runtime distributions arise where restarts are helpful while remaining agnostic about the exact definition of a mistake. Consider the probability distribution of refutation sizes to correct mistakes. It has been shown both empirically on random problems and through theoretical, probabilistic models that heavy-tails arise in the case where this distribution decays exponentially as the size of the refutation grows [24, 59]. In other words, there is an exponentially decreasing probability of making a costly (exponentially-sized) mistake.

4.8   Best-First Search

In the search tree that is traversed by a backtracking algorithm, the branches out of a node are assumed to be ordered by a value ordering heuristic, with the left-most branch being the most promising (or at least no less promising than any branch to the right). The backtracking algorithm then performs a depth-first traversal of the search tree, visiting the branches out of a node in left-to-right order. When a CSP instance is unsatisfiable and the entire search tree must be traversed, depth-first search is the clear best choice. However, when it is known or it can safely be assumed that a CSP instance is satisfiable, alternative search strategies such as best-first search become viable. In this section, I survey discrepancy-based search strategies, which can be viewed as variations on best-first search.

Harvey and Ginsberg [64, 65] were the first to propose a discrepancy-based search strategy, in an algorithm called limited discrepancy search. A discrepancy is the case where the search does not follow the value ordering heuristic and does not take the left-most branch out of a node. The idea behind limited discrepancy search is to iteratively search the tree by increasing number of discrepancies, preferring discrepancies that occur near the root of the tree. This allows the search to recover from mistakes made early in the search (see Definition 4.11). In contrast, with backtracking (or depth-first) search, mistakes made near the root of the tree can be costly to discover and undo. On the ith iteration, the limited discrepancy algorithm visits all leaf nodes with up to i discrepancies in the path from the root to the leaf. The algorithm terminates when a solution is found or the iteration is exhausted. Limited discrepancy search is called iteratively with $i = 0, 1, \ldots, k$. If $k \geq n$, where n is the depth of the search tree, the algorithm is complete; otherwise it is incomplete. Harvey and Ginsberg show both theoretically and experimentally that limited discrepancy search can be better than depth-first search on satisfiable instances when a good value ordering heuristic is available.

Korf [80] proposes a modification to the limited discrepancy algorithm so that it visits fewer duplicate nodes on subsequent iterations. On the ith iteration, Korf's algorithm visits all leaf nodes with *exactly* i discrepancies in the path from the root to the leaf. However, to achieve these savings, Korf's algorithm prefers discrepancies deeper in the tree. Korf notes that limited discrepancy search can be viewed as a variation on best-first search, where the cost of a node p is the number of discrepancies in the path from the root of the search tree to p. In best-first search, the node with the lowest cost is chosen as the next node to be extended. In Harvey and Ginsberg's proposal, ties for lowest cost are broken by choosing a node that is *closest* to the root. In Korf's proposal, ties are broken by choosing a node that is *farthest* from the root.

Walsh [133] (and independently Meseguer [95]), argues that value ordering heuristics tend to be less informed and more prone to make mistakes near the top of the search tree. Walsh proposes depth-bounded discrepancy search, which biases search to discrepancies near the top of the tree, but visits fewer redundant nodes than limited discrepancy search. On the ith iteration, the depth-bounded discrepancy search algorithm visits all leaf nodes where all discrepancies in the path from the root to the leaf occur at depth i or less. Meseguer [95] proposes interleaved depth-first search, which also biases search to discrepancies near the top of the tree. The basic idea is to divide up the search time on the branches out of a node using a variation of round-robin scheduling. Each branch—or more properly, each subtree rooted at a branch—is searched for a given time-slice using depth-first search. If no solution is found within the time slice, the search is suspended and the next branch becomes active. Upon suspending search in the last branch, the first branch again becomes active. This continues until either a solution is found or all the subtrees have been exhaustively searched. The strategy can be applied recursively within subtrees.

Meseguer and Walsh [96] experimentally compare backtracking algorithms using traditional depth-first search and the four discrepancy-based search strategies described above. On a test bed which consisted of random binary, quasigroup completion, and number partitioning CSPs, it was found that discrepancy-based search strategies could be much better than depth-first search. As with randomization and restarts, discrepancy-based search strategies are a way to overcome value ordering mistakes made early in the search.

4.9 Optimization

In some important application areas of constraint programming such as scheduling, sequencing and planning, CSPs arise which have, in addition to constraints which must be satisfied, an objective function f which must be optimized. Without loss of generality, I assume in what follows that the goal is to find a solution which minimizes f and that f is a function over all the variables of the CSP. I also assume that a variable c has been added to the CSP model and constrained to be equal to the objective function; i.e., $c = f(X)$, where X is the set of variables in the CSP. I call this the objective constraint.

To solve optimization CSPs, the common approach is to find an optimal solution by solving a sequence of CSPs; i.e., a sequence of satisfaction problems. Several variations have been proposed and evaluated in the literature. Van Hentenryck [128] proposes what can be viewed as a constraint-based version of branch-and-bound. Initially, a backtracking search is used to find any solution p which satisfies the constraints. A constraint is then added to the CSP of the form $c < f(S)$ which excludes solutions that are not better than this solution. A new solution is then found for the augmented CSP. This process is repeated until the resulting CSP is unsatisfiable, in which case the last solution found has been proven optimal. Baptiste, Le Pape, and Nuijten [9] suggest iterating on the possible values of c by either (i) iterating from the smallest value in $dom(c)$ to the largest until a solution is found, (ii) iterating from largest to smallest until a solution is no longer found, or (iii) performing binary search. Each time, of course, we are solving a satisfaction problem using a backtracking search algorithm. For these approaches to be effective, it is important that constraint propagation techniques be applied to the objective constraint. For example, see [9, Chapter 5] for propagation techniques for objective constraints for several objective functions that arise in scheduling.

4.10   Comparing Backtracking Algorithms

As this survey has indicated, many improvements to backtracking have been proposed and there are many ways that these techniques can be combined together into one algorithm. In this section, I survey work on comparing the performance of backtracking algorithms. The work is categorized into empirical and theoretical approaches. Both approaches have well-known advantages and disadvantages. Empirical comparisons allow the comparison of any pair of backtracking algorithms, but any conclusion about which algorithm is better will always be weak since it must be qualified by the phrase, "on the instances we examined". Theoretical comparisons allow categorical statements about the relative performance of some pairs of backtracking algorithms, but the requirement that any conclusion be true for all instances means that statements cannot be made about every pair of algorithms and the statements that can be made must sometimes be necessarily weak.

When comparing backtracking algorithms, several performance measures have been used. For empirical comparisons, of course runtime can be used, although this requires one to be sure that one is comparing the underlying algorithms and not implementation skill or choice of programming language. Three widely used performance measures that are implementation independent are number of constraint checks, backtracks, and nodes visited.

4.10.1   Empirical Comparisons

Early work in empirical comparisons of backtracking algorithms was hampered by a lack of realistic or hard test problems (e.g., [21, 48, 63, 93, 108, 114]). The experimental test bed often consisted of only toy problems—the ubiquitous n-queens problem first used in 1965 [57] was still being used as a test bed more than 20 years later [125]—and simple random problems. As well, often only CSPs with binary constraints were experimented upon. The focus on simple, binary CSPs was sometimes detrimental to the field and led to promising approaches being prematurely dismissed.

The situation improved with the discovery of hard random problems that arise at a phase transition and the investigation of alternative random models of CSPs (see [51] and references therein). Experiments could now be performed which compared the algorithms on the hardest problems and systematically explored the entire space of random problems to see where one algorithm bettered another (e.g., [17, 45, 126]). Unfortunately, most of the random models lack any structure or realism. The situation was further improved by the realization that important applications of constraint programming are often best modeled using global constraints and other non-binary constraints, and the construction and subsequent wide use of a constraint programming benchmark library [53].

In the remainder of this section, I review two representative streams of experiments: experiments that examine what level of constraint propagation a backtracking algorithm should perform and experiments that examine the interaction between several techniques for improving a backtracking algorithm. Many other experiments—such as those performed by authors who have introduced a new technique and then show that the technique works better on a selected set of test problems—are reported elsewhere in this survey.

Experiments on level of constraint propagation

Experiments have examined the question of what level of local consistency should be maintained during the backtracking search. Consider the representative set of experiments summarized in Table 4.2. Gaschnig [47] originally proposed interleaving backtracking search with arc consistency. Early experiments which tested this proposal concluded that an algorithm that maintained arc consistency during the search was not competitive with forward checking [48, 63, 93].

This view was maintained for about fifteen years until it was challenged by Sabin and Freuder. Sabin and Freuder [116], using hard random problems, showed that MAC could be much better than forward checking. More recently, with an increasing emphasis on applying constraint programming in practice, has come an understanding of the importance of global constraints and other intensionally represented non-binary constraints for modeling real problems. With such constraints, special purpose constraint propagation algorithms are developed and the modeler has a choice of what level of constraint propagation to enforce. It is now generally accepted that the choice of level of constraint propagation depends on the application and different choices may be made for different constraints within the same CSP.

Table 4.2: *Experiments on constraint propagation: MAC vs FC.*

	Faster?	Comment
McGregor (1979) [93]	FC	3 × faster
Haralick & Elliott (1980) [63]	FC	3 × faster
Sabin & Freuder (1994) [116]	MAC	much better
Bacchus & van Run (1995) [5]	FC	3–20 × faster
Bessière & Régin (1996) [17]	MAC	much better
Larrosa (2000) [81]	both	much better

Experiments on the interaction between improvements

Experiments have examined the interaction of the quality of the variable ordering heuristic, the level of local consistency maintained during the backtracking search, and the addition of backjumping techniques such as conflict-directed backjumping (CBJ) and dynamic backtracking (DBT). Unfortunately, these three techniques for improving a backtracking algorithm are not entirely orthogonal. Consider the representative set of experiments summarized in Table 4.3. These experiments show that, if the variable ordering is fixed and the level of constraint propagation is forward checking, conflict-directed backjumping is an effective technique. However, it can also be observed in previous experimental work that as the level of local consistency that is maintained in the backtracking search is increased and as the variable ordering heuristic is improved, the effects of CBJ are diminished [5, 17, 107, 108]. For example, it can be observed in Prosser's [108] experiments that, given a static variable ordering, increasing the level of local consistency maintained from none to the level of forward checking, diminishes the effects of CBJ. Bacchus and van Run [5] observe from their experiments that adding a dynamic variable ordering (an improvement over a static variable ordering) to a forward checking algorithm diminishes the effects of CBJ. In their experiments the effects are so diminished as to be almost negligible and they present an argument for why this might hold in general. Bessière and Régin [17] observe from their experiments that simultaneously increasing the level of local consistency even further to arc consistency and further improving the dynamic variable ordering heuristic diminishes the effects of CBJ so much that, in their implementation, the overhead of maintaining the data structures for backjumping actually slows down the algorithm. They conjecture that when arc consistency is maintained and a good variable ordering heuristic is used, "CBJ becomes useless". All of the above experiments were on small puzzles—the Zebra problem and n-queens problem—and on random CSPs which lacked any structure.

In contrast, in subsequent experiments on both random and real-world *structured* CSPs, backjumping was found to be a useful technique. Jussien, Debruyne, Boizumault [75] present empirical results that show that adding dynamic backtracking to an algorithm that maintains arc consistency can greatly improve performance. Chen and van Beek [26] present empirical results that show that, although the effects of CBJ may be diminished, adding CBJ to a backtracking algorithm that maintains arc consistency can still provide orders of magnitude speedups. Finally, CBJ is now a standard technique in the best backtracking algorithms for solving structured SAT problems [83].

Table 4.3: *Experiments on backjumping: FC vs FC-CBJ.*

	Faster?	Comment
Rosiers and Bruynooghe (1987) [114]	FC-CBJ	never worse
Prosser (1993) [108]	FC-CBJ	three times better
Frost & Dechter (1994) [45]	FC-CBJ	somewhat better
Bacchus & van Run (1995) [5]	FC-CBJ	slightly
Smith & Grant (1995) [119]	FC-CBJ	sometimes much better
Bayardo & Schrag (1996, 1997) [11, 12]	FC-CBJ	much better

4.10.2 Theoretical Comparisons

Worst-case analysis and average-case analysis are two standard theoretical approaches to understanding and comparing algorithms. Unfortunately, neither approach has proven generally successful for comparing backtracking algorithms. The worst-case bounds of backtracking algorithms are always exponential and rarely predictive of performance, and the average-case analyses of backtracking algorithms have, by necessity, made simplifying and unrealistic assumptions about the distribution of problems (e.g., [63, 105, 110]).

Two alternative approaches that have proven more successful for comparing algorithms are techniques based on proof complexity and a methodology for constructing partial orders based on characterizing properties of the nodes visited by an algorithm.

Proof complexity and backtracking algorithms

Backtracking algorithms can be compared using techniques from the proof complexity of resolution refutation proofs. The results that can be proven are of the general form: Given any CSP instance, algorithm $\mathcal{A}$ with an optimal variable and value ordering never visits fewer and can visit exponentially more nodes when applied to the instance than algorithm $\mathcal{B}$ with an optimal variable and value ordering. The optimal orderings are relative to the algorithms and thus $\mathcal{A}$ and $\mathcal{B}$ may use different orderings. I begin by briefly explaining resolution refutation proofs and proof complexity, followed by an explanation of some results of applying proof complexity techniques to the study of backtracking algorithms for CSPs.

The resolution inference rule takes two premises in the form of clauses $(A \vee x)$ and $(B \vee \neg x)$ and gives the clause $(A \vee B)$ as a conclusion. The two premises are said to be resolved and the variable x is said to be resolved away. Resolving the two clauses x and $\neg x$ gives the empty clause. Given a set of input clauses $\mathcal{F}$, a resolution proof or derivation of a clause C is a sequence of applications of the resolution inference rule such that C is the final conclusion and each premise in each application of the inference rule is either a clause from $\mathcal{F}$ or a conclusion from a previous application of the inference rule. A resolution proof that derives the empty clause is called a refutation proof, as it shows that the input set of clauses $\mathcal{F}$ is unsatisfiable.

A resolution proof of a clause C can be viewed as a directed acyclic graph (DAG). Each leaf node in the DAG is labeled with a clause from $\mathcal{F}$, each internal node is labeled with a derived clause that is justified by resolving the clauses of its two parents, and there is a single node with no successors and the label of that node is C. Many restrictions on the form of the proof DAG have been studied. For our purposes, one will suffice. A tree resolution proof is a resolution proof where the DAG of inferences forms a tree. The size of a proof is the number of nodes (clauses) in the proof DAG.

Proof complexity is the study of the size of the *smallest* proof a method can produce [28]. It is known that the smallest tree resolution refutation proof to show a set of clauses $\mathcal{F}$ is unsatisfiable can be exponentially larger than the smallest unrestricted resolution refutation proof and can never be smaller (see [13] and references therein). To see why tree proofs can be larger, note that if one wishes to use a derived clause elsewhere in the proof it must be re-derived. To see why tree proofs can never be smaller, note that every tree resolution proof is also an unrestricted resolution proof.

Why is resolution refutation proof complexity interesting for the study of backtracking algorithms? The search tree that results from applying a complete backtracking algorithm to an unsatisfiable CSP can be viewed as a resolution refutation proof. As an example of the correspondence, consider the backtracking tree that results from applying BT to the SAT problem which consists of the set of clauses $\{a \vee b \vee c, a \vee \neg c, \neg b, \neg a \vee c, b \vee \neg c\}$ Each leaf node is labeled with the clause that caused the failure, interior nodes are labeled by working from the leaves to the root applying the resolution inference rule, and the root will be labeled with the empty clause. Thus, proof complexity addresses the question of the size of the smallest possible backtrack tree; i.e., the size of the backtrack tree *if one assumes optimal variable and value ordering heuristics.*

The connection between backtracking algorithms for SAT and resolution has been widely observed and it is known that DPLL-based algorithms on unsatisfiable instances correspond to tree resolution refutation proofs. Baker [7] shows how to generalize this correspondence to the backtracking algorithm BT for general CSPs, when BT is using d-way branching. Mitchell [100], using earlier work by de Kleer [32], shows how to generalize this correspondence when BT is using 2-way branching.

Beame, Kautz, and Sabharwal [13] (hereafter Beame) use proof complexity techniques to investigate backtracking algorithms with nogood recording. Let DPLL be a basic backtracking algorithm for SAT, let DPLL+nr be DPLL with a nogood recording scheme (called FirstNewCut) added, and let DPLL+nr+restarts be DPLL with nogood recording and infinite restarts added. Beame shows that the smallest refutation proofs using DPLL can be exponentially longer than the smallest refutation proofs using DPLL+nr. In other words, DPLL with an optimal variable and value ordering never visits fewer and can visit exponentially more nodes than DPLL with nogood recording and an optimal variable and value ordering. Beame also shows that DPLL+nr+restarts is equivalent to unrestricted resolution if the learned nogoods are retained between restarts. It is an open question whether DPLL+nr is equivalent to unrestricted resolution or falls strictly between unrestricted resolution and tree resolution proofs.

Hwang and Mitchell [71] use proof complexity techniques to investigate backtracking algorithms with different branching strategies. Let BT-2-way be a basic backtracking algorithm for general CSPs using 2-way branching, and let BT-d-way be a backtracking algorithm using d-way branching. Hwang and Mitchell show that BT-d-way with an optimal variable and value ordering never visits fewer and can visit exponentially more nodes than BT-2-way with an optimal variable and value ordering.

Although a powerful technique, a limitation of the proof complexity framework is that it cannot be used to distinguish between some standard improvements to the basic chronological backtracking algorithm. For example, consider the four combinations of adding or not adding unit propagation and conflict-directed backjumping to DPLL. When using an optimal variable and value ordering each algorithm visits exactly the same number of nodes. Similar results hold for adding conflict-directed backjumping, dynamic backtracking, or forward checking to BT [7, 26, 100].

A partial order on backtracking algorithms

Backtracking algorithms can be compared by formulating necessary and sufficient conditions for a search tree node to be visited by each backtracking algorithm. These characterizations can then be used to construct a partial order (or hierarchy) on the algorithms according to two standard performance measures: the number of nodes visited and the number of constraint checks performed.

The results that can be proven are of the general form: Given any CSP instance and any variable and value ordering, algorithm $\mathcal{A}$ with the variable and value ordering never visits more nodes (and may visit fewer) when applied to the instance than algorithm $\mathcal{B}$ with the same variable and value ordering. In other words, algorithm $\mathcal{A}$ dominates algorithm $\mathcal{B}$ when the performance measure is nodes visited. A strong feature of this approach is that the results still hold ($\mathcal{A}$ still dominates $\mathcal{B}$), even if the CSP model used by both algorithms is the model that is best from algorithm $\mathcal{B}$'s point of view and even if the variable and value ordering used by both algorithms are the orderings that are best (optimal) from algorithm $\mathcal{B}$'s point of view.

Kondrak and van Beek [79] introduce the general methodology and give techniques and definitions that can be used for characterizing backtracking algorithms. Using the methodology, they formulate necessary and sufficient conditions for several backtracking algorithms including BT, BJ, CBJ, FC, and FC-CBJ. As an example of a necessary condition, it can be shown that if FC visits a node, then the parent of the node is 1-consistent (see Definition 4.3). As an example of a sufficient condition, it can be shown that if the parent of a node is 1-consistent, then BJ visits the node. The necessary and sufficient conditions can then be used to order the two backtracking algorithms. For example, to show that FC dominates BJ in terms of nodes visited, we show that every node that is visited by FC is also visited by BJ. The necessary condition for FC is used to deduce that the parent of the node is 1-consistent. Since the parent of the node is 1-consistent, the sufficient condition for BJ can then be used to conclude that BJ visits the node.

Chen and van Beek [26] extend the partial ordering of backtracking algorithms to include backtracking algorithms and their CBJ hybrids that maintain levels of local consistency beyond forward checking, including the algorithms that maintain arc consistency. To analyze the influence of the level of local consistency on the backjumping, Chen and van Beek use the notion of *backjump level*. Informally, the level of a backjump is the distance, measured in backjumps, from the backjump destination to the farthest deadend. By classifying the backjumps performed by a backjumping algorithm into different levels, CBJ is weakened into a series of backjumping algorithms which perform limited levels of backjumps. Let BJ_k be a backjumping algorithm which backjumps if the backjump level j is less than or equal to k, but chronologically backtracks if $j > k$. BJ_n is equivalent to CBJ, which performs unlimited backjumps, and BJ_1 is equivalent to Gaschnig's [48] BJ, which only does first level backjumps. Recall that the maintaining strong k-consistency algorithm (MC_k) enforces strong k-consistency at each node in the backtrack tree, where MC_1 is equivalent to FC and on binary CSPs MC_2 is equivalent to MAC. MC_k can be combined with backjumping, namely MC_k-CBJ. Chen and van Beek show that an algorithm that maintains strong k-consistency never visits more nodes than a backjumping algorithm that is allowed to backjump at most k levels. Thus, as the level of local consistency that is maintained in the backtracking search is increased, the less that backjumping will be an improvement.

Figure 4.3 shows a partial order or hierarchy in terms of the size of the backtrack tree for BJ_k, MC_k, and MC_k-CBJ. If there is a path from algorithm $\mathcal{A}$ to algorithm $\mathcal{B}$ in the figure, $\mathcal{A}$ never visits more nodes than $\mathcal{B}$. For example, for all variable orderings, MC_k never visits more nodes than BJ_j, for all $j \leq k$.

Bacchus and Grove [3] observe that the partial orderings with respect to nodes visited can be extended to partial orderings with respect to constraint checks, or other measures of the amount of work performed at each node. For example, on binary CSPs the MAC algorithm can perform $O(n^2 d^2)$ work at each node of the tree, where n is the number of variables and d is the size of the domain, whereas the FC algorithm can perform $O(nd$ work. Thus, one can conclude that on binary CSPs MAC can be at most $O(nd)$ times slower in the worst case (when the two algorithms visit the same nodes). The partial orderings with respect to nodes and constraint checks are consistent with and explain some of the empirical results reported in the literature (e.g., see the experiments reported in Tables 4.2 & 4.3).

Besides the relationships that are shown explicitly, it is important to note the ones that are implicit in the hierarchy. If there is *not* a path from algorithm $\mathcal{A}$ to algorithm $\mathcal{B}$ in the hierarchy, $\mathcal{A}$ and $\mathcal{B}$ are incomparable. To show a pair of algorithms $\mathcal{A}$ and $\mathcal{B}$ are incomparable, one needs to find a CSP and a variable ordering on which $\mathcal{A}$ is better than $\mathcal{B}$, and one on which $\mathcal{B}$ is better than $\mathcal{A}$. Examples have been given that cover all the incomparability results [4, 26, 79]. Some of the more surprising results include: CBJ and FC-CBJ are incomparable [79], CBJ and MC_k are incomparable for any fixed $k < n$ in that each can be exponentially better than the other [4], and MAC-CBJ and FC-CBJ and more generally MC_k-CBJ and MC_{k+1}-CBJ are incomparable for any fixed $k < n$ in that each can be exponentially better than the other [26].

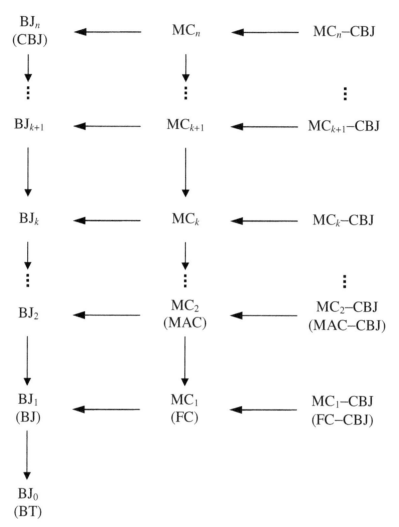

Figure 4.3: A hierarchy for BJ_k, MC_k, and MC_k-CBJ in terms of the size of the backtrack tree (adapted from [26, 79]). On binary CSPs, MC_2 is equivalent to MAC and MC_2-CBJ is equivalent to MAC-CBJ.

Acknowledgements

I would like to thank Fahiem Bacchus, Xinguang Chen, Grzegorz Kondrak, Dennis Manchak, and Jonathan Sillito for many interesting discussions and collaborations in the past on backtracking algorithms. I would also like to thank Christian Bessière and George Katsirelos for helpful comments on an early draft of this survey. This work was supported in part by the Natural Sciences and Engineering Research Council of Canada.

Bibliography

[1]   F. Bacchus. Extending forward checking. In *Proceedings of the Sixth International Conference on Principles and Practice of Constraint Programming*, pages 35–51, Singapore, 2000.

[2]   F. Bacchus. Enhancing Davis Putman with extended binary clause reasoning. In *Proceedings of the Eighteenth National Conference on Artificial Intelligence*, pages 613 – 619, Edmonton, 2002.

[3]   F. Bacchus and A. Grove. On the forward checking algorithm. In *Proceedings of the First International Conference on Principles and Practice of Constraint Programming*, pages 292–309, Cassis, France, 1995.

[4]   F. Bacchus and A. Grove. Looking forward in constraint satisfaction algorithms. Unpublished manuscript, 1999.

[5]   F. Bacchus and P. van Run. Dynamic variable ordering in CSPs. In *Proceedings of the First International Conference on Principles and Practice of Constraint Programming*, pages 258–275, Cassis, France, 1995.

[6]   S. Bain, J. Thornton, and A. Sattar. Evolving variable-ordering heuristics for constrained optimisation. In *Proceedings of the Eleventh International Conference on Principles and Practice of Constraint Programming*, pages 732–736, Sitges, Spain, 2005.

[7]   A. B. Baker. *Intelligent Backtracking on Constraint Satisfaction Problems: Experimental and Theoretical Results*. PhD thesis, University of Oregon, 1995.

[8]   L. Baptista and J. Marques-Silva. Using randomization and learning to solve hard real-world instances of satisfiability. In *Proceedings of the Sixth International Conference on Principles and Practice of Constraint Programming*, pages 489–494, Singapore, 2000.

[9]   P. Baptiste, C. Le Pape, and W. Nuijten. *Constraint-Based Scheduling: Applying Constraint Programming to Scheduling Problems*. Kluwer, 2001.

[10] R. J. Bayardo Jr. and D. P. Miranker. A complexity analysis of space-bounded learning algorithms for the constraint satisfaction problem. In *Proceedings of the Thirteenth National Conference on Artificial Intelligence*, pages 298–304, Portland, Oregon, 1996.

[11] R. J. Bayardo Jr. and R. C. Schrag. Using CSP look-back techniques to solve exceptionally hard SAT instances. In *Proceedings of the Second International Conference on Principles and Practice of Constraint Programming*, pages 46–60, Cambridge, Mass., 1996.

[12] R. J. Bayardo Jr. and R. C. Schrag. Using CSP look-back techniques to solve real-

world SAT instances. In *Proceedings of the Fourteenth National Conference on Artificial Intelligence*, pages 203–208, Providence, Rhode Island, 1997.

[13] P. Beame, H. Kautz, and A. Sabharwal. Towards understanding and harnessing the potential of clause learning. *J. of Artificial Intelligence Research*, 22:319–351, 2004. URL http://www.jair.org.

[14] J. C. Beck, P. Prosser, and R. J. Wallace. Trying again to fail first. In *Recent Advances in Constraints, Lecture Notes in Artificial Intelligence, Vol. 3419*. Springer-Verlag, 2005.

[15] U. Bertelè and F. Brioschi. *Nonserial Dynamic Programming*. Academic Press, 1972.

[16] C. Bessière, P. Meseguer, E. C. Freuder, and J. Larrosa. On forward checking for non-binary constraint satisfaction. *Artificial Intelligence*, 141:205–224, 2002.

[17] C. Bessière and J.-C. Régin. MAC and combined heuristics: Two reasons to forsake FC (and CBJ?) on hard problems. In *Proceedings of the Second International Conference on Principles and Practice of Constraint Programming*, pages 61–75, Cambridge, Mass., 1996.

[18] C. Bliek. Generalizing partial order and dynamic backtracking. In *Proceedings of the Fifteenth National Conference on Artificial Intelligence*, pages 319–325, Madison, Wisconsin, 1998.

[19] F. Boussemart, F. Hemery, C. Lecoutre, and L. Sais. Boosting systematic search by weighting constraints. In *Proceedings of the 16th European Conference on Artificial Intelligence*, pages 146–150, Valencia, Spain, 2004.

[20] D. Brélaz. New methods to color the vertices of a graph. *Comm. ACM*, 22:251–256, 1979.

[21] C. A. Brown and P. W. Purdom Jr. An empirical comparison of backtracking algorithms. *IEEE PAMI*, 4:309–315, 1982.

[22] M. Bruynooghe. Solving combinatorial search problems by intelligent backtracking. *Information Processing Letters*, 12:36–39, 1981.

[23] Y. Caseau and F. Laburthe. Improved CLP scheduling with task intervals. In *Proceedings of the Eleventh International Conference on Logic Programming*, pages 369–383, Santa Margherita Ligure, Italy, 1994.

[24] H. Chen, C. Gomes, and B. Selman. Formal models of heavy-tailed behavior in combinatorial search. In *Proceedings of the Seventh International Conference on Principles and Practice of Constraint Programming*, pages 408–421, Paphos, Cyprus, 2001.

[25] X. Chen. *A Theoretical Comparison of Selected CSP Solving and Modeling Techniques*. PhD thesis, University of Alberta, 2000.

[26] X. Chen and P. van Beek. Conflict-directed backjumping revisited. *J. of Artificial Intelligence Research*, 14:53–81, 2001. URL http://www.jair.org.

[27] V. A. Cicirello and S. F. Smith. Amplification of search performance through randomization of heuristics. In *Proceedings of the Eighth International Conference on Principles and Practice of Constraint Programming*, pages 124–138, Ithaca, New York, 2002.

[28] S. A. Cook and R. A. Reckhow. The relative efficiency of propositional proof systems. *J. Symbolic Logic*, 44:36–50, 1979.

[29] M. C. Cooper. An optimal k-consistency algorithm. *Artificial Intelligence*, 41:89–95, 1989.

[30] M. Davis, G. Logemann, and D. Loveland. A machine program for theorem-proving. *Comm. ACM*, 5:394–397, 1962.

[31] M. Davis and H. Putnam. A computing procedure for quantification theory. *J. ACM* 7:201–215, 1960.

[32] J. de Kleer. A comparison of ATMS and CSP techniques. In *Proceedings of the Eleventh International Joint Conference on Artificial Intelligence*, pages 290–296, Detroit, 1989.

[33] R. Dechter. Learning while searching in constraint satisfaction problems. In *Proceedings of the Fifth National Conference on Artificial Intelligence*, pages 178–183, Philadelphia, 1986.

[34] R. Dechter. Enhancement schemes for constraint processing: Backjumping, learning, and cutset decomposition. *Artificial Intelligence*, 41:273–312, 1990.

[35] R. Dechter and J. Pearl. Network-based heuristics for constraint satisfaction problems. *Artificial Intelligence*, 34:1–38, 1988.

[36] S. L. Epstein, E. C. Freuder, R. J. Wallace, A. Morozov, and B. Samuels. The adaptive constraint engine. In *Proceedings of the Eighth International Conference on Principles and Practice of Constraint Programming*, pages 525–540, Ithaca, New York, 2002.

[37] R. E. Fikes. REF-ARF: A system for solving problems stated as procedures. *Artificial Intelligence*, 1:27–120, 1970.

[38] J. W. Freeman. *Improvements to Propositional Satisfiability Search Algorithms* PhD thesis, University of Pennsylvania, 1995.

[39] E. C. Freuder. Synthesizing constraint expressions. *Comm. ACM*, 21:958–966, 1978.

[40] E. C. Freuder. A sufficient condition for backtrack-free search. *J. ACM*, 29:24–32, 1982.

[41] E. C. Freuder. A sufficient condition for backtrack-bounded search. *J. ACM*, 32: 755–761, 1985.

[42] E. C. Freuder and M. J. Quinn. Taking advantage of stable sets of variables in constraint satisfaction problems. In *Proceedings of the Ninth International Joint Conference on Artificial Intelligence*, pages 1076–1078, Los Angeles, 1985.

[43] E. C. Freuder and R. J. Wallace. Generalizing inconsistency learning for constraint satisfaction. In *Proceedings of the Fourteenth International Joint Conference on Artificial Intelligence*, pages 563–571, Montréal, 1995.

[44] D. Frost and R. Dechter. Dead-end driven learning. In *Proceedings of the Twelfth National Conference on Artificial Intelligence*, pages 294–300, Seattle, 1994.

[45] D. Frost and R. Dechter. In search of the best search: An empirical evaluation. In *Proceedings of the Twelfth National Conference on Artificial Intelligence*, pages 301–306, Seattle, 1994.

[46] D. Frost and R. Dechter. Look-ahead value ordering for constraint satisfaction problems. In *Proceedings of the Fourteenth International Joint Conference on Artificial Intelligence*, pages 572–578, Montréal, 1995.

[47] J. Gaschnig. A constraint satisfaction method for inference making. In *Proceedings Twelfth Annual Allerton Conference on Circuit and System Theory*, pages 866–874, Monticello, Illinois, 1974.

[48] J. Gaschnig. Experimental case studies of backtrack vs. Waltz-type vs. new algorithms for satisficing assignment problems. In *Proceedings of the Second Canadian*

Conference on Artificial Intelligence, pages 268–277, Toronto, 1978.

[49] P. A. Geelen. Dual viewpoint heuristics for binary constraint satisfaction problems. In *Proceedings of the 10th European Conference on Artificial Intelligence*, pages 31–35, Vienna, 1992.

[50] I. P. Gent, E. MacIntyre, P. Prosser, B. M. Smith, and T. Walsh. An empirical study of dynamic variable ordering heuristics for the constraint satisfaction problem. In *Proceedings of the Second International Conference on Principles and Practice of Constraint Programming*, pages 179–193, Cambridge, Mass., 1996.

[51] I. P. Gent, E. MacIntyre, P. Prosser, B. M. Smith, and T. Walsh. Random constraint satisfaction: Flaws and structure. *Constraints*, 6(4):345–372, 2001.

[52] I. P. Gent, E. MacIntyre, P. Prosser, and T. Walsh. The constrainedness of search. In *Proceedings of the Thirteenth National Conference on Artificial Intelligence*, pages 246–252, Portland, Oregon, 1996.

[53] I. P. Gent and T. Walsh. CSPlib: A benchmark library for constraints. In *Proceedings of the Fifth International Conference on Principles and Practice of Constraint Programming*, pages 480–481, Alexandria, Virginia, 1999.

[54] M. L. Ginsberg. Dynamic backtracking. *J. of Artificial Intelligence Research*, 1: 25–46, 1993. URL http://www.jair.org.

[55] M. L. Ginsberg, M. Frank, M. P. Halpin, and M. C. Torrance. Search lessons learned from crossword puzzles. In *Proceedings of the Eighth National Conference on Artificial Intelligence*, pages 210–215, Boston, Mass., 1990.

[56] M. L. Ginsberg and D. A. McAllester. GSAT and dynamic backtracking. In *Proceedings of the Second Workshop on Principles and Practice of Constraint Programming*, pages 243–265, Rosario, Orcas Island, Washington, 1994.

[57] S. Golomb and L. Baumert. Backtrack programming. *J. ACM*, 12:516–524, 1965.

[58] C. Gomes. Randomized backtrack search. In M. Milano, editor, *Constraint and Integer Programming: Toward a Unified Methodology*, pages 233–292. Kluwer, 2004.

[59] C. Gomes, C. Fernández, B. Selman, and C. Bessière. Statistical regimes across constrainedness regions. *Constraints*, 10:317–337, 2005.

[60] C. Gomes, B. Selman, and N. Crato. Heavy-tailed distributions in combinatorial search. In *Proceedings of the Third International Conference on Principles and Practice of Constraint Programming*, pages 121–135, Linz, Austria, 1997.

[61] C. Gomes, B. Selman, N. Crato, and H. Kautz. Heavy-tailed phenomena in satisfiability and constraint satisfaction problems. *J. of Automated Reasoning*, 24:67–100, 2000.

[62] C. Gomes, B. Selman, and H. Kautz. Boosting combinatorial search through randomization. In *Proceedings of the Fifteenth National Conference on Artificial Intelligence*, Madison, Wisconsin, 1998.

[63] R. M. Haralick and G. L. Elliott. Increasing tree search efficiency for constraint satisfaction problems. *Artificial Intelligence*, 14:263–313, 1980.

[64] W. D. Harvey. *Nonsystematic backtracking search*. PhD thesis, Stanford University, 1995.

[65] W. D. Harvey and M. L. Ginsberg. Limited discrepancy search. In *Proceedings of the Fourteenth International Joint Conference on Artificial Intelligence*, pages 607–613, Montréal, 1995.

[66] J. N. Hooker. Testing heuristics: We have it all wrong. *Journal of Heuristics*, 1:

33–42, 1996.

[67] J. N. Hooker and V. Vinay. Branching rules for satisfiability. *Journal of Automated Reasoning*, 15:359–383, 1995.

[68] H. H. Hoos. Heavy-tailed behaviour in randomised systematic search algorithms for SAT. Technical Report TR-99-16, UBC, 1999.

[69] J. Huang and A. Darwiche. A structure-based variable ordering heuristic for SAT. In *Proceedings of the Eighteenth International Joint Conference on Artificial Intelligence*, pages 1167–1172, Acapulco, Mexico, 2003.

[70] T. Hulubei and B. O'Sullivan. Search heuristics and heavy-tailed behaviour. In *Proceedings of the Eleventh International Conference on Principles and Practice of Constraint Programming*, pages 328–342, Sitges, Spain, 2005.

[71] J. Hwang and D. G. Mitchell. 2-way vs. d-way branching for CSP. In *Proceedings of the Eleventh International Conference on Principles and Practice of Constraint Programming*, pages 343–357, Sitges, Spain, 2005.

[72] ILOG S. A. ILOG Solver 4.2 user's manual, 1998.

[73] P. Jégou and C. Terrioux. Hybrid backtracking bounded by tree-decomposition of constraint networks. *Artificial Intelligence*, 146:43–75, 2003.

[74] U. Junker. QuickXplain: Preferred explanations and relaxations for over-constrained problems. In *Proceedings of the Nineteenth National Conference on Artificial Intelligence*, pages 167–172, 2004.

[75] N. Jussien, R. Debruyne, and B. Boizumault. Maintaining arc-consistency within dynamic backtracking. In *Proceedings of the Sixth International Conference on Principles and Practice of Constraint Programming*, pages 249–261, Singapore, 2000.

[76] K. Kask, R. Dechter, and V. Gogate. Counting-based look-ahead schemes for constraint satisfaction. In *Proceedings of the Tenth International Conference on Principles and Practice of Constraint Programming*, pages 317–331, Toronto, 2004.

[77] G. Katsirelos and F. Bacchus. Generalized nogoods in CSPs. In *Proceedings of the Twentieth National Conference on Artificial Intelligence*, pages 390–396, Pittsburgh, 2005.

[78] H. Kautz, E. Horvitz, Y. Ruan, C. Gomes, and B. Selman. Dynamic restart policies. In *Proceedings of the Eighteenth National Conference on Artificial Intelligence*, pages 674–681, Edmonton, 2002.

[79] G. Kondrak and P. van Beek. A theoretical evaluation of selected backtracking algorithms. *Artificial Intelligence*, 89:365–387, 1997.

[80] R. E. Korf. Improved limited discrepancy search. In *Proceedings of the Thirteenth National Conference on Artificial Intelligence*, pages 286–291, Portland, Oregon, 1996.

[81] J. Larrosa. Boosting search with variable elimination. In *Proceedings of the Sixth International Conference on Principles and Practice of Constraint Programming* pages 291–305, Singapore, 2000.

[82] J.-L. Lauriere. A language and a program for stating and solving combinatorial problems. *Artificial Intelligence*, 10:29–127, 1978.

[83] D. Le Berre and L. Simon. Fifty-five solvers in Vancouver: The SAT 2004 competition. In *Proceedings of the Seventh International Conference on Theory and Applications of Satisfiability Testing (SAT2004)*, pages 321–344, Vancouver, 2004. Available as: Springer Lecture Notes in Computer Science 3542, 2005.

[84] C. Lecoutre, F. Boussemart, and F. Hemery. Backjump-based techniques versus conflict-directed heuristics. In *Proceedings of the Sixteenth IEEE International Conference on Tools with Artificial Intelligence*, pages 549–557, Boca Raton, Florida, 2004.

[85] C.-M. Li and S. Gérard. On the limit of branching rules for hard random unsatisfiable 3-SAT. *Discrete Applied Mathematics*, 130:277–290, 2003.

[86] W. Li and P. van Beek. Guiding real-world SAT solving with dynamic hypergraph separator decomposition. In *Proceedings of the Sixteenth IEEE International Conference on Tools with Artificial Intelligence*, pages 542–548, Boca Raton, Florida, 2004.

[87] P. Liberatore. On the complexity of choosing the branching literal in DPLL. *Artificial Intelligence*, 116:315–326, 2000.

[88] M. Luby, A. Sinclair, and D. Zuckerman. Optimal speedup of Las Vegas algorithms. In *Proceedings of the Second Israel Symposium on the Theory of Computing and Systems*, Jerusalem, 1993.

[89] A. K. Mackworth. Consistency in networks of relations. *Artificial Intelligence*, 8: 99–118, 1977.

[90] A. K. Mackworth. On reading sketch maps. In *Proceedings of the Fifth International Joint Conference on Artificial Intelligence*, pages 598–606, Cambridge, Mass., 1977.

[91] A. M. Malik, J. McInnes, and P. van Beek. Optimal basic block instruction scheduling for multiple-issue processors using constraint programming. Technical Report CS-2005-19, School of Computer Science, University of Waterloo, 2005.

[92] J. Marques-Silva and K. A. Sakallah. GRASP – a new search algorithm for satisfiability. In *Proceedings of the International Conference on Computer-Aided Design*, pages 220–227, San Jose, Calif., 1996.

[93] J. J. McGregor. Relational consistency algorithms and their application in finding subgraph and graph isomorphisms. *Inform. Sci.*, 19:229–250, 1979.

[94] A. Meisels, S. E. Shimony, and G. Solotorevsky. Bayes networks for estimating the number of solutions to a CSP. In *Proceedings of the Fourteenth National Conference on Artificial Intelligence*, pages 185–190, Providence, Rhode Island, 1997.

[95] P. Meseguer. Interleaved depth-first search. In *Proceedings of the Fifteenth International Joint Conference on Artificial Intelligence*, pages 1382–1387, Nagoya, Japan, 1997.

[96] P. Meseguer and T. Walsh. Interleaved and discrepancy based search. In *Proceedings of the 13th European Conference on Artificial Intelligence*, pages 239–243, Brighton, UK, 1998.

[97] M. Milano and W. J. van Hoeve. Reduced cost-based ranking for generating promising subproblems. In *Proceedings of the Eighth International Conference on Principles and Practice of Constraint Programming*, pages 1–16, Ithaca, New York, 2002.

[98] S. Minton. Automatically configuring constraint satisfaction programs: A case study. *Constraints*, 1:7–44, 1996.

[99] S. Minton, M. D. Johnston, A. B. Philips, and P. Laird. Minimizing conflicts: A heuristic repair method for constraint satisfaction and scheduling problems. *Artificial Intelligence*, 58:161–206, 1992.

[100] D. G. Mitchell. Resolution and constraint satisfaction. In *Proceedings of the Ninth International Conference on Principles and Practice of Constraint Programming*,

pages 555–569, Kinsale, Ireland, 2003.

[101] R. Mohr and G. Masini. Good old discrete relaxation. In *Proceedings of the 8th European Conference on Artificial Intelligence*, pages 651–656, Munchen, Germany, 1988.

[102] U. Montanari. Networks of constraints: Fundamental properties and applications to picture processing. *Inform. Sci.*, 7:95–132, 1974.

[103] M. Moskewicz, C. Madigan, Y. Zhao, L. Zhang, and S. Malik. Chaff: Engineering an efficient SAT solver. In *Proceedings of 39th Design Automation Conference*, Las Vegas, 2001.

[104] B. A. Nadel. Constraint satisfaction algorithms. *Computational Intelligence*, 5: 188–224, 1989.

[105] B. Nudel. Consistent-labeling problems and their algorithms: Expected-complexities and theory-based heuristics. *Artificial Intelligence*, 21:135–178, 1983.

[106] S. Prestwich. A hybrid search architecture applied to hard random 3-SAT and low-autocorrelation binary sequences. In *Proceedings of the Sixth International Conference on Principles and Practice of Constraint Programming*, pages 337–352, Singapore, 2000.

[107] P. Prosser. Domain filtering can degrade intelligent backtracking search. In *Proceedings of the Thirteenth International Joint Conference on Artificial Intelligence* pages 262–267, Chambèry, France, 1993.

[108] P. Prosser. Hybrid algorithms for the constraint satisfaction problem. *Computational Intelligence*, 9:268–299, 1993.

[109] P. Prosser. MAC-CBJ: Maintaining arc consistency with conflict-directed backjumping. Research Report 177, University of Strathclyde, 1995.

[110] P. W. Purdom Jr. Search rearrangement backtracking and polynomial average time. *Artificial Intelligence*, 21:117–133, 1983.

[111] P. Refalo. Impact-based search strategies for constraint programming. In *Proceedings of the Tenth International Conference on Principles and Practice of Constraint Programming*, pages 557–571, Toronto, 2004.

[112] E. T. Richards. *Non-systematic Search and No-good Learning*. PhD thesis, Imperial College, 1998.

[113] G. Rochart, N. Jussien, and F. Laburthe. Challenging explanations for global constraints. In *CP03 Workshop on User-Interaction in Constraint Satisfaction (UICS'03)*, pages 31–43, Kinsale, Ireland, 2003.

[114] W. Rosiers and M. Bruynooghe. Empirical study of some constraint satisfaction algorithms. In P. Jorrand and V. Sgurev, editors, *Artificial Intelligence II, Methodology, Systems, Applications, Proc. AIMSA'86*, pages 173–180. North Holland, 1987.

[115] Y. Ruan, E. Horvitz, and H. Kautz. Restart policies with dependence among runs: A dynamic programming approach. In *Proceedings of the Eighth International Conference on Principles and Practice of Constraint Programming*, pages 573–586, Ithaca, New York, 2002.

[116] D. Sabin and E. C. Freuder. Contradicting conventional wisdom in constraint satisfaction. In *Proceedings of the 11th European Conference on Artificial Intelligence* pages 125–129, Amsterdam, 1994.

[117] D. Sabin and E. C. Freuder. Understanding and improving the MAC algorithm. In *Proceedings of the Third International Conference on Principles and Practice of Constraint Programming*, pages 167–181, Linz, Austria, 1997.

[118] T. Schiex and G. Verfaillie. Nogood recording for static and dynamic constraint satisfaction problems. *International Journal on Artificial Intelligence Tools*, 3:1–15, 1994.

[119] B. M. Smith and S. A. Grant. Sparse constraint graphs and exceptionally hard problems. In *Proceedings of the Fourteenth International Joint Conference on Artificial Intelligence*, pages 646–651, Montréal, 1995.

[120] B. M. Smith and S. A. Grant. Trying harder to fail first. In *Proceedings of the 13th European Conference on Artificial Intelligence*, pages 249–253, Brighton, UK, 1998.

[121] B. M. Smith and P. Sturdy. Value ordering for finding all solutions. In *Proceedings of the Nineteenth International Joint Conference on Artificial Intelligence*, pages 311–316, Edinburgh, 2005.

[122] S. F. Smith and C. Cheng. Slack-based heuristics for constraint satisfaction scheduling. In *Proceedings of the Eleventh National Conference on Artificial Intelligence*, pages 139–144, Washington, DC, 1993.

[123] G. Smolka. The OZ programming model. In *Computer Science Today*, Lecture Notes in Computer Science 1000, pages 324–343, 1995.

[124] R. M. Stallman and G. J. Sussman. Forward reasoning and dependency-directed backtracking in a system for computer-aided circuit analysis. *Artificial Intelligence*, 9:135–196, 1977.

[125] H. S. Stone and J. M. Stone. Efficient search techniques—an empirical study of the N-queens problem. *IBM J. Res. and Develop.*, 31:464–474, 1987.

[126] E. P. K. Tsang, J. E. Borrett, and A. C. M. Kwan. An attempt to map the performance of a range of algorithm and heuristic combinations. In *Proceedings of the AI and Simulated Behaviour Conference*, pages 203–216, 1995.

[127] A. Van Gelder and Y. K. Tsuji. Satisfiability testing with more reasoning and less guessing. In D. S. Johnson and M. Trick, editors, *Cliques, Coloring, and Satisfiability: Second DIMACS Implementation Challenge*, pages 559–586. American Mathematical Society, 1996.

[128] P. Van Hentenryck. *Constraint Satisfaction in Logic Programming*. MIT Press, 1989.

[129] A. P. A. van Moorsel and K. Wolter. Analysis and algorithms for restart. In *Proceedings of the IEEE Quantitative Evaluation of Systems (QEST 2004)*, pages 195–204, Enschede, The Netherlands, 2004.

[130] A. P. A. van Moorsel and K. Wolter. Meeting deadlines through restart. In *Proceedings of the 12th GI/ITG Conference on Measuring, Modelling and Evaluation of Computer and Communication Systems*, pages 155–160, Dresden, Germany, 2004.

[131] M. Vernooy and W. S. Havens. An evaluation of probabilistic value-ordering heuristics. In *Proceedings of the Australian Conference on AI*, pages 340–352, Sydney, 1999.

[132] R. J. Wallace. Factor analytic studies of CSP heuristics. In *Proceedings of the Eleventh International Conference on Principles and Practice of Constraint Programming*, pages 712–726, Sitges, Spain, 2005.

[133] T. Walsh. Depth-bounded discrepancy search. In *Proceedings of the Fifteenth International Joint Conference on Artificial Intelligence*, pages 1388–1393, Nagoya, Japan, 1997.

[134] T. Walsh. Search in a small world. In *Proceedings of the Sixteenth International*

Joint Conference on Artificial Intelligence, pages 1172–1177, Stockholm, 1999.

[135] R. Williams, C. Gomes, and B. Selman. Backdoors to typical case complexity. In *Proceedings of the Eighteenth International Joint Conference on Artificial Intelligence*, pages 1173–1178, Acapulco, Mexico, 2003.

[136] R. Zabih. Some applications of graph bandwidth to constraint satisfaction problems. In *Proceedings of the Eighth National Conference on Artificial Intelligence*, pages 46–51, Boston, Mass., 1990.

[137] Y. Zhan. Randomisation and restarts, 2001. MSc thesis, University of York.

[138] H. Zhang. A random jump strategy for combinatorial search. In *Proceedings of International Symposium on AI and Math*, Fort Lauderdale, Florida, 2002.

[139] L. Zhang, C. Madigan, M. Moskewicz, and S. Malik. Efficient conflict driven learning in a boolean satisfiability solver. In *Proceedings of the International Conference on Computer-Aided Design*, pages 279–285, San Jose, Calif., 2001.

Handbook of Constraint Programming   135
Edited by F. Rossi, P. van Beek and T. Walsh

Chapter 5

Local Search Methods

Holger H. Hoos and Edward Tsang

Local search is one of the fundamental paradigms for solving computationally hard combinatorial problems, including the constraint satisfaction problem (CSP). It provides the basis for some of the most successful and versatile methods for solving the large and difficult problem instances encountered in many real-life applications. Despite impressive advances in systematic, complete search algorithms, local search methods in many cases represent the only feasible way for solving these large and complex instances. Local search algorithms are also naturally suited for dealing with the optimisation criteria arising in many practical applications.

The basic idea underlying local search is to start with a randomly or heuristically generated candidate solution of a given problem instance, which may be infeasible, sub-optimal or incomplete, and to iteratively improve this candidate solution by means of typically minor modifications. Different local search methods vary in the way in which improvements are achieved, and in particular, in the way in which situations are handled in which no direct improvement is possible.

Most local search methods use randomisation to ensure that the search process does not stagnate with unsatisfactory candidate solutions and are therefore referred to as *stochastic local search (SLS) methods*. Prominent examples of SLS methods are randomised iterative improvement (also known as stochastic hill-climbing), evolutionary algorithms, simulated annealing, tabu search, dynamic local search and, more recently, ant colony optimisation. These classes of local search algorithms are also widely known as *metaheuristics*.

Many SLS methods are conceptually rather simple and relatively easy to implement compared to many other techniques. At the same time, they often show excellent performance and in many cases define the state-of-the-art in the respective problems.[1] Furthermore, SLS algorithms are often very flexible in that they can be easily adapted to changes in the specification of a problem. This makes them a very popular choice for solving conceptually complex application problems that are sometimes not fully formalised at the

---

[1]Still, the efficient implementation of some high-performance SLS algorithms requires considerable effort and sophisticated data structures (see, *e.g.*, [79]).

beginning of a project. Consequently, SLS algorithms are amongst the most prominent and widely used combinatorial problem solving techniques in academia and industry.

It may be noted that when taking a very broad view of constraint programming, many combinatorial problems, including scheduling, sequencing, configuration and routing problems, can be seen as constraint programming problems. Local search algorithms for these problems are widely studied by researchers from various disciplines, and the corresponding, vast body of literature would be difficult (if not impossible) to survey within a single book chapter.

Therefore, this chapter primarily provides an overview of SLS algorithms for the constraint satisfaction problem (CSP), one of the most prominent problems in constraint programming. We focus on widely known and high-performing algorithms for the general CSP and for SAT, the propositional satisfiability problem, a special case of CSP which plays an important role not only in constraint programming and reasoning research, but also in many other areas of computing science and beyond. We also briefly cover SLS algorithms for constraint optimisation problems such as MAX-CSP and MAX-SAT, the optimisation variants of CSP and SAT, respectively, and point the reader to some of the best-known frameworks and toolkits for implementing local search algorithms for constraint programming problems.

5.1   Introduction

Constraint programming is a powerful conceptual framework that can express many types of combinatorial problems. In this chapter, we mainly focus on the *finite discrete constraint satisfaction problem (CSP)*, a problem of central importance within the area of constraint programming with many applications in artificial intelligence, operations research and other areas of computing science and related disciplines.

The Constraint Satisfaction Problem (CSP)

An instance of the CSP is defined by a set of variables, a set of possible values (or *domain* for each variable and a set of *constraints* each of which involve one or more of the variables. The *Constraint Satisfaction Problem (CSP)* is to decide for a given CSP instance whether it is possible to assign to each variable a value from its respective domain such that all constraints are simultaneously satisfied. Formally, this can be expressed as follows [52]:

Definition 5.1. *A CSP instance is a triple* $P = (V, \mathcal{D}, \mathcal{C})$, *where* $V = \{x_1, \ldots, x_n\}$ *is a finite set of n variables, $\mathcal{D}$ is a function that maps each variable x_i to the set D_i of possible values it can take (D_i is called the* domain *of x_i), and $\mathcal{C} = \{C_1, \ldots, C_m\}$ is a finite set of constraints. Each constraint C_j is a relation over an ordered set* $\mathrm{Var}(C_j)$ *of variables from V, i.e., for* $\mathrm{Var}(C_j) = (y_1, \ldots, y_k)$, $C_j \subseteq \mathcal{D}(y_1) \times \cdots \times \mathcal{D}(y_k)$. *The elements of the set C_j are referred to as* satisfying tuples *of C_j, and k is called the* arity *of the constraint C_j A CSP instance P is called n-ary, if the arity of all constraints in P have arity at most n in particular,* binary CSP instances *have only constraints of arity at most two.*

P is a finite discrete CSP instance *if all variables in P have discrete and finite domains. A variable assignment of P is a mapping* $a : V \mapsto \bigcup_{i=1}^{n} D_i$ *that assigns to each variable $x \in V$ a value from its domain $\mathcal{D}(x)$. (The assignment of a value to an individual variable is called an* atomic assignment.*) Let $\mathrm{Assign}(P)$ denote the set of all possible variable*

assignments for P; then a variable assignment $a \in \mathrm{Assign}(P)$ is a solution of P if, and only if, it simultaneously satisfies all constraints in $\mathcal{C}$, i.e., if for all $C_j \in \mathcal{C}$ with, say, $\mathrm{Var}(C_j) = (y_1, \ldots, y_k)$ the assignment a maps $y_1, \ldots, y_k$ to values $v_1, \ldots, v_k$ such that $(v_1, \ldots, v_k) \in C_j$.

CSP instances for which at least one solution exists are called consistent *(or soluble)*, while instances that do not have any solutions are called inconsistent *(or insoluble)*.

The finite discrete *CSP is the problem of deciding whether a given finite discrete CSP instance P is consistent.*

The Propositional Satisfiability Problem (SAT)

The well-known satisfiability problem in propositional logic (SAT) can be seen as a prominent special case of the general CSP. Consider a propositional formula F in conjunctive normal form, *i.e.*, of the form

$$F := \bigwedge_{i=1}^{m} c_i \quad \text{with} \quad c_i := \bigvee_{j=1}^{k(i)} l_{ij}$$

where each of the l_{ij} is a propositional variable or its negation; the l_{ij} are called *literals*, while the disjunctions c_i are referred to as the *clauses* of F. The objective of the satisfiability problem is then to decide whether F is *satisfiable, i.e.*, whether there exists an assignment a of truth values *true* and *false* to the variables x_k such that every clause contains at least one literal rendered true by a. Obviously, this corresponds to a CSP instance where all variables have domains $\{true, false\}$ and for every clause c_i there is a constraint C_i between the variables appearing in c_i that is satisfied if, and only if, c_i is satisfied under the (partial) assignment of its variables. Hence, a clause with k literals corresponds to a k-ary constraint relation.

As the prototypical $\mathcal{N}P$-complete problem, SAT is of central importance to the theory of computing; it also plays an important role in circuit design and verification (see, *e.g.*, Biere et al. [6] or Gu and Puri [37]). Other practical applications of SAT include various scheduling tasks [126, 15] as well as problems from machine vision, robotics, database systems and computer graphics [38]. SAT also plays in important role in the development of algorithms; its conceptual simplicity facilitates the design, implementation and evaluation of new algorithms. Particularly with respect to local search algorithms, many ideas and techniques have been first developed for SAT, before they were generalised to more general types of CSP instances.

SAT-Encodings of CSP

CSP instances can be encoded into SAT in a number of ways (see, *e.g.*, Prestwich [84] or Hoos and Stützle [52] for an overview), and using such encodings, arbitrary CSP instances can be solved by state-of-the-art SAT solvers, including powerful local and systematic search algorithms as well as preprocessing techniques. The main appeal of this approach stems from the previously mentioned advantages of SAT for algorithm development and implementation in combination with the substantial amount of research on SAT solving techniques. SAT encodings may, however, lead to potentially significant increases in the size of problem instances and the respective search spaces; more problematically, they can obfuscate structural aspects of CSP instances that are important for efficiently solving these.

There is some evidence that the 'encode and solve as SAT' approach can work surprisingly well (see, *e.g.*, Kautz and Selman [58], Ernst et al. [24] and Hoos [48]); furthermore, it has been shown that some encodings allow SAT-solvers to directly exploit important aspects of CSP structure [5]. However, it is still unclear whether and to which extent finding good SAT-encodings is any easier than developing good native CSP algorithms — particularly in the case of local search methods, which can often benefit directly from insights and improvements achieved on SAT. It should be noted that the general issue of *modelling* (*i.e.* finding good formulations of a problem) plays an important role in constraint programming (see Chapter 11).

Local Search

Given a combinatorial problem such as the CSP, the key idea behind local search is very simple: starting at an *initial search position* (for the CSP, typically a randomly chosen, complete variable assignment), in each *step* the search process moves to a position selected from the *local neighbourhood* (typically based on a heuristic evaluation function). This process is iterated until a *termination criterion* is satisfied. To avoid stagnation of the search process, almost all local search algorithms use some form of randomisation, typically in the generation of initial positions and in many cases also in the search steps. This leads to the concept of *stochastic local search (SLS) algorithms*, which is formally defined as follows [52]:

Definition 5.2. *Given a (combinatorial) problem* Π, *a stochastic local search algorithm for solving an arbitrary problem instance* $\pi \in \Pi$ *is defined by the following components:*

- *the* search space $S(\pi)$ *of instance* π, *which is a finite set of* candidate solutions $s \in$ *(also called* search positions, locations, configurations, *or* states*) — in the case of the CSP, this is typically the set of all complete variable assignments;*

- *a set of (feasible) solutions* $S'(\pi) \subseteq S(\pi)$ *— for the CSP, this set typically consists of all solutions of the given CSP instance;*

- *a* neighbourhood relation *on* $S(\pi)$, $N(\pi) \subseteq S(\pi) \times S(\pi)$ *— this determines the positions that can be reached in one search step at any given time during the search process;*

- *a finite set of memory states* $M(\pi)$, *which, in the case of SLS algorithms that do not use memory, may consist of a single state only, and in other cases holds information about the state of the search mechanism beyond the search position (e.g., tabu tenure values in the case of tabu search);*

- *an* initialisation function $init(\pi) : \emptyset \mapsto \mathbb{D}(S(\pi) \times M(\pi))$, *which specifies a probability distribution over initial search positions and memory states — this function characterises the initialisation of the search process;*

- *a* step function $step(\pi) : S(\pi) \times M(\pi) \mapsto \mathbb{D}(S(\pi) \times M(\pi))$ *mapping each search position and memory state onto a probability distribution over its neighbouring search positions and memory states — this function specifies what happens in every search step;*

- *a* termination predicate *terminate*(π) : $S(\pi) \times M(\pi) \mapsto \mathbb{D}(\{$true, false$\})$ *mapping each search position and memory state to a probability distribution over truth values, which indicates the probability with which the search is to be terminated upon reaching a specific search position and memory state.*

In the above, $\mathbb{D}(S)$ denotes the set of probability distributions over a given set S, where formally, a probability distribution $D \in \mathbb{D}(S)$ is a function $D : S \mapsto \mathbb{R}_0^+$ that maps elements of S to their respective probabilities.

Note that this definition includes deterministic local search algorithms as special cases, in which the probability distributions used in the initialisation and step function as well as in the termination criterion are degenerate, with all probability mass concentrated on one value of the underlying domain. As previously noted, completely deterministic local search algorithms are seldom used in research or applications.

In the case of almost all local search algorithms for CSP, the search space consists of all complete variable assignments of the given CSP instance, the solution set is comprised of all satisfying assignments, and the so-called *1-exchange neighbourhood* is used, under which two assignments are direct neighbours if, and only if, they differ at most in the value assigned to one variable. In the special case of SAT, a variant of this neighbourhood relation known as the *1-flip neighbourhood* is typically used, under which two assignments are direct neighbours if, and only if, one can be obtained from the other by flipping the truth value assigned to exactly one of the variable from true to false or vice versa. In many cases the initial search position is determined by generating a variable assignment uniformly at random, and the termination criterion is satisfied if a solution is found or a given bound on the number of search steps has been exceeded.

The various local search algorithms for CSP (and SAT) differ from each other mainly with respect to their step function, which for all but the most simple (and ineffective) algorithms incorporates heuristic guidance in the form of an *evaluation function*. This function typically maps the candidate solutions of the given problem instance π onto a real number such that its global minima correspond to the solutions of π. The evaluation function is used for assessing or ranking the direct neighbours of the current search positions. A commonly used evaluation function for the CSP maps each assignment to the number of constraints violated under it. Note that solutions are characterised by evaluation function value zero, and can hence be easily recognised.

The simplest local search method that effectively uses a given evaluation function g is called *Iterative Improvement* (or *II*; also known as *hill-climbing* or *iterative descent*). In each search step, II selects an *improving position* from the current neighbourhood, *i.e.*, a position $s' \in N(s)$ with $g(s') < g(s)$, where s is the current search position. There are various commonly used heuristics for selecting such an improving neighbour. In *Iterative Best-Improvement*, a neighbour s' with minimal value $g(s')$ within $N(s)$ is chosen; if multiple such neighbours exist, one is chosen uniformly at random. In *Iterative First-Improvement*, on the other hand, the neighbourhood is evaluated in a given order, and the first improving neighbour encountered during this process is selected as the next search position. Variants of Iterative Improvement form the basis for almost all local search methods for CSP, SAT and other combinatorial problems.

procedure *MCH* (*P, maxSteps*)
   input: *CSP instance P, positive integer maxSteps*
   output: *solution of P or* "no solution found"

   a := randomly chosen assignment of the variables in P;
   for *step* := 1 **to** *maxSteps* **do**
      if a satisfies all constraints of P **then return** a **end**
      x := randomly selected variable from conflict set $K(a)$;
      v := randomly selected value from the domain of x such that
         setting x to v minimises the number of unsatisfied constraints;
      a := a with x set to v;
   end
   return "no solution found"
end *MCH*

Figure 5.1: The basic MCH algorithm; all random selections are according to a uniform probability distribution over the underlying sets.

The Min-Conflicts Heuristic

The simplest and probably most widely known iterative improvement algorithm for the CSP is the *Min Conflicts Heuristic (MCH)* [76, 77]. MCH iteratively modifies the assignment of a single variable in order to minimise the number of violated constraints, which is achieved as follows (see also Figure 5.1): Given a CSP instance P, the search process is initialised by assigning to each variable in P a value that is chosen uniformly at random from its domain. Then, in each local search step, first a CSP variable x is selected uniformly at random from the so-called *conflict set* $K(a)$, the set of all variables that appear in a constraint that is unsatisfied under the current assignment a. A new value v is then chosen from the domain of x, such that by assigning v to x, the number of unsatisfied constraints (conflicts) is minimised. If there are several values of v with that property, one of them is chosen uniformly at random. The search is terminated when a solution is found or a user-specified bound on the number of search steps has been exceeded.

A variant of the basic MCH algorithm that uses a greedy initialisation procedure has been very successfully applied to the n-Queens Problem (a prominent special case of the general CSP, for which specialized polynomial-time algorithms exist) with very large n (say, n equals a million). Furthermore, the efficacy of MCH has been demonstrated in applications to graph colouring and real-world scheduling problems [77].

Like most iterative improvement methods, MCH can get stuck in local minima of the underlying evaluation function; it is therefore *essentially incomplete* [52], *i.e.*, even if run arbitrarily long, the probability for finding a solution to soluble CSP instance may approach a value strictly smaller than one. A simple generic approach for overcoming this problem is to extend MCH with a static restart mechanism that re-initialises the search process every *maxSteps* search steps, where *maxSteps* is a user-specified parameter of the algorithm. Unfortunately, the performance of the resulting algorithm depends critically and quite sensitively on good choices of *maxSteps*, which vary substantially between different CSP instances. Substantially more effective variants of the MCH will be discussed later in this chapter.

```
procedure GSAT (F, maxTries, maxSteps)
    input: CNF formula F, positive integers maxTries and maxSteps
    output: model of F or "no solution found"

    for try := 1 to maxTries do
        a := randomly chosen assignment of the variables in formula F;
        for step := 1 to maxSteps do
            if a satisfies F then return a end
            x := randomly selected variable flipping which minimises
                    the number of unsatisfied clauses;
            a := a with x flipped;
        end
    end
    return "no solution found"
end GSAT
```

Figure 5.2: The basic GSAT algorithm; all random selections are according to a uniform probability distribution over the underlying sets.

The GSAT Algorithm

Basic GSAT [91] is a simple iterative best-improvement algorithm for SAT that uses the number of clauses unsatisfied under a given assignment as its evaluation function. The algorithm works as follows (see also Figure 5.2): Starting from a complete variable assignment chosen uniformly at random, in each local search step, a single propositional variable is flipped from *true* to *false* or vice versa. The variable to be flipped is chosen such that a maximal decrease in the number of unsatisfied clauses is achieved; if there are several variables with that property, one of them is selected uniformly at random. The iterative best-improvement search used in GSAT gets easily stuck in local minima of the evaluation function. Therefore, GSAT uses a simple static restart mechanism that re-initialises the search at a randomly chosen assignment every *maxSteps* flips. The search is terminated when a model of the given formula *F* has been found, or after *maxTries* sequences (also called 'tries') of *maxSteps* variable flips each have been performed without finding a model of *F*.

Straightforward implementations of GSAT are rather inefficient, since in each step the scores of all variables, *i.e.*, the changes in the number of unsatisfied clauses caused by the respective flips, have to be calculated from scratch. The key to efficiently implementing GSAT is to compute the complete set of scores only once at the beginning of each try, and then after each flip to update only the scores of those variables that were possibly affected by the flipped variable (details on this mechanism can be found in Chapter 6 of Hoos and Stützle [52]).

For any fixed setting of the *maxTries* parameter, GSAT is essentially incomplete [44, 47], and severe stagnation behaviour is observed on most SAT instances. Still, when it was first introduced, GSAT outperformed the best systematic search algorithms for SAT available at that time. As one of the first SLS algorithms for SAT, basic GSAT had a very significant impact on the development of a broad range of much more powerful SAT solvers, including most of the current state-of-the-art SLS algorithms for SAT. Furthermore, GSAT and its variants (described later in this chapter) also had a significant impact on the development of high-performance SLS algorithms for the CSP.

5.2   Randomised Iterative Improvement Algorithms

The main limitation of iterative improvement algorithms stems from the fact that they get stuck in local minima of the given evaluation function. A simple approach to deal with this problem is to occasionally allow non-improving search steps, *i.e.*, the selection of neighbours $s' \in N(s)$ with $g(s') \geq g(s)$ from the current neighourhood. There are numerous different mechanisms that implement this approach; many of these make use of randomised decisions in order to balance the diversification effects of worsening search steps with the search intensification provided by Iterative Improvement.

Randomised Iterative Improvement (RII) is an extension of Iterative Improvement where in each step with a fixed probability wp, a position s' is selected uniformly at random from the current neighbourhood $N(s)$ — this is called a *random walk step*; otherwise (*i.e.*, with probability $1 - wp$), a standard II step is performed. Note that using this mechanism, arbitrarily long sequences of (possibly worsening) random walk steps can be performed. Therefore, as long as the given neighbourhood graph is connected (*i.e.*, any two candidate solutions can be reached from each other by means of a sequence of search steps), RII, when run arbitrarily long, will find a solution to any soluble problem instance with probability approaching one, *i.e.*, $\lim_{t \to \infty} P_s(RT \leq t) = 1$, where $P_s(RT \leq t)$ is the probability that a solution is found in time at most t.[2] Algorithms with this property are called *probabilistically approximately complete (PAC)*.

The Min Conflicts Heuristic with Random Walk (WMCH)

By extending the Min Conflicts Heuristic with a simple random walk mechanism, a randomised iterative improvement algorithm called *WMCH* is obtained [116]. In each WMCH step, first a variable x_i is chosen uniformly at random from the conflict set (as in MCH) Then, with probability $wp \geq 0$, a random walk step is performed, *i.e.*, x_i is assigned a value from its domain D_i that has been chosen uniformly at random. In the remaining cases, that is, with probability $1 - wp$, a conflict-minimising value is chosen and assigned, as in a conventional MCH step.

The walk probability wp (also called *noise setting*) has a critical impact on the behaviour of the algorithm. For $wp = 0$, the algorithm is equivalent to the standard Min-Conflicts Heuristic and hence essentially incomplete, but for $wp > 0$, WMCH is provably probabilistically approximately complete (PAC). Intuitively, for low walk probabilities, the search process is likely to have difficulties escaping from local minima regions of the search space, while for very high walk probabilities, its behaviour starts to resemble that of an uninformed random walk, and it will increasingly lack effective heuristic guidance towards solutions. However, for suitably chosen wp settings, WMCH has been empirically observed to perform substantially better than MCH with random restart [101].

---

[2]Most local search algorithms for CSP use connected neighbourhoods; however, for more complex constraint programming problems, connected neighbourhoods that can be searched efficiently are sometimes difficult to construct.

Random walk steps in WMCH always involve a variable that appears in a currently unsatisfied constraint; they are therefore also called *conflict-directed random walk steps*. However, different from the GWSAT algorithm [92] (described in the following), which preceded and inspired WMCH, the conflict-directed random walk steps in WMCH do not necessarily render satisfied any previously unsatisfied constraint. WMCH can be varied slightly such that in each random walk step, after choosing a variable x_i involved in a currently violated constraint C, x_i is assigned a value v such that C becomes satisfied; if no such v exists, a value is chosen at random. This variant was found to perform marginally better than the random walk mechanism used in WMCH [101].

GSAT with Random Walk (GWSAT)

The basic GSAT algorithm can be significantly improved by extending it with a random walk mechanism similar to that used in WMCH. Here, in each conflict-directed random walk step, the variable to be flipped is selected uniformly at random from the set of all variables appearing in currently unsatisfied clauses. Note that as a result of any such step, at least one previously unsatisfied clause will become satisfied. This mechanism is closely related to (and in fact inspired by) the conflict-directed random walk algorithm by Papadimitriou, which has been proven to solve 2-SAT in quadratic expected time [80].

GSAT with Random Walk (GWSAT) [92] is variant of basic GSAT that in each local search step probabilistically decides between performing a basic GSAT step and a conflict-directed random walk step (as previously explained). The latter type of step is chosen with a fixed walk probability *wp*, and basic GSAT steps are performed otherwise. While for $wp = 0$, GWSAT is equivalent to basic GSAT, it has been proven to be probabilistically approximately complete (PAC) for any $wp > 0$ [47].

For suitably chosen walk probability settings (which vary between problem instances, but in many cases can be as high as 0.5), GWSAT achieves substantially better performance than basic GSAT [92]. Furthermore, it has been shown that when using sufficiently high noise settings, GWSAT does not suffer from stagnation behaviour; also, for hard SAT instances, it typically shows exponential run-time distributions (RTDs) [44, 51]. Therefore, static restarts are ineffective, and optimal speedup can be obtained by multiple independent runs parallelisation [52]. For low noise settings, stagnation behaviour is frequently observed; recently, there has been evidence that the corresponding RTDs can be characterised by mixtures of exponential distributions [46].

WalkSAT

The WalkSAT algorithm is conceptually closely related to both GWSAT and MCH; it was first published by Selman, Kautz and Cohen [92], and is now commonly known as *WalkSAT/SKC*. This algorithm was later extended into an algorithmic framework called the *WalkSAT architecture* [73], which includes the original WalkSAT/SKC algorithm as well as several other high-performance SLS algorithms for SAT as special cases (several of these will be covered in later sections of this chapter). Furthermore, variants of WalkSAT have been developed for more general classes of CSP instances as well as for constraint optimisation problems (see Section 5.6).

WalkSAT/SKC (and all other WalkSAT algorithms) are based on a 2-stage variable selection process similar to that used in MCH. In each local search step, first a clause c

is selected uniformly at random from the set of all currently unsatisfied clauses. Then, one of the variables appearing in c is flipped to obtain a new assignment. The choice of this variable is based on a heuristic scoring function $score_b(x)$ that counts the number of currently satisfied clauses that will be broken, *i.e.*, become unsatisfied, by flipping a given variable x. Using this scoring function, the following variable selection scheme is applied: If there is a variable x with $score_b(x) = 0$ in the clause c selected in stage 1, that is, if c can be satisfied without breaking another clause, x is flipped (this is called a *zero damage step*). If more than one such variable exists in c, one of them is selected uniformly at random and flipped. If no such variable exists, with a certain probability *1-p*, the variable with minimal $score_b$ value is selected (*greedy step*; ties are broken uniformly at random); in the remaining cases, that is, with probability p (the so-called *noise setting*), one of the variables from c is selected uniformly at random (*random walk step*).

Note that — like in GWSAT, but unlike in MCH — every step in WalkSAT/SKC is guaranteed to satisfy at least one previously unsatisfied clause (but may at the same time cause many others to become unsatisfied). Otherwise, WalkSAT/SKC uses the same random search initialisation, static random restart mechanism and termination criterion as GSAT.

Although it has been proven that WalkSAT/SKC with fixed *maxTries* parameter has the PAC property when applied to 2-SAT [16], it is not known whether the algorithm is PAC in the general case. In practice, WalkSAT/SKC does not appear to suffer from any stagnation behaviour when using sufficiently high (instance-specific) noise settings, in which case its run-time behaviour is characterised by exponential RTDs [44, 51, 49]. As in the case of GWSAT, stagnation behaviour is frequently observed for low noise settings, and there is some evidence that the corresponding RTDs can be characterised by mixtures of exponential distributions [46].

Typically, when using (somewhat instance-specific) optimised noise settings, Walk-SAT/SKC performs substantially better than GWSAT.[3] Furthermore, because of its two-stage variable selection scheme, WalkSAT/SKC (like all other WalkSAT algorithms and MCH variants), can be implemented efficiently without using the incremental score update technique essential for the efficient implementation of GSAT and GWSAT.

5.3   Tabu Search and Related Algorithms

The key idea behind *Tabu Search (TS)* [35, 36] is to use memory to prevent the search process from stagnating in local minima or, more generally, attractive non-solution areas of the given search space. In *Simple Tabu Search*, an iterative improvement strategy is enhanced with a short-term memory that allows it to escape from local minima. This memory is used to prevent the search from returning the most recently visited search positions for a fixed number of search steps. Simple TS can be implemented by explicitly memorising previously visited candidate solutions and ruling out any step that would lead back to those. More commonly, reversing recent search steps is prevented by forbidding the re-introduction of solution components (such as assignments of individual CSP variables) which have just been removed from the current candidate solution. A parameter

---

[3] Several techniques have been proposed for automatically tuning the noise setting for WalkSAT algorithms (see Patterson and Kautz [83], Hoos [45]).

called *tabu tenure* determines the number of search steps for which these restrictions apply. Note that forbidding possible steps using a tabu mechanism has the same effect as dynamically restricting the neighbourhood $N(s)$ of the current candidate solution s to a subset $N' \subseteq N(s)$ of *admissible neighbours*.

As an undesirable side-effect, this tabu mechanism can sometimes rule out search steps that lead to interesting, unvisited areas of the search space. Therefore, many tabu search algorithms make use of a so-called *aspiration criterion*, which specifies conditions under which the tabu status of candidate solutions or solution components is overridden. One of the most commonly used aspiration criteria overrides the tabu status of steps that lead to an improvement in the *incumbent candidate solution*, *i.e.*, the best candidate solution seen throughout the search process.

Min Conflicts Heuristic with Tabu Search (TMCH)

Extending MCH with a simple tabu search mechanism leads to the *TMCH* algorithm [101, 98]. TMCH works exactly as MCH, except that after each search step, *i.e.*, after the value of a variable x_i is changed from v to v', the variable/value pair (x_i, v) is declared tabu for the next *tt* steps, where *tt* is the *tabu tenure* parameter. While (x_i, v) is tabu, value v is excluded from the selection of values for x_i, unless assigning v to x_i leads to an improvement over the incumbent assignment (aspiration criterion).

According to empirical evidence, TMCH typically performs better than WMCH. Interestingly, a tabu tenure setting of *tt* = 2 was found to consistently result in good performance for CSP instances of different types and sizes [101].

The Tabu Search Algorithm by Galinier and Hao (TS-GH)

Although conceptually quite similar to TMCH, the tabu search algorithm by Galinier and Hao [29], *TS-GH*, typically shows much better performance. TS-GH is based on the same neighbourhood and evaluation function as MCH, but uses a different heuristic for selecting the variable/value pair involved in each search step: Amongst all pairs (x, v') for which variable x appears in a currently violated constraint and v' is any value from the domain of x, TS-GH chooses the one that leads to a maximal decrease in the number of violated constraints. If multiple such pairs exist, one of them is selected uniformly at random. As in MCH, the actual search step is then performed by assigning v' to x. This best-improvement strategy is augmented with the same tabu mechanism used in TMCH: After changing the assignment of x from v to v', the variable value pair (x, v) is declared tabu for *tt* search steps. Furthermore, the same aspiration criterion is used to enable the algorithm to perform search steps that lead to improvements over the incumbent assignment regardless of the tabu status of respective variable/value pair.

Unlike for the MCH variants discussed so far, efficient implementations of TS-GH crucially depend on an incremental update mechanism for evaluation function values similar to the one used in GSAT. The basic idea is to maintain the effects of any potential search step on the evaluation function (*i.e.*, the number of conflicts resulting from any search step) in a two-dimensional table of size $n \times k$, where n is the number of variables, and k is the size of the largest domain in the given CSP instance.

Furthermore, the tabu mechanism can be implemented efficiently as follows. For each variable/value pair (x, v) the search step number $t_{x,v}$ when x was last set to v is memorised.

When initialising the search, all the $t_{x,v}$ are set to $-tt$; subsequently, every time a variable x is set to a value v, $t_{x,v}$ is set to the current search step number t, where search steps are counted starting from 0 at the initialisation of the search process. A variable/value pair (x, v) is tabu if, and only if, $t - t_{x,v} \le tt$. By using this technique in combination with the previously described incremental update mechanism, search steps of TS-GH can be performed as efficiently as those of MCH.

TS-GH was originally introduced as an algorithm for MAX-CSP, the optimisation variant of CSP in which the objective is to find a variable assignment that satisfies a maximal number of constraints (see Section 5.6). Empirical studies suggest that when applied to the conventional CSP, TS-GH generally achieves better performance than any other MCH variant, including TMCH, rendering it one of the best SLS algorithms for the CSP currently known [101]. Unlike in the case of TMCH, the optimal setting of the tabu tenure parameter in TS-GH tends to increase with instance size; this makes it considerably harder to solve new CSP instances with peak efficiency [101].

GSAT with Tabu Search

Integrating a simple tabu search strategy into the best-improvement procedure underlying basic GSAT leads to an algorithm called *GSAT with Tabu Search (GSAT/Tabu)* [72, 98]. In GSAT/Tabu, tabu status is associated with the propositional variables in the given formula. After a variable x has been flipped, it cannot be flipped back within the next steps, where the tabu tenure, *tt*, is a parameter of the algorithm. In each search step, the variable to be flipped is selected as in basic GSAT, except that the choice is restricted to variables that are currently not tabu. Upon search initialisation, the tabu status of all variables is cleared. Otherwise, GSAT/Tabu works exactly as GSAT; in particular, it uses the same restart mechanism and termination criterion. As in the case of TMCH, to implement GSAT/Tabu efficiently, it is crucial to use incremental score updating and tabu mechanisms.

Unlike in the case of GWSAT, it is not clear whether GSAT/Tabu with fixed *maxTries* parameter has the PAC property. Intuitively, for low *tt*, the algorithm may not be able to escape from extensive local minima regions, while for high *tt* settings, all the routes to a solution may be cut off, because too many variables are tabu. However, when using instance-specific, optimised tabu tenure settings, GSAT/Tabu typically performs significantly better than GWSAT with similarly optimised parameters. This is particularly the case for large and structured SAT instances [49]; there are, however, a few exceptional cases where GSAT/Tabu performs substantially worse than GWSAT, including well-known SAT-encoded instances of logistics planning problems. Analogously to basic GSAT, GSAT/Tabu can be extended with a random walk mechanism; limited experimentation suggests that typically this hybrid algorithm does not perform better than GSAT/Tabu [98].

WalkSAT with Tabu Search

Like GSAT and MCH, WalkSAT/SKC can be extended with a simple tabu search mechanism. *WalkSAT/Tabu* [73] uses the same two stage selection mechanism and the same scoring function $score_b$ as WalkSAT/SKC and additionally enforces a tabu tenure of steps for each flipped variable. (To implement this tabu mechanism efficiently, the same approach is used as previously described for TS-GH.) If the selected clause c does not allow a zero damage step, of all the variables occurring in c that are not tabu, WalkSAT/Tabu picks the one with the highest $score_b$ value; when there are several variables with the same maximal score, one of them is selected uniformly at random. In cases where all variables appearing in the selected clause c are tabu, the variable assignment remains unchanged (a so-called *null-flip*), but the current tabu tenure values for all variables decrease exactly as after any other flip.

WalkSAT/Tabu with fixed *maxTries* parameter has been proven to be essentially incomplete [44, 47]. Although this is mainly caused by null-flips, it is not clear whether replacing null-flips by random walk steps, for instance, would be sufficient for obtaining the PAC property. In practice, however, WalkSAT/Tabu typically performs significantly better than WalkSAT/SKC, especially on structured SAT instances, such as large SAT-encoded blocks world planning problems [49].

Novelty and Variants

The *Novelty* algorithm [73] is derived from the WalkSAT framework. Like tabu search, Novelty uses a limited information on the search history to avoid search stagnation. More specifically, its variable selection mechanism is based on the intuition that repeatedly flipping back and forth the same variable should be avoided. This mechanism is based on the *age of a variable* (see also Gent and Walsh [33]), *i.e.*, the number of flips that have occurred since it was last flipped. Different from WalkSAT/SKC and WalkSAT/Tabu, Novelty and its more recent variants use the same variable scoring function as GSAT, *i.e.*, the difference in the number of unsatisfied clauses caused by the respective flip.

In each step of Novelty, after an unsatisfied clause c has been chosen uniformly at random (exactly as in WalkSAT/SKC), the variable to be flipped is selected as follows. If the variable x with the highest score does not have minimal age among the variables in c, it is always selected. Otherwise, x is only selected with a probability of *1-p*, where p is a parameter called the *noise setting*. In the remaining cases, the variable with the next lower score is selected. When sorting the variables according to their scores, ties are broken according to decreasing age. (If there are several variables with identical score and age, the reference implementation by Kautz and Selman always chooses the one that appears first in c.) Novelty (and the advanced variants described below) use the same initialisation procedure, restart mechanism and termination condition as WalkSAT/SKC.

Note that even for $p > 0$, Novelty is significantly greedier than WalkSAT/SKC, since always one of the two most improving variables from a clause is selected, where Walk-SAT/SKC may select any variable if no improvement without breaking other clauses can be achieved. Precisely for this reason, Novelty is provably essentially incomplete for fixed *maxTries* setting and has been shown to occasionally suffer from extreme stagnation on several commonly used benchmark instances [44, 49]. It may also be noted that, different from WalkSAT/SKC, the Novelty strategy for variable selection within a clause is completely deterministic for both $p = 0$ and $p = 1$. Still, in most cases, Novelty shows significantly improved performance over WalkSAT/SKC and WalkSAT/Tabu [73, 49].

R-Novelty [73], a variant of Novelty that uses a more complex variable selection mechanism, performs often, but not always, better than Novelty (for details, see McAllester et al. [73] or Chapter 6 of Hoos and Stützle [52]). Despite its use of a loop-breaking strategy designed to prevent search stagnation, this algorithm suffers from the effects of its provable essential incompleteness [44, 47], but it sometimes performs somewhat better than Novelty [73, 49].

Both Novelty and R-Novelty can be easily extended with a simple conflict-directed random walk mechanism similar to that used in GWSAT; this way, the essential incompleteness as well as the empirically observed stagnation behaviour are effectively overcome. The *Novelty*$^+$ algorithm [44, 47] selects the variable to be flipped according to the standard Novelty mechanism with probability $1 - wp$, and makes a uniform random choice from the selected clause in the remaining cases. *R-Novelty*$^+$ is obtained from R-Novelty in the same way, but does not make use of R-Novelty's loop-breaking mechanism.

Novelty$^+$ is provably PAC for $wp > 0$ and shows exponential RTDs for sufficiently high (instance-specific) settings of the primary noise parameter, p. In practice, small walk probabilities, wp, are generally sufficient to prevent the extreme stagnation behaviour occasionally observed for Novelty and to achieve substantially superior performance compared to Novelty. In fact, the algorithm's behaviour appears to be much more robust w.r.t. the wp parameter than w.r.t. the primary noise setting, p, and uniformly good performance has been observed for $wp = 0.01$ [47]. It may be noted that in cases where Novelty does not suffer from stagnation behaviour, Novelty$^+$'s performance for $wp = 0.01$ is typically almost identical to Novelty's. Similar observations hold for R-Novelty$^+$; however, there is some indication that R-Novelty$^+$ does not reach the performance of the conceptually simpler Novelty$^+$ algorithm on several classes of structured SAT instances, including SAT-encoded hard graph colouring and planning problems [49].

Adaptive Novelty$^+$ [45] is an extension of Novelty$^+$ that dynamically adapts the noise parameter during the search process and hence does not require this parameter to be tuned manually. An efficient implementation of this algorithm won first prize in the random category of the SAT 2004 SAT Solvers Competition. Novelty++, a more recent variant of Novelty, has been found to perform better than Novelty$^+$ in many cases; its performance can be further improved by hybridising the underlying variable selection mechanism with a greedy iterative improvement strategy similar to that underlying GSAT [69].

5.4   Penalty-Based Local Search Algorithms

An alternative to extending an iterative improvement strategy such that it can escape from local minima of a given evaluation function is to modify the evaluation function when the search process is about to stagnate in a local minimum [71]. This approach is also known as *Dynamic Local Search (DLS)* [52].

Penalty-based algorithms modify the evaluation function by means of *penalty weights* which are associated with solution components or other features of candidate solutions; in the case of the CSP, penalty weights are usually associated with the constraint relations of the given CSP instance and for SAT, analogously, with the clauses of the given CNF formula (in the latter case, the penalty weights are often referred to as *clause weights*). These penalty weights are modified during the search process. Various penalty-based algorithms differ in their underlying local search strategy and the mechanism used for penalty modification. The latter, in particular, can have a significant impact on the performance of the algorithm.

Penalty-based algorithms have sometimes been motivated by the intuition that by modifying the evaluation function, local minima can be eliminated or, in the case of CSP, the search process can learn to distinguish 'important' from less critical constraints, thus making it easier to find solutions (*i.e.*, global optima). There is, however, increasing evidence that the primary reason for the excellent performance of current penalty-based algorithms lies rather in the effective search diversification caused by the penalty modifications [111, 103]. The idea of diversifying search effort to different parts of the search space as needed in a specific situation has a long history in operations research – see, for example, Koopman [61] and Stone [99].

GENET and the Breakout Method

GENET [119, 107, 20, 17] was one of the earliest penalty-based algorithms in constraint satisfaction. It is based on a neural network design with nodes representing atomic variable assignments and links connecting conflicting atomic assignments. More precisely, a binary CSP instance is represented by a network in which for each variable there is a cluster of *label nodes* that correspond to the values the variable can take. Any pair of label nodes that correspond to variable assignments violating any constraint is connected by a link. A penalty weight is associated with every link in the network; at the beginning of the search process, these weights are all set to one and a random label node in each cluster is switched on.

At any stage of the search, exactly one node per cluster is switched on, that is, every variable has a unique value assigned to it, and the state of the network corresponds to a complete variable assignment. Each label node receives a signal from each of its neighboring nodes that are switched on. The strength of the signal is equal to the weight associated with the connection. For each cluster, the node that receives the least amount of inhibitory signals is switched on. Note that when all penalty weights are one, GENET resembles the Min-Conflicts Heuristic [76, 77].

Motivated by hardware implementations of neural networks, the variable whose cluster is updated in a given search step is chosen asynchronously. Implemented on a sequential machine, clusters are updated sequentially in a random order in each iteration. Whenever the network settles in a stable state, that is, when there is no change of the active node within any cluster that would reduce the total weight of edges between active nodes, the weight of all edges between active nodes are increased by one. As a result, the network may become unstable again.

The 'energy' of a network state (which is returned by the evaluation function) is the total amount of input received by all the nodes that are switched on in that state [18]. The stable states of the network correspond to the local minima of this evaluation function, and GENET reaches these by performing iterative improvement steps. If the energy is 0, then a solution to the CSP has been found.

GENET was extended to non-binary constraint satisfaction problems by using hyperedges as links in the network [119, 20, 67, 68]. Stuckey and Tam [100] used such an extension of GENET to mutate chromosomes in an evolutionary algorithm. The resulting memetic algorithm was demonstrated to be effective in solving hard CSP instances. Variants of GENET have also been used to solve challenging instances of a car sequencing problem [19].

The Breakout Method [78] is another early penalty-based algorithm for the CSP. Unlike GENET, it associates a single penalty weight with each constraint of the given CSP instance and uses an evaluation function that maps each variable assignment a to the total weighted of the constraints violated under a. Otherwise, the two algorithms are basically identical. In particular, like GENET, the Breakout Method initialises all penalty weights to one and uses iterative improvement until a local minima of its evaluation function is reached, at which point the weights of all unsatisfied constraints are incremented by one before the search is continued.

Guided Local Search (GLS)

Unlike GENET or the Breakout Method, which were designed rather specifically for constraint satisfaction problems, *Guided Local Search (GLS)* [111] is a more general penalty-based method that has been used for combinatorial decision and optimisation problems (such as SAT and TSP, respectively) [113].

As a penalty-based method, GLS associates penalties with the constraints of the given CSP instance. GLS uses an augmented evaluation function of the form

$$g'(a) = g(a) + \lambda \sum_{i=1}^{m} p_i I_i(a), \tag{5.1}$$

where a is a complete variable assignment, $g(a)$ is the evaluation function value of a (here: the number of constraints unsatisfied under a), p_i is the penalty of constraint i, and $I_i(a$ is an indicator function with value 1 if constraint i is violated under a and 0 otherwise.

All penalties are initialised to 0 at the beginning of the search, and penalty changes are applied whenever the search process reaches a local minimum of f. The penalties to be increased in a given local minimum are selected such that they maximise the *utility function*

$$util_i(a) = I_i(a) \cdot c(i)/(1 + p_i) \tag{5.2}$$

where a, $I_i(a)$, $g(a)$ and p_i are defined as in Eq. 5.1, and $c(i)$ is the cost of having constraint i unsatisfied. This cost is set to one for all constraints in a standard CSP, but by using different cost values, GLS can be easily extended to optimisation variants of the CSP with weighted constraints. This selection mechanism ensures that only penalties of currently violated constraints are increased. Secondly, the more a constraint has been penalised, the less incentive there is for penalising it again; this facilitates diversification of the search. Each penalty selected is increased by one at a time. Finally, when non-uniform constraint costs are used, this strategy keeps the search focused on satisfying higher-cost constraints. This carefully designed penalty update mechanism has been proven to be useful in various applications, including BT's scheduling problem [106] and a version of the *Radio-Link Frequency Assignment Problem* [112], an abstracted military communications problem originating from the CALMA project [8].

One of the attractive properties of GLS is that it has only one major parameter, namely λ, to tune. One good heuristic is to set the value of λ to a fraction (between 0 and 1) of the cost of the first local minimum encountered by GLS. This allows λ to be selected according to the characteristics of the given problem instance. At the time of publication, GLS was shown to be competitive with other high-performance algorithms on a widely studied set of 11 benchmark problems. More recently, GLS has been extended to incorporate random moves and aspiration [74]. The resulting algorithm, *Extended GLS*, was shown to be at least as effective as GLS, but significantly less sensitive to the value of the λ parameter for the problems it was tested on (which included SAT, Weighted MAX-SAT and the Quadratic Assignment Problem).

GSAT with Clause Weights

This early penalty-based algorithm for SAT was motivated by the observation that when performing multiple runs of basic GSAT on some types of structured SAT instances, certain clauses tend to be unsatisfied at the end of each run. The idea behind *GSAT with Clause Weights* [90] is to bias the search process towards satisfying such 'problem clauses' by associating weights with them. More precisely, weights are associated with each clause. These are initially set to one; but before each restart, the weights of all currently unsatisfied clauses are increased by $\delta = 1$. The underlying local search procedure is a variant of basic GSAT that uses a modified evaluation function $g'(F, a)$ which measures the total weight of all clauses in the given formula F that are unsatisfied under assignment a. Search initialisation, restart and termination are as in basic GSAT. (A variant called 'Averaging In' uses a modified search initialisation that introduces a bias towards the best candidate solutions reached in previous local search phases [90].)

GSAT with Clause Weights was found to perform substantially better than basic GSAT on various classes of structured SAT instances, including SAT-encoded graph colouring problems; furthermore, there is some indication that by using the same clause weighting mechanism with GWSAT, further performance improvements can be achieved [90]. To date, both of these algorithms are outperformed by WalkSAT algorithms such as Novelty[+] and by state-of-the-art penalty-based algorithms, such as SAPS (which is covered later in this section) and PAWS [102]. Several variants of GSAT with Clause Weights have been studied by Cha and Iwama [12]. Some of these use slight variations of the weight update scheme and a simple form of tabu search. However, from their limited empirical results it is doubtful that any of these variations achieves significant performance improvements over the original GSAT with Clause Weights algorithm.

Several variants of GSAT with Clause Weights that perform weight updates after each local search step have been proposed and studied by Frank [26, 27]. These are based on the idea that GSAT should benefit from discovering which clauses are most difficult to satisfy relative to recent assignments. The most basic of these variants, called *WGSAT*, uses the same weight initialisation and update procedure as GSAT with Clause Weights, but performs only a single GSAT step before updating the clause weights. A modification of this algorithm, called *UGSAT*, restricts the neighbourhood considered in each search step to the set of variables appearing in currently unsatisfied clauses [26]. (This is the same neighbourhood as used in the random walk steps of GWSAT.) While this leads to considerable speedups for naïve implementations of the underlying local search procedure, the difference for efficient implementations is likely to be insufficient to render UGSAT competitive with other GSAT variants, such as GWSAT.

Frank also studied a variant of WGSAT in which the clause weights are subject to a uniform decay over time [27]. The underlying idea is that the relative importance of clauses w.r.t. their satisfaction status can change during the search, and hence a mechanism is needed that focuses the weighted search on the most recently unsatisfied clauses. Although using this decay mechanism slightly improves the performance of WGSAT when measured in terms of variable flips, this gain is insufficient to amortise the added time complexity of the frequent weight update steps. However, similar mechanisms for focusing the search on recently unsatisfied clauses play a crucial role in state-of-the-art penalty-based algorithms for SAT that are covered later in this section.

The Discrete Lagrangian Method (DLM)

The use of penalties in dynamic local search is conceptually closely related to the use of Lagrange multipliers for solving continuous constrained optimisation problems [93, 115]. For a constrained optimisation problem in which a function $f(\vec{x})$ is to be minimised subject to equality constraints $g_i(\vec{x}) = 0$, we can define the Lagrangian function

$$L(\vec{x}, \vec{\lambda}) = f(\vec{x}) + \sum_i \lambda_i g_i(\vec{x}) \tag{5.3}$$

where the λ_i are continuous variables called *Lagrange multipliers*. Note that these play the same role as the penalty weights in the augmented evaluation function typically used in the previously discussed penalty-based algorithms. It can be shown that a local minimum satisfying all equality constraints can be obtained by finding a saddle point of L, *i.e.*, a point $(\vec{x}^*, \vec{\lambda}^*)$ such that

$$L(\vec{x}^*, \vec{\lambda}) \le L(\vec{x}^*, \vec{\lambda}^*) \le L(\vec{x}, \vec{\lambda}^*) \tag{5.4}$$

for all $(\vec{x}^*, \vec{\lambda})$ and $(\vec{x}, \vec{\lambda}^*)$ sufficiently close to $(\vec{x}^*, \vec{\lambda}^*)$. Based on this result, the problem of finding a local minimum of a constrained optimisation problem can be reduced to the problem of finding a saddle point of an unconstrained optimisation problem. This latter task can be achieved by performing iterative improvement (*e.g.*, in the form of gradient descent) on L using the variables $\vec{x}$ in combination with iterative ascent on L using the Lagrange multipliers $\vec{\lambda}$. In a local minimum $\vec{x}$ of f that does not satisfy all constraints, increasing the Lagrange multipliers has the effect of more heavily penalising violated constraints. Eventually, for some value of $\vec{\lambda}$, $L(\vec{x}, \vec{\lambda})$ is no longer a local minimum, such that further minimisation by modifying $\vec{x}$ becomes possible, resulting in fewer violated constraints.

This well-known approach for solving continuous constrained optimisation problems provided the motivation for Shang and Wah's DLM algorithm for SAT [93]. The basic idea behind this dynamic local search algorithm is to perform iterative best improvement on the same augmented evaluation function used in GSAT with clause weights (this corresponds to the minimisation of $L(\vec{x}, \vec{\lambda})$ over $\vec{x}$). Whenever a local minimum is reached, the penalties for all unsatisfied clauses are increased (this corresponds to the ascent on $L(\vec{x}, \vec{\lambda}$ by modifying $\vec{\lambda}$), until some previously worsening variable flip becomes improving, and hence the search process is no longer stuck in a local minimum. The basic version of DLM for SAT also uses a tabu mechanism equivalent to that found in GSAT/Tabu, as well as periodic decreases of all clause penalties to avoid numerical overflow. Furthermore, before the search process is started, the given formula is simplified by performing a complete pass of unit propagation.

Several extensions of the basic DLM algorithm have been shown to achieve improved performance [122, 121]; these use various memory-based mechanisms for avoiding and overcoming search stagnation more effectively (for an overview of these methods, see Hoos and Stützle [52].) All of these algorithms have a relatively large number of parameters that need to be tuned carefully in order to achieve peak performance. DLM has also been applied to weighted MAX-SAT problems [115], while extensions to non-binary problems represent an interesting research direction.

It should be noted that despite the close conceptual relationship between the approaches, important mathematical properties of Lagrangian methods for continuous optimisation do not carry over to DLM. This is primarily due to the heuristic mechanisms used by DLM for determining search steps, as opposed to the rigorous use of derivatives of the objective function in continuous Lagrangian methods.

ESG and SAPS

The *Exponentiated Subgradient (ESG) algorithm* [89] was originally motivated by sub-gradient optimisation, a well-known method for minimising Lagrangian functions that is widely used for generating lower bounds for branch-and-bound algorithms. As a penalty-based algorithms for SAT, ESG associates penalty weights with the clauses of the given CNF formula that are modified during the search process. The search is started from a randomly selected variable assignment after initialising all clause weights to one. The local search procedure underlying ESG for SAT is based on a best improvement search method that can be seen as a simple variant of GSAT; in each local search step, the variable to be flipped is selected uniformly at random from the set of all variables that appear in currently unsatisfied clauses and whose flipping leads to a maximal decrease in the total weight of unsatisfied clauses. When reaching a local minimum (*i.e.*, an assignment in which flipping any variable that appears in an unsatisfied clause would not lead to a decrease in the total weight of unsatisfied clauses), with probability η, the search is continued by flipping a variable that is uniformly chosen at random from the set of all variables appearing in unsatisfied clauses; otherwise, the local search phase is terminated.

After each local search phase, the clause weights are updated in two stages: First, the weights of all clauses are multiplied by a factor that depends on the respective satisfaction status (scaling stage): weights of satisfied clauses are multiplied by α_{sat}, weights of unsatisfied clauses by α_{unsat}. Then, all clause weights are updated using the formula $clw(c) := clw(c) \cdot \rho + (1 - \rho) \cdot \overline{w}$ (smoothing stage), where $\overline{w}$ is the average of all clause weights after scaling, and the parameter ρ has a fixed value between zero and one. The algorithm terminates when a satisfying assignment for F has been found or when a given bound on the number of search steps has been reached.

Compared to the underlying local search steps, a weight update is computationally expensive, since it involves modifications of all clause weights. Additionally, experimental evidence indicates that local search phases in ESG are typically quite short, and therefore the expensive smoothing operations have to be performed rather frequently [52, 53]. Even with the use of special implementation techniques that help ameliorate this problem, Southey and Schuurmans' highly optimised reference implementation of ESG for SAT does not always reach the performance of high-performance WalkSAT algorithms such as Novelty$^+$. Compared to DLM-2000-SAT, ESG-SAT typically requires fewer steps for finding a model of a given formula, but in terms of CPU-time, both algorithms show very similar performance [89, 53]. It may be noted that the general ESG framework has been originally proposed for the more general Boolean linear programming (BLP) problem, and it has also been applied quite successfully to combinatorial auctions winner determination problems [89].

The *Scaling and Probabilistic Smoothing (SAPS) algorithm* by Hutter et al. [53] is based on the insight that the expensive weight update scheme in ESG can be replaced by a much more efficient procedure without negative impact on the underlying search procedure. SAPS can be seen as a variant of ESG that uses a modified weight update scheme, in which the scaling stage is restricted to the weights of currently unsatisfied clauses, and smoothing is only performed with a certain probability p_{smooth}. The first of these modifications is also used in Southey and Schuurmans' efficient ESG implementation; but it is the probabilistic, and hence less frequent, smoothing that results in a substantial performance improvement over ESG and also renders superfluous the special implementation tricks that are crucial for achieving good performance in ESG. SAPS was shown to perform substantially better than ESG, DLM-2000-SAT and high-performance WalkSAT variants [53]; however, there are some types of SAT instances (in particular, hard and large SAT encoded graph colouring instances), for which SAPS does not reach the performance of Novelty$^+$.

A reactive variant of SAPS, *RSAPS* [53], automatically adjusts the smoothing probability p_{smooth} during the search, using a mechanism that is very similar to the one underlying Adaptive WalkSAT [45]. RSAPS sometimes achieves significantly better performance than SAPS; however, it still has other parameters, in particular, the scaling factor α_{unsat}, that need to be manually optimised.

5.5   Other Approaches

Besides the algorithms covered in the previous sections, many other local search methods have been applied in the context of solving CSPs. Within the confines of this chapter it is impossible to present a complete survey of the large and ever-increasing number of local search algorithms for the CSP and closely related problems, such as the Graph Colouring Problem and SAT. Therefore, the algorithms mentioned in the following were selected to illustrate some of the major approaches.

There is a large body of work on evolutionary algorithms for constraint satisfaction problems. Some of the earliest work include Tsang and Warwick [108], Paredis [82], Hao and Dorne [39], Warwick and Tsang [120] and Riff Rojas [87]; Craenen et al. [14] provides on overview and comparison of more recent evolutionary algorithms. GENET and GLS have been used as subsidiary search procedures in memetic algorithms for constraint satisfaction [100] and optimisation [43]. Galinier and Hao [30] have developed a specialised memetic algorithm for the Graph Colouring Problem (GCP) that uses short runs of an effective tabu search algorithm as its subsidiary search procedure; this algorithm is one of the most effective GCP algorithms currently known.

Hao and Dorne [39] used a specialised genetic algorithm to search the space of partial assignments. Lau [64] developed the Guided Genetic Algorithm (GGA), which applies the principle of Guided Local Search in a genetic algorithm. The idea is to use penalties to construct a fitness template, which guides crossover and mutation in a genetic algorithm such that better assignments will be chosen in the selection process with higher probability. GGA has been applied successfully to the Processor Configuration Problem [65], the General Assignment Problem in scheduling [64], and to a version of the Radio-Link Frequency Assignment Problem [66].

Constraints are used to help evolutionary algorithms search efficiently. This is done by modifying the objective functions in evolutionary computation. For example, Yu et al. [125] used penalties to guide the search away from 'poor' areas of the search space, whereas Li [70], Tsang and Li [105], and Jin [54] used incentives to guide the search towards promising areas.

Ant colony optimisation (ACO), a population-based stochastic local search method inspired by the path-finding behaviour of ants [22], has been applied with some success to the CSP [96], and in particular, to permutation constraint satisfaction problems, such as car sequencing [95], and to binary CSPs [110]. Other widely used stochastic local search methods have been applied to specific types of CSP instances. For example, there are various *simulated annealing algorithms* for the graph colouring problem (GCP) [55] and SAT [97]. Likewise, several *iterated local search algorithms* have been developed for the GCP [13, 81] and MAX-SAT [123, 94]. A generalisation of GSAT to CSP that also includes various additional SLS mechanisms, including random walk and clause penalties, was developed by Kask and Dechter [56] and later extended with a tree search mechanism based on cycle-cutsets [57]. Walser [117] has introduced a WalkSAT algorithm for Pseudo-Boolean CSP (a well-known special case of CSP), which includes a tabu mechanism as well as biased random search initialisation.

Local search does not have to be incomplete. In *Systematic Local Search* [40] and related approaches (*e.g.*, Richards et al. [86]), completeness is achieved through the recording and resolution of *no-goods* whenever the underlying local search algorithm encounters a local minimum. When a no-good is encountered, resolution is attempted: for example, if both "*P*=true and *Q*=true" and "*P*=true and *Q*=false" have been encountered, then they are replaced by "*P*=true" (a technique often used in *truth maintenance systems*; see, *e.g.*, Doyle [23]). These no-goods help Systematic Local search to escape from local optima and to achieve completeness, a desirable property which most other local search methods do not enjoy: When both "*P*=true" and "*P*=false" are found to be no-goods for any *P*, the given CSP instance has been shown to be unsatisfiable. To achieve completeness, Systematic Local Search may record an exponential number of no-goods in the worst case. However, with careful memory management, the algorithm has been demonstrated to be effective for job shop scheduling problems [21].

Constrained Local Search [85] is an example for an approach that searches over partial assignments that do not violate any constraints. Based on *dynamic backtracking* [34], Constrained Local Search conducts a depth-first search. Whenever a partial assignment cannot be further extended, a randomly chosen atomic assignment is removed from it, such that the search can be continued in a different direction. Despite its use of depth-first search, Constrained Local Search is incomplete.

Most local search algorithms for CSP use neighbourhood relations that restrict search steps to modifying the value of only one variable at a time. However, the use of larger neighbourhoods can sometimes be advantageous; for example, the swap neighbourhood, in which search steps swap the values of two variables, has been used successfully on sequencing problems in conjunction with GENET [19]. Large neighbourhoods are more commonly used in SLS algorithms for constraint optimisation problems (see next section).

5.6   Local Search for Constraint Optimisation Problems

Many real-life problems are over-constrained. For example, in a production planning application, there may be insufficient resources to complete all given jobs within their respective deadlines. In this situation, it may be desirable to find a feasible assignment of resources such that the total amount of revenue generated is maximised; this type of optimisation problem is referred to as a *maximal utility problem* [104]. In other cases, some constraints may be violated, but doing so incurs a penalty cost. The objective is then to find a solution with minimal penalty; this is known as the *minimal violation problem* [104].

These types of problems can be modelled by extending constraint satisfaction problems to include optimisation objectives. In the simplest case, the problem is represented as a CSP instance, but the objective becomes to find a variable assignment that satisfies a maximal number of constraints (*MAX-CSP*). Note that this is equivalent to finding a variable assignment that minimises the total number of violated constraints. In many cases, not all constraints are equally important. In *Weighted MAX-CSP*, this is captured by weights associated with the individual constraints, and the objective is to maximise the total weight of the satisfied constraints. More general formalisations of constraint optimisation problems include Partial CSP [28], Semi-Ring Based CSP [7] and Valued CSP [88].

A widely studied special case of MAX-CSP and Weighted MAX-CSP is the optimisation variant of SAT, *MAX-SAT*: Given a propositional formula F in conjunctive normal form, the objective in MAX-SAT is to find an assignment of truth values to the variables in F such that a maximum number of clauses in F is satisfied. In *Weighted MAX-SAT*, each clause has an associated weight, and the goal is to find an assignment that maximises the total weight of the satisfied clauses. MAX-SAT and Weighted MAX-SAT are of particular interest in algorithm development because of their conceptual simplicity in combination with the fact that any Weighted MAX-CSP instance can be transformed into a Weighted MAX-SAT instance (at the price of losing structures of the constraint graph and searching a somewhat larger space).

Local search methods are naturally suited for solving constraint optimisation problems [42]. In particular, most local search algorithms for the CSP can be directly applied to MAX-CSP, since their evaluation function directly corresponds to the optimisation objective of minimising the number of violated constraints. Moreover, these algorithms can be extended to Weighted MAX-CSP by modifying the standard evaluation function (number of constraints violated under a given assignment) such that it maps each variable assignment to the total weight of the constraints violated under it (see, *e.g.*, Lau [63]). In special cases, different evaluation functions may be useful; for example, Walser's WalkSAT algorithm for Overconstrained Pseudo-Boolean CSP with hard and soft constraints uses an evaluation function that takes into account the degree of violation of the given linear pseudo-Boolean constraint relations [118].

It is worth noting that when generalising dynamic local search methods to Weighted MAX-CSP, there is no single 'correct' way to integrate the constraint weights and the penalty values into the augmented evaluation function. Perhaps the most obvious approach is to simply add the weights and penalties over all violated constraints (see, *e.g.*, Wah and Shang [115]). An alternate solution was found to work better in GLS, where constraint weights are used for determining the penalty values to be increased after each local search phase, but do not appear in the augmented evaluation function (see Section 5.4). A similar approach is taken in Wu and Wah's DLM algorithm for Weighted MAX-SAT [122], where the clause weights are used for penalty initialisation and update, but not in the evaluation function.

Larger neighbourhoods, which allow more than one variable to be changed in a single local search step, have been more extensively studied in the context of in local search for constraint optimisation than in the case of CSP. For example, Yagiura and Ibaraki [123] have developed various types of SLS algorithms for MAX-SAT based on 2- and 3-flip neighbourhoods. Large neighbourhoods have also been used successfully in various application-relevant combinatorial optimisation problems (see, *e.g.*, Yao [124], Tsang and Voudouris [106], Ahuja et al. [2], Abdullah et al. [1]). In all of these cases, special techniques have to be used in order to search these large neighbourhoods efficiently.

Local search algorithms play a major role in solving real-life constraint optimisation problems, because in many cases, they are able to find high-quality solutions more efficiently than other approaches. For example, GLS has been incorporated into ILOG's Dispatcher system (ILOG is the market leader in commercial constraint programming software) [3, 60]. Dispatcher was specifically designed for vehicle routing, a prominent problem in Operations Research which is of central importance in the transportation business (see Chapter 23). Generally, local search algorithms can often be very usefully applied in combination with other methods. For example, branch-and-bound algorithms can benefit significantly from high-quality bounds obtained by high-performance local search methods.

5.7 Frameworks and Toolkits for Local Search

Both the development of local search algorithm for solving constraint satisfaction and optimisation problems and their practical application are often greatly facilitated by software frameworks and programming toolkits. This is particularly the case when dealing with conceptually complex constraint programming problems. Such systems can substantially ease the burden associated with achieving efficient implementations of SLS algorithms. They also facilitate software reuse and support the separation of problem formulation (modelling) and solving. In the following, we give a brief overview of some of the better known frameworks and toolkits that support SLS algorithms; while some of these are general combinatorial optimisation or constraint programming systems, others are specifically focused on local search methods.

ILOG Solver is a commercial system which provides users with a C++ library that implements state-of-the-art algorithms for constraint satisfaction and optimisation. The OPL interface to ILOG Solver supports a rich declarative syntax that can be used to define the structure of problems and heuristics [41]. *ILOG Dispatcher* is a specialised package for vehicle routing that supports a variety of local search algorithms.

The commercial *iOpt* system implements a wide range of SLS methods. Through a graphic interface, iOpt allows users to experiment with different local search strategies and to construct hybrid algorithms. It also provides an abstract class library in Java that can be used to implement local search methods [114]. Similarly, the freely available object-oriented frameworks *EasyLocal++* [31] and *HotFrame* [25] support the design and implementation of local search algorithms in C++. In these general optimisation systems, problem-independent parts of the algorithms are captured in the form of abstract classes, which are specialised by the user to implement problem-specific algorithms.

The *COMET* programming language supports both modeling and search abstractions in constraint programming. It allows users to specify and control local search algorithms using constraints, modelling and search abstractions, and it has been applied to a wide range of combinatorial problems [42]. The conceptually related *SALSA* language facilitates the concise, declarative definition of local, systematic and hybrid search algorithms [62]. Finally, the freely available *ZDC* system aims to help non-experts in constraint programming by providing them with a simple declarative language (EaCL) and a graphic user interface. It implements a number of local search algorithms, including Guided Local Search [10, 109].

Regardless of whether local search algorithms are realised within such a framework or environment or implemented 'from scratch', it is very important for the reproducibility of empirical results to ensure that their published descriptions are accurate and complete (covering also all performance-critical implementation details). Furthermore, whenever possible, reference implementations should be made available to the research community.

5.8 Conclusions and Outlook

Among the various approaches for solving constraint programming problems such as the CSP, local search methods are of considerable interest to researchers and practitioners. Although most local search algorithms are incomplete, in many cases, their performance scales better with instance size than that of complete, systematic search algorithms. Consequently, high-performance local search methods are often the only practical tool for solving large and difficult real-world problems, which often involve thousands of variable with large domains. This is especially true for decision problems where the main objective is to find feasible solutions quickly and for optimisation problems where high-quality or (near-)optimal solutions need to be obtained as efficiently as possible.

Local search methods have been shown to be very successful in solving many important classes of problems, including SAT, MAX-SAT, travelling salesman and quadratic assignment problems. Their effectiveness and efficiency has also been demonstrated for many real-world problems, including scheduling, vehicle routing and radio-frequency assignment tasks. In many of these applications, local search algorithms achieve comparable or superior performance compared to all other methods.

Although efficient local search algorithms typically incorporate problem-specific knowledge (often in the form of the neighbourhood relation and evaluation function), there are general, high-level strategies that have been shown to be effective across a broad range of combinatorial problems. Most of these general local search strategies involve randomisation to avoid search stagnation in or around local minima of the given evaluation function and are therefore captured in the general framework of Stochastic Local Search (SLS). SLS methods such as randomised iterative improvement, tabu search and dynamic local search have provided the basis for some of the most prominent and best performing algorithms for CSP and SAT. Other methods, including simulated annealing, evolutionary algorithms, ant colony optimisation and iterated local search have also been applied to these and many other constraint programming problems, and were shown to be effective for solving certain types of instances. These search strategies employ different mechanisms for balancing the exploration of the given search space (*diversification*) against the efficient exploitation of heuristic information (*intensification*). Intensification and diversification mechanism often interact in complex ways, and minor variations can have significant impact on the performance of the resulting algorithms.

For this reason, in combination with the fact that theoretical results in this area are difficult to obtain and typically very limited in their practical relevance, SLS algorithms are mostly studied empirically, by means of computational experiments. (It may be noted that a similar situation is encountered for most, if not all, other high-performance CSP

---

[4]The same applies, of course, to any other constraint programming algorithm that is evaluated empirically.

algorithms.) In the case of SLS algorithms for CSP, many empirical studies have been focused on distributions of relatively unstructured, random binary CSP instances. The same holds for MAX-CSP, and the situations for prominent special cases, such as SAT and MAX-SAT, is similar. While such instances can be useful for evaluating the efficacy of search strategies, they lack the type of structure found in many real-world problems. Consequently, there is an increasing emphasis on using structured problem instances for the empirical analysis of SLS algorithms for the CSP and related problems. This endeavour, as well as the comparability of empirical results between studies, is facilitated by public collections of benchmark problems, such as CSPLIB [32] and SATLIB [50].

Furthermore, while currently the design of new SLS algorithms largely resembles a craft in that it requires experience and intuition to a significant extent, there is substantial interest in developing more principled approaches that will facilitate the engineering of high-performance SLS algorithms. In this context, advanced empirical methods (see, *e.g.*, Chapter 4 of Hoos and Stützle [52]) in combination with frameworks that specifically support the formulation and implementation of local search algorithms (see Section 5.7) are likely to play a major role. Furthermore, our understanding of the factors causing the relative hardness of certain problem instances for a given SLS algorithm is fairly limited. The investigation of these factors, for example, by means of search space analysis, is an active research area with many open problems.

Another attractive research direction is to develop SLS algorithms that adapt their behaviour based on information collected during the search process or over runs on various problem instances. Interesting work in this area includes studies by Battiti and Tecchiolli [4], Glover [35] and Minton [75], as well as Boyan and Moore [9], Patterson and Kautz [83], Hoos [45], Mills [74], Hutter et al. [53], Burke and Newall [11] and [59].

It may be noted that in many ways, the development and understanding of SLS algorithms is significantly further advanced for SAT than for the general CSP. (The situation for MAX-SAT and MAX-CSP is analogous.) This is mostly caused by the fact that as a conceptually simpler problem, SAT for CNF formulae better facilitates the development, analysis and efficient implementation of SLS algorithms. This raises the question to which extent more efficient SLS algorithms for the general CSP can be obtained by augmenting suitably generalised high-performance SLS algorithms for SAT with specific methods for handling certain types of complex constraints known from other constraint programming approaches. Furthermore, it is likely that advanced SLS methods that have been demonstrated to be very successful in solving other combinatorial problems, such as iterated local search, variable depth search or scatter search, may still hold considerable and largely unexplored potential for solving constraint satisfaction and optimisation problems.

Overall, local search methods are among the most powerful and versatile tools for solving constraint programming problems. They give rise to a broad range of interesting research challenges, and continuing efforts to improve these methods and our understanding of them will further enhance their usefulness in a broad range of challenging real-world applications.

Bibliography

[1]   S. Abdullah, S. Ahmadi, E. Burke, and M. Dror. Applying Ahuja-Orlin's large neighbourhood for constructing examination timetabling solution. In *5th Interna-*

tional Conference on the Practice and Theory of Automated Timetabling (PATAT) pages 413–419, 2004.

[2]   R. Ahuja, O.Ergun, J. Orlin, and P. Punnen. A survey of very large scale neighborhood search techniques. *Discrete Applied Mathematics*, 123(1-3):75–102, 2002.

[3]   B. D. Backer, V. Furnon, P. Kilby, P. Prosser, and P. Shaw. Solving vehicle routing problems using constraint programming and meta heuristics. *Journal of Heuristics* 6(4):501–525, 2000.

[4]   R. Battiti and G. Tecchiolli. The reactive tabu search. *ORSA Journal on Computing* 6(2):126–140, 1994.

[5]   C. Bessière, E. Hebrard, and T. Walsh. Local consistencies in SAT. In *Theory and Applications of Satisfiability Testing, 6th International Conference (SAT 2003), Selected Revised Papers*, LNCS 2919, pages 299–314. Springer Verlag, 2004.

[6]   A. Biere, A. Cimatti, E. Clarke, and Y. Zhu. Symbolic model checking without BDDs. In *Tools and Algorithms for Construction and Analysis of Systems (TACAS '99)*, LNCS 1579, pages 193–207. Springer Verlag, Berlin, Germany, 1999.

[7]   S. Bistarelli, U. Montanari, and F. Rossi. Semiring-based constraint solving and optimization. *Journal of the ACM*, 44(2):201–236, 1997.

[8]   A. Bouju, J. Boyce, C. Dimitropoulos, G. vom Scheidt, and J. Taylor. Intelligent search for the radio link frequency assignment problem. In *International Conference on Digital Signal Processing*, Cyprus, 1995.

[9]   J. Boyan and A. Moore. Learning evaluation functions to improve optimization by local search. *Journal of Machine Learning Research*, 1:77–112, 2000.

[10]   R. Bradwell, P. M. J. Ford, E. Tsang, and R. Williams. An overview of the CACP project: modelling and solving constraint satisfaction/optimisation problems with minimal expert intervention. In *CP 2000 Workshop on Analysis and Visualization of Constraint Programs and Solvers*, 2000.

[11]   E. Burke and J. Newall. A new adaptive heuristic framework for examination timetabling problems. *Annals of Operations Research*, 129:107–134, 2004.

[12]   B. Cha and K. Iwama. Performance test of local search algorithms using new types of random CNF formulas. In *14th International Joint Conference on Artificial Intelligence*, pages 304–310. Morgan Kaufmann Publishers, San Francisco, CA, USA, 1995.

[13]   M. Chiarandini and T. Stützle. An application of iterated local search to the graph coloring problem. In *Computational Symposium on Graph Coloring and its Generalizations*, pages 112–125, Ithaca, New York, USA, 2002.

[14]   B. Craenen, A. Eiben, and J. van Hemert. Comparing evolutionary algorithms on binary constraint satisfaction problems. *IEEE Transactions on Evolutionary Computation*, 7(5):424–445, 2003.

[15]   J. Crawford and A. Baker. Experimental results on the application of satisfiability algorithms to scheduling problems. In *12th National Conference on Artificial Intelligence (AAAI-94)*, volume 2, pages 1092–1097, Seattle, Washington, USA, 1994 AAAI Press/MIT Press. ISBN 0-262-51078-2.

[16]   J. Culberson, I. Gent, and H. Hoos. On the probabilistic approximate completeness of WalkSAT for 2-SAT. Technical Report APES-15a-2000, APES Research Group, 2000.

[17]   A. Davenport. A comparison of complete and incomplete algorithms in the easy and hard regions. In *Workshop on Studying and Solving Really Hard Problems, 1st*

International Conference on Principles and Practice of Constraint Programming, pages 43–51, September 1995.

[18] A. Davenport. *Extensions and evaluation of GENET in constraint satisfaction*. PhD thesis, Department of Computer Science,University of Essex, Colchester, UK, 1997.

[19] A. Davenport and E. Tsang. Solving constraint satisfaction sequencing problems by iterative repair. In *1st International Conference on the Practical Application of Constraint Technologies and Logic Programming (PACLP)*, pages 345–357, London, April 1999.

[20] A. Davenport, E. Tsang, C. Wang, and K. Zhu. GENET: a connectionist architecture for solving constraint satisfaction problems by iterative improvement. In *12th National Conference for Artificial Intelligence*, pages 325–330, 1994.

[21] B. Dilkina, L. Duan, and W. Havens. Extending systematic local search for job shop scheduling problems. In *11th International Conference on Principles and Practice of Constraint Programming (CP 2005)*, LNCS 3709, pages 762–766. Springer-Verlag, 2005.

[22] M. Dorigo and T. Stützle. *Ant Colony Optimization*. MIT Press, Cambridge, MA, USA, 2004.

[23] J. Doyle. A truth maintenance system. *Artificial Intelligence*, 12:231–272, 1979.

[24] M. D. Ernst, T. D. Millstein, and D. S. Weld. Automatic SAT-compilation of planning problems. In *15th International Joint Conference on Artificial Intelligence*, pages 1169–1177. Morgan Kaufmann Publishers, San Francisco, CA, USA, 1997.

[25] A. Fink and S. Voß. Hotframe: A heuristic optimization framework. In *Optimization Software Class Libraries*, pages 81–154. Kluwer, 2002.

[26] J. Frank. Weighting for Godot: Learning heuristics for GSAT. In *13th National Conference on Artificial Intelligence*, pages 776–783. AAAI Press / The MIT Press, Menlo Park, CA, USA, 1996.

[27] J. Frank. Learning short-term clause weights for GSAT. In *15th International Joint Conference on Artificial Intelligence*, pages 384–389. Morgan Kaufmann Publishers, San Francisco, CA, USA, 1997.

[28] E. Freuder and R. Wallace. Partial constraint satisfaction. *Artificial Intelligence, Special Volume on Constraint Based Reasoning*, 58(1-3):21–70, 1992.

[29] P. Galinier and J.-K. Hao. Tabu search for maximal constraint satisfaction problems. In *Principles and Practice of Constraint Programming – CP 1997*, LNCS 1330, pages 196–208. Springer Verlag, Berlin, Germany, 1997.

[30] P. Galinier and J. K. Hao. Hybrid evolutionary algorithms for graph coloring. *Journal of Combinatorial Optimization*, 3(4):379–397, 1999.

[31] L. D. Gaspero and A. Schaerf. Easylocal++: an object-oriented framework for the flexible design of local-search algorithms. *Software Practice and Experience*, 33 (8):733–765, 2003.

[32] I. Gent and T. Walsh. CSPLib: a benchmark library for constraints. Technical report, APES-09-1999, 1999.

[33] I. P. Gent and T. Walsh. Towards an understanding of hill–climbing procedures for SAT. In *10th National Conference on Artificial Intelligence*, pages 28–33. AAAI Press / The MIT Press, Menlo Park, CA, USA, 1993.

[34] M. Ginsberg. Dynamic backtracking. *Journal of Artificial Intelligence Research*, 1: 25–46, 1993.

[35] F. Glover. Tabu search and adaptive memory programming — advances, applica-

tions and challenges. In *Interfaces in Computer Science and Operations Research* Kluwer Academic Publishers, 1996.

[36] F. Glover and M. Laguna. *Tabu Search*. Kluwer Academic Publishers, Boston, MA, USA, 1997.

[37] J. Gu and R. Puri. Asynchronous Circuit Synthesis with Boolean Satisfiability. *IEEE Transactions of Computer-Aided Design of Integrated Circuits and Systems*, 14(8): 961–973, 1995.

[38] J. Gu, P. Purdom, J. Franco, and B. Wah. Algorithms for the satisfiability (SAT) problem: A survey. In *Satisfiability problem: Theory and Applications*, volume 35 of *DIMACS Series on Discrete Mathematics and Theoretical Computer Science* pages 19–151. American Mathematical Society, Providence, RI, USA, 1997.

[39] J.-K. Hao and R. Dorne. A new population-based method for satisfiability problems. In *11th European Conference on Artificial Intelligence*, pages 135–139, Amsterdam, 1994. John Wiley & Sons.

[40] W. Havens and B. Dilkina. A hybrid schema for systematic local search. In *Advances in Artificial Intelligence: 17th Conference of the Canadian Society for Computational Studies of Intelligence*, LNCS 3060, pages 248–260. Springer Verlag, 2004.

[41] P. V. Hentenryck. *The OPL Optimization Programming Language*. MIT Press, Cambridge, MA, USA, 1999.

[42] P. V. Hentenryck and L. Michel. *Constraint-Based Local Search*. MIT Press, Cambridge, MA, USA, 2005.

[43] D. Holstein and P. Moscato. Memetic algorithms using guided local search, a case study. In *New ideas in optimization*, pages 235–243. McGraw Hill, 1999.

[44] H. Hoos. *Stochastic Local Search — Methods, Models, Applications*. PhD thesis, TU Darmstadt, FB Informatik, Darmstadt, Germany, 1998.

[45] H. Hoos. An adaptive noise mechanism for WalkSAT. In *18th National Conference on Artificial Intelligence*, pages 655–660. AAAI Press / The MIT Press, Menlo Park, CA, USA, 2002.

[46] H. Hoos. A mixture-model for the behaviour of SLS algorithms for SAT. In *18th National Conference on Artificial Intelligence*, pages 661–667. AAAI Press / The MIT Press, Menlo Park, CA, USA, 2002.

[47] H. Hoos. On the run-time behaviour of stochastic local search algorithms for SAT. In *16th National Conference on Artificial Intelligence*, pages 661–666. AAAI Press / The MIT Press, Menlo Park, CA, USA, 1999.

[48] H. Hoos. SAT-encodings, search space structure, and local search performance. In *16th International Joint Conference on Artificial Intelligence*, pages 296–302. Morgan Kaufmann Publishers, San Francisco, CA, USA, 1999.

[49] H. Hoos and T. Stützle. Local search algorithms for SAT: An empirical evaluation. *Journal of Automated Reasoning*, 24(4):421–481, 2000.

[50] H. Hoos and T. Stützle. SATLIB: An Online Resource for Research on SAT. In *SAT 2000*, volume 63, pages 283–292. IOS Press, Amsterdam, The Netherlands, 2000.

[51] H. Hoos and T. Stützle. Characterising the behaviour of stochastic local search. *Artificial Intelligence*, 112(1–2):213–232, 1999.

[52] H. Hoos and T. Stützle. *Stochastic Local Search: Foundations and Applications* Elsevier / Morgan Kaufmann, 2004.

[53] F. Hutter, D. A. D. Tompkins, and H. H. Hoos. Scaling and probabilistic smoothing:

Efficient dynamic local search for SAT. In *Principles and Practice of Constraint Programming – CP 2002*, LNCS 2470, pages 233–248. Springer Verlag, Berlin, Germany, 2002.

[54] N. Jin. Equilibrium selection by co-evolution for bargaining problems under incomplete information about time preferences. In *Congress on Evolutionary Computation (CEC 2005)*, pages 2661–2668, Edinburgh, September 2005.

[55] D. S. Johnson, C. R. Aragon, L. A. McGeoch, and C. Schevon. Optimization by simulated annealing: An experimental evaluation: Part II, graph coloring and number partitioning. *Operations Research*, 39(3):378–406, 1991.

[56] K. Kask and R. Dechter. GSAT and local consistency. In *14th International Joint Conference on Artificial Intelligence*, pages 616–623. Morgan Kaufmann Publishers, San Francisco, CA, USA, 1995.

[57] K. Kask and R. Dechter. A graph-based method for improving GSAT. In *13th National Conference on Artificial Intelligence*, pages 350–355. AAAI Press / The MIT Press, Menlo Park, CA, USA, 1996.

[58] H. Kautz and B. Selman. Pushing the envelope: Planning, propositional logic, and stochastic search. In *13th National Conference on Artificial Intelligence*, volume 2, pages 1194–1201. AAAI Press / The MIT Press, Menlo Park, CA, USA, 1996.

[59] M. Kern. *Parameter Adaptation in heuristic search - a population-based approach.* PhD thesis, Department of Computer Science, University of Essex, Colchester, UK, 2005.

[60] P. Kilby, P. Prosser, and P. Shaw. A comparison of traditional and constraint-based heuristic methods on vehicle routing problems with side constraints. *Constraints*, 5 (4):389–414, 2000.

[61] B. Koopman. The theory of search, part iii, the optimum distribution of searching effort. *Operations Research*, 5:613–626, 1957.

[62] F. Laburthe and Y. Caseau. SALSA: A language for search algorithms. In *4th International Conference on Principles and Practice of Constraint Programming*, LNCS 1520, pages 310–324. Springer Verlag, 1998.

[63] H. C. Lau. A new approach for weighted constraint satisfaction. *Constraints*, 7(2): 151–165, 2002.

[64] T. Lau. *Guilded Genetic Algorithm.* PhD thesis, Department of Computer Science, University of Essex, Colchester, UK, 1999.

[65] T. Lau and E. Tsang. Solving the processor configuration problem with a mutation-based genetic algorithm. *International Journal on Artificial Intelligence Tools (IJAIT)*, 6(4):567–585, December 1997.

[66] T. Lau and E. Tsang. Guided genetic algorithm and its application to radio link frequency assignment problems. *Constraints*, 6(4):373–398, 2001.

[67] J. Lee, H. Leung, and H. Won. Extending GENET for non-binary CSPs. In *17th International Conference on Tools with Artificial Intelligence*, pages 338–342, 1995.

[68] J. Lee, H. Leung, and H. Won. Towards a more efficient stochastic constraint solver. In *2nd International Conference on Principles and Practice of Constraint Programming*, pages 338–352, Cambridge, Massachusetts, USA, August 1996.

[69] C. M. Li and W. Huang. Diversification and determinism in local search for satisfiability. In *8th International Conference on Theory and Applications of Satisfiability Testing (SAT 2005)*, LNCS 3569, pages 158–172. Springer Verlag, 2005.

[70] J. Li. *FGP: A genetic programming based tool for financial forecasting.* PhD thesis,

Department of Computer Science, University of Essex, Colchester, UK, 2001.

[71] D. Luenberger, editor. *Linear and nonlinear programming*. Addison-Wesley Publishing Co., Inc., 1984.

[72] B. Mazure, L. Sais, and E. Gregoire. TWSAT: A new local search algorithm for SAT – performance and analysis. In *14th National Conference on Artificial Intelligence* pages 281–285. AAAI Press / The MIT Press, Menlo Park, CA, USA, 1997.

[73] D. McAllester, B. Selman, and H. Kautz. Evidence for invariants in local search. In *14th National Conference on Artificial Intelligence*, pages 321–326. AAAI Press / The MIT Press, Menlo Park, CA, USA, 1997.

[74] P. Mills. *Extensions to guided local search*. PhD thesis, Department of Computer Science, University of Essex, Colchester, UK, 2002.

[75] S. Minton. Automatically configuring constraint satisfaction programs, a case study. *Constraints*, 1(1&2):7–43, 1996.

[76] S. Minton, M. D. Johnston, A. B. Philips, and P. Laird. Solving large-scale constraint satisfaction and scheduling problems using a heuristic repair method. In *8th National Conference on Artificial Intelligence*, pages 17–24. AAAI Press / The MIT Press, Menlo Park, CA, USA, 1990.

[77] S. Minton, M. Johnston, A. Philips, and P. Laird. Minimizing conflicts: A heuristic repair method for constraint satisfaction and scheduling problems. *Artificial Intelligence*, 58(1–3):161–205, 1992.

[78] P. Morris. The breakout method for escaping from local minima. In *National Conference on Artificial Intelligence*, pages 40–45, 1993.

[79] D. Neto. *Efficient Cluster Compensation for Lin-Kernighan Heuristics*. PhD thesis, University of Toronto, Department of Computer Science, Toronto, Canada, 1999.

[80] C. H. Papadimitriou. On selecting a satisfying truth assignment. In *32nd Annual IEEE Symposium on Foundations of Computer Science*, pages 163–169. IEEE Computer Society Press, Los Alamitos, CA, USA, 1991.

[81] L. Paquete and T. Stützle. An experimental investigation of iterated local search for coloring graphs. In *Applications of Evolutionary Computing*, LNCS 2279, pages 122–131. Springer Verlag, Berlin, Germany, 2002.

[82] J. Paredis. Genetic state-space search for constrained optimization problems. In *13th International Joint Conference on Artificial Intelligence*, pages 967–972, 1993.

[83] D. J. Patterson and H. Kautz. Auto-walksat: A self-tuning implementation of walksat. In *LICS 2001 Workshop on Theory and Applications of Satisfiability Testing (SAT 2001)*. Elsevier, Amsterdam, The Netherlands, 2001.

[84] S. Prestwich. Local search on SAT-encoded CSPs. In *6th International Conference on Theory and Applications of Satisfiability Testing (SAT 2003)*, pages 388–399, 2003.

[85] S. Prestwich. Stochastic local search in constrained spaces. In *Practical Applications of Constraint Technology and Logic Programming (PACLP '00)*, pages 27–39, 2000.

[86] T. Richards, Y. Jiang, and B. Richards. Ng-backmarking – an algorithm for constraint satisfaction. *British Telecom Technology Journal*, 13(1):102–109, 1995.

[87] M. Riff Rojas. From quasi-solutions to solution: an evolutionary algorithm to solve CSPs. In *2nd International Conference on Principles and Practice of Constraint Programming*, pages 367–381, August 1996.

[88] T. Schiex, H. Fargier, and G. Verfaillie. Valued constraint satisfaction problems:

Hard and easy problems. In *14th International Joint Conference on Artificial Intelligence*, pages 631–639. Morgan Kaufmann Publishers, San Francisco, CA, USA, 1995.

[89] D. Schuurmans, F. Southey, and R. C. Holte. The exponentiated subgradient algorithm for heuristic Boolean programming. In *17th International Joint Conference on Artificial Intelligence*, pages 334–341. Morgan Kaufmann Publishers, San Francisco, CA, USA, 2001.

[90] B. Selman and H. Kautz. Domain-independent extensions to GSAT: Solving large structured satisfiability problems. In *13th International Joint Conference on Artificial Intelligence*, pages 290–295. Morgan Kaufmann Publishers, San Francisco, CA, USA, 1993.

[91] B. Selman, H. Levesque, and D. Mitchell. A new method for solving hard satisfiability problems. In *10th National Conference on Artificial Intelligence*, pages 440–446. AAAI Press / The MIT Press, Menlo Park, CA, USA, 1992.

[92] B. Selman, H. Kautz, and B. Cohen. Noise strategies for improving local search. In *12th National Conference on Artificial Intelligence*, pages 337–343. AAAI Press / The MIT Press, Menlo Park, CA, USA, 1994.

[93] Y. Shang and B. W. Wah. A discrete Lagrangian-based global-search method for solving satisfiability problems. *Journal of Global Optimization*, 12(1):61–99, 1998.

[94] K. Smyth, H. H. Hoos, and T. Stützle. Iterated robust tabu search for MAX-SAT. In *Advances in Artificial Intelligence, 16th Conference of the Canadian Society for Computational Studies of Intelligence*, LNCS 2671, pages 129–144. Springer Verlag, Berlin, Germany, 2003.

[95] C. Solnon. Solving permutation constraint satisfaction problems with artificial ants. In *14th European Conference on Artificial Intelligence*, pages 118–122, Berlin, Germany, August 2000.

[96] C. Solnon. Ants can solve constraint satisfaction problems. *IEEE Transactions on Evolutionary Computation*, 6(4):347–357, 2001.

[97] W. M. Spears. Simulated annealing for hard satisfiability problems. Technical report, Naval Research Laboratory, Washington D.C., USA, 1993.

[98] O. Steinmann, A. Strohmaier, and T. Stützle. Tabu search vs. random walk. In *KI-97: Advances in Artificial Intelligence*, LNAI 1303, pages 337–348. Springer Verlag, Berlin, Germany, 1997.

[99] L. D. Stone. The process of search planning: current approaches and continuing problems. *Operations Research*, 31:207–233, 1983.

[100] P. Stuckey and V. Tam. Improving evolutionary algorithms for efficient constraint satifaction. *International Journal on Artificial Intelligence Tools (IJAIT)*, World Scientific, 8(4):363–383, 1999.

[101] T. Stützle. *Local Search Algorithms for Combinatorial Problems — Analysis, Improvements, and New Applications*. PhD thesis, TU Darmstadt, FB Informatik, Darmstadt, Germany, 1998.

[102] J. Thornton, D. Pham, S. Bain, and V. Ferreira. Additive versus multiplicative clause weighting for SAT. In *19th National Conference on Artificial Intelligence*, pages 191–196. AAAI Press / The MIT Press, Menlo Park, CA, USA, 2004.

[103] D. Tompkins and H. Hoos. Warped landscapes and random acts of SAT solving. In *8th International Symposium on Artificial Intelligence and Mathematics*, 2004.

[104] E. Tsang. *Foundations of constraint satisfaction*. Academic Press, London and San

Diego, 1993.

[105] E. Tsang and J. Li. EDDIE for financial forecasting. In *Genetic Algorithms and Programming in Computational Finance*, pages 161–174. Kluwer Academic Publishers, 2002.

[106] E. Tsang and C. Voudouris. Fast local search and guided local search and their application to British Telecom's workforce scheduling problem. *Operations Research Letters*, 20(3):119–127, 1997.

[107] E. Tsang and C. Wang. A generic neural network approach for constraint satisfaction problems. In *Neural network applications*, pages 12–22. Springer-Verlag, 1992.

[108] E. Tsang and T. Warwick. Applying genetic algorithms to constraint satisfaction problems. In *9th European Conference on AI*, pages 649–654, 1990.

[109] E. Tsang, J. Ford, P. Mills, R. Bradwell, R. Williams, and P. Scott. Towards a practical engineering tool for rostering. *Annals of Operational Research, Special Issue on Personnel Scheduling and Planning*, 2006 (to appear).

[110] J. van Hemert and C. Solnon. A study into ant colony optimization, evolutionary computation and constraint programming on binary constraint satisfaction problems. In *Evolutionary Computation in Combinatorial Optimization (EvoCOP 2004)*, LNCS 3004, pages 114–123. Springer Verlag, Berlin, Germany, 2004.

[111] C. Voudouris and E. Tsang. Partial constraint satisfaction problems and guided local search. In *Practical Application of Constraint Technology (PACT'96)*, pages 337–356, London, April 1996.

[112] C. Voudouris and E. Tsang. Solving the radio link frequency assignment problem using guided local search. In *13th NATO symposium on Frequency Assignment, Sharing and Conservation Systems (Aerospace), Research and Technology Organization (RTO)*. North Atlantic Treaty Organization (NATO), 1999.

[113] C. Voudouris and E. Tsang. Guided local search, chapter 7. In *Handbook of metaheuristics*. Kluwer, 2003.

[114] C. Voudouris, R. Dorne, D. Lesaint, and A. Liret. iopt: A software toolkit for heuristic search methods. In *7th International Conference on Principles and Practice of Constraint Programming*, pages 716–729. Springer Verlag, 2001.

[115] B. Wah and Y. Shang. Discrete Lagrangian-based search for solving MAX-SAT problems. In *15th International Joint Conference on Artificial Intelligence*, pages 378–383, 1997.

[116] R. J. Wallace and E. C. Freuder. Heuristic methods for over-constrained constraint satisfaction problems. In *Over-Constrained Systems*, LNCS 1106, pages 207–216. Springer Verlag, Berlin, Germany, 1995.

[117] J. P. Walser. Solving linear pseudo-Boolean constraint problems with local search. In *14th National Conference on Artificial Intelligence*, pages 269–274. AAAI Press / The MIT Press, Menlo Park, CA, USA, 1997.

[118] J. P. Walser. *Integer Optimization by Local Search: A Domain-Independent Approach*. LNCS 1637. Springer Verlag, Berlin, Germany, 1999.

[119] C. Wang and E. Tsang. Solving constraint satisfaction problems using neural-networks. In *IEE 2nd International Conference on Artificial Neural Networks*, pages 295–299, 1991.

[120] T. Warwick and E. Tsang. Using a genetic algorithm to tackle the processors configuration problem. In *ACM Symposium on Applied Computing (SAC)*, pages 217–221, 1994.

[121] Z. Wu and B. W. Wah. An efficient global-search strategy in discrete Lagrangian methods for solving hard satisfiability problems. In *17th National Conference on Artificial Intelligence*, pages 310–315. AAAI Press / The MIT Press, Menlo Park, CA, USA, 2000.

[122] Z. Wu and B. W. Wah. Trap escaping strategies in discrete Lagrangian methods for solving hard satisfiability and maximum satisfiability problems. In *16th National Conference on Artificial Intelligence*, pages 673–678. AAAI Press / The MIT Press, Menlo Park, CA, USA, 1999.

[123] M. Yagiura and T. Ibaraki. Efficient 2 and 3-flip neighborhood search algorithms for the MAX SAT: Experimental evaluation. *Journal of Heuristics*, 7(5):423–442, 2001.

[124] X. Yao. Dynamic neighbourhood size in simulated annealing. In *International Joint Conference on Neural Networks (IJCNN'92)*, volume 1, pages 411–416. IEEE Press, Piscataway, NJ, USA, 1992.

[125] X. Yu, W. Zheng, B. Wu, and X. Yao. A novel penalty function approach to constrained optimization problems with genetic algorithms. *Journal of Advanced Computational Intelligence*, 2(6):208–213, 1998.

[126] H. Zhang. Generating college conference basketball schedules by a SAT solver. In *5th International Symposium on the Theory and Applications of Satisfiability Testing (SAT 2002)*, pages 281–291, 2002.

Chapter 6

Global Constraints

Willem-Jan van Hoeve and Irit Katriel

A *global constraint* is a constraint that captures a relation between a non-fixed number of variables. An example is the constraint $\mathtt{alldifferent}(x_1, \ldots, x_n)$, which specifies that the values assigned to the variables $x_1, \ldots, x_n$ must be pairwise distinct. Typically, a global constraint is semantically redundant in the sense that the same relation can be expressed as the conjunction of several simpler constraints. Having shorthands for frequently recurring patterns clearly simplifies the programming task. What may be less obvious is that global constraints also facilitate the work of the constraint solver by providing it with a better view of the structure of the problem.

One of the central ideas of constraint programming is the propagation-search technique, which consists of a traversal of the search space of the given constraint satisfaction problem (CSP) while detecting "dead ends" as early as possible. An algorithm that performs only the search component would enumerate all possible assignments of values to the variables until it either finds a solution to the CSP or exhausts all possible assignments and concludes that a solution does not exist. Such an exhaustive search has an exponential-time complexity in the *best case*, and this is where propagation comes in: It allows the constraint solver to prune useless parts of the search space without enumerating them. For example, if the CSP contains the constraint $x + y = 3$ and both x and y are set to 1, we can conclude that regardless of the values assigned to other variables, the partial assignment we have constructed so far cannot lead to a solution. Thus it is safe to backtrack and reverse some of our previous decisions (see also Chapter 3, "Constraint Propagation", and Chapter 4 "Backtracking Search Algorithms for CSPs").

The type of propagation that we will discuss in this chapter is called *filtering* of the variable domains. The filtering task is to examine the variables which were not assigned values yet, and remove useless values from their domains. A value is useless if it cannot participate in any solution that conforms with the assignments already made. Since it is, in general, NP-hard to determine whether or not a value in the domain of a variable is useful for the CSP, the solver filters separately with respect to each of the constraints. If a value is useless with respect to one of the constraints, then it is also useless with respect to the whole CSP, but not vice versa. In other words, filtering separately with respect to each constraint allows false-positives (keeping a value which is useless for the CSP), but not false-negatives (removing a useful value). We then arrive at a tradeoff between the *efficiency* of the filtering (i.e., the running time) and its *effectiveness* (i.e., how many useless values were identified). "Good" constraints are constraints that address this tradeoff by allowing significant filtering with a low computational cost.

A *filtering algorithm* for a constraint C is an algorithm that filters the domains of variables with respect to C. If the algorithm removes every useless value from the domain of every variable that C is defined on, we say that it achieves *complete filtering*. If it removes only some of the useless values, we say that it performs *partial filtering*.

This chapter explores the topic of globals constraints. Our goal is to familiarize the reader with the important concepts of the field, which include different types of constraints, different measures of filtering and different compromises between efficiency and effectiveness of filtering. We will illustrate each of the concepts with some examples, that is, specific global constraints and filtering algorithms. We believe that our (obviously non-exhaustive) selection of constraints and algorithms suffices to provide the reader with an overview of the state of the art of research on global constraints.

The rest of the chapter is organized as follows. Section 6.1 provides notation and preliminaries for the rest of the chapter. In Section 6.2 we describe some useful global constraints. In Section 6.3 we describe efficient algorithms that achieve complete filtering for several global constraints. In Section 6.4 we describe global optimization constraints, i.e., constraints that encapsulate optimization criteria, and filtering algorithms for them. Section 6.5 covers the topic of partial filtering algorithms, beginning with their motivation through definitions of different measures of filtering to actual examples of partial filtering algorithms. In Section 6.6 we describe complex variable types, constraints defined on them and filtering algorithms for such constraints. Finally, in Section 6.7 we review some recent ideas and directions for further research.

6.1 Notation and Preliminaries

6.1.1 Constraint Programming

The *domain* of a variable x, denoted $D(x)$, is a finite set of elements that can be assigned to x. For a set of variables X we denote the union of their domains by $D(X) = \cup_{x \in X} D(x)$

Let $X = \{x_1, \ldots, x_k\}$ be a set of variables. A *constraint* C on X is a subset of the Cartesian product of the domains of the variables in X, i.e., $C \subseteq D(x_1) \times \cdots \times D(x_k)$ A tuple $(d_1, \ldots, d_k) \in C$ is called a *solution* to C. Equivalently, we say that a solution $(d_1, \ldots, d_k) \in C$ is an assignment of the value d_i to the variable x_i, for all $1 \leq i \leq k$, and that this assignment *satisfies* C. If $C = \emptyset$, we say that it is *inconsistent*. When a constraint C is defined on a set X of k variables together with a certain set p of ℓ parameters, we will denote it by $C(X, p)$, but consider it to be a set of k-tuples (and not $k + \ell$-tuples).

A *constraint satisfaction problem* (*CSP*) is a finite set of variables X, together with a finite set of constraints C, each on a subset of X. A *solution to a CSP* is an assignment of a value $d \in D(x)$ to each $x \in X$, such that all constraints are satisfied simultaneously.

Given a constraint C defined on the variables $\{x_1, \ldots, x_k\}$, the filtering task is to shrink the domain of each variable such that it still contains all values that this variable can assume in a solution to C. An algorithm that achieves complete filtering, computes, for every $1 \leq j \leq k$,

$$D(x_j) \leftarrow D(x_j) \cap \{v_i \mid D(x_1) \times \cdots \times D(x_{j-1}) \times \{v_i\} \times D(x_{j+1}) \times \cdots \times D(x_k) \cap C \neq \emptyset\}.$$

In many applications, we wish to find a solution to a CSP that is optimal with respect to certain criteria. A *constraint optimization problem* (*COP*) is a CSP P defined on the variables $x_1, \ldots, x_n$, together with an *objective function* $f : D(x_1) \times \cdots \times D(x_n) \to \mathbb{Q}$ that assigns a value to each assignment of values to the variables. An *optimal solution* to a minimization (maximization) COP is a solution d to P that minimizes (maximizes) the value of $f(d)$. The objective function value is often represented by a variable z, together with the "constraint" `maximize` z or `minimize` z for a maximization or a minimization problem, respectively.

6.1.2 Graph Theory

Basic notions

A *graph* or *undirected graph* is a pair $G = (V, E)$, where V is a finite set of vertices and $E \subseteq V \times V$ is a multiset[1] of *unordered* pairs of vertices, called *edges*. An edge "between" $u \in V$ and $v \in V$ is denoted by $\{u, v\}$. A graph G is *bipartite* if there exists a partition $S \,\dot\cup\, T$ of V such that $E \subseteq S \times T$. We then write $G = (S, T, E)$.

A *walk* in a graph $G = (V, E)$ is a sequence $P = v_0, e_1, v_1, \ldots, e_k, v_k$ where $k \geq 0$, $v_0, \ldots, v_k \in V$, $e_1, \ldots, e_k \in E$ and $e_i = \{v_{i-1}, v_i\}$ for $1 \leq i \leq k$. If there is no confusion, P may be denoted by $v_0, v_1, \ldots, v_k$ or $e_1, e_2, \ldots, e_k$. A walk is called a *path* if $v_0, \ldots, v_k$ are distinct. A closed path, i.e., $v_0 = v_k$, is called a *circuit*.

An *induced subgraph* of a graph $G = (V, E)$ is a graph $G' = (V', E')$ such that $V' \subseteq V$ and $E' = \{\{u, v\} \mid u \in V', v \in V', \{u, v\} \in E\}$. A *component* or *connected component* of a graph $G = (V, E)$ is an induced subgraph $G' = (V', E')$ of G such that there exists a u-v path in G' for every pair $u, v \in V'$, and G' is maximal with respect to V'.

A *digraph* or *directed graph* is a pair $G = (V, A)$ where V is a finite set of vertices and $A \subseteq V \times V$ is a multiset of *ordered* pairs of vertices, called *arcs*. A pair occurring more than once in A is called a *multiple arc*. An arc from $u \in V$ to $v \in V$ is denoted by (u, v). The set of arcs incoming into a vertex u is denoted by $\delta^{in}(u) = A \cap (V \times \{u\})$ and the set of arcs outgoing from a vertex u is denoted by $\delta^{out}(u) = A \cap (\{u\} \times V)$. Similarly to undirected bipartite graphs, a directed graph $G = (V, A)$ is *bipartite* if there exists a partition $S \,\dot\cup\, T$ of V such that $A \subseteq (S \times T) \cup (T \times S)$. We then write $G = (S, T, A)$.

A *directed walk* in a directed graph $G = (V, A)$ is a sequence $P = v_0, a_1, v_1, \ldots, a_k, v_k$ where $k \geq 0$, $v_0, \ldots, v_k \in V$, $a_1, \ldots, a_k \in A$ and $a_i = (v_{i-1}, v_i)$ for $1 \leq i \leq k$. Again, if there is no confusion, P may be denoted by $v_0, v_1, \ldots, v_k$ or $a_1, a_2, \ldots, a_k$. A directed walk is called a *directed path* if $v_0, \ldots, v_k$ are distinct. A closed directed path, i.e., $v_0 = v_k$, is called a *directed circuit*.

An induced subgraph of a digraph $G = (V, A)$ is a graph $G' = (V', A')$ such that $V' \subseteq V$ and $A' = A \cap (V' \times V')$. A *strongly connected component* of a digraph $G = (V, A)$ is an induced subgraph $G' = (V', A')$ of G such that there exists a directed u-v path in G' for every pair $u, v \in V'$, and G' is maximal with respect to V'.

---

[1] A multiset is a set in which an element may occur more than once.

Matching theory

Given an undirected graph $G = (V, E)$, a *matching* in G is a set $M \subseteq E$ of disjoint edges, i.e., no two edges in M share a vertex. A matching is said to *cover* a vertex v if v belongs to some edge in M. For a set $S \subseteq V$, we say that M covers S if it covers every vertex in S. A vertex $v \in V$ is called *M-free* if M does not cover v. The *cardinality* of a matching M is the number of edges in it, $|M|$. The *maximum cardinality matching problem* is the problem of finding a matching of maximum cardinality in a graph.

Let M be a matching in a graph $G = (V, E)$. A path P in G is called M-*augmenting* if P has odd length, its ends are not covered by M, and its edges are alternatingly out of and in M. A circuit C in G is called M-*alternating* if its edges are alternatingly out of and in M. Given an M-augmenting path P, the symmetric difference[2] of M and P gives a matching M' with $|M'| = |M| + 1$. Furthermore, the existence of an M-alternating path is a *necessary* condition for the existence of a matching of larger cardinality:

Theorem 6.1 (Petersen [50]). *Let $G = (V, E)$ be a graph, and let M be a matching in G. Then M is a maximum-cardinality matching if and only if there does not exist an M-augmenting path in G.*

Hence, a maximum-cardinality matching can be found by repeatedly finding an M augmenting path in G and using it to extend M. On a bipartite graph $G = (U, W, E)$, this can be done with the following method, due to van der Waerden [67] and König [38]. Let M be the current matching. Construct the directed bipartite graph $G_M = (U, W, A)$ by orienting all edges in M from W to U and all other edges from U to W, i.e.,

$$
\begin{aligned}
A = \quad & \{(w, u) \mid \{u, w\} \in M, u \in U, w \in W\} \ \cup \\
& \{(u, w) \mid \{u, w\} \in E \setminus M, u \in U, w \in W\}.
\end{aligned}
$$

Then every directed path in G_M starting from an M-free vertex in U and ending in an M-free vertex in W corresponds to an M-augmenting path in G. By choosing $|U| \le |W$ we need to find at most $|U|$ such paths. As each path can be identified in at most $O(|A|$ time by breadth-first search, the time complexity of this algorithm is $O(|U| |A|)$.

Hopcroft and Karp [28] improved this running time to $O(|U|^{1/2} |A|)$, where we choose again $|U| \le |W|$. Instead of repeatedly augmenting M along a single M-augmenting path, the idea is to repeatedly augment M simultaneously along a collection of disjoint M-augmenting paths. Such a collection of paths can again be found in $O(|A|)$ time. By reasoning on the lengths of the alternating paths, one can show that the algorithm needs only $O(|U|^{1/2})$ iterations, leading to a total time complexity of $O(|U|^{1/2} |A|)$.

Flow theory

Let $G = (V, A)$ be a directed graph and let $s, t \in V$. A function $f : A \to \mathbb{R}$ is called a *flow from s to t*, or an *s-t flow*, if

$$
\begin{array}{llll}
(i) & f(a) \ge 0 & \text{for each } a \in A, \\
(ii) & f(\delta^{\text{out}}(v)) = f(\delta^{\text{in}}(v)) & \text{for each } v \in V \setminus \{s, t\}.
\end{array} \tag{6.1}
$$

---

[2]For two sets A and B, the *symmetric difference* $A \oplus B$ is the set of elements that belong to A or B but not both. Formally, $A \oplus B = (A \cup B) \setminus (A \cap B)$.

where for any set S of arcs, $f(S) = \sum_{a \in S} f(a)$. Property $(6.1)(ii)$ ensures *flow conservation*, i.e., for a vertex $v \neq s, t$, the amount of flow entering v is equal to the amount of flow leaving v.

The *value* of an s-t flow f is defined to be

$$\text{value}(f) = f(\delta^{\text{out}}(s)) - f(\delta^{\text{in}}(s)).$$

In other words, the value of a flow is the net amount of flow leaving s, which by flow conservation must be equal to the net amount of flow entering t.

In a flow network, each arc a is associated with a *requirement* $[d(a), c(a)]$ where $c(a) \geq d(a) \geq 0$. Viewing $d(a)$ as the "demand" of a and $c(a)$ as its "capacity", we say that a flow f is *feasible* in the network if $d(a) \leq f(a) \leq c(a)$ for every $a \in A$.

Let $w : A \to \mathbb{R}$ be a "weight" (or "cost") function for the arcs. For a directed path P in G we define $w(P) = \sum_{a \in P} w(a)$. Similarly for a directed circuit. The *weight* of any flow $f : A \to \mathbb{R}$ is defined to be

$$\text{weight}(f) = \sum_{a \in A} w(a) f(a).$$

A feasible flow f is called a *minimum-weight flow* if $\text{weight}(f) \leq \text{weight}(f')$ for any feasible flow f'. Given a digraph $G = (V, A)$ with $s, t \in V$, the *minimum-weight flow problem* is to find a minimum-weight s-t flow in G.

Let f be an s-t flow in G. The *residual graph* of G with respect to f is defined as $G_f = (V, A_f)$ where for each $(u, v) \in A$, if $f(u, v) < c(u, v)$ then $(u, v) \in A_f$ with residual demand $\max\{d(u, v) - f(u, v), 0\}$ and residual capacity $c(u, v) - f(u, v)$, and if $f(u, v) > d(u, v)$ then $(v, u) \in A_f$ with residual demand 0 and residual capacity $f(v, u) - d(v, u)$. Intuitively, if the capacity of an arc is not exceeded, then the residual demand indicates how much more flow *must* be sent along this arc for its demand to be fulfilled and the residual capacity indicates how much additional flow *can* be sent along this arc without exceeding its capacity. If the flow on an arc is strictly higher than its demand, then the residual capacity (on an arc which is oriented in the reverse direction) indicates by how much we may reduce the flow on this arc, while still fulfilling its demand.

Let P be a directed path in G_f. Every arc $a \in P$ appears in G either in the same orientation (as the arc a) or in reverse direction (as the arc a^{-1}). The characteristic vector of P is defined as follows:

$$\chi^P(a) = \begin{cases} 1 & \text{if } P \text{ traverses } a, \\ -1 & \text{if } P \text{ traverses } a^{-1}, \\ 0 & \text{if } P \text{ traverses neither } a \text{ nor } a^{-1}, \end{cases}$$

For a directed circuit C in G_f, we define $\chi^C \in \{-1, 0, 1\}^A$ similarly.

Using the above notation, a feasible s-t flow in G with minimum weight can be found using Algorithm 6.1, which is sometimes referred to as the *successive shortest paths algorithm*, due to Ford and Fulkerson [18], Jewell [31], Busacker and Gowen [11], and Iri [30]. It begins by adding the arc (t, s) to G, with demand 0 and infinite capacity. This simplifies the computations because we no longer need to consider s and t as special vertices; all we need in order to have a feasible flow is to ensure that flow conservation holds at every

---

Algorithm 6.1: Minimum-weight feasible s-t flow in $G = (V, A)$

---

set $f = \vec{0}$

add the arc (t, s) with $d(t, s) = 0, c(t, s) = \infty, w(t, s) = 0$ and $f(t, s) = 0$ to G

while *there exists an arc* (u, v) *with* $f(u, v) < d(u, v)$ **do**

    compute a directed v-u path P in G_f minimizing $w(P)$

    if *P does not exist* **then** stop (no feasible flow exists)

    else define the directed circuit $C = P, u, v$

    reset $f = f + \varepsilon\chi^C$, where ε is maximal subject to $\vec{0} \leq f + \varepsilon\chi^P \leq \vec{c}$ and

    $f(u, v) + \varepsilon \leq d(u, v)$

---

vertex. Then, the algorithm repeatedly finds an arc whose demand is not respected and adds flow along a cycle in the residual graph that contains this arc. The flow is increased maximally along this cycle, taking into account the demand and capacity requirements of the arcs on the cycle. Note that in order to meet the demand of an arc, it may be necessary to increase the flow along more than one directed cycle. It can be proved that for integer demand and capacity functions and non-negative weights, Algorithm 6.1 finds an integral feasible s-t flow with minimum weight if it exists; see for example [62, p. 175–176].

The time complexity of Algorithm 6.1 is $O(\phi \cdot \mathrm{SP})$, where ϕ is the value of the flow found and SP is the time to compute a shortest directed path in G. Although faster algorithms exist for general minimum-weight flow problems, this algorithm suffices for our purposes, because we only need to find flows of relatively small values.

Note that the van der Waerden-König algorithm for finding a maximum-cardinality matching in a bipartite graph is a special case of the above algorithm. Namely, let $G = (U, W, E)$ be a bipartite graph. Similar to the construction of the directed bipartite graph G_M in Section 6.1.2, we transform G into a directed bipartite graph G' by orienting all edges from U to W. Furthermore, we add a "source" s, a "sink" t, and arcs from s to all vertices U and from all vertices in W to t. To all arcs a of the resulting graph we assign a capacity $c(a) = 1$ and a weight $w(a) = 0$. Now the algorithm for finding a minimum-weight s-t flow in G' mimics exactly the augmenting paths algorithm for finding a maximum-cardinality matching in G. In particular, given a flow f in G' and the corresponding matching M in G, the directed graph G_M corresponds to the residual graph G'_f where s, t and their adjacent arcs have been removed. Similarly, an M-augmenting path in G_M corresponds to a directed s-t path in G'_f.

Finally, we mention a result that, as we will see, is particularly useful for designing incremental filtering algorithms. Given a minimum-weight s-t flow, we want to compute the increase that would occur in the weight of solution when an unused arc is forced to be used. The following result shows that this can be done by re-routing the flow through a minimum-cost circuit containing the unused arc, see [2, p. 338].

Theorem 6.2. *Let f be a minimum-weight s-t flow of value ϕ in $G = (V, A)$ with $f(a) = 0$ for some $a \in A$. Let C be a directed circuit in G_f with $a \in C$, minimizing $w(C)$. Then $f' = f + \varepsilon\chi^C$, where ε is subject to $d \leq f + \varepsilon\chi^C \leq c$, has minimum weight among all s-t flows g in G with $value(g) = \phi$ and $g(a) = \varepsilon$. If C does not exist, f' does not exist. Otherwise, $weight(f') = weight(f) + \varepsilon \cdot w(C)$.*

The proof of Theorem 6.2 relies on the fact that for a minimum-weight flow f in G, the residual graph G_f does not contain directed circuits with negative weight.

For further reading on network flows we recommend Ahuja et al. [2] or Schrijver [62, Chapter 6–15].

6.1.3 Linear Programming

A *linear program* consists of continuous variables and linear constraints (inequalities or equalities). The objective is to optimize a linear cost function. One of the standard forms of a linear program is

$$
\begin{array}{llllllll}
\min & c_1 x_1 & + & c_2 x_2 & + & \cdots & + & c_n x_n \\
\text{subject to} & a_{11} x_1 & + & a_{12} x_2 & + & \cdots & + & a_{1n} x_n & = & b_1 \\
& a_{21} x_1 & + & a_{22} x_2 & + & \cdots & + & a_{2n} x_n & = & b_2 \\
& \vdots & & & & & & & & \vdots \\
& a_{m1} x_1 & + & a_{m2} x_2 & + & \cdots & + & a_{mn} x_n & = & b_m \\
& x_1, \ldots, x_n \geq 0
\end{array}
$$

or, using matrix notation,

$$
\min \{ c^\mathsf{T} x \mid Ax = b, x \geq 0 \} \tag{6.2}
$$

where $c \in \mathbb{R}^n$, $b \in \mathbb{R}^n$, $A \in \mathbb{R}^{m \times n}$ and $x \in \mathbb{R}^n$. Here c represents the "cost" vector and x is the vector of variables. Every linear program can be transformed into a linear program in the form of (6.2); see for example [61, Section 7.4].

Recall that the *rank* of a matrix is the number of linearly independent rows or columns of the matrix. For simplicity, we assume in the following that the rank of A is m, i.e. there are no redundant equations in (6.2).

Let $A = (a_1, a_2, \ldots, a_n)$ where a_j is the j-th column of A. For some "index set" $I \subseteq \{1, \ldots, n\}$ we denote by A_I the submatrix of A consisting of the columns a_i with $i \in I$.

Because the rank of A is m, there exists an index set $B = \{B_1, \ldots, B_m\}$ such that the $m \times m$ submatrix $A_B = (a_{B_1}, \ldots, a_{B_m})$ is nonsingular and is therefore invertible. We call A_B a *basis* of A. Let $N = \{1, \ldots, n\} \setminus B$. If we permute the columns of A such that $A = (A_B, A_N)$, we can write $Ax = b$ as

$$
A_B x_B + A_N x_N = b,
$$

where $x = (x_B, x_N)$. Then a solution to $Ax = b$ is given by $x_B = A_B^{-1} b$ and $x_N = \vec{0}$. This solution is called a *basic solution*. A basic solution is *feasible* if $A_B^{-1} b \geq \vec{0}$. The vector x_B contains the *basic variables* and the vector x_N contains the *nonbasic variables*. If we permute c such that $c = (c_B, c_N)$, the corresponding objective value is $c^\mathsf{T} x = c_B^\mathsf{T} A_B^{-1} b + c_N^\mathsf{T} \vec{0} = c_B^\mathsf{T} A_B^{-1} b$.

Given a basis A_B, we can rewrite (6.2) into the following equivalent linear program

$$
\begin{array}{ll}
\min & c_B^\mathsf{T} A_B^{-1} b + (c_N^\mathsf{T} - c_B^\mathsf{T} A_B^{-1} A_N) x_N \\
\text{subject to} & x_B + A_B^{-1} A_N x_N = A_B^{-1} b \\
& x_B, x_N \geq 0.
\end{array} \tag{6.3}
$$

Program (6.3) represents how the objective may improve if we would replace (some) basic variables by nonbasic variables. This means that some basic variables will take value 0, while some nonbasic variables will take a non-zero value instead. If we do so, feasibility is maintained by $x_B + A_B^{-1} A_N x_N = A_B^{-1} b$. The improvement of the objective value is represented by $(c_N^\mathsf{T} - c_B^\mathsf{T} A_B^{-1} A_N) x_N$. This rewritten cost vector for x_N is called the *reduced-cost* vector and is defined on both basic and nonbasic variables as $\bar{c}^\mathsf{T} = c^\mathsf{T} - c_B^\mathsf{T} A_B^{-1} A$. We have the following (cf. [46, pp. 31–32]):

Theorem 6.3. (x_B, x_N) *is an optimal solution if and only if* $\bar{c} \geq \vec{0}$.

Apart from this result, reduced-costs have another interesting property. Namely, they represent the marginal rate at which the solution gets worse if we insert a nonbasic variable into the solution (by giving it a non-zero value). For example, if we insert nonbasic variable x_i into the solution, the objective value will increase by at least $\bar{c}_i x_i$. This property will be exploited in Section 6.5.2.

To solve linear programs one often uses the *simplex method*, invented by Dantzig [15], which employs Theorem 6.3. Roughly, the simplex method moves from one basis to another by replacing a column in A_B by a column in A_N, until it finds a basic feasible solution for which all reduced-costs are nonnegative. The method is very fast in practice, although it has an exponential worst-case time complexity. Polynomial-time algorithms for linear programs were presented by Khachiyan [36] and Karmarkar [33, 32].

For further reading on linear programming we recommend Chvátal [14] or Nemhauser and Wolsey [46].

6.2   Examples of Global Constraints

In this section we present a number of global constraints that are practically useful and for which efficient filtering algorithms exist.

6.2.1   The Sum and Knapsack Constraints

The sum constraint is one of the most frequently occurring constraints in applications. Let $x_1, \ldots, x_n$ be variables. To each variable x_i, we associate a scalar $c_i \in \mathbb{Q}$. Furthermore, let z be a variable with domain $D(z) \subseteq \mathbb{Q}$. The sum constraint is defined as

$$\mathtt{sum}(x_1, \ldots, x_n, z, c) = \left\{ (d_1, \ldots, d_n, d) \mid \forall i \; d_i \in D(x_i), d \in D(z), d = \sum_{i=1}^{n} c_i d_i \right\}.$$

We also write $z = \sum_{i=1}^{n} c_i x_i$.

The knapsack constraint is a variant of the sum constraint. Rather than constraining the sum to be a specific value, the knapsack constraint states the sum to be within a lower bound l and an upper bound u. Traditionally, one writes $l \leq \sum_{i=1}^{n} c_i x_i \leq u$. Here we represent l and u by a variable z, such that $D(z) = [l, u]$. Then we define the knapsack constraint as

$$\mathtt{knapsack}(x_1, \ldots, x_n, z, c) =$$
$$\{ (d_1, \ldots, d_n, d) \mid \forall i \; d_i \in D(x_i), d \in D(z), d \leq \textstyle\sum_{i=1}^{n} c_i d_i \} \cap$$
$$\{ (d_1, \ldots, d_n, d) \mid \forall i \; d_i \in D(x_i), d \in D(z), \textstyle\sum_{i=1}^{n} c_i d_i \leq d \},$$

which corresponds to $\min D(z) \leq \sum_{i=1}^{n} c_i x_i \leq \max D(z)$.

6.2.2 The Element Constraint

Let y be an integer variable, z a variable with finite domain, and c an array of variables, i.e., $c = [x_1, x_2, \ldots, x_n]$. The `element` constraint states that z is equal to the y-th variable in c, or $z = x_y$. More formally

$$\text{element}(y, z, x_1, \ldots, x_n) = \{(e, f, d_1, \ldots, d_n) \mid e \in D(y), f \in D(z), \forall i \ d_i \in D(x_i), f = d_e\}.$$

The `element` constraint was introduced Van Hentenryck and Carillon [24]. It can be applied to model many practical problems, especially when we want to model variable subscripts. An example is presented in Section 6.2.8 below.

6.2.3 The Alldifferent Constraint

The `alldifferent` constraint is probably the best-known, most influential and most studied global constraint in constraint programming. Apart from its simplicity and practical applicability, this is probably due to its relationship to matching theory. This important field of theoretical computer science has produced several classical results and provided the basis for efficient filtering algorithms for the `alldifferent` constraint.

Definition 6.4 (Alldifferent constraint, [39]). *Let* $x_1, x_2, \ldots, x_n$ *be variables. Then*

$$\text{alldifferent}(x_1, \ldots, x_n) = \{(d_1, \ldots, d_n) \mid \forall_i \ d_i \in D(x_i), \ \forall_{i \neq j} \ d_i \neq d_j\}.$$

A famous problem that can be modeled with `alldifferent` constraints is the n-queens problem: Place n queens on an $n \times n$ chessboard in such a way that no queen attacks another queen.

One way of modeling this problem is to introduce an integer variable x_i for every row $i = 1, 2, \ldots, n$, which ranges over column 1 to n. This means that in row i, a queen is placed in the x_i-th column. The domain of every x_i is $D(x_i) = \{1, 2, \ldots, n\}$ and we express the no-attack constraints by

$$x_i \neq x_j \quad \text{for } 1 \leq i < j \leq n, \tag{6.4}$$
$$x_i - x_j \neq i - j \quad \text{for } 1 \leq i < j \leq n, \tag{6.5}$$
$$x_i - x_j \neq j - i \quad \text{for } 1 \leq i < j \leq n, \tag{6.6}$$

The constraints (6.4) state that no two queens are allowed to occur in the same column and the constraints (6.5) and (6.6) state the diagonal cases. A more concise model can be stated as follows. After rearranging the terms of constraints (6.5) and (6.6), we transform the model into

$$\begin{aligned}
&\text{alldifferent}(x_1, \ldots, x_n), \\
&\text{alldifferent}(x_1 - 1, x_2 - 2, \ldots, x_n - n), \\
&\text{alldifferent}(x_1 + 1, x_2 + 2, \ldots, x_n + n), \\
&x_i \in \{1, 2, \ldots, n\} \text{ for } 1 \leq i \leq n.
\end{aligned}$$

6.2.4   The Global Cardinality Constraint

The *global cardinality constraint* $\text{gcc}(x_1, \ldots, x_n, c_{v_1}, \ldots, c_{v_{n'}})$ is a generalization of `alldifferent`. While `alldifferent` requires that every value is assigned to at most one variable, the `gcc` is specified on n assignment variables $x_1, \ldots, x_n$ and n' count variables $c_{v_1}, \ldots, c_{v_{n'}}$ and specifies that each value v_i is assigned to exactly c_{v_i} assignment variables. `alldifferent`, then, is the special case of `gcc` in which the domain of each count variable is $\{0, 1\}$. For any tuple $t \in D^n$ and value $v \in D$, let $occ(v, t)$ be the number of occurrences of v in t.

Definition 6.5 (Global cardinality constraint, [47]). *Let $x_1, \ldots, x_n$ be assignment variables whose domains are contained in $\{v_1, \ldots v_{n'}\}$ and let $\{c_{v_1}, \ldots, c_{v_{n'}}\}$ be count variables whose domains are sets of integers. Then*

$$\text{gcc}(x_1, \ldots, x_n, c_{v_1}, \ldots, c_{v_{n'}}) = \{(w_1, \ldots, w_n, o_1, \ldots, o_{n'}) \mid$$
$$\forall j \; w_j \in D(x_j), \forall i \; occ(v_i, (w_1, \ldots, w_n)) = o_i \in D(c_{v_i})\}.$$

An example of a problem that can be modeled with a `gcc` is the *shift assignment problem* [13, 58] in which we are given a set of workers $W = \{W_1, \ldots, W_s\}$ and a set of shifts $S = \{S_1, \ldots, S_t\}$ and the problem is to assign each worker to one of the shifts while fulfilling the constraints posed by the workers and the boss: Each worker W_i specifies in which of the shifts she is willing to work and for each shift S_i the boss specifies a lower and upper bound on the number of workers that should be assigned to this shift. In the `gcc`, the workers would be represented by the assignment variables and the shifts by the count variables. The domain of an assignment variable would contain the set of shifts that the respective worker is willing to work in and the interval corresponding to each count variable would match the lower and upper bounds specified by the boss for this shift.

6.2.5   The Global Cardinality Constraint with Costs

The *global cardinality constraint with costs* [59] combines a `gcc` and a variant of the `sum` constraint. As in Section 6.2.4, let $X = \{x_1, \ldots, x_n\}$ be a set of assignment variables and let $c_{v_1}, \ldots, c_{v_{n'}}$ be count variables. We are given a function w that associates to each pair $(x, d) \in X \times D(X)$ a "cost" $w(x, d) \in \mathbb{Q}$. In addition, the constraint is defined on a "cost" variable z with domain $D(z)$. Assuming that we want to *minimize* the cost variable z, the global cardinality constraint with costs is defined as

$$\text{cost\_gcc}(x_1, \ldots, x_n, c_{v_1}, \ldots, c_{v_{n'}}, z, w) = \{(d_1, \ldots, d_n, o_1, \ldots, o_{n'}, d) \mid$$
$$(d_1, \ldots, d_n, o_1, \ldots, o_{n'}) \in \text{gcc}(x_1, \ldots, x_n, c_{v_1}, \ldots, c_{v_{n'}}), \qquad (6.7)$$
$$\forall i \; d_i \in D(x_i), d \in D(z), \textstyle\sum_{i=1}^{n} w(x_i, d_i) \leq d\}.$$

In other words, the cost variable z represents an upper bound on the sum of $w(x_i, d_i)$ for all i. We want to find only those solutions to the `gcc` whose associated cost is not higher than this bound.

As an example of the practical use of a `cost_gcc` we extend the above shift assignment problem. It is natural to assume that different workers perform shifts differently. For example, suppose that we have a prediction of "work output" when we assign a worker to a shift. Denote this output by $O(W, S)$ for each worker W and shift S. The boss now wants to maximize the output, while still respecting the above preferences and constraints on the shifts. We can model this as

$$\texttt{cost\_gcc}(W_1, \ldots, W_n, S_1, \ldots, S_t, z, \tilde{O}),$$

where $\tilde{O}(W, S) = -O(W, S)$ for all workers W and shifts S. Namely, maximizing O is equivalent to minimizing $-O$.

6.2.6 Scheduling with Cumulative Resource Constraints

An important application area for constraint solvers is in solving NP-hard scheduling problems. Chapter 22, "Planning and Scheduling", explores the use of constraint programming for scheduling in depth. Here, we mention only one problem of this family; that of scheduling non-preemptive tasks who share a single resource with bounded capacity.

We are given a collection $T = t_1, \ldots, t_n$ of tasks, such that each task t_i is associated with four variables: Its *release time* r_i is the earliest time at which it can begin executing, its *deadline* d_i is the time by which it must complete, its *processing time* p_i is the amount of time it takes to complete and its *capacity requirement* c_i is the capacity of the resource that it takes up while it executes. In addition, we are given the capacity variable C of the resource. (The special case in which $\forall_i\ c_i = 1$ and $C = 1$ is known as the *disjunctive* case while the general case in which arbitrary capacities are allowed is the *cumulative* case.)

A solution is a schedule, i.e., a starting time s_i for each task t_i such that $r_i \le s_i \le d_i - p_i$ (the task completes before its deadline), and in addition,

$$\forall u \qquad \sum_{i | s_i \le u \le s_i + p_i} c_i \le C$$

i.e., at any time unit u, the capacity of the resource is not exceeded. Note that the starting times s_i are auxiliary variables; instead of s_i we reason about the release times r_i and deadlines d_i.
The $\texttt{cumulative}(\{r_1, \ldots, r_n\}, \{d_1, \ldots, d_n\}, \{p_1, \ldots, p_n\}, \{c_1, \ldots, c_n\}, C)$ constraint models scheduling problems as described above [1].

6.2.7 The Regular Language Membership Constraint

The $\texttt{regular}$ constraint [48] is defined on a fixed-length sequence of finite-domain variables and states that the sequence of values taken by these variables belongs to a given regular language. The $\texttt{regular}$ constraint has applications, for example, in rostering problems and sequencing problems.

Before we formally introduce the $\texttt{regular}$ constraint, we need some definitions (see [29]). A *deterministic finite automaton* (DFA) is described by a 5-tuple $M = (Q, \Sigma, \delta, q_0, F)$ where Q is a finite set of states, Σ is an alphabet, $\delta : Q \times \Sigma \to Q$ is a transition function, $q_0 \in Q$ is the initial state, and $F \subseteq Q$ is the set of final (or accepting) states. Given an input string, the automaton starts in the initial state q_0 and processes the string one symbol at the time, applying the transition function δ at each step to update the current state. The string is *accepted* if and only if the last state reached belongs to the set of final states F. Strings processed by M that are accepted are said to belong to the language defined by M, denoted by $L(M)$. As an example, the DFA M for the regular expression $aa^\star bb^\star aa^\star + cc^\star$ is shown in Figure 6.1. It accepts the strings $aaabaa$ and cc, but not $aacbba$.

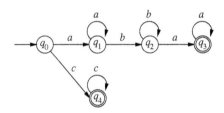

Figure 6.1: A representation of a DFA with each state shown as a circle, final states as a double circle, and transitions as arcs.

Definition 6.6 (Regular language membership constraint, [48]). *Let* $M = (Q, \Sigma, \delta, q_0$ $F)$ *be a DFA and let* $X = \{x_1, x_2, \ldots, x_n\}$ *be a set of variables with* $D(x_i) \subseteq \Sigma$ *for* $1 \leq i \leq n$. *Then*

$$\texttt{regular}(X, M) = \{(d_1, \ldots, d_n) \mid \forall i \; d_i \in D(x_i), d_1 d_2 \cdots d_n \in L(M)\}.$$

Returning to our example, consider the CSP

$$x_1 \in \{a, b, c\}, x_2 \in \{a, b, c\}, x_3 \in \{a, b, c\}, x_4 \in \{a, b, c\},$$
$$\texttt{regular}(x_1, x_2, x_3, x_4, M).$$

One solution to this CSP is $x_1 = a$, $x_2 = b$, $x_3 = a$ and $x_4 = a$.

The `regular` constraint allows us to express many relations between the variables of a sequence. For example, it is possible to express the maximum length of identical consecutive values, also known as the `stretch` constraint [49, 23]. A typical application of the `stretch` constraint is to restrict the maximum number of night shifts in a nurse scheduling problem. Pesant [48] discusses even more complicated patterns.

6.2.8 The Circuit Constraint

Before we introduce the `circuit` constraint, we need the following definition. Consider a permutation $S = s_1, \ldots, s_n$ of $\{1, \ldots, n\}$, i.e., $s_i \in \{1, \ldots, n\}$ and $s_i \neq s_j$ whenever $i \neq j$. Define the set C_S as follows:

$$1 \in C_S,$$
$$i \in C_S \Rightarrow s_i \in C_S.$$

We say that S is *cyclic* if $|C_S| = n$.

Definition 6.7 (Circuit constraint, [39]). *Let* $X = \{x_1, x_2, \ldots, x_n\}$ *be a set of variables with respective domains* $D(x_i) \subseteq \{1, 2, \ldots, n\}$ *for* $i = 1, 2, \ldots, n$. *Then*

$$\texttt{circuit}(x_1, \ldots, x_n) = \{(d_1, \ldots, d_n) \mid \forall i \; d_i \in D(x_i), d_1, \ldots, d_n \text{ is cyclic}\}.$$

To the variables in Definition 6.7 we can associate the digraph $G = (X, A)$ with arc set $A = \{(x_i, x_j) \mid j \in D(x_i), 1 \leq i \leq n\}$. An assignment $x_1 = d_1, \ldots, x_n = d_n$ corresponds to the subset of arcs $\tilde{A} = \{(x_i, x_{d_i}) \mid 1 \leq i \leq n\}$. The `circuit` constraint ensures that $\tilde{A}$ is a directed circuit.

A famous combinatorial problem that can be modeled with the `circuit` constraint is the Traveling Salesperson Problem, or TSP [40]: A salesperson needs to find a shortest route to visit n cities exactly once, and return in its starting city.

We model the TSP as follows. Let c_{ij} denote the distance between city i and j (where $1 \leq i, j \leq n$). For each city i, we introduce a variable x_i with domain $D(x_i) = \{1, \ldots, n\} \setminus \{i\}$. The value of x_i is the city that is visited by the tour immediately after city i. We also introduce for every $1 \leq i \leq n$ the variable d_i to indicate the distance from city i to city x_i. The TSP can then be modeled as follows.

$$
\begin{aligned}
&\texttt{minimize } z, \\
&\texttt{circuit}(x_1, \ldots, x_n), \\
&z = \sum_{i=1}^{n} d_i, \\
&d_i = c_{ix_i} \ \ 1 \leq i \leq n.
\end{aligned}
\tag{6.8}
$$

To perform the assignment $d_i = c_{ix_i}$, we use the constraint $\texttt{element}(x_i, d_i, c_{i*})$, where c_{i*} denotes the array $[c_{ij}]_{1 \leq j \leq n}$.

6.2.9 The Soft Alldifferent Constraint

A *soft constraint*, as opposed to a traditional *hard constraint*, is a constraint that may be violated. Instead we measure its violation, and the goal is to minimize the total amount of violation of all soft constraints. Soft constraints are particularly useful to model and solve over-constrained and preference-based problems (see Chapter 9, "Soft Constraints"). In this chapter, we follow the scheme proposed by Régin et al. [60] to soften global constraints.

A *violation measure* for a soft constraint $C(x_1, \ldots, x_n)$ is a function $\mu : D(x_1) \times \cdots \times D(x_n) \rightarrow \mathbb{Q}$. This measure is represented by a "cost" variable z, which is to be minimized. There exist several useful violation measures for soft constraints. For the soft `alldifferent` constraint, we consider two measures of violation, see [51]. The first is the *variable-based* violation measure μ_{var} which counts the minimum number of variables that need to change their value in order to satisfy the constraint. The second is the *decomposition-based* violation measure μ_{dec} which counts the number of constraints in the binary decomposition that are violated. For $\texttt{alldifferent}(x_1, \ldots, x_n)$ the latter amounts to $\mu_{\text{dec}}(x_1, \ldots, x_n) = |\{(i, j) \mid \forall i < j \ x_i = x_j\}|$.

Definition 6.8 (Soft alldifferent constraint, [51]). *Let $x_1, x_2, \ldots, x_n, z$ be variables with respective finite domains $D(x_1), D(x_2), \ldots, D(x_n), D(z)$. Let μ be a violation measure for the* `alldifferent` *constraint. Then*

$$
\begin{aligned}
&\texttt{soft\_alldifferent}(x_1, \ldots, x_n, z, \mu) = \\
&\quad \{(d_1, \ldots, d_n, d) \mid \forall i \ d_i \in D(x_i), d \in D(z), \mu(d_1, \ldots, d_n) \leq d\}
\end{aligned}
$$

is the soft `alldifferent` *constraint with respect to μ.*

As stated above, the cost variable z is minimized during the solution process. Thus, $\max D(z)$ represents the maximum value of violation that is allowed, and $\min D(z)$ represents the lowest possible value of violation.

As an example, consider the following over-constrained CSP

$$
\begin{aligned}
&x_1 \in \{a, b\}, x_2 \in \{a, b\}, x_3 \in \{a, b\}, x_4 \in \{b, c\}, \\
&\texttt{alldifferent}(x_1, x_2, x_3, x_4).
\end{aligned}
$$

We have, for instance, $\mu_{\text{var}}(a, a, b, b) = 2$, while $\mu_{\text{dec}}(a, a, b, b) = 2$, and $\mu_{\text{var}}(b, b, b, b) = 3$, while $\mu_{\text{dec}}(b, b, b, b) = 6$. We soften the `alldifferent` constraint using μ_{dec}, and transform the CSP into the following COP

$$z \in \{0, 1, \ldots, 6\},$$
$$x_1 \in \{a, b\}, x_2 \in \{a, b\}, x_3 \in \{a, b\}, x_4 \in \{b, c\},$$
$$\texttt{soft\_alldifferent}(x_1, x_2, x_3, x_4, z, \mu_{\text{dec}}),$$
$$\texttt{minimize } z.$$

A solution to this COP is $x_1 = a$, $x_2 = a$, $x_3 = b$, $x_4 = c$ and $z = 1$.

6.3 Complete Filtering Algorithms

As mentioned in Section 6.1, the filtering task with respect to a constraint C defined on a set of variables X is to remove values from the domains of variables in X without changing the set of solutions to C. We say that the filtering is complete if the removal of any additional value from the domain of any of the variables in X *would* change the set of solutions to C. Formally:

Definition 6.9 (Generalized arc consistency). *Let C be a constraint on the variables $x_1 \ldots, x_k$ with respective domains $D(x_1), \ldots, D(x_k)$. That is, $C \subseteq D(x_1) \times \cdots \times D(x_k)$. We say that C is* generalized arc consistent *(arc consistent, for short) if for every $1 \leq i \leq$ and $v \in D(x_i)$, there exists a tuple $(d_1, \ldots, d_k) \in C$ such that $d_i = v$. A CSP is arc consistent if each of its constraints is arc consistent.*

In the literature, arc consistency is also referred to as *hyper-arc consistency* or *domain consistency*. Note that arc consistency only guarantees that each individual constraint has a solution; it does *not* guarantee that the CSP has a solution.

In this section we present filtering algorithms that establish arc consistency. In general, establishing arc consistency for a non-binary constraint (or global constraint) is NP-hard (see Chapter 3, "Constraint Propagation"). For a number of global constraints, however, it is possible to establish arc consistency quite efficiently. We present such filtering algorithms in detail for the `alldifferent`, the `gcc`, and the `regular` constraints.

6.3.1 The Alldifferent Constraint

Régin [57] proposed an arc consistency algorithm for the `alldifferent` constraint which is based on matching theory.

Definition 6.10 (Value graph, [57]). *Let X be a set of variables and $D(X)$ the union of their domains. The bipartite graph $G = (X, D(X), E)$ with $E = \{\{x, d\} \mid x \in X, d \in D(x)\}$ is called the* value graph *of X.*

As an example, consider the following CSP:

$$x_1 \in \{b, c, d, e\}, x_2 \in \{b, c\}, x_3 \in \{a, b, c, d\}, x_4 \in \{b, c\},$$
$$\texttt{alldifferent}(x_1, x_2, x_3, x_4).$$

The value graph of the variables in this CSP is shown in Figure 6.2.a.

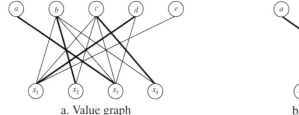
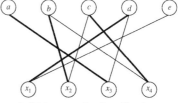

| a. Value graph | b. Value graph after filtering |

Figure 6.2: Graph representation for the `alldifferent` constraint, before and after filtering. Bold edges represent a matching, corresponding to a solution to the `alldiff-erent` constraint.

Theorem 6.11 (Régin [57])**.** *Let $X = \{x_1, x_2, \ldots, x_n\}$ be a set of variables and let G be the value graph of X. Then $(d_1, \ldots, d_n) \in$ `alldifferent`$(x_1, \ldots, x_n)$ if and only if $M = \{\{x_1, d_1\}, \ldots, \{x_n, d_n\}\}$ is a matching in G.*

Proof: By definition.   □

Note that the matching M in Theorem 6.11 covers X, and is therefore a maximum-cardinality matching.

Consider again the above CSP. A solution to this CSP, i.e., to the `alldifferent` constraint in the CSP, is $x_1 = d$, $x_2 = b$, $x_3 = a$ and $x_4 = c$. This solution corresponds to a maximum-cardinality matching in the value graph, indicated with bold edges in Figure 6.2.a.

Corollary 6.12 (Régin [57])**.** *Let G be the value graph of a set of variables $X = \{x_1, x_2, \ldots, x_n\}$. The constraint* `alldifferent`$(x_1, x_2, \ldots, x_n)$ *is arc consistent if and only if every edge in G belongs to a matching in G covering X.*

Proof: Immediate from Definition 6.9 and Theorem 6.11.   □

The following Theorem identifies edges that belong to a maximum-cardinality matching. The proof follows from [50]; see also [62, Theorem 16.1].

Theorem 6.13. *Let G be a graph and M a maximum-cardinality matching in G. An edge e belongs to some maximum-cardinality matching in G if and only if $e \in M$, or e is on an even-length M-alternating path starting at an M-free vertex, or e is on an even-length M-alternating circuit.*

Proof: Let M be a maximum-cardinality matching in $G = (V, E)$. Suppose edge e belongs to a maximum-cardinality matching N, and $e \notin M$. The graph $G' = (V, M \oplus N)$ consists of even-length paths (possibly empty) and circuits with edges alternatingly in M and N. If the paths are not of even length, either M or N can be made larger by interchanging edges in M and N along this path (a contradiction because they are of maximum cardinality).

Conversely, let M be a maximum-cardinality matching in G and let P be an even-length M-alternating path starting at an M-free vertex or an M-alternating circuit. Let be an edge such that $e \in P \setminus M$. Then $M \oplus P$ is a maximum-cardinality matching that contains e. $\qquad\qquad\qquad\square$

Using Theorem 6.13, we construct the following arc consistency algorithm. First we compute a maximum-cardinality matching M in the value graph $G = (X, D(X), E)$ This can be done in $O(m\sqrt{n})$ time, using the algorithm by Hopcroft and Karp [28], where $m = \sum_{i=1}^{n} |D(x_i)|$. Next we identify the even M-alternating paths starting at an M-free vertex, and the even M-alternating circuits in the following way.

Define the directed bipartite graph $G_M = (X, D(X), A)$ with arc set $A = \{(x, d)$ $x \in X, \{x, d\} \in M\} \cup \{(d, x) \mid x \in X, \{x, d\} \in E \setminus M\}$. In other words, edges in M are oriented from X (the variables) to $D(X)$ (the domain values) and edges not in M are oriented in reverse direction. We first compute the strongly connected components in G_M in $O(n + m)$ time [65]. Arcs between vertices in the same strongly connected component belong to an even M-alternating circuit in G, and are marked as "used". Next we search for the arcs that belong to a directed path in G_M, starting at an M-free vertex. This takes $O(m)$ time, using breadth-first search. Arcs belonging to such a path belong to an M alternating path in G starting at an M-free vertex, and are marked as "used". For all edges $\{x, d\}$ whose corresponding arc is not marked "used" and that do not belong to M, we update $D(x) = D(x) \setminus \{d\}$. Then, by Theorem 6.13, the corresponding `alldifferent` constraint is arc consistent.

It follows from the above that the `alldifferent` constraint can be checked for consistency, i.e., determined to contain a solution, in $O(m\sqrt{n})$ time and that it can be made arc consistent in $O(m)$ additional time.

In Figure 6.2.b we have shown the corresponding value graph for our example CSP, after establishing arc consistency. Note that the remaining edges are either in the matching M (for example x_1d), or on an even-length M-alternating path starting at an M-free vertex (for example ex_1dx_3a), or on an even-length M-alternating circuit (namely $x_2bx_4cx_2$).

During the whole solution process of the CSP, constraints other than `alldifferent` might also be used to remove values from variable domains. In such cases, we must update the filtering of our `alldifferent` constraint. As pointed out by Régin [57], this can be done incrementally, i.e., we can make use of our current value graph and our current maximum-cardinality matching to compute a new maximum-cardinality matching. For example, if the domain of k variables has changed, we can recompute our matching in $O(\min\{km, m\sqrt{n}\})$ time, and establish arc consistency in $O(m)$ additional time again. The same idea has been used by Barták [4] to make the `alldifferent` constraint dynamic with respect to the addition of variables during the solution process.

6.3.2   The Global Cardinality Constraint

Figure 6.3 shows an example of a `gcc` and one of its solutions. Unfortunately, it is NP-hard to filter the domains of all variables to arc consistency [53]. However, if we replace the count variables $c_{v_1}, \ldots, c_{v_{n'}}$ by constant intervals $E_i = [L_i, U_i]$ ($i = 1, \ldots, n'$), we can use a generalization of the arc consistency algorithm for the `alldifferent` constraint to efficiently filter the domains of all assignment variables to arc consistency [58]: We

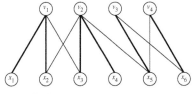

E_1	E_2	E_3	E_4
[1,3]	[1,2]	[1,1]	[1,1]

$D(x_1)$	$D(x_2)$	$D(x_3)$	$D(x_4)$	$D(x_5)$	$D(x_6)$
{1}	{1,2}	{1,2}	{2}	{2,3,4}	{3,4}

Figure 6.3: gcc example: On the left are the domains $D(x_i)$ of the assignment variables and the fixed intervals E_i that replace the count variables. On the right is the corresponding value graph with a solution marked by bold edges.

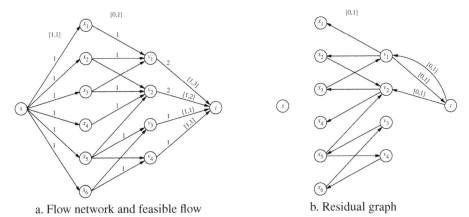

a. Flow network and feasible flow   b. Residual graph

Figure 6.4: a. The flow network for the example of Figure 6.3. The requirements of the arcs are shown as intervals above each equal-requirement group. The numbers above the arcs indicate a feasible flow. b. The residual capacity of an arc (v_i, t) indicates how many more variables can be assigned the value v_i without exceeding its capacity and the residual capacity of an arc (t, v_i) indicates how many variables which are assigned v_i can be assigned another value without going below v_i's demand.

construct the value graph G as before, orient the arcs from the variables to the values and assign to each of them a requirement of $[0, 1]$. Then, we add two vertices s and t, such that for each variable x_i there is an arc with requirement $[1, 1]$ from s to x_i, and for each value v_j, there is an arc with requirement $[L_j, U_j]$ from v_j to t (see Figure 6.4.a). The following theorem states that a solution to the gcc corresponds to an integral feasible s-t flow in this network.

Theorem 6.14 (Régin [58]). *Let $C = \text{gcc}(x_1, \ldots, x_n, c_{v_1}, \ldots, c_{v_{n'}})$ and let G be the augmented value graph described above. Then there is a one-to-one correspondence between the solutions to C and integral feasible s-t flows in G.*

Proof: Given a solution $S = (v_{i_1}, \ldots, v_{i_n}, o_1, \ldots, o_{n'})$ to the constraint, we construct a feasible flow in G as follows. For each variable x_j, $f(x_j, v_{i_j}) = 1$ and for any value $v \neq v_{i_j}$, $f(x_j, v) = 0$. For each value v_i, we set $f(v_i, t) = o_i$ and for each variable x_j we set $f(s, x_j) = 1$. It is not hard to verify that the capacities of the arcs are respected by and that flow conservation holds, so f is an integral feasible s-t flow.

Conversely, let f be a feasible flow in G. Then by the demand and capacity requirement, for every arc a from a variable vertex to a value vertex, $f(a) \in \{0, 1\}$. By flow conservation, and by our selection of capacities for the arcs from s to the variable vertex, we know that every variable vertex is incident to exactly one variable-value arc that carries flow 1.

Let $S = (v_{i_1}, \ldots, v_{i_n}, o_1, \ldots, o_{n'})$ be a tuple such that for each $1 \leq j \leq n$, the arc (x_j, v_{i_j}) is the unique arc such that $f(x_j, v_{i_j}) = 1$ and for each $1 \leq j' \leq n'$, $o_{j'}$ is the number of occurrences of the value $v_{j'}$ in $(v_{i_1}, \ldots, v_{i_n})$. To see that S is a solution to the constraint, it remains to show that every variable is assigned a value in its domain. For the assignment variables this is obvious: If a variable-value arc carries flow it must exist in the graph, and this can hold only when the value is in the domain of the variable. For the count variables, this holds, again, by flow conservation and by our choice of capacities for the arcs in the network: The value of the flow on an arc from the value vertex v_i to is, by construction of the flow network, some value f_i in E_i. By flow conservation, the amount of flow entering this value vertex is also f_i, and since flow can only enter through variable-value arcs, we get that the number of variables that are assigned the value v_i is f

$\square$

We say that the arc a belongs to a flow f if $f(a) > 0$. Once again, we conclude that:

Corollary 6.15 (Régin [58]). *Let G be the value graph of a set of variables $X = \{x_1, \ldots, x_n\}$, augmented into a flow network as described above. The constraint $\text{gcc}(x_1, \ldots, x_n$ $E_1, \ldots, E_{n'})$, where each E_i is a fixed interval, is arc consistent if and only if every variable-value arc in G belongs to some feasible integral flow in G.*

The following theorem characterizes the arcs of G that belong to feasible flows, in terms of the residual graph of G with respect to a given flow (see Figure 6.4.b). Its proof is along the same lines as the proof of Theorem 6.13 and belongs to the folklore of flow theory.

Theorem 6.16. *Let G be a graph and f a feasible flow in G. An arc belongs to some feasible flow in G if and only if it belongs to f or both of its endpoints belong to the same SCC of the residual graph of G with respect to f.*

Therefore, given a gcc whose count variables are fixed intervals, we can filter the domains of the assignment variables to arc consistency by an algorithm that follows the same approach as the arc consistency algorithm for the alldifferent constraint, except that the maximum cardinality matching computation is replaced by a feasible flow computation. If we were to use a generic flow algorithm such as Algorithm 6.1, the running time deteriorates to $O(mn)$. However, Quimper et al. [53] recently showed that the structure of the value graph can be exploited to compute the flow in $O(m\sqrt{n})$ time, using an adaptation of the Hopcroft-Karp algorithm [28] for maximum cardinality bipartite matchings.

6.3.3 The Regular Language Membership Constraint

A filtering algorithm for the regular constraint, establishing arc consistency, was presented by Pesant [48]. It makes use of a specific digraph representation of the DFA, which

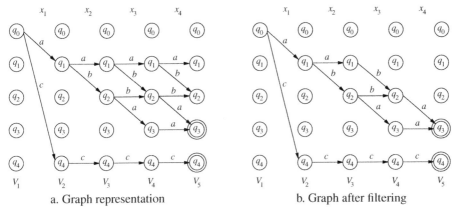

a. Graph representation   b. Graph after filtering

Figure 6.5: Graph representation for the `regular` constraint, before and after filtering. A double circle represents a final state. Arcs outgoing from a vertex which is not reachable from q_0^1 were omitted for clarity.

has similarities to dynamic programming.

Let $M = (Q, \Sigma, \delta, q_0, F)$ be a DFA and let $X = \{x_1, \ldots, x_n\}$ be a set of variables with $D(x_i) \subseteq \Sigma$ for each $1 \leq i \leq n$. We construct the digraph $\mathcal{R}$ representing `regular`(X, M) as follows. The vertex set V consists of $n + 1$ duplicates of the set of states of the DFA:

$$V = V_1 \cup V_2 \cup \cdots \cup V_{n+1},$$

where

$$\forall_{1 \leq i \leq n+1} V_i = \{q_k^i \mid q_k \in Q\}.$$

The arc set A of the graph represents the transition function δ of the DFA:

$$A = A_1 \cup A_2 \cup \cdots \cup A_n,$$

where

$$\forall_{1 \leq i \leq n} A_i = \{(q_k^i, q_l^{i+1}) \mid \delta(q_k, d) = q_l \text{ for } d \in D(x_i)\}.$$

Figure 6.5.a shows the graph $\mathcal{R}$ corresponding to the DFA in Figure 6.1.

Theorem 6.17 (Pesant [48]). *A solution to* `regular`(X, M) *corresponds to a directed path in $\mathcal{R}$ from q_0^1 in V_1 to a final state in V_{n+1}.*

Proof: Follows immediately from the construction of $\mathcal{R}$ and the definition of the `regular` constraint.   □

We apply Theorem 6.17 to establish arc consistency for the `regular` constraint:

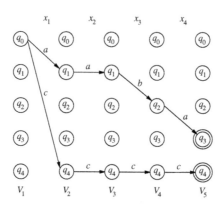

Figure 6.6: Updated graph after the removal of element a from $D(x_3)$.

Corollary 6.18 (Pesant [48]). *Let $M = (Q, \Sigma, \delta, q_0, F)$ be a DFA and let $X = \{x_1, \ldots, x_n\}$ be a set of variables with $D(x_i) \subseteq \Sigma$ for $1 \le i \le n$. The constraint* regular$(X, M$ *is arc consistent if and only if for all $x_i \in X$ and $d \in D(x_i)$, there exists an arc $a = (q_k^i, q_l^{i+1})$ such that $\delta(q_k, d) = q_l$ and a belongs to a path from q_0^1 to a final state in V_{n+1}*

Consider again the example presented in Section 6.2.7, i.e.,

$$x_1 \in \{a, b, c\}, x_2 \in \{a, b, c\}, x_3 \in \{a, b, c\}, x_4 \in \{a, b, c\},$$
$$\text{regular}(x_1, x_2, x_3, x_4, M).$$

The CSP is not arc consistent. For example, value b can never be assigned to x_1. If we make the CSP arc consistent we obtain

$$x_1 \in \{a, c\}, x_2 \in \{a, b, c\}, x_3 \in \{a, b, c\}, x_4 \in \{a, c\},$$
$$\text{regular}(x_1, x_2, x_3, x_4, M).$$

In Figure 6.5.b, the graph $\mathcal{R}$ corresponding to this example is shown after establishing arc consistency.

Corollary 6.18 implies the following filtering algorithm. First, we construct the graph $\mathcal{R}$, referred to in [48] as the "forward" phase. During this phase we omit all arcs that are not on a directed path starting in q_0^1. Then we remove all arcs that are not on a path from q_0^1 to a final state in V_{n+1}. This can be done in a "backward" phase, starting from vertices in V_{n+1} which are not final states. The total time complexity of this algorithm is dominated by the time to construct the graph, which is in $O(n \, |\Sigma| \, |Q|)$. This is also the space complexity of the algorithm.

Note that the algorithm can be made incremental. Whenever the domain of a variable has changed, we remove the corresponding arc from the graph. Then we simply perform a forward and backward phase on the affected parts of the graph, while leaving the rest unchanged. An example is given in Figure 6.6. It shows the updated graph after the removal of element b from $D(x_2)$. As a result, a is removed from $D(x_3)$.

It should be noted that this algorithm resembles the filtering algorithm for the knap-sack constraint proposed by Trick [66]. Trick's algorithm applies dynamic programming techniques to establish arc consistency on the knapsack constraint. The same algorithm can be applied to make the sum constraint arc consistent. It has a pseudo-polynomial running time however, as its complexity depends on the actual values of the domain elements of the variable which represents the sum.

6.4 Optimization Constraints

In this section we consider global constraints in the context of constraint optimization problems, or COPs. Recall that a COP contains an objective function to be optimized, and the goal is to find a solution that minimizes or maximizes its value. An *optimization constraint* is a constraint that is linked to the objective function of the problem at hand. For example, the cost_gcc is an optimization constraint. Every solution to it induces a "cost" that is represented by a variable z. The assumption is that z appears in the objective function, and is to be minimized. Whenever a solution to the COP is found, we obtain an upper bound for the variable z. Then the domain of z is filtered accordingly, and from that point on, we will only be searching for improving solutions.

Traditionally, COPs were solved in the following way. Assume that the objective function is represented by a variable z, which is to be minimized. If we find a solution to the problem, we compute its corresponding objective value opt and add the constraint $z < opt$. In that way, we search only for improving solutions. By reasoning on the domains of the variables present in the objective function, we may even detect sub-optimality before instantiating all variables, and backtrack. A major deficiency of this method, however, is that there is no inference from the domain of z to the domains of the other variables. Optimization constraints do take this two-way inference into account. They are global constraints, i.e., they specify a complex relation on a set of variables, but in addition they are also defined on a variable such as z above, which represents the value of the best solution found so far. Since we are only interested in improving solutions, a minimization (maximization) constraint is satisfied only when the value of the solution is at most (at least) z.

In this section we present complete filtering algorithms for two types of optimization constraints. First, we consider the cost_gcc, which embodies the natural extension of global constraints to optimization constraints. Next, we consider the soft_alldiffer-ent constraint, which can be applied to over-constrained and preference-based problems. In Section 6.5.2 we discuss *partial* filtering methods for optimization constraints.

6.4.1 The Global Cardinality Constraint with Costs

The filtering algorithm for the global cardinality constraint with costs (the cost_gcc) is an extension of the filtering algorithm of the gcc without costs. As in Section 6.3.2, we replace the count variables $c_{v_1}, \ldots, c_{v_{n'}}$ by constant intervals $E_1, \ldots, E_{n'}$ and filter the domains of the assignment variables.

Let $X = \{x_1, \ldots, x_n\}$, $E = \{E_1, \ldots, E_{n'}\}$ and let cost_gcc(X, E, z, w) be the constraint under consideration in this section. We extend the graph G of Section 6.3.2 by applying a "weight" function to its arcs. The weight of arc (x_i, d) is $w(x_i, d)$ for all $1 \leq i \leq n$ and $d \in D(x_i)$. To all other arcs we assign a weight 0. The filtering algorithm is based on finding a flow in the weighted version of G, which we denote by $\mathcal{C}\mathcal{G}$.

Theorem 6.19 (Régin [59]). *The constraint* cost_gcc(X, E, z, w) *is arc consistent if and only if*

   i) for all $x \in X$ *and* $d \in D(x)$ *there exists an integral feasible s-t flow* f *in* $C\mathcal{G}$ *with* $f(x, d) = 1$ *and weight*$(f) \le \max D(z)$, *and*

   ii) $\min D(z) \ge$ *weight*(f) *for some integral feasible s-t flow* f *in* $C\mathcal{G}$.

Proof: If we ignore the costs, we know from the gcc case that there is a one-to-one correspondence between integral feasible *s-t* flows and solutions to the constraint. By our choice of weights for the arcs, the weight of a flow is equal to the cost of the corresponding solution. Hence, a flow corresponds to a solution only if its weight is at most $\max D(z$ and every value in $D(z)$ (in particular, $\min D(z)$) must be larger than the weight of at least one feasible integral *s-t* flow.   □

   Theorem 6.19 gives rise to the following filtering algorithm for the cost_gcc. We first build the digraph $C\mathcal{G}$ that represents the constraint. Then, for every variable-value pair (x_i, d) we check whether the pair belongs to a solution, i.e., whether there exists a flow in $C\mathcal{G}$ that represents a solution containing $x_i = d$, with cost at most $\max D(z)$. If this is not the case, we can remove d from $D(x_i)$. Finally, we update $\min D(z)$ to be the maximum between its current value and the weight of a minimum-weight *s-t* flow of value n in $C\mathcal{G}$.

   By applying the successive shortest paths algorithm described in Section 6.1, we can compute a minimum-weight flow in $C\mathcal{G}$ in $O(n(m + n \log n))$ time. Hence, the time complexity of this filtering algorithm is $O(n^2 d(m + n \log n))$ where d is the maximum domain size. However, we can improve the efficiency by applying Theorem 6.2, as proposed by Régin [59, 56].

   The resulting, more efficient, algorithm is as follows. We first compute an initial minimum-weight flow f in $C\mathcal{G}$ representing a solution. Then for each arc $a = (u, v)$ representing (x_i, d) with $f(a) = 0$, we compute a minimum-weight directed path P from v to u in the residual graph $C\mathcal{G}_f$. Together with a, P forms a directed circuit. Because f represents a solution, it is an integer flow. This means that we can reroute one unit of flow along the circuit and obtain a flow f'. Then cost$(f') = $ cost$(f) + $ cost(P), following Theorem 6.2. If cost$(f') > \max D(z)$ we remove d from the domain of x_i.

   An initial solution is still computed in $O(n(m + n \log n))$ time, but we can reduce the time complexity to establish arc consistency. A first attempt is to compute for all arcs (x_i, d) with $f(x_i, d) = 0$ a shortest path in the residual graph. That would yield a time complexity $O((m-n)(m+n \log n))$. We can do better, however, see [59, 56]. We compute for each (variable) vertex in X the distance to all other vertices in $O(m + n \log n)$ time. Alternatively, this may be done for all (value) vertices in $D(X)$ instead. This gives us the lengths of all paths in $O(\Delta(m + n \log n))$ time, where $\Delta = \min(n, |D(X)|)$.

   In addition, this algorithm is incremental. When the domain of k variables has changed, it takes $O(k(m + n \log n))$ time to recompute a feasible flow, starting from the previous flow. Establishing arc consistency is done again in $O(\Delta(m + n \log n))$ additional time.

   Note that, by definition (6.7), we don't restrict all values of $D(z)$ to belong to a solution. This would however be the case if we had defined $\sum_{i=1}^{n} w(x_i, d_i) = d$ in (6.7). The reason for omitting this additional restriction on z is that it makes the task of establishing arc consistency NP-hard. This follows from a reduction from the "subset sum" problem (see [20]). Definition (6.7) does allow an efficient filtering algorithm, as we have seen above. In a sense, one could argue that while establishing arc consistency, the algorithm mimics the establishment of bound consistency (see Section 6.5.1) with respect to the cost variable z.

6.4.2 The Soft Alldifferent Constraint

In this section we present filtering algorithms for the `soft_alldifferent` constraint. Each of the violation measures μ_{var} and μ_{dec} gives rise to a different arc consistency problem, and we describe an algorithm for each of them.

Variable-based violation measure

Recall that the variable-based violation measure μ_{var} counts how many variables need to change their values in order for the constraint to be satisfied.

Theorem 6.20 (Petit et al. [51]). *Let G be the value graph of the variables $x_1, \ldots, x_n$ and let M be a maximum-cardinality matching in G. The constraint* `soft_alldiffer-ent`$(x_1, \ldots, x_n, z, \mu_{var})$ *is arc consistent if and only if one of the following conditions holds*

$i)$ $\min D(z) \leq n - |M| < \max D(z)$, *or*

$ii)$ $\min D(z) \leq n - |M| = \max D(z)$ *and all edges in G belong to a matching in G with cardinality $|M|$.*

Proof: We can assign $|M|$ variables to a different value. Thus we need to change the value of at least $n - |M|$ variables, i.e., $\mu_{var} \geq n - |M|$. Given an assignment with minimum violation, every change in this assignment can only increase μ_{var} by 1. Hence, if $\min D(z) \leq n - |M| < \max D(z)$ all domain values belong to a solution. On the other hand, if $n - |M| = \max D(z)$, only those edges that belong to a matching with cardinality $|M|$ belong to a solution. $\qquad\square$

The constraint `soft_alldifferent`$(x_1, \ldots, x_n, z, \mu_{var})$ can be filtered to arc consistency by an algorithm which is similar to the one in Section 6.3.1. First we compute a maximum-cardinality matching M in the value graph G in $O(m\sqrt{n})$ time, where $m = \sum_{i=1}^{n} |D(x_i)|$. If $n - |M| > \max D(z)$, the constraint is inconsistent. Otherwise, if $n - |M| = \max D(z)$, we identify all edges that belong to a maximum-cardinality matching. Here we apply Theorem 6.13, i.e., we identify the even M-alternating paths starting at an M-free vertex, and the even M-alternating circuits. This takes $O(m)$ time, as we saw in Section 6.3.1. Note that in this case vertices in X may also be M-free. Finally, we update $\min D(z) \leftarrow \max\{\min D(z), n - |M|\}$ if $\min D(z) < n - |M|$.

Decomposition-based violation measure

Recall that the decomposition-based violation measure counts the number of constraints in the binary decomposition (i.e., the set of pairwise not-equal constraints) that are violated.

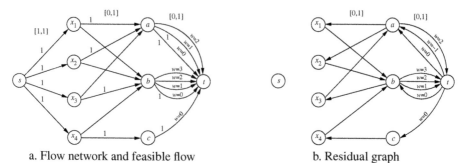

a. Flow network and feasible flow   b. Residual graph

Figure 6.7: Graph representation for the `soft_alldifferent` constraint. The requirements of the arcs are shown as intervals above each equal-requirement group. Unless
indicated otherwise, the weight w of an arc is 0. The numbers next to the arcs describe a
feasible flow with weight 1.

Once again, we construct a directed graph $\mathcal{S} = (V, A)$, this time with

$$V = \{s, t\} \cup X \cup D(X) \quad \text{and} \quad A = A_X \cup A_s \cup A_t$$

where $X = \{x_1, \dots, x_n\}$ and

$$
\begin{array}{rcl}
A_X & = & \{(x_i, d) \mid d \in D(x_i)\}, \\
A_s & = & \{(s, x_i) \mid 1 \leq i \leq n\}, \\
A_t & = & \{(d, t) \mid d \in D(x_i), 1 \leq i \leq n\}.
\end{array}
$$

Note that A_t contains parallel arcs if two or more variables share a domain value. If there
are k parallel arcs (d, t) between some $d \in D(X)$ and t, we distinguish them by numbering
the arcs as $(d, t)_0, (d, t)_1, \dots, (d, t)_{k-1}$ in a fixed but arbitrary order.

To the arcs in A_s we assign a requirement $[1, 1]$ while the arcs in $A \setminus A_s$ have requirement $[0, 1]$. We also assign a "cost" function w to the arcs. If $a \in A_s \cup A_X$, then $w(a) = 0$
If $a \in A_t$, such that $a = (d, t)_i$ for some $d \in D(X)$ and integer i, the value of $w(a) = i$.

Figure 6.7.a shows the graph $\mathcal{S}$ corresponding to the `soft_alldifferent` example
presented in Section 6.2.9.

Theorem 6.21 (van Hoeve [26]). *The constraint* `soft_alldifferent`$(x_1, \dots, x_n, z,$
$\mu_{\text{dec}})$ *is arc consistent if and only if*

   i) *every arc* $a \in A_X$ *belongs to some feasible integral flow* f *in* $\mathcal{S}$ *with* weight$(f) \leq$
      $\max D(z)$, *and*

   ii) $\min D(z) \geq$ weight(f) *for a minimum-weight s-t flow f in $\mathcal{S}$.*

Proof: Similar to the proof of Theorem 6.19. The weights on the arcs in A_t are chosen
such that the weight of a minimum-cost flow is exactly the smallest possible value of μ_{dec}
Namely, the first unit of flow entering a value $d \in D(X)$ causes no violation and chooses
the outgoing arc with weight 0. The k-th unit of flow that enters d causes $k - 1$ violations

and chooses the outgoing arc with weight $k - 1$. □

Once again, we can filter the constraint `soft_alldifferent`$(x_1, \ldots, x_n, z, \mu_{\text{dec}})$ to arc consistency by an algorithm which is similar to the one in Section 6.3.1. First we compute a minimum-cost flow f in $\mathcal{S}$. We apply the successive shortest paths algorithm, i.e., we need to compute n shortest paths in the residual graph. Because there are non-zero weights only on arcs in A_t, each shortest path computation takes $O(m)$ time, using a breadth-first search. Hence we can find f in $O(nm)$ time. If weight$(f) > \max D(z)$, we know that the constraint is inconsistent.

To identify the arcs $a = (x_i, d) \in A_X$ that belong to a feasible integral flow g with weight$(g) \leq \max D(z)$, we again apply Theorem 6.2. Thus, we search for a shortest d-x_i path in $\mathcal{S}_f$ that together with a forms a directed circuit C. We can compute all such shortest paths in $O(m)$ time, using again the fact that only arcs $a \in A_t$ contribute to the cost of such paths (more details are given in [26]).

In [27], the above algorithm was extended to other soft global constraints, such as the soft `regular` constraint and the soft `gcc` constraint. The result for the soft `regular` constraint was obtained independently in [5].

6.5 Partial Filtering Algorithms

The algorithms we have presented so far achieve perfect filtering: The removal of any additional value from the domain of any variable would change the solution set of the constraint. Sometimes, achieving this utopian goal is too costly, even intractable, and it makes sense to compromise on a weaker level of filtering. This section describes some of the approaches that have been suggested for partial filtering of global constraints.

6.5.1 Bound Consistency

Assume that the elements of the variable domains are drawn from a total order (e.g., the integers) and that the domain of each variable x_i is an interval of this total order. Thus, a domain $D(x) = [L(x), U(x)]$ is specified by a lower bound and an upper bound on the values that variable x can take.

Definition 6.22 (Bound consistency). *Let C be a constraint on the variables $x_1, \ldots, x_k$ with respective interval domains $D(x_1), \ldots, D(x_k)$. We say that C is bound consistent if for every $1 \leq i \leq k$, there exists a tuple $(d_1, \ldots, d_k) \in C$ such that $d_i = L(x_i)$ and there exists a tuple $(e_1, \ldots, e_k) \in C$ such that $e_i = U(x_i)$.*

Computing bound consistency, then, amounts to shrinking the domain intervals as much as possible without losing any solutions.

Bound consistency for `alldifferent` and `gcc`

The assumption that the domain of each variable is an interval of the values, implies that the value graph is convex:

Definition 6.23 (Convex graph). *A bipartite graph $G = (X, Y, E)$ is convex if the vertices of Y can be assigned distinct integers from $[1, |Y|]$ such that for every vertex $x \in X$, the numbers assigned to its neighbors form a subinterval of $[1, |Y|]$.*

Algorithms for computing bound consistency exploit this property of the value graph (either directly or implicitly). Naturally, filtering algorithms for `alldifferent` appeared first and the generalizations to `gcc` followed. Two parallel approaches were explored (see Table 6.1). The first is an adaption of the matching/flow method described above and the second is based on Hall's marriage theorem.

Theorem 6.24 (Hall's Marriage Theorem [22]). *A bipartite graph $G = (X, Y, E)$ has a matching covering X if and only if for any subset X' of X, we have that $|D(X')| \geq |X'|$*

In our terminology: there is a solution to an `alldifferent` constraint if and only if for every subset of the variables, the union of their domains contains enough values to match each of them with a different value. This theorem implies that if there is a set S of k variables whose domains are contained in a size-k interval I of values, then the values of I can be safely removed from the domain of any variable outside of S. It also implies that this filtering step suffices: If it cannot be applied, the `alldifferent` constraint is bound consistent.

As we saw, the flow-based approach yields both arc consistency and bound consistency algorithms. The second approach, using Hall's marriage theorem, was first applied by Leconte [41] who obtained an algorithm that computes *range consistency*, a filtering level which is stronger than bound consistency but weaker than arc consistency. Subsequently, Hall's theorem was also used in bound consistency algorithms.

	Hall's Theorem	**Matchings/Flows**	
	bound consistency	arc consistency	bound consistency
`alldifferent`	Puget [52], López-Ortiz et al. [43]	Régin [57]	Mehlhorn and Thiel [44]
`gcc`	Quimper et al. [54]	Régin [58]	Katriel and Thiel [35]

Table 6.1: The two approaches for filtering of `alldifferent` and `gcc` constraints.

In the following, n denotes the number of variables, n' denotes the number of values in the union of their domains and m denotes the sum of the cardinalities of the domains (so the value graph has $n + n'$ vertices and m edges). Since m may be as large as nn', bound consistency algorithms typically do not construct the graph explicitly.

Puget designed the first bound consistency algorithm for `alldifferent`, which is based on Hall's theorem and runs in $O(n \log n)$ time [52]. Mehlhorn and Thiel [44] later showed that since the matching and SCC computations of Régin's algorithm [57] can be performed faster on convex graphs compared to general graphs, it is possible to achieve bound consistency for `alldifferent` using the matching approach in $O(n + n')$ time plus the time required to sort the variables according to the endpoints of their domains. Katriel and Thiel [35] later generalized this algorithm for the `gcc` case. Simultaneously, Quimper et al. [54] discovered an alternative bound consistency algorithm for `gcc`, based on the Hall interval approach. The latter algorithm narrows the domains of only the assignment variables, while the former narrows the domains of the assignment variables as well as the count variables, to bound consistency.

As mentioned in Section 6.3.2, it is NP-hard to filter all variables to arc consistency. It is therefore significant that we can achieve at least *some* filtering for the domains of the count variables.

Glover's algorithm

In order to demonstrate how much simpler convex bipartite graphs are from general bipartite graphs, we describe a simple, greedy algorithm that finds a maximum cardinality matching in a convex value graph. Glover [21] was the first who suggested this algorithm as an $O(nn')$-time solution. Using sophisticated data structures, the complexity was later reduced to $O(n' + n\alpha(n))$ by Lipski and Preparata [42] and finally to $O(n' + n)$ by Gabow and Tarjan [19]. The latter solutions assume that the values are integers in the interval $[1, n']$ (which can be achieved in $O(n' \log n')$ time by sorting and relabeling them). We will restrict our description to a simple implementation of Glover's algorithm, which uses only a priority queue and does not require that the values are in $[1, n']$. This implementation runs in $O(n' + n \log n)$ time. It is much faster than the best known solution for general value graphs which, recall, runs in $O(m\sqrt{n})$ time [28].

The algorithm traverses the value vertices from smaller to larger and greedily decides, for each value vertex, whether it is to be matched and if so, with which variable vertex. For this purpose, it maintains a priority queue that contains variable vertices which are candidates for matching, sorted by the upper endpoints of their domains. When considering the value vertex v_i, the algorithm first inserts into the queue all variable vertices whose domains begin at v_i; they were not candidates for matching before, but they are now.

Next, there are two cases to consider. If the priority queue is empty, v_i will remain unmatched. Otherwise, the minimum priority variable vertex x_j is extracted, and there are two subcases. If x_j's priority is at least v_i, then it is matched with v_i. Otherwise, it should have been matched earlier, and the algorithm terminates and reports that there is no solution (the graph does not have a matching covering X, or, equivalently, the `alldifferent` constraint does not have a solution).

The intuition behind this algorithm is that it always matches the candidate variable vertex whose domain ends earliest, so when x_j is matched, any candidate vertex that remains unmatched can be matched with at least as many value vertices as x_j, but perhaps more. For a formal proof of correctness see [21] or [44].

6.5.2 Reduced-Cost Based Filtering

Next we consider a partial filtering method for optimization constraints of the following type. Let $X = \{x_1, \ldots, x_n\}$ be a set of variables with corresponding finite domains $D(x_1), \ldots, D(x_n)$. We assume that each pair (x_i, j) with $j \in D(x_i)$ induces a "cost" c_{ij}. We now extend any global constraint C on X to an optimization constraint $\mathtt{opt\_}C$ by introducing a cost variable z and defining

$$
\begin{aligned}
\mathtt{opt\_}C(x_1, \ldots, x_n, z, c) = \{(d_1, \ldots, d_n, d) \mid \\
(d_1, \ldots, d_n) \in C(x_1, \ldots, x_n), \\
\forall i \; d_i \in D(x_i), d \in D(z), \textstyle\sum_{i=1}^{n} c_{id_i} \le d\}.
\end{aligned}
$$

where we assume that z is to be minimized. For example, the `cost_gcc` is a particular instance of such constraint. We have seen that its arc consistency algorithm is efficient because of its correspondence with a minimum-weight flow. For many other optimization constraints of this type, however, such correspondence does not exist, or is difficult to identify. In such situations we may be able to apply *reduced-cost based filtering* instead, using a linear programming relaxation of the optimization constraint. This method was first introduced in this form by Focacci et al. [17], although the technique is part of the linear programming folklore under the name *variable fixing*. Note that in general, such a filtering algorithm does not establish arc consistency.

In order to apply reduced-cost based filtering, we need to infer a linear programming relaxation from the optimization constraint. First, we introduce binary variables y_{ij} for all $i \in \{1, \ldots, n\}$ and $j \in D(x_i)$, such that

$$
\begin{aligned}
x_i = j &\Leftrightarrow y_{ij} = 1, \\
x_i \neq j &\Leftrightarrow y_{ij} = 0.
\end{aligned}
\tag{6.9}
$$

To ensure that each variable x_i is assigned to a single value in its domain we state the linear constraints

$$
\sum_{j \in D(x_i)} y_{ij} = 1 \ \text{ for } i = 1, \ldots, n.
$$

The linear objective function is stated as

$$
\sum_{i=1}^{n} \sum_{j \in D(x_i)} c_{ij} y_{ij}.
$$

The next, most difficult, task is to rewrite (a part of) the optimization constraint as a system of linear constraints using the binary variables. This is problem dependent, and no general recipe exists. However, for many problems such descriptions are known, see, e.g., [55]. For example, for an `alldifferent` constraint we may add the linear constraints

$$
\sum_{i=1}^{n} y_{ij} \leq 1 \ \text{ for all } j \in \bigcup_{i=1}^{n} D(x_i)
$$

to ensure that every domain value is assigned to at most one variable.

Finally, in order to obtain a linear programming relaxation, we remove the integrality constraint on the binary variables and state

$$
0 \leq y_{ij} \leq 1 \ \text{ for } i \in \{1, \ldots, n\}, j \in D(x_i).
$$

When we solve this linear programming relaxation to optimality, we obtain a lower bound on z, and reduced-costs $\bar{c}$. Recall from Section 6.1.3 that reduced-costs estimate the increase of the objective function when we force a variable into the solution. Hence, if we enforce the assignment $x_i = j$, the objective function value will increase by at least $\bar{c}_{ij}$. Let z^* be the objective value of the current optimal solution of the linear program. Then we apply the following filtering rule:

$$
\text{if } z^* + \bar{c}_{ij} > \max D(z) \text{ then } D(x_i) \leftarrow D(x_i) \setminus \{j\}.
$$

A huge advantage of this approach is that it can be applied very efficiently. Namely, reduced-costs are obtained automatically when solving a linear program. Hence, the filtering rule can be applied without additional computational costs.

6.5.3   Intractable Global Constraints

As already noted, global constraints serve to break up the CSP into a conjunction of simpler CSPs, each of which can be filtered efficiently. We show below that if it is NP-hard to determine whether a constraint has a solution, it is also NP-hard to compute arc consistency for the constraint. The following is a special case of a Theorem due to Bessière et al. [9].

Theorem 6.25. *Let C be a constraint. If there is a polynomial-time algorithm that computes arc consistency for C then there is a polynomial-time algorithm that finds a single solution to C.*

Proof: Assume that we have an algorithm A that prunes the variable domains to arc consistency in polynomial time. Then we can find a solution to the constraint as follows:

1. Use algorithm A to compute arc consistency. The constraint has a solution if and only if all domains are now non-empty.

2. Repeat until a solution is found:

   a) Let x be a variable such that $|D(x)| > 1$ and let $v \in D(x)$.

   b) Set $D(x) \leftarrow \{v\}$

   c) Use algorithm A to compute arc consistency.

In each iteration the value of one variable is determined, so the total number of iterations is at most equal to the number of variables and the running time of the algorithm is polynomial.   □

The converse of Theorem 6.25 does not hold; there are constraints for which arc consistency is NP-hard while checking feasibility is not (see, e.g., [64]). A weaker version which does hold is stated below. The crucial point to note is that there are constraints for which it is possible to efficiently check whether the constraint has a solution, but it is NP-hard to check whether it has a solution in which a certain variable is assigned a specific value in its domain.

Theorem 6.26. *Let C be a constraint defined on the variables $X = \{x_1, \ldots, x_k\}$. If there is an algorithm A that, for any $x_i \in X$ and $d \in D(x_i)$, determines in polynomial time whether there is a solution to the constraint $C \wedge (x_i \leftarrow d)$, then there is a polynomial-time algorithm that computes arc consistency for C.*

Proof: For every variable x_i and value $d \in D(x_i)$, use algorithm A to check if there is a solution when $x_i \leftarrow d$ and remove d from $D(x_i)$ otherwise.   □

A consequence of Theorem 6.25 is that there is a very large class of practically useful global constraints for which we probably cannot achieve perfect filtering. In some cases, a possible remedy is to compromise on bound consistency; as already mentioned, bound consistency can be computed in almost-linear time for the gcc, while arc consistency, for the assignment and count variables, is NP-hard.

Filtering for the cumulative constraint

Another method to cope with NP-hardness is to *relax* the constraint. That is, to transform
our NP-hard constraint C into a constraint C' such that C' can be efficiently filtered to a
guaranteed consistency level (e.g., arc consistency or bound consistency) and $C \subset C'$, i.e.,
every solution to C is also a solution to C'. For example, the reduced-cost based filtering
method described above applies a linear programming relaxation of the constraint. Here
we will demonstrate this approach by describing a filtering algorithm for a relaxation of
the `cumulative`[3] constraint [45]. We assume for simplicity that the capacity of the
resource and the capacity requirements and processing times of the tasks are fixed, i.e.,
$|D(\mathcal{C})| = 1$ and $|D(c_i)| = |D(p_i)| = 1$ for all i. The filtering task is to increase the
minimum start times and decrease the maximum completion times of the tasks, without
losing any solutions to the constraint. We will describe the algorithm that tightens the
earliest start times; the solution for the latest completion times is symmetric. The relaxation
of the `cumulative` constraint will be defined below, but first we wish to build up the
intuition behind the definition.

Let the *energy* of task t_i be $e_i = c_i p_i$; it represents the total capacity of the resource
that is consumed by the task. For a set $\Omega \subseteq T$ of tasks, let r_Ω be the earliest release time
of a task in Ω, d_Ω the latest deadline of a task in Ω and e_Ω the sum of the energies of tasks
in Ω. Clearly, if there is a subset $\Omega \subseteq T$ of the tasks such that $e_\Omega > \mathcal{C}(d_\Omega - r_\Omega)$, the
problem is infeasible: Between time r_Ω and d_Ω, the tasks need more of the resource than
is available.

Now, let Ω be a set of tasks and $t_i \notin \Omega$ another task such that $e_{\Omega \cup \{t_i\}} > \mathcal{C}(d_\Omega -
r_{\Omega \cup \{t_i\}})$. If t_i is scheduled such that it completes executing before any task in Ω, then it
completes before d_Ω, so the total energy of the tasks scheduled in the interval $[r_{\Omega \cup \{t_i\}}, d_\Omega$
is above the capacity of the resource, a contradiction. So t_i completes execution last among
the tasks in $\Omega \cup \{t_i\}$.

Once we have found such a pair (Ω, t_i), we can use it to adjust the starting time of t_i as
follows. For each subset $\Theta \subseteq \Omega$, we examine the time interval $I = [r_\Theta, d_\Theta]$ and determine
what is the earliest time in this interval at which t_i can start executing. Since we know that
t_i cannot complete before any task in Θ, we get that if t_i is scheduled at time unit $u \in I$
then in the interval $[u, d_\Theta]$ the schedule allocates only $\mathcal{C} - c_i$ capacity units of the resource
for tasks in Θ.

Conceptually, split the resource into two parts, with capacities $\mathcal{C}_1 = \mathcal{C} - c_i$ and $\mathcal{C}_2 = c_i$
Assume that the schedule placed t_i on the second part and that t_i was the last task scheduled
there. Clearly, on the first part we can schedule at most $(\mathcal{C} - c_i)(d_\Theta - r_\Theta)$ units of energy
in the time interval I. This means that at least $rest(\Theta, c_i) = e_\Theta - (\mathcal{C} - c_i)(d_\Theta - r_\Theta)$ units
of energy must be scheduled in this time interval on the second part just to schedule all the
tasks of Θ. Even if all of this energy is scheduled as early as possible, it takes up at least
the first $\frac{1}{c_i} rest(\Theta, c_i)$ time units of the second part and therefore t_i cannot begin before
time unit $r_\Theta + \frac{1}{c_i} rest(\Theta, c_i)$.

An algorithm that performs all such adjustments to the starting times of tasks is called
an *edge-finding* algorithm (because the algorithm discovers edges in the precedence-graph
of the completion times of the tasks). The basic idea of such an algorithm is to efficiently

---

[3]The `cumulative` constraint is, in general, NP-hard. Recently, Artiouchine and Baptiste [3] developed a
bound consistency algorithm for the special case in which all processing times are equal.

identify a small number of pairs (Θ, t_i) for which the rule described above needs to be applied.

Edge-finding algorithms were first developed for the disjunctive case, which is much simpler than the most general case. The fastest algorithm runs in $O(n \log n)$ time [12]. For the cumulative case, the fastest known solution is by Mercier and Van Hentenryck [45] and runs in $O(kn^2)$ where k is the number of different capacity requirements of the tasks (a previously developed $O(n^2)$-time solution was shown to be incomplete).

After giving an outline of the algorithm, we are ready to define the constraint that it filters, i.e., the relaxation of the `cumulative` constraint. Since edge-finding algorithms existed in the scheduling literature before `cumulative` was a global constraint, this definition may seem opportunistic: We define the problem to be whatever we already know how to solve. Nevertheless, scheduling is an important application in constraint programming so we believe that the edge-finding algorithm deserves a description in constraint programming terminology: It is a bound consistency algorithm for the relaxation of the `cumulative` constraint (where the processing times and capacities of the tasks, as well as the capacity of the resource are fixed) which is satisfied if for every task t_i

$$\min\{D(r_i)\} \geq \max_{\substack{\Omega \subseteq T \\ i \notin \Omega \\ \alpha(\Omega, i)}} \quad \max_{\substack{\Theta \subseteq \Omega \\ rest(\Theta, c_i)}} \quad r_\Theta + \lceil \frac{1}{c_i} rest(\Theta, c_i) \rceil$$

where $\alpha(\Omega, i) \Leftrightarrow (\mathcal{C}(d_\Omega - r_{\Omega \cup \{i\}}) < e_{\Omega \cup \{i\}}))$.

Intractable optimization constraints

Sellmann [63, 64] suggested two forms of partial consistency, which are specifically motivated by NP-hard optimization constraints. The first is an adaptation of relaxed consistency [64] to optimization constraints. That is, we transform the constraint C into a constraint C' such that $C \subseteq C'$ and C' can be filtered efficiently. The idea is similar to the relaxation of the `cumulative` constraint described above, except that here C and C' are both optimization constraints. The reduced-cost based filtering based on a linear relaxation, which was described in Section 6.5.2, also employs this idea.

Sellmann demonstrates this technique by way of the shorter-path constraint, which is defined on a digraph G, a source vertex s and a target vertex t in G, an upper bound W and a variable P whose domain is all subsets of arcs of G (see Section 6.6.1). The constraint is satisfied if P is a set of arcs that form a path in G from s to t whose length is at most W. Since it is NP-hard to determine whether there is a path from s to t that uses a certain arc (while visiting each node at most once), it is NP-hard to compute bound consistency for the set variables P. However, it is easy to determine whether there is an "almost-path" from s to t that uses the arc (u, v) and whose length is at most the upper bound: Find the length of the shortest path from s to u and the length of the shortest path from v to t. The concatenation of these two paths through the arc (u, v) is a walk from s to t that visits every vertex at most twice. The relaxed shorter-path constraint, then, excludes from the set assigned to P any arc that does not belong to a path or almost-path from s to t in G whose length is at most W.

Sellmann's second form of partial consistency is termed *approximated consistency* [63]. Here, the idea is to use efficient approximation algorithms for NP-hard problems as components of the filtering algorithm. Recall that an α-approximation algorithm for a minimization (maximization) problem P is a polynomial-time algorithm A such that for every instance x of P, A finds a solution whose value is at most $(1 + \epsilon) \cdot Opt(P, x)$ (at least $(1 - \epsilon) \cdot Opt(P, x)$), where $Opt(P, x)$ is the value of the optimal solution to instance x of problem P. Clearly, the smaller the value of α, the better the quality of approximation. $1 + \alpha$ (resp. $1 - \alpha$) is referred to as the *approximation factor* achieved by algorithm A. For more details, see any text on approximation algorithms, such as [25, 68].

For a minimization (maximization) constraint that is defined on a variable z which holds the upper (lower) bound on the value of a solution, we say that C is ϵ-arc consistent if every value in the domain of every variable participates in a solution of value at most $z + \epsilon Opt$ (at least $z - \epsilon Opt$). The motivation behind this definition is that approximation algorithms allow us to efficiently identify problem instances whose optimal solutions are much better or much worse than the best solution found so far, but may give inconclusive replies for instances which are of comparable quality. In such cases, approximate consistency allows one-sided errors: we keep the respective value in the variable domain, to be on the safe side.

6.6 Global Variables

In recent years, some of the work of global constraints, i.e., that of providing more structured information to the solver and simplifying the syntax of CSPs, is taken up by complex variable types, which we will collectively refer to as *global variables*. Our focus in this section is on constraints defined on global variables and the design of filtering algorithms for such constraints. We will discuss two important examples: sets and graphs. Chapter 17, "Beyond Finite Domains", is devoted to the topic of complex variable types, and describes many examples and aspects that are not mentioned here.

6.6.1 Set Variables

Let us revisit the shift-assignment problem for which we used the global cardinality constraint in Section 6.2.4. We assumed that each worker is to work exactly one shift. It is more realistic, however, that we have a lower bound and an upper bound on the number of shifts that each worker is to staff. The result is known as the *symmetric cardinality constraint* [37]:

Definition 6.27. *The symmetric cardinality constraint* $\mathrm{symcc}(x_1, \ldots, x_n, c_{x_1}, \ldots, c_{x_n}, c_{v_1}, \ldots, c_{v_{n'}})$ *is defined on a collection of assignment variables* $x_1, \ldots, x_n$ *and two sets of count variables,* $c_{x_1}, \ldots, c_{x_n}$ *and* $c_{v_1}, \ldots, c_{v_{n'}}$. *It specifies that the value assigned to* x_j *is a subset of* $\{v_1, \ldots, v_{n'}\}$ *of cardinality* c_{x_j}, *and that the number of such subsets that contain* v_i *is* c_{v_i}.

We still have one variable for each worker, but the value of this variable is the *set* of shifts that the worker will staff. One way to handle this is to say that the domain contains all subsets of the shifts. This results in an exponential growth in the number of values (and hence in the size of the value graph).

An alternative is to use *set variables*. A set variable x is a variable that has a discrete domain $D(x) = [lb(x), ub(x)]$. Thus, the domain of a set variable consists of two sets, the set $lb(x)$ of *mandatory* elements and the set $ub(x) \setminus lb(x)$ of *possible* elements. The value assigned to x should be a set $s(x)$ such that $lb(x) \subseteq s(x) \subseteq ub(x)$.

For a constraint on set variables, we are not interested in arc consistency because the individual values that a set variable can take do not explicitly exist; we only have their intersection (lb) and their union (ub). Viewing the intersection as a lower bound and the union as an upper bound, we speak of bound consistency when filtering the domain of a set variable. A bound consistency computation for a constraint C defined on a set variable x requires that we:

- Remove a value v from $ub(x)$ if there is no solution to C in which $v \in s(x)$.

- Include a value $v \in ub(x)$ in $lb(x)$ if in all solutions to C, $v \in s(x)$.

To demonstrate such a computation[4], we sketch how the flow-based filtering algorithm for gcc can be adapted to compute bound consistency for the assignment variables of symcc, assuming that the domains of all count variables are fixed intervals. The flow network constructed from the value graph is almost identical, except that the requirement of an arc from s to a variable vertex reflects the cardinality requirement for the set assigned to the variable. That is, the capacity of the arc (s, x_j) is equal to the interval $D(c_{x_j})$. Then, we once again have a one-to-one correspondence between the integral s-t flows in the network and the solutions to the constraint. As before, after finding a flow we have that a non-flow arc belongs to some integral s-t flow if and only if its endpoints belong to the same SCC of the residual graph.

However, unlike in the gcc case, this does not complete the filtering task: we must also identify arcs that belong to *any* integral s-t flow, and make sure that they are in the lower bounds of the domains of the relevant set variables. It is not difficult to verify that this is exactly the set of flow arcs whose endpoints belong to different SCCs of the residual graph (recall that the requirement of an arc from a variable vertex to a value vertex is $[0, 1]$).

The bottleneck of the algorithm is the flow computation, which takes $O(mn)$ time. It is interesting to note that the cardinality of the domain of any of the set variables may well be exponential in the running time of this algorithm, which handles all of these domains at once.

6.6.2 Graph Variables

A *graph variable* [16] is simply two set variables V and E, with an inherent constraint $E \subseteq V \times V$. As with set variables, the domain $D(G) = [lb(G), ub(G)]$ of a graph variable G consists of mandatory vertices and edges $lb(G)$ (the *lower bound graph*) and possible vertices and edges $ub(G) \setminus lb(G)$ (the *upper bound graph*). The value assigned to the variable G must be a subgraph of $ub(G)$ and a super graph of the $lb(G)$.

The usefulness of graph variables depends on the existence of efficient filtering algorithms for useful constraints defined on them, i.e., constraints that force graph variables to have certain properties or certain relations between them. As a simple example, the constraint $Subgraph(G, S)$ specifies that S is a subgraph of G. Note that both S and G are

---

[4]Additional examples can be found in [8].

variables, so computing bound consistency for the *Subgraph* constraint means the following:

1. If $lb(S)$ is not a subgraph of $ub(G)$, the constraint has no solution.

2. For each $e \in ub(G) \cap lb(S)$, include e in $lb(G)$.

3. For each $e \in ub(S) \setminus ub(G)$, remove e from $ub(S)$.

The conditions above can be checked in time which is linear in the sum of the sizes of $ub(G)$ and $ub(S)$. As with set variables, we are in the interesting situation in which the number of graphs that the bound consistency algorithm reasons about may be exponential in the running-time of the algorithm.

The spanning tree constraint

As a slightly more sophisticated example, we consider the constraint $ST(G, T)$, which states that the graph T is a spanning tree of the graph G. Since a spanning tree is a subgraph, the conditions described above should be checked when computing bound consistency for ST. In addition, (1) the vertex-sets of G and T must be equal, and (2) T must be a tree.

To enforce (1), we remove from $ub(G)$ any vertex which is not in $ub(T)$ and we include in $lb(T)$ any vertex which is in $lb(G)$. As for (2), if $lb(T)$ contains a circuit then T cannot be a tree and if $ub(T)$ is not connected then T cannot be connected. In both cases, the constraint has no solution. Finally, any edge in $ub(T) \setminus lb(T)$ whose endpoints belong to the same connected component of $lb(T)$ must be removed (including it in any solution would introduce a circuit in T) and any bridge[5] in $ub(T)$ must be placed in $lb(T)$ (T cannot be connected if it is excluded).

The running time of the algorithm we described is linear in the sum of the sizes of the upper bounds of G and T. To prove that it achieves bound consistency, one needs to show that the following three conditions hold:

1. Every vertex or edge that was removed, does not participate in any solution.

2. Every remaining vertex or edge in $ub(T)$ or $ub(G)$ participates in at least one solution and every remaining vertex or edge in $ub(T) \setminus lb(T)$ or $ub(G) \setminus lb(G)$ is excluded from at least one solution to the constraint.

3. Every vertex or edge that the algorithm inserts into $lb(G)$ or $lb(T)$ participates in all solutions.

Note that in item 3 above we do not say that every element in $lb(G)$ and $lb(T)$ belongs to all solutions. This is only required of those elements that the filtering algorithm decided to include in the lower bound sets. The input may include any vertex or edge in the lower bound graph, and the filtering algorithm does not ask why: It may only remove values from variable domains, and never add them.

---

[5] A *bridge* in a graph is an edge whose removal increases the number of connected components.

6.7 Conclusion

The search for useful global constraints and the design of efficient filtering algorithms for them is an ongoing research effort that tackles many challenging and interesting problems. We have already mentioned some of the fundamental questions: What are the frequently recurring sub-problems that we would like to capture by global constraints? For a specific constraint, what is the computational complexity of filtering it to arc consistency? Should we compromise on partial consistency? We would like to briefly mention several other ideas on global constraints that have been proposed in recent years.

Given the large number of global constraints that were and will be defined, several researchers are attempting to find generic methods to specify and handle constraints. Beldiceanu et al. [7] describe a constraint solver that views a global constraint in terms of a collection of graph properties (such as the number of strongly connected components in a digraph). Then, the solver uses a database of known graph theoretic results to automatically generate new constraints that strengthen the model by allowing more filtering. They point out that out of the 227 global constraints listed in the global constraints catalog [6], about 200 can be described in terms of graph properties. Therefore, their approach seems to be widely applicable. Bessière et al. [10] defined a declarative language that can be used to specify many known constraints which model counting and occurrence problems. In this language, a constraint is specified as the conjunction of constraints, each of which can be a simple (binary) constraint on scalar or set variables, or one of two globals constraints called `range` and `roots`.

Another approach is to view the filtering task in the context of the tree search. We have already mentioned the problem of dynamic filtering, i.e., recomputing arc consistency after a small change such as the removal of a few values from variable domains. Recently, Katriel [34] pointed out that in a flow network with n nodes and m edges where every edge belongs to at least one feasible flow, there are only $O(n)$ edges whose removal would render *other* edges useless. This implies that if the filtering is random, i.e., the edge removed from the value graph of an `alldifferent` or `gcc` is always selected at random among all possibilities, the expected number of edges that need to be removed before it makes sense to recompute arc consistency is $\Theta(m/n)$. It would be interesting to evaluate experimentally whether the assumption that filtering is random is realistic, and whether delayed filtering is a good compromise between filtering efficiency and effectiveness. If this approach is to be pursued, it is necessary to either analyze each global constraint independently and determine a reasonable filtering frequency, or find a generic or automated way to do this for many global constraints.

In the area of partial filtering for NP-hard global constraints, there seems to be a lot of potential for enhancements. Here we would like to suggest the idea of approximate filtering. Recall that an approximation algorithm for an optimization problem is an algorithm that finds a solution whose value, according to the objective function of the problem, does not deviate too much from the value of the optimal solution. For a filtering problem, the objective function counts the sum of the cardinalities of the domains of the variables. An optimal solution minimizes this number, and hence an α-approximate solution, for $\alpha \geq 1$, is a solution that removes all but $\alpha\,Opt$ values from the variable domains. Formally,

Definition 6.28 (Approximate filtering). *Let $C(x_1, \ldots, x_n)$ be a constraint and assume that after filtering it to arc consistency, the sum of the cardinalities of the domains of*

$x_1, \ldots, x_n$ is Opt. An α-approximate filtering algorithm *for C is an algorithm that removes values from the domains of the variables* $x_1, \ldots, x_n$ *such that the solution set of C remains unchanged and the sum of the cardinalities of the domains of the variables is at most* $\alpha\,Opt$.

Note that approximate filtering is different from the notion of approximated consistency that was described in Section 6.5.3 in two ways. First, approximate filtering applies to any constraint while approximated consistency is defined for optimization constraints. In addition, with approximated consistency, what is being approximated is the value of the solutions to the constraint that remain, while approximate filtering directly approximates the effectiveness of the filtering algorithm.

Bibliography

[1] A. Aggoun and N. Beldiceanu. Extending CHIP in order to solve complex scheduling and placement problems. *Journal of Mathematical and Computer Modelling*, 17(7): 57–73, 1993.

[2] R.K. Ahuja, T.L. Magnanti, and J.B. Orlin. *Network Flows*. Prentice Hall, 1993.

[3] K. Artiouchine and P. Baptiste. Inter-distance Constraint: An Extension of the All-Different Constraint for Scheduling Equal Length Jobs. In P. van Beek, editor, *Proceedings of the Eleventh International Conference on Principles and Practice of Constraint Programming (CP 2005)*, volume 3709 of *Lecture Notes in Computer Science* pages 62–76. Springer, 2005.

[4] R. Barták. Dynamic Global Constraints in Backtracking Based Environments. *Annals of Operations Research*, 118(1–4):101–119, 2003.

[5] N. Beldiceanu, M. Carlsson, and T. Petit. Deriving Filtering Algorithms from Constraint Checkers. In M. Wallace, editor, *Proceedings of the Tenth International Conference on Principles and Practice of Constraint Programming (CP 2004)*, volume 3258 of *Lecture Notes in Computer Science*, pages 107–122. Springer, 2004.

[6] N. Beldiceanu, M. Carlsson, and J.X.-Rampon. Global constraint catalog. Technical Report T2005-06, Swedish Institute of Computer Science, 2005.

[7] N. Beldiceanu, M. Carlsson, J.-X. Rampon, and C. Truchet. Graph invariants as necessary conditions for global constraints. In P. van Beek, editor, *Proceedings of the Eleventh International Conference on Principles and Practice of Constraint Programming (CP 2005)*, volume 3709 of *Lecture Notes in Computer Science*, pages 92–106. Springer, 2005.

[8] C. Bessière, E. Hebrard, B. Hnich, and T. Walsh. Disjoint, partition and intersection constraints for set and multiset variables. In M. Wallace, editor, *Proceedings of the Tenth International Conference on Principles and Practice of Constraint Programming (CP 2004)*, volume 3258 of *Lecture Notes in Computer Science*, pages 138–152. Springer, 2004.

[9] C. Bessière, E. Hebrard, B. Hnich, and T. Walsh. The tractability of global constraints. In M. Wallace, editor, *Proceedings of the Tenth International Conference on Principles and Practice of Constraint Programming (CP 2004)*, volume 3258 of *Lecture Notes in Computer Science*, pages 716–720. Springer, 2004.

[10] C. Bessière, E. Hebrard, B. Hnich, Z. Kiziltan, and T. Walsh. The range and roots constraints: Specifying counting and occurrence problems. In *Proceedings of the Twen-*

tieth International Joint Conference on Artificial Intelligence (IJCAI 2005), pages 60–65. Professional Book Center, 2005.

[11] R.G. Busacker and P.J. Gowen. A Procedure for Determining a Family of Minimum-Cost Network Flow Patterns. Technical Report ORO-TP-15, Operations Research Office, The Johns Hopkins University, Bethesda, MD, 1960.

[12] J. Carlier and E. Pinson. Adjustment of heads and tails for the job-shop problem. *Euro. J. Oper. Res.*, 78:146–161, 1994.

[13] Y. Caseau, P.-Y. Guillo, and E. Levenez. A Deductive and Object-Oriented Approach to a Complex Scheduling Problem. In *Proceedings of Deductive and Object-Oriented Databases, Third International Conference (DOOD'93)*, pages 67–80, 1993.

[14] V. Chvátal. *Linear programming*. Freeman, 1983.

[15] G.B. Dantzig. Maximization of a linear function of variables subject to linear inequalities. In Tj.C. Koopmans, editor, *Activity Analysis of Production and Allocation – Proceedings of a conference*, pages 339–347. Wiley, 1951.

[16] G. Dooms, Y. Deville, and P. Dupont. CP(Graph): Introducing a Graph Computation Domain in Constraint Programming. In P. van Beek, editor, *Proceedings of the Eleventh International Conference on Principles and Practice of Constraint Programming (CP 2005)*, volume 3709 of *Lecture Notes in Computer Science*, pages 211–225. Springer, 2005.

[17] F. Focacci, A. Lodi, and M. Milano. Cost-based domain filtering. In J. Jaffar, editor, *Proceedings of the Fifth International Conference on Principles and Practice of Constraint Programming (CP 1999)*, volume 1713 of *Lecture Notes in Computer Science*, pages 189–203. Springer, 1999.

[18] L.R. Ford, Jr and D.R. Fulkerson. Constructing maximal dynamic flows from static flows. *Operations Research*, 6:419–433, 1958.

[19] H.N. Gabow and R.E. Tarjan. A linear-time algorithm for a special case of disjoint set union. In *Proceedings of the Fifteenth Annual ACM Symposium on Theory of computing (STOC 1983)*, pages 246–251. ACM, 1983.

[20] M.R. Garey and D.S. Johnson. *Computers and Intractability - A Guide to the Theory of NP-Completeness*. Freeman, 1979.

[21] F. Glover. Maximum matching in convex bipartite graphs. *Naval Research Logistics Quarterly*, 14:313–316, 1967.

[22] P. Hall. On representatives of subsets. *Journal of the London Mathematical Society*, 10:26–30, 1935.

[23] L. Hellsten, G. Pesant, and P. van Beek. A Domain Consistency Algorithm for the Stretch Constraint. In M. Wallace, editor, *Proceedings of the Tenth International Conference on Principles and Practice of Constraint Programming (CP 2004)*, volume 3258 of *Lecture Notes in Computer Science*, pages 290–304. Springer, 2004.

[24] P. Van Hentenryck and J.-P. Carillon. Generality vs. specificity: an experience with AI and OR techniques. In *Proceedings of the National Conference on Artificial Intelligence (AAAI)*, pages 660–664, 1988.

[25] D.S. Hochbaum, editor. *Approximation Algorithms for NP-Hard Problems*. Brooks / Cole Pub. Co., 1996.

[26] W.-J. van Hoeve. A Hyper-Arc Consistency Algorithm for the Soft Alldifferent Constraint. In M. Wallace, editor, *Proceedings of the Tenth International Conference on Principles and Practice of Constraint Programming (CP 2004)*, volume 3258 of *Lecture Notes in Computer Science*, pages 679–689. Springer, 2004.

[27] W.-J. van Hoeve, G. Pesant, and L.-M. Rousseau. On Global Warming: Flow-Based Soft Global Constraints. *Journal of Heuristics*, 2006. To appear.

[28] J.E. Hopcroft and R.M. Karp. An $n^{5/2}$ algorithm for maximum matchings in bipartite graphs. *SIAM Journal on Computing*, 2(4):225–231, 1973.

[29] J.E. Hopcroft and J.D. Ullman. *Introduction to automata theory, languages, and computation*. Addison-Wesley, 1979.

[30] M. Iri. A new method of solving transportation-network problems. *Journal of the Operations Research Society of Japan*, 3:27–87, 1960.

[31] W.S. Jewell. Optimal Flows Through Networks. Technical Report 8, Operations Research Center, MIT, Cambridge, MA, 1958.

[32] N. Karmarkar. A new polynomial-time algorithm for linear programming. *Combinatorica*, 4:373–395, 1984.

[33] N. Karmarkar. A new polynomial-time algorithm for linear programming. In *Proceedings of the Sixteenth Annual ACM Symposium on Theory of Computing (STOC 1984)*, pages 302–311. ACM, 1984.

[34] I. Katriel. Expected-Case Analysis for Delayed Filtering. In C. Beck and B. Smith, editors, *Proceedings of the Third International Conference on the Integration of AI and OR Techniques in Constraint Programming for Combinatorial Optimization Problems (CPAIOR 2006)*, Lecture Notes in Computer Science. Springer, 2006. To appear.

[35] I. Katriel and S. Thiel. Complete bound consistency for the global cardinality constraint. *Constraints*, 10(3):191–217, 2005.

[36] L.G. Khachiyan. A polynomial algorithm in linear programming. *Soviet Mathematics Doklady*, 20:191–194, 1979.

[37] W. Kocjan and P. Kreuger. Filtering methods for symmetric cardinality constraint. In J.-C. Régin and M. Rueher, editors, *Proceedings of the First International Conference on the Integration of AI and OR Techniques in Constraint Programming for Combinatorial Optimization Problems (CPAIOR 2004)*, volume 3011 of *Lecture Notes in Computer Science*, pages 200–208. Springer, 2004.

[38] D. König. Graphok és matrixok. *Matematikai és Fizikai Lapok*, 38:116–119, 1931.

[39] J.-L. Lauriere. A language and a program for stating and solving combinatorial problems. *Artificial Intelligence*, 10(1):29–127, 1978.

[40] E.L. Lawler, J.K. Lenstra, A.H.G. Rinnooy Kan, and D.B. Shmoys, editors. *The Traveling Salesman Problem – A Guided Tour of Combinatorial Optimization*. Wiley, 1985.

[41] M. Leconte. A bounds-based reduction scheme for constraints of difference. In *Proceedings of the Second International Workshop on Constraint-based Reasoning (Constraint 1996)*, pages 19–28, 1996.

[42] W. Lipski and F.P. Preparata. Efficient algorithms for finding maximum matchings in convex bipartite graphs and related problems. *Acta Informatica*, 15:329–346, 1981.

[43] A. López-Ortiz, C.-G. Quimper, J. Tromp, and P. van Beek. A fast and simple algorithm for bounds consistency of the alldifferent constraint. In *Proceedings of the Eighteenth International Joint Conference on Artificial Intelligence (IJCAI 2003)* pages 245–250. Morgan Kaufmann, 2003.

[44] K. Mehlhorn and S. Thiel. Faster Algorithms for Bound-Consistency of the Sortedness and the Alldifferent Constraint. In R. Dechter, editor, *Proceedings of the Sixth International Conference on Principles and Practice of Constraint Programming (CP*

2000), volume 1894 of *Lecture Notes in Computer Science*, pages 306–319. Springer, 2000.

[45] L. Mercier and P. Van Hentenryck. Edge finding for cumulative scheduling, 2005.

[46] G.L. Nemhauser and L.A. Wolsey. *Integer and Combinatorial Optimization*. Wiley, 1988.

[47] A. Oplobedu, J. Marcovitch, and Y. Tourbier. CHARME: Un langage industriel de programmation par contraintes, illustré par une application chez Renault. In *Proceedings of the Ninth International Workshop on Expert Systems and their Applications: General Conference*, volume 1, pages 55–70, 1989.

[48] G. Pesant. A Regular Language Membership Constraint for Finite Sequences of Variables. In M. Wallace, editor, *Proceedings of the Tenth International Conference on Principles and Practice of Constraint Programming (CP 2004)*, volume 3258 of *Lecture Notes in Computer Science*, pages 482–495. Springer, 2004.

[49] G. Pesant. A Filtering Algorithm for the Stretch Constraint. In T. Walsh, editor, *Proceedings of the Seventh International Conference on Principles and Practice of Constraint Programming (CP 2001)*, volume 2239 of *Lecture Notes in Computer Science*, pages 183–195. Springer, 2001.

[50] J. Petersen. Die Theorie der regulären graphs. *Acta Mathematica*, 15:193–220, 1891.

[51] T. Petit, J.-C. Régin, and C. Bessière. Specific Filtering Algorithms for Over-Constrained Problems. In T. Walsh, editor, *Proceedings of the Seventh International Conference on Principles and Practice of Constraint Programming (CP 2001)*, volume 2239 of *Lecture Notes in Computer Science*, pages 451–463. Springer, 2001.

[52] J.-F. Puget. A fast algorithm for the bound consistency of alldiff constraints. In *Proceedings of the Fifteenth National Conference on Artificial Intelligence and Tenth Innovative Applications of Artificial Intelligence Conference (AAAI / IAAI)*, pages 359–366. AAAI Press / The MIT Press, 1998.

[53] C.-G. Quimper, A. López-Ortiz, P. van Beek, and A. Golynski. Improved Algorithms for the Global Cardinality Constraint. In M. Wallace, editor, *Proceedings of the Tenth International Conference on Principles and Practice of Constraint Programming (CP 2004)*, volume 3258 of *Lecture Notes in Computer Science*, pages 542–556. Springer, 2004.

[54] C.-G. Quimper, P. van Beek, A. López-Ortiz, A. Golynski, and S.B. Sadjad. An Efficient Bounds Consistency Algorithm for the Global Cardinality Constraint. *Constraints*, 10(2):115–135, 2005.

[55] P. Refalo. Linear Formulation of Constraint Programming Models and Hybrid Solvers. In R. Dechter, editor, *Proceedings of the Sixth International Conference on Principles and Practice of Constraint Programming (CP 2000)*, volume 1894 of *Lecture Notes in Computer Science*, pages 369–383. Springer, 2000.

[56] J.-C. Régin. Cost-Based Arc Consistency for Global Cardinality Constraints. *Constraints*, 7:387–405, 2002.

[57] J.-C. Régin. A Filtering Algorithm for Constraints of Difference in CSPs. In *Proceedings of the Twelfth National Conference on Artificial Intelligence (AAAI)*, volume 1, pages 362–367. AAAI Press, 1994.

[58] J.-C. Régin. Generalized Arc Consistency for Global Cardinality Constraint. In *Proceedings of the Thirteenth National Conference on Artificial Intelligence and Eighth Innovative Applications of Artificial Intelligence Conference (AAAI / IAAI)*, volume 1, pages 209–215. AAAI Press / The MIT Press, 1996.

[59] J.-C. Régin. Arc Consistency for Global Cardinality Constraints with Costs. In J. Jaffar, editor, *Proceedings of the Fifth International Conference on Principles and Practice of Constraint Programming (CP 1999)*, volume 1713 of *Lecture Notes in Computer Science*, pages 390–404. Springer, 1999.

[60] J.-C. Régin, T. Petit, C. Bessière, and J.-F. Puget. An Original Constraint Based Approach for Solving over Constrained Problems. In R. Dechter, editor, *Proceedings of the Sixth International Conference on Principles and Practice of Constraint Programming (CP 2000)*, volume 1894 of *Lecture Notes in Computer Science*, pages 543–548. Springer, 2000.

[61] A. Schrijver. *Theory of Linear and Integer Programming*. Wiley, 1986.

[62] A. Schrijver. *Combinatorial Optimization - Polyhedra and Efficiency*. Springer, 2003.

[63] M. Sellmann. Approximated consistency for knapsack constraints. In F. Rossi, editor, *Proceedings of the Ninth International Conference on Principles and Practice of Constraint Programming (CP 2003)*, volume 2833 of *Lecture Notes in Computer Science*, pages 679–693. Springer, 2003.

[64] M. Sellmann. Cost-based filtering for shorter path constraints. In F. Rossi, editor, *Proceedings of the Ninth International Conference on Principles and Practice of Constraint Programming (CP 2003)*, volume 2833 of *Lecture Notes in Computer Science*, pages 694–708. Springer, 2003.

[65] R. Tarjan. Depth-first search and linear graph algorithms. *SIAM Journal on Computing*, 1:146–160, 1972.

[66] M.A. Trick. A Dynamic Programming Approach for Consistency and Propagation for Knapsack Constraints. *Annals of Operations Research*, 118:73–84, 2003.

[67] B.L. van der Waerden. Ein Satz über Klasseneinteilungen von endlichen Mengen. *Abhandlungen aus dem mathematischen Seminar der Hamburgischen Universität*, 5: 185–188, 1927.

[68] V. Vazirani. *Approximation Algorithms*. Springer, 2001.

Chapter 7

Tractable Structures for Constraint Satisfaction Problems

Rina Dechter

Throughout the past few decades two primary constraint processing schemes emerge—those based on *conditioning* or *search*, and those based on *inference* or *derivation*. Search in constraint satisfaction takes the form of depth-first backtracking, while inference is performed by variable-elimination and tree-clustering algorithms, or by bounded local consistency enforcing. Compared to human problem solving techniques, conditioning is analogous to guessing (a value of a variable), or reasoning by assumption. The problem is then divided into subproblems, conditioned on the instantiation of a subset of variables, each of which should be solved. On the other hand, inference corresponds to reinterpreting or making deduction from the problem at hand. Inference-based algorithms derive and record new information, generating equivalent problem representations that facilitate an easier solution.

Search and inference algorithms have their relative advantages and disadvantages. Inference-based algorithms are better at exploiting the independencies captured by the underlying constraint graph. They therefore provide a superior worst-case time-guarantee as a function of graph-based parameters. Unfortunately, any method that is time-exponential in the tree-width is also *space*-exponential in the tree-width and, therefore, not practical for dense problems.

Brute-force Search algorithms are structure-blind. They traverse the network's search space where each path represents a partial or a full solution. The linear structure of these search spaces hide the structural independencies displayed in the constraint graph and therefore, algorithms which explore these search spaces, may not be as effective. In particular they lack useful performance guarantees. On the other hand search algorithms are flexible in their memory needs and can even operate with linear memory. Also search often exhibits a much better average performance than their worst-case bounds, when augmented with various heuristics and especially when looking for a single solution. Given their complementary properties, combining inference-based and conditioning-based algorithms may better utilize the benefit of each scheme and allow improved performance guarantees, reduced space complexity and improved average performance.

This chapter focuses on structure-driven constraint processing algorithms. We will start with inference algorithms and show that their performance is controlled by graph parameters such as tree-width, induced-width and hypertree width. We then show that hybrids of search and inference can be controlled by graph-based parameters such as cycle-cutset, and w-cutset and separator-size. Finally, we present the notion of AND/OR search spaces for exploiting independencies displayed in the constraint graph during search, which, similar to inference, leads to graph-based performance bounds using parameters such as the depth of the pseudo-tree, path-width and tree-width.

7.1 Background

7.1.1 Constraint Networks and Tasks

A constraint problem is defined in terms of a set of variables taking values on finite domains and a set of functions defined over these variables. We denote variables or subsets of variables by uppercase letters (*e.g.*, X, Y, Z, S, R ...) and values of variables by lower case letters (*e.g.*, x, y, z, s). An assignment $(X_1 = x_1, \ldots, X_n = x_n)$ can be abbreviated as $x = (\langle X_1, x_1 \rangle, \ldots, \langle X_n, x_n \rangle)$ or $x = (x_1, \ldots, x_n)$. For a subset of variables S, D_S denotes the Cartesian product of the domains of variables in S. x_S and $x[S]$ are both used as the projection of $x = (x_1, \ldots, x_n)$ over a subset S. We denote functions by letters f, g h etc., and the scope (set of arguments) of the function f by $scope(f)$.

A *constraint network* $\mathcal{R}$ consists of a finite set of *variables* $X = \{X_1, \ldots, X_n\}$ each associated with a *domain* of discrete values, $D_1, \ldots, D_n$ and a set of *constraints* $\{C_1, \ldots, C_t\}$. Each of the constraints is expressed as a relation, defined on some subset of variables, whose tuples are all the simultaneous value assignments to the members of this variable subset that, as far as this constraint alone is concerned, are legal.[1] Formally, a constraint C_i has two parts: (1) the subset of variables $S_i = \{X_{i_1}, \ldots, X_{i_{j(i)}}\}$, on which it is defined, called a *constraint-scope*, and (2) a *relation*, R_i defined over S_i: $R_i \subseteq D_{i_1} \times \cdots \times D_{i_{j(i)}}$. The relation denotes all compatible tuples of D_{S_i} allowed by the constraint. Thus a constraint network $\mathcal{R}$ can be viewed as the triplet $\mathcal{R} = (X, D, C)$. The *scheme* of a constraint network is its set of scopes, namely, $scheme(\mathcal{R}) = \{S_1, S_2, \ldots, S_t\}, S_i \subseteq X$

Definition 7.1 ((operations on constraints)). *Let R be a relation on a set S of variables, let $Y \subseteq S$ be a subset of the variables. We denote by $\pi_Y(R)$ the projection of the relation R on the subset Y; that is, a tuple over Y appears in $\pi_Y(R)$ if and only if it can be extended to a full tuple in R. Let R_{S_1} be a relation on a set of variables S_1 and let R_{S_2} be a relation on a set of variables S_2. We denote by $R_{S_1} \bowtie R_{S_2}$ the natural join of the two relations. The join of R_{S_1} and R_{S_2} is a relation defined over $S_1 \cup S_2$ containing all the tuples t satisfying $t[S_1] \in R_{S_1}$ and $t[S_2] \in R_{S_2}$.*

An assignment of a unique domain value to each member of some subset of variables is called an *instantiation*. An instantiation is said to satisfy a given constraint C_i if the partial assignment specified by the instantiation does not violate C_i. An instantiation is said to

---

[1]This does not mean that the actual representation of any constraint is necessarily in the form of its defining relation, but that the relation can, in principle, be generated using the constraint's specification without the need to consult other constraints in the network.

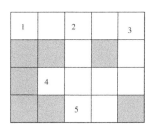

D_1 = (hoses, laser, sheet, snail, steer)

$D_2 = D_4$ = (hike, aron, keet, earn, same)

D_3 = (run, sun, let, yes, eat, ten)

D_5 = (no, be, us, it)

C_{12} = ((hoses, same), (laser,same), (sheet, earn),
           (snail, aron), (steer, earn))

(a)   (b)

Figure 7.1: A crossword puzzle and its CN representation.

be *legal* or *locally consistent* if it satisfies *all* the (relevant) constraints of the network. A consistent instantiation of *all* the variables of a constraint network is called a *solution* of the network, and the set of all solutions is a relation, ρ, defined on the set of all variables. This relation is said to be *represented* by the constraint network. Formally,

$$\rho = \{x = (x_1, \ldots, x_n) \mid \forall S_i \in scheme, \ \pi_{S_i} x \in R_i\}.$$

It can also be expressed as the join over all relations as $\rho = \bowtie_{R_i \in C} R_i$.

Example 1: Figure 7.1a presents a simplified version of a crossword puzzle (see *constraint satisfaction*). The variables are X_1 (1, horizontal), X_2 (2, vertical), X_3 (3, vertical), X_4 (4, horizontal), and X_5 (5, horizontal). The scheme of this problem is $\{\{X_1, X_2\}, \{X_1, X_3\}, \{X_4, X_2\}, \{X_4, X_3\}, \{X_5, X_2\}\}$. (We will sometime abuse notation and denote a scope such as $\{X, Y\}$ or as XY.) The domains and some constraints are specified in Figure Figure 7.1b. A tuple in the relation associated with this puzzle is the solution: $(X_1 = sheet, X_2 = earn, X_3 = ten, X_4 = aron, X_5 = no)$.

Typical tasks defined in connection with constraint networks are to determine whether a solution exists, to find one or all of the solutions, to count solutions or, when the problem is inconsistent, to find a solution that satisfies the maximum number of constraints (Max-CSP). Sometime, given a set of preferences over solutions defined via a cost function, the task is to find a consistent solution having maximum cost.

7.1.2   Graphical Representations

Graphical properties of constraint networks were initially investigated through the class of *binary constraint networks* [23]. A *binary constraint network* is one in which every *constraint scope* involves at most two variables. In this case the network can be associated with a constraint graph, where each node represents a variable, and the arcs connect nodes whose variables are explicitly constrained. Figure 7.2 shows the constraint graph associated with the crossword puzzle in Figure 7.1.

A graphical representation of higher order networks can be provided by *hypergraphs*, where again, nodes represent the variables, and *hyperarcs* or *hyperedges* (drawn as regions)

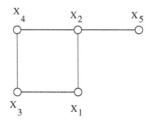

Figure 7.2: A constraint graph of the crossword puzzle.

group variables that belong to the same scope. Two variations of this representation that can be used to facilitate structure-driven algorithms are *primal-constraint graph* and *dual-constraint graph*. A *Primal-constraint graph* (a generalization of the binary constraint graph) represents variables by nodes and associates an arc with any two nodes residing in the same constraint. A *dual-constraint-graph* represents each scope by a node (also called a *c-variable*) and associates a labeled arc with any two nodes whose scopes share variables. The arcs are labeled by the shared variables.

For example, Figure 7.3 depicts the *hypergraph* (a), *primal* (b), and the *dual* (c) representations of a network with variables A, B, C, D, E, F and constraints on the scopes (ABC),(AEF), (CDE) and (ACE). The constraints themselves are symbolically given by the inequalities: $A + B \leq C, A + E \leq F, C + D \leq E, A + C \leq E$, where the domains of each variable are the integers $[2, 3, 4, 5, 6]$.

The *dual* constraint graph can be viewed as a transformation of a nonbinary network into a special type of *binary* network: the domain of the c-variables ranges over all possible value combinations permitted by the corresponding constraints, and any two adjacent c-variables must obey the restriction that their shared variables should have the same values (i.e., the c-variables are bounded by equality constraints). For instance, the domain of the c-variable ABC is {224, 225, 226, 235, 236, 325, 326, 246, 426, 336} and the binary constraint between ABC and CDE is given by the relation: $R_{ABC,CDE} = \{(224,415), (224,426)\}$. Viewed in this way, any network can be solved by binary networks' techniques. Next we summarize the above graph concepts.

Definition 7.2 (graph, hypergraph). *A graph is a pair $G = \{V, E\}$, where $V = \{X_1, ..., X_n\}$ is a set of vertices, and $E = \{(X_i, X_j)|X_i, X_j \in V\}$ is the set of edges (arcs). The degree of a variable is the number of arcs incident to it. A hypergraph is a pair $H = (V, S$ where $S = \{S_1, ..., S_t\}$ is a set of subsets of V, called hyperedges or simple edges.*

Definition 7.3 (primal graph, dual graph). *The primal graph of a hypergraph $H = (V, S)$ is an undirected graph $G = (V, E)$ such that there is an edge $(u, v) \in E$ for any two vertices $u, v \in V$ that appear in the same hyperedge (namely, there exists S_i, s.t., $u, v \in S_i$). The dual graph of a hypergraph $H = (V, S)$ is an undirected graph $G = (S, E)$ that has a vertex for each hyperedge, and there is an edge $(S_i, S_j) \in E$ when the corresponding hyper-edges share a vertex ($S_i \cap S_j \neq \emptyset$).*

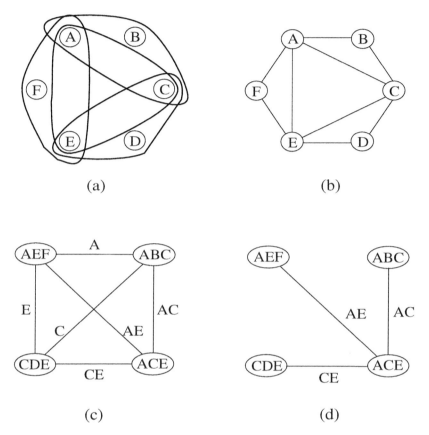

Figure 7.3: (a)Hyper, (b)Primal, (c)Dual and (d)Join-tree constraint graphs of a CSP.

7.2 Structure-Based Tractability in Inference

Almost all the known structure-based techniques rely on the observation that *binary* constraint networks whose constraint graph is a *tree* can be solved in linear time [23, 36, 17] in the number of variables. The solution of tree-structured networks are discussed next, and later it is shown how they can be used to facilitate the solution of a general constraint network.

7.2.1 Solving Tree-Networks

Given a tree-network over n variables (Fig. 7.5), the first step of the *tree-algorithm* is to generate a *rooted-directed* tree. Each node in this tree (excluding the root) has one *parent node* directed toward it and may have several *child* nodes, directed away from it. Nodes with no *children* are called *leaves*. An ordering, $d = X_1, X_2, \ldots, X_n$, is then enforced such that a parent always precedes its children. In the second step, the algorithm processes

Tree-solving
Input: A tree network $T = (X, D, C)$.
Output: A backtrack-free network along an ordering d.
1.   generate a width-1 ordering, $d = X_1, \ldots, X_n$.
2.   **let** $X_{p(i)}$ denote the parent of X_i in the rooted ordered tree.
3.   **for** $i = n$ to 1 **do**
4.   *Revise* $((X_{p(i)}), X_i)$;
5.   **if** the domain of $X_{p(i)}$ is empty, exit (no solution exists).
6.   **endfor**

Figure 7.4: Tree-solving algorithm

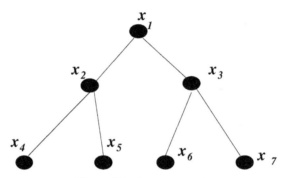

Figure 7.5: A tree network

each arc and its associated constraint from leaves to root, in an orderly layered fashion. For each directed arc from X_i to X_j it removes a value from the domain of X_i if it has *no consistent match* in the domain of X_j. Finally, after the root is processed, a backtracking algorithm is used to find a solution along the ordering d.

It can be shown that the algorithm is linear in the number of variables. In particular, backtracking search, which in general is an exponential procedure, is guaranteed to find a solution without facing any dead-ends.

The tree algorithm is sketched in Figure 7.4. The *revise* procedure revise(X_j, X_i) remove any value from the domain of X_j that has no match in the domain of X_i. The complexity of the *tree-solving* algorithm is bounded by $O(nk^2)$ steps where k bounds the domain size, because the *revise* procedure, which is bounded by k^2 steps, is executed at most n times.

Theorem 7.4. *[37] A binary tree constraint problem can be solved in $O(nk^2)$ when n is the number of variables and k bounds the domain size.*

7.2.2 Acyclic Networks

The notion of constraint trees can be extended beyond binary constraints to problems having scope higher than 2, using the notions of hypergraphs and hypertrees, leading to the creation of a class of *acyclic constraint networks*.

As noted, any constraint network $\mathcal{R} = (X, D, C)$, where $C = \{R_{S_1}, ..., R_{S_t}\}$ can be associated with a hypergraph $\mathcal{H}_\mathcal{R} = (X, H)$, where X is the set of nodes (variables), and H is the set of scopes of the constraints in C, namely $H = \{S_1, ..., S_t\}$. The dual graph of a constraint hypergraph associates a node with each constraint scope (or a hyperedge) and has an arc for each two nodes sharing variables. As noted before, this association facilitates the transformation of a non-binary constraint problem into a binary one, called the *dual problem*. Therefore, if a problem's dual graph happens to be a tree, it means that the dual constraint problem, can be efficiently solved by the tree-solving algorithm.

It turns out, however, that sometimes, even when the dual graph does not look like a tree, it is in fact a tree, if some of its arcs (and their associated constraints) are *redundant* and can be removed, leaving behind a tree structure. A constraint is considered redundant if its removal from the constraint network does not change the set of all solutions. It is not normally easy to recognize redundant constraints. In the dual representation, however, some redundancies are easy to identify: since all the constraints in the dual network enforce equalities (over shared variables), a constraint and its corresponding arc can be deleted if the variables labeling the arc are shared by every arc along an *alternate* path between the two end points. This is because the alternate path (of constraints) already enforces that equality. Removing such constraints does not alter the problem.

Example 7.5. Looking again at Figure 7.3, we see that the arc between (AEF) and (ABC) in Figure 7.3(c) is redundant because variable A also appears along the alternative path $(ABC) - AC - (ACE) - AE - (AEF)$. A consistent assignment to A is thereby ensured by these constraints even if the constraint between AEF and ABC is removed. Likewise, the arcs labeled E and C are also redundant, and their removal yields the graph in 7.3(d).

We call the property that ensures such legitimate arc removal the *running intersection property* or *connectedness* property. The running intersection property can be defined over hypergraphs or over their dual graphs, and is used to characterize equivalent concepts such as *join-trees* (defined over dual graphs) or *hypertrees* (defined over hypergraphs). An *arc subgraph* of a graph contains the same set of nodes as the graph, and a subset of its arcs.

Definition 7.6 (connectedness, join-trees, hypertrees and acyclic networks). *Given a dual graph of a hypergraph, an arc subgraph of the dual graph satisfies the* connectedness *property iff for each two nodes that share a variable, there is at least one path of labeled arcs, each containing the shared variables. An arc subgraph of the dual graph that satisfies the connectedness property is called a* join-graph. *A join-graph that is a tree is called a* join-tree. *A hypergraph whose dual-graph has a join-tree is called a* hypertree. *A constraint network whose hypergraph is a hypertree is called an* acyclic *network.*

Example 7.7. Considering again the graphs in Figure 7.3, we can see that the join-tree in Figure 7.3(d) satisfies the connectedness property. That is, the hypergraph in Figure 7.3(a) has a join-tree and is therefore a hypertree.

An acyclic constraint network can be solved efficiently. Because the constraint problem has a join-tree, its dual problem is a tree of binary constraints and can therefore be solved by the tree-solving algorithm. Note that the domains of variables in the dual problem are bounded by the number of tuples in the input constraints. In Figure 7.6, we reformulate the tree algorithm for solving acyclic problems.

Example 7.8. Consider the tree dual problem in Figure 7.3(d) and assume that the constraints are given by: $R_{ABC} = R_{AEF} = R_{CDE} = \{(0,0,1)\ (0,1,0)\ (1,0,0)\}$ and $R_{ACE} = \{(1,1,0)\ (0,1,1)\ (1,0,1)\}$. Assume the ordering $d = (R_{ACE}, R_{CDE}, R_{AEF}, R_{ABC})$ When processing R_{ABC}, its parent relation is R_{ACE}; we therefore generate $\pi_{ACE}\ (R_{ACE} \bowtie R_{ABC})$, yielding the revised relation $R_{ACE} = \{(0,1,1)\ (1,0,1)\}$. Next, processing R_{AEF} (likewise connected to R_{ACE}) we generate relation $R_{ACE} = \pi_{ACE}\ (R_{ACE} \bowtie R_{AEF}) = \{(0,1,1)\}$. Note that the revised relation R_{ACE} is now being processed. Subsequently, processing R_{CDE} we generate: $R_{ACE} = \pi_{ACE}(R_{ACE} \bowtie R_{CDE}) = \{(0,1,1)\}$ A solution can then be generated by picking the only allowed tuple for R_{ACE}, $A = 0, C = 1, E = 1$, extending it with a value for D that satisfies R_{CDE}, which is only $D = 0$, and then similarly extending the assignment to $F = 0$ and $B = 0$, to satisfy R_{AEF} and R_{ABC}

ALGORITHM ACYCLIC-SOLVING

Input: an acyclic constraint network $\mathcal{R} = (X, D, C)$, $C = \{R_1, ..., R_t\}$. S_i is the scope of R_i. A join-tree T of $\mathcal{R}$.
Output: Determine consistency, and generate a solution.
1. $d = (R_1, ..., R_t)$ is an ordering such that every relation
   appears before its descendant relations in the tree rooted at R_1.
2. **for** $j = t$ to 1, for edge (j,k) ,$k < j$, in the tree do
   $$R_k \leftarrow \pi_{S_k}(R_k \bowtie R_j)$$
   if the empty relation is created, exit, the problem has no solution.
   endfor
3. **return:** The updated relations and a solution:
   Select a tuple in R_1. After instantiating $R_1, ..., R_{i-1}$ select a tuple in R_i that is consistent with all previous assignments.

Figure 7.6: Acyclic-solving algorithm

Since the complexity of a tree-solving algorithm is $O(nk^2)$, where n is the number of variables and k bounds the domain size, the implied complexity of acyclic-solving is $O(r \cdot l^2)$ if there are r constraints, each allowing at most l tuples. However, the complexity can be improved for this special case. The join operation can be performed in time linear in the maximum number of tuples of each relation, like so: project R_j on the variables shared by R_j and its parent constraint, R_k, an $O(l)$ operation, and then prune any tuple in R_k that has no match in that projection. If tuples are ordered lexicographically, which requires $O(l \cdot logl)$ steps, the join operator has a complexity of $O(l)$, yielding an overall complexity of $O(r \cdot l \cdot logl)$ steps [13]. For a more recent analysis see [30]. In summary,

Theorem 7.9. *[13] [correctness and complexity] Algorithm acyclic-solving decides the consistency of an acyclic constraint network, and its complexity is $O(r \cdot l \cdot logl)$ steps, where r is the number of constraints and l bounds the number of tuples in each constraint relation .* $\square$

Several efficient procedures for identifying acyclic networks and for finding a representative join-tree were developed in the area of relational databases [38]. One scheme that proved particularly useful is based on the observation that a network is acyclic if, and only if, its primal graph is both *chordal* and *conformal* [6]. A graph is *chordal* if every cycle of a length of at least four has a chord, i.e., an edge joining two nonconsecutive vertices along the cycle. A graph is *conformal* if each of its maximal *cliques* (i.e. subsets of nodes that are completely connected) corresponds to a constraint scope in the original constraint networks. The *chordality* of a graph can be identified via an ordering of the graph called the *maximal cardinality ordering*, (*m-ordering*); it always assigns the next number to the node having the largest set of already numbered neighbors (breaking ties arbitrarily).

It can be shown [46] that in an m-ordered chordal graph, the parent-set of each node, namely,its earlier neighbors in the ordered graph, must be completely connected. If, in addition, the maximal cliques coincide with the scopes of the original $\mathcal{R}$, both conditions for acyclicity would be satisfied. Because for chordal graphs each node and its parent set constitutes a clique, the maximal cliques can be identified in linear time, and then a *join tree* can be constructed by connecting each maximal clique to an ancestor clique with which it shares the largest set of variables [18].

7.2.3 Tree-Decompositions, Tree-Width and Induced-Width

Since acyclic constraint networks can be solved efficiently, we naturally aim at compiling an arbitrary constraint network into an acyclic one. This can be achieved by grouping subsets of constraints into clusters, or subproblems, whose scopes constitute a hypertree, thus transforming a constraint hypergraph into a constraint hypertree. Replacing each subproblem with its set of solutions yields an acyclic constraint problem. If the transformation process is tractable the resulting algorithm is polynomial. This compilation process is called *join-tree clustering*.

The graphical input to the above scheme is the constraint hypergraph $\mathcal{H} = (X, H)$, where H is the set of scopes of the constraint network. Its output is a hypertree $\mathcal{S} = (X, S)$ and a partition of the original hyperedges into the new tree hyperedges defining the subproblems. Each subproblem is then solved, and its set of solutions is a new constraint whose scope is the hyperedge. Therefore, the result is a network having one constraint per hyperedge of the tree S, and, by construction, is acyclic.

Join-tree clustering and processing

There are various specific methods that decompose a hypergraph into a hypertree. The aim is to generate hypertrees having small-sized hyperedges because this implies small constraint subproblems. The most popular approach manipulates the constraint's primal graph and it emerges from the primal recognition process of acyclic networks described earlier. Since acyclic problems have primal graph that is chordal, the idea is to make the primal graph of a given network, which is not acyclic, chordal and then associates the maximal cliques of the resulting chordal graph with hyper-edges. Those hyperedges will be the new scopes in the targeted acyclic problem. Given an ordered graph, chordality can be enforced by recursively connecting all parents of every node starting from the last node to the first. This process leads to the notion of induced-graph, induced-width and tree-width which will be used extensively.

Definition 7.10 (induced-width,tree-width). *An* **ordered graph** *is a pair* (G, d) *denoted* G_d *where G is an undirected graph, and $d = (X_1, ..., X_n)$ is an ordering of the vertices. The* width *of a vertex in an ordered graph is the number of its earlier neighbors. The* width *of an ordered graph, $w(G_d)$, is the maximum width of all its vertices. The* induced width *of an ordered graph, $w^*(G_d)$, is the width of the induced ordered graph, denoted G_d^*, obtained by processing the vertices recursively, from last to first; when vertex X is processed, all its earlier neighbors are connected. When the identity of the graph is known we will also denote $w^*(G_d)$ by $w^*(d)$. The* induced width *of a graph, $w^*(G)$, is the minimal induced width over all its orderings [17]. It is well known that the induced width of a graph is identical to its* tree-width *[1, 18], we will therefore define tree-width of a graph as the induced-width of the graph.*

The procedure that generates the hypertree partitioning using the chordality algorithm and that then associates each cluster of constraints with its full set of solutions is called join-tree clustering (JTC) described in Figure 7.7. The first three steps of algorithm JTC manipulate the primal graph, embedding it in a chordal graph (whose maximal cliques make a hypertree), and then identifying its join-tree. Step 4 partitions the constraints into the cliques (the hypertree edges). Step 5 solves each subproblem defined by a cluster, and thus creates one new constraint for each subproblem (clique).

JOIN-TREE CLUSTERING (JTC)

Input: A constraint problem $\mathcal{R} = (X, D, C)$ and its primal graph $G = (X, E)$.
Output: An equivalent acyclic constraint problem and its join-tree: $T = (X, D, C')$
1. Select a variable ordering, $d = (X_1, ..., X_n)$.
2. **Triangulation** (create the induced graph along d and call it G^*):
      for $j = n$ to 1 by -1 **do**
      $E \leftarrow E \cup \{(i, k) | (i, j) \in E, (k, j) \in E\}$
3. **Create a join-tree of the induced graph** G^*:
   a.   Identify all maximal cliques in the chordal graph (each variable and its parents is a clique). Let $C_1, ..., C_t$ be all such cliques, created going from last variable to first in the ordering.
   b.   Create a tree-structure T over the cliques:
         Connect each C_i to a C_j $(j < i)$ with whom it shares largest subset of variables.
4. Place each input constraint in one clique containing its scope, and let
      P_i be the constraint subproblem associated with C_i.
5. Solve P_i and let R'_i be its set of solutions.
6. Return $C' = \{R'_1, ..., R'_t\}$, the new set of constraints and their join-tree, T.

Figure 7.7: Join-tree clustering

We can conclude,

Theorem 7.11. *[18] Algorithm join-tree clustering transforms a constraint network into an equivalent acyclic network.* □

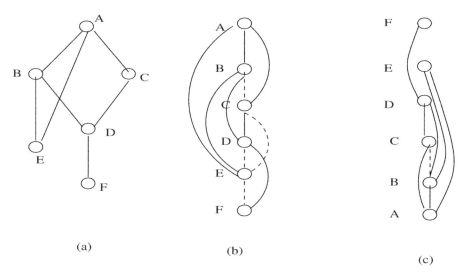

Figure 7.8: A graph (a) and two of its induced graphs (b) and (c). All arcs included.

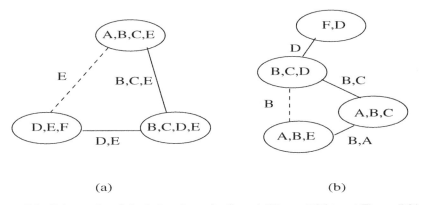

Figure 7.9: Join-graphs of the induced graphs from (a)Figure 7.8(b) and Figure 7.8(c). (All arcs included.) The corresponding join-trees are the same figures with the broken arcs removed.

Example 7.12. Consider the graph in Figure 7.8(a), and assume it is a primal graph of a binary constraint network. In this case, the primal and hypergraph are the same. Consider the ordering $d_1 = (F, E, D, C, B, A)$ in Figure 7.8(b). Performing join- tree-clustering connects parents recursively from the last variable to the first, creating the induced-ordered graph by adding the new (broken) edges of Figure 7.8(b). The maximal cliques of this induced graph are: $Q_1 = \{A, B, C, E\}$, $Q_2 = \{B, C, D, E\}$ and $Q_3 = \{D, E, F\}$ Alternatively, if ordering d_2 in Figure 7.8(c) is used, the induced graph generated has only one added edge. The cliques in this case are: $Q_1 = \{D, F\}$, $Q_2 = \{A, B, E\}$ $Q_3 = \{B, C, D\}$ and $Q_4 = \{A, B, C\}$. The corresponding join-trees of both orderings are depicted in Figure 7.9 (broken arcs are not part of the join-trees). Next, focusing on the join-tree in Figure 7.9b, JTC partition the constraints into the tree-nodes. It places the following subproblems into the nodes: $P_1 = \{R_{FD}\}$ is placed in node (FD), $P_2 = \{R_{BD}, R_{CD}\}$ is placed in node (BCD), $P_3 = \{R_{AB}, R_{AC}\}$ is placed in node (ABC) and $P_4 = \{R_{AB}, R_{BE}, R_{AE}\}$ is placed in (ABE). Next, applying steps 4 and 5 of the algorithm we solves the subproblems P_1, P_2, P_3, P_4, and replace each with R'_1, R'_2, R'_3, R'_4, where R'_i is the solution relation of P_i, yielding a desired acyclic network.

Theorem 7.13. *[18] [complexity of JTC] Given a constraint network having n variables and r constraints, the time complexity of join-tree clustering is $O(r \cdot k^{w^*(d)+1})$, and the space complexity is $O(n \cdot k^{w^*(d)+1})$ where k is the maximum domain size and $w^*(d)$ is the induced width of the ordered graph.*

Proof: Finding a tree-decomposition of a hypergraph (Step 1 of JTC) is performed over the constraint primal graph and requires $O(n^2)$ steps. The most expensive step is Step 5, which computes all the solutions of each subproblem. Since the size of each subproblem corresponds to a clique in the induced (triangulated) ordered graph, it is bounded by the induced width plus one. Solving a problem P_i having at most $w^*(d) + 1$ variables and r constraints costs $O(r_i \cdot k^{w^*(d)+1})$. Summing over all subproblems $\sum_i r_i k^{w^*(d)+1}$, yields the desired bound. The space complexity is due to the need to record the solutions for each of the n clusters having at most $w^*(d) + 1$ variables. $\square$

Once algorithm JTC delivers an acyclic problem, it can be solved by ACYCLIC-SOLVING yielding a solution. algorithm JTC followed by ACYCLIC-SOLVING provide a procedure for solving the CSP problem. We get:

Theorem 7.14 (complexity of JTC followed by ACYCLIC-SOLVING). *Given a constraint network having n variables and r constraints, the time complexity of finding a solution using join-tree clustering and ACYCLIC-SOLVING is $O(r \cdot w^*(d) \cdot logk \cdot k^{w^*(d)+1})$ and the space complexity is $O(nk^{w^*(d)+1})$, where k is the maximum domain size and $w^*(d)$ is the induced width of the ordered graph.*

Proof: JTC generates an acyclic problem having at most n relations whose sizes are bounded by $k^{w*(d)+1}$. Thus the complexity of acyclic-solving on these relations is bounded by $O(n \cdot w^*(d) \cdot logk \cdot k^{w^*(d)+1})$, which is just applying acyclic-solving when $l = O(k^{w^*(d)+1})$. $\square$

General tree-decomposition schemes

Algorithm Join-tree-clustering commits to a specific structuring algorithm that is based on chordal graphs. In this section we reformulate the notion of a tree-decomposition and

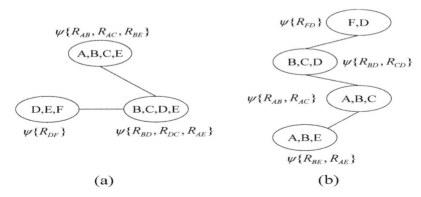

Figure 7.10: Two tree-decompositions

provide an alternative, time-space sensitive algorithm, for its processing. This exposition unifies several related schemes such as variable elimination, join-tree clustering and hypertree decomposition (to be discussed later).

Definition 7.15 (tree-decomposition). *Let $\mathcal{R} = (X, D, C)$ be a CSP problem. A tree-decomposition for $\mathcal{R}$ is a triple $< T, \chi, \psi >$, where $T = (V, E)$ is a tree, and χ and ψ are labeling functions which associate each vertex $v \in V$ with two sets, $\chi(v) \subseteq X$ and $\psi(v) \subseteq C$, that satisfy the following conditions:*

1. *For each constraint $R_i \in C$, there is at least one vertex $v \in V$ such that $R_i \in \psi(v)$, and scope$(R_i) \subseteq \chi(v)$.*

2. *For each variable $X_i \in X$, the set $\{v \in V | X_i \in \chi(v)\}$ induces a connected subtree of T. (This is the connectedness property.)*

Definition 7.16 (tree-width, hypertree-width, separator). *The tree-width of a tree-decomposition $< T, \chi, \psi >$ is $tw = \max_{v \in V} |\chi(v)| - 1$ and its hypertree width is $hw = \max_{v \in V} |\psi(v)|$. Given two adjacent vertices u and v of a tree-decomposition, the separator of u and v is defined as $sep(u, v) = \chi(u) \cap \chi(v)$. The tree-width of a CSP problem is the minimal tree-width over all its tree-decompositions.*

   Remarks: It is easy to see that the definition of a tree-decomposition of a constraint network $\mathcal{R} = (X, D, C)$ is completely determined by the hypergraph of the constraint network $\mathcal{H} = \{X, S\}$ where S is the scheme of $\mathcal{R}$: $S = \{S_i | S_i = scope(C_i)\}$. Thus a tree-decomposition of a constraint network defines a tree-decomposition of its hypergraph and its tree-width. The tree-width of a hypergraph is the minimal tree-width over all its tree-decompositions. It can be shown that the tree-width of a hypergraph is identical to the induced-width of its primal graph.

Example 7.17. Consider the binary constraint problem whose primal graph appears in Figure 7.8(a). The join-trees in Figure 7.9(a) and (b) were obtained via triangulation in orderings of Figure 7.8b and 7.8c and can be redescribed in Figure 7.10, using the two labeling functions. The χ labelings are the sets inside each node.

CLUSTER TREE-ELIMINATION (CTE)
Input: A tree decomposition $< T, \chi, \psi >$ for a problem $\mathcal{R} =< X, D, C >$.
Output: An augmented tree whose nodes are clusters containing the original constraints as well as messages received from neighbors. A decomposable problem for each node v.
Compute messages:
for every edge (u, v) in the tree, do

- Let $m_{(u,v)}$ denote the message sent by vertex u to vertex v. After node u has received messages from all adjacent vertices, except maybe from v

  – Define, $cluster_v(u) = \psi(u) \cup \{m_{(i,u)} | (i, u) \in T, \; i \neq v\}$
  – Compute and send to v:

$$m_{(u,v)} \leftarrow \pi_{sep(u,v)} (\bowtie_{R_i \in cluster_v(u)} R_i) \tag{7.1}$$

endfor
Return: A tree-decomposition augmented with constraint messages. For every node $u \in T$, return the decomposable subproblem $cluster(u) = \psi(u) \cup \{m_{(i,u)} | (i, u) \in T\}$

Figure 7.11: Algorithm cluster-tree elimination (CTE)

Once a tree-decomposition is available, algorithm *Cluster-Tree Elimination (CTE)* in Figure 7.11, can processes the decomposition. The algorithm is presented as a message-passing algorithm, where each vertex of the tree sends a constraint to each of its neighbors. If the tree contains m edges, then a total of $2m$ messages will be sent. Node u takes all the constraints in $\psi(u)$ and all the constraint messages received by u from all adjacent nodes, and generate their join projected on the various separators with its neighbors. The resulting constraint is then sent to v (remember that v is adjacent to u in the tree).

Implementing Equation 7.1: The particular implementation of equation (7.1) in CTE can vary. One option is to generate the combined relation $(\bowtie_{R_i \in cluster_v(u)} R_i)$ before sending messages to neighbor v. The other option, which we assume here, is that the message sent to each neighbor is created without recording the relation $(\bowtie_{R_i \in cluster_v(u)} R_i)$. Rather, each tuple in the join is projected on the separator immediately after being created. This will yields a better memory utilization. Furthermore, when u sends a message to v its cluster may contain the message it received from v. Thus in a synchronized message passing we can allow a single enumeration of the tuples in $cluster(u)$ when the messages are sent back towards the leaves, each of which be projected in parallel on the separators of the outgoing messages.

The output of CTE is the original tree-decomposition where each node is augmented with the constraints sent to it from neighboring nodes, called clusters. For each node the augmented set of constraints is a *minimal subproblem* relative to the input constraint problem $\mathcal{R}$. Intuitively, a subproblem of a constraint network is minimal if one can correctly answer any query on it without having to refer back to information in the whole network. More precisely, a subproblem over a subset of variables Y is minimal relative to the whole network, if its set of solutions is identical to the projection of the networks' solutions on Y.

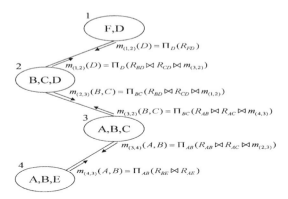

Figure 7.12: Example of messages sent by CTE

Definition 7.18 (decomposable subproblem). *Given a constraint problem* $\mathcal{R} = (X, D, C)$ *and a subset of variables* $Y \subseteq X$, *a subproblem over* Y, $\mathcal{R}_Y = (Y, D_Y, C_Y)$, *is decomposable relative to* $\mathcal{R}$ *iff* $sol(R_Y) = \pi_Y sol(\mathcal{R})$ *where* $sol(\mathcal{R})$ *is the set of all solutions of network* $\mathcal{R}$.

Convergence of CTE is guaranteed. The above description implies that the computation will proceed from leaves towards the root and back. Therefore, convergence is guaranteed after two passes, where only one constraint message is sent on each edge in each direction.

Example 7.19. Figure 7.12 shows the messages propagated over the tree-decomposition in Figure 7.10b. Since cluster 1 contains only one relation, the message from cluster 1 to 2 is the projection of R_{FD} over the separator between cluster 1 and 2, which is variable D. The message $m_{(2,3)}$ from cluster 2 to cluster 3 joins the relations in cluster 2 with the message $m_{(1,2)}$, and projects over the separator between cluster 2 and 3, which is $\{B, C\}$, and so on.

CTE can be shown to be equivalent to generating and solving an acyclic constraint problem by a tree-solving algorithm and therefore it is clearly sound [33].

Complexity of CTE

It is well known that given an induced graph having an induced-width $w^*(d)$ along an ordering d, it implies a tree-decomposition having tree-width $tw = w^*$. The opposite is also true: if there is a tree-decomposition having tree-width tw, it dictates an ordering d having induced-width $w^*(d) = tw$. Thus, from now on we will use $w^*(d)$ for both induced-width and tree-width of a given tree decomposition, while w^* or tw^* for the minimal tree-width/induced-width of a graph.

Computing the messages. Algorithm CTE can be subtly varied to influence its time and space complexities. If we first record the joined relation in Equation (7.1) and subsequently project on the separator, we will have space complexity exponential in w^*. However, we can interleave the join and project operations, and thereby make the space complexity identical to the size of the sent constraint message. The message can be computed by enumeration (or search) as follows: For each assignment v to $\chi(u)$, we can test if v is consistent with each constraint in cluster(u), and if it is, we will project the tuple v over sep, creating v_{sep}, and add it to the relation $m(sep)$.

Theorem 7.20. *[33] [Complexity of CTE] Let N be the number of vertices in a given tree decomposition of a constraint network, w^* its tree-width, sep its maximum separator size, r the number of input functions, deg the maximum degree in T, and k the maximum domain size of a variable. The time complexity of CTE is $O((r+N) \cdot deg \cdot k^{w^*+1})$ and its space complexity is $O(N \cdot k^{sep})$.*

Proof. The time complexity of processing a vertex u is $deg_u \cdot (|\psi(u)| + deg_u) \cdot k^{|\chi(u)}$ where deg_u is the degree of u, because vertex u has to send out deg_u messages, each being a combination of at most $(|\psi(u)| + deg_u)$ functions, and require the enumeration of $k^{|\chi(u)}$ combinations of values. The time complexity of CTE, $Time(CTE)$ is

$$Time(CTE) = \sum_u deg_u \cdot (|\psi(u)| + deg_u) \cdot k^{|\chi(u)|}$$

By bounding the first occurrence of deg_u by deg and $|\chi(u)|$ by the tree-width $w^* + 1$, we get

$$Time(CTE) \leq deg \cdot k^{w^*+1} \cdot \sum_u (|\psi(u)| + deg_u)$$

Since $\sum_u |\psi(u)| = r$ we can write

$$Time(CTE) \leq deg \cdot k^{w^*+1} \cdot (r+N)$$

$$= O((r+N) \cdot deg \cdot k^{w^*+1})$$

For each edge CTE will record two functions. Since the number of edges is bounded by N and the size of each function we record is bounded by k^{sep}, the space complexity is bounded by $O(N \cdot k^{sep})$.

If the cluster-tree is minimal (for any u and v, $sep(u,v) \subset \chi(u)$ and $sep(u,v) \subset \chi(v)$), then we can bound the number of vertices N by n. Assuming $r \geq n$, the time complexity of a minimal CTE is $O(deg \cdot r \cdot k^{w^*+1})$.

If $r \geq n$, this yields complexity of $O(deg \cdot r \cdot k^{w^*+1})$. It is possible to have an implementation of the algorithm whose time complexity will not depend on deg, but this improvement will be more expensive in memory [44, 33]. □

Join-tree clustering as tree-decomposition. Algorithm JTC is a specific algorithm for creating the tree-decomposition. Because it generates the full set of solutions for each node, its space complexity is exponential in $w^* + 1$, unlike CTE whose space complexity is exponential in the separator's size only. On the other hand, while the time complexity of CTE is $O(r \cdot deg \cdot k^{w^*+1})$ if $N \leq r$, the time complexity of JTC, followed by ACYCLIC SOLVING is $O(r \cdot w \cdot logk \cdot k^{w^*+1})$. Clearly, this distinction matters only if there is a substantial difference between the tree-width and the maximum separator size of a given tree-decomposition. See [33] for more details.

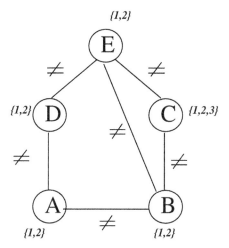

Figure 7.13: A graph coloring example

7.2.4 Variable-Elimination Schemes

We next show that variable-elimination algorithms such as Adaptive-consistency [17] can be viewed as message passing in a CTE type algorithm. Adaptive consistency, described in Figure 7.15, works by eliminating variables one by one, while deducing the effect of the eliminated variable on the rest of the problem. Adaptive-consistency can be described using the bucket data-structure. Given a variable ordering $d = A, B, D, C, E$ in a graph coloring example depicted in Figure 7.13 we process the variables from last to first, namely, from E to A. Step one is to partition the constraints into *ordered buckets*. All the constraints mentioning the last variable E are put in a bucket designated as $bucket_E$. Subsequently, all the remaining constraints mentioning D are placed in $bucket_D$, and so on. The initial partitioning of the constraints is depicted in Figure 7.14a. In general, each constraint is placed in the bucket of its latest variable.

After this initialization step, the buckets are processed from last to first by Adaptive-consistency. Processing the bucket of E, all three constraints in the buckets are solved and the solution is projected over D, C, B, recording the ternary constraint R_{DCB} which is placed in the bucket of C. Next, the algorithm process C's bucket which contains $C \neq B$ and the new constraint R_{DCB}. Joining these two constraints and projecting out C yields a constraint R_{DB} that is placed in the bucket of D, and so on.

At each step the algorithm generates a reduced but equivalent problem with one less variable expressed by the union of unprocessed buckets. Once the reduced problem is solved its solution is guaranteed to be extendible to a full solution since it accounted for the deduced constraints generated by the rest of the problem. Therefore, once all the buckets are processed, and if no inconsistency is discovered, a solution can be generated in a backtrack-free manner. Namely, a solution is assembled progressively assigning values to variables from the first variable to the last. A value of the first variable is selected satisfying all the current constraints in its bucket. A value for the second variable is then selected which satisfies all the constraints in the second bucket, and so on. Pro-

$Bucket(E)$: $E \neq D, E \neq C, E \neq B$
$Bucket(C)$: $C \neq B$
$Bucket(D)$: $D \neq A$,
$Bucket(B)$: $B \neq A$,
$Bucket(A)$:

(a)

$Bucket(E)$: $E \neq D, E \neq C, E \neq B$
$Bucket(C)$: $C \neq B \; \| \; R_{DCB}$
$Bucket(D)$: $D \neq A, \; \|, R_{DB}$
$Bucket(B)$: $B \neq A, \; \| \; R_{AB}$
$Bucket(A)$: $\| \; R_A$

(b)

Figure 7.14: A schematic execution of adaptive-consistency

Algorithm Adaptive consistency (AC)
1. **Input:** A constraint problem $R_1, \ldots R_t$, ordering $d = X_1, \ldots, X_n$.
2. **Output:** An equivalent backtrack-free set of constraints and a solution.
3. **Initialize:** Partition constraints into $bucket_1, \ldots bucket_n$. $bucket_i$ contains all relations whose scope include X_i but no higher indexed variable.
4. **For** $p = n$ *downto* 1, process $bucket_p$ as follows

    for all relations $R_1, \ldots R_m$ defined over $S_1, \ldots S_m \in bucket_p$ **do**
    (Find solutions to $bucket_p$ and project out X_p:)
$$A \leftarrow \bigcup_{j=1}^{m} S_j - \{X_i\}$$

$$R_A \leftarrow \pi_A(\bowtie_{j=1}^{m} R_j)$$

5.   if R_A is not empty, add it to the bucket of its latest variable.
    else, exit and return the empty network.

6. Return $\cup_j bucket_j$ and generate a solution: for $p = 1$ to n do
assign a value to X_p that is consistent with previous assignments and satisfies all the constraints in $bucket_p$.

Figure 7.15: Algorithm Adaptive consistency

cessing a bucket amounts to solving a subproblem defined by the constraints appearing in the bucket, and then restricting the solutions to all but the current bucket's variable. Adaptive-consistency is an instance of a general class of variable elimination algorithms called bucket-elimination that are applicable across many tasks [15].

The complexity of adaptive-consistency is linear in the number of buckets and in the time to process each bucket. Since processing a bucket amounts to solving a constraint subproblem (the computation in a bucket can be described in terms of the relational opera-tors of *join* followed by *projection*) its complexity is exponential in the number of variables mentioned in a bucket which is bounded by the *induced-width* of the constraint graph along

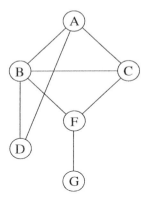

Figure 7.16: A constraint network example

that ordering [17].

Theorem 7.21 (Complexity of AC). *[15, 33] Let $w^*(d)$ be the induced width of G along ordering d. The time complexity of adaptive-consistency is $O(r \cdot k^{w^*(d)+1})$ and the space complexity is $O(n \cdot k^{w^*(d)})$.*

7.2.5 Adaptive-Consistency as Tree-Decomposition

We now show that adaptive-consistency can be viewed as a message-passing algorithm along a bucket-tree, which is a special case of tree-decomposition. Let $\mathcal{R} = (X, D, C)$ be a problem and d an ordering of its variables, $d = (X_1, ..., X_n)$. Let $B_{X_1}, ..., B_{X_n}$ be the set of buckets, each contains those constraints in C whose latest variable in d is X_i. A *bucket-tree* of $\mathcal{R}$ in an ordering d, has buckets as its nodes, and bucket B_X is connected to bucket B_Y if the constraint generated by adaptive-consistency in bucket B_X is placed in B_Y. The variables of B_{X_i} are those appearing in the scopes of any of its original constraints, as well as those received from other buckets. Therefore, in a bucket tree, every node B_X has one parent node B_Y and possibly several child nodes $B_{Z_1}, ... B_{Z_t}$.

It is easy to see that a bucket tree of $\mathcal{R}$ is a tree-decomposition of $\mathcal{R}$ where for bucket B_X, $\chi(B_X)$ contains X and its earlier neighbors in the induced graph along ordering d, while $\psi(B_X)$ contains all constraints whose highest-ordered argument is X. Therefore,

Theorem 7.22. *[33] A bucket tree of a constraint network $\mathcal{R}$ is a tree-decomposition of $\mathcal{R}$.*

Thus we can add a bottom-up message passing to adaptive-consistency yielding *Adaptive Tree Consistency* (ATC) given in Figure 7.17. In the top-down phase, each bucket receives constraint messages ρ from its children and sends ρ constraint messages to its parent. This portion is identical to AC. In the bottom-up phase, each bucket receives a ρ constraint from its parent and sends a ρ constraint to each child.

Example 7.23. Consider a constraint network defined over the graph in Figure 7.16. Figure 7.18 left shows the initial buckets along the ordering $d = (A, B, C, D, F, G)$, and the ρ constraints that will be created and passed by adaptive-consistency from top to bottom. On

Algorithm Adaptive-Tree Consistency (ATC)
Input: A problem $\mathcal{R} = (X, D, C)$, ordering d.
Output: Augmented buckets containing the original constraints and all the ρ constraints received from neighbors in the bucket-tree.
0. Pre-processing:
Place each constraint in the latest bucket, along d, that mentions a variable in its scope. Connect bucket B_X to B_Y, $Y < X$, if variable Y is the latest earlier neighbor of X in the induced graph G_d.
1. Top-down phase: (AC)
For $i = n$ to 1, process bucket B_{X_i}:
Let $\rho_1, ..., \rho_j$ be all the constraints in B_{X_i} at the time B_{X_i} is processed, including original constraints of $\mathcal{R}$. The constraint $\rho_{X_i}^Y$ sent from X_i to its parent Y, is computed by

$$\rho_{X_i}^Y(sep(X_i, Y)) = \pi_{sep(X_i,Y)} \bowtie_{i=1}^{j} \rho_i \tag{7.2}$$

2. Bottom-up phase:
For $i = 1$ to n, process bucket B_{X_i}:
Let $\rho_1, ..., \rho_j$ be all the constraints in B_{X_i} at the time B_{X_i} is processed, including the original constraints of $\mathcal{R}$. The constraints $\rho_{X_i}^{Z_j}$ for each child bucket z_j is computed by

$$\rho_{X_i}^{Z_j}(sep(X_i, Z_j)) = \pi_{sep(X_i,Z_j)}(\bowtie_{i=1}^{j} \rho_i)$$

Figure 7.17: Algorithm Adaptive-Tree Consistency (ATC)

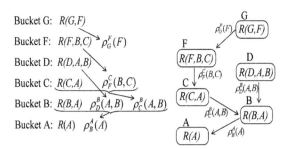

Figure 7.18: Execution of AC along the bucket-tree

its right, the figure displays the same computation as a message-passing along its bucket-tree. Figure 7.19 shows a complete execution of ATC along the linear order of buckets and along the bucket-tree. The ρ constraints are displayed as messages placed on the outgoin arcs.

Theorem 7.24 (Complexity of ATC). *[33] Let $w^*(d)$ be the induced width of G along ordering d. The time complexity of ATC is $O(r \cdot deg \cdot k^{w^*(d)+1})$, where deg is the maximum degree in the bucket-tree. The space complexity of ATC is $O(n \cdot k^{w^*(d)})$.*

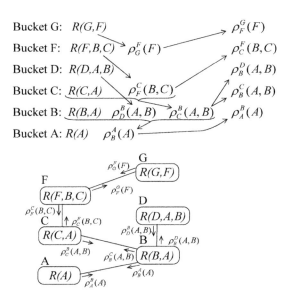

Figure 7.19: Propagation of ρ messages along the bucket-tree

7.2.6 Hypertree Decomposition

One problem with the tree-width in identifying tractability is that they are sensitive only to the primal constraint graph and not to its hypergraph structure. For example, an acyclic problem whose constraint's scope have high arity would have a high tree-width even though it can be processed in quadratic time in the input. A different graph parameter that is more sensitive to the hypergraph structure is the hypertree width [29]. It relies on a notion of hypertree decompositions for Constraint Satisfaction and it provides a stronger indicator of tractability than the tree-width.

Definition 7.25 (hypertree decomposition). *[29] A (complete) hypertree decomposition of a hypergraph $HG = (X, S)$ is a triple $< T, \chi, \psi >$, where $T = (V, E)$ is a rooted tree, and χ and ψ are labelling functions which associate with each vertex $v \in V$ two sets $\chi(v) \subseteq X$ and $\psi(v) \subseteq S$, and which satisfies the following conditions:*

1. *For each edge $h \in S$, there exists $v \in V$ such that $h \in \psi(v)$ and $scope(h) \subseteq \chi(v)$ (we say that v strongly covers h).*

2. *For each variable $X_i \in X$, the set $\{v \in V | X_i \in \chi(v)\}$ induces a (connected) subtree of T.*

3. *For each $v \in V$, $\chi(v) \subseteq scope(\psi(v))$.*

4. *For each $v \in V$, $scope(\psi(v)) \cap \chi(T_v) \subseteq \chi(v)$, where $T_v = (V_v, E_v)$ is the subtree of T rooted at v and $\chi(T_v) = \cup_{u \in V_v} \chi(u)$.*

The hypertree width hw of a hypertree decomposition is $hw = max_v |\psi(v)|$.

A hypertree decomposition of a constraint network $\mathcal{R}$ is a hypertree decomposition of its hypergraph where the vertices are the variables of $\mathcal{R}$ and the scopes of constraints are the hyperedges. The hypertree decomposition can be processed by joining all the relations in each cluster and then applying acyclic-solving procedure, or by CTE.

Processing hypertree decomposition by acyclic-solving: Once a hyper-tree decomposition is available, 1. join all the relations in each cluster, yielding a single relation on each cluster. This step takes time and space $O(m \cdot t^{hw})$ where t bounds the relation size and m is the number of edges in the hypertree decomposition, and it creates an acyclic constraint satisfaction problem. 2. Process the acyclic problem by arc-consistency. This step can be accomplished in time $O(m \cdot hw \cdot t^{hw} \cdot logt)$ because there are m arc in the hypertree decomposition, each has at most $O(t^{hw})$ tuples so acyclic-solving is $O(m \cdot t^{hw} \cdot log(t^{hw}))$ which yields the desired bound. We can summarize,

Theorem 7.26. *[29] Let m be the number of edges in the hypertree decomposition of a constraint network $\mathcal{R}$, hw be its hypertree width and t be a bound on the relation size. The hypertree decomposition can be processed by* ACYCLIC-SOLVING *in time $O(m \cdot hw \cdot logt \; t^{hw})$ and in space $O(m \cdot t^{hw})$.*

Processing hypertree decompositions by CTE: Recall that given a hypertree decomposition, each node u has to send a single message to each neighbor v. We can compute $m_{(u,v)}$ in the space saving mode as follows. 1., Join all functions $\psi(u)$ in node u yielding function $h(u)$, namely, $h(u) = \bowtie_{R \in \psi(u)} R$. This step can be done in time and space $O(t^{|\psi(u)|})$. 2. For each neighbor c of u, $c \neq v$ iterate, $h(u) \leftarrow h(u) \bowtie m_{(c,u)}$. This step can be accomplished in $O(deg \cdot hw \cdot logt \cdot t^{hw})$ time and $O(t^{hw})$ space. 3. $m_{(u,v)} \leftarrow \pi_{\chi(u) \cap \chi(v)} h(u$ We can conclude:

Theorem 7.27. *A hypertree decomposition of a constraint network can be processed by CTE in time*

$$O(m \cdot deg \cdot hw \cdot logt \cdot t^{hw})$$

and space $O(m \cdot t^{hw})$, where m is the number of edges in the hypertree decomposition, hw its hypertree width, and t is a bound on the size of the relational representation of eac function in $\mathcal{R}$.

Notice that CTE may be more space efficient than processing by generating the joins in each cluster followed by ACYCLIC-SOLVING. However, we cannot capture this saving using hw alone. If we use the *sep* parameter we could bound CTE's space complexity by $O(N \cdot k^{sep})$.

Notice that there are tree-decompositions that are not hypertree decompositions as in Definition 7.25, because hypertree decompositions require that the variable-sets labeling a vertex, will be contained in the combined scope of its labeling functions (Condition 3 of Definition 7.25). This is not required by the tree-decomposition definition. For example, consider a single n-ary constraint R. It can be mapped into a bucket-tree with n vertices. Node i contains variables $\{1, 2, ...i\}$ but no constraints, except that node n contains also the original constraints of the problem. Both join-tree and hypertree decomposition will allow just one vertex that include the function and all its variables.

Therefore, Theorem 7.27 does not apply to Definition 7.15 of tree-decomposition because the analysis assumed Condition 3 of Definition 7.25. We can overcome this problem by thinking of all uncovered variables in a node as having a universal relation with the variables as its scope. In this case we can show

Theorem 7.28. *A tree-decomposition of a constraint network $\mathcal{R}$ can be processed by CTE in time*

$$O(m \cdot deg \cdot hw^* \cdot logt \cdot t^{hw^*})$$

where t is a bound on the relation size, $hw^*(v) = (|\psi(v)| + |\{X_i|X_i \not\in scope(\psi(v))\}|)$, and $hw^* = \max_{v \in V} hw^*(v)$ and in space $O(m \cdot t^{hw*})$.

Proof. Once we add the universal relation on uncovered variables we have a restricted hypertree decomposition to which we can apply the bound of Theorem 7.27 assuming the same implementation of CTE. The number of uncovered variables in a node v is $n(v) = |\{X_i|X_i \not\in scope(\psi(v))\}|$. So the processing of a node takes time $O(t^{hw} \cdot k^{n(v)})$ where k bounds the domain size, yielding $O((max(t,k)^{hw^*})$. Assuming that $t > k$ we can use the time and space bound $O(N \cdot t^{hw^*})$. Consequently, message passing between all nodes yields overall complexity as in Theorem 7.27 when hw is replaced by hw^*. $\qquad\square$

7.2.7 Summary

This section discussed inference algorithms that transform a general constraint problem into a tree of constraints which can be solved efficiently. The complexity of the transformation process is exponentially bounded by the tree-width (or induced-width) of the constraint graph. It is also exponentially bounded by any hypertree width of the hypertree-decomposition. Thus both the induced-width and tree-width hypertree width can be used to define structure-based tractable classes. Yet, the hypertree width defines a larger tractability class because every problem with a bounded tree-width has a bounded hypertree width but not vice-versa.

7.3 Trading Time and Space by Hybrids of Search and Inference

As we noted at the introduction, search and inference have complementary properties. Inference exploit the graph structure and therefore allows structure-based time guarantees but require substantial memory. Search, does not posses good complexity time bounds yet it can operate in linear space. Therefore, using a hybrid of search and inference allows structure-driven tradeoff of space and time. Two such hybrids are presented next.

7.3.1 The Cycle-Cutset and w-Cutset Schemes

The algorithms presented in this section exploit the fact that variable instantiation changes the effective connectivity of the constraint graph. Consider a constraint problem whose graph is given in Figure 7.20a. For this problem, instantiating X_2 to some value, say a, renders the choices of values to X_1 and X_5 independent, as if the pathway $X_1 - X_2 - X_5$ were blocked at X_2. Similarly, this instantiation blocks dependency in the pathway $X_1 - X_2 - X_4$, leaving only one path between any two variables. In other words, given that X_2

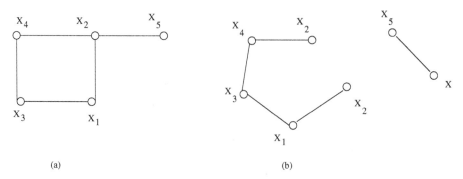

(a)   (b)

Figure 7.20: An instantiated variable cuts its own cycles.

was assigned a specific value, the "effective" constraint graph for the rest of the variables
is shown in Figure 7.20b. Here, the instantiated variable X_2 and its incident arcs are first
deleted from the graph, and X_2 subsequently is duplicated for each of its neighbors. The
constraint problem having the graph shown in Figure 7.20(a) when $X_2 = a$ is identical
to the constraint problem having the graph in Figure 7.20(b) with the same assignment
$X_2 = a$.

In general, when the group of instantiated variables constitutes a cycle-cutset; a set of
nodes that, once removed, would render the constraint graph cycle-free. The remaining
network is a tree (as shown in Figure 7.20b), and can be solved by *tree-solving* algorithm.
In most practical cases it would take more than a single variable to cut all the cycles in
the graph. Thus, a general way of solving a problem whose constraint graph contains
cycles is to identify a subset of variables that cut all cycles in the graph, find a consistent
instantiation of the variables in the cycle-cutset, and then solve the remaining problem
by the *tree algorithm*. If a solution to this restricted problem (conditioned on the cycle-
cutset values) is found, then a solution to the entire problem is at hand. If not, another
instantiation of the cycle-cutset variables should be considered until a solution is found.
If the task is to solve a constraint problem whose constraint graph is presented in Figure
7.20a, (assume X_2 has two values $\{a, b\}$ in its domain), first $X_2 = a$ must be assumed, and
the remaining tree problem relative to this instantiation, is solved. If no solution is found,
it is assumed that $X_2 = b$ and another attempt is made.

The number of times the tree-solving algorithm needs to be invoked is bounded by the
number of partial solutions to the cycle-cutset variables. A small cycle-cutset is therefore
desirable. However, since finding a minimal-size cycle-cutset is computationally hard, it
will be more practical to settle for heuristic compromises. One approach is to incorporate
this scheme within backtracking search. Because *backtracking* works by progressively
instantiating sets of variables, we only need to keep track of the connectivity status of the
constraint graph. As soon as the set of instantiated variables constitutes a cycle-cutset, the
search algorithm is switched to the tree-solving algorithm on the restricted problem, i.e.,
either finding a consistent extension for the remaining variables (thus finding a solution to
the entire problem) or concluding that no such extension exists (in which case backtracking
takes place and another instantiation tried).

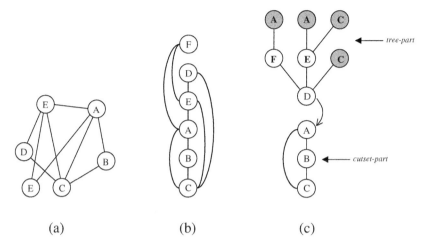

Figure 7.21: (a) a constraint graph (b) its ordered graph (c) The constraint graph of the cutset variable and the conditioned variable, where the assigned variables are darkened.

Example 7.29. Assume that backtracking instantiates the variables of the CSP represented in Figure 7.21a in the order C, B, A, E, D, F (Figure 7.21b). Backtracking will instantiate variables C, B and A, and then, realizing that these variables cut all cycles, will invoke a tree-solving routine on the rest of the problem: the tree-problem in Figure 7.21c with variables C, B and A assigned, should then be attempted. If no solution is found, control returns to backtracking which will go back to variable A.

The cycle-cutset scheme can be generalized. Rather than insisting on conditioning on a subset (cutset) that cuts all cycles and yields subproblems having induced-width 1, we can allow cutsets that create subproblems whose induced-width is higher than 1 but still bounded. This suggests a framework of hybrid algorithms parameterized by a bound w on the induced-width of subproblems solved by inference.

Definition 7.30 (w-cutset). *Given a graph G, a subset of nodes is called a w-cutset iff when the subset is removed the resulting graph has an induced-width less than or equal to w. A minimal w-cutset of a graph has a smallest size among all w-cutsets of the graph. A cycle-cutset is a 1-cutset of a graph.*

Finding a minimal w-cutset is a hard task. However, like in the special case of a cycle-cutset we can settle for a w-cutset relative to the given variable ordering. We can look for an initial set of the ordering that is a w-cutset. Then a backtracking algorithm can traverse the search space over the w-cutset and for each of its consistent assignment solve the rest of the problem by ADAPTIVE-CONSISTENCY or by CTE.

Algorithm cutset-decomposition(w) (called elim-cond in [15]) is described in Figure 7.22. It runs backtracking search on the w-cutset and adaptive-consistency on the remaining variables. The constraint problem $\mathcal{R} = (X, D, C)$ conditioned on an assignment $Y = \bar{y}$ and denoted by $\mathcal{R}_{\bar{y}}$ is $\mathcal{R}$ augmented with the unary constraints dictated by the assignment $\bar{y}$. In the worst-case, all possible assignments to the w-cutset variables need to

Algorithm cutset-decomposition(w)
Input: A constraint network $\mathcal{R} = (X, D, C)$, $Y \subseteq X$ which is a w-cutset. d is an ordering that starts with Y such that the induced-width when Y is removed, along d, is bounded by w, $Z = X - Y$.
Output: A consistent assignment, if there is one.

1. **while** $\bar{y} \leftarrow$ next partial solution of Y found by backtracking, **do**

   a) $\bar{z} \leftarrow adaptive - consistency(\mathcal{R}_{Y=\bar{y}})$.

   b) **if** $\bar{z}$ is not *false*, return solution $(\bar{y}, \bar{z})$.

2. **endwhile**.

3. **return:** the problem has no solutions.

Figure 7.22: Algorithm *cutset-decomposition(w)*

be enumerated. If c is the w-cutset size, k^c is the number of subproblems of induced-width bounded by w needed to be solved, each requiring $O((n - c)k^{w+1})$ steps.

Theorem 7.31. *[15] Algorithm cutset-decomposition(w) has time complexity of $O(n\ k^{c+w+1})$ where n is the number of variables, c is the w-cutset size and k is the domain size. The space complexity of the algorithm is $O(k^w)$.* $\square$

The special case of $w = 1$ yield the cycle-cutset decomposition algorithm whose time complexity is $O((n-c)k^{c+2})$ and it operates in linear space. Thus, the constant w can control the balance between search and inference (e.g., variable-elimination), and can affect the tradeoff between time and space.

Another approach that uses the w-cutset principle is to alternate between search and variable-elimination. Given a variable ordering for adaptive-consistency we can apply variable elimination as long as the induced-width of the variables does not exceed w. If a variable has induced-width higher than w, it will be conditioned upon. The algorithm alternates between conditioning and elimination. This scheme was used both for solving SAT problems and for optimization tasks [40, 34] and is currently used for Bayesian networks applications [20, 22]. Clearly, a cutset uncovered via the *alternating algorithm* is also a w-cutset and therefore can be used within the cutset-decomposition scheme.

Both cutset-decomposition and the alternating cutset-elimination algorithm call for a new optimization task on graphs:

Definition 7.32 (finding a minimal w-cutset). *Given a graph $G = (V, E)$ and a constant w, find a smallest subset of nodes U, such that when removed the resulting graph has induced-width less than or equal w.*

Finding a minimal w-cutset is hard, but various greedy heuristic algorithms were investigated empirically. Several greedy and approximation algorithms for the special case of cycle-cutset can be found in the literature [5]. The general task of finding a minimal w-cutset was addressed in recent papers [21, 8] both for the cutset-decomposition version

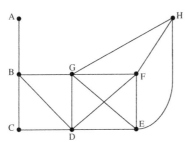

Figure 7.23: a primal constraint graph

and for the alternating version. Note that verifying that a given subset of nodes is a w-cutset can be accomplished in polynomial time (linear in the number of nodes), by deleting the candidate cutset from the graph and verifying that the remaining graph has an induced width bounded by w [1].

In summary, the parameter w can be used within the cutset-decomposition scheme to control the trade-off between search and inference. If d is the ordering used by cutset-decomposition(w) and if $w \geq w^*(d)$, the algorithm coincides with ADAPTIVE-CONSISTENCY. As w decreases, the algorithm requires less space and more time. It can be shown that the size of the smallest cycle-cutset (1-cutset), c_1^* and the smallest induced width, w^*, obey the inequality $c_1^* \geq w^* - 1$. Therefore, $1 + c_1^* \geq w^*$, where the left side of this inequality is the exponent that determines the time complexity of cutset-decomposition(w=1), while w^* governs the complexity of ADAPTIVE-CONSISTENCY. In general, if c_w^* is the size of a minimal w-cutset then,

$$1 + c_1^* \geq 2 + c_2^* \geq ...b + c_b^*, ... \geq w^* + c_{w^*}^* = w^*$$

We get a hybrid scheme controlled by w, whose time complexity decreases and its space increases as w changes from w^* to 1.

7.3.2   The Super-Bucket and Super-Cluster Schemes; Separator-Width

We now present an orthogonal approach for combining search and inference. The inference algorithm CTE that process a tree-decomposition already contains a hidden combination of variable elimination and search. It computes constraints on the separators using variable elimination and is space exponential in the separator's size. The clusters themselves can be processed by search in time exponential in the cluster size. Thus, one can trade even more space for time by allowing larger cliques but smaller separators.

Assume a problem whose tree-decomposition has tree-width r and maximum separator size s. Assume further that our space restrictions do not allow the necessary $O(k^s)$ memory required when applying CTE on such a tree. One way to overcome this problem is to combine the nodes in the tree that are connected by large separators into a single cluster. The resulting tree-decomposition has larger subproblems but smaller separators. This idea suggests a sequence of tree-decompositions parameterized by the sizes of their separators as follows.

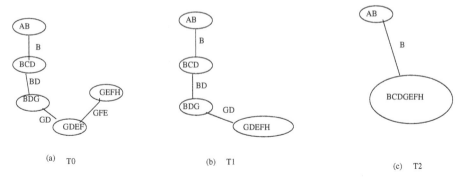

Figure 7.24: A tree-decomposition with separators equal to (a) 3, (b) 2, and (c) 1

Let T be a tree-decomposition of hypergraph $\mathcal{H}$. Let $s_0, s_1, ..., s_n$ be the sizes of the separators in T, listed in strictly descending order. With each separator size s_i we associate a secondary tree decomposition T_i, generated by combining adjacent nodes whose separator sizes are strictly greater than s_i. We denote by r_i the largest set of variables in any cluster of T_i, and by hw_i the largest number of constraints in T_i. Note that as s_i decreases, both r_i and hw_i increase. Clearly, from Theorem 7.20 it follows that,

Theorem 7.33. *Given a tree-decomposition T over n variables and m constraints, separator sizes $s_0, s_1, ..., s_t$ and secondary tree-decompositions having a corresponding maximal number of nodes in any cluster, $r_0, r_1, ..., r_t$. The complexity of CTE when applied to each secondary tree-decompositions T_i is $O(m \cdot deg \cdot exp(r_i))$ time, and $O(n \cdot exp(s_i))$ space (i ranges over all the secondary tree-decomposition).*

We will call the resulting algorithm the super-cluster tree elimination algorithm, or $SCTE(s)$. It takes a primary tree-decomposition and generates a tree-decomposition whose separator's size is bounded by s, which is subsequently processed by CTE. In the following example we assume that a naive-backtracking search processes each cluster.

Example 7.34. Consider the constraint problem having the constraint graph in Figure 7.23. The graph can be decomposed into the join-tree in Figure 7.24(a). If we allow only separators of size 2, we get the join tree T_1 in Figure 7.24(b). This structure suggests that applying CTE takes time exponential in the largest cluster, 5, while requiring space exponential in 2. If space considerations allow only singleton separators, we can use the secondary tree T_2 in Figure 7.24(c). We conclude that the problem can be solved either in $O(k^4)$ time (k being the maximum domain size) and $O(k^3)$ space using T_0, or in $O(k^5)$ time and $O(k^2)$ space using T_1, or in $O(k^7)$ time and $O(k)$ space using T_2.

Superbuckets. Since as we saw in Section 7.2.5, bucket-elimination algorithms can be extended to bucket-trees and since a bucket-tree is a tree-decomposition, by merging adjacent buckets we generate a *super-bucket-tree* (SBT) in a similar way to generating super clusters. This implies that in the top-down phase of bucket-elimination several variables are eliminated at once (see [12]). Algorithm SCTE suggests a new graph parameter.

Definition 7.35. *Given a graph G and a constant s find a tree-decomposition of G having the smallest induced-width, w_s^*. Or, find a hyper-tree decomposition having the smallest hypertree width, hw_s^*.*

A related problem of finding a tree-decomposition with a bounded tree-width w having the smallest separator, was shown to be polynomial [42]. Finding w_s^* however, is hard but it is easy for the special case of $s = 1$ as we show next.

Decomposition into non-separable components

A special tree-decomposition occurs when all the separators are singleton variables. This type of tree-decomposition is attractive because it requires only linear space. While we generally cannot find the best tree-decompositions having a bounded separators' size in polynomial time, this is a feasible task when the separators are singletons. To this end, we use the graph notion of *non-separable components* [19].

Definition 7.36 (non-separable components). *A connected graph $G = (V, E)$ is said to have a separation node v if there exist nodes a and b such that all paths connecting a and b pass through v. A graph that has a separation node is called* separable, *and one that has none is called* non-separable. *A subgraph with no separation nodes is called a* non-separable component *or a* bi-connected component.

An $O(|E|)$ algorithm exists for finding all the non-separable components and the separation nodes. It is based on a depth-first search traversal of the graph. An important property of non-separable components is that that they are interconnected in a tree-structured manner [19]. Namely, for every graph G there is a *tree SG*, whose nodes are the non-separable components $C_1, C_2, \ldots, C_r$ of G. The separating nodes of these trees are $V_1, V_2, \ldots, V_t$ and any two component nodes are connected through a separating node vertex in SG. Clearly the tree of non-separable components suggests a tree-decomposition where each node corresponds to a component, the variables of the nodes are those appearing in each component, and the constraints can be freely placed into a component that contains their scopes. Applying CTE to such a tree requires only linear space, but is time exponential in the components' sizes (see [12]).

Example 7.37. Assume that the graph in Figure 7.25(a) represents a constraint network having unary, binary and ternary constraints as follows: $\mathcal{R} = \{R_{AD}, R_{AB}, R_{DC}, R_{BC}, R_{GF}, D_G, D_F, R_{EHI}, R_{CFE}\}$. The non-separable components and their tree-structure are given in Figure 7.25(b,c). The ordering of components $d = (C_1, C_2, C_3, C_4)$ dictates super-clusters associated with variables $\{G, J, F\}, \{E, H, I\}, \{C, F, E\}$ and $\{A, B, C, D\}$. The initial partition into super-clusters and a schematic execution of CTE are displayed in Figure 7.25d.

Theorem 7.38 (non-separable components). *[24] If $\mathcal{R} = (X, D, C)$, $|X| = n$, is a constraint network whose constraint graph has non-separable components of at most size r, then the super-cluster-tree elimination algorithm, whose buckets are the non-separable components, is time exponential $O(n \cdot exp(r))$ but requires only linear in space.*

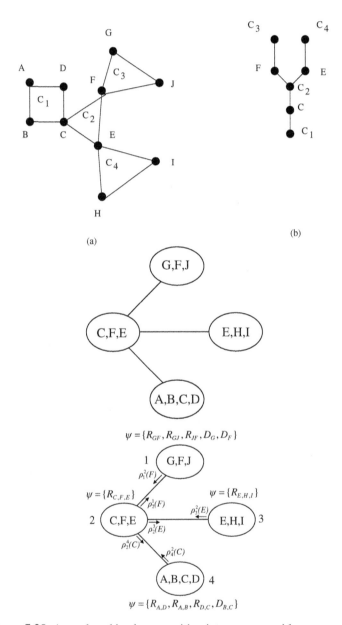

Figure 7.25: A graph and its decomposition into non-separable components.

Hinge decomposition

The non-separable component principle can be applied to the dual graph rather than to the primal constraint graph. Better yet, since the dual graph may contain redundant edges, we can first try to remove those edges to obtain a minimal dual graph (also called minimal join-graph) and then generate a tree of non-separable components. This idea is very related to another tree-decomposition principle proposed in the literature called hinge-decomposition [32]. Indeed a best hinge decomposition can be obtained in polynomial time, yielding smallest component in a bi-component tree decomposition of the dual graph whose some redundant arcs are removed. For a formal proof see [31].

7.4 Structure-Based Tractability in Search

Search algorithms typically traverse the problem's space whose paths represent a partial or full solutions. Their main virtue is that they can operate using bounded memory. Their main weakness however is that the structure of the search space hides the independencies of the constraint network. Next we show that *AND/OR search spaces* can overcome this difficulty because they display the independencies in the constraint graph and can some-time yield exponential saving compared to the traditional search space (called OR space). As a result, search algorithms can have graph-based performance guarantees like inference schemes.

7.4.1 AND/OR Search Trees

Definition 7.39 (AND/OR search tree based on DFS tree). *Given a constraint network $\mathcal{R}$ and a DFS spanning tree T of its primal graph, the AND/OR search tree of $\mathcal{R}$ based on T, denoted S_T, has alternating levels of OR nodes (labeled with variable names, e.g. X) and AND nodes (labeled with variable values, e.g. $\langle X, v \rangle$). The root of S_T is an OR node labeled with the root of T. The children of an OR node X are AND nodes, each labeled with a value of X, $\langle X, v \rangle$. The children of an AND node $\langle X, v \rangle$, are OR nodes, labeled with the variables that are children of X in T. A solution is a subtree containing the root node and for every OR node, it includes one of its child nodes and for every AND nodes it includes all its children.*

Consider the tree T in Fig. 7.26 describing a graph coloring problem over domains $\{1, 2, 3\}$. Its traditional OR search tree along the DFS ordering $d = (X, Y, T, R, Z, L, M)$ is given in Fig. 7.27, and its AND/OR search tree based on the DFS tree T with a high-lighted solution subtrees are given in Fig. 7.28.

The construction of AND/OR search trees can be guided not just DFS spanning trees but also by *pseudo-trees* which include DFS trees [25, 26, 3]. Pseudo-trees have the property that every arc of the constraint graph is a back-arc in the pseudo-tree (i.e. it doesn't connect across different branches). Clearly, any DFS tree and any chain are pseudo-trees. It is easy to see that searching an AND/OR tree guided by a pseudo-tree T is exponential in the depth m of T. Also, it is known that if a graph has a tree-width w^* it also has a pseudo-tree whose depth m satisfies $m \le w^* \cdot \log n$ [3]. In summary,

Theorem 7.40. *Given a constraint network $\mathcal{R}$ and a pseudo-tree T, its AND/OR search tree S_T is sound and complete (contains all and only solutions) and its size is $O(n \cdot k^m)$*

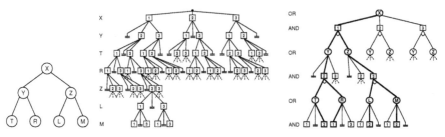

Figure 7.26: Tree T | Figure 7.27: OR search tree | Figure 7.28: AND/OR search tree

where m is the depth of its backbone pseudo-tree. Moreover, a constraint network that has a tree-width w^* has an AND/OR search tree whose size is $O(k^{w^* \cdot \log n})$.

Backjumping algorithms [28, 3] are backtracking search schemes applied to the regular OR space, which uses the problem structure to jump back from a dead-end as far back as possible. In *graph-based backjumping* (GBJ) [14] each variable maintains a graph-based induced ancestor set which ensures that no solutions are missed when jumping back to its deepest variable. Graph-based backjumping extracts knowledge about dependencies from the constraint graph alone. Whenever a dead-end occurs at a particular variable X the algorithm backs up to the most recent variable connected to X in the graph. It can be shown that backjumping in effect explores an AND/OR search space. Indeed, when *backjumping* is performed on a DFS ordering of the variables, its complexity can be bounded by $O(k^m)$ steps, m being the depth of the DFS tree. Therefore, if the graph has an induced-width w^*, there exists an ordering for which backjumping can be bounded by $O(k^{w^* \cdot logn})$.

7.4.2 AND/OR Search Graphs

It is often the case that certain states in the search tree can be merged because the subtrees they root are identical. Any two such nodes are called *unifiable*, and when merged, transform the search tree into a search graph. For example, in Fig. 7.28, the search trees below the paths $\langle X, 2 \rangle$, $\langle Y, 1 \rangle$ and $\langle X, 3 \rangle$, $\langle Y, 1 \rangle$ are identical, so the corresponding nodes are unifiable.

In general, merging all the unifiable subtrees given an AND/OR search graph yields a unique graph, called the *minimal AND/OR search graph*. Merging is applicable to the traditional OR search space as well. However, in many cases it will not be able to reach the compression we can get in AND/OR representations. Fig. 7.29 and Fig. 7.30 show a comparison between minimal OR and AND/OR search graphs for the problem in Fig. 7.26. Indeed some variable-value instantiations appear multiple times in the OR graph while just once in the AND/OR graph.

In some cases identifying unifiable nodes is easy. The idea is to extract from each path only the relevant *context* that completely determines the unexplored portion of the space. Subsequently, the subgraph is only solved once and the results are cached and indexed by the context. Searching the AND/OR graphs rather than the AND/OR tree is related to recording no-goods during backtracking search [11]. It can be shown that,

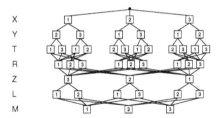

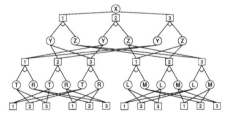

Figure 7.29: Minimal OR search graph of the tree problem in Fig. 7.26

Figure 7.30: Minimal AND/OR search graph of the tree problem in Fig. 7.26

Theorem 7.41. *[16] Given G, a pseudo-tree T of G and its induced width w^* the size of the minimal AND/OR search graph based on T is $O(n \cdot k^{w^*})$, when k bounds the domain size and n is the number of variables.*

We can show that the minimal AND/OR search graph is bounded exponentially by the primal graph's induced-width while the OR minimal search graph is bounded exponentially by its *path-width*. The path-width, pw^*, of a graph is the minimum tree-width over all tree-decompositions whose trees are chains. It is well known [10] that for any graph $w^* \le pw^* \le w^* \cdot \log n$. It is also easy to place m^* (the minimal pseudo-tree depth) yielding $w^* \le m^* \le pw^* \le w^* \cdot \log n$.

7.5 Summary and Bibliographical Notes

7.5.1 Structure-Based Tractability

Throughout this chapter several techniques that exploit the structure of the constraint network were presented. Several graph parameters stood out in the analysis. The two main classes are *width*-based and *cutset*-based. Width-based parameters capture the size of clusters required to make the graph a tree of clusters. These include the *tree-width* also known as *induced-width* w^*, (appearing in *adaptive-consistency, tree-clustering* and in searching AND/OR graphs using caching of goods and no-goods. It also includes path-width (pw) which captures the cluster size required to embed a graph in a chain of clusters, and the hypertree hw appearing in the hypertree decomposition which captures the number of constraints in a tree of clusters. Cutset-based parameters include the *cycle-cutset size* c_1 and more generally the *w-cutset size* c_w (appearing in the cutset-decomposition method, which capture the number of variables that need to be removed from the constraint graph to make its tree-width bounded by w. This concept can be extended in an obvious way to hypercutset decompositions defining cutsets for which the remaining graph has a bounded hypertree width, rather than tree-width. Other parameters that do not belong to the above two classes is 1) the *depth of a DFS-tree and a pseudo-tree m* (appearing when searching AND/OR trees and in backjumping), 2) the *size of the largest non-separable component r_1* (appearing in the decomposition to bi-connected components), 3) the size of hinges (appearing in bi-connected decomposition of a minimal dual graphs) and 4) the size of *separator*-based tree-width r_s appearing in SCTE method capturing time-space tradeoffs.

It is well known [10, 3] that for any graph $w^* \le m^* \le pw^* \le w^* \cdot \log n$. Relating width-based parameters to cutset parameters we have that $w^* \le c_i^* + i$ holds. Also graphs having bounded tree-width also have bounded hypertree width but not vice-versa. Therefore the hypertree width is the most informative parameter capturing tractability. However, when memory is bounded we can use SCTE(i) or cutset-decomposition(i) for an appropriate i so that memory of $O(k^i)$ is feasible.

7.5.2 Bibliographical Notes

Join-tree clustering was introduced in constraint processing by Dechter and Pearl [18] and in probabilistic networks by Spigelhalter et. al [35]. Both methods are based on the characterization by relational-database researchers that acyclic-databases have an underlying tree-structure, called join-tree, that allows polynomial query processing using join-project operations and easy identification procedures [6, 38, 46]. In both constraint networks and belief networks, it was observed that the complexity of compiling any knowledge-base into an acyclic one is exponential in the cluster size, which is characterized by the induced-width or tree-width. At the same time, variable-elimination algorithms developed in [7, 43] and [17] (e.g., adaptive-consistency and bucket-elimination) were also observed to be governed by the same complexity graph-parameter. In [17, 18] the connection between induced-width and tree-width was recognized through the work of [1] on tree-width and k-trees and partial k-trees, which was made explicit later in [27]. The similarity between variable-elimination and tree-clustering from the constraint perspective was analyzed [18]. Independently of this investigation, the tree-width parameter was undergoing intensive investigation in the theoretic-graph-community. It characterizes the best embedding of a graph or a hypergraph in a hypertree. Various connections between hypertrees, chordal graphs and k-trees were made by Arnborg and his colleagues [1, 2]. They showed that finding the smallest tree-width of a graph is NP-complete, but deciding if the graph has a tree-width below a certain constant k is polynomial in k. A recent analysis shows that this task can be accomplished in $O(n \cdot f(k))$ where $f(k)$ is a very bad exponential function of k [9].

The decomposition into hinges was presented in [32]. As noted any hinge-decomposition is closely related to bi-component tree decomposition of the dual graph whose redundant arcs are removed [31]. The hypertree-width parameter was introduced in [29] and shown to provide the most inclusive characterization of tractability. In recent years, research has focused on a variety of greedy and other approximation algorithms for tree-width and induced-width [4, 45]. For recent work see [39, 41]

Acknowledgements

This chapter is based in parts on Chapters 9 and 10 of [12] and on [33].

Bibliography

[1] S. A. Arnborg. Efficient algorithms for combinatorial problems on graphs with bounded decomposability - a survey. *BIT*, 25:2–23, 1985.

[2] S. A. Arnborg, D. G. Corneil, and A. Proskourowski. Complexity of finding embeddings in a k-tree. *SIAM Journal of Discrete Mathematics.*, 8:277–284, 1987.

[3] R. Bayardo and D. Miranker. A complexity analysis of space-bound learning algorithms for the constraint satisfaction problem. In *AAAI'96: Proceedings of the Thirteenth National Conference on Artificial Intelligence*, pages 298–304, 1996.

[4] A. Becker and D. Geiger. A sufficiently fast algorithm for finding close to optimal junction trees. In *Uncertainty in AI (UAI'96)*, pages 81–89, 1996.

[5] A. Becker, R. Bar-Yehuda, and D. Geiger. Random algorithms for the loop-cutset problem. In *Uncertainty in AI (UAI'99)*, pages 81–89, 1999.

[6] C. Beeri, R. Fagin, D. Maier, and M. Yannakakis. On the desirability of acyclic database schemes. *Journal of the ACM*, 30(3):479–513, 1983.

[7] U. Bertele and F. Brioschi. *Nonserial Dynamic Programming*. Academic Press, 1972.

[8] B. Bidyuk and R. Dechter. On finding w-cutset in Bayesian networks. In *Uncertainty in AI (UAI04)*, 2004.

[9] H.L. Bodlaender. Treewidth: Algorithmic techniques and results. In *MFCS-97*, pages 19–36, 1997.

[10] H.L. Bodlaender, J. R. Gilbert, H. Hasfsteinsson, and T. Kloks. Approximating treewidth, pathwidth and minimum elimination tree-height. In *Technical report RUU-CS-91-1, Utrecht University*, 1991.

[11] R. Dechter. And/or search spaces for graphical models. In *UCI Technical report*, 2005.

[12] R. Dechter. *Constraint Processing*. Morgan Kaufmann Publishers, 2003.

[13] R. Dechter. Constraint networks. *Encyclopedia of Artificial Intelligence*, pages 276–285, 1992.

[14] R. Dechter. Enhancement schemes for constraint processing: Backjumping, learning and cutset decomposition. *Artificial Intelligence*, 41:273–312, 1990.

[15] R. Dechter. Bucket elimination: A unifying framework for reasoning. *Artificial Intelligence*, 113:41–85, 1999.

[16] R. Dechter and R. Mateescu. The impact of and/or search spaces on constraint satisfaction and counting. In *Proceeding of Constraint Programming (CP2004)*, pages 731–736, 2004.

[17] R. Dechter and J. Pearl. Network-based heuristics for constraint satisfaction problems. *Artificial Intelligence*, 34:1–38, 1987.

[18] R. Dechter and J. Pearl. Tree clustering for constraint networks. *Artificial Intelligence*, pages 353–366, 1989.

[19] S. Even. Graph algorithms. In *Computer Science Press*, 1979.

[20] M. Fishelson and D. Geiger. Exact genetic linkage computations for general pedigrees. *Bioinformatics*, 2002.

[21] M. Fishelson and D. Geiger. Optimizing exact genetic linkage computations. *RECOMB*, pages 114–121, 2003.

[22] M. Fishelson, N. Dovgolevsky, and D. Geiger. Maximum likelihood haplotyping for general pedigrees. *Human Heredity*, 2005.

[23] E. C. Freuder. A sufficient condition for backtrack-free search. *Journal of the ACM*, 29(1):24–32, 1982.

[24] E. C. Freuder. A sufficient condition for backtrack-bounded search. *Journal of the ACM*, 32(1):755–761, 1985.

[25] E. C. Freuder and M. J. Quinn. Taking advantage of stable sets of variables in constraint satisfaction problems. In *Joint International Conference of Artificial Intelligence*, 1985.

[26] E. C. Freuder and M. J. Quinn. The use of lineal spanning trees to represent constraint satisfaction problems. Technical Report 87-41, University of New Hampshire, Durham, 1987.

[27] E. C. Freuder and R.J. Wallace. Partial constraint satisfaction. *Artificial Intelligence* 58(1-3):21–70, 1992.

[28] J. Gaschnig. Performance measurement and analysis of search algorithms. Technical Report CMU-CS-79-124, Carnegie Mellon University, 1979.

[29] G. Gottlob, N. Leone, and F. Scarcello. A comparison of structural CSP decomposition methods. *Artificial Intelligence*, pages 243–282, 2000.

[30] G. Gottlob, N. Leone, and F. Scarcello. The complexity of acyclic conjunctive queries. *Journal of the ACM*, pages 431–498, 2001.

[31] G. Greco and F. Scarcello. Non-binary constraints and optimal dual-graph representations. *Ijcai-03*, 2003.

[32] M. Gyssens, P. Jeavons, and D. Cohen. Decomposing constraint satisfaction problems using database techniques. *Artificial Intelligence*, 66:57–89, 1994.

[33] K. Kask, R. Dechter, J. Larrosa, and A. Dechter. Unifying tree-decompositions for reasoning in graphical models. *Artificial Intelligence*, 166(1-2):165–193, 2005.

[34] J. Larrosa and R. Dechter. Dynamic combination of search and variable-elimination in CSP and Max-CSP. *Submitted*, 2001.

[35] S.L. Lauritzen and D.J. Spiegelhalter. Local computation with probabilities on graphical structures and their application to expert systems. *Journal of the Royal Statistical Society, Series B*, 50(2):157–224, 1988.

[36] A. K. Mackworth. Consistency in networks of relations. *Artificial Intelligence*, 8(1): 99–118, 1977.

[37] A. K. Mackworth and E. C. Freuder. The complexity of some polynomial network consistency algorithms for constraint satisfaction problems. *Artificial Intelligence* 25, 1985.

[38] D. Maier. The theory of relational databases. In *Computer Science Press, Rockville, MD*, 1983.

[39] B. McMahan. Bucket elimination and hypertree decompositions. In *Institute of Information Systems (DBAI), TU, Vienna*, 2004.

[40] I. Rish and R. Dechter. Resolution vs. search; two strategies for sat. *Journal of Automated Reasoning*, 24(1/2):225–275, 2000.

[41] M. Samer. Hypertree decomposition via branch-decomposition. In *International Joint-conference of Artificial Intelligence (IJCAI05)*, pages 1535–1536, 2005.

[42] F. Scarcello, G. Greco, and N. Leone. Weighted hypertree decompositions and optimal query plans. *PODS'04*, pages 210–221, 2004.

[43] R. Seidel. A new method for solving constraint satisfaction problems. In *International Joint Conference on Artificial Intelligence (Ijcai-81)*, pages 338–342, 1981.

[44] P. P. Shenoy. Binary join trees. In *Proceedings of the 12th Conference on Uncertainty in Artificial Intelligence (UAI96)*, pages 492–499, 1996.

[45] K. Shoiket and D. Geiger. A practical algorithm for finding optimal triangulations. In *Fourteenth National Conference on Artificial Intelligence (AAAI'97)*, pages 185–190, 1997.

[46] R. E. Tarjan and M. Yannakakis. Simple linear-time algorithms to test chordality of graphs, test acyclicity of hypergraphs and selectively reduce acyclic hypergraphs. *SIAM Journal of Computation.*, 13(3):566–579, 1984.

Chapter 8

The Complexity of Constraint Languages

David Cohen and Peter Jeavons

One of the most fundamental challenges in constraint programming is to understand the computational complexity of problems involving constraints. It has been shown that the class of all constraint satisfaction problem instances is NP-hard [72], so it is unlikely that efficient general-purpose algorithms exist for solving all forms of constraint problem. However, in many practical applications the instances that arise have special forms that enable them to be solved more efficiently [11, 25, 70, 83].

One way in which this occurs is that there is some special structure in the way that the constraints overlap and intersect each other. The natural theory for discussing the structure of such interaction between constraints is the mathematical theory of hypergraphs. Much work has been done in this area, and many tractable classes of constraint problems have been identified based on structural properties (see Chapter 7). There are strong parallels between this work and similar investigations into the structure of so-called *conjunctive queries* in relational databases [41, 59].

Another way in which constraint problems can be defined which are easier to solve than in the general case is when the *types of constraints* are limited. The natural theory for discussing the properties of constraint types is the mathematical theory of relations and their associated algebras. Again considerable progress has been made in this investigation over the past few years. For example, a complete characterisation of tractable constraint types is now known for both 2-element domains [86] and 3-element domains [14]. In addition, a number of novel efficient algorithms have been developed for solving particular types of constraint problems over both finite and infinite domains [3, 8, 16, 25, 26, 28, 64].

In this chapter we will focus on the second approach. That is, we will investigate how the complexity of solving constraint problems varies with the types of constraints which are allowed. One fundamental open research problem in this area is to characterise exactly which types of constraints give rise to constraint problems which can be solved in polynomial time. This problem is important from a theoretical perspective, because it helps to clarify the boundary between tractability and intractability in a wide range of combinatorial search problems [27, 37, 49, 63]. It is also important from a practical perspective, as it allows the development of constraint programming languages which exploit the existence of diverse families of tractable constraints to provide more efficient solution techniques [70, 83].

In this chapter a set of types of constraints will be called a *constraint language*. Section 8.1 gives the basic definitions, and Section 8.2 lists some typical examples of tractable (and intractable) constraint languages.

In Section 8.3 we present the mathematical theory that leads us to the major results in the area: we will characterise the complexity of constraint languages (over finite domains) in terms of properties of associated finite algebras.

In Section 8.4 we show how the algebraic theory can be used to identify tractable constraint languages and select an appropriate algorithm. This section presents a strong conjecture for a simple algebraic characterisation of all tractable constraint languages. We will also show that a direct result of the theory is that if the decision problem for a constraint language can be solved in polynomial time, then so can the search problem. In other words, for any language for which it can be decided in polynomial time whether a solution exists, a solution can be found in polynomial time.

In Section 8.5 we consider how the algebraic theory can be extended to deal with constraint languages over infinite domains, and in Section 8.6 we consider multi-sorted constraint languages (where different variables can take their values from different sets).

Finally, in Section 8.7 we briefly consider some alternative approaches, including a constructive approach which builds new tractable constraint languages by combining simpler languages. This theory applies to constraint languages over both finite and infinite domains. This constructive approach has a rather different flavour from the more descriptive algebraic approach, and the two approaches have not yet been fully unified.

We conclude the chapter in Section 8.8 with a discussion of possible future work in this exciting area.

8.1 Basic Definitions

In this section we begin by defining the fundamental decision problem associated with any given constraint language. It is the complexity of this decision problem that is the main focus of this chapter.

The central notion in the study of constraints and constraint satisfaction problems is the notion of a *relation*.

Definition 8.1. *For any set D, and any natural number n, the set of all n-tuples of elements of D is denoted by D^n. The ith component of a tuple t will be denoted by $t[i]$.*

*A subset of D^n is called an n-ary **relation** over D. The set of all finitary relations over D is denoted by $\mathbf{R}_D$.*

*A **constraint language** over D is a subset of $\mathbf{R}_D$.*

The 'constraint satisfaction problem' was introduced by Montanari [76] in 1974 and has been widely studied [33, 37, 66, 72, 73, 74] (see Chapter 2). In this chapter we study a parameterised version of the standard constraint satisfaction problem, in which the parameter is a constraint language specifying the possible forms of the constraints.

Definition 8.2. *For any set D and any constraint language Γ over D, the **constraint satisfaction problem** $\mathrm{CSP}(\Gamma)$ is the combinatorial decision problem with*

Instance: *A triple $\langle V, D, \mathcal{C} \rangle$, where*

- *V is a set of **variables**;*
- *$\mathcal{C}$ is a set of **constraints**, $\{C_1, \ldots, C_q\}$.*
- *Each constraint $C_i \in \mathcal{C}$ is a pair $\langle s_i, R_i \rangle$, where*
  - *s_i is a tuple of variables of length n_i, called the **constraint scope**;*
  - *$R_i \in \Gamma$ is an n_i-ary relation over D, called the **constraint relation**.*

Question: *Does there exist a **solution**, that is, a function φ, from V to D, such that, for each constraint $\langle s, R \rangle \in \mathcal{C}$, with $s = \langle v_1, \ldots, v_n \rangle$, the tuple $\langle \varphi(v_1), \ldots, \varphi(v_n) \rangle$ belongs to the relation R?*

The set D, specifying the possible values for the variables, is called the **domain** of the problem. The set of solutions to a CSP instance $\mathcal{P} = \langle V, D, C \rangle$ will be denoted $\mathrm{Sol}(\mathcal{P})$.

In order to determine the computational complexity of a constraint satisfaction problem we need to specify how instances are encoded as finite strings of symbols. The *size* of a problem instance can be taken to be the length of a string specifying the variables, the domain, all constraint scopes and corresponding constraint relations. We shall assume in all cases that this representation is chosen so that the complexity of determining whether a constraint allows a given assignment of values to the variables in its scope is bounded by a polynomial function of the length of the representation. For finite domains it is most straightforward to assume that the tuples in the constraint relations are listed explicitly.

Throughout the chapter we shall be concerned with distinguishing between constraint languages which give rise to tractable problems (i.e., problems for which there exists a polynomial-time solution algorithm) and those which do not. Since many practical applications define constraint relations implicitly we ensure that our explicit representation does not affect our results by defining the notion of tractability in such a way that it only depends on finite subsets of the constraint language.

Definition 8.3. *A constraint language, Γ, is said to be **tractable** if $\mathrm{CSP}(\Gamma')$ can be solved in polynomial time, for each finite subset $\Gamma' \subseteq \Gamma$.*

*A constraint language, Γ, is said to be **NP-complete** if $\mathrm{CSP}(\Gamma')$ is NP-complete, for some finite subset $\Gamma' \subseteq \Gamma$.*

There are known to be infinitely many computational problems which are neither solvable in polynomial time nor NP-complete [67], but we shall see below that all constraint languages over domains of size 2 and 3 are known to be either tractable or NP-complete. The same dichotomy is conjectured to hold for all constraint languages over any finite domain (see Conjecture 8.52 below), although this question is still open [11, 37].

8.2 Examples of Constraint Languages

This section introduces some typical constraint languages that we will be concerned with in this chapter. For each language mentioned we simply state in this section whether it is known to be tractable or NP-complete. A more detailed discussion of many of these languages can be found later in the chapter.

Example 8.4. Let D be any *field* (that is, a set on which the operations of addition, subtraction, multiplication and division are defined, such as the rational numbers). Let Γ_{LIN} be the constraint language consisting of all those relations over D which consist of all the solutions (for a fixed ordering of the unknowns) to some system of *linear equations* over D.

Any relation from Γ_{LIN}, and therefore any instance of $\text{CSP}(\Gamma_{\text{LIN}})$, can be represented by a system of linear equations[1] over D, and so can be solved in polynomial time (e.g., by Gaussian elimination). Hence Γ_{LIN} is a tractable constraint language.   □

Example 8.5. A constraint language over a two-element set $D = \{d_0, d_1\}$ is known as a **Boolean** constraint language. Using such languages we can express the standard propositional SATISFIABILITY problem [38, 78] as a constraint satisfaction problem, by identifying the 2 elements of D with the logical values TRUE and FALSE.

It was established by Schaefer in 1978 [86] that a Boolean constraint language, Γ, is tractable if (at least) one of the following six conditions holds:

1. Every relation in Γ contains a tuple in which all entries are equal to d_0;

2. Every relation in Γ contains a tuple in which all entries are equal to d_1;

3. Every relation in Γ is definable by a conjunction of clauses, where each clause ha at most one negative literal;

4. Every relation in Γ is definable by a conjunction of clauses, where each clause ha at most one positive literal (i.e., a conjunction of **Horn clauses**);

5. Every relation in Γ is definable by a conjunction of clauses, where each clause contains at most 2 literals;

6. Every relation in Γ is the set of solutions of a system of linear equations over th finite field with 2 elements, GF(2).

In all other cases Γ is NP-complete.

This result establishes a *dichotomy* for Boolean constraint languages: any Boolean constraint language is either tractable or NP-complete. Hence this result is known as **Schaefer's Dichotomy Theorem** [86].

Similar dichotomy results have also been obtained for many other combinatorial problems over a Boolean domain which are related to the Boolean constraint satisfaction problem [63, 27].   □

Example 8.6. It follows from Schaefer's Dichotomy Theorem [86] (Example 8.5) that some Boolean constraint languages containing just a *single relation* are NP-complete.

For example, for any 2-element set $D = \{d_0, d_1\}$, let N_D be the ternary **not-all-equal** relation over D defined by

$$N_D = D^3 \setminus \{\langle d_0, d_0, d_0 \rangle, \langle d_1, d_1, d_1 \rangle\}$$
$$= \{\langle d_0, d_0, d_1 \rangle, \langle d_0, d_1, d_0 \rangle, \langle d_0, d_1, d_1 \rangle, \langle d_1, d_0, d_0 \rangle, \langle d_1, d_0, d_1 \rangle, \langle d_1, d_1, d\rangle$$

The problem $\text{CSP}(\{N_D\})$ corresponds to the NOT-ALL-EQUAL SATISFIABILITY problem [86] which is known to be NP-complete[2].

---

[1]Moreover, this system of equations can be computed from the relations in polynomial time - see [11]

[2]The standard version of NOT-ALL-EQUAL SATISFIABILITY given in [38, 78] is slightly more general, but can be shown to be polynomial-time equivalent to $\text{CSP}(\{N_D\})$.

Similarly, let T_D be the ternary **one-in-three** relation over D defined by

$$T_D = \{\langle d_0, d_0, d_1 \rangle, \langle d_0, d_1, d_0 \rangle, \langle d_1, d_0, d_0 \rangle\}.$$

The problem $\mathrm{CSP}(\{T_D\})$ corresponds to the ONE-IN-THREE SATISFIABILITY problem (with positive literals) [86, 38, 27] which is known to be NP-complete.   □

Example 8.7. The class of constraints known as **max-closed** constraints was introduced in [54] and shown to be tractable. This class of constraints has been used in the analysis and development of a number of industrial scheduling tools [70, 83].

Max-closed constraints are defined for arbitrary finite domains which are totally ordered. This class of constraints includes all of the 'basic constraints' over the natural numbers in the constraint programming language CHIP [91], as well as many other forms of constraint. The following are examples of max-closed constraints over a domain D which can be any fixed finite set of natural numbers:

$$3x_1 + x_5 + 3x_4 \geq 2x_2 + 10,$$
$$4x_1 \neq 8,$$
$$x_1 \in \{1, 2, 3, 5, 7, 11, 13\},$$
$$2x_1 x_3 x_5 \geq 3x_2 + 1,$$
$$(3x_1 \geq 7) \vee (2x_1 \geq 4) \vee (5x_2 \leq 7).$$

Hence the constraint language comprising all relations of these forms is tractable.   □

Example 8.8. Let D be any finite set, and let Γ_{ZOA} be the set of all relations of the following forms:

- All unary relations;

- All binary relations of the form $D_1 \times D_2$ for subsets D_1, D_2 of D;

- All binary relations of the form $\{\langle d, \pi(d) \rangle \mid d \in D_1\}$, for some subset D_1 of D and some permutation π of D;

- All binary relations of the form $\{\langle a, b \rangle \in D_1 \times D_2 \mid a = d_1 \vee b = d_2\}$ for some subsets D_1, D_2 of D and some elements $d_1 \in D_1, d_2 \in D_2$.

These relations were introduced in [58], where they are called **implicational relations**, and independently in [26], where they are called **0/1/all relations**.

It was shown in [26] that Γ_{ZOA} is tractable, and that for any binary relation R over D which is *not* in Γ_{ZOA}, $\Gamma_{\mathrm{ZOA}} \cup \{R\}$ is NP-complete.   □

Example 8.9. The class of binary constraints known as **connected row-convex** constraints was introduced in [35] and shown to be tractable. This class properly includes the 'monotone' relations, identified and shown to be tractable by Montanari in [76].

Let the domain D be the ordered set $\{d_1, d_2, \ldots, d_m\}$, where $d_1 < d_2 < \cdots < d_m$. The definition of connected row-convex constraints given in [35] uses a standard matrix representation for binary relations: the binary relation R over D is represented by the $m \times m$ 0-1 matrix M, by setting $M_{ij} = 1$ if the relation contains the pair $\langle d_i, d_j \rangle$, and $M_{ij} = 0$ otherwise.

A relation is said to be connected row-convex if the following property holds: the pattern of 1's in the matrix representation (after removing rows and columns containing only 0's) is connected along each row, along each column, and forms a connected 2-dimensional region (where some of the connections may be diagonal).

By [35] we see that the following examples of connected row-convex relations:

$$
\begin{pmatrix}
0&0&0&0&0&1&0&0&0&0\\
0&0&0&0&1&1&1&0&0&0\\
0&0&0&1&1&1&1&0&1&0\\
0&1&1&1&1&1&1&0&1&0\\
1&1&1&1&1&1&1&0&1&1\\
0&1&1&1&1&1&1&0&1&0\\
0&0&1&1&1&1&1&0&1&0\\
0&0&1&1&1&1&1&0&1&0\\
0&0&0&1&1&0&0&0&0&0\\
0&0&0&0&1&0&0&0&0&0
\end{pmatrix}
\begin{pmatrix}
1&1&0&0&0&0&0&0&0&0\\
1&1&0&0&0&0&0&0&0&0\\
0&0&1&1&1&0&0&0&0&0\\
0&0&1&1&1&0&0&0&0&0\\
0&0&1&1&1&0&0&0&0&0\\
0&0&1&1&1&0&0&0&0&0\\
0&0&0&0&0&1&1&1&1&1\\
0&0&0&0&0&1&1&1&1&1\\
0&0&0&0&0&1&1&1&0&0\\
0&0&0&0&0&1&1&1&0&0
\end{pmatrix}
\begin{pmatrix}
0&0&0&0&0&0&0&1&0&0\\
0&0&0&0&0&0&1&1&0&0\\
0&0&0&0&0&0&0&0&0&0\\
0&0&0&0&0&0&1&1&1&1\\
0&0&0&0&0&0&1&1&1&0\\
0&0&0&0&1&1&0&0&0&0\\
0&0&0&0&1&0&0&0&0&0\\
1&1&1&1&0&0&0&0&0&0\\
0&1&1&1&0&0&0&0&0&0\\
0&0&1&1&0&0&0&0&0&0
\end{pmatrix}
$$

form a tractable constraint language.   □

Example 8.10. The binary **inequality** relation over an ordered set D is defined as follows:

$$<_D = \{\langle d_1, d_2\rangle \in D^2 \mid d_1 < d_2\}.$$

When D is the set of natural numbers, $\mathbb{N}$, the class of constraint satisfaction problem instances $\mathrm{CSP}(\{<_D\})$ corresponds to the ACYCLIC DIGRAPH problem [4]. An instance of this problem is a directed graph G, and the question is whether G is *acyclic*, that is, contains no directed cycles. It is easy to show that a directed graph is acyclic if and only if its vertices can be numbered in such a way that every arc leads from a vertex with smaller number to a vertex with a greater one.

Since the ACYCLIC DIGRAPH problem is tractable, it follows that $\{<_\mathbb{N}\}$ is a tractable constraint language.   □

Example 8.11. The binary **disequality** relation over a set D is defined as follows:

$$\neq_D = \{\langle d_1, d_2\rangle \in D^2 \mid d_1 \neq d_2\}.$$

The class of constraint satisfaction problem instances $\mathrm{CSP}(\{\neq_D\})$ corresponds to the GRAPH COLORABILITY problem [38, 78] with $|D|$ colours. This problem is tractable when $|D| \leq 2$ or $|D| = \infty$, and NP-complete when $3 \leq |D| < \infty$.   □

Example 8.12. The ternary **betweenness** relation over an ordered set D is defined as follows:

$$B_D = \{\langle x, y, z\rangle \in D^3 \mid x < y < z \ \text{ or } \ x > y > z\}.$$

For a finite set D, the constraint language $\{B_D\}$ is tractable when $|D| \leq 4$ and is NP-complete when $|D| \geq 5$ (see Example 8.45).

For an infinite set D, the constraint language $\{B_D\}$ is NP-complete because the class of constraint satisfaction problem instances $\mathrm{CSP}(\{B_D\})$ corresponds to the BETWEENNESS problem, which is known to be NP-complete [38]. An instance of this problem is a pair $\langle A, T\rangle$ where A is a finite set and $T \subseteq A^3$; the question is whether there is a function $f : A \to \{1, \ldots, |A|\}$ such that, for every triple $\langle a, b, c\rangle \in T$, we have either $f(a) < f(b) < f(c)$ or $f(a) > f(b) > f(c)$.   □

Example 8.13. The class of constraints known as **linear Horn** constraints was introduced in [55, 62] and shown to be tractable.

The constraint relation of a linear Horn constraint is a relation over an infinite ordered set which is specified by a disjunction of an arbitrary finite number of linear disequalities and at most one weak linear inequality. The following are examples of linear Horn constraints:

$$3x_1 + x_5 - 3x_4 \leq 10,$$
$$x_1 + x_3 + x_5 \neq 7,$$
$$(3x_1 + x_5 - 4x_3 \leq 7) \vee (2x_1 + 3x_2 - 4x_3 \neq 4) \vee (x_2 + x_3 + x_5 \neq 7),$$
$$(4x_1 + x_3 \neq 3) \vee (5x_2 - 3x_5 + x_4 \neq 6).$$

Linear Horn constraints are an important class of linear constraints for expressing problems in temporal reasoning [55]. In particular, the class of linear Horn constraints properly includes the point algebra of [92], the (quantitative) temporal constraints of [60, 61] and the ORD-Horn constraints of [77]. □

8.3 Developing an Algebraic Theory

A series of papers by Jeavons and co-authors [50, 51, 52, 54] has shown that the complexity of constraint languages over a finite domain can be characterised using algebraic properties of relations (see Figure 8.1).

The first step in the algebraic approach to constraint languages exploits the well-known idea that, given an initial set of constraint relations, there will often be further relations that can be added to the set without changing the complexity of the associated problem class. In fact, it has been shown that it is possible to add all the relations that can be derived from the initial relations using certain simple rules. The larger sets of relations obtained using these rules are known as *relational clones* [34, 81]. Hence the first step in the analysis is to note that it is sufficient to analyse the complexity only for those sets of relations which are relational clones (see Section 8.3.1).

The next step in the algebraic approach is to note that relational clones can be characterised by their *polymorphisms*, which are algebraic *operations* on the same underlying set [49, 52] (see Section 8.3.2). As well as providing a convenient and concise method for describing large families of relations, the polymorphisms also reflect certain aspects of the structure of the relations that can be used for designing efficient algorithms. This link between relational clones and polymorphisms has already played a key role in identifying many tractable constraint classes and developing appropriate efficient solution algorithms for them [14, 15, 17, 19, 28, 50].

The final step in the algebraic approach links constraint languages with finite universal algebras (see Section 8.3.3). The language of finite algebras provides a number of very powerful new tools for analysing the complexity of constraints, including the deep structural results developed for classifying the structure of finite algebras [45, 75, 88].

8.3.1 Step I: From Relations to Relational Clones

As stated above, the first step in the algebraic approach is to consider what additional relations can be added to a constraint language without changing the complexity of the corresponding problem class. This technique has been widely used in the analysis of Boolean

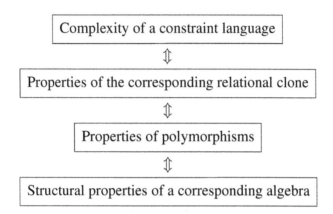

Figure 8.1: Translating questions about the complexity of constraint languages into questions about the properties of algebras.

constraint satisfaction problems [27, 86], and in the analysis of temporal and spatial constraints [36, 77, 84, 64, 65]; it was introduced for the study of constraints over arbitrary finite sets in [49].

Definition 8.14. *A constraint language* Γ **expresses** *a relation R if there is an instance* $\mathcal{P} = \langle V, D, C \rangle \in \mathrm{CSP}(\Gamma)$ *and a list* $\langle v_1, \ldots, v_n \rangle$ *of variables in V such that*

$$R = \{\langle \varphi(v_1), \ldots, \varphi(v_n) \rangle \mid \varphi \in \mathrm{Sol}(\mathcal{P})\}$$

For any constraint language Γ, the set of all relations which can be expressed by Γ will be called the **expressive power** of Γ. The expressive power of a constraint language Γ can be characterised in a number of different ways [53]. For example, it is equal to the set of all relations that can be obtained from the relations in Γ using the *relational join* and *project* operations from relational database theory [43]. It has also been shown to be equal to the set of relations definable by *primitive positive formulas* over the relations in Γ together with the equality relation, where a primitive positive formula is a first-order formula involving only conjunction and existential quantification [11]. In algebraic terminology [34, 81], this set of relations is called the **relational clone** generated by Γ, and is denoted by $\langle \Gamma \rangle$.

Example 8.15. Consider the Boolean constraint language $\Gamma = \{R_1, R_2\}$ where $R_1 = \{\langle 0, 1 \rangle, \langle 1, 0 \rangle, \langle 1, 1 \rangle\}$ and $R_2 = \{\langle 0, 0 \rangle, \langle 0, 1 \rangle, \langle 1, 0 \rangle\}$.

It is straightforward to check that all 16 binary Boolean relations can be expressed by a primitive positive formula involving R_1 and R_2. For example, the relation $R_3 = \{\langle 0, 0 \rangle, \langle 1, 0 \rangle, \langle 1, 1 \rangle\}$ can be expressed by the formula $R_3 = \exists y R_1(x, y) \wedge R_2(y, z)$ Hence $\langle \Gamma \rangle$, the relational clone generated by Γ, includes all 16 binary Boolean relations.

In fact it can be shown that, for this constraint language Γ, the set $\langle \Gamma \rangle$ consists of precisely those Boolean relations (of any arity) that can be expressed as a conjunction of unary or binary Boolean relations [82, 88]. This is equivalent to saying that the constraint language Γ expresses precisely this set of relations.   □

The link between these notions and the complexity of constraint languages is established by the next result.

Theorem 8.16 ([11, 49]). *For any constraint language Γ and any finite subset $\Gamma_0 \subseteq \langle \Gamma \rangle$ there is a polynomial time reduction from* $\mathrm{CSP}(\Gamma_0)$ *to* $\mathrm{CSP}(\Gamma)$.

Corollary 8.17. *A constraint language Γ is tractable if and only if $\langle \Gamma \rangle$ is tractable. Similarly, Γ is NP-complete if and only if $\langle \Gamma \rangle$ is NP-complete.*

This result reduces the problem of characterising tractable constraint languages to the problem of characterising tractable relational clones.

8.3.2 Step II: From Relational Clones to Sets of Operations

We have shown in the previous section that to analyse the complexity of arbitrary constraint languages over finite domains it is sufficient to consider only relational clones. This considerably reduces the variety of languages to be studied. However, it immediately raises the question of how to represent and describe relational clones. For many relational clones the only known generating sets are rather sophisticated, and in some cases no generating sets are known.

Very conveniently, it turns out that there is a well-known alternative way to represent and describe any relational clone: using *operations*.

Definition 8.18. *Let D be a set, and k a natural number. A mapping $f : D^k \to D$ is called a k-ary **operation** on D. The set of all finitary operations on D is denoted by $\mathbf{O}_D$.*

We first describe a fundamental algebraic relationship between operations and relations. Observe that any operation on a set D can be extended in a standard way to an operation on tuples of elements from D, as follows. For any (k-ary) operation f and any collection of tuples $t_1, \ldots, t_k \in D^n$, define $f(t_1, \ldots, t_k) \in D^n$ to be the tuple $\langle f(t_1[1], \ldots, t_k[1]), \ldots, f(t_1[n], \ldots, t_k[n]) \rangle$.

Definition 8.19 ([34, 75, 81, 88]). *A k-ary operation $f \in \mathbf{O}_D$ **preserves** an n-ary relation $R \in \mathbf{R}_D$ (or f is a **polymorphism** of R, or R is **invariant** under f) if $f(t_1, \ldots, t_k) \in R$ for all choices of $t_1, \ldots, t_k \in R$.*

For any given sets $\Gamma \subseteq \mathbf{R}_D$ and $F \subseteq \mathbf{O}_D$, we define the mappings Pol and Inv as follows:

$$\mathrm{Pol}(\Gamma) = \{ f \in \mathbf{O}_D \mid f \text{ preserves each relation from } \Gamma \},$$
$$\mathrm{Inv}(F) = \{ R \in \mathbf{R}_D \mid R \text{ is invariant under each operation from } F \}.$$

We remark that the mappings Pol and Inv form a *Galois correspondence* between $\mathbf{R}_D$ and $\mathbf{O}_D$ (see Proposition 1.1.14 of [81]). Brief introductions to this correspondence can be found in [34, 80], and a comprehensive study in [81]. We note, in particular, that $\mathrm{Inv}(F) = \mathrm{Inv}(\mathrm{Pol}(\mathrm{Inv}(F)))$, for any set of operations F.

It is a well-known result in universal algebra that the relational clone generated by a set of relations over a finite set is determined by the polymorphisms of those relations [81]. Here we will establish this key result using purely constraint-based reasoning.

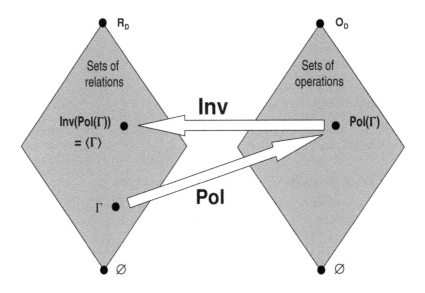

Figure 8.2: The operators Inv and Pol.

Definition 8.20. *Let Γ be a finite constraint language over a finite set D.*

*For any positive integer k, the **indicator problem of order** k for Γ is the CSP instance $\mathcal{P} = \langle V, D, \mathcal{C} \rangle \in \mathrm{CSP}(\Gamma)$ where:*

- $V = D^k$ *(in other words, each variable in $\mathcal{P}$ is a k-tuple of domain elements).*

- $\mathcal{C} = \{\langle s, R \rangle \mid R \in \Gamma$ *and s matches $R\}$.*

In this definition we say that that a list of k-tuples $s = \langle v_1, \ldots, v_n \rangle$ matches a relation R n is equal to the arity of R and for each $i \in \{1, 2, \ldots, k\}$ the n-tuple $\langle v_1[i], \ldots, v_n[i] \rangle$ is in R. Hence the CSP instance $\mathcal{P}$ has constraints from the constraint language Γ on every possible scope which matches a relation from Γ.

Note that the solutions to the indicator problem of order k for Γ are mappings from D to D that preserve each of the relations in Γ, hence they are precisely the k-ary elements of $\mathrm{Pol}(\Gamma)$.

Indicator problems are described in more detail in [48], where a number of concrete examples are given. A software system for constructing and solving indicator problems for given constraint languages is described in [39].

Theorem 8.21 ([49, 81]). *For any constraint language Γ over a finite set, $\langle \Gamma \rangle = \mathrm{Inv}(\mathrm{Pol}(\Gamma))$*

Proof. If two relations both have a polymorphism f, then their conjunction also has the polymorphism f. Similarly, if a relation has a polymorphism f, then any relation obtained by existential quantification of that relation also has the polymorphism f. Finally the equality relation has every operation as a polymorphism. It follows from these observations that for any R in the relational clone of Γ we have $\mathrm{Pol}(\{R\}) \supseteq \mathrm{Pol}(\Gamma)$. Hence $\langle \Gamma \rangle \subseteq \mathrm{Inv}(\mathrm{Pol}(\Gamma))$.

To establish the converse, let Γ be a constraint language over a finite set D, let R be an arbitrary relation in $\mathrm{Inv}(\mathrm{Pol}(\Gamma))$, and let n be the arity of R. We need to show that $R \in \langle \Gamma \rangle$, or in other words that R can be expressed using the constraint language Γ.

Let k be the number of tuples in the relation R, and construct the indicator problem $\mathcal{P}$ of order k for Γ. Choose a list of variables $t = \langle v_1, \ldots, v_n \rangle$ in $\mathcal{P}$ such that each of the n-tuples $\langle v_1[i], \ldots, v_n[i] \rangle$, for $i = 1, \ldots, k$, is a distinct element of our target relation R. Consider the relation $R_t = \{\langle f(v_1), \ldots, f(v_n) \rangle \mid f \in \mathrm{Sol}(\mathcal{P})\}$. By the observation above, the elements of $\mathrm{Sol}(\mathcal{P})$ are the k-ary polymorphisms of Γ, and these include the k projection operations which simply return one of their arguments. By the choice of t, each of these projection operations results in a distinct tuple of R being included in R_t, and so $R \subseteq R_t$. Conversely, by the choice of R, every polymorphism of Γ preserves R, and hence every element of R_t is contained in R. $\qquad\square$

Since the relational clone $\langle \Gamma \rangle$ consists of those relations that can be expressed by the constraint language Γ, we immediately obtain the following strong link between polymorphisms and expressive power.

Corollary 8.22. *A relation R over a finite set can be expressed by a constraint language Γ precisely when $\mathrm{Pol}(\Gamma) \subseteq \mathrm{Pol}(\{R\})$.*

Combining Theorem 8.16 and Theorem 8.21 we obtain the following link between polymorphisms and complexity.

Corollary 8.23. *For any constraint languages Γ, Γ_0 over a finite set, if Γ_0 is finite and $\mathrm{Pol}(\Gamma) \subseteq \mathrm{Pol}(\Gamma_0)$, then $\mathrm{CSP}(\Gamma_0)$ is reducible to $\mathrm{CSP}(\Gamma)$ in polynomial time.*

This result implies that, for any finite constraint language Γ over a finite set, the complexity of $\mathrm{CSP}(\Gamma)$ is determined, up to polynomial-time reduction, by the polymorphisms of Γ. Hence we can translate our original problem of characterising tractable constraint languages into an equivalent problem for sets of operations.

Definition 8.24. *A set of operations $F \subseteq \mathbf{O}_D$ is said to be tractable if $\mathrm{Inv}(F)$ is tractable. A set $F \subseteq \mathbf{O}_D$ is said to be NP-complete if $\mathrm{Inv}(F)$ is NP-complete.*

With this definition we have translated our basic challenge into characterising tractable sets of operations.

8.3.3   Step III: From Sets of Operations to Algebras

We have seen in the previous section that the problem of analysing the complexity of a constraint language can be translated into the problem of analysing the complexity of the set of operations which preserve all of the relations in that language. In this section we shall open the way to the use of a further set of powerful analytical tools by making the final translation step, from sets of operations to algebras.

Definition 8.25. *An **algebra** is an ordered pair $\mathcal{A} = \langle D, F \rangle$ such that D is a nonempty set and F is a family of finitary operations on D. The set D is called the* universe *of $\mathcal{A}$, and the operations from F are called* basic. *An algebra with a finite universe is referred to as a finite algebra.*

To make the translation from sets of operations to algebras we simply note that any set of operations F on a fixed set D can be associated with the algebra $\langle D, F \rangle$. Hence, we will define what it means for an algebra to be tractable by considering the tractability of the basic operations.

Definition 8.26. *An algebra* $\mathcal{A} = \langle D, F \rangle$ *is said to be tractable if the set of basic operations* F *is tractable. An algebra* $\mathcal{A} = \langle D, F \rangle$ *is said to be NP-complete if* F *is NP-complete.*

Our basic task is now translated as: characterise all tractable algebras.

It will be useful to describe an equivalence relation linking algebras that correspond to the same constraint language. As we noted earlier, the mappings Pol and Inv have the property that $\mathrm{Inv}(\mathrm{Pol}(\mathrm{Inv}(F))) = \mathrm{Inv}(F)$, so we can extend a set of operations F to the set $\mathrm{Pol}(\mathrm{Inv}(F))$ without changing the associated invariant relations. The set $\mathrm{Pol}(\mathrm{Inv}(F))$ consists of all operations that can be obtained from the operations in F, together with the set of all projection operations, by forming arbitrary compositions of operations[3]. Note that any set of operations which includes all the projection operations and is closed under composition is referred to by algebraists as a **clone** of operations. The clone of operations obtained from a set F in this way is usually referred to as the set of *term operations* over F, so we will make the following definition.

Definition 8.27. *For any algebra* $\mathcal{A} = \langle D, F \rangle$, *an operation* f *on* D *will be called a **term operation** of* $\mathcal{A}$ *if* $f \in \mathrm{Pol}(\mathrm{Inv}(F))$.
The set of all term operations of $\mathcal{A}$ *will be denoted* $\mathrm{Term}(\mathcal{A})$.

Two algebras with the same universe are called *term equivalent* if they have the same set of term operations. Since, for any algebra $\mathcal{A} = \langle D, F \rangle$, we have $\mathrm{Inv}(F) = \mathrm{Inv}(\mathrm{Term}(\mathcal{A}))$ two algebras are term equivalent if and only if they have the same set of associated invariant relations. It follows that we need to characterise tractable algebras only up to term equivalence.

We will now show that we can restrict our attention to certain special classes of algebras.

The first simplification we apply is to note that any unary polymorphism of a constraint language can be applied to all of the relations in the language without changing the complexity.

Proposition 8.28 ([52, 49]). *Let* Γ *be a constraint language over a set* D, *and let* f *be a unary operation in* $\mathrm{Pol}(\Gamma)$.
$\mathrm{CSP}(\Gamma)$ *is polynomial-time equivalent to* $\mathrm{CSP}(f(\Gamma))$, *where* $f(\Gamma) = \{f(R) \mid R \in \Gamma$ *and* $f(R) = \{f(t) \mid t \in R\}$.

If we apply Proposition 8.28 with a unary polymorphism f which has the smallest possible range out of all the unary polymorphisms of Γ, then we obtain a constraint language $f(\Gamma)$ whose unary polymorphisms are all surjective. Such a language will be called a **reduced** constraint language.

---

[3]If f is an m-ary operation on a set D, and $g_1, g_2, \ldots, g_m$ are k-ary operations on D, then the composition of f and $g_1, g_2, \ldots, g_m$ is the k-ary operation h on D defined by $h(a_1, a_2, \ldots, a_k) = f(g_1(a_1, \ldots, a_k), \ldots, g_m(a_1, \ldots, a_k))$.

Definition 8.29. *We call an algebra **surjective** if all of its term operations are surjective*[4].

It is easy to verify that a finite algebra is surjective if and only if its unary term operations are all surjective, and hence form a group of permutations. It follows that an algebra $\mathcal{A} = \langle D, F \rangle$ is surjective if and only if $\mathrm{Inv}(F)$ is a reduced constraint language. Using Proposition 8.28, this means that we can restrict our attention to surjective algebras.

The next theorem shows that for many purposes we need consider only those surjective algebras with the additional property of being idempotent.

Definition 8.30. *An operation f on D is called **idempotent** if it satisfies $f(x, \ldots, x) = x$ for all $x \in D$.*
The full idempotent reduct *of an algebra $\mathcal{A} = \langle D, F \rangle$ is the algebra $\langle D, \mathrm{Termid}(\mathcal{A}) \rangle$, where $\mathrm{Termid}(A)$ consists of all idempotent operations from $\mathrm{Term}(A)$.*

An operation f on a set D is idempotent if and only if it preserves all the relations in the set $\Gamma_{\mathrm{CON}} = \{\{\langle a \rangle\} \mid a \in D\}$, consisting of all unary one-element relations on D. Hence, $\mathrm{Inv}(\mathrm{Termid}(A))$ is the relational clone generated by $\mathrm{Inv}(F) \cup \Gamma_{\mathrm{CON}}$.

That is, considering only the full idempotent reduct of an algebra is equivalent to considering only those constraint languages in which we can arbitrarily fix variables to particular values from the domain.

Theorem 8.31 ([11]). *A finite surjective algebra $\mathcal{A}$ is tractable if and only if its full idempotent reduct $\mathcal{A}_0$ is tractable. Moreover, $\mathcal{A}$ is NP-complete if and only if $\mathcal{A}_0$ is NP-complete.*

Next we link the complexity of a finite algebra with the complexity of its sub-algebras and homomorphic images. In many cases, we can use these results to reduce the problem of analysing the complexity of an algebra to a similar problem involving an algebra with a smaller universe. In such cases we can reduce the problem of analysing the complexity of a constraint language to a similar problem for a constraint language over a smaller domain.

Definition 8.32. *Let $\mathcal{A} = \langle D, F \rangle$ be an algebra and U a subset of D such that, for any $f \in F$ and for any $b_1, \ldots, b_k \in B$, where k is the arity of f, we have $f(b_1, \ldots, b_k) \in B$. Then the algebra $\mathcal{B} = \langle B, F|_B \rangle$ is called a **sub-algebra** of $\mathcal{A}$, where $F|_B$ consists of the restrictions of all operations in F to B. If $B \neq A$, then $\mathcal{B}$ is said to be a* proper *sub-algebra.*

Definition 8.33. *Let $\mathcal{A}_1 = \langle D_1, F_1 \rangle$ and $\mathcal{A}_2 = \langle D_2, F_2 \rangle$ be such that $F_1 = \{f_i^1 \mid i \in I\}$ and $F_2 = \{f_i^2 \mid i \in I\}$, where both f_i^1 and f_i^2 are k_i-ary, for all $i \in I$.*
*A map $\Phi : \mathcal{A}_1 \to \mathcal{A}_2$ is called a **homomorphism** from $\mathcal{A}_1$ to $\mathcal{A}_2$ if*

$$f_i^1(a_1, \ldots, a_{k_i}) = f_i^2(\Phi(a_1), \ldots, \Phi(a_{k_i}))$$

holds for all $i \in I$ and all $a_1, \ldots, a_{k_i} \in \mathcal{A}_1$.
If the map Φ is surjective, then $\mathcal{A}_2$ is said to be a homomorphic image *of $\mathcal{A}_1$.*

Definition 8.34. *A homomorphic image of a sub-algebra of an algebra $\mathcal{A}$ is called a **factor** of $\mathcal{A}$.*

Theorem 8.35 ([11]). *If $\mathcal{A}$ is a tractable finite algebra, then so is every factor of $\mathcal{A}$.*
If $\mathcal{A}$ has any factor which is NP-complete, then $\mathcal{A}$ is NP-complete.

---

[4]Some authors call an algebra surjective if all of its *basic* operations are surjective. However, such algebras can have non-surjective term operations, so our definition is more restrictive.

8.4   Applications of the Algebraic Theory

8.4.1   A Pre-Processing Algorithm

The theory described in the previous section has shown that many key properties of a constraint language are determined by its polymorphisms. Hence calculating the polymorphisms of the constraint language used in a given CSP instance can be a useful step in analysing that instance.

For example, using Construction 8.20 and Proposition 8.28 we can design a pre-processing algorithm which can sometimes simplify the presentation of a constraint satisfaction problem (Algorithm 8.1).

Since the indicator problem of order 1 only has $|D|$ variables, this pre-processing step is efficient for many problems and can result in an equivalent problem instance with a considerably smaller domain.

Algorithm 8.1: Pre-processing to reduce the domain size

Input: An instance $\mathcal{P} = \langle V, D, \mathcal{C} \rangle$ of $\mathrm{CSP}(\Gamma)$ where D is finite.
Output: An equivalent instance $\mathcal{P}'$.

1. Find all unary polymorphisms of Γ by generating and solving the indicator problem of order 1 for Γ;

2. Choose a unary polymorphism f with the smallest number of values in its range;

3. If the range of f is smaller than D, apply f to each constraint relation in $\mathcal{P}$ to obtain a new problem instance $\mathcal{P}'$ over a smaller domain.

8.4.2   Tractable Cases: Using Polymorphisms as Algorithm Selectors

In many cases, it has been shown that the existence of a single polymorphism satisfying certain simple conditions is sufficient to ensure the tractability of a constraint language and to identify an appropriate polynomial-time algorithm.

Definition 8.36. *Let f be a k-ary operation on a set D.*

- *If $k = 2$ and f satisfies the identities $f(x, f(y, z)) = f(f(x, y), z)$ (associativity), $f(x, y) = f(y, x)$ (commutativity), and $f(x, x) = x$ (idempotency), then f is called a **semilattice** operation.*

- *If f satisfies the identity $f(x_1, \ldots, x_k) \in \{x_1, \ldots, x_k\}$, then f is called a **conservative** operation.*

- *If $k \geq 3$ and f satisfies the identities $f(y, x, \ldots, x) = f(x, y, x, \ldots, x) = \cdots = f(x, \ldots, x, y) = x$, then f is called a **near-unanimity** operation.*

- *If $k = 3$ and f satisfies the identities $f(y, y, x) = f(x, y, y) = x$, then f is called a **Mal'tsev** operation.*

Proposition 8.37 ([52]). *For any constraint language* Γ *over a finite set* D, *if* $\mathrm{Pol}(\Gamma)$ *contains a semilattice operation, then* Γ *is tractable, and all instances in* $\mathrm{CSP}(\Gamma)$ *can be solved by enforcing arc consistency*[5].

This result has been extended to more general *semigroup* operations in [12, 31].

Example 8.38. The Boolean constraint language consisting of all relations that can be specified by **Horn clauses**, as described in Example 8.5, has the binary polymorphism $\wedge$ (conjunction) [54], and so is tractable by Proposition 8.37. Any collection of Horn clauses can be solved by *unit resolution*, which is a specialised form of arc consistency. □

Example 8.39. The max-closed constraints defined in [54] and described in Example 8.7 all have the binary polymorphism, max, which is a semilattice operation, so they are tractable by Proposition 8.37. Any collection of max-closed constraints can be solved by enforcing arc consistency. □

Proposition 8.40 ([16]). *For any constraint language* Γ *over a finite set* D, *if* $\mathrm{Pol}(\Gamma)$ *contains a conservative commutative binary operation, then* Γ *is tractable.*

The algorithm for solving a collection of constraints preserved by a conservative commutative binary operation is based on a generalisation of local consistency techniques [16].

Proposition 8.41 ([50]). *For any constraint language* Γ *over a finite set* D, *if* $\mathrm{Pol}(\Gamma)$ *contains a* k-*ary near-unanimity operation, then* Γ *is tractable, and all instances in* $\mathrm{CSP}(\Gamma)$ *can be solved by enforcing* k-*consistency, which makes them globally consistent*[6].

In fact, it is shown in [50] that the *only* finite domain languages for which enforcing k-consistency guarantees global consistency are those which have a near-unanimity polymorphism.

Example 8.42. Let Γ be the Boolean constraint language consisting of all relations that can be specified by clauses with at most 2 literals. This language has the ternary polymorphism, d, given by $d(x, y, z) = (x \wedge y) \vee (y \wedge z) \vee (x \wedge z)$, which is a near-unanimity operation, so Γ is tractable by Proposition 8.41. A satisfying assignment for any collection of such clauses can be obtained in a backtrack-free way after enforcing path consistency. □

Example 8.43. The 0/1/all relations defined in [58, 26] and described in Example 8.8 all have the ternary polymorphism, d, given by $d(x, y, z) = x$ when $y \neq z$ and $d(x, y, z) = y$ otherwise, which is a near-unanimity operation, so they are tractable by Proposition 8.41. A solution for any collection of 0/1/all constraints can be obtained in a backtrack-free way after enforcing path consistency [26, 50]. □

Example 8.44. The connected row-convex relations defined in [35] and described in Example 8.9 all have the ternary polymorphism, m, given by $m(x, y, z) =$ "the *median* of x, y and z", which is a near-unanimity operation, so they are tractable by Proposition 8.41. A solution for any collection of connected row-convex constraints can be obtained in a backtrack-free way after enforcing path consistency [50]. □

---

[5]See Chapter 3 for a definition of this standard procedure, and a discussion of possible algorithms.
[6]See Chapter 3 for definitions and algorithms.

Example 8.45. The betweenness relation B_D on an ordered set D, described in Example 8.12, has a ternary near-unanimity polymorphism when $|D| \leq 4$, so the constraint language containing just this relation is tractable when $|D| \leq 4$, by Proposition 8.41.

The projection of B_D onto its second co-ordinate is the unary relation containing all elements of D except the largest and smallest. Hence the algebra $\langle D, \mathrm{Pol}(\{B_D\}) \rangle$ has a subalgebra of size $|D| - 2$. When $|D| \geq 5$ this subalgebra can be shown to be NP-complete. Hence, by Theorem 8.35, $\{B_D\}$ is NP-complete for finite sets D with $|D| \geq 5$.   □

Proposition 8.46 ([15, 8]). *For any constraint language Γ over a finite set D, if $\mathrm{Pol}(\Gamma)$ contains a Mal'tsev operation, then Γ is tractable.*

The algorithm for solving a collection of constraints preserved by a Mal'tsev operation is based on a generalisation of Gaussian elimination [15]. A much more straightforward version of the algorithm is given in [8]. Note that no fixed level of consistency is sufficient to solve all problems involving constraints of this type.

Example 8.47. The linear constraints described in Example 8.4 all have the ternary polymorphism p given by $p(x, y, z) = x - y + z$, which is a Mal'tsev operation, so they are tractable by Proposition 8.46. A solution for any collection of linear constraints can be obtained by a Gaussian elimination algorithm on the corresponding linear equations.   □

A unified approach to Mal'tsev operations and near-unanimity operations, which generalises Proposition 8.41 and Proposition 8.46 is given in [29].

8.4.3   Towards a Complete Classification of Complexity

We have seen that the polymorphisms of a constraint language can identify many different tractable cases and suggest an appropriate efficient solution algorithm for those cases.

However, what can be said about a constraint language Γ where $\mathrm{Pol}(\Gamma)$ does *not* contain a semilattice operation, a conservative commutative binary operation, a near-unanimity operation or a Mal'tsev operation? We cannot in general immediately conclude that Γ is intractable. However, using Rosenberg's analysis of minimal clones [85, 88], we do have the following result (adapted slightly from [49]).

Definition 8.48. *Let f be a k-ary operation on a set D.*

- *If there exists a (non-constant) unary operation g on D and an index $i \in \{1, 2, \ldots, k$ such that f satisfies the identity $f(x_1, x_2, \ldots, x_k) = g(x_i)$, then f is called an **essentially unary** operation. If g is the identity operation, then f is called a **projection***

- *If $k \geq 3$ and f satisfies the identity $f(x_1, \ldots, x_k) = x_i$ for some fixed i whenever $|\{x_1, x_2, \ldots, x_k\}| < k$, but f is not a projection, then f is called a **semiprojection***

Theorem 8.49. *For any reduced constraint language* Γ *on a finite set* D, *at least one of the following conditions must hold:*

1. $\mathrm{Pol}(\Gamma)$ *contains a constant operation;*

2. $\mathrm{Pol}(\Gamma)$ *contains a near-unanimity operation of arity 3;*

3. $\mathrm{Pol}(\Gamma)$ *contains a Mal'tsev operation;*

4. $\mathrm{Pol}(\Gamma)$ *contains an idempotent binary operation (which is not a projection);*

5. $\mathrm{Pol}(\Gamma)$ *contains a semiprojection;*

6. $\mathrm{Pol}(\Gamma)$ *contains essentially unary surjective operations only.*

If $\mathrm{Pol}(\Gamma)$ contains a constant operation, then Γ is trivially tractable, since each (non-empty) relation in Γ contains a tuple $\langle d, d, \ldots, d \rangle$, where d is the value of the constant operation. By Propositions 8.37 and 8.46, the second and third cases also guarantee tractability. Hence the first three cases in Theorem 8.49 all guarantee tractability.

In the final case of Theorem 8.49 we observe that $\mathrm{Inv}(\mathrm{Pol}(\Gamma))$ includes the disequality relation, $\neq_D$, defined in Example 8.11, and when $|D| = 2$ it includes the not-all-equal relation, N_D, defined in Example 8.6. Hence in this case we have that $\mathrm{Inv}(\mathrm{Pol}(\Gamma))$ is NP-complete for all finite sets D, so by Theorem 8.21 and Corollary 8.17 we conclude that Γ is NP-complete in this case. Hence the final case of Theorem 8.49 guarantees NP-completeness.

A similar argument gives the following slightly more general result.

Proposition 8.50 ([49])**.** *Any set of essentially unary operations over a finite set is NP-complete.*

Cases 4 and 5 of Theorem 8.49 are inconclusive, in general, although for a Boolean domain there are only two binary idempotent operations which are not projections: the two semilattice operations $\wedge$ and $\vee$ (conjunction and disjunction). Hence, over a Boolean domain, case 4 guarantees tractability by Proposition 8.37. Moreover, over a Boolean domain there are no semiprojection operations, so case 5 cannot occur. These observations mean that Theorem 8.49 is sufficient to classify the complexity of any constraint language over a Boolean domain, and hence derive Schaefer's Dichotomy Theorem [86] (see Example 8.5).

Corollary 8.51 ([11])**.** *An algebra with a 2-element universe is NP-complete if all of its basic operations are essentially unary. Otherwise it is tractable.*

The single condition described in Proposition 8.50 is the only condition needed to establish the NP-completeness of all known NP-complete constraint languages, and has been used to establish a dichotomy theorem for several broad classes of languages [11]. There is a longstanding conjecture [18] that this condition is sufficient to characterise *all* forms of intractability in constraint languages. We state this conjecture for the special case of idempotent algebras, where the only essentially unary operations are projections.

Conjecture 8.52 ([18, 11])**. *Tractable algebras conjecture:*** *A finite idempotent algebra $\mathcal{A}$ is NP-complete if it has a nontrivial factor $\mathcal{B}$ all of whose operations are projections. Otherwise it is tractable.*

By Proposition 8.28 and Theorem 8.31, the problem of determining the complexity of an arbitrary constraint language can be reduced to an equivalent problem for a certain idempotent algebra associated with the language. Therefore, this conjecture, if true, would completely solve the fundamental question of analysing the complexity of any constraint language over a finite set.

Conjecture 8.52 has been verified [11] for algebras with a 2-element universe, algebras with a 3-element universe, conservative algebras (i.e., those whose operations preserve all unary relations), and strictly simple surjective algebras (i.e. those with no non-trivial factors). If Conjecture 8.52 is true in general, then it yields an effective procedure to determine whether any finite constraint language is tractable or NP-complete, as the following result indicates.

Proposition 8.53 ([11]). *Let D be a fixed finite set. If Conjecture 8.52 is true, then for any finite constraint language Γ over D, there is a polynomial-time algorithm to determine whether Γ is NP-complete or tractable.*

In another direction, Proposition 8.50 was used in [71] to show that most non-trivial constraint languages over a finite domain are NP-complete. More precisely, let $R(n, k)$ denote a random n-ary relation on the set $\{1, \ldots, k\}$, for which the probability that $\langle a_1, \ldots, a \in R(n, k)$ is equal to 1/2 independently for each n-tuple $\langle a_1, \ldots, a_n \rangle$ where not all a_i are equal; also, set $\langle a, a, \ldots, a \rangle \notin R(n, k)$ for all a (this is necessary to ensure that $\mathrm{CSP}(\{R(n, k)\})$ is non-trivial). It is shown in [71] that the probability that $\mathrm{Pol}\,\{R(n, k)\}$ contains only projections tends to 1 as either n or k tends to infinity.

8.4.4   Search is No Harder than Decision

In this chapter we have formulated the constraint satisfaction problem as a decision problem in which the question is to decide whether or not a solution exists. However, the corresponding *search problem*, in which the question is to find a solution, is often the real practical question. Using the algebraic theory in Section 8.3, we can now show that the tractable cases of these two forms of the problem coincide.

Theorem 8.54 ([11, 20]). *Let Γ be a constraint language over a finite set. The decision problem $\mathrm{CSP}(\Gamma)$ is tractable if and only if the corresponding search problem can be solved in polynomial time.*

Proof. Obviously, tractability of the search problem implies tractability of the corresponding decision problem.

For the converse, let Γ be a tractable set of relations over a finite domain D.

Consider any instance $\mathcal{P}$ in $\mathrm{CSP}(\Gamma)$. By the choice of Γ, we can decide in polynomial time whether $\mathcal{P}$ has a solution. If it does not then the search returns with no solution.

Otherwise, using Proposition 8.28 we can transform this instance to an instance $\mathcal{P}$ over a reduced language Γ' which has a solution. Furthermore we can arrange that every solution to $\mathcal{P}'$ is a solution to $\mathcal{P}$.

Since $\mathcal{P}'$ has a solution we know that for each variable v of $\mathcal{P}'$ there must be some domain value $a \in D$ for which we can add the constraint $\langle \langle v \rangle, \{\langle a \rangle\} \rangle$ and still have a solvable instance. By considering each variable in turn, and each possible value for that variable, we can add such a constraint to each variable in turn, and hence obtain a solution to $\mathcal{P}'$. Checking for solvability for each possible value at each variable requires us to solve an instance of the decision problem $\mathrm{CSP}(\Gamma \cup \Gamma_{\mathrm{CON}})$ at most $|\mathcal{P}'|$ times. By Theorem 8.31, this can be completed in polynomial time in the size of $\mathcal{P}$. □

8.5   Constraint Languages Over an Infinite Set

Some computational problems can be formulated as constraint satisfaction problems only by using a constraint language over an *infinite* set (see Examples 8.10 and 8.12).

Many of the results of the algebraic theory described in Section 8.3 hold for both finite and infinite domains. However, Theorem 8.21 does not hold, in general, for arbitrary constraint languages over an infinite set. It is not hard to check that the inclusion $\langle \Gamma \rangle \subseteq \mathrm{Inv}(\mathrm{Pol}(\Gamma))$ still holds. However, for constraint languages over an infinite set this inclusion can be strict, as the next example[7] shows.

Example 8.55. Consider $\Gamma = \{R_1, R_2, R_3\}$ on $\mathbb{N}$, where $R_1 = \{\langle a, b, c, d \rangle \mid a = b \text{ or } c = d\}$, $R_2 = \{\langle 1 \rangle\}$, and $R_3 = \{\langle a, a+1 \rangle \mid a \in \mathbb{N}\}$. It is not difficult to show that every polymorphism of Γ is a projection, and hence $\mathrm{Inv}(\mathrm{Pol}(\Gamma))$ is the set of *all* relations on $\mathbb{N}$. However, one can check that, for example, the unary relation consisting of all even numbers does not belong to $\langle \Gamma \rangle$. □

However, if we impose some additional conditions, then the required equality does hold, as the next result indicates. A *relational structure* consists of a universe D, together with a collection of relations over D. A relational structure with a countably infinite universe is called ω-*categorical* if it is determined (up to isomorphism) by its first-order theory [46].

Theorem 8.56 ([4]). *Let $\Gamma = \{R_1, \ldots, R_k\}$ be a finite constraint language over a countably infinite set D.*
If the relational structure $\langle D, R_1, \ldots, R_k \rangle$ is ω-categorical, then $\langle \Gamma \rangle = \mathrm{Inv}(\mathrm{Pol}(\Gamma))$.

Examples of ω-categorical structures, as well as remarks on the complexity of the corresponding constraint satisfaction problems, can be found in [3], including a complete analysis of the countably infinite ω-categorical structures with a single binary relation.

8.5.1   Allen's Interval Algebra

One form of infinite-valued CSP which has been widely studied is the case where the values taken by the variables are *intervals* on some totally ordered set. This setting is used to model the temporal behaviour of systems, where the intervals represent time intervals during which events occur. The most popular such formalism is **Allen's Interval Algebra**, introduced in [1], which concerns binary qualitative relations between intervals. This algebra contains 13 basic relations (see Table 8.1), corresponding to the 13 distinct ways in which two given intervals can be related. The complete set of relations in Allen's Interval Algebra consists of the $2^{13} = 8192$ possible *unions* of the basic relations. This set of relations will be denoted Γ_{AIA}.

The constraint language Γ_{AIA} is NP-complete, and the problem of classifying the complexity of subsets of this language has attracted much attention (see, for example, [87]).

---

[7]This example is from [3], where it is credited to F. Börner.

Basic relation		Example	Endpoints
I precedes J	p	III	$I^+ < J^-$
J preceded by I	p^{-1}	JJJ	
I meets J	m	IIII	$I^+ = J^-$
J met by I	m^{-1}	JJJJ	
I overlaps J	o	IIII	$I^- < J^- < I^+$,
J overl. by I	o^{-1}	JJJJ	$I^+ < J^+$
I during J	d	III	$I^- > J^-$,
J includes I	d^{-1}	JJJJJJ	$I^+ < J^+$
I starts J	s	III	$I^- = J^-$,
J started by I	s^{-1}	JJJJJJ	$I^+ < J^+$
I finishes J	f	III	$I^+ = J^+$,
J finished by I	f^{-1}	JJJJJJ	$I^- > J^-$
I equals J	$\equiv$	IIII	$I^- = J^-$,
		JJJJ	$I^+ = J^+$

Table 8.1: The 13 basic relations in Allen's Interval Algebra.

Allen's Interval Algebra has three operations on relations: composition, intersection, and inversion. Note that these three operations can each be represented by using conjunction and existential quantification, so, for any subset Δ of Γ_{AIA}, the subalgebra Δ' generated by Δ has the property that $\Delta' \subseteq \langle\Delta\rangle$. It follows from Theorem 8.16 that $CSP(\Delta)$ and $CSP(\Delta')$ are polynomial-time equivalent. Hence it is sufficient to classify all subsets of Γ_{AIA} which are *subalgebras* of Allen's Interval Algebra.

Theorem 8.57 ([64]). *For any constraint language* $\Gamma \subseteq \Gamma_{AIA}$, *if* Γ *is contained in one of the eighteen subalgebras listed in Table 8.2, then it is tractable; otherwise it is NP-complete.*

The domain for Allen's Interval Algebra can be taken to be the countably infinite set of intervals with rational endpoints. It was noted in [4] that the relational structure associated with Allen's Interval Algebra (without its operations) is ω-categorical. Therefore, by Theorem 8.56, the complexity classification problem for subsets of Γ_{AIA} can be tackled using polymorphisms. Such an approach might provide a route to simplify the involved classification proof given in [64].

8.6 Multi-Sorted Constraint Languages

In practical constraint programming it is often the case that different variables have different domains. So far in this chapter we have considered a simplified situation in which all of the variables are assumed to have the same domain. This apparently minor simplification can have serious consequences for the analysis of the complexity of different forms of constraint; it can in fact mask the difference between tractability and NP-completeness for some languages, as we will demonstrate in this section.

The algebraic approach described in Section 8.3 has been extended to deal with the case when different variables have different domains [10], and we will now present the main results of the extended theory.

$$\mathcal{S}_{\mathsf{p}} = \{r \mid r \cap (\mathsf{pmod}^{-1}\mathsf{f}^{-1})^{\pm 1} \neq \emptyset \Rightarrow (\mathsf{p})^{\pm 1} \subseteq r\}$$
$$\mathcal{S}_{\mathsf{d}} = \{r \mid r \cap (\mathsf{pmod}^{-1}\mathsf{f}^{-1})^{\pm 1} \neq \emptyset \Rightarrow (\mathsf{d}^{-1})^{\pm 1} \subseteq r\}$$
$$\mathcal{S}_{\mathsf{o}} = \{r \mid r \cap (\mathsf{pmod}^{-1}\mathsf{f}^{-1})^{\pm 1} \neq \emptyset \Rightarrow (\mathsf{o})^{\pm 1} \subseteq r\}$$
$$\mathcal{A}_1 = \{r \mid r \cap (\mathsf{pmod}^{-1}\mathsf{f}^{-1})^{\pm 1} \neq \emptyset \Rightarrow (\mathsf{s}^{-1})^{\pm 1} \subseteq r\}$$
$$\mathcal{A}_2 = \{r \mid r \cap (\mathsf{pmod}^{-1}\mathsf{f}^{-1})^{\pm 1} \neq \emptyset \Rightarrow (\mathsf{s})^{\pm 1} \subseteq r\}$$
$$\mathcal{A}_3 = \{r \mid r \cap (\mathsf{pmodf})^{\pm 1} \neq \emptyset \Rightarrow (\mathsf{s})^{\pm 1} \subseteq r\}$$
$$\mathcal{A}_4 = \{r \mid r \cap (\mathsf{pmodf}^{-1})^{\pm 1} \neq \emptyset \Rightarrow (\mathsf{s})^{\pm 1} \subseteq r\}$$

$$\mathcal{E}_{\mathsf{p}} = \{r \mid r \cap (\mathsf{pmods})^{\pm 1} \neq \emptyset \Rightarrow (\mathsf{p})^{\pm 1} \subseteq r\}$$
$$\mathcal{E}_{\mathsf{d}} = \{r \mid r \cap (\mathsf{pmods})^{\pm 1} \neq \emptyset \Rightarrow (\mathsf{d})^{\pm 1} \subseteq r\}$$
$$\mathcal{E}_{\mathsf{o}} = \{r \mid r \cap (\mathsf{pmods})^{\pm 1} \neq \emptyset \Rightarrow (\mathsf{o})^{\pm 1} \subseteq r\}$$
$$\mathcal{B}_1 = \{r \mid r \cap (\mathsf{pmods})^{\pm 1} \neq \emptyset \Rightarrow (\mathsf{f}^{-1})^{\pm 1} \subseteq r\}$$
$$\mathcal{B}_2 = \{r \mid r \cap (\mathsf{pmods})^{\pm 1} \neq \emptyset \Rightarrow (\mathsf{f})^{\pm 1} \subseteq r\}$$
$$\mathcal{B}_3 = \{r \mid r \cap (\mathsf{pmod}^{-1}\mathsf{s}^{-1})^{\pm 1} \neq \emptyset \Rightarrow (\mathsf{f}^{-1})^{\pm 1} \subseteq r\}$$
$$\mathcal{B}_4 = \{r \mid r \cap (\mathsf{pmod}^{-1}\mathsf{s})^{\pm 1} \neq \emptyset \Rightarrow (\mathsf{f}^{-1})^{\pm 1} \subseteq r\}$$

$$\mathcal{E}^* = \left\{ r \;\middle|\; \begin{array}{l} 1)\; r \cap (\mathsf{pmod})^{\pm 1} \neq \emptyset \Rightarrow (\mathsf{s})^{\pm 1} \subseteq r, \text{ and} \\ 2)\; r \cap (\mathsf{ff}^{-1}) \neq \emptyset \Rightarrow (\equiv) \subseteq r \end{array} \right\}$$

$$\mathcal{S}^* = \left\{ r \;\middle|\; \begin{array}{l} 1)\; r \cap (\mathsf{pmod}^{-1})^{\pm 1} \neq \emptyset \Rightarrow (\mathsf{f}^{-1})^{\pm 1} \subseteq r, \text{ and} \\ 2)\; r \cap (\mathsf{ss}^{-1}) \neq \emptyset \Rightarrow (\equiv) \subseteq r \end{array} \right\}$$

$$\mathcal{H} = \left\{ r \;\middle|\; \begin{array}{l} 1)\; r \cap (\mathsf{os})^{\pm 1} \neq \emptyset \;\&\; r \cap (\mathsf{o}^{-1}\mathsf{f})^{\pm 1} \neq \emptyset \Rightarrow (\mathsf{d})^{\pm 1} \subseteq r, \text{ and} \\ 2)\; r \cap (\mathsf{ds})^{\pm 1} \neq \emptyset \;\&\; r \cap (\mathsf{d}^{-1}\mathsf{f}^{-1})^{\pm 1} \neq \emptyset \Rightarrow (\mathsf{o})^{\pm 1} \subseteq r, \text{ and} \\ 3)\; r \cap (\mathsf{pm})^{\pm 1} \neq \emptyset \;\&\; r \not\subseteq (\mathsf{pm})^{\pm 1} \Rightarrow (\mathsf{o})^{\pm 1} \subseteq r \end{array} \right\}$$

$$\mathcal{A}_{\equiv} = \{r \mid r \neq \emptyset \Rightarrow (\equiv) \subseteq r\}$$

For the sake of brevity, relations are written as collections of basic relations. So, for instance, we write (pmod) instead of $\mathsf{p} \cup \mathsf{m} \cup \mathsf{o} \cup \mathsf{d}$. We also use the symbol $\pm$, which should be interpreted as follows: a condition involving $\pm$ means the conjunction of two conditions, one corresponding to $+$ and one corresponding to $-$. For example, the condition $(\mathsf{o})^{\pm 1} \subseteq r \Leftrightarrow (\mathsf{d})^{\pm 1} \subseteq r$ means that both $(\mathsf{o}) \subseteq r \Leftrightarrow (\mathsf{d}) \subseteq r$ and $(\mathsf{o}^{-1}) \subseteq r \Leftrightarrow (\mathsf{d}^{-1}) \subseteq r$.

Table 8.2: The 18 maximal tractable subalgebras of Allen's Interval Algebra

Definition 8.58. *For any collection of sets* $\mathfrak{D} = \{D_i \mid i \in I\}$, *and any list of indices* $\langle i_1, i_2, \ldots, i_n \rangle \in I^n$, *a subset of* $D_{i_1} \times D_{i_2} \times \cdots \times D_{i_n}$, *together with the list* $\langle i_1, i_2, \ldots, i_n \rangle$, *will be called a **multi-sorted relation** over* $\mathfrak{D}$ *with arity* n *and* **signature** $\langle i_1, i_2, \ldots, i_n \rangle$.

For any multi-sorted relation R, the signature of R will be denoted $\sigma(R)$.

In the special case where $\mathfrak{D}$ contains just a single set D we will call a multi-sorted relation over $\mathfrak{D}$ a *one-sorted* relation over D.

Example 8.59. Let R be a 5-ary relation with 17 tuples defined as follows:

$$R = \{ \langle 3, 1, 2, c, b \rangle, \langle 3, 3, 2, c, b \rangle, \langle 1, 0, 2, c, b \rangle, \langle 1, 2, 2, c, b \rangle,$$
$$\langle 1, 1, 0, c, b \rangle, \langle 1, 3, 0, c, b \rangle, \langle 3, 0, 0, c, b \rangle, \langle 3, 2, 0, c, b \rangle,$$
$$\langle 3, 1, 2, c, a \rangle, \langle 3, 3, 2, c, a \rangle, \langle 1, 0, 2, c, a \rangle, \langle 1, 2, 2, c, a \rangle,$$
$$\langle 3, 1, 2, a, b \rangle, \langle 3, 3, 2, a, b \rangle, \langle 1, 1, 0, a, b \rangle, \langle 1, 3, 0, a, b \rangle, \langle 3, 3, 2, a, a \rangle \}$$

This relation can be considered in the usual way as a one-sorted relation over the set $D = \{0, 1, 2, 3, a, b, c\}$. Alternatively, it can be seen as a multi-sorted relation with signature $\langle 1, 1, 1, 2, 2 \rangle$ over the collection of sets $\mathfrak{D} = \langle D_1, D_2 \rangle$, where $D_1 = \{0, 1, 2, 3\}$ and $D_2 = \{a, b, c\}$. □

Given any set of multi-sorted relations, we can define a corresponding class of multi-sorted constraint satisfaction problems, in the following way.

Definition 8.60. *Let* Γ *be a set of multi-sorted relations over a collection of sets* $\mathfrak{D} = \{D_i \mid i \in I\}$. *The **multi-sorted constraint satisfaction problem** over* Γ, *denoted* $\mathrm{MCSP}(\Gamma)$, *is defined to be the decision problem with*

Instance: *A quadruple* $\langle V, \mathfrak{D}, \delta, \mathcal{C} \rangle$, *where*

- *V is a finite set of variables;*
- δ *is a mapping from V to I called the **domain function**;*
- $\mathcal{C}$ *is a set of constraints, where each constraint* $C \in \mathcal{C}$ *is a pair* $\langle s, R \rangle$ *such that*
  - *s, is a tuple of variables of length* n_C *called the constraint scope, and*
  - *R is an element of* Γ *with arity* n_C *and signature* $\langle \delta(s[1]), \ldots, \delta(s[n_C]) \rangle$ *called the constraint relation.*

Question: *Does there exist a solution, that is a function* φ *from V to* $\bigcup_{i \in I} D_i$ *such that, for each variable* $v \in V, \varphi(v) \in D_{\delta(v)}$, *and for each constraint* $\langle s, R \rangle \in \mathcal{C}$ *with* $s = \langle v_1, \ldots, v_n \rangle$, *the tuple* $\langle \varphi(v_1), \ldots, \varphi(v_n) \rangle$ *belongs to the multi-sorted relation* R.

It might be tempting to assume that the complexity of a set of multi-sorted relations could be determined by considering each of the domains involved separately; in other words, by separating the relations into a number of one-sorted relations, and analysing the complexity of each of these. However, in general this simple approach does not work, as the next example demonstrates.

Example 8.61. Consider the sets $D_1 = \{0, 1\}$ and $D_2 = \{a, b, c\}$, and the multi-sorted relations R_1, R_2, R_3 over $\mathfrak{D} = \{D_1, D_2\}$, each with signature $\langle 1, 2 \rangle$, where

$$R_1 = \{ \langle 1, a \rangle, \qquad R_2 = \{ \langle 0, a \rangle, \qquad R_3 = \{ \langle 0, a \rangle,$$
$$\langle 0, b \rangle, \qquad\qquad \langle 1, b \rangle, \qquad\qquad \langle 0, b \rangle,$$
$$\langle 0, c \rangle \} \qquad\qquad \langle 0, c \rangle \} \qquad\qquad \langle 1, c \rangle \}.$$

If we divide each of these multi-sorted relations into two separate one-sorted relations, then we obtain just the unary relations $\{0, 1\}$ and $\{a, b, c\}$ over the sets D_1 and D_2 respectively. Each of these unary relations individually is clearly tractable.

However, by establishing a reduction from the NP-complete problem ONE-IN-THREE SATISFIABILITY (see Example 8.6), it can be shown that the set of multi-sorted relations $\Gamma = \{R_1, R_2, R_3\}$ is NP-complete. (Details of this reduction are given in [10].) □

It is often desirable to convert a multi-sorted constraint satisfaction problem into a one-sorted problem. The most straightforward way to do this for a given multi-sorted problem instance $\langle V, \mathfrak{D}, \delta, \mathcal{C} \rangle$, is to take $\overline{D} = \bigcup_{D_i \in \mathfrak{D}} D_i$, and replace each constraint relation with a one-sorted relation over $\overline{D}$ containing exactly the same tuples.

However, this straightforward conversion method does *not* necessarily preserve the tractability of a multi-sorted constraint language Γ, as the next example indicates.

Example 8.62. Let D_1 and D_2 be two distinct supersets of a set D_0, and let Γ be the constraint language containing the single binary disequality relation $\neq_{D_0}$, as defined in Example 8.11, but now considered as a multi-sorted relation over $\{D_1, D_2\}$ with signature $\langle 1, 2 \rangle$.

Because of the signature, this constraint can only be imposed between two variables when one of them has domain D_1 and the other has domain D_2. Hence, in this case $\mathrm{MCSP}(\Gamma)$ corresponds to the problem of colouring a *bipartite graph* with $|D_0|$ colours, which is clearly tractable for any set D_0. Note that the tractability is entirely due to the signature of the relation rather than the tuples it contains.

If we convert Γ to a one-sorted constraint language by considering the relation $\neq_{D_0}$ as a one-sorted relation over the set $\overline{D} = D_1 \cup D_2$, then we obtain the usual disequality relation over D_0, which for $|D_0| > 2$ is NP-complete (see Example 8.11). □

To ensure that we do preserve tractability when converting a multi-sorted constraint language to a one-sorted constraint language, we make use of a more sophisticated conversion technique, based on the following definition.

Definition 8.63. *Let $\mathfrak{D} = \{D_1, \ldots, D_p\}$ be a finite collection of sets, and define $D^* = D_1 \times D_2 \times \cdots \times D_p$.*

For any n-ary relation R over $\mathfrak{D}$ with signature $\sigma(R) = \langle i_1, \ldots, i_n \rangle$, we define the one-sorted n-ary relation $\chi(R)$ over D^* as follows:

$$\chi(R) = \{ \langle t_1, t_2, \ldots, t_n \rangle \in (D^*)^n \mid \langle t_1[i_1], t_2[i_2], \ldots, t_m[i_m] \rangle \in R \}.$$

Note that for any one-sorted relation R, we have $\chi(R) = R$.

Example 8.64. Let R be the binary disequality relation $\neq_{D_0}$ over $\{D_1, D_2\}$ with signature $\langle 1, 2 \rangle$, as in Example 8.62. In this case $\chi(R)$ is the relation consisting of all pairs $\langle \langle a, a' \rangle, \langle b, b' \rangle \rangle \in (D_1 \times D_2) \times (D_1 \times D_2)$ such that $a, b' \in D_0$ and $a \neq b'$. □

Proposition 8.65 ([10]). *Let Γ be a multi-sorted constraint language over a finite collection of finite sets. The language Γ is tractable if and only if the corresponding one-sorted constraint language $\{\chi(R) \mid R \in \Gamma\}$ is tractable.*

To extend the algebraic results of Section 8.3 to the multi-sorted case, we need to define a suitable extension of the notion of a polymorphism. As we have shown in Example 8.61, we cannot simply separate out different domains and consider polymorphisms on each one separately; we must ensure that all of the domains are treated in a co-ordinated way. In the following definition, this is achieved by defining different *interpretations* for the same operation symbol applied to different sets.

Definition 8.66. *Let $\mathfrak{D} = \{D_i \mid i \in I\}$ be a collection of sets. A k-ary **multi-sorted operation** f on $\mathfrak{D}$ is defined by a collection of **interpretations** $\{f^{D_i} \mid i \in I\}$, where each f^{D_i} is a k-ary operation on the corresponding set D_i.*

For any multi-sorted relation R with signature $\langle i_1, \ldots, i_n \rangle$, and any collection of tuples $t_1, \ldots, t_k \in R$, define $f(t_1, \ldots, t_k)$ to be

$$\left\langle f^{D_{i_1}}(t_1[1], \ldots, t_k[1]), \ldots, f^{D_{i_n}}(t_1[n], \ldots, t_k[n]) \right\rangle.$$

Definition 8.67. *A k-ary multi-sorted operation f on $\mathfrak{D}$ is said to be a **multi-sorted polymorphism** of a multi-sorted relation R over $\mathfrak{D}$ if $f(t_1, \ldots, t_k) \in R$ for all choices of $t_1, \ldots, t_k \in R$.*

For any given multi-sorted constraint language Γ, the set of all multi-sorted polymorphisms of *every* relation in Γ is denoted $\mathrm{MPol}(\Gamma)$.

The next theorem is the main result of this section. It establishes the remarkable fact that many of the polymorphisms that ensure tractability in the one-sorted case can be combined in almost arbitrary ways to obtain new tractable multi-sorted constraint languages.

Note that a multi-sorted operation, f, is said to be *idempotent* if all of its interpretations f^D satisfy the identity $f^D(x, x, \ldots, x) = x$.

Theorem 8.68 ([10]). *Let Γ be a multi-sorted constraint language over a finite collection of finite sets $\mathfrak{D} = \{D_1, \ldots, D_n\}$.*

If, for each $D_i \in \mathfrak{D}$, $\mathrm{MPol}(\Gamma)$ contains a multi-sorted operation f_i such that

- *$f_i^{D_i}$ is a constant operation; or*

- *$f_i^{D_i}$ is a semilattice operation; or*

- *$f_i^{D_i}$ is a near-unanimity operation; or*

- *f_i is idempotent and $f_i^{D_i}$ is an affine operation,*

then $\mathrm{MCSP}(\Gamma)$ is tractable.

Example 8.69. Recall the relation R defined in Example 8.59.

If we consider R as a one-sorted relation over the domain $\{0, 1, 2, 3, a, b, c\}$, then it does not fall into any of the many known (one-sorted) tractable classes described in Section 8.4.2 above[8].

---

[8]This was established by using the program *Polyanna* described in [39], which is available from http://www.comlab.ox.ac.uk/oucl/research/areas/constraints/software/.

However if we consider R as a multi-sorted relation with signature $\langle 1, 1, 1, 2, 2 \rangle$ over the sets $D_1 = \{0, 1, 2, 3\}$ and $D_2 = \{a, b, c\}$, then we can use Theorem 8.68 to show that $\{R\}$ is tractable. To see this, it is sufficient to check that R has two multi-sorted polymorphisms $f(x, y, z)$ and $g(x, y)$, where

- f^{D_1} is the affine operation of the group $\mathbb{Z}_4$, and f^{D_2} is the (ternary) maximum operation on D_2, with respect to the order $a < b < c$ (which is idempotent).

- $g^{D_1}(x, y) = y$, and g^{D_2} is the (binary) maximum operation on D_2, with respect to the order $a < b < c$ (which is a semilattice operation).

$\square$

Further developments in the algebraic approach to multi-sorted constraints, and applications to the standard one-sorted CSP where the constraints limit the domain of each variable, are given in [10].

8.7 Alternative Approaches

8.7.1 Homomorphism Problems

An important reformulation of the CSP is the HOMOMORPHISM problem: the question of deciding whether there exists a homomorphism between two *relational structures* (see [3, 37, 41, 59]). Recall (from Section 8.5) that a relational structure is simply a set, together with a list of relations over that set.

Definition 8.70. *Let* $\mathcal{A}_1 = \langle D_1, R_1^1, R_2^1, \ldots, R_q^1 \rangle$ *and* $\mathcal{A}_2 = \langle D_2, R_1^2, R_2^2, \ldots, R_q^2 \rangle$ *be relational structures where both* R_i^1 *and* R_i^2 *are* n_i-*ary, for all* $i = 1, 2, \ldots, q$.

A mapping $\Phi : D_1 \rightarrow D_2$ *is called a **homomorphism** from* $\mathcal{A}_1$ *to* $\mathcal{A}_2$ *if it has the property that* $\langle \Phi(a_1), \ldots, \Phi(a_{n_i}) \rangle \in R_i^2$ *whenever* $\langle a_1, \ldots, a_{n_i} \rangle \in R_i^1$, *for all* $i = 1, 2, \ldots, q$.

The HOMOMORPHISM PROBLEM *for* $\langle \mathcal{A}_1, \mathcal{A}_2 \rangle$ *is to decide whether there exists a homomorphism from* $\mathcal{A}_1$ *to* $\mathcal{A}_2$.

To see that the HOMOMORPHISM PROBLEM is the same as the CSP, think of the elements in $\mathcal{A}_1$ as variables, the elements in $\mathcal{A}_2$ as values, tuples in the relations of $\mathcal{A}_1$ as constraint scopes, and the relations of $\mathcal{A}_2$ as constraint relations. With this correspondence, the solutions to this CSP instance are precisely the homomorphisms from $\mathcal{A}_1$ to $\mathcal{A}_2$.

Example 8.71. A relational structure with a single binary relation $\langle V, E \rangle$ is usually known as a (directed) **graph**.

An instance of the GRAPH H-COLORING problem consists of a finite graph G. The question is whether there is a homomorphism from G to H. When H is the complete graph on k vertices, the GRAPH H-COLORING problem corresponds to the standard GRAPH COLORABILITY problem with k colours (see Example 8.11). For an arbitrary graph $H = \langle V, E \rangle$, the GRAPH H-COLORING problem precisely corresponds to the problem CSP($\{E\}$).

For *undirected* graphs H, where the edge relation E is symmetric, the complexity of GRAPH H-COLORING has been completely characterised [44]: it is tractable if H is bipartite or contains a loop; otherwise it is NP-complete. (Note that this characterisation also follows from Conjecture 8.52, see [7].) However, if we allow H and G to be directed graphs, then the complexity of GRAPH H-COLORING has not yet been fully characterised. In fact a complete classification would answer Conjecture 8.52 since it was shown in [37] that every problem $\mathrm{CSP}(\Gamma)$ with finite Γ is polynomial-time equivalent to GRAPH H COLORING for some suitable directed graph H. $\qquad\qquad\qquad\qquad\qquad\qquad\square$

8.7.2   Constraint Languages and Logic

In the field of *descriptive complexity* [47] the computational complexity of a problem is investigated by studying the forms of *logic* which can be used to express that problem. The use of descriptive complexity techniques to analyse the complexity of constraint languages was initiated by the pioneering work of Feder and Vardi [37].

As shown in Section 8.7.1, for any finite constraint language $\Gamma = \{R_1, \ldots, R_q\}$ over a set D, the problem $\mathrm{CSP}(\Gamma)$ can be represented as the problem of deciding whether a given relational structure has a homomorphism to the relational structure $\langle D, R_1, \ldots, R_q \rangle$ Hence the class of instances of $\mathrm{CSP}(\Gamma)$ which do have a solution can be viewed as a class of relational structures (sometimes called the "yes-instances"). If this class of relational structures can be characterised in some restricted logic, then this can sometimes be used to show that $\mathrm{CSP}(\Gamma)$ is tractable, as the following example illustrates.

Example 8.72. Recall from Example 8.11 that $\mathrm{CSP}(\{\neq_D\})$ is equivalent to the problem of colouring a graph with $|D|$ colours. The class of instances which have a solution is the class of $|D|$-colourable graphs, which is a class of relational structures with a single symmetric binary relation E (specifying which vertices are connected by edges).

Now assume that $D = \{0, 1\}$. It is well-known that a graph (V, E) is 2-colourable if and only if it does not have any odd-length cycles. The property of having an odd-length cycle can be expressed in the logic programming language **Datalog** [37] using the following set of rules:

$$
\begin{aligned}
P(x, y) &: - & E(x, y) \\
P(x, y) &: - & P(x, z) \wedge E(z, u) \wedge E(u, y) \\
Q &: - & P(x, x)
\end{aligned}
$$

These rules give a recursive specification of two predicates, P and Q. Predicate $P(x, y$ holds exactly when there exists an odd-length path in (V, E) from x to y. Predicate Q, which acts as goal predicate, holds if there exists any odd-length cycle.

Hence, the class of structures for which $\mathrm{CSP}(\{\neq_{\{0,1\}}\})$ has a solution can be characterised as the set of structures (V, E) for which the goal predicate in this Datalog program does not hold. It was shown in [37] that any CSP problem whose yes-instances can be characterised by a Datalog program in this way is tractable. It has also recently been shown that any CSP problem whose yes-instances can be characterised in first-order logic can be characterised by a Datalog program in this way [2]. $\qquad\qquad\qquad\square$

The techniques of descriptive complexity can also be used to obtain a more refined description of the complexity of a constraint language. For example, Dalmau has shown [30] that if a finite constraint language Γ has a logical property which he calls "bounded path duality", then the problem $\mathrm{CSP}(\Gamma)$ is in the complexity class NL, and so can be solved very efficiently using parallel algorithms.

8.7.3 Disjunctive Combinations of Constraint Languages

Another approach to the analysis of constraint languages has been to consider how they can be built up from combinations of simpler languages whose properties are more easily analysed [25, 6]. This approach has successfully unified several important classes of tractable languages including five of the six tractable Boolean languages (Example 8.5), the max-closed constraints (Example 8.7), the 0/1/all constraints (Example 8.8), the connected row-convex constraints (Example 8.9) and the linear Horn constraints (Example 8.13). One advantage of this constructive approach is that it works equally well for both finite and infinite domains.

The key step in this approach is to define how relations can be combined disjunctively.

Definition 8.73. *Let R_1 be an n-ary relation and R_2 an m-ary relation over a common set D. The **disjunction** of R_1 and R_2, denoted $R_1 \vee R_2$, is the relation of arity $n + m$ over D defined as follows:*

$$R_1 \vee R_2 = \langle \langle x_1, \ldots, x_{n+m} \rangle \mid (\langle x_1, \ldots, x_n \rangle \in R_1) \vee (\langle x_{n+1}, \ldots, x_{n+m} \rangle \in R_2) \} \rangle$$

This definition of disjunction can be extended to constraint languages as follows.

Definition 8.74. *For any two constraint languages Γ and Δ, over the same domain D, define the constraint language $\Gamma \check{\vee} \Delta$ as follows:*

$$\Gamma \check{\vee} \Delta = \Gamma \cup \Delta \cup \{ R_1 \vee R_2 \mid R_1 \in \Gamma, R_2 \in \Delta \}$$

The constraint language $\Gamma \check{\vee} \Delta$ (pronounced Γ "or-times" Δ) contains all of the relations in Γ and Δ, together with the disjunction of each possible pair of relations from Γ and Δ.

The next example shows that when tractable constraint languages are combined using the disjunction operation defined in Definition 8.74 the resulting constraint language may or may not be tractable.

Example 8.75. Let Λ be the set of all relations over the domain {TRUE, FALSE} which can be specified by a formula of propositional logic consisting of a single *literal* (where a literal is either a variable or a negated variable).

The constraint language Λ is clearly tractable, as it is straightforward to verify in linear time whether a collection of simultaneous single literals has a solution.

Now consider the constraint language $\Lambda^{\vee 2} = \Lambda \check{\vee} \Lambda$. This set contains all Boolean constraints specified by a disjunction of (at most) 2 literals. The problem $CSP(\Lambda^{\vee 2})$ corresponds to the 2-SATISFIABILITY problem, which is well-known to be tractable [38] (see Example 8.42).

Finally, consider the constraint language $\Lambda^{\vee 3} = (\Lambda^{\vee 2}) \check{\vee} \Lambda$. This set of relations contains all Boolean relations specified by a disjunction of (at most) 3 literals. The problem $CSP(\Lambda^{\vee 3})$ corresponds to the 3-SATISFIABILITY problem, which is well-known to be NP-complete [38, 78]. □

Definition 8.76. *For any constraint language, Δ, define the set Δ^* as follows:*

$$\Delta^* = \bigcup_{i=1}^{\infty} \Delta^{\vee i}, \quad where$$

$$\Delta^{\vee 1} = \Delta$$
$$\Delta^{\vee (i+1)} = (\Delta^{\vee i}) \check{\vee} \Delta \ for \ i = 1, 2, \ldots$$

In the remainder of this section we identify a number of simple conditions on constraint languages Γ and Δ which are necessary and sufficient to ensure that various disjunctive combinations of Γ and Δ are tractable.

Definition 8.77. *For any constraint languages Γ and Δ over a common domain D, define* $\mathrm{CSP}_{\Delta \leq k}(\Gamma \cup \Delta)$ *to be the subproblem of* $\mathrm{CSP}(\Gamma \cup \Delta)$ *consisting of all instances containing at most k constraints whose relations are members of Δ.*

Using this definition, we now define what it means for one set of constraints to be 'k-independent' with respect to another.

Definition 8.78. *For any constraint languages Γ and Δ over a set D, we say that Δ is* **k-independent with respect to** *Γ if the following condition holds: any instance $\langle V, D, \mathcal{C} \rangle$ in* $\mathrm{CSP}(\Gamma \cup \Delta)$ *has a solution provided that any instance $\langle V, D, \mathcal{C}' \rangle$ in* $\mathrm{CSP}_{\Delta \leq k}(\Gamma \cup \Delta)$ *with $\mathcal{C}' \subseteq \mathcal{C}$ has a solution.*

The intuitive meaning of this definition is that the satisfiability of any set of constraints with relations chosen chosen from the set Δ can be determined by considering those constraints k at a time, even in the presence of arbitrary additional constraints from Γ.

Theorem 8.79 ([25, 6]). *Let Γ and Δ be constraint languages over a set D, such that* $\mathrm{CSP}_{\Delta \leq 1}(\Gamma \cup \Delta)$ *is tractable.*

The constraint language $\Gamma \check{\vee} \Delta^*$ is tractable if Δ is 1-independent with respect to Γ Otherwise it is NP-complete.

A polynomial-time algorithm for solving instances of $\mathrm{CSP}(\Gamma \check{\vee} \Delta^*)$, for any constraint languages Γ and Δ satisfying the conditions of Theorem 8.79 is given in [25].

Example 8.80. Let D be the set of real numbers (or the rationals). Let Γ be the constraint language over D consisting of all constraints specified by a single (weak) linear inequality (e.g., $3x_1 + 2x_2 - x_3 \leq 6$). Let Δ be the constraint language over D consisting of all constraints specified by a single linear disequality (e.g., $x_1 + 4x_2 + x_3 \neq 0$).

To show that $\mathrm{CSP}_{\Delta \leq 1}(\Gamma \cup \Delta)$ is tractable, we note that the consistency of a set of inequalities, $\mathcal{C}$, can be decided in polynomial time, using Khachian's linear programming algorithm [56]. Furthermore, for any single disequality constraint, C, we can detect in polynomial time whether $\mathcal{C} \cup \{C\}$ is consistent by simply running Khachian's algorithm to determine whether $\mathcal{C}$ implies the negation of C.

To show that Δ is 1-independent with respect to Γ, we consider the geometrical interpretation of the constraints as half spaces and excluded hyperplanes in D^n (see [62]).

Hence, we can apply Theorem 8.79 and conclude that $\Gamma \check{\vee} \Delta^*$ is tractable. This set consists of the linear Horn relations described in Example 8.13.

Note that the problem $\mathrm{CSP}(\Gamma \cup \Delta^*)$ is much simpler than $\mathrm{CSP}(\Gamma \check{\vee} \Delta^*)$ - it corresponds to deciding whether a convex polyhedron, possibly *minus* the union of a finite number of hyperplanes, is the empty set. This simpler problem was shown to be tractable in [69], using a more restrictive notion of independence which has been widely used in the development of consistency checking algorithms and canonical forms [68, 69]. However, the much larger set of linear Horn constraints is *not* independent in the sense defined in [69] (see [62]). □

Theorem 8.81 ([6]). *Let* Γ *and* Δ *be constraint languages over a set* D, *such that* $\mathrm{CSP}(\Gamma \cup \Delta)$ *is tractable.*
  The constraint language $\Gamma \cup \Delta^{\vee 2}$ *is tractable if* Δ *is 2-independent with respect to* Γ. *Otherwise it is NP-complete.*

Note that Δ is 2-independent with respect to $\emptyset$ if and only if for every $\langle V, D, \mathcal{C} \rangle \in \mathrm{CSP}(\Delta)$ which has no solution, there exists a pair of (not necessarily distinct) constraints $C_i, C_j \in \mathcal{C}$ such that $\langle V, D, \{C_i, C_j\} \rangle$ has no solution.

A polynomial-time algorithm for solving instances of $\mathrm{CSP}(\Gamma \cup \Delta^{\vee 2})$, for any constraint languages Γ and Δ satisfying the conditions of Theorem 8.81 is given in [6].

Example 8.82. Consider the class of connected row-convex constraints over a set D described in Example 8.9. In this example we will show that the tractability of connected row-convex constraints is a simple consequence of Theorem 8.81. Furthermore, by using Theorem 8.81 we are able to generalise this result to obtain tractable constraints over infinite sets of values.

Note that the 0-1 matrices defining binary connected row-convex constraints have a very restricted structure. If we eliminate all rows and columns consisting entirely of zeros, and then consider any remaining zero in the matrix, all of the ones in the same row as the chosen zero must lie one side of it (because of the connectedness condition on the row). Similarly, all of the ones in the same column must lie on one side of the chosen zero. Hence there is a complete path of zeros from the chosen zero to the edge of the matrix along both the row and column in one direction. But this means there must be a complete rectangular sub-matrix of zeros extending from the chosen zero to one corner of the matrix (because of the connectedness condition).

This implies that the whole matrix can be obtained as the intersection (conjunction) of 0-1 matrices that contain all ones except for a submatrix of zeros in one corner (simply take one such matrix, obtained as above, for each zero in the matrix to be constructed).

There are four different forms of such matrices, depending on which corner submatrix is zero, and they correspond to constraints expressed by disjunctive expressions of the four following forms:

$$(x_i \geq d_i) \quad \vee \quad (x_j \geq d_j)$$
$$(x_i \geq d_i) \quad \vee \quad (x_j \leq d_j)$$
$$(x_i \leq d_i) \quad \vee \quad (x_j \geq d_j)$$
$$(x_i \leq d_i) \quad \vee \quad (x_j \leq d_j)$$

In these expressions x_i, x_j are variables and d_i, d_j are constants.

Finally, we note that a row or column consisting entirely of zeros corresponds to a constraint of the form $(x_i \leq d_1) \vee (x_i \geq d_2)$ for an appropriate choice of d_1 and d_2.

Hence, any connected row-convex constraint is equivalent to a conjunction of expressions of these forms.

Now define Δ to be the set of all unary constraints over D specified by a single inequality of the form $x_i \leq d_i$ or $x_i \geq d_i$, for some $d_i \in D$.

It is easily shown that Δ is 2-independent with respect to $\emptyset$ and $\mathrm{CSP}(\Delta)$ is tractable, since each instance consists of a conjunction of upper and lower bounds for individual variables. Hence, by Theorem 8.81, $\Delta^{\vee}\Delta$ is tractable. By the alternative characterisation described above, this establishes that connected row-convex constraints are tractable.

Unlike the arguments used previously to establish that connected row-convex constraints are tractable [35, 50], the argument above can still be applied when the set of values D is infinite.   □

Many further examples of constraint languages over both finite and infinite domains which can be shown to be tractable by constructing them from simpler languages are given in [25].

Disjunctive combinations of constraint languages over *different* domains are discussed in [24, 13]. These papers make use of the algebraic methods discussed in Section 8.3 above.

8.8   Future Directions

We have shown in this chapter that considerable progress has been made in analysing the complexity of constraint problems with specified constraint languages. The algebraic approach described in Section 8.3 has led to a complete classification for many special cases of constraint languages, and has prompted the conjecture that *all* constraint languages can be classified as either tractable or NP-complete on the basis of their algebraic properties (Conjecture 8.52).

Even greater progress has been made in analysing the complexity of constraint problems with restricted structure, where the constraint language is unrestricted. A number of powerful structural decomposition algorithms [40], often based on ideas from relational algebra, have been developed which guarantee tractability for constraint satisfaction problems whose structure is limited to certain infinite sets of structures but whose relations are unrestricted. Furthermore, a complete classification of the complexity of constraint satisfaction problems whose structure is limited to a any set of structures with bounded arity scopes but whose relations are unrestricted is given in [42].

However, there is currently very little analytical work which combines these two approaches. One significant result of this kind shows that a certain level of local consistency (see Chapter 3), which depends on the constraint *tightness* and the maximum constraint arity, is sufficient to ensure global consistency [90]. In general, enforcing the required level of local consistency will increase the constraint arity, and so increase the required level of consistency still further, which means that this result can only be used to establish the tractability of classes of problems involving particular languages applied on particular restricted structures [90]. Other "hybrid" results of this kind, involving both structural and language properties, are discussed in [89, 79] and in Chapter 12 of [32].

In many practical problems it will be the case that some constraints fall into one tractable class and some fall into another. Can this fact be exploited to obtain an efficient solution strategy? Does this depend on the structural way in which the different forms of constraint overlap? There is currently no suitable theoretical framework to address this question. One promising approach would be to incorporate ideas of space complexity, as well as time complexity. The ability to construct solutions using only a limited amount of working space and stored information seems to be a unifying principle between many disparate techniques in constraint programming such as bucket elimination [32], hypertree decomposition [40], and several forms of tractable constraint language [52].

Another direction of future work is to extend the analysis presented here to other forms of constraint problem, such as *quantified* constraint problems, *soft* constraint problems, *overconstrained* problems, or problems where we wish to *count* the number of solutions [63]. There has been considerable progress in analysing variations of this kind for Boolean constraint problems [27]. For larger finite domains there have been some initial studies of the complexity of quantified constraint problems [5] and counting constraint problems [9] based on extensions to the algebraic theory described in this chapter: for example, it has been shown that for both of these problems the complexity of a constraint language is determined by its polymorphisms [5, 9].

A rather more substantial extension of the algebraic theory presented here is required to analyse the complexity of soft constraints, because in this form of problem the constraints are represented as functions from tuples of domain values to some measure of desirability (see Chapter 9, "Soft Constraints"). Many forms of combinatorial optimisation problems can be represented in this very general framework [27, 57]. An initial approach to analysing the complexity of such problems using algebraic techniques is developed in [21, 22] and a tractable soft constraint language is presented in [23].

Bibliography

[1]   J.F. Allen. Maintaining knowledge about temporal intervals. *Communications of the ACM*, 26:832–843, 1983.

[2]   A. Atserias. On digraph coloring problems and treewidth duality. In *Proceedings 20th IEEE Symposium on Logic in Computer Science (LICS 2005)*, pages 106–115, 2005.

[3]   M. Bodirsky and J. Nešetřil. Constraint satisfaction with countable homogeneous templates. To appear in the *Journal of Logic and Computation*.

[4]   M. Bodirsky and J. Nešetřil. Constraint satisfaction with countable homogeneous templates. In *Proceedings of Computer Science Logic and the 8th Kurt Gödel Colloquium*, volume 2803 of *Lecture Notes in Computer Science*, pages 44–57. Springer-Verlag, 2003.

[5]   F. Boerner, A. Bulatov, P. Jeavons, and A. Krokhin. Quantified constraints: Algorithms and complexity. In *Proceedings of Computer Science Logic and the 8th Kurt Gödel Colloquium*, volume 2803 of *Lecture Notes in Computer Science*, pages 58–70. Springer, 2003.

[6]   M. Broxvall, P. Jonsson, and J. Renz. Disjunctions, independence, refinements. *Artificial Intelligence*, 140(1-2):153–173, 2002.

[7]   A. Bulatov. H-coloring dichotomy revisited. *Theoretical Computer Science*, 349(1):31–39, 2005.

[8]   A. Bulatov and V. Dalmau. Mal'tsev constraints are tractable. *SIAM Journal on Computing*. (To appear).

[9]   A. Bulatov and V. Dalmau. Towards a dichotomy theorem for the counting constraint satisfaction problem. In *Proceedings 44th Symposium on Foundations of Computer Science (FOCS 2003)*, pages 562–573. IEEE Computer Society, 2003.

[10] A. Bulatov and P. Jeavons. An algebraic approach to multi-sorted constraints. In *Proceedings 9th International Conference on Constraint Programming—CP'03 (Kinsale, September 2003)*, volume 2833 of *Lecture Notes in Computer Science*, pages 183–198. Springer-Verlag, 2003.

[11] A. Bulatov, A. Krokhin, and P. Jeavons. Classifying the complexity of constraints using finite algebras. *SIAM Journal on Computing*, 34(3):720–742, 2005.

[12] A. Bulatov, Jeavons P., and M. Volkov. Finite semigroups imposing tractable constraints. In *Proceedings of the School on Algorithmic Aspects of the Theory of Semigroups and its Applications, Coimbra, Portugal, 2001*, pages 313–329. World Scientific, 2002.

[13] A. Bulatov and E. Skvortsov. Amalgams of constraint satisfaction problems. In *Proceedings of the 18th International Joint Conference on Artificial Intelligence (IJCAI 2003)*, pages 197–202. Morgan Kaufmann, 2003.

[14] A.A. Bulatov. A dichotomy theorem for constraints on a three-element set. In *Proceedings 43rd IEEE Symposium on Foundations of Computer Science (FOCS'02)* pages 649–658, Vancouver, Canada, 2002.

[15] A.A. Bulatov. Mal'tsev constraints are tractable. Technical Report PRG-RR-02-05, Computing Laboratory, University of Oxford, Oxford, UK, 2002.

[16] A.A. Bulatov. Tractable conservative constraint satisfaction problems. In *Proceedings 18th IEEE Symposium on Logic in Computer Science (LICS'03)*, pages 321–330, Ottawa, Canada, 2003. IEEE Press.

[17] A.A. Bulatov and P.G. Jeavons. Tractable constraints closed under a binary operation. Technical Report PRG-TR-12-00, Computing Laboratory, University of Oxford, Oxford, UK, 2002.

[18] A.A. Bulatov, A.A. Krokhin, and P.G. Jeavons. Constraint satisfaction problems and finite algebras. In *Proceedings 27th International Colloquium on Automata, Languages and Programming (ICALP'00)*, volume 1853 of *Lecture Notes in Computer Science*, pages 272–282. Springer-Verlag, 2000.

[19] A.A. Bulatov, A.A. Krokhin, and P.G. Jeavons. The complexity of maximal constraint languages. In *Proceedings 33rd ACM Symposium on Theory of Computing (STOC'01)*, pages 667–674, 2001.

[20] D. Cohen. Tractable decision for a constraint language implies tractable search. *Constraints*, 9:219–229, 2004.

[21] D. Cohen, M. Cooper, and P. Jeavons. A complete characterization of complexity for Boolean constraint optimization problems. In *Proceedings 10th International Conference on Constraint Programming—CP'04*, volume 3258 of *Lecture Notes in Computer Science*, pages 212–226. Springer-Verlag, 2004.

[22] D. Cohen, M. Cooper, P. Jeavons, and A. Krokhin. Soft constraints: Complexity and multimorphisms. In *Proceedings 9th International Conference on Constraint Programming—CP'03 (Kinsale, September 2003)*, volume 2833 of *Lecture Notes in Computer Science*, pages 244–258. Springer-Verlag, 2003.

[23] D. Cohen, M. Cooper, P. Jeavons, and A. Krokhin. A maximal tractable class of soft constraints. *Journal of Artificial Intelligence Research (JAIR)*, 22:1–22, 2004.

[24] D.A. Cohen, P.G. Jeavons, and R.L. Gault. New tractable classes from old. *Constraints*, 8:263–282, 2003.

[25] D.A. Cohen, P.G. Jeavons, P. Jonsson, and M. Koubarakis. Building tractable disjunctive constraints. *Journal of the ACM*, 47:826–853, 2000.

[26] M.C. Cooper, D.A. Cohen, and P.G. Jeavons. Characterising tractable constraints. *Artificial Intelligence*, 65:347–361, 1994.

[27] N. Creignou, S. Khanna, and M. Sudan. *Complexity Classification of Boolean Constraint Satisfaction Problems*, volume 7 of *SIAM Monographs on Discrete Mathemat-*

ics and Applications. Society for Industrial and Applied Mathematics, Philadelphia, PA., 2001.

[28] V. Dalmau. A new tractable class of constraint satisfaction problems. In *Proceedings 6th International Symposium on Artificial Intelligence and Mathematics*, 2000.

[29] V. Dalmau. Generalized majority-minority operations are tractable. In *Proceedings 20th IEEE Symposium on Logic in Computer Science, (LICS 2005)*, pages 438–447. IEEE Computer Society, 2005.

[30] V. Dalmau. Linear datalog and bounded path duality of relational structures. *Logical Methods in Computer Science*, 1:1–32, 2005.

[31] V. Dalmau, R. Gavaldà, P. Tesson, and D. Thérien. Tractable clones of polynomials over semigroups. In *Proceedings 11th International Conference on Constraint Programming—CP'05 (Sitges, October 2005)*, volume 3709 of *Lecture Notes in Computer Science*, pages 196–210. Springer-Verlag, 2005.

[32] R. Dechter. *Constraint Processing*. Morgan Kaufmann, 2003.

[33] R. Dechter and J. Pearl. Network-based heuristics for constraint satisfaction problems. *Artificial Intelligence*, 34(1):1–38, 1988.

[34] K. Denecke and S.L. Wismath. *Universal Algebra and Applications in Theoretical Computer Science*. Chapman and Hall/CRC Press, 2002.

[35] Y. Deville, O. Barette, and P. van Hentenryck. Constraint satisfaction over connected row convex constraints. In *Proceedings of IJCAI'97*, pages 405–411, 1997.

[36] T. Drakengren and P Jonsson. A complete classification of tractability in Allen's algebra relative to subsets of basic relations. *Artificial Intelligence*, 106:205–219, 1998.

[37] T. Feder and M.Y. Vardi. The computational structure of monotone monadic SNP and constraint satisfaction: A study through Datalog and group theory. *SIAM Journal on Computing*, 28:57–104, 1998.

[38] M. Garey and D.S. Johnson. *Computers and Intractability: A Guide to the Theory of NP-Completeness*. Freeman, San Francisco, CA., 1979.

[39] R.L Gault and P. Jeavons. Implementing a test for tractability. *Constraints*, 9:139–160, 2004.

[40] G. Gottlob, L. Leone, and F. Scarcello. A comparison of structural CSP decomposition methods. *Artificial Intelligence*, 124:243–282, 2000.

[41] G. Gottlob, L. Leone, and F. Scarcello. Hypertree decomposition and tractable queries. *Journal of Computer and System Sciences*, 64(3):579–627, 2002.

[42] M. Grohe. The complexity of homomorphism and constraint satisfaction problems seen from the other side. In *Proceedings 44th Annual IEEE Symposium on Foundations of Computer Science, (FOCS'03)*, pages 552–561, 2003.

[43] M. Gyssens, P.G. Jeavons, and D.A. Cohen. Decomposing constraint satisfaction problems using database techniques. *Artificial Intelligence*, 66(1):57–89, 1994.

[44] P. Hell and J. Nešetřil. On the complexity of H-coloring. *Journal of Combinatorial Theory, Ser.B*, 48:92–110, 1990.

[45] D. Hobby and R.N. McKenzie. *The Structure of Finite Algebras*, volume 76 of *Contemporary Mathematics*. American Mathematical Society, Providence, R.I., 1988.

[46] W. Hodges. *A Shorter Model Theory*. Cambridge University Press, 1997.

[47] N. Immerman. *Descriptive Complexity*. Texts in Computer Science. Springer-Verlag, 1998.

[48] P.G. Jeavons. Constructing constraints. In *Proceedings 4th International Conference*

on *Constraint Programming—CP'98 (Pisa, October 1998)*, volume 1520 of *Lecture Notes in Computer Science*, pages 2–16. Springer-Verlag, 1998.

[49] P.G. Jeavons. On the algebraic structure of combinatorial problems. *Theoretical Computer Science*, 200:185–204, 1998.

[50] P.G. Jeavons, D.A. Cohen, and M.C. Cooper. Constraints, consistency and closure. *Artificial Intelligence*, 101(1–2):251–265, 1998.

[51] P.G. Jeavons, D.A. Cohen, and M. Gyssens. A unifying framework for tractable constraints. In *Proceedings 1st International Conference on Constraint Programming, CP'95*, volume 976 of *Lecture Notes in Computer Science*, pages 276–291. Springer-Verlag, 1995.

[52] P.G. Jeavons, D.A. Cohen, and M. Gyssens. Closure properties of constraints. *Journal of the ACM*, 44:527–548, 1997.

[53] P.G. Jeavons, D.A. Cohen, and M. Gyssens. How to determine the expressive power of constraints. *Constraints*, 4:113–131, 1999.

[54] P.G. Jeavons and M.C. Cooper. Tractable constraints on ordered domains. *Artificial Intelligence*, 79(2):327–339, 1995.

[55] P. Jonsson and C. Bäckström. A unifying approach to temporal constraint reasoning. *Artificial Intelligence*, 102:143–155, 1998.

[56] L.G. Khachian. A polynomial time algorithm for linear programming. *Soviet Math. Dokl.*, 20:191–194, 1979.

[57] S. Khanna, M. Sudan, L. Trevisan, and D. Williamson. The approximability of constraint satisfaction problems. *SIAM Journal on Computing*, 30(6):1863–1920, 2001.

[58] L. Kirousis. Fast parallel constraint satisfaction. *Artificial Intelligence*, 64:147–160, 1993.

[59] Ph.G. Kolaitis and M.Y. Vardi. Conjunctive-query containment and constraint satisfaction. *Journal of Computer and System Sciences*, 61:302–332, 2000.

[60] M. Koubarakis. Dense time and temporal constraints with ≠. In B. Nebel, C. Rich, and W. Swartout, editors, *Principles of Knowledge Representation and Reasoning: Proceedings of the Third International Conference (KR'92)*, pages 24–35, San Mateo, CA, 1992. Morgan Kaufmann.

[61] M. Koubarakis. From local to global consistency in temporal constraint networks. In *Proceedings 1st International Conference on Constraint Programming—CP'95 (Cassis, France, September 1995)*, volume 976 of *Lecture Notes in Computer Science*, pages 53–69. Springer-Verlag, 1995.

[62] M. Koubarakis. Tractable disjunctions of linear constraints. In *Proceedings 2nd International Conference on Constraint Programming—CP'96*, volume 1118 of *Lecture Notes in Computer Science*, pages 297–307. Springer-Verlag, 1996.

[63] A. Krokhin, A. Bulatov, and P. Jeavons. Functions of multiple-valued logic and the complexity of constraint satisfaction: A short survey. In *Proceedings 33rd IEEE International Symposium on Multiple-Valued Logic (ISMVL 2003)*, pages 343–351. IEEE Computer Society, 2003.

[64] A. Krokhin, P. Jeavons, and P. Jonsson. Reasoning about temporal relations: The tractable subalgebras of Allen's interval algebra. *Journal of the ACM*, 50:591–640, 2003.

[65] A. Krokhin, P. Jeavons, and P. Jonsson. Constraint satisfaction problems on intervals and lengths. *SIAM Journal on Discrete Mathematics*, 17:453–477, 2004.

[66] P.B. Ladkin and R.D. Maddux. On binary constraint problems. *Journal of the ACM*

41:435–469, 1994.

[67] R.E. Ladner. On the structure of polynomial time reducibility. *Journal of the ACM*, 22:155–171, 1975.

[68] J-L. Lassez and K. McAloon. A constraint sequent calculus. In *Constraint Logic Programming, Selected Research*, pages 33–43. MIT Press, 1991.

[69] J-L. Lassez and K. McAloon. A canonical form for generalized linear constraints. *Journal of Symbolic Computation*, 13:1–24, 1992.

[70] D. Lesaint, N. Azarmi, R. Laithwaite, and P. Walker. Engineering dynamic scheduler for Work Manager. *BT Technology Journal*, 16:16–29, 1998.

[71] T. Łuczak and J. Nešetřil. A probabilistic approach to the dichotomy problem. Technical Report 2003-640, KAM-DIMATIA Series, Charles University, Prague, 2003.

[72] A.K. Mackworth. Consistency in networks of relations. *Artificial Intelligence*, 8:99–118, 1977.

[73] A.K. Mackworth. Constraint satisfaction. In S.C. Shapiro, editor, *Encyclopedia of Artificial Intelligence*, volume 1, pages 285–293. Wiley Interscience, 1992.

[74] A.K. Mackworth and E.C. Freuder. The complexity of constraint satisfaction revisited. *Artificial Intelligence*, 59:57–62, 1993.

[75] R.N. McKenzie, G.F. McNulty, and W.F. Taylor. *Algebras, Lattices and Varieties*, volume I. Wadsworth and Brooks, California, 1987.

[76] U. Montanari. Networks of constraints: Fundamental properties and applications to picture processing. *Information Sciences*, 7:95–132, 1974.

[77] B. Nebel and H.-J. Bürckert. Reasoning about temporal relations: a maximal tractable subclass of Allen's interval algebra. *Journal of the ACM*, 42:43–66, 1995.

[78] C.H. Papadimitriou. *Computational Complexity*. Addison-Wesley, 1994.

[79] J.K. Pearson and P.G. Jeavons. A survey of tractable constraint satisfaction problems. Technical Report CSD-TR-97-15, Royal Holloway, University of London, July 1997.

[80] N. Pippenger. *Theories of Computability*. Cambridge University Press, Cambridge, 1997.

[81] R. Pöschel and L.A. Kalužnin. *Funktionen- und Relationenalgebren*. DVW, Berlin, 1979.

[82] E.L. Post. *The two-valued iterative systems of mathematical logic*, volume 5 of *Annals Mathematical Studies*. Princeton University Press, 1941.

[83] L. Purvis and P. Jeavons. Constraint tractability theory and its application to the product development process for a constraint-based scheduler. In *Proceedings of 1st International Conference on The Practical Application of Constraint Technologies and Logic Programming - PACLP'99*, pages 63–79. Practical Applications Company, 1999.

[84] J. Renz and B. Nebel. On the complexity of qualitative spatial reasoning: A maximal tractable fragment of the Region Connection Calculus. *Artificial Intelligence*, 108:69–123, 1999.

[85] I.G. Rosenberg. Minimal clones I: the five types. In *Lectures in Universal Algebra (Proc. Conf. Szeged 1983)*, volume 43 of *Colloq. Math. Soc. Janos Bolyai*, pages 405–427. North-Holland, 1986.

[86] T.J. Schaefer. The complexity of satisfiability problems. In *Proceedings 10th ACM Symposium on Theory of Computing, STOC'78*, pages 216–226, 1978.

[87] E. Schwalb and L. Vila. Temporal constraints: a survey. *Constraints*, 3(2–3):129–149, 1998.

[88] A. Szendrei. *Clones in Universal Algebra*, volume 99 of *Seminaires de Mathematiques Superieures*. University of Montreal, 1986.

[89] P. van Beek and R. Dechter. On the minimality and decomposability of row-convex constraint networks. *Journal of the ACM*, 42:543–561, 1995.

[90] P. van Beek and R. Dechter. Constraint tightness and looseness versus local and global consistency. *Journal of the ACM*, 44:549–566, 1997.

[91] P. van Hentenryck, Y. Deville, and C-M. Teng. A generic arc-consistency algorithm and its specializations. *Artificial Intelligence*, 57:291–321, 1992.

[92] M. Vilain, H. Kautz, and P. van Beek. Constraint propagation algorithms for temporal reasoning: A revised report. In D.S. Weld and J. de Kleer, editors, *Readings in Qualitative Reasoning about Physical Systems*, pages 373–281. Morgan Kaufmann, 1989.

Chapter 9

Soft Constraints

Pedro Meseguer, Francesca Rossi, Thomas Schiex

Many real-life combinatorial problems can be naturally modelled (see Chapters 2 and 11 and [34, 2]) and often efficiently solved using constraint techniques. It is essentially a matter of identifying the decision variables of the problem and how they are related through constraints. In a scheduling problem for example, there may be as many variables as tasks, each specifying its starting time, and constraints can model the temporal relations among such variables, such as "the beginning of task 2 must occur after the end of task 1". Similar models have been designed for many problems in staff rostering, resource allocation, VLSI design and other classes of combinatorial problems. Typical solving techniques involve a search in the space of all the solutions. During such search, the constraints are not merely treated as tests, but play an active role by helping discovering inconsistencies early on, via the so-called constraint propagation, which allows one to eliminate parts of the search space and thus to make the search shorter.

In many practical cases, however, the classical constraint framework does not help. For example, it is possible that after having listed the desired constraints among the decision variables, there is no way to satisfy them all. In this case, the instance is said to be *over-constrained*, and several phases of manual model refinement are usually needed to often heuristically chose which constraints to ignore. This process, when it is feasible, is rarely formalized and always difficult and time consuming. Even when all the constraints can be satisfied, and there are several solutions, such solutions appear equally good, and there is no way to discriminate among them.

These scenarios often occur when constraints are used to formalize desired properties rather than requirements that cannot be violated. Such desired properties are not faithfully represented by constraints, but should rather be considered as *preferences* whose violation should be avoided as far as possible. *Soft constraints* provide one way to model such preferences.

As an example, consider a typical timetabling problem which aims at assigning courses and teachers to classrooms and time slots in a university. In the description of this problem there are usually many *hard* constraints, such as the size of the classrooms, the opening hours of the building, or the fact that the same teacher cannot teach two different classes at the same time. All these pieces of information are naturally modelled by constraints, all of which have to be satisfied in order to find an acceptable assignment. However, there are usually also many *soft* constraints, or preferences, which state for example the desires of the teachers (like that he prefers not to teach on Fridays), or also university policies (like that it is preferable to use smaller classrooms if possible). If all these desires would be modelled by constraints, it is easy to figure out scenarios where there is no way to satisfy all of them. On the contrary, there could be ways to satisfy all hard requirements while violating the desires as little as possible, which is what we are looking for in the real situation. Moreover, modelling the desires in a faithful way allows us to discriminate among all the solutions which satisfy the hard constraints. In fact, there could be two timetables which both satisfy the hard requirements, but where one of them satisfies better the desires, and this should be the chosen one. Similar scenarios can be found in most of the typical application fields for constraints, such as scheduling, resource allocation, rostering, vehicle routing, etc.

To cope with similar situations, classical constraints have been generalized in various ways in the past decades. Historically, first a variety of specific extensions of the basic constraint formalism have been introduced. Later, these extensions have been generalized using more abstract frameworks, which have been crucial in proving general properties and in identifying the relationship among the specific frameworks. Moreover, for each of the specific classes, algorithms for solving problems specified in the corresponding formalisms have been defined.

In this chapter we will review most of the frameworks to model soft constraints, starting from the specific ones in Section 9.2 to the general ones in Section 9.3. We will discuss the relationship among the several formalisms, and also their relationship to other preference modelling frameworks in AI. We will describe the main approaches to solve soft constraint problems, considering search methods in Section 9.5, inference strategies in Section 9.6, and approaches that combine both in Section 9.7. Many solving approaches for soft constraints are generalizations of ideas already used for hard constraint solving. Often, these generalizations are far from being direct. In those particular cases, we will analyze in detail the specific issues that arise for soft constraints. Finally, in Section 9.8 we will briefly describe some applications of soft constraints, and in Section 9.9 we will point out some promising directions for future work in the area of soft constraints.

9.1 Background: Classical Constraints

Here we summarize the main notions and associated notations that will be used in this chapter. Since soft constraints often refer to the classical case, we also present the basic concepts of classical constraint networks.

A sequence $\langle a_1, \ldots, a_k \rangle$ is a totally ordered set that allows repetition of elements. A k-tuple, or simply a tuple is a sequence of k elements. The Cartesian product of a sequence of sets $A_1, \ldots, A_k$, written $A_1 \times \cdots \times A_k$, is the set of all the k-tuples $\langle a_1, \ldots, a_k \rangle$ such that $a_1 \in A_1, \ldots, a_k \in A_k$. A variable x_i represents an unknown element of its domain D_i, that is a finite set of values. Given a sequence of distinct variables $V = \langle x_1, \ldots, x_k \rangle$ and their associated domains $D_1, \ldots, D_k$, a relation R on V is a subset of $D_1 \times \cdots \times D_k$ The arity of the relation is k and the scope of the relation is V. To make scopes explicit, we will often denote a relation R over variables V as R_V and an element of R_V as a tuple

t_V. Such a tuple t_V is called an assignment of the variables in V. The projection of a tuple t_V over a sequence of variables W, $W \subseteq V$, is the tuple formed by the values in t_V corresponding to variables in W, denoted as $t_V[W]$.

A *classical constraint network* (classical CN) is a triple $\langle X, D, C \rangle$ defined as follows:

- $X = \{x_1, \ldots, x_n\}$ is a finite set of n *variables*.

- $D = \{D_1, \ldots, D_n\}$ is the set of the *domains* corresponding to variables in X, such that D_i is the domain of x_i; d bounds the domain size.

- C is a finite set of e constraints. A constraint $c \in C$ is defined by a relation R on a sequence of variables $V \subseteq X$. V is the scope of the constraint. The relation specifies the assignments allowed by c for the variables of V. Thus, a constraint c can be viewed as a pair $\langle R, V \rangle$ also noted R_V.

Given an assignment t_V and a constraint $c = R_W$, we say that c is *completely assigned* by t_V when $W \subseteq V$. In such case, we say that t_V *satisfies* c when $t_V[W] \in R_W$. If $t_V[W] \notin R_W$, t_V *violates* c. An assignment t_V is *consistent* if it satisfies all constraints completely assigned by it. An assignment t_V is complete if $V = X$. A solution of a classical CN is a complete consistent assignment. Since all constraints must be mandatorily satisfied in a solution, we often say that they are *hard constraints*. The task of finding a solution in a classical CN is known as the *constraint satisfaction problem* (CSP), which is known to be NP-complete. In the following, we will use c to denote hard constraints, and f, g to denote soft constraints.

9.2 Specific Frameworks

In this Section we describe the first frameworks that, historically, have been proposed in the literature for modelling soft constraints. These frameworks are here called *specific* since they focus on specific interpretations of soft constraints, in terms of possibilities, priorities, costs, or probabilities.

9.2.1 Fuzzy, Possibilistic, and Lexicographic Constraints

Originally introduced by [92], and based on fuzzy set theory [42], fuzzy constraints represent the first extension of the notion of classical constraints that allowed to explicitly represent preferences. This framework has been analyzed in depth in [45, 43].

A classical constraint can be seen as the *set* of value combinations for the variables in its scope that satisfy the constraint. In the fuzzy framework, a constraint is no longer a set, but rather a *fuzzy set* [42]. This means that, for each assignment of values to its variables, we do not have to say whether it belongs to the set or not, but how much it does so. In other words, we have to use a *graded notion of membership*. This allows us to represent the fact that a combination of values for the variables of the constraint is partially permitted.

The *membership function* μ_E of a fuzzy set E associates a real number between 0 and 1 with every possible element of E. If $\mu_E(a) = 1$, then a completely belongs to the set. If $\mu_E(a) = 0$, then a does not belong to the set. Intermediary values allow for graded membership degrees. To represent classical sets, only membership degrees 0 and 1 are used.

A *fuzzy constraint network* (fuzzy CN) is a triple $\langle X, D, C \rangle$ where X and D are the set of variables and their domain, as in classical CNs, and C is a set of fuzzy constraints. A *fuzzy constraint* is a fuzzy relation R_V on a sequence of variables V. This relation, that is a fuzzy set of tuples, is defined by its membership function

$$\mu_{R_V} : \prod_{x_j \in V} D_j \quad \rightarrow \quad [0, 1]$$

The membership function of the relation R_V indicates to what extent an assignment of the variables in V belongs to the relation and therefore satisfies the constraint. Given two assignments t and t' such that $\mu_{R_V}(t) < \mu_{R_V}(t')$, we can say that t' satisfies R better than t, or that t' is preferable to t for constraint R_V. For example, if $\mu_{R_V}(t) = 0$. and $\mu_{R_V}(t') = 0.9$, then t' is preferable to t. To model an assignment t which satisfies completely the constraint, we just have to set $\mu_{R_V}(t) = 1$, while to model an assignment which violates completely the constraint, and thus it is totally unacceptable, we have to set $\mu_{R_V}(t) = 0$. Therefore, we can say that the membership degree of an assignment gives us the *preference* for that assignment. In fuzzy constraints, preference 1 is the best one and preference 0 the worst one.

In classical constraint satisfaction, when we have a set of constraints we want all of them to be satisfied. Thus, we combine constraints by taking their conjunction. Although defined differently, also in the fuzzy framework constraints are naturally combined conjunctively. Since alternative semantics have been defined [95], this approach is called *conjunctive fuzzy constraints*. The *conjunctive combination* $R_V \otimes R_W$ of two fuzzy relations R_V and R_W is a new fuzzy relation $R_{V \cup W}$ defined as

$$\mu_{R_{V \cup W}}(t) = \min(\mu_{R_V}(t[V]), \mu_{R_W}(t[W])) \quad t \in \prod_{x_i \in V \cup W} D_i$$

We can now define the preference of a complete assignment, by performing a conjunction of all the fuzzy constraints. Given any complete assignment t, its membership degree, also called *satisfaction degree*, is defined as

$$\mu_t = (\underset{R_V \in C}{\otimes} R_V)(t) = \min_{R_V \in C} \mu_{R_V}(t[V])$$

Therefore, given a complete assignment of a fuzzy CN, the preference of such an assignment is computed by considering the preference given by each constraint for that assignment, and by taking the worst one of them. In this way, we associate to a complete assignment the preference for its worst feature. This is very natural for example when we are reasoning about critical applications, such as space or medical applications, where we want to be as cautious as possible. Then, given a scenario, we usually forget about its best features and just remember its bad parts, since these are the parts we are worried about.

A *solution* of a fuzzy CN is a complete assignment with satisfaction degree greater than 0. When we compare two complete assignments, the one with the highest preference is considered to be better. Thus, the *optimal solution* of a fuzzy CN is the complete assignment whose membership degree is maximum over all complete assignments, that is,

$$\max_{t \in \prod_{x_i \in X} D_i} \min_{R_V \in C} \mu_{R_V}(t[V])$$

Going back to the medical application field, consider the situation where somebody has to undergo a medical treatment and the doctor proposes two different treatments. Each proposal is judged by considering all its features (pros and cons) and then the two proposals are compared. According to the fuzzy framework, the judgement on each proposal will be based on its worst consequence, and the proposal where such a worst consequence is less bad will be chosen. Note that this way of reasoning implies that the actual values of the membership degrees used in the fuzzy constraints are not really significant: only the relative position of each membership degree with respect to others matters in order to identify how assignments are ranked.

The fuzzy framework properly generalizes classical constraints, which are just fuzzy constraints with membership degrees 0 and 1 (that is, each assignment either totally satisfies or totally violates a constraint). So it is not surprising that, as for classical constraints, also solving fuzzy CNs is a difficult task. In fact, the task of deciding whether the best satisfaction degree (among all solutions) is larger than a given value is NP-complete, while the task of finding an optimal solution is NP-hard.

A framework which is closely related to the fuzzy one is the *possibilistic constraint framework* [99], where priorities are associated to constraints and the aim is to find an assignment which minimizes the priority of the most important violated constraint. This defines a min-max optimization task dual to the max-min task of fuzzy constraints (by just using an order inversion over membership degrees), but the two frameworks have otherwise the same expressive power. As usual for fuzzy sets, other operators besides min have also been considered for fuzzy constraint aggregation (see work by [95]), which are useful in domains where a less cautious way of reasoning is more natural.

A weakness of the conjunctive fuzzy constraint formalism is the very little discrimination between assignments induced by the min operator. In fact, assignments with the same worst preference are considered equally preferred. Consider two complete assignments t and t' of a problem with only two fuzzy constraints, and such that t satisfies these constraints with membership degrees 0.5 and 1.0 while t' satisfies them with degrees 0.5 and 0.5. Although t is obviously strictly preferable to t', the overall satisfaction degree of the two assignments are identical since $\min(0.5, 1.0) = \min(0.5, 0.5)$. A possible way to discriminate between such assignments is proposed in [47], which introduces the concept of *fuzzy lexicographic constraints*. The main idea is to consider not just the least preference value, but all the preference values when evaluating a complete assignment, and to sort such values in increasing order. When two complete assignments are compared, the two sorted preference lists are then compared lexicographically. If the least value is different, the assignment with the highest one is considered better. Otherwise, if the least value is the same, we pass to compare the next value in the increasing order, and so on. This means that assignment which have the same minimal preference, and which are thus judged equally preferable in the fuzzy framework, can now result one better than the other one. In the example above, $[0.5, 1.0]$ is strictly better than $[0.5, 0.5]$, since the least values are the same (that is, 0.5), but the next values (that is, 1 and 0.5) differ, and thus t is preferred.

9.2.2 Weighted Constraints

In many real-life problems, it is often natural to talk about costs or penalties rather than preferences. In fact, there are situations where we are more interested in the damages we get by not satisfying a constraint rather than in the advantages we obtain when we satisfy it. For example, when we want to use highways to get to a different city, we may want to find the itinerary with minimum overall cost. Also, when we want to put together a PC by buying all its parts, we want to find the combination of parts which has minimum price. A natural way to extend the classical constraint formalism to deal with these situations consists of associating a certain penalty or cost to each constraint, to be paid when the constraint is violated.

A *weighted constraint network* (weighted CN) is a triple $\langle X, D, C \rangle$, where X and D are the set of variables and their domains defined as in classical CNs, and C is a set of weighted constraints. A *weighted constraint* $\langle c, w \rangle$ is just a classical constraint c, plus a weight w (over natural, integer, or real numbers).

The *cost* of an assignment t is the sum of all $w(c)$, for all constraints c which are violated by t. An *optimal solution* is a complete assignment t with minimal cost. In the particular case when all penalties are equal to one, this is called the MAXCSP problem [48]. In fact, in this case the task consists of finding an assignment where the number of violated constraints is minimal, which is equivalent to say that the number of satisfied constraints is maximal. Moreover, if constraints are clauses over propositional variables, this becomes the well-known MAXSAT problem [85].

Originally considered in [101], this framework has been since then refined to include the fact that beyond a (possibly infinite) threshold k, costs are considered as unacceptable [65]. A *k-weighted constraint network* (k-weighted CN) is a 4-tuple $\langle X, D, C, k \rangle$ where X and D are the set of variables and their domains defined as in classical CNs, C is a set of k-weighted constraints and k is an integer. A *k-weighted constraint* $f_V \in C$ with scope V maps tuples defined on V to integers in $[0, k]$, that is,

$$f_V : \prod_{x_j \in V} D_j \quad \rightarrow \quad [0, k]$$

A *solution* is a complete assignment with cost lower than k. An *optimal solution* is a solution with minimal cost. If we define the k-bounded sum of two integers a and b as $a +^k b = \min\{a + b, k\}$, then the cost of a complete assignment t is defined as the bounded sum of all the costs obtained by applying each constraint to the projection of t on the scope of the constraint. A classical CN can be seen as a k-weighted CN where only costs 0 and k are used.

A closely related framework is the one using the so-called *probabilistic constraint* [46], whose aim is to model constraint problems where the presence of the constraints in the real-life scenario that we want to model is uncertain. Each constraint is associated to a probability that it is present in the real-life scenario. Assuming that the events (machine break, weather issues, etc.) that make the constraints present or not are independent, each constraint R can be associated with a probability p_R of its presence. The probability that a given assignment is a solution of the (unknown) real-life problem can then be computed by multiplying the probabilities that all the violated constraints are not present in the problem, that is, $\prod(1 - p_R)$.

It is easy to transform probabilities into additive costs by taking their logarithm and this allows us to reduce any probabilistic constraint instance to a weighted constraint instance [100]. Notice however that probabilistic constraints are similar to fuzzy constraints, since in both cases the values associated to the constraints are between 0 and 1, and better solutions have higher values. The main difference is that, while in fuzzy constraints the evaluation of a solution is the minimum value (over all the constraints), in probabilistic constraints it is the product of all the values.

Weighted constraints are among the most expressive soft constraint frameworks, in the sense that the task of finding an optimal solution for possibilistic, lexicographic or probabilistic frameworks can be efficiently (that is, in polynomial time) reduced to the task of finding an optimal solution for a weighted constraint instance [100].

9.3 Generic Frameworks

If we consider the specific frameworks described in the previous Section, it is easy to observe that they all follow a common structure: given a complete assignment, each constraint specifies to what extent it is satisfied (or violated) by that assignment by using a specific scale. Then, the overall degree of satisfaction (or violation) of the assignment is obtained by combining these elementary degrees of satisfaction (or violation). An optimal solution is the complete assignment with an optimal satisfaction/violation degree. Therefore, choosing the operator used to perform the combination and an ordered satisfaction/violation scale is enough to define a specific framework.

Capturing these commonalities in a generic framework is desirable, since it allows us to design generic algorithms and properties instead of a myriad of apparently unrelated, but actually similar properties, theorems and algorithms. Moreover, this offers an environment where one can study the specific frameworks and better understand their relations.

Designing such a generic framework is a matter of compromise between generality and specificity. In fact, one would like to cover as many specific frameworks as possible, while at the same time to have enough specific features to be able to prove useful properties and build efficient algorithms. The main general formalisms that have been proposed in the literature are the ones based on *semiring-based constraints* [9, 11] and *valued constraints* [100]. We will now describe both of them and discuss their relationship.

9.3.1 Semiring-Based Constraints

Semiring-based constraints rely on a simple algebraic structure, called a *c-semiring* since it is very similar to a semiring, to formalize the notion of *satisfaction degrees*, or *preference levels*. The structure is specified by a set E of satisfaction degrees, where two binary operators are defined: $\times_s$ specifies how to combine preferences, while $+_s$ is used to induce a partial ordering (actually a lattice) on E. Additional axioms, including the usual semiring axioms, are added to precisely capture the notion of satisfaction degrees in soft constraints.

A *c-semiring* is a 5-tuple $\langle E, +_s, \times_s, 0, 1 \rangle$ such that:

- E is a set, $0 \in E$, $1 \in E$.

- $+_s$ is an operator closed in E, associative, commutative and idempotent for which 0 is a neutral element and 1 an annihilator.

- $\times_s$ is an operator closed in E, associative and commutative for which 0 is an annihilator and 1 a neutral element.

- $\times_s$ distributes over $+_s$.

The minimum level 0 is used to capture the notion of absolute non-satisfaction, which is typical of hard constraints. Since a single complete unsatisfaction is unacceptable, 0 must be an annihilator for $\times_s$. This means that, when combining a completely violated constraint with a constraint which is satisfied at some level, we get a complete violation. Conversely, a complete satisfaction should not hamper the overall satisfaction degree, which explains why 1 is a neutral element for $\times_s$. In fact, this means that, when we combine a completely satisfied constraint and a constraint which is satisfied at some level l, we get exactly l. Moreover, since the overall satisfaction should not depend on the way elementary satisfactions are combined, combination (that is, $\times_s$) is required to be commutative and associative.

To define the ordering over the preference levels, operator $+_s$ is used: if $a +_s b = b$, it means that b is preferred to a, and we write this as $b \succeq_s a$. If $a +_s b = c$, and c is different from both a and b, then we say that a and b are incomparable. To make sure that this ordering has the right properties, operator $+_s$ is required to be associative, commutative and idempotent. This generates a partial order, and more precisely a lattice. In all cases, $a +_s b$ is the least upper bound of a and b in the lattice $\langle E, \succeq_s \rangle$. The fact that 1 (resp. 0) is a neutral (resp. annihilator) element for $+_s$ follows from the fact that it is a maximum (resp. minimum) element for $\succeq_s$.

Notice that the possible presence of incomparable elements means that we can choose a scale which is not totally ordered. This is useful for example when we need to reason with more than one optimization criterion, since in this case there could be situations which are naturally not comparable. For example, consider a problem which models the possible routes from one city to another one, either by using highways or roads, and assume we want to minimize cost and time, while at the same time getting the best view of the landscape. Then, it could be that a route using highways is bad in terms of cost and view, but reduces time. On the other hand, a route with roads could cost nothing and give some nice views, but could take much longer. Then these two routes would be modelled as incomparable, and imposing an order over them would be unnatural.

Finally, assume that a is better than b, and consider two complete assignments, one that satisfies a constraint at level a and the other one that satisfies the same constraint at level b. Then, if all the other constraints are satisfied equally by the two assignments, it is reasonable to expect that the assignment satisfying at level a is overall better than the one satisfying at level b. For comparable a and b, this is equivalent to saying that $(a \times_s c) +_s (b \times_s c) = (a +_s b) \times_s c$ i.e., that $\times_s$ distributes over $+_s$. In a c-semiring, this property is required in all cases, even if a and b are incomparable.

Compared to a classical semiring structure, the additional properties required by a c-semiring are the idempotency of $+_s$ (to capture a lattice ordering) and the existence of a minimum and a maximum element (to capture hard constraints). A c-semiring S is said idempotent iff $\times_s$ is idempotent ($a \times_s a = a$). In this case, $a \times_s b$ is the greatest lower bound of a and b in the distributive lattice $\langle E, \succeq_s \rangle$. Examples of idempotent operators are min, max and $\cap$.

A semiring constraint network is then a constraint network where each constraint maps the assignments of its variables to values in the c-semiring.

A *semiring constraint network* (semiring CN) is a tuple $\langle X, D, C, S \rangle$ where:

- $X = \{x_1, \ldots, x_n\}$ is a finite set of n variables.

- $D = \{D_1, \ldots, D_n\}$ is the collection of the domains of the variables in X such that D_i is the domain of x_i.

- C is a finite set of soft constraints. A soft constraint is a function f on a sequence of variables $V \subseteq X$, called the scope of the constraint, such that f maps assignments (of variables in V to values in their domains) to to semiring values, that is $f : \prod_{x_i \in V} D_i \rightarrow E$. Thus a soft constraint can be viewed as a pair $\langle f, V \rangle$ also written as f_V.

- $S = \langle E, +_s, \times_s, \mathbf{0}, \mathbf{1} \rangle$ is a c-semiring.

The *consistency level* of a complete assignment t, $val_s(t)$, is obtained by combining the individual levels of each constraint, that is,

$$val_s(t) = \underset{f_V \in C}{\times_s} f_V(t[V])$$

An *optimal solution* is a complete assignment with a consistency level higher than, equal to or incomparable with the consistency level of any other complete assignment. Because the order $\succ_s$ may be partial, the optimal solutions of a semiring CN may have different, but incomparable consistency levels.

Solving a semiring CN is a difficult task. Since semiring-based constraints properly generalize classical constraints, it is easy to prove that this task is NP-hard. If the computation of $a \times_s b$ and $a +_s b$ are time-polynomial in the size of their arguments (that is, a and b), deciding if the consistency level of a network is higher than a given threshold is an NP-complete task.

9.3.2 Valued Constraints

Valued constraints [100] are an alternative to semiring-based constraints. More precisely, one can show that valued constraints can model exactly the same scenarios as *totally ordered* semiring-based constraints. In this Section, we define precisely valued constraints and show their relation to semiring-based constraints.

Valued constraints rely on an algebraic structure called a *valuation structure*, related to a monoid. A first difference between valuation structures and c-semirings is that elements of a valuation structure represent *violation degrees* instead of satisfaction degrees, so the ordering scale is reversed. The only truly significant difference is the use of a total order $\preceq_v$ to compare such degrees. For this reason, only one operator, written $\oplus$, is needed to define how valuations combine. It plays the same role as $\times_s$ in c-semirings.

A *valuation structure* is a 5-tuple $\langle E, \oplus, \preceq_v, \bot, \top \rangle$ such that:

- E is a set, whose elements are called valuations, totally ordered by $\preceq_v$, with a maximum element $\top \in E$ and a minimum element $\bot \in E$.

- E is closed under a binary operation $\oplus$ that satisfies:

  - $\forall a, b \in E, (a \oplus b) = (b \oplus a)$. (commutativity)
  - $\forall a, b, c \in E, (a \oplus (b \oplus c)) = ((a \oplus b) \oplus c)$. (associativity)
  - $\forall a, b, c \in E, (a \preceq_v b) \rightarrow ((a \oplus c) \preceq_v (b \oplus c))$. (monotonicity)

- $\forall a \in E, (a \oplus \bot) = a.$ (neutral element)

- $\forall a \in E, (a \oplus \top) = \top.$ (annihilator)

The monotonicity axiom, which is a refinement of the distributivity axiom of c-semiring (see later), is easier to justify, since it simply says that one increased violation cannot yield an overall smaller combined violation. Other axioms have exact replicates in c-semirings.

This structure can be described as a positive totally ordered commutative monoid, a structure also known as a positive *tomonoid* [44]. When E is restricted to $[0, 1]$, this is also known in uncertainty reasoning as a triangular co-norm [61]. It is well known that this axiom set is not minimal in the sense that the annihilator axiom is actually implied by the rest $((\bot \oplus \top) = \top$ (neutral), $(\bot \oplus \top) \preccurlyeq_v (a \oplus \top)$ (minimum). Since $\top$ is maximum, we derive $(a \oplus \top) = \top$). A valuation structure S is idempotent iff $\oplus$ idempotent ($a \oplus a = a$

A *valued constraint network* (valued CN) is otherwise defined as a semiring CN except that a valuation structure replaces the c-semiring. We now show that valuation structures precisely capture the same structures as totally ordered c-semirings. To do this, we show how to transform valuation structures in equivalent totally ordered c-semirings, and vice-versa. Consider a valuation structure $S = \langle E, \oplus, \preccurlyeq_v, \bot, \top \rangle$. We define $S' = \langle E, +_s, \times_s, \mathbf{0}, \mathbf{1} \rangle$ by choosing $\mathbf{0} = \top$, $\mathbf{1} = \bot$, $\times_s = \oplus$ and by defining $a +_s b = \min_{\preccurlyeq_v}\{a, b\}$. It is easy to show that S' is a c-semiring. Then, any semiring CN defined over S' is a valued CN over S, and the two networks are equivalent, which means that, given a complete assignment, they associate to it the same preference/violation level. Conversely, consider a *totally ordered* c-semiring $S = \langle E, +_s, \times_s, \mathbf{0}, \mathbf{1} \rangle$ and define $S' = \langle E, \oplus, \preccurlyeq_v, \bot, \top \rangle$ where $\bot = \mathbf{1}$, $\top = \mathbf{0}$, $\oplus = \times_s$ and $a \preccurlyeq_v b$ iff $a +_s b = a$. It is easy to check that S' is a valuation structure. Any valued CN over S' is an equivalent semiring CN over S. This shows that the assumption of a total order is sufficient (and obviously necessary) to reduce semiring CNs to valued CNs (see [11] for more details).

9.3.3 Fundamental Operations on Soft Constraints

When processing soft constraints to find an optimal solution, there are two operations which are repeatedly used. They are called *combination* and *projection*. Combination is used, as the word says, to combine two or more constraints and obtain a new constraint which gives all the information of the original ones. On the other hand, projection is used to eliminate one or more variables from a constraint, obtaining a new constraint which gives all the information of the original one on the remaining variables.

Consider a soft constraint network (soft CN) $\langle X, D, C, S \rangle$ and two soft constraints f_V and $f'_{V'}$. Then, their *combination*, $f_V \bowtie f'_{V'}$, is the constraint $g_{V \cup V'}$ where $g(t) = f(t[V]) \times_s f'(t[V'])$. Moreover, given a constraint f_V and a set of variables $W \subseteq V$, its *projection* over W, written $f_V[W]$, is the constraint g_W defined as

$$g(t) = \sum_{t' \mid t'[W]=t} {}^{+_s} f(t')$$

In particular, when $V - W = \{x\}$, the projection over W is written $f_V[-x]$, an operation also called projecting out x from f_V.

Notice that the combination of all the constraints of a network, $\bowtie_{f \in C} f$, is a soft constraint that associates to each complete assignment its preference level $val_s(t)$. The projection of this constraint on the empty set of variables is then a constraint of zero arity $(\bowtie_{f \in C} f)[\varnothing]$ such that it is precisely equal to the level of consistency of the network.

The notion of solution of a soft CN, which has been informally stated in earlier sections, can now be defined formally using the above notions of projection and combination. A *solution* of a soft CN $\mathcal{N} = \langle X, D, C, S \rangle$ is a complete assignment t such that $(\bowtie_{f \in C} f)(t) \neq \mathbf{0}$. An *optimal solution* t is a solution such that there is no other solution t' that satisfies $val(t') \succ_s val(t)$.

As for classical CNs, the interactions between variables in a soft CN can be represented by an hyper-graph whose vertices represent variables and where an hyper-edge connects all the variables that appear in the scope of a constraint.

The *micro-structure* of a soft CN $\langle X, D, C, S \rangle$ is defined as an hyper-graph with one vertex for every value of the domain of every variable in X. For every constraint $f_V \in C$ and for every assignment t over V such that $f(t) \neq \mathbf{1}$, a labelled hyper-edge connects all the vertices that represent the values in t. The label on the hyper-edge is $f(t)$. For simplicity, if $f(t) = \mathbf{0}$ (that is, if the tuple is completely forbidden), the label may be omitted. If $f(t) = \mathbf{1}$ then the edge can be omitted. Note that this convention is inconsistent with the classical CSP representation where an absence of edge represents a forbidden tuple. When all constraints are binary, the micro-structure is a graph.

In semiring-based (or valued) constraints, $\times_s$ (or $\oplus$) is always monotonic. However, when it is strictly monotonic (that is, $\forall a, b, c \in E, (a \succ_s c), (b \neq \mathbf{0})$ then $(a \times_s b) \succ_s (c \times_s b)$), then S will be said to be strictly monotonic. If we consider two complete assignments t and t' such that for all $f_V \in C$, $f_V(t) \succeq_s f_V(t') \neq \mathbf{0}$ and for some $g_W \in C, g_W(t) \succ_s g_W(t')$, strict monotonicity guarantees that t will be preferred to t' *i.e*, $val(t) \succ_s val(t')$. This is therefore an attractive property from a rationality point of view. Note that strict monotonicity is incompatible with idempotency as soon as $|E| > 2$ [100].

9.4 Relations among Soft Constraint Frameworks

In previous sections we have defined several frameworks for modelling soft constraints, both generic and specific. Here we relate the two generic frameworks, and present the specific frameworks as particular instances of the generic ones. We also analyze their relations with other preference formalisms.

9.4.1 Comparison Between the Generic Frameworks

As noticed, semiring-based and valued constraints are very strictly related: results obtained in the semiring framework apply to the valued framework, and results obtained in the valued framework apply to the subclass of totally ordered semiring-based constraints. Apart from this semantic difference, syntactically the only (possibly disturbing) difference is that the semiring framework maximizes a satisfaction level while the valued framework minimizes a violation level.

Actually, the two frameworks are so close that we will use either of them depending on the context. Because of its generality, fundamental definitions and notions will be written in the semiring framework. For algorithms, the valued formalism will be used for simplicity and consistency with published papers. Generalization to the semiring level will be mentioned.

Semiring	$\times_s$	$+_s$	$\succeq_s$	**0**	**1**	ub_s	lb_s
Valued	$\oplus$	$\min_v$	$\preccurlyeq_v$	$\top$	$\bot$	lb_v	ub_v

Table 9.1: Translation between valued and semiring-based notations. lb_v and ub_v stand for possible lower bounds (resp., upper bounds) on violation degrees in the valued notation, which correspond respectively to upper and lower bounds on satisfaction degrees in the semiring notation.

To make the simple connection between the two framework very clear, remember that in the semiring framework, satisfaction levels are maximized and handled using $\times_s$, $+_s$ $\succeq_s$, **0**, and **1**. In the valued-based one, violation levels are minimized and handled using $\oplus$ $\min_v$, $\preccurlyeq_v$, $\top$ and $\bot$. Table 9.1 gives a simple reminder on how to pass from one notation to the other one.

9.4.2   Specific Frameworks as Soft Constraint Networks

Table 9.2 outlines the choices of E, $+_s$, and $\times_s$ needed to instantiate the semiring-based and the valued constraint formalism to get the previously outlined specific frameworks. For example, for fuzzy constraints, the membership degrees of fuzzy relations belong to $[0,1]$ and are combined with the operator min, and an optimal assignment maximizes the combined degree (*i.e.*, the largest one is preferred). The most preferred degree is therefore 1 and the worst one is 0. The corresponding semiring structure thus has $E = [0,1]$ $\times_s = \min$, $+_s = \max$ (which means $\succeq_s = \geq$).

Since all the structures in this table are totally ordered, they also are instances of the valued formalism. For example, fuzzy constraints are valued constraints which use the same set E and $\oplus = \min$ (according to the usual order over $[0,1]$). The maximum element is $\top = 0$ and the minimum element $\bot = 1$ which shows how scales are inverted in valued and semiring constraints.

For k-weighted constraints, costs are elements of $\{0,\ldots,k\}$ (where k is the maximal cost) and are combined through the bounded addition $+^k$. A minimum cost is preferred. The most preferred degree is therefore 0 and the worst one is k. The corresponding semiring structure therefore has $E = \{0,k\}$, $\times_s = +^k$, $+_s = \min$ (which means $\succeq_s = \leq$). The extreme elements are defined by $\mathbf{1} = 0$ and $\mathbf{0} = k$. In this case, the corresponding valuation structure uses the same set E and $\oplus = +^k$. The maximum element is $\top = k$ and the minimum element is $\bot = 0$.

Semiring	E	$\times_s$	$+_s$	$\succeq_s$	**0**	**1**
Classical	$\{t,f\}$	$\wedge$	$\vee$	$t \succeq_s f$	f	t
Fuzzy	$[0,1]$	min	max	$\geq$	0	1
k-weighted	$\{0,\ldots,k\}$	$+^k$	min	$\leq$	k	0
Probabilistic	$[0,1]$	xy	max	$\geq$	1	0
Valued	E	$\oplus$	$\min_v$	$\preccurlyeq_v$	$\top$	$\bot$

Table 9.2: Different specific frameworks modelled as c-semirings.

As noted above, the semiring framework allows one also to model partially ordered structures such as those induced by multi-criteria optimization. This follows directly from the fact that the product of two c-semirings is a c-semiring [10]. Other partially ordered structures are those based on on sets inclusion and intersection. For more examples and details, see [9, 100, 10, 11]. Note that, although valued CNs are incapable of directly dealing with multiple criteria, those can simply be handled by using multiple valuation structures simultaneously.

9.4.3 Fuzzy and Classical Constraints

Fuzzy constraints are the only totally ordered semiring instance with a combination operator (that is, min) which is idempotent [100]. This gives this framework a very strong connection with classical constraints, since classical constraints can be seen as fuzzy constraints on a totally ordered structures with just two preference values. Consider a conjunctive fuzzy CN $\mathcal{P} = \langle X, D, C \rangle$ and the set of all the different membership degrees used in all the fuzzy relations, defined as $F = \bigcup_{R_V \in C} (\cup_{t \in \prod_{x_j \in V} D_j} \mu_{R_V}(t))$. $\mathcal{P}$ can be decomposed into $|F|$ different classical CNs. For each level $\alpha \in F$, there is one classical CN $\mathcal{P}^\alpha = \langle X, D, C^\alpha \rangle$ with the same variables and domains as in $\mathcal{P}$. For each fuzzy constraint $f \in C$, C^α has a corresponding hard constraint f^α whose relation contains only the assignments that satisfy f with a degree higher or equal to α. This is called the α-cut of the fuzzy set [42].

With increasing values of α, each constraint in the classical CN $\mathcal{P}^\alpha$ allows less and less combinations of values. Let α^* be the maximum α such that $\mathcal{P}^\alpha$ is consistent. Then it is easy to show that the solutions of $\mathcal{P}^{\alpha^*}$ are the optimal solutions of the given fuzzy CN $\mathcal{P}$. In practice, using a dichotomic search approach, the membership degree α^* and an associated optimal solution can easily be identified by solving $O(\log(|F|))$ classical CNs.

This simple decomposition process can actually be used to extend most results on classical constraint processing (such as polynomial classes) to fuzzy constraint processing, as long as these results rely on properties preserved by this slicing approach.

9.4.4 Relations with Other AI Preference Formalisms

Soft constraints offer a very general framework to express both required and preferred properties in a combinatorial setting. However, they also make some assumptions. First, that the soft constraint statements are quantitative, that is, refer to a scale of elements which are ordered and which represent the preferences. Second, that it is reasonably easy to define the operations to combine and to aggregate preference levels. Other preference formalisms do not make these assumptions but pose different restrictions. Here we discuss the relation between soft constraints and other AI formalisms developed with a similar aim.

Partial constraint satisfaction

Inside the constraint community itself, several alternative generic formalisms have been proposed to combine constraint representation and preferences. The notion of *partial constraint satisfaction* [49, 48] was a pioneering attempt to formalize the notion of soft constraints. In order to find a solution for an over-constrained classical CN, partial constraint satisfaction tries to identify another classical CN which is both consistent and as *close* as possible to the original one. The space of networks considered to find this consistent network is defined using constraint relaxations (which amount, for example, at forgetting constraints, or at simply adding extra authorized combinations to the original ones) together with a specific metric, which is needed to identify a nearest network. The framework is very general and not totally formalized so that it cannot be truly related to semiring-based or valued constraints. It has been mainly illustrated by examples, among which a simplified variant of weighted constraint satisfaction has received the most attention.

Hierarchical constraint logic programming

In the framework of constraint logic programming, the notion of constraint hierarchies and HCLP (Hierarchical Constraint Logic Programming [13, 112]) also allows for soft constraint expressions. Here, each constraint is assigned a level (also called a *strength*) in a totally ordered hierarchy, among which the strongest level is used for hard constraints.

Once its variables are assigned, each constraint generates a cost (called an *error*) in $\mathbb{R}^+$. A solution is an assignment to all the variables which satisfies all hard constraints completely (that is, with error 0). An optimal solution is a solution which satisfies the other constraints as much as possible.

To choose between possible solutions, a *comparator* is used to eliminate assignments which are dominated. There is much freedom in the definition of comparators which again makes the comparison with semiring-based or valued constraints difficult. The so-called *global comparators* have been the most studied. In this case, at each level of the hierarchy, the errors generated by all the constraints are combined using a specific *combining function*. Then, a lexicographic order on the sequence of combined errors for successive levels in the hierarchy is used to order possible solutions.

For all existing proposals of combining functions (such as the sum of weighted errors, the maximum of weighted errors, or the sum of square of weighted errors), it is possible to show that HCLP reduces to valued and weighted CNs. However, the general definition of combining functions does not forbid the use of functions that would definitely violate fundamental semiring or valued constraint axioms (such as monotonicity).

MaxSAT

SAT (for SATisfiability) is the problem of satisfying a set of clauses in propositional logic. Each clause is a disjunction of literals, and each literal is either a variable or a negated variable. For example, a clause can be $x \vee not(y) \vee not(z)$. Satisfying a clause means giving values (either *true* or *false*) to its variables such that the clause has value *true* MAXSAT is the problem of maximizing the number of satisfied clauses.

Since the satisfiability problem in propositional logic (SAT) is a subcase of the constraint satisfaction problem using boolean variables and clauses, the problem MAXSAT [85] is clearly a particular case of the weighted constraint satisfaction problem. See [31, 55] for successful illustrations of this.

Bayesian nets

Outside the world of constraints, Bayesian networks [86] can also be considered as specific soft constraint problems where the constraints are conditional probability tables (satisfying extra properties) using $[0, 1]$ as the semiring values, multiplication as $\times_s$ and the usual total ordering on $[0, 1]$. The Most Probable Explanation (MPE) task is then equivalent to looking for an optimal solution on such problems.

CP-nets

Conditional preferences networks (CP-nets) [14] have been recently proposed to capture preferences. Beyond the usual variables and domains of constraint problems, CP-nets use conditional preferences tables to specify a total preference order on the domain of each variable depending on the values of a set of other variables. Such a set can also be empty, thus there are also variables whose preference order is not conditional on the values of other variables.

The syntax to specify a preference order over variable y given the values of variables $x_1, \ldots, x_n$ is usually written as the preference statement

$$x_1 = v_1, \ldots, x_n = v_n : y = w_1 \succ \ldots \succ y = w_k$$

where $w_1, \ldots, w_k$ are the elements in the domain of y. CP-nets are usually graphically represented by a hyper-graph, where nodes represent variables and there is one hyper-arc for each conditional preference statement. A CP-net is said to be acyclic if such a hyper-graph does not have cycles.

Preference statements in CP-nets are interpreted under the so-called *ceteris paribus* interpretation: if $x_1 = v_1, \ldots, x_n = v_n$, all else being equal, we prefer $y = w_i$ to $y = w_j$ if $i < j$. The change of value for y from w_i to w_j is then called a *worsening flip*.

A complete assignment t to the variables of a CP-net is preferred to another one, say t', if it is possible to obtain t' from t via a sequence of worsening flips. An optimal solution is then a complete assignment such that no other assignment is preferred to it. This semantics produces in general a preorder over the set of all complete assignments.

Given an arbitrary CP-net (acyclic or not), we can generate a classical CN such that its set of solutions is exactly the set of preferred solutions of the CP-net [41]. It is enough to take, for each preference statement of the form $x_1 = v_1, \ldots, x_n = v_n : y = w_1 \succ \ldots \succ y = w_k$, the constraint $x_1 = v_1, \ldots, x_n = v_n \Rightarrow y = w_1$. This means that, if we are just interested in the set of optimal solutions, classical constraints are at least as expressive as CP-nets.

However, this is not true if we are interested in maintaining the solution ordering. In this respect, CP-nets and soft constraints are incomparable since each can do something that the other one cannot do. More precisely, dominance testing (that is, comparing two complete assignments to decide which is preferred (if any)) is is an NP-complete task [40] in CP-nets. On the contrary, it is polynomial in soft constraints (if we assume $\times_s$ and $+_s$ to be polynomially computable). Thus, unless P=NP, it is not possible to generate in polynomial time a soft CN which has the same solution ordering of a given CP-net. On the other hand, given any soft CN, it is not always possible to generate a CP-net with the same ordering. This depends on the fact that CP-nets cannot represent all possible preorders, but just some of them. For example, no CP-net can generate a solution ordering where two solutions which differ for just one flip are not ordered. On the other hand, soft CNs can represent any partial order over solutions. Thus, when we are interested in the solution ordering, CP-nets and soft constraints are incomparable. The same holds also when CP-nets are augmented with a set of hard constraints.

9.4.5   Relationship with Constraint Optimization

In most implementations of classical constraint systems (see Chapter 12, 13 and 14), there are often primitives to optimize a criterion represented by one variable whose domain is totally ordered (typically an integer domain variable). For example, we may have a variable x which is linked to other variables by a constraint of the form $x = a_1.x_1 + \ldots + a_n.x_n$ representing an objective function to be optimized.

Since the central task in soft constraints is to find an assignment that optimizes a specific criterion, it is natural to consider possible formulations of soft constraint problems as classical constraint problems with a specific variable representing the optimized criterion. This can indeed be achieved.

Consider a totally ordered soft CN $\langle X, D, C, S \rangle$. We now generate a classical CN which has the variables in X plus one new variable x_V for each constraint $f_V \in C$ These extra variables have domain E (that is, the set of possible semiring values). Each original constraint $f_V \in C$ is then transformed into a classical constraint $c_{V'}$ whose scope is $V' = V \cup \{x_V\}$. The set of allowed tuples of $c_{V'}$ is obtained by taking every tuple t of the Cartesian product of the domains of the variables in V extended to V' with the semiring value $f_V(t)$.

Finally, one extra variable x_c is introduced to represent the criterion. This variable is connected to all the x_V variables using one constraint which states that $\prod_s x_V = x_c$ where $\prod_s$ uses the semiring operator $\times_s$. It is easy to check that for any assignment t of X, the only possible value for x_c is the semiring value of t. Therefore, maximizing the value of x_c leads to an optimal solution. This transformation has been first proposed in a simplified form by [87]. It is also used to model MAXSAT problems as pseudo-Boolean problems in [31].

Extra attention should be taken in practice to avoid infinite domains for the variables x_V. It is usually easy to bound them. As such, the transformation requires the addition of extra variables and the use of constraints of increased arities which may lead to limited efficiency (see Section 9.6.2 and [74, 31] for example) and strongly modifies the problem structure.

Conversely, any classical CN with an optimization criterion can obviously be represented as a soft CN: hard constraints are kept and the criterion can be transformed in a soft constraint which involves all the variables influencing the criterion.

9.4.6   Some Representational Issues

In the soft constraint models presented here, we assume that constraints are cost functions mapping tuples of domain values to semiring values. However, in actual instances, the granularity of preferences may be coarser. It is easy to see that one may decide to associate semiring values also to other kinds of objects in a constraint problem:

- Constraints: a fixed value is used when the constraint is violated, otherwise $\mathbf{1}$ is used. This scheme has been initially used in [100] for valued CNs. It is shown to be as expressive as the tuple-based scheme in [11].

- Values: only unary soft constraints are present. As shown in [66], this is surprisingly as expressive as the tuple-based scheme (by going to the dual representation) using only hard binary constraints.

- Variables: in this case, the value represents how much we care that the variable is assigned. This can be simulated using soft constraints by adding one extra value in the variable domain, which is compatible with all values of all other variables. A unary soft constraint is then used to associate a semiring level to the value.

9.5 Search

For easiness of presentation, in this Section we restrict ourselves to valued constraints, that is, *totally ordered* c-semiring structures. At the end, we will discuss how the presented algorithms can be extended to *partially ordered* c-semirings.

As in the classical case, perhaps the most direct way to solve a soft CN is searching in its state space, exploring the set of all possible assignments. Since an optimal solution is an assignment that minimizes the violation degree (or equivalently, maximizes the satisfaction degree), solving optimally a soft CN is an optimization problem, thus harder than solving classical CNs.

As usual, we differentiate between two main families of search strategies: systematic search and local search. *Systematic search* visits each state that could be a solution, or skips only states that are shown to be dominated by others, so it is always able to find an optimal solution. *Local search* does not guarantee this behavior. When it terminates, after having exhausted resources (such as time available or a limit number of iterations), it reports the best solution found so far, but there is no guarantee that it is an optimal solution. To prove optimality, systematic algorithms are required, at the extra cost of longer running times with respect to local search. Systematic search algorithms often scale worse with problem size than local search algorithms. Nevertheless, algorithms from both families can nicely cooperate to solve soft CNs, as we will see in the following.

9.5.1 Systematic Search: Branch and Bound

The state space of the problem is explored as a tree, called *the search tree*, defined as follows. A node represents a subproblem, defined by the subset of unassigned variables, its domains and constraints not completely assigned. The root represents the whole problem, while leaves represent the empty problem. Node successors are produced by selecting an unassigned variable and generating as many successors as the number of values in the variable domain. Each arc connecting a node with its successors is labelled with one of those values, meaning that this value is assigned to the selected variable. A node successor contains a subproblem of the problem in its parent node, which is obtained by removing the variable just assigned. Each path in the tree (from the root to a node) represents an assignment. Since each node has a unique path from the root, there is a one-to-one correspondence between tree nodes and assignments. For this reason, we do not differentiate between them in the following.

Depth-first branch and bound (DFBB) performs a depth-first traversal of the search tree. It keeps two bounds, lb and ub. The *lower bound* at node t, $lb(t)$, is an underestimation of the violation degree of any complete assignment below t. The *upper bound* ub is the maximum violation degree that we are willing to accept. When $ub \preceq_v lb(t)$, the subtree rooted at t can be pruned because it contains no solution with violation degree lower than ub. If it finds a complete assignment with violation degree lower than ub, this violation degree becomes the new ub; after exhausting the tree, DFBB returns the current ub. Its time complexity is $O(d^n)$, while its space complexity is $O(nd)$.

Algorithm 9.1: Depth-first branch and bound

Function DFBB $(t : tuple, ub : level) : level$
   if $(|t| = n)$ **then return** $lb(t)$;
   else
       let x_i be an unassigned variable;
       foreach $a \in D_i$ **do**
          if $(lb(t \cup \{(x_i, a)\}) \prec_v ub)$ **then**
             $ub \leftarrow \min(ub, \text{DFBB}(t \cup \{(x_i, a)\}, ub))$;
       return ub;

The efficiency of DFBB depends largely on its pruning capacity, that relies on the quality of its bounds: the higher lb and the lower ub, the better DFBB performs, since it does more pruning, exploring a smaller part of the search tree. Many efforts have been made to improve (that is, to increase) the lower bound.

Given a node, we define P and F as the sets of assigned and unassigned variables at that node. Regarding constraints, C_P (resp., C_{PF}, C_F) is the set of of constraints whose variables are completely assigned (resp., partially assigned, unassigned) at that node. Obviously, at every node we have $X = P \cup F$ and $C = C_P \cup C_{PF} \cup C_F$.

In the context of k-weighted binary constraints, lower bounds can be computed using bounded sum and by setting $k = ub$. DFBB performs the bounded sum, by taking the minimum between ub and the recursive call DFBB. The simplest lower bound is

$$lb_1(t) = \sum_{f_V \in C_P} f_V(t[V])$$

where t is the assignment tuple corresponding to the current node. A more sophisticated lower bound, that we call lb_2, includes contributions from constraints in C_{PF}. It has been implemented in the *partial forward checking* (PFC) algorithm [48]. An *inconsistency count*, ic_{ja}, is the weight contribution from C_{PF} that will be added if the current partial solution is extended with (x_j, a). A lookahead phase (similar to the lookahead done by forward checking in classical constraints, adapted to the soft case), performs the propagation from the current assignment to the domains of unassigned variables. The formal definition of lb_2 is

$$lb_2(t) = \sum_{f_V \in C_P} f_V(t[V]) + \sum_{x_j \in F} \min_a ic_{ja}$$

Another lower bound, that we call lb_3, includes contributions from constraints in C_F. Assuming a static variable ordering, a *directed arc inconsistency count*, dac_{ja}, is the weight contribution from C_F that will be added if the current partial solution is extended to a complete one including (x_j, a). This contribution is computed from variables that are arc inconsistent (see Chapter 3) with (x_j, a) and appear after x_j in the ordering. lb_3 was first implemented using these counts [110], that were nicely combined with inconsistency counts in [67], producing the expression

$$lb_3(t) = \sum_{f_V \in C_P} f_V(t[V]) + \sum_{x_j \in F} \min_a (ic_{ja} + dac_{ja})$$

Since this implementation (that assumed binary constraints) was computing lb from summations on unassigned variables, constraints had to be directed to avoid counting more than once the same constraint. This was reflected in a static variable ordering. This limitation was relaxed in a more sophisticated implementation based on the directed constraint graph on unassigned variables G^F, able to reverse its directed arcs. The new expression for this lower bound is

$$lb_3(t) = \sum_{f_V \in C_P} f_V(t[V]) + \sum_{x_j \in F} \min_a (ic_{ja} + dac_{ja}(G^F))$$

The whole algorithm, called PFC-MRDAC [71], showed a substantial improvement in performance with respect to previous approaches. A range-based version of this algorithm, suitable for problems with large domains, appeared in [89].

An alternative lower bound, that we call lb_4, is presented within the *russian doll search* (RDS) algorithm [109]. Imagine that variables are assigned by following a static order $x_1, x_2, \ldots, x_n$ and assume that they have been assigned up to x_{i-1}. Subproblem i is then defined by variables $x_i, \ldots, x_n$ and constraints among them. A lower bound for the current node is

$$lb_4(t) = \sum_{f_V \in C_P} f_V(t[V]) + \sum_{x_j \in F} \min_a ic_{ja} + \min_{t'} \sum_{f_V \in C_F} f_V(t'[V]) \qquad t' \in \prod_{x_j \in F} D_j$$

where the third term (usually called rds_i) is the optimal cost of solving subproblem i. In RDS, one search is replaced by n searches on nested subproblems, each solving optimally subproblems $n, n-1, \ldots, 1$. Solving subproblem j generates rds_j; each rds_j is stored and later reused when solving subproblem $i < j$ to compute lower bounds at different tree levels: rds_{i+1} when assigning x_i, rds_{i+2} when assigning x_{i+1}, and so on.

Since two consecutive searches of RDS differ in one variable only, the *specialized RDS* approach (SRDS) [79], computes the optimal cost of the new subproblem for each value of the new variable. While RDS performs n independent searches, SRDS increases this number up to $n\,d$. SRDS is able to compute a higher lower bound than RDS (the contribution of solving subproblem i with value a for the new variable, rds_{ia}, can be combined with ic_{ia} and take the minimum of them). Despite of performing more searches, SRDS is often superior to RDS. A further extension was presented in [81].

Most lower bound implementations are based on counters associated with variables and they aggregate two elements: the global contribution of assigned variables, and individual contributions of unassigned variables. In addition, a third element can be included: contributions of disjoint subset of unassigned variables, not recorded in the individual contributions. This new form of lower bound computation was called *partition-based* [68]. A related approach [90] proposed the *conflict-set based* lower bound.

Most of the mentioned implementations assumed binary constraints. Their generalization to non-binary constraints were presented in [80] and [90]. These lower bounds can be easily generalized by replacing k-bounded sum $+^k$ by the generic $\oplus$ operator of valued constraints. These lower bounds are presented for pedagogical reasons, since most are subsumed by lower bounds based on soft local consistency, presented in Section 9.7.2.

9.5.2   Local Search

Local search algorithms perform generic optimization of scalar functions (see Chapter 5). Therefore, any local search algorithm is suitable to optimize the function $\oplus_{f_V \in C} f_V(t[V])$ where t is a complete assignment, providing that t surpasses the consistency level considered as unacceptable (if any). Several empirical investigations about the performance of different local search methods on over-constrained problems have been done. As an example, we mention the comparison between tabu search and a hill-climbing strategy based on min-conflicts plus random walk, that appears in [51].

When solving constraint networks, local search strategies are often enhanced with some kind of constraint propagation, to discard states that cannot be solutions and to rank states that still are solution candidates. This idea has been applied to explore efficiently large neighborhoods in local search [75]. A similar approach explores neighborhoods of variable size, using limited discrepancy search [76].

In combination with DFBB, local search can be of great help for computing the initial upper bound. As preprocessing, before DFBB starts, any local search method executed for a limited period of time may provide a solution. There is no guarantee that it will be an optimal solution, but its level is an upper bound of the level of an optimal one. The DFBB algorithm can take this upper bound as its initial ub value. A good ub improves DFBB performance, since it will allow pruning from earlier levels of the search tree.

Stochastic search is other strategy that has also been used for different applications. They are based on iterative sampling, sometimes enhanced with the bias of one [15, 17] or several heuristics [18].

9.5.3   Search in Partially Ordered Semirings

We restricted search strategies to totally ordered c-semirings. The reason for this limitation is easiness of presentation of the search algorithms. On a totally ordered c-semiring, solving soft CNs becomes a scalar optimization task. An optimal solution is a single assignment with an optimal level, and there is no other complete assignment with a better level, since all levels are comparable. In a partially ordered c-semiring, several non-dominated solutions with non-comparable levels may exist. This means that search algorithms have to keep the levels of all non-dominated solutions found, and use them to prune the search tree below the current partial solution. In other words, solving soft constraint requires algorithms which are, although conceptually related, more complex to present.

There exist approaches that deal with non-comparable solutions. For example, preference-based search is a general technique to speed up search by exploiting preferences over search decisions [56]. Such a technique can be extended also to deal with multiple optimization criteria. In [57], preferences are expressed over various optimization criteria, and the search strategy looks for solutions which satisfy at best the most important criteria first, obtaining both extreme and balanced, or Pareto-optimal, solutions.

9.6   Inference

For simplicity, in this Section, we restrict ourselves to valued CNs, that is *totally ordered* c-semiring structures.

As an alternative to search strategies, inference-based algorithms can also solve soft CNs. Before considering inference in soft constraints, let us first revisit inference in the classical case.

In a classical CN $\mathcal{P}$, a constraint c is said to be a consequence of $\mathcal{P}$ (or implied by $\mathcal{P}$) iff any solution of $\mathcal{P}$ satisfies c. It is also said to be redundant because c can be added to $\mathcal{P}$ without changing its set of solutions. Inference in $\mathcal{P}$ consists in computing and adding implied constraints, producing a network which is more explicit than $\mathcal{P}$ and hopefully easier to solve. If this process is always capable of producing the zero arity implied constraint $(\bowtie_{f \in C} f)[\varnothing]$ which gives the level of consistency of the network, then inference is said to be complete. Otherwise, inference is incomplete and it has to be complemented with search. For classical CN, adaptive consistency enforcing is complete while local consistency (arc or path consistency) enforcing is incomplete.

Inference in soft constraints keeps the same basic idea: adding constraints that will make the problem more explicit without changing the set of solutions nor their levels. However, with soft constraints, the addition of a new constraint to an existing network will typically change the distribution of levels on solutions. For this reason, inference becomes more complex than simply adding implied constraints. One cannot speak of redundant constraints and we prefer the "implied" terminology.

To properly define implication between soft constraints, we first define an ordering. The main idea is that one soft constraint is tighter or smaller than another one if its requirements are stronger than the ones of the other constraint.

Consider two soft constraints f_V and f'_W. We define the *constraint ordering* $\sqsubseteq$ as the following partial order: $f_V \sqsubseteq f'_W$ if and only if, for all tuples t over $V \cup W$, $f'_W(t[W]) \preccurlyeq_v f_V(t[V])$. If $f_V \sqsubseteq f'_W$ we say that f'_W is *implied by* f_V. Notice that as expected, any cost function with constant cost $\top$ (representing inconsistency) implies any other constraint. When $V = W$, if $f \sqsubseteq f'$ and $f' \sqsubseteq f$, then $f = f'$. This order between constraints can be extended to entire networks. For two soft CNs $\mathcal{N} = \langle X, D, C, S \rangle$ and $\mathcal{N}' = \langle X', D', C', S \rangle$, we say that $\mathcal{N} \sqsubseteq_V \mathcal{N}'$ if $(\bowtie_{f \in C} f)[V] \sqsubseteq (\bowtie_{f \in C'} f)[V]$. If $\mathcal{N} \sqsubseteq_V \mathcal{N}'$ and $\mathcal{N}' \sqsubseteq_V \mathcal{N}$, we say that $\mathcal{N}$ and $\mathcal{N}'$ are *equivalent* with respect to V and we write $\mathcal{N} \equiv_V \mathcal{N}'$. If $V = X = X'$ then we just say that $\mathcal{N}$ and $\mathcal{N}'$ are *equivalent*.

When the $\oplus$ operator is idempotent, any arbitrary implied constraint can be added to a soft CN, yielding an equivalent network. However, if there is a level α that violates idempotency (such that $\alpha \oplus \alpha \neq \alpha$), the new network will not be equivalent. For this reason, three different approaches to inference in soft constraint networks can be considered:

1. When the operator $\oplus$ is idempotent, it is possible, as in classical CNs, to saturate the network by directly adding implied constraints to it. The problem remains equivalent and increasingly explicit.

2. In any case, it is possible to remove the constraints which have been used to produce the implied constraint and to put the implied constraint instead. Under simple conditions, the problem will have the same optimum as before and will also be simplified.

3. It may be possible to add the implied constraint directly to the problem and then to *extract* it from the set of constraints which have been used to produce the implied constraint. This requires additional properties from the $\oplus$ operator, but it produces an equivalent problem and not simply one with the same optimum as in the previous case.

In the Section 9.6.1, we present bucket elimination and cluster tree elimination, two fundamental approaches to perform complete inference, by using the approach 2 to compute the level of a soft CN.

In the Section 9.6.2, we detail three approaches for incomplete inference. The first one (mini-buckets) uses the same approach as above, but fails to satisfy a simple condition on the implied constraint and therefore produces problems with a modified optimum. The next one uses the approach 1 to enforce local consistency, but is restricted to idempotent $\oplus$, and the last one uses the approach 3 to enforce local consistency on a large subclass of soft CNs. These two last approaches produce equivalent problems.

9.6.1 Complete Inference

The two algorithms we are going to detail now are direct operational extensions of existing algorithms in classical CNs: it suffices to use our extended definitions of combination and projection in the original algorithms (see Chapter 7) to obtain the extended algorithms, which work for arbitrary c-semirings. This class of algorithms can actually be applied to an even larger class of problems [102].

Bucket elimination

Bucket elimination (BE) [36, 34] is a complete inference algorithm which is able to compute all optimal solutions of a soft CN (as opposed to one optimal solution, as usually done by search strategies). It is basically the extension of the *adaptive consistency* (ADC) algorithm [38] to the soft case but it was already introduced in 1972 as *variable elimination* for cost function optimization in [7]. Before describing it, we have to introduce some concepts.

Given a soft CN, a corresponding *ordered constraint graph* $G(o)$ is the primal constraint graph plus an ordering $o = x_1, x_2, \ldots, x_n$ of its variables. The *induced graph* $G^*(o)$ is the graph obtained by processing the nodes of $G(o)$ from the last one to the first one: when processing x_i, all its neighbors that precede it in the ordering are connected together, forming a clique. The *induced width* of the ordering, $w^*(o)$, is the maximum number of preceding neighbors over all the nodes of the induced graph. The induced width of the graph w^* is the minimum induced width among the possible orderings. The *bucket* B_i of variable x_i is the set of constraints having x_i as the highest indexed variable in their scope.

BE works as follows. If $\mathcal{P}$ is a soft CN with n variables, the idea is to select one variable x_i and remove it from $\mathcal{P}$, producing a soft CN $\mathcal{P}'$ with the same optimal solutions as $\mathcal{P}$, but with $X - \{x_i\}$ variables. This step is called the elimination of variable x_i. Observe that $\mathcal{P}'$ has one less variable than $\mathcal{P}$. Applying the same strategy n times, we obtain a soft CN without variables, that produces the level of the optimal solution. A polynomial procedure allows us to recover one or all optimal solutions of $\mathcal{P}$.

To eliminate variable x_i, we have to replace all constraints that mention x_i by a new constraint that summarizes the effect of these constraints, but that does not include x_i This can be done by combining all constraints mentioning x_i and projecting out x_i from the resulting constraint. If variables are processed along the ordering o, from the last to the first one, the set of all constraints mentioning x_i is precisely the bucket B_i. The new constraint that summarizes the effect of B_i in the network, but it does not mention x_i is

$$g_i = (\underset{f \in B_i}{\bowtie} f)[-x_i]$$

where $[-x_i]$ means projecting over the scope of the new constraint minus x_i. The new soft CN is obtained from the previous one by removing x_i and replacing B_i with g_i. The level of the optimal solution of the new soft CN is equal to the level of the optimal solution of the previous one because, by construction, g_i compensates for the absence of B_i. We have obtained a new soft CN, with the same optimal solutions as the original one, but with one less variable.

BE works in two phases. First, it eliminates all variables one by one, from the last one to the first one in the ordering o. When eliminating the last variable, the level of the final zero arity constraint obtained is the level of the optimal solution. In the second phase, BE constructs an optimal solution by assigning variables from the first one to the last one in the ordering o, and by reusing the intermediate constraints built to replace buckets. Variable x_i is assigned the value that has the best extension of the current partial solution $x_1, \ldots, x_{i-1}$ with respect to B_i. The solution obtained in this way is an optimal one, with the level computed in the first phase.

BE has a time complexity of $O(n(2d)^{w^*+1})$ and a space complexity of $O(nd^{w^*})$ [34]. Both are exponential in w^*, the induced width of the constraint graph, which essentially measures the graph cyclicity. The high memory cost, that comes from the high arity of intermediate constraints g_i that have to be stored as tables in memory, is the main drawback of BE in practice. When the arity of the g_i constraints remains reasonable, BE can perform very well [73]. Different approaches have been made to enhance the applicability of BE, by decreasing its memory requirements. The interested reader can consult [96, 97].

Algorithm 9.2: Bucket Elimination

Function BE $((X : var\ set,\ D : dom\ set,\ C : constr\ set))$: *level*
    foreach $i = n, \ldots, 1$ **do**
        $B_i \leftarrow \{f_V \in C | x_i \in V\}$;
        $g_i \leftarrow (\bowtie_{f_V \in B_i} c)[-x_i]$;
        remove x_i from X, replace B_i by g_i in C;
    foreach $i = 1, \ldots, n$ **do**
        $x_i \leftarrow D_i$ value that is the best extension of $x_1, \ldots, x_i$ with respect to B_i;
    return g_1;

Cluster tree elimination

Let us consider the dual graph of a soft constraint network, where nodes represent constraints, and two nodes are connected by an edge if the corresponding constraints share some variable. In such a dual graph, we are interested in clustering the nodes in a way that makes the resulting structure a tree.

A *tree decomposition* of a soft CN $\langle X, D, C, S \rangle$ is a triplet $\langle T, \chi, \psi \rangle$, where $T = \langle V, E \rangle$ is a tree. χ and ψ are labelling functions which associate with each vertex $v \in V$ two sets, $\chi(v) \subseteq X$ and $\psi(v) \subseteq C$ that satisfy the following conditions:

1. For each constraint $f_W \in C$, there is exactly one vertex $v \in V$ such that $f_W \in \psi(v)$ In addition, $W \subseteq \chi(v)$.

2. For each variable $x \in X$, the set $\{v \in V | x \in \chi(v)\}$ induces a connected subtree of T.

Tree decompositions for classical CNs often relax condition (1) by requiring that any constraint $f \in C$ must appear in *at least* one vertex $v \in V$ of the decomposition [34]. This is because in classical CNs a constraint can be repeated without causing any trouble.

The *tree width* of a tree decomposition is the maximum number of variables in a vertex minus one $tw = max_{v \in V} |\chi(v)| - 1$. If (u, v) is an edge of a tree decomposition, the *separator* of u and v is $sep(u, v) = \chi(u) \cap \chi(v)$, that is, the set of common variables between the two vertices. We will call s the maximum separator size $s = max_{(u,v) \in E} |sep(u, v)|$ The tree-width tw^* of a graph is the minimum tree-width over all possible tree decompositions. See Figure 9.7 on page 319 for an example of tree decomposition.

Cluster-tree elimination (CTE) [37, 34] is a generic algorithm able to solve classical or soft CNs. For the soft case, it takes as input a soft CN plus a tree decomposition, and it computes for every node u its minimal subproblem, that is, the subproblem whose optimal solutions are the same as the optimal solutions of the whole problem projected on $\chi(u)$.

CTE works by sending messages along edges of the tree decomposition. Given a tree decomposition $\langle \langle V, E \rangle, \chi, \psi \rangle$, every edge $(u, v) \in E$ has associated two messages: $m_{(u,v)}$ is the message from u to v, and $m_{(v,u)}$ the one from v to u. Message $m_{(u,v)}$ is a constraint computed by joining all constraints in $\psi(u)$ with all incoming CTE messages except from v, projected over the separator $sep(u, v)$. When all incoming CTE messages have arrived to u, except the one coming from v, $m_{(u,v)}$ is computed in u and sent to v.

Algorithm 9.3: Cluster tree elimination

Procedure CTE $(\langle \langle V, E \rangle, \chi, \psi \rangle$: *tree decom. of* $\langle X, D, C \rangle$ *soft CN*)
    foreach $(u, v) \in E$ *s.t. all* $m_{(i,u)}, i \neq v$ *have arrived* **do**
        $B \leftarrow \psi(u) \cup \{m_{(i,u)} \mid (i, u) \in E, i \neq v\}$;
        $m_{(u,v)} \leftarrow (\bowtie_{f \in B} f)[sep(u, v)]$;
        send $m_{(u,v)}$;

The complexity of CTE is $O(deg(r + N)d^{tw})$ in time and $O(Nd^s)$ in space, where deg is the maximum degree of T, r is the number of constraints, N is the number of nodes in the tree decomposition, tw is the tree-width and s is the separator size.

There is a close relation between algorithms BE and CTE because induced width w and tree-width tw^* exploit the same graph properties (and we have $w^* = tw^*$). The way BE processes buckets along the ordering o defines a bucket tree that is also a tree decomposition. In fact, there is a node v_i for each variable x_i, the parent of node v_i is the node v_j iff x_j is the closest preceding neighbor of x_i in the induced graph $G^*(o)$ $\chi(v_i)$ contains x_i and every preceding neighbor of x_i in $G^*(o)$; $\psi(v_i)$ is equal to the bucket B_i. Therefore, CTE can be applied to the bucket tree. In this setting, it is called the BTE algorithm, which can be seen as a two-phase algorithm. The first phase, that is, equivalent to BE, computes messages from leaves to the root in the bucket tree. The second phase computes messages from root to leaves, producing the constraints for the minimal subproblem at each node [34].

9.6.2 Incomplete Inference

Because complete inference can be extremely time and space intensive, it is often interesting to have simpler processes able of producing just a lower bound on the network consistency level. Such a lower bound can be immediately useful in branch and bound algorithms.

Mini-buckets

BE has to compute and store intermediate constraints g_i that can be of high arity, causing a high memory consumption. If we cannot afford such amount of memory, it is always possible to limit the arity of intermediate constraints, at the cost of losing optimality with respect to the returned level and the solution found.

This approach is called *mini-bucket elimination* (MBE(z)) [35], and it is an approximation scheme for BE. When eliminating variable x_i, instead of having a single bucket B_i as BE has, MBE(z) partitions B_i into subsets $B_{i_1}, \ldots, B_{i_m}$, such that the number of variables appearing in each B_{i_j} is bounded by z. Each B_{i_j} is called a mini-bucket. Parameter z limits the arity of the intermediate constraints which are

$$g_{i_j} \leftarrow (\bowtie_{f \in B_{i_j}} f)[-x_i]$$

These constraints replace mini-buckets $B_{i_1}, \ldots, B_{i_m}$. Since

$$\bigoplus_{j=1}^{m} \left((\bowtie_{f \in B_{i_j}} f)[-x_i] \right) \preccurlyeq_v (\bowtie_{f \in B_i} f)[-x_i]$$

MBE(z) computes a lower bound of the level of the optimal solution. Obviously, higher values of z increase the precision of mini-buckets, at the cost of using more memory. Both time and space complexity of MBE(z) are exponential in the z parameter.

The same idea can be applied to CTE, producing the *mini-cluster tree elimination*, MCTE(z), that is an approximation schema for the CTE algorithm. When the number of variables in a cluster is too high, it is not possible to compute a single message that captures the joint effect of all constraints of the cluster plus all incoming messages, due to memory limitations. In this case, MCTE(z) computes a lower bound of the problem by using z to limit the arity of the constraints sent in the messages.

An MCTE(z) message, noted $M_{(u,v)}$, is a set of constraints that approximate the corresponding CTE message $m_{(u,v)}$. It is computed as $m_{(u,v)}$, but instead of joining all constraints of set B, it computes a partition $P = \{B_1, B_2, \ldots, B_p\}$ of B such that the join of constraints in every B_i does not exceed arity z. We compute $M_{(u,v)}$ from P by joining all constraints in every set of the partition, projected on the set $sep(u, v)$.

Soft local consistency

Local consistency is an essential component of any constraint solver. A local consistency is a local property with an associated enforcing (often polynomial time) algorithm that transforms a classical CN into a unique and equivalent network that satisfies the property. If this equivalent network is empty, then the initial network is obviously inconsistent, allowing to detect some inconsistencies very efficiently.

A similar motivation exists for extending local consistency to soft constraints: the hope that an equivalent locally consistent network may provide a better lower bound on the network consistency level. This extension has been an incremental process and some problems are still open nowadays. The first results were obtained on fuzzy CNs [92, 104, 99]. We only consider extensions of node and arc consistency, but most results have been extended to the general notion of k-consistency [25].

For simplicity we consider binary valued CNs $\langle X, D, C, S \rangle$, although most results have been originally presented for arbitrary arities. A binary constraint involving x_i and x_j is denoted f_{ij}. Without loss of generality, we assume that networks contain one unary constraint denoted f_i for each variable $x_i \in X$, representing its domain, and one special zero-arity constraint $f_\varnothing$ with a constant value. Notice that $f_\varnothing$ is included in the computation of the consistency level of any assignment.

In such a network, a naive lower bound on the level of the network is the value of $f_\varnothing$ Local consistency enforcing will improve this naive bound.

A first operational approach.   An operational extension of local consistencies for classical CNs can be directly obtained by replacing the $\bowtie$, $\sqsubset$, and projection operators with their soft extensions (combination, constraint ordering, and projection, see 9.3.3) [9, 10].

In a classical CN (X, D, C), a variable x_i is arc consistent with respect to constraint R_{ij} when $D_i \subset (R_{ij} \bowtie D_j)[x_i]$. Generalized by using soft constraint operators, this give a first definition of arc consistency.

Given a soft idempotent CN $\mathcal{P} = \langle X, D, C, S \rangle$, a variable $x_i \in X$ is *arc consistent* with respect to a constraint f_{ij} iff for every value $a \in D_i$, $f_i \sqsubseteq (f_{ij} \bowtie f_j)[x_i]$. The variable x_i is *node consistent* when $\exists a \in D_i$ such that $f_i(a) \neq \top$. $\mathcal{P}$ is arc consistent when every variable is node consistent and arc consistent with respect to all binary constraints involving it.

The corresponding enforcing algorithm considers all variables x_i that violate the arc consistency condition ($f_i \not\sqsubseteq (f_{ij} \bowtie f_j)[x_i]$) and enforces $f_i \leftarrow f_i \bowtie ((f_{ij} \bowtie f_j)[x_i])$ (as the Revise procedure does in the classical case). Notice that this can only increase the violation degree of values in f_i. This is done iteratively until quiescence in Algorithm 9.4

Algorithm 9.4: Enforcing arc consistency in soft idempotent constraint networks.

$Q \leftarrow true$;
while Q **do**
    $Q \leftarrow false$;
    foreach $x_i \in X$ **do**
        foreach $f_{ij} \in C$ **do**
            $f \leftarrow f_i \bowtie (f_{ij} \bowtie f_j)[x_i]$;
            if $f \neq f_i$ **then** $f_i \leftarrow f; Q \leftarrow true$;

This definition and its enforcing procedure were initially formulated for arbitrary k consistency in semiring CNs in [9, 10, 12] with the following result: if $\oplus$ is idempotent, then the algorithm terminates and yields a unique equivalent arc consistent soft CN.

To see that idempotency is required for equivalence, consider a non-idempotent valuation structure. There exists $\alpha \in E$ such that $\alpha \oplus \alpha \neq \alpha$. Consider a soft CN with two variables x_1 and x_2, and two values a, b in each domain with the micro-structure illustrated in Figure 9.1. A single binary constraint f_{12} assigns level α to the pairs (a, a) and (b, b) and level $\alpha \oplus \alpha$ (denoted 2α) to the pair (b, a). After one iteration of the algorithm, $(f_{12} \bowtie f_2)[x_1]$ is equal to α on $x_1 = b$. When f_1 is modified accordingly, we get the network on the right where the pair (b, b) has now level $f_1(b) \oplus f_{12}(b, b) \oplus f_2(b) = \alpha \oplus \alpha \oplus \bot = \alpha \oplus \alpha \neq \alpha$ by assumption. Equivalence is lost.

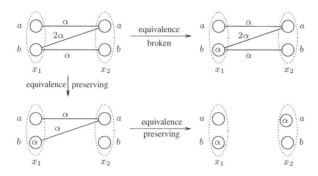

Figure 9.1: A non-idempotent network and three derived networks. On the right, the result of one iteration of Algorithm 9.4. Below, how equivalence can be preserved.

Beyond idempotent operators

To see how equivalence can be preserved, consider the network on the lower left of Figure 9.1: the implicit cost of α for the value b of x_1 has been explicited but simultaneously, we have modified f_{12} by "subtracting" one α from the levels of the pairs (b, a) and (b, b). The network obtained is equivalent to the original one and more explicit since x_1 carries some previously implicit information. The same process can be applied to value a of x_2 to get the network in the right hand side of Figure 9.1 which is equivalent to the original one.

The extra mechanism needed to perform such operations is the ability to "extract" some violation degree from any larger violation degree. This ability was used by [63] for frequency assignment problems and introduced by [98] for valued CNs.

In a valuation structure $S = \langle E, \oplus, \preceq_v, \bot, \top \rangle$, if $\alpha, \beta \in E$, $\alpha \preceq_v \beta$ and $\exists \gamma \in E$ such that $\alpha \oplus \gamma = \beta$, then γ is known as a *difference* between β and α. The valuation structure S is *fair* if for any pair of valuations $\alpha, \beta \in E$, with $\alpha \preceq_v \beta$, there exists a maximum difference of β and α. This unique maximum difference of β and α is denoted by $\beta \ominus \alpha$.

Several examples of fair and unfair structures are given in [26] and fair structures are totally analyzed in [25]. All the usual instances of valuation structures are fair, or can be transformed into a fair equivalent structure. For example, in fuzzy CNs, where $\oplus = \max$, the difference is also max since if $\beta \preceq_v \alpha$, then $\max(\alpha, \max(\alpha, \beta)) = \beta$. In k-weighted CNs, where $\oplus$ is the bounded addition, defined by $\alpha +^k \beta = \min(\alpha + \beta, k)$, the difference is $-^k$ is defined by:

$$\alpha -^k \beta = \begin{cases} \alpha - \beta & : \quad \alpha \neq k \\ k & : \quad \alpha = k \end{cases}$$

This difference allows to define a new operation on cost functions called extraction. Let f_V and f'_W be two cost functions such that $f_V \sqsubseteq f'_W$, the *extraction* of f'_W from f_V is the cost function $f_V \ominus f'_W$ with scope $V \cup W$ such that for any tuple t over $(V \cup W)$ $(f_V \ominus f'_W)(t) = f_V(t[V]) \ominus f'_W(t[W])$.

Note that $f'_W \bowtie (f_V \ominus f'_W)$ is equivalent to f_V. It becomes possible to add an implied constraint f'_W to a network and then to extract it from these to preserve equivalence. Using this approach, arc consistency has been extended to fair valued structures in [98, 26] and k-consistency in [25]. The fundamental mechanism of these local consistencies is to first build an implied constraint by combining all the constraints of a subnetwork and by projecting the resulting cost function. The projection is then added to the network and extracted from the constraint combination. Several existing local consistencies can be captured by the following notion of inference rule that preserves equivalence.

A (K, Y)-*equivalence-preserving inference rule* (EPI rule) is defined by a set of constraints $K \subset C$ and a set of variables $Y \subset X$. The application of a (K, Y)-EPI rule consists of:

1. Removing K from the network.

2. Adding $(\bowtie K)[Y]$ and $(\bowtie K) \ominus (\bowtie K)[Y]$ to the network.

Once such a rule is applied, the implicit constraint $(\bowtie K)[Y]$ is explicit and equivalence is preserved: cost has been moved from K to the scope Y. In the following, we define local consistencies as sets of EPI rules. Similarly to what Algorithm 9.4 does for idempotent structures, enforcing such a local consistency is done by the repeated application of all the EPI rules in the set until no change occurs: the network is said to satisfy the local consistency property.[1]

To illustrate this with an example, we use weighted binary CNs. Beyond its practical usefulness, [26, 25] have shown that every fair valuation structure can be decomposed in independent slices isomorphic to the valuation structure of weighted CNs, making such problems central.

Node consistency. This is the simplest level of local consistency. Node consistency [65, 69, 70] (NC) is enforced using the set of EPI rules $\{(\{f_i, f_\varnothing\}, \varnothing), \forall x_i \in X\}$. These rules are applied iteratively until quiescence, as in the classical case.

Consider the k-weighted CN in Figure 9.2 with $k = 4$ ($\oplus$ is $+^4$, $\ominus$ is $-^4$). It has three variables $X = \{x_1, x_2, x_3\}$ with values a, b. There are two constraints f_{13}, f_{23} and two non-trivial unary constraints f_1 and f_3. One optimal solution is $x_1 = x_2 = x_3 = b$ with cost 2. It also contains a dummy $f_\varnothing$ constraint of zero arity equal to 0. Applying the $(\{f_3, f_\varnothing\}, \varnothing)$ rule gives the equivalent network of Figure 9.2 on the right. It has a better obvious lower bound $f_\varnothing$ and is NC since no other rule in the set may modify the network.

Arc consistencies. Together with the NC rules, the set of rules $\{(\{f_{ij}, f_j\}, \{x_i\}), \forall f_{ij} \in C\}$ would give a natural definition of arc consistency. However, the repeated application of this set of rules is not always terminating [98]. As Figure 9.3 shows, the effect of the application of one rule may be destroyed by another one.

---

[1]Note that local consistencies may get out of this schema by building other implied constraints or by simultaneously applying several rules which can be more powerful [24].

[2]The paper [65] introduces two notions of node consistency. Our definition corresponds to NC*.

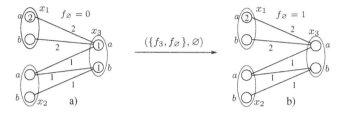

Figure 9.2: A k-weighted CN before and after node consistency enforcing.

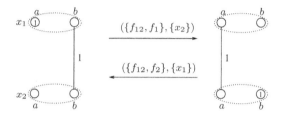

Figure 9.3: Full arc consistency can run forever.

To enforce termination, two approaches have been used. The first approach avoids the possible extraction of costs from the unary level to the binary level by simultaneously using the NC rules and $(\{f_{ij}\}, \{x_i\})$. This is called arc consistency [98, 65, 70]. Another way to enforce termination is to restrict the direction of cost moves. If a variable ordering is assumed, directional arc consistency enforcing uses the rules of NC combined with the following set of rules of full arc consistency: $\{(\{f_{ij}, f_j\}, \{x_i\}) \mid x_i < x_j\}$. Taking the union of the rules of AC and DAC defines the stronger full directional arc consistency (FDAC) [27, 69, 26].[3] Figure 9.4 shows how FDAC can be enforced on our previous network. On this simple problem, a lower bound $f_{\varnothing}$ of 2 is built (assuming order x_1, x_2, x_3).

DAC and AC are incomparable. AC and DAC are stronger than NC by definition, and FDAC is stronger than AC or DAC. If $\top = k = 1$, then k-weighted CNs become classical CNs, and NC becomes classical node consistency, AC and FDAC become classical arc consistency and DAC becomes classical directional arc consistency.

EPI rules can also be applied to weighted MAXSAT problems [31, 55]. Consider the set K of two clashing weighted 2-clauses $K = \{(\ell \vee a, u), (\neg \ell \vee b, v)\}$ where a and b are literals, u and v costs of violation. If V is the set of variables associated to literals a, b and $m = \min(u, v)$, applying the (K, V)-EPI rule returns the equivalent pair of cost functions $(\bowtie K)[V]$ and $(\bowtie K) \ominus (\bowtie K)[V]$, respectively represented by the sets of clauses $\{(a \vee b, m)\}$ and $\{(\ell \vee A, u \ominus m), (\neg \ell \vee b, v \ominus m), (\ell \vee a \vee b, m), (\neg \ell \vee a \vee b, m)\}$. This can be considered as a form of resolution principle extended to MAXSAT [91, 55].

---

[3]There are differences between the definitions given here, which correspond to [65, 69, 70], and the definitions in [26], which apply to arbitrary fair valued structures, do not use NC but, more subtly, exploit situations where $f_{ij}(a, b) \oplus f_i(a) \oplus f_j(b) = \top$.

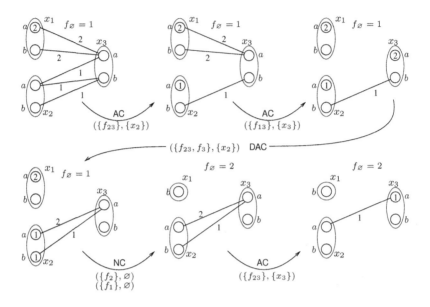

Figure 9.4: Equivalence-preserving inference rules on the network of Figure 9.2.

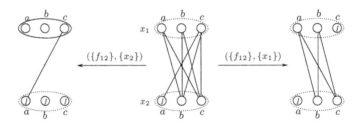

Figure 9.5: A MaxCSP and two different equivalent networks.

While most of the usual properties of local consistency in classical CNs are preserved in these definitions (equivalence, polynomial time enforcing), local consistency enforcing on non-idempotent soft CNs has a much more intricate behavior. Even for terminating properties, the uniqueness of the result of enforcing arc consistency is lost. This is shown in Figure 9.5 where each edge represents a unit cost. Applying AC rule $(\{f_{12}\}, \{x_1\})$ on the central network yields the network on the left. If we use $(\{f_{12}\}, \{x_2\})$, we get the network on the right which is AC (in fact, no more rule can be applied), but different. The left network is more interesting since enforcing NC here yields an AC network with $f_\varnothing = 1$. Finding an optimal closure has been proved to be NP-complete in [26] for integer costs.

It can be shown [98] that the lower bounds obtained by arc consistency enforcing subsume previous ad-hoc lower bounds such as directed or reversible arc consistency counts.

Stronger local consistency notions, such as existential directional arc consistency (EDAC, [32]), 3-cyclic consistency [24], and k-consistency [25] have been defined.

Soft global constraints

Important consistency enforcing algorithms in classical CNs are those associated to the so-called global constraints. Such constraints have a specific semantics and an associated algorithms that can enforce some type of local consistency on the constraint, usually much more efficiently than a generic algorithm (see Chapter 6). Several global constraints and their associated algorithms have been extended to handle soft constraints.

All these proposals have been made using the approach of [87] where a soft constraint f_S is represented as an hard constraint with an extra variable x_S representing the cost of the assignment of the other variables in S (see Section 9.4.5).

A global constraint is usually defined by three components: the precise semantics of the constraint, the level of consistency enforced on this constraint and an algorithm to enforce it. For example, a soft global constraint extends the classical all-different constraint. Two semantics have been considered for the soft version: for a given assignment of the variables involved in a soft all-different, the associated level can be either the number of variables whose value must be changed to satisfy the all-different constraint, or the number of pairs of variables that have identical values. The level of consistency enforced is classical generalized arc consistency, also called hyper-arc consistency. Enforcing algorithms based on (minimum cost) flow/matching algorithms offer efficient enforcing algorithms for these two semantics [88, 106].

Before this, [4] proposed a soft global constraint handling a variant of the One-Machine scheduling problem. Following this first proposal, a few extra soft global constraints have been proposed. Besides the previous soft all-different constraint, soft versions of the global cardinality constraint (useful for example in personnel rostering problems, see Chapter 6) and of the regular constraint (to capture regular language membership with errors) have also been proposed by [107].

The problem of just computing the cost of an assignment for a single soft global constraint has been considered in [5]. For some semantics, this problem may naturally be NP-hard, but all global constraints defined through specific graph properties can be computed in polynomial time.

9.6.3 Polynomial Classes

As for classical CNs, most polynomial classes of soft CNs can be characterized by restrictions on the (hyper)graph structure of the network, or by restrictions on the cost functions.

As observed in Section 9.6.1, the class of problems whose graph has a bounded induced width can be solved to optimality using bucket or cluster-tree elimination in polynomial time. This is an old result for optimizing combination of local cost functions which already appears in [7] where induced width is called "dimension". Note that minimizing induced width is precisely the DIMENSION problem considered in [3], where it is shown to be NP-complete (as a decision problem). This class of graphical parameters has been generalized in various ways for hyper-graphs. For more information, the reader is invited to refer to Chapter 7 and [54, 23].

The use of restriction on cost functions is more interesting. Let D and E be fixed sets. A soft constraint language over D with evaluation in E is defined to be a set of functions Γ such that each $\phi \in \Gamma$ is a function from D^e to E for some $e \in \mathbb{N}$ (e is the arity of ϕ).

The set D represents the domain of the variables (that is, the union of all domains) and the set E is the set of violation/satisfaction levels used in semiring/valued constraints. An instance of the soft constraint satisfaction problem induced by a soft constraint language Γ denoted sCSP(Γ), is simply defined as a soft CN $\langle X, D, C, S \rangle$ such that all soft constraints in C belong to Γ and S is defined over the set of satisfaction levels E. The associated question is to identify a variable assignment with maximal overall satisfaction level, as defined for semiring CNs. The soft constraint language Γ is said to be tractable when the problem sCSP(Γ) can be solved in polynomial time. All existing results we know apply only to totally ordered structures satisfying the valued network axioms, but depends crucially on the fact that the combination operator is idempotent or not.

Idempotent $\oplus$ operator. In this case, when the order on E is total, it is known that the only possible choice for $\oplus$ is min. The corresponding max-min optimization problem is the fuzzy constraint satisfaction problem considered in Section 9.2.1. As shown in Section 9.4.3, the set of optimal solutions of a fuzzy CN $\mathcal{P}$ is equal to the set of solutions of its maximum consistent α-cut $\mathcal{P}^\alpha$. If p is the number of different levels of satisfaction used in $\mathcal{P}$, then a dichotomic search for the maximum consistent α requires at most $\lceil \log_2(p) \rceil$ calls to an oracle for consistency on classical CNs. This provides a simple, but powerful result, which is capable of lifting many polynomial classes of classical CNs to fuzzy ones.

Let Γ be a soft constraint language. We note Γ^{cut} the set of relations defined by the α-cuts of all cost functions in Γ for any α. If Γ^{cut} is a tractable constraint language, then Γ is a tractable soft constraint language.

Indeed, there are at most $O(d^n)$ different satisfaction levels in any fuzzy CN. Thus an optimal solution can be identified by a sequence of $O(n \log(d))$ calls to a polynomial oracle in this case. This shows that the language of binary cost functions over domains of size is tractable if $\oplus$ is idempotent and E totally ordered. A more significant tractable language can be obtained by lifting the tractable language of simple temporal constraint satisfaction problems leading to the tractable class of semi-convex fuzzy temporal networks [60].

Non idempotent $\oplus$ operators. The weighted constraint satisfaction problem (see Section 9.2.2) provides very strong negative results for tractable languages. Indeed, when the domains are restricted to boolean domains and cost functions takes only values 0 and 1 this problems becomes the MAXSAT problem, known to be NP-complete and MAXSNP complete, which means that it has no polynomial time approximation scheme. Even restrictions to binary clauses (cost functions) or to the binary function f_{xor} (soft exclusive or) defined by $f_{xor}(x, y) = ((x \neq y)?0 : 1)$ are know to be NP-hard [28]. Tractable languages for MAXSAT and weighted MAXSAT (where cost functions can take any finite integer value) have been fully characterized by [28].

The weighted constraint satisfaction problem generalizes weighted MAXSAT by allowing to simultaneously use finite and infinite costs. Such soft Boolean constraint languages have been completely characterized and eight tractable classes have been identified (see Theorem 2 of [20]).

Compared to weighted MAXSAT, weighted CSP also allows for domains of size greater than two and this breaks some tractable MAX2SAT languages. In [21], the language of soft equality, denoted by f_{eq}, defined by $f_{eq}(x, y) = ((x = y) ? 0 : 1))$ is shown to be NP-hard for domain sizes of size 3 and more [21]. Amazingly, the non trivial language of *submodular cost functions* is a tractable language for weighted CSP [21].

A function f such that $\forall x, y, u, v, u \leq x, v \leq y$, we have: $f(u, v) + f(x, y) \leq f(u, y) + f(x, v)$ is called a submodular function. This class is relatively rich in practice and contains cost functions such as $ax + by + c$, $\sqrt{x^2 + y^2}$, $|x - y|^r (r \geq 1)$, $max(x - y, 0)^r (r \geq 1)$, etc. This class is maximal (no other function can be added to the language without making it NP-complete). An algorithm in $O(n^3 d^3)$ that can solve submodular networks is described in [21]. Other related results appear in [19, 22].

9.7 Combining Search and Inference

9.7.1 Direct Combination

As we have shown in Section 9.6, variable (or bucket) elimination is computationally and space efficient when each variable to eliminate is only connected to few other variables or when it is assigned. Once a variable is eliminated, we get a network with the same optimal cost, a smaller number of variables and constraints, and that can be solved without backtracking. Conversely, branch and bound explores the domain of every variable with limited space complexity, but with the requirement of backtracking until a provably optimal solution is found. This gives a natural way to combine both approaches: if some variable in the network has a small degree (that is, less than a constant m), we can eliminate it. Each elimination may reduce the degree of other variables and enable further eliminations. Otherwise, we can branch on a well-chosen variable (that is, one with a high degree). Once assigned, the variable becomes easy to eliminate and may enable further eliminations.

The corresponding algorithm has been described in [64] where its efficiency on problems with relatively structured or sparse graphs is shown. As variable/bucket or cluster-tree elimination, the space and time complexity of the algorithm can be a priori bounded using a parameter derived from *induced width* and parameterized by the maximum degree bound m for elimination.

9.7.2 Exploiting Stronger Bounds

The incomplete inference mechanisms all produce lower bounds which can be directly used during a branch and bound optimization.

Mini-bucket-based bounds

Intermediate constraints produced by mini-bucket elimination can be used to generate lower bounds inside branch and bound [59]. Let us assume that MBE(z) has processed the problem, from the last to first variable in an ordering o. After that, branch and bound starts following o as a static variable order. When assigning x_i, all constraints in bucket i can be evaluated, including the intermediate constraints produced by MBE(z). Their aggregation gives a lower bound on the cost of extending the current partial solution to a complete one. This lower bound can also be used as heuristic to order values of the current variable.

The previous approach can be seen as a preprocess before search starts. Since intermediate constraints have been computed along the ordering o, to use them for lower bound computation requires that branch and bound follows o as static variable ordering. However, mini-buckets can also generate lower bounds when search uses dynamic variable ordering. Instead of executing MBE(z) as preprocess, MBE(z) is executed at each node of the search space, restricted to the subproblem rooted at that node and the current partial solution. The aggregation of all constraints in the bucket of the current variable is a lower bound that, as before, can be used as heuristic to order variable values [39].

A related approach considers mini-bucket tree elimination applied to an augmented bucket tree, defined as follows. The bucket tree is the tree defined by the BE algorithm, with n vertices $\{v_1, v_2, \ldots, v_n\}$. It is augmented with $n - 1$ new vertices, $\{u_2, \ldots, u_n\}$ and $n - 1$ new arcs $\{(v_2, u_2), (v_3, u_3), \ldots, (v_n, u_n)\}$, such that $\chi(u_i) = x_i$ and $\psi(u_i) = \emptyset$ It is direct to check that the augmented bucket tree is a tree decomposition, so the MBTE(z algorithm can be applied on it. After MBTE(z) execution, constraints received in u_i can be aggregated, producing a lower bound of the singletons (pairs variable-value) of x_i. This approach can be combined with branch and bound. At each visited node of the search space, MBTE(z) is executed to compute lower bounds of each singleton of unassigned variables. These lower bounds are used for domain pruning. Since MBTE(z) is executed at each node of the search tree, the validity of the lower bounds do not depend on any variable ordering, so branch and bound can perform dynamic variable ordering. As before, these lower bounds can be used as heuristic for value ordering.

Local consistency based bounds

Branch and bound application for minimizing combined violation relies on two essential components: a lower bound $lb_v(p)$ on the violation degree of any complete assignment below the current node p, and a current upper bound ub_v which indicates the maximum violation degree which is acceptable.

The main motivation for extending local consistency to soft constraints [98] has always been to provide good lower bounds. As shown in [65], both lower and upper bounds can be directly represented in the problem associated to the current node p: a lower bound is immediately available from the constraint $f_\emptyset$, while the upper bound ub_v can be enforced by setting $\top$ to ub_v.

Local consistency enforcing is capable of improving the naive lower bound on violations defined by $f_\emptyset$ and backtracking can occur whenever this bound reaches the current value of $\top$. As in the classical case, for algorithms such as MAC (Chapter 4), the incrementality of local consistency enforcing and the fact it can inform value ordering heuristics is also essential. In soft constraints, it further provides value ordering heuristics.

Depending on the level of local consistency maintained at each node, several different algorithms are obtained. For a stronger local consistency, more work is done at each node, but less nodes are explored. Maintaining existential directional consistency [32], which is among the strongest implemented local consistency property, is apparently the best current compromise. For most problems, local consistency based bounds seem to outperform previously defined bounds.

The first combined use of local consistency and branch and bound was done on min-max (that is, fuzzy) networks since arc consistency has been defined for such networks since [92]. See for example [99, 45]. For other types of valued networks, arc consistency has been defined in [98] and combined with branch and bound in [65, 70]. The most recent algorithms described in [69, 31, 32] rely on stronger consistencies which provide even better efficiency, including on MAXSAT problems.

9.7.3 Exploiting Problem Structure

Problem structure can be exploited in several ways. Here, we will focus on the exploitation of subproblem independence and the exploitation of the locality of constraints.

Independent subproblems can be solved separately so search can be accelerated. Inside a branch and bound scheme, variables are instantiated in a particular order. At some point in search, independent subproblems become disconnected and they can be solved separately. Such independent subproblems can be identified using pseudo-tree arrangements.

A *pseudo-tree arrangement* of the constraint graph G is a rooted tree with the same set of vertices as G, where two adjacent vertices of the graph must appear in the same root-leaf branch of the pseudo-tree [50]. The interesting feature is that when assigning variables following pseudo-tree branches, independent subproblems are easily identified: when the successors of a node go to different branches, each represents an independent subproblem that can be solved separately.

A first attempt to exploit pseudo-trees inside branch and bound is the PT-BB algorithm [72]. It assigns variables following a depth-first pseudo-tree traversal, and solves separately independent subproblems. In addition to the global bounds of DFBB, it consider local upper and lower bounds, specialized for each particular subproblem. Using global and local bounds, some parts of the search space can be pruned. To cope with the issue of bad local upper bounds, this algorithm was combined with russian doll search, producing the PT-RDS algorithm. The basic idea is to performs RDS on the pseudo-tree starting from the leaves towards the root. When solving subproblem i, all its children sub-problems have already been solved. When solving subproblem $i - 1$, a local upper bound can be computed as the cost of extending the solution of subproblem i to a new variable.

The idea of pseudo-tree search is further developed in the context of *AND/OR search* [77, 78]. Developing the pseudo-tree state space, we obtain the AND/OR search tree. This tree is searched by the AOBB algorithm, that backs up costs from leaves towards the root. It maintains local upper and lower bounds at each node of the current partial solution, used to prune parts of the search space. Any lower bound computing strategy can be used.

A related approach is the *bounded backtracking* on valued CNs [105], a search strategy based on a tree decomposition. Similarly to pseudo-tree arrangements, when all the variables of a cluster (a node of the tree decomposition) have been instantiated, the child clusters become independent and can be solved separately. This property is exploited in the BDT_{val} algorithm, a branch and bound algorithm that assigns variables following an order compatible with the preorder traversal of the tree decomposition. Local upper and lower bounds are maintained and used to prune the search space.

BTD goes beyond this by caching the optimal solutions of the independent subproblems solved. When the exact same subproblem needs to be solved again, the cached value is used instead.[4] If we consider a cluster C_i in the tree decomposition and one of its son C_j, the subproblem rooted in C_j which is solved once C_i is instantiated can be identified by the assignment of the separator of C_i and C_j. If a new partial solution that includes that particular assignment for the variables of the separator is tried later, the optimal cost of the subproblem cached is reused. The justification is easy: the only connection of the subproblem with the rest of the problem passes through the separator, so with the same instantiation of the separator the subproblem will have the same optimal cost.

Bounded backtracking has time and space complexities similar to CTE. It performs search, so it can use filtering algorithms to propagate hard inconsistencies, causing domain sizes to change. Since it allows for dynamic variable ordering (compatible with the ordering of the decomposition), it can use domain-based heuristics, improving its performance with respect to the theoretical bounds.

9.8   Using Soft Constraints

There may be several different reasons for using soft constraints. The first motivation can be to just capture preferences. In this case, the essential problem is to identify (that is, to elicitate) the preferences and this is related to machine learning issues. We have assumed that soft constraints were clearly explicited, but the problem of learning soft constraints from data has also been considered [93].

As soon as preferences are captured by soft constraints added to an existing classical CN, it is possible to use such constraints to guide the search towards preferred solutions. For example, preferences over variable values (such as those usually given by users in configuration problems or produced as unary soft constraints by arc consistency enforcing) can be used as a value ordering heuristics to be used during search, so that most preferred values are tried first [108, 82, 103]. A similar technique can be used for preferences over variables. This is simple and can be very effective in practice, making soft constraints one way to express heuristic guidance.

Constraint propagation such as arc consistency can also be performed faster via the notion of preferred support, which is based on preferences over values and variables [8]. Preferences can also be used to improve several tasks beyond that of finding an optimal solution. For example, in the QUICKXPLAIN system [58], user preferences over constraints can be used to identify the most useful explanations of failures for over-constrained problems, as well as the most useful relaxations of the problem which are satisfiable. The main idea is to select, among a possibly very large number of explanations for a failure, one that involves the most preferred constraints and is minimal.

Our main focus in this Section is on solving soft constraint problems to optimality. Because the history of soft constraint technology is essentially concentrated in the last decade, it has not yet entered the arena of stable commercial solvers. But the recent progresses have lead to the design of several solvers, often targeted towards a specific type of constraint networks, either fuzzy CN, weighted CN, or weighted MAXSAT. Rather than giving an exhaustive list of solvers, we invite the reader to refer to the Soft Constraints and MAXSAT web site [30] that tries to maintain a list of complete and incomplete solvers for soft constraints together with many benchmarks from several areas. Despite their experimental

---

[4]The same idea appears in the Recursive conditioning algorithm [29] in the context of counting problems in Bayesian networks.

design, some of these solvers achieve excellent performances, sometimes outperforming commercial solvers on difficult soft constraints problems [31, 32].

Soft CNs offer a very flexible model for representing constrained problems with preferences. As a general indication of this, one may note that many usual and central problems in complexity theory such as MAXSAT, MAX CLIQUE, MAXONES, MIN VERTEX COVER, MAX CUT, MINONES, MINCOL, etc., are very straightforward to model as weighted CNs. These academic problems have often an almost direct application in various areas. For example, MIN VERTEX COVER is related to two-level logic minimization in electronic design automation, MINCOL is a simplified version of over-constrained frequency assignment, and MAX CUT has been used to solve spin glass or sport scheduling problems. Originally, however, soft constraints have been introduced to handle over-constrained problems. We now consider two application domains where such problems are frequent: resource allocation and diagnosis based on experimental (that is, real word acquired) data. In particular, we will consider resource allocation in the context of the frequency assignment problem and diagnosis in the context of bioinformatics problems.

9.8.1 Resource Allocation for Frequency Assignment

Soft constraints have been used, among others, in resource allocation problems such as satellite scheduling [6], timetabling [94] or frequency assignment [16]. In such problems, the available resources are often insufficient to answer the requirements (all expressed as hard constraints) and the problems are easily over-constrained. Actually, even when not over-constrained, optimization criteria can often be expressed as soft constraints.

The frequency assignment problem (FAP) defined by the *Centre d'Électronique de l'Armement* (CELAR) from real data is specifically interesting because of its variety and difficulty. This problem has been described in [16] and more information on frequency assignment can be found on the FAP web site [62]. A set of wireless communication connections must be assigned frequencies such that, for every connection, data transmission between the transmitter and the receiver is possible. The frequencies should be selected from a given set that may depend on the location.[5] The frequencies assigned to two different connections may incur interference resulting in a loss of quality of the signal. Two conditions are needed simultaneously in order to create interference between two signals:

- The two frequencies must be close on the electromagnetic band.

- The connections must be geographically close to each other: the signals that may interfere should have a similar level of energy at the position where they might disturb each other.

To avoid interference, when the second condition is satisfied, and depending on existing physical wave-propagation models, a sufficient distance in the frequency spectrum has to be imposed. Because the frequency resource is not infinite, some frequencies have to be reallocated and the problem of finding an assignment that satisfies all distance constraints is already NP-hard. Often, one also want to minimize some criteria. Two criteria are often considered:

---

[5]In practice, much traffic is bidirectional, so that two frequencies must be chosen for each link, one for each direction. This is often ignored by choosing two non-intersecting domains of frequency for forward and backward communication.

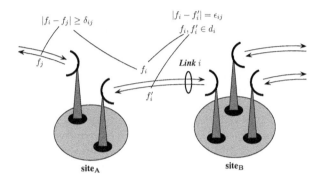

Figure 9.6: Frequency assignment

1. Minimizing the maximum frequency used allows one to use a small portion of an available spectrum, which is often allocated on a slice by slice strategy by the responsible international agencies.

2. Minimizing the number of different frequencies used allows one to rapidly find an available frequency for a new link.

When no solution exists that satisfies all distance constraints, a specific criterion overrides these possible criteria: the aim becomes interference minimization. In the CELAR case, one should minimize a weighted sum of violated distance constraints.

The problem is easy to model using one variable per link, whose domain is the set of available frequencies for the link. Constraints of the form $|f_i - f_j| \geq \delta_{ij}$ are used to specify the minimum frequency margin required between geographically close links. Because the problem may be over-constrained, these constraints are actually cost functions: a satisfactory assignment has cost $\bot = 0$ and otherwise a fixed p_{ij} cost. The aim is then to minimize the sum of all costs, which is an instance of weighted MAXCSP.

If the problem is not over-constrained (that is, there is an assignment of cost $\bot = 0$), and one wants to minimize the maximum frequency used, the problem can still be modeled as a soft fuzzy (max-min) CN where, for each variable, unary constraints associate a decreasing membership degree to increasing frequencies (for a given frequency, the same degree should be used on all variables). The alternative criteria which consists in minimizing the number of frequencies used is best modeled using a soft global constraint.

These instances have been tackled using many different combinatorial optimization techniques in 1994 (including integer linear programming techniques such as *branch and cut*). All min-max problem have been solved using constraint network technology but all over-constrained instances remained open until the first over-constrained instance was solved using a combination of graph partitioning and russian doll search [16]. The graph of the corresponding instance is visible in Figure 9.7. This very specific structure is an excellent support to algorithms exploiting tree decompositions. Some other instances have been later solved using such techniques in [63] but some problems remain open.

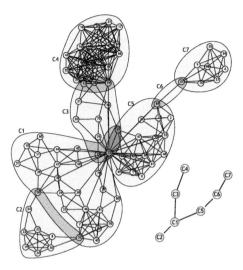

Figure 9.7: Frequency assignment graph structure of preprocessed CELAR instance 6 covered by a tree decomposition.

9.8.2 Diagnosis and Identification Problems in Bioinformatics

In diagnosis, we may build a constraint model of the normal behavior of the system that describes how the components of the system behave in "normal" conditions. For a non-working system, the observations are inconsistent with this model, and the conjunction of the model and the observation is over-constrained.

A possible approach to diagnosis in this case is to find a minimum cardinality set of components such that removing "normal behavior" constraints on these components restores consistency. Such a parsimonious approach relies on the fact that components usually work and breakage is rare. More sophisticated (for example, probabilistic) approaches can also be used. An instance of the diagnosis problem appears in bioinformatics. For other examples of uses of soft constraints in bioinformatics see [111, 53, 52] and Chapter 26.

The cell of sophisticated organisms (such as animals, plants and human beings) carry pairs of chromosomes which hold the genetic information of an individual. A position that carries some specific information on a chromosome is called a *locus* (which typically identifies the position of a gene) and the specific information contained at a locus is the *allele* carried at the locus (the m possible alleles are identified by integers from 1 to m). Since (non-sexual) chromosomes occur in (here unordered) pairs, each locus carries a pair of alleles, called the *genotype* of the individual at this locus (there are $\frac{m(m+1)}{2}$ different genotypes). Determining this genotype on a large population of individuals having parental relationships is crucial for building genetic maps, locating genes involved in diseases, resistances to diseases, etc.

A large population of related individuals, together with some (possibly partial) observation of their genotype at a locus of interest, is called a *pedigree*. The set of possible genotypes for an individual is here called its phenotype. Each individual in a pedigree is either a *founder* (that is, it has no parents in the pedigree) or not. In the latter case, parents can be identified in the pedigree. A pedigree can therefore be described using one variable by individual in the pedigree, whose domain is the set of possible pairs of alleles given the experimental data. For each non-founder, it is also known that one of his alleles comes from his father and the other from his mother. Therefore we may introduce a ternary constraint linking the two parents and each children and stating exactly this.

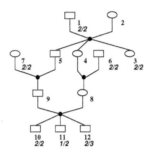

Figure 9.8: Pedigree example taken from [84] with 12 individuals.

A small example of pedigree is given in Figure 9.8. There are $n = 12$ individuals and $m = 3$ distinct alleles. Each box corresponds to a male individual, and each ellipse to a female. The arcs describe parental relations. For instance, individuals 1 and 2 have three children: 3,4, and 5. The founders are individuals 1, 2, 6, and 7. The set of possible geno-types is $G = \{1|1, 1|2, 1|3, 2|2, 2|3, 3|3\}$ where $i|j$ means that the genotype is composed by allele i and allele j. The genotype of seven individuals (that is, 1, 3, 6, 7, 10, 11 and 12) has been experimentally determined, reducing the set of possible genotypes to just one. The corresponding CN has 12 variables, with maximum domain size of 6, and 8 ternary constraints. The problem is that this pedigree is inconsistent in the sense that there is no assignment of genotypes to all individuals that satisfy all constraints. As such, pedigree consistency checking offers an interesting NP-hard problem [1] for constraint networks. The problem is easy when it is tree-structured, but this is rarely true for animal pedigree.

In practice, when the problem is inconsistent, it has to be diagnosed: likely sources of the inconsistency have to be identified and removed so that further (probabilistic) analyzes can be performed. One possible source of error lies in the genotyping process. One may want to identify a set of genotyped individuals of minimum cardinality such that removing the genotype information of these individuals (that is, allowing all possible genotypes for them) restores consistency.

This problem can be simply modeled as a weighted CN. It has the same variables and constraints as the previous classical CN (hard Mendelian constraints are modelled as cost functions taking values $\top$ and $\bot = 0$ only). However, when an individual has been genotyped, this is translated in a unary cost function that maps the observed genotype to cost $\bot$ and all other genotypes to cost 1. This represents the fact that if this is the actual genotype, then there was 1 genotyping error.

The fact that only *unary* soft constraints arise here is not a simplification in itself with respect to general weighted CSPs, since every n-ary weighted CN can be simply translated in an equivalent dual network with only unary soft constraints and hard binary constraints [66].

In the previous example of Fig. 9.8, the problem still has 12 variables, with domain size of 6. It has 8 hard ternary constraints and 7 soft unary constraints. The minimum number of typing errors is one.

In practice, the problem arises on pedigree involving thousands of animals with many loops and is better modelled by taking into account probabilistic information. As shown in [33], this can still be modelled as weighted CN for which existing general solvers are more efficient and require weaker assumptions than existing specialized tools such as Ped-Check [83, 84].

9.9 Promising Directions for Further Research

Research in the area of soft constraints, as an attempt to extend the classical constraint formalism to handle over-constraint problems and problems with preferences, started around the late 80's with Hierarchical CLP [13] and partial constraint satisfaction [49]. Then, in the early 90's specific extensions were considered, such as possibilistic constraints [99], and in 1995 the two main general frameworks (semiring-based and valued constraints) were presented [9, 100]. Since then, in the last ten years much work has been done in the area of soft constraints, and we have tried to report most of it in this chapter: significant results and improvements were obtained in search algorithms, lower bound computations, soft constraint propagation, soft global constraints, and applications. Also, a better understanding of the relationship between soft constraints and other knowledge representation formalisms has been achieved.

The future of soft constraints has many promising directions for further development. Here we point out some of them, for which we hope to see a fast development in the near future:

- Stronger local consistencies need further study in the context of soft constraints. Current experimental studies tend to prove that we have not yet reached the ideal compromise between cost and quality in existing lower bounds. This may also require global constraints, which are so conveniently exploited in classical constraint programming.

- Soft constraints can be very useful in the context of multi-agent constraint optimization and preference aggregation, which occurs often in web-based search engines. Their use in this context needs the study of reasonable preference aggregation operators and the development of distributed soft constraint solvers.

- Soft constraints are more difficult to express than classical constraints, since appropriate valuations to tuples (or constraints, or variables) have to be specified by the user. To ease the specification process, appropriate learning or elicitation tools should be developed to transform user-specified preferences into soft constraints.

- The presence of so many classes of soft constraints, and several different formalisms to express them, needs the development of ways to pass from one formalism to another one without loosing too much information. This would allow easier preference elicitation and the possibility for solver reuse.

- The study of tractable classes of soft constraints is still at its infancy. Much work is still needed to identify significant and practically useful classes of soft constraints with good computational properties.

- Preferences are more varied than those that can be currently expressed with soft constraints or other preference-based formalisms. We envision extensions of the concept of soft constraint to model also other kinds of preferences, such as bipolar, qualitative, and conditional preferences.

Another more practical issue is the practical integration of existing algorithms in popular constraint based tools which is still unsatisfactory. Significant developments in these and other lines of research will allow soft constraints to be practically and widely used in many real-life scenarios, as the main framework for the handling of over-constrained and preference-based problems.

Bibliography

[1]   L. Aceto, J. A. Hansen, A. Ingólfsdóttir, J. Johnsen, and J. Knudsen. The complexity of checking consistency of pedigree information and related problems. *J. Comput. Sci. Technol.*, 19(1):42–59, 2004.

[2]   K. R. Apt. *Principles of Constraint Programming*. Cambridge University Press, 2003.

[3]   S. Arnborg. Efficient algorithms for combinatorial problems on graphs with bounded decomposability — a survey. *BIT*, 25:2–23, 1985.

[4]   P. Baptiste, C. L. Pape, and L. Peridy. Global constraints for partial CSPs: a case-study of resource and due date constraints. In *Proc. of CP'98*, volume 1520 of *LNCS*, pages 87–101, Pisa, Italy, 1998.

[5]   N. Beldiceanu and T. Petit. Cost Evaluation of Soft Global Constraints. In *Proc. of CPAIOR'04*, volume 3011 of *LNCS*, pages 80–95, Nice, France, 2004.

[6]   E. Bensana, M. Lemaître, and G. Verfaillie. Earth observation satellite management. *Constraints*, 4(3):293–299, 1999.

[7]   U. Bertelé and F. Brioshi. *Nonserial Dynamic Programming*. Academic Press, 1972.

[8]   C. Bessière, A. Fabre, and U. Junker. Propagate the right thing: How preferences can speed-up constraint solving. In *Proc. of IJCAI'03*, pages 191–196, Acapulco, Mexico, 2003.

[9]   S. Bistarelli, U. Montanari, and F. Rossi. Constraint solving over semirings. In *Proc. of IJCAI'95*, pages 624–630, Montréal, Canada, 1995.

[10] S. Bistarelli, U. Montanari, and F. Rossi. Semiring based constraint solving and optimization. *Journal of the ACM*, 44(2):201–236, 1997.

[11] S. Bistarelli, H. Fargier, U. Montanari, F. Rossi, T. Schiex, and G. Verfaillie. Semiring-based CSPs and valued CSPs: Frameworks, properties and comparison. *Constraints*, 4:199–240, 1999.

[12] S. Bistarelli, P. Codognet, Y. Georget, and F. Rossi. Labeling and partial local consistency for soft constraint programming. In *Proc. of PADL'00*, volume 1753 of *LNCS*, pages 230–248, 2000.

[13] A. Borning, M. Mahert, A. Martindale, and M. Wilson. Constraint hierarchies and logic programming. In *Proc. of ICLP'89*, pages 149–164. MIT Press, 1989.

[14] C. Boutilier, R. I. Brafman, C. Domshlak, H. Hoos, and D. Poole. CP-nets: A Tool for Representing and Reasoning with Conditional Ceteris Paribus Preference Statements. *Journal of Artificial Intelligence Research*, 21:135–191, 2004.

[15] J. L. Bresina. Heuristic-biased stochastic sampling. In *Proc. of AAAI'96*, pages 271–278, Portland, OR, USA, 1996.

[16] B. Cabon, S. de Givry, L. Lobjois, T. Schiex, and J. Warners. Radio link frequency assignment. *Constraints*, 4:79–89, 1999.

[17] V. A. Cicirello and S. F. Smith. Amplification of search performance through randomization of heuristics. In *Proc. of CP'02*, volume 2470 of *LNCS*, pages 124–138, Ithaca, NY, USA, 2002.

[18] V. A. Cicirello and S. F. Smith. Heuristic selection for stochastic search optimization: Modeling solution quality by extreme value theory. In *Proc. of CP'04*, volume 3258 of *LNCS*, pages 197–211, Toronto, Canada, 2004.

[19] D. Cohen, M. Cooper, P. Jeavons, and A. Krokhin. Soft constraints: complexity and multimorphsims. In *Proc. of CP'03*, volume 2833 of *LNCS*, pages 244–258, Kinsale, Ireland, 2003.

[20] D. Cohen, M. Cooper, and P. Jeavons. A complete characterization of complexity for Boolean constraint optimization problems. In *Proc. of CP'04*, volume 3258 of *LNCS*, pages 212–226, Toronto, Canada, 2004.

[21] D. Cohen, M. Cooper, P. Jeavons, and A. Krokhin. A maximal tractable class of soft constraints. *Journal of Artificial Intelligence Research*, 22:1–22, 2004.

[22] D. Cohen, M. Cooper, P. Jeavons, and A. Krokhin. Identifying efficiently solvable cases of Max CSP. In *Proc. of STACS'04*, volume 2996 of *LNCS*, pages 152–163, 2004.

[23] D. Cohen, P. Jeavons, and M. Gyssens. A unified theory of structural tractability for constraint satisfaction and spread cut decomposition. In *Proc. of IJCAI'05*, pages 72–77, Edinburgh, Scotland, 2005.

[24] M. Cooper. Cyclic consistency: a local reduction operation for binary valued constraints. *Artificial Intelligence*, 155(1-2):69–92, 2004.

[25] M. Cooper. High-order consistency in Valued Constraint Satisfaction. *Constraints*, 10:283–305, 2005.

[26] M. Cooper and T. Schiex. Arc consistency for soft constraints. *Artificial Intelligence*, 154(1-2):199–227, 2004. (see arXiv.org/abs/cs.AI/0111038).

[27] M. C. Cooper. Reduction operations in fuzzy or valued constraint satisfaction. *Fuzzy Sets and Systems*, 134(3):311–342, 2003.

[28] N. Creignou, S. Khanna, and S. M. *Complexity Classications of Boolean Constraint Satisfaction Problems*. Volume 7 of SIAM Monographs on Discrete Mathematics and Applications, 2001.

[29] A. Darwiche. Recursive Conditioning. *Artificial Intelligence*, 126(1-2):5–41, 2001.

[30] S. de Givry. Soft constraint and MAXSAT web site. http://carlit.toulouse.inra.fr/cgi-bin/awki.cgi/SoftCSP.

[31] S. de Givry, J. Larrosa, P. Meseguer, and T. Schiex. Solving Max-Sat as weighted CSP. In *Proc. of CP'03*, volume 2833 of *LNCS*, pages 363–376, Kinsale, Ireland, 2003.

[32] S. de Givry, F. Heras, J. Larrosa, and M. Zytnicki. Existential arc consistency: getting closer to full arc consistency in weighted CSPs. In *Proc. of IJCAI'05*, pages 84–89, Edinburgh, Scotland, 2005.

[33] S. de Givry, I. Palhiere, Z. Vitezica, and T. Schiex. Mendelian error detection in complex pedigree using weighted constraint satisfaction techniques. In *Proc. of ICLP'05 Workshop on Constraint Based Methods for Bioinformatics*, Sitges, Spain, 2005.

[34] R. Dechter. *Constraint Processing*. Morgan Kaufmann, 2003.

[35] R. Dechter. Mini-buckets: A general scheme for generating approximations in automated reasoning. In *Proc. of IJCAI'97*, pages 1297–1303, Nagoya, Japan, 1997.

[36] R. Dechter. Bucket elimination: A unifying framework for reasoning. *Artificial Intelligence*, 113(1–2):41–85, 1999.

[37] R. Dechter and J. Pearl. Tree clustering for constraint networks. *Artificial Intelligence*, 38:353–366, 1989.

[38] R. Dechter and J. Pearl. Network-based heuristics for constraint-satisfaction problems. *Artificial Intelligence*, 34:1–38, 1988.

[39] R. Dechter, K. Kask, and J. Larrosa. A general scheme for multiple lower bound computation in constraint optimization. In *Proc. of CP'01*, volume 2239 of *LNCS* pages 346–360, Paphos, Cyprus, 2001.

[40] C. Domshlak and R. Brafman. CP-nets - Reasoning and Consistency Testing. In *Proc. of KR'02*, pages 121–132, Toulouse, France, 2002.

[41] C. Domshlak, F. Rossi, B. Venable, and T. Walsh. Reasoning about soft constraints and conditional preferences: complexity results and approximation techniques. In *Proc. of IJCAI'03*, pages 215–220, Acapulco, Mexico, 2003.

[42] D. Dubois and H. Prade. *Fuzzy sets and systems: theory and applications*. Academic Press, 1980.

[43] D. Dubois, H. Fargier, and H. Prade. Using fuzzy constraints in job-shop scheduling. In *Proc. of IJCAI'93/SIGMAN Workshop on Knowledge-based Production Planning, Scheduling and Control*, Chambery, France, 1993.

[44] K. Evans, M. Konikoff, R. Mathis, J. Maden, and G. Whipple. Totally ordered commutative monoids. *Semigroup Forum*, 62(2):249–278, 2001.

[45] H. Fargier. *Problèmes de satisfaction de contraintes flexibles et application a l'ordonnancement de production*. Thèse de doctorat, Institut de Recherche en Informatique de Toulouse (Université Paul Sabatier), Toulouse, France, 1994.

[46] H. Fargier and J. Lang. Uncertainty in constraint satisfaction problems: a probabilistic approach. In *Proc. of ECSQARU'93*, volume 747 of *LNCS*, pages 97–104, Granada, Spain, 1993.

[47] H. Fargier, J. Lang, and T. Schiex. Selecting preferred solutions in Fuzzy Constraint Satisfaction Problems. In *Proc. of the 1st European Congress on Fuzzy and Intelligent Technologies*, 1993.

[48] E. Freuder and R. Wallace. Partial constraint satisfaction. *Artificial Intelligence*, 58: 21–70, 1992.

[49] E. C. Freuder. Partial constraint satisfaction. In *Proc. of IJCAI'89*, pages 278–283, Detroit, MI, USA, 1989.

[50] E. C. Freuder and M. J. Quinn. Taking advantage of stable sets of variables in constraint satisfaction problems. In *Proc. of IJCAI'85*, pages 1076–1078, Los Angeles, CA, USA, 1985.

[51] P. Galinier and J.-K. Hao. Tabu search for maximal constraint satisfaction problems. In *Proc. of CP'97*, volume 1330 of *LNCS*, pages 196–208, Schloss Hagenberg, Austria, 1997.

[52] C. Gaspin. RNA Secondary Structure Determination and Representation Based on Constraints Satisfaction. *Constraints*, 6(2-3):201–221, 2001.

[53] C. Gaspin, S. de Givry, T. Schiex, P. Thébault, and M. Zytnicki. A new local consistency for weighted CSP applied to ncRNA detection. In *Proc. of ICLP'05 Workshop on Constraint Based Methods for Bioinformatics*, Sitges, Spain, 2005.

[54] G. Gottlob, N. Leone, and F. Scarcello. A comparison of strutural CSP decomposition methods. *Artificial Intelligence*, 124:243–282, 2000.

[55] F. Heras and J. Larrosa. Resolution in Max-SAT and its relation to local consistency in weighted CSPs. In *Proc. of IJCAI'05*, pages 193–198, Edinburgh, Scotland, 2005.

[56] U. Junker. Preference-based search for scheduling. In *Proc. of AAAI'00*, pages 904–909, Austin, TX, USA, 2000.

[57] U. Junker. Preference-based search and multi-criteria optimization. In *Proc. of AAAI'02*, pages 34–40, Edmonton, Alberta, Canada, 2002.

[58] U. Junker. Quickxplain: Preferred explanations and relaxations for over-constrained problems. In *Proc. of AAAI'04*, pages 167–172, San Jose, CA, USA, 2004.

[59] K. Kask and R. Dechter. A general scheme for automatic generation of search heuristics from specification dependencies. *Artificial Intelligence*, 129(1–2):91–131, 2001.

[60] L. Khatib, P. Morris, R. Morris, and F. Rossi. Temporal constraint reasoning with preferences. In *Proc. of IJCAI'01*, pages 322–327, Washington, USA, 2001.

[61] E. Klement, R. Mesiar, and E. Pap. *Triangular Norms*. Kluwer Academic Publishers, 2000.

[62] A. Koster. Frequency assignment problem web site. http://fap.zib.de.

[63] A. M. Koster. *Frequency assignment: Models and Algorithms*. PhD thesis, University of Maastricht, The Netherlands, 1999. Available at www.zib.de/koster/thesis.html.

[64] J. Larrosa. Boosting search with variable elimination. In *Proc. of CP'00*, volume 1894 of *LNCS*, pages 291–305, Singapore, 2000.

[65] J. Larrosa. On arc and node consistency in weighted CSP. In *Proc. of AAAI'02*, pages 48–53, Edmonton, Alberta, Canada, 2002.

[66] J. Larrosa and R. Dechter. On the dual representation of non-binary semiring-based csps. In *Proc. of the CP'00 Workshop on Modelling and Solving Soft Constraints*, 2000. http://www.math.unipd.it/~frossi/cp2000-soft/program.html.

[67] J. Larrosa and P. Meseguer. Exploiting the use of DAC in Max-CSP. In *Proc. of CP'96*, volume 1118 of *LNCS*, pages 308–322, Cambridge, MA, USA, 1996.

[68] J. Larrosa and P. Meseguer. Partition-based lower bound for Max-CSP. In *Proc. of CP'99*, volume 1713 of *LNCS*, pages 303–315, Alexandria, VI, USA, 1999.

[69] J. Larrosa and T. Schiex. In the quest of the best form of local consistency for weighted CSP. In *Proc. of IJCAI'03*, pages 239–244, Acapulco, Mexico, 2003.

[70] J. Larrosa and T. Schiex. Solving weighted CSP by maintaining arc consistency. *Artificial Intelligence*, 159(1-2):1–26, Nov. 2004.

[71] J. Larrosa, P. Meseguer, and T. Schiex. Maintaining reversible DAC for Max-CSP. *Artificial Intelligence*, 107(1):149–163, 1999.

[72] J. Larrosa, P. Meseguer, and M. Sánchez. Pseudo-tree Search with Soft Constraints. In *Proc. of ECAI'02*, pages 131–135, Lyon, France, 2002.

[73] J. Larrosa, E. Morancho, and D. Niso. On the practical applicability of bucket elimination: Still-life as a case study. *Journal of Artificial Intelligence Research*,

23:421–440, 2005.

[74]   M. Lemaître and G. Verfaillie. Daily management of an earth observation satellite : comparison of ILOG Solver with dedicated algorithms for valued constraint satisfaction problems. In *Proc. of the Third ILOG International Users Meeting*, Paris, France, 1997.

[75]   L. Lobjois, M. Lemâitre, and G. Verfaillie. Large neighbourhood search using constraint satisfaction for greedy reconstruction. In *Proc. of ECAI'00 Workshop on Modelling and Solving Constraint Problems*, 2000.

[76]   S. Loudni and P. Boizumault. Solving Constraint Optimization Problems in Anytime Contexts. In *Proc. of IJCAI'03*, pages 251–256, Acapulco, Mexico, 2003.

[77]   R. Marinescu and R. Dechter. AND/OR Tree Search for Constraint Optimization. In *Proc. of CP'04 Workshop on Preferences and Soft Constraints*, 2004.

[78]   R. Marinescu and R. Dechter. AND/OR Branch-and-Bound for Graphical Models. In *Proc. of IJCAI'05*, pages 224–229, Edinburgh, Scotland, 2005.

[79]   P. Meseguer and M. Sanchez. Specializing russian doll search. In *Proc. of CP'01* volume 2239 of *LNCS*, pages 464–478, Paphos, Cyprus, 2001.

[80]   P. Meseguer, J. Larrosa, and M. Sanchez. Lower bounds for non-binary constraint optimization problems. In *Proc. of CP'01*, volume 2239 of *LNCS*, pages 317–331, Paphos, Cyprus, 2001.

[81]   P. Meseguer, M. Sánchez, and G. Verfaillie. Opportunistic Specialization in Russian Doll Search. In *Proc. of CP'02*, volume 2470 of *LNCS*, pages 264–279, Ithaca, NY, USA, 2002.

[82]   M. Moretti, F. Rossi, E. Freuder, C. Likitvivatanavong, and R. Wallace. Explanations and optimization in preference-based configurators. In *Proc. of the Joint Workshop of the ERCIM Working Group on Constraints and the CologNet area on Constraint and Logic Programming on Constraint Solving and Constraint Logic Programming*, 2002.

[83]   J. O'Connell and D. Weeks. PedCheck: a program for identification of genotype incompatibilities in linkage analysis. *Am. J. Hum. Genet.*, 63(1):259–266, 1998.

[84]   J. O'Connell and D. Weeks. An optimal algorithm for automatic genotype elimination. *Am. J. Hum. Genet.*, 65(6):1733–1740, 1999.

[85]   C. M. Papadimitriou. *Computational Complexity*. Addison-Wesley Publishing Company, 1994.

[86]   J. Pearl. *Encyclopedia of Artificial Intelligence*, chapter Bayesian Inference Methods, pages 89–98. John Wiley & Sons, 1992.

[87]   T. Petit, J.-C. Régin, and C. Bessière. Meta-constraints on violations for over constrained problems. In *Proc. of IEEE-ICTAI'00*, pages 358–365, Vancouver, Canada, 2000.

[88]   T. Petit, J.-C. Régin, and C. Bessière. Specific filtering algorithms for over-constrained problems. In *Proc. of CP'01*, volume 2239 of *LNCS*, pages 451–463, Paphos, Cyprus, 2001.

[89]   T. Petit, J.-C. Régin, and C. Bessière. Range-based Algorithm for Max-CSP. In *Proc. of CP'02*, volume 2470 of *LNCS*, pages 280–294, Ithaca, NY, USA, 2002.

[90]   J.-C. Régin, T. Petit, C. Bessière, and J.-F. Puget. New lower bounds of constraint violations for over-constrained problems. In *Proc. of CP'01*, volume 2239 of *LNCS* pages 332–345, Paphos, Cyprus, 2001.

[91]   J. A. Robinson. A machine-oriented logic based on the resolution principle. *Journal*

of the ACM, 12(1):23–41, 1965.

[92] A. Rosenfeld, R. Hummel, and S. Zucker. Scene labeling by relaxation operations. *IEEE Trans. on Systems, Man, and Cybernetics*, 6(6):173–184, 1976.

[93] F. Rossi and A. Sperduti. Acquiring Both Constraint and Solution Preferences in Interactive Constraint Systems. *Constraints*, 9(4):311–332, 2004.

[94] H. Rudovà and K. Murray. University course timetabling with soft constraints. In *Proc. of PATAT'02*, pages 73–89, Gent, Belgium, 2002.

[95] Z. Ruttkay. Fuzzy constraint satisfaction. In *Proc. FUZZ-IEEE'94*, pages 1263–1268, Orlando, Florida, 1994.

[96] M. Sanchez, P. Meseguer, and J. Larrosa. Using Constraints with Memory to Implement Variable Elimination. In *Proc. of ECAI'04*, pages 216–220, 2004.

[97] M. Sanchez, J. Larrosa, and P. Meseguer. Tree Decomposition with Function Filtering. In *Proc. of CP'05*, volume 3709, pages 593–606, Sitges, Spain, 2005.

[98] T. Schiex. Arc consistency for soft constraints. In *Proc. of CP'00*, volume 1894 of *LNCS*, pages 411–424, Singapore, 2000.

[99] T. Schiex. Possibilistic constraint satisfaction problems or "How to handle soft constraints ?". In *Proc. of UAI'92*, pages 268–275, Stanford, CA, USA, 1992.

[100] T. Schiex, H. Fargier, and G. Verfaillie. Valued constraint satisfaction problems: hard and easy problems. In *Proc. of IJCAI'95*, pages 631–637, Montréal, Canada, 1995.

[101] L. Shapiro and R. Haralick. Structural descriptions and inexact matching. *IEEE Transactions on Pattern Analysis and Machine Intelligence*, 3:504–519, 1981.

[102] P. Shenoy. Valuation-based systems for discrete optimization. In Bonissone, Henrion, Kanal, and Lemmer, editors, *Uncertainty in AI*. North-Holland Publishers, 1991.

[103] J. Slaney, A. Binas, and D. Price. Guiding a Theorem Prover with Soft Constraints. In *Proc. of ECAI'04*, pages 221–225, Valencia, Spain, 2004.

[104] P. Snow and E. Freuder. Improved relaxation and search methods for approximate constraint satisfaction with a maximin criterion. In *Proc. of the Conf. of Canadian Society for Comput. Studies of Intelligence*, pages 227–230, 1990.

[105] C. Terrioux and P. Jégou. Bounded backtracking for the valued constraint satisfaction problems. In *Proc. of CP'03*, volume 2833 of *LNCS*, pages 709–723, Kinsale, Ireland, 2003.

[106] W. J. van Hoeve. A Hyper-Arc Consistency Algorithm for the soft AllDifferent Constraint. In *Proc. of CP'04*, volume 3258 of *LNCS*, pages 679–689, Toronto, Canada, 2004.

[107] W. J. van Hoeve, G. Pesant, and L.-M. Rousseau. On Global Warming (Softening Global Constraints). In *Proc. of CP'04 Workshop on Preferences and Soft Constraints*, Toronto, Canada, 2004.

[108] J. Váncza and A. Márkus. Solving Conditional and Conflicting Constraints in Manufacturing Process Planning. In *Proc. of CPAIOR'01 Workshop*, 2001.

[109] G. Verfaillie, M. Lemaître, and T. Schiex. Russian doll search. In *Proc. of AAAI'96*, pages 181–187, Portland, OR, USA, 1996.

[110] R. J. Wallace. Directed arc consistency preprocessing. In M. Meyer, editor, *Selected papers from the ECAI'94 Workshop on Constraint Processing*, volume 923 of *LNCS*, pages 121–137. Springer, Berlin, 1995.

[111] S. Will, A. Busch, and R. Backofen. Efficient Constraint-based Sequence Alignment

by Cluster Tree Elimination. In *Proc. of ICLP'05 Workshop on Constraint based Methods for Bioinformatics*, Sitges, Spain (see www.dimi.uniud.it/dovier/WCB05), 2005.

[112] M. Wilson and A. Borning. Hierarchical constraint logic programming. *J. Log. Program.*, 16(3):277–318, 1993.

Handbook of Constraint Programming   329
Edited by F. Rossi, P. van Beek and T. Walsh
© 2006 Elsevier B.V. All rights reserved

Chapter 10

Symmetry in Constraint Programming

Ian P. Gent, Karen E. Petrie, Jean-François Puget

Symmetry in constraints has always been important but in recent years has become a major research area in its own right. A key problem in constraint programming has long been recognised: search can revisit equivalent states over and over again. In principle this problem has been solved, with a number of different techniques. As we write, research remains very active for two reasons. First, there are many difficulties in the practical application of the techniques that are known for symmetry exclusion, and overcoming these remain important research problems. Second, the successes achieved in the area so far have encouraged researchers to find new ways to exploit symmetry. In this chapter we cover both these issues, and the details of the symmetry exclusion methods that have been conceived.

Figure 10.1: The solution to the puzzle of finding a chess position containing nine queens and a king of each colour, with the rule that no piece is on the same line (row, column or diagonal) as any queen of the opposite colour. Up to symmetry, the solution is unique.

To illustrate what we mean by symmetry, we consider the chess puzzle shown in Figure 10.1. The solution to this puzzle is unique "up to symmetry" [115], but what do we mean by symmetry in this context? By a "symmetry", we mean an operation which changes the positions of the pieces, but whose end-state obeys all the constraints if and only if the start-state does. Given a solution, which by definition satisfies all the constraints, we can find a new solution by applying any symmetry to the first solution we find. For example, given the pictured solution to the puzzle, we can swap the colours of each piece, so the black queens appear where the white queens are and vice versa. Similarly, we can rotate the chessboard by any multiple of 90 degrees to yield a new solution. Finally, we can reflect the chessboard about the horizontal axis, the vertical axis and both of the diagonal axes. Since these symmetries can be combined, there are 16 symmetries available, including the identity operation of leaving everything where it is.

Why is symmetry important? The main reason is that we can exploit symmetry to reduce the amount of search needed to solve the problem. This is of enormous potential benefit. For example, suppose we search for a solution to our chess puzzle, and the first assignment is to place a white queen in the top left hand corner. In fact, the search decision was not really to try a white queen in the top left corner, but instead the decision was to try all potential solutions with a queen of either colour in any corner of the board. Since there are 16 symmetries, we have the potential to reduce search by a factor of 16. A second reason for symmetry's importance is that many constraint problems have symmetry in them. Moreover, the act of modelling can introduce symmetries. For example, if we modelled the chess puzzle above with a variable for each queen ranging from 1 to 64 expressing its placement, there would be $2(9!)^2$ symmetric versions of each solution, as each set of queens can be permuted and the two sets swapped. Yet, this model might be desirable for effective propagation and heuristics, and so we would like to be able to deal with its symmetries effectively.

By far the most important application of symmetry in constraint programming is "symmetry breaking" in order to reduce search. The goal of symmetry breaking is never to explore two search states which are symmetric to each other, since we know the result in both cases must be the same.[1] It is common to identify three main approaches to symmetry breaking in constraint programming. The first approach is to reformulate the problem so that it has a reduced amount of symmetry, or even none at all. The second is to add symmetry breaking constraints before search starts, thereby making some symmetric solutions unacceptable while leaving at least one solution in each symmetric equivalence class. The final approach is to break symmetry dynamically during search, adapting the search procedure appropriately. This breakdown is simplistic, in that there is enormous variation within each approach, and great commonalities between approaches. However, it is a very useful informal categorisation and we will structure our discussion around it.

In the rest of this chapter we hope to answer the following questions: How do we go about achieving the search reductions that are possible? What general methods are there, and what tradeoffs are involved? How can we make it as easy as possible for the day-to-day constraint programmer to use? What research directions remain?

---

[1]The phrase "symmetry breaking" might be misleading, because not all methods actually break symmetry in the sense of creating a problem without symmetry. However, the usage is entrenched in the community and it would be even more confusing to try to change it.

10.1 Symmetries and Group Theory

The study of symmetry in mathematics is called *group theory*. We assume no background in group theory for reading this chapter, so we introduce all the concepts we need. We make no apologies for emphasising the role of group theory at this early stage, as it es-sential to understanding the role of symmetry in constraint programming. We can only introduce very briefly the key concepts, so this section should be taken only as the light-est introduction to what is one of the largest research areas in mathematics. Fortunately for most constraint programmers, a little knowledge of group theory is in fact enough to understand most of the work done to date. Sadly, introductions to group theory for math-ematicians often take for granted the link with symmetry, so we will spend a little time explaining this. We will explain group theory through *permutations*. First, nothing is lost since every group can be expressed as a set of permutations. Second, it makes it very easy to understand the link between a symmetry as an element of a group and a symmetry as an *action*. We will emphasise the notion of a group action, since this expresses how symmetries transform search states, and this is our main interest.

Example 10.1. Chessboard Symmetries
Consider a 3×3 chessboard. We label the nine squares with the numbers 1 to 9. These numbers are the *points* that will be moved by symmetries. There are eight natural symme-tries of a chessboard. We always include the *identity* symmetry, which leaves every point where it is. The identity is shown at the top left of Figure 10.2. Then, we can rotate the chessboard by 90, 180, and 270 degrees in a clockwise direction. The resulting locations of the points are shown in the rest of the top row of Figure 10.2. Finally, there are reflections in the vertical axis, in the horizontal axis, and in the two main diagonal axes, and these are shown in the bottom row.

1	2	3		7	4	1		9	8	7		3	6	9
4	5	6		8	5	2		6	5	4		2	5	8
7	8	9		9	6	3		3	2	1		1	4	7
	id				*r*90				*r*180				*r*270	

3	2	1		7	8	9		1	4	7		9	6	3
6	5	4		4	5	6		2	5	8		8	5	2
9	8	7		1	2	3		3	6	9		7	4	1
	x				*y*				*d*1				*d*2	

Figure 10.2: The 8 Symmetries of a 3×3 chessboard

The link between symmetries and permutations can be seen very simply. A permu-tation is a one-to-one correspondence between a set and itself. Each symmetry defines a permutation of the set of points. An easy way to write down permutations is in *Cauchy form*. Cauchy form is two rows of numbers. The top row is the complete set of elements, in ascending order, that the permutation acts over. The second row shows which number each element of the top rows maps to. For example, the identity symmetry and permutation maps each point to itself, and is shown in Cauchy form on the top left of Figure 10.3. The rotational symmetry by 90 degrees is shown in Cauchy form on the top right. We see that the point 1 is replaced by 7 after $r90$, 7 in turn is replaced by 9, 9 by 3, and 3 by 1. This gives a *cycle* (1 7 9 3). Another cycle is (2 4 8 6) and there is another trivial cycle just containing (5). In the main, group theorists do not use Cauchy form, preferring a notation based on the set of cycles a permutation defines.

$$id : \begin{pmatrix} 1 & 2 & 3 & 4 & 5 & 6 & 7 & 8 & 9 \\ 1 & 2 & 3 & 4 & 5 & 6 & 7 & 8 & 9 \end{pmatrix} \qquad r90 : \begin{pmatrix} 1 & 2 & 3 & 4 & 5 & 6 & 7 & 8 & 9 \\ 7 & 4 & 1 & 8 & 5 & 2 & 9 & 6 & 3 \end{pmatrix}$$

$$r180 : \begin{pmatrix} 1 & 2 & 3 & 4 & 5 & 6 & 7 & 8 & 9 \\ 9 & 8 & 7 & 6 & 5 & 4 & 3 & 2 & 1 \end{pmatrix} \qquad r270 : \begin{pmatrix} 1 & 2 & 3 & 4 & 5 & 6 & 7 & 8 & 9 \\ 3 & 6 & 9 & 2 & 5 & 8 & 1 & 4 & 7 \end{pmatrix}$$

$$x : \begin{pmatrix} 1 & 2 & 3 & 4 & 5 & 6 & 7 & 8 & 9 \\ 3 & 2 & 1 & 6 & 5 & 4 & 9 & 8 & 7 \end{pmatrix} \qquad y : \begin{pmatrix} 1 & 2 & 3 & 4 & 5 & 6 & 7 & 8 & 9 \\ 7 & 8 & 9 & 4 & 5 & 6 & 1 & 2 & 3 \end{pmatrix}$$

$$d1 : \begin{pmatrix} 1 & 2 & 3 & 4 & 5 & 6 & 7 & 8 & 9 \\ 1 & 4 & 7 & 2 & 5 & 8 & 3 & 6 & 9 \end{pmatrix} \qquad d2 : \begin{pmatrix} 1 & 2 & 3 & 4 & 5 & 6 & 7 & 8 & 9 \\ 9 & 6 & 3 & 8 & 5 & 2 & 7 & 4 & 1 \end{pmatrix}$$

Figure 10.3: Permutations representing the symmetries of a chessboard, written in Cauchy form

Example 10.2. Cyclic form

The symmetry $r90$ above contains cycles (1 3 9 7), (2 4 6 8), and (5). The *cyclic form* of $r90$ is (1 3 9 7)(2 4 6 8)(5) although cycles of length one can be omitted. The permutatio maps each point to the succeeding element of the cycle it is in, except that the last element is mapped to the first and a point in no cycle is mapped to itself. In cyclic form, we can write the symmetries of the 3×3 chessboard as shown in Figure 10.4.

$id :$	()	$r90 :$	(1 3 9 7)(2 4 6 8)
$r180 :$	(1 9)(2 8)(3 7)(4 8)	$r270 :$	(1 7 9 3)(2 4 8 6)
$x :$	(1 3)(4 6)(7 9)	$y :$	(1 7)(2 8)(3 9)
$d1 :$	(2 4)(3 7)(6 8)	ha $d2 :$	(1 9)(2 6)(4 8)

Figure 10.4: Permutations representing the symmetries of a chessboard, written in cyclic form

Comparing Figures 10.3 and 10.4 shows that the cyclic form is far more concise, especially when many points are unmoved by a permutation. One disadvantage is that it does not define exactly the set of points that the permutation is acting on: for example none of the permutations above move the point 5, so the number 5 does not appear in Figure 10.4. Also, the same permutation can be written down in many different ways, since cycles can appear in any order and each cycle can start with any element in it. However, the cyclic form is so natural for people to use that the computational group theory system GAP uses it as its input language for permutations, even though it then converts them internally into a more computationally efficient form.

Both forms of writing down permutations make it easy to see how a permutation *acts* on a point. In general, if p is a point and g a permutation, then we will write p^g to write down the point that p is moved to under g. For example, $1^{r90} = 7$, and $1^{r270} = 3$. We often extend this notation in the natural way to sets of other data structures containing points. For example, we have $\{1, 3, 8\}^{r90} = \{1^{r90}, 3^{r90}, 8^{r90}\} = \{7, 1, 6\} = \{1, 6, 7\}$: the equivalence between the last two terms is simply because sets are unordered.

There are certain key facts about permutations which provide the link between them and groups. We will explain these, then provide the fundamental definition of a group. First, it is easy to work out the composition of two permutations, which for permutations f and g we will write as $f \circ g$. The result of $f \circ g$ is calculated by taking, for each point, the result of moving that point under f and then by g. That is, for any point p, $p^{f \circ g} = (p^f)^g$. It is important to notice the order of action, i.e. we do f and then g when we write $f \circ g$, which is the other way round compared to function composition such as $\sin(\cos(x))$. Since both f and g are one-to-one correspondences, so is their composition, so the composition of two permutations is another permutation. We can calculate the composition pointwise: we simply work out what 1 moves to under f, then what the result moves to under g, and repeat for each other point.

Example 10.3. Composition of Permutations

$$r90 = \begin{pmatrix} 1 & 2 & 3 & 4 & 5 & 6 & 7 & 8 & 9 \\ 7 & 4 & 1 & 8 & 5 & 2 & 9 & 6 & 3 \end{pmatrix}$$

$$x = \begin{pmatrix} 1 & 2 & 3 & 4 & 5 & 6 & 7 & 8 & 9 \\ 3 & 2 & 1 & 6 & 5 & 4 & 9 & 8 & 7 \end{pmatrix}$$

$$r90 \circ x = \begin{pmatrix} 1 & 2 & 3 & 4 & 5 & 6 & 7 & 8 & 9 \\ 9 & 6 & 3 & 8 & 5 & 2 & 7 & 4 & 1 \end{pmatrix} = d2$$

We have already described the existence of the identity permutation, which we call id. This can be defined as the empty set of cycles for any set of points. For any permutation f there is an *inverse* permutation, such that $f \circ f^{-1} = id$. This is easily calculated: in the cyclic form we just reverse the order of each cycle; and in the Cauchy form we swap the two rows and then reorder the columns so that the first row is in numerical order.

Example 10.4. Inverse of a permutation

$$r90 = \begin{pmatrix} 1 & 2 & 3 & 4 & 5 & 6 & 7 & 8 & 9 \\ 7 & 4 & 1 & 8 & 5 & 2 & 9 & 6 & 3 \end{pmatrix}$$

$$\begin{pmatrix} 7 & 4 & 1 & 8 & 5 & 2 & 9 & 6 & 3 \\ 1 & 2 & 3 & 4 & 5 & 6 & 7 & 8 & 9 \end{pmatrix} \text{ by swapping rows}$$

$$r90^{-1} = \begin{pmatrix} 1 & 2 & 3 & 4 & 5 & 6 & 7 & 8 & 9 \\ 3 & 6 & 9 & 2 & 5 & 8 & 1 & 4 & 7 \end{pmatrix} \text{ by reordering} \quad = r270$$

Finally, we note that composition of permutations is associative. That is, $f \circ (g \circ h) = (f \circ g) \circ h$. The truth of this relies on the definition of permutation composition, i.e. that $g \circ h$ gives, for each point, the same result as applying g and then h. So, for example, $7^{(f \circ g) \circ h}$ is the result of applying f to 7, g to the result, and h to the result of that: but this is exactly the same as $7^{f \circ (g \circ h)}$, which is also found by applying f, to 7, g to the result, and h to the result of that. We now, finally, present the axioms defining a group.

Definition 10.5. *Group Axioms*
A group is a non-empty set G with a composition operator ∘ such that:
- G is closed under ∘. That is, for all $g, h \in G, g \circ h \in G$; and
- there is an identity $id \in G$. That is, for all $g \in G, g \circ id = id \circ g = g$; and
- every element g of G has an inverse g^{-1} such that $g \circ g^{-1} = g^{-1} \circ g = id$; and
- ∘ is associative. That is, for all $f, g, h \in G, (f \circ g) \circ h = f \circ (g \circ h)$.

Definition 10.6. *Order of a Group*
The order of a group G is the number of elements in the set G. It is denoted by $|G|$.

Example 10.7. The set of symmetries of a chessboard $\{id, x, y, d1, d2, r90, r180, r270$ form a group of order 8. We have that $r90^{-1} = r270$, $r270^{-1} = r90$, and all other elements g are self-inverse, i.e. $g^{-1} = g$. The group of a chessboard is non-commutative, since $d1 \circ r90 = x$ but $r90 \circ d1 = y$. In most applications in constraint programming, the group is not commutative. Note that we omitted mention of the operation associated with the group, i.e. permutation composition: this is often done where it will not cause confusion.

Note that our (entirely standard) definition of a group nowhere mentions the action done by the group element. It is vital to understand that group elements can operate in two distinct ways. First, there is the action that a group element (i.e. symmetry) has on the points that it acts on. In the chessboard example, the points were $1 \ldots 9$, and we wrote p for the result of the action of g on point p. This is what we have emphasised up to now. Second, a group element g operates by the composition operator to permute the values o other elements in the group. That is, $f \circ g$ gives another group element. The latter kind of operation is the focus of most study in group theory. In contrast, it is the group action which is of far more importance to us, since it is this action which represents the function of a symmetry on the variables and values in a constraint problem.

For permutations, the operation ∘ is composition as described above. We have already shown that there is an identity permutation, all permutations have inverses, and that composition of permutations is associative. The final condition is *closure*. We have shown that the composition of two permutations is another permutation. However, for a set of permutations to form a group, we have to have that the composition of any two permutations is in the set. This depends on the set of permutations we have chosen. There is an easy way to guarantee closure, which is to take a set of permutations and *generate* all permutations which result from composing them arbitrarily.

Definition 10.8. *The Generators of a Group*
Let S be any set of elements (for example, permutations) that can be composed by the group operation ∘ (for example, permutation composition). The set S generates G if every element of G can be written as a product of elements in S and every product of any sequence of elements of S is in G. The set S is called a set of generators for G and we write $G = \langle S \rangle$.

Example 10.9. Generators of Chessboard Symmetries
The chessboard symmetries are generated by $\{r90, d1\}$ since:

$$id = r90 \circ r90 \circ r90 \circ r90 = \begin{pmatrix} 1 & 2 & 3 & 4 & 5 & 6 & 7 & 8 & 9 \\ 1 & 2 & 3 & 4 & 5 & 6 & 7 & 8 & 9 \end{pmatrix}$$

$$r90 = r90 = \begin{pmatrix} 1 & 2 & 3 & 4 & 5 & 6 & 7 & 8 & 9 \\ 7 & 4 & 1 & 8 & 5 & 2 & 9 & 6 & 3 \end{pmatrix}$$

$$r180 = r90 \circ r90 = \begin{pmatrix} 1 & 2 & 3 & 4 & 5 & 6 & 7 & 8 & 9 \\ 9 & 8 & 7 & 6 & 5 & 4 & 3 & 2 & 1 \end{pmatrix}$$

$$r270 = r90 \circ r90 \circ r90 = \begin{pmatrix} 1 & 2 & 3 & 4 & 5 & 6 & 7 & 8 & 9 \\ 3 & 6 & 9 & 2 & 5 & 8 & 1 & 4 & 7 \end{pmatrix}$$

$$d1 = d1 = \begin{pmatrix} 1 & 2 & 3 & 4 & 5 & 6 & 7 & 8 & 9 \\ 1 & 4 & 7 & 2 & 5 & 8 & 3 & 6 & 9 \end{pmatrix}$$

$$y = d1 \circ r90 = \begin{pmatrix} 1 & 2 & 3 & 4 & 5 & 6 & 7 & 8 & 9 \\ 7 & 8 & 9 & 4 & 5 & 6 & 1 & 2 & 3 \end{pmatrix}$$

$$d2 = r90 \circ r90 \circ d1 = \begin{pmatrix} 1 & 2 & 3 & 4 & 5 & 6 & 7 & 8 & 9 \\ 9 & 6 & 3 & 8 & 5 & 2 & 7 & 4 & 1 \end{pmatrix}$$

$$x = r90 \circ d1 = \begin{pmatrix} 1 & 2 & 3 & 4 & 5 & 6 & 7 & 8 & 9 \\ 3 & 2 & 1 & 6 & 5 & 4 & 9 & 8 & 7 \end{pmatrix}$$

Given any set of permutations, we can always work with the group generated by that set, since it is by definition closed. Finding and working with generators can be a very important means of representing groups. If there are $|G|$ elements in a group, there is always a generating set of size $\log_2(|G|)$ or smaller.

Definition 10.10. *Subgroup*
A subgroup H of a group G is a subset of G that is itself a group, with the same composition operator as G. Two simple and universal examples of subgroups are that G is always a subgroup of G, as is $\{id\}$.

Example 10.11. Subgroup of Chessboard Symmetry:
The set $\{id, r90, r180, r270\}$ form a subgroup of order 4. As can be seen from Example 10.1, this can be generated by the element $r90$.

Given a subgroup H of a group G and an element g of G, the (right) *coset* $H \circ g$ is the set of elements $\{h \circ g | h \in H\}$. Two cosets of H in G constructed with different elements are either disjoint or the same, i.e. if $H \circ f \cap H \circ g \neq \emptyset$ then $H \circ f = H \circ g$. Thus the cosets of H partition the elements of G. Furthermore, all the cosets of H have size $|H|$. The number of cosets is called the *index* of H in G and is denoted by $|G : H|$. If one element is chosen from each coset of H, then a set of *coset representatives* is formed, this set is the *right transversal*. The group G is the union of the cosets formed by composing the elements of H with these coset representatives.

Example 10.12. Cosets of Chessboard Symmetries
The group G is the full chessboard symmetries, and H is the rotations of the chessboard. Then the two cosets of H are: $\{id, r90, r180, r270\}$ and $\{d1, x, d2, y\}$, where $H = H \circ id$ and $H = H \circ d1$. One set of coset representatives is $\{id, d1\}$, but there are a total of 16 possible sets of coset representatives, comprising one element from each coset.

The *orbit* of a point in G is a set of the different points that the point can be mapped to by elements of G.

Definition 10.13. *Orbit*
The orbit of a point δ in G is the set $\delta^G = \{\delta^g \mid g \in G\}$.

Example 10.14. Orbits of Points on Chessboard
Looking back at the diagram of chessboard symmetries given in Example 10.1, the orbits of a given point can be calculated. For example, the orbit of 1 is $\{1, 3, 7, 9\}$, because $1^{id} = 1$, $1^{r90} = 7$, $1^{r180} = 9$, $1^{r270} = 3$, and because all other group elements map 1 to one of these points.

The *stabiliser* of a point is the set of elements which fixes or stabilises the point. It indicates which elements can be applied to a point, which do not cause the value of the point to move.

Definition 10.15. *Stabiliser*
Let G be a permutation group acting on (amongst others) a point β. The stabiliser *of β in G is defined by: $G_\beta = \{g \in G \mid \beta^g = \beta\}$. The stabiliser G_β is a subgroup of the group G*

Example 10.16. Stabilisers of chessboard symmetries
From Figure 10.2 of chessboard symmetries, the stabiliser of any given point can be identified. For instance, the stabiliser of point 1 is $G_1 = \{id, d1\}$ as these elements map point 1 back to itself. The stabiliser of point 5 is the whole group G, i.e. $G_5 = G$, since none of the symmetries move point 5.

10.1.1 Group Theory in Constraint Programming

Whenever a constraint problem has symmetry, we can construct a group to represent the symmetry in the problem. The elements of the group permute points, dependent on the symmetries in the particular problem. The points that the elements of the group act on will typically be variable-value pairs.

Example 10.17. Representing the Symmetry of the Chess problem in Figure 10.1
Variables - The CSP has n^2 variables corresponding to the squares of the chessboard, t represent the variables requires n^2 labels
Values- There are 5 possible values for each square of the chessboard: a white queen, a black queen, a white king, a black queen, or it is empty.
Variable-Value - There are n^2 possible labels for the variables, and 5 possible labels for the variables, to represent variable-value pairs requires $5n^2$ points.

There is one particularly important group of permutations. The set S_n of *all* permutations of n objects forms a group and is called the *symmetric group* over n elements. The group S_n is of size $n!$. This group comes up frequently in constraints because we often have n objects which are indistinguishable between each other, and which are thus acted on by S_n. It also arises in combinations. For example, we will see that a commonly occurring situation is a two-dimensional matrix of variables, where we can freely permute m columns (preserving the rows) and n rows (preserving the columns). Since we can first permute the columns and then the rows, the group we have is a combination known as the *direct product $S_m \times S_n$.*

10.1.2   Computational Group Theory

Computational Group Theory is a large interdisciplinary research area in mathematics and computer science. Butler has written a text book on the algorithms used in this area [17] and Holt *et al.* [65] have recently written a handbook of computational group theory. There are two major packages for computational group theory called GAP [46] and Magma [14]. Constraint programmers using symmetry can often employ GAP or Magma as an external function. However, if that is not available or appropriate, understanding of computational group theory algorithms is important. The most important algorithm of all is the Schier Sims algorithm, for which we give an extremely brief outline.

The Schreier Sims algorithm [108] is used to construct a stabiliser chain $G_0, G_1, \ldots,$ G_n as follows:

$$
\begin{aligned}
G_0 &= G \\
\forall i \in I^n, \; G_i &= G_{i-1}
\end{aligned}
$$

By definition,

$$
G_i = \{\sigma \in G : 0^\sigma = 0 \wedge \ldots \wedge (i-1)^\sigma = i - 1\}
$$
$$
G_n \subseteq G_{n-1} \subseteq \ldots G_1 \subseteq G_0
$$

The Schreier Sims algorithm also computes set of coset representatives U_i. Those are orbits of i in G_i: $U_i = i^{G_i}$.

By definition, U_i is the set of values which i is mapped to by all symmetries in G that leave at least $0, \ldots, (i-1)$ unchanged.

In constraint programming terms the stabiliser is perhaps the most useful concept of those outlined above. The stabiliser of a variable/value pair shows what symmetry is left unbroken once that value is assigned to the given variable, during search. This is explained in more detail, with regards to GAP-SBDS, in Section 10.5.4. The stabiliser chain represents the symmetry which remains, after a collection of variables have been assigned during search.

10.2   Definitions

It might seem self-evident that in order to deal with symmetry in constraint satisfaction problems (CSPs), practitioners must first understand what is meant by symmetry. This appears not to be true: many papers on the topic do not offer a precise definition of what a symmetry is. The papers which do offer definitions often give fundamentally different ones to each other, while still identifying the same symmetries in a given problem and dealing with them correctly. There are two broad types of definition: those that define symmetry as a property of the solution set and those that define symmetry as a property that can be identified in the statement of the problem, without solving it. These will be referred to as solution symmetry and problem symmetry. In this section we give a brief survey of the definitions contained in the literature, before concentrating in more depth on recent definitions proposed by Cohen *et al* [21].

An example of a definition of solution symmetry in CSPs is given by Brown, Finkelstein & Purdom [16]: "A symmetry is a permutation that leaves invariant the set of solutions sequences to a problem." Backofen and Will [5] allow for a much broader class of problem transformations: "A symmetry S for a constraint program C_{Pr}, where a set of solutions for a given problem is denoted $\| \, C_{Pr} \, \|$, is a bijective function such that S $\| \, C_{Pr} \, \| \rightarrow \| \, C_{Pr} \, \|$." Although not explicitly stated, Backofen and Will allow a symmetry to be specified by its effect on each individual assignment of a value to a variable, this allows them to consider symmetries with regard to partial assignments.

Many definitions define restricted forms of symmetry that affect only the variables or only the values. Interchangeability, as outlined in Definition 10.18 by Freuder [39], is a limited form of solution symmetry, which only operates over values.

Definition 10.18. *Two values a, b for a variable v are fully interchangeable iff every solution to the CSP containing the assignment $\langle v, a \rangle$ remains a solution when b is substituted for a, and vice versa.*

As Freuder notes, in general identifying fully interchangeable values requires finding all solutions to the CSP. He defines local forms of interchangeability that can be identified by inspecting the problem. Definition 10.19 outlines neighbourhood interchangeability, which is a form of constraint symmetry.

Definition 10.19. *Two values a, b for a variable v are neighbourhood interchangeable iff for every constraint C on the variable v, the set of variable-value pairs that satisfies the constraint with the pair $\langle v, a \rangle$ is the same as the set of variable-value pairs that satisfies the constraints with the pair $\langle v, b \rangle$.*

Choueiry and Noubir extend the idea of interchangeability to compute another form of local interchangeability, and showed how to exploit these results in practice [19].

Benhamou [8] extends the ideas of value interchangeability slightly and distinguishes between *semantic* and *syntactic* symmetry in CSPs, corresponding to solution symmetry and problem symmetry respectively. He defines two kinds of semantic symmetry. Two values a_i and b_i for a CSP are symmetric for satisfiability if: there is a solution which contains the value a_i iff there is a solution which contains the value b_i. Two values a and b_i are symmetric for all solutions if: each solution containing the value a_i can be mapped to a solution containing the value b_i, and vice versa. If two values are symmetric for all solutions they are also symmetric for satisfiability. Identifying semantic symmetries requires solving the CSP to find all solutions, and then examining them. Benhamou defines syntactic symmetry to mean that the permutation does not change any constraint relation, defined as a set of tuples.

The notion of interchangeable values has been and is still widely used and studied, e.g. [72, 55]. However, for the purposes of this overview, we regard interchangeability as a kind of *value symmetry*. Thus, we often discuss methods below which can be applied to interchangeable values, but do not point this out explicitly.

In contrast to this value centric approach, variable centric definitions have also been proposed. In CSPs, permuting the variables in a constraint defined intensionally will in general change the constraints, e.g. the constraint $x+y = z$ is not the same as the constraint $x+z = y$. Puget [97] defines the notion of a symmetrical constraint, i.e. a constraint which is not affected by the order of the variables. For instance, the $\neq$ constraint is symmetrical. Puget's definition means that a symmetry of a CSP is a permutation of the variables which maps the set of constraints into a symmetrically equivalent set: any constraint is either unchanged by the permutation or is an instance of a symmetrical constraint and is mapped onto a constraint on the same set of variables.

A similar idea was introduced by Roy and Pachet [105]. They define the notion of *intensional permutability*. For two variables to be intensionally permutable they must have the same domain; any constraints affecting either of the two variables must affect both; and the two variables must be interchangeable in these constraints. The constraint is assumed to be defined intensionally, i.e. in terms of a formula, hence the name. An example of intensional permutability can be given by considering a linear constraint: in this case any two variables with the same coefficient and the same domain are intensionally permutable with respect to that constraint.

The definitions of symmetry given by Puget [97] and Roy & Pachet are restricted to permuting variables of the problem. Meseguer and Torras [84] give a definition of symmetry which acts on both the variables and the values of a CSP. Their definition allows both variable symmetries (that permute only the variables) and value symmetries (that permute only the values) as special cases. However, it does not fit every transformation of a CSP that we would want to recognise as a symmetry. Meseguer and Torras use the chessboard symmetries as an example, in a commonly used CSP formulation where only one piece is placed per row, the variables correspond to the rows of the chessboard and the values correspond to the columns. They show that reflection through $180°$ is a symmetry of the CSP by their definition, but four symmetries are not: reflection in the diagonals, rotation through $90°$, and $270°$.

McDonald and Smith [82] state that "a symmetry of P is a bijective function $\sigma : A \rightarrow A$ where A is some representation of a state in search e.g. a list of assigned variables, a set of current domains etc., such that the following holds: 1. Given A a partial or full assignment of P, if A satisfies the constraints C, then so does $\sigma(A)$; and 2. Similarly, if A is a nogood, then so too is $\sigma(A)$." This allows symmetries operating on both the variables and values; it gives a good intuitive view of problem symmetry space. However, due to the undefined nature of A it does not provide a rigorous definition, that could be used to identify the symmetry of a problem.

The above survey of symmetry definitions shows that symmetry definitions differ both on what aspect of the CSP they act on (only the variables, only the values or variable-value pairs) and in what they preserve (the constraints or the set of solutions). All definitions agree that symmetries map solutions to solutions; they disagree over whether this is a defining property, so that any bijective mapping of the right kind that preserves the solutions must be a symmetry, or a consequence of leaving the constraints unchanged.

Defining symmetry as preserving the set of solutions does not seem to offer a practical route to identifying symmetry in CSPs. Detecting semantic symmetries is, unsurprisingly, intractable [85, 111]: to find the full symmetry group we might need all the solutions to the CSP. On the other hand, the solution symmetry group is well-defined, whereas equivalent CSPs differing only slightly in the way that constraints are expressed, may have different problem symmetries. It may be possible, either deliberately or inadvertently, to write the constraints of a CSP in such a way that the symmetry of the problem being modelled is not apparent.

For the purpose of this chapter a definition of both solution symmetry, Definition 10.20, and a definition of problem symmetry, Definition 10.21 are given. These are in the spirit of [21], but are less formally defined.

Definition 10.20. *Solution Symmetry*
A solution symmetry is a permutation of the set of ⟨*variable*, *value*⟩ *pairs which preserves*

the set of solutions.

Definition 10.21. *Problem Symmetry*
A problem symmetry is a permutation of the set of ⟨variable, value⟩ pairs which preserves the set of constraints.

Both problem and solution symmetry allow variable and value symmetries as special cases.

In order for Definition 10.21 to be complete, a suitable interpretation of what it means to preserve the sets of constraints is needed. Any constraint c_i with scope $V_i \subseteq V$ can be defined by a set of satisfying ⟨variable, value⟩ tuples. A symmetry whose action on the set of possible ⟨variable, value⟩ tuples has been specified can be applied to the set of ⟨variable, value⟩ tuples satisfying a constraint, yielding a new set of ⟨variable, value⟩ tuples. The resulting ⟨variable, value⟩ tuples may not all relate to the same set of variables as the original constraint or each other. However, if the results of applying the symmetry to all the ⟨variable, value⟩ tuples, defining all the constraints is the same set of ⟨variable, value⟩ tuples, it can be said that the constraints are unchanged by the action of the symmetry. This definition does not require a symmetry to leave each individual constraint unchanged, but rather the set of constraints.

A recent paper by Cohen *et al.*, looks more closely at the differences between Solution Symmetry and Problem Symmetry (which they call Constraint Symmetry) [21]. Cohen *et al.* both give more rigorous definitions of the two concepts, and show the difference between the two definitions in practice.

10.3 Reformulation

Modelling has a substantial effect on how efficiently a problem can be solved. An appropriate reformulation of a model can turn an infeasible problem in practical terms into a feasible one. Modelling and reformulation are equally important for symmetry breaking. Different models of the same problem can have different symmetries; one formulation can have symmetries which are easier to deal with than another. In extreme cases, one formulation can have no symmetry at all. In other cases, the amount of symmetry can be greatly reduced from one model to another. Moreover, once a problem has been reformulated the remaining symmetries can still be dealt with before or during search, while other symmetry breaking methods can lead to great difficulties in combination with each other. Thus, reformulation of a problem can be critical in dealing with symmetries.

For a first example we mention the well known "social golfers problem", problem 10 in CSPLib, although we will only sketch the issues here since Smith goes into some detail in her chapter.[2] In this problem, 32 golfers want to play in 8 groups of 4 each week, so that any two golfers play in the same group at most once, for as many weeks as possible, the difficult case being 10 weeks. We can construct an otherwise sensible model with $32!10!8!^{10}4!^{80}$ symmetries: we can permute the 32 players; we can permute the 10 weeks; within each week we can (separately) permute the groups; and within each group we can (separately) permute the four players. In this model there are more than 10^{198} symmetric versions of each essentially different solution, and there is a very good chance that search

---

[2]"Modelling", by Barbara Smith, this Handbook.

will thrash impossibly. By remodelling, Smith reduces this number to 32!10! [113]. For each pair of players we have a variable indicating which week they play together in (or an extra variable if they never meet): the only symmetries left are the week and the player symmetries. There are still huge numbers of symmetries left, but they are of a much simpler form.

One important technique is the use of *set variables* where we have a number of indistinguishable variables. Set variables are available in most constraint solvers, and allow us to express constraints on sets' size, intersection, union, etc. In the golfers' problem, for example, one might encode the groups playing within each week as being eight set variables. Each one is constrained to be of size 4 and they are pairwise constrained to have no intersection. Because set variables are implemented with no implicit ordering between elements, we have lost the 4! symmetries in each group, reducing the total symmetries by a factor of 24^{80} in the problem. Furthermore, in the golfers' problem we can represent the constraint that two players play together no more than once, by saying that the intersection of any two groups in different weeks is of size 1 or 0. There are some theoretical and practical difficulties associated with set variables. One is that different representations of set variables by the solver have dramatically different behaviours in propagation [67]: if a solver happens to use the representation least suitable for the constraints being used, search can be dramatically increased. Another difficulty occurs when we wish to use a mixture of set and integer variables. We may have constraints on elements of a set that are most natural to express on integer variables. "Channelling" between set and integer variables can be difficult and can again lead to a failure to propagate until late in search. Alternatively, we might re-introduce integer variables to represent the elements of the set, thereby bringing back many of the symmetry problems that the set variables avoided in the first place. Despite these potential disadvantages, set variables remain a very important modelling technique to consider in any problem where a number of variables have the symmetry group S_n. Because of this, representation of set variables and propagation techniques for them are an important area of study [56, 67, 75, 106]. Another chapter in this Handbook describes set variables in detail.[3]

Another example of reformulation again illustrates the dramatic improvements that can be achieved, while even more dramatically illustrating the extent to which reformulating is an art more than a science. The all-interval series problem (problem 7 in CSPLib) is to find a permutation of the n integers from 0 to $n - 1$ so that the differences between adjacent numbers are also a permutation of the numbers from 1 to $n - 1$. There are 4 obvious symmetries in the problem: the identity, reversing the series, negating each element by subtracting it from $n - 1$, and doing both. Gent et al [54] report on a reformulation of the problem based on the observation that we can cycle a solution to the problem about a pivot to generate another solution. The location of this pivot is dependent on the assignments made. As an example, here are two solutions for $n = 11$. Differences are written underneath the numbers:

```
0 10 1 9 2 8 3 7 4 6 5          3 7 4 6 5 0 10 1 9 2 8
 10 9 8 7 6 5 4 3 2 1            4 3 2 1 5 10 9 8 7 6
```

The difference between the first number (0) on the left and last number (5) is 5. This means we can split the sequence between the 8 and 3, losing the difference 5. We can join the

---

[3]"Constraints over Structured Domains", by Carmen Gervet, this Handbook.

rest of the sequence on to the start, because the $5 - 0$ will now replace $8 - 3$. This yields exactly the solution shown on the right. In this case the pivot is between the values 8 and 3. The difference between first and last terms must always duplicate a difference in the sequence, so this operation can be applied to any solution. Because of this, we do not merely reformulate the constraint model, but actually move to solve a different problem, whose solutions lead to solutions of the original. In the reformulated problem, we find a permutation of the sequence $0, 1, \ldots n - 1$, but we now include the difference between first and last numbers, giving n differences instead of $n - 1$. The sequence has to obey two constraints: that the permutation starts $0, n - 1, 1$; and that the n differences between consecutive numbers contain all of $1, \ldots n - 1$ with one difference occurring exactly twice. [50] show that (for $n > 4$) each solution gives 8 distinct solutions to the all-interval series problem, but the reformulation has no symmetry at all. Search in this model is about 50 times faster than any competing technique.

It is possible to take advantage of different 'viewpoints' [73] of a constraint problem. To take a simple example, suppose we insist that n variables, each with the same n values, must all take different values. We can look at this problem from two points of view: we can find values for each variable, or we can find variables for each value. If there is symmetry, then value symmetry in the first viewpoint is interchanged with variable symmetry in the second viewpoint, and vice versa. This is useful if we have at hand a technique which is good at one kind of symmetry: for example Roney-Dougal *et al* [103] used this idea to break a group of variable symmetries using an efficient technique for value symmetries. Flener et al [36]. showed how value symmetries in matrix models can be transformed to variable symmetries by adding a dimension of 0/1 variables to the matrix, the new symmetries being broken using techniques described in Section 10.4.5 below. Law and Lee studied this idea theoretically and generalised it to cases where the translation is not to 0/1 variables [74].

Recently, there has been one significant advance in understanding how reformulation can be applied mechanically. Prestwich has shown that value symmetries can be eliminated automatically by a new encoding from constraints into SAT, the 'maximality encoding' [93]. This breaks all value symmetries of a special kind Prestwich calls 'Dynamic Substitutability', a variant of Freuder's value interchangeability [39]. A particular important aspect of the contribution is that Prestwich's encoding eliminates all dynamic substitutability without any detection being necessary. This means that no detection program needs to be run, nor does the constraint programmer need to specify the symmetry in any form. A disadvantage of this technique is its limitation to certain types of value symmetry. However, as mentioned above, any remaining symmetry in the translated SAT problem can be detected and broken using standard SAT techniques.

Sadly, for a method with so many advantages, there is very little we can say about reformulation because there is no fully general technique known. Not only that, but the illustrative examples above show considerable insight about their respective problems. Also, there was no guarantee (before running the relevant constraint programs) that they would lead to improved search. About the only truly general comment we can make is that the very great importance of formulating problems to reduce symmetry is not fairly reflected in the short space we devote to it in this chapter. There is a wonderful research opening for the discovery of general techniques akin to the lex-leader method for adding constraints, moving the area of reformulation from a black art to a science where questions were on tradeoffs and implementation issues, rather than the need for magical insights.

10.4 Adding Constraints Before Search

Without doubt, the method of symmetry breaking that has been most used historically involves adding constraints to the basic model. In this context, the term "symmetry breaking" is entirely appropriate. We move from a problem with a lot of symmetry to a new problem with greatly reduced symmetry – ideally with none at all. The constraints we add to achieve this are called "symmetry breaking constraints".

Constraint programmers have always added symmetry breaking constraints in an ad hoc fashion when they have recognised symmetry in a constraint problem. Often it is easy to think of constraints that break all or a large part of symmetry. For example, suppose that we have 100 variables in an array X which are indistinguishable (so that they can be freely permuted). It is straightforward, and correct, to insist that the variables are in nondecreasing order, $X[1] \leq X[2] \ldots \leq X[100]$. If we further know that all variables must be different, we can make this strictly increasing order: $X[1] < X[2] \ldots < X[100]$. If it happens that the variables take the values 1..100, then simple constraint propagation will deduce that $X[1] = 1, X[2] = 2, \ldots, X[100] = 100$. If the programmer notices this beforehand, then we can reformulate the problem to replace each variable $X[i]$ with the value i throughout our program. There are many examples where constraint programmers have added more complicated constraints to break symmetries. A typical example from the literature is adding constraints to break symmetry in the template design problem [96]. This is fine if done correctly, but can obviously lose solutions if done incorrectly. Standard methods have been developed which can make the process easier and more likely to be correct, in the situations where they apply. Even where these are not directly applicable, a knowledge of them will serve constraint programmers well, as it should simplify the derivation of correct constraints which can be added by hand.

10.4.1 The Lex-Leader Method

Puget [97] proved that whenever a CSP has symmetry, it is possible to find a 'reduced form', with the symmetries eliminated, by adding constraints to the original problem. Puget found such a reduction for three simple constraint problems, and showed that this reduced CSP could be solved more efficiently than in its original form. Following this, the key advance was to show a method whereby such a set of constraints could be generated. Crawford, Ginsberg, Luks and Roy outlined a technique, called "lex-leader" for constructing symmetry-breaking ordering constraints for variable symmetries [22]. In later work, Aloul et al also showed how the lex-leader constraints for symmetry breaking can be expressed more efficiently [2]. This method was developed in the context of Propositional Satisfiability (SAT), but the results can also be applied to CP.

The idea of lex-leader is essentially simple. For each equivalence class of solutions under our symmetry group, we will predefine one to be the canonical solution. We will achieve this by adding constraints before search starts which are satisfied by canonical solutions and not by any others.

The technique requires first choosing a static variable ordering. From this, we induce an ordering on full assignments. The ordering on full assignments is straightforward. The tuple is simply the values assigned to variables, listed in the order defined by our static ordering. Since the method is defined for variable symmetries, any permutation g converts this tuple into another tuple, and we prefer the lexicographically least of these. This method

A	B	C
D	E	F

$\rightarrow$

F	E	D
C	B	A

1.	ABCDEF $\preceq_{\text{lex}}$ ABCDEF	7. ABCDEF $\preceq_{\text{lex}}$ DEFABC
2.	ABCDEF $\preceq_{\text{lex}}$ ACBDFE	8. ABCDEF $\preceq_{\text{lex}}$ DFEACB
3.	ABCDEF $\preceq_{\text{lex}}$ BACEDF	9. ABCDEF $\preceq_{\text{lex}}$ EDFBAC
4.	ABCDEF $\preceq_{\text{lex}}$ CBAFED	10. ABCDEF $\preceq_{\text{lex}}$ FEDCBA
5.	ABCDEF $\preceq_{\text{lex}}$ BCAEFD	11. ABCDEF $\preceq_{\text{lex}}$ EFDBCA
6.	ABCDEF $\preceq_{\text{lex}}$ CABFDE	12. ABCDEF $\preceq_{\text{lex}}$ FDECAB

Figure 10.5: A 3×2 matrix containing 6 variables; and the result of swapping the two rows and reversing the columns, giving the permutation mapping ABCDEF to FEDCBA. Also shown are the 12 lex-leader constraints, including the trivial one, arising from its 12 symmetries. Note how each constraint corresponds to a permutation of the variables, as the method is defined to work for variable symmetries: the illustrated matrix transformation gives constraint 10.

is, in principle, simple to implement. Each permutation in the group gives us one $\preceq_{\text{lex}}$ constraint. So the set of constraints defined by the lex-leader method is

$$\forall g \in G, \ V \preceq_{\text{lex}} V^g \tag{10.1}$$

where V is the vector of the variables of the CSP, and $\preceq_{\text{lex}}$ is the lexicographic ordering relation. The lexicographic ordering is exactly as is standard in computer science, e.g. $AD \preceq_{\text{lex}} BC$ iff either $A < B$ or $A = B$ and $D \leq C$.

A small example illustrates the method. Consider a 3×2 matrix depicted in Figure 10.5, in a context where the rows and columns may be freely permuted. The symmetries form the group $S_3 \times S_2$, with order $3!2! = 12$. We pick the variables in alphabetical order, so the vector of the variables of the problem is ABCDEF. The 12 symmetries lead to the 12 lex-leader constraints shown in Figure 10.5, including the vacuous symmetry from the identity.

An important practical issue with the lex-leader constraints is that they do not "respect" the variable and value ordering heuristics used in search. That is, it may well be that the leftmost solution in the search tree, which would otherwise be found first, is not canonical and so is disallowed, leading to increased search. This is in contrast to techniques such as SBDS and SBDD (Sections 10.5.1 and 10.5.2), which do respect the heuristic. Simple examples have been reported where the "wrong" heuristic can lead to dramatic increases in runtime [52]. This problem is inherent in the method, but in many cases it is easy to work out what is the "right" heuristic. In particular, if the same static variable ordering is used in search as was used to construct the lex-leader ordering, and values are tried from smallest to largest, this conflict should not occur. However, this does limit the power of the constraint programmer to use dynamic variable ordering heuristics.

A less easily solved problem with lex-leader is that many groups contain an exponential number of symmetries. Lex-leader requires one constraint for each element of the group. In the case of a matrix with m rows and n columns, this is $m!n!$, which is impractical in general. Therefore there are many cases where lex-leader is applicable but impractical.

1.	*true*	7.	ABC $\preceq_{lex}$ DEF
2.	BE $\preceq_{lex}$ CF	8.	ABC $\preceq_{lex}$ DFE
3.	AD $\preceq_{lex}$ BE	9.	ABC $\preceq_{lex}$ EDF
4.	AD $\preceq_{lex}$ CF	10.	ABC $\preceq_{lex}$ FED
5.	ABDE $\preceq_{lex}$ BCEF	11.	ABCDE $\preceq_{lex}$ EFDBC
6.	ABDE $\preceq_{lex}$ CAFD	12.	ABCDE $\preceq_{lex}$ FDECA

Figure 10.6: The lex-leader constraints for the 3×2 matrix reduced on an individual basis.

2.	BE $\preceq_{lex}$ CF	9.	ABC $\preceq_{lex}$ EDF
3.	AD $\preceq_{lex}$ BE	10.	ABC $\preceq_{lex}$ FED
7.	ABC $\preceq_{lex}$ DEF	11.	ABCD $\preceq_{lex}$ EFDB
8.	ABC $\preceq_{lex}$ DFE	12.	ABC $\preceq_{lex}$ FDE

Figure 10.7: The lex-leader constraints for the 3×2 matrix reduced as a set.

However, lex-leader remains of the highest importance, because there are a number of ways it is used to derive new symmetry breaking methods. We discuss these in the following sections.

Finally we reiterate that the lex-leader method is defined only for variable symmetries: i.e. those which permute the variables but always leave the value unchanged. Thus the same restriction applies to the methods below based on lex-leader. It is not an issue in the technique's original domain, SAT, since there are only 2 values [22]. If necessary, we can add a new variable to represent the negation of each variable, and so symmetries which change values can be made into variable symmetries. Unfortunately, if we have d values, we need $d!$ versions of each variable to apply this simple idea. Therefore, a proper generalisation of lex-leader to deal with value symmetries would be valuable, even if restricted to some special cases.

10.4.2 Simplifying Lex-Leader Constraints

Lex-leader constraints can be simplified, or 'pruned' to remove redundancies [22, 77]. Following Frisch and Harvey [41], we can illustrate this using the example from Figure 10.5. The first idea is to look at each constraint individually. For example, consider constraint 2 above, ABCDEF $\preceq_{lex}$ ACBDFE. We can remove the first and fourth variables from each tuple, since clearly $A = A$ and $D = D$, giving BCEF $\preceq_{lex}$ CBFE. But if B<C the constraint is satisfied whatever the other values, and otherwise we have B=C to satisfy the constraint. In other words, if the second variables in the tuples are relevant, they must be equal. Similarly for E and F, so in fact the constraint is equivalent to BE $\preceq_{lex}$ CF. Applying this reasoning everywhere we get the constraints shown in Figure 10.6. It is interesting to note that constraints 2 and 3 show that the columns must be lexicographically ordered, and that constraint 7 forces the rows to be lexicographically ordered. We return to this observation in Section 10.4.5.

We can go further, treating the constraints as a set and not just individually. For example, $\preceq_{lex}$ is transitive, so constraints 2 and 3 imply constraint 4. A more complicated example is in constraint 11. The last elements of each tuple are E and C. But if they are relevant, we have A=E and B=F=D=C. But constraint 3 implies A≤B, from which it follows that E≤C, so the last elements of the tuple are irrelevant and may be deleted. This reasoning leads to a set of 8 constraints shown in Figure 10.7, equivalent to the original 12 [41].

Unfortunately, the approach outlined here does not get round the fundamental problem of the exponential number of symmetries. In general the number of symmetries even in the reduced set will still be exponential [77]. However, the approach does illustrate how the set of constraints can be simplified, and we will see in the next section a special case where the results are quite dramatic.

10.4.3   Symmetry with All-Different

The 'all-different' constraint occurs very commonly in constraint programming. It perhaps occurs even more often in problems with symmetry. Puget has shown that [101] if we have only variable symmetry (the only case where lex-leader is defined) on a set of n variables constrained by an all-different constraint, symmetry can be broken completely by only $n - 1$ binary constraints. This result applies to *any* group G acting on the set of variables. This remarkable result could hardly be bettered, but is in fact relatively simple.

We begin with an example, which contains only variable symmetries on a set of all-different variables, but in which the group is not a straightforward group such as S_n.

Example 10.22. Graceful Graph
We say that a graph with m edges is *graceful* if there exists a labeling f of its vertices such that:

- $0 \leq f(i) \leq m$ for each vertex i,

- the set of values $f(i)$ are all-different,

- the set of values $abs(f(i), f(j))$ for every edge (i, j) are all-different.

A straightforward translation into a CSP exists where there is a variable v_i for each vertex v_i, see [78]. The variable symmetries of the problem are induced by the automorphism of the graph. There is one value symmetry, which maps v to $m - v$, but we ignore that symmetry to leave only value symmetries. More information on symmetries in graceful graphs is available in [89]. Petrie and Smith have considered various forms of both dynamic and static symmetry breaking methods in graceful graphs [89], using these techniques they found instances of graceful graphs that were not previously known. As an example, let us consider the the graph $K_3 \times P_2$, which is shown in Figure 10.8. The group allows any of the 3! permutations of K_3, as long as the same permutation is applied to both copies of K at the same time, as well as swapping the two triangles. There are thus 12 symmetries. In fact, the group is isomorphic to that of the matrix in Figure 10.5, so the constraints are the same as we showed there.

Using the fact that the variable are subject to an all-different constraint, we can significantly reduce the number of symmetry breaking constraints. For example, consider the symmetry breaking constraint

$$ABCDEF \preceq_{\text{lex}} ACBDFE$$

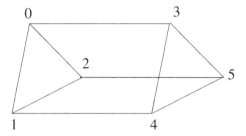

Figure 10.8: The graph $K_3 \times P_2$.

Since $A = A$ is trivially true, and since $B = C$ cannot be true because of the all-different constraint, this constraint can be simplified to just be:

$$B < C$$

This simplification is true in general and can be formalized as follows. Given a permutation g, let $s(g)$ be the smallest i such that $i^g \neq i$, and let $t(g)$ be equal to $(s(g))^g$.

Lemma 10.23. *[101]*
Given a CSP where the variables V are subject to an all-different constraint, and a variable symmetry group G for this CSP, then all variable symmetries can be broken by adding the following constraints:

$$\forall \sigma \in G, v_{s(\sigma)} < v_{t(\sigma)}$$

Note that if two permutations g and h are such that $s(g) = s(h)$ and $t(g) = t(h)$, then the corresponding symmetry breaking constraints are identical. Therefore, it is sufficient to state only one symmetry breaking constraints for each pair i, j such that there exists a permutation g with $i = s(g)$ and $j = t(h)$. The set of these pairs can be computed using the Schreier Sims algorithm [108]. In our example, these constraints are :

$$A < B, A < C, A < D, A < E, A < F, B < C$$

Note that these constraints are redundant. The constraint $A < C$ is entailed by the first and the last constraints. This remark can be used to reduce the number of constraints further by taking into account the transitivity of the $<$ constraints. The Schreier Sims algorithm gives us a stabiliser chain and sets of coset representatives U_i, as defined in Section 10.1.2. Puget uses this to prove:

Theorem 10.24. *[101]*
Given a CSP with n variables V, such that there exists an all-different constraint on these variables, then all variable symmetries can be broken by at most $n - 1$ binary constraints.

For our example, we get exactly 5 constraints: notice this is $n - 1$ in this case.

$$A < B, A < D, A < E, A < F, B < C$$

While this is only a reduction of a single constraint, that is simply because of the small size of the example. In general, Puget has reduced the number of symmetries required from a possibly $n!$ to as little as $n - 1$, for the commonly occurring case of variable symmetries in the presence of an all-different constraint. As well as its value in its own right, this shows the power of combining symmetry breaking constraints with constraints from a problem, and this remains an area ripe for exploitation.

10.4.4   Subsets of Lex Leader

The previous section showed how, in the right circumstances, a polynomial number of constraints can lead to equivalent reasoning to the full set of lex-leader constraints. Unfortunately, such a subset is not always available. Several researchers have proposed ways to state only a polynomial number of constraints without preserving complete symmetry breaking. Since the full set of lex-leader constraints leaves exactly one solution in each equivalence class, using a subset must leave *at least* one in each class, but may leave more than one. Thus, the symmetry breaking constraints do not guarantee to break all symmetries. In general the goal is to reach an acceptable tradeoff, with the greatly reduced number of constraints leading to more efficient search. In some cases, sets of symmetry breaking constraints have been proposed, and only later has it been realised that they represent a subset of the lex-leader constraints. This is a testament to the generality and naturalness of lex-leader.

Aloul et al have shown, in SAT, that very successful results can be obtained from very small subsets of lex-leader constraints, on examples such as FPGA routing problems [1]. Unlike the constraint-based work described so far, the symmetry group of the SAT problem was found using a graph-automorphism procedure on the instance. Surprisingly, the subset of symmetry breaking predicates used was simply the generators of the group found by the graph-automorphism check. It is remarkable that this gave good performance since, for example, a set of 21 generators was used in a group with 10^{16} elements. Only very special sets of generators are as effective as this, and it is not well understood what makes the generators found by graph-automorphism programs so good. While this is in a SAT context, similar results should apply to constraint programming.

Shlyakhter showed that good (though generally incomplete) subsets of lex-leader constraints could be found for acyclic digraphs, permutations, relations, and functions [109]. Apart from the individual contributions, this establishes the methodology of using the lex-leader constraints as a means of finding incomplete sets of symmetry breaking constraints, but subsets which are effective in practice. A particular case where this has proven to be of great interest is that of matrix models, to which we turn next.

10.4.5   Specialised Ordering Constraints for Matrix Models

A number of authors have taken a rather different approach to choosing appropriate constraints to break symmetry. This is based on the kind of symmetries that seem to arise very often in constraint programming. Given some class of symmetries we decide are important, we can analyse in general a subset of the lex-leader constraints which typically break a substantial number of symmetries and which can be reasoned with efficiently. The advantage of such a focus is that one can build special purpose methods for dealing with the symmetry breaking constraints, for example specialised algorithms for propagating Generalised Arc Consistency for the given set of constraints. Most work has concentrated on symmetry-breaking constraints for *matrix models*; where 'a matrix model is a constraint program that contains one or more matrices of decision variables' [36]. Matrix models are indeed very commonly occurring. For example the golfers problem can be modelled as a 3-d boolean matrix whose dimensions correspond to weeks, players and groups. A variable $x_{ijk} = 1$ iff in week i, player j plays in group k [113]. Other problems one could use as illustration are balanced incomplete block designs, steel meel slab design, progressive party problem, rack configuration, template design, and the warehouse location problem [35].

The prime example of this body of work is that on lexicographically ordering rows and columns in matrix models [36]. We deal with matrices where *rows* and *columns* are independently fully permutable. By this we mean that we can swap, at the same time, all the variables in any two rows, preserving the order of the variables within each row. Alternatively, we can swap any two columns, preserving the order of the variables within a column. This kind of symmetry occurs very commonly because we often introduce symmetry through modelling. For example, in the 3-d model of the golfers problem, the order of players, groups and weeks are arbitrary and each can be permuted freely. An $n \times m$ matrix with row and column symmetry is acted on by a group of order $n!m!$. These symmetries change the orders of rows and columns, but important relationships are preserved: specifically two elements in the same row are always in the same row, while two elements in the same column remain in the same column.

The rows in a 2-d matrix are *lexicographically ordered* if each row is lexicographically smaller (denoted $\preceq_{\text{lex}}$) than the next (if any). Adding lexicographic ordering on the rows breaks all row symmetries. Similarly, we can break all column symmetry by ordering the columns. But the interesting case is where we insist that both rows and columns should be simultaneously lexicographically ordered [36]. It is not at all obvious that this is consistent, i.e. that there is always a symmetry which will permute the rows and columns so that both sets are lexicographically ordered. In fact, we can remove solutions if we insist on the rows being in increasing order and the columns in decreasing order. However, it is always possible if we insist that all dimensions are in increasing order, and the best way to understand this is that the set of constraints are equivalent to a subset of the lex-leader constraints [109]. In general a lexicographic ordering on both the rows and the columns does *not* break all the compositions of the row and column symmetries. Nevertheless, in practice it often breaks a useful amount of symmetry. This is important, because in general it is NP-hard to find the lexicographical least representative of a matrix under row and column symmetry [22, 10].

Because of the usefulness of lex-ordering rows and columns, and the simplicity of the constraints, Frisch *et al* introduced an optimal algorithm to establish generalised arc-consistency for the $\preceq_{\text{lex}}$ constraint [40] between two vectors. Time complexity is $O(nb)$, where n is the length of the vectors and b is the time taken to adjust the bounds of an integer variable (dependent on the implementation of variables being used). This therefore gives an extremely attractive point on the tradeoff: a linear time to establish a high level of consistency on constraints which often break a lot of the symmetry in matrix models. The algorithm can be used to establish consistency in any use of $\preceq_{\text{lex}}$, so in particular is useful for any use of lex-leader constraints. Carlsson and Beldiceanu [18] showed that the propagation algorithm can be extended to generalised arc-consistency for a *chain* of vectors $V_1 \preceq_{\text{lex}} V_2 \preceq_{\text{lex}} \ldots \preceq_{\text{lex}} V_m$. This can deduce information not available if vectors are compared pairwise, and is done in linear time $O(nbm)$ if there are m vectors.

Provided care is taken, lex ordering matrices can be combined with additional constraints to break more symmetry while still taking advantage of the efficient algorithms for the lex constraints. Normally, this is done by choosing an appropriate subset of lex-leader constraints. This is an easy way to guarantee correctness provided that the same ordering of variables in the matrix is used as for the lex constraints: this means starting at the top left and going either in row order or column order. A very common technique is to insist that the top left hand corner is occupied by the (possibly equal) smallest element in the matrix: this is not guaranteed by the lex constraints themselves. If all values in the entire matrix are different, this additional constraint guarantees that all symmetry is broken [36]. There are other special cases where all symmetries are broken [36].

Other constraints have been developed in a similar way to the double-lex constraint, and applied to breaking symmetries in matrices. Kiziltan and Smith investigated the *multiset* ordering [70] following a suggestion of Frisch. The ordering is lexicographic ordering of the multiset of elements of vectors written in increasing order. More formally, we have $V_1 \preceq_{ms} V_2$ if either the smallest element of V_1 is less than the smallest element of V_2, or if the smallest elements are the same, and $V_1^- \preceq_{ms} V_2^-$, where the new vectors result from the deletion of a single occurrence of the smallest element. An advantage of the multiset ordering is that it can be placed on (say) the rows without affecting the column symmetries of a matrix. So it can for example be used even if the column symmetries do not form the group S_n. Frisch *et al* proposed a linear propagation algorithm for it, giving it similar efficiency to their algorithm for double-lex [43].

Another example of work in the same style was the introduction of the "allperm" constraint by Frisch, Jefferson and Miguel [42]. We have $V_1 \preceq_{perm} V_2$ if array V_1 is lexicographically less than any permutation of V_2. Frisch *et al* study the ways in which this may (and may not) be combined with other constraints such as double-lex and multiset. For example, it is consistent to insist that rows and columns are lex ordered, and simultaneously that the first row is $\preceq_{perm}$ all others, but we may not demand that the second row is $\preceq_{perm}$ later rows. Again, a specialised propagation algorithm was given for allperm.

We can construct 2-dimensional $2n \times 2n$ matrix model in which we insist that rows and columns are lex ordered, yet still contains full matrix symmetry in an $n \times n$ submatrix. An example for $n = 3$ is shown in Figure 10.9. The values of variables A to I are unconstrained, but if we insist that they form a latin square, the example is valid where rows are columns are ordered by the multiset ordering. If we also insist that all of A to I are ≥ 0 the example works if we insist that the first row is $\preceq_{perm}$ all other rows.

10.5   Dynamic Symmetry Breaking Methods

Dynamic symmetry breaking methods are those that operate to break symmetry during the search process. SBDD and SBDS are two such methods described in this section. In both these methods symmetry acts on variable/value pairs. Symmetry breaking by heuristic is included in this category, as although these variable and value ordering heuristics are fully defined before search commences, they are used during search. These methods are outlined in the subsequent sections.

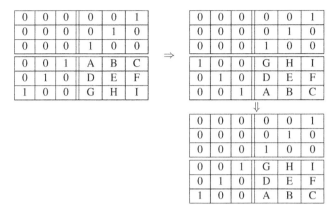

Figure 10.9: An example to show that full matrix symmetry in a bottom right submatrix can remain even when all rows and columns are lex ordered. The initial matrix (divided into quarters for clarity) is first transformed by swapping the fourth and sixth rows, and then by swapping the first and third columns. The result is still double-lex ordered but we have swapped the first and third rows of the submatrix. We can swap two columns similarly.

10.5.1 Symmetry Breaking During Search (SBDS)

Symmetry-excluding search trees were introduced by Backofen and Will [4, 5]. Gent and Smith [51] described in more detail the implementation of this technique, using the name "Symmetry Breaking During Search", but it is this latter name and its acronym "SBDS" which seems to have stuck as the general name for this method. This is perhaps slightly unfortunate since there are many other ways to break symmetry during search, most notably SBDD to be discussed in Section 10.5.2.

The basic idea of SBDS is to add constraints to a problem so that, after backtracking from a search decision, the SBDS constraints ensure that no symmetric equivalent of that decision is ever allowed. This is a *dynamic* technique, since we cannot add the constraints until we know what search decision is being made. In general terms, SBDS can work on any kind of search decision. However, for simplicity of discussion we will assume that all search decisions are of the form $var = val$, and a number of implementations of SBDS make the same assumption.

We will first illustrate with an example the kind of constraints added by SBDS. A search tree for the 8-Queens problem where the symmetry constraints added by SBDS are indicated by $\Diamond$ can be found in Figure 10.10. It is easiest to explain SBDS by going over the tree breadth-first, instead of the depth-first search the actual search algorithm would explore.

- Starting from the root, the first search decision in the search tree in Figure 10.10 is $Q[1] = 2$, i.e. the queen in row 1 goes in position 2. SBDS adds no constraints to the positive decision $Q[1] = 2$. If we backtrack at the root, we can assert $Q[1] \neq 2$. From that point on, we never want to try any state which contains any symmetric equivalent to $Q[1] = 2$. We can achieve this by adding symmetric versions of $Q[1] \neq$

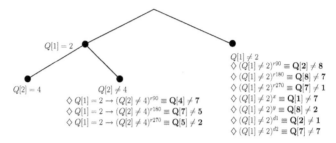

Figure 10.10: Example of SBDS on a search tree with the 8-queens problem.

2, i.e. by adding $(Q[1] \neq 2)^g$ for each g in the group, although we can omit id if the search algorithm itself asserts $Q[1] \neq 2$. The result of this in the case of the chessboard symmetries is given on the right hand branch of Figure 10.10.

- At the next level of search, on the left hand side, the next search decision is $Q[2] = 4$ Again we add no constraints to this positive decision. But if we backtrack from this, we assert $Q[2] = 4$. It would no longer be correct to ban each symmetric version of this decision, because the initial search decision $Q[1] = 2$ may have broken some of the symmetry already. In this example, $Q[1] = 2$ rules out $Q[1] = 7$, $Q[7] = 7$, $Q[2] = 1$ and $Q[8] = 2$ since those squares are on the same row, column, diagonal, and diagonal respectively. This means that no solution containing $Q[1] = 2$ can possibly have the symmetries x, y, $d1$ or $d2$. There is no need to assert any constraints for these symmetries below $Q[1] = 2$, and they are omitted from Figure 10.10.

- Still considering the same node, the more complicated case is that of the symmetries $r90$, $r180$ and $r270$. At this point in search we do not know whether or not these symmetries apply. They may hold in some future states and not in others. We cannot rule out, for example, $(Q[2] = 4)^{r90}$ for all future states, as we might lose solutions in states where $r90$ does not hold, but equally we will do redundant search if we do not rule it out in states where $r90$ does hold. SBDS solves this dilemma by adding constraints which rule out $(Q[2] = 4)^{r90}$ conditionally. This conditional constraint states that if the $r90$ is not broken (i.e. $Q[2] \neq 8$) then we have $(Q[2] \neq 4)^{r90}$, i.e. $Q[4] \neq 7$.

We can now state in general the constraints that SBDS adds, consider a node in search where the partial assignment A is to be extended by the decision $var = val$. For any problem symmetry g, we can add the constraint:

$$A \;\&\; A^g \;\&\; var \neq val \Rightarrow (var \neq val)^g \qquad (10.2)$$

To understand this constraint's soundness, note that it is equivalent to

$$(A \Rightarrow var \neq val) \Rightarrow (A \Rightarrow var \neq val)^g$$

which is almost a triviality. More significantly this equation is true before search begins, since it holds for any A, var, val and g. From this point of view we can view SBDS as making heuristic choices as to which of the (in practical terms) infinite variety of such constraints to add. Practical implementations of SBDS do not normally add the full form of (10.2). If we add the constraint at the point in search where we backtrack from the choice of $var = val$, then we know A is true and we also know that $var \neq val$, leading to the much simpler, but in context equivalent, form:

$$A^g \implies (var \neq val)^g \tag{10.3}$$

We can explain this simpler form by pointing out that it must be ensured that only unbroken symmetries are dealt with, so it is checked that A^g still holds. Then to ensure that the symmetrically equivalent subtree to the current subtree will not be explored, the $(var \neq val)^g$ is placed.

Backofen and Will proved that this method is sound in that the full non-symmetric search space will be explored [5], i.e. no solutions can be completely missed. Backofen and Will also showed that as long as all symmetries are correctly supplied, all the symmetry will be eliminated, i.e. no two solutions returned by SBDS can be equivalent.

A number of implementations of SBDS have been provided. The most publicly available to date is that in ECL^{i}PS^e [88]. These implementations always demand from the constraint programmer a separate function to implement the action of each symmetry g, in the programming language the system uses. If a problem has a large number of symmetries there may be too many for the user to identify and implement by hand. SBDS has been used successfully, despite this difficulty, with problems containing a few thousand symmetries [49]. We will see in Section 10.5.4 how computational group theory can be used to ease the burden on the programmer.

There are some important implementation issues for SBDS. A feature of SBDS is that it only breaks symmetries which are not already broken in the current partial assignment: this avoids placing unnecessary constraints. A symmetry is broken when the symmetric equivalent of the current partial assignment is not consistent with the problem constraints. Since A^g involves all values set so far, it is potentially large, so checking that a symmetry is unbroken could be expensive. However, it can be noted that if A is extended to the next partial assignment A_1 then $A_1 = A + (var = val)$ (where $var = val$ is the next decision on the search tree). Then $A_1^g = A^g + (var = val)^g$. So a Boolean variable can be constructed for each symmetry g representing whether A^g is satisfied or not: its value for A_1^g is the conjunction of its values for A^g and $var = val^g$. Hence, it can be decided incrementally whether A^g holds. Further, when the value of one of these Boolean variables becomes false, it is known that the corresponding symmetry is permanently broken, and need no longer be considered on this branch.

One problem with SBDS is that when the number of symmetries is large, than a large number of symmetry functions has to be described. In the worst case, there could be too many to be successfully compiled. This difficulty can be addressed by choosing a subset of the symmetry functions to use with SBDS. McDonald and Smith [82] explore this idea of 'partial symmetry breaking' with random subsets of symmetries, and also give an algorithm for choosing a subset of symmetry functions which should, heuristically, break a large amount of the symmetry. Unfortunately, it is infeasible to use the method in its entirety with all but the smallest problems with small symmetry groups.

SBDS has some major advantages over adding symmetry breaking constraints before search. First, the symmetries do not need to be variable symmetries, in contrast to the lex-leader method. Second, the solution found in each class of equivalent solutions is always the leftmost one in the search tree being traversed. Again in contrast to lex-leader, this means that arbitrary variable and value ordering heuristics may be used without changing either SBDS or the set of symmetry functions supplied. We say that SBDS "respects" the variable and value ordering heuristics used by the search.

10.5.2   Symmetry Breaking via Dominance Detection (SBDD)

The method of Symmetry Breaking via Dominance Detection (SBDD) was developed independently by Focacci & Milano [34], and by Fahle, Schamberger & Sellmann [33]. The title of SBDD comes from the latter of these papers, and has been adopted by the CP community as the standard name for the method. A similar algorithm was proposed by Brown, Finkelstein and Purdom in 1988 [16]. In fact, this paper describes a computational group theoretic version of this algorithm which is now familiar to the CP community as GAP-SBDD (described below in Section 10.5.5). Unfortunately, the paper by Brown *et. al.* while reasonably well known, seemed to have little influence on the constraints community, perhaps being too far ahead of its time.

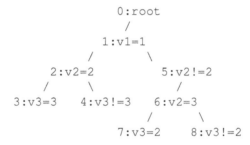

```
                        0:root
                          /
                      1:v1=1
                    /          \
            2:v2=2                5:v2!=2
           /      \                /
    3:v3=3      4:v3!=3      6:v2=3
                            /       \
                      7:v3=2       8:v3!=2
```

node	decisions	v_1	v_2	v_3	solution
0	-	1,2,3,4	1,2,3,4	1,2,3,4	
1	$v_1 = 1$	1	2,3,4	2,3,4	
2	$v_1 = 1, v_2 = 2$	1	2	3,4	
3	$v_1 = 1, v_2 = 2, v_3 = 3$	1	2	3	yes
4	$v_1 = 1, v_2 = 2, v_3 \neq 3$	1	2	4	yes
5	$v_1 = 1, v2 \neq 2$	1	3,4	2,3,4	
6	$v_1 = 1, v2 \neq 2, v_2 = 3$	1	3	2,4	
7	$v_1 = 1, v2 \neq 2, v_2 = 3, v_3 = 2$	1	3	2	yes
8	$v_1 = 1, v2 \neq 2, v_2 = 3, v_3 \neq 2$	1	3	4	yes

Figure 10.11: A partial search tree to illustrate SBDD, and a table listing the search states corresponding to each node.

SBDD operates by performing a check at every node in the search tree to see if the node about to be explored is symmetrically equivalent to one already explored, and if so prunes this branch. While a simple idea, this has the apparent problem that we will need to store the whole, exponentially sized, tree already explored. A single key idea transforms SBDD into a space-efficient method. This is that we need only store nodes at the roots of fully explored subtrees. We do not check if a node is equivalent in full to one of our stored nodes. Instead, we determine if a node is equivalent to any node which is an extension of one of the stored nodes, i.e. a node which is in a fully explored subtree. Since search has backtracked, we must have either visited the equivalent node before, or deduced for some other reason that there was no need to visit it: in either case there is no need to visit a symmetric equivalent.

Like SBDS, SBDD is based on binary branching between setting a variable and removing the value from a variable's domain. An example of how SBDD works in practice, based on the example outlined in [34], here follows. Consider a problem with three variables v_1, v_2 and v_3 subject to an 'all-different' constraint. The domain of all the variables is $\{1, 2, 3, 4\}$, and all the values can be permuted. There are 24 solutions of the problem. Figure 10.11 shows a part of the tree search that will be explored by a depth first search procedure to enumerate all solutions, assuming only a basic all-different propagation procedure. Decisions are selected in a lexicographic ordering. Nodes are represented by $n : \delta$ where n means the node is the nth node to be expanded by the search procedure, and δ is the decision or the negation of a decision for the arc between a node n and its parent. The Figure also gives for each node n the set of decisions taken on the path from the root node to n, as well as the domains of the variables corresponding to its state. Four solutions have been obtained in the illustrated search. However the solution found at node 7 is symmetrical with the one found at node 3. Those solutions are $\{v_1 = 1, v_2 = 3, v_3 = 2\}$, $\{v_1 = 1, v_2 = 2, v_3 = 3\}$ The first solution can be mapped into the second one by the symmetry swapping variables v_2 and v_3. More generally, any variable permutation is a symmetry of the problem.

SBDD is based on the notion of no-goods. No-goods are the roots of maximal sub trees that are completely traversed by a depth first search before n. Those no-goods can be found by traversing the path from the root node to n as follows. Each time the path goes from a node to its right child, then the left child of that node is a no-good: before traversing the right child of a given node a depth first search completely traverses the left sub tree of that node. Note that we use the name "no-good" although where we are searching for all solutions, fully explored trees may contain solutions. In such a case, we still wish to avoid searching any symmetric equivalent to any node in the subtree, including the solutions. In Figure 10.11, node 3 is a no-good w.r.t. node 4, node 2 is a no-good for node 5 and all the nodes in its sub tree. The no-goods w.r.t. node 8 are nodes 2 and 7.

Definition 10.25. *No-good.*
Node ν is a no-good w.r.t. n if there exists an ancestor n_a of n s.t. ν is the left hand child of n_a and ν is not an ancestor of n.

For each no-good, SBDD stores information to be compared against the current state. We use the set of decisions labeling the path from the root of the tree to the no-good [99]. We write $\delta(n)$ for this. The column labeled "decisions" in the table in Figure 10.11 gives the decision information corresponding to each node. We also use the state information at the node being searched. Specifically, we write $\Delta(S)$ for set of pairs $v_i = a_i$ for all variables v_i whose domains are reduced to a singleton. In node 8 in our example, the decisions made from the root node are $\delta(8) = \{v_1 = 1, v_2 = 3\}$, while $\Delta(8) = \{v_1 = 1, v_2 = 3, v_3 = 4\}$.

Definition 10.26. *Dominance*
We say that a node n is dominated if there exists a no-good ν w.r.t. n and a symmetry g s.t. $(\delta(\nu))^g \subseteq \Delta(n)$. We say that ν dominates n.

SBDD is then quite simple, conceptually: it never generates the children of dominated nodes, and it excludes dominated solutions. Therefore, a node n is a leaf iff it is either a solution, a failure, or a dominated node. In our example, no-good 2 dominates node 7 We have $\delta(2) = \{v_1 = 1, \; v_2 = 2\}$. Using the symmetry g which swaps variables v_2 and v_3, we obtain $(\delta(2))^g = \{v_1 = 1, v_3 = 2\}$ which is a subset of $\Delta(7) = \{v_1 = 1, \; v_3 = 2, v_2 = 3\}$.

Other definitions of dominance are possible: Definition 10.26 is from [99]. However, if we know that search always chooses $(var = val)$ before its negative $(var \neq val)$ we are free to ignore the negative decisions in $\delta(n)$ in Definition 10.26 [34, 59, 102]. For example, consider the negative decision $v_2 \neq 2 \in \delta(7)$ in Figure 10.11, and now suppose that some future node is dominated by $\delta(7)$ with $v_2 \neq 2$ removed. We can still terminate search, because every leaf node in the future subtree either has the symmetric image of $v_2 \neq 2$ or $v_2 = 2$. If the former, the node is dominated by $\delta(7)$. But if the latter, the node is dominated by $\delta(2)$ since the corresponding subtree fully explored $v_2 = 2$ and we have $\delta 7 \setminus \{v_2 \neq 2\} \cup \{v_2 = 2\} \supset \delta(2) = \{v_1 = 1, v_2 = 2\}$. The structure of search trees makes this observation general, so if positive differences are explored first, we can omit negative decisions from dominance checks.

The original definition of dominance from [33] is rather more different and based on *state inclusion*. A node n is dominated if there exists a no-good ν for n and a symmetry such that the domains of the variables in ν^g contains the domains of the variables in n. This has the disadvantage that more space is required to store no-goods. Also, it goes against the following intuition. Since we wish to establish that a set at this node is a superset of a past no-good, we would like the set at this node to be big, and the set at the no-good small: this should make it as easy as possible to pass the dominance test. On the other hand, we also want the dominance check to be as easy as possible to implement and as fast as possible to run. We might therefore be best to use a definition of dominance which fails as quickly as possible, which may be an argument in favour of state inclusion dominance. No definitive study of this issue has ever been performed, and perhaps is not possible any more than deciding what the single best heuristic is for backtrack search.

The critical issue we have glossed over so far is just *how* the dominance check is performed. The algorithm for SBDD requires a problem specific function $\Phi : (\nu, n) \rightarrow \{false, true\}$ that yields true if the previous no-good ν dominates the current partial assignment n. For problems with small symmetry groups, provision of Φ can be a greater load on the programmer than of the few symmetry functions required by SBDS. For larger groups, SBDD has the enormous advantage that it has very limited space needs. However, this does not solve the time complexity problems. For each pair ν and n, the search for amounts to solving a sub graph isomorphism problem, which is known to be NP-complete. Although SBDD requires the solution of several NP-complete problems at each node, good results have been obtained using the technique.

There seem to be three broad techniques for implementing dominance checks. First, a programmer can implement a dominance checker for a particular class of problems, for example instances of the social golfers' problem [33]. The need for this is a major problem with SBDD. Encoding a function that will recognise when a node in the search tree is symmetrically dominated by another one can be difficult, and it does not generalise between different problems with different types of symmetry. However, if such a function can be found than SBDD is a very efficient method at breaking large amounts of symmetry. Sellmann and Van Hentenryck have created a more general dominance detection function

[107]. This can lead to very efficient solutions tuned to a particular application, but this approach relies on the skill and insight of the programmer and imposes a considerable burden on them. Second, since it is an NP-complete problem, one can construct a constraint encoding of the dominance problem [99]. This is particularly interesting since it amounts to using constraint programming for computational group theory. However, it is still necessary to construct a special purpose constraint problem for each new class of problems to be solved. The third approach is to use computational group theory directly [16, 53], and we describe this further in Section 10.5.5.

An important refinement of SBDD is to notice that sometimes *failed* dominance checks can result in propagation [34, 33]. Suppose our dominance check can report that a certain variable-value pair would, if set in the current node, lead to the current node being dominated. Then we can remove that value from the domain of the variable and propagate on the result. This can perform extremely useful propagation. As usual, we have to take care that the benefits do not outweigh the costs of performing the necessary calculations. Another point to note is that the dominance check does not need to be done at every node of the search tree. As long as a check is undertaken at every leaf node then only the non-isomorphic solutions will be returned. Deciding where to apply the check is a tradeoff between the cost of checks and the search savings that result: unfortunately little is known about the best place on this tradeoff.

Like SBDS, SBDD can be shown to be a sound and complete symmetry breaking method provided that the dominance check is implemented correctly. That is, exactly one solution from each equivalence class is returned. Like SBDS, the solution found is the leftmost one in the search tree with respect to the variable and value ordering heuristics. SBDD therefore respects the variable ordering heuristic, and dynamic variable ordering may be used without any change to SBDD [33]. SBDD has also been applied to soft CSP's [11].

Harvey [59] discusses how SBDS and SBDD are related. The difference between the two algorithms is where symmetry breaking takes place. SBDS places constraints to stop nodes symmetrically equivalent nodes, to those previously explored in search, from ever being reached. On the other hand, SBDD prunes nodes having reached them and found them to be symmetrical to a previously explored part of search. In fact, it is entirely reasonable to see the difference between it and SBDS as merely one of implementation. As the set of acceptable solutions is the same in each case, an implementation of SBDS is, in a sense, an implementation of SBDD, and vice versa. This view can be a useful way of understanding the techniques in principle, but there are enormous practical differences. SBDD can outperform SBDS on many problems, as it does not post constraints, so does not have the overhead of waiting for large numbers of symmetry breaking constraints to propagate. It can successfully be used with problems which have too much symmetry for SBDS to be an appropriate technique.

10.5.3 Symmetry Excluding Heuristics

Meseguer and Torras [84] studied how symmetry can be used to guide search. Specifically, they direct search towards subspaces with a high degree of non-symmetric assignments, by breaking as many symmetries as possible with each variable assignment. The symmetry breaking heuristic proposed breaks as many symmetries as possible. Meseguer and Torras go on to propose the 'variety-maximization' heuristic which combines the smallest domain first heuristic, which can perform better than the symmetry breaking heuristic under certain conditions, with the symmetry breaking heuristic. On a simple problem the variety-maximization heuristic builds a slightly smaller search tree, than the smallest domain first heuristic, to find all solutions. Variety-maximization does notably better to find the first solution. Meseguer and Torras go on to combine the variety-maximization heuristic with symmetric value pruning by no-good recording. The size of the set of no-goods is potentially exponential, so only a subset is stored and used. The results of this combination are rather disappointing; the inclusion of symmetric value pruning does not provide a major advantage over variety-maximization alone, in any of the problems undertaken.

Using variable ordering heuristics (and indeed value ordering heuristics) to break symmetry is an attractive proposition, as it does not have the computational cost associated with the other dynamic symmetry breaking methods. Despite the work of Meseguer and Torras, there seems to be much more scope for using symmetry in heuristics than the community has exploited to date. There is also considerable scope for other ways to use symmetry heuristically. For example, if we are solving a problem with a large amount of symmetry, we might look only for solutions with some symmetry. This excludes enormous parts of the search space. On the one hand, this means that search will be incomplete, in that a negative answer does not mean there are no solutions with less symmetry. On the other hand, we might get lucky, and there may be such solutions: if there are we have all the advantage of the reduced search. While this may seem incredibly optimistic, it has been successful in practice [119].

10.5.4   SBDS with Computational Group Theory

To allow SBDS to be used in situations where there are too many symmetries to allow a function to be created for each, Gent *et al.* [52] linked SBDS in ECL^{i}PS^e with GAP (Groups, Algorithms and Programming) [46]. GAP is a system for computational algebra and in particular Computational Group Theory (CGT). There is nothing fundamental about the use of GAP or ECL^{i}PS^e, the point being that this is a co-operation between subsystems to provide constraint algorithms and to provide computational group theory algorithms. A library for GAP-SBDS is distributed with ECL^{i}PS^e.

GAP-SBDS allows the symmetry group, rather than its individual elements, to be described. GAP-SBDS operates over a set of points, where each point corresponds to a variable-value pair. One way to think of a point is in terms of a member of a $n \times m$ array, where n is the number of variables, and m is the size of the domain of each variable. The i, j-th element in the array denotes variable i and value j. The symmetry group, G, acts on these $n \times m$ points, each point being represented by a single integer. The group generators are given in ECL^{i}PS^e and passed to GAP in terms of points. This means that function are required in ECL^{i}PS^e which convert from variable/value pairs to integers representing points and vice-versa. This is a possible source of error when using the GAP-SBDS system. Even without error, to effectively use the system, the user must have some knowledge of CGT. While it is enough to write down a set of generators, even this makes the system inaccessible for many users. However, some progress has been made in this area, as we describe in Section 10.8.

The GAP-SBDS algorithm can be described in terms of Equation 10.2 from Section 10.5.1: A & A^g & $var \neq val$ $\Rightarrow$ $(var \neq val)^g$, In GAP-SBDS, the only part of this process that is controlled by GAP is $g(A)$, the other components are controlled by ECL^{i}PS^e as in the standard SBDS algorithm. $g(A)$ is calculated with the use of a right-transversal chain, a set calculated iteratively at every node in the search-tree, as the Cartesian product of every right-transversal obtained so far. More formally *RTchain* = $RT_k \times RT_{k-1} \times \ldots \times RT_1$ is defined as $p_k \circ p_{k-1} \circ \ldots \circ p_1$ where $p_i \in RT_i$. Each member of *RTchain* is a representative of the set of symmetries which agree on what to map each of the variable/value pairs in $A \wedge var \neq val$ to. This means the symmetry breaking constraint can be placed on backtracking, by transforming $var \neq val$ according to the elements in *RTchain*. However, doing this by iterating over every symmetry would be infeasible for all but relatively small groups. To counter this difficulty Gent *et al.* use lazy evaluation. The constraint $g(var \neq val)$ is only imposed when $g(A)$ is known to be true, rather than placing conditional constraints as in the original SBDS. This means that although GAP-SBDS is guaranteed to break all the symmetry, it may not break the symmetry as early in search as SBDS. This can lead to GAP-SBDS having a larger backtrack count than SBDS.

In GAP-SBDS Gent *et al.* have created an efficient implementation of SBDS, which can handle relatively large amounts of symmetry effectively. This moves the order of groups that SBDS can be be used with from the thousands to the billions. The number of symmetries is limited to this kind of scale because the number of constraints being added during search can cause space problems. Even billions is a small number when groups can grow exponentially.

10.5.5 SBDD and Computational Group Theory

We mentioned, in Section 10.5.2, that in practice SBDD can be difficult to implement. The design of the dominance detection function may be complicated, and there are no general rules for designing the function for problems with similar types of symmetry. In reality two 'similar' problems may have completely different dominance functions; there may be more than one dominance function for a problem, some of which prune more effectively than others. Gent *et al.* [53], developed GAP-SBDD to address this problem by providing a generic dominance checker, which is now available as an ECL^{i}PS^e library.

GAP-SBDD is a generic version of SBDD that uses the symmetric group of the problem, rather than an individual dominance detection function. Like GAP-SBDS, GAP-SBDD works by way of an interface between GAP and ECL^{i}PS^e and performs calculations over points, with the symmetry groups defined by a generating set of permutations. GAP-SBDD operates by maintaining both a *failSet* and a *pointSet*. The *failSet* corresponds to the set of points attributed to the positive decisions made during search to reach the root of completed subtrees. The *pointSet* denotes the set of points corresponding to variables which have been set to a fixed value on the current branch of search (both through assignments and propagation). The current node on the search tree is dominated by a complete subtree if there exists a g in the symmetry group G and a s in the *failSet* S such that $s^g \subseteq$ *pointSet*.

The dominance check is implemented using a tree data structure which encodes all the *failSets* currently applicable. Disjoint sets of points $A_1, \ldots, A_k$ and $B_0, \ldots, B_k$ can be identified, the *failSets* associated with these points are $A_1 \cup \ldots \cup A_i \cup B_i$ for each i. The right branching elements of the tree are labelled with elements of A, the left ones elements of B. Each node of the tree is associated with the sequence of labels on the path to it from the root. The dominance check is performed using a recursive search, which traverses the tree, entering each node once for every way of mapping the associated sequence of points into the current point. This is implemented in GAP with the use of stabiliser chains. While inherently just a backtracking search for an appropriate group element, the search in GAP contains a number of optimisations which cause several orders of magnitude speedup from a naive implementation [53]. As in regular SBDD, it is possible to identify cases where all but the final element of a *failSet* can be mapped into a *pointSet*, and report them back to ECL^{i}PS^e, so the value can be removed from the associated variables domain. However, like GAP-SBDS, not all possible values are identified, as this would cause too much increase in runtime.

GAP-SBDD is an efficient method for dealing with problems with large symmetry groups. In principle, the size of groups that can be used is unlimited, and certainly it has been used in practice on groups with 10^{36} elements. However, it provides no magic bullet to the inherent hardness of the dominance check. This hardness can manifest itself with individual dominance checks that take inordinate amounts of time to run. Also, it has been found that subtle differences can make enormous differences to run time. For example, while GAP-SBDD does respect the variable ordering heuristic, different heuristics on the same instance can lead to dramatic changes in the time dominance checks take. This means that the method can suffer from a lack of robustness. Nevertheless, from a very small input with no algorithmic content, GAP-SBDD constructs a complete symmetry breaking tool automatically.

10.5.6　GE-Trees

The idea of constructing GE-trees is the most recent idea to join the suite of dynamic symmetry breaking methods [103]. (GE stands for "Group Equivalence" but the abbreviation is used universally.) It differs from the others in this class, as it is more a way of considering symmetry breaking methods, than a symmetry breaking method in its own right. A GE-tree is defined as a tree in which no two nodes are symmetrically equivalent, and in which, for every solution to the problem, a symmetrically equivalent node is in the tree.[4] GE-trees are defined analogously to search trees in general: in particular, algorithms are free to stop before they construct a complete tree, for example after finding a first solution. GE-trees are intended in part to be viewed as a conceptual paradigm, to classify and compare symmetry breaking techniques. Any method of GE-tree construction will (by definition) break all problem symmetries as the search for solutions proceed. SBDS and SBDS can both be viewed as methods for constructing GE-trees, but so can lex-leader provided that all constraints it requires are used. Careful analysis of properties of GE-trees (constructed by different methods such as SBDS and SBDD, applied to the same instances) may allow the refinement and extension of existing techniques and even the development of new ones.

In some cases GE-trees are almost in the folklore. For example, consider graph colouring where each colour is indistinguishable. Many programmers have realised that the first node can be coloured arbitrarily. For the second node, we only have to consider giving it the same colour or an arbitrary different one. The third node need only be given the colours given to the first two nodes, and an arbitrary different one. The process continues until we have used all colours. This intuition can be generalised and formalised. Roney-Dougal *et al.* used the GE-tree paradigm to create a polynomial time algorithm for breaking arbitrary

---

[4]The latter condition is easy to forget but otherwise legal GE-trees could exclude some or even all solutions.

value symmetries. This can be viewed as a computational group theory-based general-isation of an algorithm presented in [64]. It is a special purpose algorithm which only creates new nodes which are guaranteed to be unique in the tree. In general this is hard, but Roney-Dougal *et al.* showed that the special nature of groups of value symmetries can be used to construct GE-trees very efficiently [103]. They report on an experimental compar-ison between this method and GAP-SBDD for problems which only have value symmetry. GE-trees are found to be the best method in all cases. This is not surprising: GAP-SBDD performs a potentially exponential search, at each node in the search tree, in order to break symmetry, compared to the low-order polynomial algorithm to break all value symmetry.

10.5.7 The STAB Method

Symmetry Breaking Using Stabilizers (STAB), like SBDS, adds symmetry breaking con-straints during search [98]. Unlike SBDS, which places constraints to break all the symme-try of the problem, STAB places symmetry breaking constraints only for symmetries that leave the partial assignment A at the current node unchanged. That is, instead of breaking symmetry in the whole group, STAB breaks symmetry in the stabiliser G_A. These con-straints take the form of lexicographic ordering constraints. Stabilisers were introduced in Section 10.1. In practice the size of stabilisers is often much smaller than the size of G. The STAB method, amounts to adding the following set of constraints at each node A.

$$V \preceq_{\text{lex}} V^g, \text{ for all } g \in G_A$$

These constraints remove all the solutions that are not lexicographically minimum with respect to the stabiliser G_A in the sub tree rooted at A.

Example 10.27. Consider a 4×5 matrix model. For simplicity we will refer to the matrix of variable by V, i.e. we identify the vector of variables with its matrix representation:

x_1	x_2	x_3	x_4	x_5
x_6	x_7	x_8	x_9	x_{10}
x_{11}	x_{12}	x_{13}	x_{14}	x_{15}
x_{16}	x_{17}	x_{18}	x_{19}	x_{20}

Consider a partial assignment A where the first 10 variables are assigned as follows:

0	0	0	1	1
0	1	1	0	0

Every symmetry for A is defined by a row permutation and a column permutation.We can state constraints for each of these symmetries, except for the identity permutation. For instance, let us state the constraint for the symmetry σ made up of the permutation $(1\ 2)$ of rows and $(2\ 4\ 3\ 5)$ on columns. The matrix $W = V^\sigma$ is

x_6	x_9	x_{10}	x_8	x_7
x_1	x_4	x_5	x_3	x_2
x_{11}	x_{14}	x_{15}	x_{13}	x_{12}
x_{16}	x_{19}	x_{20}	x_{18}	x_{17}

The symmetry breaking constraint is then, allowing for the assignment A, is then

$$[0, 0, 0, 1, 1, 0, 1, 1, 0, 0, x_{11}, x_{12}, x_{13}, x_{14}, x_{15}, x_{16}, x_{17}, x_{18}, x_{19}, x_{20}]$$
$$\preceq_{\text{lex}} [0, 0, 0, 1, 1, 0, 1, 1, 0, 0, x_{11}, x_{14}, x_{15}, x_{13}, x_{12}, x_{16}, x_{19}, x_{20}, x_{18}, x_{17}]$$

As the two vectors have the same first 10 elements, the constraint can be simplified into:

$$[x_{11}, x_{12}, x_{13}, x_{14}, x_{15}, x_{16}, x_{17}, x_{18}, x_{19}, x_{20}]$$
$$\preceq_{\text{lex}} [x_{11}, x_{14}, x_{15}, x_{13}, x_{12}, x_{16}, x_{19}, x_{20}, x_{18}, x_{17}]$$

Going back to the general case, the simplification based on identical prefixes is valid in general. Given the n-vector V, let $tail(V$,n-d) be the vector obtained by removing the first d elements of V. If A is a d-vector then constraints can be simplified into

$$tail(V, n - d) \preceq_{\text{lex}} (tail(V, n - d))^g, \text{ for all } g \in G_A$$

It should be noted that STAB is an incomplete method with regard to symmetry breaking, meaning that it does not return only the non-isomorphic solutions.

10.6   Combinations of Symmetry Breaking Methods

We have described a variety of symmetry breaking methods, each with advantages and disadvantages. It would naturally seem a good idea to combine two or more methods in order to reap all of the advantages. Unfortunately, correctly combining symmetry breaking methods has proven to be very difficult. Symmetry breaking methods try to preserve one solution from each equivalence class. How this solution is chosen depends on the method of symmetry breaking. Combining any two methods arbitrarily may mean that different solutions are ruled out by each symmetry breaking method, and so solutions are lost.

For a while it was thought by many that if the same variable and value ordering are used, then it was valid to apply several symmetry breaking methods at the same time, since none of these methods remove canonical solutions. Therefore, any combination will keep canonical solutions. For instance, one could state the Lex^2 constraints and use SBDD at the same time for matrix models. However, Smith [112] has shown this not to be the case. Harvey [60] later documented an example of this result, then showed how SBDS and SBDD can be modified so that they can be correctly combined with lexicographic ordering constraints. Unfortunately, the empirical results for this combination were disappointing. Another area which has received some study is combining a method to break variable symmetry, with a method to break value symmetry. As both of these methods are acting on different symmetry groups, this combination is intrinsically safe. Puget [101], showed how all the variable symmetry can be broken by simple ordering constraints, when there is an all-different constraint across all of the variables. He successfully combined this method with GE-trees to also break the value symmetry. Another combination which includes GE-trees has been tried [69]. This successfully combined GE-tree to break value symmetry and GAP-SBDD to break variable symmetry. This method is provably complete and sound with regard to breaking all symmetry, but is less efficient than GAP-SBDD alone on all problems tried.

In Section 10.5.7 it was noted that STAB is an incomplete method with regard to symmetry breaking, meaning that it does not return only the non-isomorphic solutions. In order to counter this drawback, Puget combined SBDD with STAB. This combined method produces good results, outperforming SBDD alone.

Another successful combination of symmetry breaking methods was completed by Petrie [90]. Petrie showed that neither of GAP-SBDS or GAP-SBDD is universally better, so combined the two methods. This was done by having one operate at the top of the search tree, than switching to the other method at a lower level. The empirical analysis of this method showed it to sometime outperform either of the methods alone. However, perhaps more importantly it was shown to be a more robust method, in that the combined method was never less efficient, than the least efficient of the two contributing systems.

10.7 Successful Applications

Many of the symmetry breaking methods outlined in the previous sections have been applied successfully to a variety of problems. We have already mentioned two successful applications: the chess puzzle at the start of the chapter, and graceful graphs. In both cases new results were obtained using symmetry breaking in constraint programming. We briefly outline some more applications, and indicate which symmetry breaking methods have been successfully applied to them. CSPLib (www.csplib.org), is an online directory of constraint problems: whenever a problem is contained within this resource, the number of the problem is given in this text to help the interested party find a detailed problem specification. The references provided are the papers which discuss symmetry breaking within the applications.

Balanced Incomplete Block Design (BIBD) generation is a standard combinatorial problem from design theory, originally used in the design of statistical experiments but since finding other applications such as cryptography. It is a special case of Block Design, which also includes Latin Square problems. BIBD's are problem 28 in CSPLib, Lam's problem, which is problem number 25 in CSPLib is that of finding a specific BIBD instance. BIBD's can be easily modelled with the use of matrices, and so many of the methods that place symmetry breaking constraints on matrices have been applied to them [44]. This problem was also used as a test bed for STAB [98] and GAP-SBDD [53].

Steel Mill Slab Design is a simplification of a real industry problem, which is to schedule the production of steel in a factory. It is problem number 38 in CSPLib. Gent *et al.* have considered conditional symmetry breaking in this problem [54]

Maximum Density Still Life problem arises from the Game of Life, invented by John Horton Conway in the 1960s and popularized by Martin Gardner in his Scientific American columns. A stable pattern, or still-life, is not changed by the rules which cause the Game of Life to iterate. The problem is to find the densest possible still-life pattern, i.e. the pattern with the largest number of live cells, that can be fitted into an $n \times n$ section of the board, with all the rest of the board dead. Maximum density still life is problem 38 in CSPLib. Smith [114] and both Bosch and Trick [12] have considered modelling and symmetry breaking in Still Life. Petrie *et al.* have studied dynamic symmetry breaking in a CP-LP hybrid, then applied this idea to this problem [90].

Social Golfers Problem is where the coordinator of a local golf club has the following problem. In her club, there are 32 social golfers, each of whom play golf once a week, and always in groups of 4. She would like you to come up with a schedule of play for these golfers, to last as many weeks as possible, such that no golfer plays in the same group as any other golfer on more than one occasion. The problem can easily be generalized to that of scheduling m groups of n golfers over p weeks, such that no golfer plays in the same group as any other golfer twice (i.e. maximum socialisation is achieved). Social Golfers is problem number 10 in CSPLib. Harvey and Winterer at the time of writing have the most efficient algorithm for this problem, which includes symmetry breaking [62].

Peaceable Coexisting Armies of Queens was introduced by Robert Bosch in his column in Optima in 1999 [13]. It is a variant of a class of problems requiring pieces to be placed on a chessboard, with requirements on the number of squares that they attack: Martin Gardner [47] discusses more examples of this class. In the "Armies of Queens" problem, we are required to place two equal-sized armies of black and white queens on a chessboard so that the white queens do not attack the black queens (and necessarily v.v.) and to find the maximum size of two such armies. Bosch asked for an integer programming formulation of the problem and how many optimal solutions there would be for a standard 8×8 chessboard. However, this problem can obviously be generalised to a $n \times n$ chessboard. Various models for this problem in conjunction with dynamic symmetry breaking, are considered by Smith *et al.*, the puzzle at the start of this chapter being a spinoff of thi research [115].

Fixed Length Error Correcting Codes are defined as follows: A fixed length error correcting code C of length n over an alphabet F is a set of strings from F^n. Given two strings from F^n we can define the distance between them. The most commonly use distance is the Hamming distance, defined as the number of positions where the strings differ. Using this we define the minimum distance of C as the minimum of the distances between distinct pairs of strings from C. Fixed Length Error Correcting codes are problem 36 in CSPLib. This problem is studied in conjunction with symmetry breaking constraints by Frisch *et al.* [42].

Peg Solitare (also known as Hi-Q) is played on a board with a number of holes. In the English version of the game, the board is in the shape of a cross with 33 holes. Pegs are arranged on the board so that at least one hole remains. A number of different problems arise from Solitaire, e.g. finding a path from the initial to a goal state, or finding the shortest number of moves to a state where no more moves are possible. Peg solitare is problem 37 in CSPLib. Jefferson *et al.* have studied on how to solve this problem using various AI paradigms, including a discussion of symmetry breaking [42].

Alien Tiles is available for play over the internet at www.alientiles.com. Alien Tiles is problem 27 in CSPLib. Gent, Smith and Linton have studied how dynamic symmetry breaking can be successfully applied to the problem of finding the hardest instance. [49].

We can see that symmetry methods are flexible enough to be applied to a great variety of problems, and we have by no means mentioned all the successful applications to date. The most successful seem to be on combinatorial puzzles such as graceful graphs. It therefore remains to be proved by the community that symmetry breaking has significant applications on industrial scale problems.

10.8   Symmetry Expression and Detection

Most research on symmetry constraints has assumed that the symmetries of a problem can be provided, in some form, by the programmer. For example, SBDS relies on programmers providing a list of functions to implement the actions of symmetries; SBDD needs a dominance check to be written; and methods such as lex-leader and GAP-SBDS need a group to be provided. Even for methods where this is not necessary, such as the use of double-lex constraints in a matrix model, a programmer has to recognise that the matrix symmetries occur and that the double-lex constraints are an appropriate technique to break them with. In recent years, increasing amounts of work have been based on the premise that this is an untenable position. Two ways of overcoming this flaw have been considered. First, it could be made easier for the programmers to write down the symmetries. Second, the symmetries could be detected automatically so there is no work at all for the programmer. This first method has been independently studied by both McDonald [48] and Harvey *et al.* [63], with a view to creating a system which produces the group needed for methods using computational group theory, without the user having to understand exactly how groups are generated. There are three main aims to these systems. The first is to get rid of the need for functions which map variable/value pairs to points (this concept is outlined in Section 10.1.1). The second is to allow the expression of the symmetry in a simple yet powerful way. The third is to create a system which requires the user to have no prior knowledge of group theory. These objectives are achieved, by providing a set of functions, which map expressions of the symmetry with regard to the variables and values (e.g. all the rows of a matrix can be interchanged) to group generators. These techniques to date are limited to the most commonly occurring kinds of symmetry, and do not allow users to express arbitrary groups.

The automatic identification of the symmetry group of some CSPs is possible through determining the automorphism group of the graph associated with the constraint problem. Puget [100] showed that this could be done in connection with the microstructure graph, which closely relates to the existential representation of the constraints. The concern with this approach is that it may not scale well (it is in the complexity class of graph isomorphism in most cases). When the problem is large, so is the graph, and the automorphism cannot be calculated in a reasonable time. Small problems can also have big graphs due to non-binary constraints, which again would mean the automorphism could not be calculated in reasonable time. To counter this potential problem Puget also introduced a method where he considered a graph related to intensional representation of each constraint. Puget found that the symmetry could be detected very efficiently, using both methods, on a variety of problems. Ramani and Markov have also has recently had some success [23], with a method closely linked to Puget's. This method undertakes graph isomorphism of the parser trees associated with the intensional representation of the constraints. Although this method is not guaranteed complete, in that it does not guarantee to find the full symmetry group, it has had some successful results in practice. It should be mentioned that in the SAT community outstanding results have been obtained using automatic symmetry detection, even on large problems [1]. This is particularly encouraging because natural structures, such as the microstructure of constraint problems, correspond to encodings into SAT. In order to know when this attractively simple method is feasible with regard to CP empirical analysis is required.

Many symmetries are also added in the modelling process, as pointed out by Frisch *et al.* [45]. If we can understand when this symmetry is added, it should be easy to pass those symmetries to symmetry-breaking methods.

10.9   Further Research Themes

We now discuss a diverse range of research using symmetry, which is unified only by not fitting easily elsewhere in this chapter. We do not to suggest that the work in this section is less important than in the rest of this chapter. Indeed, the same reasons that make this research hard to categorise makes some of it particularly innovative, and so it has significant potential for future exploration.

Symmetry and inference: Almost all research on symmetry in constraints has focussed on breaking symmetries to reduce search. When symmetry is present in a search problem, its presence is information that we can exploit in other ways. A particular example is to enhance representation and inference of constraint problems. First, we can greatly compress the size of the representation and thus enhance the representational power. Second, we can exploit knowledge of the group structure to change our algorithms for inference and propagation. This is necessary if we use a compressed representation based on the group, but also offers advantages. If we perform some work to deduce that a value can be removed, we need perform no more work to remove all symmetric equivalents of it. Similarly, if we know that a given value cannot be removed, then we need perform no more work on trying to propagate symmetric equivalents. A simple example of this idea was used to exploit the bidirectionality of constraints in arc consistency to improve AC-6 [9]. More generally, we may have arbitrary groups acting on the set of constraints. Dealing with groups correctly and efficiently raises many difficult problems. These difficulties are now being seriously attacked. By far the most significant body of work has been applied in the context of SAT, by Dixon *et al.*, in a three part journal paper spreading over almost 200 pages [27, 26, 28]. They have produced ZAP, a powerful SAT solver designed to allow concise expression of problems using group theory, while exploiting the great efficiency advances made in modern SAT solvers. At a much smaller scale, new propagation algorithms have been introduced into Constraint Programming. Gent *et al.* introduced symmetric variants of (i,j)-consistency and singleton consistency, together with algorithms for their enforcement. While implementations have been provided, it has not yet been proved that symmetry-based inference techniques will be powerful in practice. Nevertheless, the research area is of high promise, as suggested by Dixon *et al.*'s conclusion to their mammoth effort: "it is important to realize that our results only scratch the surface of what ZAP's representational shift allows" [28].

Symmetry and implied constraints: When constraints are added before search, it is possible to use them to derive 'implied' constraints. These implied (or 'redundant') constraints may greatly reduce search, in ways which are not possible using the original problem constraints [44]. We saw, in Section 10.4.3, another example where symmetry breaking and problem constraints can interact very fruitfully. Dynamic symmetry breaking techniques do not allow implied constraints to be added – at least not in the simple way that static symmetry breaking methods do. Adding implied constraints suffers from similar problems to reformulation. It can give very dramatic search reductions, but no automatic technique for adding effective implied constraints is known.

Symmetry and local search: When we know about symmetry in a constraint problem, there is no moral imperative to remove it: we can exploit the symmetry in any way we choose. Where local search is used instead of backtracking search, Prestwich pointed out that it is disadvantageous to add symmetry breaking constraints [94, 91]. While more solutions are good for *any* search method, local search suffers particularly when solutions are excluded. Since stochastic methods are designed to explore search spaces randomly, it is hard to guide them away from parts of the search space where solutions have been excluded, while each excluded solution becomes a new local optimum. In a detailed analysis, Prestwich and Roli identified two pathologies that symmetry breaking constraints caused for local search methods: global solutions have relatively smaller basins of attractions while local optima become relatively larger [95]. Since excluding symmetries seems bad for local search, can we improve it by *introducing* symmetries? Prestwich proposed this lovely idea with some success [92, 91]. Exploiting symmetry within local search algorithms remains an interesting but underdeveloped research area: Petcu and Faltings used interchangeability to guide local search away from conflicts [87], but otherwise little has been done in this direction.

Dominance and almost symmetries: Researchers have investigated cases where standard symmetry breaking methods are not applicable. For example, Beck and Prestwich studied 'dominances' in constraint problems [7]. A dominance is a transition between assignments which is guaranteed to improve (or at least make no worse) some notion of a cost function. We can see symmetries as special cases of dominances, where the cost is kept the same, and hence the transitions are invertible. Beck and Prestwich argue that dominance "should rank alongside symmetry breaking as a generic CP technique, and that it can be profitable to treat both in a uniform way." Another issue receiving recent attention is that of "almost symmetries" [37], the subject of a recent workshop [29]. The general idea is that these are symmetries which are almost, but not quite, there in the original problem. They can arise by either adding or removing constraints on the problem [58]. Examples of the former case would be symmetries which arise during search: dealing with these can be difficult, because they cause significant problems for techniques such as SBDS or SBDD [54]. The idea underlying relaxing constraints on a problem to give new symmetries is as follows [61, 81]. If the relaxed problem is highly symmetric, its reduced search space should help search. If the relaxed problem has no solutions, then neither does the original. If we do find solutions to the relaxed problem, we need additional steps to ensure that they correspond to solutions of the original.

Symmetry in other problems: Given the focus of this handbook to constraints, we have naturally restricted our discussion to constraints and SAT. However, researchers interested in symmetry in constraints should also be interested in how symmetry is tackled in other domains. For example, can we apply ideas from symmetry in constraints to other problems? Can ideas developed in other domains be applied to constraints? While we now point to some key literature in other areas, we do not even claim to provide an exhaustive list of other search problems with symmetry, much less an exhaustive or analytical study of relevant literature in those areas. In *Integer Programming*, Margot has shown how algorithms can be adapted to exploit large symmetry groups [79, 80]. New cuts are generated based on the symmetries, and large groups are handled using Schreier-Sims to represent them. In *Planning*, Fox and Long have integrated symmetry reasoning into a state-of-the-art planner, SymmetricStan [38, 37]. Fox and Long point out that symmetry detection during search, and the presence of almost-symmetry, is very important due to the nature of planning problems. It is perhaps surprising that there does not seem to be a more significant body of work in these two research areas. This is less the case in *Automated Theorem Proving*, where there is a substantial literature in adapting proof systems to deal with symmetry, e.g. [3, 71, 86, 24, 117]. There have also been substantial efforts in *Model Checking* over some years, e.g. [15, 20, 66, 110]. As in constraints, this work has tended to assume that users recognise the symmetry, and they have also been limited to simple cases of symmetry rather than using the power of computational algebra. Recently, Donaldson *et al.* have shown that more general symmetries in model checking using GAP and graph isomorphism software [30, 31, 32]. Finally, we touch only in the slightest way on the extensive mathematical literature on search with symmetry. We particularly mention McKay's *nauty* software for *Graph Isomorphism* [83] and Soicher's GRAPE package for dealing with graphs relating to groups [116]. The key algorithm is "partition backtrack" [83, 76], a very subtle intermingling of backtrack search and group-theoretic computations. The mathematical applications of such techniques are numerous: one is *Design Theory* which deals with combinatorial designs such as balanced incomplete block designs, and for which an online repository is available at www.designtheory.org [6].

10.10   Conclusions

We have presented an overview of symmetry in constraint programming. We have been unashamed in emphasising the links with group theory. The study of symmetry *is* group theory, so anyone who has ever considered symmetry in constraints has been thinking about group theory – though perhaps without realising it. We have also emphasised the ability of computational group theory to contribute methods to the efficient exploitation of symmetry in constraints. Researchers and users of constraint programming can access these techniques either through linking to the existing computational algebra packages, or by implementing their own algorithms. Again, anyone who has written code for exploiting symmetry in constraints has been, whether unconsciously or not, doing computational algebra.

The main part of this chapter is taken up by a study of symmetry breaking methods, since this is by far the largest body of research that has been undertaken on symmetry in constraints. We considered methods in three broad categories: reformulation of problems, adding symmetry breaking constraints before search, and dynamic symmetry breaking methods that operate during the search procedure. It is worth summarising in one place the very broad advantages and disadvantages of each method. It will be seen that there is no 'one-size-fits-all' method to recommend, but it should be noted that researchers have proposed solutions which at least ameliorate many of the disadvantages we mention:

- **Reformulation** is when the problem is remodelled to eliminate some or all symmetry. It can be an astonishingly efficient method of breaking symmetry, but unfortunately there is no known systematic procedure for performing the remodelling process in general. Where reformulation is possible, it can be combined easily with other methods.

- **Symmetry breaking constraints** are perhaps the most natural technique and the easiest to understand. Ideally, the new constraints should be satisfied by only one assignment in any equivalence class, but it can be difficult to find simple constraints that eliminate all the symmetry. A systematic method called 'lex-leader' is known for generating symmetry breaking constraints, when the problem only contains variable symmetry. The efficiency with which some kinds of symmetry breaking constraints can be propagated, for example in matrix models, means that adding symmetry breaking constraints can be very cost-effective even where they do not break all the symmetry. Symmetry breaking constraints do have a disadvantage in that they can interact badly with the search heuristics being used.

- **Dynamic symmetry breaking** includes many methods which adapt the search process in some way. This includes SBDS, SBDD (and the computational group theoretic versions of these methods), and STAB. Both SBDD and SBDS are complete, in that only one solution will be returned from each symmetric equivalence class. Group-theoretic versions add the advantage that only a small number of symmetries in a problem need be specified, but this is related to a disadvantage, that they often require symmetries to be expressed in a mathematical language that is unnatural for constraint programmers. A significant advantage of these methods is that they do not conflict with search heuristics. As relatively new methods, a final drawback is that they can only be used if a library package is available, or the user spends the time to adapt the search program themselves.

Quite apart from its inherent importance, we conclude by commending the study of symmetry in constraints as an enjoyable and rewarding research topic.

Acknowledgments

We thank all those who have helped us with this paper, most especially Barbara Smith, but also Gene Freuder, Carmen Gervet, Chris Jefferson, Steve Linton, Ian Miguel, and Toby Walsh. Parts of the writing of this paper were supported by EPSRC grants GR/R29673, EP/C523229/1 and GR/S30580/01 and Science Foundation Ireland grant 00/PI.1/C075.

Bibliography

[1]   F. A. Aloul, A. Ramani, I. L. Markov, and K. A. Sakallah. Solving difficult sat instances in the presence of symmetry. In *DAC*, pages 731–736. ACM, 2002. ISBN 1-58113-461-4.

[2]   F. A. Aloul, K. A. Sakallah, and I. L. Markov. Efficient symmetry breaking for boolean satisfiability. In Gottlob and Walsh [57], pages 271–276.

[3]   N. H. Arai and A. Urquhart. Local symmetries in propositional logic. In R. Dyckhoff, editor, *TABLEAUX*, volume 1847 of *Lecture Notes in Computer Science*, pages 40–51. Springer, 2000. ISBN 3-540-67697-X.

[4]   R. Backofen and S. Will. Excluding symmetries in concurrent constraint programming. In *Workshop on Modeling and Computing with Concurrent Constraint Programming held in conjunction with CP 98*, 1998.

[5]   R. Backofen and S. Will. Excluding symmetries in constraint-based search. In J. Jaffar, editor, *Principles and Practice of Constraint Programming - CP '99*, volume Lecture Notes in Computer Science 1713, pages 73–87. Springer, 1999.

[6]   R. Bailey, P. Cameron, P. Dobcsányi, J. Morgan, and L. Soicher. Designs on the web. *Discrete Math.* Forthcoming.

[7]   J. C. Beck and S. D. Prestwich. Exploiting dominance in three symmetric problems. In *Fourth International Workshop on Symmetry and Constraint Satisfaction Problems*, 2004.

[8]   B. Benhamou. Study of symmetry in constraint satisfaction problems. In *Proceedings of the 2nd workshop on Principles and Practices of Constraint Programming - PPCP'94*, pages 246–254, 2003.

[9]   C. Bessière and J.-C. Régin. Using bidirectionality to speed up arc-consistency processing. In M. Meyer, editor, *Constraint Processing, Selected Papers*, volume 923 of *Lecture Notes in Computer Science*, pages 157–169. Springer, 1995. ISBN 3-540-59479-5.

[10] C. Bessière, E. Hebrard, B. Hnich, and T. Walsh. The complexity of global constraints. In D. L. McGuinness and G. Ferguson, editors, *AAAI*, pages 112–117. AAAI Press / The MIT Press, 2004. ISBN 0-262-51183-5.

[11] S. Bistarelli and B. O'Sullivan. Combining Branch & Bound and SBDD to solve Soft CSPs. In *Proceedings of CSCLP 2004: Joint Annual Workshop of ERCIM/CoLogNet on Constraint Solving and Constraint Logic Programming*, June 2004.

[12] R. Bosch and M. Trick. Constraint programming and hybrid formulations for three Life designs. In *Proc. of CP-AI-OR'02*, pages 1396–1407, 2002.

[13] R. A. Bosch. Peaceably coexisting armies of queens. *Optima (Newsletter of the Mathematical Programming Society)*, 62:6–9, 1999.

[14] W. Bosma and J. Cannon. *Handbook of MAGMA functions*. sydneypm, Sydney University, 1993.

[15] D. Bosnacki, D. Dams, and L. Holenderski. Symmetric spin. *STTT*, 4(1):92–106, 2002.

[16] C. A. Brown, L. Finkelstein, and P. W. Purdom. Backtrack Searching in the Presence of Symmetry. In T. Mora, editor, *Applied Algebra, Algebraic Algorithms and Error-Correcting Codes*, LNCS 357, pages 99–110. Springer, 1988.

[17] G. Butler. *Fundamental Algorithms for Permutation Groups*. LNCS 559. Springer-Verlag, 1991.

[18] M. Carlsson and N. Beldiceanu. Arc-consistency for a chain of lexicographic ordering constraints, 2002.

[19] B. Y. Choueiry and G. Noubir. On the computation of local interchangeability in discrete constraint satisfaction problems. In *AAAI/IAAI*, pages 326–333, 1998.

[20] E. M. Clarke, S. Jha, R. Enders, and T. Filkorn. Exploiting symmetry in temporal logic model checking. *Formal Methods in System Design*, 9(1/2):77–104, 1996.

[21] D. A. Cohen, P. Jeavons, C. Jefferson, K. E. Petrie, and B. M. Smith. Symmetry definitions for constraint satisfaction problems. In van Beek [118], pages 17–31. ISBN 3-540-29238-1.

[22] J. Crawford, M. L. Ginsberg, E. Luks, and A. Roy. Symmetry-breaking predicates for search problems. In L. C. Aiello, J. Doyle, and S. Shapiro, editors, *KR'96: Principles of Knowledge Representation and Reasoning*, pages 148–159. Morgan

Kaufmann, San Francisco, California, 1996.

[23] P. Darga, M. Liffiton, K. Sakallah, and I.L.Markov. Exploiting Structure in Symmetry Generation for CNF. In *ACM/IEEE Design Automation Conference - DAC*, pages 530–534, 2004.

[24] T. B. de la Tour. Ground resolution with group computations on semantic symmetries. In M. A. McRobbie and J. K. Slaney, editors, *CADE*, volume 1104 of *Lecture Notes in Computer Science*, pages 478–492. Springer, 1996. ISBN 3-540-61511-3.

[25] R. L. de Mántaras and L. Saitta, editors. *Proceedings of the 16th European Conference on Artificial Intelligence, ECAI'2004, including Prestigious Applicants of Intelligent Systems, PAIS 2004, Valencia, Spain, August 22-27, 2004*, 2004. IOS Press. ISBN 1-58603-452-9.

[26] H. E. Dixon, M. L. Ginsberg, E. M. Luks, and A. J. Parkes. Generalizing boolean satisfiability ii: Theory. *J. Artif. Intell. Res. (JAIR)*, 22:481–534, 2004.

[27] H. E. Dixon, M. L. Ginsberg, and A. J. Parkes. Generalizing boolean satisfiability i: Background and survey of existing work. *J. Artif. Intell. Res. (JAIR)*, 21:193–243, 2004.

[28] H. E. Dixon, M. L. Ginsberg, D. Hofer, E. M. Luks, and A. J. Parkes. Generalizing boolean satisfiability iii: Implementation. *J. Artif. Intell. Res. (JAIR)*, 23:441–531, 2005.

[29] A. F. Donaldson and P. Gregory. Almost-symmetry in search. Technical Report TR-2005-201, University of Glasgow, 2005.

[30] A. F. Donaldson and A. Miller. Automatic symmetry detection for model checking using computational group theory. In J. Fitzgerald, I. J. Hayes, and A. Tarlecki, editors, *FM*, volume 3582 of *Lecture Notes in Computer Science*, pages 481–496. Springer, 2005. ISBN 3-540-27882-6.

[31] A. F. Donaldson, A. Miller, and M. Calder. Finding symmetry in models of concurrent systems by static channel diagram analysis. *Electr. Notes Theor. Comput. Sci.*, 128(6):161–177, 2005.

[32] A. F. Donaldson, A. Miller, and M. Calder. Spin-to-grape: A tool for analysing symmetry in promela models. *Electr. Notes Theor. Comput. Sci.*, 139(1):3–23, 2005.

[33] T. Fahle, S. Schamberger, and M. Sellmann. Symmetry breaking. In T. Walsh, editor, *Principles and Practice of Constraint Programming - CP 2001*, volume Lecture Notes in Computer Science 2239, pages 93–107. Springer, 2001.

[34] F.Focacci and M.Milano. Global cut framework for removing symmetries. In T. Walsh, editor, *Principles and Practice of Constraint Programming - CP 2001*, volume Lecture Notes in Computer Science 2239, pages 77–92. Springer, 2001.

[35] P. Flener, A. Frisch, B. Hnich, Z. Kızıltan, I. Miguel, and T. Walsh. Matrix modelling. In *Proceedings of the CP'01 Workshop on Modelling and Problem Formulation*, pages 1–7, 2001.

[36] P. Flener, A. Frisch, B. Hnich, Z. Kiziltan, I. Miguel, J. Pearson, and T. Walsh. Breaking row and column symmetries in matrix models. In P. van Hentenryck, editor, *Principles and Practice of Constraint Programming - CP 2002*, LNCS 2470, pages 462–476. Springer, 2002.

[37] M. Fox and D. Long. Extending the exploitation of symmetries in planning. In M. Ghallab, J. Hertzberg, and P. Traverso, editors, *AIPS*, pages 83–91. AAAI, 2002. ISBN 1-57735-142-8.

[38] M. Fox and D. Long. The detection and exploitation of symmetry in planning prob-

lems. In T. Dean, editor, *IJCAI*, pages 956–961. Morgan Kaufmann, 1999. ISBN 1-55860-613-0.

[39]   E. Freuder. Eliminating Interchangeable Values in Constraint Satisfaction Problems. In *AAAI-91*, pages 227–233, 1991.

[40]   A. Frisch, B. Hnich, Z. Kiziltan, I. Miguel, and T. Walsh. Global constraints for lexicographic orderings. In P. van Hentenryck, editor, *Proceedings of the Eighth International Conference on Principles and Practice of Constraint Programming* pages 93–108, 2002.

[41]   A. M. Frisch and W. Harvey. Constraints for breaking all row and column symmetries in a three-by-two matrix. In *Proceedings of the Third International Workshop on Symmetry in Constraint Satisfaction Problems"*,, September 2003.

[42]   A. M. Frisch, C. Jefferson, and I. Miguel. Constraints for breaking more row and column symmetries. In Rossi [104], pages 318–332. ISBN 3-540-20202-1.

[43]   A. M. Frisch, I. Miguel, Z. Kiziltan, B. Hnich, and T. Walsh. Multiset ordering constraints. In Gottlob and Walsh [57], pages 221–226.

[44]   A. M. Frisch, C. Jefferson, and I. Miguel. Symmetry breaking as a prelude to implied constraints: A constraint modelling pattern. In de Mántaras and Saitta [25], pages 171–175. ISBN 1-58603-452-9.

[45]   A. M. Frisch, C. Jefferson, B. Martinez-Hernández, and I. Miguel. The rules of constraint modelling. In *IJCAI*, pages 109–116, 2005.

[46]   *GAP – Groups, Algorithms, and Programming, Version 4.2*. The GAP Group, 2000. (http://www.gap-system.org).

[47]   M. Gardner. Chess queens and maximum unattacked cells. *Math Horizon*, pages 12–16, November 1999.

[48]   I. Gent and I. McDonald. NuSBDS: Symmetry Breaking made Easy. In B. Smith, I. Gent, and W. Harvey, editors, *Proceedings of the Third International Workshop on Symmetry in Constraint Satisfaction Problems*, pages 153–160, 2003. URL http://scom.hud.ac.uk/scombms/SymCon03/notes.html.

[49]   I. Gent, S. Linton, and B. Smith. Symmetry breaking in the alien tiles puzzle. Technical Report APES-22-2000, APES Research Group, October 2000. Available from http://www.dcs.st-and.ac.uk/˜apes/apesreports.html.

[50]   I. Gent, I. McDonald, and B. Smith. Conditional symmetry in the all-interval series problem. In B. Smith, I. Gent, and W. Harvey, editors, *Proceedings of the Third International Workshop on Symmetry in Constraint Satisfaction Problems*, pages 55–65, 2003.

[51]   I. P. Gent and B. M. Smith. Symmetry breaking in constraint programming. In *Proceedings of European Conference on Artificial Intelligence - ECAI 2000*, pages 599–603. IOS press, 2000.

[52]   I. P. Gent, W. Harvey, and T. Kelsey. Groups and Constraints: Symmetry Breaking During Search, 2002.

[53]   I. P. Gent, W. Harvey, T. Kelsey, and S. Linton. Generic SBDD Using Computational Group Theory. In F. Rossi, editor, *Principles and Practice of Constraint Programming - CP2003*, LNCS 2833, pages 333–347. Springer, 2003.

[54]   I. P. Gent, T. Kelsey, S. Linton, I. McDonald, I. Miguel, and B. M. Smith. Conditional symmetry breaking. In van Beek [118], pages 256–270. ISBN 3-540-29238-1.

[55]   I. P. Gent, P. Nightingale, and K. Stergiou. Qcsp-solve: A solver for quantified constraint satisfaction problems. In Kaelbling and Saffiotti [68], pages 138–143.

ISBN 0938075934.

[56] C. Gervet. Interval propagation to reason about sets: Definition and implementation of a practical language. *Constraints*, 1(3):191–244, 1997.

[57] G. Gottlob and T. Walsh, editors. *IJCAI-03, Proceedings of the Eighteenth International Joint Conference on Artificial Intelligence, Acapulco, Mexico, August 9-15, 2003*, 2003. Morgan Kaufmann.

[58] P. Gregory and A. F. Donaldson. Conclusions of the SymNET workshop on almost-symmetry in search. In *Almost-Symmetry in Search* Donaldson and Gregory [29], pages 60–61.

[59] W. Harvey. Symmetry Breaking and the Social Golfer Problem. In *Proceedings SymCon-01: Symmetry in Constraints*, pages 9–16, 2001.

[60] W. Harvey. A note on the compatibility of static symmetry breaking constraints and dynamic symmetry breaking methods. In *Proceedings SymCon-04: Symmetry and Constraint Satisfaction Problems*, pages 42–47, 2004.

[61] W. Harvey. Symmetric relaxation techniques for constraint programming. In *Almost-Symmetry in Search* Donaldson and Gregory [29], pages 50–59.

[62] W. Harvey and T. Winterer. Solving the molr and social golfers problems. In van Beek [118], pages 286–300. ISBN 3-540-29238-1.

[63] W. Harvey, T. Kelsey, and K. Petrie. Symmetry Group Expressions for CSPs. In *Proceedings SymCon-03: Third International workshop on Symmetry in Constraint Satisfaction Problems*, pages 86–96, 2003.

[64] P. V. Hentenryck, P. Flener, J. Pearson, and M. Agren. Tractable Symmetry Breaking for CSPs with Interchangeable Values. In *International Joint Conference on Artificial Intelligence - IJCAI 2003*, pages 277–282, 2003.

[65] D. F. Holt, B. Eick, and E. A. O'Brien. *Handbook of Computational Group Theory*. Chapman and Hall/CRC, 2005. ISBN 1 58488 372 3.

[66] C. N. Ip and D. L. Dill. Better verification through symmetry. *Formal Methods in System Design*, 9(1/2):41–75, 1996.

[67] C. Jefferson and A. M. Frisch. Representations of sets and multisets in constraint programming. In B. Hnich, P. Prosser, and B. Smith, editors, *The Fourth International Workshop on Modelling and Reformulating Constraint Satisfaction Problems*, pages 102–116, 2005.

[68] L. P. Kaelbling and A. Saffiotti, editors. *IJCAI-05, Proceedings of the Nineteenth International Joint Conference on Artificial Intelligence, Edinburgh, Scotland, UK, July 30-August 5, 2005*, 2005. Professional Book Center. ISBN 0938075934.

[69] T. Kelsey, S. Linton, and C. M. Roney-Dougal. New developments in symmetry breaking in search using computational group theory. In B. Buchberger and J. A. Campbell, editors, *AISC*, volume 3249 of *Lecture Notes in Computer Science*, pages 199–210. Springer, 2004. ISBN 3-540-23212-5.

[70] Z. Kiziltan and B. M. Smith. Symmetry-Breaking Constraints for Matrix Models. In *Proceedings SymCon-02: Symmetry in Constraints*, pages 1–8, 2002.

[71] B. Krishnamurthy. Short proofs for tricky formulas. *Acta Inf.*, 22(3):253–275, 1985.

[72] A. Lal, B. Y. Choueiry, and E. C. Freuder. Neighborhood interchangeability and dynamic bundling for non-binary finite CSPs. In M. M. Veloso and S. Kambhampati, editors, *AAAI*, pages 397–404. AAAI Press AAAI Press / The MIT Press, 2005. ISBN 1-57735-236-X.

[73] Y. C. Law and J. H.-M. Lee. Model induction: A new source of CSP model redun-

dancy. In *AAAI/IAAI*, pages 54–60, 2002.

[74] Y. C. Law and J. H.-M. Lee. Symmetry breaking constraints for value symmetries in constraint satisfaction. *Constraints*. Forthcoming.

[75] Y. C. Law and J. H.-M. Lee. Global constraints for integer and set value precedence. In Wallace [120], pages 362–376. ISBN 3-540-23241-9.

[76] J. S. Leon. Permutation group algorithms based on partitions, i: Theory and algorithms. *J. Symb. Comput.*, 12(4/5):533–583, 1991.

[77] E. Luks and A. Roy. The complexity of symmetry-breaking formulas. *Ann. Math. Artif. Intell.*, 41(1):19–45, 2004.

[78] I. J. Lustig and J. F. Puget. Program Does Not Equal Program: Constraint Programming and Its Relationship to Mathematical Programming. *INTERFACES*, 31 (6):29–53, 2001.

[79] F. Margot. Pruning by isomorphism in branch-and-cut. *Mathematical Programming* 94:71–90, 2002.

[80] F. Margot. Exploiting orbits in symmetric ILP. *Mathematical Programming Ser B.* 98:3–21, 2003.

[81] R. Martin. Approaches to symmetry breaking for weak symmetries. In *Almost-Symmetry in Search* Donaldson and Gregory [29], pages 37–49.

[82] I. McDonald and B. Smith. Partial symmetry breaking. In P. V. Hentenryck, editor, *Principles and Practice of Constraint Programming*, pages 431–445, 2002.

[83] B. D. McKay. Practical graph isomorphism. *Congressium Numerantium*, 30:45–87, 1981.

[84] P. Meseguer and C. Torras. Exploiting Symmetries within Constraint Satisfaction Search. *Artificial Intelligence*, 129:133–163, 2001.

[85] J. Molony. *Symmetry and Complexity in Propositional Reasoning*. PhD thesis, University of Edinburgh, 1999.

[86] N. Peltier. A new method for automated finite model building exploiting failures and symmetries. *J. Log. Comput.*, 8(4):511–543, 1998.

[87] A. Petcu and B. Faltings. Applying interchangeability techniques to the distributed breakout algorithm. In Gottlob and Walsh [57], pages 1381–1382.

[88] K. E. Petrie. *Constraint Programming, Search and Symmetry*. PhD thesis, University of Huddersfield, 2005.

[89] K. E. Petrie and B. M. Smith. Symmetry breaking in graceful graphs. In Rossi [104], pages 930–934. ISBN 3-540-20202-1.

[90] K. E. Petrie, B. M. Smith, and N. Yorke-Smith. Dynamic symmetry breaking in constraint programming and linear programming hybrids. In *In the proceedings of the Second Starting AI Researchers' Symposium - STAIRS 2004*, volume Frontiers in Artificial Intelligence and Applications 109, pages 96–106. IOS Press, 2004.

[91] S. Prestwich. Negative effects of modeling techniques on search performance. *Annals of Operations Research*, 118:137–150, 2003.

[92] S. Prestwich. Supersymmetric modeling for local search. In *Second International Workshop on Symmetry in Constraint Satisfaction Problems*, 2002.

[93] S. D. Prestwich. Full dynamic substitutability by sat encoding. In Wallace [120], pages 512–526. ISBN 3-540-23241-9.

[94] S. D. Prestwich. First-solution search with symmetry breaking and implied constraints. In *CP-01 Workshop on Modelling and Problem Formulation*, 2001.

[95] S. D. Prestwich and A. Roli. Symmetry breaking and local search spaces. In

R. Barták and M. Milano, editors, *CPAIOR*, volume 3524 of *Lecture Notes in Computer Science*, pages 273–287. Springer, 2005. ISBN 3-540-26152-4.

[96] L. G. Proll and B. M. Smith. ILP and Constraint Programming Approaches to a Template Design Problem. *INFORMS Journal on Computing*, 10:265–275, 1998.

[97] J.-F. Puget. On the satisfiability of symmetrical constraint satisfaction problems. In *Methodologies for Intelligent Systems (Proceedings of ISMIS'93)*, LNAI 689, pages 350–361. Springer, 1993.

[98] J.-F. Puget. Symmetry breaking using stabilizers. In Rossi [104], pages 585–599. ISBN 3-540-20202-1.

[99] J.-F. Puget. Symmetry breaking revisited. *Constraints*, 10(1):23–46, 2005.

[100] J.-F. Puget. Automatic detection of variable and value symmetries. In van Beek [118], pages 475–489. ISBN 3-540-29238-1.

[101] J.-F. Puget. Breaking symmetries in all-different problems. In *IJCAI*, pages 272–277, 2005.

[102] J.-F. Puget. Symmetry breaking revisited. In P. V. Hentenryck, editor, *CP*, volume 2470 of *Lecture Notes in Computer Science*, pages 446–461. Springer, 2002. ISBN 3-540-44120-4.

[103] C. M. Roney-Dougal, I. P. Gent, T. Kelsey, and S. Linton. Tractable symmetry breaking using restricted search trees. In de Mántaras and Saitta [25], pages 211–215. ISBN 1-58603-452-9.

[104] F. Rossi, editor. *Principles and Practice of Constraint Programming - CP 2003, 9th International Conference, CP 2003, Kinsale, Ireland, September 29 - October 3, 2003, Proceedings*, volume 2833 of *Lecture Notes in Computer Science*, 2003. Springer. ISBN 3-540-20202-1.

[105] P. Roy and F. Pachet. Using Symmetry of Global Constraints to Speed up the Resolution of Constraint Satisfaction Problems. In *Workshop on Non Binary Constraints, ECAI-98*, August 1998.

[106] A. Sadler and C. Gervet. Hybrid set domains to strengthen constraint propagation and reduce symmetries. In Wallace [120], pages 604–618. ISBN 3-540-23241-9.

[107] M. Sellmann and P. V. Hentenryck. Structural symmetry breaking. In Kaelbling and Saffiotti [68], pages 298–303. ISBN 0938075934.

[108] A. Seress. *Permutation group algorithms*. Number 152 in Cambridge tracts in mathematics. Cambridge University Press, 2002.

[109] I. Shlyakhter. Generating effective symmetry-breaking predicates for search problems. *Discrete Applied Mathematics*, To appear. Earlier version presented at the SAT 01 Workshop.

[110] A. P. Sistla, V. Gyuris, and E. A. Emerson. Smc: a symmetry-based model checker for verification of safety and liveness properties. *ACM Trans. Softw. Eng. Methodol.*, 9(2):133–166, 2000.

[111] A. Smaill. Symmetry in boolean constraints: Some complexity issues. In *Tenth Workshop on Automated Reasoning*, 2003.

[112] B. Smith. Personal communication to Warwick Harvey, 2004.

[113] B. M. Smith. Reducing Symmetry in a Combinatorial Design Problem. Technical report, School of Computer Studies, University of Leeds, Jan. 2001.

[114] B. M. Smith. A dual graph translation of a problem in 'Life'. In *Principles and Practice of Constraint Programming - CP2002*, LNCS 2470, pages 402–414. Springer, 2002.

[115] B. M. Smith, K. E. Petrie, and I. P. Gent. Models and symmetry breaking for 'peaceable armies of queens'. In J.-C. Régin and M. Rueher, editors, *CPAIOR*, volume 3011 of *Lecture Notes in Computer Science*, pages 271–286. Springer, 2004. ISBN 3-540-21836-X.

[116] L. H. Soicher. Computing with graphs and groups. In L. Beineke and R. Wilson, editors, *Topics in Algebraic Graph Theory*, pages 250–266. Cambridge University Press, 2004.

[117] A. Urquhart. The symmetry rule in propositional logic. *Discrete Applied Mathematics*, 96-97:177–193, 1999.

[118] P. van Beek, editor. *Principles and Practice of Constraint Programming - CP 2005 11th International Conference, CP 2005, Sitges, Spain, October 1-5, 2005, Proceedings*, volume 3709 of *Lecture Notes in Computer Science*, 2005. Springer. ISBN 3-540-29238-1.

[119] M. Vasquez and D. Habet. Complete and incomplete algorithms for the queen graph coloring problem. In de Mántaras and Saitta [25], pages 226–230. ISBN 1-58603-452-9.

[120] M. Wallace, editor. *Principles and Practice of Constraint Programming - CP 2004 10th International Conference, CP 2004, Toronto, Canada, September 27 - October 1, 2004, Proceedings*, volume 3258 of *Lecture Notes in Computer Science*, 2004. Springer. ISBN 3-540-23241-9.

Handbook of Constraint Programming
Edited by F. Rossi, P. van Beek and T. Walsh

Chapter 11

Modelling

Barbara M. Smith

Constraint programming can be a successful technology for solving practical problems; however, there is abundant evidence that how the problem to be solved is modelled as a Constraint Satisfaction Problem (CSP) can have a dramatic effect on how easy it is to find a solution, or indeed whether it can realistically be solved at all. The importance of modelling in constraint programming has long been recognized e.g. in invited talks by Freuder [14] and Puget [34].

In this chapter, it will be assumed that the problem to be solved can be represented as a CSP whose domains are finite; infinite domains are discussed in Chapter 16, "Continuous and Interval Constraints". In most of the examples, the variable domains will be sets of integers; see Chapter 17, "Constraints over Structured Domains", for more on set variables and other variable types.

A complicating factor in modelling is the interaction between the model, the search algorithm and the search heuristics. To simplify matters, it will be assumed that, having modelled the problem of interest as a CSP, the CSP will be solved using a constraint solver such as ILOG Solver, ECL^{i}PS^e, Choco, SICStus Prolog, or the like. The default complete search algorithms provided by these solvers are sufficiently similar that they provide a common context for discussing modelling. Furthermore, they are designed to solve large problems of practical significance, and for such problems, it is worth the effort of developing the best model of the problem that we can find. Some of what follows will also apply to other search techniques such as local search (covered in Chapter 5) or to other complete search algorithms, but much will not, because the search algorithm has a profound influence on modelling decisions.

In this chapter, it will be assumed that the problem to be solved is well-defined; although eliciting a correct and full problem description can be a significant proportion of the problem-solving effort, it will be assumed here that that step has been done. It will also be assumed that the problem does not involve preferences or uncertainty, which are covered in Chapters 9 and 21.

11.1   Preliminaries

In this section, the concepts needed in the rest of the chapter are defined.

A *Constraint Satisfaction Problem* (CSP) is a triple $\langle X, D, C \rangle$ where: X is a set of *variables*, $\{x_1, ..., x_n\}$; D is a set of *domains*, $D_1, ..., D_n$ associated with $x_1, ..., x_n$ respectively; and C is a set of *constraints*. Each constraint $c \in C$ is a pair $c = \langle \sigma, \rho \rangle$ where σ, the constraint *scope*, is a list of variables, and ρ, the constraint *relation*, is a subset of the Cartesian product of their domains.

The domain of a variable is the set of possible values that can be assigned to it. In this chapter, it will be assumed that the domain of a variable is a finite set.

An *assignment* is a pair (x_i, a), which means that variable $x_i \in X$ is assigned the value $a \in D_i$. A *compound assignment* is a set of assignments to distinct variables in X A *complete assignment* is a compound assignment to all variables in X.

The relation of a constraint $c = \langle \sigma_c, \rho_c \rangle$ specifies the acceptable assignments to the variables in its scope. That is, if the constraint scope σ_c is $\{x_{i_1}, x_{i_2}, ..., x_{i_k}\}$ and $\langle a_1, a_2, ..., a_k \rangle \in \rho_c$, the compound assignment assigning a_i to x_{i_k}, $1 \le i \le k$, is an acceptable assignment; we say that the assignment *satisfies* the constraint c. A solution to the CSP instance $\langle X, D, C \rangle$ is a complete assignment such that for every constraint $c \in C$, the restriction of the assignment to the scope σ_c satisfies the constraint.

The relation of a constraint may be specified *extensionally* by listing its acceptable (satisfying) tuples, or *intensionally* by giving an expression involving the variables in the constraint scope such as $x < y$ from which it can be determined whether or nor a given tuple satisfies the constraint.

The *arity* of a constraint is the size of its scope. A unary constraint is defined on a single variable, a binary constraint on two variables. There is no requirement that different constraints must have different scopes.

Given a constraint $c = \langle \sigma_c, \rho_c \rangle$, the *projection* of c onto $\tau \subset \sigma_c$ is a constraint c' whose scope is τ and whose relation is the set of tuples derived by taking each tuple in ρ_c and selecting only those components corresponding to the variables in τ.

Many forms of consistency have been defined for CSPs and individual constraints. Here, only those commonly used by constraint solvers are defined. Consistency and constraint propagation are covered fully in Chapter 3.

A binary constraint is *arc consistent* if for every value in the domain of either variable, there exists a value in the domain of the other such that the pair of values satisfies the constraint. A non-binary constraint is *generalized arc consistent* or *hyper-arc consistent* iff for any value for a variable in its scope, there exists a value for every other variable in the scope such that the tuple satisfies the constraint. *Domain propagation* on a constraint removes unsupported values (i.e. values which cannot be extended to a pair of tuple of values satisfying the constraints) from the domains of the variables in its scope until the constraint is (generalized) arc consistent.

A constraint c on variables with ordered domains (such as integers) is *bounds consistent* if for every variable x in its scope, there exists a value d_j for every other variable x_j ($1 \le j \le k$) in the scope of c, with $\min_{D_j} \le d_j \le \max_{D_j}$, such that the compound assignment $\{(x, l), (x_1, d_1), ..., (x_k, d_k)\}$ satisfies c, where l is the minimum of the domain of x, *and* similarly, values d_j' can be found with $\min_{D_j} \le d_j' \le \max_{D_j}$, such that $\{(x, u), (x_1, d_1'), ..., (x_k, d_k')\}$ satisfies c, where u is the maximum of the domain of x. (For arithmetic constraints, the values d_j, d_j' can be real values rather than integers.)

Bounds propagation on an arithmetic constraint reduces the bounds of the variables until the constraint is bounds consistent.

11.2 Representing a Problem

It is difficult to define precisely what we mean when we say that a CSP *represents* a problem P. A possible definition is that: a CSP $M = \langle X, D, C \rangle$ represents a problem P, or M is a *model* of P, if every solution of C corresponds to a solution of P and every solution of P can be derived from at least one solution to C.

The definition does not require that there is a one-to-one correspondence between the solutions of P and the solutions of M. This is because modelling a problem as a CSP often introduces symmetry, by representing entities that are indistinguishable in P by distinct variables or values in M. Hence, multiple solutions of M may correspond to the same solution to P.

Symmetry causes a further complication, because if there is symmetry in both P and M, one way to deal with it is to add constraints to M; the aim is to eliminate all but one solution in every symmetry equivalence class. The symmetry-breaking constraints exist only in M, not in P, so that multiple symmetrically-equivalent solutions to P can correspond to the same solution to M. Hence, the correspondence between the solutions to M and the solutions to P can be many-to-many. We might avoid this last complication by agreeing that symmetry-breaking constraints are a special case, intended to eliminate solutions to M and therefore also solutions to P, and that they can be ignored in considering whether M is a model of P.

A final difficulty with the definition is that it implies that any CSP models a problem that has no solutions. The definition of equivalence of CSPs given by Rossi, Petrie and Dhar [36] similarly makes any CSPs with no solutions equivalent.

In practice, in modelling a problem as a CSP, we do not rely on this definition, but choose variables and values to represent entities in P and write the constraints on these variables to represent the rules and restrictions defining the solutions to P. However, it must certainly be true that any solution to M yields exactly one solution to P, and that any solution to P corresponds to a solution to M or is symmetrically equivalent to such a solution, and that if M has no solutions, this is because P itself has no solutions.

The aim in choosing a model of a problem is to arrive at a CSP that can be solved quickly; we typically require good run-time behaviour over the range of instances to be solved. Note that the shortest run-time does not necessarily mean the least search (as measured by nodes visited or backtracks, say).

11.3 Propagation and Search

In this chapter, it will be assumed, unless stated otherwise, that the CSP will be solved by a complete search algorithm that interleaves search with constraint propagation. Such search algorithms are dealt with in Chapter 4, "Backtracking Search Algorithms for CSPs", along with variable and value ordering heuristics. The search proceeds by constructing a series of choice points, at each of which a set of mutually exclusive and exhaustive choices is constructed, involving variables whose value is not yet assigned. Common sets of choices are $\{x_i = a, x_i \neq a\}$ (binary branching); $\{x_i = 1, x_i = 0\}$ (when the variables are Boolean); $\{x_i \leq a, x_i > a\}$ (domain splitting); $\{x_i = v_1, x_i = v_2, ..., x_i = v_k\}$ where $v_1, v_2, ..., v_k$ are the values currently available in D_i (k-way branching). Choices can involve more than one variable, e.g. $\{x_i \leq x_j, x_i > x_j\}$; this is common in scheduling, for instance, where the choices might represent the two possible orders for the starting times of two activities (see Chapter 22). Although all these types of choice, and more, are possible, in the examples quoted in this chapter binary branching has been used.

The search pursues each choice in turn, first adding the constraint defining the choice to the existing constraints and propagating it, until local consistency is restored in the resulting subproblem. Typically, each type of constraint in the problem has an associated propagation algorithm, achieving the level of consistency specified for that constraint. Constraint propagation continues until no further propagation can be done, and every constraint is again in its target state of consistency. Given a target level of consistency for each constraint in C, the CSP $\langle X, D, C \rangle$ is *locally consistent* if every constraint achieves its target consistency level. If, at any stage during the search, constraint propagation results in an empty domain for some future (not-yet-assigned) variable, the search backtracks, restoring the domains to their state before the last choice was made, and exploring another of the choices created at the last choice point; if no further choices remain, the search backtracks to a previous choice point, and so on, until either a solution is found or all possible choices have been explored.

This form of search is used by default in commercial constraint solvers. It has a profound influence on the modelling process, because in taking many modelling decisions, the user needs to consider their effect on constraint propagation.

Typically, constraint solvers will enforce arc consistency (AC) on some, but not all, binary constraints and bounds consistency (BC) on arithmetic constraints. They will not usually maintain generalized arc consistency (GAC) on non-binary constraints, except for global constraints for which an efficient propagation algorithm exists. For some global constraints, the user may be able to choose the level of consistency to be maintained. For some complex constraints, the default may be to do very little consistency checking; the propagation algorithm may take action only when all but one or two of the variables in its scope have been instantiated.

These decisions in designing constraint solvers stem from a trade-off between the time and space required to maintain generalized arc consistency on all constraints and the reduction in search that could result. Puget has explained the decision to maintain only bounds consistency on arithmetic constraints in ILOG Solver by saying: "Solver is a compromise between efficiency and completeness...In the example... [of constraint propagation of arithmetic constraints] the incompleteness comes from the fact that arithmetic expressions only propagate bounds.. This is an example of the choice we made. Propagating holes in expressions would require much more memory and time than the current implementation. ¿From tests made on a very large set of examples, we found that the current compromise is by far better."

Even if we start from the assumption that the CSP will be solved using this general search algorithm, the form of the choices made at choice points, as well as the specific variable and value choices, will also affect the solution time.

Beacham, Chen, Sillito and van Beek [2] investigate the interaction between constraint models, search algorithms and search heuristics, using crossword puzzle problems. They compare three constraint models and two well-known search heuristics (minimum domain and domain/degree); the search algorithms are forward checking and a search algorithm that maintains generalized arc consistency, with three different ways of enforcing GAC. They conclude that the three choices of model, algorithm and heuristic interact, and that for the most efficient problem solving, none of the decisions can be made independently of the others.

It is a moot point whether the choice of search heuristics is part of modelling or not. It is certainly true that the performance of a model will be affected by the search heuristics, but for the purposes of this chapter, choosing the search heuristics will be excluded. However, for some types of model, there is a choice of which of the variables in the model should be used to drive the search, i.e. which variables should participate in choice points, and this will be considered as part of modelling.

11.4 Viewpoints

Different models of a problem P may result from viewing the problem P from different angles or perspectives. The term *viewpoint* was introduced informally by Geelen [19], in discussing permutation problems, and was subsequently adopted and formally defined by Law and Lee [29]. A viewpoint is a pair $\langle X, D \rangle$, where $X = \{x_1, \ldots, x_n\}$ is a set of variables, and D is a set of domains; for each $x_i \in X$, the associated domain D_i is the set of possible values for x. It must be possible to ascribe a meaning to the variables and values of the CSP in terms of the problem P, and so to say what an assignment in the viewpoint $\langle X, D \rangle$ is intended to represent in terms of P. The complete assignments defined by the viewpoint are intended to include all possible solutions of P. The constraints must then ensure that every solution to the CSP is a valid solution to P, and so are largely determined by that requirement. Hence, it is different viewpoints that give rise to fundamentally different models of a problem.

In principle, the values in the domain can be of any type. In practice, the types commonly supported by constraint solvers include integers, Booleans (perhaps only as a subtype of integers) and sets of integers. Other types have been proposed, e.g. multisets and tuples; constraint solvers may directly support these, or provide facilities to allow new types to be defined. Some of what follows may also apply to modelling using real-valued variables, and since the domains of integer variables are sometimes represented as intervals, the boundary can be blurred.

Except for some very small problems, the variables of a CSP are usually implemented using some data structure such as a list or an array. Flener, Frisch, Hnich, Kiziltan and Walsh [12] suggest that *matrix models*, based on matrices of variables, are a natural way to model many problems; indeed, almost all the examples given in this chapter use 1- or 2-dimensional matrices of variables. For some applications, other structures are important; for instance, models based on graphs are used in the network applications discussed in Chapter 25.

There are usually different viewpoints that could be chosen in modelling a problem. Although viewpoints can be combined, as will be described in section 11.9, it will be assumed for now that only one will be used. Having chosen a viewpoint, the next step is to express the constraints to ensure that the solutions to the CSP are correct, i.e. are solutions to P. However, although correctness is a minimum requirement, it is not sufficient if we are also concerned with how efficiently the CSP can be solved. A good rule of thumb in choosing a viewpoint is that it should allow the constraints to be easily and concisely expressed; we should prefer viewpoints that allow the problem to be described using as few constraints as possible, as long as those constraints have efficient, low-complexity propagation algorithms.

Nadel [30] was possibly the first to discuss different ways of modelling a problem. He lists nine different representations of the n-queens problem as a CSP (in fact, nine different viewpoints), although two of these are derived from another two simply by swapping the roles of rows and columns, and so result in identical CSPs. For instance, two of the viewpoints are:

1. the variables $r_1, .., r_n$ represent the rows of the board, and the domain of each variable is the set of integers $\{1, 2, ..., n\}$ representing the columns; an assignment $(r_i, c$ means that the queen in row i is in column c;

2. the variables $q_1, ..., q_n$ correspond to the n queens and the domain of each variable is the set of integers $\{1, 2, ..., n^2\}$, representing the squares; an assignment $(q_i, a$ means that the ith queen is on square a.

In the first viewpoint, the rule that there is only one (in fact, exactly one) queen on each row is covered by the fact that any variable can only be assigned one value. The rule that there is only one queen in each column can be expressed by the constraints $r_i \neq r_j$ for $1 \leq i < j \leq n$ or by an allDifferent constraint on $r_1, ..., r_n$.

In the second viewpoint, the rules are more awkward to express. Constraints are needed to ensure that no two queens are in the same row; if the 'row' element of a value can be extracted, there could be a constraint between every pair of variables that their row elements are not equal; the column constraints could be dealt with similarly. The diagonal constraints are more difficult to write. One possibility is to state an extensional constraint between each pair of variables, listing for each of the n^2 values, the values representing squares that are not in the same row, column or diagonal, although domain propagation would then be expensive. Furthermore, such constraints would only express that fact that there is *at most* one queen in each row or column, not that there must be *exactly* one. Although only correct solutions would be found using these constraints, the model would allow partial solutions in which the queens already placed attack all the squares on a row or column, since there is nothing explicit in the constraints to forbid this. Hence, a model based on the second viewpoint would be less efficiently solved than the model based on the first viewpoint.

11.5   Expressing the Constraints

Once we have arrived at a viewpoint that allows the constraints to be easily and concisely expressed, there are often choices in exactly how to write the constraints; an example has already been seen in the first viewpoint for the n-queens problem, where there is a choice between binary $\neq$ constraints and an allDifferent constraint.

The way in which the constraints are written affects the efficiency of the resulting model, because it affects how the constraints will propagate during the search. Harvey and Stuckey [22] observe that, "An unnerving and not well studied property of propagation based solvers, is that the form of a constraint may change the amount of information that propagation discovers." They illustrate this with the constraints $c_1 \equiv (x = y)$, $c_2 \equiv (x + y = z)$ and $c_3 \equiv (2y = z)$, where x, y and z are integer variables. If $C = \{c_1, c_2$

and $C' = \{c_1, c_3\}$, C and C' are equivalent, in the sense that they have the same solutions. However, if C and C' are made locally consistent, then in C', the domain of z (using AC) or its upper and lower bounds (using BC) will be even integers, but this is not necessarily true of C.

Unfortunately, to arrive at a good model of P, it is essential to be aware of the range of constraints supported by the constraint solver and the level of consistency enforced on each and to have some idea of the complexity of the corresponding propagation algorithms. This is, of course, a long way from the declarative ideal. In this section, some of the choices available when writing constraints are discussed.

11.5.1   Combining Constraints

Combining constraints with the same scope can be a way of expressing them more concisely. The conjunction of two constraints with the same scope allows only the tuples that are allowed by both. Enforcing the same level of local consistency on a conjunction $c_1 \wedge c_2$ as on c_1 and c_2 separately will remove at least as many domain values. However, it may or may not reduce the run-time, depending on how time-consuming it is to enforce local consistency on the conjunction and on the separate constraints.

An example can be found in the n-queens problem. Using the first viewpoint listed earlier (the standard CSP model for this problem), the variables $x_1, x_2, ..., x_n$ representing rows 1 to n of the board, and the values are $\{1, 2, ..., n\}$, representing the columns. The rule that two queens cannot be on the same column or diagonal can most simply be written using more than one constraint between each pair of variables x_i and x_j, $i < j$. For instance:

- $x_i \neq x_j$

- $x_i - x_j \neq j - i$

- $x_j - x_i \neq j - i$

Figure 11.1 shows a state that might be arrived at during search, when $n = 6$. Two variables, x_1 and x_2, have already been assigned, and the crossed squares are no longer available, because queens placed there would conflict with the two already placed; the corresponding values will have been removed from the domains of the remaining variables x_3, x_4, x_5, x_6. A queen cannot now be placed in row 5, column 3, because it would conflict

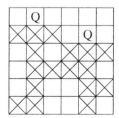

Figure 11.1: A search state in the 6-queens problem

with both remaining places for a queen in the 3rd row. However, the three constraints between x_3 and x_5 are arc consistent; the value 3 for x_5 is supported by the value 1 for x_3 as far as the first constraint is concerned, and by the value 3 for x_3 as far as the second constraint is concerned. If the conjunction of the three constraints were expressed as a single constraint, domain propagation would delete 3 from the domain of x_5. (However, since the conjunction is unlikely to be expressible as a single constraint using the standard constraints provided by constraint solvers, it might require writing a special constraint or forcing AC in some other way. Simply writing a single constraint as a conjunction of the separate constraints will not guarantee that the solver will enforce GAC on it, and it may in fact do *less* consistency checking than on the separate constraints.)

Katsirelos and Bacchus [28] discuss improving constraint propagation by enforcing GAC on conjunctions of constraints, rather than the individual constraints. If c_1 and c_2 are two constraints in a CSP, domain propagation on their conjunction $c_1 \wedge c_2$ removes at least as many domain values as domain propagation on c_1 and c_2 separately. If the scopes of c_1 and c_2 are disjoint, then domain propagation on the conjunction is equivalent to domain propagation on the separate constraints, but the larger the overlap in the scopes, the larger the potential domain pruning from conjoining the constraints. Katsirelos and Bacchus use Bessière and Régin's GAC-schema algorithm [4] in their experiments: for that algorithm, if the scope of c_1 is a subset of the scope of c_2, it is less time-consuming to enforce GAC on the conjunction than on the individual constraints. They propose, as a heuristic, to combine constraints which share all or most of their variables. They use the Golomb ruler problem, discussed in more detail in section 11.9, as an example. They model the problem as a CSP by using the positions of the m 'ticks' on the ruler as the variables $x_1, ..., x_m$ The constraints are that $|x_j - x_i| \neq |x_l - x_k|$, for $1 \leq i, j, k, l \leq m$. In this model, there are seven constraints of this kind over any set of four variables (four quaternary and three ternary). They show that combining the quaternary and ternary constraints on each set of four such variables reduces the number of backtracks slightly and the run-time a lot, compared to using the individual constraints; they maintain GAC on constraints in either case. (Note that this is not the model usually used for the Golomb ruler problem, so that their results are not comparable with others.)

11.5.2 Eliminating Variables

Harvey and Stuckey [22] give a number of theorems on rewriting linear constraints and how bounds propagation or domain propagation will be affected. For instance, one theorem concerns using a two-variable linear equation to substitute for one of these variables in a linear constraint: suppose $c_1 \equiv (\sum_{i=1}^{n} a_i x_i \text{ op } d)$, where op $\in \{=, \leq, \neq\}$ and $c_2 \equiv (b_j x_j + b_k x_k = e), j \neq k, b_j \neq 0, b_k \neq 0$. Let c_3 be the constraint resulting from using c_2 to remove x_j in c_1. Then bounds propagation on $\{c_3, c_2\}$ is stronger than bounds propagation on $\{c_1, c_2\}$. (i.e. each variable domain in the first case is a subset of its domain in the second case). The same is true for domain propagation.

11.5.3 Global Constraints

Constraint solvers provide a range of *global constraints*, developed to replace particular sets of constraints that occur frequently. Global constraints are the subject of Chapter 6. They allow a single constraint on any number of variables to replace a set of constraints, and provide a propagation algorithm that typically enforces GAC on the constraint.

There is sometimes a choice as to what level of consistency will be maintained on the global constraint. A frequently occurring global constraint is the allDifferent constraint, and it does provide such a choice. A constraint allDifferent($x_1, x_2, ..., x_n$) can either be treated as if it had been written as $n(n-1)/2$ binary $\neq$ constraints on which AC is maintained; or bounds consistency (BC) can be maintained on the global constraint; or generalized arc consistency (GAC) can be maintained. Maintaining a higher level of consistency takes more time; on the other hand, if more values can be removed from the domains of the variables, the search effort will be reduced and this will save time. Whether or not the time saved outweighs the time spent depends on the problem. In the case of the allDifferent constraint, experience suggests that if the number of values in the union of the domains of $x_1, x_2, ..., x_n$ is n or not much greater, maintaining GAC is likely to be worthwhile; but if the number of values is much greater than n, so that the allDifferent constraint is looser, it is less likely that domain propagation will remove more values than the $\neq$ constraints, and so it may not be cost-effective (see for instance [31]).

11.5.4 Extensional Constraints

Some constraint solvers give the user the option to enforce GAC on any constraint. CHIP, for instance, had the facility to enforce arc consistency on arbitrary constraints defined by Prolog predicates, and this was used in solving a microcode labelling problem, described in [47]. ILOG Solver provides a table constraint, in which the set of allowed (or not allowed) tuples can be explicitly listed. SICStus Prolog similarly has a `case` constraint that allows the solutions to the constraint to be specified as a directed acyclic graph.

Cheng and Yap [7] demonstrate the usefulness of the SICStus Prolog `case` constraint in Maximum Density Still Life, a problem derived from the Game of Life. The game is played on a squared board and in the problem considered, each cell of the board is either alive or dead according to the state of its eight neighbouring cells. The original model has a Boolean variable for each cell, with the value 1 representing 'alive' and 0 representing 'dead'. The constraint between a variable and the variables representing the neighbouring cells is complex: the value of the cell is 1 if the sum of the neighbouring variables is exactly 3, or 0 if their sum is < 2 or > 4. The aim is to find a configuration of live and dead cells on an $n \times n$ board that satisfies the constraints and maximizes the number of live cells. Cheng and Yap use the `case` constraint to represent the constraint between the cells in a $3 \times n$ 'super-row'. They use the fact that the variables in the problem are Boolean to construct a Binary Decision Diagram of the constraint and convert the BDD to a DAG. For a good ordering of the variables, the size of the resulting BDD increases only linearly with n, so that maintaining consistency of the `case` constraint remains efficient.

It can be useful to be able to express even binary constraints extensionally and ensure that arc consistency is maintained. For instance, in the Black Hole patience game [20], a pack of playing cards has to be arranged in sequence, in such a way that successive cards in the sequence have consecutive values, so that for instance a five can only be followed by a four or a six (of any suit). An ace can be either a high or a low value, and so can be followed by a two or a king. (There are other conditions on the sequence that are not relevant here.) The viewpoint used in solving Black Hole games using CP in [20] has a variable x_i for each position i in the sequence, $1 \le i \le 52$; the domain of each variable is $\{1, .., 52\}$, representing the cards, where the values 1 to 13 represent the ace to king of spades respectively, 14 to 26 represent the ace to king of hearts, and so on. To ensure a correct sequence, there must be a binary constraint between x_i and x_{i+1} for $1 \le i \le 51$; for instance, if x_i is assigned the value 15 (representing the two of hearts), the possible values for x_{i+1} are 1, 3, 14, 16, 27, 29, 40, 42, representing the aces and threes. The constraint is expressed extensionally by listing the possible values for x_{i+1} for each possible value of x_i, using the table constraint in ILOG Solver, which maintains AC on the constraint.

11.5.5   Reified Constraints and Meta-Constraints

A reified constraint associates a 0/1 variable x with a constraint c, so that x takes the value 1 if the constraint c is satisfied and 0 otherwise. More or less equivalently, in terms of expressivity, a meta-constraint is a constraint over constraints. Fernandez and Hill [11] discuss representing a *self-referential puzzle* introduced by Henz [23] in a variety of constraint programming languages, using reified constraints and meta-constraints.

More significantly, they can be used to express disjunctions of constraints. For instance, the condition that constraint c_1 or constraint c_2 (or both) must be satisfied can be expressed by associating the constraints with the variables x_1 and x_2 respectively and adding the constraint that $x_1 + x_2 \ge 1$.

Van Hentenryck and Deville [48] introduced the cardinality operator to express such disjunctive conditions; it allows upper and lower bounds to be stated on the number of constraints in a set that must be satisfied. Of course, it is not sufficient simply to allow disjunctive conditions to be expressed; changes to the domains of the variables involved must also be propagated efficiently. The implementation of reified constraints in constraint logic programming is discussed in Chapter 12.

11.6   Auxiliary Variables

In the last section, different ways of writing constraints on the variables in the chosen viewpoint were discussed. However, more choices are available, and the potential for more efficient models, if other variables can be introduced.

Auxiliary variables are variables introduced into a model, either because it is difficult to express the constraints at all in terms of the existing variables, or to allow the constraints to be expressed in a form that would propagate better, i.e. lead to more domain reductions.

An early example appears in a paper on the car sequencing problem (problem 1 in CSPLib) by Dincbas, Simonis and van Hentenryck [9]. A number of cars are to be made on a production line: each of them may require one or more options which are installed at different stations on the line. The option stations have lower capacity than the rest of the production line, e.g. a station may be able to cope with at most one car out of every two. The cars are to be arranged in a production sequence so that these capacities are not exceeded.

In [9], the initial viewpoint has variables s_i, $1 \le i \le n$, where n is the number of cars to be produced, and therefore the length of the production sequence. The value of s represents the car to be produced in position i in the sequence, or more precisely the *class* of car, since cars requiring the same set of options can be considered as identical.

It is straightforward to express some of the constraints required to model the problem in this viewpoint, for instance, that the number of variables assigned a specific value is equal to the number of cars in the corresponding class. However, the option capacities are difficult to express using these variables alone.

Dincbas *et al.* introduce auxiliary Boolean variables o_{ij}, $1 \leq i \leq n$, $1 \leq j \leq m$, such that $o_{ij} = 1$ iff the car in the ith slot in the sequence requires option j. The constraints expressing the option capacities are expressed in terms of these variables; suppose that the capacity of option 1 is one car in every two. Then the capacity of the option can be enforced using the constraints:

$$o_{i,1} + o_{i+1,1} \leq 1 \text{ for } 1 \leq i < n$$

Constraints are also needed to express the relationship between the auxiliary variables and the original variables. In this case, this could be done by the constraints $o_{ij} = \lambda_{s_i,j}$, $1 \leq i \leq n$, $1 \leq j \leq m$, where the constant $\lambda_{kj} = 1$ iff car class k requires option j.

Usually, auxiliary variables are not sufficient to define a viewpoint, i.e. it would not be possible to build a model of the problem using only the auxiliary variables. However, the auxiliary variables in the car sequencing problem could constitute a viewpoint; every valid production sequence can be specified as a complete assignment to these variables.

It is sometimes worthwhile to use auxiliary variables as search variables, alongside the original variables. An example occurs in a network design problem arising from the deployment of synchronous optical networks (SONET) [43]. The network contains a number of client nodes and a number of SONET rings. A SONET ring joins a number of nodes; a node is installed on a ring using an add-drop multiplexer (ADM). There are known demands (in terms of numbers of channels) between pairs of nodes; in a simplified version of the problem, the level of demand is ignored, but if there is a traffic demand between two nodes, there must be a ring that they are both installed on. Each node can be installed on more than one ring, and there is a maximum number of nodes that can be installed on each ring. The objective is to minimise the total number of ADMs required, while satisfying all the demands.

The viewpoint used in [43] has variables x_{ik}, $1 \leq i \leq n$, $1 \leq k \leq m$, where n is the number of nodes and m is the number of available rings. $x_{ik} = 1$ if node i is assigned to ring k, 0 otherwise.

A number of auxiliary variables are introduced, representing for instance the number of rings that each node is on. It was found to be a successful search strategy to assign this last set of variables first, before assigning the variables x_{ik}. In terms of the underlying problem, although deciding *how many* rings each node is on is not sufficient to specify the network, it greatly simplifies the remaining problem of deciding *which* rings each node is on.

Note that if the auxiliary variables would constitute a viewpoint in their own right, and we assign values to these variables as well as the viewpoint variables, the resulting model might be more appropriately considered as combining two viewpoints, as in section 11.9.

11.7 Implied Constraints

Implied constraints, also called redundant constraints, are constraints which are implied by the constraints defining the problem. They do not change the set of solutions, and hence are logically redundant. The aim in adding implied constraints to the CSP is to reduce the search effort to solve the problem.

A necessary condition for an implied constraint to be useful in reducing search is that it forbids one or more compound assignments that the existing constraints will allow (given the level of propagation that will be maintained on the individual constraints during search).

A compound assignment forbidden by an implied constraint cannot lead to a solution, since it does not change the set of solutions. Without the implied constraint, such an assignment may occur during the search, and determining that it cannot be completed may take a very long time.

Dincbas, Simonis and van Hentenryck [9] used implied constraints in solving the car sequencing problem described earlier. In section 11.6, the constraints on the variables o_{ij} enforcing the option capacities are given. These constraints only express that fact that the option capacities cannot be exceeded; there is nothing to prevent a partial sequence of cars from using a particular option *below* capacity. However, a certain number of cars requiring each option have to be fitted into the sequence, so that going below capacity in one part of the sequence may make it impossible to avoid exceeding the capacity elsewhere. Hence, there are implied constraints which have not yet been expressed.

For instance, suppose there are 30 cars, and 12 of them require option 1, with capacity 1 car in any 2. Then at least one of the cars in slots 1 to 8 of the production sequence must require option 1; otherwise 12 of cars 9 to 30 will require option 1, which violates the capacity constraint. Similarly, cars 1 to 10 must include at least two option 1 cars, ... , and cars 1 to 28 must include at least 11 of the option 1 cars. Dincbas *et al.* added implied constraints of this kind for each option and for all sub-sequences starting with slot 1. Without these constraints, partial sequences in which one or more option stations are under-utilized can be formed, and eventually the search will have to backtrack when it is found that the sequence cannot be completed without exceeding the option capacity. The implied constraints prevent wasted search of unsatisfiable subproblems.

11.7.1   Implied Constraints and Search Order

Ensuring that each implied constraint forbids an assignment that would be allowed otherwise is not sufficient to guarantee that the added constraints will reduce the search effort. It may be that the assignments forbidden by a proposed implied constraint would never occur during the search anyway, given the search order. Hence, in backtracking search, the order in which the variables are assigned can affect whether it will be beneficial to add an implied constraint or not.

For instance, Borrett & Tsang [5] discuss adding an implied constraint between variables q and r when binary constraints between p and q and between p and r already exist in the CSP. The constraint c_{qr} could be derived by composing the constraints c_{pq} and c_{pr} - effectively, making this triple of variables path consistent. Borrett & Tsang show that using a simple backtracking algorithm (i.e. one doing no constraint propagation), if the three variables p, q and r are assigned in that order, the implied constraint c_{qr} will have no effect on the number of nodes visited. On the other hand, if the CSP already contains the constraints c_{pr} and c_{qr}, then adding the constraint c_{pq} can reduce the number of nodes visited, given the same search order.

Similarly, in the car sequencing problem, the usefulness of the implied constraints used by Dincbas *et al.* depends on the search order [39]. In the example given earlier, at least one car in slots i to $i+7$ of the sequence must require option 1, for any value of i from 1 to 23; hence, as well as the constraint added by Dincbas *et al.*, there are many other equally valid constraints. Overall, there are potentially very many implied constraints imposing a lower limit on the number of cars requiring a particular option in *any* sub-sequence of length k. However, if the search builds up the sequence of cars consecutively from slot

1, only the implied constraints on the first k cars affect the search. The other possible implied constraints would always be consistent, but checking this whenever one of the variables involved is assigned a value would slow down the search. On the other hand, if the variables were assigned in a different order, a different set of implied constraints would be useful.

11.7.2 Implied Constraints v. Global Constraints

Following the work of Dincbas *et al.* on the car sequencing problem, Régin and Puget [35] later developed a global constraint specifically for sequence problems, using the car sequencing problem as a test case. They noted that "our filtering algorithm subsumes all the implied constraints" used by Dincbas *et al.* The global constraint makes the effort of devising and implementing implied constraints redundant, in this case. It may often be true that implied constraints are only useful because a suitable global constraint does not (yet) exist. On the other hand, many implied constraints are simple and cheap to propagate, whereas global constraints are often time-consuming to propagate. Moreover, it is only worth the effort of implementing a global constraint if it can be used for a significant class of problems; for a one-off problem, where good implied constraints can be found, the implied constraints are likely to be more cost-effective.

11.7.3 Implied Constraints from Subproblems

Van Beek and Wilken [46] use implied constraints in finding minimum length instruction schedules for the object code produced by a compiler. The implied constraints are lower bounds on the number of steps between a pair of instructions, found by considering subproblems; if a consistency check in the subproblem shows that the current lower bound on the distance between two instructions cannot be achieved, a constraint increasing the bound can be added. Van Beek and Wilken comment that generating powerful implied constraints in this way was the key to being able to solve very large real instruction scheduling problems. In the SONET problem, described in section 11.6, implied constraints were also derived (in that case by hand) from considering subproblems; the SONET constraints are lower bounds on the auxiliary variables that represent the number of times that each node is installed on a ring. These examples suggest that subproblems might also be a useful source of tighter variable bounds in other cases.

11.7.4 Finding Implied Constraints

Implied constraints can often be explained as projections of a conjunction of a few of the problem constraints onto a subset of the variables in the union of their scopes. These constraints can be seen as partially enforcing some higher level of consistency in the problem. Although the search algorithm only enforces consistency on single constraints, there are forms of consistency that take all the constraints on a subset of the variables and find inconsistent tuples. Enforcing consistency on subsets of the constraints is computationally expensive, even if only done before search; if it generated the equivalent of useful implied constraints, it would likely also generate a much larger number that would not be useful during the search. Furthermore, consistency enforcing generates sets of forbidden tuples; these would be presented to the constraint solver as extensional non-binary constraints, which are time-consuming to propagate. This does not at present appear a promising route to generating implied constraints automatically; it is not sufficiently selective, and implied constraints need to be expressed in form that can propagate efficiently, like other problem constraints.

Alternatively, adding implied constraints to a CSP is often inspired by a search taking an unacceptably long time to solve a problem, and discovering on examining the search tree in detail that assignments that are obviously incorrect are being considered; implied constraints are generalizations that state explicitly what is incorrect about these assignments and other potential failed assignments of the same kind. On this view, implied constraints are akin to nogoods (inconsistent compound assignments) that are uncovered during search. However, individual nogoods have little effect on the search, and if there are enough of them to be useful, checking them will hinder the constraint solver. An advantage is that they do take account of the search heuristics. Again, automatically generating implied constraints from nogoods identified during the search would require some means of expressing the constraints in a form that can propagate efficiently.

Some attempts have been made to generate implied constraints automatically, by looking for logical consequences of the existing constraints. Hnich, Richardson and Flener [26] classify implied constraints, and discuss automatically generating implied constraints of each type. Some of the types that they identify have been discussed separately here; for instance, one of the types is a global constraint (such as an allDifferent constraint) used to replace a set of constraints (a clique of $\neq$ constraints). Other types require introducing new variables. However, two of their types fit closely the implied constraints discussed in this section: variable elimination (using one constraint to eliminate a variable in its scope from other constraints involving that variable) and constraints over a new scope (using a set of constraints to derive a new constraint over a subset of the union of their scopes). Hnich _et al._ describe using PRESS (PRolog Equation Solving System) to try to derive implied constraints from linear and nonlinear arithmetic constraints; in their test cases, it can find some implied constraints of the variable elimination type, and also implied linear constraints derived from nonlinear constraints, but not the other types.

Frisch, Miguel and Walsh [18] also make some initial steps towards automating the generation of implied constraints by developing _methods_ (analogous to methods in proof planning) that can be applied to the set of constraints in a CSP to derive new constraints. One is the `eliminate` method, which attempts to eliminate variables or terms from non-linear constraint, to give a constraint of lower arity that may propagate better. For example:

$$\frac{A}{BC} + \frac{D}{EF} + \frac{G}{HI} = 1 \text{ with } \frac{A}{BC} \leq \frac{D}{EF} \leq \frac{G}{HI} \text{ yield: } 3\frac{A}{BC} \leq 1$$

Neither of these approaches addresses the interaction of the search heuristics and the implied constraints, but if a class of implied constraints can be identified for a type of problem, such as the car sequencing problem, it would be possible to identify the constraints that are useful during search, and discard the rest. Simonis _et al._ [38] discuss using visualization tools in a constraint solver to assess the value of implied constraints, by examining the progress of the search in detail. This makes it possible to check that the implied constraints work well with the search heuristics or to find out which of the implied constraints are effective.

11.8 Reformulations of CSPs

In the last sections, different ways of improving a model were discussed; the changes to the model keep the same viewpoint but change or add to the constraints, or expand the viewpoint by adding auxiliary variables. The alternative way to change the model is to change the viewpoint. This may require literally looking at the problem from a different perspective and developing some insight into the problem. However, some transformations from one viewpoint to another are standard or are useful in specific problem classes.

There is an established and continuing body of work on transforming CSPs into satisfiability problems (e.g. [49]). This work will not be discussed here, because its aim is fundamentally different; rather than developing a model that can be solved more efficiently as a CSP, using a constraint solver, it aims to solve the underlying problem more efficiently as a SAT problem, using a SAT solver.

11.8.1 Non-Binary to Binary translations

Early search algorithms for CSPs only dealt with binary constraints; as a result, there are some standard transformations of a CSP with non-binary constraints into a binary CSP [1]. The *hidden variable* transformation adds a new variable h_i to the CSP for each non-binary constraint, c_i; the values of h_i correspond to tuples of variables in the scope of c_i. The original constraint c_i is replaced by binary constraints between h_i and the variables in the scope of c_i; each value of h_i implies a value for each variable in the scope of c_i, and the binary constraints enforce this correspondence. In the terminology of this chapter, the hidden variables would be classed as auxiliary variables, rather than a change of viewpoint.

The *dual graph* translation of a non-binary CSP replaces the original constraints by new variables, and so produces a new CSP based on a different viewpoint. The dual variable d_i represents the constraint c_i, and its values represent the tuples satisfying c_i. There is a binary constraint between two dual variables d_i and d_j if the scopes of c_i and c_j have a non-empty intersection; the binary constraint forbids pairs of values which would assign different values to any of the shared variables.

Bacchus and van Beek [1] investigate these transformations empirically, using a forward checking algorithm: when applied to the original non-binary model, the algorithm checks a k-ary constraint whenever all but one variable in its scope has been assigned. They show that both the hidden variable and dual graph transformation can outperform the original model; however, given constraint solvers that have better ways of dealing with many types of non-binary constraint, these transformations have been little used in practice.

An exception is the use of dual variables to replace 9-ary constraints in the Maximum Density Still Life problem, described earlier in section 11.5.4. In [42], the 9-ary constraints between a cell and its eight neighbours are replaced by dual variables, exactly as in the dual graph transformation. Unlike the dual graph transformation, the original variables are also kept, although only in order to express the objective, that the number of live cells should be maximized. The dual variables represent 3×3 'supercells'; one advantage of the dual graph translation, as well as replacing the cumbersome 9-ary constraints, is that it allows the supercells rather than the cells to be the search variables. Hence, the dual graph translation in this case corresponds to a genuinely different perspective on the problem.

A similar transformation has been used by Hnich, Prestwich and Selensky [25] in modelling the covering test problem (problem 45 in CSPLib), arising in software testing. The covering test problem is: for a given tuple (t, k, g, b) find a *covering array* $CA(t, k, g)$ of size b or show that none exists. The covering array has k columns and b rows, and in every subset of t columns every possible t-tuple over the alphabet $Z_g = \{0, 1, 2, ..., g-1\}$ must occur in at least one row. A solution for $t = 3$, $k = 5$, $g = 2$, $b = 10$ is shown in Figure 11.2. Every triple of values from $\{0, 1\}$, from $(0, 0, 0)$ to $(1, 1, 1)$, occurs in the first three columns of the array, and this is true of every other subset of three columns as required.

1	2	3	4	5
0	0	0	0	0
0	0	0	1	1
0	0	1	0	1
0	1	0	0	1
0	1	1	1	0
1	0	0	0	1
1	0	1	1	0
1	1	0	1	0
1	1	1	0	0
1	1	1	1	1

Figure 11.2: A covering array $CA(3, 5, 2)$ of size 10.

A natural way to model the problem is to introduce a $b \times k$ matrix of integer variables, x_{ri}, for $1 \leq r \leq b$ and $1 \leq i \leq k$, such that $x_{ri} = m$ if the value in column i and row r of the array is m. However, it is hard to express the constraints that in every subset of columns, every possible t-tuple must occur.

To make these constraints easier to express, Hnich *et al.* introduced *compound variables*, analogous to the variables of the dual graph transformation, to represent every t tuple of columns in each row. In the case of a binary alphabet, each compound variable has domain $\{0, ..., 2^t\}$. There are still non-binary constraints on these variables: there is a global cardinality constraint on the compound variables corresponding to a given t-tuple in each row, to ensure that every value between 0 and $2^t - 1$ is assigned at least once. In addition, just as in the dual graph translation, there are binary constraints between the compound variables corresponding to a row that if they have columns in common, in terms of the original variables, they must agree on the values that they give to their shared variables.

These examples show that the dual variables of the dual graph translation can be practically useful in rewriting non-binary constraints, even without eliminating the non-binary constraints completely.

11.8.2 Permutation Problems

A well-studied class of problem with two standard viewpoints is the class of permutation problems. A CSP is a permutation problem if the union of the domains has the same number of elements as there are variables and each variable must be assigned a different value. Any solution assigns a permutation of the values to the variables. Other constraints in the problem determine which permutations are acceptable solutions.

Each possible value is assigned to exactly one variable and each variable is assigned exactly one value. The *dual* viewpoint was identified by Geelen [19]; it switches the roles of the variables and values. For example, the usual CSP model of the n-queens problem in which the variables represent the rows and the values represent the columns is a permutation problem; the dual model has the variables representing the columns and the values representing the rows. In this instance, the two viewpoints give the same CSP, so that one is not better than the other. In many permutation problems, however, the constraints are easier to express and propagate better in one viewpoint than the other. For example, the problem of finding an $n \times n$ magic square, containing the numbers 1 to n^2 arranged so that the sum of every row and column is the same, can be expressed as a permutation problem; we can either find the number to go in each cell of square, or decide which cell to put each number in. However, the constraints on the row and column sums are much easier to express in the first viewpoint than the second.

As described in the next section, rather than choosing one viewpoint or its dual, we can combine the two; much recent work on permutation problems has investigated this possibility.

11.8.3 Boolean Models

Another possible viewpoint for a permutation problem has a Boolean variable x_{ij} for every possible variable-value combination (or value-variable combination in the dual viewpoint). For instance, in the n-queens problem, the variables x_{ij}, $1 \le i, j \le n$ correspond to the squares of the board. The assignment $(x_{ij}, 1)$ means that there is a queen on the square in row i and column j, and $(x_{ij}, 0)$ means that there is not.

Similarly, a Boolean viewpoint can be derived from and CSP viewpoint with integer or set variables. For any assignment (x_i, j) in an integer viewpoint, there is a Boolean variable b_{ij} in the Boolean viewpoint; the assignment $(b_{ij}, 1)$ corresponds to the assignment (x_i, j), whereas any other assignment to x_i corresponds to $(b_{ij}, 0)$. For any assignment (X_i, S) in a viewpoint with set variables, and for any value $j \in S$, the Boolean variable b_{ij} is assigned the value 1.

The variables of the Boolean viewpoint are closely similar to the variables of the direct encoding of a CSP into SAT [49]. However, the Boolean viewpoint usually gives a less efficient CSP than the integer or set model. The transformation to a Boolean viewpoint is described here to emphasize that there is always a choice of models in representing a problem as a CSP; in practice, it is often more useful to try to convert an initial Boolean model into one with integer or set variables.

11.8.4 Different Perspectives

So far in this section, the examples of changing viewpoint have involved reformulating an existing viewpoint. However, for some problems, it may be possible to find a new viewpoint by viewing the problem from a different angle; this is potentially valuable, because the constraints expressed in a radically different viewpoint may express different insights into the problem and so show different ways of solving it.

A problem where many different viewpoints have been devised is the 'open stacks' problem, set for the first Constraint Modelling Challenge, in connection with the Modelling and Solving Problems with Constraints workshop at IJCAI'05. The submissions to the Challenge can be found at `www.dcs.st-and.ac.uk/~ipg/challenge`. The problem, as stated for the Challenge, is: "A manufacturer has a number of orders from customers to satisfy; each order is for a number of different products, and only one product can be made at a time. Once a customer's order is started (i.e. the first product in the order has been made) a stack is created for that customer. When all the products that a customer requires have been made, the order is sent to the customer, so that the stack is closed. Because of limited space in the production area, the number of stacks that are in use simultaneously i.e. the number of customer orders that are in simultaneous production, should be minimized."

A wide variety of viewpoints were represented amongst the Challenge entries. Perhaps the most obvious viewpoint has variables representing positions in the production sequence and values representing the products; this creates a permutation problem, so that this viewpoint also has a dual. One insight into the problem is that although ostensibly requiring a sequence of the products, it can in fact be solved by sequencing the customers; this gives a viewpoint where the variables are the positions in a sequence of customers; the value of the ith variable is the ith customer to have their order completed. Other viewpoints focus on the stacks: one has variables representing the customers, and the value assigned to a variable is the stack area that customer will use. Also focussing on the stacks, another viewpoint has a Boolean variable for each pair of customers: the value 0 means that they share a stack location, and 1 means that they do not. This last viewpoint relates very directly to the objective, since minimizing the maximum number of open stacks is equivalent to maximizing the number of customers that can share a stack location. Several other viewpoints also feature in the entries.

Different viewpoints can be used individually as the basis of a model of the problem. However, a more interesting approach is to combine different viewpoints; this will be discussed in the next section. When the viewpoints being combined are based on different insights into the problem, this potentially allows all these insights to contribute to solving the problem, rather than forcing the modeller to choose just one.

11.9   Combining Viewpoints

If two viewpoints $V_1 = \langle X_1, D_1 \rangle, V_2 = \langle X_2, D_2 \rangle$ for the same problem have been identified, a complete model of the problem can be constructed from each viewpoint, say $M_1 = \langle X_1, D_1, C_1 \rangle$, $M_2 = \langle X_2, D_2, C_2 \rangle$. Hence, the models are *mutually redundant* It can be beneficial to combine the two models rather than to choose between them. The combined model has variables $X_1 \cup X_2$ and (in the simplest form of combination) constraints $C_1 \cup C_2 \cup C_c$, where C_c is a set of *channelling constraints*. The channelling constraints express the relationship between the two sets of variables, X_1, X_2, in such a way that assignments in either viewpoint can be translated into assignments in the other. This idea was introduced by Cheng, Choi, Lee and Wu [6].

The potential advantage of combining viewpoints in this way comes from propagating the constraints of the two models during the search for a solution. The search variables can be the variables of one of the viewpoints, say X_1 (this is discussed further below). As search proceeds, propagating the constraints C_1 removes values from the domains of the variables in X_1. The channelling constraints may then allow values to be removed from the domains of the variables in X_2. Propagating these value deletions using the constraints of the second model, C_2, may remove further values from these variables, and again these removals can be translated back into the first viewpoint by the channelling constraints. The net result can be that more values are removed within viewpoint V_1 than by the constraints C_1 alone, leading to reduced search. Cheng *et al.* give a detailed account of how the propagation in a combined model works, using the n-queens problems as a case study.

Law and Lee [29] discuss a process they term *model induction*; this uses two viewpoints, without combining them, and provides an insight into why multiple viewpoints can be useful. Given two viewpoints $\langle X, D \rangle$ and $\langle X', D' \rangle$, the constraints of the second viewpoint are translated into constraints in the first viewpoint, using the channelling constraints. The new constraints can be merged into the existing constraints with the same scope in the first viewpoint. Law and Lee showed that this brings new information into the first viewpoint and can speed up search.

In section 11.8, permutation problems were defined and the dual viewpoint described. In solving a permutation problem, it is often beneficial to combine the two viewpoints. In a permutation problem with k variables $x_1, x_2, ..., x_k$, the domain of each variable is $\{1, 2, ..., k\}$. The dual variables are $d_1, d_2, ..., d_k$, also with domains $\{1, 2, ..., k\}$. The channelling constraints defining the relationship between the variables of the two viewpoints are: $(x_i = j) \equiv (d_j = i)$, $\forall i, j,\ 1 \leq i \leq k, 1 \leq j \leq k$. (Note that these can be more efficiently represented by a global *inverse* constraint [3] rather than n^2 binary constraints, although the binary constraints give the same propagation.)

Hnich, Smith and Walsh [27] consider both permutation problems and injection problems (which are similar, but have more values than variables). Several possible combined models for injection problems are investigated, in some cases using dummy values for the dual variables, to allow for the values that are not assigned to the original variables.

Cheng *et al.* [6] also give an example of combining an integer variable viewpoint with a set variable viewpoint in a nurse rostering problem; the problem can be viewed as either allocating shifts to nurses or as allocating nurses to shifts. The first viewpoint has an integer variable n_{ij} for each nurse i and day j; its value represents the shift that nurse i works on day j. The second viewpoint has a set variable S_{kj} for each shift k and day j; its value represents the set of nurses that work shift k on day j. The channelling constraints to combine the viewpoints are $(n_{ij} = k) \equiv (i \in S_{kj})$.

As well as the *inverse* constraint already mentioned, a number of other global constraints such as the *element* constraint relate two sets of variables and so can often be seen as channelling constraints between the variables of two viewpoints. (See Chapter 6, "Global Constraints".)

However, although it is not necessary for channelling constraints to be binary, they must ensure that assignments in one viewpoint can trigger constraint propagation in the other when only a few variables have been assigned. If constraint propagation via the channelling constraints can only occur when a complete assignment has been made (i.e. therefore when a solution has already been found) there is no benefit from the combination.

11.9.1   Selecting Constraints

It is clearly safe to combine two or more models of a problem into a single combined model, containing the variables and the constraints of both models, together with the channelling constraints. The constraints of either model will ensure that the solutions to the CSP correspond to the solutions to the problem, so that this will also be true of the combined model.

However, it is often unnecessary to include all the constraints of both models, and the search will be speeded up if some of the constraints are dropped.

In many cases, a motivation for combining viewpoints is that some of the constraints are hard to express (and propagate weakly) in one viewpoint and some are hard to express in the other. The combined model allows the constraints to be expressed in the most convenient viewpoint. In this situation, it often happens that the two complete models, one for each viewpoint, only exist in theory; the only model actually constructed is the combined model, with a mixture of constraints expressed in each viewpoint.

In the Golomb ruler example, the requirement that the pairwise differences between the marks on the ruler are all distinct can be expressed in terms of either viewpoint: either as the 4-ary constraints $x_j - x_i \neq x_l - x_k$ or as a single global constraint allDifferent(d_{12}, d_{13} ..., $d_{m-1,m}$). These are equally correct in ensuring that the solutions meet the condition; however, they are not equivalent in terms of propagation. [44] shows empirically that the allDifferent constraint (or a clique of $\neq$ constraints) gives much better results than the 4-ary constraints (if GAC is not maintained on the 4-ary constraints).

For permutation problems, where two viewpoints with variables $x_1, x_2, ..., x_n$ and $d_1, d_2, ..., d_n$ can be combined as described earlier, with the channelling constraints $x_i = j) \equiv (d_j = i)$, these channelling constraints are sufficient to ensure that the values assigned to $x_1, x_2, ..., x_k$ (and so also those assigned to $d_1, d_2, ..., d_k$) are distinct [27]. Hence, the constraints $x_i \neq x_j, 1 \leq i < j \leq n$ or allDifferent($x_1, x_2, ..., x_n$), required in the original model, are no longer needed in the combined model to ensure correct solutions. Maintaining arc consistency on the binary channelling constraints can prune more values than binary $\neq$ constraints on these variables, though fewer than GAC on the allDifferent constraint. Enforcing AC on a set of binary $\neq$ constraints, representing an allDifferent constraint, removes a value from the domain of a variable if that value is the only one value in the domain of another variable (e.g. because it has been assigned that value). Enforcing AC on the channelling constraints does the same pruning as the $\neq$ constraints, and in addition removes all values but one from the domain of a variable (and thereby effectively assigns the remaining value to the variable) if the remaining value does not appear in the domain of any other variable in $\{x_1, x_2, ..., x_k\}$. Hence, in a combined model of a permutation problem, binary $\neq$ constraints between the variables of either viewpoint are a waste of effort; an allDifferent constraint on one set of variables is not needed for correctness but in some problems may do sufficient additional pruning to give a smaller run-time than the channelling constraints alone.

[40] introduced the idea of a *minimal dual model* of a permutation problem: this has both sets of variables, the constraints (excluding the allDifferent constraint) of only one model and the channelling constraints. For some permutation problems, the constraints of one model are strictly stronger than those of the other, so that including both sets of constraints gives no benefit in terms of reducing search, and incurs an overhead in run-time. In [40], it is demonstrated empirically that for Langford's problem (problem 24 in CSPLib),

the minimal dual model generates the same search as a model using all constraints of both models, but has a much shorter run-time.

Choi, Lee and Stuckey [8] investigate theoretically when some of the constraints in one viewpoint are *propagation redundant* in a model which also has the constraints of another viewpoint and the channelling constraints. A constraint is propagation redundant if the propagation that it would cause is subsumed by the propagation resulting from other constraints in the model. Propagation redundant constraints can clearly be removed from the model, and should be removed since they only add an unnecessary overhead. (Note that unlike many other changes to a model, removing propagation redundant constraints does not depend on the search heuristics.) Choi *et al.* suggest that their approach can be automated.

11.9.2 Choice of Search Variables

When combining two (or more) viewpoints of a problem, there is a choice of which set of variables to use to drive the search. Since each viewpoint could be the basis for a model of the problem, assigning values to either set of variables would be sufficient to solve the problem. This is obviously true if the combined model contains all the constraints of both individual models; the combined model could be treated as either of the original models, together with some extra baggage. It is still true if the combined model does not contain all the constraints of both models, provided that every condition defining the solutions to the underlying problem is expressed as a constraint in one or other viewpoint.

For instance, in Langford's problem the constraints expressed in one viewpoint propagate better than those in the other, but searching on the variables of the second viewpoint, in a combined model, leads to solutions with less search effort [27].

Another possibility is to use both sets of variables together as search variables. This makes most sense if the variables are of the same type and if the variable ordering is dynamic; the next variable can then be chosen from either set, according to the state of the search (although one could imagine a static ordering which chose alternately from each set of variables, say). When a variable from either set is assigned a value, the channelling constraints ensure that the corresponding dual variable is immediately assigned a value too. Hence, although the number of search variables may appear to be twice as large as it need be, only half of them will be specifically assigned during the search. This search strategy, choosing the variable with smallest domain, has been successfully used with problems that can be modelled as permutation problems, by Hnich, Smith and Walsh [27].

11.9.3 Multiple Viewpoints

Models in which more than two viewpoints are combined are possible. Given that combining mutually redundant models can lead to additional constraint propagation, Cheng *et al.* [6] suggested that "it seems reasonable to combine and implement as many mutually redundant models as one can dream of." Dotú, del Val and Cebrián [10] investigated this empirically in solving instances of the quasigroup completion problem, considered as a multiple permutation problem. A quasigroup completion instance requires completion of an $n \times n$ Latin square when some entries have already been filled.

The initial model has variables x_{ij}, $1 \leq i, j \leq n$ representing the cell in row i, column j. The domain of every variable is the set $\{1, ..., n\}$. Since the values in every row and in every column of the Latin square must form a permutation of the values 1 to n, two other models that are duals of this are possible: in one the variables r_{ik}, $1 \leq i, k \leq n$ represent the column in which the value k appears in row i; in the other, the variables c_{jk}, $1 \leq j, k \leq n$ represent the row in which the value k appears in column j. There are three sets of channelling constraints that link each pair of models, for instance $(x_{ij} = k) \equiv (r_{ik} = j)$ Dotú *et al.* found that overall, a model combining three viewpoints linked by three sets of channelling constraints performed well.

11.10   Symmetry and Modelling

Symmetry in CSPs, and symmetry breaking, is a large topic in its own right and dealt with in Chapter 10, but some aspects of symmetry and its interaction with modelling are worth discussing here.

As already mentioned, modelling a problem P as a CSP may introduce symmetry, by using distinct variables and/or values to represent entities that are indistinguishable in P.

An example is the second viewpoint for the n-queens problem, given earlier, which has a variable for each queen. This introduces an unnecessary notion of the 1st queen, the 2nd queen and so on, so that different solutions to the CSP can correspond to exactly the same layout of the board, but with the queen labelled 1 swapped with the queen labelled 2. Neither of the other two viewpoints given has this symmetry (although the n-queens problem has inherent symmetry which does appear in the other viewpoints). This illustrates that introducing symmetry can sometimes easily be avoided by choosing another viewpoint.

The golfers problem (problem 10 in CSPLib) is another case in which some viewpoints introduce symmetry. One instance of the problem is stated as: *32 golfers want to play in 8 groups of 4 each week, in such a way that any two golfers play in the same group at most once. How many weeks can they do this for?* The problem can be generalised to different sizes and numbers of groups. To model the problem of finding a schedule for n weeks, using integer variables, a possible viewpoint has 0/1 variables x_{ijkl}, where $x_{ijkl} = 1$ if player i is the jth player in the kth group in week l, and 0 otherwise. However, the players within each group, the groups within each week, the weeks within the schedule and the players themselves could all be permuted in any solution to give an equivalent solution.

The first symmetry (the players within the group) can be eliminated by using set variables to represent the groups: the set variable G_{kl} represents the kth group in week l, and the value of this variable represents the set of players forming that group. The constraints on these variables are that:

- the cardinality of each set is 4;

- the sets in any week do not overlap, i.e. for all l, the sets G_{kl}, $k = 1, ..., 8$ have an empty intersection;

- any two sets in different weeks have at most one member in common.

Constraint solvers that support set variables provide cardinality constraints, and constraints on the intersection of set variables, to allow such constraints to be expressed. Using set variables rather than integer variables is a common way to avoid introducing symmetry in this way: where the order of objects within a group is immaterial, the group can be modelled as a set rather than as a sequence, which would introduce symmetrically equivalent sequences.

The model of the car sequencing problem described by Dincbas, Simonis and van Hentenryck [9], discussed in section 11.6, is also a reformulation to avoid symmetry. The statement of the problem asks for a sequence of the cars to be produced, so that one obvious way to model it would be as a permutation problem, in which the variables are the slots in the sequence and the values are the cars, or v.v. However, two cars requiring the same options are effectively identical, so that this model would allow symmetrically equivalent sequences in which identical cars are swapped. Dincbas *et al.* avoid this by introducing classes of identical cars. This requires additional constraints to ensure that the correct number of cars in each class appear in the sequence.

Both ideas can be useful in other contexts, such as staff rostering. Suppose a crew is required for each shift. Some or all of the crew can often be treated as a set, e.g. if staff are not allocated specific roles, and the only requirement is that a minimum number must be provided, they can be represented as a set. If staff with identical skills can be treated as interchangeable in constructing a roster, it may only be necessary to count how many staff within each skill-set have been allocated.

In [41], further models of the golfers problem are given which eliminate more of the symmetry. The first has an integer variable for each pair of players, i_1, i_2: the value assigned to the variable p_{i_1,i_2} represents the week in which this pair of players plays together, with a dummy value in case they never play together. This viewpoint does not distinguish between the players within a group, or between the groups within a week. To allow the constraints to be expressed concisely, auxiliary set variables were also introduced, for each player i and each week l, representing the set of players that player i plays with in week l.

A final model presented in [41] also eliminates the symmetry due to the fact that the weeks of the schedule are interchangeable, although it only deals with the special cases of the golfers problem in which every player plays every other player at some point during the schedule. For each pair of players i_1, i_2, it has a set variable representing the group of players that the pair plays with, and another representing the other pairs of players that play together in the week that i_1 and i_2 play together. Unfortunately, the model has a very large number of variables, but it proved better than the earlier models for solving small instances. Note that it still has some of the original symmetry, due to the interchangeability of the players. This work does demonstrate that designing models with the intention of reducing the symmetry can sometimes be successful, although the resulting model may become rather complex.

11.10.1 Symmetry-Breaking Constraints

When there is symmetry in the chosen model of a problem (either symmetry introduced in modelling, or inherent in the problem), one possible way to eliminate or reduce it is to add symmetry-breaking constraints. Devising such constraints is beyond the scope of this chapter, but it is worth pointing out here that as a side-effect, such constraints often allow implied constraints to be derived that would not otherwise be possible.

This was observed in the template design problem [33] (problem 2 in CSPLib). The problem is to design templates for printing large sheets of card with items such as cat-food boxes. An order quantity is specified for each product, such as different flavours of cat-food. The overall objective is to minimize the total number of sheets that have to be printed (and so minimize waste), while fulfilling the order quantities for each product.

The t templates to be used are numbered in the model, but in practice are interchangeable; constraints are added to the model to eliminate this symmetry. The variable r_i represents the number of sheets of card to be printed from template i, and the symmetry-breaking constraints specify that $r_i \leq r_{i+1}$, for $1 \leq i < t$.

The objective is to minimize $p = \sum_i r_i$, i.e. the total number of sheets of card to be printed, and the number of templates needed, t, is at most 4 in the instances studied. Implied constraints can be added, derived from the symmetry-breaking constraints. For instance, if there are two templates, at most half the sheets are printed from one template and at least half from the other. Because of the symmetry-breaking constraints, we can add: if $t = 2$, $r_1 \leq p/2$ and $r_2 \geq p/2$; if $t = 3$, $r_1 \leq p/3$; $r_2 \leq p/2$ and $r_3 \geq p/3$; and so on.

Deriving implied constraints from symmetry-breaking constraints has been discussed in more detail by Frisch, Jefferson and Miguel [15]. They show, for instance, that adding lexicographic ordering constraints on the rows and columns to reduce the symmetry in CSP representing the Balanced Incomplete Block Design problem (prob28 in CSPLib) allows powerful implied constraints and a considerable simplification of the other constraints, giving for some instances a huge reduction in the time to solve the problem. In many problems, there are several distinct ways of adding constraints to give the same reduction in the symmetry; Frisch *et al.* suggest that in some cases the choice could be guided by considering the implied constraints that can then be derived.

11.11   Optimization Problems

Tsang [45] defines a Constraint Satisfaction Optimization Problem (CSOP) as follows:

A CSOP $\langle X, D, C, f \rangle$ is defined as a CSP $\langle X, D, C \rangle$ together with an optimization function f which maps every solution to a numerical value. The task in a CSOP is to find the solution T such that the value of $f(T)$ is either maximized or minimized, depending on the requirements of the problem.

If P is an optimisation problem, and $M_O = \langle X, D, C, f \rangle$ is a CSOP that models P then every solution of C can be translated into exactly one solution of P and at least one optimal solution of P can be derived from a solution to C. (There is no requirement in this case that every optimal solution to P should be found as a solution of C.)

Typically, a CSOP is solved in a branch-and-bound fashion, adding a constraint whenever a solution T is found that the value of the optimization function must be better than $f(T)$ in any future solution. This constraint provides an increasingly tight bound and can prune the search for future solutions; eventually, if it is proved that no solution satisfying the current bound exists, the last solution found has been proved optimal. The adaptation of the branch-and-bound principle from operational research was described by van Hentenryck [47].

Often, however, an optimization problem is represented and solved as a CSP or as a sequence of CSPs. This is especially appropriate when the optimization function measures some feature of the CSP structure, typically the number of variables. Hnich, Prestwich and Selensky [25], for instance, describe modelling a problem in software testing in which the objective is to construct a set of test vectors with specified coverage properties: the objective is to minimize the number of test vectors required. The CSP has a matrix of variables to represent the test vectors and hence the optimization function is the number of rows in the matrix. A sequence of CSPs is constructed, adding a row to the matrix each time, and the first CSP in the sequence that has a solution represents an optimal solution to the problem.

Even when the optimization function can easily be represented by an additional variable within the CSP, the problem may be represented as a CSP rather than a CSOP. For instance, in [43], the objective in the SONET problem described in 11.6 is represented as a variable, and assigned first during the search. The values of the objective variable are assigned in ascending order, and hence the first solution found has the smallest possible value of the objective variable, i.e. is optimal. For the problem described, this was found (empirically) to be more efficient than a branch-and-bound approach. However, it would only be feasible if there were only a few values between the smallest value in the domain of the objective variable, after initial constraint propagation, and the optimal value.

In an optimization problem, a compound assignment that satisfies the constraints can be forbidden if it can be shown that for any solution that this assignment would lead to, there must be another solution that is equally good or better. Dominance rules are constraints that forbid compound assignments that are dominated in this way; they are similar to implied constraints, in their effect, but are not logical consequences of the constraints C and do not necessarily preserve the set of optimal solutions. Prestwich and Beck [32], on the other hand, consider dominance rules as strongly related to conditional symmetry in satisfaction problems.

Getoor, Ottosson, Fromherz and Carlson [21] describe a scheduling application (optimal on-line scheduling of photo-copiers and similar machines) in which dominance rules play an important part. (Note that Getoor *et al.* use the term redundant constraint.) They classify the types of dominance rule that they found, including lower and upper bounds on the schedule length for a job, derived by relaxing some of the constraints to give a simpler problem.

Useful dominance rules can often be very simple and obvious. This can also be true of implied constraints, but in satisfaction problems, the search heuristics tend to guide the search away from obviously wrong compound assignments; in optimization problems, the search at some point has to prove that there is no solution, unless there is a good bound on the objective that makes the proof trivial. In proving that a problem has no solution by exhaustive search, every possibility allowed by the constraints has to be explored.

For instance, in the SONET problem, described earlier [43], it is obviously suboptimal to have a SONET ring with only one node on it, since installing a node on a ring contributes to the cost, but the only reason to install a node on a ring is to allow it to communicate with another node on that ring. A constraint that every ring must have at least two nodes on it, and that there must be traffic between them, rules out these solutions and makes a significant difference to the search.

Optimization problems arising in scheduling, and the importance of propagating the value of the objective to prune the search, are discussed in Chapter 22.

11.12 Supporting Modelling and Reformulation

As will be clear from this chapter, there can often be many different ways to model a problem. Ideally, an automatic modelling system should generate the best model; but given the interaction between the model, the search algorithm and the search heuristics, there is not likely to be a single best model. We could envisage a system that generates a number of different models of a problem, and can advise that one is better than another under certain circumstances. Flener, Pearson and Ågren [13] describe a system that refines a specification to a model that uses matrices of Boolean variables. Systems that generate alternative models from a specification of the problem are described by Hnich [24], and in two related papers by Frisch, Hnich, Miguel, Smith & Walsh [16] and Frisch, Jefferson, Martinez Hernandez and Miguel [17]. The system described in the last papers can generate models with multiple viewpoints, linked by channelling constraints. [17] presents empirical results based on a number of problems, comparing the models produced with those described in the literature. For instance, the system generated 27 models of the SONET problem, described earlier; even so, this did not include all of those described in [43]. Comparing the models generated, other than empirically, is still a gap.

A completely different route to formalizing modelling is by identifying common *patterns* that can be transferred from one problem to another. Flener *et al.* [12] advocated a need to "identify, formalise and document these patterns of formulation and solution". Walsh [50] relates the idea to design patterns in architecture and software engineering. This seems the most effective support available for modellers at present; for instance, since the paper by Cheng *et al.* [6], the use of multiple viewpoints linked by channelling constraints has become commonplace, and dual viewpoints of permutation problems in particular have been thoroughly studied and understood.

Although there is some progress towards identifying a range of possible ways of modelling a problem, there is less progress towards identifying good models, except by trying them empirically. In the early days of constraint programming, models were sometimes compared by estimating the sizes of their search spaces, i.e. the product of the domain sizes. This could be a good indication of the search effort if the search algorithm simply did generate and test, but it is too simplistic for any more sophisticated search algorithm. Since the choice of model interacts with the choices of search algorithm and search heuristics, models can only be compared in the context of the other choices. Simonis *et al.* [38] describe the use of visualization tools to examine the progress of the search in detail and to compare the performance of different models; in principle, such tools can also be used to identify inefficiencies in the search and to guide further improvements to the model.

Some modelling advice has been devised; for instance, Simonis [37] gives '30 Golden Rules' for modelling. There are a few specific guidelines in the CP folk-lore, e.g. "Avoid Boolean models", and more generally, "Reduce the number of variables" or "Reduce the number of constraints". These guidelines are worth discussing, because although they have a grain of truth, they should not be taken too literally:

- *Reduce the number of variables.* Clearly, reducing the number of variables conflicts with using multiple viewpoints and/or auxiliary variables, which have been demonstrated to be a good approach to modelling. Furthermore, increasing the number of search variables, by assigning values to the extra variables, can reduce search. Even so, it is likely that a model which requires fewer variable assignments to describe the solutions to the problem will be a better model; hence, an integer model is likely to be better than a Boolean model of the same problem. However, this is only true if the variables chosen allow the constraints to be expressed in a way that propagates well; it would be easy, for instance, to artificially reduce the number of variables by making a single variable in the new model stand for a pair of variables in the old model, but in general, this will not result in a better model.

- *Reduce the number of constraints.* Again, this conflicts with introducing implied constraints, if taken literally. However, rewriting a set of constraints in a more compact form is likely to be beneficial, if the resulting constraints can propagate efficiently; this covers, for instance, combining constraints with the same scope or using a global constraints to replace a set of constraints. As before, however, simply conjoining constraints for the sake of reducing their number will not result in a better model if the new constraints cannot propagate efficiently.

One could equally well reverse this advice, to say "*Add* more variables and constraints". New variables (whether auxiliary variables or a complete new viewpoint), and constraints on these variables, that make explicit knowledge of the underlying problem that was not hitherto expressed, can allow the problem to be solved more easily.

However, with any changes to the model, whether the changes are adding variables and constraints or removing them, one caveat should be borne in mind: changes to the model that reduce search may not always reduce run-time. It may be necessary to test a model empirically in order to see whether a proposed change will in fact lead to solutions being found more quickly.

Bearing in mind this caveat (and also the interaction between the model, the search algorithm and the search heuristics), the best advice at present seems to be to aim for a rich model, using multiple viewpoints, auxiliary variables and implied constraints, incorporating as much insight into the problem as possible. The more we understand the problem and build that understanding into the model, the better we will be able to solve it.

Acknowledgements

I should like to thank Pascal van Hentenryck, Jimmy Lee, Jeff Choi and Yat Chiu Law for useful comments, and Ian Miguel for his help. This material is based on works supported by the Science Foundation Ireland under Grant No. 00/PI.1/C075.

Bibliography

[1] F. Bacchus and P. van Beek. On the Conversion Between Non-Binary and Binary Constraint Satisfaction Problems. In *Proceedings AAAI'98*, pages 311–318, 1998.

[2] A. Beacham, X. Chen, J. Sillito, and P. van Beek. Constraint programming lessons learned from crossword puzzles. In *Proceedings of the 14th Canadian Conference on Artificial Intelligence*, pages 78–87, 2001.

[3] N. Beldiceanu. Global constraints as graph properties on structured network of elementary constraints of the same type. Technical Report Technical Report T2000/01, SICS, 2000.

[4] C. Bessière and J. Régin. Enforcing arc consistency on global constraints by solving subproblems on the fly. In *Proceedings CP'99*, pages 103–117, 1999.

[5] J. E. Borrett and E. P. Tsang. A Context for Constraint Satisfaction Problem Formulation Selection. *Constraints*, 6:299–327, 2001.

[6]   B. M. W. Cheng, K. M. F. Choi, J. H. M. Lee, and J. C. K. Wu. Increasing constraint propagation by redundant modeling: an experience report. *Constraints*, 4:167–192, 1999.

[7]   K. C. K. Cheng and R. H. C. Yap. Applying Ad-hoc Global Constraints with the case Constraint to Still-Life. *Constraints*, 11, 2006. (To appear).

[8]   C. W. Choi, J. H. M. Lee, and P. J. Stuckey. Removing Propagation Redundant Constraints in Redundant Modeling. *ACM Transactions on Computational Logic* 2006. (To appear).

[9]   M. Dincbas, H. Simonis, and P. van Hentenryck. Solving the car-sequencing problem in constraint logic programming. In Y. Kodratoff, editor, *Proceedings ECAI-88*, pages 290–295, 1988.

[10] I. Dotú, A. del Val, and M. Cebrián. Redundant Modeling for the QuasiGroup Completion Problem. In F. Rossi, editor, *Principles and Practice of Constraint Programming - CP 2003*, LNCS 2833, pages 288–302. Springer, 2003.

[11] A. Fernández and P. M. Hill. A comparative study of eight constraint programming languages over the Boolean and finite domains. *Constraints*, 5:275–301, 2000.

[12] P. Flener, A. M. Frisch, B. Hnich, Z. Kiziltan, I. Miguel, and T. Walsh. Matrix Modelling: Exploiting Common Patterns in Constraint Programming. In *Proceedings of the International Workshop on Reformulating Constraint Satisfaction Problems - Towards Systematisation and Automation*, 2002.

[13] P. Flener, J. Pearson, and M. Ågren. Introducing ESRA, a relational language for modelling combinatorial problems. In M. Bruynooghe, editor, *LOPSTR'03: Revised Selected Papers*, LNCS 3018, pages 214–232. Springer, 2004.

[14] E. C. Freuder. Modeling: The Final Frontier. In *Proceedings PACLP99, the 1st International Conference on the Practical Applications of Constraint Technologies and Logic Programming*, pages 15–21, 1999. Keynote address.

[15] A. Frisch, C. Jefferson, and I. Miguel. Symmetry-breaking as a Prelude to Implied Constraints: A Constraint Modelling Pattern. In *Proceedings of ECAI 2004*, pages 171–175, 2004.

[16] A. M. Frisch, B. Hnich, I. Miguel, B. M. Smith, and T. Walsh. Transforming and Refining Abstract Constraint Specifications. In J.-D. Zucker and L. Saitta, editors, *Abstraction, Reformulation and Approximation, 6th International Symposium, Proceedings SARA 2005*, LNCS 3607, pages 76–91. Springer, 2005.

[17] A. M. Frisch, C. Jefferson, B. Martinez Hernandez, and I. Miguel. The Rules of Constraint Modelling. In *Proceedings IJCAI05*, pages 311–318, 2005.

[18] A. M. Frisch, I. Miguel, and T. Walsh. Extensions to proof planning for generating implied constraints. In *Proceedings of Calculemus-01*, pages 130–141, 2001.

[19] P. A. Geelen. Dual Viewpoint Heuristics for Binary Constraint Satisfaction Problems. In B. Neumann, editor, *Proceedings ECAI'92*, pages 31–35, 1992.

[20] I. Gent, C. Jefferson, I. Lynce, I. Miguel, P. Nightingale, B. Smith, and A. Tarim. Search in the Patience Game 'Black Hole'. Technical Report CPPod-10-2005, CPPod Research Group, 2005. Available from http://www.dcs.st-and.ac.uk/s˜cppod/publications/reports/.

[21] L. Getoor, G. Ottosson, M. Fromherz, and B. Carlson. Effective Redundant Constraints for Online Scheduling. In *Proceedings of AAAI'97*, pages 302–307, 1997.

[22] W. Harvey and P. J. Stuckey. Improving Linear Constraint Propagation by Changing Constraint Representation. *Constraints*, 8:173 – 207, 2003.

[23] M. Henz. Don't Be Puzzled! In *Proceedings of Workshop on Constraint Programming Applications*, Aug. 1996.

[24] B. Hnich. *Function Variables for Constraint Programming*. PhD thesis, University of Uppsala, 2003.

[25] B. Hnich, S. D. Prestwich, and E. Selensky. Constraint-Based Approaches to the Covering Test Problem. In B. Faltings, A. Petcu, F. Fages, and F. Rossi, editors, *Recent Advances in Constraints, Joint ERCIM/CoLogNet International Workshop on Constraint Solving and Constraint Logic Programming, CSCLP 2004, Revised Selected and Invited Papers*, LNCS 3419, pages 172–186. Springer, 2005.

[26] B. Hnich, J. Richardson, and P. Flener. Towards Automatic Generation and Evaluation of Implied Constraints. Technical Report Technical report 2003-014, Department of Information Technology, Uppsala University, Sweden, 2003.

[27] B. Hnich, B. M. Smith, and T. Walsh. Dual Models of Permutation and Injection Problems. *Journal of Artificial Intelligence Research*, 21:357–391, 2004.

[28] G. Katsirelos and F. Bacchus. GAC on conjunctions of constraints. In T. Walsh, editor, *Principles and Practice of Constraint Programming - CP 2001*, LNCS 2239, pages 610–614. Springer, 2001.

[29] Y. C. Law and J. H. M. Lee. Model Induction: a New Source of CSP Model Redundancy. In *Proceedings of the 18th National Conference on Artificial Intelligence (AAAI-2002)*, pages 54–60, 2002.

[30] B. A. Nadel. Representation Selection for Constraint Satisfaction: A Case Study Using n-Queens. *IEEE Expert*, 5:16–23, June 1990.

[31] K. E. Petrie and B. M. Smith. Symmetry Breaking in Graceful Graphs. Technical Report APES-56-2003, APES Research Group, 2003. Available from http://www.dcs.st-and.ac.uk/~apes/apesreports.html.

[32] S. Prestwich and J. C. Beck. Exploiting dominance in three symmetric problems. In *Fourth International Workshop on Symmetry and Constraint Satisfaction Problems*, 2004.

[33] L. G. Proll and B. M. Smith. ILP and Constraint Programming Approaches to a Template Design Problem. *INFORMS Journal on Computing*, 10:265–275, 1998.

[34] J.-F. Puget. Constraint programming next challenge: Simplicity of use. In M. Wallace, editor, *Principles and Practice of Constraint Programming - CP 2004*, LNCS 3258, pages 5 – 8. Springer, 2004. Invited talk.

[35] J.-C. Régin and J.-F. Puget. A Filtering Algorithm for Global Sequencing Constraints. In G. Smolka, editor, *Principles and Practice of Constraint Programming - CP97*, LNCS 1330, pages 32–46. Springer-Verlag, 1997.

[36] F. Rossi, C. Petrie, and V. Dhar. On the Equivalence of Constraint Satisfaction Problems. In *Proceedings of ECAI-90*, pages 550–556, 1990.

[37] H. Simonis. Finite Domain Constraint Programming Methodology. Tutorial presented at the PACT 2000 conference. (Available as a Powerpoint presentation from the author.), 2000.

[38] H. Simonis, T. Cornelissens, V. Dumortier, G. Fabris, F. Nanni, and A. Tirabosco. Using Constraint Visualisation Tools. In P. Deransart, M. V. Hermenegildo, and J. Maluszynski, editors, *Analysis and Visualization Tools for Constraint Programming*, LNCS 1870, pages 321–356. Springer, 2000.

[39] B. M. Smith. Succeed-first or Fail-first: A Case Study in Variable and Value Ordering Heuristics. In M. Wallace, editor, *Proceedings PACT97, 3rd International Conference*

on the Practical Application of Constraint Technology, pages 321–330. The Practical
Application Company, 1997.

[40] B. M. Smith. Modelling a Permutation Problem. Research Report 2000.18, School
of Computer Studies, University of Leeds, 2000.

[41] B. M. Smith. Reducing Symmetry in a Combinatorial Design Problem. In *Proceedings of CP-AI-OR'01, the International Workshop on Integration of AI and OR Techniques in Constraint Programming for Combinatorial Optimization Problems* 2001.

[42] B. M. Smith. A Dual Graph Representation of a Problem in 'Life'. In P. van Hentenryck, editor, *Principles and Practice of Constraint Programming - CP 2002*, LNCS 2470, pages 402–414. Springer, 2002.

[43] B. M. Smith. Symmetry and Search in a Network Design Problem. In R. Bartak and M. Milano, editors, *Integration of AI and OR Techniques in Constraint Programming for Combinatorial Optimization Problems, Proceedings of CPAIOR 2005 (2nd International Conference)*, LNCS 3524, pages 336–350. Springer, 2005.

[44] B. M. Smith, K. Stergiou, and T. Walsh. Using auxiliary variables and implied constraints to model non-binary problems. In *Proceedings AAAI-2000 (Conference of the American Assocation for Artificial Intelligence)*, pages 182–187, 2000.

[45] E. Tsang. *Foundations of Constraint Satisfaction*. Academic Press, 1993.

[46] P. van Beek and K. Wilken. Fast optimal instruction scheduling for single-issue processors with arbitrary latencies. In T. Walsh, editor, *Principles and Practice of Constraint Programming - CP 2001*, LNCS 2239, pages 625–639. Springer, 2001.

[47] P. van Hentenryck. *Constraint Satisfaction in Logic Programming*. MIT Press, 1989.

[48] P. van Hentenryck and Y. Deville. The Cardinality Operator: A New Logical Connective and Its Application to Constraint Logic Programming. In *Proceedings of the 8th International Conference on Logic Programming (ICLP-91)*, pages 745–759, 1991.

[49] T. Walsh. SAT v CSP. In *Proceedings CP'2000*, pages 441–456, 2000.

[50] T. Walsh. Constraint patterns. In F. Rossi, editor, *Principles and Practice of Constraint Programming - CP 2003*, LNCS 2833, pages 53–64. Springer, 2003. Invited talk.

Part II

Extensions, Languages, and Applications

Handbook of Constraint Programming
Edited by F. Rossi, P. van Beek and T. Walsh

Chapter 12

Constraint Logic Programming

Kim Marriott, Peter J. Stuckey, Mark Wallace

Constraint Logic Programming (CLP) is the merger of two declarative paradigms: constraint solving and logic programming. As both constraint solving and logic programs are based on mathematical relations the merger is natural and convenient. CLP encourages experimentation and fast algorithm development by narrowing the gap between the logic and the solving algorithms. This is because CLP can express both conceptual and design models and, even more importantly, CLP can also express mappings from conceptual to design models. By a *conceptual* model of a problem, we mean its precise formulation in logic, and by the *design* model of the problem we mean its algorithmic formulation, which maps to a sequence of steps for solving it. A single problem may have many different conceptual models, and many different design models.

The first important characteristic of constraint logic programs is that they allow succinct, natural conceptual modeling of satisfaction and optimization problems.

Example 12.1. For example, the cryptarithmetic problem

SEND + MORE = MONEY

where each letter represents a different digit, is naturally conceptually modeled by the following CLP program: (we will use the concrete syntax of ECLiPSe [20] throughout this chapter)

```
smm(S,E,N,D,M,O,R,Y) :-
    [S,E,N,D,M,O,R,Y] :: 0..9,
                    1000 * S + 100 * E + 10 * N + D
                  + 1000 * M + 100 * O + 10 * R + E
    #= 10000 * M + 1000 * O + 100 * N + 10 * E + Y,
    M #>= 1, S #>= 1,
    alldifferent([S,E,N,D,M,O,R,Y]).
```

The first line initiates a rule to define a new predicate (or user-defined constraint) *smm* which has the variables of the problem as arguments. The remainder of the rule defines *smm* in terms of other constraints. The second line defines that each variable is an integer in the range 0 to 9 (i.e. they are digits), the third to fifth constrains them to satisfy the cryptarithmetic constraint, the sixth line constrains both M and S to be non-zero, and the seventh uses a global constraint *alldifferent* to ensure that all the digits are different.

This example demonstrates the ability to define application specific constraints and the use of data structures such as lists. As we shall see in Section 12.3, CLP languages are much more expressive than most other approaches for defining constraint problems, in particular the standard framework of constraint satisfaction problems (CSPs) or mathematical modeling languages such as GAMS or OPL. They allow local variables and recursive definitions that together allow one to express problems with an unbounded number of variables. They can also represent solutions without necessarily fixing all variables. This enables CP languages to support interactive problem solving. For example the user can control search, by posting search decisions one at a time, and observing the resulting partial solution calculated by the CLP program, before deciding what to do next.

The second characteristic of CLP languages is that they allow the programmer to define search strategies for solving their model. This is a core component of the design model. This is possible because CLP languages inherit backtracking search from logic programming. When combined with reflection predicates that provide information about the current solver state, this allows the programmer to specify sophisticated, efficient, problem specific search strategies.

Example 12.2. The most basic search procedure in a CLP system is called "labeling" and can be defined by the following two rules:

```
labeling([]).
labeling([V|Rest]) :-
    indomain(V),
    labeling(Rest).
```

This recurses through a list of variables and uses the predicate `indomain(V)` to non-deterministically set each variable V to each of its possible values in turn.

We can solve the original cryptarithmetic problem by combining this search predicate with the model above in the goal

```
smm(S,E,N,D,M,O,R,Y), labeling([S,E,N,D,M,O,R,Y]).
```

This gives a design model for the problem assuming the existence of an underlying finite domain constraint solver. When this goal is evaluated by the CLP system it will return the answer $S = 9, E = 5, N = 6, D = 7, M = 1, O = 0, R = 8, Y = 2$. We explore programmer-defined search further in Section 12.5,

The third characteristic of modern CLP languages, such as ECLiPSe [20] or SICStus Prolog [99], is that they allow the programmer to (at least partially) define how the underlying constraint solver processes the constraints. This of course is the core part of the design model. A variety of mechanisms have been utilized including disjunction, reification, indexicals, constraint handling rules and generalized propagation. We shall discuss this more in Section 12.4, also see Chapter 14 "Finite Domain Constraint Programming Systems".

Finally, a fourth characteristic of constraint logic programming is that the CLP paradigm is generic in the choice of the primitive constraints and constraint solving technology. Our example above uses bounded integer constraints: one CLP system might use propagation-based methods to solve these, while another might use a mixed integer programming (MIP) solver, while a third might use local search techniques. Another CLP system might not provide bounded integer constraints, but instead provide linear constraints over the reals and use simplex or interior point solving techniques. The key to this genericity is the CLP Schema [50, 55]. This provides a common operational and declarative semantics for all CLP languages, regardless of the constraints. We shall detail the semantic foundation of CLP languages in Section 12.2.

As well as covering semantic foundations (Section 12.2), conceptual modeling (Section 12.3), design modeling (Section 12.4), and search (Section 12.5), we provide a brief history of CLP in Section 12.1, discuss its impact on other research fields in Section 12.6 before concluding with our thoughts on the future of CLP and important directions for future research.

12.1 History of CLP

12.1.1 The Origins of CLP

The core ideas behind constraint logic programming were developed by three largely independent research teams: that of Colmeraur in Marseilles; that of Jaffar and Lassez in Melbourne (Australia) (then IBM T.J. Watson Research Center at Yorktown Heights); and the CHIP team led by Dincbas at the European Computer-Industry Research Center (ECRC) in Munich.

Constraint logic programming emerged as a generalization of logic programming. In the CLP view of logic programming, standard logic programming languages such as Prolog provide a single kind of constraint, syntactic equality solved with unification. However, syntactic equality is quite restrictive and a major thrust of logic programming research in the early 1980s was devoted to developing and formalizing equational logic programming languages in which unification was generalized to handle different kinds of equality. One of the aims of this research was to combine the logic and functional paradigms. See for example the collection of papers in [32].

Another major thrust was the development of languages in which Prolog's fixed left-to-right literal selection strategy was generalized to allow goals to be delayed until their arguments were sufficiently instantiated, thus allowing more flexible dynamic evaluation. The limitations of a fixed literal selection strategy were recognized early in the development of logic programming languages. Absys1 [38] a precursor to Prolog provided dynamic scheduling as did the logic programming languages IC-Prolog [23], Prolog-II [25] and MU-Prolog [73]. Thus, for example, in MU-Prolog `wait` declarations can be used to specify that evaluation of a particular predicate must "wait" until its arguments are non-variable. Based on this, MU-Prolog provided syntactic disequations and arithmetic predicates that provide simple constraint solving using local propagation techniques.

The CLP paradigm, in which arbitrary constraints are allowed, was the natural consequence of these two research directions. The actual term Constraint Logic Programming was coined by Jaffar and Lassez [50] in 1986(7) and they gave a schema and semantics for the CLP class of languages. This was an extension of their work on semantic schema for equational logic programs [53] and semantics for disequations [52]. With others, they developed the language CLP($\mathcal{R}$) [54] a language extending Prolog by providing arithmetic constraints. This used an incremental Simplex algorithm for solving linear constraints and delayed evaluation of non-linear arithmetic constraints until they became linear or sufficiently ground. The utility of $CLP(\mathcal{R})$ was demonstrated by using it for financial modeling and for a variety of engineering applications.

Colmeraur and his team developed Prolog II [27] in the early 1980s and then Prolog III [26] in the late 1980s. Prolog II provided equations and disequations over rational trees and was the first logic programming language explicitly described as using constraints. It also provided "freeze" the first kind of dynamic scheduling. Prolog III was a true CLP language extending Prolog II by providing constraints over the Booleans, linear arithmetic over the rational numbers, and constraints over lists (sequences). It was used for applications such as chemical reasoning.

The team at ECRC (notably Dincbas, van Hentenryck and Simonis) developed CHIP [34] in the period 1985-1988. It was developed for solving combinatorial optimization problems for industry by marrying Prolog's backtracking search with consistency techniques from artificial intelligence research. It was the first CLP language to explicitly provide finite domain constraints. It provided a limited form of dynamic scheduling by way of demons. Showcase applications included circuit diagnosis, scheduling and cutting stock problems.

Although constraint logic programming originated in logic programming related ideas also arose in the artificial intelligence and operations research communities. Sutherland's SKETCHPAD [107] was one of the first computer systems to employ constraints. Other notable precursors to CLP include research at MIT into languages and systems for constraint solving, for example the language CONSTRAINTS [106]. This research was motivated by electrical circuit analysis and design. Steele [106] was probably the first to point out the conceptual similarity between constraint solving and logic programming. Other precursors are languages and systems such as REF-ARF [37] and ALICE [62] designed to solve CSP style problems. ALICE allows models to be written using abstract functions which may be injective, bijective, etc. Constraint solving is handled by consistency methods as well as by reasoning about abstract functions. Mathematical modeling languages such as AMPL [7] and symbolic algebra manipulation packages such as MATLAB [69] also share some similarities with CLP languages allowing one the specify problems in a high level mathematical way and solve them (using an external solver in the case of modeling languages; and using algebraic and numerical solving approaches supported by the algebra packages). Precursors to CLP are discussed more fully in [51]

12.1.2 Subsequent CLP Research Directions

The CLP Schema provided a generic way of building new programming languages: simply take a class of constraints and some solver for these constraints and pop these into a rule-based language. It was a simple, appealing recipe and in the first few years of CLP research there was an explosion in the number of CLP languages.

The languages LOGIN [5] and LIFE [4] provided equality over feature trees and closely related structures. The languages clp(FD) (later GNU-Prolog [43]), Echidna [100] and Flang provided finite domain constraints. BNR-Prolog [78] provides Boolean constraints, finite domain constraints and real interval arithmetic, Trilogy [119] provided strings, integer and real arithmetic constraints. CAL [3] and RISC-CLP [46] provided more powerful constraint solving over non-linear arithmetic constraints.

One of the most important directions in CLP research has been to move away from the original "black box" view of the underlying constraint solver of the first CLP languages, where the solver simply answered satisfiability questions, to languages and systems which provide the programmer with a "glass box" view of the underlying constraint solving in which the programmer can extend, combine and even write new solvers [118].

A recent direction in CLP research has been the investigation of hybrid-constraint solving techniques which combine propagator-based solving techniques with linear programming and MIP solving techniques and with local search techniques [90, 121]. Such approaches have proven to be extremely useful in solving industrial applications [89, 123, 28, 81]. The CLP language ECLiPSe [20] was expressly designed to support the development of such hybrid constraint solving techniques. It has demonstrated that constraint logic programming provides a good basis for programming and experimenting with different constraint solving techniques.

12.2 Semantics of Constraint Logic Programs

CLP languages extend logic-based programming languages by allowing constraints with a pre-defined interpretation. The key insight of Jaffar and Lassez's CLP Scheme is that for these languages, the operational semantics, declarative semantics and the relationship between these can be parameterized by a choice of constraints, solver and an algebraic and logical semantics for the constraints. Our presentation of the main results follows:

We assume that the reader is familiar with the basics of first-order logic. See for example [98, 35].

We let $\exists_W F$ denote the logical formula $\exists V_1 \exists V_2 \cdots \exists V_n F$ where variable set $W = \{V_1, \ldots, V_n\}$, and we let $\tilde{\exists}_W F$ denote the restriction of the logical formula F to the variables in W. That is, $\tilde{\exists}_W F$ is $\exists_{vars(F) \backslash W} F$, where the function $vars$ takes a syntactic object and returns the set of free variables occurring in it. We let $\tilde{\exists} F$ denote the existential closure of F and $\tilde{\forall} F$ denote the universal closure of F.

A *renaming* is a bijective mapping between variables. We naturally extend renamings to mappings between logical formulas, rules, and constraints. Syntactic objects s and s' are said to be *variants* if there is a renaming ρ such that $\rho(s) = s'$.

The CLP scheme defines a class of languages, $CLP(\mathcal{C})$, which are parametric in the choice of *constraint domain* $\mathcal{C}$. The constraint domain $\mathcal{C}$ is a pre-interpretation defining the "built-in" primitive constraints and functions, and their interpretation. It contains the following components:

- The *constraint domain signature*, $\Sigma_{\mathcal{C}}$, which defines a set of function and predicate symbols and associates an arity with each symbol. This implicitly defines the *terms* of the constraint language, built from function symbols and variables, and the *primitive constraints* which are the *atoms* defined by $\Sigma_{\mathcal{C}}$, i.e. predicates symbol with term arguments.

- The *domain of computation*, $\mathcal{D}_{\mathcal{C}}$, which is the intended interpretation of the constraints. It consists of a set D and a mapping from the symbols in $\Sigma_{\mathcal{C}}$ to relations and functions over D which respects the arities of the symbols.

- The *constraint theory* $\mathcal{T}_{\mathcal{C}}$, which is a possibly infinite set of formulae that describe the logical semantics of the constraints $\Sigma_{\mathcal{C}}$.

- A *solver*, $solv_{\mathcal{C}}$, which maps each conjunction of primitive constraints to one of *true*, *false* or *unknown*, indicating that the solver can determine the conjunction i satisfiable, unsatisfiable or it cannot tell.

The solver provides an operational semantics for the constraints, while the domain of computation provides an algebraic interpretation and the constraint theory provides a logical interpretation.

We assume that:

- The binary predicate symbol "=" is in $\Sigma_{\mathcal{C}}$, that = is interpreted as identity in $\mathcal{D}_C$ and that $\mathcal{T}_{\mathcal{C}}$ contains the standard equality axioms for =.

- The solver does not take variable names into account, that is, for all renamings ρ $solv_{\mathcal{C}}(c) = solv_{\mathcal{C}}(\rho(c))$.

- The domain of computation, solver and constraint theory *agree* in the sense that $\mathcal{D}_C$ is a model of $\mathcal{T}_{\mathcal{C}}$, and for any primitive constraint c, if $solv_{\mathcal{C}}(c) = $ *false* then $\mathcal{T}_{\mathcal{C}} \models \neg \tilde{\exists} c$, and if $solv_{\mathcal{C}}(c) = $ *true* then $\mathcal{T}_{\mathcal{C}} \models \tilde{\exists} c$.

The example constraint domain we saw in the cryptarithmetic problem (Example 12.1) consists of equality = over the uninterpreted functors (Herbrand terms) e.g. constructors for lists: [ ] (the empty list) and $[\cdot|\cdot]$ (cons), and bounded integer constraints constructed from the usual integer constants e.g. 0, -1, 15, 167, ..., integer functions $+$, $-$, $*$, and integer comparison relations #=, #>=, #>, #<, #<= and the constraint :: restricting a list of integer variables to a particular set of integers. The solver is incomplete (that is it sometimes returns *unknown*), and uses unification to solve equalities over the uninterpreted functors and propagation methods to solve the integer constraints.

12.2.1 Syntax of Constraint Logic Programs

Constraint logic programs are statements in logic (more precisely definite clauses) which extend a constraint domain by defining new constraints in terms of the primitive constraints. Constraint logic programs over the domain $\mathcal{C}$ are termed $CLP(\mathcal{C})$ programs.

A *constraint logic program* (CLP), or *program*, is a finite set of rules. A *rule* is of the form $H :\!- B$ where H, the *head*, is an atom and B, the *body*, is a finite, non-empty sequence of literals. We let $\square$ denote the empty sequence. We shall write rules of the form $H :\!- \square$ simply as H. A *literal* is either an atom or a primitive constraint. An *atom* has the form $p(t_1, ..., t_n)$ where p is a user-defined predicate symbol and the t_i are terms from the constraint domain. For simplicity we assume that predicate symbols have a unique arity.

We use the standard CLP convention that variables start with upper case letters, while predicates and functions begin with lower case letters.

Example 12.3. The following simple CLP program defines the relation $max(x, y, z) \leftrightarrow z = \max\{x, y\}$.

```
max(X,Y,Z)  :- X #>= Y,  Z #= X.    %% M1
max(X,Y,Z)  :- Y #>= X,  Z #= Y.    %% M2
```

Both the atom max(X,Y,Z) and the primitive constraint X #>= Y are literals. There are two rules with head max(X,Y,Z). The body of the first rule is X #>= Y, Z #= X The rules have names M1 and M2 given as comments which we shall use later.

The CLP schema provides an operational, algebraic and logical semantics for the user-defined constraints in a CLP program which extends that of the underlying constraint domain.

12.2.2 Operational Semantics

The operational semantics allows us to compute with the predicates defined by the program. In essence the operational semantics defines a way of repeatedly unfolding the user-defined constraints in a goal (or conjunction of literals) until a conjunction of primitive constraints is reached.

The *definition of a user-defined predicate p in program P, defn$_P$(p)*, is the set of variants of rules in P such that the head of each rule has form $p(s_1, ..., s_n)$. To side step renaming issues, we assume that each time *defn$_P$* is called it returns variants with distinct new variables.

The operational semantics is given in terms of the "derivations" from goals. Derivations are sequences of reductions between "states", where a *state* is a tuple $\langle G\,|\,c\rangle$ which contains the current literal sequence or "goal" G and the current constraint store c (a conjunction of primitive constraints). At each reduction step, the leftmost literal in the goal is rewritten as follows. If the literal is a primitive constraint, and it is consistent with the current constraint store, then it is added to it. If it is inconsistent then the derivation "fails". If the literal is an atom, it is reduced using one of the rules in its definition.

A state $\langle L_1, L_2, ..., L_m\,|\,c\rangle$ can be *reduced* as follows:

1. If L_1 is a primitive constraint and $solv(c \wedge L_1) \neq false$, it is reduced to

$$\langle L_2, ..., L_m\,|\,c \wedge L_1\rangle$$

   .

2. If L_1 is a primitive constraint and $solv(c \wedge L_1) = false$, it is reduced to $\langle \square\,|\,false\rangle$.

3. If L_1 is an atom, then it is reduced to

$$\langle s_1 = t_1, ..., s_n = t_n, B, L_2, ..., L_m\,|\,c\rangle$$

for some $(A\ \text{:-}\ B) \in defn_P(p)$ where L_1 is of form $p(s_1, ..., s_n)$ and A is of form $p(t_1, ..., t_n)$.

4. If L_1 is an atom and $defn_P(p) = \emptyset$, it is reduced to $\langle \square\,|\,false\rangle$ where L_1 is of form $p(s_1, ..., s_n)$.

A *derivation* from a goal G in a program P is a sequence of states $S_0 \Rightarrow S_1 \Rightarrow \cdots \Rightarrow S_n$ where S_0 is $\langle G\,|\,true\rangle$ and there is a reduction from each S_{i-1} to S_i, using rules in P. The *length* of a derivation of the form $S_0 \Rightarrow S_1 \Rightarrow \cdots \Rightarrow S_n$ is n. A derivation from G is *finished* if the last goal cannot be reduced. The last state in a finished derivation from G must have the form $\langle \square\,|\,c\rangle$. If c is *false* the derivation is said to be *failed*. Otherwise the derivation is *successful*. The *answers* of a goal G for program P are the constraints $\bar{\exists}_{vars(G)}c$ where there is a successful derivation from G to final state with constraint c.

In many implementations of CLP languages the answer is simplified into a logically equivalent constraint, perhaps by removing existentially quantified variables, before being shown to the user.

Example 12.4. Consider the execution of the goal `max(A,B,C), B #= 2` with the CLP program from Example 12.3. One successful derivation is:

$$\langle \texttt{max(A,B,C), B \#= 2} \mid true \rangle$$
$$\Downarrow M1$$
$$\langle \texttt{A = X, B = Y, C = Z, X \#>= Y, Z \#= X, B \#= 2} \mid true \rangle$$
$$\Downarrow$$
$$\langle \texttt{B = Y, C = Z, X \#>= Y, Z \#= X, B \#= 2} \mid A = X \rangle$$
$$\Downarrow$$
$$\langle \texttt{C = Z, X \#>= Y, Z \#= X, B \#= 2} \mid A = X \wedge B = Y \rangle$$
$$\Downarrow$$
$$\langle \texttt{X \#>= Y, Z \#= X, B \#= 2} \mid A = X \wedge B = Y \wedge C = Z \rangle$$
$$\Downarrow$$
$$\langle \texttt{Z \#= X, B \#= 2} \mid A = X \wedge B = Y \wedge C = Z \wedge X \geq Y \rangle$$
$$\Downarrow$$
$$\langle \texttt{B \#= 2} \mid A = X \wedge B = Y \wedge C = Z \wedge X \geq Y \wedge Z = X \rangle$$
$$\Downarrow$$
$$\langle \square \mid A = X \wedge B = Y \wedge C = Z \wedge X \geq Y \wedge Z = X \wedge B = 2 \rangle$$

The corresponding answer projected on to the original variables A, B, and C is $A \geq 2 \wedge B = 2 \wedge C = A$.

Apart from returning answers to a goal, execution of a constraint logic program may also return the special answer *no* indicating that the goal has "failed" in the sense that all derivations of the goal are failed.

Definition 12.5. *If a state or goal G has a finite set of derivations all of which are failed, G is said to* finitely fail.

Example 12.6. There are two possible derivations for the goal `A #= 1, max(A,2,1)` with the CLP program from Example 12.3. The first is :

$$\langle \text{A \#= 1, max(1,2,1)} \,|\, true \rangle$$
$$\Downarrow$$
$$\langle \text{max(A,2,1)} \,|\, A = 1 \rangle$$
$$\Downarrow M1$$
$$\langle \text{A = X, 2 = Y, 1 = Z, X \#>= Y, Z \#= X} \,|\, A = 1 \rangle$$
$$\Downarrow$$
$$\langle \text{2 = Y, 1 = Z, X \#>= Y, Z \#= X} \,|\, A = 1 \wedge A = X \rangle$$
$$\Downarrow$$
$$\langle \text{1 = Z, X \#>= Y, Z \#= X} \,|\, A = 1 \wedge A = X \wedge 2 = Y \rangle$$
$$\Downarrow$$
$$\langle \text{X \#>= Y, Z \#= X} \,|\, A = 1 \wedge A = X \wedge 2 = Y \wedge 1 = Z \rangle$$
$$\Downarrow$$
$$\langle \Box \,|\, false \rangle$$

The second is:

$$\langle \text{A \#= 1, max(1,2,1)} \,|\, true \rangle$$
$$\Downarrow$$
$$\langle \text{max(A,2,1)} \,|\, A = 1 \rangle$$
$$\Downarrow M2$$
$$\langle \text{A = X, 2 = Y, 1 = Z, Y \#>= X, Z \#= Y} \,|\, A = 1 \rangle$$
$$\Downarrow$$
$$\langle \text{2 = Y, 1 = Z, Y \#>= X, Z \#= Y} \,|\, A = 1 \wedge A = X \rangle$$
$$\Downarrow$$
$$\langle \text{1 = Z, Y \#>= X, Z \#= Y} \,|\, A = 1 \wedge A = X \wedge 2 = Y \rangle$$
$$\Downarrow$$
$$\langle \text{Y \#>= X, Z \#= Y} \,|\, A = 1 \wedge A = X \wedge 2 = Y \wedge 1 = Z \rangle$$
$$\Downarrow$$
$$\langle \text{Z \#= Y} \,|\, A = 1 \wedge A = X \wedge 2 = Y \wedge 1 = Z \wedge Y \geq X \rangle$$
$$\Downarrow$$
$$\langle \Box \,|\, false \rangle$$

Hence the goal is finitely failed.

Examining the operational semantics defined above, it is clear that the only use of the solver is to determine whether the constraint $c \wedge L_1$ is unsatisfiable where L_1 is a new primitive constraint and the constraint solver has just previously determined that the current constraint store c is not unsatisfiable. For this reason a significant component of CLP system research has been the design of *incremental* constraint solving algorithms specialised to answer this kind of problem. We return to this topic in Section 12.4.1.

It is important to recognize that, because the solver can be incomplete, a successful derivation may give an answer which is unsatisfiable since the solver may not be powerful enough to recognize that the constraint is unsatisfiable. When dealing with incomplete solvers it is useful to identify a class of goals for which the solver in known to be complete. We say a solver is *complete* for a set of constraints if it returns either *true* or *false*. We say a CLP program is *solver complete* for a goal G if the solver is complete for all answers to G. Typically constraint logic programs are written so that they are solver complete for the goals of interest.

For finite domain solvers, there is no guarantee that inconsistencies will be detected until all the variables in a constraints are *fixed*, that is, explicitly constrained to take a single value. However there *is* a guarantee in this case: the solver will fail if the ground constraint is inconsistent and succeed otherwise, corresponding to the answers *false* and *true* respectively. This is the reason for using the labeling predicate with the program from Example 12.1 since this assigns a value to all variables in the problem.

For a simplex based linear inequality solver which handles non-linear constraints by delaying them until enough variables are fixed for them to become linear (such as that used in CLP(R) [54]), the solver is complete as long as no delayed non-linear constraints remain.

12.2.3   The Semantics of Success

In this section we give an algebraic and a simple logical semantics for the answers to a CLP program and show that these semantics accord with the operational semantics (and each other).

Simple logical semantics

We can view each rule in a CLP program, say

$$A \;:\text{-}\; L_1, \dots, L_n$$

as representing the implication

$$\tilde{\forall}(A \leftarrow L_1 \wedge \dots \wedge L_n)$$

and the program is understood to represent the conjunction of its rules.

Example 12.7. For example, the `max` program represents

$$(\forall X \forall Y \forall Z. max(X, Y, Z) \leftarrow (X \geq Y \wedge Z = X)) \wedge$$
$$(\forall X \forall Y \forall Z. max(X, Y, Z) \leftarrow (Y \geq X \wedge Z = Y))$$

Note that from this formula we can infer that $max(1, 2, 2)$ holds, but we cannot infer negative consequences such as $\neg max(1, 2, 1)$.

The *logical semantics* of a $CLP(\mathcal{C})$ program P is the theory obtained by adding the rules of P to the constraint theory of the constraint domain $\mathcal{C}$.

We can show that the operational semantics is sound and complete with respect to the logical semantics where soundness means that the answers are logical consequences of the information in the program and completeness means that the answers returned by the operational semantics "cover" all of the constraints which imply the goal.

Theorem 12.8. *(Logical Soundness of Success) Let $\mathcal{T}_{\mathcal{C}}$ be the constraint theory for constraint domain $\mathcal{C}$ and P be a $CLP(\mathcal{C})$ program. If goal G has answer c, then*

$$P, \mathcal{T}_{\mathcal{C}} \models \bar{\exists}_{vars(G)}c \to G.$$

Theorem 12.9. *(Logical Completeness of Success) Let $\mathcal{T}_{\mathcal{C}}$ be the constraint theory for constraint domain $\mathcal{C}$ and P be a $CLP(\mathcal{C})$ program. Let G be a goal and c a constraint. If $P, \mathcal{T}_{\mathcal{C}} \models c \to G$ then G has answers $c_1, \ldots, c_n$ such that*

$$\mathcal{T}_{\mathcal{C}} \models c \to (\bar{\exists}_{vars(G)}c_1 \vee \ldots \vee \bar{\exists}_{vars(G)}c_n).$$

Algebraic semantics

We now turn our attention to the algebraic semantics. Such a semantics requires us to find a model for the program which is the "intended" interpretation of the program. Clearly, the intended interpretation of a CLP program should not change the interpretation of the primitive constraints or function symbols: All it should do is to extend this intended interpretation by providing an interpretation for each user-defined predicate symbol in P.

Definition 12.10. *A $\mathcal{C}$-interpretation for a $CLP(\mathcal{C})$ program P is an interpretation which agrees with the constraint interpretation $D_{\mathcal{C}}$ on the interpretation of the symbols in $\mathcal{C}$.*

Definition 12.11. *A $\mathcal{C}$-model of a $CLP(\mathcal{C})$ program P is a $\mathcal{C}$-interpretation which is a model of P.*

Since the meaning of the primitive constraints is fixed by $\mathcal{C}$ we can identify each $\mathcal{C}$-interpretation with the subset of the $\mathcal{C}$-base of P, written $\mathcal{C}$-base$_P$, which it makes true where $\mathcal{C}$-base$_P$ is the set

$$\{p(d_1, \ldots, d_n) \mid \begin{array}{l} p \text{ is an } n\text{-ary user-defined predicate in } P \text{ and} \\ \text{each } d_i \text{ is a domain element of } D_{\mathcal{C}} \end{array}\}.$$

Every program has a least $\mathcal{C}$-model, denoted $lm(P, \mathcal{C})$ which is usually regarded as the intended interpretation of the program since it is the most conservative $\mathcal{C}$-model. This result is analogous to that for logic programs in which the algebraic semantics of a logic program is given by its least Herbrand model. The proof of existence of the least model is almost identical to that for logic programs,

Theorem 12.12. *(Algebraic Soundness of Success) Let P be a $CLP(\mathcal{C})$ program. If goal G has answer c, then $lm(P, \mathcal{C}) \models \bar{\exists}_G c \to G$.* □

Soundness of the algebraic semantics ensures that the operational semantics only returns solutions which are solutions to the goal. However, we would also like to be sure that the operational semantics is complete in the sense that the answers "cover" all solutions to the goal.

Theorem 12.13. *(Algebraic Completeness of Success)*
Let P be a $CLP(\mathcal{C})$ program and G be a goal. If for valuation θ

$$lm(P, \mathcal{C}) \models_{\theta} G.$$

then G has an answer c such that $D_{\mathcal{C}} \models_{\theta} \bar{\exists}_{vars(G)}c$.

12.2.4 Fixpoint Semantics

The standard proof for algebraic completeness of success relies on a fixpoint semantics to bridge the gap between the algebraic and the operational semantics. This semantics is also of independent interest so we will introduce it. For a more detailed treatment the reader is referred to [55].

The fixpoint semantics is based on the "immediate consequence operator" which maps the set of "facts" in a $\mathcal{C}$-interpretation to the set of facts which are implied by the rules in the program. In a sense, the function captures the Modus Ponens rule of inference. This semantics generalizes the T_P semantics for logic programs. The T_P^{Term} operator is due to van Emden and Kowalski [108] (who called it T). Apt and van Emden [10] later used the name T_P which has become standard.

Definition 12.14. *Let P be a $CLP(\mathcal{C})$ program. The* immediate consequence function *for P is the function $T_P^{\mathcal{C}}$. Let I be a $\mathcal{C}$-interpretation, and let σ range over valuations for $\mathcal{C}$ Then $T_P^{\mathcal{C}}(I)$ is defined as*

$$\{\sigma(A) \mid A \; :- \; L_1, \ldots, L_n \text{ is a rule in } P \text{ for which } I \models_\sigma L_1 \wedge \ldots \wedge L_n\}$$

This is quite a compact definition. It is best understood by noting that

$$I \models_\sigma L_1 \wedge \cdots \wedge L_n$$

iff for each literal L_i either L_i is a primitive constraint and $\mathcal{C} \models_\sigma L_i$ or L_i is a user-defined predicate, say $p(t_1, \ldots, t_m)$, and $p(\sigma(t_1), \ldots, \sigma(t_m)) \in I$.

Since $T_P^{\mathcal{C}}$ is monotonic on the complete lattice $\mathcal{C}$-base$_P$ it has a least and greatest fixpoint which we denote by $lfp(T_P^{\mathcal{C}})$ and $gfp(T_P^{\mathcal{C}})$, respectively.

The key result relating the algebraic semantics and the fixpoint semantics is that the least model of a program P is the least fixpoint of $T_P^{\mathcal{C}}$.

Theorem 12.15. *Let P be a $CLP(\mathcal{C})$ program. $lm(P, \mathcal{C}) = lfp(T_P^{\mathcal{C}})$.*

12.2.5 Semantics for Finite Failure

We have seen that in the operational semantics for CLP programs, goals can also finitely fail. Intuitively, we would like a logical semantics such that if goal G finitely fails, then $\neg G$ is a consequence of the semantics. Unfortunately, this is not true for the simple logical semantics given in Section 12.2.3 since, as we have previously observed, it does not have negative consequences. We now refine our logical and an algebraic semantics to provide a semantics for finite failure.

We use a second logical semantics of the program called the Clark completion [21]. The Clark completion captures the reasonable assumption that the programmer really wants the rules defining a predicate to be an "if and only if" definition—the rules should cover all of the cases which make the predicate true.

Definition 12.16. *The* definition *of n-ary predicate symbol p in the program P, is the formula*

$$\forall X_1 \ldots \forall X_n \, p(X_1, \ldots, X_n) \leftrightarrow B_1 \vee \ldots \vee B_m$$

where each B_i corresponds to a rule in P of the form $p(t_1, \ldots, t_n)$:- $L_1, \ldots, L_k$ and B_i is

$$\exists Y_1 \ldots \exists Y_j \ (X_1 = t_1 \wedge \ldots \wedge X_n = t_n \wedge L_1 \ldots \wedge L_k)$$

where $Y_1, \ldots, Y_j$ are the variables in the original rule and $X_1, \ldots, X_n$ are variables that do not appear in any rule. Note that if there is no rule with head p, then the definition of p is simply

$$\forall X_1 \ldots \forall X_n \ p(X_1, \ldots, X_n) \leftrightarrow false$$

as $\bigvee \emptyset$ is naturally considered to be false.

   The (Clark) *completion, $P^\star$, of a constraint logic program P is the conjunction of the definitions of the user-defined predicates in P.*

Example 12.17. For example the (simplified) completion of the `max` program from Example 12.3 is

$$\forall X \forall Y \forall Z.max(X, Y, Z) \leftrightarrow (X \geq Y \wedge Z = X) \vee (Y \geq X \wedge Z = Y)$$

With this interpretation we can determine that $\neg max(1, 2, 1)$.

   The completion semantics refines the logical semantics given earlier. In particular, both semantics agree on the positive logical consequences of the program:

Theorem 12.18. *Let $\mathcal{T}_C$ be the constraint theory for constraint domain C and let P be a $CLP(C)$ program and G a goal. Then, $P^\star, \mathcal{T}_C \models \tilde{\exists} G$ iff $P, \mathcal{T}_C \models \tilde{\exists} G$* □

   Thus, the completion semantics provides a logical semantics for success. Further, it provides a logical semantics for finite failure:

Theorem 12.19. *(**Logical Soundness of Finite Failure**) Let $\mathcal{T}_C$ be the constraint theory for constraint domain C and let P be a $CLP(C)$ program. If goal G finitely fails then $P^\star, \mathcal{T}_C \models \neg\tilde{\exists} G$.* □

   We would also like to prove that the operational implementation of finite failure is complete for this logical semantics. A goal is said to be *finitely evaluable* for a program if it has no infinite derivations.

Theorem 12.20. *(**Logical Completeness of Finite Failure for a Finitely Evaluable Goal**) Let $\mathcal{T}_C$ be a theory for constraint domain C, let P be a $CLP(C)$ program, and let G be a goal. If*

$$P^\star, \mathcal{T}_C \models \neg\tilde{\exists} G$$

then G finitely fails provided G is finitely evaluable and P is solver complete for G.

   The reason for requiring finite evaluability is that if there is an infinite derivation the fixed left-to-right evaluation order may mean that the unsatisfiability of the derivation is not found.

Example 12.21. Consider the program P,

```
q :- q.
```

and the goal $G \equiv X = 2, q, X \neq 2$. Clearly

$$P^\star, \mathcal{T}_C \models \neg\tilde{\exists}G$$

but G will not finitely fail.

However the requirement for finite evaluability can be weakened to only require that processing of literals in (infinite) derivations is *fair* in the sense that no literal in the goal remains ignored forever. Of course, this is not true for the standard operational semantics. However, in practice the programmer is usually only interested in finitely evaluable goals.

Our algebraic semantics for success was provided by the least $\mathcal{C}$-model of P. This model also provides an algebraic semantics for finite failure of finitely evaluable goals. If we take a program's completion as the logical formula which captures the *true* meaning of the program then the intended interpretation of the program should also be a $\mathcal{C}$ interpretation which is a model for the completion.

Definition 12.22. *Let P be a $CLP(\mathcal{C})$ program. We denote the least $\mathcal{C}$-model of $P^\star$ by* $lm(P^\star, \mathcal{C})$.

Fortunately, $lm(P^\star, \mathcal{C}) = lm(P, \mathcal{C})$, thus our algebraic semantics can also be understood as being the least $\mathcal{C}$-model of $P^\star$.

Soundness of finite failure for the algebraic semantics is an immediate consequence of the soundness of finite failure for the logical semantics, as any intended interpretation of the constraint domain is a model of the constraint theory.

Theorem 12.23. *(Algebraic Soundness of Finite Failure) Let P be a $CLP(\mathcal{C})$ program. If goal G finitely fails then:* $lm(P^\star, \mathcal{C}) \models \neg\tilde{\exists}G$. □

Theorem 12.24. *(Algebraic Completeness of Finite Failure for a Finitely Evaluable Goal) Let P be a $CLP(\mathcal{C})$ program, and let G be a finitely evaluable goal. If $lm(P^\star, \mathcal{C}) \models \neg\tilde{\exists}G$ then G finitely fails provided P is solver complete for G.*

Algebraic completeness of finite failure for non-finitely evaluable goals is difficult to achieve. Even if we demand literal processing is fair we also require that the program is canonical and the result only holds for ground goals and only with respect to the *greatest* $\mathcal{C}$-model of $P^\star$. See [55] for details.

12.2.6 Extending the Semantics

Negation and general CLP programs

One of the major directions in logic programming research has been to extend the basic Horn clause framework to allow negative literals in the body of a rule. The simplest operational semantics for such negative literals is to use *negation as failure rule* of Clark [21] in which a negative literal succeeds if the literal finitely fails. This is called SLDNF. This is in accord with our earlier discussion of finite failure of a goal. As long all variables in the negative literal have a fixed value by the time it is evaluated it is possible to show that this operational semantics is sound w.r.t. the program completion semantics [21]. Proving completeness is considerably more problematic. One difficulty for instance is that the program completion may be inconsistent: Consider the program

```
p :- not p.
```

whose completion is $p \Leftrightarrow \neg p$. For more details the reader is referred to the survey paper of Apt and Bol [8].

Most CLP languages provide negation as implemented by negation as failure. But for this to be logically correct the programmer must ensure that the negative literal is ground by the time it is evaluated and that the program is solver complete for the negative literal. In essence the CLP system is providing a rather weak solver for negative literals. In practice such negation is not very useful except for data structure manipulation.

A stronger operational semantics for negation that fits well with the CLP framework is *constructive negation*. This was introduced for logic programming by Chan [61, 19] and is related to intensional negation [11, 12] and to Sato and Tamaki's earlier compile-time technique for generating the negation of a predicate [93]. Stuckey [104] generalized constructive negation to CLP and it was further studied by Fages [36]. The idea is that negative literals are allowed to construct answers. Recall the code for max given in Example 12.3

```
max(X,Y,Z) :- X #>= Y, Z #= X.    %% M1
max(X,Y,Z) :- Y #>= X, Z #= Y.    %% M2
```

The literal not max(X,Y,Z) is evaluated by unfolding the definition of *max* and negating this and transforming into a disjunction of conjuncts of literals:

$$\neg((X \geq Y \wedge Z = X) \vee (Y \geq X \wedge Z = Y))$$

which is equivalent to

$$(X \not\geq Y \wedge Y \not\geq X) \vee (X \not\geq Y \wedge Z \neq Y) \vee (Z \neq X \wedge Y \not\geq X) \vee (Z \neq X \wedge Z \neq Y).$$

The system then tries each of the conjuncts in turn. Unfortunately, efficient implementation of constructive negation is not straightforward so current systems do not support it. It requires the underlying solver to support negated constraints and universally quantified variables because of local variables and iterative unfolding of negated literals because of recursion.

In practice, most CLP systems are designed so that the primitive constraints are closed under negation and so allow the programmer to explicitly program the required negative literal.

Example 12.25. We can define the negation of the max predicate explicitly as:

```
not_max(X,Y,Z) :- X #< Y, Z #\= Y.
not_max(X,Y,Z) :- Z #\= X, Y #< X.
not_max(X,Y,Z) :- Z #\= X, Z #\= Y.
```

where #\= encodes disequality ($\neq$).

Abductive CLP programming was recently introduced by Kakas *et. al.* [57] and generalizes abductive logic programming (see the review by Kakas *et. al.* [56]). This is based on a dual view to the standard deductive operational semantics for CLP. The idea is that the goal is an observation which must be explained by additional hypothesis which are obtained by running the CLP program backwards. Somewhat related is inductive (constraint) logic programming in which the idea is to infer a logic program or CLP program which best explains some data/observations. Muggleton and De Raedt [72] provides an overview of inductive logic programming while the papers of Sebag and Rouveirol [96] and Padmanabhuni and Ghose [82] generalize it to a CLP context.

Answer set programming (ASP) is a form of logic programming devised for improved handling of negation, for programs that can be interpreted on small constraint domains. While ASP supports only = as a built-in constraint, it has proven to be an elegant formalism for modelling CSP. Programs are evaluated by model generation, as opposed to the query reduction detailed above for CLP. Intuitively, program clauses are used both for generating the search space and for constraining it. Efficient constraint solving is achieved through specialized propositional satisfaction solvers, but there is little support for search control [65].

Optimization

The classical semantics for CLP is restricted to answering satisfaction questions. Modern CLP languages provide minimization subgoals of the form `minimize(G, E)` [1] which require the system to find solutions of goal G which minimize the expression E.

In order to answer such minimization subgoals the underlying solver needs to provide strong enough minimization capabilities. In analogy to solver completeness, we say a program is *minimization complete* for goal G and expression E if the solver can determine the minimum value E can take for each answer c of G. In other words, it can determine $\min\{\theta(E) \mid D_C \models_\theta c\}$ if one exists. We assume that if a solver is minimization complete for a goal it is also solver complete.

In practice this usually means that each answer c of G should fix all the variables of E which makes the minimization calculation trivial since there is only one value $\theta(E)$. For solvers based on linear real constraints where the expression E was a linear expression we can use a linear programming algorithm to determine the value of this expression. Hence a CLP(R) program will be minimization complete for goal G and expression E if each answer c of G is such that for c all nonlinear constraints have enough fixed variables to become linear, and the expression E is linear once we simplify away the variables fixed by c.

The operational semantics can be extended to handle minimization subgoals as follows: A state $\langle L_1, \dots, L_m \mid c \rangle$ can be reduced as follows:

5. If L_1 is a minimization subgoal $minimize(G, E)$ there are two cases.

   a) If there is at least one answer c' of $\langle G \mid c \rangle$ where $m = \min\{\theta(E) \mid D_C \models_\theta c'\}$ and for all other answers c'' of $\langle G \mid c \rangle$ we have that $\min\{\theta(E) \mid D_C \models_\theta c''\} \geq$

---

[1] They also provide maximization subgoals `maximize(G,E)`, but from a semantic viewpoint these are equivalent to `minimize(G,-E)`.

m then it is reduced to

$$\langle G, L_2 \ldots, L_m \mathbin{\mathbf{I}} c \wedge E = m \rangle$$

b) If $\langle G \mathbin{\mathbf{I}} c \rangle$ is finitely failed or has an answer c' where $\min\{\theta(E) \mid D_C \models_\theta c'\}$ is unbounded, then it is reduced to $\langle \Box \mathbin{\mathbf{I}} false \rangle$.

Note that if the sub-derivation $\langle G \mathbin{\mathbf{I}} c \rangle$ does not terminate then there will be no minimization derivation step.

In practice this is not precisely the operational semantics used by most CLP systems since these may use information about the current best minimum value m to prune exploration of the remaining search space. We discuss this more fully in Section 12.5.3. However this idealized semantics captures the basic operational behavior of minimization.

It impossible to ascribe a logical or algebraic semantics to (this form of) minimization subgoals in general (see [68] for a more complete treatment of the semantics of optimization). For this chapter we restrict ourselves to the case that minimization is only used as the topmost goal. In practice this is usual.

We define the logical reading of $minimize(G, E)$ to be the formula

$$\exists M (G \wedge E = M \wedge \neg \bar{\exists}_{\{M\}} (G \wedge E < M))$$

and denote this by $mt(minimize(G, E))$. This captures that we want the answers to the minimization goal to be those solutions to G for which there is no other solution to G which makes the value of E smaller.

Both the logical and algebraic semantics are sound and complete with respect to this logical reading assuming that the goal to be minimized is finitely evaluable:

Theorem 12.26. *(Soundness and Completeness for Minimization)*
Let P be a $CLP(\mathcal{C})$ program, G be a finitely evaluable goal and E an expression, where P is minimization complete for G and E. Let $\mathcal{T}_\mathcal{C}$ be the constraint theory for constraint domain $\mathcal{C}$ and $\mathcal{D}_\mathcal{C}$ the interpretation. Then,

$$P^\star, \mathcal{T}_\mathcal{C} \models mt(minimize(G, E)) \leftrightarrow (\bar{\exists}_V c_1 \vee \ldots \vee \bar{\exists}_V c_n)$$

and

$$lm(P^\star, \mathcal{C}) \models mt(minimize(G, E)) \leftrightarrow (\bar{\exists}_V c_1 \vee \ldots \vee \bar{\exists}_V c_n)$$

where $c_1, \ldots, c_n$ are the answers of $minimize(G, E)$ and $V = vars(minimize(G, E))$.

12.3 CLP for Conceptual Modeling

Constraint logic programs provide an ideal conceptual modeling language since they provide a very expressive subset of first-order logic including existential quantification, and implications defining new constraints in terms of conjunctions and disjunctions of other constraints. We first demonstrate how CLP can be used to model constraint satisfaction problems (CSP) and then discuss how CLP provides considerably more concise and powerful ways of modeling problems than does the standard CSP formulation.

12.3.1   Formulating Standard CSPs

The standard class of constraint satisfaction problems (CSPs), studied in many of the chapters in this book, admits a fixed finite set of variables V, upon which are imposed a number of constraints. A unary *domain* constraint is imposed upon each variable, restricting the set of values it can take. The remaining constraints involve more than one variable. Each n-ary constraint has a *definition*, formally expressed as a set of n-tuples, and a *scope* which is a sequence of n variables from the set V. CLP offers a direct conceptual model for all CSPs in this class.

As we have seen CLP provides a very natural way to express logical combinations of constraints. Briefly, if the constraint $C1$ is the conjunction of $C2$ and $C3$, this can be expressed in CLP as `C1 :- C2, C3`. If, on the other hand, the constraint $C1$ is the disjunction of $C2$ and $C3$ then in CLP we can write

```
C1 :- C2.
C1 :- C3.
```

These two constructs allow us to naturally model CSPs.

Example 12.27. Consider the CSP which has variables X, Y, Z, with respective domains $\{1, 2, 3\}, \{2, 3, 4\}, \{1, 3\}$, and it has two constraints, $c1$ and $c2$. The constraint $c1$ has scope $\langle X, Y \rangle$ and definition $\langle 1, 2 \rangle, \langle 1, 3 \rangle, \langle 2, 3 \rangle$, and the constraint $c2$ has scope $\langle X, Z \rangle$ and definition $\langle 1, 1 \rangle, \langle 2, 2 \rangle, \langle 3, 3 \rangle$. This CSP is captured by the following program:

```
solve(X,Y,Z) :-
        X :: [1,2,3], Y :: [2,3,4], Z :: [1,3],
        c1(X,Y), c2(X,Z).

c1(1,2). c1(1,3). c1(2,3).

c2(1,1). c2(2,2). c2(3,3).
```

We have arbitrarily named the main predicate `solve`. The definition of the predicate `solve/3` comprises a domain constraint for each of the variables X, Y and Z, a constraint $c1$ on the variables X and Y, and a constraint $c2$ on the variables X and Z. The definition of $c1$ and $c2$ are given below.

In fact the above model of CSPs is a logic program whose execution requires no constraint solving beyond simple equality testing. As we shall see CLP languages allow us define the same problem in a manner that will execute far more efficiently than the model above.

12.3.2   Defining Constraints

The standard CSP formulation, in which a constraint is defined as a set of tuples, abstracts away from one of the key modeling issues in CP: how to define each constraint.

CLP systems typically provide equality and disequality as well as standard mathematical functions and relations, as illustrated in Example 12.1 in the Introduction as built-in, that is, primitive constraints. These built-in constraints also typically include so called *global constraints.* Standard examples are `alldifferent` [110, 87] also used in Example 12.1 and `cumulative` [2] which is useful in scheduling applications. Global constraints are complex, compound constraints which are useful in high-level modeling and which are logically equivalent to combination of simpler constraints but for which better operational behavior (such as more propagation) is possible if they are implemented as a single constraint rather than as a combination of simpler constraints. See Chapter 6 "Global Constraints" for a detailed discussion of global constraints.

As we have seen in Section 12.2, the code for `max` given in Example 12.3

```
max(X,Y,Z)  :-  X #>= Y,  Z #= X.
max(X,Y,Z)  :-  Y #>= X,  Z #= Y.
```

directly encodes the logical formula:

$$max(X,Y,Z) \leftrightarrow ((X \geq Y \wedge Z = X) \vee (Y \geq X \wedge Z = Y))$$

Note however that the use of multiple rules implies that search will be required to solve the constraint.

CLP programs allow local variables in constraints. These are implicitly existentially quantified.

Example 12.28. For example the following constraint requires that X is an even number.

```
even(X)  :-  X #= 2*Y.
```

Y is a local variable. Logically this corresponds to the constraint $\exists Y.(X = 2 \times Y)$.[2]

Note that local variables do not need to be given an initial domain. This example also illustrates a constraint whose "extent" is infinite. The number of solutions to the evenness constraint is unbounded, so it cannot be represented extensionally as we represented `c1` and `c2` in Example 12.27 above.[3]

This ability to encapsulate a CSP as a constraint, and to make any of the variables local to that constraint, makes it possible to construct complex CSPs from simple ones. In particular by keeping variables as "local" as possible, it is possible to minimize the worst case complexity for solving the complex CSP [70].

Moving further away from the standard CSP, we can define constraints recursively. The following program is an example of a constraint logic program over the reals.

Example 12.29. The *mortgage* constraint was introduced in [49]. The *mortgage* constraint relates the principal borrowed *Principal*; the interest rate paid on it in each time period *Interest*; the amount paid back in each time period *Payment*; the total number of time periods until the mortgage is paid off *Time*, and the *Balance* owing at the end of the mortgage.[4]

---

[2] *In ECLiPSe the relations symbols beginning with # (e.g. #>= and #=) constrain the variables involved to be integers. Hence in this code X must be even, since Y is an integer.*
[3] *Of course given a finite domain for X we could represent it finitely, but then we need a possibly different representation for each usage.*
[4] *In ECLiPSe the relation symbols beginning with \$ allow the variables involved to be real or integer. Hence for* mortgage *the variables involved are real numbers, except for* Time *which must be an integer.*

```
mortgage(Principal,Interest,Payment,Time,Balance) :-
    Time #>= 1,
    NewPrincipal $= Principal*(1+Interest) - Payment,
    NewTime #= Time - 1,
    mortgage(NewPrincipal,Interest,Payment,NewTime,Balance).
mortgage(Principal,Interest,Payment,Time,Balance) :-
    Time #= 0,
    Balance $= Principal.
```

In this version of the constraint:

1. The interest rate is the same in every time period

2. The payment is the same in every time period

3. The balance is the amount owing at the end of the last time period

Note that the number of primitive constraints collected in the constraint store will depend on the *Time* parameter. If *Time* takes the value n in the solution then $3n + 2$ primitive constraints will have been collected.

12.3.3   Data Structures

One of the strengths of CLP languages is that they inherit constraint solving over finite trees (i.e. terms) from logic programming languages. These provide standard data structures such as records, lists and trees. Such data structures are important because they allow the conceptual model and other constraints to be parametric in the number of variables. This is important because for many CSP problems and many constraints, the number of variables depends on the runtime data.

Lists are often used in global constraints, such as `alldifferent` used in the smm program of Example 12.1. In CLP the `alldifferent` constraint takes a single argument which is a list of variables. Typically this constraint is built-in, so there is no need to provide its definition in a conceptual model. If we wish to impose the constraint that, say, three variables X, Y and Z must take distinct values we write `alldifferent([X,Y,Z])` The syntax `[X,Y,Z]` denotes a list, with elements X, Y and Z.

Example 12.30. The well-known N-queens problem is to place N queens on an $N \times N$ chess board, so that no queen can take another. Below we given a CLP program defining `nqueens/2`, which defines the constraints for the N-queens problems where N is the first (integer) argument. Since each queen must be placed on a different row, we use a model in which there is a single variable for each queen, representing the column it must occupy. The first goal in the definition of `nqueens/2` below is `length(Queens,N)` This creates a list of N variables where the ith variable in the list represents the column occupied by the queen on the ith row. The syntax `Queens :: 1..N` is a shorthand which constrains each variable in the list `Queens` to take an integer value between 1 and N. The constraint `alldifferent(Queens)` ensures that all the queens are on different columns, while the constraint `safe(Queens)` is a recursively defined constraint which ensures that all the queens are on different diagonals.

```
nqueens(N,Queens) :-
    length(Queens,N),
    Queens :: 1..N,
    alldifferent(Queens),
    safe(Queens).

safe([Q1|Queens]) :-
    noattack(Queens, Q1, 1),
    safe(Queens).
safe([]).

noattack([Q2|Queens],Q1,Diff) :-
    Q1 + Diff #\= Q2,
    Q1 - Diff #\= Q2,
    Diff1 #= Diff + 1,
    noattack(Queens,Q1,Diff1).
noattack([],_,_).
```

The definition of safe/1 breaks its argument list into the first queen Q1 and the remaining queens Queens, checks the queen Q1 is on a different diagonal from the remaining queens Queens using noattack/3, and then calls itself recursively on the remaining queens.

The noattack check itself iterates over each of the remaining queens in turn, incrementing a counter Diff, as it goes through the list of remaining queens. The counter therefore reflects the number of rows between the first queen Q1 and the other queen Q2. Consequently the constraints Q1+Diff #\= Q2 and Q1-Diff #\= Q2 ensure that Q1 and Q2 are on different diagonals.

While space does not allow a complete introduction to programming in CLP, it is hoped that this small example program can provide a flavor of the conceptual modeling power of CLP. The reader is referred to [67, 110] for more examples.

Real constraint problems are rarely presented neatly as a set of decision variables under a set of constraints. Like the n-queens example above, they are often presented in an implicit form, from which the actual decision variables and constraints have to be extracted when the runtime data becomes available. For this purpose the additional data structures and programming constructs provide by CLP are required.

12.3.4 Optimization and Soft Constraints

Constraint problems arising in real applications are rarely just satisfaction problems. They are almost always optimization problems, where the number of resources is to be minimized or the value of activities carried out with the available resources is to be maximized.

This is modeled in a CLP conceptual model using the construct minimize(G,E) introduced in Section 12.2.6. Since the semantics of multiple, possibly nested minimization goals is unclear, CLP languages typically require that only one variable minimization goal is allowed. Historically this restriction to a single minimization goal has been achieved by associating the optimization requirement with the search component of the CLP design model, to be covered in the next section. We will follow historical precedence and also describe optimization in the next section.

Industrial applications of CP often allow constraints to be violated, i.e. treated as soft constraints, and maintain a measure of their violation to be included in the optimization expression. This is modeled in CLP by adding an extra argument to the constraint, and incorporating it in the expression to be optimized.

The following constraint succeeds without penalty if its arguments have different values, but incurs a penalty of one if they are the same:[5]

```
soft_diff(X,Y,0) :- X #\= Y.
soft_diff(X,X,1).
```

12.4   CLP for Design Modeling

Constraint logic programming not only provides a conceptual modeling language but also a design modeling language since the primitive constraints expressed in the conceptual model can be directly executed using the underlying constraint solver(s).

12.4.1   Constraint Solvers

One of the distinguishing features of CLP languages is that constraints are generated dynamically, and tests for satisfaction on the partially generated constraints controls subsequent execution and constraint generation. The `mortgage` program of Example 12.29 clearly illustrates this, the program will not terminate if we do not repeatedly check satisfiability during the derivation. This contrasts to say mathematical modeling languages in which constraint solving only takes place after the constraints are generated.

Incremental constraint solvers keep an internal solver state which represents the constraints encountered so far in the derivation. As new constraints are added the solver state is updated and checked for unsatisfiability. When the solver detects that the current state is unsatisfiable execution returns to the last state with an unexplored child state. The solver-state must be restored to a state equivalent to the solver-state at that point and continue execution on the unexplored derivation. This is called *backtracking*.

Example 12.31. Consider execution of the goal A #= 1, max(A,2,1) as shown in Example 12.6. The first derivation is tried, and on failure the solver-state represents the unsatisfiable constraint $A = 1 \land A = X \land 2 = Y \land 1 = Z \land X \geq Y$. Execution now backtracks to the state $\langle \text{max(A,2,1)} \mid A = 1 \rangle$ and the solver-state must be returned to represent the constraint $A = 1$.

As a consequence constraint logic programming has been the birthplace of a number of constraint solving algorithms for supporting incremental backtracking constraint solving. In Prolog II an incremental algorithm for solving equations and disequations was developed [27].

In $CLP(\mathcal{R})$ incremental Simplex algorithms were developed [54, 105] that, opposed to dual Simplex methods standard in operations research, handled strict inequalities, and detected all variables fixed by the constraints in order to help evaluate non-linear constraints. The solvers essentially use a dual Simplex method to be incremental. The incremental Simplex algorithms are complete when the constraints in the solver are linear, or all the

---

[5]As we shall see in the next section `soft_diff` is a *reified* disequality constraint.

non-linear constraints have had enough of the variables involved fixed by linear constraints to become linear. Similar approached were also developed in [113]

Finite domain solvers utilizing artificial intelligence techniques were first incorporated in CHIP [34]. Essentially the finite domain solver maintains a record of the possible values of each variable, its *domain*, and implements constraints as *propagators* that are executed when the domain of the variables involved change. Each propagator possibly reduces the domains of the variables involved in the constraint. The process is repeated until no propagator can change a domain of a variable. The solvers are incremental since adding a new constraint simply involves scheduling its propagators, and then remembering the propagators for later rescheduling. Finite domain solvers are guaranteed to be complete when every variable is fixed to a unique value.

Another important class of domain constraints are interval domains over floating point numbers. In this case propagation based techniques are also used to solve arithmetic constraints over the floating point numbers. The use of floating point intervals for constraint solving was suggested by Cleary [24] and independently by Hyvönen [48]. The first implementation in a CLP system was in BNR Prolog, and is discussed in [76, 77].

CLP solvers need to support backtracking. Typically backtracking is supported by *trailing* (inherited from the WAM machine of Prolog [122, 6]) or *copying* [94]. Trailing records changes made to the solver state, and then undoes the changes on backtracking. Copying simply copies the solver state, and backtracks by moving back to an old copy. There is also *semantic backtracking* [116] which rebuilds the previous state (or at least one that is semantically equivalent) using a set of high-level descriptions of changes. For a comparison of backtracking approaches see [95]

12.4.2 Understanding Solver Incompleteness

An important consideration in using a constraint logic programming system as a design modeling language is understanding the incompleteness of the solver as well as the interaction of its modeling capabilities with search.

The design modeler will want to ensure that each goal of interest is solver complete, that is, we are guaranteed the solver answers *true* or *false* at the end of each derivation.

When using a linear inequality solver based on the Simplex algorithm [54] for example the design model must ensure that any primitive constraints sent to the solver eventually become linear. Consider the `mortgage` example program, the nonlinear constraints for *NewPrincipal* can be ensured to become linear by using `mortgage` in a manner where *Interest* is eventually fixed, for example.

When using a finite domain propagation solver (e.g. [34]) or interval reasoning constraint solver (e.g. [78]) the design model must eventually ensure that every variable is fixed to reach a solver complete constraint store. For `mortgage` this can be ensured by eventually fixing *Interest* and *Payment* and one of *Principal* or *Balance* (since the remaining variables will be fixed by propagation).

The considerations of incompleteness of the solver must be matched against its modeling and search capabilities. For example a Simplex-based solver is complete for linear constraints, while interval reasoning is not. Nevertheless the interval reasoner returns variable bounds which Simplex does not. These bounds can be exploited for search, when constraints are posted to the interval solver. At each search node a variable is chosen, and its interval partitioned into subintervals which are explored on the different branches under the node. The intervals provide a stopping condition for the search: when all the intervals have a sufficiently small width. This kind of search is not possible if constraints are only posted to the Simplex-based solver.[6] For example the goal `mortgage(100,I,60,2,0)` will not lead to solver complete constraints for either solver, but with the interval solver we can enter a search process seeking a solution for I to an accuracy of 0.001 (`locate([I],0.001)` in ECLiPSe notation), which will determine the unique answer $I = 0.131$. Since the constraints are non-linear, it is not possible with a Simplex-based solver to follow a similar process of narrowing down the variable intervals.

12.4.3 Modeling and Disjunction

As we have seen, the basic approach to modeling disjunction in CLP languages, is to use multiple rules. The advantage of this form of disjunction is that it can be used with any underlying solver, but the disadvantage is that it usually leads to large search spaces.

Consider the `solve` predicate from Example 12.27. We can model the domain constraint `::` as

```
X :: L :- member(X,L).
```

```
member(X,[X|_]).
member(X,[_|R]) :- member(X,R).
```

The `member(X,L)` predicate effectively sets the variable X to each value in the list L in turn. Now all domain constraints are managed by the backtracking through derivations in the CLP system using only a solver that can test for term equality. The disadvantage of this approach is that we will search through $3 \times 3 \times 2 \times 3 \times 3 = 162$ derivations to find the two solutions. Note that since the Herbrand equation solver is complete all states only contain solver complete constraints.

Finite domain propagation solvers allow us express the "disjunctive" domain constraint directly without using multiple rules. A finite domain solver running the `solve` predicate from Example 12.27 will only require $3 \times 3 = 9$ derivations to be explored to find the 2 solutions. Here since the $c1$ and $c2$ constraints fix all the variables, again all derivations eventually lead to solver complete constraints.

But there are far better ways of handling the constraints $c1$ and $c2$. We can model them using a specific construct called a *table* which is handled by a finite domain propagation solver [84]. This ensures during search that the variables remain arc-consistent for the subproblem $c1 \wedge c2$. Alternatively we can model them in the usual way using multiple rules, but model the problem in a special way. The CLP syntax makes it easy to wrap a goal, or any part of it, in a higher-order predicate that can be used to control how it should be evaluated.

Example 12.32. Supposing the control predicate `prop` is implemented so that it handles its argument using constraint propagation. Then we can rewrite Example 12.27 as follows:

---

[6]Unless the problem is handled by maximising and minimising each variable in turn, which is computationally very much more costly than interval reasoning.

```
solve(X,Y,Z) :-
        X :: [1,2,3], Y :: [2,3,4], Z :: [1,3],
        prop( c1(X,Y) ), prop( c2(X,Z) ).

c1(1,2). c1(1,3). c1(2,3).

c2(1,1). c2(2,2). c2(3,3).
```

CLP languages have offered different control predicates, with different names and control behaviours. Some of these will be presented in section 12.4.6 below.

12.4.4 Reified Constraints

Most finite domain constraint solvers allow the user to add an extra Boolean argument to the simple primitive constraints, that enforces or prohibits the constraint according to the value of the Boolean.[7] For example the constraint `1 #= (X #= Y)` enforces the constraint $X = Y$ and is equivalent to the constraint `X #= Y`. On the other hand the constraint `0 #= (X #= Y)` prohibits $X = Y$ and is equivalent to `X #\= Y`. Hence `soft_diff(X,Y,B)` is equivalent to `B #= (X #= Y)`, but the reified constraint does not use multiple rules to define the "disjunctive" constraint.

CLP languages introduced reified constraints to finite domain constraint solvers, originally using a *cardinality* combinator [112] . They are now a standard feature of finite domain constraint solvers.

Let us represent a reified constraint as $c[B]$, where c is the original constraint, and B is the extra Boolean variable. The ideal behavior of the reified constraint $c[B]$ is to propagate domain reductions on its variables as follows:

- If, with the current domains, c is unsatisfiable, then propagate $B = 0$.

- If the constraint is satisfied by every combination of values from the domains of its variables, then propagate $B = 1$.

- If $B = 0$, then impose the constraint $\neg c$.

- If $B = 1$, then impose c

Some reified constraints in some CLP systems have weaker propagation than this, but all systems propagate a fixed Boolean value as soon as all the variables in c are instantiated.

Reified primitive constraints can be straightforwardly extended to reify logical combinations of primitive constraints using conjunction, disjunction, and implication. For example we can model conjunction $(c_1 \land c_2)[B]$ as $c1[B1] \land c2[B2] \land B = B1 \times B2$, and implication $(c_1 \rightarrow c_2)[B]$ as $c1[B1] \land c2[B2] \land B2 \geq B1$. The power of reified constraints is that they allow logical combinations of constraints to be expressed.

Example 12.33. We can re-define the *max* constraint of Example 12.3 using reification as follows:

---

[7]The facility can also be provided for linear inequalities in a integer linear programming solver where the variables have known finite possible ranges.

```
max(X,Y,Z) :- 1 #= ((X #>= Y and Z #= X) or
                     (Y #>= X and Z #= Y)).
```

Unfortunately, most CLP languages do not allow reification of non-primitive constraints and so the constraint must instead be defined by:

```
max(X,Y,Z) :-
        B11 #= (X #>= Y), B12 #= (Z #= X),
        B1 #= B11 * B12,
        B21 #= (Y #>= X), B22 #= (Z #= Y),
        B2 #= B21 * B22,
        B1 + B2 #>= 1.
```

Here $B11$ represents whether $X \geq Y$ holds, while $B12$ represents whether $Z = X$ holds. $B1$ represents the conjunction of $B1$ and $B2$, i.e. that the first rule holds. Similarly $B2$ represents the second rule similarly. Finally, at least one of $B1$ and $B2$ must be true. Systems that support reification of non-primitive constraints automatically convert the first form into the second.

The difference between this definition of max and the original definition is important. Both definitions have the same meaning, but they have very different operational behavior. The original definition selects the first clause in the definition of max, and imposes the constraints that $X \geq Y$ and $Z = X$. Only if the problem is insoluble under these constraints, or failure occurs for some other reason, does the CLP system try the other clause in the definition of max on *backtracking*.

By contrast, the definition using reified constraints does not make any "guesses" in order to satisfy the max goal. It imposes all the primitive reified constraints in the definition, and they propagate finite domain reductions according to their built-in propagation behavior. But one needs to be careful: the reified constraints do not propagate strongly as one might expect, as we shall see in the next example.

In the design model, to separate search from constraint propagation, it is necessary to avoid introducing any choice points into the definitions of the constraints.

12.4.5   Redundant Constraints

Since we are dealing with incomplete solvers, we must take care to understand exactly how completely our solver will deal with the design model that we create. In many cases we can add information to the solver that is logically redundant, but since the solver is incomplete, allows the solver to infer more information.

Example 12.34. Using the reified design model for max/3 from Example 12.33 we might expect that after the goal [X,Y,Z] :: 1..10, max(X,Y,Z), X #>= 4 the solver would reduce the domain of Z to 4..10. But it does not, since neither $B1$ or B can be fixed to 0 or 1, no information can be inferred by the reified model.

We can improve the design model of max to ensure this happens by adding the redundant constraints Z #>= X, Z #>= Y to the model. These are logically implied by the reified description but give different propagation behavior.

Note that another form of redundant constraints can also be usefully used in design modeling with CLP. When a predicate requires multiple rules in order to be expressed we can add redundant information in order to make information that is true of all disjunctive rules defining the constraint visible immediately.

Example 12.35. The constraint `Time #>= 1` in the *mortgage* program of Example 12.29 is redundant in the sense that in any success of mortgage using this rule the constraint must hold. If we omit it we will not change the answers to the program. But many goals, for example

```
10 #>= Time, mortgage(100, 0.1, Time, 20, Balance)
```

that would terminate for the original program will not terminate for the modified program since the first clause can succeed recursively infinitely many times with `Time` constrained to become more and more negative.

Before leaving this subsection, it should be noted that no definition of max in terms of reified constraints can maintain bounds or arc consistency.

Example 12.36. The troublesome case is illustrated by the following goal:

```
X :: 3..8,  [Y,Z] :: 1..10, max(X,Y,Z), Y #=< 6.
```

We would expect that the domain of Z would be reduced to 3..8. Unfortunately, it is still unknown whether $X \geq Y$ or $X < Y$ and consequently none of the reified constraints can propagate information about the upper bound of Z.

In the next section we shall therefore introduce facilities for propagating information that cannot be expressed simply as a conjunction of the built-in constraints introduced previously in this section.

12.4.6 Specifying Constraint Behavior

CLP systems offer many built-in constraints whose behavior is predefined. These include a wide variety of global constraints: Beldiceanu lists over 60 global constraints in [13].

However, there is no expectation that CLP systems could ever have built-in all the (global) constraints that will ever be needed. Accordingly CLP provides facilities to define new constraints, and specify their behavior. One of the most important directions in CLP research has been to move away from the original "black box" view of the underlying constraint solver of the first CLP languages to languages and systems which provide the programmer with a "glass box" view of the underlying constraint solving in which the programmer can extend, combine and even write new solvers [118].

One simple mechanism for supporting this inherited from logic programming languages is *dynamic scheduling*. Dynamic scheduling in CLP languages simply allows an atom to have an attached delay condition (usually in terms of arguments being fixed or non-variable) which prevents its execution until the current constraint store makes the condition true. Prolog-II [27] was the first system to incorporate dynamic scheduling using the `freeze` meta-predicate. Most modern CLP languages provide dynamic scheduling facilities. The use of dynamic scheduling for writing constraint solvers appears in the paper of Kawamura *et al* [59]. However the power of dynamic scheduling is essentially limited to writing local propagation based solvers or extensions where some variable become fixed allows us to fix other variables.

Holzbaur [45] has demonstrated that *attributed variables* are simple, powerful low-level method for extending logic programming languages with constraint solvers. These allow the programmer to associate arbitrary attributes with variables, i.e. named properties that can be used as storage locations as well as to extend the default unification algorithm when such variables are unified with other terms or with each other. Attributed variables are based on suspension (variables) provided in SICStus Prolog to support dynamic scheduling [18] and were introduced by Le Houitouze [47] and are very similar to meta-structures, introduced by Neumerkel [74] to allow user defined unification. They are provided in SICStus Prolog, ECLiPSe as well as other Prologs.

Support for solver extension is particularly useful for propagation-based finite domain solvers as it allows the programmer to introduce new global constraints with better propagation behavior. Almost all finite domain propagation solvers defined in CLP languages offer support for building new propagators by providing hooks into the underlying data structures and queuing mechanisms.

A higher level language construct for creating finite domain propagators, called indexicals, was first proposed in [117, 118] and then popularized by [33, 17]. An indexical is a primitive constraint of form of X *in* r, where X is a domain variable and r is a range expression. More complex finite domain arithmetic constraints are compiled into indexicals. For instance $X \leq Y$ is compiled to X *in* $-\infty..max(Y)$, Y *in* $min(X)..\infty$. This not only simplifies the implementation of finite domain solvers, but also allows the programmer to extend the finite domain solver by defining new constraints in terms of indexicals. Indexicals are provided in many recent CLP languages including GNU-Prolog [43] and SICStus Prolog.

Example 12.37. An indexical definition for the `max/3` predicate (using SICStus Prolog syntax since ECLiPSe does not support indexicals) is:

```
max(X,Y,Z) +:
    Z #>= X,
    Z #>= Y,
    Z in dom(X) \/ dom(Y).
```

The indexical constraint for Z ensures that it takes any possible value from the union of possible values of X and Y. Hence it will provide the propagation missing in Example 12.36.

Indexicals were inspired by concurrent constraint programming (CCP) languages [92] and in fact can be understood to be a CCP language called cc(FD) [117, 118]. In general this idea of defining a constraint solvers using CCP has proven very powerful. Such approaches include residuation [103] and action rules [124] .

CHR (Constraint Handling Rules) [41, 40] extend this approach by allowing the left-hand side of a rule to have multiple constraints. It can be used to program not only constraint propagators but also constraint reasoning rules. CHR resembles a production system. In CHR, the left-hand side of a rule specifies a pattern of constraints in the constraint store and the right-hand side specifies new constraints to replace those on the left-hand side or to be added into the store. Constraint handling rules were introduced by Frühwirth [41] and are described more fully in [40] and Chapter 13 "Constraints in Procedural and Functional Languages". CHRs are provided in CLP languages ECLiPSe, SICStus, and HAL [42].

Recent research has examined how to automatically define constraint handling rules [9, 1] given a disjunctive definition of a constraint using multiple rules. The constraint handling rules generated are guaranteed to perform all the inferences possible of a certain form, thus providing a powerful form of automating the construction of design model for a constraint.

The last approaches we discuss for defining constraint behaviors are based on defining the constraint using multiple clauses (which is the conceptual model of the constraint) and then mapping this definition, automatically, to a design model.

Generalized propagation [63] is one mechanism for doing this. As we saw earlier in Section 12.4.3, generalized propagation executes a multiple clause definition to extract the information that is true of all possible solutions. As more information is known about the arguments of the constraint re-execution will find less solutions and thus propagate more information that is true of all of them.

Example 12.38. The *max* example can be defined straightforwardly using generalized propagation as:

```
max(X,Y,Z)  :- max_basic(X,Y,Z) infers most.

max_basic(X,Y,Z)  :- X #>= Y, Z #= X.
max_basic(X,Y,Z)  :- Y #>= X, Z #= Y.
```

This version of `max/3` will infer the maximum possible information expressible as domains for any goal. Consider the goal from Example 12.36, initially when `max` is run the domain of X is 2..8. It will execute the two branches finding two answers: the first where Y has domain 1..8 and Z has domains 3..8 and the second where Y and Z are in 3..10. So the domain of Z is updated by the generalized propagator to $3..8 \cup 3..10 = 3..10$. When the domain of Y changes to 1..6 as a result of `Y #=< 6` the generalized propagator for `max` is re-executed this time determining that in the first answer Z has domain 3..8 and now in the second answer it has domain 3..6 so the domain is updated to 3..8. Note how the generalized propagation definition extracts both the information from the redundant constraints $Z \geq X \wedge Z \geq Y$ as well as the information about the maximal value.

Another form of generalized propagation is simply to construct all the ground solutions of the constraint and then define an arc consistency propagator on this table of ground values. The resulting table is used to construct an arc consistency propagator using an arc consistency algorithm such as AC3 or AC6. This was illustrated previously for the constraints *solve* program of Example 12.32.

The different forms of generalisation are selected by a parameter, so for Example 12.32 we use `Goal infers ac` instead of `prop(Goal)`.

12.5 Search in CLP

Search is an implicit part of constraint logic programming. Execution searches through the possible derivations in a depth-first left right manner. Because of this it is relatively straightforward to define specific search routines in constraint logic programs.

The aim of search is to overcome the incompleteness of the solver or its weakness in modeling the constraints required by the user (hence requiring multiple rules). In the first case the constraint programmer will add search predicates to enforce that the derivations are eventually solver complete. In the second case the constraint programmer should make use of disjunctive definitions that efficiently determine solutions.

The first case is the more usual case. For finite domain propagation solvers the search routine will almost always involve ensuring that enough variables are eventually fixed to enforce solver completeness.

CLP is a form of declarative programming, so we can say what a search predicate means, logically. A complete search routine finds all different ways of solving the problem, on backtracking. Logically, therefore, a complete search routine does not constrain its variables in any way that was not already implied by the constraints in the program. Given a variable X is defined with an initial domain $l..u$, the built in predicate indomain(X) is equivalent to $x = l \vee x = l+1 \vee \cdots \vee x = u$. The labeling predicate labeling shown in Example 12.2 is logically equivalent to *true*, since it just applies indomain to each of the variables in the list of its argument.

However, the search routine does something very important. Each path in the search *does* impose extra constraints on the variables that were not imposed at the root of the tree. Because the constraints at each leaf of the search tree are decided by the solver, this allows us to ensure the goal is solver complete.

In summary, a complete search routine elicits a disjunction of conjunctions of constraints that is logically equivalent to the input problem constraints. Instantiating variables, is just one way of adding constraints that drive the solver to a state where it will answer *true* or *false*.

There is a wide variety of possible search procedures we can write. In a finite domain example we typically have choices on which order to treat the variables, which order to treat values, whether we should explore the search tree in a depth-first or iterative-deepening manner. There are many kinds of search such as limited discrepancy search. All of these are programmable using constraint logic programs and reflection predicates.

12.5.1 Reflection

Programmable search is one of the most powerful features of constraint programming. In order to program search in CLP *reflection predicates* are provided which allow the constraint programmer to query the current state of the constraint store.

For finite domain propagation and interval reasoning solvers the most important reflection predicates return information about the current domains of variables. Information such as the current lower bound on a variable domain, current upper bound, the set of current possible domain values for a variable, as well as aggregate data such as the number of current possible domain values. For ECLiPSe ic solver some reflection predicates are e.g. get_min(X,L) which returns the minimum possible value L of a variable X get_domain_size(X,S) which returns the number of values S in the current domain of variable X, is_in_domain(X,V) which succeeds if V is a value in the current domain of variable X.

It is difficult to give any logical reading of the reflection predicates. Their use is usually restricted to programming search strategies, where the meaning of the program will not be affected by their interpretation (since the entire search will be logically equivalent to *true*), but of course the efficiency of the search in finding solutions will be highly dependent on their usage.

12.5.2 Search Control

Search can be specified in most CLP languages (and other constraint programming paradigms) by a single parameterized procedure with parameters for

- variable choice

- value choice

- method

The "method" specifies how the search tree is explored (for example depth-first), and alternative forms of incomplete search (for example bounded backtracking).

This makes it very simple to invoke standard (complete or incomplete) search routines, which instantiate variables in some order (which may be dynamic such as *first fail* where we pick the variable with the least number of remaining values), to values in their domains. CLP systems typically offer a parameterised search routine where the choices can be expressed as parameter values.

CLP is a "higher-order" language, that allows goals to be passed as arguments to other predicates. This makes CLP search very flexible. For example it enables the programmer to define a highly problem-specific variable choice routine, and pass it to the search procedure as an argument.

Example 12.39. We can define our own value selection strategy, in this case trying the median value, and then removing it from the domain, programmed using reflection predicates.

```
indomain_median(V) :-
    get_domain_as_list(V,List),
    median(List,M),
    choose(V,M).

choose(V,M)  :- V #= M.
choose(V,M)  :- V #\= M, indomain_median(V).
```

The code `indomain_median` gets the domain of V as a list D using the reflection predicate `get_domain_as_list`, finds the median M of the list D, and either sets V to M or removes M from the domain of the list and repeats. The definition of `median(List,M)` is omitted.

Again, because CLP supports a higher order syntax, such a user-defined value selection strategy can be passed to a generic search routine as a parameter.

In the remainder of this section we shall explore ways in which CLP offers more than just a set of search parameters. In particular we shall be looking at routines that program a specific search, search without necessarily instantiating variables, and at repair search.

Search states and choices

Heuristics are key to efficient search. Good heuristics depend on access to all aspects of the current search state. In CLP this information is typically linked to the decision variables.

Naturally the user can define whatever heuristic works best for the problem at hand. For scheduling it is sometimes best to choose the "start time" variable with the earliest available time in its domain. This does not fit into the "generic" variable choice and value choice search used previously, but we can straightforwardly program this heuristic using reflection predicates.

Example 12.40. An example of a programmed search strategy used in scheduling is to set the variable with the least possible value to this value or constrain it to be greater than this value. It can be programmed using reflection predicates as:

```
label_earliest([]).
label_earliest([X0|Xs]) :-
    get_min(X0, L0),
    find_earliest(Xs, X0, L0, X, L, R),
    try_earliest(X,L,R).

find_earliest([], X, L, X, L, []).
find_earliest([X1|Xs], X0, L0, X, L, [X0|R]) :-
    get_min(X1,L1),
    L1 #< L0,
    find_earliest(Xs, X1, L1, X, L, R).
find_earliest([X1|Xs], X0, L0, X, L, [X1|R]) :-
    get_min(X1,L1),
    L1 #>= L0,
    find_earliest(Xs, X0, L0, X, L, R).

try_earliest(X,L,R) :-
    X #= L,
    label_earliest(R).
try_earliest(X,L,R) :-
    X #> L,
    label_earliest([X|R]).
```

The code label_earliest finds the variable with the least minimum value using the predicate find_earliest, and then either sets it to its minimal value (and removes the variable from further consideration since it is now fixed), or sets it to be greater than the minimal value (and continues considering it) using try_earliest. The code for find_earliest(Xs, X0, L0, X, L, R) finds the variable X in $Xs \cup \{X0\}$ (given $X0$ has minimum domain value $L0$) with the least minimum domain value L, where R is the remaining set of variables $Xs \cup \{X0\} - \{X\}$.

To further illustrate the power of CLP we now consider a specific kind of heuristic information. This is a tentative value associated with each future variable. One very widely used method of constructing tentative values is to solve a relaxed problem, in which the awkward constraints are switched off and it is easy to find an optimal solution. The "linear relaxed" problem is very often used because efficient solvers are available for linear problems of a huge size (millions of variables and hundreds of thousands of constraints). One optimal solution is returned and the variable values in this solution are installed as tentative values to support a CLP search heuristic.

The variable chosen for labeling is typically the one whose tentative value most violates the relaxed constraints.

These heuristics often support more sophisticated choices than simply labeling a variable. For example the linear relaxation may not even return an integer value for a finite domain constraint (since finite domains cannot be expressed in terms of linear constraints). If the tentative value is, say 1.5, the choice made at the search node might be $X \leq 1$ on one branch and $X \geq 2$ on the other. This kind of choice is very easy to express in CLP by defining a branch predicate with two clauses:

```
branch(Var,Tent) :-
    Up is ceiling(Tent),
    Var #>= Up.
branch(Var,Tent) :-
    Down is floor(Tent),
    Var #=< Down.
```

Here Var is the chosen variable, and $Tent$ is its current tentative value. The added constraints $Var \geq Up$ and $Var \leq Down$ are posted to the constraint solver used by the programmer. This may be a linear constraint solver, a finite domain solver, or a continuous interval solver, for example. The key point is that for the search to do its job, the constraints imposed at each search step should accumulate until the constraint store becomes solver complete.

Posting inequalities is the standard form of choice for problems involving continuous decision variables. These problems arise on robotics, chemistry and many complex scientific and engineering applications. The constraints in these kinds of applications are typically non-linear and can only be handled by sophisticated "global optimization" techniques.[8] Constraint programming with interval solvers are proving very effective for solving such problems [111, 79].

Unfortunately, posting inequalities does not guarantee that solver completeness is reached after any reasonable number of steps. Instead, at the leaves of the search tree we require the variables to fall within a "sufficiently small interval". The answer returned by a CLP system is a conjunction of constraints which entail the goal. However in case the goal is not solver complete, there is no guarantee that this conjunction is satisfiable. In this case, therefore, the constraints comprise not only an interval for each constraint, but also further constraints on the variables for which the solver can neither decide if they are entailed nor if they are disentailed by the interval constraints. It *is* however guaranteed that no solutions lie outside the final intervals returned on all the branches of the search tree.

Local search

The tentative values used as heuristics for tree search, as introduced above, can also be used in a different way for local search. Many CLP systems support a facility for propagating changes to the tentative values. To enforce the constraint $Z = X + Y$, these systems recompute a new tentative value for Z whenever the tentative values of X or Y are updated. Moreover for other constraints a measure of the degree of violation can be propagated on

---

[8]See http://www.mat.univie.ac.at/~neum/glopt.html.

updates to the variables occurring in the constraints in the same way. This approach was pioneered in the Localizer system [115].

To search for a solution, these CLP systems allow the programmer to simply change the tentative values associated with one or more variables, propagating the changes automatically. These updates can be used to compute the quality of the new tentative variable assignment, in terms of the degree of constraint violation, or simply the tentative value of a global cost variable. This facility supports a wide variety of local search mechanisms from hill climbing, to simulated annealing and tabu search [114]. For more information on local search, see Chapter 5 "Local Search Methods".

12.5.3   Optimization and Search

We finish off the section by remarking on the interaction between search and optimization in constraint logic programming. Mostly optimization search in constraint logic programming is simply a combination of the search primitives discussed above with an optimization subgoal such as `minimize/2` introduced in Section 12.2.6.

There are typically at least two forms of minimization subgoal provided in CLP systems. The usual default minimization is a form of branch and bound, that once a new answer is found with a better minimal value, effectively imposes a new constraint requiring solutions to be smaller than the new best value obtained, and continues the search. The second approach is to restart the search from the beginning whenever a new minimum value is found, including a new constraint requiring solutions to be better than the new best value. This may have better behavior than the branch and bound methods when the variable choice heuristics are strongly influenced by the new bound.

Minimization exploits the higher-order syntax of CLP: any search goal can be given as the first argument to the higher-order predicate `minimize/2`. After execution, the second argument is instantiated to the minimum.

12.6   Impact of CLP

Research initiated in CLP, and covered in this volume

CLP provides a powerful and practical framework for thinking about constraint satisfaction and optimization problems. Indeed it was within the CLP paradigm that many of the concepts and research directions described in this handbook were first introduced. For example global constraints were introduced in CLP [14]; it was within the CLP paradigm that multiple cooperating constraint solvers were introduced [15]; it is within the CLP community that much of the research has taken place exploring the interface between Operations Research and Artificial Intelligence [120]; recently modeling languages for local search have also emerged from CLP [115].

Constraint databases

Much early CLP-inspired research was based on the idea that if constraints could so successfully be added to the logic programming paradigm, then why not add them to other (usually declarative) paradigms. Two important outcomes of this were constraint databases and concurrent constraint logic programming.

The paper [50] gave both a logical reading for a CLP program and a fixpoint semantics which provided a theoretical bottom-up evaluation mechanism for CLP programs. A natural consequence of this is to think of a CLP program as a kind of database, in the same way as logic programs can be considered to be deductive databases. Kanellakis, Kuper and Revesz [58] were the first to formally define a constraint database in terms of "generalized tuples" which extended standard relational databases by allowing tuples in the database to have attributes implicitly defined by associated constraints. The topic of constraint databases is now a fertile research area. The recent book by Revesz [88] provides a good introduction and overview.

Concurrent constraint programming

The concurrent constraint programming languages were another major offshoot of CLP. They generalized research on concurrent logic languages to handle constraints. Clark and Gregory introduced committed choice and don't care non-determinism into Prolog [22]. For more information about concurrent logic languages see the survey by Shapiro [97]. Maher generalized concurrent logic languages to the constraint setting by recognizing that the synchronization operator used in concurrent logic languages can be thought of as constraint entailment [66]. The formal properties of concurrent constraint programming languages have been widely studied since then. In particular, Saraswat has provided elegant theoretical semantics for these languages [92] and was responsible for the term "concurrent constraint programming." A number of concurrent constraint programming languages have been designed and implemented [44, 118], but arguably their greatest impact has been in the implementation of constraint solvers in CLP systems. One notable exception to this is the Mozart [71] implementation of the Oz language which combines concurrent constraint programming with distribution and object oriented programming. For more details on Oz see Chapter 13 "Constraints in Procedural and Concurrent Languages".

Constraints and other programming paradigms

Given the success of CLP it was also natural to investigate the combination of solving constraints with the other major declarative programming language paradigm–functional programming. The first approach is due to Darlington *et al* [30]. The paper of Crossley *et al* [29] describes the constrained lambda calculus approach in which only definite values can be communicated from the constraint store. The Oz programming language has been developed by Smolka. In addition to incorporating functional and concurrent constraint programming, it also provides objects. It is introduced in [101, 102].

Combining constraints with term rewriting began with augmented term rewriting introduced by Leler in [64]. Constrained term rewriting generalizes ordered rewriting systems. An introduction is given by Kirchner [60]. Constraints have also been integrated into type inference by Odersky *et. al.* [75] and Bürckett has given a resolution-based proof mechanism for full logic that incorporates constraint solving [16].

Combining constraints with imperative programming languages has not been investigated very fully. Kaleidoscope [39] developed by Borning and others, is one of the few examples of such languages. The combination does not seem very successful because of the conflict between the imperative programmer's desire to fully know the state of every variable during execution and the constraint programming view of complex flow of information.

Much more successful have been object-oriented constraint solving toolkits. In the toolkit approach the programmer is limited in their handling of constraints and constrained variables by the abstract data type provided by the toolkit. CHARME [80] and ILOG SOLVER [84] are commercial constraint-solving toolkits for finite domain constraints. They are both off shoots of the CLP language CHIP developed at ECRC and use similar propagation based constraint solving techniques. An object oriented Lisp based toolkit called PECOS [85] was the precursor to ILOG SOLVER.

CLP and problem modelling

One recent impact of CLP languages has been on mathematical modeling languages. Mathematical modeling languages were first introduced in the 1970's, replacing matrix generators as the way of specifying large linear programs. The majority of mathematical modeling languages are designed for real linear arithmetic constraints with real linear optimization functions, since these are the constraints supported by the underlying solvers used by the modeling languages. Mixed integer constraints are supported by later modeling languages. AMPL [7] fits in this category and also provides additional forms of modeling such as facilities for modeling graphs. There has been some research on extending MIP based modeling languages to support CP-like global constraints [86] and more ambitiously to support both CP and MIP solvers. Of particular note is the OPL modeling language [109] which dramatically extends mathematical modeling languages by providing CP-like global constraints and search as well as sophisticated data structures. Again the interested reader is referred to Chapter 13 "Constraints in Procedural and Concurrent Languages."

Industrial applications

Finally, CLP and CP constraint solving toolkits are widely used in industrial applications. One of the first industrial applications of CLP was for the container port of Hong Kong in 1990. Since then several constraint-based technology companies have emerged in Europe, America and Asia. ILOG, is a major such company with revenues of 125Million dollars per annum. ILOG's website claims that "Because only ILOG can boast a technology portfolio that includes both ILOG CPLEX for mathematical programming and ILOG CP for constraint programming—the proven foundation of planning and scheduling systems—8 of the Top 10 ERP/SCM vendors have embedded ILOG's core technologies".

CLP is used by major companies for production scheduling transport scheduling, financial planning and a host of resource planning and scheduling applications. CLP is not only used for traditional resource planning and scheduling but for the new generation of companies and applications: Cisco uses CLP for its internet routing products, and Cadence—the electronic design automation company—is a major user of constraint technology.

12.7   Future of CLP and Interesting Research Questions

It is almost exactly 20 years since the CLP paradigm was introduced. It has been an important component in the success of CP, providing the initial reason for the "programming" component. One impact has been on logic programming. CLP is now a cornerstone of logic programming theory, systems and applications. Standard logic programming systems, such as GNU-Prolog and SICStus Prolog now provide constraint solving libraries. It has also received substantial interest from researchers into computational logic and has had considerable impact on database research, and we believe an increasing impact on modeling language design.

It is worth summarizing the strengths of CLP. CLP languages are fully-fledged programming languages meaning that they provide the constraint programmer with great power for modeling problems, for specifying problem specific search heuristics and for experimenting with hybrid constraint solving techniques. They provide powerful and flexible search control and modern CLP languages provide a variety of techniques, such as attributed variables, indexicals, CHRs, for extending the constraint solver.

However, CLP languages have some drawbacks, which are driving the current research programs in this area.

First, some features inherited from logic programming—and more particularly Prolog—need to be learnt and comprehended for modeling and especially for writing search or hybrid solvers. It is awkward to use recursion rather than iteration, compile time checking is limited, there is an unwieldy syntax for arrays, overloading of standard mathematical operators is not supported and standard mathematical syntax is not available for modeling problems. There is no sharp distinction between the conceptual and the design model, and the data is part of the program. The difficulty of programming in CLP languages was identified as a problem in [91].

One solution is to modify and extend the syntax of CLP languages to be closer to standard mathematical modeling. For instance, the CLP language ECLiPSe provides iteration allowing conceptual modeling closer to traditional modeling languages. Arguably, the modeling language OPL can be viewed as a (very) restricted CLP language. Although this seems easy, there is considerable tension between the aims of designing a simple, mathematical like modeling language, and a language expressive enough to allow the programmer to specify problem-specific constraint solving techniques. Another approach is to explore the use of a problem-domain specific visual front ends. Yet a third, is to build a modeling language on top of the CLP systems.

A major strength of CLP is a simple, elegant declarative semantics which brings together logical, algebraic and operational viewpoints. As a result CLP is a powerful and precise language for modelling problems. With the facilities for constraint solving and search control, CLP is also a clean and powerful tool for solving problems. In this respect, however, the declarative semantics serves little purpose: a highly efficient program can have the same declarative semantics as a hopelessly inefficient one.

Programming semantics for CLP which allows design models to be compared for efficiency is now required. This semantics must account for optimisation, reflection, search, and constraint handling. Work on semantics for propagators is partially addressing this issue but much more work is required to build CLP semantics that enables us to directly compare CLP models with the same declarative semantics so that we can predict which will use more computational resources and under what circumstances.

The chronological backtracking search model of CLP languages needs to be combined with local search techniques in which the search state is updated by local changes. The combination of backtrack-based tree search and local search is an exciting research area.

With the flexibility of CLP comes a runtime overhead, which especially penalises the implementation of constraint solvers within the CLP language itself. The goal of increasing efficiency of CLP languages has been addressed for many years. Approaches include better compilation, local and global analysis, and programmer mode and type declarations [42]. On the other hand the declarative nature of CLP makes it naturally parallelisable [83, 31]. Many feel that the coming generation of hardware will be dependent on parallelism for continued speed improvements, and that declarative paradigms like CLP will therefore become increasingly important.

Bibliography

[1] S. Abdennadher and C. Rigotti. Automatic generation of rule-based solvers for intentionally defined constraints. *International Journal of Artificial Intelligence Tools* 11(2):283–302, 2002.

[2] A. Aggoun and N. Beldiceanu. Extending CHIP in order to solve complex scheduling problems. In *Proc. JFPL*, Lille, 1992.

[3] A. Aiba, K. Sakai, Y. Sato, D. J. Hawley, and R. Hasegawa. Constraint logic programming language CAL. In *Proceedings of the International Conference on Fifth Generation Computer Systems*, pages 263–276, December 1988.

[4] H. Aït-Kaci and P. Lincoln. LIFE: A natural language for natural language. Technical Report ACA-ST-074-88, MCC, 1988.

[5] H. Aït-Kaci and R. Nasr. LOGIN: A logic programming language with built-in inheritance. *Journal of Logic Programming*, 3(3):187–215, 1986.

[6] Hassan Aït-Kaci. *Warren's Abstract Machine: A Tutorial reconstruction*. MIT Press, 1991.

[7] AMPL. Ampl: A modeling language for mathematical programming. www.ampl.com.

[8] K. Apt and R. Bol. Logic programming and negation: A survey. *Journal of Logic Programming*, 19/20:9–71, 1994.

[9] K. Apt and E. Monfroy. Constraint programming viewed as rule-based programming. *Theory and Practice of Logic Programming*, 1(6):713–750, 2001.

[10] K. Apt and M. van Emden. Contributions to the theory of logic programming. *JACM*, 29:841–862, 1982.

[11] R. Barbuti, P. Mancarella, D. Pedreschi, and F. Turini. Intensional negation of logic programs: Examples and implementation techniques. In *TAPSOFT, Vol.2. Proceedings of the International Joint Conference on Theory and Practice of Software Development,*, volume 250 of *Lecture Notes in Computer Science*, pages 96–110. Springer, 1987.

[12] R. Barbuti, P. Mancarella, D. Pedreschi, and F. Turini. A transformational approach to negation in logic programming. *Journal of Logic Programming*, 8(3):201–228, 1990.

[13] N. Beldiceanu. Global constraints as graph properties on a structured network of elementary constraints of the same type. In Rina Dechter, editor, *CP*, volume 1894 of *Lecture Notes in Computer Science*, pages 52–66. Springer, 2000. ISBN 3-540-41053-8.

[14] N. Beldiceanu and E. Contjean. Introducing global constraints in CHIP. *Mathematical and Computer Modelling*, 12:97–123, 1994.

[15] H. Beringer and B. De Backer. Combinatorial problem solving in constraint logic

programming with cooperating solvers. In *Logic Programming: Formal Methods and Practical Applications*, pages 245–272. Elsevier, 1995.

[16] H.-J. Bürckert. A resolution principle for constrained logics. *Artificial Intelligence*, 66:235–271, 1994.

[17] B. Carlson, M. Carlsson, and D. Diaz. Entailment of finite domain constraints. In *Logic Programming — Proceedings of the Eleventh International Conference on Logic Programming*, pages 339–353. MIT Press, 1196.

[18] M. Carlsson. Freeze, indexing, and other implementation issues in the WAM. In *Proceedings of the Fourth International Conference on Logic Programming*, pages 40–58. MIT Press, 1987.

[19] D. Chan. Constructive negation based on the completed database. In *Proceedings, 5th Int. Conf. and Symp. on Logic Programming*, pages 111–125. MIT Press, 1988.

[20] A. M. Cheadle, W. Harvey, A. Sadler, J. Schimpf, K. Shen, and M. Wallace. ECL^{i}PS^e. Technical Report 03-1, IC-Parc, Imperial College London, 2003.

[21] K. Clark. Negation as failure. In H. Gallaire and J. Minker, editors, *Logic and Databases*, pages 293–322. Plenum Press, 1978.

[22] K. Clark and S. Gregory. A relational language for parallel programming. In *Proc. ACM Conference on Functional Languages and Computer Architecture*, pages 171–178. ACM Press, 1981.

[23] K. Clark and F. McCabe. IC-Prolog - language features. In K. Clark and S. Tarnlund, editors, *Logic Programming*, pages 122–149. Academic Press, 1982.

[24] J. Cleary. Logical arithmetic. *Future Computing Systems*, 2(2):125–149, 1987.

[25] A. Colmerauer. PROLOG II reference manual and theoretical model. Technical report, Groupe Intelligence Artificielle, Université Aix – Marseille II, October 1982.

[26] A. Colmerauer. Opening the PROLOG-III universe. *BYTE Magazine*, 12(9), August 1987.

[27] A. Colmerauer. Equations and inequations on finite and infinite trees. In *Proceedings of the International Conference on Fifth Generation Computer Systems*, pages 85–99, Tokyo, 1984.

[28] W. Cronholm and Ajili F. Hybrid branch-and-price for multicast network design. In *Proceedings of the 2nd International Network Optimization Conference (INOC 2005),*, pages 796–802, 2005.

[29] J. Crossley, L. Mandel, and M. Wirsing. First-order constrained lambda calculus. In F. Baader and K. U. Schulz, editors, *Frontiers of Combining Systems 96—First International Workshop*, pages 339–356. Kluwer, 1996.

[30] J. Darlington, Y.-K. Guo, and H. Pull. A new perspective on integrating functional and logic languages. In *Fifth Generation Computer Systems*, pages 682–693, Tokyo, Japan, 1992.

[31] M. Garcia de la Banda, M.Hermenegildo, and K. Marriott. Independence in CLP languages. *ACM Transactions on Programming Languages and Systems*, 22(2): 296–339, 2000.

[32] D. DeGroot and G. Lindstrom, editors. *Logic Programming: Relations, Functions, and Equations*, 1985. Prentice-Hall.

[33] D. Diaz and P. Codognet. A minimal extension of the WAM for clp(FD). In D.S. Warren, editor, *Logic Programming: Proceedings of the 10th International Conference*, pages 774–792, Budapest, Hungary, June 1993. MIT Press.

[34] M. Dincbas, P. Van Hentenryck, H. Simonis, and A. Aggoun. The constraint logic

programming language CHIP. In *Proc. Second Int. Conf. Fifth Generation Computer Systems*, pages 249–264, 1988.

[35] H. Enderton. *A Mathematical Introduction to Logic.* Academic Press, 1972.

[36] F. Fages. Constructive negation by pruning. *Journal of Logic Programming*, 32(2): 85–118, 1997.

[37] R.E. Fikes. REF-ARF: A system for solving problems stated as procedures. *Artificial Intelligence Journal*, 1(1), 1970.

[38] A. Foster and E. Elcock. Absys1: An incremental compiler for assertions: An introduction. In B. Melzer and D. Mitchie, editors, *Machine Intelligence 4*. Edinburgh University Press, 1969.

[39] B. Freeman-Benson and A. Borning. The design and implementation of Kaleidoscope'90: A constraint imperative programming language. In *Proc. IEEE Int. Conf. Computer Languages*, pages 174–180. IEEE Computer Soc. Press, 1992.

[40] T. Frühwirth. Theory and practice of constraint handling rules. *Journal of Logic Programming*, 37:95–138, 1998.

[41] T. Frühwirth. Constraint simplification rules. In A. Podelski, editor, *Constraint Programming: Basics and Trends*, volume 910 of *LNCS*. Springer-Verlag, 1995.

[42] M. García de la Banda, B. Demoen, K. Marriott, and P.J. Stuckey. To the gates of HAL: a HAL tutorial. In *Proceedings of the Sixth International Symposium on Functional and Logic Programming*, volume 2441 of *LNCS*, pages 47–66. Springer-Verlag, 2002.

[43] GNU Prolog. www.gnu.org/software/gprolog/gprolog.html.

[44] D. Gudeman, K. De Bosschere, and S. Debray. jc: An efficient and portable implementation of Janus. In K. Apt, editor, *Logic Programming: Proceedings of the 1992 Joint International Conference and Symposium*, pages 399–413, Washington, November 1992. MIT Press.

[45] C. Holzbaur. *Specification of Constraint Based Inference Mechanisms through Extended Unification.* PhD thesis, Dept. of Medical Cybernetics & AI, University o Vienna, October 1990.

[46] H. Hong. Non-linear constraint solving over real numbers in constraint logic programming (introducing RISC-CLP). Technical Report 92-08, Research Institute for Symbolic Computation, Johannes Kepler University, Linz, Austria, 1992.

[47] S. Le Huitouze. A new data structure for implementing extensions to Prolog. In *Proceedings of the Conference on Programming Language Implementation and Logic Programming*, pages 136–150. Springer, 1990.

[48] E. Hyvönen. Constraint reasoning based on interval arithmetic. In *Proceedings of the Eleventh International Joint Conference on Artificial Intelligence*, pages 193–199, Detroit, 1989.

[49] J. Jaffar and J.-L. Lassez. Constraint logic programming. In *POPL*, pages 111–119, 1987.

[50] J. Jaffar and J.-L. Lassez. Constraint logic programming. In *Proceedings of the 14th ACM Symposium on Principles of Programming Languages*, pages 111–119, Munich, Germany, January 1987. ACM Press.

[51] J. Jaffar and M. Maher. Constraint logic programming: A survey. *Journal of Logic Programming*, 19/20:503–582, 1994.

[52] J. Jaffar and P. Stuckey. Semantics of infinite tree logic programming. *Theoretical Computer Science*, 42(4):141–158, 1986.

[53] J. Jaffar, J.-L. Lassez, and M. Maher. A logic programming language scheme. In D. DeGroot and G. Lindstrom, editors, *Logic Programming: Relations, Functions and Equations*, pages 441–468. Prentice Hall, 1986.

[54] J. Jaffar, S. Michaylov, P.J. Stuckey, and R.H.C. Yap. The CLP($\mathcal{R}$) language and system. *ACM Transactions on Programming Languages and Systems*, 14(3):339–395, 1992.

[55] J. Jaffar, M. Maher, K. Marriott, and P.J. Stuckey. The semantics of constraint logic programs. *Journal of Logic Programming*, 37(1–3):1–46, 1998.

[56] A. Kakas, R. Kowalski, and F. Toni. Abductive logic programming. *Journal of Logic Programming*, 2(6):719–770, 1992.

[57] A. Kakas, A. Michael, and C. Mourlas. Aclp: Abductive constraint logic programming. *Journal of Logic Programming*, 44(1-3):129–177, 2000.

[58] P. Kanellakis, G. Kuper, and P. Revesz. Constraint query languages. *Journal of Computer and System Science*, 51(1):26–52, 1995.

[59] T. Kawamura, H. Ohwada, and F. Mizoguchi. CS-Prolog: A generalized unification based constraint solver. In K. Furukawa et al, editor, *Sixth Japanese Logic Programming Conference*, volume 319 of *LNCS*, pages 19–39. Springer Verlag, 1987.

[60] H. Kirchner. Some extensions of rewriting. In H. Comon and J.-P. Jouannaud, editors, *Term Rewriting*, volume 909 of *LNCS*, pages 54–73. Springer Verlag, 1994.

[61] K. Kunen. Negation in logic programming. *Journal of Logic Programming*, 4: 289–308, 1987.

[62] J.-L. Laurière. A language and a program for stating and solving combinatorial problems. *Artificial Intelligence*, 10:29–127, 1978.

[63] T. Le Provost and M. Wallace. Generalised constraint propagation over the CLP scheme. *Journal of Logic Programming*, 16(3):319–360, 1993.

[64] W. Leler. *Constraint Programming Languages: Their Specification and Generation*. Addison–Wesley, 1988.

[65] V. Lifschitz. Introduction to answer set programming. URL http://www.cs. utexas.edu/users/vl/mypapers/esslli.ps. 2004.

[66] M. Maher. Logic semantics for a class of committed-choice programs. In J.-L. Lassez, editor, *Logic Programming: Proceedings of the 4th International Conference*, pages 858–876, Melbourne, Australia, May 1987. MIT Press.

[67] K. Marriott and P.J. Stuckey. *Programming with Constraints: an Introduction*. MIT Press, 1998.

[68] K. Marriott and P.J. Stuckey. Semantics of constraint logic programs with optimization. *ACM Letters on Programming Languages and Systems*, 2(1–4):197–212, 1993.

[69] MATLAB. Matlab. www.mathworkds.com.

[70] U. Montanari and F. Rossi. Perfect relaxation in constraint logic programming. In *ICLP*, pages 223–237, 1991.

[71] Mozart. Mozart-oz. www.mozart-oz.org.

[72] S. Muggleton and L. De Raedt. Inductive logic programming: Theory and methods. *Journal of Logic Programming*, 19/20:629–679, 1994.

[73] L. Naish. The MU-PROLOG 3.2db reference manual. Technical report, Department of Computer Science, University of Melbourne, Victoria, Australia, 1985.

[74] U. Neumerkel. Extensible unification by metastructures. Metaprogramming in Logic (META'90), 1990.

[75] Martin Odersky, Martin Sulzmann, and Martin Wehr. Type inference with constrained types. *TAPOS*, 5(1):35–55, 1999.

[76] W. Older and A. Vellino. Extending Prolog with constraint arithmetic on real intervals. In *Proceedings of the Canadian Conference on Electrical and Computer Engineering*, pages 14.1.1–14.1.4, 1990.

[77] W. Older and A. Vellino. Constraint arithmetic on real intervals. In F. Benhamou and A. Colmerauer, editors, *Constraint Logic Programming: Selected Research*, pages 175–195. MIT Press, 1993.

[78] W. Older and A. Vellino. Constraint arithmetic on real intervals. In F. Benhamou and A. Colmerauer, editors, *Constraint Logic Programming: Selected research*, chapter 10. MIT Press, 1993.

[79] W. J. Older and F. Benhamou. Programming in CLP(BNR). In *PPCP*, pages 228–238, 1993.

[80] A. Oplobedu, J. Marcovitch, and Y. Tourbier. Charme: Un langage industriel de programmation par contraintes, illustré par une application chez renault. In *Ninth International Workshop on Expert Systems and their Applications: General Conference, Volume 1*, pages 55–70, Avignon, May 1989. EC2.

[81] W. Ouaja and Richards E. B. A hybrid multicommodity routing algorithm for traffic engineering. *Networks*, 43(3):125–140, 2004.

[82] S. Padmanabhuni, J.-H. You, and A. Ghose. A framework for learning constraints: Preliminary report. In *Learning and Reasoning with Complex Representations, PRICAI'96 Workshops on Reasoning with Incomplete and Changing Information and on Inducing Complex Representations*, volume 1359 of *Lecture Notes in Computer Science*, pages 133–147. Springer, 1998.

[83] S. Prestwich and S. Mudambi. Improved branch and bound in constraint logic programming. In U. Montanari and F. Rossi, editors, *Constraint Programming: Proceedings of the 1st International Conference*, volume 976 of *LNCS*, pages 533–548. Springer Verlag, 1995.

[84] J.-F. Puget. A C++ Implementation of CLP. In *Proceedings of SPICIS'94*, Singapore, November 1994.

[85] J.-F. Puget. PECOS: A High Level Constraint Programming Language. In *Proceedings of SPICIS'92*, Singapore, September 1992.

[86] P. Refalo. Linear formulation of constraint programming models and hybrid solvers. In *Principles and Practice of Constraint Programming (CP'2000)*, number 1894 in LNCS, pages 369–383. Springer, 2000.

[87] J.-C. Regin. A filtering algorithm for constraints of difference in CSPs. In *Proc. AAAI*, pages 362–367, 1994.

[88] P. Revesz. *Introduction to Constraint Databases*. Springer, 2002.

[89] R. Rodosek and M. G. Wallace. A generic model and hybrid algorithm for hoist scheduling problems. In *CP '98: Proceedings of the 4th International Conference on Principles and Practice of Constraint Programming*, pages 385–399, London, UK, 1998. Springer-Verlag.

[90] R. Rodosek, M. G. Wallace, and M. Hajian. A new approach to integrating mixed integer programming with constraint logic programming. *Annals of Operations research*, 86:63–87, 1999.

[91] F. Rossi. Constraint (logic) programming: A survey on research and applications. In *New Trends in Constraints*, volume 1865 of *Lecture Notes in Computer Science*

pages 40–74. Springer, 1999.

[92] V. Saraswat. *Concurrent Constraint Programming*. ACM Distinguished Dissertation Series. MIT Press, 1993.

[93] Taisuke Sato and Hisao Tamaki. Transformational logic program synthesis. In *FGCS*, pages 195–201, 1984.

[94] C. Schulte. Comparing trailing and copying for constraint programming. In Danny De Schreye, editor, *Proceedings of the International Conference on Logic Programming*, pages 275–289. MIT Press, 1999.

[95] Christian Schulte. *Programming Constraint Services*, volume 2302 of *Lecture Notes in Artificial Intelligence*. Springer-Verlag, 2002.

[96] M. Sebag and C. Rouveirol. Polynomial-time learning in logic programming and constraint logic programming. In *Inductive Logic Programming Workshop*, volume 1314 of *Lecture Notes in Computer Science*, pages 105–126. Springer, 1997.

[97] E. Shapiro. The family of concurrent logic programming languages. *ACM Computing Surveys*, 21(3):412–510, 1989.

[98] J.R. Shoenfield. *Mathematical Logic*. Addison-Wesley, 1967.

[99] SICStus Prolog. www.sics.se/sicstus/.

[100] G. Sidebottom and W. Havens. Hierarchical arc consistency for disjoint real intervals in constraint logic programming. *Computational Intelligence*, 8(4):601–623, 1992.

[101] G. Smolka. The Oz programming model. In J. van Leeuwen, editor, *Computer Science Today*, Lecture Notes in Computer Science, vol. 1000, pages 324–343. Springer-Verlag, Berlin, 1995.

[102] G. Smolka. An Oz primer. Technical report, Programming Systems Lab. DFKI, Available at `http://www.ps.uni-sb.de/oz/`, 1995.

[103] G. Smolka. Residuation and guarded rules for constraint logic programming. Technical report, Digital Equipment Paris Research Laboratory Research Report, June 1991.

[104] P.J. Stuckey. Negation and constraint logic programming. *Information and Computation*, 118(1):12–33, 1995.

[105] P.J. Stuckey. Incremental linear constraint solving and detection of implicit equalities. *ORSA Journal of Computing*, 3(4):269–274, 1991.

[106] G. Sussman and G. Steele. CONSTRAINTS — a language for expressing almost–hierarchical descriptions. *Artificial Intelligence*, 14(1):1–39, 1980.

[107] I. Sutherland. Sketchpad: A man-machine graphical communication system. In *Proceedings of the Spring Joint Computer Conference*, pages 329–346. IFIPS, 1963.

[108] M. van Emden and R. Kowalski. The semantics of predicate logic as a programming language. *JACM*, 23:733–742, 1976.

[109] P. Van Hentenryck. *The OPL Optimization Programming Language*. MIT Press, 1999.

[110] P. Van Hentenryck. *Constraint Satisfaction in Logic Programming*. MIT Press, 1989.

[111] P. Van Hentenryck. A gentle introduction to Numerica. *Artificial Intelligence*, 103: 209–235, 1998.

[112] P. Van Hentenryck and Y. Deville. The cardinality operator: A new logical connective for constraint logic programming. In F. Benhamou and A. Colmerauer, editors, *Constraint Logic Programming: Selected Research*, pages 383–403. MIT

Press, 1993.

[113] P. Van Hentenryck and T. Graf. Standard forms for rational linear arithmetics in constraint logic programming. *Annals of Mathematics and Artificial Intelligence*, 5: 303–319, 1992.

[114] P. Van Hentenryck and L. Michel. *Constraint-Based Local Search*. MIT Press, 2005.

[115] P. Van Hentenryck and L. Michel. Localizer: A modeling language for local search. *Constraints*, 5:41–82, 2000.

[116] P. Van Hentenryck and R. Ramachandran. Backtracking without trailing in $CLP(\Re_{Lin})$. *ACM Transactions on Programming Languages and Systems*, 17(4): 635–671, July 1995.

[117] P. Van Hentenryck, V. Saraswat, and Y. Deville. Constraint processing in cc(FD). Technical report, unpublished manuscript, 1992.

[118] P. Van Hentenryck, V. Saraswat, and Y. Deville. Design, implementation and evaluation of the constraint language cc(fd). In A. Podelski, editor, *Constraint Programming: Basics and Trends*, number 910 in LNCS. Springer-Verlag, 1995.

[119] P. Voda. The constraint language trilogy: Semantics and computations. Technical report, Complete Logic Systems, North Vancouver, BC, Canada, 1988.

[120] M. Wallace and F. Ajili. Hybrid problem solving in ECLiPSe. In *Constraint and Integer Programming Toward a Unified Methodology*, volume 27 of *Operations Research/Computer Science Interfaces Series*, chapter 6. Springer, 2004.

[121] M. G. Wallace and J. Schimpf. Finding the right hybrid algorithm - a combinatorial meta-problem. *Annals of Mathematics and Artificial Intelligence*, 34(4):259 – 269, 2002.

[122] D. H. D. Warren. An Abstract Prolog Instruction Set. Technical report, SRI International, Artificial Intelligence Center, October 1983.

[123] T. H. Yunes, A. V. Moura, and C. C. de Souza. Hybrid column generation approaches for urban transit crew management problems. *Transportation Science*, 39 (2):273–288, 2002.

[124] N.-F. Zhou. Programming finite-domain constraint propagators in action rules. *Theory and Practice of Logic Programming*, 5, 2005.

Handbook of Constraint Programming
Edited by F. Rossi, P. van Beek and T. Walsh

Chapter 13

Constraints in Procedural and Concurrent Languages

Thom Frühwirth, Laurent Michel, and Christian Schulte

This chapter addresses the integration of constraints and search into programming languages from three different points of views. It first focuses on the use of constraints to model combinatorial optimization problem and to easily implement search procedures, then it considers the use of constraints for supporting concurrent computations and finally turns to the use of constraints to enable open implementations of constraints solvers.

The idea of approaching hard combinatorial optimization problems through a combination of search and constraint solving appeared first in logic programming. The genesis and growth of constraint programming within logic programming is not surprising as it catered to two fundamental needs: a declarative style and non-determinism.

Despite the continued support of logic programming for constraint programmers, research efforts were initiated to import constraint technologies into other paradigms (in particular procedural and object-oriented paradigms) to cater to a broader audience and leverage constraint-based techniques in novel areas. The first motivation behind a transition is a desire to ease the adoption of a successful technology. Moving constraints to a platform and paradigm widely accepted would facilitate their adoption within existing software systems by reducing resistance to the introduction of technologies and tools perceived as radically different. A second motivation is that constraints are versatile abstractions equally well suited for modeling and supporting concurrency. In particular, concurrent computation can be seen as agents that communicate and coordinate through a shared constraint store. Third, constraint-based techniques can leverage the semantics of a target application domain to design specialized constraints or search procedures that are more effective than off-the-shelves constraints. The ability, for domain specialists, to *easily* create, customize and extend both constraints solvers and search is therefore a necessity for adaptability.

The continued success and growth of constraints depends on the availability of flexible, extensible, versatile and easy to use solvers. It is contingent on retaining performance that rival or exceed the ad-hoc methods they supplant. Therefore, efficiency remains a key objective, often at odds with flexibility and ease of use.

Meeting these broad objectives, namely ubiquity, flexibility, versatility and efficiency within traditional paradigms that lack support for declarative programming creates unique challenges. First, a flexible tool must support mechanisms to let users define new constraints either through combinators or from first principles. The mechanisms should focus on the specification of *what* each constraint computes (its declarative semantics) rather than *how* it computes it (operational semantics) to retain simplicity without sacrificing efficiency. Second, search procedures directly supported by language abstractions, i.e., nondeterminism in logic programming, must be available in traditional languages and remain under end-user control. Also, search procedures should retain their declarative nature and style to preserve simplicity and appeal. Finally, a constraint tool must bridge the semantic gaps that exists between a high-level model, its implementation and the native abstractions of the host language to preserve clarity and simplicity while offering a natural embedding in the target language that does not force its users to become logic programming experts.

Many answers to these challenges have been offered and strike different trade-offs. Each answer can be characterized by features that address a subset of the objectives. Some constraint tools favored ease of adoption and efficiency over preserving declarativeness and flexibility. Others focused on the creation of new *hybrid*, multi-paradigm languages and platforms that preserved declarative constructions, adopt constraints and concurrency as first class citizens in the design, and preserve efficiency with a lesser emphasis on targeting existing platforms. A third option focusing on flexibility and declarative constructions brought rule-based systems where new solvers over entirely new domains can be easily constructed, extended, modified and composed.

This chapter provides insights into the strengths, weaknesses and capabilities of systems that fall in one of these three classes: toolkits for procedural and object-oriented languages, hybrid systems and rule-based systems.

13.1   Procedural and Object-Oriented Languages

Over the last decade, constraint programming tools have progressively found their way into mainstream paradigms and languages, most notably C++. This transformation, however, is not obvious and creates many challenges. To understand the nature of the difficulty, it is useful to step back and consider the initial motivations. To apprehend the interactions between constraint toolkits and their procedural or object-oriented host languages, it is useful to separate two key components of constraint programming, i.e., *modeling with constraints* and *programming the search*. Each component brings its own challenges that vary with the nature of the host language. Section 13.1.1 reviews the design objectives and inherent challenges before turning to the issue of constraint-based modeling in section 13.1.2, and search programming in section 13.1.3. Finally, section 13.1.4 discusses pragmatic issues that permeate throughout all integration attempts.

13.1.1   Design Objectives

Modern constraint-based languages strive to simplify the task of writing models that are readable, flexible and easy to maintain. This is naturally challenging as programs for complex problems often requires ingenuity on the part of the developer to express multiple orthogonal concerns and encode them efficiently within a language that imposes its own limitations. Logic programming is the cradle of constraint programming for good reasons as it offers two important supports: a declarative framework on which to build constraints as generalizations of unification; and non-determinism to support search procedures, and, in particular, depth-first search.

The challenges

Nonetheless, logic programming imposes a few limitations. First, it does not lend itself to the efficient implementation of extensible toolkits. Early on, efficiency considerations as well as simplicity pushed logic programming systems to implement all constraints as "built-ins" of the language giving rise to closed *black-box* solvers. Second, it does not easily accommodate search procedures that deviate from the depth-first strategy. It therefore raises significant challenges for potential users of strategies like BFS, IDFS [70] or LDS [50] to name a few. Third, its target audience comprises almost exclusively computer-savvy programmers, who feel comfortable writing recursive predicates for tasks as mundane as generating constraints and constraint expressions. This relative difficulty does not appeal to a much larger group of potential users of the technology: the mathematical programming community. Mathematical solvers (LP, IP, MIP [56, 46]) and their modeling languages [34, 26, 104] indeed offer facilities that focus on modeling and, to a large extent, relieve their users from most (all) programming efforts.

The past two decades saw improvements on one or more of these fronts. The next paragraphs briefly review two trends *related to* procedural and object-oriented languages.

Libraries and glass-box extensibility. Ilog Solver [58] is a C++ library implementing a finite domain solver and is thus a natural example of an object-oriented embodiment. The embedding of a solver within a C++ library offers opportunities to address the extensibility issues as both decision variables and constraints can be represented with object hierarchies that can be refined and extended. However the move to C++, a language that does not support non-deterministic computation, has increased the challenges one faces to write, debug and maintain search procedures. Note that CHR [39] supports glass-box extensibility through user-definable rules and is the subject of Section 13.3.

From programming to modeling. Numerica [111] is a modeling language for highly non-linear global optimization. It was designed to address the third limitation and make the technology of Newton [112] (a constraint logic programming language) available to a much broader audience of mathematical programmers. The objective behind Numerica was to improve the modeling language to a point where executable models were expressed at the level of abstraction of their formal counterparts typically found in scientific papers. The approach was further broadened with novel modeling languages for finite domain solvers supporting not only the statement of constraints but also the specification of advanced search procedures and strategies. OPL [105, 104, 114] embodies those ideas in a rich declarative language while OplScript [108] implements a procedural language for the composition of multiple OPL models. Note that OPL is an interpreted language whose virtual machine is implemented in terms of ILOG SOLVER constructions. The virtual machine itself is non trivial given the semantic gap between OPL and ILOG SOLVER.

At the same time, a finite domain solver was implemented in LAURE [21] and then moved to CLAIRE [63], a language compiled to C++ that simplified LAURE's constructions to make it accessible to a broader class of potential users. CLAIRE was later enhanced with SALSA [63], a declarative and algebraic extension that focused on the implementation of search procedures.

13.1.2   Constraint Modeling

Constraint modeling raises two concerns: the ease of use and expressiveness of the toolkit and its underlying extensibility. Each concern is intrinsically linked to the host language and has a direct impact on potential end users. This section discusses each one in turn.

Ease of use and expressiveness

The constraint modeling task within a procedural or an object-oriented language presents interesting challenges. It is desirable to obtain a *declarative* reading of a *high-level* model statement that exploits the facilities of the host language (e.g., static and strong typing in C++). The difficulty is to leverage the language to simplify programs and raise their modeling profile to a sufficient level of abstraction. Note that modeling languages (e.g., OPL) tightly couple the toolkit and the language to obtain the finest level of integration that preserves a complete declarative reading of models despite an apparent procedural style. Indeed, OPL looks procedural but is actually declarative as it is side effect free (i.e., it has no destructive assignments).

Aggregation and combinators.   Consider the classic magic series puzzle. The problem consists of finding a sequence of numbers $S = (s_0, s_1, \cdots, s_{n-1})$ such that s_i represents the number of occurrences of i within the sequence S. For instance, $(6, 2, 1, 0, 0, 0, 1, 0,0,0)$ is a sequence of length 10 with 6 occurrences of 0, 2 occurrences of 1, 1 occurrence of and finally 1 occurrence of 6. Clearly, any solution must satisfy the following property

$$\sum_{k=0}^{n-1}(s_k = i) = s_i \ \forall i \in \{0, 1, 2, \cdots, n-1\}$$

To solve the problem with a constraint programming toolkit, it is first necessary to state the n constraints shown above. Each constraint is a linear combination of the truth value (interpreted as 0 or 1) of elementary constraints of the form $s_k = i$. The difficulty is therefore to construct a toolkit with automatic reification of constraints and with seamless aggregation primitives, i.e., summations, products, conjunctions or disjunctions to name a few that facilitate the combination of elementary primitives.

Figure 13.1 illustrates the differences between the OPL and ILOG SOLVER statements for the magic series problem. The ILOG SOLVER model constructs an expression iteratively to build the cardinality constraint for each possible value. It also relies on convenience functions like `IloScalProd` to create the linear redundant constraint. The OPL model is comparatively simpler as the mathematical statement maps directly to the model. It is worth noting that the level of abstraction shown by the OPL model is achievable within C++ libraries with the same level of typing safety as demonstrated in [72]. Finally, both systems implement constraint combinators (e.g., cardinality) and offer global constraints

ILOG SOLVER   OPL

```
1. int main(int argc,char* argv[]){    1. int n<<"Number of Variables:";
2.    IloEnv env;int n;cin>>n;          2. range Dom 0..n-1;
3.    try {                             3. var Range s[Dom];
4.       IloModel m(env);               4. solve {
5.       IloIntVarArray s(env,n,0,n);   5.    forall(i in Dom)
6.       IloIntArray c(env,n);          6.       s[i] = sum(j in Dom) (s[j]=i);
7.       for(int i=0;i<n;i++) {         7.    sum(j in Dom) s[j]*j = n;
8.          IlcIntExp e = s[0] == i;    8. };
9.          for(int k=1;k<n;k++)
10.            e += s[k] == i;
11.         m.add(s[i] == e);
12.      }
13.      for(int i=0;i<n;i++) c[i]=i;
14.      m.add(IloScalProd(s,c) == n);
15.      solve(m,env,vars);
16.   } catch(IloException& ex) ...
17.}
```

Figure 13.1: The Magic Series statements.

that capture common substructures, simplify some of the modeling effort, and can exploit the semantics of constraints for better performance.

Typing. A seamless toolkit integration depends on the adherence to the precepts and conventions of the host language. For instance, C++ programmers often expect static and strong typing for their programs and rely on the C++ compiler to catch mistakes through type checking. From a modeling point of view the ability to rely on types and, in particular, on finite domain variables defined over domains of specific types is instrumental is writing clean and simple models. Consider the stable marriage problem. The problem is to pair up men and women such that the pairings form marriages and satisfy stability constraints based on the preferences of all individuals. A marriage between m and w is stable if and only if whenever m prefers a woman k over his wife w, k also happens to prefer her own husband over m so that m and w have no reason to part. The OPL model is shown in Figure 13.2. The fragment husband[wife[m]] = m illustrates that the type of values in the domain of wife[m] is an enumerated type Women that happens to be equal to the type of the index for the array husband. Similarly, the type of each entry of the husband array is Men and therefore equal to the type of the right hand side of the equality constraint. To the modeler, the result is a program that can be statically type checked.

Matrices. From an expressiveness point of view, the ability to index arrays with finite domain variables is invaluable to write concise and elegant models. It is equally useful on matrices, especially when its absence implies a non trivial reformulation effort to derive for an expression $m[x, y]$ a *tight* reformulation based on an element constraint. The reformulation introduces a ternary relation $R(i, j, k) = \{\langle i, j, k \rangle \mid i \in D(x) \land j \in D(y) \land k \in 0..|D(x)| \cdot |D(y)| - 1\}$ that, for each pair of indices $i \in D(x)$ and $j \in D(y)$, maps the entry $m[i, j]$ to its location k in an array a. Then, $m[x, y]$ can be rewritten as $a[z]$ with the addition of the constraint $(x, y, z) \in R$ where z is a fresh variable.

```
1.  enum Women ...;
2.  enum Men ...;
3.  int rankW[Women,Men] = ...
4.  int rankM[Men,Women] = ...
5.  var Women wife[Men];
6.  var Men husband[Women];
7.  solve {
8.     forall(m in Men)     husband[wife[m]] = m;
9.     forall(w in Women)   wife[husband[w]] = w;
10.    forall(m in Men & o in Women)
11.       rankM[m,o] < rankM[m,wife[m]] => rankW[o,husband[o]] < rankW[o,m];
12.    forall(w in Women & o in Men)
13.       rankW[w,o] < rankW[w,husband[w]] => rankM[o,wife[o]] < rankM[o,w];
14. }
```

Figure 13.2: The OPL model for Stable Marriage.

Note that if the language supports a rich parametric type system (e.g., C++), it is possible to write templated libraries that offer both automatic reformulations and static/strong typing as shown in [72].

Extensibility

Extensibility is crucial to the success of toolkits and libraries alike. It affects them in at least two respects. First, the toolkit or library itself should be extensible and support the addition of user-defined constraints and user-defined search procedures. This requirement is vital to easily develop domain specific or application specific constraints and blend them seamlessly with other pre-defined constraints. Given that constraints are compositional and implemented in terms of filtering algorithms that task should be easily handled. Second, it is often desirable to embed the entire constraint program within a larger application to facilitate its deployment.

Solver extensibility.   Object orientation is a paradigm for writing extensible software through a combination of polymorphism, inheritance, and delegation. In the mid 90s, the first version of ILOG SOLVER [79, 80] was developed to deliver an extensible C++ library. The extensibility of its modeling component stems from a reliance on abstract classes (interfaces) for constraints to specify the API that must be supported to react to events produced by variables. For instance an ILOG SOLVER integer variable can expose notifications for three events whenDomain, whenRange, whenValue to report a change in the domain, the bounds, or the loss of a value. A constraint subscribes to notifications from specific variables to respond with its demon method. Figure 13.3 illustrates a user-defined equality constraint implementing bound consistency. Its post method creates two demons and attaches them to the variables. Both demons are implemented with a macro (last line) that delegates the event back to the constraint. The demon method propagates the constraint by updating the bound of the other variable. The extension mechanism heavily depends on the specification of a *filtering algorithm* rather than a set of *indexicals* (e.g., clp(FD) [28]) or *inference rules* (e.g., CHR [39]) and therefore follows a far more pro-

```
1.  class MyEqual : public IlcConstraintI {
2.    IlcIntVar _x,_y;
3.  public:
4.    MyEqual(IloSolver s,IlcIntVar x,IlcIntVar y)
5.      : IlcConstraintI(s),_x(x),_y(y) {}
6.    void post() {
7.      _x.whenValue(equalDemon(getSolver(),this,_x));
8.      _y.whenValue(equalDemon(getSolver(),this,_y));
9.    }
10.   void demon(IlcIntVar x) {
11.     IlcIntVar other = (x == _x) ? _y : _x;
12.     other.setMin(x.getMin());
13.     other.setMax(x.getMax());
14.   }
15. };
16. ILCCTDEMON1(equalDemon,MyEqual,demon,IlcIntVar,var);
```

Figure 13.3: ILOG SOLVER custom constraint.

cedural mind-set that requires a fair level of understanding to identify relevant events and variables and produce a filtering procedure.

Solver embedding. Extensibility also matters for the deployment of constraint-based technology. In this respect, the integration of a CP toolkit within a mainstream object-oriented language is a clear advantage as models can easily be encapsulated within reusable classes linked within larger applications. Modeling languages present an additional difficulty but can nonetheless be integrated through component technology (COM or CORBA) [57] or even as web-services as illustrated by the OSiL efforts [33].

13.1.3 Programming the Search

The second component of a constraint programming model is concerned with the search. The search usually addresses two orthogonal concerns. First, *what* is the topology of the search tree that is to be explored. Second, *how* does one select the next node of the search tree to be explored. Or, given a search tree, what is the order used to visit its nodes? Both can be thought of as declarative specifications but are often mixed to accommodate the implementation language. The integration of the two elements in procedural and object-oriented languages is particularly challenging, given the lack of language abstractions to manipulate the search control flow.

Search tree specification

OPL is a classic example of declarative specification of the search tree. It supports statements that specify the order in which variables and values must be considered. OPL provides default strategies and does not require the user to implement his own. However, as problems become more complex, it is critical to provide this ability. Figure 13.4 illustrates on the left-hand side the naive formulation for the $n-$queens model. The constraints are stated for all pairs of indices i and j in Dom such that $i < j$. The right-hand side shows the search procedure. Lines 10-14 specify the search tree with a variable and a value ordering . It simply scans the variables in the order indicated by Dom (ascending) and, for each variable i, it non-deterministically chooses a values v from Dom and attempts to impose the additional constraint queen[i] = v. On failure, the non-deterministic choice is reconsidered and the next value from Dom is selected.

```
1.  int n = ...; range Dom 1..n;          10. search {
2.  var Dom queen[Dom];                    11.   forall(i in Dom)
3.  solve {                                12.     tryall(v in Dom)
4.    forall(ordered i,j in Dom){          13.       queen[i] = v;
5.      queen[i] <> queen[j];              14. }
6.      queen[i]+i <> queen[j]+j;
7.      queen[i]-i <> queen[j]-j;
8.    }
9.  }
```

Figure 13.4: The OPL queens model.

Implementing a search facility in an object-oriented language like C++ or Java is hard for a simple reason: the underlying language has no support for non-determinism and therefore no control abstractions for making choices like tryall. To date, all libraries have used some form of embedded *goal interpreter* whose purpose is to evaluate an *and-or tree* data structure reminiscent of logic programming predicates where non-determinism is expressed with or-nodes and conjunction with and-nodes. The approach was used in ILOG SOLVER and more recently in CHOCO, a Java-based toolkit. Figure 13.5 shows a goal-based implementation of the $n-$queens search tree. ILOG SOLVER also provides pre-defined search tree specifications for the often-used methods.

```
1.  ILCGOAL4(Forall,IloIntVarArray,x,IloInt,i,IloInt,low,IloInt,up) {
2.    if (i <= up)
3.      return IlcAnd(Tryall(getSolver(),x[i],low,up),
4.                    Forall(getSolver(),x,i+1,low,up));
5.    else return IlcGoalTrue(getSolver());
6.  }
7.  ILCGOAL3(Tryall,IloIntVar,x,IloInt,v,IloInt up) {
8.    if (x.isBound()) return 0;
9.    else if (v > up) fail();
10.   else return IlcOr(x=v,IlcAnd(x!=v,Tryall(getSolver(),x,v+1)));
11. }
12. ...
13. solver.solve(Forall(queens,1,1,n));
```

Figure 13.5: An ILOG SOLVER implementation of a search tree specification.

Lines 1 through 6 define a goal that performs the same variable selection as line 11 of the OPL model. Lines 7-11 define a goal to try all the possible values for the chosen variable and correspond to lines 12 and 13 of the OPL model. The two macros ILCGOAL4 and ILCGOAL3 define two classes (ForallI and TryallI) together with convenience functions (Forall and Tryall) to instantiate them[1]. The block that follows each macro

---

[1]Observe that the code in Figure 13.5 always uses the convenience functions and never directly refer to the underlying implementation class

is the body of the goal whose purpose is to construct the And-Or tree on the fly.

Observe that the implementation of the search procedure is now broken down into several small elements that are not textually close. A few observation are in order

- A goal-based solution relies on an embedded goal interpreter and is therefore incompatible with C++ development tools like a debugger. For instance, tracing the execution is hard as there is no access to the state of the interpreter (e.g., current instruction, parameters' value, etc..). To compensate, recent versions of ILOG SOLVER provide debugging support through instrumented libraries to inspect and visualize the state of the search tree.

- Every single operation that must occur during the search (e.g., printing, statistic gathering, visualizations) must be wrapped up in user-defined goals that are inserted into the search tree description.

- It is non-trivial to modularize entire search procedures in *actual C++ functions or classes* to reuse search fragments. Again, the only option is to write a function or class that will *inline* a goal data structure representing the search procedure to insert. Note that a deep copy of the entire goal (the entire function) is required each time to simulate the parameter passing as there is no call mechanism per se.

- The body of a goal's implementation is both delicate and subtle as there is a temporal disconnection between the execution of its various components. For instance, one may be tempted to optimize the `Forall` goal shown in Figure 13.5 to eliminate the creation of a fresh goal instance for each recursive goal and favor a purely recursive solution as in

```
ILCGOAL4(Forall,IloIntVarArray,x,IloInt,i,IloInt,low,IloInt,up) {
    if (i <= up) {
        IloInt i0 = i; i = i + 1;
        return IlcAnd(Tryall(getSolver(),x[i0],low,up),this);
    } else return IlcGoalTrue(getSolver());
}
```

However, this would be wrong. Indeed, i is an instance variable of the goal that is merely re-inserting itself back into the query resulting in making $i = i + 1$ visible to the next invocation. However, on backtrack i is *not* restored to its original value. Consequently, one must compensate wit a *reversible* integer (`IlcRevInt`). Yet, this is insufficient as the modification ($i = i + 1$) should occur *inside* the `Tryall` choice point and it is thus necessary to add a goal to increment i as in

```
ILCGOAL4(Forall,IloIntVarArray,x,IlcRevInt&,i,IloInt,low,IloInt,up) {
    if (i <= up) {
        return IlcAnd(IlcAnd(Tryall(getSolver(),x[i],low,up),
                             IncrementIt(i)),this);
    } else return IlcGoalTrue(getSolver());
}
```

Finally, note how the arguments to goal instantiations are evaluated when the parent goal executes, *not* when the goal itself is about to execute. For instance, a goal that follows `IncrementIt(i)` should not expect i to be incremented yet.

Standard search procedures are not limited to static variable/value ordering but often rely on dynamic heuristics in order to select the next variable/value to branch on. Such heuristics can be implemented both within modeling languages and libraries.

Variable selection heuristic.   In OPL, the variable selection heuristic is specified with
a clause in the `forall` statement that associates with the selection a measure of how
desirable the choice is. For instance, the fragment

```
forall(i in Dom ordered by increasing dsize(queens[i])) ...
```

indicates that the queens should be tried in increasing order of domain size. Note that
OPL supports more advanced criteria based on lexicographic ordering of tuple-values to
automate a useful but tedious task. For instance, the fragment

```
forall(i in Dom ordered by increasing <dsize(queens[i]),abs(i - n/2)>)
   tryall(v in Dom)
     queen[i] = v;
```

implements a middle variable selection heuristic that considers first the variable with the
smallest domain and breaks ties by choosing the variable closest to the middle of the board.
   ILOG SOLVER is equally capable at the expense of a few small additions to user-defined
goals. Indeed, the key change is that the index of the next variable to consider is no longer
a static expression (the i of the Forall goal in Figure 13.5), but is instead computed at the
beginning of the goal. Note that the selection is re-done at each invocation of the Forall
and can skip over bound variables.

Value selection heuristic.   OPL provides an ordering clause for its `tryall` that matches
the variable ordering clause of the `forall` both in syntax and semantics. For instance the
statement

```
tryall(v in Domain ordered by increasing abs(v - n/2)) ...
```

would consider the values from *Domain* in order of increasing distance from the middle of
the board. ILOG SOLVER goals for the value selection operate similarly with one caveat:
The value selection goal must track (with an additional data structure) the already tried
values to focus on only the remaining values, a task hidden by OPL's implementation.

Control flow primitives.   For the search, the most significant difference between a mod
eling language and a library is, perhaps, the availability of traditional control statements.
As pointed out earlier, ILOG SOLVER's level of abstraction for programming the search is
the underlying and-or tree. OPL, provides traditional control primitives such as iterations
(`while` loops), selections (`select`), local bindings (`let` expressions) and branchings
(`if-then-else`). Consider for instance the simple OPL fragment shown in Figure 13.6
which, upon failure, adds the negation of the failed constraint. The distance between a
goal-based specification and a high-level procedure is significant.

Exploration strategies

The specification of the search tree was concerned with *what* was going to be explored.
Exploration strategies are concerned with *how* the dynamic search tree is going to be explored. Many strategies are possible, ranging from the standard depth first search to complex combination of iterated limited searches. Even though an exploration strategy sounds
like a very algorithmic endeavor, it is both possible and desirable to produce a declarative

```
1.  search {
2.    forall(in in Dom)
3.      while (not bound(queens[i])) do
4.        let v = dmin(queens[i]) in
5.          try
6.            queens[i] = v | queens[i] <> v
7.          endtry;
8.  }
```

Figure 13.6: Traditional Control Abstractions Example in OPL.

specification and let the search engine implement it automatically. This is especially true in the context of a procedural (or object-oriented) language as a procedural specification would force programmers to explicitly address the issue of non-determinism (and its implementation). This section briefly reviews two approaches based on OPL [113] (or ILOG SOLVER [78]) and COMET [73].

OPL and ILOG SOLVER strategy specifications. The key ingredient to specify an exploration strategy is to provide a search node management policy. Each time a choice is considered during the search, it creates search nodes corresponding to the various alternatives. Once created, the exploration must *select* the node to explore next and *postpone* the less attractive ones. The *evaluation* of a node's attractiveness is, of course, strategy dependent. But once the attractiveness function and the postponement rules are encapsulated in a strategy object, the exploration algorithm becomes completely generic with respect to the strategy.

```
1.SearchStrategy dfs() {
2.  evaluated to - OplSystem.getDepth();
3.  postponed when OplSystem.getEvaluation()>OplSystem.getBestEvaluation();
4.}

5.applyStrategy dfs()
6.  forall(i in Dom)
7.    tryall(v in Dom)
8.      queen[i] = v;
```

Figure 13.7: Exploration Strategy in OPL.

Consider the statement in Figure 13.7. It first defines a DFS strategy and uses it to explore the search tree. The specification contains two elements: the evaluation function that defines the node's attractiveness and the postponement rule that states when to delay. Each time the exploration produces a node, it is subjected to the strategy to evaluate its attractiveness and decide its fate. To obtain DFS, it suffices to use the opposite of the node's depth as its attractiveness and to postpone a node whenever it is shallower than the "best node" available in the queue. The system object (OplSystem gives access to enough statistic about the depth, right depth, number of failures, etc..) to implement advanced strategies like LDS or IDS to name a few. When the strategy is expressed as a node management policy, one can implement the same mechanism in a library.

COMET strategy specifications. COMET is an object-oriented programming language for constraint-based local search offering control abstractions for non-determinism [71, 106]. These abstractions are equally suitable for local search methods (low overhead) and complete methods.

COMET uses first-class continuations to represent and manipulate the state of the program's control flow. COMET's `tryall` is semantically equivalent to OPL's `tryall` Search strategies can be expressed via policies for the management of the captured continuations and embedded in `Search Controllers` that parameterize the search.

```
1. DFS sc();                           1. class DFS implements SearchController {
2. exploreall<sc> {                    2.    Stack _s; Continuation _exit;
3.    forall(i in Dom) {               3.    DFS() { _s = new Stack();}
4.       tryall<sc>(v in Dom){         4.    void start(Continuation c) {_exit = c;
5.          queen[i] = v;              5.    void exit() { call(_exit);}
6.       }                             6.    void addChoice(Continuation c) {
7.    }                                7.       _s.push(c);
8. }                                   8.    }
                                       9.    void fail() {
                                       10.      if (_s.empty()) exit();
                                       11.      else call(_cont.pop());
                                       12.   }
                                       13.}
```

Figure 13.8: Exploration strategies with COMET.

The code fragment on the left hand side of Figure 13.8 is a COMET procedure whose semantics are identical to the OPL statement from Figure 13.7. The key difference is the search controller (`sc`) of type `DFS` whose implementation is shown on the right hand side. The statements parameterized by `sc` (`exploreall` and `tryall`) delegate to the search controller the management of the continuations that represent search nodes. To derive DFS, it suffices to store in a stack the continuations produced by the branches in the `tryall`. When a failure occurs (e.g., at an inconsistent node), the fail method transfers the control to the popped continuation. If there is none left, the execution resumes after the `exploreall` thanks to a call to the `_exit` continuation.

COMET completely decouples the node management policy from the exploration algorithm, allows both a declarative and an operational reading of the search specification and provides a representation of the control flow's state that is independent of the underlying computation model.

13.1.4 Pragmatics

The integration of a constraint programming toolkit within a purely procedural or object-oriented language presents challenges for the modeling and implementation of the search.

Constraint modeling

Constraint modeling is relatively easy *if* the host language supports first-class expressions or syntactic sugar to simulate them. If operators cannot be overloaded (like in Java), the expression of arithmetic and set-based constraint is heavier. See Figure 13.9 for a Java fragment setting up the queens problem in the CHOCO solver.

```
1.   Problem p = new Problem();
2.   IntVar[] queens = new IntVar[n];
3.   for(int i = 0; i < n; i++)
4.      queens[i] = p.makeEnumIntVar("queen" + i, 1, n);
5.   for (int i=0; i<n; i++) {
6.      for (int j=i+1; j<n; j++) {
7.         p.post(p.neq(queens[i], queens[j]));
8.         p.post(p.neq(queens[i],p.plus(queens[j], j-i)));
9.         p.post(p.neq(queens[i],p.minus(queens[j], j-i)));
10.     }
11. }
```

Figure 13.9: The n−queens problem in CHOCO.

Search implementation

The lack of support for non-determinism is far more disruptive. One extreme solution is to close the specification of the search and only offer pre-defined procedures. The clear advantage is an implementation of non-determinism that can be specialized to deliver good performance.

A second option, used with ILOG SOLVER [58], is to embed in the library a goal oriented interpreter. With a carefully crafted API addressing the issues listed below, it is possible to open the interface to support user-defined extensions.

Control transfer. The interface between the goal-based search and the rest of the program must be as seamless as possible.

Mixed memory models. Multiple memory models must coexist peacefully (traditional C Heap, logical variables Heap, traditional execution stack, search stack or trail to name a few) to avoid leaks or dangling pointer issues.

Debugging support. A significant part of the program runs inside an embedded interpreter which renders the native debugging facilities virtually useless. This must be mitigated with the inclusion of dedicated and orthogonal debugging tools to instrument the goal interpreter.

Control abstractions. The native control abstraction tend to be ineffective to express search procedures and underscore the importance of hiding or isolating the semantic subtleties associated with the goal interpreter. Note that the level of abstraction of search procedures can be lifted closer to OPL as demonstrated in [72]. However, this implementation retains a goal-like interpreter that also fails to integrate with existing tools.

13.2 Concurrent Constraint Programming

At the end of the 1980s, concurrent constraint logic programming (CCLP) integrated ideas from concurrent logic programming [97] and constraint logic programming (CLP):

• Maher [65] proposed the ALPS class of committed-choice languages.

- The ambitious Japanese Fifth-Generation Computing Project relied on a concurrent logic language based on Ueda's GHC [103].

- The seminal work of Saraswat [82] introduced the *ask-and-tell* metaphor for constraint operations and the concurrent constraints (CC) language framework that permits both don't-care and don't-know non-determinism.

- Smolka proposed a concurrent programming model Oz that subsumes functional and object-oriented programming [101].

Implemented concurrent constraint logic programming languages include AKL, CIAO, CHR, and Mozart (as an implementation of Oz).

13.2.1 Design Objectives

Processes are the main notion in concurrent and distributed programming. They are building blocks of *distributed systems*, where data and computations are physically distributed over a network of computers. *Processes* are programs that are executed concurrently and that can interact with each other. Processes can either execute local actions or *communicate* and *synchronize* by sending and receiving messages. The communicating processes build a *process network* which can change dynamically. For concurrency it does not matter if the processes are executed physically in parallel or if they are interleaved sequentially. Processes can intentionally be non-terminating. Consider an operating system which should keep on running or a monitoring and control program which continuously processes incoming measurements and periodically returns intermediate results or raises an alarm.

In CCLP, concurrently executing processes communicate via a shared constraint store. The processes are defined by predicates and are called *agents*, because they are defined by logical rules and often implement some kind of artificially intelligent behavior. Constraints take the role of (partial) messages and variables take the role of communication channels. Usually, communication is asynchronous. Running processes are CCLP goals that place and check constraints on shared variables.

This communication mechanism is based on *ask-and-tell* of constraints that reside in the common constraint store. *Tell* refers to imposing a constraint (as in CLP). Ask is an inquiry whether a constraint already holds. *Ask* is realized by an *entailment* test. It checks whether a constraint is implied by the current constraint store. Ask and tell can be seen as generalizations of read and write from values to constraints. The ask operation is a *consumer* of constraints (even though the constraint will not be removed), the tell operation is a *producer* of constraints.

For a process, decisions that have been communicated to the outside and actions that have affected the environment cannot be undone anymore. *Don't-know non-determinism* (Search) must be encapsulated in this context. Also, failure should be avoided. Failure of a goal atom (i.e., a single process) always entails the failure of the entire computation (i.e., all participating processes). In applications such as operating or monitoring systems this would be fatal.

13.2.2 The CC Language Framework

We concentrate on the committed-choice fragment of Saraswat's CC language framework [83, 84, 81]. The abstract syntax of CC is given by the following EBNF grammar:

Declarations $D ::= p(\tilde{t}) \leftarrow A \mid D, D$

Agents $\quad A ::= \textit{true} \mid tell(c) \mid \sum_{i=1}^{n} ask(c_i) \rightarrow A_i \mid A \| A \mid \exists x p(\tilde{t}) \mid p(\tilde{t})$

where $\tilde{t}$ stands for a sequence of terms, x for a variable, and where c and the c_i's are constraints. Instead of using existential quantification ($\exists$), projection is usually implicit in implemented CC languages by using local variables as in CLP.

Each predicate symbol p is defined by exactly one declaration. A *CC program P* is a finite set of declarations.

The operational model of CC is described by a transition system. States are pairs consisting of agents and the common constraint store. The transition relation is given by the transition rules in Fig. 13.10.

Tell $\qquad \langle tell(c), d \rangle \rightarrow \langle \textit{true}, c \wedge d \rangle$

Ask $\qquad \langle \sum_{i=1}^{n} ask(c_i) \rightarrow A_i, d \rangle \rightarrow \langle A_j, d \rangle \quad$ if $CT \models d \rightarrow c_j$ $(1 \leq j \leq n)$

Composition $\qquad \dfrac{\langle A, c \rangle \rightarrow \langle A', c' \rangle}{\begin{array}{l} \langle (A \| B), c \rangle \rightarrow \langle (A' \| B), c' \rangle \\ \langle (B \| A), c \rangle \rightarrow \langle (B \| A'), c' \rangle \end{array}}$

Unfold $\qquad \langle p(\tilde{t}), c \rangle \rightarrow \langle A \| tell(\tilde{t} = \tilde{s}), c \rangle \qquad$ if $(p(\tilde{s}) \leftarrow A)$ in program P

Figure 13.10: CC transition rules

Tell $tell(c)$ adds the constraint c to the common constraint store. The constraint *true* always holds.

Ask *Don't care non-determinism* between choices is expressed as $\sum_{i=1}^{n} ask(c_i) \rightarrow A_i$. One nondeterministically chooses one c_i which is implied by the current constraint store d, and continues computation with A_i.

Composition The $\|$ operator enables parallel composition of agents. Logically, it is interpreted as conjunction.

Unfold Unfolding replaces an agent $p(\tilde{t})$ by its definition according to its declaration.

A finite CC derivation (computation) can be successful, failed or deadlocked depending on its final state. If the derivation ends in a state with unsatisfiable constraints it is called *failed*. Otherwise, the constraints of the final state are satisfiable. If its agents have reduced to *true*, then it is *successful*, else it is *deadlocked* (i.e., the first component contains at least one suspended agent). Deadlocks come with concurrency. They are usually considered programming errors or indicate a lack of sufficient information to continue computation.

13.2.3   Oz and AKL as Concurrent Constraint Programming Languages

The concurrent constraint programming model establishes a clean and simple model for synchronizing concurrent computations based on constraints. On the other hand, CLP (see Chapter 12, "Constraint Logic Programming") provides support for modeling and solving combinatorial problems based on constraints. The obvious idea to integrate both models to yield a single and uniform model for concurrent and parallel programming and problem solving however has proven itself as challenging. Besides merging concurrency and problem solving aspects, the CCP model only captures synchronization based on a single shared constraint store. Other common aspects such as controlling the amount of concurrency in program execution and exchanging messages between concurrently running computations are not dealt with.

These challenges and issues have been one main motivation for the development of AKL and Oz as uniform programming models taking inspirations from both CCP and CLP. The development of AKL started before that of Oz, and naturally Oz has been inspired by many ideas coming from AKL. Later, the two development teams joined forces to further develop Oz and its accompanying programming system Mozart [77]. As Oz integrates all essential ideas but parallel execution from AKL, this section puts its focus on Oz and mentions where important ideas have been integrated from AKL. Achieving parallelism has been an additional motivation in AKL, this resulted in a parallel implementation of AKL [76, 75].

Currently Oz and Mozart are used in many different application areas where the tight combination of concurrency and problem solving capabilities has shown great potential. Education is one particular area where many different programming paradigms can be studied in a single language [115]. Oz as a multi-paradigm language is discussed in [117].

13.2.4   Expressive Concurrent Programming

The concurrent constraint programming model does not specify which amount of concurrency is necessary or useful for program execution. This is clearly not practical: the amount of concurrency used in program execution makes a huge difference in efficiency. The rationale is to use as little concurrency as possible and as much concurrency as necessary.

Experiments with Oz for the right amount of concurrency range from an early ultra-concurrent model [52], over a model with implicit concurrency control [100] to the final model with explicit concurrency control. Explicit concurrency control means that execution is organized into threads that are explicitly created by the programmer. Synchronization then is performed on the level of threads rather than on the level of agents as in the CCP model.

Many-to-one communication. Variables in concurrent constraint programming offer an elegant mechanism for one-to-many communication: a variable serves as a communication channel. Providing more information on that variable by a tell amounts to message sending on that variable. The variable then can be read by many agents with synchronization through entailment on the arrival of the message.

With constraints that can express lists (such as constraints over trees) programs can easily construct streams (often referred to as open-ended lists). A stream is defined by a current tail being a yet unconstrained variable t. Sending a message m tells the constraint $t = \mathrm{cons}(m, t')$ (expressing that the message m is the first element of the stream t followed by elements on the stream t') where t' is a new variable for the new current tail of the stream.

This idea for stream-based communication is very useful for programming concurrent applications [97, 82]. However, it has a serious shortcoming: it does not support many-to-one communication situations where more than a single sender exists. The tail can be only constrained at most once by a tell. Hence all potential senders need to know and update the current tail of a stream.

AKL introduced *ports* to solve this problem and allow for general message-passing communication [62]. The importance of supporting general message-passing communication is witnessed by concurrent programming languages where communication is entirely based on message passing, for example Erlang [13].

A port provides a single point of reference to a stream of messages. It stores the current tail of the stream that is associated with a port. Ports provide a send operation. The send operation takes a port and a message, appends the message to the tail of the port's stream, and updates the stream's tail as described above.

Naming entities. Ports in AKL require that they can be referred to for a send operation. Modeling a port as a constraint in the concurrent constraint programming framework is impossible. The very idea of a port is that its associated tail changes with each send operation. Changing the tail is in conflict with a monotonically growing constraint store.

A generic solution to this problem has been conceived in Oz by the introduction of *names* [100]. A name can be used similar to a constant in a constraint. Additionally, the state of a computation now also has an additional compartment that maps names to entities (such as ports). For example, using a name n for a port means that constraints can be used to refer to the port by using the name n. The additional compartment then stores that n refers to a port and the current tail associated with that port. Names are provided in a way that they cannot be forged and are unique, more details are available in [100].

Mutable state. Ports are not primitive in Oz. Ports are reduced to cells as a primitive that captures mutable state. As discussed above, a cell is referred to by a name and the only operation on a cell is to exchange its content. From cells, ports can be obtained straightforwardly [101].

More expressive programming. Oz incorporates extensions to the concurrent constraint model to increase its expressive power for programming. It adds first-class procedures by using names to refer to procedural abstractions (closures). By this, the aspect of giving procedures first-class status is separated from treating them in the underlying constraint system. The constraint system is only concerned with names referring to procedural abstractions but not with their denotation. This approach also supports functional computation by simple syntactic transformations [101].

The combination of names, first-class procedures, and cells for mutable state constitute the ingredients necessary for object-oriented computing. Here names are used as references to objects, mutable object state is expressed from cells, and classes are composed

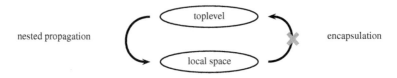

Figure 13.11: Nested propagation and encapsulation for spaces.

from first-class procedures. This setup allows for full-fledged concurrent object-oriented programming including object-based synchronization and class-based inheritance [51].

Distributed programming.   The basic idea of distribution in Oz is to abstract away the network as much as possible. This means that all network operations are invoked implicitly by the system as an incidental result of using particular language operations. Distributed Oz has the same language semantics as Oz by defining a distributed semantics for all language entities such as variables or objects based on cells.

Network transparency means that computations behave the same independent of the site they compute on, and that the possible interconnections between two computations do not depend on whether they execute on the same or on different sites. Network transparency is guaranteed in Distributed Oz for most entities.

An overview on the design of Distributed Oz is [48]. The distributed semantics of variables is reported in [49]; the distributed semantics of objects is discussed in [116].

13.2.5   Encapsulation and Search

The main challenge in combining concurrency with problem solving is that constraint-based computations used for problem solving are *speculative* in nature: their failure is a regular event. Using backtracking for undoing the effect of a failed speculative computation is impossible in a concurrent context. Most computations including interoperating with the external world cannot backtrack. The essential idea to deal with speculative computations in a concurrent context is to *encapsulate* speculative computation so that the failure of an encapsulated computation has no effect on other computations.

Computation spaces.   The idea of encapsulation has been pioneered by AKL, where en capsulation has been achieved by delegating computations to so-called deep guards (to be discussed later in more detail). Oz generalizes this idea as follows. Computations (roughly consisting of threads of statements and a constraint store) are contained in a *computation space*. Encapsulation in Oz then is achieved by delegating speculative computations to *local* computation spaces. The failure of a local space leaves other spaces unaffected.

Computation spaces can then be nested freely resulting in a tree of nested computation spaces as sketched in Figure 13.11. Encapsulation prevents that constraints told by computations in local computation spaces are visible in spaces higher up in the space tree. Nested propagation makes sure that constraints told in computation spaces are propagated to nested spaces.

```
NewSpace  :  Script → Space
Ask       :  Space → Status
Access    :  Space → Solution
Clone     :  Space → Space
Commit    :  Space × Int → Unit
Inject    :  Space × Script → Unit
```

Figure 13.12: Operations on first-class computation spaces.

Stability. Given a setup with local spaces for encapsulation, it is essential to have a criteria when a computation is not any longer speculative. A ground-breaking idea introduced by Janson and Haridi in the context of AKL is *stability* [61, 47, 60]. A speculative computation becomes *stable*, if it has entirely reduced to constraints and that these constraints are entailed or disentailed (that is, the constraints do not make any speculative assumptions themselves) by the constraints from computation spaces higher up in the space tree.

Stability naturally generalizes the notion of entailment by capturing when arbitrary computations are not any longer speculative. In particular, both entailment and stability are monotonic conditions: a stable computation space remains stable regardless of other computations.

Deep guards. Stability has been first used as a control criteria for combinators using so-called *deep guards*. A combinator can be disjunction, negation, or conditional, for example. In the concurrent constraint programming model guards (that is, ask statements) are *flat* as they are restricted to constraints. Deep guards allow arbitrary statements (agents) of the programming language. Similar to how entailment defines when and how computation can proceed for a flat guard, stability defines when and how computation can proceed for a deep guard.

First-class computation spaces. Local computation spaces together with stability as control regime serve as the foundation for both search and combinators in Oz. A general idea in Oz is that important abstractions such as procedures, classes, and objects are available as first-class citizens in the language. As discussed in Section 13.2.4, this is achieved by names that separate reference to entities from the entities proper.

Similarly, local computation spaces are available as first-class computation spaces. Having spaces available first-class, search and combinators become programmable within Oz as programming language.

The operations on first-class computation spaces are listed in Figure 13.12. `NewSpace` takes a script (a procedure that defines the constraint problem to be solved) and returns a space that executes the script. `Ask` synchronizes until computation in the space has reached a stable state. It then returns the status of the space, that is, whether the space is `failed`, `solved`, or has `alternatives`. Alternatives are then resolved by search. `Access` returns the solution stored in a space. `Clone` returns a copy of a space. `Commit` selects an alternative of a choice point. `Inject` adds constraints to a space. How the operations are employed for programming search becomes is sketched briefly below.

```
fun {All S}
   case {Ask S}
   of failed then nil
   [] solved then [{Access S}]
   [] alternatives then C={Clone S} in
      {Commit S 1} {Commit C 2}
      {Append {All S} {All C}}
   end
end
```

Figure 13.13: Depth-first exploration for all solutions.

Programming search. Most constraint programming systems (see Chapter 14, "Finite Domain Constraint Programming Systems") have in common that they offer a fixed and small set of search strategies. The strategies covered are typically limited to single, all, and best-solution search. Search cannot be programmed, which prevents users to construct new search strategies. Search hard-wires depth-first exploration, which prevents even system developers to construct new search strategies. With first-class computation spaces, Oz provides a mechanism to easily program arbitrary search engines featuring arbitrary exploration strategies.

Figure 13.13 conveys that programming search based on first-class computation spaces is easy. The figure contains a formulation of depth-first exploration that returns all solutions. All takes a space S containing the problem to be solved as input. It returns either the empty list, if no solution is found, or a singleton list containing the solution. If a space needs to be resolved by search, the space is copied (by application of Clone) and exploration follows the left alternative (Commit S 1) and later the right alternative (Commit C 2). Append then appends the solutions obtained from exploring both S and C.

The complete search engine is obtained by adding space creation according to the problem P (specified by a procedure P) to be solved:

```
fun {SearchAll P}
   {All {NewSpace P}}
end
```

First-class computation spaces not only cover many standard search engines but have been applied to interactive visual search [94], parallel search [92], and recomputation-based search [95]. A complete treatment of search with first-class computation spaces is [93]. Abstractions similar to first-class computation spaces are also used in the C++ based libraries Figaro [54] and Gecode [44].

Programming combinators. First-class computations spaces can also be used to program deep-guard combinators such as disjunction, negation, blocking implication, for example. Here the motivation is the same as for programming search: the user is not restricted to a fixed set of combinators but can devise application-specific combinators when needed. By this they generalize the idea of deep-guard combinators introduced in AKL. Programming combinators is covered in [91] and more extensively in [93].

13.3   Rule-Based Languages

Rule-based formalisms are ubiquitous in computer science, from theory to practice, from modelling to implementation, from inference rules and transition rules to business rules. Executable rules are used in declarative programming languages, in program transformation and analysis, and for reasoning in artificial intelligence applications. Rules consist of a data description (pattern) and a replacement statement for data matching that description. Rule applications cause localized transformations of a shared data structure (e.g., constraint store, term, graph, database). Applications are repeated until no more change happens.

Constraint Handling Rules (CHR) is a rule-based programming language in the tradition of constraint logic programming, the only one specifically developed for the implementation of constraint solvers. It is traditionally an extension to other programming languages but has been used increasingly as a general-purpose programming language, because it can embed many rule-based formalisms and describe algorithms in a declarative way.

The next section discusses design objectives and related work. Then we give an overview of syntax and semantics of CHR [35, 42] as well as of properties for program analysis such as confluence and operational equivalence. Then we give constraint solvers written in CHR, for Booleans, minima, arithmetic equations, finite and interval domains and lexicographic orders.

13.3.1   Design Objectives

Constraint solver programming.   In the beginning of CLP, constraint solving was hardwired in a built-in constraint solver written in a low-level procedural language. While efficient, this so-called *black-box* approach makes it hard to modify a solver or build a solver over a new domain, let alone debug, reason about and analyse it. Several proposals have been made to allow more for flexibility and costumization of constraint solvers (called *glass-box*, sometimes *white-box* or even *no-box* approaches):

- Demons, forward rules and conditionals of the CLP language CHIP [29], allow defining propagation of constraints in limited ways.

- Indexicals, clp(FD) [25], allow implementing constraints over finite domains at a medium level of abstraction.

- Given constraints connected to a Boolean variable that represents their truth [16, 98] allow expressing any logical formula over primitive constraints.

- Constraint combinators, cc(FD) [110], allow building more complex constraints from simpler constraints.

All approaches extend a solver over a given, specific constraint domain, typically finite domains. The goal then was to design a programming language specifically for writing constraint solvers. Constraint Handling Rules (CHR) [35, 42, 11, 87] is a concurrent committed-choice constraint logic programming language consisting of guarded rules that transform multi-sets of relations called constraints until no more change happens.

Underlying concepts.   CHR was motivated by the inference rules that are traditionally used in computer science to define logical relationships and fixpoint computation in the most abstract way.

In CHR, one distinguishes two main kinds of rules: *Simplification rules* replace constraints by simpler constraints while preserving logical equivalence, e.g., $X \leq Y \wedge Y \leq X \Leftrightarrow X = Y$. *Propagation rules* add new constraints that are logically redundant but may cause further simplification, e.g., $X \leq Y \wedge Y \leq Z \Rightarrow X \leq Z$. Obviously, conjunctions in the head of a rule and propagation rules are essential in expressing constraint solving succinctly.

Given a logical calculus and its transformation rules for deduction, its (conditional) inference rules directly map to propagation rules and its (biconditional) replacement rules to simplification rules. Also, the objects of logic, the (constraint) theories, are usually specified by implications or logical equivalences, corresponding to propagation and simplification rules.

Given a state transition system, its transition rules can readily be expressed with simplification rules. In this way, dynamics and changes (e.g., updates) can be modelled, possibly triggered by events and handled by actions. This justifies the use of CHR as a general purpose programming language.

Design influences.   The design of CHR has many roots and combines their attractiv features in a novel way. Logic programming (LP), constraint logic programming (CLP) [66, 42] and concurrent committed-choice logic programming (CCP) [96, 81] are direct ancestors of CHR. Like automated theorem proving, CHR uses formulae to derive new information, but only in a restricted syntax (e.g., no negation) and in a directional way (e.g., no contrapositives) that makes the difference between the art of proof search and an efficient programming language.

CHR adapts concepts from term rewriting systems [14] for program analysis, but goes beyond term rewriting by working on conjunctions of relations instead of nested terms, and by providing in the language design propagation rules, logical variables, built-in constraints, implicit constraint stores, and more. Extensions of rewriting, such as rewriting Logic [69] and its implementation in Maude [24] and Elan [19] have similar limitations as standard rewriting systems for writing constraints. The functional language Bertrand [64] uses augmented term rewriting to implement constraint-based languages.

Executable rules with multiple head atoms were proposed in the literature to model parallelism and distributed agent processing as well as objects [15, 12], but not for constraint solving. Other influences for the design of CHR were the Gamma computation model and the chemical abstract machine [15], and, of course, production rule systems like OPS5 [20].

Independent developments related to the concepts behind CHR were the multi-paradigm programming languages CLAIRE [22], and OZ [99] as well as database research: constraint and deductive databases, integrity constraints, and event-condition-action rules.

Expressiveness.   The paper [102] introduces CHR machines, analogous to RAM an Turing machines. It shows that these machines can simulate each other in polynomial time, thus establishing that CHR is Turing-complete and, more importantly, that every algorithm can be implemented in CHR with best known time and space complexity, something that is not known to be possible in other pure declarative programming languages like Prolog.

Applications. Recent CHR libraries exist for most Prolog systems, e.g., [55, 85], Java [10, 119, 118, 67], Haskell [23] and Curry. Standard constraint systems as well as novel ones such as temporal, spatial or description logic constraints have been implemented in CHR. Over time CHR has proven useful outside its original field of application in constraint reasoning and computational logic[2], be it agent programming, multi-set rewriting or production rule systems: Recent applications of CHR range from type systems [31] and time tabling [5] to ray tracing and cancer diagnosis [11, 87]. In some of these applications, conjunctions of constraints are best regarded as interacting collections of concurrent agents or processes. We will not discuss CHR as a general-purpose programming language for space reasons.

Abstract syntax

We distinguish between two different kinds of constraints: *built-in (pre-defined) constraints* which are solved by a built-in constraint solver, and CHR *(user-defined) constraints* which are defined by the rules in a CHR program. Built-in constraints include syntactic equality $=$, *true*, and *false*. This distinction allows to embed and utilize existing constraint solvers as well as side-effect-free host language statements. Built-in constraint solvers are considered as black-boxes in whose behavior is trusted and that do not need to be modified or inspected. The solvers for the built-in constraints can be written in CHR itself, giving rise to a hierarchy of solvers [88].

A CHR *program* is a finite set of rules. There are three kinds of rules:

$$
\begin{aligned}
&\textit{Simplification rule:} &&\textit{Name } @ \, H \Leftrightarrow C \mid B \\
&\textit{Propagation rule:} &&\textit{Name } @ \, H \Rightarrow C \mid B \\
&\textit{Simpagation rule:} &&\textit{Name } @ \, H \setminus H' \Leftrightarrow C \mid B
\end{aligned}
$$

Name is an optional, unique identifier of a rule, the *head* H, H' is a non-empty conjunction of CHR constraints, the *guard* C is a conjunction of built-in constraints, and the *body* B is a goal. A *goal* is a conjunction of built-in and CHR constraints. A trivial guard expression "*true*" can be omitted from a rule.

Simpagation rules abbreviate simplification rules of the form $H \wedge H' \Leftrightarrow C \mid H \wedge B$, so there is no further need to discuss them separately.

Operational semantics

At runtime, a CHR program is provided with an initial state and will be executed until either no more rules are applicable or a contradiction occurs.

The operational semantics of CHR is given by a transition system (Fig. 13.14). Let P be a CHR program. We define the transition relation $\mapsto$ by two computation steps (transitions), one for each kind of CHR rule. *States* are goals, i.e., conjunctions of built-in and CHR constraints. States are also called *(constraint) stores*. In the figure, all upper case letters are meta-variables that stand for conjunctions of constraints. The constraint theory CT defines the semantics of the built-in constraints. G_{bi} denotes the built-in constraints of G.

---

[2]Integrating deduction and abduction, bottom-up and top-down execution, forward and backward chaining, tabulation and integrity constraints.

Simplify

If $(r@H \Leftrightarrow C \mid B)$ is a fresh variant with variables $\bar{x}$ of a rule named r in P

and $CT \models \forall\, (G_{bi} \rightarrow \exists \bar{x}(H{=}H' \wedge C))$

then $(H' \wedge G) \mapsto_r (B \wedge G \wedge H{=}H' \wedge C)$

Propagate

If $(r@H \Rightarrow C \mid B)$ is a fresh variant with variables $\bar{x}$ of a rule named r in P

and $CT \models \forall\, (G_{bi} \rightarrow \exists \bar{x}(H{=}H' \wedge C))$

then $(H' \wedge G) \mapsto_r (H' \wedge B \wedge G \wedge H{=}H' \wedge C)$

Figure 13.14: Computation steps of Constraint Handling Rules

Starting from an arbitrary initial goal, CHR rules are applied exhaustively, until a fixpoint is reached. A simplification rule $H \Leftrightarrow C \mid B$ *replaces* instances of the CHR constraints H by B provided the guard C holds. A propagation rule $H \Rightarrow C \mid B$ instead *adds* B to H. If new constraints arrive, rule applications are restarted. Computation stops in a failed final state if the built-in constraints become inconsistent. Trivial non-termination of the **Propagate** computation step is avoided by applying a propagation rule at most once to the same constraints (see the more concrete semantics in [1]).

In more detail, a rule is *applicable*, if its head constraints are matched by constraints in the current goal one-by-one and if, under this matching, the guard of the rule is implied by the built-in constraints in the goal. Any of the applicable rules can be applied, and the application cannot be undone, it is committed-choice.

A *computation (derivation)* of a goal G is a sequence $S_0, S_1, \ldots$ of states with $S_i \mapsto S_{i+1}$ beginning with the *initial state (query, problem)* $S_0 = G$ and ending in a final state or not terminating. A *final state (answer, solution)* is one where either no computation step is possible anymore or where the built-in constraints are inconsistent.

Example 13.1. We define a CHR constraint for a partial order relation $\leq$:

```
reflexivity    @ X≤X ⇔ true
antisymmetry   @ X≤Y ∧ Y≤X  ⇔ X=Y
transitivity   @ X≤Y ∧ Y≤Z  ⇒ X≤Z
```

The CHR program implements reflexivity, antisymmetry, transitivity and redundancy in a straightforward way.

Operationally the rule `reflexivity` removes occurrences of constraints that match X≤X. The rule `antisymmetry` means that if we find X≤Y as well as Y≤X in the current goal, we can replace them by the logically equivalent X=Y. The rule `transitivity` propagates constraints. It adds the logical consequence X≤Z as a redundant constraint, but does not remove any constraints.

A computation of the goal A≤B $\wedge$ C≤A $\wedge$ B≤C proceeds as follows (rules are applied to underlined constraints):

```
A≤B ∧ C≤A ∧ B≤C            ↦ transitivity
A≤B ∧ C≤A ∧ B≤C ∧ C≤B      ↦ antisymmetry
A≤B ∧ C≤A ∧ B=C            ↦ antisymmetry
A=B ∧ B=C
```

Starting from a circular relationship, we have found out that the three variables must be the same.

Refined, parallel and compositional semantics. The high-level description of the operational semantics of CHR given here does not explicitly address termination at failure and of propagation rules, and leaves two main sources of non-determinism: the order in which constraints of a query are processed and the order in which rules are applied (rule scheduling). As in Prolog, almost all CHR implementations execute queries from left to right and apply rules top-down in the textual order of the program. This behavior has been formalized in the so-called *refined semantics* [32] that was proven to be a concretization of the standard operational semantics given in [1]. In [41] a *parallel* execution model for CHR is presented.

Search. Search in CHR is usually provided by the host language, e.g., by the built-in backtracking of Prolog or by search libraries in Java. In addition, in all Prolog implementations of CHR, the disjunction of Prolog can be used in the body of CHR rules. This was formalized in the language CHR$^\vee$ [7, 8]. An early implementation of CHR in Eclipse Prolog also featured so-called labeling declarations [35], that allowed Prolog clauses for CHR constraints. These can be directly translated into CHR$^\vee$, which we will use to define labeling procedures.

Pragmatics. When writing CHR programs, manuals such as [55] suggest to prefer simplification rules and to avoid propagation rules and multiple heads (although indexing often helps to find partner constraints in constant time [85]). One will often modify and compose existing CHR and other programs. Some possibilities are: Flat composition by taking the union of all rules [4]; hierarchical composition by turning some CHR constraints into built-in constraints of another constraint solver [90]; extending arbitrary solvers with CHR [30]. CHR are usually combined with a host language. In the host language, CHR constraints can be posted; in the CHR rules, host language statements can be included as built-in constraints.

Declarative semantics

Owing to the tradition of logic and constraint logic programming, CHR features – besides an operational semantics – a *declarative semantics*, i.e., a direct translation of a CHR program into a first-order theory. In the case of constraint solvers, this strongly facilitates proofs of a program's faithful handling of constraints.

The *logical reading (meaning) of simplification and propagation rules* is given below.

$$H \Leftrightarrow C \mid B \quad \forall (C \to (H \leftrightarrow \exists \bar{y}\, B))$$
$$H \Rightarrow C \mid B \quad \forall (C \to (H \to \exists \bar{y}\, B))$$

The sequence $\bar{y}$ are the variables that appear only in the body B of a rule.

The *logical reading of a* CHR *program* is the conjunction of the logical readings of its rules united with the constraint theory CT that defines the built-in constraints. The *logical reading of a state* is just the conjunction of its constraints. State transitions preserve logical equivalence, i.e., all states in a computation are logically the same. From this result, soundness and completeness theorems follow that show that the declarative and operational semantics coincide strongly, in particular if the program is confluent [9].

Linear-logic semantics.   The classical-logic declarative semantics, however, does not suffice when CHR is used as a general-purpose concurrent programming language. Many algorithms do not have a correct first-order logic reading, especially when they crucially rely on change through updates. This problem has been demonstrated in [41, 86] and led to the development of an alternative declarative semantics. It is based on a subset of *linear logic* [45] that can model resource consumption. It therefore more accurately describes the operational behavior of simplification rules [18].

Program properties and their analysis

One advantage of a declarative programming language is the ease of program analysis. The paper [27] introduces a fix-point semantics which characterizes the input/output behavior of a CHR program and which is *and*-compositional. It allows to retrieve the semantics of a conjunctive query from the semantics of its conjuncts. Such a semantics can be used as a basis to define incremental and modular program analysis and verification tools. An abstract interpretation framework for CHR is introduced in [89]. The basic properties of termination, confluence and operational equivalence are traditionally analysed using specific techniques as discussed below. Time complexity analysis is discussed in [36], but details often rely on problem specific techniques.

Minimal states.   When analysing properties of CHR programs that involve the infinitely many possible states, we can sometimes restrict ourselves to a finite number of so-called minimal states. For each rule, there is a minimal, most general state to which it is applicable. This state is the conjunction of the head and the guard of the rule. Removing any constraint from the state would make the rule inapplicable. Every other state to which the rule is applicable contains the minimal state. Adding constraints to the state cannot inhibit the applicability of a rule because of the *monotonicity property* of CHR [9].

Termination.   A CHR program is called *terminating*, if there are no infinite computations. Since CHR is Turing-complete, termination is undecidable. For CHR programs that mainly use simplification rules, simple well-founded orderings are often sufficient to prove termination [37, 36]. For CHR programs that mainly use propagation rules, results from bottom-up logic programming [43] as well as deductive and constraint databases apply. In general, termination analysis is difficult for non-trivial interactions between simplification and propagation rules.

Confluence.   In a CHR program, the result of computations from a given goal will always have the same meaning. However the answer may not be syntactically the same. The confluence property of a program guarantees that any computation for a goal results in the same final state no matter which of the applicable rules are applied.

The papers [1, 9] give a decidable, sufficient and necessary condition for confluence: A terminating CHR program is confluent if and only if all its critical pairs are joinable. For checking confluence, one takes two rules (not necessarily different) from the program.

The minimal states of the rules are overlapped by equating at least one head constraint from one rule with one from the other rule. For each *overlap*, we consider the two states resulting from applying one or the other rule. These two states form a so-called *critical pair*. One tries to *join* the states in the critical pair by finding two computations starting from the states that reach a common state. If the critical pair is not joinable, we have found a counterexample for confluence of the program.

Example 13.2. Recall the program for $\leq$ of Example 13.1. Consider the rules for reflexivity and antisymmetry and overlap them to get the following critical state and computations.

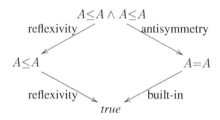

The resulting critical pair is obviously joinable. The example also shows that multiplicities matter in CHR.

Any terminating and confluent CHR program has a consistent logical reading [9, 1] and will automatically implement a concurrent any-time (approximation) and on-line (incremental) algorithm.

Completion. Completion is the process of adding rules to a non-confluent program until it becomes confluent. Rules are built from a non-joinable critical pair to allow a transition from one of the states into the other while maintaining termination.

Example 13.3. Given the $\leq$ solver, assume we want to introduce a $<$ constraint by adding just one rule about the interaction between these two types of inequalities.

$$X \leq Y \wedge Y \leq X \quad \Leftrightarrow \quad X = Y \quad \text{(antisymmetry)}$$
$$X \leq Y \wedge Y < X \quad \Leftrightarrow \quad \textit{false} \quad \text{(inconsistency)}$$

The resulting program is not confluent.

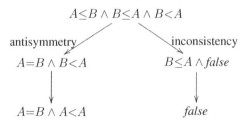

Completion uses the two non-joinable states to derive an interesting new rule, discovering irreflexivity of $<$.

$$X < X \Leftrightarrow \textit{false}$$

In contrast to other completion methods, in CHR we generally need more than one rule to make a critical pair joinable: a simplification rule and a propagation rule [3].

Operational equivalence. A fundamental and hard question in programming language semantics is when two programs should be considered equivalent. For example correctness of program transformation can be studied only with respect to a notion of equivalence. Also, if modules or libraries with similar functionality are used together, one may be interested in finding out if program parts in different modules or libraries are equivalent. In the context of CHR, this case arises frequently when constraint solvers written in CHR are combined. Typically, a constraint is only partially defined in a constraint solver. We want to make sure that the operational semantics of the common constraints of two programs do not differ.

Two programs are operationally equivalent if for each goal, all final states in one program are the same as the final states in the other program. In [2], the authors gave a decidable, sufficient and necessary syntactic condition for operational equivalence of terminating and confluent CHR programs[3]: The minimal states of all rules in both programs are simply run as goals in both programs, and they must reach a common state. An example for operational equivalence checking can be found with the minimum example in Section 13.3.2.

13.3.2　Constraint Solvers

We introduce some constraint solvers written in CHR, for details and more solvers see [38, 42]. We will use the concrete ASCII syntax of CHR implementations in Prolog: Conjunction $\wedge$ is written as comma ','. Disjunction $\vee$ is written as semi-colon ';'. Let '=<' and '<' be built-in constraints now.

Boolean constraint solver

Boolean algebra (propositional logic) constraints can be solved by different techniques [68]. The logical connectives are represented as Boolean constraints, i.e., in relational form. For example, conjunction is written as the constraint and(X,Y,Z), where Z is the result of anding X and Y. In the following terminating and confluent Boolean constraint solver [42], a local consistency algorithm is used. It simplifies one Boolean constraint at a time into one or more syntactic equalities whenever possible. The rules for propositional conjunction are as follows.

```
and(X,Y,Z) <=> X=0 | Z=0.
and(X,Y,Z) <=> Y=0 | Z=0.
and(X,Y,Z) <=> X=1 | Y=Z.
and(X,Y,Z) <=> Y=1 | X=Z.
and(X,Y,Z) <=> X=Y | Y=Z.
and(X,Y,Z) <=> Z=1 | X=1,Y=1.
```

The above rules are based on the idea that, given a value for one of the variables in a constraint, we try to determine values for other variables. However, the Boolean solver goes beyond propagating values, since it also propagates equalities between variables. For example, and(1,Y,Z),neg(Y,Z) will reduce to false, and this cannot be achieved by value propagation alone.

---

[3]To the best of our knowledge, CHR is the only programming language in practical use that admits decidable operational equivalence.

Search.   The above solver is incomplete. For example, the solver cannot detect inconsistency of `and(X,Y,Z),and(X,Y,W),neg(Z,W)`. For completeness, constraint solving has to be interleaved with search. For Boolean constraints, search can be done by trying the values 0 or 1 for a variable. The generic labeling procedure `enum` traverses a list of variables.

```
enum([]) <=> true.
enum([X|L]) <=> indomain(X), enum(L).

indomain(X) <=> (X=0 ; X=1).
```

Minimum constraint

The CHR constraint `min(X,Y,Z)` means that Z is the minimum of X and Y.

```
r1 @ min(X,Y,Z) <=> X=<Y  | Z=X.
r2 @ min(X,Y,Z) <=> Y=<X  | Z=Y.
r3 @ min(X,Y,Z) <=> Z<X   | Y=Z.
r4 @ min(X,Y,Z) <=> Z<Y   | X=Z.
r5 @ min(X,Y,Z) ==> Z=<X, Z=<Y.
```

The first two rules `r1` and `r2` correspond to the usual definition of `min`. But we also want to be able to compute backwards. So the two rules `r3` and `r4` simplify `min` if the order between the result Z and one of the input variables is known. The last rule `r5` ensures that `min(X,Y,Z)` unconditionally implies `Z=<X, Z=<Y`. Rules such as these can be automatically generated from logical specifications [6].

Example 13.4.   Redundancy from a propagation rule is useful, as the goal `min(A,2,2)` shows. To this goal only the propagation rule is applicable, but to the resulting state the second rule becomes applicable:

$$\begin{array}{ll} & \texttt{min(A,2,2)} \\ \mapsto_{r5} & \texttt{min(A,2,2),2=<A} \\ \mapsto_{r2} & \texttt{2=<A} \end{array}$$

In this way, we find out that for `min(A,2,2)` to hold, `2=<A` must hold.
Another interesting derivation involving the propagation rule is:

$$\begin{array}{ll} & \texttt{min(A,B,M),A=<M} \\ \mapsto_{r5} & \texttt{min(A,B,M),A=M,M=<B} \\ \mapsto_{r1} & \texttt{A=M, M=<B} \end{array}$$

It can be shown that the program is terminating and confluent. For example, the only overlap of the minimal states for the first two rules, `r1` and `r2` is `min(X,Y,Z),X=Y`. For both rules, their application leads to logically equivalent built-in constraints `X=Y, Y=Z`.

Operational equivalence.   We would like to know if these two CHR rules defining the user-defined constraint `min` with differing guards

```
min(X,Y,Z) <=> X=<Y  | Z=X.
min(X,Y,Z) <=> Y<X   | Z=Y.
```

are operationally equivalent with these two rules

```
min(X,Y,Z) <=> X<Y  | Z=X.
min(X,Y,Z) <=> Y=<X | Z=Y.
```

or if the union of the rules results in a better constraint solver for `min`.

Already the minimal state of the first rule of the first program, `min(X,Y,Z),X=<Y` shows that the two programs are not operationally equivalent, since it can reduce to `Z=X` in the first program, but is a final state for the second program, since `X=<Y` does not apply any of the guards in the second program. Thus the union of the two programs allows for more constraint simplification. In the union, the two rules with the strict guards can be removed as another operational equivalence test shows that they are redundant.

Linear polynomial equation solving

Typically, in arithmetic constraint solvers, incremental variants of classical variable elimination algorithms [59] like Gaussian elimination for equations and Dantzig's Simplex algorithm for equations are implemented.

A conjunction of equations is *in solved form* if the left-most variable of each equation does not appear in any other equation. We compute the solved form by eliminating multiple occurrences of variables. In this solved form, all determined variables (those that take a unique value) are discovered.

```
eliminate @ A1*X+P1 eq 0 \ P2X eq 0 <=>
                         find(A2*X,P2X,P2) |
                         normalize(A2*(-P1/A1)+P2,P3),
                         P3 eq 0.

constant  @ B eq 0 <=> number(B) | zero(B).
```

The `constant` rule says that if the polynomial contains no more variables, then the number B must be zero. The `eliminate` rule performs variable elimination. It takes any pair of equations with a common occurrence of a variable, X. In the first equation, the variable appears left-most. This equation is used to eliminate the occurrence of the variable in the second equation. The first equation is left unchanged. In the guard, the built-in `find(A2*X,P2X,P2)` tries to find the expression A2*X in the polynomial P2X, where X is the common variable. The plenum P2 is P2X with A2*X removed. The constraint `normalize(E,P)` transforms an arithmetic expression E into a linear polynomial P.

The solver is complete, so no search is necessary. It is terminating but not confluent due to the `eliminate` rule: Consider two equations with the same left-most variable, then the rule can be applied in two different ways. The solver produces the solved form as can be shown by contradiction: If a set of equations is not in solved form, then the `eliminate` rule is applicable. The solver is concurrent by nature of CHR: It can reduce pairs of equations in parallel or eliminate the occurrence of a variable in all other equations at once.

Finite domains

Here, variables are constrained to take their value from a given, finite set. Choosing integers for values allows for arithmetic expressions as constraints. Influential CLP languages with finite domains are CHIP [29], clp(FD) [25] and cc(FD) [110].

The *domain constraint* X *in* D means that the variable X takes its value from the given finite domain D. For simplicity, we start with the *bounds consistency* algorithm for interval constraints [109, 17]. The implementation is based on interval arithmetic. In the solver, in, le, eq, ne, and add are CHR constraints, the inequalities <, >, =<, >=, and <> are built-in arithmetic constraints, and min, max, +, and − are built-in arithmetic functions. X in A..B constrains X to be in the interval A..B. The rules for local consistency affect the interval constraints (in) only, the other constraints remain unaffected.

```
inconsistency @ X in A..B <=> A>B | false.
intersect@ X in A..B, X in C..D <=> X in max(A,C)..min(B,D).

le @ X le Y, X in A..B, Y in C..D <=> B>D |
        X le Y, X in A..D, Y in C..D.
le @ X le Y, X in A..B, Y in C..D <=> C<A |
        X le Y, X in A..B, Y in A..D.


eq @ X eq Y, X in A..B, Y in C..D <=> A<>C |
        X eq Y, X in max(A,C)..B, Y in max(C,A)..D.
eq @ X eq Y, X in A..B, Y in C..D <=> B<>D |
        X eq Y, X in A..min(B,D), Y in C..min(D,B).
```

The CHR constraint X le Y means that X is less than or equal to Y. Hence, X cannot be larger than the upper bound D of Y. Therefore, if the upper bound B of X is larger than D, we can replace B by D without removing any solutions. Analogously, one can reason on the lower bounds to tighten the interval for Y. The eq constraint causes the intersection of the interval domains of its variables provided the bounds are not yet the same.

Example 13.5. Here is a sample computation involving le:

```
            U in 2..3, V in 1..2, U le V
    ↦le    V in 1..2, U le V, U in 2..2
    ↦le    U le V, U in 2..2, V in 2..2.
```

Finally, $X+Y=Z$ is represented as add(X,Y,Z).

```
add @ add(X,Y,Z), X in A..B, Y in C..D, Z in E..F <=>
        not (A>=E-D,B=<F-C,C>=E-B,D=<F-A,E>=A+C,F=<B+D) |
        add(X,Y,Z),
        X in max(A,E-D)..min(B,F-C),
        Y in max(C,E-B)..min(D,F-A),
        Z in max(E,A+C)..min(F,B+D).
```

For addition, we use interval addition and subtraction to compute the interval of one variable from the intervals of the other two variables. The guard ensures that at least one interval becomes smaller whenever the rule is applied. Here is a sample computation involving add:

```
U in 1..3, V in 2..4, W in 0..4, add(U,V,W)   ↦add
add(U,V,W), U in 1..2, V in 2..3, W in 3..4
```

For termination, consider that the rules `inconsistency` and `intersection` from above remove one interval constraint each. We assume that the remaining rules deal with non-empty intervals only. This holds under the refined semantics and can be enforced by additional guard constraints on the interval bounds. Then in each rule, at least one interval in the body is strictly smaller than the corresponding interval in the head, while the other intervals remain unaffected. The solver is confluent, provided the intervals are given. The solver also works with intervals of real numbers of a chosen granularity, so that to ensure termination rules are not applied anymore to domains which are considered too small.

Enumeration domains.   Besides intervals, finite domains can be explicit enumerations of possible values. The rules for enumeration domains are analogous to the ones for interval domains and implement arc consistency [74], for example:

```
inconsistency @ X in [] <=> false.
intersect@ X in L1,X in L2 <=> intersect(L1,L2,L3) | X in L3.
```

Search.   We implement the search routine analogous to the one for Boolean constraints. For interval domains, search is usually done by splitting intervals in two halves. This splitting is repeated until the bounds of the interval are the same.

```
indomain(X), X in A..B <=> A<B |
                (X in A..(A+B)//2, indomain(X) ;
                 X in (A+B)//2+1..B, indomain(X)).
```

The guard ensures termination. For enumeration domains, each value in the domain (implemented as a list) is tried. $X=V$ is expressed as `X in [V]`.

```
indomain(X), X in [V|L] <=> L=[_|_] |
                (X in [V] ; X in L, indomain(X)).
```

The guard ensures termination. Calling `indomain(X)` in the second disjunct ensures that subsequently, the next value for X from the list L will be tried.

N-queens.   The famous n-queens problem asks to place n queens $q_1, \ldots, q_n$ on an $n * n$ chess board, such that they do not attack each other. The problem can be solved with a CHR program, where N is the size of the chess board and Qs is a list of N queen position variables.

```
solve(N,Qs) <=> makedomains(N,Qs), queens(Qs), enum(Qs).
queens([Q|Qs]) <=> safe(Q,Qs,1), queens(Qs).
safe(X,[Y|Qs],N) <=> noattack(X,Y,N), safe(X,Qs,N+1).
```

Instead of implementing `noattack` with the usual three finite domain inequality constraints, we can use `noattack` directly:

```
noattack(X,Y,N), X in [V], Y in D <=>
            remove(D,[V,V+N,V-N],D1) | Y in D1.
noattack(Y,X,N), X in [V], Y in D <=>
            remove(D,[V,V+N,V-N],D1) | Y in D1.
```

The constraint between three lists `remove(D,L,D1)` holds if `D1` is `D` without the values in `L` and at least one value has been removed.

Lexicographic order global constraint

A lexicographic order $\preceq_{lex}$ (`lex`) allows to compare sequences by comparing the elements of the sequences proceeding from start to end. Given two sequences l_1 and l_2 of variables of the same length n, $[x_1, \ldots, x_n]$ and $[y_1, \ldots, y_n]$, then $l_1 \preceq_{lex} l_2$ if and only if $n=0$ or $x_1 < y_1$ or $x_1 = y_1$ and $[x_2, \ldots, x_n] \preceq_{lex} [y_2, \ldots, y_n]$.

The solver [40] consists of three pairs of rules, the first two corresponding to base cases of the recursion (garbage collection), then two rules performing forward reasoning (recursive traversal and implied inequality), and finally two for backward reasoning, covering a not so obvious special case when the lexicographic constraint has a unique solution.

```
l1 @ [] lex [] <=> true.
l2 @ [X|L1] lex [Y|L2] <=> X<Y | true.
l3 @ [X|L1] lex [Y|L2] <=> X=Y | L1 lex L2.
l4 @ [X|L1] lex [Y|L2] ==> X=<Y.

l5 @ [X,U|L1] lex [Y,V|L2] <=> U>V | X<Y.
l6 @ [X,U|L1] lex [Y,V|L2] <=> U>=V, L1=[_|_] |
                  [X,U] lex [Y,V], [X|L1] lex [Y|L2].
```

The implementation is short and concise without giving up on linear time worst case time complexity. It is incremental and concurrent by nature of CHR. It is provably correct and confluent. It is independent of the underlying constraint system. In [40], also completeness of constraint propagation is shown, i.e., given a `lex` constraint and an inequality, all implied inequalities are generated by the solver.

13.4 Challenges and Opportunities

The integration of constraint technology in more traditional or hybrid paradigms has been a source of significant progress. Nonetheless, it is still shy of a comprehensive solution that addresses all the motivating objectives. It has, however, created flexible platforms particularly well-suited for experimenting with novel research ideas and directions. This section considers some of these opportunities.

13.4.1 Cooperative Solvers

Cooperative solvers are already a reality. Linear Programming and Integer Programming solvers have been used in conjunction with constraint solvers and the combination often proved quite effective. New solvers are developed regularly either for domain specific needs or as vertical extensions. In all cases, hybridization raises many issues: How should solvers communicate? How do solvers compose? What is the composite's architecture (side-by-side, master-slave, concurrent,...)? What are the synchronization triggers and events (variable bounds, heuristic information, objective function, impacts,...)? Should the solvers operate on redundant statements of the same problems or on disjoint subset of constraints they are better suited for? Can solver-specific formulations be derived from a unique master statement? Can the formulations be automatically refined over time?

13.4.2 Orthogonal Computation Models

Recent developments in constraint-based local search [107] clearly indicate that constraint-based solvers can be developed for radically different computation models. From a declarative standpoint, local search solvers rely on constraints to specify the properties of solutions and write elegant, high-level, and reusable search procedures which automatically exploit the constraints to guide the search. From a computational standpoint, the solver incrementally maintains properties (e.g. truth value, violation degree, variable and value based violations) under non-monotonic changes to the decision variables that always have a tentative value assignment. This organization is a fundamental departure from classic domain-based consistency and filtering techniques found in traditional finite domain solvers.

The fundamental differences are related to the nature of the underlying computational models. How can these solvers be effectively hybridized? What steps are required for an efficient integration of the computation models that does not result in severe performance degradation for either? Once the two technologies coexist, how can the solvers be composed? How can each solver benefit from results produced by its counter-part? Which form of collaboration is most effective?

13.4.3 Orthogonal Concerns

As solvers sophistication increases, it becomes difficult to anticipate the behavior of a solver on a given problem formulation. The advances in solver technology (efficiency, flexibility, openness) should be matched with equal progress in supporting abstractions for model designers. For Rapid application development, it is essential to assist the developers of optimization models. Improvements should include better debugging tools (where debugging occurs at the abstraction level of the model), explanation tools for post-mortem analysis, but also tracing tools for live analysis of the solver's behavior during the search process. Tools like the Oz Explorer [94] or the tree visualizer of OplStudio [114] provide initial insights into the dynamics of the search but fail to relate this behavior to modeling abstractions (constraints) and their interplay. Novel tools should also support the exploration of alternative model formulation and search heuristics to quickly identify successful strategies, a task which becomes increasingly burdensome given the large number of potential heuristics that ought to be considered.

13.5 Conclusion

Constraint solving and handling has moved from logic programming into more common programming paradigms and faced the challenges that it found there.

- Generalizing search from built-in backtracking of Prolog to flexible search routines as in OPL, Oz and SALSA.

- User friendliness by providing well-known metaphors resulting in modelling languages such as OPL and Comet.

- Integration into advanced multi-paradigm languages such as CLAIRE and Oz.

- The move from black-box solvers to glass-box solvers, that can be customized and analysed more easily, with constraint handling rules (CHR) at the extreme end of the spectrum.

These issues will remain a topic of research and development in constraint programming for the near future, but impressive first steps have been done.

Acknowledgments

Christian Schulte is partially funded by the Swedish Research Council (VR) under grant 621-2004-4953.

Bibliography

[1] S. Abdennadher. Operational semantics and confluence of constraint propagation rules. In *3rd International Conference on Principles and Practice of Constraint Programming*, LNCS 1330. Springer, 1997.

[2] S. Abdennadher and T. Frühwirth. Operational equivalence of constraint handling rules. In *Fifth International Conference on Principles and Practice of Constraint Programming, CP99*, LNCS 1713. Springer, 1999.

[3] S. Abdennadher and T. Frühwirth. On completion of constraint handling rules. In *4th International Conference on Principles and Practice of Constraint Programming, CP98*, LNCS 1520. Springer, 1998.

[4] S. Abdennadher and T. Frühwirth. Integration and optimization of rule-based constraint solvers. In M. Bruynooghe, editor, *Logic Based Program Synthesis and Transformation - LOPSTR 2003, Revised Selected Papers*, LNCS 3018. Springer, 2004.

[5] S. Abdennadher and M. Marte. University course timetabling using Constraint Handling Rules. *Journal of Applied Artificial Intelligence*, 14(4):311–326, 2000.

[6] S. Abdennadher and C. Rigotti. Automatic generation of chr constraint solvers. *Theory Pract. Log. Program.*, 5(4-5):403–418, 2005. ISSN 1471-0684. doi: http: //dx.doi.org/10.1017/S1471068405002371.

[7] S. Abdennadher and H. Schütz. Model generation with existentially quantified variables and constraints. In *6th International Conference on Algebraic and Logic Programming*, LNCS 1298. Springer, 1997.

[8] S. Abdennadher and H. Schütz. CHR$^\vee$: A flexible query language. In *Flexible Query Answering Systems*, LNAI 1495. Springer, 1998.

[9] S. Abdennadher, T. Frühwirth, and H. Meuss. Confluence and semantics of constraint simplification rules. *Constraints Journal, Special Issue on the 2nd International Conference on Principles and Practice of Constraint Programming*, 4(2): 133–165, 1999.

[10] S. Abdennadher, E. Krämer, M. Saft, and M. Schmauss. Jack: A java constraint kit. In *Electronic Notes in Theoretical Computer Science*, volume 64, 2000.

[11] S. Abdennadher, T. Frühwirth, and C. Holzbaur. Editors, Special Issue on Constraint Handling Rules. *Theory and Practice of Logic Programming*

(TPLP), 5(4–5), 2005. URL http://www.informatik.uni-ulm.de/pm/
mitarbeiter/fruehwirth/tplp-chr/index.html.

[12]   J.-M. Andreoli and R. Pareschi. Linear objects: logical processes with built-in inheritance. In *7th International Conference on Logic programming (ICLP)*, pages
495–510, Cambridge, MA, USA, 1990. MIT Press. ISBN 0-262-73090-1.

[13]   J. Armstrong, R. Virding, and M. Williams. *Concurrent Programming in Erlang*
Prentice-Hall International, Englewood Cliffs, NY, USA, 1993.

[14]   F. Baader and T. Nipkow. *Term Rewriting and All That*. Cambridge Univ. Press,
1998.

[15]   J.-P. Banatre, A. Coutant, and D. L. Metayer. A parallel machine for multiset transformation and its programming style. *Future Generation Computer Systems*, 4:
133–144, 1988.

[16]   F. Benhamou. Interval constraint logic programming. In A. Podelski, editor, *Constraint Programming: Basics and Trends*, LNCS 910, pages 1–21. Springer, 1995.

[17]   F. Benhamou and W. J. Older. Applying interval arithmetic to real, integer, and
boolean constraints. *The Journal of Logic Programming*, 32(1), 1997.

[18]   H. Betz and T. Frühwirth. A linear-logic semantics for constraint handling rules.
In P. van Beek, editor, *11th Conference on Principles and Practice of Constraint
Programming CP 2005*, volume 3709 of *Lecture Notes in Computer Science*, pages
137–151. Springer, Oct. 2005. URL http://www.informatik.uni-ulm.
de/pm/mitarbeiter/fruehwirth/Papers/llchr-final0.pdf.

[19]   P. Borovansky, C. Kirchner, H. Kirchner, P. E. Moreau, and M. Vittek. ELAN:
A logical framework based on computational systems. In *Proc. of the First
Int. Workshop on Rewriting Logic*, volume ENTCS 4(1). Elsevier, 2004. URL
citeseer.ist.psu.edu/borovansky97elan.html.

[20]   L. Brownston, R. Farrell, E. Kant, and N. Martin. *Programming expert systems
in OPS5: an introduction to rule-based programming*. Addison-Wesley Longman
Publishing Co., Inc., Boston, MA, USA, 1985. ISBN 0-201-10647-7.

[21]   Y. Caseau, P.-Y. Guillo, and E. Levenez. A Deductive and Object-Oriented Approach to a Complex Scheduling Problem. In *Proc. of DOOD'93*, Phoenix, AZ,
December 1989.

[22]   Y. Caseau, F.-X. Josset, and F. Laburthe. Claire: combining sets, search and rules to
better express algorithms. *Theory Pract. Log. Program.*, 2(6):769–805, 2002. ISSN
1471-0684. doi: http://dx.doi.org/10.1017/S1471068401001363.

[23]   W.-N. Chin, M. Sulzmann, and M. Wang. A type-safe embedding of constraint handling rules into haskell. Technical report, School of Computing, National University
of Singapore, Singapore, 2003.

[24]   M. Clavel, F. Durán, S. Eker, P. Lincoln, N. Martí-Oliet, J. Meseguer, and J. F.
Quesada. Maude: specification and programming in rewriting logic. *Theor. Com-
put. Sci.*, 285(2):187–243, 2002. ISSN 0304-3975. doi: http://dx.doi.org/10.1016/
S0304-3975(01)00359-0.

[25]   P. Codognet and D. Diaz. Compiling constraints in clp(FD). *Journal of Logic
Programming*, 27(3):185–226, 1996.

[26]   *Mosel: An   Overview.*   Dash   Optimization   White   Paper,   2004.
http://www.dashoptimization.com/home/products/products_mosel.html.

[27]   G. Delzanno, M. Gabbrielli, and M. C. Meo. A compositional semantics for chr.
In *PPDP '05: Proceedings of the 7th ACM SIGPLAN international conference on*

Principles and practice of declarative programming, pages 209–217, New York, NY, USA, 2005. ACM Press. ISBN 1-59593-090-6. doi: http://doi.acm.org/10. 1145/1069774.1069794.

[28]   D. Diaz and P. Codognet. A minimal extension of the WAM for CLP(FD). In *Proceedings of the Tenth International Conference on Logic Programming (ICLP-93)*, pages 774–792, Budapest (Hungary), June 1993.

[29]   M. Dincbas, P. Van Hentenryck, H. Simonis, A. Aggoun, T. Graf, and F. Berthier. The constraint logic programming language CHIP. In *International Conference on Fifth Generation Computer Systems*, pages 693–702. Institute for New Generation Computer Technology, 1988.

[30]   G. J. Duck, P. J. Stuckey, M. G. de la Banda, and C. Holzbaur. Extending arbitrary solvers with constraint handling rules. In *PPDP '03: Proceedings of the 5th ACM SIGPLAN international conference on Principles and practice of declaritive programming*, pages 79–90, New York, NY, USA, 2003. ACM Press. ISBN 1-58113-705-2. doi: http://doi.acm.org/10.1145/888251.888260.

[31]   G. J. Duck, S. L. P. Jones, P. J. Stuckey, and M. Sulzmann. Sound and decidable type inference for functional dependencies. In *ESOP*, pages 49–63, 2004.

[32]   G. J. Duck, P. J. Stuckey, M. G. de la Banda, and C. Holzbaur. The Refined Operational Semantics of Constraint Handling Rules. In B. Demoen and V. Lifschitz, editors, *20th International Conference on Logic Programming (ICLP)*, LNCS. Springer, 2004.

[33]   R. Fourer, K. Martin, and J. Ma. Modeling systems & optimization services. Book in preparation.

[34]   R. Fourer, D. Gay, and B. Kernighan. *AMPL: A Modeling Language for Mathematical Programming*. The Scientific Press, San Francisco, CA, 1993.

[35]   T. Frühwirth. Theory and Practice of Constraint Handling Rules, Special Issue on Constraint Logic Programming. *Journal of Logic Programming*, 37(1–3):95–138, 1998. URL http://www.pst.informatik.uni-muenchen.de/personen/fruehwir/drafts/jlp-chr1.ps.Z.

[36]   T. Frühwirth. As Time Goes By: Automatic Complexity Analysis of Simplification Rules. In *8th International Conference on Principles of Knowledge Representation and Reasoning*, Toulouse, France, 2002.

[37]   T. Frühwirth. Proving termination of constraint solver programs. In E. M. K.R. Apt, A.C. Kakas and F. Rossi, editors, *New Trends in Constraints*, LNAI 1865. Springer, 2000.

[38]   T. Frühwirth. Constraint systems and solvers for constraint programming. *Special Issue of Archives of Control Sciences (ACS) on Constraint Programming for Decision and Control*, 2006. URL http://www.informatik.uni-ulm.de/pm/mitarbeiter/fruehwirth/Papers/acs-systems3.pdf. To appear.

[39]   T. Frühwirth. Constraint handling rules. In A. Podelski, editor, *Constraint Programming: Basics and Trends*, LNCS 910. Springer, March 1995.

[40]   T. Frühwirth. Complete propagation rules for lexicographic order constraints over arbitrary domains. In *Recent Advances in Constraints, CSCLP 2005*, LNAI. Springer, 2006. To appear.

[41]   T. Frühwirth. Parallelizing union-find in constraint handling rules using confluence. In M. Gabbrielli and G. G., editors, *Logic Programming: 21st International Con-*

ference, ICLP 2005, volume 3668 of *Lecture Notes in Computer Science*, pages 113–127. Springer, Oct. 2005. URL http://www.informatik.uni-ulm. de/pm/mitarbeiter/fruehwirth/Papers/puf0.pdf.

[42] T. Frühwirth and S. Abdennadher. *Essentials of Constraint Programming*. Springer, 2003.

[43] H. Ganzinger and D. McAllester. A new meta-complexity theorem for bottom-up logic programs. In *International Joint Conference on Automated Reasoning*, LNCS 2083, pages 514–528. Springer, 2001.

[44] Gecode Team. Gecode (generic constraint development environment), 2005. Available from www.gecode.org.

[45] J.-Y. Girard. Linear logic: Its syntax and semantics. *Theoretical Computer Science* 50:1–102, 1987.

[46] C. Guéret, C. Prins, M. Sevaux, and S. Heipcke. *Applications of Optimization with XpressMP*. Dash Optimization Ltd., 2002.

[47] S. Haridi, S. Janson, and C. Palamidessi. Structural operational semantics for AKL. *Future Generation Computer Systems*, 8:409–421, 1992.

[48] S. Haridi, P. Van Roy, P. Brand, and C. Schulte. Programming languages for distributed applications. *New Generation Computing*, 16(3):223–261, 1998.

[49] S. Haridi, P. Van Roy, P. Brand, M. Mehl, R. Scheidhauer, and G. Smolka. Efficient logic variables for distributed computing. *ACM Transactions on Programming Languages and Systems*, 21(3):569–626, May 1999.

[50] W. Harvey and M. Ginsberg. Limited Discrepancy Search. In *Proceedings of the 14th International Joint Conference on Artificial Intelligence*, Montreal, Canada, August 1995.

[51] M. Henz. *Objects for Concurrent Constraint Programming*, volume 426 of *International Series in Engineering and Computer Science*. Kluwer Academic Publishers, Boston, MA, USA, Oct. 1997.

[52] M. Henz, G. Smolka, and J. Würtz. Oz—A programming language for multi-agent systems. In *13th International Joint Conference on Artificial Intelligence*, volume 1, pages 404–409, Chambéry, France, 1993. Morgan Kaufmann Publishers. Revised version appeared as [53].

[53] M. Henz, G. Smolka, and J. Würtz. Object-oriented concurrent constraint programming in Oz. In V. Saraswat and P. Van Hentenryck, editors, *Principles and Practice of Constraint Programming*, pages 29–48. The MIT Press, Cambridge, MA, USA, 1995.

[54] M. Henz, T. Müller, and K. B. Ng. Figaro: Yet another constraint programming library. In I. de Castro Dutra, V. S. Costa, G. Gupta, E. Pontelli, M. Carro, and P. Kacsuk, editors, *Parallelism and Implementation Technology for (Constraint) Logic Programming*, pages 86–96, Las Cruces, NM, USA, Dec. 1999. New Mexico State University.

[55] C. Holzbaur and T. Frühwirth. *Constraint Handling Rules Reference Manual for Sicstus Prolog*. Vienna, Austria, July 1998. URL http://www.sics.se/isl/ sicstus/sicstus_34.html.

[56] Ilog CPLEX 6.0. Reference Manual. Ilog SA, Gentilly, France, 1998.

[57] Ilog OPL Studio 3.0. Reference Manual. Ilog SA, Gentilly, France, 2000.

[58] Ilog Solver 4.4. Reference Manual. Ilog SA, Gentilly, France, 1998.

[59] J.-L. J. Imbert. Linear constraint solving in clp-languages. In A. Podelski, editor,

Constraint Programming: Basics and Trends, LNCS 910. Springer, 1995.

[60] S. Janson. *AKL - A Multiparadigm Programming Language*. PhD thesis, SICS Swedish Institute of Computer Science, SICS Box 1263, S-164 28 Kista, Sweden, 1994. SICS Dissertation Series 14.

[61] S. Janson and S. Haridi. Programming paradigms of the Andorra kernel language. In V. Saraswat and K. Ueda, editors, *Logic Programming, Proceedings of the 1991 International Symposium*, pages 167–186, San Diego, CA, USA, Oct. 1991. The MIT Press.

[62] S. Janson, J. Montelius, and S. Haridi. Ports for objects. In *Research Directions in Concurrent Object-Oriented Programming*. The MIT Press, Cambridge, MA, USA, 1993.

[63] F. Laburthe and Y. Caseau. SALSA: A Language for Search Algorithms. In *Fourth International Conference on the Principles and Practice of Constraint Programming (CP'98)*, Pisa, Italy, October 1998.

[64] W. Leler. *Constraint programming languages: their specification and generation*. Addison-Wesley Longman Publishing Co., Inc., Boston, MA, USA, 1988. ISBN 0-201-06243-7.

[65] M. J. Maher. Logic semantics for a class of committed-choice programs. In J.-L. Lassez, editor, *4th International Conference on Logic Programming*, pages 858–876, Cambridge, Mass., 1987. MIT Press.

[66] K. Marriott and P. J. Stuckey. *Programming with Constraints: An Introduction*. MIT Press, Cambridge, Mass., 1998.

[67] L. Menezes, J. Vitorino, and M. Aurelio. A High Performance CHRv Execution Engine. In *Second Workshop on Constraint Handling Rules, at ICLP05*, Sitges, Spain, October 2005.

[68] S. Menju, K. Sakai, Y. Sato, and A. Aiba. A study on boolean constraint solvers. In F. Benhamou and A. Colmerauer, editors, *Constraint Logic Programming: Selected Research*, pages 253–268. MIT Press, Cambridge, Mass., 1993.

[69] J. Meseguer. Conditional rewriting logic as a unified model of concurrency. *Theor. Comput. Sci.*, 96(1):73–155, 1992. ISSN 0304-3975. doi: http://dx.doi.org/10.1016/0304-3975(92)90182-F.

[70] P. Meseguer. Interleaved Depth-First Search. In *Proceedings of the 15th International Joint Conference on Artificial Intelligence*, Nagoya, Japan, August 1997.

[71] L. Michel and P. Van Hentenryck. A Constraint-Based Architecture for Local Search. In *Conference on Object-Oriented Programming Systems, Languages, and Applications.*, pages 101–110, Seattle, WA, USA, November 4-8 2002. ACM.

[72] L. Michel and P. Van Hentenryck. A Modeling Layer for Constraint-Programming Libraries. *INFORMS Journal on Computing*, 2004. in press.

[73] L. Michel and P. Van Hentenryck. Non-deterministic control for hybrid search. In *CPAIOR'05: Proceedings of the 2nd International Conference on the Integration of Constraint Programming, Artificial Intelligence and Operations Research"*, pages 1–15, Prague, Czech Republic, 2005. Springer-Verlag.

[74] R. Mohr and G. Masini. Good old discrete relaxation. In *8th European Conference on Artificial Intelligence*, pages 651–656, Munich, Germany, 1988.

[75] J. Montelius. *Exploiting Fine-grain Parallelism in Concurrent Constraint Languages*. PhD thesis, SICS Swedish Institute of Computer Science, SICS Box 1263, S-164 28 Kista, Sweden, Apr. 1997. SICS Dissertation Series 25.

[76] J. Montelius and K. A. M. Ali. An And/Or-parallel implementation of AKL. *New Generation Computing*, 13–14, Aug. 1995.

[77] Mozart Consortium. The Mozart programming system, 1999. Available from `www.mozart-oz.org`.

[78] L. Perron. Search procedures and parallelism in constraint programming. In *CP '99: Proceedings of the 5th International Conference on Principles and Practice of Constraint Programming*, pages 346–360, London, UK, 1999. Springer-Verlag. ISBN 3-540-66626-5.

[79] J.-F. Puget. A C++ Implementation of CLP. In *Proceedings of SPICIS'94*, Singapore, November 1994.

[80] J.-F. Puget and M. Leconte. Beyond the Glass Box: Constraints as Objects. In *Proceedings of the International Symposium on Logic Programming (ILPS-95)*, pages 513–527, Portland, OR, November 1995.

[81] V. Saraswat. *Concurrent Constraint Programming*. MIT Press, Cambridge, Mass., 1993.

[82] V. A. Saraswat. *Concurrent Constraint Programming*. ACM Doctoral Dissertation Awards: Logic Programming. The MIT Press, Cambridge, MA, USA, 1993.

[83] V. A. Saraswat and M. Rinard. Concurrent constraint programming. In *POPL '90: Proceedings of the 17th ACM SIGPLAN-SIGACT symposium on Principles of programming languages*, pages 232–245, New York, NY, USA, 1990. ACM Press. ISBN 0-89791-343-4. doi: http://doi.acm.org/10.1145/96709.96733.

[84] V. A. Saraswat, M. Rinard, and P. Panangaden. The semantic foundations of concurrent constraint programming. In *POPL '91: Proceedings of the 18th ACM SIGPLAN-SIGACT symposium on Principles of programming languages*, pages 333–352, New York, NY, USA, 1991. ACM Press. ISBN 0-89791-419-8. doi: http://doi.acm.org/10.1145/99583.99627.

[85] T. Schrijvers. Analyses, optimizations and extensions of constraint handling rules, Ph.D. Thesis. Technical report, Department of Computer Science, K.U.Leuven, Belgium, June 2005.

[86] T. Schrijvers and T. Frühwirth. Optimal union-find in constraint handling rules, programming pearl. *Theory and Practice of Logic Programming (TPLP)*, 6(1), 2006. URL http://arxiv.org/abs/cs.PL/0501073.

[87] T. Schrijvers and T. Frühwirth. CHR Website, `www.cs.kuleuven.ac.be/~dtai/projects/CHR/`, 2006.

[88] T. Schrijvers, B. Demoen, G. Duck, P. Stuckey, and T. Frühwirth. Automatic implication checking for chr constraints. In *6th International Workshop on Rule-Based Programming*, Apr. 2005. URL http://www.cs.kuleuven.ac.be/~dtai/publications/files/41606.pdf.

[89] T. Schrijvers, P. J. Stuckey, and G. J. Duck. Abstract interpretation for constraint handling rules. In *PPDP '05: Proceedings of the 7th ACM SIGPLAN international conference on Principles and practice of declarative programming*, pages 218–229, New York, NY, USA, 2005. ACM Press. ISBN 1-59593-090-6. doi: http://doi.acm.org/10.1145/1069774.1069795.

[90] T. Schrijvers, B. Demoen, G. Duck, P. Stuckey, and T. Frühwirth. Automatic Implication Checking for CHR Constraints. *Electronic Notes in Theoretical Computer Science, Proceedings of 6th International Workshop on Rule-Based Programming, Nara, Japan, 2005*, 147(1):93–111, January 2006.

[91] C. Schulte. Programming deep concurrent constraint combinators. In E. Pontelli and V. S. Costa, editors, *Practical Aspects of Declarative Languages, Second International Workshop, PADL 2000*, volume 1753 of *Lecture Notes in Computer Science*, pages 215–229, Boston, MA, USA, Jan. 2000. Springer-Verlag.

[92] C. Schulte. Parallel search made simple. In N. Beldiceanu, W. Harvey, M. Henz, F. Laburthe, E. Monfroy, T. Müller, L. Perron, and C. Schulte, editors, *Proceedings of TRICS: Techniques foR Implementing Constraint programming Systems, a post-conference workshop of CP 2000*, number TRA9/00, pages 41–57, 55 Science Drive 2, Singapore 117599, Sept. 2000.

[93] C. Schulte. *Programming Constraint Services*, volume 2302 of *Lecture Notes in Artificial Intelligence*. Springer-Verlag, Berlin, Germany, 2002.

[94] C. Schulte. Oz Explorer: A visual constraint programming tool. In L. Naish, editor, *Proceedings of the Fourteenth International Conference on Logic Programming*, pages 286–300, Leuven, Belgium, July 1997. The MIT Press.

[95] C. Schulte. Programming constraint inference engines. In G. Smolka, editor, *Proceedings of the Third International Conference on Principles and Practice of Constraint Programming*, volume 1330 of *Lecture Notes in Computer Science*, pages 519–533, Schloß Hagenberg, Linz, Austria, Oct. 1997. Springer-Verlag.

[96] E. Shapiro. The family of concurrent logic programming languages. *ACM Computing Surveys*, 21(3):413–510, 1989.

[97] E. Shapiro. The family of concurrent logic programming languages. *ACM Computing Surveys*, 21(3):413–510, 1989.

[98] G. A. Sidebottom. A language for optimizing constraint propagation, Ph.D. Thesis. Technical report, Simon Fraser University, Canada, 1993.

[99] G. Smolka. The Oz programming model. In J. van Leeuwen, editor, *Computer Science Today*, LNCS 1000, Berlin, Heidelberg, New York, 1995. Springer.

[100] G. Smolka. A foundation for higher-order concurrent constraint programming. In J.-P. Jouannaud, editor, *1st International Conference on Constraints in Computational Logics*, volume 845 of *Lecture Notes in Computer Science*, pages 50–72, München, Germany, Sept. 1994. Springer-Verlag.

[101] G. Smolka. The Oz programming model. In J. van Leeuwen, editor, *Computer Science Today*, volume 1000 of *Lecture Notes in Computer Science*, pages 324–343. Springer-Verlag, Berlin, 1995.

[102] J. Sneyers, T. Schrijvers, and B. Demoen. The Computational Power and Complexity of Constraint Handling Rules. In *Second Workshop on Constraint Handling Rules, at ICLP05*, Sitges, Spain, October 2005.

[103] K. Ueda. Guarded horn clauses. In *Concurrent Prolog*, pages 140–156, Cambridge, MA, USA, 1988. MIT Press. ISBN 0-262-19255-1.

[104] P. Van Hentenryck. Constraint and Integer Programming in OPL. *Informs Journal on Computing*, 14(4):345–372, 2002.

[105] P. Van Hentenryck. *The OPL Optimization Programming Language*. The MIT Press, Cambridge, Mass., 1999.

[106] P. Van Hentenryck and L. Michel. Nondeterministic Control For Hybrid Search. In *Proceedings of the Second International Conference on the Integration of AI and OR Techniques in Constraint Programming for Combinatorial Optimisation Problems (CP-AI-OR'04)*, Prague, Czech Republic, 2005. Springer-Verlag.

[107] P. Van Hentenryck and L. Michel. *Constraint-Based Local Search*. The MIT Press,

Cambridge, Mass., 2005.

[108] P. Van Hentenryck and L. Michel. *New Trends in Constraints*, chapter OPL Script: Composing and Controlling Models. Lecture Note in Artificial Intelligence (LNAI 1865). Springer Verlag, 2000.

[109] P. van Hentenryck, Y. Deville, and C.-M. Teng. A generic arc-consistency algorithm and its specializations. *Artificial Intelligence*, 57:291–321, 1992.

[110] P. van Hentenryck, V. A. Saraswat, and Y. Deville. Constraint processing in cc(FD). In A. Podelski, editor, *Constraint Programming: Basics and Trends*, LNCS 910. Springer, 1995.

[111] P. Van Hentenryck, L. Michel, and Y. Deville. *Numerica: a Modeling Language for Global Optimization*. The MIT Press, Cambridge, Mass., 1997.

[112] P. Van Hentenryck, L. Michel, and F. Benhamou. Newton: Constraint programming over nonlinear constraints. *Sci. Comput. Program.*, 30(1-2):83–118, 1998. ISSN 0167-6423. doi: http://dx.doi.org/10.1016/S0167-6423(97)00008-7.

[113] P. Van Hentenryck, L. Perron, and J.-F. Puget. Search and Strategies in OPL. *ACM Transactions on Computational Logic*, 1(2):1–36, October 2000.

[114] P. Van Hentenryck, L. Michel, F. Paulin, and J. Puget. *Modeling Languages in Mathematical Optimization*, chapter The OPL Studio Modeling System. Kluwer Academic Publishers, 2003.

[115] P. Van Roy and S. Haridi. *Concepts, Techniques, and Models of Computer Programming*. The MIT Press, Cambridge, MA, USA, 2004.

[116] P. Van Roy, S. Haridi, P. Brand, G. Smolka, M. Mehl, and R. Scheidhauer. Mobile objects in Distributed Oz. *ACM Transactions on Programming Languages and Systems*, 19(5):804–851, Sept. 1997.

[117] P. Van Roy, P. Brand, D. Duchier, S. Haridi, M. Henz, and C. Schulte. Logic programming in the context of multiparadigm programming: the Oz experience. *Theory and Practice of Logic Programming*, 3(6):715–763, Nov. 2003.

[118] P. V. Weert, T. Schrijvers, and B. Demoen. The K.U.Leuven JCHR System. In *Second Workshop on Constraint Handling Rules, at ICLP05*, Sitges, Spain, October 2005.

[119] A. Wolf. Adaptive Constraint Handling with CHR in Java. In *7th International Conference on Principles and Practice of Constraint Programming (CP 2001)*, LNCS 2239. Springer, 2001.

Chapter 14

Finite Domain Constraint Programming Systems

Christian Schulte and Mats Carlsson

One of the main reasons why constraint programming quickly found its way into applications has been the early availability of usable constraint programming systems. Given the wide range of applications using constraint programming it is obvious that one of the key properties of constraint programming systems is their provision of widely reusable services for constructing constraint-based applications.

A constraint programming system can be thought of as providing a set of reusable services. Common services include constraint propagation, search, and services for interfacing to the system. This chapter looks in more detail at which services are provided by a constraint programming system and in particular what are the key principles and techniques in constructing and coordinating these services.

To give the chapter a clear focus and a reasonably uniform presentation, we mostly restrict our attention to propagation-based finite domain constraint programming systems. That is, systems that solve problems using constraint propagation involving variables ranging over some finite set of integers. The focus on finite domain constraint programming systems coincides with both practical relevance and known principles and techniques: systems at least offer services for finite domains; much of the known principles and techniques have been conceived and documented for finite domains.

Essential for a system in providing the services mentioned above are some important abstractions (or objects) to be implemented by a system: variables, implementations for constraints, and so on. Important abstractions for propagation, search, and interfacing are as follows.

Constraint propagation. To perform constraint propagation a system needs to implement *variables* ranging over finite domains. Constraints expressing a relation among variables are implemented by *propagators*: software abstractions which by execution perform constraint propagation. Finally, a *propagation engine* coordinates the execution of propagators in order to deliver constraint propagation for a collection of constraints.

Search. Search in a finite domain constraint programming system has two principal dimensions. The first dimension is concerned with how to describe the search tree, typically achieved by a *branching* or *labeling*. The second dimension is concerned with how to explore a search tree, this is typically achieved by an *exploration strategy* or *search strategy* Any system implementing search must provide a *state restoration* service which maintains computation states for the nodes of the search tree.

Interfacing. A system must provide access to the services mentioned above so that applications can use them. Depending on the underlying constraint programming system, the services can be tightly integrated into some host language (such as Prolog) or being provided by some library (pioneered by ILOG Solver as a C++-based library).

Different levels of interfaces can be observed with different systems. Clearly, all systems offer at least interfaces which allow to use the system-provided services in applications. Even though the constraints, search engines, and so on provided by a system are sufficient for many applications, some applications might require more. For these applications, a system must be extensible by new propagators for possibly new constraints, new branching strategies, and new exploration strategies.

Chapter structure. The structure of this chapter is as follows. The next section gives a simple architecture for finite domain constraint programming systems. It describes *what* a system computes and *how* computation is organized in principle. The following two Sections 14.2 and 14.3 describe how systems implement this architecture. Section 14.2 describes how propagation is implemented while the following section describes how search is implemented. An overview over existing finite domain constraint programming systems is provided by Section 14.4. The last section of this chapter summarizes the key aspects of a finite domain constraint programming system and presents current and future challenges.

14.1 Architecture for Constraint Programming Systems

This section defines a simple architecture of a finite domain constraint programming system. The section describes *what* results a system computes and *how* it computes them. The focus is on the basic entities and principles that are used in systems; the actual implementation techniques used in systems are discussed in the following sections.

Much of the content follows the presentation in [58]. Essential parts of the architecture described here have been first identified and discussed by Benhamou in [13].

14.1.1 Propagation-Based Constraint Solving

This section defines terminology and *what* a system actually computes.

Domains. A *domain* D is a complete mapping from a fixed (countable) set of variable $\mathcal{V}$ to finite sets of integers. A domain D is *failed*, if $D(x) = \emptyset$ for some $x \in \mathcal{V}$. A variable $x \in \mathcal{V}$ is *fixed* by a domain D, if $|D(x)| = 1$. The *intersection* of domains D_1 and D_2 denoted $D_1 \sqcap D_2$, is defined by the domain $D(x) = D_1(x) \cap D_2(x)$ for all $x \in \mathcal{V}$.

A domain D_1 is *stronger* than a domain D_2, written $D_1 \sqsubseteq D_2$, if $D_1(x) \subseteq D_2(x)$ for all $x \in \mathcal{V}$.

We use range notation $[l, u]$ for the set of integers $\{n \in \mathbb{Z} \mid l \leq n \leq u\}$.

Assignments and constraints. An *integer assignment* a is a mapping of variables to integer values, written $\{x_1 \mapsto n_1, \ldots, x_k \mapsto n_k\}$. We extend the assignment a to map expressions and constraints involving the variables in the natural way.

Let vars be the function that returns the set of variables appearing in an assignment. In an abuse of notation, we define an assignment a to be an element of a domain D, written $a \in D$, if $a(x_i) \in D(x_i)$ for all $x_i \in \text{vars}(a)$.

The *minimum* and *maximum* of an expression e with respect to a domain D are defined as $\min_D e = \min\{a(e) \mid a \in D\}$ and $\max_D e = \max\{a(e) \mid a \in D\}$.

A *constraint* c over variables $x_1, \ldots, x_n$ is a set of assignments a such that $\text{vars}(a) = \{x_1, \ldots, x_n\}$. We also define $\text{vars}(c) = \{x_1, \ldots, x_n\}$.

Propagators. A constraint is defined extensionally by a collection of assignments for its variables. Typical systems do not compute with these extensional representations directly for two reasons:

1. Representing all possible assignments of a constraint might take too much space to be feasible (exponential space in the number of variables). In particular, space becomes an issue if $\text{vars}(c)$ contains more than two variables.

2. Common constraints have a certain *structure* (such as representing a linear equation constraint or an alldifferent constraint). Representing a constraint extensionally will make it difficult or even impossible to take advantage of this underlying structure.

Constraint propagation systems *implement* a constraint c by a collection of *propagators*. Propagators are also known as filters (implemented by some *filtering algorithm*) and *narrowing operators* [13]. A propagator p is a function that maps domains to domains. In order to make constraint propagation well-behaved (to be discussed in Section 14.1.2), propagators are *decreasing* and *monotonic*.

- A propagator p must be a *decreasing* function: $p(D) \sqsubseteq D$ for all domains D. This property is obvious and guarantees that constraint propagation only removes values.

- A propagator p must be a *monotonic* function: $p(D_1) \sqsubseteq p(D_2)$ whenever $D_1 \sqsubseteq D_2$. That is, application of p to stronger domains also yields stronger domains.

Propagators must faithfully implement constraints. A propagator p is *correct* for a constraint c iff it does not remove any assignment for c. That is, for all domains D

$$\{a \in D\} \cap c = \{a \in p(D)\} \cap c$$

This is a very weak restriction, for example the identity propagator i with $i(D) = D$ for all domains D is correct for all constraints c.

A propagator must also provide sufficient propagation to distinguish solutions from non-solutions. Hence, a set of propagators P is *checking* for a constraint c, if for domains D where all variables $\text{vars}(c)$ are fixed the following holds: $p(D) = D$ for all $p \in P$, iff the unique assignment $a \in D$ where $\text{vars}(a) = \text{vars}(c)$ is a solution of c ($a \in c$). In other words, all domains D corresponding to a solution of a constraint c on its variables are required to be a fixpoint of the propagator p.

A set of propagators P *implements* a constraint c, if all $p \in P$ are correct for c and P is checking for c. We denote this fact by $P = \text{prop}(c)$.

Systems consider sets of propagators rather than a single propagator as implementations of constraints to have more freedom in implementing a constraint. For example, a common way to implement simple constraints is by indexicals (to be discussed in Section 14.2.5): a collection of indexical propagators is used to implement a single constraint. On the other hand, systems provide global constraints with the idea that a single propagator implements a constraint involving many variables.

Note that only very little propagation is required for a set of propagators to be checking (as the term suggests, checking is sufficient; no actual propagation is required). The level of consistency provided by a propagator set is irrelevant to this model. Consistency levels only provide a convenient way to refer to the strength of propagators. As far as achieving good propagation is concerned, it does not matter whether a propagator set corresponds to a predefined consistency level. What matters is that the propagator set offers a good compromise between strength and cost of propagation.

To simplify our presentation we assume that propagators are defined for all variables $\mathcal{V}$ In a system, a propagator p will be only interested in some variables: the variables $\text{vars}(c$ of the constraint c that is implemented by p. Two sets of variables which are important are the *input* and *output* variables.

The *output* variables $\text{output}(p) \subseteq \mathcal{V}$ of a propagator p are the variables changed by the propagator: $x \in \text{output}(p)$ if there exists a domain D such that $p(D)(x) \neq D(x)$.

The *input* variables $\text{input}(p) \subseteq \mathcal{V}$ of a propagator p is the smallest subset $V \subseteq \mathcal{V}$ such that for all domains D_1 and D_2: $D_1(x) = D_2(x)$ for all $x \in V$ implies that $D'_1(x) = D'_2(x)$ for all $x \in \text{output}(p)$ where $D'_1 = D_2 \sqcap p(D_1)$ and $D'_2 = D_1 \sqcap p(D_2)$. Only the input variables are useful in computing the application of the propagator to the domain. We say that a propagator p *depends* on a variable x, if $x \in \text{input}(p)$.

Example 14.1 (Propagators). For the constraint $c \equiv x_1 \leq x_2 + 1$ the function p_1 defined by $p_1(D)(x_1) = \{n \in D(x_1) \mid n \leq \max_D x_2 + 1\}$ and $p_1(D)(x) = D(x), x \neq x_1$ is a correct propagator for c. Its output variables are $\{x_1\}$ and its input variables are $\{x_2\}$. Let $D_1(x_1) = \{1, 5, 8\}$ and $D_1(x_2) = \{1, 5\}$, then $p_1(D_1) = D_2$ where $D_2(x_1) = D_2(x_2) = \{1, 5\}$.

The propagator p_2 defined as $p_2(D)(x_2) = \{n \in D(x_2) \mid n \geq \min_D x_1 - 1\}$ is another correct propagator for c. Here and in the following we assume that a propagator is defined as identity for variables not mentioned in the definition. Its output variables are $\{x_2\}$ and input variables $\{x_1\}$.

The set $\{p_1, p_2\}$ is checking for c. For example, the domain $D(x_1) = D(x_2) = \{2$ corresponding to a solution of c is a fixpoint of both propagators. The non-solution domain $D(x_1) = \{2\}, D(x_2) = \{0\}$ is not a fixpoint (of either propagator).

Now we are in the position to describe what a constraint programming system computes. A *propagation solver* for a set of propagators P and some initial domain D $\text{solv}(P, D)$, finds the greatest mutual fixpoint of all the propagators $p \in P$. In other words, $\text{solv}(P, D)$ returns a new domain defined by

$$\text{solv}(P, D) = \text{gfp}(\lambda d. \text{iter}(P, d))(D) \qquad \text{iter}(P, D) = \bigsqcap_{p \in P} p(D)$$

---

propagate(P_f, P_n, D)
1:   $N \leftarrow P_n$
2:   $P \leftarrow P_f \cup P_n$
3: **while** $N \neq \emptyset$ **do**
4:     $p \leftarrow \mathsf{select}(N)$
5:     $N \leftarrow N - \{p\}$
6:     $D' \leftarrow p(D)$
7:     $M \leftarrow \{x \in \mathcal{V} \mid D(x) \neq D'(x)\}$
8:     $N \leftarrow N \cup \{p' \in P \mid \mathrm{input}(p') \cap M \neq \emptyset\}$
11:   $D \leftarrow D'$
12: **return** D

Figure 14.1: Basic propagation engine **propagate**.

where gfp denotes the greatest fixpoint w.r.t $\sqsubseteq$ lifted to functions.

14.1.2   Performing Propagation

A constraint programming system is concerned with performing propagation and search. In this section, we consider the propagation engine and postpone the discussion of search to Section 14.1.5.

The *propagation engine* **propagate** shown in Figure 14.1 computes $\mathrm{solv}(P, D)$ for a given set of propagators P and a domain D. Note that lines 9 and 10 are left out for an extension to be discussed later. The engine **propagate** takes two sets of propagators as input where P_f contains propagators already known to be at fixpoint for D. This is an important feature to obtain incremental propagation during search. If no fixpoint knowledge on propagators is available, it is safe to execute **propagate**$(\emptyset, P, D)$.

The algorithm uses a set N of propagators to apply (N stands for *not* known to be at fixpoint). Initially, N contains all propagators from P_n. Each time the while loop is executed, a propagator p is deleted from N, p is applied, and the set of *modified variables* M is computed. All propagators that share input variables with M are added to the set of propagators not known to be at fixpoint. Adding a propagator p to the set N is called *scheduling p*.

An invariant of the engine is that at the while statement $p(D) = D$ for all $p \in P - N$. The loop terminates, since in each iteration either a propagator is removed from N or a strictly smaller domain D' is computed (as a propagator is a decreasing function and there are only finitely many domains). After termination, the invariant yields that $D' = $ **propagate**(P_f, P_n, D) is a fixpoint for all $p \in P_f \cup P_n$, that is **propagate**$(P_f, P_n, D) = \mathrm{solv}(P_f \cup P_n, D)$.

As mentioned, the fact that a propagator is a decreasing function is essential for termination. The fact that a propagator is monotonic guarantees that **propagate**(P_f, P_n, D) actually computes $\mathrm{solv}(P_f \cup P_n, D)$ and that the order in which propagators are executed does not change the result of **propagate**(P_f, P_n, D). The propagation engine (assuming $P_f = \emptyset$) is more or less equivalent to the propagation algorithm of Apt [7, Section 7.1.3].

The engine is geared at simplicity, one particular simplification being that it does not pay particular attention to failed domains. That is, even though the domain D becomes failed, propagation continues until a domain is computed that is both failed and a fixpoint for all propagators in P. A concrete system might optimize this, as is discussed in Section 14.1.6.

Note that **propagate** leaves undefined how a propagator p is selected from N. Strategies for selecting propagators are discussed in Section 14.2.1.

Example 14.2 (Propagation). Consider the propagator p_1 for the constraint $x_1 \leq x_2$ defined by

$$\begin{aligned} p_1(D)(x_1) &= \{n \in D(x_1) \mid n \leq \max_D x_2\} \\ p_1(D)(x_2) &= \{n \in D(x_2) \mid n \geq \min_D x_1\} \end{aligned}$$

Also consider the propagator p_2 for the constraint $x_1 \geq x_2$ defined analogously.

Let us start propagation for the domain D_0 with $D(x_1) = \{0, 2, 6\}$ and $D(x_2) = \{-1, 2, 4\}$ by executing **propagate**$(\emptyset, \{p_1, p_2\}, D_0)$. This initializes both P and N to $\{p_1, p_2\}$.

Let us assume that p_1 is selected for propagation. Then, p_1 is removed from N and yields $D'(x_1) = \{0, 2\}$ and $D'(x_2) = \{2, 4\}$. The set of modified variables M is $\{x_1, x_2$ and hence after this iteration N is $\{p_1, p_2\}$.

In the second iteration, let us assume that p_2 is selected for propagation. This yields $D'(x_1) = D'(x_2) = \{2\}$. Again, the set of modified variables M is $\{x_1, x_2\}$ and hence N is $\{p_1, p_2\}$.

Assume that in the next iteration p_1 is selected. Now D is already a fixpoint of p_1 and the set of modified variables M is empty. This in turn means that N is just $\{p_2\}$ after this iteration.

The last iteration selects p_2 for execution, does not modify the domain, and N becomes empty. Hence, **propagate**$(\emptyset, \{p_1, p_2\}, D_0)$ returns a domain D with $D(x_1) = D(x_2) = \{2\}$.

14.1.3 Improving Propagation

The propagation engine shown in Figure 14.1 is naive in that it does not exploit additional information about propagators. Improved engines being the base for existing systems try to avoid propagator execution based on the knowledge whether a domain is a fixpoint for a propagator.

In the following we discuss common properties of propagators, which help to avoid useless execution. How a system implements these properties (or detects these properties) is discussed in Section 14.2.

Idempotent propagators. Assume that a propagator p has actually made the domain stronger, that is, $D' \neq D$. This means that there exists a variable $x \in \mathcal{V}$ for which $D'(x) \subset D(x)$. Assume further that $x \in \text{input}(p)$. Hence p will be included in N.

Quite often, however, propagators happen to be idempotent: a propagator p is idempotent, if the result of propagation is a fixpoint of p. That is, $p(p(D)) = p(D)$ for all domains D.

Hence, to avoid inclusion of an idempotent propagator p, the following lines can be added to the propagation engine after line 8:

9: **if** (p idempotent) **then**
10:     $N \leftarrow N - \{p\}$

Example 14.3 (Idempotent propagators). The propagators p_1 and p_2 from Example 14.2 are both idempotent as can be seen easily.

Taking this into account, propagation takes only three iterations. If the same selection of propagators is done as above, then N is $\{p_2\}$ after the first iteration and $\{p_1\}$ after the second iteration.

Note that in particular all domain consistent propagators are idempotent.

Entailment.   An idempotent propagator can be exempted from being included in N directly after p has been applied. A much stronger property for a propagator p is *entailment*. A propagator p is *entailed* by a domain D, if all domains D' with $D' \sqsubseteq D$ are fixpoints of p, that is $p(D') = D'$. This means that as soon as a propagator p becomes entailed, it can be safely deleted from the set of propagators P.

Example 14.4 (Entailed propagator). Consider the propagator p_1 for the constraint $x_1 \leq x_2$ from Example 14.2. Any domain D with $\max_D x_1 \leq \min_D x_2$ entails p_1.

Propagator rewriting.   During propagation the domain D might fix some variables in $\text{input}(p) \cup \text{output}(p)$ of a propagator p. Many propagators can be replaced by simpler propagators after some variables have become fixed.

Example 14.5 (Propagator rewriting for fixed variables). Consider the propagator p with $p \in \text{prop}(c)$ where $c \equiv x_1 + x_2 + x_3 \leq 4$:

$$p(D)(x_1) = \{n \in D(x_1) \mid n \leq \max_D(4 - x_2 - x_3)\}$$

Assume that propagation has computed a domain D which fixes x_2 to 3 (that is, $D(x_2) = \{3\}$). Then p can be replaced by the simpler (and most likely more efficient) propagator p' defined by:

$$p'(D)(x_1) = \{n \in D(x_1) \mid n \leq \max_D(1 - x_3)\}$$

A propagator p can always be rewritten to a propagator p' for a domain D, if $p(D') = p'(D')$ for all domains D' with $D' \sqsubseteq D$. This means that propagator rewriting is not only applicable to domains that fix variables.

This is for example exploited for the "type reduction" of [52] where propagators are rewritten as more knowledge on domains (there called types) becomes available. For example, the implementation of $x_0 = x_1 \times x_2$ will be replaced by a more efficient one, when all elements in $D(x_1)$ and $D(x_2)$ are non-negative.

14.1.4   Propagation Events

For many propagators it is simple to decide whether they are still at a fixpoint for a changed domain based on *how* the domain has changed. How a domain changes is described by *propagation events* (or just *events*).

Example 14.6 (Disequality propagators). Consider the propagator p with $\{p\} = \text{prop}(c$
for the constraint $c \equiv x_1 \neq x_2$:

$$
\begin{aligned}
p(D)(x_1) &= D(x_1) - \text{single}(D(x_2)) \\
p(D)(x_2) &= D(x_2) - \text{single}(D(x_1))
\end{aligned}
$$

where $\text{single}(N)$ for a set N is defined as N if $|N| = 1$ and $\emptyset$ otherwise.

Clearly, any domain D with $|D(x_1)| > 1$ and $|D(x_2)| > 1$ is a fixpoint of D. That is, p only needs to be applied if x_1 or x_2 are fixed.

Similarly, the propagator p_1 from Example 14.1 only needs to be applied to a domain D if $\max_D x_2$ changes and p_2 from the same example needs to be applied to a domain D if $\min_D x_1$ changes.

Assume that the domain D changes to the domain $D' \sqsubseteq D$. The usual events defined in a constraint propagation system are:

- $\text{fix}(x)$: the variable x becomes fixed.

- $\text{minc}(x)$: the minimum of variable x changes.

- $\text{maxc}(x)$: the maximum of variable x changes.

- $\text{any}(x)$: the domain of variable x changes.

Clearly the events overlap. Whenever a $\text{fix}(x)$ event occurs then a $\text{minc}(x)$ event, a $\text{maxc}(x)$ event, or both events must also occur. If any of the first three events occur then an $\text{any}(x)$ event occurs. This is captured by the following definition of $\text{events}(D, D')$ for domains $D' \sqsubseteq D$:

$$
\begin{aligned}
\text{events}(D, D') &= \{\text{any}(x) \mid D'(x) \subset D(X)\} \\
&\cup \{\text{minc}(x) \mid \min_{D'} x > \min_D x\} \\
&\cup \{\text{maxc}(x) \mid \max_{D'} x < \max_D x\} \\
&\cup \{\text{fix}(x) \mid |D'(x)| = 1 \text{ and } |D(x)| > 1\}
\end{aligned}
$$

Events satisfy an important monotonicity condition: suppose domains $D'' \sqsubseteq D' \sqsubseteq D$ then

$$
\text{events}(D, D'') = \text{events}(D, D') \cup \text{events}(D', D'').
$$

So an event occurs on a change from D to D'' iff it occurs in the change from D to D' or from D' to D''.

Example 14.7 (Events). Let $D(x_1) = \{1, 2, 3\}$, $D(x_2) = \{3, 4, 5, 6\}$, $D(x_3) = \{0, 1\}$ and $D(x_4) = \{7, 8, 10\}$ while $D'(x_1) = \{1, 2\}$, $D'(x_2) = \{3, 5, 6\}$ $D'(x_3) = \{1\}$ and $D'(x_4) = \{7, 8, 10\}$. Then $\text{events}(D, D')$ is

$$
\{\text{maxc}(x_1), \text{any}(x_1), \text{any}(x_2), \text{fix}(x_3), \text{minc}(x_3), \text{any}(x_3)\}
$$

For a propagator p, the set $\text{es}(p) \subseteq \{\text{fix}(x), \text{minc}(x), \text{maxc}(x), \text{any}(x) \mid x \in \mathcal{V}\}$ of events is an *event set* for p if the following two properties hold:

1. For all domains D' and D with $D' \sqsubseteq D$ and $D(x) = D'(x)$ for all $x \in \mathcal{V}-\text{input}(p)$ if $p(D) = D$ and $p(D') \neq D'$, then $\text{es}(p) \cap \text{events}(D, D') \neq \emptyset$.

2. For all domains D with $p(D) \neq p(p(D))$: $\mathrm{es}(p) \cap \mathrm{events}(D, p(D)) \neq \emptyset$.

The first clause of the definition captures the following. If the domain D is a fixpoint and the stronger domain D' (stronger only on the input variables) is not a fixpoint for a propagator p, then an event occurring from changing the domain D to D' must be included in the event set $\mathrm{es}(p)$. The second clause refers to the case when a propagator p does not compute a fixpoint (that is, $p(d) \neq p(p(D))$). In this case, an event must occur when the domain changes from D to $p(D)$. Note that the second clause never applies to an idempotent propagator.

An event set plays an analogous role to the set of input variables: if an event from the event set occurs when going from a domain D to a domain D', the propagator is no longer guaranteed to be at a fixpoint and must be re-applied.

Note that the definition of an event set is rather liberal as the definition does not require the event set to be the smallest set: any set that guarantees re-application is allowed. In particular, for any propagator p the set $\{\mathrm{any}(x) \mid x \in \mathrm{input}(p)\}$ is an event set: this event set makes propagation behave as if no events at all are considered. However, an implementation will try to use event sets that are as small as possible.

Example 14.8 (Event sets). The propagator p_1 from Example 14.2 depends on the event set $\{\mathrm{minc}(x_1), \mathrm{maxc}(x_2)\}$. The propagator p from Example 14.6 depends on the event set $\{\mathrm{fix}(x_1), \mathrm{fix}(x_2)\}$.

Now it is obvious how the propagation engine from Figure 14.1 can take advantage of events: instead of considering the set of modified variables and the input variables of a propagator for deciding which propagators are to be included into N, consider the events and an event set for a propagator. In other words, replace line 8 by:

8: $N \leftarrow N \cup \{p' \in P \mid \mathrm{es}(p') \cap \mathrm{events}(D, D') \neq \emptyset\}$

14.1.5 Performing Search

A constraint programming system evaluates $\mathrm{solv}(P, D)$ during search. We assume an execution model for solving a constraint problem with a set of constraints C and an initial domain D_0 as follows. We execute the procedure $\mathsf{search}(\emptyset, P, D_0)$ for an initial set of propagators $P = \bigcup_{c \in C} \mathrm{prop}(c)$. This procedure (shown in Figure 14.2) serves as an architecture of a constraint programming system.

The procedure requires that D be a fixpoint for all propagators in P_f (f for fixpoint). The propagators included in P_n do not have this requirement (n for not at fixpoint). This partitioning of propagators is used for incremental propagation with respect to recursive calls to search (as discussed below).

The somewhat unusual definition of search is quite general. The default *branching* strategy (also known as *labeling* strategy) for many problems is to choose a variable x such that $|D(x)| > 1$ and explore $x = \min_D x$ or $x \geq \min_D x + 1$. This is commonly thought of as changing the domain D for x to either $\{\min_D x\}$ or $\{n \in D(x) \mid n > \min_D x\}$. Branching based on propagator sets for constraints allows for more general strategies, for example $x_1 \leq x_2$ or $x_1 > x_2$.

```
  search(P_f, P_n, D)
1:  D ← propagate(P_f, P_n, D)
2:  if D is failed domain then
3:     return false
4:  if ∃x ∈ V.|D(x)| > 1 then
5:     choose {c_1, ..., c_m} where C ∧ D ⊨ c_1 ∨ ··· ∨ c_m
6:     for all i ∈ [1, m] do
7:        if search(P_f ∪ P_o, prop(c_i), D) then
8:           return true
9:     return false
10: return true
```

Figure 14.2: Architecture of constraint programming system.

Note that search has two dimensions: one describes how the search tree looks and the other describes how the search tree is explored. In the above architecture the selection of the c_i together with the selection of propagators $\mathrm{prop}(c_i)$ for the c_i describes the shape of the search tree. The sets $\mathrm{prop}(c_i)$ we refer to as *alternatives* and the collection of all alternatives is called *choice point*. Completely orthogonal is how the search tree is explored. Here, the architecture fixes exploration to be depth-first. Exploration is discussed in more detail in 14.3.

Note that search performs incremental propagation in the following sense: when calling propagate only the propagators $\mathrm{prop}(c_i)$ for the alternatives are not known to be at a fixpoint.

14.1.6 Implementing the Architecture

This section discusses general approaches to implementing the architecture for a constraint programming system introduced above. The focus is on what needs to be implemented and how the architecture (as an abstraction of a system) relates to a real system.

Detecting failure and entailment. In our architecture, failure is only detected inside search after returning from propagate by testing whether the domain obtained by propagation is failed. It is clear that a system should optimize detecting failure such that no propagation is wasted if a domain becomes failed and that no inspection of a domain is required to detect failure.

A typical way to make the detection of failure or entailment of a propagator more efficient is to let the propagator not only return a domain but also some status information describing whether propagation has resulted in a failed domain or whether the propagator has become entailed.

Implementing domains. The architecture describes that a propagator takes a domain as input and returns a new domain. This is too memory consuming for a real system. Instead, a system maintains a single data structure implementing one domain and propagators update this single domain when being applied.

Inspecting propagate in Figure 14.1 it becomes clear that maintaining a single domain is straightforward to achieve. The only reason for having a domain D and D' is in order to be able to identify the modified variables M.

State restoration. For propagation, systems maintain a single domain as has been argued above. However, a single domain becomes an issues for search: when calling search recursively as in Figure 14.2 and a domain is not transferred as a copy, backtracking (that is, returning from the recursive call) needs to restore the domain.

State restoration is not limited to domains but also includes private states of propagators and also whether propagators have become entailed. State restoration is a key service required in a constraint programming system and is discussed in Section 14.3.2 in detail.

Finding dependent propagators. After applying a propagator, propagate must compute the events (similar to the set of modified variables) in order to find all propagators that depend on these events. Clearly, this requires that a system be able to compute the events and find the dependent propagators efficiently.

Variables for propagators. In addition to the fact that propagators update a single domains rather than returning domains, implementations need to be careful in how many variables are referenced by a propagator. In our architecture, propagators are defined for all variables in $\mathcal{V}$. However, from the above discussion it is clear that a propagator p is only concerned with variables $\text{input}(p) \cup \text{output}(p)$. Quite often, the variables in $\text{input}(p) \cup \text{output}(p)$ are called the *parameters* of p.

A system will implement a propagator p such that it maintains its $\text{input}(p) \cup \text{output}(p)$ in some datastructure, typically as an array or list of variables. While most of the properties discussed for our architecture readily carry over to this extended setup, the case of multiple occurrences of the same variable in the datastructure maintained by a propagator needs special attention.

Multiple variable occurrences and unification. Depending on the actual system, multiple occurrences may both be common and appear dynamically. Here, dynamic means that variable occurrences for a propagator p might become the same during some computation not performed by p itself. This is typically the case when the constraint programming system is embedded in a constraint logic programming host language featuring *unification* for logical variables. Unification makes two variables x and y equal without the requirement to assign the variables a particular value. In this case the variables x and y are also said to be *aliased*.

The main issues with multiple occurrences of the same variable are that they make (a) detection of idempotence and (b) achieving good propagation more difficult, as is discussed in Section 14.2.3.

Private state. In our architecture, propagators are functions. In systems, propagators often need to maintain some *private state*. Private state is for example used to achieve incrementality, more information is given in Section 14.2.3.

14.2   Implementing Constraint Propagation

In this section, we detail the software architecture introduced on an abstract level in Section 14.1. This architecture can be roughly divided into *domain variables*, data structures implementing the problem variables; *propagators*, coroutines implementing the problem constraints by executing operations on the variables that it constrains; and *propagation services*, callable by the propagators in order to achieve the overall fixpoint computation.

Domain variables and propagators form a bipartite graph: every propagator is linked to the domain variables that it constrains, and every domain variable is linked to the propagators that constrain it.

In the following, we will not discuss issues related to the state restoration policy used, this is discussed in Section 14.3.2.

14.2.1   Propagation Services

From an operational point of view, a constraint programming system can be described in terms of coroutines (propagators) and events (domain changes). Propagators raise events, which leads to other propagators being resumed, until a fixpoint is reached. The management of events and selection (scheduling) of propagators are the main tasks of the propagation services.

Events.   Most integer propagation solvers use the events defined in Section 14.1.4, although some systems collapse $minc(x)$ and $maxc(x)$ into a single event (for example, ILOG Solver [32]). Choco [36] maintains an event queue and interleaves propagator execution with events causing more propagators to be added to the queue.

Other events than those discussed in Section 14.1.4 are also possible. For example, $neq(x, n)$: the variable x can no longer take the value n, that is, $n \in D(x)$ and $n \notin D'(x)$ for domains D and D'. These events have been used in e.g. B-Prolog [75].

Selecting the next propagator.   It is clear that the number of iterations performed by the propagation engine shown in Figure 14.1 depends also on which propagator is selected to be applied next. The selection policy is system-specific, but the following guiding principles can be observed:

- Events providing much information, for example fix events, yield quicker reaction than events providing less information. This captures selecting propagators according to expected *impact*.

- Propagators with low complexity, e.g. small arithmetic propagators, are given higher priority than higher complexity propagators. This captures selecting propagators according to *cost*.

- Starvation is avoided: no event or propagator should be left unprocessed for an unbounded amount of time (unless there is a propagator of higher priority or higher impact to run). This is typically achieved by selecting propagators for execution in a last-in last-out fashion (that is, maintaining the set N in Figure 14.2 as a queue).

Most systems have some form of static priorities, typically using two priority levels (for example, SICStus Prolog [35], Mozart [43]). The two levels are often not entirely based on cost: in SICStus Prolog all indexicals (see Section 14.2.5) have high priority and global constraints lower priority. While ECL^{i}PS^e [14, 28] supports 12 priority levels, its finite domain solver also uses only two priority levels where another level is used to support constraint debugging. A similar, but more powerful approach is used by Choco [36] using seven priority levels allowing both LIFO and FIFO traversal.

Schulte and Stuckey describe a model for dynamic priorities based on the complexity of a propagator in [58]. They describe how priorities can be used to achieve staged propagation: propagators dynamically change priority to first perform weak and cheap propagation and only later perform stronger and more complex propagation. Another model for priorities in constraint propagation based on composition operators is [25]. This model runs all propagators of lower priority before switching propagation back to propagators of higher priority.

Prioritizing particular operations during constraint propagation is important in general. For (binary) arc consistency algorithms, ordering heuristics for the operations performed during propagation can reduce the total number of operations required [72]. For interval narrowing, prioritizing constraints can avoid slow convergence, see for example [38].

14.2.2 Variable Domains

In a reasonable software architecture, propagators do not manipulate variable domains directly, but use the relevant propagation services. These services return information about the domain or update the domain. In addition, they handle failure (the domain becomes empty) and control propagation.

Value operations. A *value operation* on a variable involves a single integer as result or argument. We assume that a variable x with $D = \mathrm{dom}(x)$ provides the following value operations: x.getmin() returns $\min(D)$; x.getmax() returns $\max(D)$; x.hasval(n) returns $n \in D$; x.adjmin(n) updates $\mathrm{dom}(x)$ to $\{m \in D \mid m \geq n\}$; x.adjmax(n) updates $\mathrm{dom}(x)$ to $\{m \in D \mid m \leq n\}$; and x.excval(n) updates $\mathrm{dom}(x)$ to $\{m \in D \mid m \neq n\}$. These operations are typical for finite domain constraint programming systems like Choco, ILOG Solver, ECL^{i}PS^e, Mozart, and SICStus Prolog. Some systems provide additional operators such as for fixing values.

Iterators. It is quite common for a propagator to iterate over all values of a given variable. Suppose that i is a value iterator for some variable providing the following operations: i.done() tests whether all values have been iterated; i.value() returns the current value; and i.next() moves to the next value.

Domain operations. A *domain operation* supports simultaneous access or update of multiple values of a variable domain. If the multiple values form a consecutive interval $[n, m]$, such operations need only take n and m as arguments. Many systems provide general sets of values by supporting an abstract set type, e.g. Choco, ECL^{i}PS^e, Mozart and SICStus Prolog. Schulte and Tack describe in [60] domain operations based on generic range and value iterators. Other systems like ILOG Solver only allow access by iteration over the values of a variable domain.

Subscription. When a propagator p is created, it *subscribes* to its input variables. Subscription guarantees that p is executed whenever the domain of one of its variables changes according to an event. Options for representing the subscriber set of a given variable x include the following:

1. A single suspension list of pairs $E_i.p_i$ where E_i denotes the event set for which propagator p_i requires execution. When an event on x occurs, the list is traversed and the relevant propagators are selected for execution. Obviously, a lot of pairs that do not match the event could be scanned.

2. Multiple suspension lists of propagators for different events. On subscription, the propagator is placed in one of the lists. When an event on x occurs, all propagators on the relevant lists are selected for execution. Typically, there is one list for each event type $e \in \{\text{fix}(x), \text{minc}(x), \text{maxc}(x), \text{any}(x)\}$ plus one list for propagators whose event set contains both $\text{minc}(x)$ and $\text{maxc}(x)$. This is the design used in Choco, ECL^{i}PS^e, Mozart, and SICStus Prolog. Other systems collapse $\text{minc}(x$ and $\text{maxc}(x)$ into a single event $\text{minmaxc}(x)$ (for example, ILOG Solver [32] and Gecode [24]).

3. An array of propagators, partitioned according to the various events. When an event on x occurs, all propagators in the relevant partitions are selected for execution. This representation is particularly attractive if the possible events are $e \in \{\text{fix}(x), \text{minmaxc}(x), \text{any}(x)\}$, in which case the relevant partitions form a single interval.

Domain representation. Popular representations of $D = \text{dom}(X)$ include range sequences and bit vectors. A *range sequence* for a finite set of integers I is the shortest sequence $s = \{[n_1, m_1], \ldots, [n_k, m_k]\}$ such that I is covered $\left(I = \cup_{i=1}^{k}[n_i, m_i]\right)$ and the ranges are ordered by their smallest elements ($n_i \leq n_{i+1}$ for $i \leq i < k$). Clearly, a range sequence is unique, none of its ranges is empty, and $m_i + 1 < n_{i+1}$ for $1 \leq i < k$ A *bit vector* for a finite set of integers I is a string of bits such that the ith bit is 1 iff $i \in I$

Table 14.1 compares the worst-case complexity of the basic operations for these representations. Range sequences are usually represented as singly or doubly linked lists. Bit vectors are typically represented as a number of consecutive memory words, with an implementation defined size limit, usually augmented with direct access to $\min(D)$ and $\max(D)$. Range sequence thus seem to be more scalable to problems with large domains.

14.2.3 Propagators

A propagator p is a software entity with possibly private state (we allow ourselves to refer to the function as well as its implementation as propagator). It (partially) implements a constraint c over some variables or *parameters*. The task of a propagator is to observe its parameters and, as soon as a value is removed from the domain of a parameter, try to remove further values from the domains of its parameters. The algorithm employed in the

Table 14.1: Complexity of basic operations for range sequences of length r and bit vectors of size v augmented with explicit bounds.

Operations	Range sequence	Bitvector
x.getmin()	$O(1)$	$O(1)$
x.getmax()	$O(1)$	$O(1)$
x.hasval(n)	$O(r)$	$O(1)$
x.adjmin(n)	$O(r)$	$O(1)$
x.adjmax(n)	$O(r)$	$O(1)$
x.excval(n)	$O(r)$	$O(v)$
i.done()	$O(1)$	$O(v)$
i.value()	$O(1)$	$O(1)$
i.next()	$O(1)$	$O(v)$

process is called a *filtering algorithm*. Thus, the filtering algorithm is repeatedly executed in a coroutining fashion.

The main work of a filtering algorithm consists in computing values to remove and to perform these value removals via the value and domain operations described above. The events raised by these operations cause other propagators to be scheduled for execution.

Life cycle. The life cycle of a propagator p is depicted in Figure 14.3. When a constraint c is posted, its parameters are checked and subscribed to, p is created, its private state is allocated, and it is scheduled for execution. If the constraint c is implemented by more than one propagator, all propagators implementing c are created likewise.

One run of p has one of three possible outcomes:

- p may realize that the constraint has no solution, e.g. by a domain becoming empty. The parameters are unsubscribed to, the private state is deallocated, and the current search node fails.

- p may discover that the constraint holds no matter what of the remaining values are taken by the parameters. The parameters are unsubscribed to and the private state is deallocated,

- None of the above. p is moved to the set of suspended propagators, and will remain there until the relevant events are raised.

Idempotent propagators. Suppose a propagator p runs and removes some values. This raises some events, which would normally reschedule p for execution, as p subscribes to the very variables whose domains it just pruned. But suppose now that p is idempotent. Then by definition running p again would be useless. Thus, idempotence is a desirable property of propagators: if p is known to be idempotent, then p itself can be excluded from the set of propagators scheduled for execution by events raised by p.

However, guaranteeing idempotence may be a serious difficulty in the design of a filtering algorithm—it is certainly more convenient to not guarantee anything and instead

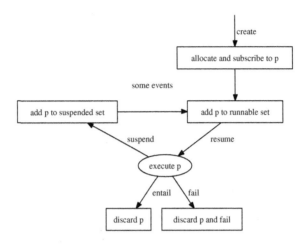

Figure 14.3: Life cycle of propagator p

leave the fixpoint computation to the propagation loop, at the cost of some redundant runs of p. Also, if the same variable occurs multiple times in the parameters, there is usually no straightforward way to guarantee idempotence.

Most systems do not require of propagators to be idempotent; some optimize the scheduling of propagators that are known to be idempotent. Mozart, as an exception, only supports idempotent propagators [45].

Schulte and Stuckey describe *dynamic idempotence* in [58] as a generalization: a propagator p signals after application whether the new domain is a fixpoint of p (similar to signaling failure or entailment as described above).

Multiple value removals.   Suppose a propagator p runs and multiple values are removed by multiple operations from the same variable x. It would be very wasteful to traverse the suspension list(s) of x and schedule subscribing propagators for each removal. A much more reasonable design is to perform such traversal once per modified parameter, at the end of executing p. Therefore, the value and domain operations described above usually do not perform such scheduling. Instead, propagators call the relevant propagation services near the end of the filtering algorithm.

This is already manifest in the **propagate** function described in Section 14.1.2: it records the modified variables (or the events that occurred) and schedules the propagators only after the propagator has been applied.

Amount of information available.   When a propagator p is resumed, it is usually interested in knowing which values have been deleted from which parameters since last time. The propagation services may provide part of this information, or even all of it. Of course, there is a trade-off between the efforts spent by the propagation services maintaining this information and the efforts spent by the propagators discovering it. One can distinguish three levels of granularity of the information provided to p:

coarse p is told that something has changed, but not what. This is the information provided in SICStus Prolog and Mozart.

medium p is told which parameters have been changed. This is the information provided in CHIP.

fine p is told which parameters have been changed, as well as the set of removed values. This is the information provided in ILOG Solver.

Use of private state. The private state that each propagator maintains can be used for a number of things:

auxiliary data structures Many filtering algorithms contain as components algorithms operating on specific data structures (digraphs, bipartite graphs, heaps etc.). The private state stores such data structures.

incrementality When a propagator is resumed, it is often the case that a single parameter has been changed, and that a single change has been made to it. Many filtering algorithms can exploit this fact and be incremental, i.e. perform its computation based on a previous state and changes made since that state was saved. An incremental computation is typically an order of magnitude cheaper than computing from scratch, but if many changes have been made, it is not necessarily the case.

domain information Suppose that the propagation services do not provide fine-grained information when a propagator is resumed. Nevertheless, by maintaining in its private state a copy of the parameter domains, or some suitable abstraction, the propagator can compute the required information.

fixed parameters It is often useful for a propagator of arity m to maintain a partitioning of its parameters X into two sets X_f, whose values have been fixed, and X_v, whose values have not yet been fixed. Most filtering algorithms focus their attention on the set X_v. This partitioning is easily achieved by a simple array A of pointers or indices, such that X_f occupies array elements $A[1, \ldots, k]$ and X_v array elements $A[k + 1, \ldots, m]$, where $k = |X_f|$. As a parameter is fixed, the relevant array elements are simply swapped and k is incremented.

Multiple variable occurrences. The same variable may occur multiple times among the parameters of a propagator p, initially as well as dynamically due to unification. This by itself does not cause problems, except, as noted above, any guarantees of idempotence are usually given under the assumption that no variable aliasing occurs.

Some propagators may also use variable aliasing in order to propagate more. For example, suppose that in a propagator for the constraint $x - y = z$, x and y are aliased. The propagator can then conclude $z = 0$, no matter what value is taken by x and y. Harvey and Stuckey discuss multiple occurrences of the same variable for linear integer constraints introduced by substitution in [29] and show how the amount of propagation changes with allowing substitution.

14.2.4 Daemons

So far, we have been assuming that an element of a suspension list is just a passive data structure pointing at a propagator p to schedule for execution. One can extend this design by associating with such elements a procedure called a *daemon*, which has access to p and its private state. If during traversal of the suspension list a daemon is encountered, instead of scheduling the propagator for execution, the daemon is simply run. This design is motivated by the following reasons:

- If the propagation services do not tell propagators which parameters have been changed, the daemon can maintain that information, since a daemon is always associated with a given parameter.

- Scheduling and resuming a propagator often involves larger overhead than running a daemon. If there is some simple test to determine whether the propagator can propagate anything, then the daemon can run that test, and if successful, schedule the propagator for execution.

- If there is some information in the private state that needs to be updated incrementally as the parameters are modified, daemons are a convenient mechanism for doing so.

Systems using daemons include CHIP, SICStus Prolog, and ILOG Solver.

14.2.5 Indexicals

Indexicals [66, 19, 15], also known as projection constraints [62], are a popular approach to implement simple propagators using a high-level specification language.

An indexical is a propagator with a single output variable and is defined in terms of a range expression. A constraint $c(x_1, \ldots, x_n)$ is then implemented by n indexicals p_i Each indexical p_i is defined by x_i in r_i where r_i is a range expression (to be explained later). Each of the indexicals p_i has the input variables $\{x_1, \ldots, x_n\}$.

Executing an indexical p of the form x_i in r_i with a current domain D computes the projection $\hat{c}_i$ of c onto x_i from $D(x_1), \ldots, D(x_{i-1}), D(x_{i+1}), \ldots, D(x_n)$. The domain returned by p is $p(D)(x_i) = D(x_i) \cap \hat{c}_i$ and $p(D)(x_j) = D(x_j)$ for all $1 \leq i \neq j \leq n$.

Indexicals can be seen as a programming interface for fine-grained control over propagation. They do not provide for the integration of sophisticated filtering algorithms for global constraints. Figure 14.4 shows a subset of the range expressions used in SICStus Prolog.

Example 14.9. To illustrate the use of indexicals for controlling the amount of propagation, consider the constraint $x = y + c$ where c is assumed to be a constant. This may be expressed with indexicals maintaining arc consistency:

$$(x \text{ in } \mathrm{dom}(y) + c, \; y \text{ in } \mathrm{dom}(x) - c)$$

or with indexicals maintaining bounds consistency:

$$(x \text{ in } \min(y) + c \,..\, \max(y) + c, \; y \text{ in } \min(x) - c \,..\, \max(x) - c)$$

$$
\begin{aligned}
R & ::= & T \mathinner{..} T \mid R \cap R \mid R \cup R \mid R \mathrel{?} R \mid \backslash R \\
  & \mid & R + T \mid R - T \mid R \bmod T \mid \mathrm{dom}(x) \\
  & \mid & \text{a finite subset of } \mathbb{Z} \\[6pt]
T & ::= & N \mid T + T \mid T - T \mid T * T \mid \lceil T/T \rceil \mid \lfloor T/T \rfloor \mid T \bmod T \\
  & \mid & \min(x) \mid \max(x) \mid \mathrm{card}(x) \\[6pt]
N & ::= & x \mid i, \text{ where } i \in \mathbb{Z} \mid \infty \mid -\infty
\end{aligned}
$$

Figure 14.4: Range expressions in SICStus Prolog indexicals

As discussed in [66, 19, 15], range expressions for indexicals must comply with certain monotonicity rules to make sense logically and operationally (corresponding to the properties that hold true for propagators and for propagators being the implementation of a constraint).

14.2.6 Reification

A *reified constraint* (also known as *meta constraint*) $c \leftrightarrow b$ reflects the truth value of the constraint c onto a 0/1-variable b. So if c is entailed (disentailed) by the constraint store, b is constrained to 1 (0), and if $b = 1$ ($b = 0$), c ($\neg c$) is posted.

One way of providing reification of a class of constraints is by extending the indexical mechanism, as proposed in [66] and implemented in SICStus Prolog [15]. Indexicals as described above are used for posting a constraint c. For reification, however, we also need to be able to post $\neg c$, and to check whether c is entailed or disentailed. This can be done by introducing *checking indexicals*. A checking indexical has the same format as a regular one, x_i in r_i, but instead of updating the domain for x_i, it checks whether $D(x_i) \subseteq \hat{c}_i$ holds for a given domain D.

14.3 Implementing Search

This section describes how systems implement search. As introduced in Section 14.1, a system needs to implement branching, state restoration, and exploration. The section discusses each of these issues in turn.

14.3.1 Branching

How a system implements branching depends in particular on whether the system is based on a programming language that has search built-in (such as Prolog or Oz). In this case, a branching strategy is expressed easily from the primitive of the language that controls search. In Prolog-based systems, for example, several clauses of a predicate then define the branching strategy. With relation to Figure 14.2, each clause corresponds to one of the alternatives $\mathrm{prop}(c_i)$.

Other languages provide special constructs that allow to express several alternatives. OPL, for example, offers a `try`-statement with several clauses corresponding to the alternatives [69]. A similar approach is taken in Oz, where a `choice`-statement serves the same purpose [63, 54]. For Oz, Schulte gives in [54] a reduction to a primitive that only allows one to assign an integer to a variable.

If the underlying language does not have search built-in (such as for libraries built on top of C++) systems provide some other means to describe a choice point. ILOG Solver [32], for example, provides the concept of a choice point (some data structure), which consists of several alternatives called *goals*. Goals themselves can be composed from several subgoals.

A common pattern for branching strategies is to select a particular not-yet fixed variable x according to some criteria. A common example is first-failure branching, which selects a variable with smallest domain. Here it is important to understand what the strategy does in case of ties: which one of the possibly many variables with a smallest domain is selected. For example, Wallace, Schimpf, et al. note in [71] that comparing search in systems can be particularly difficult due to a different treatment of ties in different systems.

14.3.2   State Restoration

As described in Section 14.1.6 search requires that a previous state of the system can be restored. The state includes the domain of the variables, propagators (for example, propagators that became entailed need to be restored), and private state of propagators.

Exploration (to be discussed in Section 14.3.3) creates a search tree where the nodes of the search tree correspond to the state of the system. In relation to **search** as shown in Figure 14.2, a new node is defined by each recursive invocation of **search**.

Systems use basically three different approaches to state restoration (the term state restoration has been coined by Choi, Henz, et al. in [18]):

copying   A copy of a node is created before the node is changed.

trailing   Changes to nodes are recorded such that they can be undone later.

recomputation   If needed, a node is recomputed from scratch.

Expressiveness.   The main difference as it comes to expressiveness is the number of nodes that are simultaneously available for further exploration. With copying, all nodes that are created as copies are directly ready for further exploration. With trailing, exploration can only continue at a single node at a time.

In principle, trailing does not exclude exploration of multiple nodes. However, they can be explored in an interleaved fashion only and switching between nodes is a costly operation.

Having more than a single node available for exploration is essential to search strategies like concurrent, parallel, or breadth-first.

Trailing.   A trailing-based system uses a trail to store undo information. Prior to performing a state-changing operation, information to reconstruct the state is stored on the trail. In a concrete implementation, the state changing operations considered are updates of memory locations. If a memory update is performed, the location's address and its old content is stored on the trail. To this kind of trail we refer as single-value trail. Starting exploration from a node puts a mark on the trail. Undoing the trail restores all memory locations up to the previous mark. This is essentially the technology used in Warren's Abstract Machine [74, 8].

In the context of trailing-based constraint programming systems two further techniques come into play:

time-stamping With finite domains, the domain of a variable can be narrowed multiple times. However it is sufficient to trail only the original value, intermediate values need no restoration: each location needs to appear at most once on the trail. Otherwise memory consumption is no longer bounded by the number of changed locations but by the number of state-changing operations performed. To ensure this property, time-stamping is used: as soon as an entity is trailed, the entity is stamped to prevent it from further trailing until the stamp changes again.

The time-stamp changes every time a new mark is put on the trail. Note that time-stamping concerns both the operations and the data structures that must contain the time-stamp.

multiple-value trail A single-value trail needs $2n$ entries for n changed locations. A multiple value trail uses the optimization that if the contents of $n > 1$ successive locations are changed, $n + 2$ entries are added to the trail: one for the first location's address, a second entry for n, and n entries for the locations' values.

For a discussion of time-stamps and a multiple value trail in the context of the CHIP system, see [1, 3].

Copying. Copying needs for each data structure a routine that creates a copy and also recursively copies contained data structures. A system that features a copying garbage collector already provides almost everything needed to implement copying. For example in the Mozart implementation of Oz [43], copying and garbage collection share the same routines parameterized by a flag that signals whether garbage collection is performed or whether a node is being copied.

By this all operations on data structures are independent of search with respect to both design and implementation. This makes search in a system an orthogonal issue.

Discussion. Trailing is the predominating approach used for state restoration in finite domain constraint programming systems. Clearly, all Prolog-based systems use trailing but also most other systems with the exception of Oz/Mozart [43], Figaro [31], and Gecode [24].

Trailing requires that all operations be search-aware: search is not an orthogonal issue to the rest of the system. Complexity in design and implementation is increased: it is a matter of fact that a larger part of a system is concerned with operations rather than with basic data structure management. A good design that encapsulates update operations will avoid most of the complexity. To take advantage of multiple value trail entries, however, operations require special effort in design and implementation.

Semantic backtracking as an approach to state restoration that exploits the semantics of an underlying solver for linear constraints over the reals is used in CLP(R) [33] and also in [65]. Semantic backtracking stores constraints that are used to reestablish an equivalent state of the system rather than trailing all changes to the underlying constraints. By this the approach can be seen as a hybrid between trailing and recomputation. A similar technique is used by Régin in [51], where the author describes how to maintain arc consistency by restoring equivalent states rather than identical states.

Recomputation. Recomputation trades space for time, a node is reconstructed on demand by redoing constraint propagation. The space requirements are obviously low: only the path in the search tree leading to the node must be stored. Basing exploration on recomputation alone is infeasible. Suppose a complete binary search tree of height n, which has 2^n leafs. To recompute a single leaf, n exploration steps are needed. This gives a total of $n2^n$ exploration steps compared to $2^{n+1} - 2$ exploration steps without recomputation (that is, the number of arcs).

The basic idea of combining recomputation with copying or trailing is as follows: copy (or start trailing) a node from time to time during exploration. Recomputation then can start from the last copied (or trailed) node on the path to the root. The implementation of recomputation is straightforward, see [56, 54] for example.

If exploration exhibits a failed node it is quite likely that not only a single node is failed but that an entire subtree is failed. It is unlikely that only the last decision made in exploration was wrong. This suggests that as soon as a failed node occurs during exploration, the attitude for further exploration should become more pessimistic. *Adaptive recomputation* [54] takes a pessimistic attitude by creating intermediate copies as follows: during recomputation an additional copy is created at the middle of the path for recomputation.

Performance of recomputation depends critically on the amount of information stored for the path. In naive recomputation, the path is stored as a list of integers identifying which alternative (that is, the i in $\mathrm{prop}(c_i)$) needs to be recomputed. While this makes the space requirements for recomputation problem independent, n fixpoints need to be computed for a path of length n.

In *batch recomputation* [18], the alternatives $\mathrm{prop}(c_i)$ are stored. To recompute a node it is sufficient to compute a single fixpoint. Batch recomputation is shown to be considerably more efficient than naive recomputation in [18]. *Decomposition-based search* as a similar idea to batch recomputation is reported by Michel and Van Hentenryck in [41]. Here also the alternatives rather than just integers are stored for recomputation.

14.3.3 Exploration

The architecture for search in a finite domain constraint programming system described in Section 14.1.5 only considers left-most depth-first exploration of the search tree. Clearly, systems offer more exploration strategies to allow for example search for a best solution. A few systems also provide abstractions from which new exploration strategies can be programmed.

Predefined exploration strategies. All Prolog-based languages systems support single- and all-solution search following depth-first exploration as sketched in Section 14.1.5. Best-solution search is controlled by a single cost variable and amounts to search for a solution with smallest or largest cost. CLP-based systems offer an interactive toplevel for controlling exploration that allows the user to prompt for multiple solutions. The interactive toplevel cannot be used within programs. $\mathrm{ECL}^i\mathrm{PS}^e$ provides visual search through the Grace tool [39] and other strategies such as LDS [30] and time and resource bounded search.

ILOG Solver [32] and OPL [64] offer LDS [30], DDS [73], and IDFS [40]. Best-solution search in ILOG Solver also uses a cost variable. To avoid recomputation of the best solution, the program must be modified to explicitly store solutions. Search in ILOG Solver is incremental in that solutions can be computed on request.

Programming exploration. The first system to offer support for programming explo-ration has been Oz/Mozart. Schulte and Smolka introduce the solve combinator in [57], which allows to program exploration based on the idea of having a first-class representation of nodes in the search tree. Schulte describes computation spaces as a refinement [56, 54] of the solve combinator, which also allows to program strategies supporting recomputa-tion and parallel execution. Computation spaces have been used to realize user-controlled interactive search [55] and parallel search on networked computers [53]. Curry [27] offers the same programming model as the solve combinator.

Another system providing support for programming exploration is ILOG Solver [32] (OPL [64] offers an equivalent model for programming exploration). Programming ex-ploration in ILOG Solver is based on limits and node evaluators [47, 69]. Programmable limits allow to stop exploration (time limit, for example). Node evaluators map search tree nodes to priorities. Node priorities determine the exploration order of nodes. Additionally, a special priority discards nodes.

ILOG Solver supports switching between arbitrary nodes in the search tree by full recomputation. For example, best-first search needs to switch between arbitrary nodes. To limit the amount of switching, Solver uses an additional threshold value. Only if the cost improvement exceeds the threshold, nodes are switched. This results in an approximation of best-first search. Fully interactive exploration is not feasible with full recomputation.

SALSA [37] is a language for the specification of search algorithms that cover ex-ploration strategies for tree search as well as neighborhood-based search (local search). SALSA requires a host language that supports search (for example, Claire [16]) as compi-lation target.

14.4 Systems Overview

This section discusses different approaches used for finite domain programming systems and a brief overview of existing systems.

14.4.1 Approaches

Several approaches and systems have been suggested to solve combinatorial problems with finite domain constraints. Historically, many systems have been implemented by embed-ding into an existing Prolog host system. There are many reasons for such an approach:

1. Much of the required infrastructure of the constraint solver is provided by the host language: data structures, memory management, support for search and backtrack-able updates.

2. The high level and declarative nature of Prolog makes it a reasonable choice of language for expressing combinatorial problems.

From the point of view of writing applications in mainstream object-oriented programming languages such as C++ and Java, although they can readily interface to modules written in other languages, providing a constraint solver as a class library is arguably a more attractive approach. This requires a larger implementation effort to provide the necessary infrastructure, but also gives more opportunities for optimization, as there are no design constraints imposed by a host system.

14.4.2 Prominent Systems

This section gives a brief overview of some finite domain constraint programming systems. As it is impossible to cover all systems that exist or have existed, we have selected systems that introduced some new ground-breaking ideas or that are prominent in other ways. The systems are partitioned into autonomous systems and library systems.

Autonomous systems

B-Prolog [75].   Extends a Prolog virtual machine with instructions for constraint propagation. Introduces action rules, a generalization of indexicals.

cc(FD) [66, 67, 68].   A representative of the concurrent and glass-box constraint programming research directions. Significant contributions include indexicals and constraint combinators.

clp(FD) [22, 19].   A representative of the approach of extending a Prolog virtual machine [74] with instructions for constraint propagation. Uses indexicals. Precursor of GNU Prolog.

CHIP [1, 2, 3].   A Prolog system with a constraint solver written in C. A pioneer in the global constraints research area [4, 11]. Provides a rich set of global constraints. Also available as C/C++ libraries.

ECL^{i}PS^e [70, 5, 14].   A Prolog system with constraint solving based on a general coroutining mechanism and attributed variables. A pioneer in the areas of integration with MIP solvers such as CPLEX and XPRESS-MP and using hybrid methods for constraint solving [61].

GNU Prolog [20, 21].   The successor of clp(FD), compiles Prolog programs with constraints to native binaries, extending a Prolog virtual machine [74] with instructions for constraint propagation. Uses indexicals.

Mozart [63, 43].   A development platform based on the Oz language, mixing logic, constraint, object-oriented, concurrent, distributed, and multi-paradigm programming. Search in Mozart is based on copying and recomputation.

Nicolog [62]. Extends a Prolog virtual machine with instructions for constraint propagation. Introduces *projection constraints*, extending indexicals with conditional expressions and tests.

PaLM [34]. PaLM (Propagation and Learning with Move) is a constraint programming system, based on the Choco constraints library. Its most important contributions are its explanation-based features, which can be used to control the search as well as provide answers to questions such as:

- Why does my problem not have any solution?

- Why can variable x not take value a in a solution?

- Why is variable x currently assigned to a?

SICStus Prolog [35, 15]. A Prolog system with constraint solving based on a general coroutining mechanism and attributed variables. Constraint solver written in C using global constraints as well as indexicals.

Library systems

CHIP [1, 2, 3]. C/C++ library version of the CHIP constraint solver as described above.

Choco [36]. A constraint solver kernel, originally written in the Claire programming language. A more recent Java version is available. Designed to be a platform for CP research, allowing for easy extensions and experimentation with event handling and scheduling policies. A library of global constraints, Iceberg, is available.

FaCiLe [9]. A constraint programming library written in OCaml, featuring constraints over integer as well as integer set finite domains.

Gecode [24, 58, 60]. A constraint solver library implemented in C++. Designed to be not used directly for modeling but for interfacing to systems offering modeling support (for example, Alice [6] an extension to Standard ML, interfaces to Gecode). Gecode is based on copying and recomputation rather than trailing.

ILOG Solver and JSolver [32]. A constraint solver library tightly integrated into the C++ and Java languages. Features constraints over integer as well as integer set finite domains. A pioneer in constraint solver libraries and in integrating constraint and object-oriented programming.

14.5 Outlook

Finite-domain constraint programming systems have proven useful tools for solving many problems in a wide range of application areas. As witnessed by this chapter many useful techniques for the implementation of constraint systems are available, both for constraint propagation as well as for search.

However, due to the change of available hardware platforms, the advent of new methods for problem solving and new constraints and propagators, and new requirements for systems, it is quite clear that the development of constraint programming systems will be faced with many new and difficult challenges. Some of the challenges are as follows.

Parallelism. Search for constraint programming offers great potential for parallelism: rather than exploring a single node at a time, explore several nodes of the search tree in parallel. There has been considerable work in the area of parallel search in general and parallel search for logic programming in particular [17, 26], however only little attention has been given to parallel search for constraint programming: only few systems support parallel search (ECL^{i}PS^e [44, 50], ILOG Solver [47], and Mozart [53, 54]) and only little experience in using parallel search for solving real-life problems is available [46, 48].

This is in sharp contrast to the fact that solving constraint problems is difficult and parallel computers are commodities. Networked computers are available everywhere and are mostly being idle. Pretty much all desktop machines sold in the next few years will feature processors providing parallel execution by multiple processing cores. The challenge for systems is to exploit the resources provided by parallel computers and making their useful exploitation simple.

Hybrid architectures. Propagation-based constraint programming is clearly not the only approach for solving combinatorial optimization problems. Other approaches such as integer programming and local search have shown their potential and even hybrid approaches are emerging. The questions for a system is how to best combine and provide services based on different approaches. One of the key questions is of course how tight the integration can and should be. Shen and Schimpf discuss the integration of linear integer solvers in ECL^{i}PS^e in [61].

Correctness. The last decade has seen the advent of an ever increasing number of powerful filtering algorithms used in propagators for the implementation of global constraints. However, implementing these propagators is typically complex and it is far from obvious that an implementation is actually correct for a given constraint. Additionally, taking advantage of properties such as idempotence and entailment add additional complexity to the implementation.

Ideally, a system should only offer propagators that are known to be correct. So far, a systematic methodology for proving correctness of these algorithms is missing. Worse still, even approaches for the systematic testing with sufficient coverage for propagators are not available. Correctness is important as the usefulness of constraint programming relies on the very fact that what is computed by a system is actually a solution to the problem solved.

Open interfaces. Today's development and deployment of constraint-based applications is often system specific: a programmer develops a constraint-based solution to a problem and integrates it into some larger software system. Development is system-specific as the model used can not easily be ported or adapted to a different system. Deployment is system-specific as many systems (notably language-based systems) require quite some effort for integrating constraint-based components into larger software systems.

The challenge is to devise open interfaces such that the same model can be used with many different systems without any porting effort and that the integration into software systems is easy. The former issue is partly addressed by using *modeling languages* such as OPL [64] or ESRA [23], for example. Modeling languages, however, only address part of the challenge as different systems offer vastly different services (think of what collection of global constraints systems support).

Richer coordination. One of the beauties of constraint programming is the simplicity of how constraint propagation can be coordinated: propagators are connected by variables acting as simple communication channels enjoying strong properties such as being decreasing. The beauty comes at the price of making communication low-level: only value removal is communicated.

The challenge is to provide richer communication to achieve stronger propagation. A potential candidate for communication are graph properties expressing information on a collection of constraints. Another approach, which chooses propagators for constraints to minimize propagation effort while retaining search effort, is based on properties that characterize the interaction among several constraints sharing variables [59].

Acknowledgments

The authors are grateful to Peter Stuckey for much of the material in Section 14.1, which is based on joint work by Peter Stuckey and Christian Schulte. Martin Henz, Mikael Lagerkvist, and Peter Stuckey provided helpful comments, which considerably improved this chapter. The authors thank Pascal Van Hentenryck for convincing them to give an invited tutorial at CP 2002 on finite domain constraint programming systems, which has served as a starting point for this chapter. Christian Schulte is partially funded by the Swedish Research Council (VR) under grant 621-2004-4953.

Bibliography

[1] Abderrahmane Aggoun and Nicolas Beldiceanu. Time Stamps Techniques for the Trailed Data in Constraint Logic Programming Systems. In S. Bourgault and M. Dincbas, editors, *Actes du Séminaire 1990 de programmation en Logique*, pages 487–509, Trégastel, France, May 1990. CNET, Lannion, France.

[2] Abderrahmane Aggoun and Nicolas Beldiceanu. Overview of the CHIP Compiler System. In Koichi Furukawa, editor, *Proceedings of the Eight International Conference on Logic Programming*, pages 775–788, Paris, France, June 1991. The MIT Press.

[3] Abderrahmane Aggoun and Nicolas Beldiceanu. Overview of the CHIP compiler system. In Frédéric Benhamou and Alain Colmerauer, editors, *Constraint Logic Programming: Selected Research*, pages 421–437. The MIT Press, Cambridge, MA, USA, 1993.

[4] Abderrahmane Aggoun and Nicolas Beldiceanu. Extending CHIP in order to solve complex scheduling and placement problems. *Journal of Mathematical and Computer Modelling*, 17(7):57–73, 1993.

[5]   Abderrahmane Aggoun, David Chan, Pierre Dufresne, Eamon Falvey, Hugh Grant, Warwick Harvey, Alexander Herold, Geoffrey Macartney, Micha Meier, David Miller, Shyam Mudambi, Stefano Novello, Bruno Perez, Emmanuel Van Rossum, Joachim Schimpf, Kish Shen, Periklis Andreas Tsahageas, and Dominique Henry de Villeneuve. ECLiPSe 5.0. User manual, IC Parc, London, UK, November 2000.

[6]   Alice Team. The Alice system, 2003. Programming Systems Lab, Universität des Saarlandes. Available from www.ps.uni-sb.de/alice/.

[7]   Krzysztof R. Apt. *Principles of Constraint Programming*. Cambridge University Press, 2003.

[8]   Hassan Aït-Kaci. *Warren's Abstract Machine: A Tutorial Reconstruction*. Logic Programming Series. The MIT Press, Cambridge, MA, USA, 1991.

[9]   Nicolas Barnier and Pascal Brisset. FaCiLe: a functional constraint library. *ALP Newsletter*, 14(2), May 2001. Available from www.recherche.enac.fr/opti/facile/.

[10] Peter Van Beek, editor. *Eleventh International Conference on Principles and Practice of Constraint Programming*. Lecture Notes in Computer Science. Springer-Verlag, Sitges, Spain, October 2005.

[11] Nicolas Beldiceanu and Evelyne Contejean. Introducing global constraints in CHIP. *Journal of Mathematical and Computer Modelling*, 20(12):97–123, 1994.

[12] Nicolas Beldiceanu, Warwick Harvey, Martin Henz, François Laburthe, Eric Monfroy, Tobias Müller, Laurent Perron, and Christian Schulte. Proceedings of TRICS: Techniques foR Implementing Constraint programming Systems, a post-conference workshop of CP 2000. Technical Report TRA9/00, School of Computing, National University of Singapore, 55 Science Drive 2, Singapore 117599, September 2000.

[13] Frederic Benhamou. Heterogeneous Constraint Solving. In *Proceedings of the Fifth International Conference on Algebraic and Logic Programming (ALP'96), LNCS 1139*, pages 62–76, Aachen, Germany, 1996. Springer-Verlag.

[14] Pascal Brisset, Hani El Sakkout, Thom Frühwirth, Warwick Harvey, Micha Meier, Stefano Novello, Thierry Le Provost, Joachim Schimpf, and Mark Wallace. ECLiPSe Constraint Library Manual 5.8. User manual, IC Parc, London, UK, February 2005.

[15] Mats Carlsson, Greger Ottosson, and Björn Carlson. An open-ended finite domain constraint solver. In Hugh Glaser, Pieter H. Hartel, and Herbert Kuchen, editors, *Programming Languages: Implementations, Logics, and Programs, 9th International Symposium, PLILP'97*, volume 1292 of *Lecture Notes in Computer Science*, pages 191–206, Southampton, UK, September 1997. Springer-Verlag.

[16] Yves Caseau, François-Xavier Josset, and François Laburthe. CLAIRE: Combining sets, search and rules to better express algorithms. In Danny De Schreye, editor, *Proceedings of the 1999 International Conference on Logic Programming*, pages 245–259, Las Cruces, NM, USA, November 1999. The MIT Press.

[17] Jacques Chassin de Kergommeaux and Philippe Codognet. Parallel logic programming systems. *ACM Computing Surveys*, 26(3):295–336, September 1994.

[18] Chiu Wo Choi, Martin Henz, and Ka Boon Ng. Components for state restoration in tree search. In Toby Walsh, editor, *Proceedings of the Seventh International Conference on Principles and Practice of Constraint Programming*, Lecture Notes in Computer Science, vol. 2239. Springer Verlag, 2001.

[19] Philippe Codognet and Daniel Diaz. Compiling constraints in clp(FD). *The Journal of Logic Programming*, 27(3):185–226, June 1996.

[20] Daniel Diaz and Philippe Codognet. GNU prolog: Beyond compiling Prolog to C. In Enrico Pontelli and Vítor Santos Costa, editors, *Practical Aspects of Declarative Languages, Second International Workshop, PADL 2000*, volume 1753 of *Lecture Notes in Computer Science*, pages 81–92, Boston, MA, USA, January 2000. Springer-Verlag.

[21] Daniel Diaz and Philippe Codognet. Design and implementation of the GNU prolog system. *Journal of Functional and Logic Programming*, 2001(6), 2001.

[22] Daniel Diaz and Philippe Codognet. A minimal extension of the WAM for clp(FD). In David S. Warren, editor, *Proceedings of the Tenth International Conference on Logic Programming*, pages 774–790, Budapest, Hungary, June 1993. The MIT Press.

[23] Pierre Flener, Justin Pearson, and Magnus Ågren. Introducing ESRA, a relational language modelling combinatorial problems. In Maurice Bruynooghe, editor, *Logic Based Program Synthesis and Transformation: 13th International Symposium*, volume 3108 of *Lecture Notes in Computer Science*, pages 214–229, Uppsala, Sweden, August 2004. Springer-Verlag.

[24] Gecode. Gecode: Generic constraint development environment, 2005. Available from www.gecode.org.

[25] Laurent Granvilliers and Eric Monfroy. Implementing constraint propagation by composition of reductions. In *ICLP'03*, volume 2916 of *Lecture Notes in Computer Science*, pages 300–314. Springer-Verlag, 2003.

[26] Gopal Gupta, Enrico Pontelli, Khayri Ali, Mats Carlsson, and Manuel Hermenegildo. Parallel execution of Prolog programs. *ACM Transactions on Programming Languages and Systems*, 23(4):472–602, July 2001.

[27] Michael Hanus. A unified computation model for functional and logic programming. In Neil D. Jones, editor, *The 24th Symposium on Principles of Programming Languages*, pages 80–93, Paris, France, January 1997. ACM Press.

[28] Warwick Harvey. Personal communication, April 2004.

[29] Warwick Harvey and Peter J. Stuckey. Improving linear constraint propagation by changing constraint representation. *Constraints*, 7:173–207, 2003.

[30] William D. Harvey and Matthew L. Ginsberg. Limited discrepancy search. In Chris S. Mellish, editor, *Fourteenth International Joint Conference on Artificial Intelligence*, pages 607–615, Montréal, Québec, Canada, August 1995. Morgan Kaufmann Publishers.

[31] Martin Henz, Tobias Müller, and Ka Boon Ng. Figaro: Yet another constraint programming library. In Inês de Castro Dutra, Vítor Santos Costa, Gopal Gupta, Enrico Pontelli, Manuel Carro, and Peter Kacsuk, editors, *Parallelism and Implementation Technology for (Constraint) Logic Programming*, pages 86–96, Las Cruces, NM, USA, December 1999. New Mexico State University.

[32] ILOG S.A. *ILOG Solver 6.0: Reference Manual*. Gentilly, France, October 2003.

[33] Joxan Jaffar, Spiro Michaylov, Peter J. Stuckey, and Roland H. C. Yap. The CLP(R) language and system. *Transactions on Programming Languages and Systems*, 14(3): 339–395, 1992.

[34] Narendra Jussien and Vincent Barichard. The PaLM system: explanation-based constraint programming. In Beldiceanu et al. [12], pages 118–133.

[35] Intelligent Systems Laboratory. SICStus Prolog user's manual, 3.12.1. Technical report, Swedish Institute of Computer Science, Box 1263, 164 29 Kista, Sweden, April 2005.

[36] François Laburthe. CHOCO: implementing a CP kernel. In Beldiceanu et al. [12], pages 71–85.

[37] François Laburthe and Yves Caseau. SALSA: A language for search algorithms. In Michael Maher and Jean-François Puget, editors, *Proceedings of the Fourth International Conference on Principles and Practice of Constraint Programming*, volume 1520 of *Lecture Notes in Computer Science*, pages 310–324, Pisa, Italy, October 1998. Springer-Verlag.

[38] Olivier Lhomme, Arnaud Gotlieb, and Michel Rueher. Dynamic optimization of interval narrowing algorithms. *The Journal of Logic Programming*, 37(1–3):165–183, 1998.

[39] Micha Meier. Debugging constraint programs. In Montanari and Rossi [42], pages 204–221.

[40] Pedro Meseguer. Interleaved depth-first search. In Pollack [49], pages 1382–1387.

[41] Laurent Michel and Pascal Van Hentenryck. A decomposition-based implementation of search strategies. *ACM Transactions on Computational Logic*, 5(2):351–383, 2004.

[42] Ugo Montanari and Francesca Rossi, editors. *Proceedings of the First International Conference on Principles and Practice of Constraint Programming*, volume 976 of *Lecture Notes in Computer Science*. Springer-Verlag, Cassis, France, September 1995.

[43] Mozart Consortium. The Mozart programming system, 1999. Available from `www.mozart-oz.org`.

[44] Shyam Mudambi and Joachim Schimpf. Parallel CLP on heterogeneous networks. In Pascal Van Hentenryck, editor, *Proceedings of the Eleventh International Conference on Logic Programming*, pages 124–141. The MIT Press, Santa Margherita Ligure, Italy, 1994.

[45] Tobias Müller. *Constraint Propagation in Mozart*. Doctoral dissertation, Universität des Saarlandes, Fakultät für Mathematik und Informatik, Fachrichtung Informatik, Im Stadtwald, 66041 Saarbrücken, Germany, 2001.

[46] Claude Le Pape, Laurent Perron, Jean-Charles Régin, and Paul Shaw. Robust and parallel solving of a network design problem. In *Eigth International Conference on Principles and Practice of Constraint Programming*, volume 2470 of *Lecture Notes in Computer Science*, pages 633–648, Ithaca, NY, USA, September 2002. Springer-Verlag.

[47] Laurent Perron. Search procedures and parallelism in constraint programming. In Joxan Jaffar, editor, *Proceedings of the Fifth International Conference on Principles and Practice of Constraint Programming*, volume 1713 of *Lecture Notes in Computer Science*, pages 346–360, Alexandra, VA, USA, October 1999. Springer-Verlag.

[48] Laurent Perron. Practical parallelism in constraint programming. In Narendra Jussien and François Laburthe, editors, *Proceedings of the Fourth International Workshop on Integration of AI and OR Techniques in Constraint Programming for Combinatorial Optimisation Problems (CP-AI-OR'02)*, pages 261–275, Le Croisic, France, March, 25–27 2002.

[49] Martha E. Pollack, editor. *Fifteenth International Joint Conference on Artificial Intelligence*. Morgan Kaufmann Publishers, Nagoya, Japan, August 1997.

[50] Steven Prestwich and Shyam Mudambi. Improved branch and bound in constraint logic programming. In Montanari and Rossi [42], pages 533–548.

[51] Jean-Charles Régin. Maintaining arc consistency algorithms during the search without additional cost. In Beek [10], pages 520–533.

[52] Pierre Savéant. Constraint reduction at the type level. In Beldiceanu et al. [12], pages 16–29.

[53] Christian Schulte. Parallel search made simple. In Beldiceanu et al. [12], pages 41–57.

[54] Christian Schulte. *Programming Constraint Services*, volume 2302 of *Lecture Notes in Artificial Intelligence*. Springer-Verlag, Berlin, Germany, 2002.

[55] Christian Schulte. Oz Explorer: A visual constraint programming tool. In Lee Naish, editor, *Proceedings of the Fourteenth International Conference on Logic Programming*, pages 286–300, Leuven, Belgium, July 1997. The MIT Press.

[56] Christian Schulte. Programming constraint inference engines. In Gert Smolka, editor, *Proceedings of the Third International Conference on Principles and Practice of Constraint Programming*, volume 1330 of *Lecture Notes in Computer Science*, pages 519–533, Schloß Hagenberg, Linz, Austria, October 1997. Springer-Verlag.

[57] Christian Schulte and Gert Smolka. Encapsulated search in higher-order concurrent constraint programming. In Maurice Bruynooghe, editor, *Logic Programming: Proceedings of the 1994 International Symposium*, pages 505–520, Ithaca, NY, USA, November 1994. The MIT Press.

[58] Christian Schulte and Peter J. Stuckey. Speeding up constraint propagation. In Mark Wallace, editor, *Tenth International Conference on Principles and Practice of Constraint Programming*, volume 3258 of *Lecture Notes in Computer Science*, pages 619–633, Toronto, Canada, September 2004. Springer-Verlag.

[59] Christian Schulte and Peter J. Stuckey. When do bounds and domain propagation lead to the same search space? *Transactions on Programming Languages and Systems*, 27(3):388–425, May 2005.

[60] Christian Schulte and Guido Tack. Views and iterators for generic constraint implementations. In Beek [10], pages 817–821.

[61] Kish Shen and Joachim Schimpf. Eplex: An interface to mathematical programming solvers for constraint logic programming languages. In Beek [10], pages 622–636.

[62] Gregory Sidebottom. *A Language for Optimizing Constraint Propagation*. PhD thesis, Simon Fraser University, 1993.

[63] Gert Smolka. The Oz programming model. In Jan van Leeuwen, editor, *Computer Science Today*, volume 1000 of *Lecture Notes in Computer Science*, pages 324–343. Springer-Verlag, Berlin, 1995.

[64] Pascal Van Hentenryck. *The OPL Optimization Programming Language*. The MIT Press, Cambridge, MA, USA, 1999.

[65] Pascal Van Hentenryck and Viswanath Ramachandran. Backtracking without trailing in clp(r-lin). *ACM Trans. Program. Lang. Syst.*, 17(4):635–671, 1995.

[66] Pascal Van Hentenryck, Vijay Saraswat, and Yves Deville. Constraint processing in cc(FD). Manuscript, 1991.

[67] Pascal Van Hentenryck, Vijay Saraswat, and Yves Deville. Design, implementation and evaluation of the constraint language cc(FD). In Andreas Podelski, editor, *Constraint Programming: Basics and Trends*, volume 910 of *Lecture Notes in Computer Science*, pages 293–316. Springer-Verlag, 1995.

[68] Pascal Van Hentenryck, Vijay Saraswat, and Yves Deville. Design, implementation, and evaluation of the constraint language cc(FD). *The Journal of Logic Programming*,

37(1–3):139–164, October 1998.

[69] Pascal Van Hentenryck, Laurent Perron, and Jean-François Puget. Search and strategies in OPL. *ACM Transactions on Computational Logic*, 1(2):285–320, October 2000.

[70] Mark Wallace, Stefano Novello, and Joachim Schimpf. Eclipse: A platform for constraint logic programming. Technical report, IC-Parc, Imperial College, London, GB, August 1997.

[71] Mark Wallace, Joachim Schimpf, Kish Shen, and Warwick Harvey. On benchmarking constraint logic programming platforms. *Constraints*, 9(1):5–34, 2004.

[72] Richard J. Wallace and Eugene C. Freuder. Ordering heuristics for arc consistency algorithms. In *Ninth Canadian Conference on Artificial Intelligence*, pages 163–169, Vancouver, Canada, 1992.

[73] Toby Walsh. Depth-bounded discrepancy search. In Pollack [49], pages 1388–1393.

[74] David H. D. Warren. An abstract Prolog instruction set. Technical Note 309, SRI International, Artificial Intelligence Center, Menlo Park, CA, USA, October 1983.

[75] Neng-Fa Zhou. Programming finite-domain constraint propagators in action rules. *Theory and Practice of Logic Programming*, 6(1):1–26, 2006. To appear.

Handbook of Constraint Programming
Edited by F. Rossi, P. van Beek and T. Walsh

Chapter 15

Operations Research Methods in Constraint Programming

John N. Hooker

A number of operations research (OR) methods have found their way into constraint programming (CP). This development is entirely natural, since OR and CP have similar goals.

OR is essentially a variation on the scientific practice of mathematical modeling. It describes phenomena in a formal language that allows one to deduce consequences in a rigorous way. Unlike a typical scientific model, however, an OR model has a prescriptive as well as a descriptive purpose. It represents a human activity with some freedom of choice, rather than a natural process. The laws of nature become constraints that the activity must observe, and the goal is to maximize some objective subject to the constraints.

CP's constraint-oriented approach to problem solving poses a prescriptive modeling task very similar to that of OR. CP historically has been less concerned with finding optimal than feasible solutions, but this is a superficial difference. It is to be expected, therefore, that OR methods would find application in solving CP models.

There remains a fundamental difference, however, in the way that CP and OR understand constraints. CP typically sees a constraint as a procedure, or at least as invoking a procedure, that operates on the solution space, normally by reducing variable domains. OR sees a constraint set as a whole cloth; the solution algorithm operates on the entire problem rather than the constraints in it. Both approaches have their advantages. CP can design specialized algorithms for individual constraints or subsets of constraints, thereby exploiting substructure in the problem that OR methods are likely to miss. OR algorithms, on the other hand, can exploit global properties of the problem that CP can only partially capture by propagation through variable domains.

15.1 Schemes for Incorporating OR into CP

CP's unique concept of a constraint governs how OR methods may be imported into CP. The most obvious role for an OR method is to apply it to a constraint or subset of constraints in order to reduce variable domains. Thus if the constraints include some linear inequalities, one can minimize or maximize a variable subject to those inequalities, thereby possibly reducing the variable's domain. The minimization or maximization problem is a linear programming (LP) problem, which is an OR staple.

This is an instance of the most prevalent scheme for bringing OR into CP: create a *relaxation* of the CP problem in the form of an OR model, such as an LP model. Solution of the relaxation then contributes to domain reduction or helps guide the search. Other OR models that can play this role include mixed integer linear programming (MILP) models (which can themselves be relaxed), Lagrangean relaxations, and dynamic programming models. OR has also formulated specialized relaxations for a wide variety of common situations and provides tools for relaxing global constraints.

A relaxation provides several benefits to a CP solver. (a) It can tighten bounds on a variable. (b) Its solution may happen to be feasible in the original problem. (c) If not, the solution can guide the search in a promising direction. (d) The solution may allow one to filter domains in other ways, for instance by using reduced costs or Lagrange multipliers, or by examining the state space in dynamic programming. (e) In optimization problems, the solution can provide a bound on the optimal value that can be used to prune the search tree. (f) More generally, by pooling relaxations of several constraints in a single OR-based relaxation, one can exploit global properties of the problem that are only partially captured by constraint propagation.

Other hybridization schemes decompose the problem so that CP and OR can attack the parts of the problem to which they are best suited. To date, the schemes receiving the most attention have been branch-and-price algorithms and generalizations of Benders decomposition. CP-based branch and price typically uses CP for "column generation"; that is, to identify variables that should be added dynamically to improve the solution during a branching search. Benders decomposition often uses CP for "row generation"; that is, to generate constraints (nogoods) that direct the main search procedure.

OR/CP combinations of all three types can bring substantial computational benefits. Table 15.1 lists a sampling of some of the more impressive results. These represent only a small fraction, however, of hybrid applications; over 70 are cited in this chapter.

Even this collection omits entire areas of OR/CP cooperation. One is the use of concepts from operations research to design filters for certain global constraints, such as the application of matching and network flow theory to all-different, cardinality, and related constraints, and particularly to "soft" versions of these constraints. These ideas are covered in Chapter 6 and are therefore not discussed here. Two additional areas are heuristic methods and stochastic programming, both of which have a long history in OR. These are discussed in Chapters 5 and 21, respectively.

15.2   Plan of the Chapter

This chapter surveys the three hybridization schemes mentioned above: relaxation, branch-and-price methods, and Benders decomposition.

Sections 15.3–15.9 are devoted to relaxation, and of these the first four deal primarily with linear relaxations. Section 15.3 summarizes the elementary theory of linear programming (LP), which is used repeatedly in the chapter, and the role of LP in domain filtering. Section 15.4 briefly describes the formulation of MILP models. These are useful primarily because one can find LP relaxations for a wide variety of constraints by creating a MILP

Table 15.1: Sampling of computational results for methods that combine CP and OR.

Problem	Contribution to CP	Speedup
CP plus relaxations similar to those used in MILP		
Lesson timetabling [51]	Reduced-cost variable fixing using an assignment problem relaxation.	2 to 50 times faster than CP.
Minimizing piecewise linear costs [105]	Convex hull relaxation of piecewise linear function	2 to 200 times faster than MILP. Solved two instances that MILP could not solve.
Boat party & flow shop scheduling [77]	Convex hull relaxation of disjunctions, covering inequalities	Solved 10-boat instance in 5 min that MILP could not solve in 12 hours. Solved flow shop instances 3 to 4 times faster.
Product configuration [121]	Convex hull relaxation of element constraints, reduced cost variable fixing.	30 to 40 times faster than MILP (which was faster than CP).
Automatic digital recording [113]	Lagrangean relaxation	1 to 10 times faster than MILP (which was faster than CP).
Stable set problems [66]	Semi-definite programming relaxation.	Significantly better suboptimal solutions than CP in fraction of the time.
Structural design [23]	Linear quasi-relaxation of nonlinear model with discrete variables.	Up to 600 times faster than MILP. Solved 2 problems in < 6 min that MILP could not solve in 20 hours.
Scheduling with earliness and tardiness costs [14]	LP relaxation.	Solved 67 of 90 instances, while CP solved only 12.
CP-based branch and price		
Traveling tournament scheduling [44]	Branch-and-price framework.	First to solve 8-team instance.
Urban transit crew management [133]	Branch-and-price framework.	Solved problems with 210 trips, while traditional branch and price could accommodate only 120 trips.
Benders-based integration of CP and MILP		
Min-cost multiple machine scheduling [81]	MILP master problem, CP feasibility subproblem	20 to 1000 times faster than CP, MILP.
Min-cost multiple machine scheduling [120]	Updating of single MILP master (branch and check)	Additional factor of 10 over [81]
Polypropylene batch scheduling [122]	MILP master problem, CP feasibility subproblem.	Solved previously insoluble problem in 10 min.
Call center scheduling [16]	CP master, LP subproblem.	Solved twice as many instances as traditional Benders.
Min cost and min makespan planning & cumulative sched. [71]	MILP master problem, CP optimization subproblem	100 to 1000 times faster than CP, MILP. Solved significantly larger instances.
Min no. late jobs and min tardiness planning & cumulative sched. [72]	MILP master problem, CP . optimization subproblem with LP relaxation	Min late jobs 100-1000 times faster than MILP, CP; min tardiness significantly faster, better solutions when suboptimal.

model for them and dropping the integrality restrictions on the variables. Section 15.5 is a brief introduction to cutting planes, which can strengthen LP relaxations. Section 15.6 describes linear relaxations for some popular global constraints, while Section 15.7 provides continuous relaxations for piecewise linear constraints and disjunctions of nonlinear systems. Sections 15.8 and 15.9 deal with Lagrangean relaxation and dynamic programming, which can also provide useful relaxations.

Sections 15.10 and 15.11 are devoted to the remaining hybridization schemes discussed here, branch-and-price methods and Benders decomposition. The final section briefly explores the possibility of full CP/OR integration.

15.3   Linear Programming

Linear programming (LP) has a number of advantages that make it the most popular OR model discussed here. Although limited to linear inequalities (or equations) with continuous variables, it is remarkably versatile for representing real-world situations. It is even more versatile as a relaxation. It has an elegant duality theory that lends itself to sensitivity analysis and domain filtering. Finally, the LP problem is extremely well solved. It is rare for a practical LP instance, however large, to present any difficulty for a state-of-the-art solver.

LP relaxation provides all of the benefits of relaxation that were mentioned earlier. In particular, a solution that is infeasible in the original problem can guide the search by suggesting how to branch. If a variable x_j is required to be integral in the original problem, then an nonintegral value $\bar{x}_j$ in the solution of the LP relaxation suggests branching by requiring $x_j \leq \lfloor \bar{x}_j \rfloor$ in one branch and $x_j \geq \lceil \bar{x}_j \rceil$ in the other. Rounding of LP solutions, a technique widely used in approximation algorithms, can also be used a guide to backtracking [58].

Semidefinite programming [4, 129] generalizes LP and has been used in a CP context as a relaxation for the stable set problem [66]. It can also serve as a basis for approximation algorithms [57].

15.3.1   Optimal Basic Solutions

Without loss of generality an LP problem can be written

$$
\begin{aligned}
& \min \; cx \\
& Ax \geq b, \; x \geq 0, \; x \in \Re^n
\end{aligned}
\tag{15.1}
$$

where A is an $m \times n$ matrix. This can be read, "minimize cx subject to the constraints $Ax \geq b$, $x \geq 0$." In OR terminology, any $x \in \Re^n$ is a *solution* of (15.1), and any $x \geq$ for which $Ax \geq b$ is a *feasible* solution. The problem is *infeasible* if there is no feasible solution. It is *unbounded* if (15.1) is feasible but has no optimal solution.

The feasible set of (15.1) is a polyhedron, and the vertices of the polyhedron correspond to *basic* feasible solutions. Since the objective function cx is linear, it is intuitively clear that some vertex is optimal unless the problem is unbounded. It is useful to develop this idea algebraically.

The LP problem is first rewritten in equality form

$$\min \ cx$$
$$Ax = b, \ x \geq 0, \ x \in \Re^n \tag{15.2}$$

An inequality constraint $ax \geq a_0$ can always be converted to an equality constraint by introducing a surplus variable $s_0 \geq 0$ and writing $ax - s_0 = a_0$.

Assume for the moment that (15.2) is feasible. Suppose further that $m \leq n$ and A has rank m. If A is partitioned as $[B \ N]$, where B is any set of m independent columns, then (15.2) can be written

$$\min \ c_B x_B + c_N x_N$$
$$B x_B + N x_N = b, \quad x_B, x_B \geq 0 \tag{15.3}$$

The variables x_B that correspond to the columns of B are designated *basic* variables because B is a basis for $\Re^m$. One can solve the equality constraints for x_B in terms of the nonbasic variables x_N:

$$x_B = B^{-1}b - B^{-1}N x_N \tag{15.4}$$

Thus any feasible solution of (15.4) has the form $(x_B, x_N) = (B^{-1}b - B^{-1}N x_N, x_N)$ for some $x_N \geq 0$. Setting $x_N = 0$ yields a basic solution $(B^{-1}b, 0)$, which corresponds to a vertex of the feasible polyhedron if $B^{-1}b \geq 0$.

Substituting (15.4) into the objective function of (15.3) allows cost to be expressed as a function of the nonbasic variables x_N:

$$c_B B^{-1}b + (c_N - c_B B^{-1}N)x_N$$

Thus $c_B B^{-1}b$ is the cost of the basic solution $(B^{-1}b, 0)$. The row vector $r = c_N - c_B B^{-1}N$ contains the *reduced costs* associated with the nonbasic variables x_N. Since every feasible solution of (15.3) can be obtained by setting x_N to some nonnegative value, the cost can be smaller than $c_B B^{-1}b$ only if at least one reduced cost is negative. So the basic solution $(B^{-1}b, 0)$ is optimal if $r \geq 0$.

15.3.2 Simplex Method

Given a basic feasible solution $(B^{-1}b, 0)$, the *simplex method* can find a basic optimal solution of (15.3) or show that (15.3) is unbounded. If $r \geq 0$, the solution $(B^{-1}b, 0)$ is already optimal. Otherwise increase any nonbasic variable x_j with negative reduced cost r_j. If the column of $B^{-1}N$ in (15.4) that corresponds to x_j is nonnegative, then x_j can increase indefinitely without driving any component of x_B negative, which means (15.3) is unbounded. Otherwise increase x_j until some basic variable x_i hits zero. This creates a new basic solution. The column of B corresponding to x_i is moved out of B and the column of N corresponding to x_j is moved in. B^{-1} is quickly recalculated and the process repeated.

The procedure terminates with an optimal or unbounded solution if one takes care not to cycle through solutions in which one or more basic variables vanish (*degeneracy*). A starting basic feasible solution can be obtained by solving a "Phase I" problem in which the objective is to minimize the sum of constraint violations. The starting basic variables in the Phase I problem are temporary slack or surplus variables added to represent the constraint violations that result when the other variables are set to zero.

More than half a century after its invention by George Dantzig, the simplex method is still the most widely used method in state-of-the-art solvers. *Interior point* methods are competitive for large problems and are also available in commercial solvers.

15.3.3 Duality and Sensitivity Analysis

The *dual* of a linear programming problem (15.1) is

$$\max \lambda b$$
$$\lambda A \leq c, \quad \lambda \geq 0, \quad \lambda \in \Re^m \tag{15.5}$$

The dual can be understood as seeking the tightest lower bound v on the objective function cx that can be inferred from the constraints $Ax \geq b$, $x \geq 0$. One consequence of the Farkas Lemma, a classical result of mathematical programming, is that $cx \geq v$ can be inferred from a feasible system $Ax \geq b, x \geq 0$ if and only if some nonnegative linear combination $\lambda Ax \geq \lambda b$ of $Ax \geq b$ dominates $cx \geq v$. Since $\lambda Ax \geq \lambda b$ dominates $cx \geq$ when $\lambda A \leq c$ and $\lambda b \geq v$, (15.5) is simply the problem of finding the tightest lower bound v. The dual (15.5) and the *primal* problem (15.1) therefore have the same optimal value if both are feasible and unbounded (*strong duality*).

The dual provides sensitivity analysis, which in turn leads to domain filtering. Note first that the value λb of any dual feasible solution provides a lower bound on the value cx of any primal feasible solution (*weak duality*). This is because $\lambda b \leq \lambda Ax \leq cx$, where the first inequality is due to $Ax \leq b$ and $\lambda \geq 0$, and the second inequality to $\lambda A \geq$ and $x \geq 0$. Now suppose x^* is optimal in the primal and λ^* is optimal in the dual. If the right-hand side b of the primal constraints is perturbed to obtain a new problem with constraints $Ax \geq b + \Delta b$, only the objective function of the dual changes, specifically to $\lambda(b + \Delta b)$. Thus λ^* is still dual feasible and provides a lower bound $\lambda^*(b + \Delta b)$ on the optimal value of the perturbed primal problem. In other words, the perturbation increases the optimal value $\lambda^* b$ of the original problem by at least $\lambda^* \Delta b$.

The dual multipliers in λ^* are readily available when the primal is solved. In fact, $\lambda^* = c_B B^{-1}$, as can be verified by writing the dual of (15.3). These multipliers indicate the sensitivity of the optimal cost to small changes in b. In addition the reduced costs are closely related to the dual multipliers, since $r = c_N - c_B B^{-1} N = c_N - \lambda^* N$. The reduced cost of a single nonbasic variable x_j is $r_j = c_j - \lambda^* A_j$, where A_j is the column of N (and of A) corresponding to x_j.

A related property of the dual solution is *complementary slackness*, which means that a dual variable can be positive only if the corresponding primal constraint is tight in an optimal solution. Thus if x^* and λ^* are optimal in the primal and dual, respectively, then $\lambda^*(Ax^* - b) = 0$. This is because $\lambda^* b = cx^*$, by strong duality, which together with $\lambda^* b \leq \lambda^* Ax^* \leq cx^*$ implies $\lambda^* b = \lambda^* Ax^*$ or $\lambda^*(Ax^* - b) = 0$.

15.3.4 Domain Filtering

The dual solution can help filter variable domains. Suppose that the LP problem (15.1) is a relaxation of a problem that is being solved by CP. There is an upper bound U on the cost cx. For instance, U might be the cost of the best feasible solution found so far in a cost minimization problem, and there is no need to consider solutions with cost greater than U. Suppose (15.1) has optimal value v^*, and the optimal dual solution is λ^*. Suppose further that $\lambda_i^* > 0$, which means the constraint $A^i x \geq b_i$ is tight (i.e., $A^i x^* = b_i$), due to complementary slackness. If the solution of (15.1) were to change, the left-hand side of the ith constraint $A^i x \geq b_i$ of (15.1) could change, say by an amount Δb_i. This would affect the optimal value of (15.1) as much as changing the constraint $A^i x \geq b_i$ to $A^i x \geq b_i + \Delta b_i$, which is to say it would increase the optimal value by at least $\lambda_i^* \Delta b_i$. Since the optimal value cannot rise to a value greater than U, one must have that $\lambda_i^* \Delta b_i \leq U - v^*$, or $\Delta b_i \leq (U - v^*)/\lambda_i$. Since $\Delta b_i = A^i x - A^i x^* = A^i x - b_i$, this yields the valid inequality

$$A^i x \leq b_i + \frac{U - v^*}{\lambda_i} \tag{15.6}$$

for each constraint i of (15.1) with $\lambda_i^* > 0$. The inequality (15.6) can now be propagated, which is particularly useful if some of the variables x_j have integer domains in the original problem.

One can reduce the domain of a particular nonbasic variable x_j by considering the nonnegativity constraint $x_j \geq 0$. Since the reduced cost of x_j measures the effect on cost of increasing x_j, the dual multiplier associated with $x_j \geq 0$ is the reduced cost $r_j = c_j - \lambda^* A_j$. So (15.6) becomes $x_j \leq (U - v^*)/r_j$. If x_j has an integer domain in the original problem, one can say $x_j \leq \lfloor (U - v^*)/r_j \rfloor$.

CP applications of reduced-cost-based filtering include the traveling salesman problem with time windows [96], product configuration [121], fixed charge network flows [86], lesson timetabling [51], and the traveling salesman problem with time windows [51]. The additive bounding procedure [50], which uses reduced costs, has been applied to limited discrepancy search [91].

15.3.5 Example: Traveling Salesman with Time Windows

A traveling salesman problem with time windows provides an example of domain filtering [51]. Suppose a salesman (or delivery truck) must make several stops, perhaps subject to such additional constraints as time windows. The objective is to minimize the total travel time, which has upper bound U. The *assignment problem relaxation* of the constraint set is

$$\min \sum_{ij} c_{ij} x_{ij}$$
$$\sum_{j} x_{ij} = \sum_{j} x_{ji} = 1, \text{ all } i, \qquad x_{ij} \in \{0, 1\}, \text{ all } i, j \tag{15.7}$$

where c_{ij} is the travel time from stop i to stop j. Variable x_{ij} is 1 when the salesman visits stop j immediately after stop i and is zero otherwise. One can now solve an LP relaxation of (15.7) obtained by replacing $x_{ij} \in \{0, 1\}$ with $0 \leq x_{ij} \leq 1$. If r_{ij} is the reduced cost associated with x_{ij} and v^* the optimal value of (15.7), then x_{ij} can be fixed to zero if $(U - v^*)/r_{ij} < 1$. This particular LP problem can be solved very rapidly, since there are specialized methods (e.g. the Hungarian algorithm) for assignment problems.

Solving the LP relaxation of an assignment problem (15.7) actually solves the problem itself, since every basic solution of (15.7) is integral. This is due to the total unimodularity of the matrix of constraint coefficients, which means that every square submatrix has a determinant of 1, -1, or 0.

15.4   Mixed Integer/Linear Modeling

A *mixed integer/linear programming* (MILP) problem is an LP problem with the additional restriction that certain variables must take integer values. It is a (pure) integer/linear programming (ILP) problem when all the variables are integer-valued, and a 0-1 linear programming problem when all the variables have domain $\{0, 1\}$.

MILP problems are solved by a *branch-and-bound* search mechanism. An LP relaxation of the problem is solved at each node of a search tree. If the optimal value of the relaxation is greater than or equal to the value of the best candidate solution found so far, the search backtracks. Otherwise, if all variables in the LP solution are integral, then it becomes a candidate solution. If one or more variables are nonintegral, the search branches on one of the nonintegral variables by splitting its domain. Cutting planes are commonly added at the root node and possibly at other nodes, resulting in a *branch-and-cut* method.

Although MILP problems are generally much harder to solve that LP problems, the solution technology has been the subject of intense development for at least three decades. Commercial solvers have achieved orders-of-magnitude speedups through the right combination of cutting planes, branching heuristics, and preprocessing.

The primary role of MILP in CP, however, is to provide an LP relaxation of a constraint or subset of constraints. One formulates an MILP model and drops the integrality condition. MILP is a highly versatile modeling language if one is sufficiently ingenious. Writing a model with a "good" LP relaxation, however, is often more an art than a science [124]. A good relaxation is generally viewed as one whose optimal value is close to that of the MILP problem.

15.4.1   MILP Representability

It is known precisely what sort of feasible set can be represented by an MILP model. A subset S of $\Re^n$ is MILP-representable if and only if S is the union of finitely many polyhedra, all of which have the same recession cone. The *recession cone* of a polyhedron P is the set of directions in which P is unbounded, or more precisely, the set of vectors $r \in \Re^n$ such that, for some $u \in P$, $u + \alpha r \in P$ for all $\alpha \geq 0$.

The intuition behind this fact can provide a tool for writing MILP models when S has a fairly simple structure. Since S is a union of polyhedra, it is described by a disjunction of linear systems:

$$\bigvee_{k \in K} A^k x \leq b^k \tag{15.8}$$

in which each system $A^k x \leq b^k$ represents a polyhedron. To obtain an MILP model of (15.8), one can introduce 0-1 variables y_k that take the value 1 when the kth disjunct holds:

$$A^k x^k \leq b^k y_k, \ k \in K$$
$$x = \sum_{k \in K} x^k, \ \sum_{k \in K} y_k = 1 \tag{15.9}$$
$$x, x^k \in \Re^n, \ y_k \in \{0, 1\}, \ k \in K$$

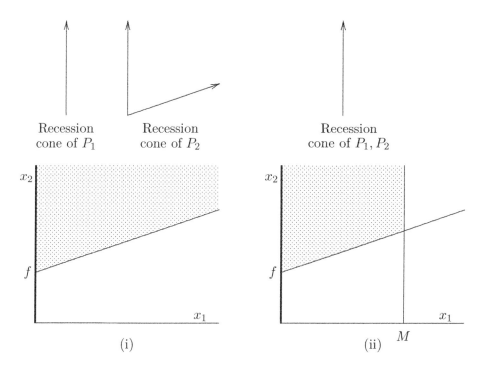

Figure 15.1: *(i) Feasible set of a fixed charge problem, consisting of the union of polyhedra P_1 (heavy line) and P_2 (shaded area). (ii) Feasible set of the same problem with the bound $x_1 \leq M$, where P_2' is the shaded area.*

Note that the vector x of continuous variables is disaggregated into variables x^k. Thus when $y_\ell = 1$ and the other y_ks are zero, the constraints force $x = x^\ell$ and therefore require x to satisfy $A^\ell x \leq b^\ell$.

There are a number of devices for writing MILP formulations when (15.10) does not yield a practical model. A comprehensive discussion of these may be found in [127].

15.4.2 Example: Fixed Charge Function

MILP representability is illustrated by the fixed charge function, which occurs frequently in modeling. Suppose the cost x_2 of producing quantity x_1 is bounded below by zero when the production quantity x_1 is zero, and $f + cx_1$ otherwise, where f is the fixed cost and c the unit variable cost. If S is the set of feasible points (x_1, x_2), then S is the union of two polyhedra P_1 and P_2 (Fig 15.1a). The recession cone of P_1 is P_1 itself, and the recession cone of P_2 is the set of all vectors (x_1, x_2) with $x_2 \geq cx_1 \geq 0$. Since these cones are not identical, S is not MILP-representable.

However, in practice one can put a sufficiently large upper bound M on x_1. Now the recession cone of each of the resulting polyhedra P_1, P_2' (Fig. 15.1b) is the same (namely,

P_1), and the feasible set $S' = P_1 \cup P_2'$ is therefore MILP-representable. P_1 is the polyhedron described by $x_1 \leq 0$, $x_1, x_2 \geq 0$, and P_2' is described by $cx_1 - x_2 \leq -f$, $x_1 \leq M$, $x_1 \geq 0$. So (15.9) becomes

$$
\begin{array}{llll}
x_1^1 \leq 0 & cx_1^2 - x_2^2 \leq -fy_2 & x_1 = x_1^1 + x_1^2 & y_1 + y_2 = 1 \\
x_1^1, x_2^2 \geq 0 & 0 \leq x_1 \leq My_2 & x_2 = x_2^1 + x_2^2 & y_1, y_2 \in \{0,1\}
\end{array}
\tag{15.10}
$$

As often happens, (15.10) simplifies. Only one 0-1 variable appears, which can be renamed y. Since x_1^1 is forced to zero, $x_1 = x_1^2$, and the resulting model is $x_2 \geq fy + cx_1$, $x_1 \leq My$. Obviously y encodes whether the quantity produced is zero or positive, in the former case ($y = 0$) forcing $x_1 = 0$, and in the latter case incurring the fixed charge f. "Big M" constraints like $x_1 \leq My$ are common in MILP models.

15.4.3   Relaxing the Disjunctive Model

The disjunctive model (15.10) has the advantage that its continuous relaxation, obtained by replacing $y_i \in \{0,1\}$ with $0 \leq y_i \leq 1$, is a *convex hull relaxation* of (15.8)—the tightest possible linear relaxation. The convex hull of a set $S \in \Re^n$ is the intersection of all half planes that contain S. The LP relaxation of (15.10) is a convex hull relaxation in the sense that the projection of its feasible set onto the original variables x_1, x_2 is the convex hull of the feasible set of (15.8).

A model of (15.8) with fewer variables is

$$
\begin{aligned}
& A^k x \leq b^k + M^k(1 - y_k), \ k \in K \\
& \sum_{k \in K} y_k = 1, \ x \in \Re^n, \ y_k \in \{0,1\}, \ k \in K
\end{aligned}
\tag{15.11}
$$

where each component of M^k is a valid upper bound on the corresponding inequality of $A^k \leq b^k$. The kth disjunct is enforced when $y_k = 1$. The LP relaxation of (15.11) is not in general a convex hull relaxation, but (15.11) is a correct model even if the polyhedra described by the systems $A^k x \geq b^k$ do not have the same recession cone. The LP relaxation of (15.10), incidentally, is a valid convex hull relaxation of (15.10) even when the polyhedra do not have the same recession cone.

The LP relaxation of (15.11) simplifies when each system $A^k \leq b^k$ is a single inequality $a^k x \leq a_k$ and $0 \leq x \leq m$ [13]. The variables y_k drop out and the relaxation becomes

$$
\left(\sum_{k \in K} \frac{a^k}{M_k} \right) x \leq \sum_{k \in K} \frac{b_k}{M_k} + |K| - 1, \ 0 \leq x \leq m
$$

where $M_k = b_k - \sum_j \min\{0, a_j^k\} m_j$.

15.5   Cutting Planes

Cutting planes, variously called *cuts* or *valid inequalities*, are linear inequalities that can be inferred from an integer or mixed integer constraint set. Cutting planes are added to

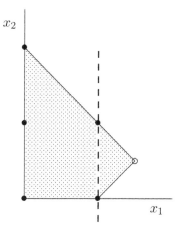

Figure 15.2: *Feasible set (shaded area) of the LP relaxation of a system $x_1 + x_2 \leq 2$, $x_1 - x_2 \leq 0$ with domains $x_j \in \{0, 1, 2\}$, and a cutting plane $x_1 \leq 1$ (dashed line).*

the constraint set to "cut off" noninteger solutions of its LP relaxation, thus resulting in a tighter relaxation.

Cutting planes can also exclude redundant partial assignments (redundant compound labels), even if is not their intended purpose. In some cases they may achieve consistency of one kind or another, even though the concept of consistency never developed in the OR community. It is therefore likely that cutting planes reduce backtracking in branch-and-bound algorithms by excluding redundant partial assignments, quite apart from their role in strengthening relaxations.

For example, $x_1 \leq 1$ is a cutting plane for the system $x_1 + x_2 \leq 2$, $x_1 - x_2 \leq 1$ in which each x_j has domain $\{0, 1, 2\}$. As Fig. 15.2 shows, $x_1 \leq 1$ is valid because it cuts off no feasible (0-1) points. Yet it cuts off part of the feasible set of the LP relaxation and therefore strengthens the LP relaxation, in fact resulting in a convex hull relaxation. Adding the cut also achieves arc consistency for the constraint set, since it reduces x_1's domain to $\{0, 1\}$.

A few basic types of cutting planes are surveyed here. General references on cutting planes include [93, 99, 130], and the role of cutting planes in CP is further discussed in [20, 22, 38, 52, 69, 77]. CP-based application of cutting planes include the orthogonal Latin squares problem [6], truss structure design [23], processing network design [60, 77], single-vehicle routing [110], resource-constrained scheduling [40], multiple machine scheduling [22], boat party scheduling [77], and the multidimensional knapsack problem [100]. Cutting planes for disjunctions of linear systems have been applied to factory retrofit planning, strip packing, and zero-wait job shop scheduling [111].

15.5.1   Chvátal-Gomory Cuts

One can always generate a cutting plane for an integer linear system $Ax \leq b$ by taking a nonnegative linear combination $uAx \leq ub$ of the inequalities in the system and rounding down all fractions that result. This yields the cut $\lfloor uA \rfloor x \leq \lfloor ub \rfloor$, where $u \geq 0$. For example, one can obtain the cut $x_1 \leq 0$ from $x_1 + x_2 \leq 1$ and $x_1 - x_2 \leq 0$ (Fig. 15.2) by giving each a multiplier of $\frac{1}{2}$ in the linear combination.

After generating a cut of this kind, one can add it to $Ax \leq b$ and repeat the process. Any cut generated recursively in this fashion is a *Chvátal-Gomory cut*. A fundamental result of cutting plane theory is that every cut is a Chvátal-Gomory cut [31].

A subset of Chvátal-Gomory cuts are enough to achieve consistency. If two particular types of cuts, *resolvents* and *diagonal sums*, are recursively derived from 0-1 inequalities that are dominated by inequalities in $Ax \leq b$, then every inequality implied by $Ax \leq$ (up to equivalence) is implied by one of the generated cuts; see [67, 70] for details. This fact leads to a logic-based method for 0-1 linear constraint solving [12]. The derivation of resolvents alone is enough to achieve strong n-consistency and therefore hyperarc consistency.

15.5.2   General Separating Cuts

Since it is impractical to generate all Chvátal-Gomory cuts, a more common approach is to identify one or more cuts that exclude or "cut off" a nonintegral solution of the current LP relaxation. These are known as *separating cuts* because they separate the nonintegral solution from the convex hull of the original problem's feasible set. For instance, if the LP relaxation of the example in Fig. 15.2 has the solution $(\frac{3}{2}, \frac{1}{2})$, then $x_1 \leq 1$ is a separating cut.

A general-purpose separating cut can be generated by solving the LP relaxation of an integer system in equality form (15.2) to obtain a basic solution $(\hat{b}, 0)$, where $\hat{b} = B^{-1}b$ If x_i is any basic variable with a nonintegral value in this solution, the valid inequality

$$x_i \leq \lfloor \hat{b}_i \rfloor - \lfloor \hat{N}_i \rfloor x_N \tag{15.12}$$

cuts off $(\hat{b}, 0)$. Here $\hat{N} = B^{-1}N$, and $\hat{N}_i$ refers to the ith row of $\hat{N}$. This cut is popularly known as a *Gomory cut*.

For many years Gomory cuts were believed to be ineffective, but now it is known that they can be very useful if sufficiently many are generated. Multiple cuts can be obtained by generating one for each nonintegral x_i, or perhaps by re-solving the LP with cuts added and generating further Gomory cuts.

Gomory cuts have an analog for MILP systems, known as *separating mixed integer rounding cuts* [94], that are equally important in practice. Let the MILP system in equality form be $A_1 y + A_2 x = b$ with $x, y \geq 0$ and y integer. Let B and N be basic and nonbasic columns in the LP relaxation as before, and suppose that a basic variable y_i is nonintegral. Define J to be the set of indices j for which y_j is basic and K to be the set of indices for which x_j is basic. Also let $J_1 = \{j \in J \mid \text{frac}(\hat{N}_{ij}) \geq \text{frac}(\hat{b}_i)\}$ and $J_2 = J \setminus J_1$ where $\text{frac}(\alpha) = \alpha - \lfloor \alpha \rfloor$ is the fractional part of α. Then the following is a mixed integer rounding cut that cuts off the nonintegral solution:

$$y_i \geq \lfloor \hat{b}_i \rfloor - \sum_{j \in J_1} \lceil \hat{N}_{ij} \rceil y_j - \sum_{j \in J_2} \left(\lfloor \hat{N}_{ik} \rfloor + \frac{\mathrm{frac}(\hat{N}_{ij})}{\mathrm{frac}(\hat{b}_i)} \right) y_j - \frac{1}{\mathrm{frac}(\hat{b}_i)} \sum_{j \in K} \hat{N}_{ij}^+ x_j$$

where $\hat{N}_{ij}^+ = \max\{0, \hat{N}_{ij}\}$.

15.5.3 Knapsack Cuts

Knapsack cuts, also known as *lifted covering inequalities*, are defined for an integer linear inequality $ax \leq \alpha$ with $a \geq 0$. (One can always obtain $a \geq 0$ by replacing each x_j that has a negative coefficient with $U_j - x_j$, where U_j is an upper bound on x_j.) Knapsack cuts do not affect consistency, since they are generated for one constraint at a time, but they tighten the LP relaxation and are often useful in practice.

Suppose first that $ax \leq \alpha$ is a 0-1 inequality. A *cover* for $ax \leq \alpha$ is an index set $J \in \{1, \ldots, n\}$ for which $\sum_{j \in J} a_j > \alpha$. A cover is *minimal* if no proper subset it is a cover. If J is a cover, the *covering inequality* $\sum_{j \in J} x_j \leq |J| - 1$ is obviously valid for $ax \leq \alpha$. (Only minimal covers need be considered, since nonminimal covering inequalities are redundant of minimal ones.) For example, $J = \{1, 2, 3, 4\}$ is a minimal cover for the inequality

$$5x_1 + 5x_2 + 5x_3 + 5x_4 + 8x_5 + 3x_6 \leq 17$$

and gives rise to the covering inequality $x_1 + x_2 + x_3 + x_4 \leq 3$.

A covering inequality can often be strengthened by adding variables to the left-hand side; that is, by *lifting* the inequality into a higher dimensional space. *Sequential lifting* is presented here, in which terms are added one at a time; there are also techniques for adding several terms simultaneously [93]. If $\sum_{j \in J} x_j \leq |J| - 1$ is a covering inequality, then $\pi_k x_k + \sum_{j \in J} x_j \leq |J| - 1$ is also valid for $ax \leq \alpha$, provided

$$\pi_k \leq |J| - 1 - \max \left\{ \sum_{j \in J} x_j \;\middle|\; \sum_{j \in J} a_j x_j \leq \alpha - a_k, \; x_j \in \{0, 1\} \text{ for } j \in J \right\}$$

For example, $x_1 + x_2 + x_3 + x_4 \leq 3$ can be lifted to $x_1 + x_2 + x_3 + x_4 + 2x_5 \leq 3$. If it is lifted further by adding x_6, the inequality is unchanged since $\pi_6 = 0$. The order of lifting can affect the outcome; if x_6 is added before x_5, the resulting cut is $x_1 + x_2 + x_3 + x_4 + x_5 + x_6 \leq 3$. Lifted inequalities are useful only when they can be generated quickly, as when the covering inequality has only a few variables, or the problem has special structure. The coefficients π_k can be computed sequentially by dynamic programming [93].

Covering inequalities can also be derived for an inequality $ax \geq \alpha$ with general integer variables. Here J is a cover if $\sum_{j \in J} a_j \bar{x}_j > \alpha$, where $\bar{x}_j$ is an upper bound on x_j. Any cover J yields the covering inequality $\sum_{j \in J} x_j \leq \alpha / \max_{j \in J}\{a_j\}$. Lifting is possible but more difficult than in the 0-1 case.

15.6 Relaxation of Global Constraints

Linear relaxations for a few common global constraints are presented here: element, all-different, circuit and cumulative. Some relaxations are continuous relaxations of MILP models, and others are derived directly without recourse to an MILP model. These and other relaxations are surveyed in [70, 106].

15.6.1   Element Constraint

An element constraint has the form

$$\text{element}(x, (t_1, \ldots, t_m), v) \tag{15.13}$$

and requires that $v = t_x$. (15.13) implies the disjunction $\bigvee_{k \in D_x} (v = t_k)$, where D_x is the current domain of x. This disjunction can be given an MILP model (15.10), which leads immediately to a convex hull relaxation of (15.13). If each t_k is a constant, then the relaxation is trivial: $\min_{k \in D_x}\{t_k\} \le v \le \max_{k \in D_x}\{t_k\}$. However, if each t_k is a variable with interval domain $[L_k, U_k]$, (15.10) yields a more interesting convex hull relaxation:

$$L_j y_k \le t_j^k \le U_j y_k, \ j, k \in D_x$$

$$v = \sum_{k \in D_x} t_k^k, \quad \sum_{k \in D_x} y_k = 1$$

$$t_k = \sum_{j \in D_x} t_k^j, \ y_k \ge 0, \ k \in D_x$$

Since this relaxation contains a large number of variables t_i^k, one may wish to use the simpler relaxation

$$\sum_{k \in D_x} t_k - (|D_x| - 1)U_{\max} \le v \le \sum_{k \in D_x} t_k - (|D_x| - 1)L_{\min} \tag{15.14}$$

$$L_k \le t_k \le U_k, \ k \in D_x$$

where $L_{\min} = \min_{k \in D_x}\{L_k\}$ and $U_{\max} = \max_{k \in D_x}\{U_k\}$. This is a convex hull relaxation when $L_k = L_{\min}$ and $U_k = U_{\max}$ for all k [70]. One can also use the LP relaxation of (15.11). Another relaxation is

$$\left(\sum_{k \in D_x} \frac{1}{U_{\max} - L_k}\right) v \le \sum_{k \in D_x} \frac{t_k}{U_{\max} - L_k} + |D_x| - 1$$

$$\left(\sum_{k \in D_x} \frac{1}{U_k - L_{\min}}\right) v \ge \sum_{k \in D_x} \frac{t_k}{U_k - L_{\min}} - |D_x| + 1$$

$$L_k \le t_k \le U_k, \ k \in D_x$$

This is in general not redundant of (15.14), unless of course (15.14) is a convex hull relaxation.

15.6.2   All-Different Constraint

The constraint

$$\text{all-different}(y_1, \ldots, y_n)) \tag{15.15}$$

requires that $y_1, \ldots, y_n$ be distinct. If the domain D_{y_i} of each y_i is a finite set of real numbers and $\bigcup_{i=1}^n D_{y_i} = \{a_1, \ldots, a_m\}$, (15.15) can be given the MILP formulation:

$$y_i = \sum_{j=1}^m a_j x_{ij}, \quad \sum_{j=1}^m x_{ij} = 1, \quad i \in \{1, \ldots, n\}$$

$$\sum_{i=1}^n x_{ij} \geq 1, \ j \in \{1, \ldots, m\} \tag{15.16}$$

$$x_{ij} = 0, \text{ all } i, j \text{ with } j \notin D_{y_i}$$

where the binary variable $x_{ij} = 1$ when $y_i = j$. A continuous relaxation can be obtained by replacing $x_{ij} \in \{0, 1\}$ with $x_{ij} \geq 0$. This is a convex hull relaxation, in the sense that the projection of its feasible set onto the variables y_i is the convex hull of the feasible set of (15.15).

The MILP formulation (15.16) is convenient for some problems and not for others. Suppose for instance the problem is to find a minimum-cost assignment of jobs to workers, where c_{ij} is the cost of assigning job j to worker i. The constraint (15.15) requires that every worker get a different job, and the problem is to minimize $\sum_{i=1}^n c_{iy_i}$ subject to (15.15). MILP solves the problem by minimizing $\sum_{ij} c_{ij} x_{ij}$ subject to (15.16).

However, if one wishes to find a minimum-cost route in a traveling salesman problem, the objective function becomes nonlinear in the integer model. (15.15) is a correct model for this problem only if y_i is the ith stop visited, rather than the stop visited immediately after i as in (15.7). So if c_{ij} is the travel time from i to j as before, the problem is to minimize $\sum_{i=1}^n c_{y_i y_{i+1}}$ subject to (15.15), where y_{n+1} is identified with y_1. The integer model must minimize the nonlinear expression $\sum_{ijk} c_{jk} x_{ij} x_{i+1,k}$ subject to (15.16). However, there are linear 0-1 models for this problem, the most popular of which is presented in the next section.

If D_{y_i} is the same set of numbers $\{a_1, \ldots, a_m\}$ for each i, with $a_1 \leq \cdots \leq a_m$, a convex hull relaxation [70, 75, 128] can be written in the original variables:

$$\sum_{j=1}^{|J|} a_j \leq \sum_{j \in J} x_j \leq \sum_{j=m-|J|+1}^m a_j, \text{ all } J \subset \{1, \ldots, n\}$$

There are exponentially many constraints, but one can start by using only the constraints

$$\sum_{j=1}^n a_j \leq \sum_{j=1}^n x_j \leq \sum_{j=m-n+1}^m a_j$$

and bounds on the variables, and then generate separating cuts as needed. Let $\bar{x}$ be the solution of the current relaxation of the problem, and renumber the variables so that $\bar{x}_1 \leq \cdots \leq \bar{x}_n$. Then for each $i = 2, \ldots, n-1$ one can generate the cut

$$\sum_{j=1}^i x_j \geq \sum_{j=1}^i a_j$$

if $\sum_{j=1}^{i} \bar{x}_j < \sum_{j=1}^{i} a_j$. Also for each $i = n-1, \ldots, 2$ generate the cut

$$\sum_{j=i}^{n} x_j \leq \sum_{j=m-n+i}^{m} a_j$$

if $\sum_{j=i}^{n} \bar{x}_j > \sum_{j=m-n+i}^{m} a_j$. There is no separating cut if $\bar{x}$ lies within the convex hull of the alldiff feasible set.

Relaxation of multiple all-different constraints is discussed in [5] and of two overlapping all-different constraints in [34].

15.6.3   Circuit Constraint

The constraint

$$\text{circuit}(y_1, \ldots, y_n) \tag{15.17}$$

requires that $z_1, \ldots, z_n$ be a permutation of $1, \ldots, n$, where each $z_i = y_{z_{i-1}}$ (and z_0 is identified with z_n). The domain D_{y_i} of each y_i is a subset of $\{1, \ldots, n\}$. The elements $1, \ldots, n$ may be viewed as vertices of a directed graph G that contains an edge (i, j) whenever $j \in D_{y_i}$. An edge (i, j) is selected when $y_i = j$, and (15.17) requires that the selected edges form a hamiltonian circuit.

The circuit constraint can be modeled with a traveling salesman formulation. Let the 0-1 variable x_{ij} (for $i \neq j$) take the value 1 when $y_i = j$:

$$\sum_{j=1}^{n} x_{ij} = \sum_{j=1}^{n} x_{ji} = 1, \ i \in \{1, \ldots, n\} \tag{a}$$

$$\sum_{(i,j) \in \delta(S)} x_{ij} \geq 1, \ \text{all } S \subset \{1, \ldots, n\} \text{ with } 2 \leq |S| \leq n-2 \tag{b}$$

$$(15.18)$$

Here $\delta(S)$ is the set of edges (i, j) of G for which $i \in S$ and $j \notin S$. If $j \notin D_{y_i}$, the formulation (15.18) omits variable x_{ij}. Constraints (a) comprise the assignment relaxation (15.7) already discussed. The *subtour elimination constraints* (b) exclude circuits within proper subsets S of $\{1, \ldots, n\}$ by requiring that at least one edge connect a vertex in S to one outside S.

The traveling salesman problem minimizes $\sum_i c_{ix_i}$ subject to (15.17). Its MILP formulation minimizes $\sum_{ij} c_{ij} x_{ij}$ subject to (15.18) and $x_{ij} \in \{0, 1\}$. There are exponentially many subtour elimination constraints in this formulation, but one can begin with a relaxation of the problem (such as the assignment relaxation) and add separating cuts as needed. If $\bar{x}$ is a solution of the current relaxation, let the *capacity* of edge (i, j) be $\bar{x}_{ij}$. Select a proper subset S of the vertices for which the total capacity of edges leaving S is a minimum. The subtour elimination constraint (15.18b) corresponding to S is a separating cut if the minimum capacity is less than 1. There are fast algorithms for finding S ([49, 103]).

If $j \in D_{y_i}$ if and only if $i \in D_{y_j}$, and $c_{ij} = c_{ji}$, for every pair i, j, the problem becomes the *symmetric* traveling salesman problem and can be given a somewhat more compact model that uses a 2-*matching* relaxation. The OR literature has developed different (albeit related) analyses and algorithms for the symmetric and asymmetric problems; see [61] for a comprehensive discussion.

Several families of cutting planes have been developed to strengthen the LP relaxation. By far the most widely used are *comb inequalities*. Suppose H is a subset of vertices of G, and $T_1, \ldots, T_m$ are pairwise disjoint sets of vertices (where m is odd), such that $H \cap T_k$ and $T_k \setminus H$ are nonempty for each k. H is the *handle* of the comb and each T_i is a *tooth*. Then the following is a comb inequality for the asymmetric problem:

$$\sum_{(i,j)\in\delta(H)} x_{ij} + \sum_{k=1}^{m} \sum_{(i,j)\in\delta(T_k)} x_{ij} \geq \tfrac{1}{2}(3m+1)$$

One can get some intuition as to why the cut is valid by considering a comb with three teeth and six vertices. Various proofs of validity are given in [97]. The comb inequalities are facet-defining when G is a complete graph.

15.6.4   Cumulative Constraint

The fundamental constraint for cumulative scheduling is

$$\text{cumulative}(s, p, c, C) \tag{15.19}$$

where variables $s = (s_1, \ldots, s_n)$ represent the start times of jobs $1, \ldots, n$. Parameters $p = (p_1, \ldots, p_n)$ are the processing times and $c = (c_1, \ldots, c_n)$ the resource consumption rates. Release times and deadlines are implicit in the domains $[R_j, D_j]$ of the variables s_j. The constraint (15.19) requires that the total resource consumption rate at any time be less than or equal to C. That is, $\sum_{j \in J_t} c_j \leq C$ for all t, where $J_t = \{j \mid s_j \leq t < s_j + p_j\}$.

The most straightforward MILP model discretizes time and introduces a 0-1 variable x_{jt} that is 1 when job j starts at time t. The variable appears for a particular pair j, t only when $R_j \leq t \leq D_j - p_j$. The model is

$$
\begin{aligned}
\sum_{j} \sum_{t' \in T_{jt}} c_j x_{jt'} &\leq C, \text{ all } t \qquad (a) \\
\sum_{t} x_{jt} &= 1, \quad \text{all } j \qquad\qquad (b)
\end{aligned}
\tag{15.20}
$$

where each $x_{ij} \in \{0, 1\}$ and $T_{jt} = \{t' \mid t - p_j < t' \leq t\}$. Constraints (a) enforce the resource limit, and (b) requires that each job start at some time.

Model (15.20) is large when there are a large number of discrete times. In such cases it may be advantageous to use one of two discrete-event formulations that employ continuous-time variables, although these models provide weaker relaxations. In each model there are $2n$ events, each of which can be the start of a job or the finish of a job. The continuous variable s_k is the time of event k.

In one model, the 0-1 variable $x_{jkk'}$ is 1 if event k is the start of job j and event k' is the finish of job j. The inventory variable z_k keeps track of how much resource is being consumed when event k occurs; obviously one wants $z_k \leq C$. The model for (15.19) is

$$z_k = z_{k-1} + \sum_j \sum_{k'>k} c_j x_{jkk'} - \sum_j \sum_{k'<k} c_j x_{jk'k}, \text{ all } k \qquad (a)$$

$$z_0 = 0, \quad 0 \leq z_k \leq C, \text{ all } k \qquad (b)$$

$$\sum_k \sum_{k'>k} x_{jkk'} = 1, \text{ all } j \qquad (c)$$

$$s_{k'} - s_k \geq \sum_j p_j x_{jkk'}, \text{ all } k, k' \text{ with } k < k' \qquad (d) \qquad (15.21)$$

$$s_k \geq \sum_j \sum_{k'>k} x_{jkk'} R_j, \text{ all } k \qquad (e)$$

$$t_k \leq D_{\max} \left(1 - \sum_j \sum_{k'<k} x_{jk'k} \right) + \sum_j \sum_{k'<k} x_{jk'k} D_j, \text{ all } k \quad (f)$$

where each $x_{jkk'} \in \{0,1\}$ and $D_{\max} = \max_j\{D_j\}$. Constraint (a) keeps track of how much resource is being consumed, and (b) imposes the upper limit. Constraint (c) makes sure that each job starts once and ends once. Constraint (d) presents jobs from overlapping, and (e) enforces the release times. Constraint (f) uses a big-M construction (where $D_{\max}$ is the big-M) to enforce the deadlines.

Model (15.21) can grow quite large if there are too many events, due to the triply indexed variables $x_{jkk'}$. An alternative is to use separate variables for start-events and finish-events, which requires that the deadlines be enforced in a different way. This reduces the triple index to a double index at the cost of producing a weaker relaxation. Let the 0-1 variable x_{jk} be 1 when event k is the start of job j, and $y_{jk} = 1$ when event k is the finish of job j. The new continuous variable f_j is the finish time of job j.

$$z_k = z_{k-1} + \sum_j c_j x_{jk} - \sum_j c_j y_{jk}, \text{ all } k \qquad (a)$$

$$z_0 = 0, \quad z_k \leq C, \text{ all } k \qquad (b)$$

$$\sum_k x_{jk} = 1, \quad \sum_k y_{jk} = 1, \text{ all } j \qquad (c)$$

$$\sum_j x_{jk} + y_{jk} = 1, \text{ all } k \qquad (d)$$

$$s_{k-1} \leq s_k, \quad x_{jk} \leq \sum_{k'<k} y_{jk'}, \text{ all } k > 1 \qquad (e)$$

$$s_k \geq \sum_j R_j x_{jk}, \text{ all } k \qquad (f)$$

$$s_k + p_j x_{jk} - D_{\max}(1 - x_{jk}) \leq f_j$$
$$\leq s_k + D_{\max}(1 - y_{jk}), \text{ all } j, k \quad (g)$$
$$f_j \leq d_j, \text{ all } j \qquad (h)$$

where each $x_{jk}, y_{jk} \in \{0,1\}$. Constraints (a) and (b) perform the same function as before Constraints (c) and (d) require that each job start once and end once but not as the same event. Constraints (e) are redundant but may tighten the relaxation. One constraint requires the events to occur in chronological order, and one requires a job's start-event to have a smaller index than its finish-event. Constraint (f) observes the release times. The new element is constraint (g). The first inequality defines the defines the finish time f_j of each job by forcing it to occur no earlier than p_j time units after the start time. The second inequality forces the time associated with the finish-event to be no earlier than the finish time. Finally, constraint (h) enforces the deadlines.

A fourth relaxation uses only the original variables s_j [75]. Let $J = \{j_1, \ldots, j_m\}$ be any subset of the jobs $\{1, \ldots, n\}$, indexed so that $p_{j_1} c_{j_1} \leq \cdots \leq p_{j_m} c_{j_m}$. Then

$$\sum_{j \in J} s_j \geq m R_{\min} + \frac{1}{C} \sum_{i=1}^{m} (m - i + 1) p_{j_i} c_{j_i} - \sum_{i=1}^{m} p_{j_i}$$

$$\sum_{j \in J} s_j \leq m D_{\max} - \frac{1}{C} \sum_{i=1}^{m} (m - i + 1) p_{j_i} c_{j_i}$$

where $R_{\min} = \min_i \{R_{j_i}\}$ and $D_{\max} = \max_i \{D_{k_i}\}$. A relaxation can be created by using these inequalities for selected subsets of jobs. One need only consider subsets J of the form $\{j \mid [R_j, D_j] \subset [R_i, D_k]\}$ for pairs i, k with $R_i < D_k$. Larger subsets tend to yield much stronger inequalities.

15.7 Relaxation of Piecewise Linear and Disjunctive Constraints

Specialized relaxations can be devised for a number of additional constraints that commonly occur in modeling. Two such constraints are bounds on piecewise linear, semicontinuous cost functions, and disjunctions of nonlinear inequality systems. There are also convex hull relaxations (not discussed here) for various logical constraints [70], such as cardinality rules requiring that if at least k of a given set of propositions are true, then at least ℓ of another set are true ([132], generalized in [10]).

15.7.1 Semicontinuous Piecewise Linear Functions

Piecewise linear functions are often useful in modeling, partly because they can approximate nonlinear functions. A semicontinuous piecewise linear function $f(x)$ can be written

$$f(x) = \frac{U_k - x}{U_k - L_k} c_k + \frac{x - L_k}{U_k - L_k} d_k \quad \text{for } x \in [L_k, U_k], \quad k = 1, \ldots, m$$

and is illustrated in Fig. 15.3.

The function $f(x)$ can be given an MILP model by replacing all occurrences of $f(x)$ with a new continuous variable v and writing

$$v = \sum_k \lambda_k a_k + \mu_k b_k, \quad x = \sum_k \lambda_k L_k + \mu_k U_k, \quad \sum_k \lambda_k + \mu_k = 1, \quad \sum_k y_k = 1$$

$$0 \leq \lambda_k \leq y_k, \quad 0 \leq \mu_k \leq y_k, \quad \text{all } k$$

where each $y_k \in \{0, 1\}$. An LP relaxation is obtained by replacing $y_j \in \{0, 1\}$ by $0 \leq y_j \leq 1$. The MILP model for continuous piecewise linear functions is slightly simpler; see [127]. An MILP model is used with a probe backtrack algorithm in [2].

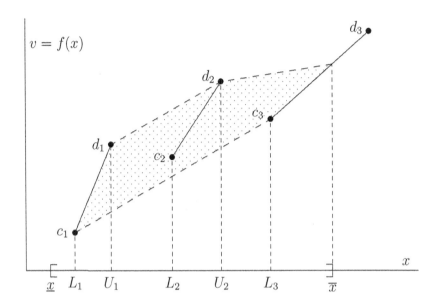

Figure 15.3: *Semicontinuous piecewise linear function $f(x)$ (solid line segments) and its convex hull relaxation (shaded area), where $[\underline{x}, \overline{x}]$ is the current domain of x.*

Computational studies [101, 102, 105] suggest that it is often more efficient to write a convex hull relaxation directly in the original variables and dispense with the auxiliary variables λ_k, μ_k, y_k. One simply writes an inequality in v, x to represent each edge of the convex hull, illustrated in Fig. 15.3.

15.7.2   Disjunctions of Nonlinear Systems

Methods for relaxing disjunctions of linear systems were presented in Section 15.4.3. They have proved useful for relaxing problems that combine discrete and continuous linear elements. Many applications, however, mix discrete and continuous *nonlinear* elements. Fortunately, the convex hull relaxation for the linear case can be generalized to the convex nonlinear case. It has been used to solve several chemical process engineering problems [89, 90, 104, 112, 125]

The task is to relax

$$\bigvee_{k \in K} g^k(x) \leq 0 \tag{15.22}$$

where $g^k(x)$ is a vector of convex functions and $x \in \Re^n$. It is assumed that x and each $g^k(x)$ are bounded, and in particular that $L \leq x \leq U$. A convex hull relaxation for (15.22) can be derived by writing x as a convex combination of points $\hat{x}^k$ that respectively satisfy the disjuncts of (15.22):

$$x = \sum_{k \in K} \beta_k \hat{x}^k, \quad \sum_{k \in K} \beta_k = 1$$

$$g^k(\hat{x}^k) \leq 0, \quad \beta_k \geq 0, \quad L \leq \hat{x}^k \leq U, \quad \text{all } k \in K$$

Using the change of variable $x^k = \beta_k \hat{x}^k$ and multiplying the nonlinear constraints by β_k yields a continuous relaxation for (15.22):

$$x = \sum_{k \in K} x^k, \quad \sum_{k \in K} \beta_k = 1$$

$$\beta_k g^k \left(\frac{x^k}{\beta_k} \right) \leq 0, \quad \beta_k \geq 0, \quad \beta_k L \leq x^k \leq \beta_k U, \quad \text{all } k \in K \tag{15.23}$$

It can be shown that the functions $\beta_k g^k(x^k/\beta_k)$ are convex and moreover that (15.23) is a convex hull relaxation of (15.22) [89, 119]. Since β_k can vanish, it is common in practice to introduce a perturbation ϵ, which preserves convexity. The nonlinear constraints of (15.23) become

$$(\beta_k + \epsilon) g^k \left(\frac{x^k}{\beta_k + \epsilon} \right) \leq 0, \quad \text{all } k \in K$$

One can also relax (15.22) with a big-M relaxation similar to the LP relaxation of (15.11):

$$g^k(x) \leq M^k(1 - \beta_k), \quad \beta_k \geq 0, \quad \text{all } k \in K$$

$$\sum_{k \in K} \beta_k = 1$$

where each component of M^k is an upper bound on the corresponding function in $g^k(x)$.

15.8   Lagrangean Relaxation

Many relaxations are formed simply by removing constraints. *Lagrangean relaxation* refines this process by imposing a penalty for violation of the deleted constraints, provided they have inequality form.   This tends to make the minimum value of the relaxed problem larger and may therefore provide a tighter bound on the optimal value of the original problem.

A Lagrangean relaxation is actually a family of relaxations, since one can choose the penalty (i.e., the Lagrange multiplier) for each constraint violation. The problem of selecting the multipliers that result in the tightest bound is the *Lagrangean dual*.

Since solution of the Lagrangean dual tends to be time consuming, the general practice in CP applications is to solve it only at the root node and use the resulting Lagrange multipliers at all subsequent nodes. These multipliers not only define a relaxation that can be quickly solved or propagated, but they allow domain filtering in the same fashion as the dual multipliers of an LP relaxation. In fact, dual multipliers are a special case of Lagrange multipliers.

Lagrangean relaxation is particularly useful in CP when a full linear relaxation is incompatible with the very rapid processing of search tree nodes that often characterizes CP methods. In such cases one may be able to solve a Lagrangean dual of the LP at the root node, which is itself an LP problem, to obtain a weaker but specially-structured LP relaxation that can be solved quickly at the remaining nodes.

CP-based Lagrangean methods have been applied to network design [36], automatic digital recording [113], traveling tournament problems [17], the resource-constrained shortest path problem [54], and the general problem of filtering domains [85].

15.8.1   The Lagrangean Dual

Lagrangean relaxation is applied to problems of the form

$$
\begin{aligned}
&\min f(x) \\
&g_i(x) \leq 0, \quad i = 1, \ldots, m \\
&x \in S, \quad x \in \Re^n
\end{aligned}
\tag{15.24}
$$

where $x \in S$ represents an arbitrary constraint set but in practice is carefully chosen to have special structure. Lagrangean relaxation *dualizes* the constraints $g_i(x) \leq 0$ by penalizing their violation in the objective function:

$$
\begin{aligned}
&\min \theta(x, \lambda) = f(x) + \sum_{i-1}^{m} \lambda_i g_i(x) \\
&x \in S, \quad x \in \Re^n
\end{aligned}
\tag{15.25}
$$

where each $\lambda_i \geq 0$ is a *Lagrange multiplier*. The motivation for using the relaxation is that the special structure of the constraints $x \in S$ makes it easy to solve. The term "penalty" is not quite right for the expression $\lambda_i g_i(x)$, however, since a penalty should vanish when the solution is feasible; $\lambda_i g_i(x)$ can go negative when x is feasible, resulting in a "saddle" function.

Clearly $\theta(x, \lambda) \leq f(x)$ for any x that is feasible in the relaxation (15.25), since $\lambda \geq$ and each $g_i(x) \leq 0$. Thus for any $\lambda \geq 0$, the optimal value $\theta(\lambda)$ of the Lagrangean relaxation (15.25) is a lower bound on the optimal value v^* of the original problem (15.24) (*weak duality*). The tightest lower bound on v^* is obtained by solving the *Lagrangean dual* problem: maximize $\theta(\lambda)$ subject to $\lambda \geq 0$. The amount by which this bound falls short of v^* is the *duality gap*.

15.8.2   Solving the Dual

Since the Lagrangean function $\theta(\lambda)$ is concave, it can be maximized by finding a local maximum. A popular approach is *subgradient optimization*, which begins with a starting value $\lambda^0 \geq 0$ and sets each $\lambda^{k+1} = \lambda^k + \alpha_k \sigma^k$, where σ^k is a subgradient of $\theta(\lambda)$ at $\lambda = \lambda^k$. Conveniently, if $\theta(\lambda^k) = f(x^k, \lambda)$, then $(g_1(x^k), \ldots, g_m(x^k))$ is a subgradient. The stepsize α_k should decrease as k increases, but not so quickly as to cause premature convergence. A simple option is to set $\alpha_k = \alpha_0/k$, or perhaps $\alpha_k = \alpha_0(\bar{\theta} - \theta(\lambda^k))/||\sigma^k||$ where $\bar{\theta}$ is a dynamically adjusted upper bound on the maximum value of $\theta(\lambda)$. The stepsize is highly problem-dependent and must be tuned for every problem class. Solution methods are further discussed in [11, 98].

Typically the Lagrangean dual is solved only at the root node. As one descends into the search tree, branching adds constraints to the problem, and the dual solution λ^* ceases to be optimal. Nonetheless the optimal value of the Lagrangean relaxation, with λ set to λ^* and branching constraints added, continues to be a valid lower bound of the optimal solution. In fact there is no need to obtain optimal λ_is even at the root node, and frequently the subgradient algorithm is terminated early.

One must take care that branching constraints do not destroy the special structure of the Lagrangean relaxation. For instance, one may wish to branch by fixing one or variables rather than adding inequality constraints.

15.8.3 Special Case: Linear Programming

The Lagrangean dual of an LP problem is easy to solve, since it is equivalent to the LP dual. Suppose the original problem (15.24) is an LP problem

$$\min cx$$
$$Ax \geq b, \quad Dx \geq d, \quad x \geq 0 \tag{15.26}$$

in which the linear system $Dx \geq d$ has some kind of special structure. If $Ax \geq b$ is dualized, then $\theta(\lambda)$ is the optimal value of

$$\min \theta(x, \lambda) = cx + \lambda(b - Ax) = (c - \lambda A)x + \lambda b$$
$$Dx \geq d, \quad x \geq 0 \tag{15.27}$$

Suppose x^* is an optimal solution of the original LP problem (15.26), and (λ^*, μ^*) is an optimal dual solution in which λ^* corresponds to $Ax \geq b$ and μ^* to $Dx \geq d$. Thus

$$cx^* = \lambda^* b + \mu^* d \tag{15.28}$$

by strong duality. It will be shown below that $\theta(\lambda^*) = cx^*$. This implies that λ^* is an optimal dual solution of the Lagrangean dual problem, since $\theta(\lambda)$ is a lower bound on cx^* for any $\lambda \geq 0$.

One can therefore solve the Lagrangean dual of (15.26) at the root node by solving its LP dual. If (λ^*, μ^*) solves the LP dual, then λ^* solves the Lagrangean dual in which $Ax \geq b$ is dualized. At subsequent nodes one solves the specially structured LP problem (15.27), with λ set to the value λ^* obtained at the root node, to obtain a valid lower bound on the value of the LP relaxation at that node.

To see that $\theta(\lambda^*) = cx^*$, note first that x^* is feasible in

$$\min_{x \geq 0} \{(c - \lambda^* A)x \mid Dx \geq d\} \tag{15.29}$$

and μ^* is feasible in its LP dual

$$\max_{\mu \geq 0} \{ud \mid \mu D \leq c - \lambda^* A\} \tag{15.30}$$

where the latter is true because (λ^*, μ^*) is dual feasible for (15.26). But the corresponding objective function value of (15.29) is

$$(c - \lambda^*)x^* = cx^* + \lambda^*(b - Ax^*) - \lambda^* b = cx^* - \lambda^* b$$

where the second equation is due to complementary slackness. This is equal to the value $\mu^* d$ of (15.30), due to (15.28). So $cx^* - \lambda^* b$ is the optimal value of (15.29), which means that cx^* is the optimal value $\theta(\lambda^*)$ of (15.27) when $\lambda = \lambda^*$.

15.8.4   Domain Filtering

Lagrangean duality provides a generalization of the filtering mechanism based on LP dual-ity. Suppose that there is an upper bound U on the cost $f(x)$ in (15.24), and let $v^* = \theta(\lambda^*$ be the optimal value of the Lagrangean dual. Let x^* solve (15.25) when $\lambda = \lambda^*$, so that $\theta(\lambda^*) = \theta(\lambda^*, x^*)$, and suppose further that $g_i(x^*) = 0$. If the solution of (15.24) were to change, function $g_i(x)$ could decrease, say by an amount Δ_i. This would in-crease the optimal value of (15.24) as much as changing the the constraint $g_i(x) \leq 0$ to $g_i(x) + \Delta_i \leq 0$. The function $\theta(\lambda)$ for the altered problem is $\theta'(\lambda) = \min_{x \in S}\{\theta'(\lambda, x)\}$ where $\theta'(\lambda, x) = f(x) + \sum_j \lambda_j g_j(x) + \lambda_i \Delta_i$. Since $\theta'(\lambda^*, x)$ differs from $\theta(\lambda^*, x)$ only by a constant, any x that minimizes $\theta(\lambda^*, x)$ also minimizes $\theta'(\lambda^*, x)$. So

$$\theta'(\lambda^*) = \theta'(\lambda^*, x^*) + \lambda_i^* \Delta_i = v^* + \lambda_i^* \Delta_i$$

is a lower bound on the optimal value of the altered problem, by weak duality. Thus one must have $v^* + \lambda^* \Delta_i \leq U$, or $\Delta_i \leq (U - v^*)/\lambda_i^*$. Since $\Delta_i = g_i(x^*) - g_i(x) = -g_i(x)$ this yields a valid inequality parallel to (15.6) that can be propagated:

$$g_i(x) \geq -\frac{U - v^*}{\lambda_i^*} \tag{15.31}$$

If constraint i imposes a lower bound L on a variable x_j (i.e., $-x_j + L \leq 0$), then (15.31) becomes $x_j \leq L + (U - v^*)/\lambda_i^*$. This can be used to reduce the domain of x_j if $\lambda_i^* > 0$, and similarly if there is an upper bound on x_j.

15.8.5   Example: Generalized Assignment Problem

The *generalized assignment problem* is an assignment problem (15.7) with the complicat-ing constraint that the jobs j assigned to each resource i satisfy $\sum_j \alpha_{ij} x_{ij} \leq \beta_i$. Let's suppose that an LP relaxation of the problem is to be solved at each node of the search tree to obtain bounds. If solving this LP with a general-purpose solver is too slow, the complicating constraints can be dualized, resulting in a pure assignment problem with cost function $\sum_{ij}(c_{ij} - \lambda_i^* \alpha_{ij})x_{ij}$. The optimal multipliers λ_i^* can be obtained at the root node by solving the full LP relaxation.

At subsequent nodes one can solve the Lagrangean relaxation very quickly with the Hungarian algorithm. The relaxation provides a weak bound, but the dual variables allow useful domain filtering. The search branches by setting some x_{ij} to 0 or 1, which in turn can be achieved by giving x_{ij} a very large or very small cost in the objective function of the Lagrangean relaxation, thus preserving the problem structure.

15.9   Dynamic Programming

Dynamic programming (DP) exploits recursive or nested structure in a problem. A DP model provides one more opportunity for an OR-based relaxation of a CP problem, and the DP model can itself be relaxed to reduce time and space consumption. Since DP models express the optimal value as a recursively defined function, they can often be coded in a CP modeling language. DP models are also particularly amendable to filtering discrete domains, including cost-based filtering.

15.9.1 Recursive Optimization

Given the problem of minimizing $f(x)$ subject to $x \in S$, a DP model defines a sequence of *state variables* $s_1, \ldots, s_n$. The original variables $x = (x_1, \ldots, x_n)$ are viewed as a sequence of *controls*. Each control x_k brings about a transition from state s_k to state $t_k(x_k, s_k)$. The optimization problem is viewed as finding a minimum-cost sequence of controls.

The key property of a DP model is that each state s_k must contain enough information to determine the set $X_k(s_k)$ of feasible controls and the cost $g_k(s_k, x_k)$ of applying each control x_k, without knowing how one got to state s_k. Thus if each $x_k \in X_k(s_k)$ and each $s_{k+1} = t_k(x_k, s_k)$, then $x \in S$ and $f(x) = \sum_{k=1}^{n} g_k(s_k, x_k)$.

This structure immediately leads to recursive equations, known as *Bellman's equations*, that solve the problem. The computation works backward from a final state s_{n+1}:

$$f_k(s_k) = \min_{x_k \in X_k(s_k)} \{g_k(s_k, x_k) + f_{k+1}(t(x_k, s_k))\}, \quad k = n, \ldots, 1 \quad (15.32)$$

where s_1 is the initial state and $f_1(s_1)$ is the optimal value $min\{f(x) \mid x \in S\}$. The cost $f_k(s_k)$ is interpreted as the minimum cost of going from state s_k to a final state. The final costs $f_{n+1}(s_{n+1})$ are given as *boundary conditions*.

A DP algorithm compiles a table of each $f_k(s_k)$ for all values of s_k based on the previously computed table of $f_{k+1}(s_{k+1})$. At each stage k the set $X_k^*(s_k)$ of controls that yield the minimum in (15.32) for each s_k is recorded. When $f_1(s_1)$ is obtained, the algorithm works forward to obtain an optimal solution $(x_1^*, \ldots, x_n^*)$ and optimal sequence of states $s_1^*, \ldots, s_n^*$ by letting each x_k^* be any element of $X_k^*(s_k^*)$ and each $s_k^* = g_k(x_{k-1}^*, s_{k-1}^*)$, where $s_1^* = s_1$.

For instance, suppose one wishes to find a shortest path from every vertex of a directed acyclic graph (V, E) to vertex $n + 1$. If the length of edge (i, j) is c_{ij} with $c_{ii} = 0$, the recursion is $f_k(i) = \min_{j \in E(i)} \{c_{ij} + f_{k+1}(j)\}$, where $E(i) = \{i\} \cup \{j \mid (i, j) \in E\}$. The cost $f_k(i)$ is interpreted as the length of the shortest path from vertex i to vertex $n + 1$ having $n - k + 1$ or fewer edges. The boundary condition is $f_{n+1}(n + 1) = 0$.

The art of dynamic programming lies in identifying state variables s_k that do not have too many possible values. Only certain problems have a recursive structure that can be exploited in this manner, but many examples of these can be found in [19, 42]

15.9.2 Domain Filtering

An important special case arises when DP is applied to finding feasible solutions of a constraint C, since this allows one to achieve hyperarc consistency for C. In this case one can view the objective function $f(x)$ as equal to 1 when x violates C and 0 otherwise. The boundary conditions are defined by letting $f_{n+1}(s_{n+1})$ be 0 for all final states s_{n+1} that satisfy C and 1 for all other states. All other costs $g_k(s_k, x_k) = 0$. So if $f_k(s_k) = 0$, $X_k^*(s_k)$ is the set of all controls x_k that can lead to a feasible solution when they are applied in state s_k. This means $\bigcup_{s_k \mid f_k(s_k)=0} X_k^*(s_k)$ is the set of values of x_k that can lead to a feasible solution, and hyperarc consistency is achieved by reducing the domain of x_k to this set.

15.9.3 Example: Cost-Based Filtering

Suppose that a cost constraint $ax \leq b$ is given, and one wishes to filter the variable domains D_{x_k}. A classical DP recursion for finding all feasible solutions defines the state variable s_k to be the sum $\sum_{j<k} a_j x_j$ of the first $k-1$ terms on the left-hand side of $ax \leq b$. The recursion is

$$f_k(s_k) = \min_{x_k \in D_{x_k}} \{f_{k+1}(s_k + a_k x_k)\}$$

with the boundary condition $f_{n+1}(s_{n+1}) = 0$ for $s_{n+1} \leq b$ and $f_{n+1}(s_{n+1}) = 1$ for $s_{n+1} > b$. Note that $g_k(s_k, x_k) = 0$ in this recursion.

If the absolute value of the coefficients a_k is bounded, then the number of states (values of s_k for all k) is polynomially bounded and the DP recursion has polynomial complexity.

DP therefore provides a pseudopolynomial algorithm that achieves hyperarc consistency for $ax \leq b$. For instance, if $ax \leq b$ is $4x_1 + 2x_2 + 3x_3 \leq 12$ and each $D_{x_k} = \{1, 2\}$ then possible states s_k are illustrated in Fig. 15.4. Every solution (x_1, x_2, x_3) defines a path $s_1 \to s_2 \to s_3 \to s_4$ through the network. Heavy lines show paths that correspond to optimal solutions (i.e., $f(x) = 0$) and therefore feasible solutions of $4x_1 + 2x_2 + 3x_3 \leq 12$ For instance, $f_3(6) = f_3(8) = 0$ since $s_3 = 4x_1 + 2x_2$ can be either 6 or 8 in an optimal solution, but $f_3(s_3) = 1$ for all other s_3.

One can read the filtered domains from the network. For instance, the filtered domain of x_3 is $\bigcup_{s_3|f(s_3)=0} X_3^*(s_3) = X_3^*(6) \cup X_3^*(8) = \{1, 2\} \cup \{1\} = \{1, 2\}$. The reduced domains of x_1 and x_2 are $\{1\}$ and $\{1, 2\}$, respectively. This idea is developed further in [123].

15.9.4 State Space Relaxation

When the state variables s_k have too many values, *state space relaxation* can reduce the number of values and make the problem easier to solve. State space relaxation in effect uses a hash code for the states; it defines a function $\phi(s_k)$ that maps many values of s_k to the same state. Every control $x_k \in X_k(s_k)$ is mapped to a control that takes the system from $\phi(s_k)$ to $\phi(g_k(s_k, x_k))$. The cost function $\hat{g}_k$ for the relaxation must satisfy $\hat{g}_k(\phi(s_k), \phi(y_k)) \leq g_k(s_k, x_k)$. The optimal value of the relaxed problem is a lower bound on the optimal value of the original recursion.

This can be illustrated by relaxing a DP formulation of the traveling salesman problem on a graph (V, E). The objective is to minimize $\sum_i c_{x_i x_{i+1}}$ subject to alldiff$(x_1, \ldots, x_n)$ and $(x_i, x_{i+1}) \in E$. Let x_1 be the first customer visited after leaving home base i_0, and fix the last customer visited x_n to be home base. The classical DP formulation defines state variable s_k to be (i, V_k), where V_k is any set of $n - k + 1$ vertices and $i \in V_k$. The cost $f_k(i, V_k)$ is interpreted as the cost of the minimum-cost tour that starts at i and covers all the vertices in V_k. If $E_i = \{j \mid (i, j) \in E\}$, the recursion is

$$f_k(i, V_k) = \min_{x_k \in (V_k \cap E_i) \setminus \{i\}} \{c_{ix_k} + f_{k+1}(x_k, V_k \setminus \{i\})\} \tag{15.33}$$

with boundary condition $f_n(i, \{i\}) = c_{ii_0}$ for all vertices i with $i_0 \in E_i$ and $f_n(i, \{i\}) = \infty$ for all other i.

The recursion (15.33) is not computationally useful because there are exponentially many states (i, V_k). However, this DP model can be relaxed, for example by mapping all

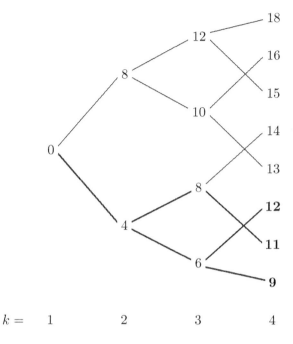

Figure 15.4: *States s_k for the constraint $4x_1 + 2x_2 + 3x_3 \leq 12$ with $x_j \in \{1, 2\}$. Edges leaving state 0 correspond to $x_1 = 1, 2$, and similarly for other edges. Costs associated with the terminal states ($k = 4$) are 0 for the boldface states and 1 for the others. Heavy lines correspond to paths that lead to optimal solutions (i.e. solutions feasible for $4x_1 + 2x_2 + 3x_3 \leq 12$).*

states (i, V_k) for a given k to $\phi(i, V_k) = (i, k)$. The cost of a transition from (i, k) to $(j, k+1)$ is the same as that from any (i, V_k) to any (j, V_{k+1}), namely c_{ij}. The recursion (15.33) becomes

$$\hat{f}_k(i) = \min_{x_k \in E_i} \left\{ c_{ix_k} + \hat{f}_{k+1}(x_k) \right\} \tag{15.34}$$

with the same boundary condition as before. A CP solution of (15.34) and other issues are discussed in [53].

15.9.5 Nonserial Dynamic Programming 1

DP is based on the principle that each state s_k depends only on the previous state s_{k-1} and control x_{k-1}. In *nonserial dynamic programming* (NSDP), a state may depend on several previous states.

NSDP has been known in OR for more than 30 years [18]. Essentially the same idea has surfaced in a number of contexts, including Bayesian networks [88], belief logics [115,

117], pseudoboolean optimization [35], location theory [28], k-trees [7, 8], and bucket elimination [39].

In the simplest form of NSDP, the state variables s_k are the original variables x_k. This is the form most relevant to CP, since it permits solution of a constraint set C in time that is directly related to the width of the dependency graph G of C.

The *width* of a directed graph G is the maximum in-degree of vertices of G. The *induced width* of G with respect to an ordering of vertices $1, \ldots, n$ is the width of G' with respect to this ordering, where G' is constructed as follows. Remove vertices $n, n-1, \ldots,$ from G one a time, and when each vertex i is removed, add edges as necessary so that the vertices adjacent to i at the time of its removal form a clique. Then G' consists of G plus all edges added in this process.

The dependency graph G for constraint set C contains a vertex for each variable x_j of C and an edge (x_i, x_j) when x_i and x_j occur in a common constraint. Let S_k be the set of vertices in $\{1, \ldots, k-1\}$ that are adjacent to k in G', and let x^i be the set of variables in constraint $C_i \in C$. Define the cost function $c_i(x^i)$ to be 1 if x^i violates C_i and 0 otherwise. Then the NSDP recursion again works backward:

$$f_k(S_k) = \min_{x_k \in D_{x_k}} \left\{ \sum_{i \in I_k} c_i(x^i) + \sum_{j \in J_k} f_j(S_j) \right\}, \quad k = 1, \ldots, n \qquad (15.35)$$

where I_k is the set of indices i for which x^i contains x_k but none of $x_{k+1}, \ldots, x_n$. J_k is the set of indices $j \in \{k+1, \ldots, \ldots, n\}$ for which S_j contains x_k but none of $x_{k+1}, \ldots, x_n$ Note that the computation of $f_k(S_k)$ may use previously computed costs $f_i(S_i)$ for several $i \in \{k+1, \ldots, n\}$. The process gets started by computing $f_n(S_n)$, which requires no previous results. The optimal value $\sum_{k|S_k=\emptyset} f_k(\emptyset)$ is 0 if and only if C has a feasible solution. A feasible solution is recovered by recording for each k the set $X_k^*(S_k)$ of values of x_k that achieve the minimum value of zero in (15.35). The for $k = 1, \ldots n$ one can select any $x_k^* \in X_k^*(S_k^*)$, where S_k^* contains the previously selected values for $x_j \in S_k$.

The complexity of the recursion (15.35) is at worst proportional to nD^{w+1}, where D is the size of the largest variable domain, and w is the size of the largest set S_k. But w is the width of G' and therefore the induced with of G with respect to the ordering $x_1, \ldots, x_n$ So the complexity of solving a constraint set C by NSDP is at worst exponential in the induced width of C's dependency graph with respect to the reverse order of recursion. These ideas are further discussed in [70].

15.10 Branch-and-Price Methods

Branch and price is a well-known OR technique that is applied to MILP problems with a very large number of variables. In fact, the MILP model is sometimes reformulated so as to have exponentially many variables, since this may simplify the model while yet allowing solution by branch and price.

The basic idea is to solve the MILP initially with only a few variables, and add variables to the problem as they are needed to improve on the current solution. A subproblem is solved to identify promising variables. Since a variable is added to the problem by adding a column to the MILP constraint matrix, this approach is often known as *column generation*

Complicating constraints can be dealt with implicitly by restricting what sort of columns can be generated by the subproblem.

It is in the column generation phase that CP can be useful, since the subproblem may have complicated constraints that make it more amenable to solution by CP rather than OR methods. CP-based branch and price has proved successful in several applications that involve assignment of resources under complex constraints.

15.10.1 The Algorithm

Branch and price is applied to an MILP problem

$$\min cy$$
$$Ay = b, \quad y \geq 0, \quad y_\ell \text{ integer for } \ell \in I \tag{15.36}$$

where $I \subset \{1, \ldots, n\}$. The algorithm is a branch-and-bound search that solves the LP relaxation at each node of the search tree by column generation.

The column generation procedure begins with an LP relaxation that contains a subset of the variables:

$$\min \sum_{\ell \in L} c_\ell y_\ell$$
$$\sum_{\ell \in L} A_\ell y_\ell = b; \quad y_\ell \geq 0, \quad \ell \in L \tag{15.37}$$

where A_ℓ is column ℓ of A and $L \subset \{1, \ldots, n\}$. If $\lambda^* = (\lambda_1^*, \ldots, \lambda_m^*)$ is the optimal dual solution of (15.37), then any nonbasic variable y_ℓ has reduced cost $c_\ell - \lambda^* A_\ell$ (see Section 15.3). A subproblem is solved to find a column (c_ℓ, A_ℓ) with the smallest reduced cost. Thus the subproblem minimizes $z_0 - \sum_{i=1}^m \lambda_i^* z_i$ subject to $(z_0, z_1, \ldots, z_m) \in Z$, where Z is the set of all columns (c_ℓ, A_ℓ). If a column with negative reduced cost is found, it is added to (15.37). The process is repeated until no column with negative reduce cost is found in the subproblem, whereupon (15.37) is solved. If all goes well, only a small fraction of the columns of A will have been generated.

15.10.2 Example: Generalized Assignment Problem

Most applications of branch and price involve an assignment problem with complicating constraints. One example is the generalized assignment problem, which again is an assignment problem (15.7) with the complicating constraint that the jobs j assigned to each resource i satisfy $\sum_j \alpha_{ij} x_{ij} \leq \beta_i$.

The problem is reformulated for branch and price by letting k index all possible assignments of jobs to a given resource i that satisfy $\sum_j \alpha_{ij} x_{ij} \leq \beta_i$. The 0-1 variable $y_{ik} = 1$ if the kth assignment to resource i is selected. So if $\delta_{ijk} = 1$ when job j is assigned to resource i in assignment k, an LP relaxation of the problem has the form (15.36) with

$\ell = (i, k)$:

$$\min \sum_{ik} \left(\sum_j c_{ij} \delta_{ijk} \right) y_{ik}$$

$$\sum_{ik} \delta_{ijk} y_{ik} = 1, \quad \text{all } j \qquad (a)$$

$$\sum_k y_{ik} = 1, \quad \text{all } i \qquad (b)$$

$$y_{ik} \geq 0, \quad \text{all } i, k$$

(15.38)

If dual variables λ_j are associated with constraints (a) and μ_i with constraints (b), the reduced cost of a variable y_{ik} in (15.38) is

$$\sum_j c_{ij} \delta_{ijk} - \sum_j \lambda_j \delta_{ijk} - \mu_i = \sum_j (c_{ij} - \lambda_j) \delta_{ijk} - \mu_i$$

The subproblem of finding a variable y_{ik} with negative reduced cost can be solved by examining each resource i separately and solving the 0-1 knapsack problem

$$\min \sum_j (c_{ij} - \lambda_j) z_j - \mu_i$$

$$\sum_j \alpha_{ij} z_j \leq \beta_i; \quad z_j \in \{0, 1\}, \quad \text{all } j$$

0-1 knapsack problems can be solved by a number of methods [95], including CP [48].

15.10.3   Other Applications

One of the most successful applications of CP-based branch and price is to airline crew assignment and crew rostering [26, 47, 82, 87, 114]. In [47], for example, a path constraint is used to obtain a permissible roster with a negative reduced cost. The search tree is pruned by solving a relaxation of the problem (a single-source shortest path problem) so as to obtain a lower bound on the reduced cost.

CP-based branch and price has also been applied to transit bus crew scheduling [133], aircraft scheduling [59], vehicle routing [109], network design [27], employee timetabling [41], physician scheduling [55], and the traveling tournament problem [43, 44]. Several implementation issues are discussed in [45, 108].

15.11   Benders Decomposition

Benders decomposition was developed in the context of mathematical programming, but the root idea has much wider application. It solves a problem by enumerating, in a *master problem*, possible values of a pre-selected subset of variables. Each set of values that might be assigned to these variables defines the *subproblem* of finding the best values for the remaining variables. Solution of the subproblem generates a nogood, known as a *Benders cut*, that excludes that particular assignment to the master problem variables, and perhaps other assignments that can be no better. The master problem is re-solved with the new Benders cut in order to find a better solution, and the process continues until no further improvement is possible.

Benders decomposition can profitably combine OR and CP, since one approach can be applied to the master problem and one to the subproblem, depending on which best suits the problem structure. This sort of combination has yielded substantial speedups in computation.

15.11.1 Benders Decomposition in the Abstract

In classical Benders decomposition, the subproblem is a linear or nonlinear programming problem [15, 56], and the Benders cuts are generated using dual or Lagrange multipliers. However, if one recognizes that LP duality is a special case of a more general *inference duality*, the concept of a Benders cut can be generalized [70, 80]. In fact the basic idea of Benders decomposition is best seen in this more general setting and then specialized to the classical case.

Benders decomposition applies to problems of the form

$$
\begin{aligned}
&\min f(x,y) \\
&(x,y) \in S, \quad x \in D_x, \quad y \in D_y
\end{aligned}
\tag{15.39}
$$

Each iteration k of the Benders algorithm begins with a fixed value x^k for x and solves a subproblem for the best y:

$$
\begin{aligned}
&\min f(x^k,y) \\
&(x^k,y) \in S, \quad y \in D_y
\end{aligned}
\tag{15.40}
$$

Solution of the subproblem yields an optimal solution y^k and an optimal value $v_k = f(x^k, y^k)$. The solution process is analyzed to identify a proof that $f(x^k, y) \geq v_k$; such a proof can be regarded as solving the inference dual of (15.40). (The inference dual of an LP problem is the classical LP dual.) If x^k is changed to some other value x, this same proof may still show that $f(x,y)$ is bounded below by some function $B_k(x)$. This yields the Benders cut $z \geq B_k(x)$, where $B_k(x^k) = v_k$ and z is a variable indicating the optimal value of the original problem (15.39).

At this point one solves the master problem, which contains the Benders cuts so far generated.

$$
\begin{aligned}
&\min z \\
&z \geq B_i(x), \quad i = 1, \ldots k, \quad x \in D_x
\end{aligned}
\tag{15.41}
$$

The solution x^{k+1} of (15.41) begins the next iteration. Since the master problem (15.41) is a relaxation of the original problem and the subproblem (15.40) a restriction if it, the optimal value z_{k+1} of the master problem is a lower bound on the optimal value of (15.39), and the optimal value of any subproblem is an upper bound. The algorithm terminates with an optimal solution when the two bounds converge; that is, when $z_{k+1} = \min_{i \in \{1,\ldots,k\}} \{v_i\}$. They converge finitely under fairly weak conditions, for instance if the domain D_x is finite, as it is in examples considered here.

15.11.2   Classical Benders Decomposition

The historical Benders decomposition applies to problems of the form

$$\min f(x) + cy$$
$$g(x) + Ay \geq b, \ \ x \in S, \ \ y \geq 0, \ \ x \in D_x, \ \ y \in \Re^n$$

The subproblem (15.40) is the LP problem

$$\min f(x^k) + cy$$
$$Ay \geq b - g(x^k), \ \ y \geq 0, \ \ y \in \Re^n \tag{15.42}$$

Suppose first that (15.42) has optimal value v^k and an optimal dual solution λ^k. By strong duality $v^k - f(x^k) = \lambda^k(b - g(x^k))$, which means

$$B_k(x) = f(x) + \lambda^k(b - g(x)) \tag{15.43}$$

is the tightest lower bound on cost when $x = x^k$. That is, λ^k specifies a proof of the lower bound v^k by defining a linear combination $\lambda^k Ay \geq \lambda^k(b - g(x^k))$ that dominates $cy \geq v^k - f(x^k)$. But since λ^k remains dual feasible when x^k in (15.42) is replaced by any x, (15.43) remains a lower bound on cost for any x; that is, λ^k specifies a proof of the lower bound $B_k(x)$. This yields the Benders cut

$$z \geq f(x) + \lambda^k(b - g(x)) \tag{15.44}$$

If the dual of (15.42) is unbounded, there is a direction or ray λ^k along which its solution value can increase indefinitely. In this case the Benders cut is $\lambda^k(b - g(x)) \leq 0$ rather than (15.44). The Benders cuts $z \geq B_k(x)$ in the master problem (15.41) therefore take the form (15.44) when the subproblem dual is bounded in iteration k, and the form $\lambda^k(b - g(x)) \leq$ when the subproblem dual is unbounded. The master problem can be solved by any desired method, such as branch and bound if it is an MILP problem.

15.11.3   Example: Planning and Scheduling

A basic planning and scheduling problem illustrates the use of nonclassical Benders to combine MILP and CP [71].   Each n jobs must be assigned to one of m facilities for processing. Each job j has processing time p_{ij} and uses c_{ij} units of resource on facility i. Every job has release time 0 and deadline d. Jobs scheduled on any facility i may run simultaneously so long as the total resource consumption at any one time is no greater than C_i (cumulative scheduling). The objective is to minimize makespan (i.e., finish the last job as soon as possible).

If job j has start time s_j on machine y_j, the problem can be written

$$\min z$$
$$z \geq s_j + p_{y_j j}, \ \ 0 \leq s_j \leq d - p_{y_j j}, \ \ \text{all } j$$
$$\text{cumulative}\big(s^i(y), p^i(y), c^i(y), C_i\big), \ \ \text{all } i$$

where $s^i(y) = (s_j \mid y_j = i)$ and similarly for $p^i(y), c^i(y)$.

The master problem assigns jobs to facilities and is well suited for MILP solution. The subproblem schedules jobs assigned to each facility and is suitable for a CP approach.

Given an assignment y^k obtained by solving the master problem, the subproblem separates into an independent scheduling problem for each facility i:

$$\min z_i$$
$$z_i \geq s_i + p_{ij}, \ \ 0 \leq s_j \leq d - p_{ij}, \ \ \text{all } j \in J_{ki}$$
$$\text{cumulative}(s^i(y^k), p^i(y^k), c^i(y^k), C_i)$$

where $J_{ki} = \{j \mid y_j^k = i\}$ is the set of jobs assigned to facility i. Let z_{ik} be the optimal makespan obtained in the subproblem P_i for facility i. A Benders cut can be constructed by reasoning as follows.

First let $\hat{P}_i$ be the problem that results when jobs in set R are removed from problem P_i, and let $\hat{z}$ be the optimal makespan for $\hat{P}_i$. Then

$$\hat{z} \geq z_{ik} - \Delta \tag{15.45}$$

where $\Delta = \sum_{j \in R} p_{ij}$. To see this, construct a solution S for P_i by scheduling the jobs in R sequentially after the last job in the optimal solution of $\hat{P}_i$. The resulting makespan is $\hat{z} + \Delta$. If $\hat{z} + \Delta \leq d$, then S is feasible for P_i, so that $z_{ik} \leq \hat{z} + \Delta$ and (15.45) follows. On the other hand, if $\hat{z} + \Delta > d$, then (15.45) follows because $z_{ik} \leq d$.

Since the master problem will be solved by MILP, it is convenient to write the Benders cuts in terms of 0-1 variables x_{ij}, where $x_{ij} = 1$ when $y_j = i$. In subsequent iterations of the Benders algorithm, the jobs in J_{ki} that are removed from facility i are those for which $x_{ij} = 0$. So (15.45) yields the following lower bound on the minimum makespan z for facility i, which is also a lower bound on the minimum makespan z for the problem as a whole:

$$z \geq z_{ik} - \sum_{j \in J_{ki}} p_{ij}(1 - x_{ij}) \tag{15.46}$$

Each Benders cut $z \geq B_k(x)$ in the master problem is therefore actually a set of inequalities (15.46), one for each facility i. The master problem becomes

$$\min z$$
$$\sum_i x_{ij} = 1, \ \ \text{all } j \tag{a}$$
$$z \geq z_{i\ell} - \sum_{j \in J_{i\ell}} p_{ij}(1 - x_{ij}), \ \ \text{all } i, \ell = 1, \ldots, k \tag{b}$$
$$z \geq \frac{1}{C_i} \sum_{j=1}^n c_{ij} p_{ij} x_{ij}, \ \ \text{all } i \tag{c}$$

$$\tag{15.47}$$

The expression (c) is a simple relaxation of the subproblem, which can be important to obtain good computational performance.

The Benders cuts (b) in (15.47) use only the solution of the subproblem and no information regarding the solution process. If additional information is available from the CP solver, one can trace which jobs play no role in proving optimality. These jobs can be removed from the sets $J_{i\ell}$ in the Benders cuts as described in [74], resulting in stronger cuts. The solution of the master problem can be accelerated by updating the solution of the previous master, as proposed in [70] and implemented in [120].

15.11.4   Other Applications

Classical Benders can be applied in a CP context when the subproblem is an LP problem, leaving CP to solve the master problem. This approach was used in [46] to solve minimal perturbation scheduling problems in which the sequencing is decided in the master problem and the assignment of start times in the subproblem. A similar approach was applied to scheduling the workforce in a telephone call center [16].

Most applications, however, have used nonclassical Benders methods in which CP or logic-based techniques solve the subproblem. CP is a natural approach to solving the inference dual of the subproblem, since inference techniques play a major role in CP solvers. Explanations [25, 83, 84, 118] for CP solutions are particularly relevant, since an explanation is in effect a proof of correctness or optimality and therefore solves the inference dual.

Nonclassical Benders was first used to solve circuit verification problems [80], and underlying theory was developed in [70, 78]. Application to CP-based planning and scheduling was proposed in [70] and has been implemented for min-cost planning and disjunctive scheduling [81] (later extended to multistage problems [63]), and planning and cumulative scheduling to minimize cost and makespan [71, 30] as well as tardiness [72]. Similar methods were applied to dispatching of automated guided vehicles [34], steel production scheduling [62], batch scheduling in a chemical plant [92] and polypropylene batch scheduling in particular [122]. CP was used to solve the master problem in a nonclassical Benders approach to real-time scheduling of computer processors [24]. In [131] a traffic diversion problem is solved with a Benders method that has an LP subproblem but generates specialized cuts that are not based on dual variables.

Nonclassical Benders methods for integer programming are studied in [29, 78] and for the propositional satisfiability problem in [70, 78].

15.12   Toward Integration of CP and OR

Importing OR into CP is part of a trend that has been taking shape over the last decade: the integration of OR and CP, or at least portions of them, into a unified approach to problem solving. Several paradigms for integration have emerged.

One general scheme is *double modeling*: some (or all) constraints are formulated in a CP model, some in an MILP model, and some in both. The two models then exchange information during the solution process (e.g., [64, 107, 126]). The relaxation and decomposition strategies discussed here may be seen as special cases in which one of the two models is subservient to the other (see also [37]).

Double modeling, however, is perhaps more a matter of cooperation than unification. Schemes that move closer to full integration point to underlying commonality between CP and OR. Types of commonality include: the role of logical inference in CP and OR [68, 70]; the parallel between CP's filtering algorithms and domain store on the one hand, and MILP's cutting planes and linear constraint store on the one hand [20, 21, 69]; formulability in a single modeling framework based on conditional constraints [76, 77, 116];

analogous roles of duality [79]; and a common search-infer-and-relax algorithmic structure [9, 73]. The ultimate goal is to view OR and CP as special cases of a single methodology.

The evolution of ideas in this area, as well as growing interest in integrated methods, can be traced in the development of such hybrid solvers as ECL^iPS^e, OPL Studio, Mosel, SCIP, and SIMPL. ECL^iPS^e [107] is a Prolog-based constraint logic programming system that provides an interface with linear and MILP solvers. The CP solver in ECL^iPS^e communicates tightened bounds to the MILP solver, while the MILP solver detects infeasibility and provides a bound on the objective function that is used by the CP solver. The optimal solution of the linear constraints in the problem can be used as a search heuristic. Recent developments are described in [3].

OPL Studio [65] provides an integrated modeling language that expresses both MILP and CP constraints. It sends the problem to a CP or MILP solver depending on the nature of constraints. A script language allows one to implement cooperation between the CP and MILP solvers.

Mosel [32, 33] is "both a modeling and programming language" that interfaces with various solvers, including MILP and CP solvers. SCIP [1] is a programming language that gives the user "total control" of a solution process that can involve both CP and MILP solvers. SIMPL [9] uses a high-level modeling language in which the choice of constraints and their parameters determine how techniques interact at the micro level.

There will perhaps always be a role for specialized solvers. However, one can also foresee a future in which today's general-purpose CP-based and OR-based solvers evolve into integrated systems in which there is no longer a clear distinction, nor any need to make a distinction, between CP and OR components.

Bibliography

[1]   T. Achterberg. SCIP: A framework to integrate constraint and mixed integer programming. ZIB-report, Konrad-Zuse-Zentrum für Informationstechnik Berlin, 2004.

[2]   F. Ajili and H. El Sakkout. LP probing for piecewise linear optimization in scheduling. In C. Gervet and M. Wallace, editors, *Proceedings of the International Workshop on Integration of Artificial Intelligence and Operations Research Techniques in Constraint Programming for Combintaorial Optimization Problems (CPAIOR 2001)*, Ashford, U.K., 2001.

[3]   F. Ajili and M. Wallace. Hybrid problem solving in ECLiPSe. In M. Milano, editor, *Constraint and Integer Programming: Toward a Unified Methodology*, pages 169–206. Kluwer, Dordrecht, 2004.

[4]   F. Alizadeh. Interior point methods in semidefinite programming with applications to combinatorial optimization. *SIAM Journal of Optimization*, 5:13–51, 1995.

[5]   G. Appa, D. Magos, and I. Mourtos. Linear programming relaxations of multiple all-different predicates. In J. C. Régin and M. Rueher, editors, *Integration of AI and OR Techniques in Constraint Programming for Combinatorial Optimization Problems (CPAIOR 2004)*, volume 3011 of *Lecture Notes in Computer Science*, pages 364–369. Springer, 2004.

[6]   G. Appa, I. Mourtos, and D. Magos. Integrating constraint and integer programming for the orthogonal Latin squares problem. In P. Van Hentenryck, editor, *Principles*

and Practice of Constraint Programming (CP2002), volume 2470 of Lecture Notes in Computer Science, pages 17–32. Springer, 2002.

[7]   S. Arnborg, D. G. Corneil, and A. Proskurowski. Complexity of finding embeddings in a k-tree. SIAM Journal on Algebraic and Discrete Mathematics, 8:277–284, 1987.

[8]   S. Arnborg and A. Proskurowski. Characterization and recognition of partial k-trees. SIAM Journal on Algebraic and Discrete Mathematics, 7:305–314, 1986.

[9]   I. Aron, J. N. Hooker, and T. H. Yunes. SIMPL: A system for integrating optimization techniques. In J. C. Régin and M. Rueher, editors, Integration of AI and OR Techniques in Constraint Programming for Combinatorial Optimization Problems (CPAIOR 2004), volume 3011 of Lecture Notes in Computer Science, pages 21–36. Springer, 2004.

[10] E. Balas, A. Bockmayr, N. Pisaruk, and L. Wolsey. On unions and dominants of polytopes. Mathematical Programming, 99:223–239, 2004.

[11] F. Barahona and R. Anbil. The volume algorithm: Producing primal solutions with a subgradient algorithm. Mathematical Programming, 87:385–399, 2000.

[12] P. Barth. Logic-based 0-1 Constraint Solving in Constraint Logic Programming Kluwer, Dordrecht, 1995.

[13] N. Beaumont. An algorithm for disjunctive programs. European Journal of Operational Research, 48:362–371, 1990.

[14] C . Beck and P. Refalo. A hybrid approach to scheduling with earliness and tardiness costs. Annals of Operations Research, 118:49–71, 2003.

[15] J. F. Benders. Partitioning procedures for solving mixed-variables programming problems. Numerische Mathematik, 4:238–252, 1962.

[16] T. Benoist, E. Gaudin, and B. Rottembourg. Constraint programming contribution to Benders decomposition: A case study. In P. Van Hentenryck, editor, Principles and Practice of Constraint Programming (CP2002), volume 2470 of Lecture Notes in Computer Science, pages 603–617. Springer, 2002.

[17] T. Benoist, F. Laburthe, and B. Rottembourg. Lagrange relaxation and constraint programming collaborative schemes for traveling tournament problems. In C. Gervet and M. Wallace, editors, Proceedings of the International Workshop on Integration of Artificial Intelligence and Operations Research Techniques in Constraint Programming for Combintaorial Optimization Problems (CPAIOR 2001) Ashford, U.K., 2001.

[18] U. Bertele and F. Brioschi. Nonserial Dynamic Programming. Academic Press, new York, 1972.

[19] D. P. Bertsekas. Dynamic Programming and Optimal Control, volume 1 and 2. Athena Scientific, Nashua, NH, 2001.

[20] A. Bockmayr and T. Kasper. Branch-and-infer: A unifying framework for integer and finite domain constraint programming. INFORMS Journal on Computing 10:287–300, 1998.

[21] A. Bockmayr and T. Kasper. Branch-and-infer: A framework for combining CP and IP. In M. Milano, editor, Constraint and Integer Programming: Toward a Unified Methodology, pages 59–88. Kluwer, Dordrecht, 2004.

[22] A. Bockmayr and N. Pisaruk. Detecting infeasibility and generating cuts for mixed integer programming using constraint programming. In M. Gendreau, G. Pesant, and L.-M. Rousseau, editors, Proceedings of the International Workshop on Inte-

gration of Artificial Intelligence and Operations Research Techniques in Constraint Programming for Combintaorial Optimization Problems (CPAIOR 2003), Montréal, 2003.

[23] S. Bollapragada, O. Ghattas, and J. N. Hooker. Optimal design of truss structures by mixed logical and linear programming. *Operations Research*, 49:42–51, 2001.

[24] H. Cambazard, P.-E. Hladik, A.-M. Déplanche, N. Jussien, and Y. Trinquet. Decomposition and learning for a hard real time task allocation problem. In M. Wallace, editor, *Principles and Practice of Constraint Programming (CP2004)*, volume 3258 of *Lecture Notes in Computer Science*, pages 153–167. Springer, 2004.

[25] H. Cambazard and N. Jussien. Identifying and exploiting problem structures using explanation-based constraint programming. In R. Barták and M. Milano, editors, *Integration of AI and OR Techniques in Constraint Programming for Combinatorial Optimization Problems (CPAIOR 2005)*, volume 3524 of *Lecture Notes in Computer Science*, pages 94–109. Springer, 2005.

[26] A. Chabrier. A cooperative CP and LP optimizer approach for the pairing generation problem. In *Proceedings of the International Workshop on Integration of Artificial Intelligence and Operations Research Techniques in Constraint Programming for Combintaorial Optimization Problems (CPAIOR 1999)*, Ferrara, Italy, 2000.

[27] A. Chabrier. Heuristic branch-and-price-and-cut to solve a network design problem. In M. Gendreau, G. Pesant, and L.-M. Rousseau, editors, *Proceedings of the International Workshop on Integration of Artificial Intelligence and Operations Research Techniques in Constraint Programming for Combintaorial Optimization Problems (CPAIOR 2003)*, Montréal, 2003.

[28] D. Chhajed and T. J. Lowe. Solving structured multifacility location problems efficiently. *Transportation Science*, 28:104–115, 1994.

[29] Y. Chu and Q. Xia. Generating benders cuts for a class of integer programming problems. In J. C. Régin and M. Rueher, editors, *Integration of AI and OR Techniques in Constraint Programming for Combinatorial Optimization Problems (CPAIOR 2004)*, volume 3011 of *Lecture Notes in Computer Science*, pages 127–141. Springer, 2004.

[30] Y. Chu and Q. Xia. A hybrid algorithm for a class of resource-constrained scheduling problems. In R. Barták and M. Milano, editors, *Integration of AI and OR Techniques in Constraint Programming for Combinatorial Optimization Problems (CPAIOR 2005)*, volume 3524 of *Lecture Notes in Computer Science*, pages 110–124. Springer, 2005.

[31] V. Chvátal. Edmonds polytopes and a hierarchy of combinatorial problems. *Discrete Mathematics*, 4:305–337, 1973.

[32] Y. Colombani and S. Heipcke. Mosel: An extensible environment for modeling and programming solutions. In N. Jussien and F. Laburthe, editors, *Proceedings of the International Workshop on Integration of Artificial Intelligence and Operations Research Techniques in Constraint Programming for Combinatorial Optimization Problems (CPAIOR 2002)*, Le Croisic, France, 2002.

[33] Y. Colombani and S. Heipcke. Mosel: An overview. White paper, Dash Optimization, 2004.

[34] A. I. Corréa, A. Langevin, and L. M. Rousseau. Dispatching and conflict-free routing of automated guided vehicles: A hybrid approach combining constraint programming and mixed integer programming. In J. C. Régin and M. Rueher, editors,

Integration of AI and OR Techniques in Constraint Programming for Combinatorial Optimization Problems (CPAIOR 2004), volume 3011 of *Lecture Notes in Computer Science*, pages 370–378. Springer, 2004.

[35] Y. Crama, P. Hansen, and B. Jaumard. The basic algorithm for pseudoboolean programming revisited. *Discrete Applied Mathematics*, 29:171–185, 1990.

[36] W. Cronholm and Farid Ajili. Strong cost-based filtering for Lagrange decomposition applied to network design. In M. Wallace, editor, *Principles and Practice of Constraint Programming (CP2004)*, volume 3258 of *Lecture Notes in Computer Science*, pages 726–730. Springer, 2004.

[37] E. Danna and Claude Le Pape. Two generic schemes for efficient and robust cooperative algorithms. In M. Milano, editor, *Constraint and Integer Programming: Toward a Unified Methodology*, pages 33–58. Kluwer, Dordrecht, 2004.

[38] I. de Farias, E. L. Johnson, and G. L. Nemhauser. Branch-and-cut for combinatorial optimization problems without auxilliary variables. In C. Gervet and M. Wallace, editors, *Proceedings of the International Workshop on Integration of Artificial Intelligence and Operations Research Techniques in Constraint Programming for Combintaorial Optimization Problems (CPAIOR 2001)*, Ashford, U.K., 2001.

[39] R. Dechter. Bucket elimination: A unifying framework for several probabilistic inference algorithms. In *Proceedings of the Twelfth Annual Conference on Uncertainty in Artificial Intelligence (UAI 96)*, pages 211–219, Portland, OR, 1996.

[40] S. Demassey, C. Artiques, and P. Michelon. A hybrid constraint propagation-cutting plane procedure for the RCPSP. In N. Jussien and F. Laburthe, editors, *Proceedings of the International Workshop on Integration of Artificial Intelligence and Operations Research Techniques in Constraint Programming for Combinatorial Optimization Problems (CPAIOR 2002)*, Le Croisic, France, 2002.

[41] S. Demassey, G. Pesant, and L.-M. Rousseau. Constraint-programming based column generation for employee timetabling. In R. Barták and M. Milano, editors, *Integration of AI and OR Techniques in Constraint Programming for Combinatorial Optimization Problems (CPAIOR 2005)*, volume 3524 of *Lecture Notes in Computer Science*, pages 140–154. Springer, 2005.

[42] E. V. Denardo. *Dynamic Programming: Models and Applications*. Dover Publications, Mineola, NY, 2003.

[43] K. Easton, G. Nemhauser, and M. Trick. The traveling tournament problem description and benchmarks. In T. Walsh, editor, *Principles and Practice of Constraint Programming (CP2001)*, volume 2239 of *Lecture Notes in Computer Science*, pages 580–584. Springer, 2001.

[44] K. Easton, G. Nemhauser, and M. Trick. Solving the traveling tournament problem: A combined integer programming and constraint programming approach. In *Proceedings of the International Conference on the Practice and Theory of Automated Timetabling (PATAT 2002)*, 2002.

[45] K. Easton, G. Nemhauser, and M. Trick. CP based branch and price. In M. Milano, editor, *Constraint and Integer Programming: Toward a Unified Methodology*, pages 207–231. Kluwer, Dordrecht, 2004.

[46] A. Eremin and M. Wallace. Hybrid Benders decomposition algorithm in constraint logic programming. In T. Walsh, editor, *Principles and Practice of Constraint Programming (CP2001)*, volume 2239 of *Lecture Notes in Computer Science*, pages 1–15. Springer, 2001.

[47] T. Fahle, U. Junker, S. E. Karish, N. Kohn, M. Sellmann, and B. Vaaben. Constraint programming based column generation for crew assignment. *Journal of Heuristics*, 8:59–81, 2002.

[48] T. Fahle and M. Sellmann. Constraint programming based column generation with knapsack subproblems. In *Proceedings of the International Workshop on Integration of Artificial Intelligence and Operations Research Techniques in Constraint Programming for Combintaorial Optimization Problems (CPAIOR 2000)*, pages 33–44, Paderborn, Germany, 2000.

[49] M. Fischetti, A. Lodi, and P. Toth. Solving real-world atsp instances by branch-and-cut. In M. Jünger, G. Reinelt, and G. Rinaldi, editors, *Combinatorial Optimization—Eureka, You Shrink!, Papers Dedicated to Jack Edmonds*, volume 2570 of *Lecture Notes in Computer Science*, pages 64–77. Springer, 2003.

[50] M. Fischetti and P. Toth. An additive bounding procedure for combinatorial optimization problems. *Operations Research*, 37:319–328, 1989.

[51] F. Focacci, A. Lodi, and M. Milano. Cost-based domain filtering. In J. Jaffar, editor, *Principles and Practice of Constraint Programming (CP1999)*, volume 1713 of *Lecture Notes in Computer Science*, pages 189–203. Springer, 1999.

[52] F. Focacci, A. Lodi, and M. Milano. Cutting planes in constraint programming: An hybrid approach. In R. Dechter, editor, *Principles and Practice of Constraint Programming (CP2000)*, volume 1894 of *Lecture Notes in Computer Science*, pages 187–201. Springer, 2000.

[53] F. Focacci and M. Milano. Connections and integrations of dynamic programming and constraint programming. In C. Gervet and M. Wallace, editors, *Proceedings of the International Workshop on Integration of Artificial Intelligence and Operations Research Techniques in Constraint Programming for Combintaorial Optimization Problems (CPAIOR 2001)*, Ashford, U.K., 2001.

[54] T. Gellermann, M. Sellmann, and R. Wright. Shorter-path constraints for the resource constrained shortest path problem. In R. Barták and M. Milano, editors, *Integration of AI and OR Techniques in Constraint Programming for Combinatorial Optimization Problems (CPAIOR 2005)*, volume 3524 of *Lecture Notes in Computer Science*, pages 201–216. Springer, 2005.

[55] B. Gendron, H. Lebbah, and G. Pesant. Improving the cooperation between the master problem and the subproblem in constraint programming based column generation. In R. Barták and M. Milano, editors, *Integration of AI and OR Techniques in Constraint Programming for Combinatorial Optimization Problems (CPAIOR 2005)*, volume 3524 of *Lecture Notes in Computer Science*, pages 217–227. Springer, 2005.

[56] A. M. Geoffrion. Generalized benders decomposition. *Journal of Optimization Theory and Applications*, 10:237–260, 1972.

[57] M. X. Goemans and D. P. Williamson. Improved approximation algorithms for maximum cut and satisfiability problems using using semidefinite programming. *Journal of the ACM*, 42:1115–1145, 1995.

[58] C. P. Gomes and D. B. Shmoys. The promise of LP to boost CSP techniques for combinatorial problems. In N. Jussien and F. Laburthe, editors, *Proceedings of the International Workshop on Integration of Artificial Intelligence and Operations Research Techniques in Constraint Programming for Combinatorial Optimization Problems (CPAIOR 2002)*, Le Croisic, France, 2002.

[59]   M. Grönkvist. Using constraint propagation to accelerate column generation in aircraft scheduling. In M. Gendreau, G. Pesant, and L.-M. Rousseau, editors, *Proceedings of the International Workshop on Integration of Artificial Intelligence and Operations Research Techniques in Constraint Programming for Combintaorial Optimization Problems (CPAIOR 2003)*, Montréal, 2003.

[60]   I. E. Grossmann, J. N. Hooker, R. Raman, and H. Yan. Logic cuts for processing networks with fixed charges. *Computers and Operations Research*, 21:265–279, 1994.

[61]   G. Gutin and A. P. Punnen, editors. *The Traveling Salesman Problem and Its Variations*. Kluwer, Dordrecht, 2002.

[62]   I. Harjunkoski and I. E. Grossmann. A decomposition approach for the scheduling of a steel plant production. *Computers and Chemical Engineering*, 25:1647–1660, 2001.

[63]   I. Harjunkoski and I. E. Grossmann. Decomposition techniques for multistage scheduling problems using mixed-integer and constraint programming methods. *Computers and Chemical Engineering*, 26:1533–1552, 2002.

[64]   S. Heipcke. Integrating constraint programming techniques into mathematical programming. In H. Prade, editor, *Proceedings, 13th European Conference on Artificial Intelligence*, pages 259–260. Wiley, New York, 1999.

[65]   P. Van Hentenryck, I. Lustig, L. Michel, and J. F. Puget. *The OPL Optimization Programming Language*. MIT Press, Cambridge, MA, 1999.

[66]   W. J. Van Hoeve. A hybrid constraint programming and semidefinite programming approach for the stable set problem. In F. Rossi, editor, *Principles and Practice of Constraint Programming (CP2003)*, volume 2833 of *Lecture Notes in Computer Science*, pages 407–421. Springer, 2003.

[67]   J. N. Hooker. Generalized resolution for 0-1 linear inequalities. *Annals of Mathematics and Artificial Intelligence*, 6:271–286, 1992.

[68]   J. N. Hooker. Logic-based methods for optimization. In A. Borning, editor, *Principles and Practice of Constraint Programming (CP2002)*, volume 874 of *Lecture Notes in Computer Science*, pages 336–349. Springer, 1994.

[69]   J. N. Hooker. Constraint satisfaction methods for generating valid cuts. In D. L. Woodruff, editor, *Advances in Computational and Stochastic Optimization, Logic Programming and Heuristic Search*, pages 1–30. Kluwer, Dordrecht, 1997.

[70]   J. N. Hooker. *Logic-Based Methods for Optimization: Combining Optimization and Constraint Satisfaction*. Wiley, New York, 2000.

[71]   J. N. Hooker. A hybrid method for planning and scheduling. In M. Wallace, editor, *Principles and Practice of Constraint Programming (CP2004)*, volume 3258 of *Lecture Notes in Computer Science*, pages 305–316. Springer, 2004.

[72]   J. N. Hooker. Planning and scheduling to minimize tardiness. In *Principles and Practice of Constraint Programming (CP2005)*, volume 3709 of *Lecture Notes in Computer Science*, pages 314–327. Springer, 2005.

[73]   J. N. Hooker. A search-infer-and-relax framework for integrating solution methods. In R. Barták and M. Milano, editors, *Integration of AI and OR Techniques in Constraint Programming for Combinatorial Optimization Problems (CPAIOR 2005)* volume 3524 of *Lecture Notes in Computer Science*, pages 243–257. Springer, 2005.

[74]   J. N. Hooker. A hybrid method for planning and scheduling. *Constraints*, to appear.

[75]   J. N. Hooker. *Integrated Methods for Optimization*. To appear.

[76] J. N. Hooker, H.-J. Kim, and G. Ottosson. A declarative modeling framework that integrates solution methods. *Annals of Operations Research*, 104:141–161, 2001.

[77] J. N. Hooker and M. A. Osorio. Mixed logical/linear programming. *Discrete Applied Mathematics*, 96–97:395–442, 1999.

[78] J. N. Hooker and G. Ottosson. Logic-based Benders decomposition. *Mathematical Programming*, 96:33–60, 2003.

[79] J. N. Hooker, G. Ottosson, E. S. Thornsteinsson, and H.-J. Kim. A scheme for unifying optimization and constraint satisfaction methods. *Knowledge Engineering Review*, 15:11–30, 2000.

[80] J. N. Hooker and H. Yan. Logic circuit verification by benders decomposition. In V. Saraswat and P. Van Hentenryck, editors, *Principles and Practice of Constraint Programming: The Newport Papers*, pages 267–288, Cambridge, MA, 1995. MIT Press.

[81] V. Jain and I. E. Grossmann. Algorithms for hybrid MILP/CP models for a class of optimization problems. *INFORMS Journal on Computing*, 13:258–276, 2001.

[82] U. Junker, S. E. Karish, N. Kohl, B. Vaaben, T. Fahle, and M. Sellmann. A framework for constraint programming based column generation. In J. Jaffar, editor, *Principles and Practice of Constraint Programming (CP1999)*, volume 1713 of *Lecture Notes in Computer Science*, pages 261–275. Springer, 1999.

[83] N. Jussien. The versatility of using explanations within constraint programming. Research report, École des Mines de Nantes, France, 2003.

[84] N. Jussien and S. Ouis. User-friendly explanations for constraint programming. In *Eleventh Workshop on Logic Programming environments (WLPE 2001)*, Paphos, Cyprus, 2001.

[85] M. O. Khemmoudj, H. Bennaceur, and A. Nagih. Combining arc consistency and dual Lagrangean relaxation for filtering CSPs. In R. Barták and M. Milano, editors, *Integration of AI and OR Techniques in Constraint Programming for Combinatorial Optimization Problems (CPAIOR 2005)*, volume 3524 of *Lecture Notes in Computer Science*, pages 258–272. Springer, 2005.

[86] H.-J. Kim and J. N. Hooker. Solving fixed-charge network flow problems with a hybrid optimization and constraint programming approach. *Annals of Operations Research*, 115:95–124, 2002.

[87] N. Kohl. Application of OR and CP techniques in a real world crew scheduling system. In *Proceedings of the International Workshop on Integration of Artificial Intelligence and Operations Research Techniques in Constraint Programming for Combintaorial Optimization Problems (CPAIOR 2000)*, Paderborn, Germany, 2000.

[88] S. L. Lauritzen and D. J. Spiegelhalter. Local computations with probabilities on graphical structures and their application to expert systems. *Journal of the Royal Statistical Society B*, 50:157–224, 1988.

[89] S. Lee and I. Grossmann. Generalized disjunctive programming: Nonlinear convex hull relaxation and algorithms. *Computational Optimization and Applications*, 26:83–100, 2003.

[90] S. Lee and I. E. Grossmann. Global optimization of nonlinear generalized disjunctive programming with bilinear equality constraints: Applications to process networks. *Computers and Chemical Engineering*, 27:1557–1575, 2003.

[91] A. Lodi and M. Milano. Discrepancy-based additive bounding. In M. Gendreau, G. Pesant, and L.-M. Rousseau, editors, *Proceedings of the International Workshop*

on Integration of Artificial Intelligence and Operations Research Techniques in Constraint Programming for Combintaorial Optimization Problems (CPAIOR 2003) Montréal, 2003.

[92]   C. T. Maravelias and I. E. Grossmann. Using MILP and CP for the scheduling of batch chemical processes. In J. C. Régin and M. Rueher, editors, *Integration of AI and OR Techniques in Constraint Programming for Combinatorial Optimization Problems (CPAIOR 2004)*, volume 3011 of *Lecture Notes in Computer Science* pages 1–20. Springer, 2004.

[93]   H. Marchand, A. Martin, R. Weismantel, and L. Wolsey. Cutting planes in integer and mixed integer programming. *Discrete Applied Mathematics*, 123:397–446, 2002.

[94]   H. Marchand and L. A. Wolsey. Aghgregation and mixed integer rounding to solve mips. *Operations Research*, 49:363–371, 2001.

[95]   S. Martello and P. Toth. *Knapsack Problems: Algorithms and Computer Implementations*. Wiley, New York, 1990.

[96]   M. Milano and W. J. van Hoeve. Reduced cost-based ranking for generating promising subproblems. In P. Van Hentenryck, editor, *Principles and Practice of Constraint Programming (CP2002)*, volume 2470 of *Lecture Notes in Computer Science*, pages 1–16. Springer, 2002.

[97]   D. Naddef. Polyhedral theory and branch-and-cut algorithms for the symmetric TSP. In G. Gutin and A. P. Punnen, editors, *The Traveling Salesman Problem and Its Variations*, pages 29–116. Kluwer, Dordrecht, 2002.

[98]   A. Nedic and D. P. Bertsekas. Incremental subgradient methods for nondifferentiable optimization. *SIAM Journal on Optimization*, 12:109–138, 2001.

[99]   G. L. Nemhauser and L. A. Wolsey. *Integer and Combinatorial Optimization*. Wiley, New York, 1999.

[100] M. Osorio and F. Glover. Logic cuts using surrogate constraint analysis in the multi-dimensional knapsack problem. In C. Gervet and M. Wallace, editors, *Proceedings of the International Workshop on Integration of Artificial Intelligence and Operations Research Techniques in Constraint Programming for Combintaorial Optimization Problems (CPAIOR 2001)*, Ashford, U.K., 2001.

[101] G. Ottosson, E. Thorsteinsson, and J. N. Hooker. Mixed global constraints and inference in hybrid IP-CLP solvers. In *Proceedings of CP99 Post-Conference Workshop on Large-Scale Combinatorial Optimization and Constraints* http://www.dash.co.uk/wscp99, pages 57–78, 1999.

[102] G. Ottosson, E. Thorsteinsson, and J. N. Hooker. Mixed global constraints and inference in hybrid CLP-IP solvers. *Annals of Mathematics and Artificial Intelligence* 34:271–290, 2002.

[103] M. Padberg and G. Rinaldi. An efficient algorithm for the minimum capacity cut problem. *Mathematical Programming*, 47:19–36, 1990.

[104] R. Raman and I. E. Grossmann. Modeling and computational techniques for logic based integer programming. *Computers and Chemical Engineering*, 18:563–578, 1994.

[105] P. Refalo. Tight cooperation and its application in piecewise linear optimization. In J. Jaffar, editor, *Principles and Practice of Constraint Programming (CP1999)* volume 1713 of *Lecture Notes in Computer Science*, pages 375–389. Springer, 1999.

[106] P. Refalo. Linear formulation of constraint programming models and hybrid

solvers. In R. Dechter, editor, *Principles and Practice of Constraint Programming (CP2000)*, volume 1894 of *Lecture Notes in Computer Science*, pages 369–383. Springer, 2000.

[107] R. Rodošek, M. Wallace, and M. Hajian. A new approach to integrating mixed integer programming and constraint logic programming. *Annals of Operations Research*, 86:63–87, 1997.

[108] L.-M. Rousseau. Stabilization issues for constraint programming based column generation. In J. C. Régin and M. Rueher, editors, *Integration of AI and OR Techniques in Constraint Programming for Combinatorial Optimization Problems (CPAIOR 2004)*, volume 3011 of *Lecture Notes in Computer Science*, pages 402–408. Springer, 2004.

[109] L. M. Rousseau, M. Gendreau, and G. Pesant. Solving small VRPTWs with constraint programming based column generation. In N. Jussien and F. Laburthe, editors, *Proceedings of the International Workshop on Integration of Artificial Intelligence and Operations Research Techniques in Constraint Programming for Combintaorial Optimization Problems (CPAIOR 2002)*, Le Croisic, France, 2002.

[110] R. Sadykov. A hybrid branch-and-cut algorithm for the one-machine scheduling problem. In J. C. Régin and M. Rueher, editors, *Integration of AI and OR Techniques in Constraint Programming for Combinatorial Optimization Problems (CPAIOR 2004)*, volume 3011 of *Lecture Notes in Computer Science*, pages 409–415. Springer, 2004.

[111] N. W. Sawaya and I. E. Grossmann. A cutting plane method for solving linear generalized disjunctive programming problems. Research report, Department of Chemical Engineering, Carnegie Mellon University, 2004.

[112] N. W. Sawaya and I. E. Grossmann. Computational implementation of non-linear convex hull reformulations. Research report, Department of Chemical Engineering, Carnegie Mellon University, 2005.

[113] M. Sellmann and T. Fahle. Constraint programming based Lagrangian relaxation for a multimedia application. In C. Gervet and M. Wallace, editors, *Proceedings of the International Workshop on Integration of Artificial Intelligence and Operations Research Techniques in Constraint Programming for Combintaorial Optimization Problems (CPAIOR 2001)*, Ashford, U.K., 2001.

[114] M. Sellmann, K. Zervoudakis, P. Stamatopoulos, and T. Fahle. Crew assignment via constraint programming: Integrating column generation and heuristic tree search. *Annals of Operations Research*, 115:207–225, 2002.

[115] G. Shafer, P. P. Shenoy, and K. Mellouli. Propagating belief functions in qualitative markov trees. *International Journal of Approximate Reasoning*, 1:349–400, 1987.

[116] H. M. Sheini and K. A. Sakallah. A SAT-based decision procedure for mixed logical/integer linear problems. In R. Barták and M. Milano, editors, *Integration of AI and OR Techniques in Constraint Programming for Combinatorial Optimization Problems (CPAIOR 2005)*, volume 3524 of *Lecture Notes in Computer Science*, pages 320–335. Springer, 2005.

[117] P. P. Shenoy and G. Shafer. Propagating belief functions with local computation. *IEEE Expert*, 1:43–52, 1986.

[118] M. H. Sqalli and E. C. Freuder. Inference-based constraint satisfaction supports explanation. In *National Conference on Artificial Intelligence (AAAI 1996)*, pages 318–325, 1996.

[119] R. Stubbs and S. Mehrotra. A branch-and-cut method for 0-1 mixed convex programming. *Mathematical Programming*, 86:515–532, 1999.

[120] E. Thorsteinsson. Branch and check: A hybrid framework integrating mixed integer programming and constraint logic programming. In T. Walsh, editor, *Principles and Practice of Constraint Programming (CP2001)*, volume 2239 of *Lecture Notes in Computer Science*, pages 16–30. Springer, 2001.

[121] E. Thorsteinsson and G. Ottosson. Linear relaxations and reduced-cost based propagation of continuous variable subscripts. *Annals of Operations Research*, 115:15–29, 2001.

[122] C. Timpe. Solving planning and scheduling problems with combined integer and constraint programming. *OR Spectrum*, 24:431–448, 2002.

[123] M. Trick. A dynamic programming approach for consistency and propagation for knapsack constraints. In C. Gervet and M. Wallace, editors, *Proceedings, Integration of AI and OR Techniques in Constraint Programming for Combinatorial Optimization Problems (CPAIOR 2001)*, pages 113–124, Ashford, U.K., 2001.

[124] M. Trick. Formulations and reformulations in integer programming. In R. Barták and M. Milano, editors, *Integration of AI and OR Techniques in Constraint Programming for Combinatorial Optimization Problems (CPAIOR 2005)*, volume 3524 of *Lecture Notes in Computer Science*, pages 366–379. Springer, 2005.

[125] A. Vecchietti, S. Lee, and I. E. Grossmann. Characterization and formulation of disjunctions and their relaxations. In *Proceedings of Mercosul Congress on Process Systems Engineering (ENPROMER 2001)*, volume 1, pages 409–414, Santa Fe, Chile, 2001.

[126] M. Wallace, M. S. Novello, and J. Schimpf. ECLiPSe: A platform for constraint logic programming. *ICL Systems Journal*, 12:159–200, 1997.

[127] H. P. Williams. *Model Building in Mathematical Programming, 4th Ed.* Wiley, New York, 1999.

[128] H. P. Williams and H. Yan. Representations of the all_different predicate of constraint satisfaction in integer programming. *INFORMS Journal on Computing* 13:96–103, 2001.

[129] H. Wolkowicz, R. Saigal, and L. Vandenberghe, editors. *Handbook of Semidefinite Programming*. Kluwer, Dordrecht, 2000.

[130] L. A. Wolsey. *Integer Programming*. Wiley, New York, 1998.

[131] Q. Xia, A. Eremin, and M. Wallace. Problem decomposition for traffic diversions. In J. C. Régin and M. Rueher, editors, *Integration of AI and OR Techniques in Constraint Programming for Combinatorial Optimization Problems (CPAIOR 2004)* volume 3011 of *Lecture Notes in Computer Science*, pages 348–363. Springer, 2004.

[132] H. Yan and J. N. Hooker. Tight representations of logical constraints as cardinality rules. *Mathematical Programming*, 85:363–377, 1995.

[133] T. H. Yunes, A. V. Moura, and C. C. de Souza. Hybrid column generation approaches for urban transit crew management problems. *Transportation Science*, to appear.

Chapter 16

Continuous and Interval Constraints

Frédéric Benhamou and Laurent Granvilliers

Continuous Constraint Solving

Continuous constraint solving has been widely studied in several fields of applied mathematics and computer science. In computer algebra [13, 16, 24, 25], continuous constraints are viewed as formulas from first-order logic interpreted over the real numbers. The symbolic algorithms transform the constraint systems within the same equivalence class in the interpretation domain according to some simplification ordering. These techniques, for instance Gröbner bases and quantifier elimination, are mainly devoted to polynomial constraints and require a preprocessing of the non-polynomial functions. Exact computations are guaranteed, provided that rational numbers in infinite precision or algebraic numbers are used. These algorithms generally run in exponential time and space and reaching good practical complexities is a main challenge.

In numerical analysis [119], continuous constraints are viewed as equations or inequalities between real functions. The numerical methods mainly implement fixed-point operators processing (linear) relaxations of the nonlinear systems. The computations are approximate whenever floating-point numbers are used. In this area, the quality of the algorithms is determined by the convergence rate, the tightness of the relaxations, and the method for controlling rounding errors. Interval analysis [98] is a set extension of numerical analysis such that the floating-point numbers are replaced with the intervals. The interval approximations are defined so as to enclose the computed real quantities and the algorithms are said to be *complete*.

In constraint programming, continuous constraints are viewed as relations. The complete solving of nonlinear systems is implemented by exhaustive search techniques that compute solution space coverings by means of multi-dimensional boxes. The search is commonly accelerated through propagation-based algorithms. In this framework, the constraint projections can be computed by constraint inversion and interval evaluation steps. We often employ the term *interval constraints* to emphasize that continuous constraints are solved by means of interval-based techniques. One of the main advantages of this approach is that it does not require specific properties of the systems. Moreover, the propagation framework is general enough to allow the use of more specific techniques like numerical or symbolic algorithms [2].

Continuous and interval constraints are generally contrasted with non negative integer or more generally discrete constraints. These last constraints, sometimes also called finite domain constraints, are generally studied in the Constraint Satisfaction Problems (CSP) framework and are basic components of most current constraint-based languages, including CHIP [36], Eclipse [128], GNU Prolog [35], ILOG Solver [107] and Choco [85]. In reality, continuous and discrete constraints are two areas of constraint programming that have much in common. One of the main purposes of this paper, besides the introduction of interval constraints, is to discuss their similarities, their differences and their complementarities.

Introduced in the mid eighties by Cleary [21], interval constraints have been developed with several objectives in mind:

- Extend the CLP and CSP technologies to continuous, non linear constraints;

- Design efficient and sound propagation-based methods over the reals;

- Study, compare and combine these methods with numerical analysis approaches;

- Provide a theoretical and algorithmic propagation-based framework to mix discrete and continuous constraints.

Nearly two decades later, most of these objectives were met, at least in part, considering that this technology is now routinely used in a number of nonlinear global optimization software packages and has made its way into several application areas including robotics and design.

A Brief History

Back in the mid eighties, the constraint programming community originated from the meeting of researchers in declarative programming paradigms such as (Constraint) Logic Programming [70, 71] and researchers in Artificial Intelligence, mostly coming from the CSP world. Although working on computation domains presenting opposite finiteness properties (Herbrand terms vs finite domains) both communities shared a view of the universe that was relational, symbolic and ruled by fixed point operators.

Prolog II, designed by Colmerauer [27], is generally considered as the first CLP language. The constraints of Prolog II are equations and disequalities over terms. The next generation of CLP languages, Prolog III [26], CHIP [36] and CLP($\Re$) [72], went a step further by introducing constraints over new computation domains including rational and real numbers, integers, Boolean and lists. It is in fact remarkable that in these three languages, one of the common computational domains is the set of rational or real numbers. Moreover the numerical constraints are made of linear constraints, with a delay mechanism to process nonlinear constraints. In other words, the first constraint logic programming languages introduced, among other things, continuous constraints as first class citizens.

At this point, the designers of CHIP showed that the finite domain technology they had developed (roughly arc consistency embedded in a Prolog-like language, see [123]) was particularly efficient on a number of difficult combinatorial problems. This basically paved the way to the most successful research area in constraint programming of the last two decades[1].

Meanwhile, on the continuous front, Cleary [21] independently combined results from interval analysis [98] to address the non-relational processing of numerical equations in standard Prolog. He then modified the Prolog engine to introduce a relational form of interval arithmetic. This work was rapidly followed by the implementation of BNR Prolog by Older and Vellino [105] and its sequel CLP(BNR) where mixed continuous/discrete and reified constraints were introduced [6]. In parallel, several works by different researchers among whose Hyvönen [68], Lhomme [88] and Faltings [37] explored the extension of Constraint Satisfaction Problems to continuous domains. Another branch of similar research emerged in Russia (see for example [122]), following the pioneering work on sub-definite models developed by Narin'yani [100].

The second milestone in the interval constraint research is centered on the design and development of Numerica by Van Hentenryck et al. [125]. The language combined a modeling language adapted to nonlinear constraints and various algorithmic improvements that led to a number of massive speedups. The central algorithm of Numerica [8, 124] was later improved in [9] and most of the current interval constraint solvers implement some variants of this algorithm. It was shown in [124] that these techniques were particularly effective to solve problems where local methods are either inefficient or not adapted (e.g. involving singularities, multiple solutions or inconsistencies). One spectacular result concerns a benchmark called "the transistor problem" and is described in [108].

Finally, more recent advances in interval and continuous constraints include inner approximations and quantified continuous constraints [22], and new application domains like control theory and robotics [79], computer graphics and graphical interfaces [10, 66], and engineering design [117].

Chapter Structure

The purpose of Section 16.1 is to present the basic ideas of the continuous constraint programming approach and to discuss the shift from discrete to continuous constraints. The general solving framework is introduced in Section 16.2 and specific cases like quantified constraint solving and global optimization are motivated. Interval consistency techniques for continuous constraints are described in Section 16.3. Interval methods from interval analysis are presented in Section 16.4. In Section 16.5, we discuss the possible hybridizations of symbolic and numerical techniques within the constraint programming approach. Section 16.6 is focused on quantified constraint solving. In particular, we show that consistency techniques can be used to process first order constraints and not only existentially quantified conjunctive constraints. A few software packages and applications are described in Section 16.7 and we finally conclude in Section 16.8.

---

[1]It is remarkable that, in the expression "constraint programming", the meaning of the term "programming" has very consistently evolved with the research area, starting from a "programming language" flavor to reach a semantics closer to what we have in "mathematical programming".

16.1   From Discrete to Continuous Constraints

In this section, we introduce interval constraint techniques, dedicated to continuous constraints solving and based on interval consistency techniques [21, 32, 105]. Our goal here is to present the main intuitions by way of examples. Let us consider nonlinear equations of the form $f(x_1, \ldots, x_n) = 0$, where f is a real function. We also assume that the domain of every variable x_k is a closed interval of real numbers I_k. As a consequence, the search space, that is the set of potential solutions, is a Cartesian product of intervals called an interval box (or simply a box). If $x = (x_1, \ldots, x_n)$, we denote as I_x the box $I_1 \times \cdots \times I_n$

As is the case with discrete CSPs, the main goal of (interval) consistency techniques is to eliminate values of variables that do not belong to constraint solutions. For example, a relational definition of (generalized) *arc consistency* can be stated as follows [90, 129]. Given $k \in \{1, \ldots, n\}$, the set of real numbers

$$\{a_k \in I_k : \qquad \exists a_1 \in I_1, \ldots, \exists a_{k-1} \in I_{k-1},$$
$$\exists a_{k+1} \in I_{k+1}, \ldots, \exists a_n \in I_n \ f(a_1, \ldots, a_n) = 0\} \qquad (16.1)$$

defines the values of I_k that are consistent with the constraint, that is an arc consistent domain for x_k which corresponds to the projection of the constraint over x_k. In a continuous context, due to the finiteness of machine arithmetic, this set is in general uncomputable. As a consequence, arc consistency must be weakened over the real numbers. The basic idea of interval consistencies is to define a superset of the set (16.1) using interval numbers [98]. These techniques are said to be complete since no constraint solution is lost. The following example shows various instantiations of (16.1):

Example 16.1. Let $y - x^2 = 0$ be a constraint and let $y \in [1, 2]$. Each of the following pair represents an initial domain of x and the corresponding arc consistent set for x:

$$([0, 1], \{1\}) \quad ([-1, 1], \{-1, 1\}) \quad ([0, 2], [1, \sqrt{2}]) \quad ([-1, 2], \{-1\} \cup [1, \sqrt{2}])$$

We notice that the set (16.1) cannot always be represented using machine arithmetic since $\sqrt{2}$ is not a machine number. Moreover, the set can be connected or disconnected. To handle these problems, several approximation notions are defined, based on floating point intervals. The issue is then to devise efficient computational methods. ☐

Hull consistency is a complete approximation of arc consistency obtained by replacing the set defined in equation (16.1) with the smallest enclosing interval, which is called the interval hull. The domain reduction rules combine interval arithmetic and constraint inversion steps, as illustrated by the following example:

Example 16.2. Let $y - x^2 = 0$ be a constraint, and let $x \in [0, 2]$ and $y \in [-1, 2]$. Given the smallest machine number $a \geqslant \sqrt{2}$, the reduction rules are defined as follows:

$$\begin{cases} I_y & := & [0, 2] & = & I_y \ \cap \ I_x^2 \\ I_x & := & [0, a] & = & I_x \ \cap \ \sqrt{I_y} \end{cases}$$

The key point is to express every variable as a function of the other variables. This is immediate for y while it needs an inversion of the square operation for x. Interval arithmetic is used for the evaluation step, which allows one to control rounding operations in order to compute a superset of the set defined by equation (16.1). ☐

The solving method is a search algorithm that maintains local consistency at each node of the search tree. The local consistency of a set of constraints is computed by constraint propagation using the reduction rules. This process is convergent and computes a set of locally consistent domains in finite time, since the set of intervals is finite and the reductions rules are contracting and monotonic [2].

Example 16.3. Let $c_1 : y - x^2 = 0$ and $c_2 : y - x - 1 = 0$ be two constraints, and let $(x, y) \in [-4, 4]^2$. The following sequence describes a propagation process such that a constraint is used to reduce one variable domain at every step:

$$(c_1, y \in [0, 4]), \quad (c_1, x \in [-2, 2]), \quad (c_2, y \in [0, 3]),$$
$$(c_2, x \in [-1, 2]), \quad (c_1, x \in [-1, 1.73\ldots]), \quad \ldots$$

The final hull consistent set is the product $[-1, 1.61\ldots] \times [0, 2.61\ldots]$. □

In the spirit of numerical computations, the approximate solutions have to be known in general at a given precision $\varepsilon > 0$. The precision of an interval $[a, b]$ can be defined by the real number $(b - a)$. In this framework, the search tree must be made of inconsistent terminal nodes, consistent terminal nodes such that the precision of every interval is smaller than ε, and non-terminal nodes, which are processed by splitting. Bisecting the largest domain is a good heuristic on average.

Example 16.4. Let $\{y - x^2 = 0, y - x - 1 = 0\}$ be a set of constraints, and let $(x, y) \in [-4, 4]^2$. This problem has two solutions. Given a precision of 10^{-8}, two approximate solutions can be computed:

$$[-0.61\ldots, -0.61\ldots] \times [0.38\ldots, 0.38\ldots] \quad and \quad [1.61\ldots, 1.61\ldots] \times [2.61\ldots, 2.61\ldots]$$

Each approximate solution encloses one solution. This is a good case since interval computations are complete but not necessarily sound. Soundness can be obtained in particular cases by means of theorems from real analysis, e.g., Brouwer's [15] and Miranda's [94]. Let us remark that the hull of the solution set is much tighter than the hull consistent domain of Example 16.3, which comes from the weakness of local consistency. □

To conclude, the shift from discrete to continuous domains requires an approximation domain, new reduction rules and splitting heuristics. Interval arithmetic provides good properties, since every computation is convergent and complete. In the following, we will describe advanced interval-based techniques such as the combination of consistency techniques and numerical operators from interval analysis.

16.2 The Branch-and-Reduce Framework

The problem of solving constraint-based mathematical models over the real numbers is uncomputable in general [111]. It is only possible to calculate approximations to the solutions by using machine arithmetic. Along these lines, the main goal of interval-based techniques is to solve combinatorial problems defined as relaxations of the exact continuous problems [98]. More precisely, we address the problem of covering solution sets with finite sets of interval boxes of reasonable precision. This problem is NP-hard in the general case. Our goal is to design solving techniques whose practical time complexity is better

Table 16.1: The general branch-and-reduce algorithm for solving constraint problems.

BranchAndReduce(C : *constraint model, I : interval box, ...*)
begin
    $L := \{I\}$ % set of interval boxes
    repeat
        J := **Choose**(L)   % choice of a current box
        K := **Reduce**(C, J)   % reduction of the current box
        L := **Branch**(L, K)   % branching operation on the covering
        L := **Revise**(L)   % simplification of the current covering
    until L is terminal
    return L % covering of the solutions of C within I
end

than the exponential worst case. Another important issue related to numerical computations is to prove the existence of solutions within an interval box in order to provide safe results.

The problem of covering the solution set of a constraint-based model within an interval box can be handled by branch-and-reduce algorithms [1, 61, 98, 101, 125]. The main principle of these algorithms is to recursively refine the initial interval box, which is trivially a covering. At least two solving procedures must be implemented. A *branching* procedure splits an interval box from the covering in such a way that the result is a covering of the box (a partition in the best case). A *reduction* procedure narrows down an interval box in such a way that no solution belongs to the eliminated sub-boxes. Furthermore, for an optimization problem, a *bounding* procedure computes lower and upper bounds of the objective function within feasible boxes. This leads to the elimination of interval boxes for which the evaluation of the objective is out of the bounds. A general branch-and-reduce scheme is presented in Table 16.1, where the revise function may implement a bounding procedure or more generally a simplification algorithm. The algorithm stops when the current covering is declared to be final according to some criteria such as precision, cardinality of the covering, and computation time. This scheme can be specialized to process different problems:

- Solving a constraint system with isolated solutions can be based on interval numerical operators or constraint propagation techniques (see Sections 16.4 and 16.3). In general, the algorithm stops when the size of every domain from the covering is smaller than a given threshold. A simple branching heuristics is the bisection of the largest domain.

- Solving a constraint system having a continuum of solutions, for example a set of inequality constraints, is more complex since it requires managing *inner* boxes included in the continuum. Inner boxes can be computed using interval-based operators applied on the negations of the constraints [4]. An efficient representation inspired from computational geometry has been introduced in [127]. When computing inner approximations, a main issue is to avoid separating continuums in order to minimize the covering size. To this end, specific branching operators can be implemented.

- Solving a quantified formula requires the propagation of interval boxes through connectives and quantifiers [109]. For instance, a conjunction of constraints leads to domain intersection; a disjunction leads to domain union; the existential quantifier amounts to computing a projection. The main problem is to design numerical operators that are able to eliminate the quantifiers. For instance, it can be very difficult to compute inner boxes with respect to existentially quantified equations. These questions will be discussed in Section 16.6.

- Globally solving a constrained optimization problem requires maintaining reliable bounds on the objective function over the feasible solution space [61]. These bounds are typically obtained by processing linear relaxations [121]. Furthermore, new bounds can be reliably obtained only over regions that must contain at least one solution. To this end, existence proof algorithms based on theorems from fixed-point theory have been proposed [15, 82], see Section 16.4.3. Finally, the ordering of boxes to be processed and the branching method are two important components of the algorithm since the goal is to quickly find boxes that give good values of the objective in order to prune the rest of the search space [30].

16.3 Consistency Techniques

The approximation of consistency properties over the real numbers introduces several difficult problems such as the computation over sets of values, the control of numerical errors, the inversion of nonlinear functions, and the acceleration of slow convergence. Several techniques based on interval arithmetic [1, 98] have been proposed to handle these problems. Interval arithmetic is an efficient and reliable implementation of set computations that allows the propagation of interval domains through nonlinear constraints. These techniques have been pioneered in [21, 32, 68, 105].

In this section, we consider nonlinear constraints from a real-based structure such as equations and inequality constraints involving arithmetic operations and elementary functions over the real numbers. In this framework, integer values can be processed as specific real values.

16.3.1 Interval Arithmetic

Interval arithmetic is the arithmetic of interval numbers. Every *interval* $[a, b]$ is defined as a set of real numbers $\{a \leqslant x \leqslant b\}$. The set of intervals $\mathbf{I}$ is a lattice for set inclusion. Furthermore, interval arithmetic is defined as a set extension of real arithmetic. Given a real operation $\circ \in \{+, -, \times\}$, the corresponding interval operation is defined by

$$(I, J) \mapsto \blacklozenge \{x \circ y : x \in I,\ y \in J\}$$

where the symbol $\blacklozenge$ stands for the hull of a set of real numbers. These operations are implemented by computations over the interval bounds, as follows:

$$
\begin{aligned}
[a, b] \ + \ [c, d] &= [a + b, c + d] \\
[a, b] \ - \ [c, d] &= [a - d, b - c] \\
[a, b] \ \times \ [c, d] &= [\min(ac, ad, bc, bd), \max(ac, ad, bc, bd)]
\end{aligned}
$$

Elementary functions are defined in the same way.

Interval arithmetic can be used to compute the range of a real function over a domain. The so-called interval evaluation algorithm is the standard term evaluation procedure using interval arithmetic, where every variable is replaced with its domain. The result is a superset of the range of the function, which is equal to the exact set if every variable in the function expression occurs only once [98]. This process is the base case of a general approach to approximating a real function by an interval function:

Definition 16.5. *An interval function* $F : \mathbf{I}^n \rightarrow \mathbf{I}$ *is an interval extension of a function* $f : \mathbf{R}^n \rightarrow \mathbf{R}$ *if for every* $I \in \mathbf{I}^n$ *the inclusion* $\{f(x) : x \in I\} \subseteq F(I)$ *holds.*

There exist many kinds of interval extensions based on symbolic transformations or numerical relaxations such as Bernstein forms, Horner forms or Taylor expansions [17, 18, 65, 110].

In practice, the interval bounds are represented by machine numbers such as floating-point numbers [69, 99]. Since the interval domain is finite it follows that an interval cannot be indefinitely reduced. The bounds must be rounded: every lower bound is downward rounded, and every upper bound is upward rounded. By so doing, every computed interval is larger than the exact set, which is the price to pay for completeness.

16.3.2   Computing Projections from Tree Representations

Hull consistency is a direct approximation of arc consistency. More precisely, if the hull of the set defined by equation (16.1) is equal to I_k, then the domain of x_k is hull consistent; otherwise, the domain can be reduced. The goal is to compute the largest hull consistent domain included in I_k. However, this set is uncomputable in general due to the accumulation of rounding errors in interval computations. It can also be difficult to isolate variables in complex constraints. As a consequence, hull consistency is generally computed over a decomposition of the constraints.

The decomposition is a symbolic procedure that transforms every constraint into a set of constraints having at most one operation symbol. Given a constraint c, the decomposition C is obtained from c by introducing a set of new variables V such that the equivalence $c \iff \exists V C$ holds.

Example 16.6. Let $xy - z^2 = 1$ be a constraint. The main idea is to introduce a new variable for every operation symbol:

$$\{v_1 = xy, \ v_2 = z^2, \ v_3 = v_1 - v_2, \ v_3 = 1\}$$

The projection of this set over the variables x, y, z is trivially equivalent to the initial constraint.   □

Consistency over the decomposed set of constraints is obtained by constraint propagation. Every constraint is processed by a projection operator until no domain can be modified, as shown in Section 16.1. This strategy is optimal if the constraint network is a tree, which happens when every variable occurs only in one constraint [34, 40, 97]. This situation seldom arises in practice for the whole network. However, the set of constraints computed after the decomposition of one constraint is a tree if no variable occurs twice. This remark has led to a specialized algorithm to compute hull consistency [9, 49, 52]. The main idea is to propagate the variable domains from the leaves to the root, and from the root to the leaves in the tree-representation of the constraint. The bottom-up phase is an evaluation of the terms using interval arithmetic. The top-down phase is a projection of the constraint over every term.

Example 16.7. Let $xy - z^2 = 1$ be a constraint and let $\{v_1 = xy, v_2 = z^2, v_3 = v_1 - v_2, v_3 = 1\}$ be its decomposition. Let $x \in [-1, 1]$, $y \in [0, 2]$ and $x \in [-4, 4]$. The bottom-up phase is just an evaluation of the new variables:

$$
\begin{array}{l|ll}
v_1 = xy & I_{v_1} := I_x \times I_y & := [-2, 2] \\
v_2 = z^2 & I_{v_2} := I_z^2 & := [0, 16] \\
v_3 = v_1 - v_2 & I_{v_3} := I_{v_1} - I_{v_2} & := [-18, 2]
\end{array}
$$

The top-down phase is a projection of the constraint onto every variable:

$$
\begin{array}{l|ll}
v_3 = 1 & I_{v_3} := I_{v_3} \cap [1, 1] & := [1, 1] \\
v_1 = v_2 + v_3 & I_{v_1} := I_{v_1} \cap (I_{v_2} + I_{v_3}) & := [1, 2] \\
v_2 = v_1 - v_3 & I_{v_2} := I_{v_2} \cap (I_{v_1} - I_{v_3}) & := [0, 1] \\
z = \sqrt{v_2} & I_z := I_z \cap \sqrt{I_{v_2}} & := [-1, 1] \\
x = v_1/y & I_x := I_x \cap (I_{v_1}/I_y) & := [0.5, 1] \\
y = v_1/x & I_y := I_y \cap (I_{v_1}/I_x) & := [1, 2]
\end{array}
$$

It is clear that the new variables are used for intermediary computations in order to exchange information between the user variables. In practice, their introduction is then unnecessary.

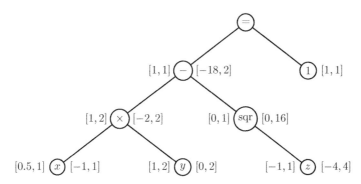

This computation is depicted in the previous figure where each node is labelled by the interval evaluation of the corresponding term (right-hand interval) and the constraint projection onto the term (left-hand interval). □

This strategy can be seen as a single operator for processing a complex constraint, which has been called HC4revise. It has been shown in [49] that this operator is idempotent only if the approximation domain is the set of unions of intervals. The use of unions of intervals has been discussed in [3, 9], but its practical efficiency is still doubtful. This operator can also be used in the general case, when some variables have many occurrences, with no guarantee of optimality. To improve accuracy in the general case, three issues have to be tackled: multiple occurrences of variables, locality of reasoning and propagation strategies.

Example 16.8. Set computations may be imprecise when the variables have many occurrences in one constraint. Let $x + x = 0$ be a constraint and let $x \in [-1, 1]$. The reduction rule is $I_x := I_x \cap (-I_x)$, which is useless. However, the constraint is equivalent to $x = 0$ In this case, the occurrences of x are handled as different variables, and no elimination of values happens as in the real domain. This problem will be addressed in Section 16.3.3. □

Example 16.9. Local consistency reasoning may be weak when the variables occur in many constraints. Let $x + y = 0$ and $x - y = 0$ be two constraints and let $(x, y) \in [-1, 1]^2$ These domains are hull consistent with respect to both constraints. However, the constraint system is equivalent to $x = y = 0$. In this case, the constraints are handled independently, and no reduction is performed with respect to the conjunction of constraints. This problem will be addressed in Section 16.3.4. □

16.3.3 Box Consistency

Box consistency is a relaxation of hull consistency [8]. The principle is to replace the constraint satisfaction test over the real domain with a refutation procedure over the interval domain. More precisely, let us examine the definition of arc consistency. A value $a_k \in I$ is inconsistent, and so does not belong to the set (16.1), if we have

$$\forall a_1 \in I_1, \ldots, \forall a_{k-1} \in I_{k-1}, \forall a_{k+1} \in I_{k+1}, \ldots, \forall a_n \in I_n \ f(a_1, \ldots, a_n) \neq 0.$$

An equivalent statement is that the range of f over the domain $I_1 \times \cdots \times I_{k-1} \times \{a_k\} \times I_{k+1} \times \cdots \times I_n$ is nonzero. The key idea is to compute a superset of this range using any interval extension F of f. Once computed, a value can be eliminated if any superset of the range is nonzero. The definition of box consistency then follows. If we have

$$I_k = \blacklozenge\{a_k \in I_k : 0 \in F(I_1, \ldots, I_{k-1}, \blacklozenge\{a_k\}, I_{k+1}, \ldots, I_{n-1})\} \qquad (16.2)$$

then the domain of x_k is box consistent. Otherwise, the goal is to find the extreme values in I_k that are consistent. The standard implementation uses a bisection search procedure, which exploits the monotonicity property of interval evaluation.

Example 16.10. Let $y - x^2 = 0$ be a constraint and let $(x, y) \in [0, 1] \times [0, 4]$. The left bound of I_y is box consistent since 0 belongs to the interval $0 - I_x^2 = [-1, 0]$. On the contrary, the right bound is inconsistent. Then the domain of y can be divided to find the rightmost consistent value, as follows:

$$
\begin{array}{ccccccl}
[2, 4] & - & I_x^2 & = & [1, 4] & \rightarrow & [2, 4] \quad \textit{eliminated} \\
[0, 2] & - & I_x^2 & = & [-1, 2] & & \\
[1, 2] & - & I_x^2 & = & [0, 2] & & \\
[1.5, 2] & - & I_x^2 & = & [0.5, 2] & \rightarrow & [1.5, 2] \quad \textit{eliminated} \\
\cdots & & & & \cdots & & \cdots
\end{array}
$$

The final computed domain is the interval $I_y = [0, 1]$. However, it is clear that the search converges slowly. The univariate interval Newton method described in Section 16.4 can be used to accelerate the convergence [8]. □

The main capability of box consistency is the ability to handle the elimination problem of set computations. In fact, computing hull consistency is equivalent and cheaper when the considered variable occurs only once in the constraint [23, 9].

Example 16.11. Once again, let us consider the constraint $x + x = 0$ and let $x \in [-1, 1]$. The refutation procedure fails for the whole domain since 0 belongs to the interval $[-1, 1] + [-1, 1] = [-2, 2]$. However, it succeeds for every sub-domain that does not contain 0. In this case, the domain can be reduced to 0. $\qquad \square$

16.3.4 Strong Consistencies

Strong consistency techniques are designed to compute the projections of sets of constraints over the variables [39, 96]. The goal is to combine the constraints in order to improve the precision of domain reductions. These techniques can be organized in a hierarchy, from local consistencies such as hull consistency and box consistency to the strongest global consistency, which corresponds to the projection of the whole set of constraints.

The principle of 3B consistency [88] is to eliminate a variable value if the set of constraints is not locally consistent when the variable takes this value. More precisely, a constraint system S is 3B consistent if for every variable x, for every bound $x = a$, the system $S \cup \{x = a\}$ is locally consistent.

Example 16.12. Let $x + y = 0$ and $x - y = 0$ be two constraints and let $(x, y) \in [-1, 1]^2$. This domain is hull consistent. However, it is not 3B consistent. For instance, for $x = -1$, the constraints implies that $y = 1$ and $y = -1$, which may be detected by constraint propagation. $\qquad \square$

The reduction of a variable domain can be implemented by a search procedure similar to the box consistency algorithm. However, the sub-domains are eliminated by a constraint propagation approach using a local consistency technique on the whole constraint system. This approach has been experimented with using hull consistency and box consistency [88, 108]. But the practical time complexity may be prohibitive with respect to some local consistency alone if all the variables are processed.

Example 16.13. Let $x + y = 0$ and $x - y = 0$ be two constraints and let $(x, y) \in [-1, 1]^2$. In this case, the propagation algorithm using hull consistency is able to eliminate any subdomain of x or y if it does not contain 0. For instance, if we have $x \in [0.5, 1]$ then the propagation on y gives

$$I_y := I_y \cap I_x \cap -I_x = \varnothing.$$

As a consequence, the sub-domain $[0.5, 1]$ of x can be removed. The search procedure converges towards a small domain enclosing the solution $x = y = 0$. $\qquad \square$

The notion of kB consistency is a generalization of 3B consistency [88] defined by induction as follows. A constraint system S is kB consistent (for $k \geq 3$) if for every variable x, for every bound $x = a$, the system $S \cup \{x = a\}$ is $(k - 1)$B consistent. There were several other attempts at enforcing strong consistency algorithms over nonlinear constraints [37, 67, 68]. A nice implementation of global (hull) consistency has been realized by combining local consistency, complete search, and local search [29]. In [38], local extrema of ternary constraints as well as intersection points between constraints are computed using gradient-based numerical methods applied on the constraint curves. In [117], every ternary constraint is represented by a set of consistent regions of the 3D space. That allows the combination of constraints using Boolean operations, and then to implement strong consistency algorithms. This approach has been used to solve engineering problems, but it must be limited to weak precisions.

16.3.5 Acceleration Techniques

Constraint propagation is an iterative algorithm that applies local consistency operators until equilibrium. It is known that the final domain does not depend on the order of application of the operators [2]. However, the convergence speed is determined by the strategy as well as the kind of operators associated with the constraints [54].

The creation of the set of operators from the set of constraints may depend on several parameters such as the form of constraints, the form of the constraint network, the size of domains, etc. For instance, the combination of hull consistency and box consistency in the BC4 algorithm is based on a theorem that states that these techniques are equivalent if the variables have at most one occurrence per constraint [9]. Since computing hull consistency is cheaper than computing box consistency, the strategy is as follows: for every constraint c, the HC4revise operator is created if there exists a variable occurring once in c; the box consistency operator is used for every variable occurring at least twice in c. Doing so, we have a family of algorithms adapted to the form of constraints.

Example 16.14. Given $(x, y) \in [-10, 10]$, let us consider the constraint $c : x^2 + y^2 = 1$ and two equivalent forms $c_1 : xx + y^2 = 1$ and $c_2 : xx + yy = 1$. The following table show the results of the constraint propagation algorithm when the different operators are used. In each case, we give the reduced domain and the number of computed interval operations.

	Hull consistency		Box consistency		BC4	
c	$[-1, 1]^2$	15	$[-1, 1]^2$	1178	$[-1, 1]^2$	15
c_1	$[-10, 10]^2$	16	$[-1, 1] \times [-\sqrt{2}, \sqrt{2}]$	1238	$[-1, 1] \times [-\sqrt{2}, \sqrt{2}]$	625
c_2	$[-10, 10]^2$	17	$[-10, 10]^2$	40	$[-10, 10]^2$	40

The domains are the same for constraint c since the variables occur once in c but the hull consistency technique is much faster. The box consistency technique is more powerful for c_1 because the many occurrences of y are efficiently handled. In this case, the combination is as powerful but cheaper since hull consistency is used for x. Finally, there is no reduction for c_2 since no operator is able to handle two variables having multiple occurrences. □

It has been observed that local computations can be weakened during constraint propagation while maintaining the global convergence [88]. The goal is to prevent slow convergence arising with respect to one constraint and to alternate more often the reductions for different constraints. This strategy has been used to accelerate box consistency [56]. The dichotomous search algorithm has been modified in order to stop when intervals of size $w > 0$ at domain bounds cannot be eliminated. Moreover, a globally converging strategy is used to decrease the value of w until $w = 0$.

Example 16.15. The system $(x - 2)x(x + 1) = (x - 1)x(x + 2) = 0$ with $x \in [-10, 10]$ can be solved by box consistency alone. The computed domains are $[-1, 2]$ with the first constraint, $[0, 1]$ with the second constraint, and then $[0, 0]$ using the first constraint. Every local zero in $\{-1, 1, 2\}$ is computed at the highest precision, which is useless. The accelerated strategy is one order of magnitude faster. □

The elimination of cycles during propagation is a long studied topic that has been considered for nonlinear constraints [89]. During a cycle, some variable domains may be reduced by several different operators, which do not lead to the same amount of reductions. A good strategy is then to select the best operators, to apply them until equilibrium, and then to propagate the domain modifications through the other operators. A parallel version of this algorithm has been successfully implemented in [53].

Another approach consists in accelerating the convergence of domain bounds [86]. Given a sequence of reduced domains $[a_0, b_0] \supseteq [a_1, b_1] \supseteq \cdots$, the idea is to accelerate the sequences $a_0 \leqslant a_1 \leqslant \cdots$ and $b_0 \geqslant b_1 \geqslant \cdots$ independently. Well-known numerical methods such as Aitken's Δ^2 are applied to compute approximate limits a and b of the two sequences. It can then be interesting to prove that the domains $[a_0, a)$ and $(b, b_0]$ are inconsistent. This heuristic has been shown to be useful in implementing 3B consistency.

16.4 Numerical Operators

Interval analysis has been defined as an extension of numerical analysis over the intervals [98]. In general, the main goal is to implement complete and efficient set computations in order to enclose the solution set of a given problem. In this section, we are interested in constraint solving techniques. The basic principle of the direct interval methods is to replace real arithmetic with interval arithmetic. The main idea of the iterative methods is to extend the classical operators so as to compute tight enclosures. More precisely, given an initial point $x_0 \in \mathbf{R}^n$ and an operator ϕ, the general expression of an iterative method is as follows:

$$\left\{ \begin{array}{l} x_0 \\ x_{k+1} := \phi(x_k), \quad k \geqslant 0. \end{array} \right.$$

A finite sequence of approximate solutions is computed from the initial point until some precision criterion is verified. Given an initial set $I_0 \in \mathbf{I}^n$ and the interval counterpart Φ of ϕ, the corresponding interval-based iterative method is as follows:

$$\left\{ \begin{array}{l} I_0 \\ I_{k+1} := I_k \cap \Phi(I_k), \quad k \geqslant 0. \end{array} \right.$$

A finite sequence of nested intervals is computed until stabilization. The result is an interval enclosing the solution set of the given problem within I_0.

16.4.1 The Newton Method

Let $f : \mathbf{R} \to \mathbf{R}$ be a function which is continuous on a closed interval $[a, b]$ and differentiable on its interior (a, b). The mean value theorem states that for all $x, x_0 \in [a, b]$ there exists $c \in \mathbf{R}$ strictly lying between x and x_0 such that

$$f(x) - f(x_0) = f'(c)(x - x_0). \tag{16.3}$$

It follows that any root x of f verifies the relation

$$x = x_0 - f(x_0)/f'(c), \ f'(c) \neq 0. \tag{16.4}$$

The classical Newton method is obtained from (16.4) by approximating c by x_0. The interval Newton method follows from the following membership relation:

$$x \in \{x_0 - f(x_0)/f'(y) : y \in (a, b), \ f'(y) \neq 0\}. \tag{16.5}$$

Since the set (16.5) can be enclosed by means of interval arithmetic and interval extensions of the functions, we obtain the following interval Newton step:

$$I_{k+1} := I_k \cap (x_k - F(x_k)/F'(I_k)), \ 0 \notin F'(I_k), \ k \geqslant 0. \tag{16.6}$$

The result of this iteration is a sequence of nested intervals enclosing the solution set. The necessary condition is that the computed range of the derivative of f does not contain the zero value. The point x_k is generally taken as the midpoint of the current interval I_k. Geometrically, this method amounts to approximating a function around a point x_k by a cone whose shape is determined by the range of the derivative of f over I_k.

Example 16.16. Let $f(x) = x^2 - 2$ be a function and let $x \in [1, 10]$. Since the derivative is non-zero on the given domain, the Newton method can be applied:

$$I_x := [1, 10] \cap (4.5 - (4.5^2 - 2)/(2 \times [1, 10])) = [1, 3.5825]$$

After 5 iterations, an enclosure of $\sqrt{2}$ with 8 significant digits is computed:

$$I_x := [1.414213559529903, 1.414213565673288]$$

In the vicinity of the solution, the Newton method converges with order 2, i.e., the size of a thin interval is approximately the square of the size of the previously computed one. □

16.4.2   Solving Linear Systems

A heavily studied topic in interval analysis is the solving of linear systems of equations, see for instance [1, 101, 61, 113]. Let $\mathbf{A} \in \mathbf{I}^{n \times n}$ be an interval matrix and let $B \in \mathbf{I}^n$ be an interval vector. The solution set of the interval linear system $\mathbf{A}x = B$ is defined by

$$\Sigma(\mathbf{A}, B) := \{x \in \mathbf{R}^n : Ax = b \text{ for some } A \in \mathbf{A}, \ b \in B\}.$$

Informally speaking, any solution of a real system included in the interval system must belong to $\Sigma(\mathbf{A}, B)$. It has been shown that the problem of exactly enclosing this solution set is NP-hard [112]. In practice, the goal is to compute good enclosures.

As an example, we describe the interval Gauss-Seidel method. Every row i of the linear system can be rewritten as

$$x_i = \frac{1}{A_{ii}} \left[B_i - \sum_{j \neq i} A_{ij} x_j \right].$$

If we have interval bounds I_j on x_j then new bounds on x_i are computed as

$$I_i := I_i \cap \frac{1}{A_{ii}} \left[B_i - \sum_{j \neq i} A_{ij} I_j \right] \tag{16.7}$$

provided that A_{ii} does not contain the zero value. The interval Gauss-Seidel method iterates the step (16.7) from $i := 1$ to n until stabilization. We remark that this procedure is very similar to constraint propagation using hull consistency to invert the linear equations. The main difference is that hull consistency is generally applied on every variable with respect to every constraint, which can be more precise but also more expensive.

If we have $0 \in A_{ii}$ the classical interval division returns the interval $(-\infty, +\infty)$ and the step is useless. In this case, several techniques may lead to tighter bounds:

- The extended interval division can be more precise depending on the value of the numerator [64, 80]. This operation corresponds to the computation of the projection of the constraint $x = y/z$ over x using unions of intervals.

- Another row can be used to prune the domain of x_i. The general problem is then to choose a good transversal in the system, namely the row which leads to the largest reduction for a given variable [48].

- The system can be transformed before solving. In fact, it is recommended to multiply it by a well-chosen matrix called a preconditioner [62]. In practice, a good preconditioner is the inverse of the midpoint matrix of coefficients of I.

Rigorously solving linear programming problems with interval data is a difficult problem, see for instance [75]. The main basic idea is to use the classical Simplex algorithm to determine optimal points and then to use interval methods to verify the optimality and to compute rigorous error bounds [74, 102].

16.4.3 Solving Nonlinear Systems

In the general case, completely solving nonlinear systems requires an exhaustive search by means of branch-and-reduce algorithms. In this framework, interval methods can be used to early prune the search space by removing infeasible regions. In the following, we will present the multivariate interval Newton method for solving systems of nonlinear equations [63, 98, 101, 103] and reformulation-linearization techniques [87, 118] that can be used for nonlinear equations and inequalities. Another well-known method is the Krawczyk operator [83]. The main idea of these techniques is to iterate an inner step where a linear relaxation of the nonlinear system is determined and solved using linear interval methods.

Let $f : \mathbf{R}^n \to \mathbf{R}^n$ be a vector of continuously differentiable nonlinear functions and let $x \in \mathbf{R}^n$ be bounded by $I \in \mathbf{I}^n$. The multivariate interval Newton method is an iterative method for solving the problem $f(x) = 0$, $x \in I$, which is an obvious extension of the univariate Newton method presented in Section 16.4.1. Let J_f be a matrix of interval extensions of the partial derivatives of f and let F be an interval extension of f. Given $x_0 \in I$, an enclosure of the solution set can be obtained by solving the following interval linear system on x:

$$J_f(I)(x - x_0) = -F(x_0)$$

Given $y = x - x_k$ (initially $y = x - x_0$), the inner step of the iterative method trivially follows:

$$\begin{cases} I_y & := & I_k - x_k \\ I_y & := & \text{solve system } J_f(I_k)y = -F(x_k) \\ N(I_k, x_k) & := & I_y + x_k \end{cases}$$

The interval linear system on y is generally solved by means of the interval Gauss-Seidel method. Many strategies can be implemented according to the precision of the inner step, the precision of the computed enclosure, and the Gauss-Seidel strategy. The following properties hold:

- $N(I_k, x_k)$ is an enclosure of the solution set. As a consequence, the new domain can be computed as

$$I_{k+1} := N(I_k, x_k) \cap I_k.$$

  In particular, if the resulting domain is empty, then the problem has no solution.

- If $N(I_k, x_k) \subseteq I_k$, then there exists an $x \in I_k$ such that $f(x) = 0$. This existence property is derived from the fixed-point theory [15, 41].

Example 16.17. Let us consider the system $x_1^2 + x_2^2 = 1/16$, $x_2 = 4x_1^2$ with $x \in [0, 0.25]^2$. We describe the first step of the Newton method. The following linear relaxation is created after preconditioning:

$$\begin{pmatrix} [0, 2] & [-0.5, 0.5] \\ [-1, 1] & [0.5, 1.5] \end{pmatrix} y = \begin{pmatrix} 5/32 \\ 3/32 \end{pmatrix}$$

with $y \in [-0.125, 0.125]^2$. Then the domain y_2 can be reduced during the Gauss-Seidel method:

$$I_{y_2} := \left[-\frac{1}{8}, \frac{1}{8}\right] \cap \left(\frac{1}{[0.5, 1.5]}\left(\frac{3}{32} - [-1, 1]\left[-\frac{1}{8}, \frac{1}{8}\right]\right)\right) = \left[-\frac{1}{16}, \frac{1}{8}\right]$$

Then the new domain of x_2 can immediately be computed:

$$I_{x_2} := \left(\left[-\frac{1}{16}, \frac{1}{8}\right] + \frac{1}{8}\right) \cap \left[0, \frac{1}{4}\right] = \left[\frac{1}{16}, \frac{1}{4}\right]$$

It can be observed that the initial system is arc consistent. In this case, the Newton method is clearly more powerful.   □

Rectangular systems can be also be tackled by Newton-like methods. The most common approach is to fix the variables to which the system is least sensitive using for instance the midpoint values [61].

The purpose of reformulation-linearization techniques is to rewrite nonlinear systems using convex and concave linear approximations and to solve them by means of linear methods [87, 118]. As an example, we describe the simple case of quadratic equations defined as sums of linear terms and quadratic terms x^2 and xy. The first step is to replace the quadratic terms by new variables $w = x^2$ and $z = xy$. The second step is to constrain the new variables. Given $x \in [a, b]$ and $y \in [c, d]$, the following constraints are verified:

$$w \geqslant 2ax - a^2, \ w \geqslant 2bx - b^2, \ w \leqslant (a + b)x - ab,$$
$$z \geqslant cx + ay - ac, \ z \leqslant dx + ay - ad, \ z \geqslant dx + by - bd, \ z \leqslant cx + by - bc$$

Finally, the resulting set of linear constraints can be solved. For instance, the Simplex algorithm can be used to minimize and to maximize every variable in order to reduce its domain.

Example 16.18. Once again, let us consider the system $x_1^2 + x_2^2 = 1/16, x_2 = 4x_1^2$ with $x \in [0, 0.25]^2$. The nonlinear system can be rewritten as follows using $z_1 = x_1^2$ and $z_2 = x_2^2$:

$$z_1 + z_2 = 0.0625, \quad x_2 = 4z_1,$$
$$0 \leqslant x_1 \leqslant 0.25, \quad 0 \leqslant x_2 \leqslant 0.25,$$
$$z_1 \geqslant 0, \quad z_1 \geqslant 0.5x_1 - 0.0625, \quad z_1 \leqslant 0.25x_1,$$
$$z_2 \geqslant 0, \quad z_2 \geqslant 0.5x_2 - 0.0625, \quad z_2 \leqslant 0.25x_2$$

After solving the four optimization problems, new bounds are obtained:

$$x \in [0.125, 0.209] \times [0.125, 0.167].$$

The new bounds can then be used for the next iteration. We may remark that these bounds are much tighter than the ones given by the Newton method (see Example 16.17). □

To conclude, we may say that the strategy remains a main issue, since solving $2n$ linear systems to reduce n domains may be expensive. More generally, this is the problem of designing efficient hybrid methods by combining different solvers, which will be discussed in the next section.

16.5 Hybrid Techniques

There is no unique algorithm for efficiently solving constraints over the real numbers. Conversely, every algorithm is parametrized by an input model, time and space complexities, efficiency conditions, and properties on the output. Depending on the context, it can be useful to combine several algorithms in a super algorithm [57]. However, the work of designing hybrid strategies may be very difficult since that may demand a lot of experience on the algorithms to be combined. In the following, we will present some features leading to combine symbolic methods, numerical methods, and consistency techniques for real constraint solving and optimization.

16.5.1 Symbolic and Consistency Techniques

Consistency techniques are known to be subject to the locality problem. Informally speaking, the propagation of local consistency-based reductions may not lead to a tight enclosure of the solution set. An objective is then to symbolically transform the constraints in order to strengthen constraint propagation techniques.

The elementary approach is to share common expressions occurring in the constraints [52, 125]. This can be done by introducing a new variable for every shared expression. In order to keep the dimension of the problem, a more efficient method is to represent the constraint network as a directed acyclic graph (DAG). In this case, stronger consistency reasoning can be obtained by propagating domain modifications through the DAG. However, that requires a slight reshaping of classical algorithms since some information must be attached to the nodes of the graph.

Example 16.19. Consider the unsatisfiable constraint system $xy = 1, xy = -1$ and let $(x, y) \in [-1, 1]^2$. This problem is trivially bound consistent: for example, given $x = 1$ there exist $y_1 = 1$ and $y_2 = -1$ such that $xy_1 = 1$ and $xy_2 = -1$. Now, sharing the expression xy leads to check the consistency of the relation $1 = -1$, which trivially fails. □

A more difficult approach is to rewrite the constraints [5, 91, 95]. The main principle is to symbolically create constraint relaxations and then to apply symbolic algorithms. For example, one would apply Gaussian elimination on linear systems of equations or Gröbner bases on polynomial systems of equations. These algorithms may be used to calculate quasi-triangular systems that can be easily solved by constraint propagation. However, the control of symbolic processing is a main issue. For example, the linear relaxations are mostly rectangular (there are more variables than constraints) and it may be difficult to eliminate the linear variables. More difficult, computing a Gröbner basis may require exponential time and space, which is not realistic for implementing efficient symbolic-numeric algorithms.

Example 16.20. Gaussian elimination is powerful when the linear relaxations are not very rectangular. For example, consider the system

$$x_k - \frac{1}{2n} \sum_{i=1}^{n} \left(x_i^3 + k \right) = 0, \quad 1 \leqslant k \leqslant n$$

with the initial domain $[-10^8, +10^8]^n$. A linear relaxation is obtained if each term x_i^3 is abstracted by one variable y_i. After applying Gaussian elimination on the linear system, new equivalent system is obtained by replacing y_i by x_i^3:

$$x_{k+1} = x_1 + \frac{k}{2n}, \quad 1 \leqslant k \leqslant n - 1, \quad x_1 - \frac{1}{2n} \sum_{i=1}^{n} \left(\left(x_1 + \frac{i-1}{2n} \right)^3 + k \right) = 0$$

The original system is very hard for constraint propagation techniques even for low dimensions (e.g., $n = 4$). Conversely, the new system, which is triangular, is immediately solved. □

The principle of symbolic algorithms is to combine and then to simplify the constraints. However, the simplification of nonlinear constraints is not trivial in general. A weaker approach is to combine the constraints only if they can be simplified enough [55]. For example, consider two constraints $f[s] = 0$ and $g[t] = 0$ where s and t are terms occurring in f and g. A combination procedure may create a redundant constraint $h[s, t] = 0$ only if the combination of s and t in h can be rewritten. This approach requires that simplificatio rules are known in order to guide the combination strategy.

16.5.2 Symbolic and Interval Methods

The main tool of interval analysis is the computation of the range of a real function over a domain. However, a computed interval can be much larger than the true range, which is known as the overestimation problem of interval arithmetic.

Example 16.21. The range of $x - x$ over $[0, 1]$ can be estimated as $[0 - 1, 1 - 0] :=$ $[0, 1] - [0, 1]$. The problem comes from the fact that the two occurrences of x are considered as different variables, since different values are used during evaluation. A trivial simplification can lead to computing 0.   □

A main issue is then to rewrite a function in order to compute tight enclosures of its range. Various techniques have been proposed such as Horner forms, Bernstein polynomials, or Taylor models [18, 65, 11]. Another approach is based on affine arithmetic [33, 93]. The main idea is to define an interval $[a, b]$ by the affine expression such as

$$\frac{b+a}{2} + \frac{b-a}{2} \cdot \varepsilon, \quad \varepsilon \in [-1, 1].$$

The evaluation procedure is defined to manage the linear variables ε. For example, the range of $x - x$ over $[0, 1]$ is computed as

$$0 := \left(0 + \frac{2}{2} \cdot \varepsilon\right) - \left(0 + \frac{2}{2} \cdot \varepsilon\right).$$

However, the nonlinearities are incompatible with affine expressions. In this case, it is necessary to compute linear relaxations. The efficiency of this approach clearly depends on the quality of the relaxations.

16.5.3 Interval and Consistency Techniques

The behaviors and requirements of interval methods and consistency techniques are very different. Informally, the efficiency of interval methods is related to the combination of linear constraint relaxations and the good rates of convergence near the solutions. Consistency techniques are able to quickly reduce large domains by means of constraint projections and to exploit the constraint network structure in order to implement fast propagation algorithms. Their cooperation naturally follows.

The purpose of box consistency is to calculate the extreme zeros of an equation $f(x) = 0$ over a domain. The master algorithm is a bisection procedure implementing an interval test to remove the inconsistent sub-domains. The goal is to accelerate the search having an exponential time complexity in the worst case. To this end, the uni-dimensional Newton method can be used to prune any sub-domain provided that the derivative of f is nonzero [8].

Example 16.22. Let $x^2 - 2 = 0$ be a constraint and let $x \in [0, 4]$. If the interval test is implemented by interval evaluation, five domains are created during the search: $[0, 4]$, $[0, 2]$, and $[1, 2]$ are declared to be consistent, and $[2, 4]$ and $[0, 1]$ are rejected. Then the Newton method is applied on $[1, 2]$ since the range of the derivative is $[2, 4]$. The result is a tight enclosure of the square root of 2.   □

The hybridization of constraint propagation and the multidimensional interval Newton method can be efficient for solving nonlinear systems. In this case, constraint propagation is very useful during the early phases of domain reductions and the Newton method is efficient only for small domains. In this spirit, the master algorithm of Numerica is an iteration of constraint propagation using box consistency before applying the Newton method, until reaching a sufficient precision [125].

16.5.4 Towards a General Framework

The hybridization of symbolic algorithms, interval methods and constraint propagation is a general framework to solving continuous nonlinear constraints. The symbolic algorithms can be used to rewrite the constraints according to properties or requirements of the numerical tools. For example, constraint propagation is improved provided that redundant constraints are generated and the constraint network is represented as a DAG. The DAG allows the sharing of numerical computations such as the interval evaluations of functions and derivatives [52].

More generally, the analysis of constraint systems must be the first phase of general purpose solving tools. In particular, the solving strategy strongly depends on static characteristics such as the form of the constraints and the shape of the constraint network. For example, the structure of the network can be detected by decomposition algorithms [12]. We believe that the design of intermediary languages based on symbolic constraint transformations may lead to important components of solving strategies.

16.6 First Order Constraints

16.6.1 Extending Interval Constraints

Among the possible generalizations of the interval constraint framework, some extend the expressive power (modeling) while others improve the efficiency (solving). The first category includes optimization, differential equations, mixed constraints, and quantified continuous constraints. The second category is mainly concerned with solver cooperation and in particular numerical-symbolic cooperation. The optimization aspect was for example developed in the design and implementation of the systems Numerica [125] and Baron [121]. Some of the most important aspects reside in the appropriate combinations of continuous constraint propagation, interval analysis and branch and bound techniques. The use of interval constraints for ordinary differential equations solving was addressed, for instance, in [28, 73, 104]. It was shown in [6] that mixed constraints (constraints involving real and integer variables) are a special case of a general framework for numerical constraints but there is a need for specific, efficient algorithms and implementations. Concerning solver cooperation for continuous constraints, some results are presented in the survey paper [57]. We will focus here on the last of these extensions, quantified continuous constraints.

16.6.2 Quantified Continuous Constraints

As we mentioned, constraints can be defined as first order formulas over a given domain (here the real numbers). Yet, practically, they are most often restricted to atomic constraints. In this last case, models are generally defined as existentially quantified conjunctions of atomic constraints. In a number of problems ranging from robust control and camera control to motion planning, this existential definition of models is not satisfactory. Let us take an example from robotics: given a mobile robot arm, find all points that do not collide with the robot hand. Since we want to avoid collision *for all positions of the hand* the variables defining the hand position of the robot in the model are universally quantified.

The general problem is undecidable when it involves transcendental functions like the sine and the exponential [120], and doubly exponential when restricted to polynomials [31]. In this context, a number of authors, from computer algebra, numerical analysis or constraint programming, have devised techniques to approximate the solution set or to handle specific instances.

For example, a strongly related problem from control theory is called the "guaranteed tuning problem" [78] and amounts to finding the values for some tuning parameter such that a set of inequalities can be verified for all the possible values of some perturbation vector. More precisely, given I a box of feasible values for some tuning parameter vector x and J, a box of feasible values for some perturbation vector p, find the set

$$S = \{x \in I : \forall p \in J \ f(x, p) \geqslant 0\}.$$

One of the first approaches to solve arbitrarily quantified constraints over the real numbers was developed by Collins and called cylindrical algebraic decomposition [24]. The presentation of this method is beyond the scope of this paper, but let us mention that it is restricted to polynomials.

Another track of research, which is of major interest for constraint programming based techniques, relies on the computation of sub-pavings of real relations. Given a relation, a sub-paving is a set of boxes that covers the relation. These boxes can be separated in three categories: the set of boxes that are proved to be included in the relation, the set of boxes that are proved not to intersect the relation, and the remaining set of boxes that may be accumulated on the frontier. Boxes from these different sets can be used to compute outer and inner approximations of solution sets and, combined with local consistency notions, to reason about quantifiers. The computation of these sub-pavings is essentially based on search methods. To compute these sub-pavings, some authors have used Bernstein polynomials [43], ternary constraint octree representations [117] or inner approximation expansion [22]. In [76, 77] a combination of recursive splitting, interval evaluations and properties of interval arithmetic is used to compute sub-pavings and address some forms of quantified constraints. The introduction of universal quantifiers is then based on interval inclusion tests. An interval inclusion test uses simple interval inferences to prove that a formula of the type $(\forall x \in I) f(x) \diamond 0$, where x is an nary vector of variables over $\mathbb{R}$, I a box, f a vector of continuous real functions in $\mathbf{R}^n \to \mathbf{R}^m$. For example, the constraint $(\forall x_1 \in [-2, 2])(\forall x_2 \in [3, 5]), x_1 + x_2 > 0$ can be shown true since evaluating the natural interval extension gives $[-2, 2] + [3, 5] = [1, 7]$ and every value in $[1, 7]$ is greater than 0.

To go a step further some authors have used properties of interval consistencies. As we have seen, interval constraint algorithms can discard inconsistent boxes and separate them from boxes possibly containing solutions. Based on this property, in [10] an algorithm computes interval-based pruning of negated inequalities and recursively construct an inner approximation of the solution space. This algorithm is then used to approximate constraint sets containing exactly one universally quantified variable.

This idea was generalized in [109] to handle arbitrary first order inequalities over the reals. In this paper the main idea is to design an algorithm whose inputs are a quantified constraint C with n free variables, a box $I \subseteq \mathbf{R}^n$ and a positive real number ε. The outputs of the algorithm are two sets of boxes A and B verifying that all points of A are in the solution set of C and all points of B are not in the solution set of C. Furthermore, the precision of the approximation is parameterized with ε and the volume of the space

$I \setminus (A \cup B)$ is smaller than ε. To compute these sets of boxes, the proposed algorithm is built on a branch and prune architecture. Branching is done by interval bisections on the domains of the free variables but also on the domains of the quantified variables (e.g., $\exists x \in I$ can be replaced with $\exists x \in I_1 \vee \exists x \in I_2$). Pruning is achieved recursively on atomic, conjunctive, disjunctive formulas and on formulas of the form $\exists x \in I \, C$ or $\forall x \in I \, C$. The main idea is to use standard pruning operators implementing consistency properties to narrow down the boxes wrt. the formula and to apply the same algorithm on the negation of the formula to compute an inner approximation of the solution set.

Finally another related area concerns the use of modal intervals [42] for quantified constraints. As stated in [46], modal interval theory can be viewed as a useful interpretation of an extension of interval arithmetic called directed interval arithmetic, or Kaucher arithmetic [81]. Directed interval arithmetic is obtained as an extension of the set of standard intervals by improper intervals and a corresponding extension of the definitions of the interval arithmetic operations.

A modal interval $\dot{I} = (I, Q)$, where I is a real interval and $Q \in \{\exists, \forall\}$, defines a set of real intervals in the following way:

$$
\begin{aligned}
(I, \exists) &= \{K \in \mathbf{I} : (\exists x) \, x \in I \models x \in K\} &= \{K \in \mathbf{I} : I \cap K \neq \varnothing\} \\
(I, \forall) &= \{K \in \mathbf{I} : (\forall x) \, x \in I \models x \in K\} &= \{K \in \mathbf{I} : I \subseteq K\}
\end{aligned}
$$

Directed (or generalized) intervals and modal intervals being isomorphic (see for example [46]) one can use the equivalent following definition:

$$
\dot{I} = [a, b] = \left\{ \begin{array}{ll} ([a, b]', \exists) & \text{if } a \leqslant b \\ ([a, b]', \forall) & \text{if } a \geqslant b \end{array} \right.
$$

where $[a, b]' = [b, a]' = \{x \in \mathbf{R} : \min(a, b) \leqslant x \leqslant \max(a, b)\}$. This formulation is very useful for simplifying a number of definitions, proofs and computations on modal intervals. For example, inclusion, union and intersection of modal intervals are defined in a natural way over the sets of real intervals but the practical definitions are based on generalized interval arithmetic. Modal interval extensions of continuous real functions, also called semantic extensions are defined as follows. Let f be a continuous function over the reals and let $\dot{F}$ be a modal interval function. The function $\dot{F}$ is a semantic interval extension of f on $\dot{I}$ if and only if we have

$$
(\forall K \in \mathbf{I})(K \in \dot{I} \models f(K) \in \dot{F}(\dot{I})).
$$

Then, $\dot{F}$ is a semantic interval extension of f if it is a semantic interval extension of f for all modal interval $\dot{I}$. The extension to n-ary real continuous functions is done in the usual way.

A very important semantic extension in modal interval analysis is the *-semantic extension of a continuous function f to a modal interval vector $\dot{I} = ((I_1, Q_1), \ldots, (I_n, Q_n))$ defined by:

$$
f^*(\dot{I}) = [\min_{I \in I_E} \max_{I \in I_F} f(x), \max_{I \in I_E} \min_{I \in I_F} f(x)]
$$

where E and F are respectively the sets of indexes corresponding to the proper (existential) and improper (universal) components of $\dot{I}$.

Finally, the fundamental link between modal interval analysis and first order interval constraints is established by the so-called *-semantic theorem from [59]. Let f be a real n-ary function, $\dot{I} = ((I_1, Q_1), \ldots, (I_n, Q_n))$ a modal interval vector and $\dot{J} = (J, Q_j)$ a modal interval. Slightly simplified, the theorem states that following two conditions are equivalent:

1. $f^*(\dot{I}) \subseteq \dot{J}$;

2. $(\forall x_E \in I_E)(Q_j z \in J)(\exists x_A \in I_A)(f(x) = z)$

When $z = 0$, one can fix $J = [0, 0]$ and this theorem shows that proving a formula of the form:

$$(\forall x \in I)(\exists y \in J) \, f(x, y) = 0$$

is equivalent to the computation of the *-semantic extension of the function f. Based on this theorem, some recent works have extended this idea to solve several classes of quantified equations and inequalities [116, 126].

To conclude, computing guaranteed inner and outer approximations of first order constraints over the reals has many applications in areas like engineering, robotics, design, and computer graphics. Current results on this field are basically based on combinations of interval propagation and other techniques, and in particular methods from computer algebra and interval analysis results.

16.7 Applications and Software packages

16.7.1 Applications

Interval constraints have recently been used in various application fields with different goals: to prove that a given problem is not satisfiable, to compute a numerical enclosure of the solution set, or to derive global optima according to some objective function.

In engineering conceptual design, the goal is to generate classes of solutions that satisfy a given high-level specification of the product to be designed [117, 106]. The architecture of the product can be described by compositions of components, while some parts have several possible design options. To this end several formalisms such as dynamic and composite discrete constraint satisfaction problems have been devised [44]. Another approach is to express the problem as a first-order formula involving conjunctions and disjunctions of constraints. On top of these configuration constraints, product dimensioning is often related to physical requirements and can be processed by numerical constraint solving. The general goal is to solve mixed problems involving dimensioning continuous parameters and discrete configuration choices. An example of a design support software based on interval consistency techniques is the design platform CE [130]. This platform has recently been used to realize aeronautical systems.

In robotics constraint-based techniques have successfully been used to compute the workspace of manipulators, i.e. the space of configurations [19, 92]. For instance one interesting result is the computation of the discrete set of solutions of the well-known Gough-Stewart parallel platform. In this framework there are many geometric constraints, which can be efficiently processed by combinations of consistency techniques and linear relaxations [118]. An important challenge is to compute non-singular trajectories in the workspace. In general, singularities are described by nonlinear constraints and their negations have to be taken into account to keep the allowed regions. Since a trajectory is derived from a connected set of regions, path algorithms can be implemented. Similar techniques have been exploited in biological engineering to determine the structure of proteins [84].

In automatic control there are many interesting problems for constraint-based approaches such as parameter estimation and state estimation [77, 79]. Parameter estimation is the problem of computing the parameters of a given model according to experimental data of the observed system. If the data are associated with an upper bound of the error of measurement then interval constraints can be used to determine the range of the parameters. In this framework the efficiency of interval-based constraint propagation is strongly related to the number of measurements obtained from different sensors. In fact different measurements of the same phenomenon may lead to redundant constraints and consequently to more powerful local consistency reasonings. Another challenge is to cope with invalid data. In this case the constraint satisfaction problem can be relaxed in order to maximize the number of data that fit into the model.

In image synthesis and animation numerical constraints have been used to tackle camera control applications [10, 45]. For instance, given a 3D animated scene, consider the problem of computing a 3D camera trajectory that fulfills a given specification of the final movie, involving for instance time-dependent camera positions, positions of objects on the screen, and relative positions of objects. This general problem involves 3D geometric constraints to be verified in a time interval, which implies the time variable is universally quantified. Since the solution set is huge in general, solutions can be filtered according to objective criteria modeling for instance realistic motions of the camera. More recent work has been focused on characterizing semantic decompositions of the space [20]. Decompositions are computed by geometric techniques based on implicit surfaces and numerical solutions are further derived from decompositions using local and global numerical algorithms.

16.7.2 Software Packages

The interval constraint software packages are based on several components such as an interval arithmetic library, a constraint propagation engine and a search module. This framework is general enough to plug in various techniques such as projection algorithms, numerical operators and even optimization procedures. We describe a few systems in the following.

- The interval arithmetic libraries provide operations and elementary functions on intervals defined by their bounds. The bounds are generally implemented by floating-point numbers. Bound types are defined as parameters in modern libraries like Boost [14] and Gaol [47]. There also exist multi-precision interval packages [58] such as MPFI. A generic interface definition between those libraries and constraint solving procedures like projections has been proposed in [50] but the implementation can be quite inefficient.

- Intlab [114] is a main software achievement of the interval analysis community. Like C-XSC [60], it provides an interval arithmetic library and a collection of interval algorithms derived from real analysis. To our knowledge, constraint programming techniques have not yet been integrated into these packages. Addressing this issue is an important challenge if one wants constraint technology to become a standard tool, in particular in engineering and applied sciences.

- Interval methods are at the core of many constraint programming systems. Two language types are generally distinguished: the constraint language, devoted to numerical constraints, and the host language that can be derived from different programming paradigms such as logic programming and object-oriented programming. CLP(BNR) [105], derived from BNR-Prolog, was the first constraint logic programming system which implemented Cleary's algorithms. The same techniques have been implemented in the object-oriented software ILOG Solver [107]. A cooperative hybrid strategy has been defined in Prolog IV [7], using consistency techniques and linear algebraic algorithms that communicate through fixed variables. More recent tools include Eclipse [128], RealPaver [51], Constraint Explorer [130] and ICOS [87].

- Interval consistency techniques have been shown to be powerful for constrained global optimization. They are particularly useful in the early steps of the search by pruning infeasible regions at a low cost. Numerica [125] was one of the first languages to prove that the approach can be very efficient for actual applications. Its core solving algorithm mainly combines box consistency, a multidimensional interval Newton operator and local optimization algorithms. Consistency techniques have been further implemented in GlobSol [82] and BARON [115]. The former is well-known in the interval community. The latter is a leading mixed integer nonlinear programming software package. In this tool, relaxation techniques are used to compute bounds on the objective function but interval arithmetic is not implemented.

16.8 Conclusion

This chapter is primarily devoted to giving a broad overview on the basics of continuous and interval constraint solving and to showing the main similarities and differences with discrete constraints. Based on the same theoretical framework (fixed point computations over complete lattices) the algorithmic approach differs in taking much of its foundations in numerical analysis when discrete constraints rely on graph theory and integer programming. We have shown how a number of algorithms from interval analysis and the domain reduction-propagation-search cycle from constraint programming can be integrated to tackle non-trivial problems from a variety of domains. These domains extend the number of areas in which constraint programming may have a real technological impact. Finally, interval constraint programming appears to be a promising approach for the integration, in an efficient and flexible way, of continuous optimization and discrete constraint programming. This leads to many promising research tracks like global continuous constraints, mixed integer-real constraints programming and soft interval constraints. Any significant progress in these areas is likely to have important applications in engineering and decision support systems.

Acknowledgements

We are indebted to many researchers with whom we have worked and have had fruitful discussions on continuous and intervals constraints these last years. In particular, we would like to thank wholeheartedly Pedro Barahona, Alexandre Goldsztejn, Luc Jaulin, Michel

Rueher, Peter van Beek and Pascal Van Hentenryck for their careful reading and their numerous remarks on previous versions of this chapter.

Bibliography

[1]   Götz Alefeld and Jürgen Herzberger. *Introduction to Interval Computations*. Academic Press, 1983.

[2]   Krzysztof R. Apt. The Essence of Constraint Propagation. *Theoretical Computer Science*, 221(1-2):179–210, 1999.

[3]   Heikel Batnini, Claude Michel, and Michel Rueher. Mind the Gaps: A New Splitting Strategy for Consistency Techniques. In P. G. Van Beek, editor, *Proceedings of International Conference on Principles and Practice of Constraint Programming* volume 3709 of *Lecture Notes in Computer Science*, pages 77–91. Springer, 2005.

[4]   Frédéric Benhamou and Frédéric Goualard. Universally Quantified Interval Constraints. In R. Dechter, editor, *Proceedings of International Conference on Principles and Practice of Constraint Programming*, volume 1894 of *Lecture Notes in Computer Science*, pages 67–82, Singapore, 2000. Springer.

[5]   Frédéric Benhamou and Laurent Granvilliers. Automatic Generation of Numerical Redundancies for Non-Linear Constraint Solving. *Reliable Computing*, 3(3):335–344, 1997.

[6]   Frédéric Benhamou and William J. Older. Applying Interval Arithmetic to Real, Integer and Boolean Constraints. *Journal of Logic Programming*, 32(1):1–24, 1997.

[7]   Frédéric Benhamou and Touraivane. Prolog IV: Langage et Algorithmes. In J.-J. Chabrier, editor, *Journées Francophones de Programmation en Logique*, pages 51–65, Dijon, France, 1995. Teknea.

[8]   Frédéric Benhamou, David McAllester, and Pascal Van Hentenryck. CLP(Intervals) Revisited. In M. Bruynooghe, editor, *Proceedings of International Symposium on Logic Programming*, pages 124–138, Ithaca, New York, USA, 1994. MIT Press.

[9]   Frédéric Benhamou, Frédéric Goualard, Laurent Granvilliers, and Jean-François Puget. Revising Hull and Box Consistency. In D. De Schreye, editor, *Proceedings of International Conference on Logic Programming*, pages 230–244, Las Cruces, New Mexico, USA, 1999. The MIT Press.

[10]   Frédéric Benhamou, Frédéric Goualard, Eric Languénou, and Marc Christie. Interval Constraint Solving for Camera Control and Motion Planning. *ACM Transactions on Computational Logic*, 5(4):732–767, 2004.

[11]   Martin Berz and Georg Hoffstaetter. Computation and Application of Taylor Polynomials with Interval Remainder Bounds. *Reliable Computing*, 4:83–97, 1998.

[12]   Christian Bliek, Bertrand Neveu, and Gilles Trombettoni. Using Graph Decomposition for Solving Continuous CSPs. In M. J. Maher and J.-F. Puget, editors, *Proceedings of International Conference on Principles and Practice of Constraint Programming*, volume 1520 of *Lecture Notes in Computer Science*, pages 102–116, Pisa, Italy, 1998. Springer.

[13]   Alexander Bockmayr and Volker Weispfenning. *Handbook of Automated Reasoning*, chapter Solving Numerical Constraints, pages 752–842. Elsevier Science Publishers, 2001.

[14]   Hervé Brönnimann, Guillaume Melquiond, and Sylvain Pion. The Boost Interval

Arithmetic Library. *Theoretical Computer Science*, Special Issue on Real Numbers and Computers, 2006. To appear.

[15]   Luitzen Egbertus Jan Brouwer. Über Abbildung von Mannigfaltigkeiten. *Mathematische Annalen*, 71:97–115, 1912.

[16]   Bruno Buchberger. Gröbner Bases: an Algorithmic Method in Polynomial Ideal Theory. In N. K. Bose, editor, *Multidimensional Systems Theory*, pages 184–232. D. Reidel Publishing Company, 1985.

[17]   Ole Caprani and Kaj Madsen. Mean Value Forms in Interval Analysis. *Computing*, 25:147–154, 1980.

[18]   Martine Ceberio and Laurent Granvilliers. Horner's Rule for Interval Evaluation Revisited. *Computing*, 69(1):51–81, 2002.

[19]   Damien Chablat, Philippe Wenger, Félix Majou, and Jean-Pierre Merlet. An Interval Analysis Based Study for the Design and the Comparison of 3-DOF Parallel Kinematic Machines. *International Journal of Robotics Research*, 23(6):615–624, 2004. Forthcoming.

[20]   Marc Christie and Jean-Marie Normand. A Semantic Space Partitionning Approach to Virtual Camera Control. In J. Marks and M. Alexa, editors, *Proceedings of the Annual Eurographics Conference*, volume 24 of *Computer Graphics Forum*, pages 247–256, 2005.

[21]   John G. Cleary. Logical Arithmetic. *Future Computing Systems*, 2(2):125–149, 1987.

[22]   Hélène Collavizza, François Delobel, and Michel Rueher. Extending Consistent Domains of Numeric CSPs. In T. Dean, editor, *Proceedings of International Joint Conference on Artificial Intelligence*, pages 406–413, Stockholm, Sweden, 1999. Morgan Kaufmann.

[23]   Hélène Collavizza, François Delobel, and Michel Rueher. Comparing partial consistencies. *Reliable Computing*, 5(3):213–228, 1999.

[24]   George E. Collins. Quantifier elimination for real closed fields by cylindrical algebraic decomposition. In *Proceedings of the 2nd GI Conference on Automata Theory and Formal Languages*, pages 134–183, London, UK, 1975. Springer-Verlag.

[25]   Georges E. Collins and Hoon Hong. Partial Cylindrical Algebraic Decomposition for Quantifier Elimination. *Journal of Symbolic Computation*, 12:299–328, 1991.

[26]   Alain Colmerauer. An Introduction to Prolog III. *Communications of the ACM*, 33 (7):69–90, 1990.

[27]   Alain Colmerauer. Equations and Inequations on Finite and Infinite Trees. In Institute for New Generation Computer Technology, editor, *Proceedings of International Conference on Fifth Generation Computer Systems*, pages 85–99, Tokyo, Japan, 1984. OHMSHA Ltd. Tokyo and North-Holland.

[28]   Jorge Cruz and Pedro Barahona. Constraint Satisfaction Differential Problems. In Francesca Rossi, editor, *Proceedings of International Conference on Principles and Practice of Constraint Programming*, volume 2833 of *Lecture Notes in Computer Science*, pages 259–273, Kinsale, Ireland, 2003. Springer.

[29]   Jorge Cruz and Pedro Barahona. Global Hull Consistency with Local Search for Continuous Constraint Solving. In P. Brazdil and A. Jorge, editors, *Proceedings of Portuguese Conference on Artificial Intelligence*, volume 2258 of *Lecture Notes in Computer Science*, pages 349–362, Porto, Portugal, 2001. Springer.

[30]   Tibor Csendes and Dietmar Ratz. Subdivision Direction Selection in Interval Math-

ods for Global Optimization. *SIAM Journal on Numerical Analysis*, 34(3):922–938, 1997.

[31] James H. Davenport and Joos Heintz. Real quantifier elimination is doubly exponential. *Journal of Symbolic Computation*, 5:29–35, 1988.

[32] Ernest Davis. Constraint Propagation with Interval Labels. *Artificial Intelligence* 32:281–331, 1987.

[33] Luis H. de Figueiredo and Jorge Stolfi. Adaptive Enumeration of Implicit Surfaces with Affine Arithmetic. *Computer Graphics Forum*, 15(5):287–296, 1996.

[34] Rina Dechter and Judea Pearl. Network-based Heuristics for Constraint Satisfaction Problems. *Artificial Intelligence*, 34:1–38, 1988.

[35] Daniel Diaz and Philippe Codognet. GNU Prolog: Beyond Compiling Prolog to C. In E. Pontelli and V. Santos Costa, editors, *Proceedings of International Workshop on Practical Aspects of Declarative Languages*, volume 1753 of *Lecture Notes in Computer Science*, pages 81–92, Boston, MA, USA, 2000. Springer.

[36] Mehmet Dincbas, Pascal Van Hentenryck, Helmut Simonis, Abderrahmane Aggoun, Thomas Graf, and Françoise Berthier. The constraint logic programming language chip. In Institute for New Generation Computer Technology, editor, *Proceedings of International Conference on Fifth Generation Computer Systems*, pages 693–702, Tokyo, Japan, 1988. OHMSHA Ltd. Tokyo and Springer-Verlag.

[37] Boi Faltings. Arc Consistency for Continuous Variables. *Artificial Intelligence*, 65 (2):363–376, 1994.

[38] Boi Faltings and Esther Gelle. Local Consistency for Ternary Numeric Constraints. In M. E. Pollack, editor, *Proceedings of International Joint Conference on Artificia Intelligence*, pages 392–397, Nagoya, Japan, 1997. Morgan Kaufmann.

[39] Eugene C. Freuder. Synthesizing Constraint Expressions. *Communications of the ACM*, 21(11):958–966, 1978.

[40] Eugene C. Freuder. A sufficient condition for backtrack-free search. *Journal of the ACM*, 29:29–32, 1982.

[41] Andreas Frommer, Bruno Lang, and Marco Schnurr. A Comparison of the Moore and Miranda Existence Tests. *Computing*, 72:349–354, 2004.

[42] Ernest Gardenes, Miguel A. Sainz, Lambert Jorba, Remei Calm, Rosa Estela, Honorino Mielgo, and Albert Trepat. Modal intervals. *Reliable Computing*, 7(2):77–111, 2001.

[43] Jürgen Garloff and Birgit Graf. Solving Strict Polynomial Inequalities by Bernstein Expansion. In N. Munro, editor, *Symbolic Methods in Control System Analysis and Design*, pages 339–352. The Institution of Electrical Engineers, London, 1999.

[44] Esther Gelle and Boi Faltings. Solving Mixed and Conditional Constraint Satisfaction Problems. *Constraints*, 8:107–141, 2003.

[45] Michael Gleicher and Andrew P. Witkin. Through-the-lens Camera Control. In J. J. Thomas, editor, *Proceedings of Annual Conference on Computer Graphics and Interactive Techniques*, pages 331–340, Chicago, IL, USA, 1992. ACM.

[46] Alexandre Goldsztejn. *Définition et Applications des Extensions des Fonctions Réelles aux Intervalles Généralisés: Nouvelle Formulation de la Théorie des Intervalles Modaux et Nouveaux Résultats*. PhD thesis, Université de Nice, 2005. In French.

[47] Frédéric Goualard. *Gaol: NOT Just Another Interval Library*. University of Nantes, France, 2005. http://sourceforge.net/projects/gaol/.

[48] Frédéric Goualard. On Considering an Interval Constraint Solving Algorithm as a Free-steering Nonlinear Gauss-Seidel Procedure. In A. Omicini and R. L. Wainwright, editors, *Proceedings of ACM Symposium of Applied Computing*, pages 31434–1438, Santa Fe, New Mexico, USA, 2005. ACM Press.

[49] Frédéric Goualard and Laurent Granvilliers. Controlled Propagation in Continuous Numerical Constraint Networks. In A. Omicini and R. L. Wainwright, editors, *Proceedings of ACM Symposium of Applied Computing*, pages 377–382, Santa Fe, New Mexico, USA, 2005. ACM Press.

[50] Laurent Granvilliers. An Interval Component for Continuous Constraints. *Journal of Computational and Applied Mathematics*, 162(1):79–92, 2004.

[51] Laurent Granvilliers. On the Combination of Interval Constraint Solvers. *Reliable Computing*, 7(6):467–483, 2001.

[52] Laurent Granvilliers and Frédéric Benhamou. Progress in the Solving of a Circuit Design Problem. *Journal of Global Optimization*, 20(2):155–168, 2001.

[53] Laurent Granvilliers and Gaétan Hains. A Conservative Scheme for Parallel Interval Narrowing. *Information Processing Letters*, 74:141–146, 2000.

[54] Laurent Granvilliers and Eric Monfroy. Implementing Constraint Propagation by Composition of Reductions. In C. Palamidessi, editor, *Proceedings of International Conference on Logic Programming*, volume 2916 of *Lecture Notes in Computer Science*, pages 300–314, Mumbai, India, 2003. Springer.

[55] Laurent Granvilliers and Mina Ouabiba. Combination of Nonlinear Terms in Interval Constraint Satisfaction Techniques. In B. Buchberger and J. A. Campbell, editors, *Proceedings of International Conference on Artificial Intelligence and Symbolic Computation*, volume 3249 of *Lecture Notes in Computer Science*, pages 118–131, Linz, Austria, 2004. Springer.

[56] Laurent Granvilliers, Frédéric Goualard, and Frédéric Benhamou. Box Consistency through Weak Box Consistency. In W. Meng, editor, *Proceedings of IEEE Conference on Tools with Artificial Intelligence*, pages 373–380, Chicago, USA, 1999. IEEE Computer Society.

[57] Laurent Granvilliers, Eric Monfroy, and Frédéric Benhamou. Symbolic-Interval Cooperation in Constraint Programming. In G. Villard, editor, *Proceedings of International Symposium on Symbolic and Algebraic Computation*, pages 150–166, London, Ontario, Canada, 2001. ACM Press.

[58] Markus Grimmer, Knut Petras, and Nathalie Revol. Multiple Precision Interval Packages: Comparing Different Approaches. In R. Alt, A. Frommer, R. B. Kearfott, and W. Luther, editors, *Numerical Software with Result Verification*, volume 2991 of *Lecture Notes in Computer Science*, pages 64–90. Springer, 2004.

[59] SIGLA/X Group. Modal Intervals. In *Proceedings of Workshop on Applications of Interval Analysis to Systems and Control*, pages 139–207, 1999.

[60] Rolf Hammer, Matthias Hocks, Ulrich Kulisch, and Dietmar Ratz. *C++ Toolbox for Verified Computing*. Springer-Verlag, 1995.

[61] Eldon Robert Hansen. *Global Optimization using Interval Analysis*. Marcel Dekker, 1992.

[62] Eldon Robert Hansen. Interval Arithmetic in Matrix Computations. *SIAM Journal of Numerical Analysis*, 2:308–320, 1965.

[63] Eldon Robert Hansen and Saumyendra Sengupta. Bounding Solutions of Systems of Equations using Interval Analysis. *BIT*, 21(2):203–211, 1981.

[64]   Timothy J. Hickey, Qu Ju, and Maarten H. van Emden. Interval Arithmetic: From
       Principles to Implementation. *Journal of the ACM*, 48(5):1038–1068, 2001.
[65]   Hoon Hong and Volker Stahl. Bernstein Form is Inclusion Monotone. *Computing*
       55:43–53, 1995.
[66]   Hiroshi Hosobe. A Modular Geometric Constraint Solver for User Interface Ap-
       plications. In B. Mynatt, editor, *Proceedings of Annual ACM Symposium on User
       Interface Software and Technology*, pages 91–100, Orlando, Florida, USA, 2001.
       ACM.
[67]   Eero Hyvönen. Constraint Reasoning based on Interval Arithmetic. The Tolerance
       Propagation Approach. *Artificial Intelligence*, 58:71–112, 1992.
[68]   Eero Hyvönen. Constraint Reasoning Based on Interval Arithmetic. In N. S. Sridha-
       ran, editor, *Proceedings of International Joint Conference on Artificial Intelligence*
       pages 1193–1198, Detroit, MI, USA, 1989. Morgan Kaufmann.
[69]   IEEE. *IEEE Standard for Binary Floating-Point Arithmetic*. Institute of Electrical
       and Electronics Engineers, 1985. IEEE Std 754-1985, Reaffirmed 1990.
[70]   Joxan Jaffar and Jean-Louis Lassez. Constraint Logic Programming. In M. J.
       O'Donnell, editor, *Proceedings of ACM Symposium on Principles of Programming
       Languages*, pages 111–119, Munich, Germany, 1987. ACM Press.
[71]   Joxan Jaffar and Michael Maher. Constraint Logic Programming: A Survey. *Journal
       of Logic Programming*, 19–20:503–581, 1994.
[72]   Joxan Jaffar, Spiro Michaylov, Peter Stuckey, and Roland Yap. The CLP($\Re$) lan-
       guage and system. *ACM Transactions on Programming Languages and Systems*, 14
       (3):339–395, 1992.
[73]   Micha Janssen, Pascal Van Hentenryck, and Yves Deville. A Constraint Satisfaction
       Approach for Enclosing Solutions to Parametric Ordinary Differential Equations.
       SIAM Journal on Numerical Analysis, 40(5):1896–1939, 2002.
[74]   Christian Jansson. Rigorous Lower and Upper Bounds in Linear Programming.
       SIAM Journal on Optimization, 14(3):914–935, 2004.
[75]   Christian Jansson and Siegfried M. Rump. Rigorous Solution of Linear Program-
       ming Problems with Uncertain Data. *Methods and Models of Operations Research*
       35:87–111, 1991.
[76]   Frank Jardillier and Eric Languénou. Screen-space constraints for camera move-
       ments: the virtual cameraman. *Computer Graphics Forum*, 17(3):175–186, 1998.
[77]   Luc Jaulin and Eric Walter. Set Inversion via Interval Analysis for Nonlinear
       Bounded-Error Estimation. *Automatica*, 29(4):1053–1064, 1993.
[78]   Luc Jaulin and Eric Walter. Guaranteed tuning, with application to robust control
       and motion planning. *Automatica*, 32(9):1217–1221, 1996.
[79]   Luc Jaulin, Michel Kieffer, Olivier Didrit, and Eric Walter. *Applied Interval
       Analysis: With Examples in Parameter and State Estimation, Robust Control and
       Robotics*. Springer, 2001.
[80]   William Kahan. A More Complete Interval Arithmetic. Technical report, University
       of Toronto, Canada, 1968.
[81]   Edgar W. Kaucher. Interval Analysis in the Extended Interval Space IR. *Computing
       Supplementum*, 2:33–49, 1980.
[82]   Ralf Baker Kearfott. *Rigorous Global Search: Continuous Problems*. Nonconvex
       Optimization and Its Applications. Kluwer Academic Publishers, 1996.
[83]   Rudolf Krawczyk.   Newton-Algorithmen zur Bestimmung von Nullstellen mit

Fehlerschranken. *Computing*, 4:187–201, 1969.

[84] Ludwig Krippahl and Pedro Barahona. Applying Constraint Programming to Protein Structure Determination. In J. Jaffar, editor, *Proceedings of International Conference on Principles and Practice of Constraint Programming*, volume 1713 of *Lecture Notes in Computer Science*, pages 289–302, Alexandria, Virginia, USA, 1999. Springer.

[85] François Laburthe and the OCRE project team. CHOCO: implementing a CP kernel. In *Proceedings of International Workshop on Techniques for Implementing Constraint Programming Systems*, 2000.

[86] Yahia Lebbah and Olivier Lhomme. Accelerating Filtering Techniques for Numeric CSPs. *Artificial Intelligence*, 139(1):109–132, 2002.

[87] Yahia Lebbah, Claude Michel, Michel Rueher, David Daney, and Jean-Pierre Merlet. Efficient and Safe Global Constraints for handling Numerical Constraint Systems. *SIAM Journal on Numerical Analysis*, 42(5):2076–2097, 2005.

[88] Olivier Lhomme. Consistency Techniques for Numeric CSPs. In R. Bajcsy, editor, *Proceedings of International Joint Conference on Artificial Intelligence*, pages 232–238, Chambéry, France, 1993. Morgan Kaufmann.

[89] Olivier Lhomme, Arnaud Gotlieb, and Michel Rueher. Dynamic Optimization of Interval Narrowing Algorithms. *Journal of Logic Programming*, 37(1–2):165–183, 1998.

[90] Alan K. Mackworth. Consistency in Networks of Relations. *Artificial Intelligence*, 8(1):99–118, 1977.

[91] Philippe Marti and Michel Rueher. A Distributed Cooperating Constraints Solving System. *International Journal on Artificial Intelligence Tools*, 4(1-2):93–113, 1995.

[92] Jean-Pierre Merlet. Solving the Forward Kinematics of a Gough-type Parallel Manipulator with Interval Analysis. *International Journal of Robotics Research*, 23(3): 221–236, 2004.

[93] Frédéric Messine. Extensions of Affine Arithmetic: Application to Global Optimization. *Journal of Universal Computer Science*, 8(11):992–1015, 2002.

[94] C. Miranda. Un'osservatione su un teorema di Brouwer. *Boll. Un. Mat. Ital.*, 3(2): 5–7, 1940.

[95] Eric Monfroy, Michael Rusinowitch, and René Schott. Implementing Non-Linear Constraints with Cooperative Solvers. In K. M. George, J. H. Carroll, D. Oppenheim, and J. Hightower, editors, *Proceedings of ACM Symposium on Applied Computing*, pages 63–72, Philadelphia, PA, USA, 1996. ACM Press.

[96] Ugo Montanari. Networks of Constraints: Fundamental Properties and Applications to Picture Processing. *Information Science*, 7(2):95–132, 1974.

[97] Ugo Montanari and Francesca Rossi. Constraint Relaxation may be Perfect. *Artificial Intelligence*, 48(2):143–170, 1991.

[98] Ramon Edgar Moore. *Interval Analysis*. Prentice-Hall, Englewood Cliffs, NJ, 1966.

[99] Jean-Michel Muller. *Elementary Functions: Algorithms and Implementation*. Birkhäuser, 1997.

[100] Alexander S. Narin'yani. Subdefinite Models and Operations with Subdefinite Values. *Preprint, USSR academy of sciences, Siberian Division*, 400, 1982.

[101] Arnold Neumaier. *Interval Methods for Systems of Equations*. Cambridge University Press, 1990.

[102] Arnold Neumaier and Oleg Scherbina. Safe Bounds in Linear and Mixed-Integer

Programming. *Mathematical Programming A*, 99:283–296, 2004.

[103] Karl Nickel. On the Newton Method in Interval Analysis. MRC Report 1136, Mathematics Research Center, University of Wisconsin, Madison, 1971.

[104] William J. Older. Application of relational interval arithmetic to ordinary differential equations. In *Proceedings of the first Workshop on Constraint Languages and their Use in Problem Modelling*, pages 60–69, Ithaca, New York, 1994.

[105] William J. Older and André Vellino. Extending Prolog with Constraint Arithmetic on Real Intervals. In *Proceedings of IEEE Canadian Conference on Electrical and Computer Engineering*, New York, 1990. IEEE Computer Society Press.

[106] Barry O'Sullivan. *Constraint-Aided Conceptual Design*. PhD thesis, University College Cork, 1999.

[107] Jean-François Puget and Michel Leconte. Beyond the Glass Box: Constraints as Objects. In J. W. Lloyd, editor, *Proceedings of International Symposium of Logic Programming*, pages 513–527, Portland, USA, 1995. MIT Press.

[108] Jean-François Puget and Pascal Van Hentenryck. A Constraint Satisfaction Approach to a Circuit Design Problem. *Journal of Global Optimization*, 13(1):75–93, 1998.

[109] Stephan Ratschan. Approximate Quantified Constraint Solving by Cylindrical Box Decomposition. *Reliable Computing*, 8(1):21–42, 2002.

[110] Helmut Ratschek and Jon Rokne. About the Centered Form. *SIAM Journal of Numerical Analysis*, 17(3):333–337, 1980.

[111] David Richardson. Some Unsolvable Problems Involving Elementary Functions of a Real Variable. *Journal of Symbolic Logic*, 33:514–520, 1968.

[112] Jiri Rohn. Enclosing Solutions of Linear Interval Equations is NP-hard. *Computing* 53:365–368, 1994.

[113] Jiri Rohn, Siegfried M. Rump, and Tetsuro Yamamoto, editors. *Linear Algebra in Self-Validating Methods*, volume 324 of *Linear Algebra and its Applications* Elsevier Science, 2001.

[114] Siegfried M. Rump. *Developments in Reliable Computing*, chapter INTLAB - INTerval LABoratory, pages 77–104. Kluwer Academic Publishers, 1999.

[115] Nikolaos V. Sahinidis. BARON: A General Purpose Global Optimization Software Package. *Journal of Global Optimization*, 8(2):201–205, 1996.

[116] Miguel Sainz, Pau Herrero, Joaquim Armengol, and Joseph Vehi. An extended interval inclusion test for proving first order logic formulas over the reals. Technical report, Universitat de Girona, 2005.

[117] Djamila Sam-Haroud and Boi Faltings. Consistency Techniques for Continuous Constraints. *Constraints*, 1:85–118, 1996.

[118] Hanif D. Sherali and Warren P. Adams. *A Reformulation-Linearization Technique for Solving Discrete and Continuous Nonconvex Problems*. Kluwer Academic Publishers, Dordrecht/Boston/London, 1999.

[119] Josef Stoer and Roland Bulirsch. *Introduction to Numerical Analysis*. Springer, 1991.

[120] Alfred Tarski. *A decision method for elementary algebra and geometry*. Univ. of California Press, 1951.

[121] Mohit Tawarmalani and Nikolaos V. Sahinidis. Global Optimization of Mixed-Integer NonLinear Programs: A Theoretical and Computational Study. *Mathematical Programming A*, 99(3):563–591, 2004.

[122] Vitaly Telerman and Dmitry Ushakov. Subdefinite Models as a Variety of Constraint Programming. In B. Manaris and P. Marquis, editors, *Proceedings of International Conference on Tools with Artificial Intelligence*, pages 157–164, Toulouse, France, 1996. IEEE Computer Society.

[123] Pascal Van Hentenryck. *Constraint Satisfaction in Logic Programming*. Logic Programming Series. MIT Press, Cambridge, MA, 1989.

[124] Pascal Van Hentenryck, David McAllester, and Deepak Kapur. Solving Polynomial Systems Using a Branch and Prune Approach. *SIAM Journal of Numerical Analysis*, 34(2):797–827, 1997.

[125] Pascal Van Hentenryck, Laurent Michel, and Yves Deville. *Numerica: a Modeling Language for Global Optimization*. MIT Press, 1997.

[126] Pau Herrero Vinas, Miguek A. Sainz, Josep Vehi, and Luc Jaulin. Quantified Set Inversion Algorithm with Applications to Control. *Reliable Computing*, 11(5):369–382, 2005.

[127] Xuan-Ha Vu, Djamila Sam-Haroud, and Marius-Calin Silaghi. Approximation Techniques for Nonlinear Problems with Continuum of Solutions. In S. Koenig and R. C. Holte, editors, *Proceedings of International Symposium on Abstraction, Reformulation and Approximation*, volume 2371 of *Lecture Notes in Computer Science*, pages 224–241. Springer, 2002.

[128] Marc Wallace, Stefano Novello, and Joachim Schimpf. ECLiPSe : A Platform for Constraint Logic Programming. *ICL Systems Journal*, 12(1):159–200, 1997.

[129] David L. Waltz. Generating Semantic Descriptions from Drawings of Scenes with Shadows. In P. H. Winston, editor, *The Psychology of Computer Vision*. McGraw Hill, 1975.

[130] Laurent Zimmer, Alexis Anglada, Marc Christie, and Laurent Granvilliers. Constraint Explorer: a Modelling and Sizing Tool for Engineering Design. In *Proceedings of World Multi-Conference on Systemics, Cybernetics and Informatics*, Orlando, USA, 2004.

Handbook of Constraint Programming
Edited by F. Rossi, P. van Beek and T. Walsh
© 2006 Elsevier B.V. All rights reserved

Chapter 17

Constraints over Structured Domains

Carmen Gervet

*The computer will be the most marvellous
of all tools as soon as program writing and
debugging will be no longer necessary*
—Jean-Louis Laurière (1976)

A wide range of combinatorial search problems find a natural formulation in the language of sets, multisets, strings, functions, graphs or other structured objects. Bin-packing, set partitioning, set covering, combinatorial design problems, circuits and mapping problems are some of them. They are NP-complete problems originating from areas as diverse as combinatorial mathematics, operations research or artificial intelligence. These problems deal essentially with the search for discrete structured objects. While a high-level modeling approach seems more natural, many solutions have exploited the effectiveness of finite domains or mixed integer programming solvers. In this chapter we present higher level modeling facilities utilizing constraints over structured domains.

What is a structured object? Let us consider the example of a bin-packing problem. The main constrained objects are the different bins, each describing a collection of unordered distinct elements, subject to disjointness constraints among them, weight constraints reflecting on each bin capacity and possible cardinality restrictions on the number of items allowed in each bin. Informally, such objects are structured in the sense that they involve more than one element *in a specific setting*.

When Fikes introduced the notion of finite domain in 1970 [31], the idea was to approximate the range of an unknown integer (an integer variable) and to prune inconsistent values from such a domain that cannot belong to any solution. Already in the description of the language REF-ARF, Fikes proposed directions for future work such as: *"considering the addition to the program of capabilities for handling unordered sets"*. Mid-eighties the seminal work of Van Hentenryck et al. integrated consistency techniques over finite integer domains into logic programming [90], and gave birth to the first finite domain constraint logic programming language CHIP (Constraint Handling In Prolog) [23], leading to a new generation of academic and industrial constraint programming systems. The successes of CHIP and its peers also raised the questions of the languages limitations. While Finite Domain (FD) solvers grew in efficiency, it remained that models lacked generic and natural formulations when representing structured objects, making the programming effort more cumbersome and sometimes ad-hoc.

As an example, let us consider the structured object, "set", constrained to be subset of a known base set. A finite domain approach would consider two possible representations:

- a list of FD variables taking their value from a finite set of integers that represents the base set. This approach requires the removal of order and multiplicity among the elements of the list, which is achieved by adding ordering constraints. For example the list $[X_1, X_2, X_3] :: [0..5], X_1 < X_2 < X_3$ represents a set of 3 elements subset of the set $\{0, 1, 2, 3, 4, 5\}$. If the size of the set is unknown some dummy FD variables are also necessary. Clearly this does not make easy the modeling of additional set constraints such as intersection, or union.

- a list of 0-1 FD variables. This second formulation is equivalent to the semantics of a finite set subset of a known set. It uses 0-1 variables, and originates from 0-1 Integer Programming (ILP). Basically, this approach exploits the one-to-one correspondence that exists between a subset s of a known set S and a Boolean algebra. The correspondence is defined by the characteristic function:

$$f : y_i \rightarrow \{0, 1\} \quad f(y_i) = 1 \text{ iff } i \in s$$

In other words, a 0-1 variable is associated with each element in the base set S and takes the value 1 if and only if the element belongs to the unknown set s. Set constraints are then simply represented within the Boolean algebra with arithmetic operators. The main drawback of this representation is that it looses the semantics and structure of the problem addressed. Operationally it can benefit from global reasoning from mathematical programming, but in a constraint programming environment lacks conciseness and does not best exploit the problem structure. We give further on some comparisons between 0-1 and set models.

Approach. This chapter is not intended to give a complete coverage of all results available in softwares and systems that embed constraints over structured domains. Instead we try to cover a number of significant research topics in more detail. This should give a context and picture for the research and its methodology, provide the most important references, and enable the reader to study research papers on the topic.

17.1 History and Applications

Before the research field of "constraint programming" even existed, the seminal work of Laurière in 1976 proposes constrained structured objects in the design and development of ALICE [61]. Laurière's idea was to combine generality and efficiency in addressing combinatorial problems. He defines an input language, purely descriptive, with high level objects such as functions and relations between two known sets, constrained by some properties, such as injection and bijection. ALICE was a pioneer in the use of structured objects to model combinatorial problems.

In a parallel line of research, most proposals to extend constraint reasoning over new structured domains came as extensions of the logic programming system, Prolog. Logic programming is a powerful programming framework which enables the user to state non-deterministic programs in relational form [56, 20]. The extension to Constraint Logic Programming (CLP) combines the positive features of logic programming with constraint solving techniques, where the concept of constraint solving replaces the unification procedure in logic programming and provides, among others, a uniform framework for handling new structured domains. Previous chapters have presented in depth the state of the art in the precursors constraint domains (rationals, Boolean algebra, finite integer domains, real intervals). This chapter is interested in discrete and structured domains such as strings, finite sets in different forms, relations, maps and graphs.

In 1989 Walinsky presented CLP(Σ^*), an instance of the CLP scheme over the computation domain of strings, represented as regular sets [92]. The practical motivation was to incorporate strings into logic programming to strengthen the standard string-handling features (e.g. concat, substring). It constitutes the first attempt to compute regular sets by means of constraints like the membership relation. For example A in (X.''ab''.Y) states that any string assigned to variable A must contain the substring ab. This approach was further developed by Golden and Pang in 2003 [42] even though they did not seem aware of Walinsky's work. Their main contribution is to use finite automata to represent regular sets. Both approaches consider possibly infinite sets of strings. More recently Pesant proposed a global constraint on a fixed length sequence of finite domain variables with application to rostering and car sequencing problems [74].

The most widely studied structured domain is most definitely that of sets. The motivations to embed sets in constraint based languages are quite diverse and address different issues ranging from program analysis, software prototyping and specification, set theory axiomatization and combinatorial problem solving. The terminology of "set constraints" is worth a few words even though it does not relate directly to constraint satisfaction problems. Heintze and Jaffar [46] coined the term of set constraints in 1990 to handle a class of sets of trees (possibly infinite) and to deal with relations of the form $s_1 \subseteq s_2$ where s_1 and s_2 denote specific set expressions, possibly recursive, defined over trees. This line of research applies to program analysis systems ([6, 2] among others) which was pioneered by John Reynolds in 1969 [81]. Besides the terminology of set constraints, these systems do not relate to constraint programming over a specific computation domain, as they do not interpret set operations but rather show the expressiveness of "set constraints" for the analysis of programs developed in logic or functional programming. For further information, please refer to survey articles such as [72].

Ironically it was about the same time that the notion of *finite sets* was embedded as a high level programming abstraction in logic-based and then constraint (logic) based languages, in quite a different setting. We refer to the term set to denote a finite set. A set is basically a collection of distinct elements commonly described by $\{x_1, ..., x_n\}$. The use of a logic-based language as the underlying framework came from proposals in database query languages where the aim was to strengthen typical existing set facilities of languages like Prolog (e.g. setof, bagof) to handle sets of terms and complex data structures. In this line of work sets have been embedded in [10, 57, 87, 25]. All these languages converge on one aspect: representing a set variable by a set constructor so as to nest objects in a natural manner. This constructor is specified either by an extensional representation $\{x_1, ..., x_n\}$ ([10, 57]) or by an iterative one $\{x\} \cup E$ where E can be unified with a set of terms containing possibly set variables (concept of sets of finite depth, or hereditarily finite sets in $\{\log \}$ [25], CLPS [63], and [89]).

Even though these languages use constraints to reason upon sets, they do face the NP-completeness of the equality relation over constructed sets (as a particular case of Associative, Commutative and Idempotent (ACI) relation [65]). The main reason is the absence of a unique most general unifier when unifying constructed sets. For example, the equality $\{X, Y\} = \{3, 4\}$ derives two solution sets: $\{X = 3, Y = 4\}$ and $\{X = 4, Y = 3\}$ neither of which is more general than the other. This means that the satisfaction of the ACI axioms, introduces nondeterminism in the unification procedure by deriving disjunctions of a finite number of equalities.

While such approaches did not offer a practical solution to set unification they were not essentially motivated by effective solving of combinatorial problems. In 1992, a new class of finite set constraint solvers was designed to expand the modeling facilities of finite domain solvers when tackling set-based combinatorial search problems (e.g. bin packing, set partitioning, combinatorial designs or more recently network design). The idea was developed independently by Puget [75, 76], and Gervet [37, 38]. The objective was to propose a high-level modeling language which enabled us to model a set-based combinatorial problem as a set domain CSP – where set variables range over set intervals – and which tackled set constraints by using consistency techniques. A set domain is a collection of known sets of arbitrary elements like $\{\{1, 2\}, \{1, 4\}, \{1, 5\}\}$. It is specified by a set interval, $[\{1\}, \{1, 2, 4, 5\}]$, where the lower bound contains the *definite* elements of the set, and the upper bound extends it with possible elements. Gervet formalized the concepts and ideas when presenting the `Conjunto` language in [39, 40]. Though implementation details vary, at their core the set constraint solvers of `solver` [77], ECL^iPS^e[86], `MOZART-OZ` [67, 69], `FACILE` [7], `B-Prolog` [94], `CHOCO` [58], all have the subset bounds as domain representation. The availability of all these solvers both in academia and industry, has enabled the design of new models and solutions to problems from combinatorial mathematics [8], VLSI circuit verification and warehouse location [3], as well as network design problems (e.g. weight setting [29], SONET [88, 85]).

However, it has also raised the question of the limitations of the core `Conjunto`-like set interval solver, leading to further research in this area. Research advances in finite set solvers include: i) the extension of the core subset bound solver with new inferences relative to the set cardinality constraint (mainly described in `Cardinal` [3] and `OZ` [68]), ii) the development of global set constraint propagators, iii) the search for more expressive set domain representations.

Regarding global set constraints propagators, Sadler and Gervet investigated the case of n-ary constraints on fixed cardinality sets such as `atmost1`, `distinct`, stating respectively that n sets of known cardinality should intersect pairwise in atmost one element, or not be equal [82]. This first attempt was followed by challenging results both theoretically and algorithmically. Walsh in [93] addresses the question of whether such global constraints could infer anything more than their decompositions and with Bessière et al. started a systematic investigation of determining the tractability of a range of global set constraints [14]. New global propagators were presented for the `disjoint` and `partition` constraints for sets of known cardinality, independently by Sadler and Gervet in [83] and Bessière et al. in [13]. Such constraints have been present in Ilog `SOLVER` with similar algorithms [50].

Regarding the effectiveness of finite set intervals, Lagoon and Stuckey propose in [60] a radically different approach to the standard subset domain bounds. They show that Reduced Ordered Binary Decision Diagrams (ROBDDs) can be used to represent full domains efficiently. The same year, the set interval representation was also reconsidered by Sadler and Gervet in [84] in order to make better use of the cardinality information and break set symmetries in problems such as combinatorial designs [85]. They define a hybrid set domain whereby the conventional subset domain is enriched with a lexicographic domain that shows to better exploit the cardinality information and symmetry breaking constraints. As this chapter was compiled, Gervet and Van Hentenryck proposed a length-lex representation of set domains that encodes directly cardinality and lexicographic information, and shows promise in reaching powerful and cost effective pruning [41].

Other structured objects have been considered to expand the modeling facilities of finite domain constraints. Multisets (sets where an element may occur more than once), commonly referred to as *bags*, have been embedded in few constraint languages and seem an adequate choice of model for template design problems [54]. Existing approaches to multiset reasoning make use of constructors or domains. For example `CLPS` uses multiset constructors while `SOLVER` uses multiset domains. In [93], Walsh formalizes the idea of multiset domains and discusses the expressiveness of different domain representations. Quimper and Walsh also recently proposed in [78] to use efficient enumeration procedures (see Knuth [55]) to extend the use of some global constraint on large domains over sets, but also tuples represented as lists of integer variables.

Finally, higher level structured domains have recently been re-discovered (graph and map variables) or proposed (ontologies, lattices). The proposals follow two main trends: i) high level constructors that are part of a specification or modelling language compiled into an executable code such as the works of Flener et al. [32] leading to the modeling language `ASRA` [32], and the PhD thesis of Hnich in $\mathcal{L}$ [48], ii) high level computation domains to reason with and about relations and graphs as in `Conjunto`[39], `CP(Graph)` [24], and `CP(Graph + Map)` [22], and order-sorted domains introduced by Caseau and Puget [17], as well as ontology domains introduced by Laburthe [59]. Fernández and Hill generalized all interval reasoning approaches over structured domains that are lattices into a single framework, deriving the $clp(\mathcal{L})$ language [30].

17.2 Constraints over Regular and Constructed Sets

Most of the recent proposals (late eighties) to embed strings or constructed sets as a high level programming abstraction aim at extending a logic-based language and thus assume such a language as the underlying framework. In this section we review the major approaches which embed strings and constructed sets in constraint programming.

17.2.1 Regular Sets

CLP(Σ^*). This language represents an instance of the CLP scheme over the computation domain of regular sets[92]. A regular set is a finite set composed of strings which are generated from a finite alphabet Σ. CLP(Σ^*) has been designed and implemented to provide a logic-based formalism for incorporating strings into logic programming in a more expressive manner than the standard string-handling features (eg. `concat`, `substring`). A CLP(Σ^*) program is a Prolog program enriched with regular set terms and built-in constraints.

Operations on regular sets comprise concatenation $R_1.R_2$, disjunction or union $R_1 +$ R_2 (i.e., $R_1 \cup R_2$) and the closure operator R_1^* which describes the least set R' such that $R' = \epsilon + (R', R_1)$. These operations allow us to build any regular expression when combined with the identity elements under concatenation (1) and union ($\emptyset$). This language provides an atomic constraint over set expressions which is the membership constraint of the form x in e where x is either a variable or a string and e is a regular expression. For example A in $(X."ab".Y)$ states that any string assigned to variable A must contain the substring ab.

The satisfiability of membership constraints over regular sets clearly poses the problem of termination. In the above example, if Y is a free variable there is an infinite number of instances for A. The solver guarantees termination by: (i) applying a scheduling strategy which selects the constraints capable of generating a finite number of instances, (ii) applying a satisfiability procedure based on deduction rules which check and transform the selected atomic constraints. The non selected ones are simply floundered.

The selected constraints x in e are such that either e is a string or e is a variable and x string. The conditional deduction rules over each of these constraints infer a new constraint or a simplified one if a given condition is satisfied. Each condition represents a possible form of selected set constraints.

As an example, the following rules describe the derivation of concatenated expressions under idempotent substitutions:

$$\frac{\left(\begin{array}{c} w = w_1.w_2 \\ \sigma_1 \vdash "w_1'' \text{ in } e_1 \\ \sigma_2 \vdash "w_2'' \text{ in } e_2 \end{array} \right)}{\sigma_1 \cup \sigma_2 \vdash "w'' \text{ in } e_1.e_2} \quad \text{and} \quad \frac{\left(\begin{array}{c} \sigma_1 \vdash X_1 \text{ in } e_1 \\ \sigma_2 \vdash X_2 \text{ in } e_2 \end{array} \right)}{[X = (X_1\sigma_1).(X_2\sigma_2)] \vdash X \text{ in } e_1.e_2}$$

The σ_i are idempotent substitutions, which means that given two substitutions σ_1 and σ_2, $\sigma_1 \cup \sigma_2$ produces the most general idempotent substitution if one exists that is more specific than the two previous ones.

Soundness and completeness of the deduction rules are guaranteed only if there are no variables within the scope of any closure expression e^* in addition to the criteria of constraint selection. This approach constitutes a first attempt to compute regular sets by means of constraints like the membership relation. The complexity of the satisfiability procedure is not given, but infinite computations are avoided thanks to the use of floundering.

Regular sets and finite automata.   The key challenges when reasoning about string constraints effectively are 1) to represent infinite string sets without actually requiring infinite space, and 2) to enforce constraints over infinite string sets without exhaustively listing the consistent values [42]. To do so one would use regular languages, i.e. sets of strings accepted by regular expressions or finite automata, which are widely used for instance in string matching or lexical analysis.

Constraints over the string variables extend the ones presented in CLP(Σ^*) with constraints on the length of a string length. Two different representations of regular languages are used: regular expressions and finite automata (FAs) [49]. Regular expressions that represent a regular language over an alphabet Σ, are used as input and are converted to FAs, which are used computationally. This system has been used within a constraint based planner for NASA. The solver performs set operations on Finite Automata to prune the string domains and reach a consistent state. All of the set operations and string constraints are either linear or quadratic in the size of the FAs representing the string domain. However, the FA can grow exponentially with the number of operations, i.e. the number of constraints that contain the variable whose domain is represented by the FA. Ultimately how the FA grows will depend on the nature of the problem at hand.

Such languages allow variables to range over an infinite set of strings. This is suitable for their motivational problems but is not a requirement in all application domains involving strings.

The use of membership constraints for sequences of finite domain variables also exists in the constraint programming literature to address in particular combinatorial search problems such as rostering and car sequencing. The objective is usually to identify or enforce patterns of values, specified over finite domain variables. The approaches are commonly embedded as global constraints with associated propagator. We refer the reader to the `sequence` constraint (constrains the number of times a certain pattern of length l appears in a sequence of variables) introduced in [80], solver's `IlcTableConstraint` [50] (takes a sequence of n finite-domain variables and a set of n-tuples representing the valid assignments of values to these variables), or the more recent `regular(x,M)` constraint [74]. This constraint is a regular language membership constraint that constrains "any sequence of values taken by the finite domain variables of x to belong to the regular language recognized by M". It reasons upon strings of the regular language that have a given length n which is powerful enough for its purpose.

The embedding and use of regular sets in constraint (logic) programming has a clear diversity from enhancing the string manipulation of Prolog to enforcing patterns of values in combinatorial search problems.

17.2.2 Constraints over Constructed Sets

The first steps towards embedding sets in constraint programming first assumed a logic-based language as the underlying framework. This follows from the declarative nature of logic programming, which well combines with set constructs, and its nondeterminism which is suited to stating set-based programs. The presented languages are the main ones relating to constraint reasoning. More literature exists relating solely to logic programming.

{log} and CLP($\mathcal{SET}$). {log} [25, 26, 27] has been designed and implemented mainly for theorem proving. Consequently, it embeds an axiomatized set theory whose properties guarantee soundness and completeness of the language.

Set terms are constructed using the interpreted functors `with` and `{}`, e.g. $\emptyset$ `with` x `with` ($\emptyset$ `with` y `with` z) = $\{\{z,y\},x\}$. The language includes a limited collection of predicates ($\in, =, \neq, \notin$) as set constraints. The axiomatized set theory consists of a set of axioms which describe the behaviour of the constructor `with`. For example the *extensionality axiom* shows how to decide if two sets can be considered equal:

v `with` $x = w$ `with` $y \rightarrow$
$\qquad (x = y \wedge v = w) \vee (x = y \wedge v$ `with` $x = w) \vee$
$\qquad (x = y \wedge v = w$ `with` $y) \vee \exists z \, (v = z$ `with` $y \wedge w = z$ `with` $x)$

Using the axioms, a set of properties are derived describing the permutativity (right associativity) and absorption of the `with` constructor. For example, the permutativity property is depicted by:

$(x$ `with` $y)$ `with` $z = (x$ `with` $z)$ `with` y (permutativity)

The complete solver consists of a constraint simplification algorithm defined by a set of derivation rules with respect to each primitive constraint. A derivation rule for the equality constraint is, for example:

h `with` $\{t_n, ..., t_0\} = k$ `with` $\{s_m, ..., s_o\}$

If h and k are not the same variables then select non-deterministically one action among a set of possible substitutions (minimal set of unifiers). The nondeterministic satisfaction procedure of constructed sets reduces a given constraint to a collection of constraints in a suitable form by introducing choice points in the constraint graph itself. This leads to a hidden exponential growth in the search tree. In this approach, completeness of the solver is required if one aims at performing theorem proving. Thus, there is no possible compromise here between completeness and efficiency. The soundness and completeness of its solver allow us to use it for theorem proving and problem specification.

$\{\log\}$ has been revisited from a LP to a CLP framework in order to provide a uniform framework for the handling of set constraints $(\in, =, \neq, \notin)$. The CLP counterpart called CLP($\mathcal{SET}$) is described in [28]. The design and implementation of $\{\log\}$ and subsequently CLP($\mathcal{SET}$) have settled the theoretical foundations for embedding constructed sets of the form $\{x\} \cup S$ into (constraint) logic programming.

CLPS. The CLPS language (Constraint Logic Programming with Sets) was designed for prototyping combinatorial search problem dealing with sets, multisets, or sequences. It is based on a three sorted logic, the three sorts being: sets, multisets and sequences of finite depth (eg. $s = \{\{\{e, a\}\}, c\}$ is a set of depth three) [63]. The concept of depth is equivalent for each sort.

In CLPS, set expressions are built from the usual set operator symbols $(\cup, \cap, \setminus, \#)$. Set variables are constructed either iteratively by means of the set constructor $\{x\} \cup$ or by extension by grouping elements within braces (eg. $\{x_1, ..., x_n\}$). The language also embeds finite integer domains and allows set elements to range over a finite domain. Sequences and multisets are built using, respectively, the constructors $sq\{...\}$ and $m\{...\}$ Basic constraints are relations from $\{\in, =, \notin, \neq, \subseteq\}$ interpreted in the usual mathematical way together with a depth (::) and a type checking operator.

The satisfiability problem for sets, sequences and multisets is $\mathcal{N}P$-complete [65]. To cope with this, CLPS provides several methods whose use depends on the characteristics of the CLPS program at hand. The solver makes use of various techniques comprising: (i) a set of semantical-consistency rules, (ii) an arc-consistency algorithm of type AC-3 [66] combined with a local search procedure (forward checking) and (iii) a transformation procedure which transforms the set constraint system into an equivalent mathematical model based on integer linear programming [47]. The rules in (i) check the consistency of each set constraint with respect to homogeneity of types, depth and cardinality. For example the system

$\{x\} = \{y, z\}$ is semantically-consistent if $y = z$

A semantically-consistent system of set constraints is then solved in two stages. The solver first divides the system in two independent subsets: 1) the first one, SC_{fd}, contains set constraints whose constrained sets are sets of integer domain variables, 2) the other one, written SC_v contains sets and set constraints where set elements are free variables or known values. The solver applies (ii) and (iii) respectively to check satisfiability over SC_{fd} and SC_v.

An interesting component is the resolution of SC_v using (iii). A system SC_v is satisfiable if its equivalent integer linear programming form is satisfiable [47]. To check satisfiability, the system provides a correct and complete procedure which transforms the set constraint system into an equivalent mathematical model based on integer linear programming. This procedure consists in flattening each set constraint and reducing the system of flattened formulas to an equivalent system of linear equations and disequations over finite domain variables. The derived system is then solved using consistency techniques. The flattening algorithm works by adding additional variables to reach forms from $(x = y, \; x \in y, \; x = \{x_1, ..., x_n\}, x = y \cup z, \; x = y \cap z, \; x = y \setminus z$, etc.). The reduction to linear form is performed by associating to each set variable x_i a new variable C_{xi} which represents its cardinality and to each pair of variables $(x_i, \; x_j)$ a new binary variable Q_{ij} denoting possible set equality constraints. If there are n constraints the complexity of the reduction procedure is in $\mathcal{O}(n^3)$.

The proposed solving methods are among the most appropriate for handling set constraints over constructed sets. They fit the application domain of the language which aimed initially at combinatorial problem prototyping. Unfortunately the nondeterminism in the unification of set/multisets/strings constructs prevents an efficient pruning of the domains attached to set elements (in case they represent domain variables). The focus is put on the expressive power of the language rather than on the efficient solving.

Since its first release, the CLPS kernel has been extended in many ways. In particular, new solvers on constructed terms for multisets and sequences have been defined based on PQR-trees and proved to be appropriate for modelling and solving scheduling problems with a reasonable efficiency [9]. The application domain of CLPS has since migrated and a new solver called CLPS-B has been designed and implemented to animate and generate test sequences from B and Z formal specifications [15]. The B method, developed by Abrial, forms part of a formal specification model based on first order logic extended to set constructors and relations, (see [1] for a description of the B method).

17.3   Constraints over Finite Set Intervals

As we mentioned earlier on, many combinatorial search problems find a natural formulation in the language of sets. The embedding of finite set intervals in constraint programming languages builds upon the successes of finite domain constraint satisfaction problem (CSP) in order to allow for natural and concise modeling of a set-based combinatorial search problems as set domain CSP – where set variables range over finite set domain – and set constraints are handled using consistency techniques. The motivations differ slightly from the previous languages since the approach compromises expressiveness (sets don't contain variables) with efficiency (trivial deterministic unification of finite sets). We present the main components of the finite set solver, since it is available in most CP languages and lead to much further research and improvements in recent years. Comprehensive theoretical and practical descriptions can be found in [39, 77, 40].

Notations.   Set variables will be represented by the letters x, y, z, s, set constants by the letters a, b, c, d, natural numbers by the letters m, n and integer variables by v, w. All these symbols can be subscripted.

17.3.1 Subset Domain Bounds and Convex Closure Operator

A set domain can be specified in extension as a collection of known sets of arbitrary elements like $\{\{a, b\}, \{c, d\}, \{e\}\}$. However, such domains can be large (e.g., if $s \subseteq \{1, \ldots, 100\}$, its domain contains 2^{100} elements). A common approach to tackling large domains is to approximate the domain reasoning by an interval reasoning as in many FD solvers. This is why the notion of set domain has been approximated by a *set interval specified by its upper and lower bounds*, defined by some appropriate ordering on the domain values. In this case the partial ordering under set inclusion is considered. This enables the use of consistency techniques [66] by reasoning in terms of interval variations, when dealing with a system of set constraints. The set interval $[\{\}, \{a, b, c, d, e\}]$ represents the convex closure of the set domain above.

The core idea is to approximate the domain of a set variable by a closed interval denoted $[glb, lub]$, specified by its unique least upper bound glb, and unique greatest lower bound lub, under set inclusion. Any such interval within a powerset lattice is necessarily convex allowing us to perform correct computations over the set intervals. This approach finds similarities with other interval reasoning approaches like real intervals or Booleans (see [71, 11]).

The glb of the set domain contains the *definite* elements of s and the lub contains in addition *possible* elements of s.

Example 17.1. The constraint $s \in [\{3, 1\}, \{3, 1, 5, 6\}]$ means that the elements $3, 1$ belong to s and that 5 and 6 are possible elements of s.

Regarding set expressions, the domain of a union or intersection of sets is not a set interval because it is not a convex subset of the $\mathcal{P}(\{1, 2, 3, 4, 5, 6\})$, the domain of discourse (e.g. $I = [\{1\}, \{1, 3\}] \cup [\{\}, \{2, 6\}]$, $\{1, 3\}, \{6\} \in I$ but $[\{\}, \{1, 3, 6\}] \not\subseteq I$). It is possible to maintain such disjunctions of domains during the computation, but this leads to a combinatorial explosion. This handling of "holes" can be avoided by considering the convex closure of a set expression domain. To do so one needs a convex closure operation over a subset of a powerset lattice equipped with set inclusion ordering.

Convex closure operation.   Let $\mathcal{D}_S$ be the powerset lattice $\langle \mathcal{P}(\mathcal{H}_u), \subseteq \rangle$ with the partial order $\subseteq$ where $\mathcal{P}(s)$ denotes the powerset of s and the universe of discourse $\mathcal{H}_u$ refers to the Herbrand universe. To ensure that any set domain is a set interval, we define a convex closure operation which associates to any $\mathcal{D}_S$ its convex closure as being a set interval.

Definition 17.2. *Given any subset* $x = \{a_1, \ldots, a_n\}$ *of* $\mathcal{D}_S$ *we have:*

$$conv\,(x) = \overline{x} = [\bigcap_{a_i \in x} a_i, \bigcup_{a_i \in x} a_i]$$

The convex closure of the set $\{\{3,2\},\{3,4,1\},\{3\}\}$ belonging to $\mathcal{P}(D_S)$ is the set interval $[\{3\},\{1,2,3,4\}]$.

The operations $\bigcap_{a_i \in x} a_i$ and $\bigcup_{a_i \in x} a_i$ derive respectively $glb(x)$ and $lub(x)$. The operation $\widetilde{conv}(x) = \overline{x} = [glb(x), lub(x)]$ satisfies the properties of extension ($x \subseteq \overline{x}$), idempotence ($\overline{x} = \overline{\overline{x}}$), and monotony (if $x \subseteq y$, then $\overline{x} \subseteq \overline{y}$)

The existence of limit elements for any set $\{a,b\}$ belonging to D_S allows us to define a notion of set domain as a convex subset of D_S, that is a set interval $[a \cap b, a \cup b]$.

Set interval calculus.   The powerset algebra D_S interprets the set function symbols $\cup, \cap$, $\setminus$ in their usual set theoretical sense (*i.e.*, $\emptyset$ is the empty set, $\setminus$ the set difference, etc.). The interpreted set union and intersection symbols have the usual algebraic properties (commutativity, associativity, idempotence, absorption). By making use of the convex closure operation we ensure that the union and intersection of set intervals yield intervals as well. The resulting set interval calculus is described as follows:

$$\overline{[a,b] \cup [c,d]} = [a \cup c, b \cup d]$$
$$\overline{[a,b] \cap [c,d]} = [a \cap c, b \cap d]$$
$$\overline{\mathcal{P}(D_s)} = \mathcal{P}(D_s) \text{ and } \overline{\emptyset} = \emptyset$$

With regard to the set difference operation $[a,b] \setminus [c,d]$, its set theoretical definition is $x \setminus y = x \cap y'$ where y' is the complement of y. The complement of a set interval is characterized only by the fact that it does not contain the elements in the lower bound (e.g. c in this case). So the convex closure of a set interval difference is:

$$\overline{[a,b] \setminus [c,d]} = [a \setminus d, b \setminus c]$$

17.3.2   Set Constraints and Graduations

Primitive set constraints apply to set variables or ground sets. They constrain at most two set variables or a set variable and an integer (for graduated constraints). They can be of the form $S \in [a,b], S \subseteq S_1, S = S_1 \cup S_2, S = S_1 \cap S_2, S = S_1 \setminus S_2, e \in S, e \notin S, |S| \geq c, |S| \leq c$.

Many more constraints can be specified but will be rewritten in term of the primitive ones. For instance, n-ary constraints of the form $s_1 \cup s_2 \subseteq s_3 \cap s_4$. Th reason is that the partial solving of constraints requires us to express each set variable in terms of the others. Since there is no inverse operation for $\cup, \cap, \setminus$ there is no way to move all the operation symbols on one side of the constraint relation. So it is necessary to decompose n-ary constraints into primitive ones unless some global reasoning is sought with dedicated propagators (see next section). The decomposition approach is similar to the relational form of arithmetic constraints over real intervals [18].

To increase the expressiveness of a set solver, and in particular to be able to deal with optimization functions, we apply graduation functions to sets. A graduation maps a no quantifiable term to an integer value denoting a measure of the term. The set cardinality is one example of such a function. Another one is the weight function that sums the element values of the set. Both can then be restricted by arithmetic constraints. The following definitions give necessary conditions to consider graduations for a given set.

Definition 17.3. *A set S provided with an order relation $\preceq$ is graduated if there exists a function f from S to $\mathcal{Z}$ (positive and negative integers) which satisfies:*

$x \prec y \Rightarrow f(x) < f(y)$ *($\prec$ is a strict ordering, $<$ the arithmetic inequality)*

x *precedes* $y \Rightarrow f(x) = f(y) + 1$

An element x_i precedes an element x_{i+1} if in the chain of elements $x = x_0 \prec x_1 \prec \ldots \prec x_n = y$ in S there is no other element between them.

f *is the graduation of S.*

The existence of a graduation of a set which does not correspond to a chain (e.g. a set of set intervals) is guaranteed for the closed set intervals under set inclusion [40]. Furthermore, if there exists one such graduation of a set, then there exists an infinite number of graduations of this set. The weight function is a case in point.

Definition 17.4. *A graduation f is a function from $[\mathcal{D}_S, \subseteq]$ to $\mathcal{Z}$ (set of positive and negative integers) which maps each element $x \in D_S$ to a unique m such that $f(x) = m$.*

The convex closure of a graduation f is required to deal with elements from ΩD_S. The closure function, written $\overline{f}$, maps elements from ΩD_S to a subset of the powerset $\mathcal{P}(\mathcal{Z})$ containing intervals of positive and negative integers. This subset is designated by $\Omega \mathcal{Z}$.

Example 17.5. *Let s be a set and $|s|$ its cardinality (a positive integer). Consider the constraint $s \in [\{\}, \{1, 2\}]$. The cardinality function is approximated by $\overline{||}$. Intuitively we have $\overline{||}(s) = [0, 2]$.*

Definition 17.6. *Let $f : D_S \rightarrow \mathcal{Z}$. The function $\overline{f} : \Omega D_S \rightarrow \Omega \mathcal{Z}$ is derived from f as follows:*

$$\overline{f}([a, b]) = [f(a), f(b)]$$

Property 17.7. *If $x \in [a, b]$ then $f(x) \in \overline{f}([a, b])$.*

This property guarantees that the output of the function $\overline{f}$ applied to a set domain contains the actual graduation value of the concerned set variable.

17.3.3   Local Consistency

Local consistency for the primitive constraints individually ensure that the set interval calculus holds. This can be captured in the following definition of bound consistency for constraints over combined domains [13].

Definition 17.8. *A constraint is Bound Consistent (denoted BC), iff for each set (holds also for multiset domain variables), its $lub(s)$ (respectively $glb(s)$) is the union (respectively intersection) of all the values for s that belong to a valid assignment, and for each integer variable x there is a valid assignment that satisfies the constraint for the max and min values in the domain of x. An assignment is valid if the value given to each set (or multiset) is within its domain bounds, and the value given to each integer variable is between the min and max in its domain.*

For the sole case of set and multiset variables, BC can be defined using the characteristic function for each set variable (or occurrence representation for multiset variables). A set constraint is BC if its characteristic function is bounds consistent in the common finite domain terminology [93].

17.3.4 Enforcing BC

The consistency notion defines conditions to be satisfied by set domain bounds, and integer domains so that a set constraint is BC. If such conditions are not satisfied this means that elements in the domain are irrelevant. BC can be inferred by moving such elements "out of the boundaries of the domain" which means pruning the bounds of the domain. The essential point is that a refinement of both bounds allows us to prune a domain. Reducing the set of possible values a set could take can be achieved either by extending the collection of *definite* elements of a set *i.e.*, adding elements to the glb of a set domain, or by reducing the collection of *possible* elements *i.e.*, removing elements from the lub of a set domain. Both computations are deterministic. The inference rules are presented as deterministic rewrite rules that operate when the conditions are met:

$$\frac{\text{conditions}}{\text{constraint store changes}}$$

For set constraints

Consider the constraint $s \subseteq s_1$ such that $s \in [a, b], s_1 \in [c, d]$. Inferring its local consistency amounts to possibly extending the lower bound of the domain of s_2 and to possibly reducing the upper bound of the domain of s_1. This is depicted by the following inference rule:

I1. $$\frac{b' = b \cap d, \quad c' = c \cup a}{\{s \in [a, b], \ s_1 \in [c, d], \ s \subseteq s_1\} \longmapsto \{s \in [a, b'], s_1 \in [c', d], \ s \subseteq s_1\}}$$

When s, s_1 denote set expressions, the relational forms are created and the following additional inference rule is necessary to deal with the projection functions. For each projection function $\overline{\rho_i}$ describing the domain of an s_i appearing in a set expression, we have:

I2. $$\frac{a'_i = a_i \cup c, \quad b'_i = b_i \cap d}{\{s_i \in [a_i, b_i], \ \overline{\rho_i} = [c, d]\} \longmapsto \{s_i \in [a'_i, b'_i]\}}$$

For primitive graduated constraints

The constraint $f(s) \in [m, n]$ such that $s \in [a, b]$ describes a mapping from an element belonging to a partially ordered set to an element belonging to a totally ordered set. Consequently, it might occur that two distinct elements in $[a, b]$ have the same valuation in $[m, n]$. This implies that inferring the local consistency of this constraint might require refining $[a, b]$ only if a single element in $[a, b]$ satisfies the constraint. If this element exists, it corresponds necessarily to one of the domain bounds since they are uniquely defined and are strict subset (or superset), of any element in the domain. Thus, the value of the graded function mapped onto them cannot be shared. The inference mechanism is depicted by the following rules. $min()$ and $max()$ are functions which take as input a collection of integers and return respectively the minimal and maximal integer value of this collection.

I3. $$\frac{[m', n'] = [max(m, f(a)), min(n, f(b))]}{\{s \in [a, b], f(s) \in [m, n]\} \longmapsto \{s \in [a, b], f(s) \in [m', n']\}}$$

I4.
$$\frac{n = f(a)}{\{\,s \in [a,b]\,,f(s) \in [m,n]\}\;\longmapsto\;\{s = a\,\}}$$

I5.
$$\frac{m = f(b)}{\{\,s \in [a,b]\,,f(s) \in [m,n]\}\;\longmapsto\;\{s = b\,\}}$$

By their definition, the inference rules are correct (all possible solutions are kept), contracting (final domains are subset of the initial domains), idempotent (the smallest domains have been computed the first time) and inclusion monotone (smaller initial domains yield smaller final domains). The consistency of a system of constraints results from the consistency of each constraint appearing in it. A generic algorithm is used to call the relevant inference rules dedicated to enforcing BC. It reduces the set bounds until a fixed point is reached. In the case of set intervals, the algorithm resembles the relaxation algorithm used by CLP(Intervals) systems [62] commonly referred to as fixed point algorithm [11], see Chapter 16, "Continuous and interval constraints".

17.3.5   Illustrative Model

We illustrate a 0-1 model versus a subset-bound set model of a simple bin packing problem [39]. Bin packing problems belong to the class of set partitioning problems. A multiset of n integers is given $\{w_1, ..., w_n\}$ and specifies the weight elements to partition. Another integer W_{max} is given and represents the weight capacity. The aim is to find a partition of the n integers into a minimal number of m bins (or sets) $\{s_1, .., s_k\}$ such that in each bin the sum of all integers does not exceed W_{max}. This problem is usually stated in terms of arithmetic constraints over 0-1 variables and solved using MIP techniques or finite domain constraint programming. It requires one matrix (a_{ij}) to represent the elements of each set, one vector x_j to represent the selected subsets s_k and one vector w_i to represent the weights of the elements a_{ij}. The set model uses a `weight` graded constraint that sums the weights of the items in a set domain.

IP abstract formulation

$$\sum_{j=1}^{m} a_{ij}\, x_j = 1 \; \forall i \in \{1, .., n\}$$

where:
$x_j = 0..1 \;(1 \text{ if } s_j \in \{s_1, .., s_k\})$
$a_{ij} = 0..1 \;(1 \text{ if } i \in s_j)$
$\sum_{i=1}^{n} a_{ij}\, w_i \leq W_{max} \; \forall j \in \{1, ..., m\}$

set abstract formulation

$$s_1 \cap s_2 = \{\},\, s_1 \cap s_3 = \{\},\, ..,\, s_{n-1} \cap s_m = \{\}$$
$$s_1 \cup s_2 \cup ... \cup s_m = \{(1, w_1), .., (n, w_n)\}$$

$s_j \in [\{\}, \{(1, w_1), .., (n, w_n)\}]$
`weight`$(i, w_i) = w_i;$
$\forall s_j,\, \sum_{i=1}^{\#glb(s_j)} \texttt{weight}(i, w_i) \leq W_{max}$

Under these assumptions, the program to solve is to minimize the number of bins:
$\min x_0 = \sum_{j=1}^{m} x_j$ $\min x_0 = \#\{s_j \mid s_j \neq \{\}\}$

17.3.6   Multiset Domains

Multisets can also be used to model the bin packing problem by considering essentially the weights and not the items. They were introduced in the previous section in the context of constructed sets. We present here approaches towards introducing multiset objects that are specified using domains, as they can be naturally seen as extensions to set domains where the occurrence needs to be taken into account. Multiset domains are not present in many languages yet, but can be found in SOLVER under the name *bags* [50]. As described in [54], the main difference between set and multiset domains in a Constraint Satisfaction Problem sense lies in the maintenance of the occurrence functions. And in fact multisets can be solely defined by means of the occurrence function. Let $occ(m, s)$ be the number of occurrences of m in the multiset s. Multiset operations such as union, intersection, difference, etc, are defined by properties of the occurrence function. We have:

$$occ(m, s_1 \cup s_2) = max(occ(m, s_1), occ(m, s_2))$$
$$occ(m, s_1 \cap s_2) = min(occ(m, s_1), occ(m, s_2))$$
$$occ(m, s_1 \setminus s_2) = max(0, occ(m, s_1) - occ(m, s_2))$$
$$s_1 = s_2 \text{ iff } \forall m, occ(m, s_1) = occ(m, s_2)$$
$$s_1 \subseteq s_2 \text{ iff } \forall m, \ occ(m, s_1) \leq occ(m, s_2)$$

Just like sets, different representations are possible for multiset domains. The subset bound representation can be generalized to sets allowing multiple occurrence of elements, and the characteristic function can be generalized to the occurrence vector. Also the list of finite domain variables commonly used to represent sets in Finite Domain (FD) solvers can be used for multisets with the difference that the variables are not constrained to be distinct but each element should appear in a number of variables describing its occurrence. We can compare the expressiveness of the different representations in terms of the multiset values it represents. For instance, the occurrence representation is more expressive than the bound representation (see proofs in [93]). The FD list, also referred to as cardinality representation, is incomparable to either.

Example 17.9. A multiset m_{s1} with possible values $\{\{1, 1, 2\}\}, \{\{2, 2, 2\}\}$ can be represented by the "occurrence" vector of integer variables $[x_1, x_2]$ with:

$$x_1 = \ occ(1, ms) \in 0..2, \text{ and } x_2 = \ occ(2, ms) \in 1..3$$
The bound representation for this multiset domain is specified by:
$$m_{s1} \in [\{1, 1, 2\}..\{2, 2, 2\}]$$
The FD list representation for the same multiset variable is specified by:
$$[y_1, y_2, y_3], \ y_1 \in 1..2, \ y_2 \in 1..2, \ y_3 = 2$$

Enforcing BC is done by applying inference rules similar to the ones for set constraints taking into account the semantics of the occurrence element (see [93]).

17.4   Influential Extensions to Subset Bound Solvers

`Conjunto` and its peers provide a natural and concise modeling facility for set-based CSPs, space efficient in the representation of large domains, integrated with finite domain solvers through graded function constraints. However, the growing use of such solvers has raised some important shortfalls over the past years, the main ones being the loose approximation of the subset bounds when the actual domains are *sparse*, and the passive use of the cardinality information, ubiquitous in set-based combinatorial problems, and the breaking of problem symmetries. We present the most influential approaches towards improving finite set solvers.

So far, there has been four research directions to strengthen constraint propagation of the first subset bound solvers, built upon `Conjunto` inference rules. These comprise (1) additional cardinality inferences to enrich a subset bound solver; (2) a hybrid set domain that complements the conventional subset domain with lexicographic bounds; (3) a set solver based on a full domain representation using Reduced Ordered Binary Decision Diagrams (ROBDD); (4) global constraint propagators over subset bounds. This section surveys the four of them.

17.4.1 Cardinal

The `Cardinal` solver [3] is a finite set solver in the `Conjunto` style (i.e. subset bound solver) with enhancements to strengthen the use of the cardinality information. `Conjunto` uses the cardinality (and other graded functions like weight) in a unidirectional way, meaning that when a set domain gets refined its cardinality is pruned. The possible inferences from the cardinality to the set have not been considered, mainly due to the practical objective of the language then to remain cost effective in addressing large set-based CSPs (bin-packing, partitioning). However, finite set solvers have a wider applicability. In particular Azevedo applies subset bound solvers to tackle digital circuit diagnosis [4, 3]. For such problems active use of the cardinality information is essential.

Conventional Boolean representations of digital signals consider a pair: a set of faults on which the signal depends, and a Boolean value that the signal takes if there were no faults at all. Both are variables. For instance, $X = \{\{f/0, g/0\}, \{i/1\}\} - 0$ means that signal X is normally 0 but if both gates f and g are stuck-at-0 or gate i is stuck-at-1, then its actual value is 1. Thus $\emptyset$-N represents a signal with constant value N, independent of any fault [4]. The idea of using sets to represent digital circuits is to join the two domains in one by using a transformation, based on a single set domain that approximates both with minimal loss of information. A set representing a pair S-0 is simply represented by the set S, while the pair S-1 is represented by the set $\overline{S}$. The set S can have values $\emptyset$ or D (known set) and is thus given a set interval domain $[0, D]$ whose corresponding cardinality should ideally have only the two possible values $\{0, |D|\}$. Such disjunctive cardinality domains, mapped to sparse set domains, makes the subset bound approximation very loose and ineffective.

New inferences rules are added to the solver to strengthen constraint propagation over the cardinality information, and would benefit such combinatorial problems in particular [4]. Additional cardinality inferences are associated with each basic set operation. To illustrate the pruning power of `Cardinal`, we consider the set difference operation. The following example shows the benefits of additional inference rules using the cardinality information:

Example 17.10. Let s_1, s_2 and s_3 be three set variables such that we have the following system of constraints:

$$s_1, s_2 \subseteq \{a, b, c, d\}, |s_1| = 2, s_3 = s_2 \setminus s_1$$

While traditional subset bound solvers do not infer any information, the `Cardinal` system would infer that $|s_3| \leq 2$. Then any further constraint upon the cardinality of s such as $|s_3| = 3$ would lead to a failure.

The inference rules defined to achieve bounds consistency for the cardinality variables c_1, c_2, c_3 amount to adding new constraints on the cardinality variables to the constraint store. In the case of the set difference constraint we have:

$$c_3 \geq c_1 - c_2$$
$$c_3 \leq c_1 - |glb(s_1) \cap glb(s_2)|$$
$$c_3 \leq |lub(s_1) \cup lub(s_2)| - c_2$$

Note that the `Cardinal` solver first infers arc consistency over the cardinality bounds, at constraint set up which can be useful when cardinality domains are disjunctive like in digital circuits models, but costly in the general case. Thus it maintains bounds consistency over these bounds to remain effective while strengthening constraint propagation. For each primitive set constraints as the set difference above, an inference rule leading to AC for the cardinality domains is first applied.

$$c_3 \in \{n \mid \exists i \in D_1, j \in D_2, \max(i - j, i - |lub(s_1) \cap lub(s_2)|) \leq n$$
$$n \leq \min(i - |glb(s_1) \cap glb(s_2)|, |lub(s_1) \cup lub(s_2)| - j)\}$$

Example 17.11 ([3]). Consider two sets s_1 and s_2 that can only be $\emptyset$ or $\{f, g, h, i\}$ (i.e. cardinality 0 or 4). To find the initial cardinality domain of their difference $s_3 = s_1 \setminus s_2$, we examine cardinality pairs $\langle 0, 0 \rangle, \langle 0, 4 \rangle, \langle 4, 0 \rangle, \langle 4, 4 \rangle$ and conclude that the set difference cardinality is also the pair $\langle 0, 4 \rangle$.

The `Cardinal` solver has been implemented atop ECL^iPS^e [86] and is fully described in [3, 5]. This solver has shown how finite set solvers can be competitive on problems which were the realm of Boolean algebra. It has demonstrated the expressiveness of finite sets and their applicability to digital circuit design in particular.

17.4.2   Lexicographic Bounds

The ubiquity of the set cardinality information goes beyond digital circuit design and encompasses the large class of combinatorial design problems (e.g. see [19] for a survey) for which set-based CSP models are ideally suited. Examples are sport scheduling, Steiner systems, error-correcting codes. Traditional subset bound solvers have difficulty with such problems as they do not make strong use of the set cardinality information. `Cardinal` offers more in terms of cardinality inferences but such inferences do not propagate onto the subset bounds except for instantiation. This issue is addressed in [84], by extending the domain representation to more closely approximate the true domain of a set variable. This is a complementary approach to `Cardinal` that strengthens the propagation of finite set constraints in a tractable way.

The idea is to consider a set domain ordering that better exploits the cardinality information, and that is also effective at breaking symmetries (when using symmetry breaking constraints) [85]. The new bound representation for set domains is based on an ordering different from the set inclusion (subset order). It is a lexicographic ordering with *lexicographic bounds* specified by $\langle \text{inf}, \text{sup} \rangle$. This ordering relation defines a *total* order on sets of natural numbers, in contrast to the *partial* order $\subseteq$. We use the symbols $\preceq$ (and $\prec$) to denote a total strict (respectively non-strict) lexicographic order.

Definition 17.12. *Let $\preceq$ be a total order on sets of integers defined as follows:*

$$s_1 \preceq s_2 \text{ iff } s_1 = \emptyset \vee m_1 < m_2 \vee (m_1 = m_2 \wedge s_1 \setminus \{M_1\} \preceq s_2 \setminus \{m_2\})$$
$$\text{where } m_1 = max(s_1) \text{ and } m_2 = max(s_2)$$

Example 17.13. Consider the sets $\{1,2,3\}, \{1,3,4\}, \{1,2\}, \{3\}$, the list that orders these sets w.r.t. $\preceq$ is $[\{1,2\}, \{3\}, \{1,2,3\}, \{1,3,4\}]$.

A common use of this ordering is in search problems to break symmetries (e.g. [21] on SAT clauses or [33, 36] on vectors of FD variables). However, this is not the use to which this ordering is put here. It is used on *ground* sets as a means to approximate the domain of a finite set variable by upper and lower bounds w.r.t. this order.

A lex bound domain overcomes one major weakness of the subset bounds, in that the lex bounds denote possible solution sets that satisfy the cardinality restrictions imposed on the set variable.

Example 17.14. Consider a variable X ranging over a subset domain $[\{1,2\}, \{1,2,3,4\}$ such that X is of size 3. The subset bounds are not a possible instance for X as the domain cannot be pruned to satisfy the cardinality restriction. The lexicographic bounds on the other hand are $[\{1,2,3\}, \{1,2,4\}]$, denoting the min and max sets of size 3 (w.r.t. to the ordering) containing $\{1,2\}$.

Despite its success allowing cardinality constraint to filter the domain more actively, the lex bound representation is unable to always represent certain critical constraints. Primary amongst these constraints is the inclusion or exclusion of a single element. Such constraints are not always representable in the domain because the lex bounds represent possible set instances and not definite and potential elements of a set. In the example above there are sets in between the lex bounds that do not contain $\{1,2\}$, such as $\{4,1\}$. It is the inability to capture such fundamental constraints efficiently in the domain which lead to a hybrid domain of both subset and lexicographic bounds.

The lexicographic ordering for sets is not the only possible definition, nor is it, perhaps, the most common when talking about sets. Its use comes from two reasons: 1) for sets of cardinality 1 it is equivalent to the $\leq$ ordering of FD variables and 2) usefully, it extends the $\subseteq$ ordering and we have:

Theorem 17.15. *[84]* $\forall s_1, s_2 \in \mathcal{P}(U) : s_1 \subseteq s_2 \Rightarrow s_1 \preceq s_2$

Theorem 17.15 is used in the hybrid domain to make inferences between the two bounds representations for set variables.

A collection of inference rules have been defined to propagate primitive set constraints with respect to the lex bounds, subset bounds and cardinality bounds. A prototype hybrid solver has been implemented in ECL^{i}PS^e atop the ic_sets library. First results showed spectacular improvements over traditional subset bound solvers, on the network design SONET problem [85] and more pruning but at a substantial computational cost on some combinatorial design problems such as the Steiner triple problems and binary error correcting codes. The main novelty of the approach is the introduction of a new domain representation whose bounds account for the cardinality restrictions and can be used for effective symmetry breaking (using symmetry breaking constraints).

17.4.3 ROBDDs

The problem of efficient finite set reasoning in a constraint logic programming context can also be addressed from a radically different perspective as described in [60]. The idea was first motivated by rejecting the belief that the very large number of values of a finite set domain precludes a precise and un-approximated representation, and instead to show how Reduced Order Binary Decision Diagrams (ROBDDs) can be used to represent full set domains and set constraints in a compact manner. Using existing efficient libraries to represent and manipulate these compact data structures, Lagoon and Stuckey demonstrate techniques for combining ROBDDs in ways that correspond to basic finite set constraints (e.g. \, ∩, ∪, ‖) which minimize the size of the resulting ROBDD [60]. An ROBDD is a *canonical function representation (up to reordering)* of a Binary Decision Diagram which permits and efficient implementation of many Boolean function operations [16].

Let s be a set variable, and let $\{1, .., N\}$ be its domain of possible values. The ROBDD domain representation makes use of the characteristic function that defines the one-to-one correspondence between a subset s of a known set S and a Boolean algebra:

$$f : x_i \to \{0, 1\} \text{ such that } f(x_i) = 1 \text{ iff } i \in s$$

Hence a set variable s is represented by a vector of Boolean variables $< x_1, .., x_N >$. Now if we consider an assignment A of values to variables, each x_i will take value one if and only if $i \in s$. The i's are first drawn from a universe of discourse. Such an assignment can be represented as a Boolean formula $B(A)$:

$$B(A) = \bigwedge_{i \in U} y_i \text{ where } y_i = \begin{cases} x_i & \text{if } i \in A \\ \neg x_i & \text{otherwise} \end{cases}$$

Each known set can be seen as an assignment, hence the full domain of a set variable $D(s)$ can itself be represented by a Boolean formula $B(D(s))$. This formula is a disjunction of $B(A)$ over all possible sets A in $D(s)$ [45]:

$$B(D(s)) = \bigvee_{A \in D(s)} B(A) \text{ where } B(A) \text{ is defined above}$$

Example 17.16. Let $U = \{1, 2, 3\}$ and let s be a set variable with $D(s) = \{\{1\}, \{1,3\}, \{2,3\}\}$. We associate Boolean variables $\{v_1, v_2, v_3\}$ with s given U. $D(s)$ is the Boolean formula $(v_1 \wedge \neg v_1 \wedge \neg v_3) \vee (v_1 \wedge \neg v_2 \wedge v_3) \vee (\neg v_1 \wedge v_2 \wedge v_3)$. The three solutions to this formula correspond to the elements of D(s).

While such a formula can be constructed using an ROBDD, in practice the approach only ever constructs the ROBDD for a domain implicitly through constraint propagation. The ROBDDs are used to model the constraint themselves. Indeed any set constraint can be converted to a Boolean formula.

Example 17.17. Let $U = \{1, 2, 3\}$, and the constraint $s_1 \subseteq s_2$. Assume that the Boolean variables associated with s_1 and s_2 respectively are v_1, v_2, v_3 and w_1, w_2, w_3. The inclusion constraint can be represented by the Boolean formula: $(v_1 \to w_1) \wedge (v_2 \to w_2) \wedge (v_3 \to w_3)$. This formula can be represented by two different ROBDDs depending on the variable ordering.

ROBDDs are ordered and thus require an ordering of the Boolean variables used. The order can have a drastic effect on the size of the ROBDDs when constraints are represented, i.e. when there is a specific relationship between elements of the universe.

The Boolean approach allows the ROBDD-based modeling to be extended to handling integer and multiset constraint problems as well as some global set constraints (comprehensive description in [45]). While initially motivated by using a full set domain representation that do not approximate the possible set values, ROBDD have also been used to model less strict consistency notions and domain approximations, such as set bounds, cardinality bounds and lexicographic bounds consistency; with a thorough comparative evaluation of the different domain representations [44, 45].

The ROBDD-based solver offers a flexible modelling facility and has shown high performance results on several standard combinatorial design constraint problems. However, it does require the use of Boolean formula and variables to model such problems.

17.4.4   Global Set Constraints

The above works strengthen constraint propagation in complementary ways by revising the concept of set domain or enriching the local inference rules. A more traditional approach in constraint programming to offer a better tradeoff "natural formulation"/efficiency consists in deriving global propagators for a class of symbolic constraints, see Chapter 6, on Global Constraints. This was not considered in finite set solvers till recently, at least in published academic articles, but is now contributing interesting results.

Global reasoning on a class of symbolic set constraints, first considered some n-ary constraints like the `atmost1` (sets intersecting pairwise in atmost one element), or its complement, the `distinct` constraint (sets that differ pairwise in atleast one element) over sets of fixed cardinality [82]. Such constraints and other n-ary constraints like `union` and `disjoint` have been used in set-based constraint languages but essentially as syntactic abstractions of collections of binary or ternary constraints, solved with local consistency techniques. The ubiquity of set intersection in conjunction with cardinality restrictions in set-based combinatorial problems drove the research agenda towards more efficient propagators.

Example 17.18.

$[s_1, s_2, s_3] \in \{\{\}..\{a, b, c, d\}\}$
$|s_1| = |s_2| = |s_3| = 2$
`disjoint`$(\{s_1, s_2, s_3\}$

BC on this system of constraints does not detect inconsistency. However, if the cardinality constraints are combined with the disjointness constraint one can see that there are no solutions by doing a simple pigeon hole test. This can be deduced if we consider the set of constraints globally. In fact, the representation of sets within powersets specified as set intervals can be used to derive some global inferences based on combinatorial analysis formulas. A simple satisfiability test can first be checked (ie. pigeon hole test), determining whether a set of 4 elements can be partitioned into 3 sets of 2 which fails ($\frac{4}{3} \neq 2$). A more elaborate test that does not require the sets to have same cardinalities derives an upper bound on the number of possible partitions of 4 elements into 3 sets of cardinality 2. Such numbers are known as a Stirling number $\frac{4!}{(2!)^3(3!)} = \frac{1}{2}$ [12]. If it is less than one, the problem is unsatisfiable since there isn't a single possible partition. However if the number is greater than one we would know how many different partitions there are.

There exist some counting functions that determine the maximum number of configurations allowed in a superset S, given some shared properties, see [82]. When considering the values of these functions on can then investigate how and when they can be used effectively, first to detect unsatisfiability but also to prune further irrelevant set values in an a priori manner. The counting functions provide a mathematical information that is not easily deducible in logic. They enable the definition of a set of inference rules to strengthen propagation on global constraints such as atmost1 , distinct over fixed cardinality sets. Such rules do not infer BC but are tractable.

Decomposition and complexity

The problematic of deriving inference rules without a clear idea of how much we do or can infer, and how far we can go towards global reasoning raises fundamental theoretical issues. This lead to a systematic study of several aspects of global constraints and global set and multiset constraints in particular. The approach determined whether decomposition hinders Bounds Consistency (BC), and when it does whether there exists a polynomial algorithm to infer BC on the considered global constraint [93, 13].

For instance, BC on the n-ary disjoint is equivalent to BC on its decomposition into binary constraints (pairwise empty intersection). Basically, this holds because any set can be assigned the empty set. However, when the set cardinalities are constrained (and not zero), –which is frequent in combinatorial design problems for example– the equivalence no longer holds. It was also proved that decomposition of the   atmost1 constraint hinders propagation and that enforcing BC on this constraint is NP-hard.

We summarize the complexity results in Table 17.1. Decomposable implies polynomial, since existing algorithms to infer BC on a set of binary or ternary set constraints are indeed polynomial. Results hold for both set and multiset domains unless specified otherwise. The acronyms stand for: NE (non empty), FC (fixed cardinality). The constraints are classified in terms of the intersection constraints and cardinality restrictions involved. For example the atmost1 constraint corresponds to pairwise intersect in at most one element ($k = 1$) for fixed cardinality sets, which is the second column of first table.

If now we add the union constraint ($\bigcup_i s_i = s$) to the intersection ones we obtain covering problems. The first left column above becomes a partition constraint for which results are known. The other columns are yet open problems.

$|s_i \cap s_j| = 0$ Partition is decomposable and *polynomial*
$\quad\quad + \forall k, |s_k| > 0$, NEpartition is not decomposable but *polynomial*
$\quad\quad + \forall k, |s_k| = c_k$, FCpartition also referred to as partition
$\quad\quad$ is not decomposable and is *polynomial on sets, NP-hard on multisets*

It is important to note that the global constraints applied to multisets versus sets diverge on the two most important constraints (from an application point of view): fixed cardinality disjoint and partition constraints. We describe below the existing algorithms to infer BC when the constraints apply to sets, however doing so over multisets has been proved to be NP-hard [13].

Table 17.1: Summary of complexity results (based on [13]).

$\forall k...$	$\lvert s_i \cap s_j \rvert = 0$	$\lvert s_i \cap s_j \rvert \leq k$	$\lvert s_i \cap s_j \rvert \geq k$	$\lvert s_i \cap s_j \rvert = k$
-	Disjoint decomposable *polynomial*	Intersect$_{\leq k}$ decomposable *polynomial*	Intersect$_{\geq k}$ decomposable *polynomial*	Intersect$_{= k}$ not decomp. *NP-hard*
$\lvert s_k \rvert > 0$	NEdisjoint not decomposable *polynomial*	NEintersect$_{\leq k}$ decomposable *polynomial*	NEintersect$_{\geq k}$ decomposable *polynomial*	NEintersect$_{= k}$ not decomp. *NP-hard*
$\lvert s_k \rvert = c_k$	FCdisjoint disjoint not decomposable *polynomial on sets* *NP-hard on multisets*	FCintersect$_{\leq k}$ atmost1 not decomposable *NP-hard*	FCintersect$_{\geq k}$ not decomposable *NP-hard*	FCintersect$_{= k}$ not decomp. *NP-hard*

Algorithms for the disjoint and partition constraints

The basic case of disjoint and partition is decomposable for the reasons we gave above. However, when sets have fixed cardinality, decomposition of these constraints hinders constraint propagation and thus deriving a global propagator is necessary to ensure BC. We describe how these constraints have been solved in the literature. Two lines of work have been undertaken to derive similar algorithms for the global disjoint and partition

Based upon counting functions from design theory, the first approach derived four global conditions which must hold for disjoint sets of fixed cardinality [83]. Using an extension of Hall's theorem [43], the authors proved that these conditions, if satisfied, were sufficient to ensure BC. The actual proof procedure constitutes the basis of the algorithm which actually corresponds to an augmenting network in a max-flow problem, and is similar to a combination of a flow/matching and a Strongly Connected Component (SCC) algorithm (see [83]). Interestingly this implementation corresponds closely to the GAC algorithm for the Global Cardinality Constraint (GCC) [79], see Chapter 6, "Global Constraints", and we show the reasons why below. This algorithm also holds for the partition constraint since the only pruning achievable on the disjoint is when one can identify minimal partitions within the constraint (i.e strongly connected components). So one needs to identify partitions in order to do any global pruning on the disjoint constraint.

Using the GCC constraint.
The GCC constraint applies to a family of finite domain variables with set of values in B. It constrains the number of times (cardinality) an element of B can be assigned among the different variables.

The use of the GCC constraint to resolve the disjoint and partition constraints is offered in ILOG solver and Configurator [50, 51] and has been recently described in [13].

The main idea is to formulate each of the two global set constraint with a *dual FD model* based upon the GCC constraint. The semantics of the disjoint constraint is as follows. Let $\mathtt{disjoint}(s_1, .., s_i, .., s_m)$ constrains the set variables s_i such that $\forall i \in B, s_i \in A, |s_i| = c$. The disjointness constraint ensures that no element of A (domain of the s_i) is added to two different set variables.

This constraint has an equivalent formulation in the language of finite integer variables where one seeks to assign a set identifier to a FD variable. This formulation is called dual because the initial set variables become values and the set elements become variables. The equivalent dual formulation uses the GCC constraint, as presented below.

Consider the $\mathtt{GCC}(\{y_1, .., y_j, .., y_n\}, B', C)$ constraint such that $\forall j \in A, y_j \in B'$ (with $B' = B \cup \varepsilon$ with ε being a dummy value for the case where j is unassigned). The global cardinality constraint limits to $C[j] = 1$ in the disjoint case, the number of times an element i from B' is assigned to a variable y_j (ranges between $0..\infty$ for the dummy variable). We have $n = m \times c$ FD variables. The dummy value is necessary since there might be some values in A that don't belong to any set at all. The set model and dual FD model with GCC constraint are equivalent. A solution to the first model can be mapped to a solution of the second model and vice versa by applying the following one-to-one mapping:

$$\text{for } i \in A : y_j = i \textbf{ iff } j \in s_i$$

Thus a solution is consistent with the set model if and only if its dual FD representation is consistent with the GCC model. The complexity of both the GCC and set based algorithm is in $\mathcal{O}(m^2 c)$, with m the number of sets and c their cardinality [83, 13].

Further remarks.

- Note that the equivalence between the two models holds because the constraints represent an injective mapping from a set of elements into a set of sets (each element belongs to at most one set). As soon as an element can belong to more than one set we have a surjective mapping and the dual approach based on bipartite graph, and network flow model would not apply.

- This dual approach also holds for the $\mathtt{partition}$ constraints over fixed cardinality sets with the only difference that all elements must be assigned and thus the dummy value is removed.

More recently, the application of existing global constraints over finite domain variables to other domains has been considered. For instance, the $\mathtt{all-different}$ and GCC global constraints have been extended to variables whose values are multisets, sets or tuples [78]. Note that a tuple is represented as a list of finite domain variables as opposed to having a tuple domain with tuples as elements. The issue for such domains is the large domain size. A binomial representation is proposed to address this aspect. Existing global propagators are used in combination with efficient enumeration algorithms for large domains.

17.5   Constraints over Maps, Relations and Graphs

17.5.1   ALICE Legacy

As mentioned earlier, the seminal work of Laurière was motivated by a need to *state com-binatorial problems simply by constraining relation and graph objects over finite sets* [61]. It aimed at clearly separating the problem statement from its solving. The motivation was to allow a combinatorial search problem to be formulated in the most concise and natural manner.

The constrained object was not associated with a domain (set of values the relation can take) and was not "pruned" using consistency techniques, rather it was mapped to an internal representation based on a bipartite graph structure. Operations were performed on this structure.

In ALICE, constraints are expressed in a mathematical language based on relation the-ory and some notions of graph theory. The searched objects are functions which should satisfy a set of constraints. The solver combines a depth-first search method with sophis-ticated constraint manipulation techniques and a set of powerful heuristics. The lack of flexibility of this seminal system both in the language representation and the solving strat-egy motivated the design and implementation of CHIP.

It has also motivated numerous works in the development of high level specification languages for combinatorial problems. Such proposals have been revived in the past years and we can now see two clear trends in the design of high level constraint languages over maps, relations and graphs objects:

- a class of *programming languages* over new constraint domains, where functions relations or graphs become constrained objects. The resolution algorithms depend then upon the representation of the new constrained objects. Most of these works are still novel and currently mapped down to finite set solvers as we will see below.

- a class of *modeling languages* offering high level constructs such as functions, maps and sequences to model combinatorial problems in a concise manner. Such ap-proaches do not reason directly about the constrained object to solve the specified problem. Instead, the formulation is compiled into a lower language benefiting usu-ally from existing solvers.

17.5.2   Constraint Programming Beyond Sets

The extension of constraint solvers with high modelling and programming facilities has lead to the definition of new constraint domains over binary relations, graph and maps essentially. We will present their main components.

Relation variables.   When dealing with sets, it sounds quite natural to deal with relations as well. The `Conjunto` language —mainly designed to handle finite set constraints— also provides relations at the language level to extend the expressive power of the language when dealing for example with circuit problems and matching problems originating from Operations research. Relation terms are basically built using set terms.

A relation $\mathcal{R}$ is commonly represented as a set of ordered pairs (x_i, y_j) such that x_i belongs to the DS-domain d of $\mathcal{R}$ and y_j to its AS-range[1] a. In other words, a relation $\mathcal{R}$ on two ground sets d and a is a subset of the Cartesian product $d \times a$. Keeping this representation to deal with relations as specific set terms containing pairs of elements can be very costly in memory. Indeed, the statement of the Cartesian product referring to a relation requires us to consider explicitly a huge set of pairs. This is very inconvenient. Instead, a relation in Conjunto is represented as a specific data structure which is characterized by two ground sets (DS-domain and AS-range) and a list containing the successor sets attached to each element of DS-domain.

Considering one successor set per element splits the domain of a relation into a collection of set domains. The resulting value of a relation is clearly the union of the successor sets. This approach is close to the one introduced in ALICE which dealt essentially with functions. However, in ALICE there is no explicit notion of set domain.

Definition 17.19. *Let a relation be* $r \subseteq d \times a$. *The successor set* s *of an element* $x \in d$ *is the set* $s = \{y \in a \mid (x, y) \in r\}$.

The definition of constraints applied to relation variables abstracts from stating directly constraints over the set DS-domain and AS-range or over the successor sets. The following injection, map, surjection, bijection constraints over a relation r have been embedded in Conjunto. We illustrate some of them below. They are represented using the cardinality operation $| |$, the usual set operation symbols $(\cup, \cap)$ and the arithmetic inequality $(\geq)$.

Constraints	Interpretation
r bin_r d --> a	$r = \text{birel}(l, d, a)$ where $l = \{s_i \mid \forall i \in d, \ s_i \in \{\}..a\}$
(i, j) in_r r	if $i \in d, j \in a$ then $j \in s_i$
funct(r)	$\forall i \in d, \ |s_i| = 1$
inj(r)	$|d| \leq |a|, \ |d| = n$
	$s_1 \cap s_2 = \emptyset, \ s_1 \cap s_3 = \emptyset, \ \dots, \ s_{n-1} \cap s_n = \emptyset$
	$\forall i \in d, \ |s_i| = 1$
surj(r)	$|d| \geq |a|, \ |d| = n$
	$s_1 \cup s_2 \dots \cup s_n = a$
	$\forall i \in d, \ |s_i| = 1$

These constraints do not require any specific solver since the reasoning is based on the successor set variables. Such constraints were used to prototype partitioning problems.

Graph and map variables. In the same line of work, the CP(Graph) language has been designed to tackle combinatorial problems involving "subgraph findings" common in the fields of communication networks, route planning and more recently bio-informatics [24].

CP(Graph) deals more specifically with graphs and graph constraints and represents a graph domain by considering its nodes and arcs, that is a graph $g = (sn, sa)$ is defined by a set of nodes sn and a set of arcs $sa \subseteq sn \times sn$. It handles both directed and undirected graphs and offers a set of kernel constraints used to derive other graph constraints.

Similarly to subset bound solvers, CP(Graph) builds upon a partial ordering among graphs to reason upon graph domains. We have, given $g_1 = (sn_1, sa_1)$ and $g_2 = (sn_2, sa_2)$:

---

[1] DS-domain and AS-range stand respectively for departure and arrival sets

$g_1 \subseteq g_2$ iff $sn_1 \subseteq sn_2 \wedge sa_1 \subseteq sa_2$

Graph domains are represented by the lattice of graphs partially ordered by set inclusion and specified by a graph interval $[g_L, g_U]$ such that g_L is the greatest lower bound and g_U the least upper bounds of the lattice. It also considers the arcs and nodes as set variables. The use of additional node and arc variables adds expressiveness to the language when describing complex graph constraints.

Dooms et al. show that any complex graph constraint can be expressed using a combination of the following kernel graph constraints:

- $Arcs(g, sa) \in [sa_L, sa_U]$ where sa describes the set of arcs of g that range over the subset bound domain
- $Nodes(g, sn) \in [sn_L, sn_U]$ where sn describes the set of nodes of g that range over a subset bound domain
- $ArcNode(a, n_1, n_2)$ states that the arc variable a is an arc between two nodes n_1 and n_2

A set of propagation rules allows to infer arc consistency over these constraints. The expressiveness of the constraints allows `CP(Graph)` to define more complex graph constraints based upon the kernel constraints. We illustrate some of them. The functional form of the kernel constraints is used to ease readability.

The $SubGraph(g_1, g_2)$ constraint can be specified by:

$$SubGraph(g_1, g_2) \equiv Nodes(g_1) \subseteq Nodes(g_2) \wedge Arcs(g_1) \subseteq Arcs(g_2)$$

The $InNeighbors(g, n, sn)$ constrains sn to be the nodes in g for which an inward arc incident to n is present.

$$InNeighbors(g, n, sn) \equiv sn \subseteq Nodes(g) \wedge (|sn| > 0 \Leftrightarrow n \in Nodes(G)$$
$$\wedge \forall i \in Nodes(g_U) : n \in sn \Leftrightarrow (i, n) \in Arcs(G)$$

Clearly even tough the kernel allow us to express any graph constraints, such formulations might not be effective. Thus CP(Graph) also offers global graph constraints based on existing results from literature in the field, see Chapter 6, "Global Constraints".

Recent advances in CP(Graph) include its extension to manipulate *map* terms as well in CP(Graph + Map)[22]. The main application of CP(Map) is for graph pattern problems. The language extends the relation terms of `Conjunto` (built upon domain and range limited to ground sets) where domain and range become variables. As the departure set of the map is not a ground set, instead of using a list of successor sets, `CP(Map)` uses an indexed array. As maps are functions and not general relations, the domain variables stored in this indexed array are not finite sets but finite domain variables.

17.5.3   High Level Modeling/Specification Languages

Recent proposals have considered Map variables as high level type constructors, simplifying the modeling of combinatorial optimization problems, which would then be compiled into another programming language. We outline recent results in this related area of constraint modeling. The language ASRA defines a relation or map variable from a set v to a set w, where supersets of v and w must be known [32]. While the map variables and constraints are used to model a constraint problems, the resolution of the model is handled by another system. In this proposal, the derived model are compiled into OPL[91]. This idea can also be found in the language $\mathcal{L}$ where v and w are ground sets[48]. Finally, relation and map variables are also described in [35] as a useful abstraction in constraint modelling. Rules are proposed for refining constraints on these complex variables into constraints on finite integer and set variables.

17.6 Constraints over Lattices and Hierarchical Trees

Proposals for higher computation domains have been made recently which deserve attention. These include the generalization of existing interval based approaches to propose a generic framework for defining and solving interval constraints on any set of domains (finite or infinite) that are lattices [30]. The approach is based on the use of a single form of constraint similar to that of an indexical used by Constraint Logic Programming for finite domains and on a particular generic definition of an interval domain built from an arbitrary lattice. They provide the theoretical foundations for this framework and a schematic procedure for the operational semantics. Examples are provided that illustrate how new (compound) constraint solvers can be constructed from existing solvers using lattice combinators and how different solvers (possibly on distinct domains) can communicate and hence, cooperate in solving a problem.

Another challenging domain is that of order-sorted domains and ontologies. Both proposals are driven by industrial needs. The first one shows how constraint satisfaction techniques can be extended to address order-sorted domains, from class taxonomies with an object oriented perspective [17]. The use of ontologies, is itself motivated by applications for the configuration of product and services, for instance in the e-commerce [59]. This second approach defines a constraint domain where all values that a variable may take are organized into a hierarchy. Such hierarchies are often called ontologies or thesauri in Artificial Intelligence. Both approaches are quite close. The objective is to define a system that would allow the use of order-sorted domains in constraint programming for modeling purposes. The outlined algorithmic approach to reason about ontologies follows the bound and convex interval reasoning of finite set intervals. Other approaches to deal with hierarchies have essentially used the standard CSP formalism and constrain the values of properties as opposed to the entities in a hierarchy itself [34].

17.7 Implementation Aspects

We present some of the core implementation issues mainly relating to subset bound solvers since they are the main practical language implementations and are used by higher level constructs as well. For example the `CP(Graph)` prototype is built over the FD and finite set solver of `OZ`.

17.7.1 Existing Subset Bound Solvers

Subset bound solvers can be found atop different types of kernel languages such as Prolog enriched with constraint solving and replacing the standard Prolog variable by an attributed variable [52] subject to a dedicated unification algorithm. Prolog based set solvers can be found in ECL^{i}PS^e, B-Prolog and Cardinal for instance. Other kernel systems are based on object oriented language such as C^{++}(SOLVER), concurrent object-oriented language like OZ (MOZART), a functional language OCaml (FACILE), and java (the open source Choco system) to name the main ones. Each offers different modeling and resolution facilities.

17.7.2   Set Data Structures

Most existing finite set solvers make use of the subset bound representation for space and computational efficiency reasons. The ROBDD proposal investigates the use of binary decision diagram to represent set domains, allowing for full domains as well as intervals.

The internal representation of sets plays a role in the time complexity of the different set operations on the domains since such operations cannot be considered constant unlike arithmetic operations over integers. For the bound representation we can use 2 sorted lists one for each bound, an array of 0-1 variables (both bounds in a single array) or bitmaps representing the characteristic function of the set. The same structures can be used for ground set representations if the two bounds are stored separately as well as more elaborate ones such as binomial trees or binary trees.

Since set operations on domains are performed by reasoning on either or both bounds we give hereafter the time complexity for basic set operations on ground sets. When one structure is used to embed both bounds the same reasoning applies. Let s be the set with largest domain such that $d = |lub(s)| + |glb(s)|$. The cardinality information is usually maintained dynamically as part of the set variable data structure.

ROBDDs correspond to directed acyclic graphs. Recall that the ROBDD approach transforms set constraints into Boolean operations and can model domain reasoning as well as interval reasoning. The complexity of basic set operations depends on the ordering of the Boolean variables. For a given constraint we can generate an exponential as well as a linear representation in a Boolean formula. We consider N as the size of the set domain which can potentially correspond to $2^{lub(s)}$. The main thing is that each basic set operation generates an ROBDD. So the complexity issue relates to the size of the generated ROBDD.

17.7.3   Complexity of Set Operations

For bound domains the corresponding initial ROBDD corresponds to the size of the lower bound independent of the upper bound size and any update can be represented in O($glb(s) \mid +N- \mid lub(s) \mid$). For an extensive domain representation the size of the initial ROBDD is linear relative to N [60]. The size of the ROBDD for the different basic set operations is given below where N is the size of the largest set domain and k a bound on the cardinality. The cardinality constraint is quite tricky to express in Boolean formula and requires a quadratic number of formula defined recursively hence the complexity results.

The strength of hash tables is the constant time on average to retrieve information. "+" represents the "capacity" of the backing (the number of buckets).

Alternative approaches exist based on the representation of a ground set. They are used mainly for dynamic set operations (add, remove, and sometimes union) and correspond to tree structures (B-tree, binary search tree, binomial tree). The worst case time complexity for ground sets operations is usually measured by the height of the tree. For sets of cardinality c we have: $h = \log c$ where h is the height of the tree. For such structures the efficiency lies in the membership test $\mathcal{O}(\log c)$, union is in $O(c \log c)$.

	$=$	$\subseteq$	$\cup$	$\cap$	$\backslash$	$\in$	$\|\|$
sorted list	$O(d)$	$O(glb(s))$	$O(d)$	$O(d)$	$O(d)$	$O(\|\,glb(s)\,\|)$	$O(1)$
0-1 array	(1)	(d)	$O(d)$	$O(d)$	$O(d)$	$O(1)$	$O(1)$
hash table	$O(1)$	$O(k+)$	$O(k+)$	$O(k+)$	$O(k+)$	$O(1)$	$O(1)$
ROBDD	$O(N)$	$O(N)$	$O(N)$	$O(N)$	$O(N)$	$O(1)$	$O(k(N-k))$

17.8 Applications

Each structured domain was developed to address particular application needs. For instance, the graph domain was motivated by a problem for biochemical network analysis [24]. The order-sorted and ontology domains were driven by industrial problems, for instance in the area of e-commerce for ontologies.

The structured domain which has been the most widely developed and used is certainly that of finite sets. The reason is probably that sets are the underlying structured objects for the other domains. Set solvers have been used to tackle small and large size benchmark and "real-world" problems ranging from bin packing ([39]), set partitioning ([40, 70, 68]), digital circuit and warehouse location [3], combinatorial design ([8, 60, 45]), and network design ([29, 88, 85]) among others. Recently, combinatorial designs have shown to have a wide applicability in error-correcting codes, sport scheduling, Steiner systems and more recently networking and cryptography (e.g. see [19] for a survey). Set constraints have shown their adequacy for such problems, and powerful models have been derived combined with symmetry breaking techniques and heuristic techniques. We draw particular attention, to the solving of the challenging Kirkman school girl problem in few seconds, with an elaborate approach which uses a set model extended with redundant constraints and symmetry breaking techniques[8]. More discussions on symmetry breaking and modeling aspects can be found respectively in Chapter 10, "Symmetry in Constraint Programming", and Chapter 11 "Modelling".

Another application area of increasing interest for constraint practitioners, is network design. Various successful set-based models have been proposed to tackle the network design SONET problem from a constraint programming perspective [88, 85]. They demonstrate the strength of applying dual models, redundant constraints and symmetry breaking techniques to set models.

17.9 Further Topics

Constraint reasoning over structured domains has mainly been motivated by the development of high level modeling and specification languages that ease the formulation of complex combinatorial problems while retaining efficiency.

Research on high level specification languages has long existed but is now growing in constraint programming [32, 48, 15]. Many constraint programming languages –both in academia and industry– utilizing structured domains have been proposed, demonstrating important progress (e.g. graphs [24], order-sorted domains [17], ontologies [59], multi-sets [93], and lattices [30]). Much progress has also been made on improving language effectiveness, in particular with respect to set solvers (e.g. cardinality inferences [5], the use of ROBDDs [45], more expressive domain representations [84, 41], global propagators [82, 13, 51]). This research area is extremely active.

Finally, a programming language that allows practitioners to state the problem in a natural and concise form without needing to worry about the solution method does not yet exist. However, certain steps have been taken towards this goal. In particular, a high level problem formulation allows language designers and programmers, to see the actual problem structure and components, and consequently to identify combinations of constraints that best exploit the problem structure.

Acknowledgements

The author is thankful to Jean-François Puget for his comments during the preparation of this chapter. The author was partially supported by the Royal Academy of Engineering, on a Global Research Award.

Bibliography

[1] J-R. Abrial. The B Book - Assigning Programs to Meanings. *Cambridge University Press*, ISBN = 0521496195, 1996.

[2] A. Aiken. Set Constraints: Results, Applications andFuture Directions. In *Proceedings of PPCP'04*, 1994.

[3] F. Azevedo. *Constraint Solving over Multi-Valued Logics. Application to Digital Circuits*. Frontiers in Artificial Intelligence and Applications, 2003.

[4] F. Azevedo and P. Barahona. Cardinal: an extended set solver. in *Proceedings of Computational Logic*, 2000.

[5] F. Azevedo. Cardinal: A Finite Set Constraints Solver. In Constraint journal, (to appear), 2006.

[6] L. Bachmaier, H. Ganzinger, and U. Waldmann. Set Constraints are the Monadic Class. In *Proceedings of LICS*-1993.

[7] N. Barnier and P. Brisset. Facile: A Functional Constraint Library. In *CICLOPS'01* workshop, help alongside with CP-2001.

[8] N. Barnier and P. Brisset. Solving the Kirkman's Schoolgirl Problem in a Few Seconds. In M. Wallace, editor, *Proceedings of CP*-2004.

[9] P. Baptiste, B. Legeard, and H. Zidoum. Sequence Constraint Solving in Constraint Logic Programming. In *ICTAI*-1994.

[10] C. Beeri, S. Naqvi, O. Shmueli, and S. Tsur. Set constructors in a logic database language. In *Journal of Logic Programming*, pages 181–232, 1991.

[11] F. Benhamou. Interval Constraint Logic Programming. In A. Podelski, editor, *Constraint Programming: Basics and Trends*, LNCS 910, 1995.

[12] C. Berge. Principle of combinatorics. Volume 72 of Mathematics in science and engineering. Academic Press, 1971.

[13] C. Bessière, B. Hnich, E. Hébrard, and T. Walsh. Disjoint, Partition and Intersection Constraints for Sets and Multiset Variables. In M. Wallace, editor, *Proceedings of CP*-2004, LNCS 3258.

[14] C. Bessière, B. Hnich, E. Hébrard, and T. Walsh. The Tractability of Global Constraints. In M. Wallace, editor, *Proceedings of CP*-2004, LNCS 3258.

[15] F. Bouquet, B. Legeard, and F. Peureux. CLPS-B: A Constraint Solver to Animate a B Specification. *International Journal on Software Tools for Technology Transfer, STTT*. 6:2, pp 143–157, Springer Verlag, 2004.

[16] R.E. Bryant. *Symbolic Boolean Manipulation with Ordered Binary-Decision Diagrams*. ACM Comput. Surv., 24(3), 293–318, 1992.

[17] Y. Caseau and J.-F. Puget. Constraints on Order-Sorted Domains. In *ECAI workshop*, 1996.

[18] J.G. Cleary. Logical arithmetic. *In Future Generation Computing Systems*, chapter 2(2),1987.

[19] Colbourn, Dinitz, and Stinson. Applications of Combinatorial Designs to Communications, Cryptography, and Networking. In *Surveys in Combinatorics, London Mathematical Society Lecture Note Series 187*. Cambridge University Press, 1999.

[20] A. Colmerauer, H. Kanoui, and M. Van Caneghem. Prolog, bases théoriques et développements actuels. *T.S.I. (Techniques et Sciences Informatiques)*, 2(4),1983.

[21] J. Crawford, M. Ginsberg, E.M. Luks, and A. Roy. Symmetry breaking predicates for search problems. In *Fifth Int. Conf. on Knowledge Rep. and Reasoning*, 1996.

[22] Y. Deville, G. Dooms, S. Zampelli, and P. Dupont. CP(Graph + Map) for Approximate Graph Matching. In *Proceedings of BeyondFD'05, First International Workshop on CP beyond FD*, held alongside CP-2005.

[23] M. Dincbas, H. Simonis, and P. Van Hentenryck et al. The Constraint Logic Programming Language CHIP. In *Proceedings of FGCS*-1988.

[24] G. Dooms, Y. Deville, and P. Dupont. CP(Graph): Introducing a Graph Computation Domain in Constraint Programming. In *Proceedings of CP*-2004.

[25] A. Dovier, E. G. Omodeo, E. Pontelli, and G. Rossi. {log}: A Logic Programming Language with Finite Sets. In *Proceedings of ICLP*-1991.

[26] A. Dovier. *Computable Set Theory and Logic Programming*. PhD Thesis TD-1/96, Universitàdegli Studi di Pisa, dip. di Informatica, March 1996.

[27] A. Dovier, E. G. Omodeo, E. Pontelli, and G. Rossi. {log}: A Language for Programming in Logic with Finite Sets. *In Journal of Logic Programming*, 28(1), 1996.

[28] A. Dovier, C. Piazza, E. Pontelli, and G. Rossi. Sets and Constraint Logic Programming. *In ACM Transaction on Programming Language and Systems*, 22(5) 2000.

[29] A. Eremin, F. Ajili, and R. Rodosek . A Set-based Approach to the Optimal IGP Weight Setting Problem. In *Proceedings of INOC*-2005.

[30] A.J. Fernandez and P.M. Hill. An Interval Constraint System for Lattice Domains. *in ACM Transactions on Programming Languages and Systems (TOPLAS)*, 26(1), ACM Press, 2004.

[31] R. E. Fikes. Ref-arf: A system for solving problems stated as procedures. *Artificial Intelligence*, 1:27–120, 1970.

[32] P. Flener, B. Hnich, Z. Kiziltan. Compiling high level type constructors in constraint programming. In *Proceedings of PADL*-2001, LNCS 1990.

[33] P. Flener, A. Frisch, B. Hnich, Z. Kiziltan, I. Miguel, J. Pearson, and T. Walsh. Breaking row and column symmetries in matrix models. In *Proceedings of CP*-2002,

LNCS.

[34] D. W. Fowler, D. Sleeman, G. Wills, T. Lyon, and D. Knott The Designers' Workbench: Using Ontologies and Constraints for Configuration. In 24th *International Conference on Innovative Techniques and Applications of AI*, 2004.

[35] A.M. Frisch, C. Jefferson, B.M. Hernandez, and I. Miguel. The Rules of Constraint Modelling. In *Proceedings of IJCAI*-2005.

[36] I.P. Gent, P. Prosser, and B.M. Smith. A 0/1 encoding of the gaclex for pairs of vectors. In *ECAI/W9 Modelling and Solving Problems with Constraints*, 2002.

[37] C. Gervet. New Structures of Symbolic Constraint Objects: Sets and Graphs. In *Third Workshop on Constraint Logic Programming (WCLP'93)*, 1993.

[38] C. Gervet. Sets and Binary Relation Variables Viewed as Constrained Objects. In *Workshop on Logic Programming with Sets*, held alongside ICLP-1993.

[39] C. Gervet. Conjunto : Constraint Logic Programming with Finite Set Domains. In M. Bruynooghe, editor, *Proceedings of ILPS*-1994.

[40] C. Gervet. Interval Propagation to Reason about Sets: Definition and Implementation of a Practical Language. *In Constraints journal* 1(3), 1997.

[41] C. Gervet and P. Van Hentenryck. A New Set Domain Representation Using Length-Lex Ordering. Technical Report, TR-06-02, Brown University, 2006.

[42] K. Golden and W. Pang. Constraint Reasoning over Strings. In *Proceedings of CP* 2003.

[43] P. Hall. On Representatives of Subsets. *Journal of London Mathematical Society*, 10, 1935.

[44] P. Hawkins, V. Lagoon, and P.J. Stuckey. Set bounds and (split) set domain propagation using ROBDDs. In G. Webb and X. Yu, editors, *Proceedings of AI'04: Australian Joint Conference on Artificial Intelligence*, LNCS 3339, 2004.

[45] P. Hawkins, V. Lagoon, and P. Stuckey. Solving Set Constraint Satisfaction Problems using ROBDDs. *Journal of Artificial Intelligence Research* 24, 2005.

[46] N. Heintze and J. Jaffar. A Decision Procedure for a Class of SetConstraints. In *Proceedings of the Fifth Annual IEEE Symposium on Logic in Computer Science* 1990.

[47] M. Hibti, H. Lombardi, and B. Legeard. Deciding in HFS-Theory via Linear Integer Programming with Application to Set Unification. In *Proceedings of LPAR*-1993.

[48] B. Hnich. *Function variables for Constraint Programming.* PhD thesis, Uppsala University,Department of Information Science, 2003.

[49] J. Hopcraft and J. Ullman. *Introduction to Automata Theory, Languages and Computation.* Addison-Wesley, Philippines, 1979.

[50] Ilog. User's manual. ILOG Solver 6.0 Sept., 2003.

[51] Ilog. User's manual. ILOG Configurator 2.3, 2004.

[52] S. Le Huitouze. A New Datastructure for Implementing Extensions to Prolog. In *Proceedings of PLILP*-1990, LNCS 456.

[53] D. Kapur and P. Narendran. NP-completeness of the set unification and matching problems. In *Proceedings of CADE*, 1986.

[54] Z. Kiziltan and T. Walsh. Constraint Programming with Multisets. In *Proceedings of the SymCon-02 workshop*, held alongside CP-2002.

[55] D. Knuth. The Art of Programming, Volume 4, Pre-Fascicle 2a: Generating all tuples.

[56] R.A. Kowalski. Predicate Logic as a Programming Language. In *Proceedings of IFIP*-1974.

[57] G. Kuper. *Logic Programming with Sets*, volume 41 of *1*, Academic Press, 1990.

[58] F. Laburthe. CHOCO: Implementing a CP Kernel. http://www.choco-constraints.net/, 2000. In *Proceedings of TRICS*, held alongside CP-2000.

[59] F. Laburthe. Constraints over Ontologies. In F. Rossi, editors, *Proceedings of CP-2003*.

[60] V. Lagoon and P.J. Stuckey. Set domain propagation using ROBDDs. In M. Wallace, editor, *Proceedings CP-2004*, LNCS 3258.

[61] J. L. Laurière. A Language and a Program for Stating and Solving Combinatorial Problems. *Artificial Intelligence*, 10, 1978.

[62] J.H.M. Lee and H. van Emden. Interval Computation as Deduction in CHIP. In *Journal of Logic Programming*, 16 (3-4), Elsevier, 1993.

[63] B. Legeard and E. Legros. Short overview of the CLPS System. In *Proceedings of PLILP-1991*.

[64] C.C. Lindner and A. Rosa. *Topics on Steiner Systems*, volume 7 of *Annals of Discrete Mathematics*. North Holland, 1980.

[65] M. Livesey and J. Siekmann. Unification of Sets and Multisets. Memo seki-76-ii, University of St. Andrews (Scotland) and Universität Karlsruhe (Germany) Department of Computer Science, 1976.

[66] A. K. Mackworth. Consistency in networks of relations. *Artificial Intelligence*, 1977.

[67] Mozart/Oz, http://www.moxart-oz.org/.

[68] T. Müller. Constraint Propagation in Mozart. PhD dissertation, Universität des Saarlandes, Naturwissenschaftlich-Technische Fakultät I, Fachrichtung Informatik, SaarbrÄucken, Germany, 2001.

[69] T. Müller and M. Müller. Finite Set Constraints in Oz. In *Workshop Logische Programmierung*, Burkhard Freitag and Dietmar Seipel, editors, 13, 1997.

[70] T. Müller. Solving Set Partitioning Problems with Constraint Programming. In *Proceedings of PAPPACT-1998*.

[71] W. Older and A. Vellino. Constraint Arithmetic on Real Intervals. In F. Benhamou and A. Colmerauer, editors, *Constraint Logic Programming: Selected Papers*. MIT Press, 1993.

[72] L. Pacholski and A. Podelski. Set Constraints: a Pearl in Research and Constraints. Tutorial at CP-1997.

[73] K. J. Perry, K. V. Palem, K. MacAloon, and G. M. Kuper. The Complexity of Logic Programming with Sets. *Computer Science*, 1986.

[74] G. Pesant. A Regular Language Membership Constraint for Finite Sequences of Variables. In *Proceedings of CP-2004*.

[75] J-F. Puget. PECOS a High Level Constraint Programming Language In *Proceedings of Spicis*, 1992.

[76] J-F. Puget. Set Constraints and Cardinality Operator: Application to Symmetrical Combinatorial Problems. In *Third Workshop on Constraint Logic Programming (WCLP'93)*, 1993.

[77] J.F. Puget. Finite set intervals. In *Workshop on set constraints*, held alongside CP-1996.

[78] C.-G. Quimper and T. Walsh. Beyond Finite Domains: the All Different and Global Cardinality Constraints. in *Proc. of CP-2005*, 2005.

[79] J.C. Régin. Generalized arc consistency for global cardinality constraints. In *Proceedings of AAAI-1996*, AAAI Press/The MIT Press.

[80] J.C. Régin and J.-F. puget. A Filtering Algorithm for Global Sequencing Constraints. In *Proceedings of CP*-1997, LNCS.

[81] J.C. Reynolds. Automatic Computation of Data Set Definitions. *In Information Processing*, 68, 1969.

[82] A. Sadler and C. Gervet. Global Reasoning on Sets. In *FORMUL'01 workshop on modelling and problem formulation* held alongside CP-2001.

[83] A. Sadler and C. Gervet. Global Filtering for the Disjointness Constraint on Fixed Cardinality Sets. Technical report ICPARC-04-02, March 2004.

[84] A. Sadler and C. Gervet. Hybrid Set Domains to Strengthen Constraint Propagation and Reduce Symmetries. In M. Wallace, editor, *Proceedings of CP*-2004, LNCS.

[85] A. Sadler. Strengthening Finite Set Constraint Solvers through Active Use of Problem Structure, Symmetries and Cardinality Information. PhD thesis, University of London, Imperial College, April 2005.

[86] J. Schimpf, A. Cheadle, W. Harwey, A. Sadler, K. Shen, and M. Walllace. ECL^{i}PS^e Technical report 03-1, IC-Parc, Imperial College London, 2003.

[87] O. Shmueli, S. Tsur, and C. Zaniolo. Compilation of set terms in the logic data language (LDL). *The Journal of Logic Programming*, 12(12):89–119, 1992.

[88] B. M. Smith. Symmetry and Search in a Network Design Problem. In *Proceedings of CP-AI-OR*-2005, LNCS 3524, Springer, 2005.

[89] F. Stolzenburg. Membership-constraints and complexity in logic programming with sets. In Franz Baader and Klaus U. Schulz, editors, *Frontiers in Combining Systems* Kluwer Academic, 1996.

[90] P. Van Hentenryck. *Constraint Satisfaction in Logic Programming*. Logic Programming Series. The MIT Press, 1989.

[91] P. Van Hentenryck. *The OPL Optimization Programming Language*. The MIT Press, 1999.

[92] C. Walinsky. CLP(Σ^*): Constraint Logic Programming with Regular Sets. In *Proceedings of ICLP*-1989.

[93] T. Walsh. Consistency and Propagation with Multiset Constraints: A Formal Viewpoint. In *Proceedings of CP*-2003, LNCS.

[94] N.F. Zhou. B-Prolog http://www.probp.com/.

Handbook of Constraint Programming   639
Edited by F. Rossi, P. van Beek and T. Walsh
© 2006 Elsevier B.V. All rights reserved

Chapter 18

Randomness and Structure

Carla Gomes and Toby Walsh

This chapter covers research in constraint programming (CP) and related areas involving random problems. Such research has played a significant role in the development of more efficient and effective algorithms, as well as in understanding the source of hardness in solving combinatorially challenging problems.

Random problems have proved useful in a number of different ways. Firstly, they provide a relatively "unbiased" sample for benchmarking algorithms. In the early days of CP, many algorithms were compared using only a limited sample of problem instances. In some cases, this may have lead to premature conclusions. Random problems, by comparison, permit algorithms to be tested on statistically significant samples of hard problems. However, as we outline in the rest of this chapter, there remain pitfalls waiting the unwary in their use. For example, random problems may not contain structures found in many real world problems, and these structures can make problems much easier or much harder to solve. As a second example, the process of generating random problems may itself be "flawed", giving problem instances which are not, at least asymptotically, combinatorially hard.

Random problems have also provided insight into problem hardness. For example, the influential paper by Cheeseman, Kanefsky and Taylor [12] highlighted the computational difficulty of problems which are on the "knife-edge" between satisfiability and unsatisfiability [84]. There is even hope within certain quarters that random problems may be one of the links in resolving the P=NP question.

Finally, insight into problem hardness provided by random problems has helped inform the design of better algorithms and heuristics. For example, the design of a number of branching heuristics for the Davis Logemann Loveland satisfiability (DPLL) procedure has been heavily influenced by the hardness of random problems. As a second example, the rapid randomization and restart (RRR) strategy [45, 44] was motivated by the discovery of heavy-tailed runtime distributions in backtracking style search procedures on random quasigroup completion problems.

18.1   Random Constraint Satisfaction

We begin by introducing the random problems classes studied in constraint satisfaction, and discussing various empirical and theoretical results surrounding them.

18.1.1   Models A to D

Most experimental and theoretical studies use one of four simple models of random constraint satisfaction problems. In each, we generate a constraint graph G, and then for each edge in this graph, we choose pairs of incompatible values for the associated conflict matrix. The models differ in how we generate the constraint graph and how we choose incompatible values. In each case, we can describe problems by the tuple $\langle n, m, p_1, p_2 \rangle$ where n is the number of variables, m is the uniform domain size, p_1 is a measure of the density of the constraint graph, and p_2 is a measure of the tightness of the constraints.

model A: we independently select each one of the $n(n-1)/2$ possible edges in G with probability p_1, and for each selected edge we pick each one of the m^2 possible pairs of values, independently with probability p_2, as being incompatible;

model B: we randomly select exactly $p_1 n(n-1)/2$ edges for G, and for each selected edge we randomly pick exactly $p_2 m^2$ pairs of values as incompatible;

model C: we select each one of the $n(n-1)/2$ possible edges in G independently with probability p_1, and for each selected edge we randomly pick exactly $p_2 m^2$ pairs of values as incompatible;

model D: we randomly select exactly $p_1 n(n-1)/2$ edges for G, and for each selected edge we pick each one of the m^2 possible pairs of values, independently with probability p_2, as being incompatible;

Whilst p_1 and p_2 can be either a probability or a fraction, similar results are observed with the four different models. Most experimental studies typically fix n and m, and vary p_1 and/or p_2. Typical parameter ranges include $\langle 10, 10, p_1, p_2 \rangle$, $\langle 20, 10, p_1, p_2 \rangle$, $\langle 10 - 200, 3, p_1, 1/9 \rangle$, and $\langle 10 - 200, 3, p_1, 2/9 \rangle$. The penultimate of these parameter ranges resembles graph 3-colouring. See Table 1 in [27] for a more extensive survey.

18.1.2   Phase Transition

Random problems generated in this way exhibit phase transition behaviour similar to that seen in statistical mechanics [12]. Loosely constrained problems are almost surely satisfiable. As we increase the parameters and constrain the problems more, problems become almost surely unsatisfiable. As n increase, the transition between satisfiable and unsatisfiable problems becomes sharper and sharper. In the limit, it is a step function [22]. Using a Markov first moment method, the location of this phase transition can be predicted to occur where the expected number of solutions is approximately 1 [73, 80]. Associated with this rapid transition in satisfiability of problems, is a peak in problem hardness for a wide range both of systematic and local search methods [12, 67, 73, 80]. Such problems are on the "knife-edge" between satisfiability and unsatisfiability [84]. It is very hard to tell if they are satisfiable or unsatisfiable. If we branch on a variable, the resulting subproblem is smaller but otherwise tends to look similar. We can only determine if the current subproblem is satisfiable deep in the search tree. See Figure 18.1 for some graphs displaying the "easy-hard-easy" pattern associated with phase transitions.

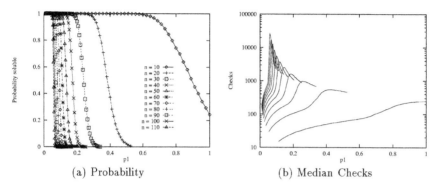

(a) Probability   (b) Median Checks

Figure 18.1: Phase transition for Model B problems with $\langle n, 3, p_1, 2/9 \rangle$ (a) percentage satisfiability and (b) median search effort for FC-CBJ with the fail-first heuristic against p_1, and n from 10 to 110. Graphs taken from [27].

Whilst the hardest problems typically occur close to this rapid transition in satisfiability, hard problems can occur elsewhere. In particular, in the easy and satisfiable region, problems can occasionally be very hard to solve, especially for systematic search procedures like forward checking [32, 47, 46]. Such exceptionally hard problems (EHPs) appear to be a consequence of early branching mistakes. Better branching heuristics, more informed backtracking mechanisms, greater constraint propagation and restart strategies can all reduce the impact of EHPs greatly. Since curves of median search effort may disguise the appearance of EHPs, experimentalists are encouraged to look for outliers.

18.1.3   Constrainedness

Williams and Hogg introduced the first comprehensive theoretical model of such phase transition behaviour for constraint satisfaction problems [86]. More recently, Gent et al. presented a theory that works across a wide range of problems and complexity classes including constraint satisfaction and satisfiability problems [30]. This theory is based around the definition of the "constrainedness" of a problem using the parameter κ. For an ensemble of problems:

$$\kappa = 1 - \frac{\log_2(\langle Sol \rangle)}{N}$$

Where $\langle Sol \rangle$ is the expected number of solutions for a problem in the ensemble, and N is the number of bits needed to represent a solution (or equivalently the log base 2 of the size of the state space). For instance, for model B, this is:

$$\kappa = \frac{n-1}{2} p_1 \log_m \left(\frac{1}{1-p_2} \right)$$

This constrainedness parameter, κ lies in the interval $[0, \infty)$. For $\kappa < 1$, problems are under-constrained and are typically easy to show satisfiable. For $\kappa > 1$, problems are over-constrained and are typically relatively easy to show unsatisfiable. For $\kappa \approx 1$, problems are critically constrained and exhibit a sharp transition in satisfiability. For instance, for random constraint satisfaction problem, graph k-colouring problems, number partitioning, and travelling salesperson problems, a rapid phase transition in problem satisfiability has been observed around $\kappa \approx 1$ [27].

Exact theoretical results about the location of the phase transition and of the hardness of random constraint satisfaction problems have been harder to obtain than either empirical results or approximate results using "theories" like that of constrainedness. One exception is work in resolution complexity. Most of the standard backtracking algorithms like forward checking and conflict-directed backjumping explore search trees bounded in size by the size of a corresponding resolution refutation. Resolution complexity results can thus be used to place (lower) bounds on problem hardness. For example, random constraint problems almost surely have an exponential resolution complexity when the constraint tightness is small compared to the domain size [68, 66, 25, 89].

18.1.4   Finite-Size Scaling

The scaling of the phase transition with problem size can be modelled using finite-size scaling methods taken from statistical mechanics [60, 30]. In particular, around some critical value of constrainedness κ_c, problems of all sizes are indistinguishable except for a simple change of scale given by a power law in N. Once rescaled, macroscopic properties like the probability that a problem is satisfiable obey simple equations. For example, the probability of satisfiability can be modelled with the simple equation:

$$prob(Sol > 0) \quad = \quad f\left(\frac{\kappa - \kappa_c}{\kappa_c} N^{1/\nu}\right)$$

Where f is some universal function, $\frac{\kappa - \kappa_c}{\kappa_c}$ plays the roles of the reduced temperature $\frac{T - T_c}{T_c}$ as it rescales around the critical point, and $N^{1/\nu}$ is a simple power law that describes the scaling with problem size. See Figure 18.2 for some graphs which illustrate this finite-size scaling. Finite-size scaling is used in statistical mechanics to describe systems like Ising magnets with 10^{20} or more atoms (and thus with $2^{10^{20}}$ or so states). It is remarkable therefore that similar mathematics can be used to describe a constraint satisfaction problem with tens or hundreds of variables and therefore just 2^{100} or so states.

Finite-size scaling also appears to be useful to model the change in problem hardness with problem size and problem constrainedness [31]. Finally, parameters like κ and proxies for them which are cheaper to compute appear useful as branching heuristics [27]. A good heuristic is to branch on the "most constrained" variable. This will encourage propagation and tend to give a new subproblem to solve which is much smaller.

18.1.5   Flaws and Flawless Methods

Random problems may contain structures which make them artificially easy. One issue is trivial flaws which a polynomial algorithm could easily discover. In a binary constraint satisfaction problem, the assignment of a value to a variable is said to be flawed if there exists another variable that cannot be assigned a value without violating a constraint. The

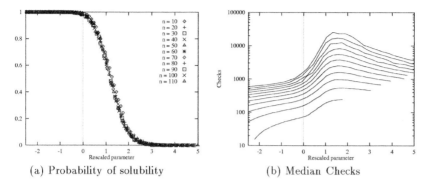

(a) Probability of solubility   (b) Median Checks

Figure 18.2: Finite-size scaling of the phase transition for Model B problems with $\langle n, 3, p_1, 2/9 \rangle$. (a) percentage satisfiability and (b) median search effort for FC-CBJ with the fail-first heuristic against the rescaled parameter, $\frac{\kappa - \kappa_c}{\kappa_c} N^{1/\nu}$ for $\kappa_c = 0.625$ and $\nu = 2.3$. Graphs taken from [27].

value is supported otherwise. A variable is flawed iff each value is flawed. A problem with a flawed variable cannot have a solution. Achlioptas et al. [4] identify a potential shortcoming of all four random models. They prove that if $p_2 \geq 1/m$ then, as n goes to infinity, there almost surely exists a flawed variable. Such problems are not intrinsically hard as a simple arc-consistency algorithm can solve them in polynomial time.

Fortunately, such flaws are unlikely in the size of problems used in practice [27]. We can also define parameters for existing methods and new generation methods which prevent flaws. For example:

model B: the parameter scheme $m = n^\alpha$, $p_1 = \beta \log(n)/(n-1)$ for some constants α, β [91, 89]; Xu and Li also present a similar parameter scheme for model D in which domain size grows polynomially with the number of variables; such problems are guaranteed to have a phase transition and to give problems which almost surely have an exponential resolution complexity;

model D: Smith proposes a somewhat more complex scheme which increases m and the average degree of the constraint graph with n [81];

model E: a new generation method in which we select uniformly, independently and with repetition, exactly $pm^2 n(n-1)/2$ nogoods out of the $m^2 n(n-1)/2$ possible for some fixed p [4];

modified models A to D: we ensure the conflict matrix of each constraint is flawless by randomly choosing a permutation π_i of 1 to m, and insist that (i, π_i) is a good before we randomly pick nogoods from the other entries in the conflict matrix; each value is thereby guaranteed to have some support [27].

Model E is very similar to the one studied by Williams and Hogg [86]. One possible shortcoming of Model E is that it generates problems with a complete constraint graph for quite small values of p. It is hard therefore to test the performance of algorithms on sparse problems using Model E [27].

The modified versions of models A to D are guaranteed not to contain trivial flaws which would be uncovered by enforcing arc-consistency. However, more recent results have shown that such problems may still be asymptotically unsatisfiable and can be solved in polynomial time using a path consistency algorithm [25]. In response, Gao and Culberson propose a method to generate random problems which are weakly path-consistent, and which almost surely have an exponential resolution complexity.

18.1.6 Related Problems

Phase transition behaviour has also been observed in other problems associated with constraint satisfaction problems. This includes problems in both higher and lower complexity classes. For example, phase transition behaviour has been observed in polynomial problems like establishing the arc-consistency of random constraint satisfaction problems [29]. The probability that the problem can be made arc-consistent goes through a rapid transition, and this is associated with a peak for the complexity of coarse grained arc-consistency algorithms. As a second example, phase transition behaviour has been observed in PSPACE-complete problems like the satisfiability of quantified Boolean formulae. We have to be again carefully of generating flawed problems, but if we do, there is a rapid transition in satisfiability, and this is associated with a complexity peak for many search algorithms [37]. As a third and final example, phase transition behaviour has been observed in PP-complete problems like deciding if a Boolean formulae can be satisfied by at least the square-root of the total number of assignments [8].

18.2   Random Satisfiability

One type of constraint satisfaction problem with a special but very simple structure is propositional satisfiability (SAT). In a SAT problem, variables are only Boolean, and constraints are propositional formulae, typically clauses. Many problems of practical and theoretical importance can be easily mapped into SAT. Random SAT problems have been the subject of extensive research. As a result, some of our deepest understanding has come in this area.

18.2.1   Random k-SAT

There exist a number of different classes of random SAT problem. One such problem class is the "constant probability" model in which each variable is included in a clause with a fixed probability. However, this gives problems which are often easy to solve. Following [67], research has focused on the random k-SAT problem class. A random k-SAT problem in n variables consists of m clauses, each of which contains exactly k Boolean variables drawn uniformly and at random from the set of all possible k-clauses. A rapid transition in satisfiability is observed to occur around a fixed ratio of clauses to variables and this appears to be correlated with a peak in search hardness [67]. Such problems are routinely used to benchmark SAT algorithms.

For random 2-SAT, which is polynomial, the phase transition has been proven to occur at exactly $m/n = 1$ [14, 38]. For random k-SAT for $k \geq 3$, exact results have been harder to obtain. For $k = 3$, the phase transition occurs between $3.42 \leq m/n \leq 4.51$ Experiments suggest that the transition is at $m/n = 4.26$. Asymptotically, the satisfiability transition is "sharp" (that is, it is a step function) [22]. A very recent result proves that the threshold is at $2^k \log(2) - O(k)$, confirming "approximate" results from statistical mechanics using replica methods [5]. Finite-size scaling methods can again be used to model the sharpening of the phase transition with problem size [60].

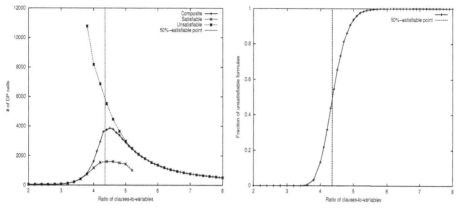

Figure 18.3: Median search cost for DPLL to solve 50 variable random 3-SAT problems and fraction of unsatisfiable clauses, both plotted against the ratio of clauses to variables. Graphs adapted from [67].

At least one note of caution needs to be sounded about the using random 3-SAT as the distribution of solutions is highly skewed. In particular, at the phase transition, the expected number of solutions is exponentially large [57]. Thus, whilst many problems have no solutions, a few problems will have exponentially many.

18.2.2 Backbone

A possible "order parameter" for such phase transitions is the backbone. For a satisfiable problem, the backbone is the fraction of variables which take fixed values in all satisfying assignments. Such variables must be assigned correctly if we are to find a solution. For an unsatisfiable problem, the backbone is the fraction of variables which take fixed values in all assignments which maximize the number of satisfied clauses. A satisfiable problem with a large backbone is likely to be hard to solve for systematic methods like DPLL since there are many variables to branch incorrectly upon. For random 3-SAT, the backbone size jumps discontinuously at the phase transition, suggesting that it behaves like a first-order (or discontinuous) phase transition in statistical mechanics. For random 2-SAT, on the other hand, the backbone size varies smoothly over the phase transition suggesting that it behaves like a second-order (or continuous) phase transition. However, the order (or continuity) of the phase transition does not appear to be directly connected to the problem complexity as there are NP-complete problems with second-order (or continuous) phase transitions.

18.2.3 2+p-SAT

Significant insight into phase transition behaviour has come from "interpolating" between random 2-SAT (which is polynomial and quite well understood theoretically) and random 3-SAT (which is NP-hard and much less well understood theoretically). The random 2+p SAT problem class consists of SAT problems with a mixture of $(1 - p)m$ clauses with 2 variables and pm clauses with 3 variables, each clause drawn uniformly and at random from the space of all possible clauses of the given size. For $p = 0$, we have random 2-SAT. For $p = 1$, we have random 3-SAT. For $0 < p < 1$, we have problems with a mixture of both 2-clauses and 3-clauses. From the perspective of worst-case complexity, 2+p-SAT is rather unexciting. For any fixed $p > 0$, the problem class is NP-complete. However, problems appear to be behave polynomially for $p < 0.4$ [69, 3]. It is only for $p \geq 0.4$ that problems appear hard to solve. This increase in problem hardness has been correlated with a rapid transition in the size of the backbone, and with a change from a continuous to a discontinuous phase transition [69]. For $0 \leq p \leq 0.4$, the satisfiability phase transition for random 2+p-SAT occurs at a simple lower bound, $1/(1-p)$ constructed by simply considering the satisfiability of the embedded 2-SAT subproblem. In other words, the 2-clauses alone determine satisfiability. It is not perhaps so surprising therefore that average search costs appears to be polynomial. Note that, having made some branching decisions on a 3-SAT problem, DPLL is effectively solving a 2+p-SAT subproblem. The performance of such procedures can thus be modelled by mapping trajectories through p and m/n space [15].

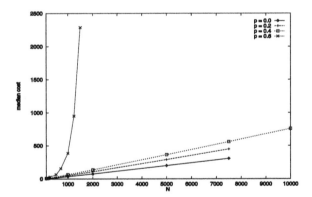

Figure 18.4: Median computational cost for DPLL to solve random 2+p-SAT problems plotted against the number of variables, N for a range of values of p. Graph adapted from [15].

18.2.4 Beyond k-SAT

Phase transition behaviour has been observed in other satisfiability problems including:

1 in k-SAT: each "clause" contains k literals, exactly one of which must be true. This was the first problem NP-complete class in which the exact location of its satisfiability phase transition was proven [1]. For all $k \geq 3$, random 1 in k-SAT problems have a sharp, second-order or continuous phase transition at $m/n = 2/k(k-1)$.

NAE-SAT: each "clause" contains k literals, all of which cannot take the same truth value. For $k = 3$, the phase transition for random NAE SAT problems occurs somewhere between $1.514 < m/n < 2.215$ [1]. Empirical results put the phase transition at around $m/n \approx 2.1$. A NAE SAT problem can be mapped into a SAT problem with twice the number of clauses. Although these clauses are correlated, it is remarkable that these correlations appear to be largely irrelevant and the phase transition occurs at almost exactly half the clause to variable ratio of the random 3-SAT phase transition.

XOR SAT: each "clause" contains k literals, an odd number of which must be true in any satisfying assignment. For $k = 3$, random NAE SAT has a sharp threshold in the interval $0.8894 \leq m/n \leq 0.9278$ [17]. Experiments put the transition at $m/n \approx 0.92$, whilst statistical mechanical calculations put it at $m/n = 0.918$ [21].

non-clausal SAT: formulae have a fixed shape (a given structure of and and or connectives) which are labelled with literals at random [71]. This model displays a phase transition in satisfiability with an associated easy-hard-easy pattern in search cost.

quantified SAT: in a quantified Boolean formula (QBF) we have variables which are both existentially quantified and universally quantified. If we generate random QBF formulae, we need to throw out clauses containing just universally quantified variables (as these are trivially unsatisfiable). If we eliminate such "flaws", there is a rapid phase transition, and an associated complexity peak [37]

18.2.5 Satisfiable Problems

Random problems have been a driving force in the design of better algorithms. To benchmark incomplete local search procedures, standard random problem generators are unsuitable as they produce both satisfiable and unsatisfiable instances. We could simply filter out unsatisfiable instances using a complete method. However, we are then unable to benchmark incomplete search methods on problems that are beyond the reach of complete methods. Designing generators, on the other hand, that generate only satisfiable problems has proven surprisingly difficult.

One approach is to "hide" at least one solution in a problem instance. For example, we can choose a random truth assignment $T \in \{0, 1\}^n$ and then generate a formula with n variables and αm random clauses, rejecting any clause that violates T. Unfortunately, this method is highly biased to generating formulas with many assignments. They are much easier for local search methods like Walksat [74] than formulas of comparable size obtained by filtering a random 3-SAT generator. More sophisticated versions of this "1-hidden assignment" scheme provide improvements but still lead to biased samples [7]. Achlioptas et al. [6] proposed a "2-hidden assignment" approach in which clauses that violate both T and its complement are rejected. Whilst DPLL solvers find such problems as hard as regular random 3-SAT problems, local search methods find them easy. An improved approach, called "q-hidden" [56], hides a single assignment but biases the distribution so that each variable is as likely to appear positively as as negatively, and the formula no longer points toward the satisfying assignment T. Indeed, we can even make it more likely that a variable occurrence disagrees with T, so that the formula becomes "deceptive" and points away from the hidden assignment. Empirical results suggest that the q-hidden model produces formulas that are much harder for Walksat.

Recently Xu et al [90] gave modifications of the random models B and D to generate "forced" solvable instances whose hardness is comparable to "unforced" solvable instances, based on the theoretical argument that the number of expected solutions in both cases is identical. They also provide empirical results showing that the unforced solvable instances, unforced solvable and unsolvable instances, and forced solvable instances exhibit a similar hardness pattern. In section 18.3 we will discuss a quite different strategy for generating guaranteed satisfiable random instances for structured CSP problems.

18.2.6   Optimization Problems

Phase transition behaviour has also been identified in a range of optimization problems. Some of our best understanding has come in satisfiability problems related to optimization like MAX-SAT (for example, [94, 79]. However, insight has also come from other domains like number partitioning [34, 36] and the symmetric and asymmetric travelling salesperson problems [35, 96, 95]. The simplest view is that optimization problems naturally push us to the phase boundary [33]. For systematic backtracking algorithms like branch and bound, we essentially solve a pair of decision problems right at the phase transition: we first find a solution to the decision problem with an optimal objective and then prove that the decision problem with any smaller objective is unsatisfiable. A more sophisticated view is that optimization problems like MAX-SAT can be viewed as bounded by a sequence of decision problems at successive objective values [94].

The concept of backbone has also been generalized to deal with optimization problems [78]. As with decision problems, transitions in problem hardness have been correlated with rapid transitions in backbone size [78, 94, 95]. These views suggest that there is a relatively simple connection between the hardness of decision and the corresponding optimization problem. Indeed, by solving (easy) decision problems away from the phase boundary, we can often predict the cost of finding optimal solutions [77].

18.3   Random Problems with Structure

Uniform random problems like random k-SAT are unlikely to contain structures found in many real world problems. Such structures can make problems much easier or much harder to solve. Researchers have therefore looked at ways of generating structured random problems. For example, the question of the existence of discrete structures like quasigroups with particular properties gives some of the most challenging search problems [76]. However, such problems may be too uniform and highly structured when compared to messy real-world problems. In order to bridge this gap, a number of random problem classes have been proposed that incorporate structures rarely seen in purely uniform random problems. For example, Gomes and Selman [39] proposed the quasigroup completion problem (QCP). As another example, Walsh proposed small-world search problems [85].

18.3.1 Quasigroup Completion

An order n quasigroup, or *Latin Square* , is defined by $n \times n$ multiplication in which each row and column is a permutation of the n symbols. A *partial* Latin square with p pre-assigned cells is an $n \times n$ matrix in which p cells of the matrix have been assigned symbols such that no symbol occurs repeated in a row or a column. The Quasigroup Completion Problem (QCP) is to determine if the remaining $n^2 - p$ cells (or "holes") can be assigned to obtain a complete Latin square (see Figure 18.5). QCP is NP-complete [16]. The structure in QCP is similar to that found in real-world domains like scheduling, timetabling, routing, and experimental design. One problem that directly maps onto the QCP is that of assigning wavelengths to routes in fiber-optic networks [61].

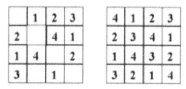

Figure 18.5: Quasigroup Completion Problem of order 4, with 5 holes.

To generate a random QCP instance, we randomly select p cells and assign each a symbol. We have a choice in the level of consistency enforced between such assignments to eliminate "obvious" inconsistencies. The most commonly used model enforces forward checking [39]. Shaw et al [75] studied a model which enforces generalized arc consistency on the all-different constraints on the rows and the columns of the matrix. This gives harder problems but biases the sampling. Empirical studies have identified phase transition behaviour in QCP [39]. The computationally hardest instances again lie at the phase transition. almost all unsolvable ("over-constrained" region). Figure 18.6 shows the computational cost (median number of backtracks) and phase transition in solvability for solving QCP instances of different orders.

18.3.2 Quasigroup with Holes

The QCP model generates both satisfiable and unsatisfiable instances. A different model, the Quasigroup With Holes problem (QWH), generates *only* satisfiable instances with good computational properties [2]. QWH instances are generated by starting with a full quasigroup and "punching" holes into it. Achlioptas et al [2] proposed the following QWH generator: (1) Generate a complete Latin square uniformly from the space of all Latin squares using a Markov chain; (2) punch a fraction p of "holes" into the full Latin square (*i.e.*, unassign some of the entries) in a uniform way. The resulting partial Latin square is guaranteed to be satisfiable. Achlioptas et al [2] demonstrated a rapid transition in the size of the backbone of QWH instances, coinciding with the hardest problem instances for *both* incomplete and complete search methods. Note that this transition is different from the standard transition in satisfiability as QWH *only* contains satisfiable instances. The location of this transition appears to scale as $n^2 - p/n^{1.55}$ [2].

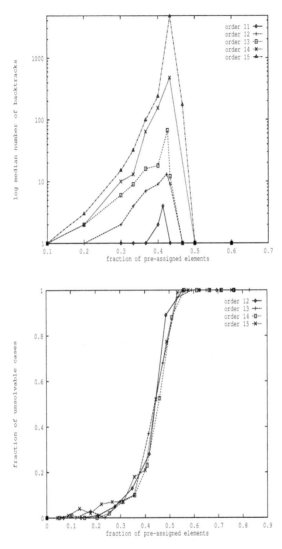

Figure 18.6: Top panel: computational cost of solving QCP instances (order 11–15). X-axis: fraction of pre-assigned cells; Y-axis - median number of backtracks for solution (log scale). Bottom panel: phase transition in solvability for QCP instances (order 12–15). X-axis: fraction of pre-assigned cells; Y-axis - fraction of instances for which the partial Latin square could not be completed into a full Latin square. (Each data point was computed based on 100 instances. Graphs from [39].)

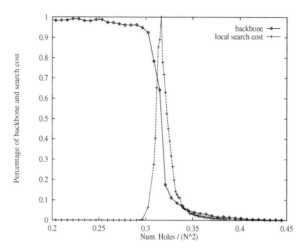

Figure 18.7: Backbone phase transition with cost profile for QWH. Graph from [2].

18.3.3 Other Structured Problems

A number of other random problem classes with structure have been studied. For instance, Walsh looked at search problems like graph coloring where the underlying graph has a "small-world" structure [85]. Although small-world graphs are sparse, their nodes tend to be clustered and the path length between any two nodes short. Walsh showed that a small-world structure often occurs in graphs associated with many real-world search problems. Unfortunately the cost of coloring random graphs with a small-world structure can have a heavy-tailed distribution (see next section) in which a few runs are exceptionally long. However, the strategy of randomization and restarts can eliminate these heavy tails.

To generate random small-world graphs, Walsh merged together random graphs with a structured ring lattice [85]. Inspired by this method, Gent *et al.* proposed a general method called *morphing* to introduce structure or randomness into a wide variety of problems [28]. They show that a mixture of structure and randomness can often make search problems very hard to solve. A little structure added to a random problem, or a little randomness added to a structured problem may be enough to mislead search heuristics. They argue that morphing provides many of the advantages of random and structured problem classes without some of the disadvantages. As in random problem classes, we can generate large, and statistically significant samples with ease. However, unlike random problems, morphed problems can contain many of the structures met in practice.

18.4 Runtime Variability

Broadly speaking, random problems tend to display "easy-hard-easy" patterns in difficulty. However, there has been some research into variability within this simple picture, and into ways such variability can be exploited.

18.4.1 Randomization

A randomized complete algorithm can be viewed as a probability distribution on a set of deterministic algorithms. Behaviour can vary even on a single input, depending on the random choices made by the algorithm. The classical adversary argument for establishing lower bounds on the run-time of a deterministic algorithm is based on the construction of a input on which the algorithm performs poorly. While an adversary may be able to construct an input that foils one (or a small fraction) of the deterministic algorithms in the set, it is more difficult to devise inputs that are likely to defeat a randomly chosen algorithm. Furthermore, as we will discuss below, the introduction of a "small" random element allows one to run the randomized method on the *same* instance several times, isolating the variance inherent in the search procedure from e.g., the variance that would result from considering different instances.

There are several opportunities to introduce randomization in a backtrack search method. For example, we can add randomization to the branching heuristic for tie-breaking [41, 43]. Even this simple modification can dramatically change the behavior of a search algorithm. If the branching heuristic is particular decisive, it may rarely need to tie-break. In this case, we can tie-break between some of the top ranked choices. The look-ahead and look-back procedures can also be randomized. Lynce *et al.* random backtracking which randomizes the backtracking points, and unrestricted backtracking which combines learning to maintain completeness [64, 65]. Another example is restarts of a deterministic backtrack solver with clause learning: each time the solver is restarted, with the additional learned clauses, it behaves quite differently from the previous run, appearing to behave "randomly" [70, 65].

18.4.2 Fat and Heavy Tailed Behavior

The study of the runtime distributions instead of just medians and means often provides a better characterization of search methods and much useful information in the design of algorithms. For instance, complete backtrack search methods exhibit *fat* and *heavy-tailed* behavior [47, 41, 23]. *Fat-tailedness* is based on the *kurtosis* of a distribution. This is defined as μ_4/μ_2^2 where μ_4 is the fourth central moment about the mean and μ_2 is the second central moment about the mean, *i.e.*, the variance. If a distribution has a high central peak and long tails, than the kurtosis is large. The kurtosis of the standard normal distribution is 3. A distribution with a kurtosis larger than 3 is *fat-tailed* or *leptokurtic* Examples of distributions that are characterized by fat-tails are the exponential distribution, the lognormal distribution, and the Weibull distribution. Heavy-tailed distributions have "heaver" tails than fat-tailed distributions; in fact they have some infinite moments. More precisely, a random variable X is heavy-tailed if it has Pareto like decay in its distribution, i.e:

$$1 - F(x) = P[X > x] \sim Cx^{-\alpha}, \ x > 0,$$

where $\alpha > 0$ and $C > 0$ are constants. When $1 < \alpha < 2$, X has infinite variance, and infinite mean and variance when $0 < \alpha <= 1$. The log-log plot of $1 - F(x)$ of a Pareto-like distribution (i.e., the survival function) shows linear behavior with slope determined by α.

Backtrack search methods exhibit dramatically different statistical regimes across the constrainedness regions of random CSP models [11]. Figure 18.8 illustrates the phenomenon. In the first regime (the bottom two curves in figure 18.8, $p \leq 0.07$), we see

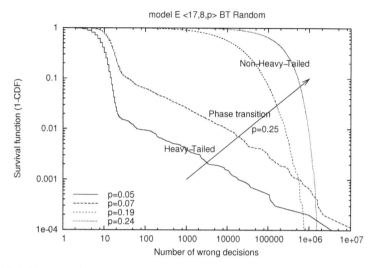

Figure 18.8: Heavy-tailed (linear behavior) and non-heavy-tailed regime in the runtime of instances of model E $\langle 17, 8, p \rangle$. CDF stands for Cumulative Density Function. Graphs adapted from [11].

heavy-tailed behavior. This means that the runtime distributions decay slowly. When we increase the constrainedness of our model towards the phase transition (higher p), we encounter a different statistical regime in the runtime distributions, where the heavy-tails disappear. In this region, the instances become inherently hard for the backtrack search algorithm, all the runs become homogeneously long, the variance of the backtrack search algorithm decreases and the tails of its survival function decay rapidly (see top two curves in figure 18.8, with $p = 0.19$ and $p = 0.24$; tails decay exponentially).

Heavy-tailed behavior in combinatorial search has been observed in several other domains, in both random instances and real-world instances: QCP [41], scheduling [45], planning[44], graph coloring [85, 55], and inductive logic programming [92]. Several formal models generating heavy-tailed behavior in search have been proposed [13, 87, 88, 55, 11, 51]. If a runtime distribution of a backtrack search method is heavy-tailed, it will produce runs over several orders of magnitude, some extremely long but also some extremely short. Methods like randomization and restarts try to exploit this phenomenon. (See section 18.4.4.)

18.4.3 Backdoors

Insight into heavy-tailed behaviour comes from considering backdoor variables. These are variables which, when set, give us a polynomial subproblem. Intuitively, a small backdoor set explains how a backtrack search method can get "lucky" on certain runs, where backdoor variables are identified early on in the search and set the right way. Formally, the definition of a backdoor depends on a particular algorithm, referred to as *sub-solver*, that solves a tractable subcase of the general constraint satisfaction problem [87].

Definition 18.1. *A sub-solver A given as input a CSP, C, satisfies the following:*

• *(Trichotomy) A either rejects the input C, or "determines" C correctly (as unsatisfiable or satisfiable, returning a solution if satisfiable),*

• *(Efficiency) A runs in polynomial time,*

• *(Trivial solvability) A can determine if C is trivially true (has no constraints) or trivially false (has a contradictory constraint),*

• *(Self-reducibility) if A determines C, then for any variable x and value v, then A determines $C[v/x]$.*[1]

For instance, A could be an algorithm that performs unit propagation, or arc consistency, or hyper-arc consistency for the *alldiff* constraint, or an algorithm that solves a linear programming problem, or any algorithm satisfying the above four properties. Using the definition of sub-solver we can now formally define the concept of backdoor set. Let A be a sub-solver, and C be a CSP. A nonempty subset S of the variables is a *backdoor* in C for A if for some $a_S : S \to D$, A returns a satisfying assignment of $C[a_S]$. Intuitively, the backdoor corresponds to a set of variables, such that when set correctly, the sub-solver can solve the remaining problem. A stronger notion of the backdoor, considers both satisfiable and unsatisfiable (inconsistent) problem instances. A nonempty subset S of the variables is a *strong backdoor* in C for A if for all $a_S : S \to D$, A returns a satisfying assignment or concludes unsatisfiability of $C[a_S]$. From a logical perspective, there is no formal connection between the backbone and the backdoor of a problem. Indeed, whilst it is possible to exhibit problems where they are identical, it is also possible to exhibit problems where they are disjoint. In practice, the overlap between backbones and backdoors appears to be slight [59].

Cutsets [18] are a particular kind of backdoor sets. A cutset is a set of variables such that, once they are removed from the constraint graph, the remaining graph has a property that enables efficient reasoning, an *induced width* of at most a constant bound b; for example, if $b = 1$ then the graph is cycle-free, i.e., it can be viewed as a tree, and therefore it can be solved using directed arc consistency. Backdoor sets can thus be seen as a generalization of cutsets, i.e., any cutset is a backdoor set. Backdoors are more general than the notion of cutsets since they consider *any* kind of polynomial time sub-solver. Note that, while cutsets (and W-cutsets) use a notion of tractability based solely on the topology of the underlying constraint graph, backdoor sets rely on a polynomial time solver to define the notion of tractability. A related issue is the fact that backdoor sets factor in the values of variables and the semantics of constraints (via the propagation triggered by the polytime solver) and therefore backdoor sets can be significantly smaller than cutsets. For example, if we have a constraint graph that contains a clique of size k, the cutset has at least $k - 2$ variables, while the backdoor set can be substantially smaller. Another example, considering CNF theories, is that while a Horn theory can have a cutset of size $O(n)$, the backdoor with respect to unit propagation has size 0 - unit propagation immediately detects (in)consistency of Horn theories. Stated differently, given two CNF theories, one of them a Horn theory and the other one an arbitrary CNF theory but with the same constraint graph as the Horn theory, there is no difference between the two theories from the perspective of

---

[1]*We use the notation $C[v/x]$ to denote the simplified CSP obtained from a CSP, C, by setting the value of variable x to value v.*

cutsets, but the difference between them from the perspective of backdoors is likely to be substantial.

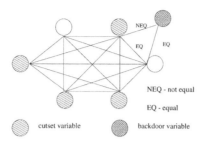

NEQ - not equal

EQ - equal

cutset variable   backdoor variable

Figure 18.9: Cutset vs. backdoor sets. Any cutset is a backdoor set. However, backdoor sets can be considerably smaller since they factor in the semantics of the constraints, via the propagation triggered by the sub-solver. Any clique of size k has a cutset of size $k - 2$. In this picture, the size of the cutset is 4 while the size of the backdoor set is 1 if the sub-solver performs forward checking or anything stronger.

A key issue is therefore the size of the backdoor set. Random formulas do not appear to have small backdoor sets. For example, for random 3-SAT problems, the backdoor set appears to be a constant fraction (roughly 30%) of the total number of variables [53]. This may explain why the current DPLL based solvers have not made significant progress on hard randomly generated instances. Seizer considers the parameterized complexity of the problem of whether a SAT instance has a weak or strong backdoor set of size k or less for DPLL style sub-solvers, i.e., subsolvers based on unit propagation and/or pure literal elimination [82]. He shows that detection of weak and strong backdoor sets is unlikely to be fixed-parameter tractable. Nishimura et al. [72] provide more positive results for detecting backdoor sets where the sub-solver solves Horn or 2-cnf formulas, both of which are linear time problems. They prove that the detection of such a strong backdoor set is fixed-parameter tractable, whilst the detection of a weak backdoor set is not. The explanation that they offer for such a discrepancy is quite interesting: for strong backdoor sets one only has to guarantee that the chosen set of variables gives a subproblem with the chosen syntactic class; for weak backdoor sets, one also has to guarantee satisfiability of the simplified formula, a property that cannot be described syntactically.

Empirical results based on real-world instances suggest a more positive picture. Structured problem instances can have surprisingly small sets of backdoor variables, which may explain why current state of the art solvers are able to solve very large real-world instances. For example the logistics-d planning problem instance, (log.d) has a backdoor set of just 12 variables, compared to a total of nearly 7,000 variables in the formula, using the polytime propagation techniques of the SAT solver, Satz [62]. Hoffmann et al proved the existence of *strong* backdoor sets of size just $O(\log(n))$ for certain families of logistics planning problems and blocks world problems domains [54].

Even though, computing backdoor sets is typically intractable, even if we bound the size of the backdoor [82], heuristics and techniques like randomization and restarts may nevertheless be able to uncover a small backdoor in practice [87, 59, 52]. For example one can obtain a complete randomized restart strategy that runs in polynomial time when

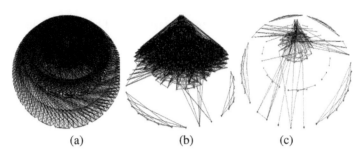

(a)	(b)	(c)

Figure 18.10: Constraint graph of a real-world instance from the logistics planning do-main. The instance in the plot has 843 vars and 7,301 clauses. One backdoor set for this instance w.r.t. unit propagation has size 16 (not necessarily the minimum backdoor set). (a) Constraint graph of the original constraint graph of the instance. (b) Constraint graph after setting 5 variables and performing unit propagation on the graph. (c) Constraint graph after setting 14 variables and performing unit propagation on the graph.

the backdoor set contains at most $\log(n)$ variables [87]. Dequen and Dubois introduced a heuristic for DPLL based solvers that exploits the notion of backbone that outperforms other heuristics on random 3-SAT problems [19, 20].

18.4.4 Restarts

One way to exploit heavy-tailed behaviour is to add restarts to a backtracking procedure. A sequence of short runs instead of a single long run may be a more effective use of compu-tational resources. Gomes et al. proposed a rapid randomization and restart (RRR) to take advantage of heavy-tailed behaviour and boost the efficiency of complete backtrack search procedures [44]. In practice, one gradually increases the cutoff to maintain completeness ([44]). Gomes et al. have proved formally that a restart strategy with a fix cutoff eliminates heavy-tail behavior and therefore all the moments of a restart strategy are finite [43].

When the underlying runtime distribution of the randomized procedure is fully known, the optimal restart policy is a fixed cutoff [63]. When there is no *a priori* knowledge about the distribution, Luby *et al.* also provide a *universal strategy* which minimizes the expected cost. This consists of runs whose lengths are powers of two, and each time a pair of runs of a given length has been completed, a run of twice that length is immediately executed. The universal strategy is of the form: $1, 1, 2, 1, 1, 2, 4, 1, 1, 2, 4, 8, \cdots$. Although the universal strategy of Luby *et al.* is provably within a constant log factor of the the optimal fixed cutoff, the schedule often converges too slowly in practice. Walsh introduced a restart strategy, inspired by Luby *et al.*'s analysis, in which the cutoff value increases geometrically [85]. The advantage of such a strategy is that it is less sensitive to the details of the underlying distribution. State-of-the-art SAT solvers now routinely use restarts. In practice, the solvers use a default cutoff value, which is increased, linearly, every given number of restarts, guaranteeing the completeness of the solver in the limit ([70]). Another important feature is that they learn clauses across restarts. The work on backdoor sets also provides formal results on restart strategies. In particular, even though finding a small set of backdoor variables is computationally hard, the presence of a small backdoor in a problem provides a concrete computational advantage in solving it with restarts [87].

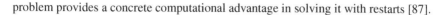

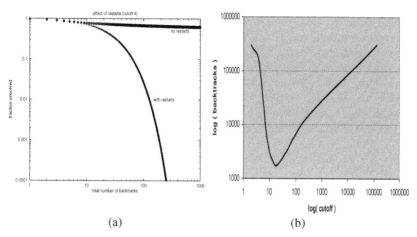

(a)   (b)

Figure 18.11: Restarts: (a) Tail $(1 - F(x))$ as a function of the total number of backtracks for a QCP instance, log-log scale; the left curve is for a cutoff value of 4; and, the right curve is without restarts. (b) The effect of different cutoff values on solution cost for the logistics.d planning problem. Graph adapted from [41, 43].

In reality, we will be somewhere between full and no knowledge of the runtime distribution. [48] introduce a Bayesian framework for learning predictive models of randomized backtrack solvers based on this situation. Extending that work, [58], considered restart policies that can factor in information based on real-time observations about a solver's behavior. In particular, they introduce an *optimal* policy for dynamic restarts that considers observations about solver behavior. They also consider the dependency between runs. They give a dynamic programming approach to generate the optimal restart strategy, and combine the resulting policy with real-time observations to boost performance of backtrack search methods.

Variants of restart strategies include randomized backtracking [64], and the random jump strategy [93] which has been used to solve a dozen previously open problems in finite algebra. Finally, one can also take advantage of the high variance of combinatorial search methods by combining several algorithms into a "portfolio," and running them in parallel or interleaving them on a single processor [50, 40, 42].

18.5   History

Research in this area can be traced back at least as far as Erdös and Rényi's work on phase transition behaviour in random graphs [10]. One of the first observations of a complexity peak for constraint satisfaction problems was Gaschnig in his PhD thesis where he used $\langle 10, 10, 1, p_2 \rangle$ model B problems (these resemble 10-queens problems) [26]. Fu and Anderson connected phase transition behaviour with computational complexity [24], as did Huberman and Hogg [49]. However, it was not till 1991, when Cheeseman, Kanefsky and Taylor published an influential paper [12] that research in this area accelerated rapidly.

Cheeseman et al. correlated complexity peaks for search algorithms with rapid transitions in problem satisfiability. They conjectured that all NP-complete problems display such phase transition behaviour and that this is correlated with the rapid change in solution probability. More recently, phase transition behaviour has been correlated with rapid changes in the size of the backbone. However, problem classes have been identified like Hamiltonian Cycle whose phase transition does not seem to throw up hard instances [83], as well as NP-complete problem classes which do not have any backbone [9]. Cheeseman, Kanefsky and Taylor also conjectured that polynomial problems do not have such phase transition behaviour or if they do it occurs only for a bounded problem size (and hence bounded cost) [12]. However, as we noted, even polynomial problems like establishing arc-consistency display similar phase transition behaviour [29]. Another polynomial problem class which displays phase transition behaviour is 2-SAT [38, 14].

18.6   Conclusions

As the many examples in this chapter have demonstrated, research into random problems has played a significant role in our understanding of problem hardness, and in the design of efficient and effective algorithms to solve constraint satisfaction and optimization problems. We need to take care when using random problems as there are a number of pitfalls awaiting the unwary. For example, random problems may lack structures found in real world problems. Research into areas like random quasigroup completion attempts to address such issues directly. As a second example, random problems may be generated with "flaws". However, if care is taken, such flaws can easily be prevented. There are many areas that look promising for future research. For example, we are only starting to understand the connection (if any) between the backbone and backdoor [59]. As another example, random problems capturing structural properties of real world problems [54] are starting to provide insight into key issues like backdoors. As a final example, search methods inspired by insights from random problems like randomization and restarts offer a promising new way to tackle hard computational problems. What is certain, however, is that random problems will continue to be a useful tool in understanding (and thus tackling) problem hardness.

Bibliography

[1]   D. Achlioptas, A. Chtcherba, G. Istrate, and C. Moore. The phase transition in 1-in-SAT and NAE SAT. In *Proceedings of the 12th Annual ACM-SIAM Symposium on Discrete Algorithms (SODA'01)*, pages 719–720, 2001.

[2]   D. Achlioptas, C. Gomes, H. Kautz, and B. Selman. Generating Satisfiable Instances. In *Proceedings of the Seventeenth National Conference on Artificial Intelligence (AAAI-00)*, New Providence, RI, 2000. AAAI Press.

[3]   D. Achlioptas, L.M. Kirousis, E. Kranakis, and D. Krizanc. Rigorous results for (2+p)-SAT. *Theoretical Computer Science*, 265(1-2):109–129, 2001.

[4]   D. Achlioptas, L.M. Kirousis, E. Kranakis, D. Krizanc, M.S.O. Molloy, and Y.C. Stamatiou. Random constraint satisfaction: A more accurate picture. In G. Smolka, editor, *Proceedings of Third International Conference on Principles and Practice of Constraint Programming (CP97)*, pages 107–120. Springer, 1997.

[5] D. Achlioptas and Y. Peres. The threshold for random k-SAT is $2^k \log(2) - o(k)$. *Journal of the AMS*, 17(4):947–973, 2004.

[6] D. Achlioptas, H. Jia, and C. Moore. Hiding satisfying assignments: Two are better than one. In *Proceedings of AAAI 2004*. AAAI, 2004.

[7] Y. Asahiro, K. Iwama, and E. Miyano. Random generation of test instances with controlled attributes. Contributed to the DIMACS 1993 Challenge archive, 1993.

[8] D.D. Bailey, V. Dalmau, and P.G. Kolaitis. Phase transitions of PP-complete satisfiability problems. In *Proceedings of the 17th IJCAI*, pages 183–189. International Joint Conference on Artificial Intelligence, 2001.

[9] A.J. Beacham. The complexity of problems without backbones. Master's thesis, Department of Computing Science, University of Alberta, 2000.

[10] B. Bollobás. *Random Graphs*. London, Academic Press, 1985.

[11] C. Gomes and C. Fernandez and B. Selman and C. Bessiere. Statistical Regimes Across Constrainedness Regions. In M. Wallace, editor, *Proceedings of 10th International Conference on Principles and Practice of Constraint Programming (CP2004)*. Springer, 2004.

[12] P. Cheeseman, B. Kanefsky, and W.M. Taylor. Where the really hard problems are. In *Proceedings of the 12th IJCAI*, pages 331–337. International Joint Conference on Artificial Intelligence, 1991.

[13] H. Chen, C. Gomes, and B. Selman. Formal Models of Heavy-tailed Behavior in Combinatorial Search. In T. Walsh, editor, *Proceedings of 7th International Conference on Principles and Practice of Constraint Programming (CP2001)*, pages 408–421. Springer, 2001.

[14] V. Chvatal and B. Reed. Mick gets some (the odds are on his side). In *Proceedings of the 33rd Annual Symposium on Foundations of Computer Science*, pages 620–627. IEEE, 1992.

[15] S. Cocco and R. Monasson. Trajectories in phase diagrams, growth processes and computational complexity: how search algorithms solve the 3-satisfiability problem. *Physical Review Letters*, 86(8):1654–1657, 2001.

[16] C. Colbourn. The complexity of completing partial Latin squares. *Discrete Applied Mathematics*, 8:25–30, 1984.

[17] N. Creognou, H. Daude, and O. Dubois. Approximating the satisfiability threshold for random k-XOR-formulas. Technical Report LATP/UMR6632 01-17, Laboratoire d'Informatique Fondamentale de Marseille, 2001.

[18] R. Dechter. Enhancement schemes for constraint processing: Backjumping, learning and cutset decomposition. *Artificial Intelligence*, 41(3):273–312, 1990.

[19] G. Dequen and O. Dubois. Kcnfs: An efficient solver for random k-SAT formulae. In *Proceedings of Sixth International Conference on Theory and Applications of Satisfiability Testing (SAT-03)*, 2003.

[20] O. Dubois and G. Dequen. A backbone search heuristic for efficient solving of hard 3-SAT formulae. In *Proceedings of the 18th IJCAI*. International Joint Conference on Artificial Intelligence, 2003.

[21] S. Franz, M. Leone, F. Ricci-Tersenghi, and R. Zecchina. Exact solutions for diluted spin glasses and optimization problems. *Phys. Rev. Letters*, 87(12):127209, 2001.

[22] E. Friedgut and J. Bourgain. Sharp thresholds of graph properties and the k-SAT problem. *Journal of the American Mathematical Society*, 12(4):1017–1054, 1999.

[23] D. Frost, I. Rish, and L. Vila. Summarizing CSP Hardness with Continuous Prob-

ability Distributions. In *Proceedings of the 14th National Conference on AI*, pages 327–333. American Association for Artificial Intelligence, 1997.

[24] Y. Fu and P. Anderson. Application of statistical mechanics to NP-complete problems in combinatorial optimisation. *J. Phys. A*, 19:1605–1620, 1986.

[25] Y. Gao and J. Culberson. Consistency and random constraint satisfaction problems. In M. Wallace, editor, *Proceedings of 10th International Conference on Principle and Practice of Constraint Programming (CP2004)*. Springer, 2004.

[26] J. Gaschnig. Performance measurement and analysis of certain search algorithms. Technical report CMU-CS-79-124, Carnegie-Mellon University, 1979. PhD thesis.

[27] I.P. Gent, E. MacIntyre, P. Prosser, B.M. Smith, and T. Walsh. Random constraint satisfaction: Flaws and structure. *Constraints*, 6(4):345–372, 2001.

[28] I.P. Gent, H. Hoos, P. Prosser, and T. Walsh. Morphing: Combining structure and randomness. In *Proceedings of the 16th National Conference on AI*. American Association for Artificial Intelligence, 1999.

[29] I.P. Gent, E. MacIntyre, P. Prosser, P. Shaw, and T. Walsh. The constrainedness of arc consistency. In *3rd International Conference on Principles and Practices o Constraint Programming (CP-97)*, pages 327–340. Springer, 1997.

[30] I.P. Gent, E. MacIntyre, P. Prosser, and T. Walsh. The constrainedness of search. In *Proceedings of the 13th National Conference on AI*, pages 246–252. American Association for Artificial Intelligence, 1996.

[31] I.P. Gent, E. MacIntyre, P. Prosser, and T. Walsh. The scaling of search cost. In *Proceedings of the 14th National Conference on AI*, pages 315–320. American Association for Artificial Intelligence, 1997.

[32] I.P. Gent and T. Walsh. Easy Problems are Sometimes Hard. *Artificial Intelligence* 70:335–345, 1994.

[33] I.P. Gent and T. Walsh. Phase transitions from real computational problems. In *Proceedings of the 8th International Symposium on Artificial Intelligence*, pages 356–364, 1995. URL http://apes.cs.strath.ac.uk/papers/ISAI95crc.ps.gz.

[34] I.P. Gent and T. Walsh. Phase transitions and annealed theories: Number partitioning as a case study. In *Proceedings of 12th ECAI*, 1996.

[35] I.P. Gent and T. Walsh. The TSP phase transition. *Artificial Intelligence*, 88:349–358, 1996.

[36] I.P. Gent and T. Walsh. Analysis of heuristics for number partitioning. *Computational Intelligence*, 14(3):430–451, 1998.

[37] I.P. Gent and T. Walsh. Beyond NP: the QSAT phase transition. In *Proceedings of the 16th National Conference on AI*. American Association for Artificial Intelligence, 1999.

[38] A. Goerdt. A threshold for unsatisfiability. In I. Havel and V. Koubek, editors, *Mathematical Foundations of Computer Science*, Lecture Notes in Computer Science, pages 264–274. Springer Verlag, 1992.

[39] C. Gomes and B. Selman. Problem Structure in the Presence of Perturbations. In *Proceedings of the Fourteenth National Conference on Artificial Intelligence (AAAI-97)*, pages 221–227, New Providence, RI, 1997. AAAI Press.

[40] C. P. Gomes and B. Selman. Algorithm Portfolio Design: Theory vs. Practice. In *Proceedings of the Thirteenth Conference On Uncertainty in Artificial Intelligence (UAI-97)*, Linz, Austria., 1997. Morgan Kaufman.

[41] C. Gomes, B. Selman, and N. Crato. Heavy-tailed Distributions in Combinatorial Search. In G. Smolka, editor, *Proceedings of Third International Conference on Principles and Practice of Constraint Programming (CP97)*, pages 121–135. Springer, 1997.

[42] C. Gomes and B. Selman. Algorithm portfolios. *Artificial Intelligence*, 126:43–62, 2001.

[43] C. Gomes, B. Selman, N. Crato, and H. Kautz. Heavy-tailed phenomena in satisfiability and constraint satisfaction problems. *Journal of Automated Reasoning*, 24 (1/2):67–100, 2000.

[44] C. Gomes, B. Selman, and H. Kautz. Boosting Combinatorial Search Through Randomization. In *Proceedings of the 15th National Conference on Artificial Intelligence (AAAI-98)*. American Association for Artificial Intelligence, 1998.

[45] C. Gomes, B. Selman, K. McAloon, and C. Tretkoff. Randomization in backtrack search: Exploiting heavy-tailed profiles for solving hard scheduling problems. In *The Fourth International Conference on Artificial Intelligence Planning Systems (AIPS'98)*, 1998.

[46] S. Grant and B.M. Smith. Where the *Exceptionally* Hard Problems Are. In *Proceedings of the CP-95 workshop on Really Hard Problems*, 1995. Available as University of Leeds, School of Computer Studies Research Report 95.35.

[47] T. Hogg and C.P. Williams. The Hardest Constraint Problems: a Double Phase Transition. *Artificial Intelligence*, 69:359–377, 1994.

[48] E. Horvitz, Y. Ruan, C. Gomes, H. Kautz, B. Selman, and D. Chickering. A bayesian approach to tackling hard computational problems. In *Proceedings of 17th Annual Conference on Uncertainty in Artificial Intelligence (UAI-01)*, pages 235–244, 2001.

[49] B.A. Huberman and T. Hogg. Phase Transitions in Artificial Intelligence Systems. *Artificial Intelligence*, 33:155–171, 1987.

[50] B. Huberman, R. Lukose, and T. Hogg. An economics approach to hard computational problems. *Science*, (265):51–54, 1993.

[51] T. Hulubei and B. O'Sullivan. Optimal Refutations for Constraint Satisfaction Problems. In *Proc. of the 19th International Joint Conference on Artificial Intelligence (IJCAI-05)*, 2005.

[52] T. Hulubei and B. O'Sullivan. The impact of search heuristics on heavy-tailed behaviour. *Constraints*, 11(2), 2006.

[53] Y. Interian. Backdoor sets for random 3-SAT. In *Proceedings of 6th International Conference on Theory and Applications of Satisfiability Testing*, 2003.

[54] J. Hoffmann and C. Gomes and B. Selman. Structure and problem hardness: Asymmetry and DPLL proofs in SAT-based planning. In *Proceedings of the Second International Workshop on Constraint Propagation and Implementation, CP 2005*, 2005.

[55] H. Jia and C. Moore. How much backtracking does it take to color random graphs? Rigorous results on heavy tails. In M. Wallace, editor, *Proceedings of 10th International Conference on Principles and Practice of Constraint Programming (CP2004)*. Springer, 2004.

[56] H. Jia, C. Moore, and D. Strain. Generating hard satisfiable formulas by hiding solutions deceptively. In *Proceedings of AAAI 2005*. AAAI, 2005.

[57] A. Kamath, R. Motwani, K. Palem, and P. Spirakis. Tail bounds for occupancy and the satisfiability threshold conjecture. *Randomized Structure and Algorithms*, 7:59–80, 1995.

[58] H. Kautz, E. Horvitz, Y. Ruan, C. Gomes, and B. Selman. Dynamic restart policies. In *Proceedings of the 18th National Conference on AI*, pages 674–681. American Association for Artificial Intelligence, 2002.

[59] P. Kilby, J. Slaney, S. Thiebaux, and T. Walsh. Backbones and backdoors in satisfiability. In *Proceedings of the 20th National Conference on AI*. AAAI, 2005.

[60] S. Kirkpatrick and B. Selman. Critical behaviour in the satisfiability of random Boolean expressions. *Science*, 264:1297–1301, 1994.

[61] S. R. Kumar, A. Russell, and R. Sundaram. Approximating Latin square extensions. *Algorithmica*, 24:128–138, 1999.

[62] C.M. Li and Anbulagan. Heuristics based on unit propagation for satisfiability problems. In *Proceedings of the 15th IJCAI*, pages 366–371. International Joint Conference on Artificial Intelligence, 1997.

[63] M. Luby, A. Sinclair, and D. Zuckerman. Optimal speedup of Las Vegas algorithms. *Information Processing Letters*, 47:173–180, 1993.

[64] I. Lynce, L. Baptista, and J. Marques-Silva. Stochastic systematic search algorithms for satisfiability. In *Proceedings of LICS workshop on Theory and Applications of Satisfiability Testing (SAT 2001)*, 2001.

[65] I. Lynce and J. Marques-Silva. Complete unrestricted backtracking algorithms for satisfiability. In *Fifth International Symposium on the Theory and Applications of Satisfiability Testing (SAT'02)*, 2002.

[66] D. Mitchell. The resolution complexity of constraint satisfaction. In *Proceedings of 8th International Conference on Principles and Practice of Constraint Programming (CP2002)*. Springer, 2002.

[67] D. Mitchell, B. Selman, and H. Levesque. Hard and Easy Distributions of SAT Problems. In *Proceedings of the 10th National Conference on AI*, pages 459–465. American Association for Artificial Intelligence, 1992.

[68] M. Molloy and M. Salavatipour. The resolution complexity of random constraint satisfaction problems. In *Proceedings of 44th Symposium on Foundations of Computer Science (FOCS 2003)*. IEEE Computer Society, 2003.

[69] R. Monasson, R. Zecchina, S. Kirkpatrick, B. Selman, and L. Troyansky. 2+p SAT: Relation of typical-case complexity to the nature of the phase transition. *Random Structures and Algorithms*, 15(3-4):414–435, 1999.

[70] W. Moskewicz, C.F. Madigan, Y. Zhao, L. Zhang, and S. Malik. Chaff: Engineering an efficient SAT solver. In *Proceedings of Design Automation Conference*, pages 530–535, 2001.

[71] J.A. Navarro and A. Voronkov. Generation of hard non-clausal random satisfiability problems. In *Proceedings of the 20th National Conference on AI*, pages 436–442. American Association for Artificial Intelligence, 2005.

[72] N. Nishimura, P. Ragde, and S. Szeider. Detecting backdoor sets with respect to horn and binary clauses. In *Proceedings of SAT 2004*. AAAI, 2004.

[73] P. Prosser. Binary constraint satisfaction problems: Some are harder than others. In *Proceedings of the 11th ECAI*, pages 95–99. European Conference on Artificial Intelligence, 1994.

[74] B. Selman, H. Kautz, and B. Cohen. Noise strategies for improving local search. In *Proceedings of 12th National Conference on Artificial Intelligence*, pages 337–343, 1994.

[75] P. Shaw, K. Stergiou, and T. Walsh. Arc Consistency and Quasigroup Completion. In

Proceedings of the ECAI-98 workshop on non-binary constraints, 1998.

[76] J. Slaney, M. Fujita, and M. Stickel. Automated reasoning and exhaustive search: quasigroup existence problems. *Computers and Mathematics with Applications*, 29: 115–132, 1995.

[77] J. Slaney and S. Thiébaux. On the hardness of decision and optimisation problems. In *Proceedings of the 13th ECAI*, pages 244–248. ECAI, 1998.

[78] J. Slaney and T. Walsh. Backbones in optimization and approximation. In *Proceedings of 17th IJCAI*. IJCAI, 2001.

[79] J. Slaney and T. Walsh. Phase transition behavior: from decision to optimization. In *Proceedings of the 5th International Symposium on the Theory and Applications of Satisfiability Testing, SAT 2002*, 2002.

[80] B.M. Smith. The phase transition in constraint satisfaction problems: A closer look at the mushy region. In *Proceedings of the 11th ECAI*. European Conference on Artificial Intelligence, 1994.

[81] B.M. Smith. Constructing an asymptotic phase transition in random binary constraint satisfaction. *Theoretical Computer Science*, 265:265–283, 2000.

[82] S. Szeider. Backdoor sets for DLL solvers. *Journal of Automated Reasoning*, 2006. Special issue, SAT 2005. To appear.

[83] B. Vandegriend and J. Culberson. The Gn,m phase transition is not hard for the Hamiltonian Cycle problem. *Journal of Artificial Intelligence Research*, 9:219–245, 1998.

[84] T. Walsh. The constrainedness knife-edge. In *Proceedings of the 15th National Conference on AI*. American Association for Artificial Intelligence, 1998.

[85] T. Walsh. Search in a small world. In *Proceedings of 16th IJCAI*. International Joint Conference on Artificial Intelligence, 1999.

[86] C. Williams and T. Hogg. Exploiting the deep structure of constraint problems. *Artificial Intelligence*, 70:73–117, 1994.

[87] R. Williams, C. Gomes, and B. Selman. Backdoors to typical case complexity. In *Proceedings of 18th IJCAI*. International Joint Conference on Artificial Intelligence, 2003.

[88] R. Williams, C. Gomes, and B. Selman. On the connections between backdoors, restarts, and heavy-tailedness in combinatorial search. In *Proceedings of Sixth International Conference on Theory and Applications of Satisfiability Testing (SAT-03)*, 2003.

[89] K. Xu, F. Boussemart, F. Hemery, and C. Lecoutre. A simple model to generate hard satisfiable instances. In *Proceedings of the 19th International Conference on AI*. International Joint Conference on Artificial Intelligence, 2005.

[90] K. Xu, F. Boussemart, F. Hemery, and C. Lecoutre. A simple model to generate hard satisfiable instances. In *Proceedings of IJCAI 2005*. IJCAI, 2005.

[91] K. Xu and W. Li. Exact phase transitions in random constraint satisfaction problems. *Journal of Artificial Intelligence Research*, 12:93–103, 2000.

[92] F. Zelezny, A. Srinivasan, and D. Page. Lattice-search runtime distributions may be heavy-tailed. In *Proceedings of the Twelfth International Conference on Inductive Logic Program*, 2002.

[93] H. Zhang. A random jump strategy for combinatorial search. In *Proceedings of International Symposium on AI and Math*, Fort Lauderdale, Florida, 2002.

[94] W. Zhang. Phase transitions and backbones of 3-SAT and Maximum 3-SAT. In

T. Walsh, editor, *Proceedings of 7th International Conference on Principles and Practice of Constraint Programming (CP2001)*. Springer, 2001.

[95] W. Zhang. Phase transitions and backbones of the asymmetric traveling salesman problem. *JAIR*, 21:471–497, 2004.

[96] W. Zhang and R.E. Korf. A study of complexity transitions on the asymmetric traveling salesman problem. *Artificial Intelligence*, 81(1-2):223–239, 1996.

Chapter 19

Temporal CSPs

Manolis Koubarakis

Reasoning with temporal constraints has been a hot research topic for the last twenty years. The importance of this topic has been recognized in many areas of Computer Science and Artificial Intelligence e.g., planning [4], scheduling [23], natural language understanding [91], knowledge representation [79], spatio-temporal databases and geographical information systems [62], constraint databases [89], medical information systems [102], computer-aided verification [5], multimedia presentations [2] etc.

Temporal reasoning is an area that has greatly benefited by the application of techniques from constraint programming ever since the early papers by James Allen and others [3, 107, 31, 108, 34]. The CSP framework introduced in Chapter 2 of this handbook is immediately applicable for representing and reasoning about temporal information, and so are the algorithms of Chapters 3, 4 and 5. Temporal CSPs have been proved to be a robust framework where general CSP results such as the ones surveyed in Chapters 7 and 8 of this handbook could be applied profitably. Moreover, specific results about temporal CSPs have often provided the motivation for deriving general results about CSPs. Temporal CSPs have been studied in depth, not only because of intellectual curiosity, but mostly due to their importance for applications such as planning, scheduling, temporal databases and others mentioned above. In many cases, the problems studied come straight from the application front and developed solutions are immediately put into practical use.

In this chapter, we survey work on temporal CSPs starting from the papers that appeared in the early nineties [3, 107, 31, 108, 34] and continue with contributions that have been published as recently as last year. We have covered all of the influential works, but due to space, we have sometimes been brief in our presentation. Our presentation is sometimes historical; we hope this will turn out to be useful for the readers. For more information on temporal CSPs and temporal reasoning in general, the reader can read the Handbook of Temporal Reasoning in Artificial Intelligence [41] or the original papers that have appeared in the literature.

The rest of this chapter is organized as follows. Section 19.1 introduces some preliminary concepts of temporal reasoning and temporal CSPs. Section 19.2 introduces the most influential temporal reasoning formalisms based on constraint networks that have been proposed in the literature and relevant algorithmic problems. Then, Section 19.3 discusses efficient constraint satisfaction algorithms for these formalisms. Section 19.4 introduces the application need for more expressive queries over temporal constraint networks (especially queries combining temporal and non-temporal information) and surveys various proposals that address this need. Sections 19.5 and 19.6 introduce the scheme of indefinite constraint databases that is, up to today, the most comprehensive proposal for querying hybrid representations consisting of a relational database component and a constraint network component. In the case of temporal CSPs, the constraint network can be used to store temporal constraints on various temporal objects, and the relational database to store facts referring to these objects. Finally, Section 19.7 concludes the chapter and points out some open problems.

19.1   Preliminaries

In this section, we introduce the topic of representing and reasoning about temporal information, and discuss the representational choices that have been made in the temporal reasoning literature. We also introduce some basic concepts of CSPs that will subsequently be used throughout the chapter.

19.1.1   Temporal Representation and Reasoning: Basic Concepts

In everyday life, most people are able to communicate their knowledge and understanding of temporal phenomena without any major difficulties. However, quite different intuitions surface as soon as people undertake to construct a formal temporal representation. The literature distinguishes among three approaches for representing temporal phenomena: the *change-based* approach (exemplified by situation calculus [74] or event calculus [64]), the *time-based* approach (exemplified by various temporal logics [106]) or temporal database models [62]) and their combination [86]. Research on temporal CSPs adopts a time-based approach to temporal representation and inference. Time is introduced explicitly via an appropriate set of times (called the *time structure*) and change is manifested when propositions become true or false at different elements of this set. Once one adopts this approach, the time structure must be precisely defined. The relevant issues here are:

- What are the elements of the time structure? *Points, intervals* or *both*? Research in temporal CSPs has usually adopted some set of numbers P (e.g., the rationals) to be the set of points and pairs $(x, y) \in P$ such that $x < y$ to be the set of intervals. Conventional time unit systems have also been studied (e.g., see the TUS system of [70]).

- Is time *totally ordered, partially ordered, branching* or *cyclic*? Research in temporal CSPs usually assumes time to be totally ordered. There has recently been some interesting work on CSPs for other models of time e.g., partially ordered time, branching time etc. [16].

- Is time *discrete* or *dense*? The issue here is whether there exists a unit of time which cannot be decomposed. Discrete time is usually considered to be isomorphic to the integers ($\mathbb{Z}$). Proponents of dense time have a choice between rationals ($\mathbb{Q}$) and reals

(ℝ). Various kinds of temporal CSPs have been studied that deal nicely with all three cases.

- Is time *bounded* or *unbounded*? Time is unbounded when for every element of the time structure there is a "previous" and a "next" element. Temporal CSPs can easily handle both cases.

Once one adopts an ontology and a structure for time, one usually turns to another, equally important, consideration: what are the kinds of temporal knowledge that must be represented? There are many kinds of temporal information that are useful in applications:

- *Definite temporal information.* We have definite temporal information when the time associated with an event or fact is known to be equal to an *absolute time* i.e., a point or interval on the time line. In other words, the time associated with an event or fact is known to full precision in the desired level of granularity. For example, the sentences "The car was on service throughout March 25th, 1993" and "The car has gone for service every March 25th for the years 1993-2000" give definite temporal information with respect to the time line of the Gregorian calendar. Note that the information in the second sentence is *periodic*.

- *Indefinite or indeterminate temporal information.* We have indefinite temporal information when the time associated with an event or fact is either unknown or has not been fully specified. The time associated with an event or fact can be under-specified in various ways [39]:

  - The time associated with an event or fact might be specified via a *qualitative relationship* (different than equality) to some absolute time. As an example, consider the sentence "John became manager *after* March, 1993".

  - The time associated with an event or fact might be specified via a *relationship* to the time associated with another event or fact. In this case, the two times can be related through a *qualitative, metric* (or *quantitative*) or *mixed temporal constraint.* For example, consider the statements "The explosion occurred *after* John left the scene" (qualitative temporal information), "The explosion occurred *5 to 10 minutes after* John left the scene" (metric temporal information), and "The explosion occurred *5 to 10 minutes after* John left the scene *while* he was getting into his car" (mixed temporal information).

  - The granularity of the system time line does not match the precision to which the time associated with an event or fact is known. As an example, consider storing the information "John was hired on January 25, 1993" in a system with time-stamps in the granularity of a second.

  - Dating techniques can be imperfect. All clocks have inherent imprecision.

Temporal CSPs are an expressive framework and they can represent all the above types of temporal information.

19.1.2 Background on CSPs

The area of temporal CSPs was initiated by James Allen in his seminal paper [3]. Allen proposed to represent qualitative temporal knowledge by interval constraint networks. An *interval constraint network* (see Figure 19.1) is a directed graph where nodes represents intervals and edges are labelled with vectors (i.e., disjunctions) of the thirteen binary qualitative interval relations presented in [3]. Following [3], many researchers concentrated on CSPs (or, equivalently, constraint networks) as a means for representing and reasoning about temporal knowledge. Their proposals are surveyed in Section 19.2 of this chapter.

In this chapter, the equivalent terms *CSP, constraint network* and *set (conjunction) of constraints* will be used interchangeably. We now define formally some of the concepts from the standard CSP literature that we will use in this chapter. We use $dom(x_i)$ to refer to the domain of variable x_i.

Definition 19.1. *Let C be a set of constraints in variables $x_1, \ldots, x_n$. The* solution set *of C, denoted by $Sol(C)$, is the following relation:*

$$\{(v_1, \ldots, v_n) \in dom(x_1) \times \cdots \times dom(x_n) : \text{ for every } c \in C, (v_1, \ldots, v_n) \text{ satisfies } c\}$$

Each member of $Sol(C)$ is called a solution *of C.*

Definition 19.2. *A set of constraints is called* consistent *or* satisfiable *if and only if its solution set is non-empty.*

We now define the standard concepts of i-consistency, strong i-consistency and global consistency (or decomposability).

Let C be a set of constraints in variables $x_1, \ldots, x_n$. For any i such that $1 \leq i \leq n$ $C(x_1, \ldots, x_i)$ will denote the set of constraints in C involving *only* variables $x_1, \ldots, x_i$.

Definition 19.3. *Let C be a set of constraints in variables $x_1, \ldots, x_n$ and $1 \leq i \leq n$. C is called i-*consistent *iff for every $i - 1$ distinct variables $x_1, \ldots, x_{i-1}$, every valuation $u = \{x_1 \leftarrow v_1, \ldots, x_{i-1} \leftarrow v_{i-1}\}$ such that $v_1 \in dom(x_1), \ldots, v_{i-1} \in dom(x_{i-1})$ and u satisfies the constraints $C(x_1, \ldots, x_{i-1})$, and every variable x_i different from $x_1, \ldots, x_{i-1}$ there exists a value $v_i \in dom(x_i)$ such that u can be extended to a valuation $u' = u \cup \{x_i \leftarrow v_i\}$ which satisfies the constraints $C(x_1, \ldots, x_{i-1}, x_i)$. C is called* strong i-*consistent if it is j-consistent for every j, $1 \leq j \leq i$. C is called* globally consistent *or* decomposable *iff it is i-consistent for every i, $1 \leq i \leq n$.*

We now define the standard concept of minimal set of constraints. Minimal sets of constraints are especially important in temporal CSPs because they make explicit all implied *binary* constraints (e.g., the strictest constraints between the endpoints of an interval or the constraints capturing the strictest qualitative relation between two points etc.). In a constraint network representation of binary constraints, the concept of minimal constraint set is equivalent to the concept of *minimal network*.

Definition 19.4. *A set of constraints C will be called* minimal *if any instantiation of two variables, which satisfies the constraints involving these variables only, can be extended to a solution of C.*

In temporal CSPs, the variables are used to represent time elements (points or intervals), the domains are time structures (usually $\mathbb{Z}, \mathbb{Q}$ or $\mathbb{R}$ for time points, and the set of intervals over $\mathbb{Z}, \mathbb{Q}$ or $\mathbb{R}$ for time intervals), and the constraints represent temporal relationships. Section 19.2 presents various temporal CSP frameworks with appropriate choices for variables, domains and temporal constraints.

The following reasoning problems have been traditionally associated with CSPs:

- Deciding whether a set of constraints is consistent.

- Finding a solution or all the solutions of a consistent constraint set.

- Computing the minimal set of constraints equivalent to a given one.

- Determining if a set of constraints is i-consistent, strong i-consistent or globally consistent.

The above reasoning problems have also been the main focus of algorithms for temporal CSPs proposed in the literature. These algorithms are surveyed in Section 19.3 of this chapter.

19.2 Constraint-Based Formalisms for Reasoning About Time

In this section we initiate our survey of temporal representation and reasoning formalisms based on constraint networks. We distinguish the proposed formalisms depending on the kind of temporal information they allow: qualitative, metric or mixed temporal information.

19.2.1 Qualitative Temporal Reasoning

As we already said earlier, the first important paper that proposed to represent qualitative temporal information by CSPs was [3] by James Allen. In [3], Allen introduced a formalism for reasoning about intervals in time. An *interval* i is a pair (i^-, i^+) where i^- and i^+ are *endpoints* on the real line and $i^- < i^+$ holds. Allen's formalism is based on thirteen mutually exclusive *binary relations* which can capture all the possible ways two intervals can be related. These *atomic* relations are

$$before, \; meets, \; overlaps, \; during, \; starts, \; finishes, \; equals$$

and their inverses (*equals* is its own inverse). Figure 19.2 defines these relations in terms of endpoint constraints, and gives a shorthand notation and pictorial representation for them.

Allen's formalism has received a lot of attention and has been the formalism of choice for representing qualitative interval information. Whenever the interval information to be represented is indefinite, a disjunction of some of the thirteen atomic relations can be used to represent what is known. There are 2^{13} such disjunctions representing qualitative relations between two intervals. Each one of these relations will be denoted by the set of its constituent basic relations e.g., $\{b, bi, d, m\}$. The *empty* relation will be denoted by $\bot$, and the *universal* relation will be denoted by $\top$. The set of all 2^{13} relations expressible in Allen's formalism will be denoted by $\mathcal{IA}$. The operations of intersection ($\cap$), complement ($\cdot^{-1}$) and composition ($\circ$) can be defined on $\mathcal{IA}$ as follows:

$$(\forall x, y)(x \, r^{-1} \, y \Leftrightarrow y \, r \, x)$$

$$(\forall x, y)(x \, (r \cap r') \, y \Leftrightarrow (x \, r \, y \wedge x \, r' \, y))$$

$$(\forall x, y)(x \, (r \circ r') \, y \Leftrightarrow (\exists z)(x \, r \, z \wedge z \, r' \, y))$$

The set $\mathcal{IA}$ equipped with these operations forms an algebra [82], called the *interval algebra*.

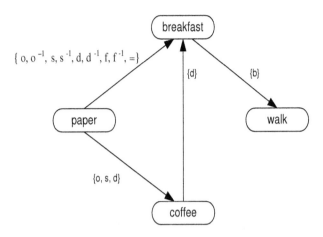

Figure 19.1: An $\mathcal{IA}$ network

Example 19.5. Let us consider the following text [103]:

> Fred was reading the paper while eating his breakfast. He put the paper down
> and drank the last of his coffee. After breakfast, he went for a walk.

If we use $breakfast, paper, walk$ and $coffee$ to stand for appropriate time intervals, the
information included in the above sentences is captured by the $\mathcal{IA}$ network of Figure 19.1.

In [3], Allen presented a constraint propagation algorithm for $\mathcal{IA}$ networks based on
path consistency which runs in $O(n^3)$ time where n is the number of intervals in the network. When constraints are propagated, some temporal knowledge that has been implicit
before is made explicit. Later on, Vilain and Kautz showed that Allen's constraint propagation algorithm is not complete because deciding the consistency of a set of $\mathcal{IA}$ constraints
is an NP-complete problem and so is computing the minimal network [107].

In the same paper, Vilain and Kautz introduced the *point algebra* $\mathcal{PA}$ which allows
one to relate two time points using the binary qualitative relations $<$, $>$ and $=$ and their
disjunctive combinations (see Figure 19.2). [107] also identified the *pointisable subclass*
$\mathcal{PIA}$ of $\mathcal{IA}$ which consists of all elements of $\mathcal{IA}$ that can be expressed as a conjunction
of binary constraints using only elements of $\mathcal{PA}$.

In [107], Vilain and Kautz claimed that Allen's constraint propagation algorithm computes the minimal network for $\mathcal{PA}$. Subsequently, van Beek pointed out that this result is
true only for the subset of $\mathcal{PA}$ which does not include the *disequality* relation $\neq$; this is the
convex point algebra $C\mathcal{PA}$ [101, 108, 104]. The same result is true for the *continuous endpoint subclass* $C\mathcal{EIA}$ of $\mathcal{IA}$ which consists of all elements of $\mathcal{IA}$ that can be expressed as
a conjunction of binary constraints using only elements of $C\mathcal{PA}$ [101, 108, 104]. Van Beek
also pointed out that enforcing strong 4-consistencyin an $\mathcal{PIA}$ or $\mathcal{PA}$ network results in
an equivalent minimal network [101, 108, 104]. However, enforcing strong 4-consistency
does not result in global consistency for these networks. As shown by Koubarakis in
[57], strong 5-consistency is necessary and sufficient for achieving global consistency in
$\mathcal{PIA}$ and $\mathcal{PA}$. Van Beek has also presented two efficient algorithms for $\mathcal{PA}$ and $\mathcal{PIA}$

Basic Relation	Symbol	Pictorial Representation	Endpoint Constraints
i before j	*b*	iiiiiiii	$i^- < j^-$, $i^- < j^+$,
j after i	b^{-1}	jjjjjjjjj	$i^+ < j^-$, $i^+ < j^+$
i meets j	*m*	iiiiiiii	$i^- < j^-$, $i^- < j^+$,
j met-by i	m^{-1}	jjjjjjjjjj	$i^+ = j^-$, $i^+ < j^+$
i overlaps j	*o*	iiiiiiii	$i^- < j^-$, $i^- < j^+$,
j overlapped-by i	o^{-1}	jjjjjjjjjjj	$i^+ > j^-$, $i^+ < j^+$
i during j	*d*	iiiiiiii	$i^- > j^-$, $i^- < j^+$,
j includes i	d^{-1}	jjjjjjjjjjjjjjjjjj	$i^+ > j^-$, $i^+ < j^+$
i starts j	*s*	iiiiiiiii	$i^- = j^-$, $i^- < j^+$,
j started-by i	s^{-1}	jjjjjjjjjjjjjjjj	$i^+ > j^-$, $i^+ < j^+$
i finishes j	*f*	iiiiiiiiii	$i^- > j^-$, $i^- < j^+$,
j finished-by i	f^{-1}	jjjjjjjjjjjjjjjjjj	$i^+ > j^-$, $i^+ = j^+$
i equals j	$=$	iiiiiiiiiii	$i^- = j^-$, $i^- < j^+$,
		jjjjjjjjjjj	$i^+ > j^-$, $i^+ = j^+$

Basic Relation	Symbol	Pictorial Representation	Point Constraints
p before i	*b*	p	$p < i^-$
i after p	b^{-1}	iiiiiiiii	
p starts i	*s*	p	$p = i^-$
i started-by p	s^{-1}	iiiiiiiii	
p during i	*d*	p	$i^- < p < i^+$
i includes p	d^{-1}	iiiiiiiii	
p after i	*a*	p	$i^+ < p$
i before p	a^{-1}	iiiiiiiii	

Basic Relation	Symbol	Pictorial Representation	
p before q	$<$	p	
q after p	$>$		q
p equals q	$=$	p	
		q	
p after q	$>$	q	
q before p	$<$		p

Figure 19.2: Interval-to-interval, point-to-interval and point-to-point relations

networks: an $O(n^2)$ algorithm for consistency checking and finding a solution, and an $O(\max mn^2, n^3)$ for computing the minimal network [103]. The parameter n here is again the number of nodes in the network, while m is the number of edges labelled with $\neq$.

The work by Vilain, Kautz and van Beek [108] motivated the search for new subclasses of $\mathcal{IA}$ that are tractable. The most widely studied subclass discovered so far is the *Ord-Horn subclass* $\mathcal{H}$ introduced by Nebel and Bürckert in [82]. $\mathcal{H}$ consists of all relations $r \in \mathcal{A}$ which satisfy the following condition. If i and j are intervals, $i\ r\ j$ can be equivalently expressed as a conjunction of Ord-Horn constraints on the endpoints of i and j. An *Ord-Horn constraint* is a disjunction $d_1 \vee \cdots \vee d_n$ where at most one of the d_i's is an inequality of the form $x \leq y$, the rest of the d_i's are disequations of the form $x \neq y$, and x and y are variables ranging over the real numbers.

It is interesting to notice that $\mathcal{H}$, the most expressive tractable subclass of $\mathcal{IA}$ among the ones introduced above, consists of 868 relations i.e., it covers more than 10% of $\mathcal{A}$. $\mathcal{H}$ is *maximal* i.e., it cannot be extended without losing tractability [82].

Recently, Krokhin, Jeavons and Jonsson showed that there are *exactly* 18 maximal tractable subclasses of $\mathcal{IA}$; reasoning in any subset of $\mathcal{IA}$ not included in these subclasses is NP-complete [65]. This is an important *dichotomy* result: it classifies all subproblems of an NP-complete problem as either tractable or NP-complete. It is important to point out that this result is proved analytically while previous work had resorted to systematic computerized analysis (see e.g., [38]).

Koubarakis [59] has demonstrated that, in general, there is no low level of local consistency that can achieve global consistency of $\mathcal{H}$ constraints. Earlier, Bessière, Isli and Ligozat [12] had presented some subclasses of $\mathcal{H}$ for which path consistency achieves global consistency.

Gerevini [42] considers $\mathcal{PA}$ and $\mathcal{H}$ and studies *incremental* algorithms for checking consistency, maintaining a solution and maintaining the minimal network. The algorithms of [42] improve the static algorithms for these problems by a factor of $O(n)$ or $O(n^2)$ when a sequence of $O(n^2)$ operations (assertions or relaxations of constraints) are processed. In related work, Delgrande and Gupta [36] consider the problem of updating chains of $\leq$ or $<$ relations.

In [75], Meiri defines the *qualitative algebra* $\mathcal{QA}$, an expressive formalism for qualitative temporal reasoning on points and intervals. In $\mathcal{QA}$, one is able to express binary constraints of the form $o_i\ r_1\ o_j \vee \cdots \vee o_i\ r_k\ o_j$ where o_i, o_j are points or intervals and $r_1, \ldots, r_k$ are:

- interval-to-interval relations from $\mathcal{IA}$

- point-to-point relations from $\mathcal{PA}$

- *point-to-interval* or *interval-to-point* relations [109]. These five, mutually exclusive relations and their inverses can hold between a point and an interval. They are shown pictorially in Figure 19.2.

[75] presents several results on $\mathcal{QA}$ and its subclasses including how to combine it with metric information (see Section 19.2.3 below). Recently, [50] presented a dichotomy theorem which gives a *complete* classification of all subclasses of $\mathcal{QA}$ as either tractable or NP-complete.

The expressive power of the qualitative temporal reasoning algebras defined in this section can be summarized as follows (the symbol $\subset$ should be read as "contains" or "is less expressive than") :

$$\mathcal{CPA} \subset \mathcal{PA} \subset \mathcal{QA} \text{ and } \mathcal{CEIA} \subset \mathcal{PIA} \subset \mathcal{H} \subset \mathcal{IA} \subset \mathcal{QA}$$

19.2.2 Metric Temporal Reasoning

Dechter, Meiri and Pearl studied metric temporal information using *disjunctive binary difference (DBD) constraints*[1] of the form

$$a_1 \leq x_i - x_j \leq b_1 \vee \cdots \vee a_n \leq x_i - x_j \leq b_n$$

where x_i, x_j are real variables representing time points and $a_1, \ldots, a_n, b_1, \ldots, b_n$ are real numbers [34]. To deal with these constraints, [34] introduced $\mathcal{DBD}$ *networks* where nodes represent variables and arcs represent binary constraints.

Example 19.6. Let us consider the following text [34]:

John goes to work either by car (30-40 minutes) or by bus (at least 60 minutes). Fred goes to work either by car (20-30 minutes) or in a car pool (40-50 minutes). Today John left home between 7:10 and 7:20, and Fred arrived at work between 8:00 and 8:10. We also know that John arrived at work about 10-20 minutes after Fred left home.

Let x_0 be a special time point (real variable) denoting the "beginning of time" (7:00 in our case). Let x_1, x_2, x_3, x_4 be real variables such that $[x_1, x_2]$ is the interval corresponding to John's travel to work, and $[x_3, x_4]$ is the interval corresponding to Fred's travel to work. The left part of Figure 19.3 shows a $\mathcal{DBD}$ network capturing the temporal relations in the above text.

Deciding consistency of $\mathcal{DBD}$ networks is NP-complete [34]. An important tractable subcase occurs when all constraints have a *single* disjunct i.e., they are of the form $a \leq x_i - x_j \leq b$. We will call these constraints simply *binary difference (BD) constraints*. For the class of $\mathcal{BD}$ constraints, deciding consistency and at the same time computing the minimal network can be done in $O(n^3)$ time (where n is the number of variables) by running any all-pairs shortest-paths algorithm (e.g., Floyd-Warshall [29]) on an equivalent weighted, directed graph representation of the constraints called the *distance graph* [34]. The right part of Figure 19.3 shows the distance graph equivalent to the $\mathcal{BD}$ constraint network obtained from the $\mathcal{DBD}$ constraint network on the left part of the figure after dropping the interval $[60, infty]$ from the edge (x_1, x_2) and $[20, 30]$ from the edge (x_3, x_4).

For the class of $\mathcal{BD}$ constraints, computing the shortest-paths among all pairs of nodes in the distance graph is equivalent to enforcing path consistency in the original network. Notice also that path consistency is necessary and sufficient for achieving global consistency for the class of $\mathcal{BD}$ constraints [34]. Deciding consistency only can alternatively be

---

[1]In this section, we deviate from the usual terminology of the literature and name classes of metric temporal constraints by referring to what relationships they can express (e.g., difference, disjunctions etc.). In this way, we avoid using names formed with adjectives such as simple, complex etc. that do not say much about the expressivity of the particular constraint class they are used to name.

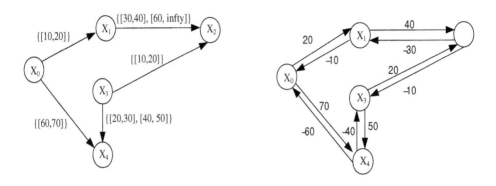

Figure 19.3: A $\mathcal{DBD}$ network (left) and a distance graph for a part of it (right)

achieved by a single-source shortest-paths algorithm (e.g., Bellman-Ford [29]) in $O(nE)$ time where n is the number of nodes and E the number of edges in the distance graph. Alternatively, one can use a *directional path consistency* algorithm on the given network which runs in $O(nW^*(d)^2)$ time where $W^*(d)$ is the maximum number of parents that a node possesses in the resulting network [34].

The framework of difference constraints of [34] has been influential in much future work in this area. For example, Koubarakis [57] and, independently, Gerevini and Christani [43] have introduced the class of *binary difference constraints with disequations* ($\mathcal{BD}^{\neq}$) by extending the class of $\mathcal{BD}$ constraints to include disequations of the form $x - y \neq r$ (r is a real constant). Deciding consistency in $\mathcal{BD}^{\neq}$ can be checked in $O(n^3)$ time by trivially modifying any all-pairs shortest path algorithm used for the class of $\mathcal{BD}$ constraints so that it reports inconsistencies resulting from any disequation $x - y \neq r$ and any (implied) equality of the form $x - y = r$. Computing the minimal network for $\mathcal{BD}^{\neq}$ constraints can be done in $O(\max mn^2, n^3)$ where n is the number of variables and m is the number of disequations [57, 43]. [57] has also shown that strong 5-consistency is the necessary and sufficient condition for achieving global consistency in the case of $\mathcal{BD}^{\neq}$ constraints. Recently, [63] extended this result to the class of *unit two-variable per inequality/disequation* ($UTVPI^{\neq}$) constraints. In addition to terms of the form $x - y$, this class allows terms of the form $x + y$ and the same comparison operators as $\mathcal{BD}^{\neq}$.

Extensions to the framework of [33] also explored more practical directions. For example, [13] has shown how to extend this framework so that *multiple time granularities* are supported.

A related but more expressive class of temporal constraints which has also been studied widely in the literature is the class of n-ary disjunctive difference constraints. An *n-ary disjunctive difference* ($\mathcal{NDD}$) constraint is a formula of the form

$$a_1 \leq x_1 - y_1 \leq b_1 \vee \cdots \vee a_n \leq x_n - y_n \leq b_n$$

where $x_1, y_1, \ldots, x_n, y_n$ are real variables representing time points and $a_1, \ldots, a_n, b_1, \ldots, b_n$ are real numbers [6, 96, 97].

Example 19.7. The following are examples of $\mathcal{NDD}$ constraints:

$$x_1 - y_1 \leq 2, \quad x_1 - y_1 \leq 5 \vee -2 \leq x_2 - y_2 \leq 2 \vee x_3 - y_3 \leq 4,$$

$$0 \leq x_4 - y_4 \vee 2 \leq x_5 \leq 5$$

Disjunctive constraints with disjuncts having different pairs of variables cannot be expressed in the $\mathcal{DBD}$ constraints framework of [34].

Example 19.8. Let I, J be intervals, I^-, J^- their beginning points and I^+, J^+ their ending points. The following $\mathcal{NDD}$ constraints express the fact that intervals I and J have duration between 5 and 10 minutes and they cannot overlap.

$$5 \leq I^+ - I^- \leq 10, \quad 5 \leq J^+ - J^- \leq 10, \quad I^+ - J^- \leq 0 \vee J^+ - I^- \leq 0$$

Example 19.9. Let I and J be intervals corresponding to the execution of operations O_I and O_J. O_I and O_J will be executed on a machine that can handle only one operation at a time and has a set up time of 2 minutes. Let I^-, J^- be the beginning points of I and J and I^+, J^+ their ending points.

The following is an appropriate constraint on the scheduling of operations O_I and O_J:

$$I^+ - J^- \leq -2 \vee J^+ - I^- \leq -2$$

Deciding the consistency of a set of $\mathcal{NDD}$ constraints is also NP-complete. *Boolean combinations of binary difference ($\mathcal{BCBD}$) constraints* have also been studied recently [98].

The quest for tractability of metric temporal CSPs received a big push forward when Koubarakis [59] and Jonsson and Bäckström [49] independently introduced the class of Horn-disjunctive linear constraints. A *linear constraint* ($\mathcal{LIN}$) is a formula of the form $\left(\sum_{i=1}^{n} a_i x_i \right) \theta r$ where $a_1, ..., a_n, r$ are rational constants, $x_1, ..., x_n$ are variables and θ is $\leq$ or $<$. We freely use $\geq, >$ and $=$ as well. A *Horn-disjunctive linear ($\mathcal{HDL}$) constraint* is a disjunction $d_1 \vee \cdots \vee d_n$ where each d_i is a weak linear inequality or a linear disequation, and the number of inequalities among $d_1, \ldots, d_n$ does not exceed one.

Example 19.10. The following are examples of $\mathcal{HDL}$ constraints:

$$3x_1 + x_5 - 3x_4 \leq 10, \quad x_1 + x_3 + x_5 \neq 7,$$

$$3x_1 + x_5 - 4x_3 \leq 7 \vee 2x_1 + 3x_2 - 4x_3 \neq 4 \vee x_2 + x_3 + x_5 \neq \frac{5}{2},$$

$$4x_1 + x_3 \neq 3 \vee 5x_2 - 3x_5 + x_4 \neq 6$$

Deciding the consistency of a set of $\mathcal{HDL}$ constraints can be done in PTIME [56, 59, 49]. The main intuition behind this result is that disequations can be dealt with independently from one another for the purposes of consistency checking.

There are currently no relevant maximality results regarding the tractability of $\mathcal{HDL}$ constraints. [16] give two such maximal tractable subclasses of the class of disjunctions of $\mathcal{PA}$ relations.

[15] demonstrates how to implement efficiently consistency checking for $\mathcal{HDL}$ constraints when disjuncts are constrained to be of the form $x_i - x_j \leq a$ or $x_i - x_j \neq a$.

The properties of the class of $\mathcal{HDL}$ constraints have partly motivated Cohen et al. [27] to study questions of tractability for constraints that are obtained as *disjunctions of simpler constraints* with certain useful properties (e.g., independence, guaranteed satisfaction etc.). The importance of such results is that they are obtained in an *abstract CSP framework* and turn out to be useful for many kinds of specific CSPs e.g., temporal, spatial, etc. For some of the results in this area, the reader should see [26, 17] and Chapter 8 of this handbook

Recently, Kumar [68] pioneered the use of *randomized* algorithms for temporal CSPs. [68] initially presents a randomized algorithm for $\mathcal{BD}$ constraints. Then, the intuitions derived from this class are used to develop a strongly-polynomial deterministic algorithm, and a simple randomized algorithm for a restricted class of $\mathcal{NDD}$ constraints, denoted by $\mathcal{RNDD}$, which includes the following three types of constraints:

$$l_{ij} \le x_i - y_j \le u_{ij}, \quad a_1 \le x_i \le b_1 \vee \cdots \vee a_n \le x_i \le b_n, \quad l_i \le x_i \le u_i \vee l_j \le x_j \le u$$

The expressive power of the metric temporal CSPs defined in this section can be summarized as follows:

$$\mathcal{LIN} \subset \mathcal{HDL}, \quad \mathcal{BD} \subset \mathcal{BD}^{\ne} \subset \mathcal{DBD} \subset \mathcal{NDD} \subset \mathcal{BCBD}, \quad \mathcal{BD}^{\ne} \subset \mathcal{HDL},$$

and $\mathcal{BD} \subset \mathcal{RNDD} \subset \mathcal{NDD}$

19.2.3 Qualitative and Metric Temporal Reasoning Combined

Meiri [75] has combined the expressive power of the qualitative algebra $\mathcal{QA}$ and the $\mathcal{DBD}$ constraint framework of [34] to come up with a framework of binary mixed temporal constraint networks where nodes are points or intervals and constraints are qualitative from $\mathcal{QA}$ or quantitative from $\mathcal{DBD}$. Independently, Kautz and Ladkin [53] have proposed a very similar framework that combines qualitative constraints from the interval algebra $\mathcal{IA}$ and the $\mathcal{BD}$ constraints of [34].

Example 19.11. Let us consider the following text [75]:

> John and Fred work for a company that has local and main offices in Los Angeles. They usually work at the local office, in which case it takes John less than 20 minutes and Fred 15-20 minutes to get to work. Twice a week, John works at the main office, in which case his commute to work takes at least 60 minutes. Today John left home between 7:00-7:05 a.m. and Fred arrived at work 7:50-7:55 a.m. We also know that Fred and John met at a traffic light on their way to work.

Let x_0 be the real variable denoting the "beginning of time" (7:00 again). Let $J = [x_1, x_2]$ be the time interval corresponding to John's travel to work, and $F = [x_3, x_4]$ be the time interval corresponding to Fred's travel to work where x_1, x_2, x_3, x_4 are real variables representing the interval endpoints. Figure 19.4 shows a constraint network capturing the temporal relations in the above text.

More recently, Krokhin et al. presented another framework that combines qualitative and metric temporal reasoning [66]. In this case, the objects of interest are intervals and qualitative information is expressed in $\mathcal{IA}$. In addition, metric temporal information on interval endpoints can be expressed using $\mathcal{HDL}$ constraints. The important result of [66] is

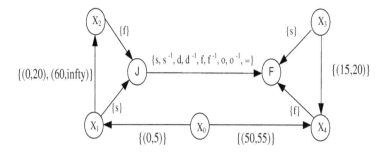

Figure 19.4: A network with qualitative and metric temporal constraints

a dichotomy theorem that settles the standard tractability question for the proposed framework by completely characterizing all subproblems that are tractable; all the remaining
ones are shown to be NP-complete. Since the framework of [66] subsumes the framework
of [53], the tractability question for this framework has also been settled. The exact characterization of all tractable classes of the framework of [75] remains an open problem.

Qualitative reasoning about *durations* has also been considered in [80] and other papers
and a formalism called *point-duration* networks has been defined. Point-duration networks
start from $\mathcal{PA}$ networks and enrich them with binary comparisons of the times elapsed
between pairs of points (i.e., durations of intervals). The comparison of these durations is
also done using the relations of $\mathcal{PA}$. Similarly, Pujari et al. [84] have defined a similar
framework called $\mathcal{INDU}$ for reasoning about intervals using $\mathcal{IA}$ and interval durations using $\mathcal{PA}$. It is not clear up to now, how far one can go with these two duration frameworks
since, as pointed out in [10], the framework is not closed under the composition operation. Recently, Renz and Ligozat [88] discussed this issue in a general CSP context and
differentiated between composition as defined in Section 19.2.1 for $\mathcal{IA}$ (and most other
frameworks studied here) and *weak* composition. In general, the frameworks of [80, 84]
are not as well developed currently as the rest of the frameworks surveyed in this chapter
so we will not deal with them any further in this chapter.

19.3   Efficient Algorithms for Temporal CSPs

In the previous section, we have surveyed work on temporal CSPs, complexity results and
algorithms for deciding consistency, computing the minimal network and enforcing global
consistency. In typical temporal reasoning applications (e.g., planning and scheduling) the
databases of temporal constraints to be handled are very large thus *scalability* of temporal
reasoning algorithms becomes important. Unfortunately, the algorithms of Section 19.2
are *not* scalable. Even for the case of tractable temporal reasoning formalisms such as
$\mathcal{PA}$, typical algorithms [103] require $O(n^2)$ space and $O(\max mn^2, n^3)$ time to answer
queries. Researchers in temporal reasoning quickly recognized this problem and imple-

mented efficient reasoners for various formalisms described in Section 19.2. This is the
work that we survey in this section.

19.3.1   Efficient Algorithms for Qualitative Temporal CSPs

The work on efficient algorithms for qualitative temporal constraints can be distinguished
into two categories: scalable algorithms for constraint classes with PTIME reasoning problems (especially $\mathcal{PA}$) and backtracking or local search algorithms for classes with NP-
complete reasoning problems (especially $\mathcal{IA}$).

Efficient algorithms for $\mathcal{PA}$

Len Schubert, Alfonso Gerevini and colleagues implemented and experimentally evaluated
the temporal reasoners TimeGraph I and II for handling constraints expressed in $\mathcal{PA}$ [44].
The main idea in TimeGraph II, which is the most advanced version, is to represent sets of
$\mathcal{PA}$ constraints by directed labelled graphs, partition these graphs into *chains* (i.e., linearly
ordered points) where constant time reasoning is possible, and use a *meta-graph* to reason
about points belonging to different chains. TimeGraph II also handles binary disjunctions
of $\mathcal{PA}$ constraints using an intelligent backtracking algorithm [44]. TimeGraph I and II
have been used in various planning and natural language understanding projects e.g., [91].
    The work of [45] has also addressed scalability for $\mathcal{PA}$ networks using an approach
which also relies heavily on an underlying directed graph structure. In this case, *spanning
trees* are the basic data structure where efficient reasoning with respect to the $\leq$ relation is
performed. The algorithms of [45] are incomplete for $\mathcal{PA}$ since they cannot handle cases
involving the relation $\neq$ [44]. The work of [45] has been extended with metric constraints
and has been utilized in the temporal reasoner of the IxTeT temporal planner [69].
    [37] further extend the ideas of TimeGraph II by relying on *series-parallel graphs*
(instead of chains) as their basic efficient data structure. [37] provides new intuitions regarding the techniques of TimeGraph II, and shows experimentally what improvements are
possible when series-parallel graphs become the basic data structure.

Efficient algorithms for $\mathcal{IA}$

Ladkin and Reinfeld [72] were the first to implement and evaluate experimentally backtracking algorithms for solving $\mathcal{IA}$ constraints. The backtracking algorithm of [72] has
the following characteristics: a preprocessing step based on path consistency, instantiation
of disjunctions by any set of $\mathcal{IA}$ relations for which path consistency is complete, chronological backtracking, and forward checking using path consistency. [105] improves [72]
with a more efficient version of path consistency and heuristics for dynamic variable ordering. [81] shows that performance improvements can be obtained if we use the class $\mathcal{H}$ for
instantiating disjunctions in the backtracking algorithm of [72]. [72] and [81] also studied
the phase transition of the problem of solving $\mathcal{IA}$ constraints.
    [99] shows how to solve $\mathcal{IA}$ consistency checking problems using local search. In [99],
a given $\mathcal{IA}$ problem with m interval variables is first translated into an equivalent (with respect to satisfiability) problem where the endpoints of the intervals are constrained to range
over the integers $1, \ldots, 2m$. Then, this problem is solved using the discrete Langrangia
method.

Let us now turn our attention to efficient algorithms for metric temporal CSPs. Here attention has been focused on $\mathcal{BD}$, $\mathcal{DBD}$ and $\mathcal{NDD}$ constraints. For $\mathcal{BD}$ constraints, the emphasis has been on improving existing polynomial time algorithms as well as devising incremental versions of such algorithms that are important in applications (e.g., planning or scheduling). Since the reasoning problems for classes $\mathcal{DBD}$ and $\mathcal{NDD}$ have exponential complexity, the emphasis there has been on backtracking algorithms and local search algorithms with influences from CSP and SAT solvers.

19.3.2   Efficient Algorithms for $\mathcal{BD}$ and $\mathcal{DBD}$ Constraints

[21] and [22] has considered incremental algorithms for networks of $\mathcal{BD}$ constraints. The idea in these algorithms is that when a new constraint is added or retracted, a constraint propagation algorithm is not run from scratch, but only some processing *local* to the insertion or deletion takes place. [21] concentrates on incremental arc-consistency algorithms for $\mathcal{BD}$ constraints while [22] presents an incremental version of the well-known Bellman-Ford algorithm for the single-source shortest-paths problem [29]. Similarly, [24] has presented an incremental version of the directional path consistency algorithm of [33].

Recently, Xu and Choueiry [111] presented an efficient algorithm for deciding the consistency of $\mathcal{BD}$ constraints. This algorithm essentially improves the partial path consistency algorithm of [14] (which operates on a triangulated constraint graph) and applies it to the case of $\mathcal{BD}$ constraints. [111] demonstrates experimentally that this algorithm improves on many of its competitors that have appeared in the literature [34] in the case of large and sparse constraint graphs.

[92, 32] consider checking the consistency of $\mathcal{DBD}$ constraints using backtracking algorithms that operate on the equivalent *meta-CSP* (i.e., the CSP with variables corresponding to disjunctions and values corresponding to $\mathcal{BD}$ disjuncts) and utilize local consistency algorithm like path consistency for preprocessing and forward checking. [92] points out that enforcing path consistency in networks of $\mathcal{DBD}$ constraints can result in the creation of an exponential number of intervals. Then, it develops alternative local processing algorithms that compute looser constraints than path consistency but do so in polynomial time. Finally, [92] demonstrates that significant savings are achieved when these local processing algorithms are combined with backtracking to check the consistency of sets of $\mathcal{DBD}$ constraints.

Xu and Choueiry [110] show alternative ways to improve on chronological backtracking algorithms for $\mathcal{DBD}$ constraints [92, 32]. Their techniques include utilizing the algorithm of [111] to check the consistency of the set of $\mathcal{BD}$ constraints considered at each node of the search tree, exploiting the constraint topology, having good variable-ordering heuristics, and reducing the domains with a special form of arc consistency [25]. More recently, [95] have also investigated using the incremental all-pairs-shortest-path algorithm of [22] instead of [111] at each node of the search tree.

TMM (Time Map Manager) is another important temporal reasoning system with support for $\mathcal{BD}$ constraints [31]. The main contribution of TMM is *not* its CSP features but rather its querying facilities, its good support for *temporal persistence* and *causality*, and its sophisticated indexing algorithms for handling large databases of temporal propositions [30]. TMM will be again discussed in Section 19.4.

19.3.3   Efficient Algorithms for $\mathcal{N}\mathcal{D}\mathcal{D}$ Constraints and Extensions

The papers [97, 6, 100, 83, 98, 7] have tackled the problem of checking the consistency
of sets of $\mathcal{N}\mathcal{D}\mathcal{D}$ constraints efficiently. As it is explained nicely in [7], all these works
propose algorithms that consist of the following basic steps:

- *Generation step:* Generate all possible sets of $\mathcal{B}\mathcal{D}$ constraints that satisfy the disjunctions.

- *Consistency checking step:* Check consistency of these sets.

The papers [97, 100, 83] do the generation step by solving a meta-CSP with variables
corresponding to disjunctions and values corresponding to $\mathcal{B}\mathcal{D}$ disjuncts. The papers [6, 98,
7] do the generation step by solving the corresponding propositional satisfiability problem
(where $\mathcal{B}\mathcal{D}$ disjuncts are represented by propositional variables). The consistency checking
step in both cases is carried out using various incremental algorithms for $\mathcal{B}\mathcal{D}$ constraints
e.g., incremental directional path consistency [24] or incremental full path consistency
[77].

Stergiou and Koubarakis [97] were the first to discuss various backtracking algorithms
(chronological backtracking, backjumping and forward checking with backjumping) and
related heuristics for $\mathcal{N}\mathcal{D}\mathcal{D}$ constraints. [97] presents theoretical results that characterize
these algorithms in terms of number of search tree nodes visited and consistency checks
performed by extending [54] where backtracking algorithms for binary CSPs are com-
pared ($\mathcal{N}\mathcal{D}\mathcal{D}$ constraints are n-ary). [97] also evaluate the performance of their algorithms
experimentally using randomly generated hard problems.

Armando et al. [6] subsequently showed how to improve the results of [97] by an
algorithm, called TSAT, which is built on top of a SAT solver that implements the Davis-
Putnam procedure efficiently. The SAT solver produces the sets of $\mathcal{B}\mathcal{D}$ constraints to be
checked for consistency. In addition, TSAT has a preprocessing step that produces a more
accurate SAT encoding than the obvious one, and a constraint propagation step as in the
forward checking algorithm of [97].

[83] presents CSPi, an extension of the forward checking algorithm of [97] with a
semantic branching step and a heuristic method for reducing the number of forward checks
performed. The semantic branching step, which is available for free in SAT methods such
as [6], is as follows. If the current valuation (set of $\mathcal{B}\mathcal{D}$ disjuncts) $\{c_1, c_2, \ldots, c_i\}$ cannot
be extended by another disjunct c_{i+1} so that we reach a satisfying valuation, then CSPi
adds $\neg c_i$ to the current valuation and proceeds to choose another literal from the $(i+1)$-th
disjunction. [83] shows that CSPi improves on [97] and is competitive with TSAT.

[100] adopts the CSP framework of [97] and improves it by introducing no-good
recording as well as the other pruning techniques introduced by earlier literature (a different form of the backjumping used in [97], semantic branching as used in [83] and removal
of subsumed variables as used in [83]). The resulting system, called Epilitis, is shown to
dominate all earlier algorithms [97, 6, 83].

[98] was the earliest paper to deal with deciding $\mathcal{B}\mathcal{C}\mathcal{B}\mathcal{D}$ constraints. The approach of
[98] is to transform a given $\mathcal{B}\mathcal{C}\mathcal{B}\mathcal{D}$ formula ϕ into a propositional logic formula and then
use the SAT solver Chaff [78] to decide it. The transformation involves essentially the
following two steps:

- Introduce a new propositional variable for each $\mathcal{BD}$ constraint in ϕ, and transform ϕ into a new propositional logic formula ϕ'.

- Conjoin to ϕ' a new propositional logic formula that encodes transitive relations among variables derived from the original $\mathcal{BD}$ constraints.

Finally, [7] presents the system TSAT++ which is able to deal with Boolean combinations of difference constraints using a SAT-based approach (in particular, the SIMO solver [46]) and a powerful combination of preprocessing, constraint propagation, branching and intelligent backtracking techniques. [7] demonstrates that TSAT++ is more efficient than the systems of [97, 6, 100, 83, 98] presented above, but also MathSAT [8] which is able to deal with Boolean combinations of linear constraints. The performance analysis of [7] is based on randomly generated hard problems and instances of real-world applications.

Recently, Schwartz and Pollack studied incremental algorithms for $\mathcal{NDD}$ constraints [93]. They consider three update operations (tightening the bound of a $\mathcal{BD}$ constraint, add a $\mathcal{BD}$ constraint or add an $\mathcal{NDD}$ constraint) and present incremental algorithms to handle these updates using techniques from dynamic CSPs such as no-good recording and oracles.

Finally, [76] shows how to solve $\mathcal{NDD}$ constraints using local search. Contrary to earlier complete algorithms using a meta-CSP approach [97, 100, 83], the algorithm of [76] searches over the space defined by the original CSP using an algorithm which derives from GSAT [94] and Tabu search [47].

19.4 More Expressive Queries for Temporal CSPs

When constraint networks are used to represent temporal information (see Section 19.2), their nodes represent the times when certain facts are true, or when certain events take place, or when events start or end. By labeling nodes with appropriate natural language expressions (e.g., *breakfast* or *walk* in Example 19.5) and arcs by temporal relations, temporal constraint networks can be queried in useful ways. The typical query targeted by most of the algorithms discussed in Sections 19.2 and 19.3 is: "What is the strictest temporal relationship between intervals (or points) A and B?". This query is typically answered by consulting the minimal network corresponding to the given temporal constraints.

Van Beek [102] was the first to consider more expressive queries for databases with temporal constraints. In [102], a database is a set of $\mathcal{IA}$ constraints among appropriately named interval constants (representing *events*). The first class of queries considered by [102] is *modal* (possibility or certainty) queries. A *certainty (resp. possibility) query* is a formula of the form

$$OP \ \phi(e_1, \dots, e_n)?$$

where OP is $\Box$ (resp. $\Diamond$), and ϕ is a Boolean combination of $\mathcal{IA}$ constraints that use event constants $e_1, \dots, e_n$. As an example, consider the query "Is it possible that event *walk* happened after event *breakfast*?".

The second class of queries considered by [102] is aggregation queries. An *aggregation query* is of the form

$$x_1, \dots, x_n : x_1 \in E \wedge \cdots \wedge x_n \in E \wedge OP \ \phi(x_1, \dots, x_n)$$

where E is the set of all events in the database, OP is the modal operator $\Diamond$ or $\Box$, and ϕ is a Boolean combination of $\mathcal{IA}$ constraints that use variables $x_1, \ldots, x_n$. As an example, consider the query "What are the known events that come after event $breakfast?$".

The temporal reasoning system LATER [18, 28] is another proposal for querying temporal CSPs in sophisticated ways. LATER allows users to define symbolic time points and time intervals and assert temporal constraints relating them with other symbolic objects, or time constants representing conventional *dates, times* and *durations*. LATER offers a practical temporal reasoning framework that includes vocabulary for expressing many useful qualitative and metric temporal constraints. Only certain kinds of disjunctive relations are allowed so that the expressive power of LATER does not become greater than the expressive power of $\mathcal{BD}$ constraints [19]. The complete set of LATER functions and predicates can be found in [18].

The following types of queries are supported by LATER [18]:

1. Queries *extracting temporal information* (e.g., when, how long, duration and relation queries).

2. Modal queries as in [102].

3. *Hypothetical queries.* These queries allow one to query the database using queries of types 1 and 2 under the assumption that certain additional temporal constraints hold.

Although [102] and LATER offer expressive languages for querying databases of temporal constraints, queries combining *non-temporal* as well as temporal information (e.g., "*Who* is certainly having breakfast before taking a walk?") cannot be asked in these systems, even though the knowledge required to answer them might have been available in the first place. This problem arises because temporal CSPs do not have the required expressive power for representing all kinds of knowledge needed in a real application.

This situation has been understood by temporal reasoning researchers, and application-oriented systems where temporal reasoners were *combined* with general-purpose data and knowledge representation frameworks have been proposed (and in most cases implemented). These proposals include EPILOG[2], Shocker[3], TMM [31], Telos [79], and the relational temporal constraint databases of [55] and [20]. EPILOG and Shocker use the temporal reasoners Timegraph I and II, Telos uses a subclass of $\mathcal{IA}$, TMM uses $\mathcal{BD}$ constraints, the proposal of [55] uses $\mathcal{BD}$ constraints and the system of [20] uses LATER.

In the rest of this chapter, we study the *scheme of indefinite constraint databases* proposed by Koubarakis [58, 63], as the formalism that unifies the proposals of [102, 55, 18, 20]. This formalism is a *scheme* because it can be instantiated with various kinds of constraints defined by a first-order language (e.g., temporal, spatial etc. [63]). When the constraints chosen are temporal, the resulting formalism can be used to represent temporal constraints on various temporal objects, and the relational database can be used to store facts referring to these objects.

Sections 19.5 and 19.6 show that in order to be able to answer queries in this scheme, we must be prepared to go from temporal CSPs to *first-order theories of temporal constraints* as studied in [71, 58]. We identify *variable elimination* (and its logical analogue

---

[2] See http://www.cs.rochester.edu/research/epilog/.
[3] See http://www.cs.rochester.edu/research/cisd/projects/kr-tools/.

quantifier elimination) as the main technical tool needed by the proposed framework. We then show that query evaluation in the proposed formalism can be viewed as quantifier elimination in a first-order language of temporal constraints.

The indefinite constraint database scheme has been presented in the past as a constraint-based extension of the relational data model [58] or as a constraint-based extension of an equivalent subset of first-order logic [63]. We follow the second approach in this chapter using material directly from [63].

19.5 First-Order Temporal Constraint Languages

We start by introducing some concepts useful for the developments in forthcoming sections. We will deal with many-sorted first-order languages [40]. For each first-order language $\mathcal{L}$, we will define a structure $\mathcal{M}_{\mathcal{L}}$ that will give the *intended interpretation* of formulas of $\mathcal{L}$ (this is called the *intended structure* for $\mathcal{L}$). The theory $Th(\mathcal{M}_{\mathcal{L}})$ (i.e., the set of sentences of $\mathcal{L}$ that are true in $\mathcal{M}_{\mathcal{L}}$) will also be considered. Finally, for each language $\mathcal{L}$ a special class of formulas called $\mathcal{L}$-*constraints* will be defined.

Ladkin [71] and Koubarakis [58, 63] have defined various first-order temporal constraint languages where the atomic formulas come from the temporal CSP frameworks defined in Section 19.2. As an example, we define below the first-order languages PA, IA and LIN that are based on the classes of $\mathcal{PA}, \mathcal{IA}$ and $\mathcal{LIN}$ constraints respectively.[4]

19.5.1 The Languages PA and IA

The language PA is a simple first-order language that we can use for talking about points in time. The logical symbols of PA include: parentheses, a countably infinite set of variables, the equality symbol $=$ and the standard sentential connectives. There is only one non-logical symbol: the predicate symbol $<$.

The intended structure $\mathcal{M}_{PA}$ has the set of rational numbers $\mathbb{Q}$ as its domain, and interprets predicate symbol $<$ as the relationship "less than" over the rational numbers. We will freely use other defined predicates like $\leq$ and $\neq$. We define PA-*constraints* to be exactly the constraints of the class $\mathcal{PA}$.

In a similar way, we can define the first-order language IA which has as atomic formulas the interval constraints expressible in the class $\mathcal{IA}$ (see [60, 61] for a precise definition).

19.5.2 The Language LIN

The language LIN is the first order language of linear constraints. The logical symbols of LIN include: parentheses, a countably infinite set of variables, the equality symbol $=$ and the standard sentential connectives. The non-logical symbols of LIN include: a countably infinite set of constants (one for each rational numeral), the binary function symbols $+$ and $*$ (the symbol $*$ can only be applied to a variable and a constant) and the binary predicate symbol $<$.

---

[4] We use the calligraphic type style to write classes of constraints and italic type style to write the corresponding first-order language.

The intended structure $\mathcal{M}_{LIN}$ has the set of rational numbers $\mathbb{Q}$ as its domain. $\mathcal{M}_{LIN}$ assigns to each constant symbol an element of $\mathbb{Q}$, to function symbol $+$ the addition operation for rational numbers, to function symbol $*$ the multiplication operation for rational numbers, and to predicate symbol $<$ the relation "less than" over $\mathbb{Q}$. We define LIN *constraints* to be the constraints of the class $\mathcal{LIN}$.

19.5.3   Quantifier and Variable Elimination

In this section we define the operations of quantifier and variable elimination. Quantifier elimination is an operation from mathematical logic [40]. Variable elimination is an algebraic operation [90]. As we will see below, quantifier elimination algorithms utilize variable elimination algorithms as subroutines. In the scheme of indefinite constraint databases to be introduced in Section 19.6, the operation of quantifier elimination is very useful because it can be used for query evaluation. [35] discuss variable elimination and related concepts for arbitrary CSPs.

Definition 19.12. *Let Th be a theory in some first-order language $\mathcal{L}$. Th admits elimination of quantifiers* iff *for every formula ϕ there is a disjunction ϕ' of conjunctions of $\mathcal{L}$-constraints such that $Th \models \phi \equiv \phi'$.*

This definition is stronger than the traditional one where ϕ' is simply required to be quantifier-free [40]. We require ϕ' to be in the above form because we do not want to deal with negations of $\mathcal{L}$-constraints.

Let Th be a theory in some first order language $\mathcal{L}$, and let ϕ be a formula. If Th admits elimination of quantifiers, then a quantifier-free formula ϕ' equivalent to ϕ can be computed in the following standard way [40]:

1. Compute the prenex normal form $(Q_1 x_1) \cdots (Q_m x_m)\psi(x_1, \ldots, x_m)$ of ϕ.

2. If Q_m is $\exists$ then let $\theta_1 \vee \cdots \vee \theta_k$ be a disjunction equivalent to $\psi(x_1, \ldots, x_m)$ where the θ_i's are conjunctions of $\mathcal{L}$-constraints. Then *eliminate variable x_m* from each θ to compute θ'_i using a *variable elimination* algorithm for $\mathcal{L}$-constraints. The resulting expression is $\theta'_1 \vee \cdots \vee \theta'_k$.

   If Q_m is $\forall$ then let $\theta_1 \vee \cdots \vee \theta_k$ be a disjunction equivalent to $\neg\psi(x_1, \ldots, x_m)$ where the θ_i's are conjunctions of $\mathcal{L}$-constraints. Then *eliminate variable x_m* from each θ to compute θ'_i as above. The resulting expression is $\neg(\theta'_i \vee \cdots \vee \theta'_k)$.

3. Repeat step 2 to eliminate all remaining quantifiers and obtain the required quantifier-free formula.

Step 2 of the above algorithm assumes the existence of a variable elimination algorithm for conjunctions (or, equivalently, *sets*) of $\mathcal{L}$-constraints. The operation of variable elimination can be defined as follows.

Definition 19.13. *The operation of* variable elimination *takes as input a set C of $\mathcal{L}$ constraints with set of variables X and a subset Y of X, and returns a new set of constraints C' such that $Sol(C') = \Pi_{X \setminus Y}(Sol(C))$ where Π_Z is the standard operation of projection of a relation on a subset Z of its set of columns.*

For the class of LIN-constraints defined above variable elimination can be performed using Fourier's algorithm. Fourier's algorithm can be summarized as follows [90]. Any weak linear inequality involving a variable x can be written in the form $x \leq r_u$ or $x \geq r_l$ i.e., it gives an upper or a lower bound on x. Thus if we are given two linear inequalities, one of the form $x \leq r_u$ and the other of the form $x \geq r_l$, we can eliminate x and obtain the inequality $r_l \leq r_u$. Obviously, $r_l \leq r_u$ is a logical consequence of the given inequalities. In addition, any solution of $r_l \leq r_u$ can be extended to a solution of the given inequalities (simply by choosing for x any value between the values of r_l and r_u). Following this observation, Fourier's elimination algorithm forms all pairs $x \leq r_u$ and $x \geq r_l$, eliminates x and returns the resulting constraints. The generalization of this algorithm to strict linear inequalities is obvious.

Example 19.14. Let us consider the following set of LIN-constraints:

$$x_3 \leq x_1, \ x_5 < x_1, \ x_1 - x_2 \leq 2, \ x_4 \leq x_5$$

The elimination of variable x_1 using Fourier's algorithm results in the following new set:

$$x_3 - x_2 \leq 2, \ x_5 - x_2 < 2, \ x_4 \leq x_5.$$

The following theorem will be useful below. The result for PA and IA are due to [71].

Theorem 19.15. *The theories $Th(\mathcal{M}_{PA})$, $Th(\mathcal{M}_{IA})$ and $Th(\mathcal{M}_{LIN})$ admit quantifier elimination.*

The presentation of preliminary concepts is now complete. We can therefore proceed to define the scheme of indefinite constraint databases.

19.6 The Scheme of Indefinite Constraint Databases

In this section, we present the scheme of indefinite constraint databases originally proposed in [58]. We follow the spirit of the original proposal but use first-order logic instead of relational database theory.

We assume the existence of a many-sorted first-order language $\mathcal{L}$ with a fixed intended structure $\mathcal{M}_{\mathcal{L}}$. Let us also assume that $Th(\mathcal{M}_{\mathcal{L}})$ *admits quantifier elimination* (Section 19.5.3 has defined this concept precisely). For the purposes of this section, $\mathcal{L}$ can be a language like PA, IA and LIN that can be used to talk about temporal objects (i.e., points or intervals).

Let us now consider, as an example, the information contained in the following two sentences:

> Mary took a walk in the park. After walking around for a while, she met Fred and started talking to him.

The information in the above sentences is about activities (e.g., walking, talking), constraints on the times of their occurrence (e.g., after) and, finally, other information about real-world entities (e.g., names of persons). Temporal CSPs as discussed in Section 19.2 can be used to represent such information.

In the scheme of indefinite constraint databases (and in similar formalisms like [31, 18]) information like the above is represented by utilizing a first-order temporal language like

LIN and extending it to represent non-temporal information. Let us now show how to do this formally in an abstract setting by considering an arbitrary many-sorted first-order language $\mathcal{L}$ with the properties discussed above.

19.6.1 From $\mathcal{L}$ to $\mathcal{L} \cup \mathcal{E}\mathcal{Q}$ and $(\mathcal{L} \cup \mathcal{E}\mathcal{Q})^*$

Let $\mathcal{E}\mathcal{Q}$ be a fixed first-order language with only equality (=) and a countably infinite set of constant symbols. The intended structure $\mathcal{M}_{\mathcal{E}\mathcal{Q}}$ for $\mathcal{E}\mathcal{Q}$ interprets = as equality and constants as "themselves". $\mathcal{E}\mathcal{Q}$ is a very simple language which can only be used to represent knowledge about things that are or are not equal. $\mathcal{E}\mathcal{Q}$-constraints or *equality constraints* are formulas of the form $x = v$ or $x \neq v$ where x is a variable, and v is a variable or a constant.

We now consider the language $\mathcal{L} \cup \mathcal{E}\mathcal{Q}$. The set of sorts for $\mathcal{L} \cup \mathcal{E}\mathcal{Q}$ will contain the special sort $\mathcal{D}$ (for terms of $\mathcal{E}\mathcal{Q}$) and all the sorts of $\mathcal{L}$. The intended structure for $\mathcal{L} \cup \mathcal{E}\mathcal{Q}$ is $\mathcal{M}_{\mathcal{L}\cup\mathcal{E}\mathcal{Q}} = \mathcal{M}_{\mathcal{L}} \cup \mathcal{M}_{\mathcal{E}\mathcal{Q}}$.

The following lemma is straightforward.

Lemma 19.16. *If theory* $Th(\mathcal{M}_{\mathcal{L}})$ *admits quantifier elimination then the same holds for* $Th(\mathcal{M}_{\mathcal{L}\cup\mathcal{E}\mathcal{Q}})$.

Finally, we define a new first-order language $(\mathcal{L} \cup \mathcal{E}\mathcal{Q})^*$ by augmenting $\mathcal{L} \cup \mathcal{E}\mathcal{Q}$ with a countably infinite set of *database predicate symbols* $p_1, p_2, \ldots$ of various arities. These predicate symbols can be used to represent information about our application domain. The arguments of these predicates will be constants and variables constrained by formulas of $\mathcal{L} \cup \mathcal{E}\mathcal{Q}$. The indefinite constraint databases and queries defined below are formulas of $(\mathcal{L} \cup \mathcal{E}\mathcal{Q})^*$.

In the following example and all the examples of subsequent sections, we assume $\mathcal{L}$ to be the language LIN defined in Section 19.5. The language $LIN \cup \mathcal{E}\mathcal{Q}$ is now multi-sorted with sorts $\mathcal{D}$ (for the constants of $\mathcal{E}\mathcal{Q}$) and $\mathcal{Q}$ (for the rational constants of LIN).

Example 19.17. Let $walk$ be a ternary database predicate symbol with arguments of sor $\mathcal{D}$, $\mathcal{Q}$ and $\mathcal{Q}$ respectively. The following is a formula of the language $(LIN \cup \mathcal{E}\mathcal{Q})$ capturing the fact that somebody took a walk during some unknown interval of time:

$$(\exists x/\mathcal{D})(\exists t_1/\mathcal{Q})(\exists t_2/\mathcal{Q})(t_1 < t_2 \wedge walk(x, t_1, t_2))$$

19.6.2 Databases and Queries

In this section, the symbols $\bar{x}, \bar{y}, \bar{x}_i, \bar{y}_i$, etc. will denote vectors of variables while $\bar{\omega}$ will stand for a vector of Skolem constants. In addition, the symbols $\bar{T}$ and $\bar{T}_i$ will denote vectors of sorts of $\mathcal{L}$. Similarly, the symbol $\bar{\mathcal{D}}$ will denote a vector with all its components being the sort $\mathcal{D}$.

Indefinite constraint databases and queries are special formulas of $(\mathcal{L} \cup \mathcal{E}\mathcal{Q})^*$ and are defined as follows [63].

Definition 19.18. *An* indefinite constraint database *is a formula* $DB(\bar{\omega})$ *of* $(\mathcal{L} \cup \mathcal{E}\mathcal{Q})^*$ *of the following form:*

$$\bigwedge_{i=1}^{m} (\forall \bar{x}_i/\bar{\mathcal{D}})(\forall \bar{t}_i/\bar{T}_i)(\bigvee_{j=1}^{l_i} Local_j(\bar{x}_i, \bar{t}_i, \bar{\omega}) \equiv p_i(\bar{x}_i, \bar{t}_i)) \ \wedge \ ConstraintStore(\bar{\omega}$$

where

- $Local_j(\bar{x}_i, \bar{t}_i, \bar{\omega})$ *is a conjunction of $\mathcal{L}$-constraints in variables $\bar{t}_i$ and Skolem constants $\bar{\omega}$, and $\mathcal{E}\mathcal{Q}$-constraints in variables $\bar{x}_i$.*

- $ConstraintStore(\bar{\omega})$ *is a conjunction of $\mathcal{L}$-constraints in Skolem constants $\bar{\omega}$.*

The second component of the above formula defining a database is a *constraint store*. This store is a conjunction of $\mathcal{L}$-constraints i.e., a CSP. $\bar{\omega}$ is a vector of *Skolem constants* denoting time entities (e.g., points and intervals) about which *only partial knowledge* is available. This partial knowledge has been coded in the constraint store as a CSP using the language $\mathcal{L}$.

The first component of the database formula is a set of equivalences *completely defining* the database predicates p_i. This is an instance of the well-known technique of predicate completion in first-order databases [85].

These equivalences may refer to the Skolem constants of the constraint store. In temporal reasoning applications, the constraint store will contain the temporal constraints usually captured by a CSP, while the predicates p_i will encode, in a flexible way, the events or facts usually associated with the variables of this CSP.

For a given database DB the first conjunct of the database formula will be denoted by $EventsAndFacts(DB)$, and the second one by $ConstraintStore(DB)$. For clarity, we will sometimes write sets of conjuncts instead of conjunctions. In other words, a database DB can be seen as the following pair of sets of formulas:

$$(EventsAndFacts(DB),\ ConstraintStore(DB)).$$

We will feel free to use whichever definition of database fits our needs in the rest of this section.

The new machinery in the indefinite constraint database scheme (in comparison with relational or Prolog databases) is the Skolem constants in $EventsAndFacts(DB)$ and the constraint store which is used to represent "all we know" about these Skolem constants. Essentially this proposal is a combination of constraint databases (without indefinite information) as defined in [52], and the marked null values proposal of [48, 1]. Similar ideas can also be found in the first-order databases of [85].

Let us now give some examples of indefinite constraint databases. The constraint language used is LIN but the constraints are simpler than full linear: rational order constraints, difference constraints and bounds on variables.

Example 19.19. The following is an indefinite constraint database which formalises the information in the paragraph considered at the beginning of this section.

$$(\{\ (\forall x/\mathcal{D})(\forall t_1, t_2/\mathcal{Q})((x = Mary \wedge t_1 = \omega_1 \wedge t_2 = \omega_2) \equiv walk(x, t_1, t_2)),$$
$$(\forall x/\mathcal{D})(\forall y/\mathcal{D})(\forall t_3, t_4/\mathcal{Q})$$
$$((x = Mary \wedge y = Fred \wedge t_3 = \omega_3 \wedge t_4 = \omega_4) \equiv talk(x, y, t_3, t_4))\ \},$$
$$\{\ \omega_1 < \omega_2,\ \omega_1 < \omega_3,\ \omega_3 < \omega_2,\ \omega_3 < \omega_4\ \}\ )$$

This database contains information about the events $walk$ and $talk$ in which Mary and Fred participate. The temporal information expressed by order constraints is indefinite since we do not know the exact constraint between Skolem constants ω_2 and ω_4.

Example 19.20. Let us consider the following planning database used by a medical labo-ratory for keeping track of patient appointments for the year 2006.

$$(\{ (\forall x, y/\mathcal{D})(\forall t_1, t_2/\mathcal{Q})$$
$$(((x = Smith \land y = Chem1 \land t_1 = \omega_1 \land t_2 = \omega_2) \lor$$
$$(x = Smith \land y = Chem2 \land t_1 = \omega_3 \land t_2 = \omega_4) \lor$$
$$(x = Smith \land y = Radiation \land t_1 = \omega_5 \land t_2 = \omega_6)) \equiv treatment(x, y, t_1, t_2)) \},$$
$$\{ \omega_1 \geq 0, \ \omega_2 \geq 0, \ \omega_3 \geq 0, \ \omega_4 \geq 0, \ \omega_5 \geq 0, \ \omega_6 \geq 0,$$
$$\omega_2 = \omega_1 + 1, \ \omega_4 = \omega_3 + 1, \ \omega_6 = \omega_5 + 2, \ \omega_2 \leq 91, \ \omega_3 \geq 91, \ \omega_4 \leq 182,$$
$$\omega_3 - \omega_2 \geq 60, \ \omega_5 - \omega_4 \geq 20, \ \omega_6 \leq 213 \})$$

Since we use LIN, the set of rationals $\mathbb{Q}$ is our time line. The year 2006 is assumed to start at time 0 and every interval $[i, i + 1)$ represents a day (for $i \in \mathbb{Z}$ and $i \geq 0$). Time intervals will be represented by their endpoints. They will always be assumed to be of the form $[B, E)$ where B and E are the endpoints.

The above database represents the following information:

1. There are three scheduled appointments for treatment of patient Smith. This is rep-resented by three conjuncts in the disjunction defining the extension of predicate *treatment*.

2. Chemotherapy appointments must be scheduled for a single day. Radiation appoint-ments must be scheduled for two consecutive days. This information is represented by constraints $\omega_2 = \omega_1 + 1$, $\omega_4 = \omega_3 + 1$, and $\omega_6 = \omega_5 + 2$.

3. The first chemotherapy appointment for Smith should take place in the first three months of 2006 (i.e., days 0-91). This information is represented by the constraints $\omega_1 \geq 0$ and $\omega_2 \leq 91$.

4. The second chemotherapy appointment for Smith should take place in the second three months of 2006 (i.e., days 92-182). This information is represented by con-straints $\omega_3 \geq 91$ and $\omega_4 \leq 182$.

5. The first chemotherapy appointment for Smith must precede the second by at least two months (60 days). This information is represented by constraint $\omega_3 - \omega_2 \geq 60$

6. The radiation appointment for Smith should follow the second chemotherapy ap-pointment by at least 20 days. Also, it should take place before the end of July (i.e., day 213). This information is represented by constraints $\omega_5 - \omega_4 \geq 20$ and $\omega_6 \leq 213$.

Let us now define queries. The concept of query defined here is more expressive than the query languages for temporal CSPs discussed in Section 19.4 above, and it is similar to the concept of query in TMM [31].

Definition 19.21. *A first order modal query over an indefinite constraint database is an expression of the form* $\bar{x}/\bar{\mathcal{D}}, \bar{t}/\bar{\mathcal{T}} : OP \ \phi(\bar{x}, \bar{t})$ *where* OP *is the modal operator* $\Diamond$ *or* $\Box$ *and* ϕ *is a formula of* $(\mathcal{L} \cup \mathcal{E}\mathcal{Q})^*$. *The constraints in formula* ϕ *are only* $\mathcal{L}$*-constraints and* $\mathcal{E}\mathcal{Q}$*-constraints.*

Modal queries will be distinguished in certainty queries ($\square$) and possibility queries ($\lozenge$) as in [102].

Example 19.22. The following query refers to the database of Example 19.19 and asks "Who was the person who possibly had a conversation with Fred during this person's walk in the park?":

$$x/\mathcal{D}: \lozenge(\exists t_1, t_2, t_3, t_4/\mathcal{Q})\, (walk(x, t_1, t_2) \wedge talk(x, Fred, t_3, t_4) \wedge t_1 < t_3 \wedge t_4 < t_2)$$

Let us observe that each query can only have *one* modal operator which should be placed in front of a formula of $(\mathcal{L} \cup \mathcal{E}\mathcal{Q})^*$. Thus we do not have a full-fledged modal query language. Such a query language can be interesting in a formal framework dealing with indefinite information, but we will not consider this issue further in this chapter.

We now define the concept of an answer to a query.

Definition 19.23. *Let q be the query $\bar{x}/\bar{\mathcal{D}}, \bar{t}/\bar{\mathcal{T}}: \lozenge\phi(\bar{x}, \bar{t})$ over an indefinite constraint database DB. The answer to q is a pair $(answer(\bar{x}, \bar{t}), \emptyset)$ such that*

1. *$answer(\bar{x}, \bar{t})$ is a formula of the form*

$$\bigvee_{j=1}^{k} Local_j(\bar{x}, \bar{t})$$

   where $Local_j(\bar{x}, \bar{t})$ is a conjunction of $\mathcal{L}$-constraints in variables $\bar{t}$ and $\mathcal{E}\mathcal{Q}$-constraints in variables $\bar{x}$.

2. *Let V be a variable assignment for variables $\bar{x}$ and $\bar{t}$. If there exists a model M of DB which agrees with $\mathcal{M}_{\mathcal{L}\cup\mathcal{E}\mathcal{Q}}$ on the interpretation of the symbols of $\mathcal{L} \cup \mathcal{E}\mathcal{Q}$, and M satisfies $\phi(\bar{x}, \bar{t})$ under V then V satisfies $answer(\bar{x}, \bar{t})$ and vice versa.*

We have chosen the notation $(answer(\bar{x}, \bar{t}), \emptyset)$ to signify that *an answer is also a database* which consists of a single predicate defined by the formula $answer(\bar{x}, \bar{t})$ and the empty constraint store. In other words, no Skolem constant (i.e., no uncertainty) is present in the answer to a modal query. Although our databases may contain uncertainty, we know for sure what is possible and what is certain.

Example 19.24. The answer to the query of Example 19.22 is $(x = Mary, \emptyset)$.

The definition of answer in the case of certainty queries is the same as Definition 19.23 with the second condition changed to:

2. *Let M be any model of DB which agrees with $\mathcal{M}_{\mathcal{L}\cup\mathcal{E}\mathcal{Q}}$ on the interpretation of the symbols of $\mathcal{L} \cup \mathcal{E}\mathcal{Q}$. Let V be a variable assignment for variables $\bar{x}$ and $\bar{t}$. If M satisfies $\phi(\bar{x}, \bar{t})$ under V then V satisfies $answer(\bar{x}, \bar{t})$ and vice versa.*

Definition 19.25. *A query is called* closed *or yes/no if it does not have any free variables. Queries with free variables are called* open.

Example 19.26. The query of Example 19.22 is open. The following is its corresponding closed query:

$$: \lozenge(\exists x/\mathcal{D})(\exists t_1, t_2, t_3, t_4/\mathcal{Q})\, (walk(x, t_1, t_2) \wedge talk(x, Fred, t_3, t_4) \wedge t_1 < t_3 \wedge t_4 < t_2)$$

By convention, when a query is closed, its answer can be either $(true, \emptyset)$ (which means *yes*) or $(false, \emptyset)$ (which means *no*).

Example 19.27. The answer to the query of Example 19.26 is $(true, \emptyset)$ i.e., yes.

Example 19.28. Let us consider the database of Example 19.20 and the query "Find all appointments for patients that can possibly start at the 92th day of 2006". This query can be expressed as follows:

$$\{ x, y/\mathcal{D} : \; \Diamond(\exists t_1, t_2/\mathcal{Q})(treatment(x, y, t_1, t_2) \wedge t_1 = 92) \}$$

The answer to this query is the following:

$$((x = Smith \wedge y = Chem2) \vee (x = Smith \wedge y = Radiation), \; \emptyset)$$

19.6.3 Query Evaluation is Quantifier Elimination

Query evaluation over indefinite constraint databases can be viewed as quantifier elimination in the theory $Th(\mathcal{M}_{\mathcal{L} \cup \mathcal{E} \mathcal{Q}})$. $Th(\mathcal{M}_{\mathcal{L} \cup \mathcal{E} \mathcal{Q}})$ admits quantifier elimination. This is a consequence of the assumption that $Th(\mathcal{M}_{\mathcal{L}})$ admits quantifier elimination (see beginning of this section) and the fact that $Th(\mathcal{M}_{\mathcal{E} \mathcal{Q}})$ admits quantifier elimination (proved in [52]). The following theorem is essentially from [58] and [63].

Theorem 19.29. *Let DB be the indefinite constraint database*

$$\bigwedge_{i=1}^{m} (\forall \bar{x}_i/\bar{\mathcal{D}})(\forall \bar{t}_i/\bar{\mathcal{T}}_i)(\bigvee_{j=1}^{l_i} Local_j(\bar{x}_i, \bar{t}_i, \bar{\omega}) \equiv p_i(\bar{x}_i, \bar{t}_i)) \; \wedge \; ConstraintStore(\bar{\omega}$$

and q be the query $\bar{y}/\bar{\mathcal{D}}, \bar{z}/\bar{\mathcal{T}} : \; \Diamond\phi(\bar{y}, \bar{z})$. The answer to q is $(answer(\bar{y}, \bar{z}), \; \emptyset)$ where $answer(\bar{y}, \bar{z})$ is a disjunction of conjunctions of $\mathcal{E}\mathcal{Q}$-constraints in variables $\bar{y}$ and $\mathcal{L}$ constraints in variables $\bar{z}$ obtained by eliminating quantifiers from the following formula of $\mathcal{L} \cup \mathcal{E} \mathcal{Q}$:

$$(\exists \bar{\omega}/\bar{\mathcal{T}}')(ConstraintStore(\bar{\omega}) \wedge \psi(\bar{y}, \bar{z}, \bar{\omega}))$$

In this formula the vector of Skolem constants $\bar{\omega}$ has been substituted by a vector of appropriately quantified variables with the same name ($\bar{\mathcal{D}}'$ is a vector of sorts of $\mathcal{L}$). $\psi(\bar{y}, \bar{z}, \bar{\omega})$ is obtained from $\phi(\bar{y}, \bar{z})$ by substituting every atomic formula with database predicate p by an equivalent disjunction of conjunctions of $\mathcal{L}$-constraints. This equivalent disjunction is obtained by consulting the definition

$$\bigvee_{j=1}^{l_i} Local_j(\bar{x}_i, \bar{t}_i, \bar{\omega}) \equiv p_i(\bar{x}_i, \bar{t}_i)$$

of predicate p_i in the database DB.

If q is a certainty query then $answer(\bar{y}, \bar{z})$ is obtained by eliminating quantifiers from the formula

$$(\forall \bar{\omega}/\bar{\mathcal{T}}')(ConstraintStore(\bar{\omega}) \implies \psi(\bar{y}, \bar{z}, \bar{\omega}))$$

where $ConstraintStore(\bar{\omega})$ and $\psi(\bar{y}, \bar{z}, \bar{\omega})$ are defined as above.

Example 19.30. Using the above theorem, the query of Example 19.22 can be answered by eliminating quantifiers from the formula:

$$(\exists \omega_1, \omega_2, \omega_3, \omega_4/\mathcal{Q})$$
$$(\omega_1 < \omega_2 \wedge \omega_1 < \omega_3 \wedge \omega_3 < \omega_2 \wedge \omega_3 < \omega_4 \wedge$$
$$(\exists t_1, t_2, t_3, t_4/\mathcal{Q})((x = Mary \wedge t_1 = \omega_1 \wedge t_2 = \omega_2) \wedge$$
$$(x = Mary \wedge t_3 = \omega_3 \wedge t_4 = \omega_4) \wedge t_1 < t_3 \wedge t_4 < t_2)$$

The result of this elimination is the formula $x = Mary$.

Koubarakis and Skiadopoulos [58, 63] have studied the complexity of query answering in the scheme of indefinite constraint databases for various temporal and spatial constraint languages $\mathcal{L}$. Their results precisely outline the frontier between tractable and possibly intractable query answering problem. [63] shows that if one wants to be able to answer modal queries in PTIME, it is no longer sufficient to have a constraint class (e.g., $\mathcal{BD}$) with PTIME reasoning problems (e.g., consistency checking for $\mathcal{BD}$ can be done in $O(n^3)$ time); further conditions should be imposed on queries and databases.

19.7 Conclusions

We have surveyed work on temporal CSPs starting from early papers such as [3, 107, 31, 108, 34] and continuing with influential contributions that have been published as recently as last year. There are certain topics of work in temporal CSPs that we did not cover due to limited space. These include:

- Temporal CSPs for non-totally-ordered time e.g., partially ordered time, branching time etc. [16].

- Representing *periodic* temporal information by constraints [51].

- *Non-convex* intervals and their CSPs [9].

- *Soft constraints* or *preferences* in temporal CSPs [67].

- *Overconstrained* temporal CSPs [73].

- Connections with *spatial* CSPs [87].

We expect research on temporal CSPs to continue healthily in the years to come due to their importance in applications. In our opinion, the following topics are likely to be in the front line of future developments:

- New algorithmic techniques for temporal constraint solving e.g., randomized algorithms [68] or local search [76, 11].

- Theory and algorithms for combining temporal CSPs and optimization concepts [67, 73].

- Theory and algorithms for quantified formulas with temporal constraints [71, 58, 63].

- Tractability results for the classes where this question has not been answered completely e.g., [75].

- Integration with spatial CSPs to deal with spatio-temporal scenarios [62].

Acknowledgements

I would like to thank Peter van Beek, Kostas Stergiou, Spiros Skiadopoulos, Peter Jonsson and Berthe Choueiry for comments on various versions of this chapter.

Bibliography

[1]   S. Abiteboul, P. Kanellakis, and G. Grahne. On the Representation and Querying of Sets of Possible Worlds. *Theoretical Computer Science*, 78(1):159–187, 1991.

[2]   S. Adali, L. Console, M. L. Sapino, M. Schenone, and P. Terenziani. Representing and reasoning with temporal constraints in multimedia presentations. In *TIME* pages 3–12, 2000.

[3]   J. Allen. Maintaining Knowledge about Temporal Intervals. *Communications of the ACM*, 26(11):832–843, November 1983.

[4]   J. Allen, H. Kautz, and R. Pelavin, editors. *Reasoning About Plans*. Morgan-Kaufmann, 1991.

[5]   R. Alur. Timed automata. In *CAV*, pages 8–22, 1999.

[6]   A. Armando, C. Castellini, and E. Giunchiglia. SAT-based procedures for temporal reasoning. In *ECP*, pages 97–108, 1999.

[7]   A. Armando, C. Castellini, E. Giunchiglia, and M. Maratea. A SAT-based decision procedure for the Boolean combination of difference constraints. In *SAT*, 2004.

[8]   G. Audemard, P. Bertoli, A. Cimatti, A. Kornilowicz, and R. Sebastiani. A SAT based approach for solving formulas over Boolean and linear mathematical propositions. In *CADE*, pages 195–210, 2002.

[9]   P. Balbiani, J.-F. Condotta, and G. Ligozat. Reasoning about generalized intervals: Horn representability and tractability. In *TIME*, pages 23–30, 2000.

[10]   P. Balbiani, J.-F. Condotta, and G. Ligozat. On the consistency problem for the INDU calculus. In *TIME*, pages 203–211, 2003.

[11]   M. Beaumont, J. Thornton, A. Sattar, and M. J. Maher. Solving over-constrained temporal reasoning problems using local search. In *PRICAI*, pages 134–143, 2004.

[12]   C. Bessière, A. Isli, and G. Ligozat. Global consistency in Interval Algebra networks: Tractable subclasses. In *ECAI*, pages 3–7, 1996.

[13]   C. Bettini, X. S. Wang, and S. Jajodia. Solving multi-granularity temporal constraint networks. *Artificial Intelligence*, 140(1/2):107–152, 2002.

[14]   C. Bliek and D. Sam-Haroud. Path consistency on triangulated constraint graphs. In *IJCAI*, pages 456–461, 1999.

[15]   M. Broxvall. A method for metric temporal reasoning. In *AAAI/IAAI*, pages 513–518, 2002.

[16]   M. Broxvall and P. Jonsson. Point algebras for temporal reasoning: Algorithms and complexity. *Artificial Intelligence*, 149(2):179–220, 2003.

[17]   M. Broxvall, P. Jonsson, and J. Renz. Disjunctions, independence, refinements. *Artificial Intelligence*, 140(1/2):153–173, 2002.

[18] V. Brusoni, L. Console, B. Pernici, and P. Terenziani. LaTeR: an efficient, general purpose manager of temporal information. *IEEE Expert*, 12(4):56–64, August 1997.

[19] V. Brusoni, L. Console, and P. Terenziani. On the computational complexity of querying bounds on differences constraints. *Artificial Intelligence*, 74(2):367–379, 1995.

[20] V. Brusoni, L. Console, P. Terenziani, and B. Pernici. Qualitative and Quantitative Temporal Constraints and Relational Databases: Theory, Architecture, and Applications. *IEEE Transactions on Knowledge and Data Engineering*, 1(6):948–968, 1999.

[21] R. Cervoni, A. Cesta, and A. Oddi. Managing dynamic temporal constraint networks. In *AIPS*, pages 13–18, 1994.

[22] A. Cesta and A. Oddi. Gaining efficiency and flexibility in the simple temporal problem. In *TIME*, 1996.

[23] A. Cesta, A. Oddi, and S. F. Smith. A constraint-based method for project scheduling with time windows. *Journal of Heuristics*, 8(1):109–136, 2002.

[24] N. Chleq. Efficient algorithms for networks of quantitative temporal constraints. In *Proceedings of CONSTRAINTS-95*, pages 40–45, Melbourne Beach, Florida, USA, April 1995.

[25] B. Y. Choueiry and L. Xu. An efficient consistency algorithm for the temporal constraint satisfaction problem. *AI Communications*, 17(4):213–221, 2004.

[26] D. Cohen, P. Jeavons, P. Jonsson, and M. Koubarakis. Building tractable disjunctive constraints. *Journal of the ACM*, 47(5):826–853, 2000.

[27] D. A. Cohen, P. Jeavons, and M. Koubarakis. Tractable disjunctive constraints. In *CP*, pages 478–490, 1997.

[28] L. Console and P. Terenziani. Efficient processing of queries and assertions about qualitative and quantitative temporal constraints. *Computational Intelligence*, 15 (4):442–465, 1999.

[29] T. Cormen, C. Leiserson, and R. Rivest. *Introduction to Algorithms*. MIT Press, 1990.

[30] T. Dean. Using temporal hierarchies to efficiently maintain large temporal databases. *Journal of the ACM*, 36(4):687–718, 1989.

[31] T. Dean and D. McDermott. Temporal Data Base Management. *Artificial Intelligence*, 32(1):1–55, 1987.

[32] R. Dechter. *Constraint Processing*. Morgan Kaufmann, 2003.

[33] R. Dechter, I. Meiri, and J. Pearl. Temporal Constraint Networks. In *KR*, pages 83–93, 1989.

[34] R. Dechter, I. Meiri, and J. Pearl. Temporal Constraint Networks. *Artificial Intelligence*, 49(1-3):61–95, 1991.

[35] R. Dechter and P. van Beek. Local and global relational consistency. *Theoretical Computer Science*, 173(1):283–308, 1997.

[36] J. P. Delgrande and A. Gupta. Updating $\leq$, $<$-chains. *Information Processing Letters*, 82(5):261–268, 2002.

[37] J. P. Delgrande, A. Gupta, and T. V. Allen. A comparison of point-based approaches to qualitative temporal reasoning. *Artificial Intelligence*, 131(1-2):135–170, 2001.

[38] T. Drakengren and P. Jonsson. A complete classification of tractability in allen's algebra relative to subsets of basic relations. *Artificial Intelligence*, 106(2):205–219, 1998.

[39] C. Dyreson and R. Snodgrass. Valid-time Indeterminacy. In *ICDE*, pages 335–343, 1993.

[40] H. Enderton. *A Mathematical Introduction to Logic*. Academic Press, 1972.

[41] M. Fisher, D. Gabbay, and L. Vila, editors. *Handbook of Temporal Reasoning in Artificial Intelligence*. Elsevier, 2005.

[42] A. Gerevini. Incremental qualitative temporal reasoning: Algorithms for the Point Algebra and the ORD-Horn class. *Artificial Intelligence*, 166(1-2):37–80, 2005.

[43] A. Gerevini and M. Cristani. Reasoning with Inequations in Temporal Constraint Networks. Technical report, IRST - Instituto per la Ricerca Scientifica e Tecnologica, Povo TN, Italy, 1995. A shorter version appears in the Proceedings of the Workshop on Spatial and Temporal Reasoning, IJCAI-95.

[44] A. Gerevini and L. Schubert. Efficient Algorithms for Qualitative Reasoning about Time. *Artificial Intelligence*, 74:207–248, 1995.

[45] M. Ghallab and M. Alaoui. Managing Efficiently Temporal Relations through Indexed Spanning Trees. In *IJCAI*, pages 1297–1303, 1989.

[46] E. Giunchiglia, M. Maratea, and A. Tacchella. Look-ahead vs. look-back techniques in a modern SAT solver. In *SAT*, 2003.

[47] F. Glover and M. Laguna. *Tabu Search*. Dordrecht, 1997.

[48] T. Imielinski and W. Lipski. Incomplete Information in Relational Databases. *Journal of ACM*, 31(4):761–791, 1984.

[49] P. Jonsson and C. Bäckström. A unifying approach to temporal constraint reasoning. *Artificial Intelligence*, 102:143–155, 1998.

[50] P. Jonsson and A. A. Krokhin. Complexity classification in qualitative temporal constraint reasoning. *Artificial Intelligence*, 160(1-2):35–51, 2004.

[51] F. Kabanza, J.-M. Stevenne, and P. Wolper. Handling Infinite Temporal Data. *Journal of Computer and System Sciences*, 51(1):3–17, 1995.

[52] P. Kanellakis, G. Kuper, and P. Revesz. Constraint Query Languages. *Journal of Computer and System Sciences*, 51:26–52, 1995.

[53] H. Kautz and P. Ladkin. Integrating Metric and Qualitative Temporal Reasoning. In *AAAI*, pages 241–246, 1991.

[54] G. Kondrak and P. van Beek. A theoretical evaluation of selected backtracking algorithms. *Artificial Intelligence*, 89(1-2):365–387, 1997.

[55] M. Koubarakis. Database Models for Infinite and Indefinite Temporal Information. *Information Systems*, 19(2):141–173, March 1994.

[56] M. Koubarakis. Tractable Disjunctions of Linear Constraints. In *CP*, pages 297–307, Boston, MA, August 1996.

[57] M. Koubarakis. From Local to Global Consistency in Temporal Constraint Networks. *Theoretical Computer Science*, 173:89–112, February 1997.

[58] M. Koubarakis. The Complexity of Query Evaluation in Indefinite Temporal Constraint Databases. *Theoretical Computer Science*, 171:25–60, January 1997. Special Issue on Uncertainty in Databases and Deductive Systems, Editor: L.V.S. Lakshmanan.

[59] M. Koubarakis. Tractable disjunctions of linear constraints: basic results and applications to temporal reasoning. *Theoretical Computer Science*, 266(1-2):311–339, 2001.

[60] M. Koubarakis. Querying temporal constraint networks: A unifying approach. *Applied Intelligence*, 17(3):297–311, 2002.

[61] M. Koubarakis. Indefinite temporal databases with temporal information: Representational power and computational complexity. In M. Fisher, D. Gabbay, and L. Vila, editors, *Handbook of Temporal Reasoning in Artificial Intelligence*. Elsevier, 2005.

[62] M. Koubarakis, T. K. Sellis, A. U. Frank, S. Grumbach, R. H. Güting, C. S. Jensen, N. A. Lorentzos, Y. Manolopoulos, E. Nardelli, B. Pernici, H.-J. Schek, M. Scholl, B. Theodoulidis, and N. Tryfona, editors. *Spatio-Temporal Databases: The CHOROCHRONOS Approach*, volume 2520 of *Lecture Notes in Computer Science*, 2003. Springer.

[63] M. Koubarakis and S. Skiadopoulos. Querying Temporal and Spatial Constraint Networks in PTIME. *Artificial Intelligence*, 123(1-2):223–263, 2000.

[64] R. Kowalski and M. Sergot. A Logic-based Calculus of Events. *New Generation Computing*, 1(4):67–95, 1986.

[65] A. A. Krokhin, P. Jeavons, and P. Jonsson. Reasoning about temporal relations: The tractable subalgebras of Allen's interval algebra. *Journal of the ACM*, 50(5): 591–640, 2003.

[66] A. A. Krokhin, P. Jeavons, and P. Jonsson. Constraint satisfaction problems on intervals and lengths. *SIAM Journal on Discrete Mathematics*, 17(3):453–477, 2004.

[67] T. K. S. Kumar. A polynomial-time algorithm for simple temporal problems with piecewise constant domain preference functions. In *AAAI*, pages 67–72, 2004.

[68] T. K. S. Kumar. On the tractability of restricted disjunctive temporal problems. In *ICAPS*, pages 110–119, 2005.

[69] P. Laborie and M. Ghallab. Planning with sharable resource constraints. In *IJCAI*, pages 1643–1649, 1995.

[70] P. Ladkin. Primitives and Units for Time Specification. In *AAAI*, pages 354–359, 1986.

[71] P. Ladkin. Satisfying First-Order Constraints About Time Intervals. In *AAAI*, pages 512–517, 1988.

[72] P. B. Ladkin and A. Reinefeld. Effective solution of qualitative interval constraint problems. *Artificial Intelligence*, 57(1):105–124, 1992.

[73] M. H. Liffiton, M. D. Moffitt, M. E. Pollack, and K. A. Sakallah. Identifying conflicts in overconstrained temporal problems. In *IJCAI*, pages 205–211, 2005.

[74] J. McCarthy and P. J. Hayes. Some Philosophical Problems From the Standpoint of Artificial Intelligence. In B. Meltzer and D. Mitchie, editors, *Machine Intelligence*, pages 463–502. Edinburg University Press, 1969.

[75] I. Meiri. Combining qualitative and quantitative constraints in temporal reasoning. *Artificial Intelligence*, 87(1-2):343–385, 1996.

[76] M. D. Moffitt and M. E. Pollack. Applying local search to disjunctive temporal problems. In *IJCAI*, pages 242–247, 2005.

[77] R. Mohr and T. C. Henderson. Arc and path consistency revisited. *Artificial Intelligence*, 28(2):225–233, 1986.

[78] M. Moskewicz, C. Madigan, Y. Zhao, L. Zhang, and S. Malik. Chaff: Engineering an efficient SAT solver. In *39th Design Automation Conference (DAC)*, 2001.

[79] J. Mylopoulos, A. Borgida, M. Jarke, and M. Koubarakis. Telos: A Language for Representing Knowledge About Information Systems. *ACM Transactions on Information Systems*, 8(4):325–362, October 1990.

[80] I. Navarrete, A. Sattar, R. Wetprasit, and R. Marín. On point-duration networks for temporal reasoning. *Artificial Intelligence*, 140(1/2):39–70, 2002.

[81] B. Nebel. Solving hard qualitative temporal reasoning problems: Evaluating the efficiency of using the ORD-Horn class. *Constraints*, 1(3):175–190, 1997.

[82] B. Nebel and H.-J. Bürckert. Reasoning about temporal relations: A maximal tractable subclass of Allen's interval algebra. *Journal of the ACM*, 42(1):43–66, January 1995.

[83] A. Oddi and A. Cesta. Incremental forward checking for the disjunctive temporal problem. In *ECAI*, pages 108–112, 2000.

[84] A. K. Pujari, G. V. Kumari, and A. Sattar. INDU: An interval and duration network. In *Australian Joint Conference on Artificial Intelligence*, pages 291–303, 1999.

[85] R. Reiter. Towards a logical reconstruction of relational database theory. In M. Brodie, J. Mylopoulos, and J. Schmidt, editors, *On Conceptual Modelling: Perspectives from Artificial Intelligence, Databases and Programming Languages* pages 191–233. Springer Verlag, 1984.

[86] R. Reiter. *Knowledge in Action: Logical Foundations for Specifying and Implementing Dynamical Systems.* MIT Press, 2001.

[87] J. Renz. A Spatial Odyssey of the Interval Algebra: 1. Directed Intervals. In *IJCAI* pages 51–56, 2001.

[88] J. Renz and G. Ligozat. Weak composition for qualitative spatial and temporal reasoning. In *CP*, pages 534–548, 2005.

[89] P. Revesz. *Introduction to Constraint Databases.* Springer, 2002.

[90] A. Schrijver, editor. *Theory of Integer and Linear Programming.* Wiley, 1986.

[91] L. Schubert and C. Hwang. Episodic logic meets Little Red Riding Hood: A comprehensive, natural representation for language understanding. In L. Iwanska and S. Shapiro, editors, *Natural Language Processing and Knowledge Representation: Language for Knowledge and Knowledge for Language*, pages 111–174. MIT/AAAI Press, 2000.

[92] E. Schwalb and R. Dechter. Processing disjunctions in temporal constraint networks. *Artificial Intelligence*, 93:29–61, 1997.

[93] P. Schwartz and M. E. Pollack. Two approaches to semi-dynamic disjunctive temporal problems. In *ICAPS Workshop on Constraint Programming for Planning and Scheduling*, 2005.

[94] B. Selman, H. J. Levesque, and D. G. Mitchell. A new method for solving hard satisfiability problems. In *AAAI*, pages 440–446, 1992.

[95] Y. Shi, A. Lal, and B. Y. Choueiry. Evaluating consistency algorithms for temporal metric constraints. In *AAAI*, pages 970–971, 2004.

[96] S. Staab. From binary temporal relations to non-binary ones and back. *Artificial Intelligence*, 128(1-2):1–29, 2001.

[97] K. Stergiou and M. Koubarakis. Backtracking algorithms for disjunctions of temporal constraints. *Artificial Intelligence*, 120(1):81–117, 2000.

[98] O. Strichman, S. A. Seshia, and R. E. Bryant. Deciding separation formulas with SAT. In *CAV*, pages 209–222, 2002.

[99] J. Thornton, M. Beaumont, A. Sattar, and M. J. Maher. A local search approach to modelling and solving Interval Algebra problems. *Journal of Logic and Computation*, 14(1):93–112, 2004.

[100] I. Tsamardinos and M. E. Pollack. Efficient solution techniques for disjunctive temporal reasoning problems. *Artificial Intelligence*, 151(1-2):43–89, 2003.

[101] P. van Beek. Approximation Algorithms for Temporal Reasoning. In *IJCAI*, pages

1291–1296, 1989.

[102] P. van Beek. Temporal Query Processing with Indefinite Information. *Artificial Intelligence in Medicine*, 3:325–339, 1991.

[103] P. van Beek. Reasoning About Qualitative Temporal Information. *Artificial Intelligence*, 58:297–326, 1992.

[104] P. van Beek and R. Cohen. Exact and Approximate Reasoning about Temporal Relations. *Computational Intelligence*, 6:132–144, 1990.

[105] P. van Beek and D. W. Manchak. The design and experimental analysis of algorithms for temporal reasoning. *Journal of Artificial Intelligence Research*, 4:1–18, 1996.

[106] J. van Benthem. *The Logic of Time*. D. Reidel Publishing Company, 1983.

[107] M. Vilain and H. Kautz. Constraint Propagation Algorithms for Temporal Reasoning. In *AAAI*, pages 377–382, 1986.

[108] M. Vilain, H. Kautz, and P. van Beek. Constraint Propagation Algorithms for Temporal Reasoning: A Revised Report. In D. Weld and J. de Kleer, editors, *Readings in Qualitative Reasoning about Physical Systems*, pages 373–381. Morgan Kaufmann, 1989.

[109] M. B. Vilain. A system for reasoning about time. In *AAAI*, pages 197–201, 1982.

[110] L. Xu and B. Y. Choueiry. Improving backtrack search for solving the TCSP. In *CP*, pages 754–768, 2003.

[111] L. Xu and B. Y. Choueiry. A new efficient algorithm for solving the simple temporal problem. In *TIME*, pages 212–222, 2003.

Chapter 20

Distributed Constraint Programming

Boi Faltings

Constraint satisfaction and optimization problems often involve multiple participants. For example, producing an automobile involves a supply chain of many companies. Scheduling production, delivery and assembly of the different parts would best be solved as a constraint optimization problem ([35]). A more familiar task for most of us is *meeting scheduling*: arrange a set of meetings with varying participants such that no two meetings involving the same person are scheduled at the same time, while respecting order and deadline constraints ([18, 22]). Another application that has been studied in detail is coordinating a network of distributed sensors ([2]).

Such problems can of course be solved by gathering all constraints and optimization criteria into a single large CSP, and then solving this problem using a centralized algorithm. In practice there are many cases where this is not feasible, because it is impossible to bound the problem to a manageable set of variables.

For example, in meeting scheduling, once two people are planning a common meeting, this meeting is potentially in conflict with many other meetings either of them are planning and whose times are decided in parallel. A centralized solver does not know beforehand which of these potential conflicts will become important, and thus will have to gather information about all of them. Since any two people in the world are connected through on average six degrees, this constraint problem is likely to involve a substantial part of the world's population! In contrast, in a distributed solution, changes need to propagate only when there are conflicts between meetings. As such conflicts can usually be resolved by local adjustments, propagation will be limited and the problem can usually be solved with a reasonable amount of effort. This is a typical application where *distributed* algorithms for constraint satisfaction are attractive.

As an another example, consider a configuration system for vacations that composes information obtained from the internet. Even though there are only a finite number of elements to be composed, the number of information sources that could be considered is unboundedly large. Thus, even with a small number of variables it may be impossible for a constraint solver to know the entire space of admissible values and tuples for variables and constraints. Fortunately, the semantics of CSP allows to prove the validity of a solution even without knowing the entire problem. The *open constraint satisfaction* formulation addresses this form of distributed CSP.

There are also other reasons why distributed constraint satisfaction may be necessary:

- cost of formalization: when problem solving is centralized, each participant will have to formulate its constraints on all imaginable options beforehand. This may be excessively complex: a part supplier, for example, might have to give all feasible delivery dates and quantities beforehand, requiring it to explicitly plan and evaluate a huge number of different scenarios.

  In contrast, when using open constraint satisfaction, agents are asked to evaluate only a minimal number of constraints. Furthermore, if solving is distributed they can use whatever software they have for this purpose.

- privacy: in a meeting scheduling scenario, the fact that person A is also meeting with person B may be private information that A wants to keep from another person C. When problem solution is centralized, the solver will see all meetings and constraints, and thus gains valuable private information that can easily be leaked or stolen.

  In contrast, a distributed solution can be constructed in such a way that agents only reveal information piecemeal when evaluating constraints, and other agents only see information they are required to see for the solving process.

- dynamicity: the problem may change dynamically in that new agents appear while others disappear. When a centralized solver is used, these changes would have to be managed by the central server, which may not be feasible.

- brittleness: a centralized solver creates a central point of failure that leads to brittleness of the entire system. In contract, when solving is distributed among different agents, it allows load balancing and redundant and thus fault-tolerant computation among different agents, leading to more reliable systems. Also, parallel execution might make the entire process more efficient.

A distributed algorithm involves a considerable amount of message exchange, which means that the overall solution may well be slower than a centralized process. In general, distributed techniques work well only when the problem is sparse and loose, i.e. each variable has constraints with only few other variables, and for each constraint there are many value combinations that satisfy it. When problems are dense and tight, usually the distributed solution requires so much information exchange among the agents that it would be much more efficient to communicate the problem to a central solver.

The topic has been studied for quite some time; Sycara et al. ([35]) has considered heuristics for distributed constrained search, and Dechter ([5]) has considered the feasibility of distributed constraint satisfaction in a network of identical agents. Since then, a considerable range of techniques has been developed.

This chapter gives an overview of the main techniques that have been developed for constraint satisfaction and optimization in distributed settings. It first covers methods for synchronous and asynchronous distributed solving by backtracking, local search and dynamic programming. It then describes methods for open constraint programming and optimization, and finally considers the issues of self-interest and privacy. In the interest of a coherent description, I unified different algorithms, and thus occasionally present concepts with different names and simplifications. I believe that the algorithms illustrate the main techniques of the field in a concise and coherent manner.

20.1 Definitions

In this section, we formally define two variations to the standard formulation of constraint satisfaction problems. The first, which we call *distributed* constraint satisfaction, formalizes the fact that constraint solving happens under the control of different independent agents. The second, called *open* constraint satisfaction, formalizes the fact that information about the CSP is distributed among different agents.

A distributed constraint satisfaction problem is commonly defined as follows:

Definition 20.1. *A* distributed *constraint satisfaction problem (DisCSP) is a tuple* $< X$, $D, C, A >$ *where:*

- $X = \{x_1, .., x_n\}$ *is a set of n variables.*

- $D = \{d_1, .., d_n\}$ *is a set of n domains.*

- $C = \{c_1, .., c_m\}$ *is a set of m constraints.*

- $A = \{a_1, .., a_n\}$ *is a set of n agents, not necessarily all different.*

The main difference to a classical CSP, as defined in Chapter 1, is that every variable x_i is controlled by a corresponding agent a_i, meaning that this agent sets the variable's value. When an agent controls more than one variable, this would be modelled by a single variable whose values are combinations of values of the original variable. It is further assumed that agent a_i knows x_i's domain d_i and all constraints involving x_i, and that it can reliably communicate with all other agents. The values of n and m need not be known to any agent, thus allowing for problems of unbounded size as mentioned in the introduction. The main challenge is to develop distributed algorithms that solve the CSP by exchanging messages among the agents in A.

As in Chapter 1, each constraint c_j is a pair $< r_{s_j}, s_j >$ where s_j is a tuple of variables and r_{s_j} is a cost function $s_j \Rightarrow \{0, 1\}$ that maps every value combination of s_j into 0 if it is consistent, and 1 if it is not. A *solution* to the DisCSP is an assignment of values to all variables that is consistent for all relations.

A distributed constraint satisfaction problem can be extended to a distributed constraint optimization problem by letting the functions r_{s_j} map to $\Re^+$, representing a cost. A solution to the optimization problem is an assignment of values to all variables such that the sum of the costs of all constraints is minimized. Hard constraints can be incorporated by mapping consistent value combinations to cost 0, and inconsistent ones to cost ∞ (in practice, some very large number). It is possible to extend this formulation to general soft constraints (see Chapter 9) but little work has been done on that.

Note that the assumption that each agent controls a variable and knows all the constraints involving that variable may not be applicable to all situations. For example, in meeting scheduling agents usually do not have unilateral power to fix the time of a meeting, and do not know the constraints of the other participants. Silaghi et al. ([28]) have proposed an alternative formulation where each agent applies its constraints find an agreement on the value of variables. Their *asynchronous aggregation search* (AAS) algorithm shows how the asynchronous backtracking techniques for distributed search can be modified to accommodate this formulation which can be more appropriate for applications.

The definition of open constraint satisfaction problems is somewhat more complex, since we need to take into account the fact that the problem itself varies. The definition thus follows that given for dynamic constraint satisfaction (Chapter 21), except that here its is the variable domains rather than the set of constraints that vary, and that the domains are monotonically increasing:

Definition 20.2. *An* open constraint satisfaction problem *(OCSP) is a possibly unbounded, partially ordered set* $\{CSP(0), CSP(1), ...\}$ *of constraint satisfaction problems, where CSP(i) is defined by a tuple* $< X, D(i), C >$ *where*

- $X = \{x_1, x_2, ..., x_n\}$ *is a set of n variables,*

- $D(i) = \{d_1(i), d_2(i), ..., d_n(i)\}$ *is the set of domains for CSP(i), with $d_k(0) = \{\}$ for all k, and*

- $C = \{(x_i, x_j), (x_k, x_l), ...\}$ *is a set of m binary constraints, given by the pairs of variables they involve and intensional relations between them.*

The set is ordered by the relation $\prec$ *where* $CSP(i) \prec CSP(j)$ *if and only if* $(\forall k [1..n]) d_k(i) \subseteq d_k(j)$ *and* $(\exists k \in [1..n]) d_k(i) \subset d_k(j)$.

An assignment *to an OCSP is a combination of value assignments from the corresponding domains to all variables. An assignment is* consistent *in instance* $CSP(i)$ *if and only if all intensional constraints are satisfied. A* solution *of an OCSP is an assignment that is consistent for some instance* $CSP(i)$ *and any instance* $CSP(j) \succ CSP(i)$.

Open CSP can be extended to open constraint optimization problems (OCOP) by adding a set of cost functions:

- $W(i) = \{w_1(i), w_2(i), ..., w_n(i)\}$ is a set of cost (weight) functions on the domains in D, where $w_i : d_i \rightarrow \Re^+$ gives the cost associated with each value in the domain d_i.

Note that in order to not require all costs to be known, they are associated with variable domains rather than constraints. Note also that the two variants can be combined, i.e. it is possible to have an open CSP where control of the variables is distributed among different agents.

In this chapter, we consider only unary and binary constraints. Most algorithms for DisCSP can be generalized to n-ary constraints.

20.2   Distributed Search

20.2.1   Synchronous Backtracking

The simplest algorithm for solving constraint satisfaction problems is backtrack search. In backtrack search, a partial assignment of values to a subset of variables $\{x_1, .., x_k\}$ is iteratively extended by adding an assignment to another variable x_{k+1} such that all constraints with already assigned variables are satisfied. When no such extension is possible, the algorithm backtracks and changes one or more of the earlier assignments.

The backtrack search algorithm can be readily extended to a distributed algorithm by passing the partial assignments from agent to agent. Thus, agent a_k passes the partial assignment $\{x_1 = v_1, .., x_k = v_k\}$ to a_{k+1} who adds a consistent assignment for x_{k+1}, if possible, or otherwise returns a message to a_k signalling the need to backtrack. This is basically a centralized backtrack algorithm where the thread of control passes to different agents during the execution. Such an algorithm is described for example in [40].

Most of the well-known search techniques for centralized backtracking also apply to synchronous distributed backtracking:

- forward checking and higher degrees of consistency can be implemented by letting each agent a_i maintain a label that contains the admissible values for its variable x_i. Constraint propagation between different variables is implemented by sending messages between the corresponding agents.

- the variable ordering can be chosen statically or dynamically according to various heuristics, again by exchanging messages among agents.

- backjumping can be implemented by passing the backtrack not to the last involved agent, but to the one that is responsible for the variable to be backtracked to.

Considerable efficiency gains can be obtained by exploiting the parallelism inherent in the agents. Synchronous search can be extended with *asynchronous forward checking* ([17]). Here, forward checking is executed in parallel by sending messages to all agents that are responsible for unassigned variables, rather than treating them sequentially. This parallelism can also be extended to subsequent propagation that achieves higher degrees of consistency.

In *dynamic distributed backjumping* ([20]), instantiation continues in parallel with forward checking, and agents are informed of domain wipeouts by nogood messages. An additional heuristic identifies potential conflicts with variable assignments and orders values to avoid these conflicts. These two modifications bring improvements of about 1-2 orders of magnitude in cycles, constraint checks and number of messages.

However, synchronous backtracking has essentially the same restrictions as centralized solutions, except that there may be a small advantage in privacy in that constraints do not have to be communicated to any other parties. Furthermore, they do not exploit the potential for parallel execution among the different agents, as essentially only one agent is active at any one time.

20.2.2 Asynchronous Backtracking

Most of the research effort in distributed constraint satisfaction has focussed on asynchronous distributed search algorithms. These are characterized by the fact that all agents are active in parallel and only coordinate as needed to ensure consistency of the constraints their variables are involved in.

The first category of asynchronous search algorithms are *asynchronous backtracking* algorithms that perform a systematic exploration of the entire search space. The first of

---

Algorithm 20.1: ABT-opt: Asynchronous backtracking adapted for optimization.

1: **Procedure** receive-add-link(xj)
2: add xj.agent to self.lower-agents
3: **call**(receive-ok(xj.agent,self.x))

1: **Procedure** receive-ok(var)
2: **for** ng ∈ nogoods **do**
3:     **if** ∃vc ∈ conds(ng) vc.agent=var.agent ∧ vc.v ≠ var.v **then**
4:         eliminate ng from nogoods
5: replace v ∈ self.agentview s.th. v.agent = var.agent by var
6: adjust-value

1: **Procedure** receive-nogood(new-ng)
2: **for** var ∈ new-ng.cond **do**
3:     **if** (cv ← x ∈ self.agentview s.th. x.agent = var.agent) = NIL **then**
4:         add var to self.agentview
5:         **call**(var.agent,receive-add-link(self.x))
6:     **else**
7:         **if** cv.v ≠ var.v **then**
8:             **return**
9: **for** ng ∈ self.nogoods s.th. ng.v = new-ng.v ∧ new-ng.tag ∩ ng.tag = ng.tag **do**
10:     eliminate ng from self.nogoods
11: self.nogoods ← self.nogoods ∪{new-ng}
12: adjust-value

1: **Procedure** adjust-value
2: old-value ← self.x.v ; self.cost ← ∞
3: **for** v ∈ self.domain **do**
4:     δ ← r(v) ; LB ← 0 ; tag ← { self } ; exact ← true
5:     **for** xj ∈ self.agentview **do**
6:         δ ← δ + r(xj,v)
7:     **for** ng ∈ self.nogoods s.th. ng.v = v **do**
8:         LB ← LB + ng.cost
9:         tag ← tag ∪ ng.tag
10:         exact ← exact ∧ ng.exact
11:     exact ← exact ∧ (tag ∩ self.lower-agents = self.lower-agents)
12:     **if** δ + LB ≤ self.cost **then**
13:         self.x.v ← v ; self.cost ← δ + LB; self.tag ← tag; self.exact ← exact
14: **if** (self.cost ≠ 0) ∨ self.exact **then**
15:     **if** (self.agentview = φ) ∧ self.exact **terminate(self.cost)**
16:     xj ← lowest priority variable in self.agentview
17:     **call**(xj.agent,receive-nogood(nogood(xj.v,
        agentview\xj,self.tag,self.cost,self.exact))
18: **if** self.x.v ≠ old-value **then**
19:     **for** a ∈ self.lower-agents **do**
20:         **call**(a,receive-ok(self.x))

```
self:
```

x	own `variable`
domain (constant)	domain of the own variable
r (constant)	`r(xj,vi)` gives the cost $r_{\{xj,self.x\}}(xj.v, vi)$ (associated with the constraint with `xj`) and `r(vi)` gives the cost $r_{\{self.x\}}(vi)$ if there is unary constraint on the own variable, and 0 otherwise
agentview	set of `variables`
lower-agents	set of pointers to agents
nogoods	set of `nogoods`
cost	estimate of the cost of self and lower priority variables
tag	set of agents, used to keep track of received nogoods
exact	true if cost is exact and false if only a lower bound

```
variable:
```

v	value
agent	pointer to responsible agent

```
nogood:
```

v	variable value that nogood refers to
cond	set of `variable`
tag	set of pointers to agents
cost	cost of the nogood
exact	true/false depending on whether cost is exact or only a lower bound.

```
1: Procedure ABT-opt
2: self.x.v ← NIL; self.lower-agents ← {lower priority agents sharing a constraint}
3: self.agentview ← {higher priority variables sharing a constraint}
4: adjust-value
```

Figure 20.1: Data structures and main procedure for ABT-opt.

these algorithms, Asynchronous Backtracking(ABT), was published by Yokoo et al. ([37], and it has become a reference in the field on which many other algorithms are built. It was formulated for binary constraints and here we will also assume that all constraints are binary.

Figure 20.1 shows the data structures used for the ABT algorithm. Each agent has a data structure `self` that contains its own variable, constants that represent the domain of its variable as well as the constraints it has with other variables, and several fields that are used to store the current state of the search. The other data structures are `variables` and `nogoods` that will be explained in more detail below.

Algorithm 20.1 shows the main procedures of the ABT algorithm. Its presentation is slightly adapted so that it can also be used for optimization, following ([31]) and ([34]). It uses the construct **call** to indicate that the agent sends a message to another agent, thus invoking the receiving agent's procedure for receiving this message. These invocations are

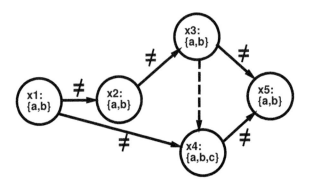

Figure 20.2: Example of a distributed constraint satisfaction problem. Circles represent different agents, directed arrows represent constraints between variables. Here, all constraints are inequality constraints. The dashed arrow indicates a link that might have to be added during the execution and is not part of the problem.

made asynchronously, i.e. they do not return any values and the invoking process does not wait for them to finish. However, it is assumed that no invocations are lost, all invocations by the same agent are handled in the order in which they were made, and no agents crash

ABT explores a backtrack search tree with a fixed variable ordering that we assume to be $x_1, x_2, .., x_n$, without loss of generality. The ordering is assumed to be known to all agents, and establishes *priorities* in that a variable x_i has priority over another variable x whenever $i < j$. Note that this does not imply that any agent has knowledge of the entire problem: the order could be established for example by assigning each agent a unique number (e.g. serial number of the processor and the process id of the agent) and letting the ordering be identical to this numbering.

The variable ordering is used to decide a direction for each constraint: the agent controlling the first variable in the ordering is called the *value-sending* agent, and the other is called the *constraint-evaluating* agent.

As an example, consider the problem shown in Figure 20.2, where variables are assumed to be ordered according to their index. The constraints are thus directed as indicated by the arrows.

The algorithm is initially called by invoking each agent with the procedure ABT-opt shown at the bottom of Figure 20.1. This initializes the own value, identifies the initial set of lower priority agents, and initializes the agentview to the higher priority variables, which are initialized with values that could be randomly chosen. The agent then picks an own value by calling adjust-value, which also causes it to be sent in OK messages to the lower priority agents. Once all these messages have been received, every agent has a correct agentview. During the search, agents continue to set their value asynchronously whenever they receive new information.

When an agent receives an OK message, it is invoked through the procedure receive ok. The agent keeps a record of nogoods that identify assignment combinations that have

---

[1]When agents do crash, the algorithm still terminates, but the constraints enforced by crashed agents are not necessarily satisfied in the final result.

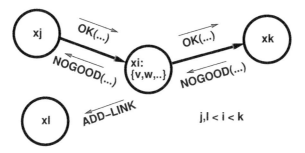

Figure 20.3: Messages used in asynchronous backtracking. The agent responsible for x_i receives OK messages from higher priority agents a_j $(j < i)$ and nogood message from lower priority agents a_k $(k > i)$ when their variables have common constraints with x_i. It may send add-link messages to request the value of other higher priority variables x_l.

been found to lead to inconsistencies or costs as explained further below. In order to avoid a combinatorial explosion in its memory requirements, the agent first eliminates any nogoods that are no longer valid given the new assignment. It then integrates the received value into its agentview. This is a data structure that keeps track of all values of higher priority agents that are relevant for its search.

Next, it adjusts its own value to optimally satisfy the constraints. This is done in the procedure adjust-value. It first evaluates the constraints with earlier variables to determine which values in its domain cause the least amount of inconsistency. For each value v in the domain, the variable δ is used to compute a lower bound on the cost that this value would imply. We assume here that the constant r returns a value of 0 if the combination given as an argument is allowed by the constraint, and 1 otherwise, so that the cost measures the number of constraint violations. The agent first sums the number of constraint violations with higher priority variables given in agentview(Steps 5-6). In LB, it adds any nogoods that may exist on the value, indicating violations in lower priority variables(Steps 7-10). The tag and exact variables are used for termination detection and are explained later (see 20.2.4).

The agent computes the number of violations in cost as δ + LB, and chooses the value with the smallest cost(Steps 12-13). Ideally, this cost is 0, in which case it has found a consistent value. If no consistent value can be found, the minimum cost is > 0, and the agent sends a nogood to the lowest higher-priority agent in its agent view(Steps 14-17). Finally, if this leads to choosing a different value, it is sent to the lower priority agents via OK messages(Steps 18-20).

In the example, assume that all variables are initially set to a. We consider one possible execution where all messages take about the same time, so that it can be understood as a sequence of parallel rounds. However, such synchrony is not required to obtain the correct results. In the first round, agents receive the following messages and make the following changes:

	message(s)	action
a_2	OK(x_1=a)	$x_2 \leftarrow$ b
a_3	OK(x_2=a)	$x_3 \leftarrow$ b
a_4	OK(x_1=a)	$x_4 \leftarrow$ b
a_5	OK(x_3=a)	$x_5 \leftarrow$ b
	OK(x_4=a)	

which leads to a second round:

	message(s)	action
a_3	OK(x_2=b)	$x_3 \leftarrow$ a
a_5	OK(x_3=b)	$x_5 \leftarrow$ a
	OK(x_4=b)	

and a third round:

	message(s)	action
a_5	OK(x_3=a)	inconsistent!

If no value consistent with the agent view can be found, as is the case for a_5, the agent can conclude that the current agent view is responsible for this failure. It constitutes a *nogood*: a combination of assignments that makes it impossible to assign a value to the variable, and thus cannot be part of any solution of the CSP. The nogood is constructed as a *resolvent* of all constraints and existing nogoods. It is sent in a nogood message to the agent responsible for the lowest priority variable in the nogood.

Nogoods are generated whenever an agent a_i does not find a consistent value for its variable x_i. In this case, each value in d_i entails at least one constraint violation, i.e. the minimum cost for all values is > 0. In this case, the agent concludes that its current agent view does not allow any solution, and passes this up as a nogood to the lowest priority agent in its agentview.

Here, d_5 has possible values a and b. where:

$$x_3 = a \;\Rightarrow\; x_5 \neq a$$
$$x_4 = b \;\Rightarrow\; x_5 \neq b$$

Thus, the minimum cost is equal to 1, so that the current agent view, $(x_3 = a, x_4 = b)$ is passed up as a nogood with v = b, cond = $(x_3 = a)$, tag = x_5 and cost = 1 to a_4 the lowest priority agent in the agent view.

For each of the values $v \in d_i$, agent a_i stores one or more nogoods whose cost field gives a lower bound on the cost that will be incurred by variables in the field nogood.tag

$$(x_j = v_j \land x_k = v_k \land ... \land x_i = v) \Rightarrow cost(\text{nogood.tag}) \geq \text{nogood.cost}$$

which, assuming that x_i is the lowest-priority variable, is written in explanatory form as:

```
nogood.cond ⊆ self.agentview ∧ nogood.v = self.x.v ⇒
cost-sum(nogood.tag) ≥ nogood.cost
```

and stored with agent a_i. In the version of ABT shown here, agents ensure that all nogoods for the same value refer to disjoint tags and that they are all applicable in the current agent view.

An agent receives a `nogood` by being invoked through the `receive-nogood` message. Note that an agent may receive a nogood that contains variables that it previously had no constraint with, and thus are not part of its agent view. In order to decide whether the nogood is applicable, it thus has to add a link with this variable so that it will be informed whenever it changes. This is done using an `add-link` message(Steps 2-5).

An agent applies its nogoods when checking for consistency of its current value assignment. It has to only apply those nogoods that are consistent with the current agent view. In fact, any nogoods that are no longer consistent with the agent view can be discarded as they will in any case be rediscovered should the agent view again become compatible with it. This means that the amount of storage required at each agent grows at most linearly with the size of the domain and the number of variables. As a consequence, when an agent receives a nogood which is no longer applicable to the current agentview, it discards it(Steps 7-8).

Next, it eliminates all existing nogoods that already cover part or all of the variables covered by the nogood just received, as indicated by the tags. These may exist because the agent may have already received nogoods resulting from partial propagation among the lower-priority agents. Finally, it adds the nogood to the nogood list, and adjusts its current value. This may result in further nogood messages being passed to higher priority agents(Steps 9-10).

In this example, a_4 has now received a nogood that involves x_3, and it can no longer evaluate its applicability. Thus, it sends an `add-link` message to a_3 and is informed that the current value of x_3 is a, so that the nogood is indeed applicable and its own value is no longer consistent. Thus, a_4 now searches for a new value for x_4 and finds value c, which now makes the entire problem consistent, and no further messages result.

Bessière et al. [3] show that adding links can be skipped if after sending a nogood of nonzero value, all nogoods involving a variable that is not linked with the current one are immediately discarded. If they are indeed required, they will eventually be rediscovered, but the algorithm will repeat a portion of the search and thus become less efficient.

Algorithm 20.1 terminates when the highest priority agent derives a nogood that is either exact or has non-zero cost. In the first case, the algorithm has found an assignment without constraint violation and thus a solution to the CSP. In the second case, the problem has no solution. The termination is initiated by a procedure **terminate** that should also inform the other agents that the process is now terminated. For more detail see Section 20.2.4.

When agents operate asynchronously, it can happen that some agents change value faster than others. This can lead to an agent receiving several OK messages for the same variable before processing them. In this case, only the last message has to be kept. Timestamps can be used to identify this when message delivery times are not predictable.

20.2.3 Asynchronous Distributed Constraint Optimization

Constraint optimization most commonly uses the branch-and-bound algorithm. This algorithm is difficult to adapt to an asynchronous, distributed setting because it requires agreement among all agents on a global upper bound on the solution cost. However, optimization can be carried out purely on the basis of lower bound propagation.

As has been observed in [31], the asynchronous backtracking algorithm (Algorithm 20.1) can also be used for constraint optimization by assuming that constraints no longer

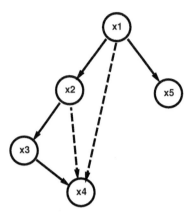

Figure 20.4: DFS tree ordering.

just return values of 0 (consistent) and 1 (inconsistent), but a more general cost measure in $\Re^+$. The algorithm works exactly as in the constraint satisfaction problem. However, while in the case of constraint satisfaction, most of the time a variable's nogood ends up having a value of 0 and is thus not transmitted, in this case most nogoods will have a positive cost and thus travel up the hierarchy.

To show the correctness of the optimization, consider in more detail the computation of local costs. An agent responsible for variable x_i the local cost $\delta(v)$ of value v of its own variable as

$$\delta(v) = r_{\{x_i\}}(v) + \sum_{x_j \in agentview} r_{\{x_i, x_j\}}(v, v_j)$$

i.e. the cost of this value at the variable itself plus the sum of all costs for the constraints with higher priority variables. It uses this value to compute for each value v the *lower bound*

$$LB(x_i = v) = \delta(v) + \sum_{ng \in compatible-nogoods(x_i=v)} ng.cost$$

as the sum of the local value and all nogoods for this value that are compatible with the current agent view. It always chooses its own value as the value v that minimizes the lower bound. If this is different from the current value, it sends OK message to lower priority agents.

The nogoods that agents receive express lower bounds on the total cost of constraints evaluated by lower priority agents. They supersede any earlier nogoods that refer to the same or a subset of the variables. Thus, Algorithm 20.1 checks for this in lines 9 and 10 of procedure receive-nogood and discards any obsolete nogoods.

However, it would still be possible for several nogoods to refer to the same variable and thus for the corresponding costs to be summed up multiple times. When we only consider constraint *satisfaction*, this is not a problem because it is not necessary to compute the exact number of violations, but only to detect that some violation is present. However, in optimization such overlaps lead to inaccurate results.

We now show that if agents are ordered in a *DFS tree* order, such overlaps can never occur. A DFS tree is a rooted and directed spanning tree of the constraint graph such that any edge not in the tree, called a *back edge*, can only exist between an ancestor and a descendant in the tree, but never to a sibling or descendant of a sibling. Figure 20.4 shows an example of a DFS tree consisting of 5 nodes. Tree-edges are shown as solid lines, and back-edges as dashed lines. Any graph can be ordered as a DFS tree, for example using depth-first search traversal to find the tree-edges and order. This process can also be carried out as a distributed algorithm.

In a DFS tree, backedges from a node x_i can only lead to nodes x_j that are on the path from the root to x_i. Since agents always send nogoods to their lowest-priority ancestor, no nogood can ever be sent between agents connected by a back-edge, but only along tree edges. Thus, there is always a unique path from any agent to any other agent, and so a given variable x_k can participate in only one chain of nogoods. This means that the nogoods sent by the children always give an exact bound on the actual cost of the lower priority agents.

Thus, ordering the agents as a DFS tree simplifies the algorithm and guarantees non-overlapping nogoods. A similar observation underlies the AND/OR search trees discovered recently ([15]).

This algorithm is essentially the ADOPT algorithm described in [19]. However, ADOPT also includes a mechanism of *backtrack thresholds* to avoid excessive recomputation of nogoods. It addresses the problem that the algorithm frequently recomputes earlier partial solutions as the bounds change.

Consider a variable x_i and three states s_1, s_2 and s_3 such that all higher-priority variables have identical values, but x_i changes first from a to b, then back to a since the nogood for b turns out to be bigger than that of a. When x_i changes state, all lower-priority variables discard their nogoods. Thus, when x_i changes back to a, they will again have to search to re-establish the solution they had already reached earlier. However, x_i's ancestor still has a nogood for value a, and can indicate this as the cost of the best solution that the lower-priority agents must find. The lower-priority agents can use this information to speed up their search that reconstructs the optimal solution for value a. Backtrack thresholds involve some further bookkeeping issues that are addressed in detail in the ADOPT algorithm ([19]).

20.2.4 Termination Detection

In the context of the ABT algorithm as we have described it here, termination detection can be achieved by also propagating upper bounds on the quality of the solution. This has been first proposed in the ADOPT algorithm ([19]). Note first that in ABT-opt, when all agents below x_k have received all nogood messages, the lower bound computation returns the exact cost of the subproblem below the sending agent. Thus, we include in the nogood an extra field that indicates if the nogood is exact or not. This is then used by higher priority agents to see if their costs are exact: only if they have received exact nogoods covering all lower priority agents will their costs become exact as well. Note that exact nogoods are passed on even when their cost is zero so that the receiving agents can tell whether their cost is exact.

Finally, when the highest-priority agent derives an exact nogood, the algorithm terminates. In a constraint satisfaction problem, if the cost is non-zero, the problem has no consistent solution. Otherwise, the current assignment to all variables is a consistent or optimal solution.

20.2.5 Soundness, Termination and Completeness of ABT

Soundness and termination of the ABT algorithm can be proven inductively as follows. Consider variable x_k and assume as inductive hypothesis that as long as variables $x_1..x_{k-}$ do not change value, variables $x_k..x_n$ will converge in finite time on an assignment whose cost is minimal given the values of $x_1..x_{k-1}$, and that this cost is transmitted to x_k as a nogood with the exact field set to `true`.

Clearly, the inductive hypothesis holds for x_n since there are no lower priority variables, it chooses its optimal value instantly and transmits its exact cost to its parent.

Now consider variable x_k. It will change value only when the nogood for its current value increases so that its cost becomes greater than that of another value. As the nogoods form lower bounds on the optimal costs, they cannot increase beyond this optimal cost. Since each nogood is the sum of costs taken from a finite set, this implies a bounded number of increases. Thus, x_k must eventually reach quiescence, and by the inductive hypothesis, it will receive exact nogoods with the costs of the optimal assignments for $x_{k+1}..x_n$. Since the algorithm chooses the value of x_k to minimize the cost of $x_k..x_n$ given the value of $x_1..x_{k-1}$, x_k can only stabilize on the optimal value and then sends an exact nogood with the optimal cost of $x_k..x_n$ given the values of its ancestors. Thus, it also satisfies the inductive hypothesis. By induction, the hypothesis also holds for x_1, which proves soundness and termination of the algorithm.

For the constraint satisfaction case, completeness follows from termination and the fact that the algorithm finds an optimal solution. If there is an assignment that satisfies all constraints, it has cost 0 and so the algorithm will terminate with an assignment that has cost 0 and violates no constraints.

20.2.6 Performance Evaluation

The complexity of constraint satisfaction algorithms is commonly measured by counting the number of constraint checks. In asynchronous search algorithms, a more accurate measure of the expected execution time is to count the number of *concurrent constraint checks*, given as the smallest number of cycles required when each agent can execute a constraint check in parallel, thus considering the interdependency of their execution. Meisels et al. ([16]) presents an algorithm called CCA for computing the number of concurrent constraint checks during a simulation run of an algorithm.

In a distributed execution, sending a message often takes much longer than a constraint check. For example, sending a message through e-mail can take minutes, amounting to millions of constraint checks. Thus, many researchers measure message complexity as the main measure of expected execution time. Here again, one can simply count the total number of messages, or obtain a measure of *concurrent messages* that more accurately reflects the interdependencies among them.

An issue here is also the size of messages, as some algorithms may be able to package information into fewer but larger messages. This applies particularly to techniques based on dynamic programming, described later in this chapter.

It has been customary in distributed systems research to show a graph of complexity vs. the ratio between the time required to send a message and the time required for a constraint check. This measure has been used in the original paper on ABT ([37]) and in several other algorithm evaluations, and is the most comprehensive performance measure since it also makes apparent parallelism between message delivery and computation.

20.3   Improvements and Variants

20.3.1   Agents Controlling Constraints Instead of Variables

In ABT, it was assumed that each variable is under the control of an agent, and that this agent knows all constraints relevant to that variable. In many applications, variables are public knowledge and it is necessary to generate a consensus among agents as to their value. On the other hand, agents are free to set constraints as they wish.

Silaghi et al. ([28]) have shown how ABT can be adapted to this situation. It involves treating a dual problem where agents exchange constraints or parts of constraints rather than variable assignments. To represent them efficiently, their *asynchronous aggregation search*(AAS) algorithm uses aggregations of values that are described next.

20.3.2   Value Aggregation to Reduce Message Traffic

When variables in a DisCSP have large domains, it is often the case that several values behave the same with respect to constraints. It is then more useful to aggregate them into a single value that can be treated in a single message.

This idea is developed in the AAS algorithm ([28, 33]). AAS is similar to ABT, but uses the dual of the original problem so that agents are now responsible for constraints, and variables are shared between agents that have constraints on them. Each agent decomposes the space of value combinations of a constraint into equivalent groups such that all value combinations within them have the same cost. These can be considered the values of the dual variables, and the algorithm then performs the ABT algorithm on this dual problem. Some complications occur since the decompositions may have to be refined during search. On randomly generated problems, aggregation brings improvements of several orders of magnitude in search efficiency ([33]).

20.3.3   Distributed Consistency Maintenance

One of the most successful techniques in (centralized) CSP is consistency, in particular arc consistency. They can be adapted to asynchronous settings as well, but labels now have to refer to the context of higher priority variables that has been used to generate them so that they can be reset whenever this context is no longer valid.

The MHDC algorithm ([33]) maintains arc consistency during distributed search in AAS by adding a separate type of message called a *propagate* message. It again results in very significant performance gains on randomly generated problems.

20.3.4   Asynchronous Weak-Commitment Search

An important weakness of ABT is that it uses a static variable order, which is known to lead to inefficient search in CSP. In asynchronous weak-commitment search (AWC) [38]), agent priorities are dynamically adjusted so that whenever a backtrack occurs, the agent initiating the backtrack becomes the highest priority agent. This focusses the search on the most difficult parts of the problem space, and AWC is reported to be significantly (at least 1 order of magnitude) more efficient than ABT. However, a major drawback is that AWC is complete only when all nogoods are stored, leading to exponential storage requirements.

20.3.5   Asynchronous Reordering

Reordering is one of the most powerful techniques for speeding up search algorithms for constraint satisfaction and optimization. In asynchronous search, reordering is significantly more complex as there is no central view of the problem.

A first algorithm that uses reordering is AWC, described above. AWC needs to store an exponential number of nogoods to be complete and is thus not considered practical.

However, it is possible to allow a more limited form of reordering if agents are only allowed to change the orders of lower priority agents. Such reorderings do not affect the validity of the nogoods that have been received from these agents, and thus termination in a finite number of steps after the last reordering is still guaranteed. This has been proposed by Silaghi et al. ([29]) in the ABTR algorithm and more recently by Zivan and Meisels ([42]) in the ABT_DO algorithm.

In these algorithms, each agent can impose a new ordering of the agents below itself, and inform these lower-priority agents of the new order. When an agent receives a message informing it of a new order, it adjusts its `agent-view` to add all agents that now have a higher priority, and discards all nogoods that mention agents that now have a lower priority.

When several agents propose reorderings, their priority is decided using a signature scheme. It consists of a set of counters, one for each position in the ordering: $(c_1 . . c_n)$ When the k-th agent in the current ordering proposes a new order, the signature of this new order is derived from the old one by keeping all $c_i, i < k$ the same, increasing c_k by 1, and setting all $c_j, j > k$ to 0. Priority between orderings can now be decided by comparing their signatures lexicographically, i.e. letting l be the first position where two signatures differ, the signature with a higher c_l has higher priority.

Note that given the restrictions on allowable orders, the highest priority agent can never leave its position. Silaghi et al. ([30]) show a protocol based on proxy agents that allows general reorderings, but at the expense of a more complex algorithm where roles are exchanged between agents.

Both Silaghi et al. [29] and Zivan and Meisels ([42]) report gains in efficiency for certain reordering heuristics; however, these gains are not nearly as significant as what can be observed in centralized algorithms.

20.3.6   Storing Nogoods

One of the main problems with asynchronous search is that in order to limit the amount of storage required, nogoods are erased as soon as they become inapplicable due to changes in the agent view. This means that the algorithms derive the same information over and over again. Much efficiency can be gained by systematically storing all nogoods that are discovered during search. This is particularly interesting when variables are ordered as a DFS tree so that nogoods form tight bounds on the cost of possible solutions. It has been shown experimentally ([33]) that such storage can tremendously increase the efficiency of asynchronous backtracking algorithms.

The amount of memory required for systematically storing all nogoods can be bounded using the following consideration. The maximum number of nogoods that need to be stored at an agent is equal to the size of its own domain times the number of possible contexts, i.e. assignment combinations to higher-priority variables that are the target of edges or back-edges from lower-priority variables. It can be shown ([24]) that for any variable, the number of variables in this context can never exceed the *induced width* of the DFS tree ordering. Thus, the maximum amount of space required at any agent is exponential in the induced width of this ordering.

In many practical distributed problems, this width is actually not very large. For example, in meeting scheduling, most meetings are between people in similar groups. It has been shown ([22]) that this leads to graphs with relative low induced width. Other examples, such as sensor networks, also typically have low induced width.

20.3.7 Cooperative Mediation

Another way to deal with the complexity of distributed optimization problems is to detect particularly difficult parts and solves those in a centralized fashion. The *optimal asynchronous partial overlay* (OptAPO) algorithm ([14]) dynamically calls upon certain agents to mediate by determining the optimal solution for itself and its neighbours using a centralized branch-and-bound algorithm. When message delivery is slow, as is usually the case, this can bring significant performance increases over algorithms based on asynchronous backtracking such as ADOPT.

20.3.8 Distributed Dynamic Programming

A fundamental problem with distributed backtracking algorithms is that they explore the search space sequentially by changing variable assignments. As variables are distributed, each change in assignment requires message exchange between agents. Since the search space has exponential size in the number of variables, the algorithms inevitably require an exponentially growing number of messages. Messages are costly and slow to send, so this is usually unacceptable.

Dynamic programming techniques such as *bucket elimination* ([7]) are interesting as they allow exploring all assignments in parallel. Thus, instead of sequentially exploring all assignments of a variable x_i and passing this on to a lower-priority variable x_j, variable x_j sends a single message to x_i that gives the optimal cost for each of the possible values of x_i. In the DPOP algorithm ([24]), agents are arranged in a DFS tree, as described above, and each agent communicates with its direct parent/children in the tree. Children send UTIL messages to their parents, while parents send VALUE messages to their children. Each UTIL message specifies, for each possible value combination of the parent and possibly a number of ancestors the optimal cost for the sending variable and all its descendants in the pseudotree. Value messages are similar to OK messages in that they specify the value assigned to the parent variable.

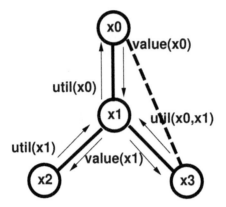

Figure 20.5: Example of a distributed optimization problem and its solution using DPOP.

Agents use the following rules:

1. an agent that has received UTIL messages from all its children and VALUE messages from all its parents decides on its optimal value and sends VALUE messages to all its children.

2. otherwise, if it has received UTIL messages from all its children it constructs a UTIL message to its parent.

Figure 20.5 shows an example of a distributed constraint optimization problem solved using the DPOP algorithm. Assume that each variable can take values w(hite) and b(lack), and that we have the following constraints:

$$c(x_0, x_3) = x_0 \begin{array}{c|cc} & x_3 & \\ & w & b \\ \hline w & 3 & 0 \\ b & 3 & 3 \end{array} \qquad c(x_0, x_1) = x_0 \begin{array}{c|cc} & x_1 & \\ & w & b \\ \hline w & 1 & 0 \\ b & 2 & 2 \end{array}$$

$$c(x_1, x_2) = x_1 \begin{array}{c|cc} & x_2 & \\ & w & b \\ \hline w & 1 & 0 \\ b & 0 & 1 \end{array} \qquad c(x_1, x_3) = x_1 \begin{array}{c|cc} & x_3 & \\ & w & b \\ \hline w & 2 & 0 \\ b & 0 & 2 \end{array}$$

Initially, only agents a_2 and a_3 satisfy the second behavior rule and send the following messages to their parent a_1:

$$UTIL(x_1) = \begin{array}{cc} & x_1 \\ \hline w & b \\ 0 & 0 \end{array} \qquad UTIL(x_0, x_1) = x_0 \begin{array}{c|cc} & x_1 & \\ & w & b \\ \hline w & 0 & 2 \\ b & 3 & 3 \end{array}$$

They give the lowest costs that can be obtained for these values of x_1 and x_0 given the best choices for x_2 and x_3, and are obtained by combining the constraints on x_2 and x_3

respectively, using the bucket elimination operation ([7]). As soon as these messages have been received by a_1, a_1 also satisfies the second behavior rules and generates the following UTIL message to its parent a_0:

$$UTIL(x_0) = \begin{array}{c} x_0 \\ \hline \begin{array}{cc} w & b \\ \hline 1 & 3 \end{array} \end{array}$$

a_0 has no parents and has received UTIL messages from all its children, so it satisfies the first behavior rule, decides its value to be w and sends this to a_1 as a VALUE message. a_1 now has all the required information to decide on its best value, w, and sends VALUE messages ($x_0 = w, x_1 = w$) to x_2 and x_3 who can finally decide on their own values b. Propagation then stops since no agent satisfies any of the rules. All agents know that they have decided on the optimal value so that no further termination detection is necessary.

It is interesting to consider solving the same example as above using asynchronous backtracking. When nogoods are systematically stored for all combinations of higher-priority agents, agents exchange exactly the same information as in dynamic programming, but through a sequence of nogoods. The memory required in each agent to store all nogoods is identical to the size of the largest message in dynamic programming. When nogoods are not stored systematically, a high price is paid for rediscovering nogoods over and over again. Thus, in the distributed case we can understand backtracking and dynamic programming as two related approaches.

In the DPOP algorithm, the number of messages grows only linearly with the size of the problem. However, messages may become very large. It can be shown ([24]) that the maximum message size is exponential in the induced width of the pseudotree ordering used. This growth can be dealt with using a technique similar to that of mini-bucket elimination ([8]). Here, we need to identify higher priority variables that are involved in the highest-dimensional messages. These variables will then change their values incrementally while informing the lower-priority agents, similar to what is done in asynchronous backtracking. While this reintroduces the problem of message explosion due to the state changes of these variables, growth is much more moderate since in a problem with low width, there are only few such variables.

The dynamic programming formulation also has several other advantages:

- it is possible to limit memory consumption by dropping dimensions of UTIL messages, and propagate upper and lower bounds ([25]). This allows computing solutions that are optimal within these bounds.

- it is possible to stop propagation of UTIL messages when the differences between values are insignificant, either because they have no influence on the rest of the problem or because their influence can be bounded by an approximation tolerance ([25]).

- for settings where the problem undergoes dynamic changes, it is possible to incrementally adapt the solution using a self-stabilization technique ([23]): each agent that observes a change initiates new UTIL messages that propagate through the network and initiate changes wherever necessary. All agents know simultaneously when the new optimal value has been reached and can change to this value without any further synchronization mechanism, thus achieving super-stabilization. Such a

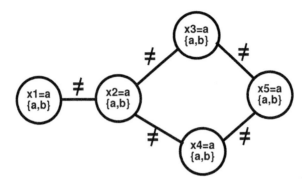

Figure 20.6: Distributed local search.

property is interesting for using distributed optimization as a method for controlling a distributed system.

It can be argued that for problems with high width constraint graphs, the distributed CSP approach does not offer significant advantages and would be solved better by centralizing the problem. As the search is likely to explore a large portion of the possible states, agents need to reveal information about their constraints to many other agents and so there is little privacy advantage. Furthermore, due to the high cost of message exchange, it is unlikely that the parallelism inherent in the distributed algorithm will bring any practical advantage.

20.4   Distributed Local Search

Recall that local search (see Chapter 5) works by starting with an initial configuration where values are assigned to all variables, and then makes incremental modifications to reduce the number of inconsistencies or minimize the cost of the configuration. Each modification is applied to individual variables or small sets of variables. Because of this local nature, they can be carried out by a single agent. This makes local search extremely well suited to distributed implementation.

Researchers have considered distributed local search algorithms where moves are restricted to modifications of single variables, and each variable is controlled by a single agent. Figure 20.6 shows an example of such a problem. We assume that initially, all variables are set to the value a, and thus all inequality constraints are violated.

The basic algorithm is *hill-climbing*: make local changes to the variables such that the number of constraint violations is reduced as much as possible. However, changes must be coordinated so that neighbouring agents in the constraint graph never change value at the same time. Otherwise, in the example each agent would change its local value to b, but not reduce constraint violations at all.

Algorithm 20.2 implements distributed hill-climbing with coordination. It requires synchronous execution with two rounds of message exchange with the set of neighbours $N(x)$ in each cycle: first, to exchange the actual values, and later to exchange the best improvements. Note that each agent only has to know $N(x)$, but nothing about the rest of the problem, so that in spite of synchronous execution this algorithm can still be applied to unbounded problems.

Algorithm 20.2: Distributed local search algorithm.

1: v(x) ← initial-value; tc1(x) ← 0; tc2(x) ← 0
2: **repeat**
3:   send current value v(x) to all neighbours in N(x)
4:   receive current values v(xj) from all xj ∈ N(x)
5:   currentCost ← $\sum_{x_j \in n(x)}$ c(x,xj=v(xj))
6:   **if** currentCost $\neq$ 0 **then** tc1(x) ← 0 **else** tc1(x) ← tc1(x)+1
7:   dmax ← 0; vmin ← NIL
8:   **for** v ∈ d **do**
9:     δ ← currentCost − $\sum_{x_j \in n(x)}$ c(x=v,xj=v(xj))
10:     **if** δ > dmax **then**
11:       dmax ← δ; vmin ← v
12:   **if** dmax $\neq$ 0 **then** tc2(x) ← 0 **else** tc2(x) ← tc2(x)+1
13:   send improvement dmax and termination counts tc1(x), tc2(x) to all xj ∈ N(x)
14:   receive improvements dm(xj) and tc1(xj), tc2(xj) from all xj ∈ N(x)
15:   **for** xj ∈ N(x) **do**
16:     **if** dm(xj) > dmax ∨ (dm(xj)=dmax ∧ xj ≻ self) **then**
17:       vmin ← NIL
18:     tc1(x) ← min(tc1(x),tc1(xj)+1); tc2(x) ← min(tc2(x),tc2(xj)+1)
19:   **if** vmin $\neq$ NIL **then**
20:     v(x) ← vmin
21: **until** tc2(x) > max-dist
22: **if** tc1(x) > max-dist **then** success **else** failure

---

Thus, if an agent finds a neighbour that obtains a bigger improvement than itself, it will not change its value. The effect of this simple coordination is that no neighbours ever change value simultaneously. For the example, a consistent solution is achieved in the first round of execution:

var	current-cost	vmin	dmax	change
x_1	1	b	1	-
x_2	3	b	3	b
x_3	2	b	2	-
x_4	2	b	2	-
x_5	2	b	2	b

Note that only x_2 and x_5 change values: x_2 wins over its neighbours because it has the best improvement, and x_5 because it has the highest index. Since they are not neighbours, they can change in the same cycle.

To detect termination, Algorithm 20.2 uses two termination counters `tc1` and `tc2`. `tc1` measures the minimum distance of any variable that could be involved in a constraint violation. `tc2` measures the minimum distance of any variable that could be unable to make further improvement. Agents extend their knowledge by exchanging counters in the second message exchange (Steps 13-14), and update their distances by taking the minimum of their values in (Step 18).

The algorithm must terminate when no agent can find any improvement. This is the case when the distance of any such agent is larger than the maximum distance of any agent in the constraint graph, given by the constant max-dist. This constant must be global knowledge of the problem, but can be an overestimation without affecting the correctness of the algorithm. If at termination the minimum distance of an agent with a violation, tcl(x), also exceed this distance, then a consistent solution has been found (Step 22).

It is well-known that hillclimbing algorithms can easily get stuck in local minima where no local improvement is possible, but the best solution has not yet been found. Two types of solutions to this problem have been given for distributed local search.

The first solution is distributed stochastic search, where with some probability the algorithm also accepts changes that do not result in an improvement in the quality of the configuration. A detailed description and analysis of several such algorithms is given in [44]. The implementation of these techniques is a straightforward modification of the hillclimbing procedure given above. One way to do this is to insert a step following the computation of δ in Step 9:

9a. **if** $\delta \leq 0$ **then** with probability p, $\delta \leftarrow 1$

where the probability might be varied as optimization progresses.

Another solution is to adjust the problem topology using the breakout algorithm [39, 13]. Here, we associate with each constraint a weight that is initially set to 1 and varies over time. In the hillclimbing procedure, we do not simply sum the costs, but multiply each constraint by its weight.

Whenever the main loop of the algorithm terminates (Step 21) and the algorithm has not found a consistent solution (tcl(x) $\leq$ max-dist), the agent increases the weight of all currently violated constraints by 1. This has the effect of making the current optimum less attractive and thus driving the search to a different configuration in subsequent moves. Then, the procedure is restarted from the beginning. This process repeats until either a consistent solution is found or some timeout limit is reached. Basharu et al. ([1]) report that resetting weights periodically or in response to observing agent behavior further improves performance.

While the breakout algorithm often performs quite well at getting search out of local optima, there are simple situations that it fails to solve, as pointed out in [43]. Figure 20.7 shows an example of such a situation. Here, each node represents a variable that must be colored either black or white, and each arc is an inequality constraint between neighbouring nodes. Note that the problem is solvable by coloring the nodes alternatively black and white. Assume that the breakout algorithm starts in the configuration shown on the top left. There are conflicts between nodes 2 and 3, and between nodes 6 and 7, that both cannot be eliminated by a local change. Thus, a breakout step increases the constraint weights from 1 to 2, as indicated in the next step on the right. Now, the algorithm can make an improvement in the weighted sum of constraint violations by changing the color of nodes 2 and 6. However, this generates a similar situation to the initial one, with 2 local minima. The algorithm again increases the weight, makes changes to variables 1 and 5, and the cycle continues until finally we reach the same situation as the initial one, except that all constraint weights have increased by 1. Thus, the breakout algorithm will never find a solution to this problem, but infinitely cycle and increase the constraint weights.

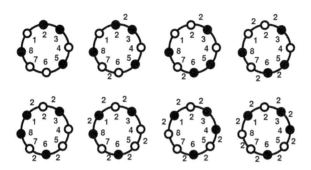

Figure 20.7: Problem that is unsolvable for the distributed breakout algorithm.

Note that such a behavior can be detected by the fact that constraint weights are continuously increasing in some subproblem. In fact, if there is a subproblem that the breakout algorithm is unable to solve - either because it has no solution or because of the algorithm's incompleteness - it must be the case that during each breakout cycle, at least one of the constraints has its weights increased. If the subproblem is small, it is possible to identify this subproblem and then solve it using a complete backtrack search algorithm. Such schemes, as described in [9], can be applied to solve large-scale distributed CSP with hundreds of variables.

20.5   Open Constraint Programming

In open constraint programming, the set of variables may be bounded and commonly known, but variable domains and admissible constraint tuples are distributed among a possibly unboundedly large set of information sources, so that the problem can never be completely centralized. Using transformations such as hidden-variable encoding (see Chapter 11), constraints can be treated as tuple-valued variables. It is therefore sufficient to consider distributed variable domains.

As an example of a problem requiring such an approach, consider a configuration system for financial portfolios. It can obtain information about available financial products from a large set of information sources. Furthermore, many of these products are themselves configured on demand by their providers. It is thus not possible to place a bound on the space of possible parts that can be considered in such a configuration.

The challenge in open constraint programming is to solve such a problem without knowing the complete domains. Algorithms are defined based on a model where variable domains are discovered incrementally by querying a mediator. We say that an algorithm for open constraint programming is complete if it always terminates with a solution when there is one; however, a complete algorithm may never terminate when there are unboundedly large domains. Note that a more restricted version that requires domains to be finite has been proposed as *interactive* constraint satisfaction in [6].

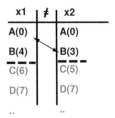

Figure 20.8: The principle underlying open constraint optimization.

Open constraint satisfaction   Open constraint satisfaction is feasible since by the semantics of constraint satisfaction, a solution to a CSP remains a solution even when values are added to the domains of one or more variables:

Lemma 20.3. *Let A be a consistent assignment to an instance $CSP(i)$ of an OCSP. Then A is also a consistent assignment to all instances $CSP(j), CSP(i) \prec CSP(j)$ of the same OCSP.*

Proof. As the domains of $CSP(i)$ are contained in those of $CSP(j)$, A is also an assignment in $CSP(j)$. As the constraints remain the same, it remains consistent.   □

Thus, if we find a consistent assignment to an instance $CSP(i)$, we have found a solution to the OCSP, and do not need to examine any further values.

Algorithms for open constraint satisfaction incrementally query information sources for additional domain values until they find either a solution, or detect a subproblem where all domains have been completely obtained and that has no solution. The key issue is to query values in a balanced way so that the problem becomes solvable as quickly as possible, and to detect unsolvable problems even in the presence of unbounded domains without falling into infinite queries of these values. Centralized algorithms for open CSP can be found in [12].

Open constraint optimization   In open constraint optimization, a solution is not just any variable assignment that satisfies the constraints, but an assignment that maximizes a utility (or, equivalently, minimizes a cost). We assume that utilities are given by additional soft constraints that are formulated on the values of individual, possibly tuple-valued variables.

Open constraint optimization is feasible under the condition that queries to the mediator always return the most preferred values or value combinations first. It is shown in [12] that if this condition does not hold, it is not possible to prove that a solution is optimal without retrieving the entire domains of variables, and thus not possible to have a general algorithm for solving open constraint optimization problems.

The reason for this fact is illustrated by Figure 20.8. It shows a COP with just two variables x_1 and x_2, connected by an inequality constraint. The variables can take different values with their costs shown in parentheses. The optimal solution is $x_1 = a, x_2 = b$ with a total cost of $0 + 3 = 3$. To show that this solution is indeed optimal, it is sufficient to know the first two values of each domain, since:

- any solution that would use a value of x_1 beyond the second value (b) would have cost of at least 4 for x_1 and 0 for x_2 (cost of the best possible value), yielding a sum of 4 which is more than the 3 we get in the proposed solution.

- any solution that would use a value of x_2 beyond the second value (b) would have cost of at least 3 for x_2 and 0 for x_1, yielding a total of 3 which again is no better than the proposed solution.

Based on this principle, it is possible to construct algorithms that determine the optimal solution without querying the entire variable domains. While there can not be any deterministic algorithm that always examines only the minimal number of values necessary to prove optimality, it is possible to come close to this limit using techniques based on the A^* algorithm ([12]).

Algorithm 20.3: fo-opt: an incremental algorithm for solving OCOP.

1: **Function fo-opt**(OCOP)
2: **For** i $\in$ {1..n}, d_i ← (**more**(x_i))
3: OPEN ← {(first(d_1),..,first(d_n))}
4: **loop**
5:     M ← {a $\in$ OPEN|cost(a) = $\min_{b \in OPEN}$ cost(b)}
6:     a ← lexicographically smallest element of M
7:     remove a from OPEN
8:     **if** consistent(a) **then**
9:        **return** a
10:     **else**
11:        c ← c(x_k,...,x_l) such that max(k,...,l) is the smallest and c is violated in a (first violated constraint)
12:        **for** j $\in$ vars(c) **do**
13:           **if** a(j) = last(d_j) **then**
14:              d_j ← append(d_j,**more**(x_j))
15:           nxj ← succ(a(j),d_j)
16:           b ← (a(1),..,a(j-1),nxj,a(j+1),..,a(n))
17:           **if** b $\notin$ OPEN **then**
18:              OPEN ← OPEN ∪{b}

Algorithm 20.3 is an example of such an algorithm. Search nodes are complete (but possibly inconsistent) assignments to all variables. Initially, the algorithm uses the function **more** to query the best value for all variables, and thus becomes the initial search node.

Following the best-first search heuristic, the OPEN list of nodes is kept ordered by decreasing utility, and the best node is chosen to be expanded next(Steps 5-7). When this node is a consistent assignment, an optimal solution has been found(Steps 8-9).

Successors to a search node could be generated by assigning one of the variables the next best value, thus giving each node n successors. When the domain is not sufficiently known, it is queried to obtain the new value. However, as shown in [12], it is only necessary to generate successors that include new values for the variables involved in the first violated constraint, where constraints are ordered according to the highest variable they involve, according to some fixed ordering. This leads to a significantly lower memory consumption as well as a much smaller number of value queries, and significantly improves the performance of the algorithm which now comes close to the minimal number of queries. Algorithm 20.3 thus picks out the first violated constraint in Step 11 and generates the successors in Step 15. Note that the function **more** is used to query the next best domain value if necessary.

Algorithm 20.3 is guaranteed to produce the optimal solution because search nodes are explored in the order of non-increasing utility. Thus, when a consistent solution is found, it will necessarily be the one with the minimum possible cost.

While Algorithm 20.3 is a centralized algorithm, open constraint optimization can also be carried out by distributed algorithms. In particular, [27] shows how open constraint optimization can be integrated with the DPOP algorithm (Section 20.3.8) to produce a distributed constraint optimization algorithm that can deal with unbounded domains and exchanges significantly less information than the DPOP, ADOPT and ABT algorithms.

20.6   Further Issues

20.6.1   Incentive-Compatibility

Agents may have conflicting interests regarding the solution to a distributed CSP. If they are allowed to post any hard or soft constraints they like, it is in their best interest to enforce their preferences by exaggerating their constraints. If all agents adopt this behavior, the solution computed by the algorithm will no longer be meaningful. Another problem is that agents can manipulate the outcome by not correctly executing the distributed optimization algorithm ([21]).

Both problems can be avoided by mechanisms where agents are required to pay a tax corresponding to the constraints they impose on others. The tax is calculated so that it is in the best interest of agents to report their constraints truthfully. Such mechanisms are called *truthful* or *incentive-compatible* mechanisms.

Another property that is important in multi-agent settings is that of *individual rationality*. It means that each agent is better off by participating in the joint mechanism rather than remaining on its own. If a tax scheme is used, it means that the amount of tax an agent may be forced to pay is never greater than the gain it gets out of influencing the choice of the algorithm.

A well-known mechanism for incentive-compatibility is the *Vickrey-Clarke-Groves tax*(VCG) mechanism. It can be shown that it is the only general mechanism that guarantees both incentive-compatibility and individual rationality for all agents. Its application for multi-agent decision making has first been proposed in [10] and its application to distributed CSP described in [11]. [26] describes in detail how the DPOP algorithm can be combined with a completely distributed VCG tax mechanism, resulting in a scheme that is completely resistant to manipulation.

In the VCG mechanism, each agent pays the difference in cost to all other agents between the optimal solution when it is present and the solution when it is not:

$$ payment(A) = \sum_{r_k \in R - R_A} r_k(v_R^*) - r_k(v_{R-R_A}^*) $$

where R is the set of all relations, R_A is the set of relations imposed by agent A, and v_R^*, $v_{R-R_A}^*$ are the solutions that minimize the sum of costs in R and $R - R_A$, respectively. The tax must be paid to an uninterested party (charity).

The following argument shows why this tax makes it optimal for an agent to tell the truth:

- suppose that agent A overstates the importance of his constraints. Then it will gain an advantage for those cases where his claimed cost is higher than his real cost. However, it turns out that in these cases, he will also have to pay a tax which is higher than the benefit it gets out of having his solution chosen - consequently, this behavior is not rational for the agent.

- suppose on the other hand that the agent understates its costs. Then it will save the tax in those cases where it would fall between its stated and its true cost for the value that is chosen. However, in all these cases the tax would be lower than the loss it incurs by having this value chosen, so again it is not individually rational for the agent to act this way.

It has been shown ([21, 26]) that VCG taxes can also eliminate the potential for agents to manipulate the outcome by unfaithfully executing a distributed search algorithm.

The VCG tax mechanism applies only to constraint optimization with soft constraints. A hard constraint can cause an unbounded amount of utility loss to the remaining agents, and thus by the principle of VCG taxes an unbounded amount of tax for the agent that imposes it. Such a tax may be considered to violate that agent's individual rationality. Therefore, in general hard constraints should only be used to model commonly verifiable knowledge.

20.6.2 Privacy

One of the possible motivations for using distributed constraint satisfaction is to protect the privacy of agents' constraints. The ultimate protection is achieved when solving a CSP using cryptographic techniques. Here, no agent learns anything about other agents' constraints except that a certain combination of assignments - the final solution - is consistent with all constraints.

Secure distributed constraint satisfaction, as described by Yokoo in [41], is based on cryptographic techniques that achieve three properties:

1. constraints are encrypted, and consistency of a value assignment is decided without decrypting the constraints;

2. values are permuted in a random-looking way so that no agent can tell what value corresponds to what position;

3. algorithms search the entire search space so that no information can be drawn from the time it takes to find a solution.

Each agent encrypts all its constraints by generating a constraint matrix that includes encrypted versions of the elements 1 (consistent) and another number z (inconsistent). Using randomized encryption techniques, each of these is made to look like a completely random number so that an observer cannot tell whether two cells contain identical elements.

When the algorithm checks for the consistency of an assignment, it collects the relevant constraint entries and multiplies them together. Thanks to a second property of the encryption scheme, that of being homomorphic, the product of the encrypted numbers is equivalent to the encryption of their product. Thus, the product can subsequently be decrypted and checked for whether it contains a 1 - meaning that all constraints were 1, and thus satisfied - or another number, meaning that at least one constraint was not satisfied. This decryption must in fact be done by passing the result through all involved agents, and thus invariably leads to a very large number of messages.

To ensure that no agent can know what values were found consistent or inconsistent, the scheme furthermore involves a *permutation* of all domain values. Each agent permutes all constraint matrices referring to its own values with the same permutation of domain values, and applies a renewed randomization of the encryption so that the permutation cannot be discovered by comparing values.

Search can use a centralized or decentralized algorithm, but each constraint check requires a cooperative decryption of the result of multiplying the relevant constraints. When a consistent solution is found, each agent can apply the permutation of its domain in reverse and thus finds out what its value was.

In subsequent work it has been noted that since the computation time of the search algorithm reveals information about the constraints, and that even this protocol is not entirely secure. For an example of a protocol that is also secure against this kind of attack, see [32].

Cryptographic privacy protection is very costly to implement, and so far has not been used in practical applications of realistic size. In principle, all distributed CSP algorithms provide some level of privacy protection, since constraints are only revealed to neighbouring agents, and even here only when backtracking is required. An analysis of privacy loss is found for example in [36]. Researchers have also explored whether constraints could be shared by participants, allowing them to be enforced even though no agent knows the entire constraint ([4]).

20.7   Conclusion

Many applications of constraint satisfaction and optimization occur in settings with multiple agents and may even be unbounded. In that case, it is no longer feasible to solve them by centralizing all problem information on a single server. Distributed constraint satisfaction techniques address such naturally unbounded problems. The localized nature of constraint satisfaction is a major advantage in such settings; classical optimization techniques such as linear programming are not easily applied in a distributed and possibly asynchronous manner.

Unboundedness can occur in two ways. The first is that the set of variables and constraints involved in the problem is not bounded. This is the classical distributed constraint satisfaction problem, and it occurs for example in meeting scheduling. The second is that the admissible values and value tuples are unbounded. This is the *open* constraint satisfaction problem, and it occurs for example in product or supply chain configuration. This chapter has presented an overview of the main algorithms that have been developed for these scenarios.

Applications of distributed constraint satisfaction algorithms are just beginning to appear. Since many of these problems were impossible to solve by computer before, the technology is in fact an enabler for future applications that are now beginning to be explored.

Bibliography

[1] M. Basharu, I. Arana and H. Ahriz: "Solving DisCSPs with Penalty Driven Search," *Proceedings of the 20th AAAI*, pp. 47-52, 2005

[2] R. Béjar, C. Domshlak, C. Fernández, C. Gomes, B. Krishnamachari, B. Selman, and M. Valls: "Sensor networks and distributed CSP: communication, computation and complexity," *Artificial Intelligence* **161**(1-2), pp. 117-147, 2005

[3] C. Bessière, A. Maestre, I. Brito and P. Meseguer: "Asynchronous backtracking without adding links: a new member in the ABT family," *Artificial Intelligence* **161**(1-2), pp. 7-24, 2005

[4] I. Brito and P. Meseguer: "Distributed Forward Checking," *Proceedings of the 9th CP*, Springer LNCS 2833, pp. 801-806, 2003

[5] Z. Collin, R. Dechter and S. Katz: "On the Feasibility of Distributed Constraint Satisfaction," *Proceedings of the 12th IJCAI*, pp. 319-324, Sydney, 1991

[6] R. Cucchiara, M. Gavanelli, E. Lamma, P. Mello, M. Milano, and M. Piccardi: "Constraint propagation and value acquisition: why we should do it interactively," *Proceedings of the 16th IJCAI*, pp.468-477, 1999

[7] R. Dechter: "Bucket elimination: A unifying framework for reasoning," *Artificial Intelligence* **113**, pp.41-85, 1999

[8] R. Dechter and I. Rish: "Minibuckets: A general scheme for approximating inference," *Journal of ACM*, pp. 107-153, 2003

[9] C. Eisenberg and B. Faltings: "Hybrid Solving Method for Large-Scale Distributed Constraint Satisfaction Problems, in W. Zhang and V. Sorge (eds.): *Distributed Problem Solving and Reasoning in Multi-agent Systems*, IOS Press, pp. 19-33, 2004

[10] E. Ephrati and J. S. Rosenschein: "The Clarke tax as a consensus mechanism among automated agents," *Proceedings of the 9th AAAI*, pp. 173-178, 1991

[11] B. Faltings: "Incentive-compatible Open Constraint Optimization," *Proceedings of the 4th ACM Conference on Electronic Commerce*, 2003

[12] B. Faltings and S. Macho-Gonzalez: "Open Constraint Programming," *Artificial Intelligence* **161**(1-2), pp. 181-208, 2005

[13] K. Hirayama, M. Yokoo, "Coordinated Multi-agent Local Search", *Artificial Intelligence* **161**(1-2), pp. 89-116, 2005

[14] R. Mailler and V. Lesser: "Solving Distributed Constraint Optimization Problems Using Cooperative Mediation," *Proceedings of the 3rd AAMAS*, pp. 438-445, 2004

[15] R. Marinescu and R. Dechter: "AND/OR Branch-and-Bound for Graphical Models," *Proceedings of the 19th IJCAI*, pp. 224-229, 2005

[16] A. Meisels, E. Kaplansky, I. Razgon and R. Zivan: "Comparing Performance of Distributed Constraints Processing Algorithms," *Proceedings of 3rd Workshop on Distributed Constraint Reasoning* pp. 86-93, 2002

[17] A. Meisels and R. Zivan: "Asynchronous Forward-Checking for DisCSPs," in W. Zhang and V. Sorge (eds.): *Distributed Problem Solving and Reasoning in Multi-agent Systems*, IOS Press, pp. 93-107, 2004

[18] P. J. Modi, M. Veloso: "Multiagent Meeting Scheduling with Rescheduling," *5th Workshop on Distributed Constraint Reasoning*, 2004

[19] P. J. Modi, W.-M. Shen, M. Tambe, and M. Yokoo: "An Asynchronous Complete Method for Distributed Constraint Optimization," *Artificial Intelligence* **161**(1-2), pp. 149-180, 2005

[20] V. Nguyen, D. Sam-Haroud and B. Faltings: "Dynamic Distributed Backjumping," *Recent Advances in Constraints*, Springer LNAI 3419, pp. 71-85, 2005

[21] D. C. Parkes and J. Shneidman: "Distributed implementations of Vickrey-Clarke-Groves mechanisms," *Proceedings of the 3rd AAMAS*, pp. 261-268, 2004

[22] A. Petcu and B. Faltings: "An Efficient Constraint Optimization Method for Large Multiagent Systems, " *AAMAS Workshop on large-scale multi-agent systems*, 2005.

[23] A. Petcu and B. Faltings: "Superstabilizing, Fault-containing Multiagent Combinatorial Optimization," *Proceedings of the 20th AAAI*, pp. 1406-1411, 2005

[24] A. Petcu and B. Faltings: "A Scalable Method for Multiagent Constraint Optimization," *Proceedings of the 19th ICJAI*, pp 266-271, 2005

[25] A. Petcu and B. Faltings: "Approximations in Distributed Optimization," *Proceedings of the 11th CP*, Springer LNCS 3709, pp. 802-806, 2005

[26] A. Petcu, B. Faltings and D. Parkes: "MDPOP: Faithful Distributed Implementation of Efficient Social Choice Problems," *Proceedings of the 5th AAMAS*, 2006

[27] A. Petcu and B. Faltings: "ODPOP: An Algorithm for Open Distributed Constraint Optimization," *AAMAS 06 Workshop on Distributed Constraint Reasoning*, 2006

[28] M. Silaghi, D. Sam-Haroud and B. Faltings: "Asynchronous Search with Aggregations," *Proceedings of the 17th AAAI*, pp. 917-922, 2000

[29] M. Silaghi, D. Sam-Haroud and B. Faltings: "ABT with Asynchronous Reordering," *Proceedings of 2nd A-P Conference on Intelligent Agent Technology* IEEE press, pp. 54-63, 2001

[30] M. Silaghi, D. Sam-Haroud and B. Faltings: "Hybridizing ABT and AWC into a polynomial space, complete protocol with reordering," EPFL Technical Report 01/364, 2001

[31] M. Silaghi: "Asynchronously Solving Distributed Problems with Privacy Requirements," Ph.D. Thesis 2601, EPFL, 2002

[32] M. Silaghi: "Meeting Scheduling System Guaranteeing n/2-Privacy and Resistant to Statistical Analysis (Applicable to any DisCSP)," *Proceedings of the 3rd International Conference on Web Intelligence*, IEEE press, pp. 711-715, 2004

[33] M. Silaghi and B. Faltings: "Asynchronous Aggregation and Consistency in Distributed Constraint Satisfaction," *Artificial Intelligence* **161**(1-2), pp. 25-54, 2005

[34] M. Silaghi and M. Yokoo: "Nogood-based Asynchronous Distributed Optimization (ADOPT-ng)," *Proceedings of the 5th AAMAS*, 2006

[35] K. Sycara, S.F. Roth, N. Sadeh-Koniecpol, and M.S. Fox: "Distributed Constrained Heuristic Search," IEEE Transactions on Systems, Man, and Cybernetics, **21**(6), pp. 1446-1461, 1991

[36] R. J. Wallace and E. C. Freuder: "Constraint-based reasoning and privacy/efficiency tradeoffs in multi-agent program solving," *Artificial Intelligence* **161**(1-2), pp. 209-227, 2005

[37] M. Yokoo, E. H. Durfee, T. Ishida, and K. Kuwabara: "Distributed Constraint Satisfaction for Formalizing Distributed Problem Solving", *Proceedings of the 12th ICDCS*, pp.614-621, 1992.

[38] M. Yokoo: "Weak-commitment Search for Solving Constraint Satisfaction Problems", *Proceedings of the 12th AAAI*, pp.313–318, 1994.

[39] M. Yokoo, K. Hirayama: "Distributed Breakout Algorithm for Solving Distributed Constraint Satisfaction Problems" *Proceedings of the 2nd ICMAS*, pp.401–408, 1996

[40] M. Yokoo, E. H. Durfee, T. Ishida, and K. Kuwabara: "Distributed Constraint Satisfaction Problem: Formalization and Algorithms," *IEEE Trans. on Knowledge and Data Engineering* **10**(5), 1998

[41] M. Yokoo, K. Suzuki, and K. Hirayama, "Secure Distributed Constraint Satisfaction: Reaching Agreement without Revealing Private Information", *Artificial Intelligence* **161**(1-2), pp. 229-246, 2005

[42] R. Zivan and A. Meisels: "Dynamic Ordering for Asynchronous Backtracking on DisCSPs," *Proceedings of the 11th CP*, Springer LNCS 3709, pp. 32-46, 2005

[43] W. Zhang and L. Wittenburg: "Distributed breakout revisited," *Proceedings of the 18th AAAI*, pp.352-357, 2002

[44] W. Zhang, G. Wang, Z. Xing and L. Wittenberg: "Distributed stochastic search and distributed breakout: Properties, comparison and applications to constraint optimization problems in sensor networks," *Artificial Intelligence* **161**(1-2), pp. 55-87, 2005

Chapter 21

Uncertainty and Change

Kenneth N. Brown and Ian Miguel

Constraint Programming (CP) has proven to be a very successful technique for reasoning about assignment problems, as evidenced by the many applications described elsewhere in this book. Much of its success is due to the simple and elegant underlying formulation: describe the world in terms of decision variables that must be assigned values, place clear and explicit restrictions on the values that may be assigned simultaneously, and then find a set of assignments to all the variables that obeys those restrictions. Thus, CP makes two assumptions about the problems it tackles:

1. There is no *uncertainty* in the problem definition: each problem has a crisp and complete description.

2. Problems are not *dynamic*: they do not change between the initial description and the final execution of the solution.

Unfortunately, these two assumptions do not hold for many practical and important applications. For example, scheduling production in a factory is, in practice, fundamentally dynamic and uncertain: the full set of jobs to be scheduled is not known in advance, and continues to grow as existing jobs are being completed; machines break down; raw material is delivered late; employees become ill; jobs take longer than expected; or processes have inherently random aspects, and so some jobs may have to be repeated. Alternatively, in engineering or architectural design, the constraints themselves are not known with certainty — this may be because the designer is not aware of the detail of the constraints, or because the constraints are inherently vague — or may be changing because the designer is exploring the problem space, reformulating the problem as the consequences of each modelling decision become clearer.

Current constraint solving tools provide very little support for explicit reasoning about uncertain and dynamic problems. In many cases, an approximated deterministic and static model may suffice, and provides the user with enough information about the structure of the problem to make good enough decisions. In other cases, though, the user is required to re-formulate the problem repeatedly, in response to each change or to each discovery of more detail of the problem. What support should CP tools offer in those situations? For many problems, all that may be required is a sufficiently fast solver, reacting to the changes with new solutions, or producing many initial solutions to different formulations in the case of uncertainty. At other times, for dynamic problems, the new solutions should be as close as possible to the previous ones, to minimise the cost of change. More advanced methods should generate solutions that are robust to the likely changes, or that are sufficiently flexible to allow the changes to be accommodated. Particular attention should also be paid to time limits, since the dynamic changes may occur too quickly to allow exhaustive analysis — in that case, time-bounded or anytime reasoning is required.

In this chapter, we consider the uses and extensions of constraint programming for handling problems subject to change and uncertainty. We classify the research into two broad categories based on the problem type:

(i) uncertain problems, which require a single solution; and

(ii) Dynamically changing problems, which require multiple solution stages.

Within (ii), we consider three further sub-categories:

(ii-a) problems where the solver simply reacts each time the problems change;

(ii-b) problems where the solving process is adapted to record information about the problem structure, which can be used during the reaction phase; and

(ii-c) problems where the solver proactively searches for solutions that anticipate the expected changes.

We will begin by briefly reviewing the definitions of constraint satisfaction and optimisation problems, and presenting a small example problem which we will use throughout the chapter. We will then consider each of the categories and sub-categories in turn. Finally, we will conclude with a discussion of challenges for future research.

21.1 Background and Definitions

The finite-domain *constraint satisfaction problem* (CSP) consists of a triple $\langle X, D, C \rangle$ where X is a set of variables, D is a set of domains, and C is a set of constraints. Each $x_i \in X$ is associated with a finite domain $D_i \in D$ of potential values. An *assignment* to a variable x_i is the selection of a value v_i from its domain D_i. A constraint $c \in C$ constraining variables $x_i, \ldots, x_j$, specifies a subset of the Cartesian product $D_i \times \ldots \times D$ indicating mutually-compatible variable assignments. A tuple of values $v = (v_i, \ldots, v_j)$ *satisfies* a constraint c over $x_i, \ldots, x_j$ if $v \in c$. A *partial assignment* to a problem is a collection of assignments to a subset of the variables in the problem, and a complete assignment is an assignment for every variable. A *solution* is a complete assignment that satisfies all constraints. A *constrained optimisation problem* is a CSP with some objective function, which is to be optimised.

21.2 Example: Course Scheduling

To illustrate the various problems and techniques, we will use as a basis the following simple example (adapted from [22]) throughout the chapter. Consider the task of scheduling

		Type	
i↘j	L(1)	P(2)	T(3)
D a y s 1	x_{11}	x_{12}	x_{13}
2	x_{21}	x_{22}	x_{23}
3	x_{31}	x_{23}	x_{33}

$$\forall i \; \sum_{j=1}^{3} x_{ij} \geq 2 \qquad \text{sessions per day} \quad (21.1)$$

$$\forall j \; \sum_{i=1}^{3} x_{ij} \in \{1, 2, \ldots, 5\} \qquad \text{no. of session type} \; (21.2)$$

$$\sum_{i=1}^{3} \sum_{j=1}^{3} x_{ij} \in \{10, 11, 12\} \qquad \text{total sessions} \qquad (21.3)$$

Figure 21.1: Course Scheduling Problem

a short course over three days consisting of a number of lectures, practical sessions, and tutorial sessions. The constraints are that there must be at least two sessions a day and, over the three days, there must be between 1 and 5 of each type of session and between 10 and 12 sessions in total. This problem can be cast as a CSP by using 9 variables, x_{ij} with i and j in $\{1, 2, 3\}$, where i denotes the day and j the session type with 1 = lecture, 2 = practical, 3 = tutorial. Each variable has domain $\{0, 1, 2, 3, 4, 5\}$ denoting the number of sessions of the corresponding type on a particular day. The constraints are expressed on these variables as presented in Figure 21.1. Figure 21.2 presents one possible solution to this problem in which there are two lectures, three practical and five tutorial sessions over the three days.

		Type	
i↘j	L(1)	P(2)	T(3)
D a y s 1	1	0	1
2	1	1	0
3	0	2	4

Figure 21.2: A Solution to Course Scheduling Problem

21.3 Uncertain Problems

First we consider problems where a complete crisp description of the problem will not be revealed at all, and so we must produce a single initial solution that cannot be changed. In order to produce the solutions, we have to consider how the imprecision in the problem description is expressed. We consider three cases: *(i)* the problem itself is intrinsically imprecise — for example, where the price of a configuration must be 'cheap', where 'cheap'

$$\forall i \sum_{j=1}^{3} x_{ij} \geq 2 \qquad \textit{sessions per day}$$

$$\sum_{i=1}^{3} \sum_{j=1}^{3} x_{ij} \in \{10, 11, 12\} \qquad \textit{total sessions}$$

		Sums of Assignment Tuples					
		1	2	3	4	5	Otherwise
lectures	$\sum_{i=1}^{3} x_{i1}$	0.4	0.6	0.8	1.0	0.8	0
practicals	$\sum_{i=1}^{3} x_{i2}$	0.6	0.8	1.0	0.8	0.6	0
tutorials	$\sum_{i=1}^{3} x_{i3}$	0.6	0.8	1.0	0.8	0.6	0

Figure 21.3: The Fuzzy Course Scheduling Problem. Fuzzy constraints show satisfaction degrees for different possible assignment tuples.

is defined by a fuzzy membership function, *(ii)* we have a set of possible realisations of the problem, one of which will be the final version of the problem, and *(iii)* we have probability distributions over the full realisations — for example, a distribution over the values that might be available to us, or over the legal tuples in the constraints. Secondly, for *(ii)* and *(iii)*, we also consider problems where the description will eventually be revealed, but requires an instant response. In such cases, we can extend the techniques to include contingencies — families of solutions, one of which will be selected depending on the revealed problem.

21.3.1   Fuzzy Problems

Fuzzy constraint satisfaction [22] (see also Chapter 9) captures imprecision in the definition of a constraint by allowing constraints to be partially satisfied, as well as completely satisfied or completely unsatisfied. To continue the above example, a constraint specifying that an expression in certain cost variables must be "cheap", rather than being satisfied or violated, can be satisfied to a greater or lesser extent according to the assignments to the cost variables. This allows us to capture notions such as "fairly cheap" and "relatively expensive".

In a fuzzy constraint satisfaction problem, a constraint $c(x_i, \ldots, x_j)$ is represented by a fuzzy relation, which is in turn defined by a *membership function* that associates a degree of satisfaction in a totally ordered scale (usually [0, 1], with 0 and 1 representing complete violation and complete satisfaction respectively) with each tuple in $D_i \times \ldots \times D_j$. The conjunction of two fuzzy relations is usually interpreted as the minimum membership value assigned by either relation. To produce a satisfaction degree for a given partial or complete assignment, the conjunction operator is used to aggregate the satisfaction degrees of all constraints on the assigned variables. This allows us to rank different assignments and therefore search for optimal solutions to a fuzzy CSP.

To illustrate, we consider a fuzzy version of the course scheduling problem given in Figure 21.1. Professor A is to give the lectures in the course. She prefers to give four

Constraint	Assignment Sum	Sat Degree
Sessions per Day	2, 4, 4	1.0
Total Sessions	10	1.0
Lectures	3	0.8
Practicals	3	1.0
Tutorials	4	0.8
Overall Satisfaction Degree: 0.8		

Type

Days \ i j	L(1)	P(2)	T(3)
1	1	0	1
2	1	1	0
3	0	2	4

Constraint	Assignment Sum	Sat Degree
Sessions per Day	2, 4, 4	1.0
Total Sessions	10	1.0
Lectures	4	1.0
Practicals	3	1.0
Tutorials	3	1.0
Overall Satisfaction Degree: 1.0		

Type

Days \ i j	L(1)	P(2)	T(3)
1	1	0	1
2	2	1	1
3	1	2	1

Figure 21.4: Sub-optimal and Optimal Solutions to the Fuzzy Course Scheduling Problem

of these sessions. Dr B is organising the practical sessions, and he prefers to give about three of these. Finally, Dr C is responsible for the tutorial sessions, and also prefers that there should be about three of these. These preferences are captured in fuzzy constraints on the lecture, practical and tutorial session variables, as presented in Figure 21.3. Note that constraints on the number of sessions per day and the total number of sessions remain as hard constraints. Hard constraints are simple to represent with fuzzy constraints: the satisfaction degree of each assignment tuple is either 0 or 1.

Figure 21.4 presents two solutions to the fuzzy course scheduling problem. The first is the same as the solution to the crisp course scheduling problem given in Figure 21.2. This solution has satisfaction degree 0.8 because there are three lecture sessions (from Figure 21.2, the satisfaction degree of the constraint on the number of lectures is therefore 0.8) and three tutorial sessions (also satisfaction degree 0.8). Hence, the fuzzy conjunction of the satisfaction degrees of all the constraints is 0.8. The second solution has satisfaction degree 1.0 and is therefore optimal. The reader will be able to confirm that the satisfaction degree of each constraint is 1.0.

21.3.2 Problems with Possible Realisations

For problems with a set of possible realisations, we first need to consider the ways in which the problem definition could be incomplete — i.e. what is missing from the original description that will be revealed. Based on the definition in 21.1, this could be:

1. The complete set of variables is not known;

2. The domains of the variables are not completely specified; or

3. The constraints are not completely specified — either the full set of constraints is not known, or the individual constraints are not fully described.

In fact, we could reformulate the definition of a CSP so that only the constraints need to be specified explicitly (the domains would be unary constraints restricting values from a universal set, and the variables are implicitly defined to be those appearing anywhere in the constraint set), and thus formally we only need to consider uncertainty in the constraint set. In practice, the different types of uncertainty are treated separately, to model specific features of different application domains, and give rise to different formalisms and algorithms.

In *Mixed CSPs* [27], we model the case where some of the variables are not controlled by the solver, but will be assigned by some external source (which may be a user, another agent, later knowledge discovery, or a random process). Thus the variables of the problem are divided into two classes: controlled decision variables and uncontrollable parameters. The decision variables are normal CSP variables, but the parameters will be set by the external source (and thus essentially fix the domains of those variables to a singleton set). The possible realisations of the problem are then defined by the sets of possible values that the parameters may take. Constraints restrict the assignments of values to variables in the normal way. A *pure* decision is an assignment of values to all the decision variables, which should be a solution to one or more of the possible realisations. If there are no constraints on the realisations (i.e. the parameters are independent), then it is NP-complete to determine whether there exists a single pure decision which is a solution to all realisations in a binary mixed CSP. For cases where the true realisation will be revealed, a *conditional* decision associates different assignments of values to different realisations, and an *optimal* conditional decision has a solution for each possible realisation. Fargier *et al* [27] give an anytime algorithm for finding conditional decisions.

As an example, consider the course scheduling problem as before, but now we assume that the number of tutorials on day 1 (x_{13}) will be decided later (based on the availability of tutors). That is, the variable x_{13} becomes an uncontrollable parameter. Suppose we know that x_{13} can take one of two possible values, 0 or 1. Figure 21.5a shows a pure decision for all the other variables that satisfies both possible realisations. Suppose now that the number of lectures on day 2 (x_{21}) will also be fixed at a later date, and that the value of x_{21} may be 0, 1 or 2, independently of the value of x_{13}. There are now six possible realisations, based on the possible values of (x_{13}, x_{21}): $\{(0,0), (0,1), (0,2), (1,0), (1,1), (1,2)\}$. No single pure decision is possible (since it will not be possible to satisfy the constraint on the total number of sessions); however, figure 21.5b shows an optimal conditional decision, by associating a decision with each possible realisation.

To cover problems with uncertain data, Yorke-Smith and Gervet define *Uncertain CSPs* [77], in which the constraints are uncertain — specifically, they use an algebraic representation of the constraints, with uncertainty over the coefficients. Their goal is to define the *certainty closure*, the set of all solutions to possible realisations of the constraints, and then to search for specific types of closure, including a *covering set*, which contains at least one solution for each realisation, or the *most robust solution*, which is a solution to the greatest number of realisations. Their suggested solution method is to transform the UCSP into a standard CSP, such that the set of all solutions to the CSP is equivalent to the desired closure of the UCSP.

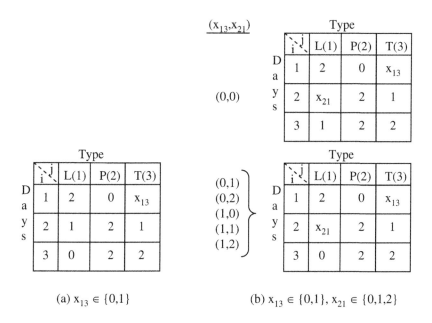

(a) $x_{13} \in \{0,1\}$ (b) $x_{13} \in \{0,1\}$, $x_{21} \in \{0,1,2\}$

Figure 21.5: *mixed* CSP: *(a)* a pure decision; *(b)* an optimal conditional decision.

Suppose in our course scheduling problem, the full workload requirements have not been revealed to us; specifically, the total number of sessions may be required to be either 10 or 12, and the required length of a practical may be either 1 or 2 hours, but the constraints on the hours per day, and the hours of each session type remain the same. The original problem could then be represented as presented in Figure 21.6, where w_1 and w_3 are known to be 1, but the values of w_2 and t are unknown, but taken from the sets $\{1,2\}$ and $\{10,12\}$ respectively. Therefore, there are 4 possible realisations: $\{w_2 = 1, t = 10\}$, $\{w_2 = 1, t = 12\}$, $\{w_2 = 2, t = 10\}$ and $\{w_2 = 2, t = 12\}$. A covering set is shown in Figure 21.7, where the first solution is the most robust solution.

21.3.3 Probability-Based Problems

The next step on from problems with possible realisations is to consider problems where there is a probability distribution over those realisations. Two different formalisms have been proposed with the name *probabilistic CSPs*. The first [25] involves uncertainty over the constraints that appear in the problem, associating a probability with each single constraint, representing the (independent) probability that that constraint is active. The aim is to find an assignment of values to variables which has the highest probability of being a solution to the true problem. For example (Fig. 21.8), suppose we have three possible additional constraints on the practicals in our timetabling problem: the number of practicals must be not less than the number of lectures, with a probability of 0.6; the number of

$$\forall i \sum_{j=1}^{3} w_j x_{ij} > 2 \tag{21.4}$$

$$\forall j \sum_{i=1}^{3} w_j x_{ij} \in \{1, \ldots, 5\} \tag{21.5}$$

$$\sum_{i=1}^{3} \sum_{j=1}^{3} w_j x_{ij} = t \tag{21.6}$$

Figure 21.6: The Uncertain Course Scheduling Problem

practicals on day 3 must be greater than the number of practicals on day 1, with probability 0.5; and the total number of practicals must be no higher than 2, with a probability of 0.2.

There is no assignment with a probability of 1.0 of being a solution; an assignment with maximal probability of being a solution is shown in figure 21.9. This first type of probabilistic CSP could be thought of as the probabilistic equivalent of uncertain CSPs described above, assigning a probability distribution to the values of coefficients in the constraints. Probabilistic CSPs can be represented using the two general soft constraint frameworks *valued* CSP [69] and *semi-ring*[12] CSP described in Chapter 9, "Soft Constraints".

The second type of probabilistic CSPs [26] correspond to mixed CSPs, with the addition of a probability distribution over the possible assignments to the uncontrollable parameters. The aim here is to find a pure decision with maximal probability of being a solution to the full problem. A branch and bound algorithm based on forward checking is described. Again, we can also consider conditional decisions, and an algorithm is given for generating them. Consider now the same problem as described in Figure 21.5, but with two probability distributions over the values of $x_{13} : \{0 : 0.3, 1 : 0.7\}$ and $x_{21} : \{0 : 0.5, 1 : 0.4, 2 : 0.1\}$ Again, no decision can have a probability of 1.0 of being a solution to the full problem (since the two realisations $\langle x_{13} = 1, x_{21} = 2 \rangle$ and $\langle x_{13} = 0, x_{21} = 0 \rangle$ cannot be satisfied by the same assignment due to the total sessions constraint; figure 21.10 shows a maximal pure decision, with total probability of 0.93 of being a solution (failing only on the realisation $\langle x_{13} = 1, x_{21} = 2 \rangle$).

1-stage stochastic CSPs [76] are similar to (the second) probabilistic CSPs, but wit the difference that a problem is defined to be θ-satisfiable if there exists a (pure) decision with a probability higher than θ of being a solution. The complexity of 1-stage stochastic CSPs is shown to be NP^{PP}-complete. Stochastic CSPs in general encompass multiple stages and will be discussed further in Section 21.4.3.

21.4   Problems that Change

Now we consider problems that are subject to change over time, and where the opportunity exists to respond to each change via a new solution step. The changes may be imposed by a user, an external agent or the environment. Typically, this occurs during the execution of

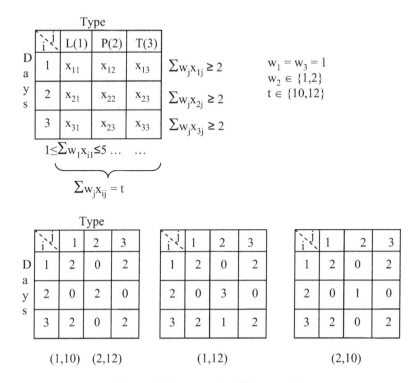

Figure 21.7: *uncertain* CSP: a covering set.

a solution, but in certain cases change may be so rapid that it occurs even as a solution to the original problem is being sought.

Dynamic CSPs ([17], see Figure 21.11) view a changing problem as a sequence of CSPs linked by *restrictions* and *relaxations* (also known as *retractions*), where constraints are respectively added to, and removed from, one problem in the sequence to obtain the next. There are three key concerns in solving dynamic CSPs. The first is to minimise

$$\sum_{i=1}^{3} x_{i2} \geq \sum_{i=1}^{3} x_{i1} \quad (P = 0.6) \tag{21.7}$$

$$x_{32} > x_{12} \quad (P = 0.5) \tag{21.8}$$

$$\sum_{i=1}^{3} x_{i2} \leq 2 \quad (P = 0.2) \tag{21.9}$$

Figure 21.8: The Probabilistic Course Scheduling Problem

		1	2	3
D	1	1	0	2
a	2	1	1	1
y s	3	0	2	2

(Type)

Figure 21.9: *probabilistic* CSP$_1$: a maximal solution.

the need for change, and thus to find *robust*[1] solutions that are likely to remain solutions even after the change has occurred, or to need only minor 'repairs'. The second is to minimise the cost of change, if a change to the solution is required. Hence, we seek *stable* solutions following a change. This is a significant concern in many applications and can stem, for example, from the cost of retooling or simply from the inconvenience to end users. The third is to minimise the reaction time, obtaining a new solution as quickly as possible. The three concerns are often opposed to each other, and thus the particular solution technique implemented will depend on the application. We consider three cases, based on the requirements of the problem and on the knowledge we have of the future changes. Sub-section 21.4.1 assumes no knowledge of the future, and attempts to re-use aspects of the old solution when computing the new solutions. Subsection 21.4.2 also assumes no fore-knowledge of the changes, but attempts to re-use some of the previous reasoning process when generating a new solution. Finally, sub-section 21.4.3 considers problems where the modeller has some uncertain knowledge of the future changes, and examines techniques which are robust to those likely changes. Typically, this involves problems which grow over time, or where the problem structure is gradually revealed.

---

[1]The term 'flexibility' is also used to describe robustness. For consistency, we use 'robust' throughout.

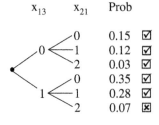

x_{13}	x_{21}	Prob	
	0	0.15	☑
0	1	0.12	☑
	2	0.03	☑
	0	0.35	☑
1	1	0.28	☑
	2	0.07	☒

		1	2	3
D	1	2	0	x_{13}
a	2	x_{21}	1	1
y s	3	0	2	2

(Type)

Figure 21.10: *probabilistic* CSP$_2$: a maximal solution.

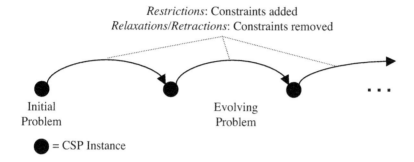

Figure 21.11: Dynamically Changing Problem Represented as a Sequence of Static CSPs.

21.4.1 Pure Reaction

We will begin by assuming no knowledge of how the problem is likely to change. Naively, each new problem can be solved from scratch. However, efficient solvers exploit the past history of problems and solutions to guide them in solving the new problem, while attempting to minimise the cost of changeover. *Local Repair* methods maintain all assignments from the solution to the previous problem to use as a starting point. The initial assignment is then progressively modified until an acceptable solution to the current problem is obtained.

Minton *et al* [52] describe a local repair method that searches through the space of possible repairs. This search is guided by the *min-conflicts* heuristic that seeks to minimise the number of unsatisfied constraints after each step. The heuristic repair method can be used naturally in a non-systematic (hill-climbing) or systematic (backtracking) search strategy. In the following example, we will illustrate systematic heuristic repair. Reconsider the solution to the Course Scheduling Problem given in Figure 21.2. This solution, although satisfying the constraints given in Figure 21.1, does have a very busy final day. Therefore, the next time the course is run, a new constraint is added that places a maximum on the number of sessions per day. Figure 21.12 presents this variant of the problem, which we will call the *Balanced Course Scheduling Problem*.

Heuristic repair performs a standard backtracking search, with a value ordering heuristic that prefers the assignment that conflicts least with the values assigned by the solution to the previous problem to future variables. Consider solving the Balanced Course Scheduling Problem having obtained the solution to the original Course Scheduling Problem given in Figure 21.2. We use a variable ordering scheme that assigns lecture, then practical then tutorial variables in ascending day order. We also assume that ties are broken by preferring an assignment that matches the previous solution. The current assignments to x_{11} and x_{21} do not conflict with any of the future variables, and so are left unchanged. Consider now the assignment of x_{31}. This variable cannot be assigned 4 or 5, since this would violate constraint (21.2). The remaining values all conflict with the values assigned by the previous solution to x_{32} and x_{33} and constraint (21.10). Since the value 0 is closest to satisfying

$$\forall i \sum_{j=1}^{3} x_{ij} \geq 2 \qquad \textit{sessions per day}$$

$$\forall j \sum_{i=1}^{3} x_{ij} \in \{1, 2, \ldots, 5\} \qquad \textit{no. of session type}$$

$$\sum_{i=1}^{3} \sum_{j=1}^{3} x_{ij} \in \{10, 11, 12\} \qquad \textit{total sessions}$$

$$\forall i \sum_{j=1}^{3} x_{ij} \leq 4 \qquad \textit{max sessions per day} \qquad (21.10)$$

Figure 21.12: The Balanced Course Scheduling Problem

the constraint[2], it is assigned to x_{31}. The search proceeds in this manner as presented in Figure 21.13.

The *Local Changes* algorithm [73] is also a local repair method, but it uses a mor sophisticated search strategy than Minton *et al*'s heuristic repair to focus on resolving the conflicts in a particular sub-problem. Local Changes partitions the variable set X

---

[2]As noted in [52], for non-binary constraints the measure of conflict depends on the nature of the constraint itself.

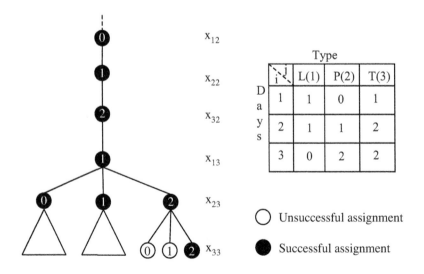

Figure 21.13: Partial Search Tree for Balanced Course Scheduling Problem using Min-conflicts Heuristic

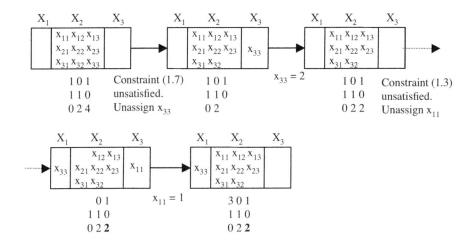

Figure 21.14: Solving the Balanced Course Scheduling Problem using Local Changes

into three subsets, X_1, X_2 and X_3: variables in X_1 have fixed assignments (this is to ensure termination, as will be shown); variables in X_2 have assignments, but which may be modified; variables in X_3 are unassigned. When solving a new problem in a dynamic sequence, all variables are in X_2, with assignments taken from the solution to the previous problem in the sequence. Hence, when solving the Balanced Course Scheduling Problem, search begins with X_2 containing all nine x_{ij} variables, assigned as shown in Figure 21.2.

If this assignment satisfies all constraints, then there is already a solution to the current problem and Local Changes terminates. Otherwise, it unassigns at least one variable for each unsatisfied constraint (placing each in X_3) and attempts to repair their assignments in order to resolve the conflict. Returning to the solution of the Balanced Course Scheduling Problem, as depicted in Figure 21.14, the only constraint that is unsatisfied is the instance of constraint (21.10) concerning day 3. The choice of which of the variables constrained by constraint (21.10) is heuristic. Assume x_{33} is chosen, unassigned and therefore moved into X_3. Local Changes now recurses over X_3, re-assigning the variables to repair the conflicts.

In the example, X_3 contains only x_{33}, which is selected for re-assignment. We assume a reasonably informed value heuristic, assigning $x_{33} = 2$. However, this assignment does not satisfy Constraint (21.3). At this point, Local Changes fixes the assignment of x_{33}, moving it into X_1 and attempts to repair the problem with respect to this choice. The fixing step is to avoid an endless cycle of repairs. If the problem cannot be solved with respect to this assignment, Local Changes will backtrack over it and try another assignment. In the example, x_{11} is re-assigned to 3, producing a solution to the problem. We have demonstrated the operation of Local Changes on a standard dynamic CSP. The algorithm has also been extended to work with fuzzy dynamic CSPs [51] (see Section 21.3.1).

The use of a local repair technique promotes stability by tending to find a solution to the new problem that is close to the solution of the previous problem, as demonstrated by the Min-conflicts and Local Changes examples above. There is no guarantee, however, that the solution will be optimally stable. The alternative is to make stability an explicit criterion when solving each problem in a dynamic sequence, and insist that each new solution is optimally stable. The algorithm RB-AC [66] follows exactly this approach, starting with the solution to the previous problem in the sequence and iteratively testing whether re-assigning one variable, two variables, three variables, and so on, is sufficient to solve the current problem. Petcu and Faltings [59] also search explicitly for stable solutions, but do not restrict stability to mean simply the number of assignments in common. Instead, special stability constraints are added that must be satisfied in order for the solution to be stable. Similarly, El Sakkout and Wallace [23] define linear *minimal perturbation* functions for dynamic scheduling problems. Following a change the minimal perturbation function is defined with respect to the solution to the previous problem and used as an objective for the new problem. Bartak *et al* [2] extend this formulation to support over-constrained problems.

21.4.2   Preparing to React by Recording Information

While maintaining our assumption that we have no information about how the problem is likely to change, it is still possible to prepare for these changes by recording information during the search for a solution that is likely to be useful when solving the changed problem, under the reasonable assumption that the latest problem in a dynamic sequence will retain some structure in common with the previous problems.

For each problem in a dynamic sequence, the *oracles* approach [71] records the path taken to the solution. For every new problem in the sequence, search begins from scratch, but these oracles are used to guide the search and prune the search space. Consider first constraint restriction. Figure 21.15 presents a partial search tree for the solution given in Figure 21.2 to the Course Scheduling Problem.

Having solved the Course Scheduling Problem, to solve the Balanced Course Scheduling Problem using the oracles approach, search begins from scratch, using the solution path from Figure 21.15 as the oracle. The search branch down to x_{22} is identical to that explored in finding the previous solution. However, when considering x_{32}, it is possible to prune the sub-tree rooted with $x_{32} = 1$ without exploring it (see Figure 21.15): since there was no solution in this sub-tree for the less-constrained previous problem there cannot be a solution in the sub-tree following constraint restriction. Search continues in this way, as presented in Figure 21.15 following the oracle and pruning fruitless sub-trees until the constraints added cause failure, at which point the search defaults to chronological backtracking while recording a new oracle for future use.

When both restriction and relaxation/retraction are allowed, to retain soundness the oracle chosen must be associated with a previously-solved problem that is less constrained (i.e. contains a subset of the constraints) than the current problem. Van Hentenryck and Provost [71] show how to select an oracle that prunes maximally without sacrificing soundness. Having identified such an oracle, it is used exactly as in the foregoing example.

A popular and powerful approach to preparing for change is to record *explanations* Jussien [42] defines explanations informally as "subsets of constraints justifying solver events". Usually, the solver events are constraint additions, either unary (value removals) or higher arity. Crucially, explanations support change to the problem structure *during*

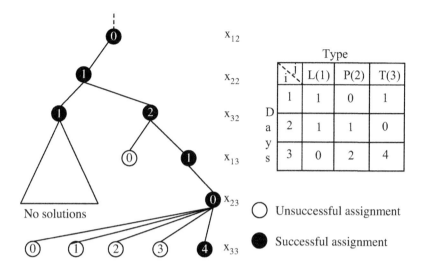

Type			
i↘j	L(1)	P(2)	T(3)
1	1	0	1
2	1	1	0
3	0	2	4

○ Unsuccessful assignment

● Successful assignment

Figure 21.15: Partial Search Tree for Course Scheduling Problem

search, as well after a solution has been found and is being executed. Note, however, that supporting changes during systematic search requires a more sophisticated search strategy than simple chronological backtracking, such as Dynamic Backtracking [33, 44] or the Local Changes algorithm discussed in the previous sub-section.

A significant amount of attention in the literature has been devoted to employing explanations in maintaining arc consistency (the reader is directed to Chapter 3 for an explanation of arc consistency) in the face of changes to the problem. Specifically, the problem is assumed to be in an arc consistent state, a change to the problem structure occurs and the goal is to restore arc consistency. Since it is common practice to maintain arc consistency during search, following a change it is natural to restore arc consistency before proceeding. We might also wish to maintain the problem in an arc consistent state, rather than solve it immediately. For instance, Debruyne [15] describes how a bioinformatics problem is configured through a process of interaction with a biologist. The biologist adds or removes constraints from the problem until the current problem is acceptable to him/her. The problem is sufficiently difficult to make solving it following each change impractical, but if enforcing arc consistency does not show that the current problem is unsolvable then this is a good indicator that the problem has solutions. Boyd and Bowen also use explanations to support a similar interactive process [13].

As has been pointed out by many authors, constraint restriction alone is simple to deal with in this setting: a standard arc consistency algorithm can be run as normal following the addition of new constraints. Constraint relaxation/retraction is, however, more difficult to support. This is because value removals resulting from enforcing arc consistency before constraint retraction may no longer be valid. Hence, following retraction, some values typically must be reinstated. Explanations are used to support the identification of these values.

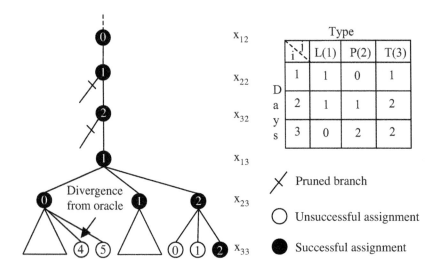

Figure 21.16: Partial Search Tree for Balanced Course Scheduling Problem using Oracles

One common explanation scheme for this purpose, as embodied by the algorithms DnAC-4 [9], DnGAC4 [10], DnAC-6 [15] as well as the work of Prosser *et al* [64], is based on recording *justifications* for value removals similar to those used in truth maintenanc schemes [21]. This is simply the constraint c whose revision caused the value v to be removed from the domain of some variable x. If c is subsequently retracted, v is tentatively restored to x's domain (tentatively because there may be alternative justifications for its removal). Of course the reinstatement of v calls into question all values v' removed from the domains of other variables, specifically where the removal is justified by a constraint involving x. If a constraint check reveals that a v' is supported by v, it is also tentatively restored. This process propagates through the network, restoring values as appropriate. The final step is to run a modified arc consistency algorithm, which removes all tentatively restored values for which it can find an alternative justification.

One variant of this scheme, appearing in the AC|DC algorithm [56] and its descendants [55, 70, 1] saves space by extracting explanations directly from the constraint graph. Another, such as [16], strengthens the justifications recorded to the set of original problem constraints that imply a value removal. The tradeoff is the time and space required to record explanations versus the time required to react to a change in the problem. Although maintaining arc consistency was the original focus of much of this research, explanations have also been used to support the re-use of nogoods discovered during search [68], and have been generalised to arbitrary constraint propagators in, for example, the PaLM system [16] and Constraint Logic Programming [32].

To illustrate, we present a simple example of the utility of explanations. Returning to the original Course Scheduling problem from Figure 21.1, consider that the different session types are indistinguishable — in any (non-)solution, the assignments to one column of variables representing a session can be exchanged with another to produce a (non-)solution.

This is a *symmetry* (see Chapter 10)[3], which can be exploited by imposing an ordering on the session types, for instance by insisting that the sum of the columns is non-decreasing:

$$\sum_{i=1}^{3} x_{i1} \le \sum_{i=1}^{3} x_{i2} \le \sum_{i=1}^{3} x_{i3} \qquad \textit{Order Constraints on Session Types} \qquad (21.11)$$

From the total sessions constraint (21.3), one can reason that the session type with the smallest number of assigned sessions can have at most 4 sessions assigned. The ordering constraints (21.11) allow us to identify this session type as the lectures. Hence we can add the implied constraint:

$$\sum_{i=1}^{3} x_{i1} \le 4 \qquad \textit{Lectures — Revised Maximum} \qquad (21.12)$$

The explanation for constraint (21.12) is the pair of constraints (21.3) and (21.11). Consider now the transition to the Balanced Course Scheduling Problem. Assuming that the ordering constraints to exploit symmetry are retained, the explanation for constraint (21.12), and therefore the constraint itself, remains valid. The saving made is that the cost of deriving the implied constraint is incurred only once, but the benefit, in terms of reducing search following changes to the problem, remains for as long as its explanation is valid.

21.4.3 Predicting Changes

In many real-world problem domains, we have some uncertain knowledge of what the changes might be. For example, in a scheduling problem, we may know the characteristics of all jobs set for production, even if we don't know when the work can begin; a dispatch service may have extensive histories of previous work requests and thus can predict the pattern of future request; or in a manufacturing environment, we may have knowledge of the reliability of a process, and thus can compute the probability of errors. In all of these cases, we can improve our initial solutions by reasoning about the likely changes. In general, we wish to produce *robust* solutions that, when change occurs, are likely to remain solutions or can be modified at little cost.

In *recurrent* CSP [75], changes to problems are assumed to be temporary and recurring — for example, the occasional temporary loss of a resource due to reliability problems. The authors assume that they have no *a priori* knowledge of the changes, and thus must learn the distribution by monitoring changes while solutions are being executed. They propose a min-conflicts [52] repair-based method, to recover solutions when the changes happen, and as they learn the distribution of the changes, they penalise solutions which use values that are frequently lost. In their *supersolutions* framework [37], Hebrard *et al.* address a similar problem, in that values may be unavailable when the solution is executed. Their aim is to find initial solutions that are robust to this loss, or that can be repaired with a small number of changes. They define the concept of an (a, b)-*super solution*, which is a solution to the original problem which, if any a value assignments are lost, can be repaired by reassigning the relevant variables plus another b variables. In particular, a $(1, 0)$-super

---

[3]The reader will have noticed that the days are also indistinguishable, but we focus on the session types for simplicity.

$$\forall i \ D_i = \{y_{ij} : j = 1\ldots 6\}, count(D_i, \phi) \le 4 \qquad (21.13)$$
$$S = \{y_{ij} : i = 1\ldots 3, j = 1\ldots 6\} \qquad (21.14)$$
$$count(S, L) \in \{1, 2, \ldots, 5\} \qquad (21.15)$$
$$count(S, P) \in \{1, 2, \ldots, 5\} \qquad (21.16)$$
$$count(S, T) \in \{1, 2, \ldots, 5\} \qquad (21.17)$$
$$count(S, \phi) \in \{6, 7, 8\} \qquad (21.18)$$

Figure 21.17: The Extended Course Scheduling Problem

solution is essentially robust to the loss of any single value — for each variable, there is a backup value which could be assigned without violating any of the constraints.

As an example, consider a more detailed version of the course scheduling problem. We now assume there are six possible time slots each day (giving 18 variables y_{ij}, where $i \in \{1, 2, 3\}$ and $j \in \{1, \ldots, 6\}$), which we may fill will a lecture (L), a practical (P) or a tutorial (T), or leave empty (ϕ). The new model is given in Figure 21.17, where we assume a constraint $count(S, v)$, which counts the number of times a variable from the set S takes the value v.

We now assume that after we construct and advertise the timetable, we may be told that certain time slots cannot be filled with sessions of a given type (for example, because of room changes elsewhere). Can we find a $(1, 0)$-supersolution — that is, a solution that can be adapted by reassigning only the affected variable? Figure 21.18a shows one such supersolution — any class (L,P or T) can be replaced by another class, and any empty slot can be filled by a class. Figure 21.18b shows a solution that is not a $(1, 0)$-supersolution, since if we lose the value T from y_{14}, then we cannot find another satisfying solution reassigning only that time slot (since we cannot satisfy the constraint on the number of tutorials).

Periods

i\j	1	2	3	4	5	6
D 1	L	P	P	T	0	0
a y 2	L	P	T	0	0	0
s 3	L	L	T	0	0	0

i\j	1	2	3	4	5	6
1	L	P	P	T	0	0
2	L	P	P	0	0	0
3	L	L	P	0	0	0

(a)   (b)

Figure 21.18: *supersolutions*: *(a)* $(1, 0)$-supersolution; *(b)* not a $(1, 0)$-supersolution.

Finding an (a, b)-super solution is shown to be NP-complete for any fixed a. The authors develop a MAC algorithm for finding $(1, 0)$-super solutions, and extend it to a branch-and-bound algorithm for finding the most robust solution when a $(1, 0)$-super solution does not exist (the most robust solution is defined to be one in which a maximal number of variables can be repaired without violating any constraints). This work has been extended [38] to consider $(1, b)$-super solutions, with the ability to place restrictions on the repairs that are considered — for example, to model scheduling problems, where values represent the times at which activities start, the repairs are restricted to using higher values representing later times, so that the repair can be carried out when the break arises during execution. The supersolutions concept has then further extended [39] to include the probability of a value assignment being lost, and the cost of making the repair: specifically, a (α, β)-*weighted supersolution* is one in which any set of value assignments with a total probability greater then α of being lost can be repaired by changing any variables at a total cost of less then β. Weighted supersolutions have been defined to model combinatorial auctions, where each winning bid has a probability of being withdrawn.

Stochastic CSPs [76] (introduced in subsection 21.3.3) allow us to model problems with multiple phases: first the solver must assign a set of variables, then the environment reveals the values of a set of parameters, the solver must then assign another set, and so on. The values of the parameters are assumed to be described by probability distributions. The solution to a multi-stage stochastic CSP is then a tree, in which the assignment of values to the later decision variables are conditional on the previous decisions and the revealed values of the parameters. This allows us to model, for example, production planning, in which the volume to be manufactured in the 2nd quarter depends on the volume manufactured in the 1st quarter, on the realised demand for the 1st quarter, and on the uncertain demand in the future. In the general case, multi-stage stochastic CSPs are $PSPACE$-complete. This work is then extended to use scenario-based semantics [50], and allows chance constraints, which must be satisfied over a proportion of the scenarios. The framework has been implemented as *Stochastic OPL*, in which multiple futures are represented as separate scenarios which are then reformulated as a single larger CSP.

Branching CSP [30] also considers multiple phases, but models problems which grow by the uncertain addition of variables and their associated constraints — for example, online scheduling, where new tasks arrive as the existing tasks are being executed. The model of future arrivals is a probabilistic tree, in which the arrival of any variable is conditional on the preceding arrival sequence. Each variable that arrives may be accepted and assigned a value which does not violate any constraint over the arrived variables, or rejected and assigned no value; a specified utility is gained for each variable that is accepted. The aim is then to assign values to nodes in the tree, such that no constraint is violated and expected utility is maximised. The solution is thus a policy, specifying actions for each possible arrival sequence. Branching CSP has similarities to Markov Decision Problems [65], since the arrivals tree is essentially a finite horizon markov process; however, it is complicated by the fact that choice available at each node is constrained by the previous choices, and formulating the problem as an MDP may require exponentially many states. The Branching CSP algorithms use backtrack search and constraint propagation to reduce this combinatorial explosion [29].

Consider now a special case of the course scheduling problem, in which the resource allocator must decide on initial room requests, but should also cater for new timetabling requests. For simplicity, we consider a simpler problem (Figure 21.19), with one room suitable for lectures, and one for practicals, and three time periods. We assume one initial request: (A) a one hour lecture to be followed by a later one-hour practical. There are also three other requests that we might receive: (B) a two-hour practical, (C) a one-hour lecture followed immediately by a one-hour practical, or (D) another single one-hour lecture. Each requests must be given a time slot immediately or rejected. Each request generates revenue, if it is allocated a time slot; rejected requests generate no revenue. The constraints and the probability tree are shown in the figure. Our immediate task is to decide whether to accept or reject requests A and B, and to allocate times, but ultimately we want a policy for the tree which maximises expected revenue. One example policy is also shown in the figure, which maximises expected revenue by immediately rejecting the unprofitable A, allowing the more profitable B or C, or both, to be accommodated if they arrive.

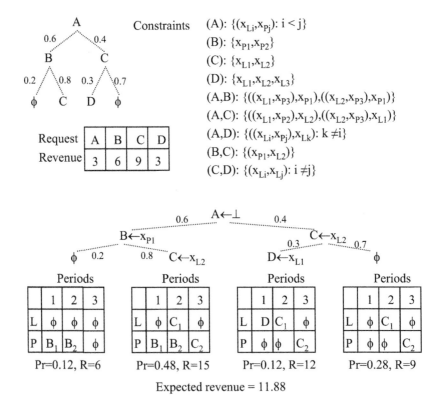

Figure 21.19: A branching CSP problem and solution

Bent and van Hentenryck [6, 7] also consider problems which grow over time by the addition of tasks. However, rather than have an explicit probability distribution over the future states, they assume that they have a black-box generator which can generate samples of the future. At each stage in the process, they generate a number of samples, and use the results of optimisation on the samples to make a decision for the current time step. They consider a number of approaches, including: *expectation*, in which each possible decision is evaluated over all samples, and the one with the highest expected value is selected; *con-*

sensus, in which each sample is solved to optimality, and from the solutions the immediate decision which occurs most often is selected; and *regret*, in which each sample is again solved to optimality, and then the possible decisions are evaluated with respect to how much of the objective value would be lost compared to the other decisions. The expectation method produces the best results, but is infeasible for real problems because of the number of optimisations required. The regret method approaches the quality of expectation when there is time to optimise, but is similar to consensus when only a small number of samples are possible, and thus is particularly effective in real-time situations or where the underlying optimisation problem is hard. In common with the approaches that use explicit probability distributions, there is a question as to where the underlying distribution for the black-box generator comes from; the authors have proposed an online learning method [8], which gradually constructs the distribution as it receives requests. [5] also considers problems that grow, examining a number of different approaches to generating robust initial solutions and regular updates

The most significant application area for constraint problems that change is scheduling. Many practical scheduling problems can be expressed as Simple Temporal Problems [20], in which constraints specify single intervals between two time points, and solved in polynomial time. [74] considers an extension in which the durations of some tasks are uncertain, and hence some timepoints are decision variables, while others are uncontrollable (using the same terminology as for mixed CSP [27]). The aim is then to find a policy for executing tasks: problems are defined to be *strongly controllable* if a single decision (i.e. an assignment of a value to each decision variable) will produce an executable schedule regardless of the eventual values of the uncontrollable timepoints; and *weakly controllable* if there exists a decision for each possible realisation of the timepoints. The work was further extended [54] to include *dynamically controllable* problems, for which there exists an online policy: the values assigned to the decision variables need depend only on the observed timepoints in order to get an executable schedule. Checking whether a problem is strongly or dynamically controllable is in P, but weak controllability is in $co - NP$. This work has recently been extended to include soft temporal constraints [78], and it is shown that this does not increase the complexity class: in particular, a polynomial algorithm is presented for generating online execution algorithms that optimise over the soft constraints.

Uncertainty in the duration of tasks is a significant issue in more general scheduling problems. [14] examines the introduction of slack time to handle such uncertainty in job-shop problems. They consider three variations: adding extra time to the duration of every task, modifying the constraints to ensure that slack time exists between tasks, and modifying the constraints dependent on the location of the task in the problem. For a given constraint $Y_{st} \geq X_{st} + dur(x)$, the first would change the value of $dur(x)$ to $dur(x) + \sigma(x)$, while the latter two would change the constraint by adding the term $slack(x)$ to the right hand side. The resultant problem can then be solved using existing scheduling algorithms. Experimental evidence shows that the latter two consistently outperform a simple right-shift reactive solution in terms of tardiness, while the former is significantly poorer, but can give better predictions of execution time in problems with high levels of uncertainty. More recent work [3, 4] considers the problem of producing schedules with a given probability of being executed inside a time limit, and with good probabilistic makespans. The authors develop branch and bound algorithms with Monte Carlo simulation at each node, and heuristic algorithms which generate deterministic problems from the means and variances of the task durations. The heuristic algorithms are shown to scale well with larger problems.

For project scheduling problems, Policella *et al* [61] consider notions of robustness based on initial solutions that are partial orders of tasks. They assume that some pairs of tasks have minimum separation constraints, and that each task occupies a known amount of resource. They consider dynamic changes to the problem in the form of partial resource unavailability, or changes in task duration. Their aim is to produce a partial ordering of the tasks such that any allocation of start times consistent with it also satisfies the time and resource constraints. A partial order is then deemed to be robust if it can absorb changes to the problem details during execution — that is, start times can still be assigned with violating the partial order or the problem constraints. Their approach is first to generate a single schedule with fixed start times, and then to "robustify" it by generating a partial order from it. Previous research has shown that this approach can generate more robust schedules than starting with a least commitment approach [62]. The partial orders are based on chains of precedence constraints for individual units of the resource, and greater robustness is obtained by generating independent chains.

Finally, we note some recent research integrating constraint programming techniques with belief networks, for reasoning about a combination of probabilistic and deterministic information. Belief networks have been studied in AI for many years, and represent the probabilistic dependencies between random variables. They can be used to find the most probable value of a variable, given a set of observations of other variables, and can be used to update beliefs as observations are made incrementally. Constraints can be integrated into the networks by representing them implicitly as conditional probability tables on boolean random variables [58], mapping valid combinations to *true* with probability 1.0, and invalid combinations to *false*. However, this loses the benefits of constraint-based search and propagation. [18] instead represent the constraints explicitly, and show how variable elimination methods can be significantly faster on such representations for computing the probability that a given tuple is a solution. That approach, however, requires large amounts of space. Therefore [19] instead develop search algorithms, which combine constraint propagation with search over AND/OR graphs, requiring only linear space.

21.5   Pseudo-dynamic Formalisms

In this section we describe extensions to classical CSP that, while closely related to dynamic CSPs by name or definition, have important differences that we should be careful to recognise.

We begin by emphasising the difference between dynamic CSPs and what are now known [67] as *conditional* CSPs [53][4]. In a conditional CSP, the whole problem is known statically, but parts of it are made active or inactive depending on the assignments of certain variables. For example, in configuring a car it is only necessary to decide the details of a sunroof if the decision has been made that a sunroof is to be fitted. Conditional CSPs are a natural way to model both configuration [53] (see Chapter 24) and planning problems [45] (see Chapter 22).

---

[4]The potential for confusion stems from the fact that this work was originally presented with the title 'Dynamic Constraint Satisfaction Problems', where 'dynamic' is refers to the fact that the structure of the problem changed based on decisions made during search

Open Constraint Satisfaction Problems (OCSPs [24]) assume a distributed environment and an *open-world* setting, in which the set of variables and constraints is known statically but the variable domains and tuples allowed by the constraints are incrementally discovered by querying different information sources in a network. This is a natural representation for, for example, many e-commerce problems where suppliers might be queried as necessary as to the specifications and possible configurations of their products. Returning to our running example of course scheduling, one might imagine scheduling a larger course, or multiple courses, taught by several people. In this case, the people involved might be queried to discover acceptable numbers of sessions they were willing to teach and constraints on their timetabling. If the problem remained unsolvable, further queries could be made, and so on.

Open CSP makes the further assumption that information-gathering queries are by far the most expensive individual operation that the solver performs, hence the emphasis is on producing a solution with a minimal number of queries. Faltings and Macho-Gonzalez show that, since domains and allowed tuples increase monotonically with each new query, it is unnecessary to know the entire problem structure in order to solve the problem — a solution to a partially-discovered problem is guaranteed to be a solution to the whole problem [24]. They give the *o-search* algorithm to solve OCSPs that improves over the naive approach of simply gathering all domain values and constraint tuples before solving the problem by interleaving querying and solving: new domain values and constraint tuples are sought only if the currently known sub-problem has no solution. The *fo-search* algorithm refines *o-search* by only gathering new domain values and constraint tuples for the portion of the currently-known sub-problem identified as being responsible for the sub-problem having no solution.

OCSP has also been extended to fuzzy CSPs (see Section 21.3.1) and to optimisation problems [24]. In both cases to be able to find an optimal solution without knowing the whole problem structure there is a monotonicity assumption: domain elements and tuples are returned in non-increasing order of membership degree / non-decreasing order of cost. This is a realistic assumption — the participants in the open course scheduling example described above are likely to be happy to respond to queries with their most preferred option first.

Open CSP is very closely related to Interactive CSP (ICSP [47]) in which again domain elements are acquired incrementally in solving a problem. The key difference is that, since at least one of the solution algorithms presented (*Interactive Forward Checking*) acquires *all* domain values for a particular variable that are consistent with respect to the current assignment, there is an implicit assumption that variable domains are finite. OCSP is also closely related to dynamic CSP, since the incremental addition of domain elements and constraint tuples can be viewed as a sequence of problems linked by the relaxation/retraction of unary constraints disallowing the acquired domain elements [49].

21.6 Challenges and Future Trends

As we have seen, there have been many attempts to extend constraint reasoning to handle dynamic and uncertain problems. The attempts all appear to be isolated, with little commonality between them; they define different problem types, and different types of objectives. In particular, it is difficult to compare techniques, since each is typically addressing its own problem variation, and testing them requires generators of the uncertain and dynamic aspects. There is a need for general purpose, parameterisable, problem generators and execution simulators. Such tools should allow the different types of uncertainty and change to be expressed, and should allow the temporal nature of the changes to be described. An initial scheme for a generator for scheduling problems has been proposed [60]. Tools of this sort would be a start on the road to classifying techniques, and identifying which methods are best suited to which problem types. A common library of problems would be useful in itself, to give an indication of the range and frequency of the different problem types in practical applications. For example, CSPLib[5], an otherwise invaluable repository of benchmark constraint problems, contained no problems with explicit uncertainty or dynamism.

A related challenge is to bring all the different frameworks together. There are some foundational approaches, like Dynamic CSP [17], but nothing as yet with a similar coverage to semiring CSP [12] or valued CSP [69] for soft constraints. Can we find a single framework that encompasses all the different features proposed so far? One such framework has recently been proposed [63], and the question remains open as to whether such a framework should have a rich language allowing the direct expression of many different features, or a simpler more restricted language which would require the reformulation of problems.

On an abstract level, there are three main solution techniques: extending the representational power and reasoning methods to represent uncertain and dynamic problems explicitly, and generate their solutions; reformulating problems into large deterministic problems, and generating the solutions using existing techniques; or generating scenarios or samples, and then solving each one using standard deterministic techniques. It is an open question as to where the boundary lies, to allow us to decide which technique should be applied to which class and size of problem. In particular, more tractability results are required for the different formulations.

In general, constraint solving under change and uncertainty is in its infancy. Closer links need to be established with the existing techniques in other areas of artificial intelligence, mathematics and optimisation, including belief networks [40], MDPs [65] and POMDPs [57], queuing theory [35], stochastic processes [41], stochastic programming [11], Monte Carlo methods [28], stochastic satisfiability [48], decision theory [34] and fuzzy logic [46]. See Halpern [36] for an overview of uncertainty reasoning in general.

Finally, the biggest challenge is to integrate dynamic and uncertain reasoning methods with industrial strength constraint programming tools — as has begun to be the case with, for example, the PaLM system [43]. This would allow the approaches discussed in this chapter and future techniques to be put into practice for real-world decision and optimisation problems, without requiring users to write their own search and propagation algorithms. Towards this goal, Fromherz and Conley [31] describe a general constraint solver design to support a dynamic environment. Further progress is likely to be made by integrating principled simulation and sampling techniques first — see for example [50] — since they will allow existing CP tools to be used without modification.

---

[5]http://www.csplib.org, 29th September, 2005

21.7 Summary

Many real and important problems involve change and uncertainty. Solutions are required that take account of vagueness in the problem description, or that minimise the effect of the uncertainty on the solution. Basic approaches to handling change include rapid reaction through re-specifying the problems and re-solving when the changes occur, preparing to change by maintaining explanations and data structures that will allow the solver to avoid repeating work, or proactively generating solutions that are robust, by explicitly reasoning about the possible changes. A number of different techniques have been developed, and they have demonstrated that constraint programming methods can be extended to handle many different forms of dynamism and uncertainty, and that many exemplar problems can be solved efficiently. Constraint programming toolkits need to be extended with facilities to handle such problems. Further work is required to establish which of the techniques and frameworks are practical candidates, and to integrate this body of research with the many other research fields which deal with change and uncertainty. Finally, for an alternative viewpoint on the material in this chapter, the reader is directed to the survey by Verfaillie and Jussien [72].

Acknowledgments

We thank the anonymous referee for useful comments on a draft of this chapter. Ken Brown's work was supported in part by grants 03/CE3/I405 (SFI Centre for Telecommunications Value-chain Research) and SC/2003/81 (Enterprise Ireland). Ian Miguel is supported by a UK Royal Academy of Engineering/EPRSC Research Fellowship.

Bibliography

[1] R. Bartak and P. Surynek. An improved algorithm for maintaining arc consistency in dynamic constraint satisfaction problems. In *FLAIRS'05: Proceedings of the Eighteenth International Florida Artificial Intelligence Research Society Conference*, pages 161–166. AAAI Press, 2005.

[2] R. Bartak, T. Muller, and H. Rudova. A new approach to modeling and solving minimal perturbation problems. In *Recent Advances in Constraints*, volume 3010, pages 223–249. Springer Lecture Notes in Artificial Intelligence, 2004.

[3] J. C. Beck and N. Wilson. Job shop scheduling with probabilistic durations. In *ECAI'04: Proceedings of the Sixteenth European Conference on Artificial Intelligence*, pages 652–656. IOS Press, 2004.

[4] J. C. Beck and N. Wilson. Proactive algorithms for scheduling with probabilistic durations. In *IJCAI'05: Proceedings of the Nineteenth International Joint Conference on Artificial Intelligence*, pages 1201–1206. Professional Book Center, 2005.

[5] T. Benoist, E. Bourreau, Y. Caseau, and B. Rottembourg. Towards stochastic constraint programming: A study of online multichoice knapsack with deadlines. In *CP'01: Proceedings of the Seventh International Conference on Principles and Practice of Constraint Programming*, volume 2239, pages 61–76. Springer Lecture Notes in Computer Science, 2001.

[6] R. Bent and P. van Hentenryck. The value of consensus in online stochastic scheduling. In *ICAPS'04: Fourteenth International Conference on Automated Planning and Scheduling*, pages 219–226. AAAI Press, 2004.

[7] R. Bent and P. van Hentenryck. Regrets only! online stochastic optimization under time constraints. In *AAAI'04: Proceedings of the Nineteenth National Conference on Artificial Intelligence*, pages 501–506. AAAI Press, 2004.

[8] R. Bent and P. van Hentenryck. Online stochastic optimization without distributions. In *ICAPS'05: Fifteenth International Conference on Automated Planning and Scheduling*, pages 171–180. AAAI Press, 2005.

[9] C. Bessiere. Arc-consistency in dynamic constraint satisfaction problems. In *AAAI'91: Proceedings of the Ninth National Conference on Artificial Intelligence* pages 221–226. AAAI Press/MIT Press, 1991.

[10] C. Bessiere. Arc-consistency for non-binary dynamic CSPs. In *ECAI'92: Proceedings of the Tenth European Conference on Artificial Intelligence*, pages 23–27. John Wiley and Sons, 1992.

[11] J. R. Birge and F. V. Louveaux. *Introduction to Stochastic Programming*. Springer Verlag, 1997.

[12] S. Bistarelli, U. Montanari, and F. Rossi. Constraint solving over semi-rings. In *IJCAI'95: Proceedings of the Fourteenth International Joint Conference on Artificial Intelligence*, pages 624–630. Morgan Kaufmann, 1995.

[13] D.B. Boyd and J. Bowen. Using dependency records to generate design coordination advice in a constraint-based approach to concurrent engineering. *Computers in Industry*, 33(2):191–199, 1997.

[14] A. J. Davenport, C. Gefflot, and J. C. Beck. Slack-based techniques for robust schedules. In *ECP'01: Proceedings of the Sixth European Conference on Planning*, pages 7–18, 2001.

[15] R. Debruyne. Arc-consistency in dynamic CSPs is no more prohibitive. In *ICTAI'96: Proceedings of the Eighth International Conference on Tools with Artificial Intelligence*, pages 299–307. IEEE Computer Society, 1996.

[16] R. Debruyne, G. Ferrand, N. Jussien, W. Lesaint, S. Ouis, and A. Tessier. Correctness of constraint retraction algorithms. In *FLAIRS'03: Proceedings of the Sixteenth International Florida Artificial Intelligence Research Society Conference*, pages 172–176. AAAI Press, 2003.

[17] R. Dechter and A. Dechter. Belief maintenance in dynamic constraint networks. In *AAAI'88: Proceedings of the Ninth National Conference on Artificial Intelligence* pages 37–42. AAAI Press/MIT Press, 1988.

[18] R. Dechter and D. Larkin. Hybrid processing of belief and constraints. In *UAI'01: Proceedings of the Seventeenth Annual Conference on Uncertainty in Artificial Intelligence*, pages 112–119. Morgan Kaufmann, 2001.

[19] R. Dechter and R. Mateescu. Mixtures of deterministic-probabilistic networks and their and/or search space. In *UAI'04: Proceedings of the Twentieth Annual Conference on Uncertainty in Artificial Intelligence*, 2004.

[20] R. Dechter, I. Meiri, and J. Pearl. Temporal constraint networks. *Artificial Intelligence*, 49:61–95, 1991.

[21] J. Doyle. A truth maintenance system. *Artificial Intelligence*, 12:231–272, 1979.

[22] D. Dubois, H. Fargier, and H. Prade. Possibility theory in constraint satisfaction problems. *Applied Intelligence*, 6:287–309, 1996.

[23] H. El Sakkout and M. Wallace. Probe backtrack search for minimal perturbation in dynamic scheduling. *Constraints*, 5(4):359–388, 2000.

[24] B. Faltings and S. Macho-Gonzalez. Open constraint programming. *Artificial Intelligence*, 161, 2005.

[25] H. Fargier and J. Lang. Uncertainty in constraint satisfaction problems: a probalistic approach. In *ECSQARU'93: Proceedings of the Second European Conference on Symbolic and Qualitative Approaches to Reasoning with Uncertainty*, volume 747, pages 97–104. Springer Lecture Notes in Computer Science, 1995.

[26] H. Fargier, J. Lang, R. Martin-Clouaire, and T. Schiex. A constraint satisfaction framework for decision under uncertainty. In *UAI'95: Proceedings of the Eleventh Conference on Uncertainty in Artificial Intelligence*, pages 167–174. Morgan Kaufmann, 1995.

[27] H. Fargier, J. Lang, and T. Schiex. Mixed constraint satisfaction: a framework for decision problems under incomplete knowledge. In *AAAI'96: Proceedings of the Thirteenth National Conference on Artificial Intelligence*, pages 175–180. AAAI Press/MIT Press, 1996.

[28] G. S. Fishman. *Monte Carlo: Concepts, Algorithms and Applications*. Springer Verlag, 1996.

[29] D. Fowler and K. Brown. Branching constraint satisfaction problems and markov decision problems compared. *Annals of Operations Research*, 118:85–110, 2003.

[30] D. W. Fowler and K. N. Brown. Branching constraint satisfaction problems for solutions robust under likely changes. In *CP2000: Proceedings of the Sixth International Conference on Principles and Practice of Constraint Programming*, volume 1894, pages 500–504. Springer Lecture Notes in Computer Science, 2000.

[31] M. Fromherz and J. Conley. Issues in reactive constraint solving. In *COTIC'97: Proceedings of the Workshop on Concurrent Constraint Programming for Time Critical Applications*, 1997.

[32] Y. Georget, P. Codognet, and F. Rossi. Constraint retraction in CLP(FD): Formal framework and performance results. *Constraints*, 4(1):1–41, 1999.

[33] M. Ginsberg. Dynamic backtracking. *Journal of Artificial Intelligence Research*, 1: 25–46, 1993.

[34] P. Goodwin and G. Wright. *Decision Analysis for Management Judgment (3e)*. Wiley, 2004.

[35] D. Gross and C. M. Harris. *Fundamentals of Queueing Theory (3e)*. Wiley, 1998.

[36] J. Halpern. *Reasoning about Uncertainty*. MIT Press, 2003.

[37] E. Hebrard, B. Hnich, and T. Walsh. Super solutions in constraint programming. In *CPAIOR'04: Proceedings of the First International Conference on Integration of AI and OR Techniques in Constraint Programming for Combinatorial Optimisation Problems*, volume 3011, pages 157–172. Springer Lecture Notes in Computer Science, 2004.

[38] E. Hebrard, B. Hnich, and T. Walsh. Robust solutions for constraint satisfaction and optimization. In *ECAI'04: Proceedings of the Sixteenth European Conference on Artificial Intelligence*, pages 186–190. IOS Press, 2004.

[39] A. Holland and B. OŚullivan. Weighted super solutions for constraint programs. In *AAAI'05: Proceedings of the Twentieth National Conference on Artificial Intelligence*, pages 378–383. AAAI Press/MIT Press, 2005.

[40] F. V. Jensen. *Bayesian Networks and Decision Graphs*. Springer, 2001.

[41] P. W. Jones and P. Smith. *Stochastic Processes*. Oxford University Press, 2001.

[42] N. Jussien. The versatility of using explanations within constraint programming. Technical Report 03-04-INFO, Ecole des Mines de Nantes, 2003.

[43] N. Jussien and V. Barichard. The PaLM system: Explanation-based constraint programming. In *TRICS'00: Proceedings of the International Workshop on Techniques for Implementing Constraint Programming Systems*, pages 118–133, 2000.

[44] N. Jussien, R. Debruyne, and P. Boizumault. Maintaining arc-consistency within dynamic backtracking. In *CP'2000: Proceedings of the Sixth International Conference on Principles and Practice of Constraint Programming*, volume 1894, pages 249–261. Springer Lecture Notes in Computer Science, 2000.

[45] S. Kambhampati. Planning graph as a (dynamic) CSP: Exploiting EBL, DDB and other CSP search techniques in graphlan. *Journal of Artificial Intelligence Research* 12:1–34, 2000.

[46] G. Klir and Yuan B. *Fuzzy sets and fuzzy logic: theory and applications*. Prentice Hall, 1995.

[47] E. Lamma, P. Mello, M. Milano, R. Cucchiara, M. Gavanelli, and M. Piccardi. Constraint propagation and value acquisition: Why we should do it interactively. In *IJCAI'99: Proceedings of the Sixteenth International Joint Conference on Artificial Intelligence*, pages 467–473. Morgan Kaufmann, 1999.

[48] M. Littman, S. Majercik, and T. Pitassi. Stochastic boolean satisfiability. *Journal of Automated Reasoning*, 27(3):251–296, 2001.

[49] S. Macho-Gonzalez and P. Meseguer. Open, interactive and dynamic CSP. In *Proceedings of the International Workshop on Constraint Solving under Change and Uncertainty*, pages 13–17, 2005.

[50] S. Manander, A. Tarim, and T. Walsh. Scenario-based stochastic constraint programming. In *IJCAI'03: Proceedings of the Eighteenth International Joint Conference on Artificial Intelligence*, pages 257–262. Morgan Kaufmann, 2003.

[51] I. Miguel and Q. Shen. Fuzzy rrDFCSP and planning. *Artificial Intelligence*, 148 (1–2):11–52, 2003.

[52] S. Minton, M.D. Johnston, A.B. Philps, and P. Laird. Minimizing conflicts: A heuristic repair method for constraint satisfaction and scheduling problems. *Artificial Intelligence*, 58:161–205, 1992.

[53] S. Mittal and B. Falkenhainer. Dynamic constraint satisfaction problems. In *AAAI'90: Proceedings of the Eighth National Conference on Artificial Intelligence*, pages 25–32. AAAI Press/MIT Press, 1990.

[54] P. Morris, N. Muscettola, and T. Vidal. Dynamic control of plans with temporal uncertainty. In *IJCAI'01: Proceedings of the Seventeenth International Joint Conference on Artificial Intelligence*, pages 494–502. Morgan Kaufmann, 2001.

[55] M. Mouhoub. Arc consistency for dynamic CSPs. In *KES'03: Proceedings of the Seventh International Conference on Knowledge-based Intelligent Information and Engineering Systems*, volume 2773, pages 393–400. Springer Lecture Notes in Computer Science, 2003.

[56] B. Neveu and P. Berlandier. Maintaining arc consistency through constraint retraction. In *ICTAI'94: Proceedings of the Sixth International Conference on Tools with Artificial Intelligence*, pages 426–431. IEEE Computer Society, 1994.

[57] L. Pack Kaelbling, M. Littman, and A. Cassandra. Planning and acting in partially observable stochastic domains. *Artificial Intelligence*, 101:99–134, 1998.

[58] J. Pearl. *Probabilistic Reasoning in Intelligent Systems*. Morgan Kaufmann, 1988.

[59] A. Petcu and B. Faltings. Optimal solution stability in continuous-time optimization. In *DCR'05: Proceedings of the Sixth International Workshop on Distributed Constraint Reasoning*, pages 207–221, 2005.

[60] N. Policella and R. Rasconi. Looking for a common scheduling perturbations benchmark. In *Changes'05: Proceedings of the International Workshop on Constraint Solving under Change and Uncertainty, Sitges*, pages 23–27, 2005.

[61] N. Policella, A. Oddi, S. F. Smith, and A. Cesta. Generating robust partial order schedules. In *CP'04: Proceedings of the Tenth International Conference on the Principles and Practice of Constraint Programming*, volume 3258, pages 406–511. Springer Lecture Notes in Computer Science, 2004.

[62] N. Policella, S. F. Smith, and A. Cesta, A.and Oddi. Generating robust schedules through temporal flexibility. In *ICAPS'04: Fourteenth International Conference on Automated Planning and Scheduling*, pages 209–218. AAAI Press, 2004.

[63] C. Pralet, G. Verfaillie, and T. Schiex. Composite graphical models for reasoning about uncertainties, feasibilities, and utilities. In *Soft'05: Proceedings of the Seventh International Workshop on Preferences and Soft Constraints, Sitges*, pages 104–118, 2005.

[64] P. Prosser, C. Conway, and C. Muller. A constraint maintenance system for the distributed resource allocation problem. *Intelligent Systems Engineering*, 1(1), 1992.

[65] M. L. Puterman. *Markov Decision Processes: Discrete Stochastic Dynamic Programming*. Wiley, 1994.

[66] N. Roos, Y. Ran, and J. van den Herik. Combining local search and constraint propagation to find a minimal change solution for a dynamic CSP. In *AIMSA'00: Proceedings of the Ninth International Conference on Artificial Intelligence: Methodology, Systems, and Applications*, volume 1904, pages 272–282. Springer Lecture Notes in Computer Science, 2000.

[67] M. Sabin and E. Freuder. Detecting and resolving inconsistency and redundancy in conditional constraint satisfaction problems. In *Proceedings of the CP'98 Workshop on Constraint Problem Reformulation*, 1998.

[68] T. Schiex and G. Verfaillie. Nogood recording for static and dynamic constraint satisfaction problems. *International Journal of Artificial Intelligence Tools*, 3(2): 187–207, 1994.

[69] T. Schiex, H. Fargier, and G. Verfaillie. Valued constraint satisfaction problems: Hard and easy problems. In *IJCAI'95: Proceedings of the Fourteenth International Joint Conference on Artificial Intelligence*, pages 631–637. Morgan Kaufmann, 1995.

[70] P. Surynek and R. Bartak. A new algorithm for maintaining arc consistency after constraint retraction. In *CP'04: Proceedings of the Tenth International Conference on Principles and Practice of Constraint Programming*, volume 3258, pages 767–771. Springer Lecture Notes in Computer Science, 2004.

[71] P. van Hentenryck and T. L. Provost. Incremental search in constraint logic programming. *New Generation Computing*, 9:257–275, 1991.

[72] G. Verfaillie and N. Jussien. Constraint solving in uncertain and dynamic environments: A survey. *Constraints*, 10(3):253–281, 2005.

[73] G. Verfaillie and T. Schiex. Solution reuse in dynamic constraint satisfaction problems. In *AAAI'94: Proceedings of the Twelfth National Conference on Artificial Intelligence*, pages 307–312. AAAI Press, 1994.

[74] T. Vidal and H. Fargier. Handling contingency in temporal constraint networks: From consistency to controllabilities. *Journal of Experimental and Theoretical Artificial Intelligence*, 11:23–45, 1999.

[75] R. J. Wallace and E. C. Freuder. Stable solutions for dynamic constraint satisfaction problems. In *CP'98: Proceedings of the Fourth International Conference on Principles and Practice of Constraint Programming*, volume 1520, pages 447–461. Springer Lecture Notes in Computer Science, 1998.

[76] T. Walsh. Stochastic constraint programming. In *ECAI'02: Proceedings of the Fifteenth European Conference on Artificial Intelligence*, pages 111–115. IOS Press, 2002.

[77] N. Yorke-Smith and C. Gervet. Certainty closure: A framework for reliable constraint reasoning with uncertainty. In *CP'03: Proceedings of the Ninth International Conference on Principles and Practice of Constraint*, volume 2833, pages 769–783. Springer Lecture Notes in Computer Science, 2003.

[78] N. Yorke-Smith, K. B. Venable, and F. Rossi. Temporal reasoning with preferences and uncertainty. In *IJCAI'03: Proceedings of the Eighteenth International Joint Conference on Artificial Intelligence*, pages 1385–1386. Morgan Kaufmann, 2003.

Chapter 22

Constraint-Based Scheduling and Planning

Philippe Baptiste, Philippe Laborie, Claude Le Pape, Wim Nuijten

Solving a scheduling problem generally consists in allocating scarce resources to a given set of activities over time. Planning can be seen as a generalization of scheduling where the set of activities to be scheduled is not known in advance. The additional complexity of planning thus lies in the fact one also has to decide on the set of activities that will be scheduled. Constraint-Based Scheduling is the discipline that studies how to solve scheduling problems by using Constraint Programming (CP). Constraint-Based Planning in turn is the discipline that studies how to solve planning problems by CP. As the use of CP in scheduling is more mature, we first turn to Constraint-Based Scheduling after which we will come back to Constraint-Based Planning.

Constraint-Based Scheduling has over the years grown into one of the most successful application areas of CP. One of the key factors of this success lies in the fact that a combination was found of the best of two fields of research that pay attention to scheduling, namely *Operations Research* (OR) and *Artificial Intelligence* (AI). Traditionally, a lot of the attention in OR has been paid to rather "pure" scheduling problems that are based on relatively simple mathematical models. For solving the problem at hand, the combinatorial structure of the problem is heavily exploited, leading to improved performance characteristics. We could say that an OR approach often aims at achieving a high level of *efficiency* in its algorithms. However, when modeling a practical scheduling problem using these classical models, one is often forced to discard degrees of freedom and side constraints that exist in the practical scheduling situation. Discarding degrees of freedom may result in the elimination of interesting solutions, regardless of the solution method used. Discarding side constraints gives a simplified problem and solving this simplified problem may result in impractical solutions for the original problem.

In contrast, AI research tends to investigate more general scheduling models and tries to solve the problems by using general problem-solving paradigms. We could say an AI approach tends to focus more on the *generality of application* of its algorithms. This, however, implies that AI algorithms may perform poorly on specific cases, compared to OR algorithms.

So, on one hand we have OR which offers us *efficient* algorithms to solve problems that in comparison have a more limited application area. On the other hand we have AI that offers us algorithms that are more *generally applicable*, but that might suffer from somewhat poor performance in the specific cases an efficient OR algorithm exists. An important way to combine the two was found by incorporating OR algorithms inside *global* constraints. Such algorithms are able to take into account a set of constraints from a global point of view in an efficient way. The typical scheduling example of a global constraint is the constraint that propagates on the combination of all activities requiring capacity from a shared resource. The basics of many of the algorithms inside global constraints, certainly in the early stages of the field, can be found in OR. By applying the locality principle [70], such specialized algorithms can work side by side with general propagation algorithms that take care of the rest of the constraints. In this way one can preserve the general modeling and problem-solving paradigm of CP while the integration of efficient propagation algorithms improves the overall performance of the approach. Stated in another way, efficient OR algorithms integrated in a CP approach allow the user to benefit from the efficiency of OR techniques in a flexible framework. Translated to the area of Constraint-Based Scheduling two strengths emerge: i) natural and flexible modeling of scheduling problems as Constraint Satisfaction Problems (CSPs) [72] and ii) powerful propagation of temporal and resource constraints. All this said, we want to remark that over the years the distinction between AI and OR is often becoming less and less clear and is also deemed less and less important.

Let us now step from Constraint-Based Scheduling to Constraint-Based Planning. There are basically two approaches for applying CP to planning:

- The first approach (see Section 22.2.2) dates back to the first attempts to build non-linear plans in the 70s [62, 17, 53] and consists in refining a partial plan made of a temporal network of activities. Similarly to Constraint-Based Scheduling, constraint propagation can be used in this temporal network to propagate temporal, state, and resource constraints. These approaches are flexible enough to handle *complex and realistic* planning problems [66]. Although in these approaches the idea of constraint propagation has been present since the beginning, it is only in recent years that efficient global propagation algorithms, partially inspired from the ones available in Constraint-Based Scheduling have been designed [75].

- The second approach (see Section 22.2.1) consists in compiling the planning problem into a CSP and use CSP or SAT solvers as a blackbox to solve the problem [6, 73, 23, 51]. These approaches work on a simplification of the real planning problem expressed in a STRIPS-like formalism and tend to focus on *efficiency* rather than on generality of application. Several ideas stemming from this approach can be used to provide efficient global constraint propagation algorithms and heuristics to guide the search [75].

Although the use of CP in planning is, due to the problem complexity, less mature than its use in scheduling, Constraint-Based Planning thus follows the same pattern as

Constraint-Based Scheduling where CP is used as a framework for integrating efficient special purpose algorithms into a flexible and expressive paradigm.

Besides the strengths mentioned above, we want to mention two more reasons that contributed to the success of Constraint-Based Scheduling: a natural fit of expressing scheduling specific heuristics with CP tree search, and a proven good potential of combining the CP approach with solution techniques as Local Search, Large Neighborhood Search, and Mixed Integer Programming. The first allows to both exploit all the work done on scheduling heuristics in the past as to write new scheduling heuristics with easy to understand scheduling semantics. The second allows to get improved performance in the cases where that is needed. The same strengths should also benefit Constraint-Based Planning.

The remainder of this chapter is organized as follows. Section 22.1 presents CP models for scheduling together with descriptions of propagation techniques for constraints used in these models. Section 22.2 does the same for planning problems. As over the years dedicated global constraint propagation techniques for resource constraints have received a lot of attention, they are discussed in more detail in Section 22.3. In Section 22.4 constraint propagation techniques on optimization criteria are discussed, after which Section 22.5 pays attention to the search procedures that are used in Constraint-Based Planning and Scheduling to solve resource constraints. Finally in Section 22.6 conclusions are presented together with identification of potential future research directions.

22.1 Constraint Programming Models for Scheduling

In this section we give an overview of the kind of scheduling problems that are studied by the Constraint-Based Scheduling community. We present the different components together with a description of how these components can be modeled as a part of a CSP.

Throughout this chapter we use the following notation. Let $\{A_1, \ldots, A_n\}$ be a set of n activities and $\{R_1, \ldots, R_m\}$ a set of m resources. Let's for now consider a basic scheduling problem where each of the activities has a processing time and requires a certain capacity from one or several resources. The resources have a given capacity that can not be exceeded at any point in time. There may furthermore be a set of temporal constraints between activities and an objective function. The problem to be solved is to decide when to execute each activity to optimize the objective function, while respecting both temporal and resource constraints. Later on in this section several extensions are discussed, but for now this basic scheduling problem suffices for the discussion.

22.1.1 Activities

When looking at the type of activities in a problem, we distinguish *non-preemptive scheduling*, *preemptive scheduling*, and *elastic scheduling*. In non-preemptive scheduling, activities cannot be interrupted. Each activity must execute without interruption from its start time to its end time. In preemptive scheduling, activities can be interrupted at any time, *e.g.*, to let some other activities execute. In elastic scheduling the amount of resource assigned to an activity A_i can, at any time t, assume any value between 0 and the resource capacity, provided that the sum over time of the assigned capacity equals a given value called *energy*. The equivalent notion of energy in the case of a non-preemptive activity is the product of its processing time and the capacity required.

A non-preemptive scheduling problem can be efficiently encoded as a CSP in the following way. For each activity three variables are introduced, $start(A_i)$, $end(A_i)$, and $proc(A_i)$. They represent the start time, the end time, and the processing time of A respectively. We are not aware of CP approaches not using this encoding.

With r_i the release date and d_i the deadline of activity A_i as defined in the initial data of the scheduling problem, $[r_i, d_i]$ is the time window in which A_i has to execute. Based on that the initial domains of $start(A_i)$ and $end(A_i)$ are $[r_i, lst_i]$ and $[eet_i, d_i]$, respectively. Here lst_i and eet_i stand for the latest start time and the earliest end time of A_i. For convenience, we also use this notation to denote the current domains of $start(A_i)$ and $end(A_i)$ i.e., the domains when we are in the process of propagating constraints. Of course in that case instead of the initial release date and deadline, r_i and d_i denote the current earliest start time and latest end time

The processing time of the activity is defined as the difference between the end time and the start time of the activity: $proc(A_i) = end(A_i) - start(A_i)$. p_i denotes the smallest value in the domain of $proc(A_i)$. All data related to an activity are summarized in Figure 22.1. Light gray is used to depict the time window $[r_i, d_i]$ of an activity and dark gray is used to represent the processing time of the activity.

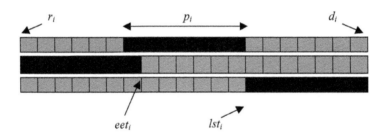

Figure 22.1: Data related to an activity

Preemptive scheduling problems are more difficult to represent since a schedule is more complex than a simple set of start and end times of activities. We discuss two possibilities. One can either associate a set variable (i.e., a variable the value of which will be a set) $set(A_i)$ with each activity A_i, or alternatively define a 0-1 variable $X(A_i, t)$ for each activity A_i and time t. $set(A_i)$ represents the set of times at which A_i executes, while $X(A_i, t)$ takes value 1 if and only if A_i executes at time t. The processing time $proc(A_i$ of A_i is defined as the number of time points t at which A_i executes, i.e., as $|set(A_i)|$. In practice, the $X(A_i, t)$ variables are not represented explicitly as the value of $X(A_i, t)$ is 1 if and only if t belongs to $set(A_i)$.

Assuming time is discretized, $start(A_i)$ and $end(A_i)$ can be defined by $start(A_i) = \min_{t \in set(A_i)} t$ and $end(A_i) = \max_{t \in set(A_i)} t + 1$. Notice that in the non-preemptive case, $set(A_i) = [start(A_i), end(A_i))$, with the interval $[start(A_i), end(A_i))$ closed on the left and open on the right so that $|set(A_i)| = end(A_i) - start(A_i) = proc(A_i)$.

These constraints are easily propagated by maintaining a lower bound and an upper bound for the set variable $set(A_i)$. The lower bound $lb(set(A_i))$ is a series of disjoint intervals ILB_i^u such that each ILB_i^u is constrained to be included in $set(A_i)$. The upper bound $ub(set(A_i))$ is a series of disjoint intervals IUB_i^v such that $set(A_i)$ is constrained to be included in the union of the IUB_i^v. If the size of the lower bound (*i.e.*, the sum of the sizes of the ILB_i^u) becomes larger than the upper bound of $proc(A_i)$ or if the size of the upper bound (*i.e.*, the sum of the sizes of the IUB_i^v) becomes smaller than the lower bound of $proc(A_i)$, a contradiction is detected. If the size of the lower bound (or of the upper bound) becomes equal to the upper bound (respectively, lower bound) of $proc(A_i)$, $set(A_i)$ receives the lower bound (respectively, the upper bound) as its final value. Minimal and maximal values of $start(A_i)$ and $end(A_i)$, *i.e.*, earliest and latest start and end times, are also maintained. Each of the following rules, considered independently one from another, is used to update the bounds of $set(A_i)$, $start(A_i)$ and $end(A_i)$. Let t be any point in time, then

$$t < r_i \Rightarrow t \notin set(A_i)$$
$$t \in lb(set(A_i)) \Rightarrow start(A_i) \leq t$$
$$d_i \leq t \Rightarrow t \notin set(A_i)$$
$$t \in lb(set(A_i)) \Rightarrow t < end(A_i)$$
$$[\forall_{u<t}\, u \notin ub(set(A_i))] \Rightarrow t \leq start(A_i)$$
$$[\forall_{u \geq t}\, u \notin ub(set(A_i))] \Rightarrow end(A_i) \leq t$$
$$start(A_i) \leq \max\{u \mid \exists_{S \subseteq ub(set(A_i))}\, |S| = p_i \wedge \min(S) = u\}$$
$$end(A_i) \geq \min\{u \mid \exists_{S \subseteq ub(set(A_i))}\, |S| = p_i \wedge \max(S) = u - 1\}$$

Needless to say, whenever any of these rules leads to a situation where the lower bound of a variable is larger than its upper bound, a contradiction is detected.

In the following, we may occasionally use the notations $X(A_i, t)$ and $set(A_i)$ for an activity A_i that cannot be interrupted. In such a case, the following rules are also applied:

$$X(A_i, t) = 0 \wedge t < eet_i \Rightarrow start(A_i) > t$$
$$X(A_i, t) = 0 \wedge lst_i \leq t \Rightarrow end(A_i) \leq t$$

Elastic activities are discussed in the following section.

22.1.2 Resource Constraints

When looking at the type of resources found in a problem, we distinguish *disjunctive scheduling* and *cumulative scheduling*. In a disjunctive scheduling problem, all resources are of capacity 1 (such resources are often called *machines*) and thus can execute at most one activity at a time. In a cumulative scheduling problem, resources exist that can execute several activities in parallel, of course provided that the resource capacity is not exceeded.

Resource constraints represent the fact that activities require some amount of resource throughout their execution. Given an activity A_i and a resource R whose capacity is $cap(R)$, generally a variable $cap(A_i, R)$ is introduced that represents the amount of resource R required by activity A_i. Where no confusion is possible we will often omit "R" and use $cap(A_i)$ to denote $cap(A_i, R)$. For fully elastic activities, the $cap(A_i, R)$ variable is not meaningful and a variable $E(A_i, R)$ that represents the *energy* required by the activity on the resource R is introduced. Note that for non-elastic activities, we have

$E(A_i, R) = cap(A_i, R)proc(A_i)$. To represent a schedule, a set of variables $E(A_i, t, R)$ is required that denote the number of units of the resource R used by activity A_i at time t In all cases, we have the constraint stating that enough resource capacity must be allocated to activities to cover the energy requirement:

$$E(A_i, R) = \sum_t E(A_i, t, R)$$

If A_i is not an elastic activity, there are some strong relations between $E(A_i, t, R)$ and $X(A_i, t)$:

$$E(A_i, t, R) = X(A_i, t)cap(A_i, R)$$

For elastic activities, we have a weaker relation between the variables:

$$[E(A_i, t, R) > 0] \Leftrightarrow [X(A_i, t) > 0]$$

Generally speaking, the resource constraint can be written as follows. For each point in time t

$$\sum_{i=1}^n E(A_i, t, R) \le cap(R) \tag{22.1}$$

Depending on the scheduling situation, (22.1) can be rewritten. In the non-preemptive case, (22.1) leads for all times t to

$$\sum_{A_i | start(A_i) \le t < end(A_i)} cap(A_i, R) \le cap(R)$$

In the preemptive case, (22.1) leads for all times t to

$$\sum_{A_i | start(A_i) \le t < end(A_i)} X(A_i, t)cap(A_i, R) \le cap(R)$$

22.1.3   Temporal Constraints

Temporal relations between activities can be expressed by linear constraints between start and end variables of activities. For instance, a standard precedence constraint between two activities A_1 and A_2 stating that A_2 is to be started after A_1 is ended can be modeled by the linear constraint $end(A_1) \le start(A_2)$. In general, with both x and y a start or end variable and d an integer, temporal relations can be expressed by constraints of the type $x - y \le d$

When the temporal constraint network is sparse, as it is usually the case in scheduling, such constraints can be easily propagated using a standard arc-B-consistency algorithm [49]. In addition, a variant of Ford's algorithm (see for instance [37]) proposed by Cesta and Oddi [15] can be used to detect any inconsistency between such constraints, in time polynomial in the number of constraints and independent of the domain sizes.

When the temporal network is dense or when it is useful to compute and maintain the minimal and maximal delay between any pair of time points in the schedule, path consistency can be enforced on the network [21] for example by applying Floyd-Warshall's All-Pairs-Shortest-Path algorithm [27].

22.1.4 Extensions of the Basic Model

Although the model presented until now covers quite a number of scheduling problems, in this section we pay attention to extensions that are frequently found in industrial applications.

Alternative resources

In some scheduling situations an activity A_i can be scheduled on any one resource from a set S of resources. We say that S is the set of *alternative resources* for A_i. A common way to model this is to for each activity A_i introduce a variable $altern(A_i)$ representing the chosen resource among the resource alternatives. To simplify notation, we assume that resources are numbered from 1 to m and that $altern(A_i)$ denotes the variable whose value represents the index of the resource on which A_i is executed. We remark that quite commonly the processing time of the activity depends on the resource on which the given activity is executed, *i.e.*, the resources are unrelated. The same goes for the cost of executing the activity, *i.e.*, different alternatives can have different costs. Another commonly found type of constraints reasons on interdependencies of resource allocations, *e.g.*, a constraint like "if A_1 is scheduled on resource R_1 then A_3 has to be scheduled on resource R_2". These constraints are used to model things like alternative production lines.

Alternative resource constraints are propagated as if the activity A_i were split into $|domain(altern(A_i))|$ fictive activities A_i^u where each activity A_i^u requires resource R_u [47]. Following this notation r_i^u denotes the earliest start time of A_i^u, *etc.* The alternative resource constraint maintains the constructive disjunction between the alternative activities A_i^u for $u \in domain(altern(A_i))$, *i.e.*, it ensures that:

$$
\begin{aligned}
r_i &= \min\{r_i^u \mid u \in domain(altern(A_i))\} \\
lst_i &= \max\{lst_i^u \mid u \in domain(altern(A_i))\} \\
eet_i &= \min\{eet_i^u \mid u \in domain(altern(A_i))\} \\
d_i &= \max\{d_i^u \mid u \in domain(altern(A_i))\} \\
lb(proc(A_i)) &= \min\{lb(proc(A_i^u)) \mid u \in domain(altern(A_i))\} \\
ub(proc(A_i)) &= \max\{ub(proc(A_i^u)) \mid u \in domain(altern(A_i))\}
\end{aligned}
$$

Constraint propagation will deduce new bounds for alternative activities A_i^u on the alternative resource R_u. Whenever the bounds of an activity A_i^u turn out to be incoherent, the resource R_u is simply removed from the set of possible alternative resources for activity A_i, *i.e.*, $domain(altern(A_i))$ becomes $domain(altern(A_i)) - \{u\}$.

In some approaches the fictive activities A_i^u are actually generated together with a way to express that only one of them per original activity A_i will really require one of the alternative resources. In this context the generated activities A_i^u are often referred to as *optional* activities. See below for a discussion on optional activities.

Setup times and setup costs

Setup times and setup costs are of great importance in industrial applications. They are found abundantly and the correct treatment of them is often crucial, both because they are a mandatory component to express the problem in the required detail as it is needed to find good solutions with respect to them as they represent a substantial part of the real-life cost. The setup time (also transition time) $setup(A_1, A_2)$ between two activities A_1 and A_2 is defined as the amount of time that must elapse between the end of A_1 and the start of A_2 when A_1 immediately precedes A_2 on a given resource. A setup cost $setupCost(A_1, A_2$ can also be associated to the transition between A_1 and A_2. The objective of the scheduling problem can be to find a schedule that minimizes the sum of the setup costs.

In a vast majority of problems activities subjected to setups are to be scheduled on the same machine (the semantics of setups is much more complex on resources of capacity greater than 1). Setup considerations can be combined with alternative resources. In such a case, two parameters are associated to each tuple (A_i, A_j, R_u): the setup time $setup(A_i, A_j, R_u)$ and the setup cost $setupCost(A_i, A_j, R_u)$ between activities A_i and A if A_i and A_j are scheduled sequentially on the same machine R_u. The attached constraint is that $start(A_j^u) \geq end(A_i^u) + setup(A_i, A_j, R_u)$. There may furthermore exist a setup time $setup(-, A_i, R_u)$ (with corresponding cost $setupCost(-, A_i, R_u)$) that has to elapse before the start of A_i when A_i is the first activity on R_u and, similarly, a teardown time $setup(A_i, -, R_u)$ (with corresponding cost $setupCost(A_i, -, R_u)$) that has to elapse after the end of A_i when A_i is the last activity on R_u. Section 22.4.2 pays attention to constraint propagation methods for setup times and setup costs constraints.

Breakable activities and calendars

In [58] a problem is described that has a lot of properties frequently found in industrial applications. One such property is the fact resources can be governed by a *calendar* under which activities scheduled on the resource are executed. Such a calendar thus defines the execution conditions for activities and consists of a list of breaks and a *productivity profile* An activity scheduled on the resource at hand can be interrupted by breaks smaller than the maximal break duration mBD. An activity is thus *breakable* when $mBD > 0$ and *not breakable* when $mBD = 0$. The productivity profile defines the efficiency of the activity execution. If an activity is scheduled in a time interval with productivity $p\%$, $p\%$ of a processing time unit is executed per time unit. A productivity below 100% thus means that per time unit less than one processing time unit is executed which in turn implies that the duration of an activity will exceed its processing time. For productivities exceeding 100% obviously the inverse holds. The processing time of an activity is therefore equal to the integral, from start to end, of the productivity. We refer to [65] for a more extensive discussion on breakable activities and productivity profiles.

A CP model for this consists in introducing a *duration variable* per activity and redefining the meaning of the processing time variable. The duration variable $dur(A_i)$ of an activity is then defined as the difference between the end time and the start time of the activity: $dur(A_i) = end(A_i) - start(A_i)$. The processing time variable is defined as the time it will take to execute the activity when it is not interrupted by breaks and all along the execution the productivity is exactly 100%. All four activity variables *start*, *end*, *dur* and *proc* are governed by the break constraint and the productivity profile constraint of the resource on which the activity is executed. For sake of clarity we do not use this meaning for the processing time variable in the rest of this chapter, *i.e.*, the processing time is defined as the difference between the end time and the start time of an activity.

Optional activities/leaving activities unperformed

Whether coming from alternative resources (see above) or directly present in the model, in many scheduling problems activities exist for which it is not yet decided whether they will be executed on a resource or not. Such activities are often referred to as *optional* activities.

Modeling an optional activity is often obtained by allowing the processing time variable to take on the value 0. Care is to be taken then that non-standard precedence constraints are not still active. If for instance an optional activity A_1 is part of a chain of activities and a precedence constraint of the type $end(A_1) + d \leq start(A_2)$ is defined, setting the processing time variable to become 0 and keeping the precedence constraint active will still induce a possibly unwanted delay d between the predecessors of A_1 and A_2. Another way to model optional activities is to introduce a variable per activity expressing whether the activity really exists or not. This is obviously a more direct way of modeling but requires the adaptation of propagation algorithms to deal with this additional variable and concept [78].

In industrial scheduling problems one often finds the possibility of subcontracting an activity A_i, this against a certain incurred cost $cost_i$. This means that the activity does not use resource capacity but does take time. A way to model this is to allow the capacity variable $cap(A_i)$ to take on the value 0 and to introduce a variable $cost$ representing the cost together with the constraint $cap(A_i) = 0 \Rightarrow cost = cost_i$. Another way to model this is to introduce an alternative resource corresponding to the subcontracting alternative. This can be interesting if subcontracting is subject to a different calendar than in-house production, which of course is not uncommon. The cost of the alternative would correspond to $cost_i$. On the "subcontracting" resource one would in this case not enforce the capacity constraint, even though this model can easily be extended to enforce the capacity constraint to model restricted subcontracting possibilities.

In [58] a model is described where one can decide that an activity will be left *unperformed*, meaning that the activity will not require capacity, but will obey potential temporal constraints, etc., and will also obey the calendar of the chosen resource. This corresponds to the situation where one wants to include the possibility to temporarily increase the production capacity in its own production facility, this of course against a certain cost. Other useful constraints included are *performance compatibility constraint* between two activities expressing that either they are both performed or they are both unperformed.

State resources

A state resource represents a resource of infinite capacity, the state of which can vary over time. Each activity may, throughout its execution, require a state resource to be in a given state (or in any of a given set of states). Consequently, two activities may not overlap if they require incompatible states of a state resource during their execution. Adaptations of the Timetable Constraint (see Section 22.3.2) and Disjunctive Constraint (see Section 22.3.1) are used as basic propagation algorithms on those resources.

Reservoirs

A reservoir resource is a multi-capacity resource that can be consumed and/or produced by activities. A reservoir has an integer maximal capacity and may have an initial level. As an example of a reservoir you can think of a fuel tank. Note that a cumulative resource can be seen as a special case of a reservoir that is consumed at the beginning of the activity and produced in the same quantity at the end of the activity when the activity releases the resource.

The Timetable Constraint presented in Section 22.3.2 can be generalized to the case of reservoirs and is classically used as the basic propagation algorithm on those resources. However, we will see in Section 22.3.3 that other techniques are available to provide additional propagation.

22.1.5 Objective Function

Finally, *decision* problems and *optimization* problems are distinguished. In decision problems, one has only to determine whether a schedule exists that meets all constraints. In optimization problems, an objective function has to be optimized. In this chapter we concentrate on problems where there is one objective function, *i.e.*, we do not consider cases where multiple objective functions are defined.

The commonly used way of modeling an objective function is simply by introducing a variable *criterion* that is constrained to be equal to the value of the objective function. Although the minimization of the makespan, *i.e.*, the end time of the schedule, is commonly used, other criteria are of great practical interest *e.g.*, the sum of setup times or costs, the number of late activities, the maximal or average tardiness or earliness, storage costs, alternative costs, the peak or average resource utilization, etc. We will come back to these criteria later.

Many of the classical scheduling criteria take into account a due date δ_i that one would like to meet for each activity. In contrast to a deadline d_i which is mandatory, a due date δ can be seen as a preference. In the following, C_i denotes the completion time of activity A_i. Lateness L_i of A_i is defined as the difference between the completion time and the due date of A_i, *i.e.*, $L_i = C_i - \delta_i$. The tardiness T_i of A_i is defined as $\max(0, L_i)$, while earliness of A_i is defined as $\max(0, -L_i)$. The notation U_i is used to denote a unit penalty per late job, *i.e.*, U_i equals 0 when $C_i \le \delta_i$ and equals 1 otherwise. See also Figure 22.2.

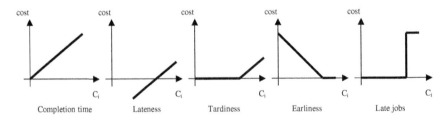

Figure 22.2: Some scheduling related objective functions

The commonly studied criteria F are either formulated as a sum or as a maximum. A weight per activity w_i may be used to give more importance to some activities. We mention the following well-known optimization criteria:

- Makespan: $F = C_{\max} = \max C_i$

- Total weighted flow (or completion) time: $F = \sum w_i C_i$
- Maximum tardiness: $F = T_{\max} = \max T_i$
- Total weighted tardiness: $F = \sum w_i T_i$
- Total weighted number of late jobs: $F = \sum w_i U_i$

For these simple cases which are the most often studied in the literature, the objective function is thus a function of the end variables of the activities.

$$criterion = F(end(A_1), \ldots, end(A_n))$$

In that case, the objective constraint is a simple arithmetic expression on which arc-B-consistency can be easily achieved.

Considering the objective constraint and the resource constraints independently is not a problem when F is a maximum such as $C_{\max}$ or $T_{\max}$. Indeed, the upper bound on *criterion* is directly propagated on the completion time of each activity, *i.e.*, latest end times are tightened efficiently. The situation is much more complex for sum functions such as $\sum w_i C_i$, $\sum w_i T_i$, or $\sum w_i U_i$. For these functions, efficient constraint propagation techniques must take into account the resource constraints and the objective constraint simultaneously. We pay attention to propagation for sum functions in Section 22.4. There we will also pay attention to objective functions that are not a function of the end variables of the activities like sum of setup times and sum of setup costs.

Once all constraints of the problem are added, the most commonly used technique to look for an optimal solution is to solve successive decision variants of the problem. Several strategies can be considered to minimize the value of *criterion*. One way is to iterate on the possible values, either from the lower bound of its domain up to the upper bound until one solution is found, or from the upper bound down to the lower bound determining each time whether there still is a solution. Another way is to use a dichotomizing algorithm, where one starts by computing an initial upper bound $ub(criterion)$ and an initial lower bound $lb(criterion)$ for *criterion*. Then

1. Set $D = \left\lfloor \dfrac{lb(criterion) + ub(criterion)}{2} \right\rfloor$

2. Constrain *criterion* to be at most D. Then solve the resulting CSP, *i.e.*, determine a solution with *criterion* $\leq D$ or prove that no such solution exists. If a solution is found, set $ub(criterion)$ to the value of *criterion* in the solution; otherwise, set $lb(criterion)$ to $D + 1$.

3. Iterate steps 1 and 2 until $ub(criterion) = lb(criterion)$.

22.2 Constraint Programming Models for Planning

While the previous section presented CP models for scheduling, in this section we pay attention to CP models for planning as studied by the Constraint-Based Planning community. In this section and in general throughout this chapter we assume that the readers are familiar with basic planning techniques and terminology. For more information on such planning techniques and terminology, we refer to [36].

A general formulation of the planning problem defines three inputs in some formal language:

1. A description of the initial state and expected changes of the world,

2. A description of the agent's goal (*i.e.*, what behavior is desired), and

3. A description of the possible actions that can be performed. This last description is often called a domain theory.

The planner's output is a feasible sequence of actions referred to as a *plan* which, when executed in any world satisfying the initial state and undergoing the expected changes, will achieve the agent's goal.

22.2.1   CSPs for Planning-Graph Techniques

The classical STRIPS [26] representation describes the initial state of world with a complete set of ground propositions. The representation is restricted to goals of attainment, and these goals are defined as a conjunction of propositions; all world states satisfying the goal formula are considered equally good. A domain theory completes a planning problem. In the STRIPS representation, each operator is described with a conjunctive precondition and conjunctive effect that define a transition function from states to states. An action is a fully grounded operator. An action can be executed in any state s satisfying the precondition formula. The effect of executing an action in a state s is described by eliminating from each proposition of the action delete-list and adding to s each proposition from the action add-list. The add-list and delete-list of the action are called the effect of the action. This defines the so called classical planning problem.

For instance in a blocks world domain, the propositions for describing the state of the world are shown in Table 22.1. The operators of this planning domain move a clear block onto another clear block or the table as shown in Table 22.2.

$clear(X)$:	**There is no block on block X.**
$onT(X)$:	**Block X is on the table.**
$on(X, Y)$:	**Block X is on block Y.**

Table 22.1: Propositions for the blocks world domain

In this section, we will consider the planning problem with initial state: $[on(C, A) \wedge onT(A) \wedge onT(B)]$ and goal state: $[on(A, B) \wedge on(B, C)]$ depicted in Figure 22.3.

In recent years, researchers have investigated the reformulation of planning problems as constraint satisfaction problems (CSPs) in an attempt to use powerful algorithms for constraint satisfaction to find plans more efficiently [73, 23, 51]. In these approaches, each CSP typically represents the problem of finding a plan with a fixed number of steps. A solution to the CSP can be mapped back to a plan; if no solution exists, the number of steps permitted in the plan is increased and a new CSP is generated.

Graphplan [6] works on STRIPS domains by creating a planning graph which represents the set of propositions which can be achieved after a number of steps along with mutual exclusion (mutex) relationships between propositions and actions. Mutually exclusive actions are actions that cannot be executed in the same step. Two actions in the same

BB(X,Y,Z)	**Move X from atop Y to atop Z**
preconditions:	$clear(X) \wedge clear(Z) \wedge on(X,Y)$
add-list:	$clear(Y) \wedge on(X,Z)$
delete-list:	$clear(Z) \wedge on(X,Y)$
TB(X,Y)	**Move X from the table to atop Y**
preconditions:	$clear(X) \wedge clear(Y) \wedge onT(X)$
add-list:	$on(X,Y)$
delete-list:	$clear(Y) \wedge onT(X)$
BT(X,Y)	**Move X from atop Y to the table**
preconditions:	$clear(X) \wedge on(X,Y)$
add-list:	$onT(X) \wedge clear(Y)$
delete-list:	$on(X,Y)$

Table 22.2: Operators for the blocks world domain

Initial state   Goal state

Figure 22.3: A planning problem

step are mutex if either of the actions deletes a precondition or add-effect of the other. Two propositions p and q in the same step are mutex if all possible actions for establishing proposition p are exclusive with all possible actions for establishing proposition q. If two actions a and b have some mutex precondition then they are mutex. Note that the persistence of a proposition between two steps is considered as a particular type of action called a *persistence* action.

This planning graph is then searched for a plan which achieves the goals from the initial state and that is mutex-free in each step. The planning graph corresponding to our blocks world example with 3 developed steps is shown in Figure 22.4. Note that this planning graph is not complete, some mutex are missing in all steps and some actions are missing in step 2.

While the original algorithm performed backward search, the plan graph can also be transformed into a CSP which can be solved by any CSP solver.

In [23], variables of this CSP are propositions distinguished by step. Values are possible actions for establishing those propositions with a special dummy value ($\perp$) stating that the proposition is inactive. Constraints say that preconditions of actions that are used to establish active propositions cannot be inactive and mutex action/proposition pairs must be satisfied. For instance, a constraint $on\_A\_B\_G = TB\_A\_B \Rightarrow (onT\_A_3 \neq \perp \wedge clear\_A_3 \neq \perp \wedge clear\_B_3 \neq \perp)$ means that if proposition on_A_B in the goal state is to be established by action TB_A_B, then, it means that propositions onT_A, $clear\_A$ and $clear\_B$ must hold in step 3, that is, they must have been established by some action. A fragment of the CSP corresponding to the planning graph of Figure 22.4 is shown in Table 22.3.

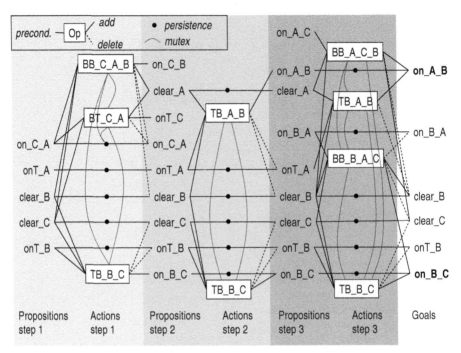

Figure 22.4: Planning graph with 3 steps

Variables:	$on\_C\_A_1, onT\_A_1, clear\_B_1, clear\_C_1, onT\_B_1,$
	$on\_C\_B_2, clear\_A_2, onT\_C_2, on\_C\_A_2, onT\_A_2, clear\_B_2, clear\_C_2, onT\_B_2, on\_B\_C_2,$
	$on\_A\_C_3, on\_A\_B_3, clear\_A_3, on\_B\_A_3, onT\_A_3, clear\_B_3, clear\_C_3, onT\_B_3, on\_B\_C_3,$
	$on\_A\_B_G, on\_B\_C_G,...$
Domains:	$on\_C\_A_1 : \{Init\}, onT\_A_1 : \{Init\}, clear\_B_1 : \{Init\}, clear\_C_1 : \{Init\}, onT\_B_1 : \{Init$
	$on\_C\_B_2 : \{BB\_C\_A\_B, \perp\}, clear\_A_2 : \{BB\_C\_A\_B, BT\_C\_A, \perp\}, onT\_C_2 : \{BT\_C\_A, \perp\}$
	$on\_C\_A_2 : \{Persist, \perp\}, onT\_A_2 : \{Persist, \perp\}, clear\_B_2 : \{Persist, \perp\},$
	$clear\_C_2 : \{Persist, \perp\}, on\_B\_C_2 : \{TB\_B\_C, \perp\}, onT\_B_2 : \{Persist, \perp\}, ...$
	$on\_A\_B_G : \{BB\_A\_C\_B, TB\_A\_B, Persist, \perp\}, on\_B\_C_G : \{TB\_B\_C, BB\_B\_A\_C, \perp\}$
Constraints:	**activity preconditions**
	$on\_A\_B\_G = TB\_A\_B \Rightarrow (onT\_A_3 \neq \perp \wedge clear\_A_3 \neq \perp \wedge clear\_B_3 \neq \perp)$
	$on\_A\_B\_G = BB\_A\_C\_B \Rightarrow (on\_A\_C_3 \neq \perp \wedge clear\_A_3 \neq \perp \wedge clear\_B_3 \neq \perp)$
	...
Constraints:	**mutexes**
	$on\_C\_B_2 = BB\_C\_A\_B \Rightarrow onT\_C_2 \neq BT\_C\_A$
	...
Constraints:	**goal state**
	$on\_C\_B_G \neq \perp, on\_A\_B_G \neq \perp$

Table 22.3: Fragment of the generated CSP problem for 3 steps

If no solution is found, the planning graph is extended by adding an additional step and the CSP is extended accordingly until it is feasible. In the example, the CSP with 3 steps is feasible and a solution is: step 1: BT_C_A, step 2: TB_B_C, step 3: TB_A_B.

In [51], a slightly different CSP model is used with only boolean variables, one variable for each proposition in each step and one variable for each action in each step. Some redundant constraints (other than mutex) are identified and added to the CSP model. For instance the fact that an action cannot be immediately followed by its opposite action in a plan of optimal length.

In general, the reformulated problem is solved using classical CSP techniques (arc-consistency, dynamic variable ordering, memoization) and does not require specific constraint propagation techniques this is the reason why we will not focus on this family of approaches in the sequel of this chapter.

22.2.2 CSPs in Plan-Space Search

A second growing trend in planning is the extension of planning systems to reason about both time and resources. STRIPS is simply not expressive enough to represent more realistic planning problems. This demand for increased sophistication has led to the need for more powerful techniques to reason about time and resources during planning.

In Constraint-Based Planning, each search node represents a partial plan and consists of a set of time intervals, connected by constraints. The partial plan may be incomplete, in that constraints are not necessarily satisfied and pending choices have not been made. The planning process then involves modifying a partial plan until it has been turned into a complete and valid plan. Traditional search-based methods accomplish this by trying different options for completing partial plans, and backtracking when constraints are found to be violated. Constraint reasoning methods, such as propagation and consistency checks can be used to help out in that process.

The scheduling community has used constraint satisfaction techniques to perform this sort of reasoning. The main difference between constraint-based planning and scheduling is that, in planning, the set of activities of the plan is not completely known a-priori and must be determined during the search. The rules that govern the insertion of new activities in the plan are expressed as implicit or explicit constraints and, although they slightly differ from one planning system to the other [35, 42, 18, 40, 32], they all have the same flavor.

To fix the ideas, we will use in this section the IxTeT formalism [35, 42]. In this planning language the state of the world is described by a set of multi-valued state attributes together with a set of resource attributes. Each state attribute describes a particular feature of the world, for instance the position of a block. A resource is an object (or a set of objects) that can be simultaneously shared by several actions provided its maximal capacity is not exceeded. Operators (or tasks) are temporal structures composed of a set of events describing the changes of the world induced by the task (event), a set of assertions on state attributes describing conditions that must remain true during some time intervals (hold) and a set of resource usage (use, produce, consume) describing how the task uses some resources. All the above statements refer to time points that can be constrained with respect to the time interval [start,end] of the task. An example of model for the blocks world domain is shown in Table 22.4. Note that the domain is represented here with a finer grain than the STRIPS definition in Section 22.2.1: the operator is defined with internal time points, delays between these time points (duration) are expressed together with resource requirements (here, the task requires one hand from the two hands that are available to move the blocks). Beside resource usage, note that state attributes are very similar to state resources used in scheduling (see section 22.1.4) in that no task requiring a given state attribute to take different value can overlap in time.

constant	blocks = {a, b, c}; positions = {a, b, c, table, hand};
attribute	clear(?x) { ?x in blocks; **?value in** {yes, no}; } on(?x) { ?x in blocks; **?value in** positions; }
resource	hands() { **capacity** = 2; }

task	TB(?x, ?y)(**start, end**) {
	// **Move ?x from the table to atop ?y**
	timepoint t1, t2;
	event(clear(?x):(yes,no), **start**);
	event(on(?x):(table,hand), t1);
	event(on(?x):(hand,?z), t2);
	event(clear(?z):(yes,no), t2);
	hold(on(?x):hand, (t1, t2));
	event(clear(?x):(no,yes), **end**);
	hold(clear(?x):no, (**start, end**));
	use(hands(): 1, (**start, end**));
	(t1 - **start**) **in** [00:10, 00:20];
	(t2 - t1) **in** [00:15, 00:25];
	(**end** - t2) **in** [00:10, 00:20];
	}

Table 22.4: Part of the blocks world domain in IxTeT

A partial plan is a set of tasks together with a set of constraints between the tasks variables (including temporal constraints between the task time points). The initial plan only contains a fake start task that asserts all the state attributes of the initial state and a fake end task that has the goal as (non-established) preconditions. A partial plan is complete and valid if and only if each instantiation of all the variables of the partial plan lead to a feasible fully-grounded plan where (1) the change of state attributes over time is non-ambiguously defined by and consistent with the events and assertions of the tasks of the plan and (2) resource constraints are satisfied. Figure 22.5 shows an example of a partial plan.

Partial plans are iteratively refined at each search node until the partial plan is complete and valid. Three types of plan refinements are considered:

- Non-established conditions are those events or assertions that are still not established by a task or the initial state. For instance, in the partial plan of Figure 22.5, the condition $clear(A) : yes$ related with the event at the start time point of task $TB(A, B$ is still not established. Non-established conditions can be established by an existing event in the plan or by inserting a new task. In the case of the example, a new task $BT(C, A)$ could be added before the start of task $TB(A, B)$ to establish the condition.

- Possible conflicts between unordered events/assertions are pairs of statements that may require the same state attribute to take different values at the same moment.

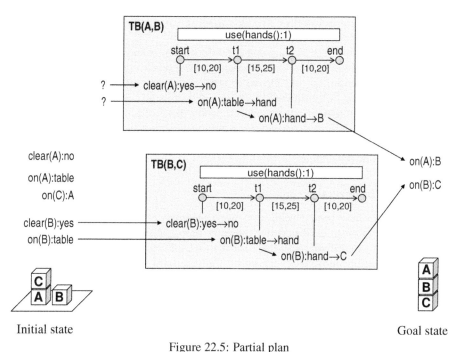

Figure 22.5: Partial plan

These incompatibility constraints can be solved by posting precedence constraints to order the conflicting events/assertions.

- Possible resource conflicts are subsets of resource requirements that may overlap in time and would in this case over-consume the resource. This would be the case of the two tasks in the example if the maximal capacity of the resource *hands* is 1. These resource conflicts can be solved by ordering the tasks or, in case the resource can be produced, by inserting a task that produces the resource.

In Constraint-Based Planning, the partial plan is usually represented as a CSP with variables representing the task time points together with non-temporal variables appearing in the task definition as well as special variables representing the tasks that can be used to establish conditions in the partial plan. Specialized constraint propagation algorithms can be used to reduce the domain of variables or to deduce new temporal constraints. As far as time and resources are concerned, these propagation algorithms are essentially the same as the ones developed for pure scheduling problems, which will be described in Section 22.3. Indeed, unless stated otherwise, all the algorithms described in Section 22.3 can be implemented so as to accept other tasks and variables as the search evolves. We also sketch in that section how some of these algorithms can be adapted to propagate on state attributes. See [75] for recent advances in the field of using Constraint Programming in Plan-Space Search.

22.3   Constraint Propagation for Resource Constraints

Resource constraints represent the fact that activities require some amount of resource throughout their execution. In this section propagation for resource constraints is described for unary resources (machines), cumulative resources, and reservoirs. As we will see, the propagation of resource constraints is a purely deductive process that allows to deduce inconsistencies and to tighten the temporal characteristics of activities and resources. Throughout this section, we will concentrate on non-preemptive scheduling. We refer the reader to [5] for the generalization of the described constraint propagation techniques to preemptive and elastic scheduling.

22.3.1   Unary Resources

Several mechanisms have been developed to propagate unary resource constraints. Here we restrict the discussion to the disjunctive constraint propagation scheme and to the well-known edge-finding algorithm. Also note that the time tabling mechanism described in Section 22.3.2 can be applied to unary resources. We refer to [5] for a detailed introduction and comparison of several other constraint propagation techniques.

Disjunctive constraint propagation

Two activities A_i and A_j requiring the same unary resource cannot overlap in time. So either A_i precedes A_j or A_j precedes A_i. If n activities require the resource, one thus has $n(n-1)/2$ (explicit or implicit) of such disjunctive constraints. Variants exist in the literature [24, 8, 44, 68, 74, 4], but in most cases the propagation consists of maintaining arc-B-consistency on the formula:

$$[end(A_i) \leq start(A_j)] \vee [end(A_j) \leq start(A_i)]$$

Enforcing arc-B-consistency on this formula is done as follows. Whenever the earliest end time of A_i exceeds the latest start time of A_j, A_i cannot precede A_j; hence A_j must precede A_i. The time bounds of A_i and A_j are consequently updated with respect to the new temporal constraint $end(A_j) \leq start(A_i)$. Similarly, when the earliest end time of A_j exceeds the latest start time of A_i, A_j cannot precede A_i. When neither of the two activities can precede the other, a contradiction is detected.

In Constraint-Based Planning, the disjunctive constraint can easily be adapted to propagate conflicts between mutually exclusive statements [75].

Edge-finding

The edge-finding constraint propagation technique consists of deducing that some activities from a given set Ω must, can, or cannot, execute first (or last) in Ω. Such deductions lead to new ordering relations ("edges" in the graph representing the possible orderings of activities) and new time bounds, *i.e.*, strengthened earliest start times and latest end times of activities.

In the following, r_Ω, d_Ω, and p_Ω denote the smallest of the earliest start times, the largest of the latest end times, and the sum of the minimal processing times of the activities in Ω, respectively. Let $A_i \ll A_j$ ($A_i \gg A_j$) mean that A_i executes before (after) A_j and

$A_i \ll \Omega$ ($A_i \gg \Omega$) mean that A_i executes before (after) all the activities in Ω. Once again, variants exist [9, 10, 11, 12, 54, 7, 52, 59, 77] but the following rules capture the "essence" of the edge-finding propagation technique:

$$\forall_\Omega \, \forall_{A_i \notin \Omega} \, [d_{\Omega \cup \{A_i\}} - r_\Omega < p_\Omega + p_i] \Rightarrow [A_i \ll \Omega]$$
$$\forall_\Omega \, \forall_{A_i \notin \Omega} \, [d_\Omega - r_{\Omega \cup \{A_i\}} < p_\Omega + p_i] \Rightarrow [A_i \gg \Omega]$$
$$\forall_\Omega \, \forall_{A_i \notin \Omega} \, [A_i \ll \Omega] \Rightarrow [end(A_i) \leq \min_{\emptyset \neq \Omega' \subseteq \Omega} (d_{\Omega'} - p_{\Omega'})]$$
$$\forall_\Omega \, \forall_{A_i \notin \Omega} \, [A_i \gg \Omega] \Rightarrow [start(A_i) \geq \max_{\emptyset \neq \Omega' \subseteq \Omega} (r_{\Omega'} + p_{\Omega'})]$$

If n activities require the resource, there are a priori $O(n * 2^n)$ pairs (A_i, Ω) to consider. Still, it is easy to see that when a rule is applied for some set Ω, the same rule provides even better deductions for the superset $\Omega' = \{A_i \mid [r_i, d_i) \subseteq [r_\Omega, d_\Omega)\}$. This makes that one can restrict the rules to sets Ω_I made of all activities whose time window belongs to some interval I. As there are no more that $O(n^2)$ such intervals I, we have a straightforward polynomial algorithm, running in cubic time, to implement the edge-finding rules. Algorithms that perform all the time bound adjustments in $O(n^2)$ are presented in [10, 56, 54]. Another variant of the edge-finding technique is presented in [11]. It runs in $O(n \log n)$ but requires much more complex data structures. [77] presents another variant running in $O(n \log n)$ that requires less complex data structures than the ones used in [11].

Techniques similar to edge-finding have been proposed to propagate groups of mutex relations in planning [75].

"Not-first" and "not-last" rules

"Not-first" and "not-last" propagation rules have also been developed as a "negative" counterpart to edge-finding. These rules deduce that an activity A_i cannot be the first (or the last) to execute in $\Omega \cup \{A_i\}$.

$$\forall_\Omega \, \forall_{A_i \notin \Omega} \, [d_{A_i} - r_\Omega < p_\Omega + p_i] \Rightarrow [end(A_i) \leq \max_{B \in \Omega} lst_B]$$
$$\forall_\Omega \, \forall_{A_i \notin \Omega} \, [d_\Omega - r_{A_i} < p_\Omega + p_i] \Rightarrow [start(A_i) \geq \min_{B \in \Omega} eet_B]$$

The corresponding time bound adjustments can be made in $O(n^2)$ [3, 71].

Conjunctive reasoning between temporal and resource constraints

The above given propagation techniques reason on the time bounds of activities on one unary resource. In [57, 69] propagation techniques are presented that reason on the combination of time bounds of activities on multiple unary resources and the temporal constraints linking these activities. Even though these techniques have led to good computational results, they have not yet been studied much. Propagation techniques that reason on the combination of activity time bounds and temporal constraints on one cumulative resource or reservoir have been studied. We discuss these techniques in the Section 22.3.3.

22.3.2 Cumulative Resources

Cumulative resource constraints represent the fact that activities A_i use some amount $cap(A_i)$ of resource throughout their execution. Many algorithms have been proposed for the propagation of the non-preemptive cumulative constraint. A limited subset of these algorithms is presented in this section. In the remainder of this chapter, c_i denotes the minimal value of $cap(A_i)$, *i.e.*, the minimal capacity required by A_i.

Timetable constraint

First we consider the timetable mechanism, widely used in Constraint-Based Scheduling tools, that allows to propagate the resource constraint in an incremental fashion. The "timetable" is used to maintain information about resource utilization and resource availability over time. Resource constraints are propagated in two directions. From resources to activities, to update the time bounds of activities (earliest start times and latest end times) according to the availability of resources; and from activities to resources, to update the timetables according to the time bounds of activities. Although several variants exist [44, 31, 45, 67, 50] the propagation mainly consists of maintaining for any time arc-B-consistency on the formula:

$$\sum_{A_i \mid start(A_i) \leq t < end(A_i)} cap(A_i) \leq cap(R)$$

Disjunctive constraint

Let A_i and A_j be two activities such that $c_i + c_j > cap(R)$. As such they cannot overlap in time and thus either A_i precedes A_j or A_j precedes A_i, *i.e.*, the disjunctive constraint holds between these activities. In general the disjunctive constraint achieves arc-B-consistency on the formula

$$[cap(A_i) + cap(A_j) \leq cap(R)] \vee [end(A_i) \leq start(A_j)] \vee [end(A_j) \leq start(A_i)]$$

Energy reasoning

Energy based constraint propagation algorithms compare the amount of energy provided by a resource over some interval $[t_1, t_2)$ to the amount of energy required by activities that have to be processed over this interval. [25] proposes the following definition of the required energy consumption that takes into account the fact that activities cannot be interrupted. Given an activity A_i and a time interval $[t_1, t_2)$, $W_{Sh}(A_i, t_1, t_2)$, the "Left-Shift / Right-Shift" required energy consumption of A_i over $[t_1, t_2)$ is c_i times the minimum of the three following durations.

- $t_2 - t_1$, the length of the interval;

- $p_i^+(t_1) = \max(0, p_i - \max(0, t_1 - r_i))$, the number of time units during which A executes after time t_1 if A_i is left-shifted, *i.e.*, scheduled as soon as possible;

- $p_i^-(t_2) = \max(0, p_i - \max(0, d_i - t_2))$, the number of time units during which A_i executes before time t_2 if A_i is right-shifted, *i.e.*, scheduled as late as possible.

This leads to $W_{Sh}(A_i, t_1, t_2) = c_i \min(t_2 - t_1, p_i^+(t_1), p_i^-(t_2))$. In Figure 22.6 an example is given where the required energy consumption of A_1 over $[2, 7)$ is 8. Indeed, at least 4 time units of A_1 have to be executed in $[2, 7)$; *i.e.*, $W_{Sh}(A, 2, 7) = 2 \min(5, 5, 4) = 8$.

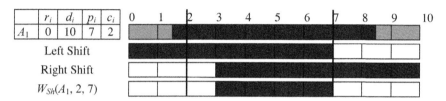

Figure 22.6: Left-Shift / Right-Shift.

The Left-Shift / Right-Shift overall required energy consumption $W_{Sh}(t_1, t_2)$ over an interval $[t_1, t_2)$ is then defined as the sum over all activities A_i of $W_{Sh}(A_i, t_1, t_2)$. The Left-Shift / Right-Shift slack $S_{Sh}(t_1, t_2)$ over $[t_1, t_2)$ is defined as $C(t_2 - t_1) - W_{Sh}(t_1, t_2)$. It is obvious that if there is a feasible schedule then $S_{Sh}(t_1, t_2) \geq 0$ for all t_1 and t_2 such that $t_2 \geq t_1$.

It is shown in [5] how the values of W_{Sh} can be used to adjust activity time bounds. Given an activity A_i and a time interval $[t_1, t_2)$ with $t_2 < d_i$, it is examined whether A_i can end before t_2. If there is a time interval $[t_1, t_2)$ such that

$$W_{Sh}(t_1, t_2) - W_{Sh}(A_i, t_1, t_2) + c_i p_i^+(t_1) > C(t_2 - t_1)$$

then a valid lower bound of the end time of A_i is

$$t_2 + \frac{1}{c_i}(W_{Sh}(t_1, t_2) - W_{Sh}(A_i, t_1, t_2) + c_i p_i^+(t_1) - C(t_2 - t_1))$$

Similarly, when

$$W_{Sh}(t_1, t_2) - W_{Sh}(A_i, t_1, t_2) + c_i \min(t_2 - t_1, p_i^+(t_1)) > C(t_2 - t_1),$$

A_i cannot start before t_1 and a valid lower bound of the start time of A_i is

$$t_2 - \frac{1}{c_i}(C(t_2 - t_1) - W_{Sh}(t_1, t_2) + W_{Sh}(A_i, t_1, t_2)).$$

[5] presents a $O(n^3)$ algorithm to compute these time bound adjustments for all n activities. It is first shown there are $O(n^2)$ intervals $[t_1, t_2)$ of interest. Given an interval and an activity, the adjustment procedure runs in $O(1)$. As such the obvious overall complexity of the algorithm is thus $O(n^3)$. An interesting open question is whether there is a quadratic algorithm to compute all the adjustments on the $O(n^2)$ intervals under consideration. Another open question at this point is whether the characterization of the $O(n^2)$

time intervals in [5] can be sharpened in order to eliminate some intervals and reduce the practical complexity of the corresponding algorithm. Finally, it seems reasonable to think that the time bound adjustments could be sharpened. Even though the energy tests can be limited (without any loss) to a given set of intervals, it could be that the corresponding adjustment rules cannot.

22.3.3 Conjunctive Reasoning between Temporal and Resource Constraints

The propagation algorithms described in the previous section reason on the time bounds of activities (r_i, lst_i, eet_i, d_i) and do not directly take into account the precedence constraints that may exist between them. We describe in this section two recently proposed propagation algorithms respectively on cumulative resources and reservoirs. Like previous propagation algorithms, both of them are used to discover new time bounds and/or new precedence relations. The main originality lies in the fact that they analyze the relative position of activities (precedence relations in the precedence graph) rather than their absolute position only, as was the case for the previously discussed propagation techniques. As a consequence, they allow a much stronger propagation when the time windows of activities are large and when the current schedule contains a lot of precedence relations, which is typically the case when integrating planning and scheduling.

Precedence graph

The algorithms presented in this section require that a temporal network representing the relations between the time points of all activities (start and end times) using the Point Algebra [76] is maintained during search. We denote the set of qualitative relations between time points by $\{\emptyset, \prec, \preceq, =, \succ, \succeq, \neq, ?\}$. The temporal network is in charge of maintaining the transitive closure of those relations.

If s_i and e_i denote the start and end time-point of activity A_i, the initial set of relations consist of the precedences $s_i \prec e_i$ for each activity A_i and $x_i \preceq x_j$ or $x_i \prec x_j$ for each precedence constraint $x_i \leq x_j + d_{ij}$ depending on the value of d_{ij}. For instance, for a precedence constraint $end(A_i) \leq start(A_j)$ between two activities A_i and A_j, the initial precedence graph contains the relation $e_i \preceq s_j$.

During search additional precedence relations can be added as decisions or as the result of constraint propagation.

Energy precedence constraint

The *energy precedence* propagation [41] for an activity A_i on a cumulative resource R ensures that for each subset ϕ of predecessor activities of activity A_i the resource provides enough energy to execute all activities in ϕ between r_ϕ and s_i. More formally, it performs the following deduction rule

$$\forall_{\phi \subseteq \{A_j | e_j \preceq s_i\}} \; start(A_i) >= r_\phi + \lceil E_\phi / cap(R_k) \rceil$$

where E_ϕ is the sum of the minimal value of $E(A_j, R_k)$ (minimal energy) over all A in ϕ. The propagation of the energy precedence constraint can be performed for all the activities on a resource and for all the subsets ϕ with a total worst-case time complexity of $O(n(p + log(n))$ where n is the number of activities on the resource and p the maximal number of predecessors of a given activity in the temporal network ($p < n$).

Balance constraint

On a reservoir resource, if x is the start or end time of an activity that changes the reservoir level, we denote by $q(x)$ the integer variable representing the relative change of the reservoir level due to the activity. By convention, $0 < q(x)$ represents a production event and $q(x) < 0$ a consumption event. The basic idea of the *balance constraint* [41] is to for each event x compute an upper and lower bound on the reservoir level at the time of x. Using the temporal network, an upper bound on the reservoir level at date $x - \epsilon$ just before x can be computed assuming that:

- All the production events y that *may* be executed strictly before x are executed strictly before x and produce as much as possible, *i.e.*, produce $ub(q(y))$ (denoted by $q_{max}(y)$). Let $Poss^{\preceq}(x) = \{y \mid \neg(x \prec y)\}$ denote the set of events that may be executed before or at the same time as x.

- All the consumption events y that *need* to be executed strictly before x are executed strictly before x and consume as little as possible, *i.e.*, consume $q_{max}(y)$[1]. Let $Nec^{\prec}(x) = \{y \mid (y \prec x)\}$ denote the set of events that necessarily execute strictly before x.

- All the consumption events that *may* execute simultaneously or after x are executed simultaneously or after x.

More formally, if P is the set of production events and C the set of consumption events, the upper bound can be computed as follows:

$$L^<_{max}(x) = \sum_{y \in P \cap Poss^{\preceq}(x)} q_{max}(y) + \sum_{y \in C \cap Nec^{\prec}(x)} q_{max}(y) \qquad (22.2)$$

For symmetry reasons, we describe only the propagation based on $L^<_{max}(x)$. Using this bound, the balance constraint is able to discover four types of information: dead ends, new bounds for required capacity variables, new bounds for time variables, and new precedence relations.

- Discovering dead ends. This is the most trivial propagation. Whenever $L^<_{max}(x) < 0$, we know that the level of the reservoir will surely be negative just before event x so the search has reached a dead end.

- Discovering new bounds on required capacity variables. Suppose there exists a consumption event $y \in Nec^{\prec}(x)$ such that $q_{max}(y) - q_{min}(y) > L^<_{max}(x)$. If y would consume a quantity q such that $q_{max}(y) - q > L^<_{max}(x)$ then, simply by replacing $q_{max}(y)$ by q in (22.2), we see that the level of the reservoir would be negative just before x. Thus, we can deduce that $q(y) \geq q_{max}(y) - L^<_{max}(x)$.

- Discovering new bounds on time variables.

  $\backslash Nec^{\prec}(x)$ consists of the set of events that may but need not necessarily execute strictly before x, *i.e.*, they can also execute at the same time as or after x. Let $P(x)$

---

[1]For a consumption event, $q < 0$ and thus, q_{max} really corresponds to the smallest consumption of the event.

denote the set of production events in $Poss^{\preceq}(x) \setminus Nec^{\prec}(x)$. The reasoning behind the deduction here is that if the maximal reservoir level of all events necessarily executed strictly before x is negative, then some production events in $P(x)$ need to be scheduled before x, more specifically x needs to be scheduled after a sufficient number of these production events to not have a negative reservoir level. More formally, let's rewrite (22.2) as follows:

$$L_{max}^{<}(x) = \sum_{y \in Nec^{\prec}(x)} q_{max}(y) + \sum_{y \in P \cap (Poss^{\preceq}(x) \setminus Nec^{\prec}(x))} q_{max}(y)$$

The first term of this equation is the sum of the maximal production and minimal consumption of the events that necessarily execute strictly before x, thus giving the maximal reservoir level. As $L_{max}^{<}(x) \geq 0$, we know that if this term is negative, it means that some production events in $P(x)$ will have to be executed strictly before x in order to produce at least:

$$\Delta_{min}^{<}(x) = - \sum_{y \in Nec^{\prec}(x)} q_{max}(y)$$

We suppose the production events $(y_1, \cdots, y_i, \cdots, y_p)$ in $P(x)$ are ordered by non-decreasing minimal time $t_{min}(y)$. $t_{min}(y)$ is either the earliest start time or earliest end time, depending on whether y is a start or end time. Let k be the index in $[1, p]$ such that:

$$\sum_{i=1}^{k-1} q_{max}(y_i) < \Delta_{min}^{<}(x) \leq \sum_{i=1}^{k} q_{max}(y_i)$$

If event x is executed at a date $t(x) \leq t_{min}(y_k)$, not enough producers will be able to execute strictly before x in order to ensure a positive level just before x. Thus, $t_{min}(y_k) + 1$ is a valid lower bound of $t(x)$.

- Discovering new precedence relations. There are cases where one can perform an even stronger propagation. $P(x)$ is again the set of production events in $Poss^{\preceq}(x)$ $Nec^{\prec}(x)$. If there is one production event y in $P(x)$ that is needed to produce before x to not get a negative reservoir level, a precedence relation can be deduced between y and x. So, suppose there exists a production event y in $P(x)$ such that:

$$\sum_{z \in P(x) \cap Poss^{\preceq}(y)} q_{max}(z) < \Delta_{min}^{<}(x)$$

Then, if we had $t(x) \leq t(y)$, we would see that again there is no way to produce $\Delta_{min}^{<}(x)$ before event x as the only events that could produce strictly before event x are the ones in $P(x) \cap Poss^{\preceq}(y)$. Thus, we can deduce the necessary precedence relation: $t(y) < t(x)$. Note that a weaker version of this propagation has been proposed in [16] that runs in $O(n^2)$ and does not analyze the precedence relations between the events of $P(x)$.

The balance algorithm can be executed for all the events x on a reservoir with a global worst-case complexity in $O(n^2)$ if the propagation that discovers new precedence relations is not turned on, and in $O(n^3)$ for a full propagation. In practice, there are many ways to shortcut this worst case and in particular, it has been noticed that the algorithmic cost of the extra propagation that discovers new precedence relations was in general negligible. Unlike all the other propagation algorithms we have seen in this section 22.3, the balance constraint cannot directly be applied in planning problems because it assumes that the set or producer and consumer events is completely known. The extension of the balance constraint to planning problems is discussed in [41].

22.4   Constraint Propagation on Optimization Criteria

As said in Section 22.1.5, the commonly used way of modeling an objective function is by introducing a variable *criterion* that is constrained to be equal to the value of the objective function. In cases where the objective function F is a function of the end variables of the activities and F is a maximum such as $C_{\max}$ or $T_{\max}$, considering the objective constraint and the resource constraints independently is not a problem. Indeed, the upper bound on *criterion* is directly propagated on the end time of each activity, *i.e.*, latest end times are tightened efficiently.

The situation is more complex for sum functions such as $\sum w_i C_i$, $\sum w_i T_i$, or $\sum w_i U_i$, and for objective functions that are not a function of the end variables of the activities like sum of setup times and sum of setup costs. For several of these cases, dedicated constraint propagation techniques have been developed often taking the resource constraints and the objective function simultaneously into account.

In this section we describe such dedicated constraint propagation techniques for two objective functions in more detail: weighted number of late activities ($\sum w_i U_i$) and sum of setup times and setup costs. For more general considerations on cost-based constraint propagation we refer to [28].

22.4.1   Weighted Number of Late Activities

In this section we pay attention to constraint propagation for the objective function $\sum w_i U_i$, i.e., minimizing the weighted number of late activities, as described in [5].

The basis for this constraint propagation is formed by calculating a good lower bound on the weighted number of late activities. Such a lower bound is obviously also a lower bound for the variable *criterion*. Relaxing non-preemption is a well-known technique to obtain good lower bounds in scheduling. Unfortunately, the preemptive problem remains NP-Hard. A "relaxed preemptive lower bound", *i.e.*, a slightly stronger relaxation than the preemptive relaxation, can be used. As explained below, it can be computed in $O(n^2 \log n)$.

Let us recall a well-known result for the One-Machine Scheduling Problem (*i.e.*, the problem of scheduling activities on a unary resource). Its preemptive relaxation is polynomial and has the very interesting property that there exists a feasible preemptive schedule if and only if over any interval $[t_1, t_2)$, the sum of the processing times of the activities in $\{A_i \mid [t_1 \leq r_i] \wedge [d_i \leq t_2]\}$ is at most $t_2 - t_1$. It is well-known that relevant values for t_1 and t_2 are respectively the release dates and the deadlines [8].

A decision variable x_i per activity is introduced that equals 1 when the activity is on-time and 0 otherwise. Notice that if $d_i \leq \delta_i$, A_i is on-time in any solution, *i.e.*, $x_i = 1$ In such a case we adjust the value of δ_i to d_i (this has no impact on solutions) so that due dates are always smaller than or equal to deadlines. We also assume that there is a preemptive schedule that meets all deadlines (if not, the resource constraint does not hold and a backtrack occurs). The following Mixed Integer Program (MIP) [64] computes the minimum weighted number of late activities in the preemptive case:

$$\min \sum_1^n w_i(1 - x_i)$$

$$u.c. \quad \begin{cases} \forall_{t_1} \; \forall_{t_2 > t_1} \; \sum_{S(t_1,t_2)} p_i + \sum_{P(t_1,t_2)} p_i x_i \leq t_2 - t_1 \\ \forall_{i \in \{1,\dots,n\}} \; x_i \in \{0,1\} \end{cases} \quad (22.3)$$

where $S(t_1, t_2)$ is the set of activities that are sure to execute between t_1 and t_2 and where $P(t_1, t_2)$ is the set of activities that are preferred to execute between t_1 and t_2.

$$\begin{aligned} S(t_1, t_2) &= \{A_i \mid r_i \geq t_1 \wedge d_i \leq t_2\} \\ P(t_1, t_2) &= \{A_i \mid r_i \geq t_1 \wedge d_i > t_2 \wedge \delta_i \leq t_2\} \end{aligned}$$

Actually, it is easy to see that the relevant values of t_1 correspond to the release dates and those of t_2 to the due dates and deadlines. Hence, there are $O(n^2)$ constraints in the MIP. We now focus on the *continuous relaxation* of (22.3) in which for any activity A_i such that $r_i + p_i > \delta_i$, *i.e.*, for any late activity, the constraint $x_i = 0$ is added.

$$\min \sum_1^n w_i(1 - x_i)$$

$$u.c. \quad \begin{cases} \forall_{t_1 \in \{r_i\}} \; \forall_{t_2 \in \{d_i\} \cup \{\delta_i\} \mid t_2 > t_1} \; \sum_{S(t_1,t_2)} p_i + \sum_{P(t_1,t_2)} p_i x_i \leq t_2 - t_1 \\ \forall_i \; r_i + p_i > \delta_i \Rightarrow x_i = 0 \\ \forall_{i \in \{1,\dots,n\}} \; x_i \in [0, 1] \end{cases} \quad (22.4)$$

The linear program (22.4) can be solved with an LP solver and we can use reduced costs to prove that some activities can, must or cannot end before their due date. In [5] an $O(n^2 \log n)$ algorithm is described solving the same problem.

22.4.2   Sum of Setup Times and Sum of Setup Costs

In this section we pay attention to constraint propagation of setup time and setup cost constraints. We discuss the constraint propagation as described in [30]. We also refer to [29, 28] that extend work of Brucker and Thiele [7] in the context of CP. To simplify the presentation, we only consider the case where there are no cumulative resources. We do include the possible presence of alternative resources (see Section 22.1.4).

The basis for the constraint propagation of setup times and setup costs described in this section is formed by using a *routing problem* as a relaxation of the scheduling problem. In this problem, one has a set of *start* nodes, a set of *internal* nodes, and a set of *end* nodes. Each internal node i represents an activity A_i. When having m alternative machines, one is looking for m disjoint *routes* or *paths* in the graph defined by these three sets. Each route corresponds to a different machine, starting in the start node of the machine, traversing a sequence of internal nodes, and ending in the end node of the machine. More precisely, let $I = \{1, \ldots, n\}$ be a set of n nodes, and $E = \{n + 1, \ldots, n + m\}$ and $S = \{n + m + 1, \ldots, n + 2 * m\}$ two sets of m nodes. Nodes in I represent internal nodes, nodes in S represent start nodes, and nodes in E represent end nodes. A global constraint is defined ensuring that m different routes $\rho_1, \ldots, \rho_m$ exist such that all internal nodes are visited exactly once by a route starting from a node in S and ending in a node in E. Start nodes $n + m + 1, \ldots, n + 2 * m$ belong to routes $\rho_1, \ldots, \rho_m$, respectively. End nodes $n + 1, \ldots, n + m$ belong to routes $\rho_1, \ldots, \rho_m$, respectively. Moreover, sets of possible routes can be associated to each internal node.

In the CP model three variables per node are defined. Variables $next_i$ and $prev_i$ identify the nodes visited directly after and directly before node i, respectively. Variables $route_i$ identify the route node i belongs to. Variables $next_i$ and $prev_i$ take their values in $\{1, \ldots, n + 2m\}$. Variables $route_i$ take their values in $\{1, \ldots, m\}$. Each start and end node has its route variable bound, *i.e.*, $route_{n+1} = 1, \ldots, route_{n+m} = m$, $route_{n+m+1} = 1$, $\ldots, route_{n+2m} = m$. In order to have a uniform treatment of all nodes inside the constraint, each start node $n + m + u$ has its $prev_{n+m+u}$ variable bound to the corresponding end node ($prev_{n+m+u} = n + u$), and each end node $n + u$ has its $next_{n+u}$ variable bound to the corresponding start node ($next_{n+u} = n + m + u$). There furthermore exists a setup cost c_{ij}^u that expresses that if node j is visited directly after node i on a route u ($next_i = j, route_i = route_j = u$), a cost c_{ij}^u is induced. A feasible solution is defined as an assignment of distinct values to each next variable, while avoiding sub-tours (tours containing only internal nodes), and respecting the constraints

$$next_i = j \iff prev_j = i$$
$$next_i = j \implies route_i = route_j$$

The problem is then to find an optimal feasible solution, *i.e.*, a feasible solution that minimizes

$$\sum_{i=1}^{n} c_{i\,next_i}^u \tag{22.5}$$

As said, the routing problem described constitutes a relaxation of the global scheduling problem. If an internal node i has its next variable assigned to another internal node j, activity A_i directly precedes activity A_j. If an internal node i has its next variable assigned to an ending node $n+u$, activity A_i is the last activity scheduled on machine R_u. The setup cost function c_{ij}^u of the routing problem corresponds to the setup times $setup(A_i, A_j, R_u)$ or setup costs $setupCost(A_i, A_j, R_u)$ between activities (see Section 22.1.4). As such the minimization of the total setup cost (22.5) in the routing problem corresponds to the minimization of the sum of setup times or setup costs in the scheduling problem.

Route optimization constraint

One of the basic ideas of the constraint propagation in [30] is to create a global constraint having a propagation algorithm aimed at removing those assignments from variable domains which do not improve the best solution found so far. Domain reduction is achieved by optimally solving an Assignment Problem [22] which is a relaxation of the routing problem described and thus also of the global scheduling problem. The Assignment Problem is the graph theory problem of finding a set of disjoint sub-tours such that all the vertices in a graph are visited and the overall cost is minimized.

In the routing problem we look for a set of m disjoint routes each of them starting from a start node and ending in the corresponding end node covering all nodes in a graph, *i.e.*, considering that each end node is connected to the corresponding start node, we look for a set of m disjoint tours each of them containing a start node. This problem can be formulated as an Assignment Problem on the graph defined by the set of nodes in the routing problem and the set of arcs (i, j) such that $j \in domain(next_i)$. The cost on arc (i, j) is the minimal setup cost (or time), *i.e.*,

$$\min_{u \in domain(route_i) \cap domain(route_j)} setupCost(A_i, A_j, R_u).$$

The value of the optimal solution of the Assignment Problem is obviously a lower bound on the value of the optimal solution of the routing problem. The *primal-dual* algorithm described in [34] provides an optimal integer solution for the Assignment Problem. Besides this optimal assignment with the corresponding lower bound LB on the original problem, a reduced cost matrix $\bar{c}$ is obtained. Each $\bar{c}_{ij}$ estimates the additional cost to be added to LB if variable $next_i$ takes the value j. These results can be used both in constraint propagation as in the definition of search heuristics. The lower bound LB is trivially linked to the *criterion* variable representing the objective function through the constraint $LB \leq criterion$. More interesting is the propagation based on reduced costs. Given the reduced cost matrix $\bar{c}$, it is known that $LB_{next_i=j} = LB + \bar{c}_{ij}$ is a valid lower bound for the problem where $next_i$ takes the value j. Therefore we can impose

$$LB_{next_i=j} > ub(criterion) \Rightarrow next_i \neq j$$

For more details on the use of reduced costs for setup constraints we refer to [30]. We remark that reduced cost fixing appears to be particularly suited for CP. In fact, while reduced cost fixing is extensively used in OR frameworks, it is usually not exploited to trigger other constraints, but only in the following lower bound computation, *i.e.*, the following node in the search tree. When embedded in a CP framework, the reduced cost fixing produces domain reductions which usually trigger propagation from other constraints in the problem through shared variables.

Precedence graph constraint

Linking the routing model and the scheduling model is done thanks to a *precedence graph constraint*. This constraint maintains for each machine R_u an extended precedence graph G_u that allows to represent and propagate temporal relations between pairs of activities on the machine as well as to dynamically compute the transitive closure of those relations. More precisely, G_u is a graph whose vertices are the alternative activities A_i^u that may execute on machine R_u (see Section 22.1.4). A node A_i^u is said to *surely contribute* if machine R_u is the only possible machine on which A_i can be processed. Otherwise, if activity A can also be processed on other machines, the node A_i^u is said to *possibly contribute*. Two kinds of edges are represented on G_u:

- A *precedence edge* between two alternative activities $A_i^u \rightarrow A_j^u$ means that if machine R_u is chosen for both activities A_i and A_j, then A_j will have to be processed after A_i on R_u.

- A *next edge* between two alternative activities $A_i^u \Rightarrow A_j^u$ means that if machine R_u is chosen for both activities A_i and A_j then A_j will have to be processed directly after A_i on R_u. No activity may be processed on R_u between A_i and A_j.

The first role of the precedence graph is to incrementally maintain the closure of this graph when new edges or vertices are inserted, *i.e.*, to deduce new edges given the ones already present in the graph. The following five rules [30] are used by the precedence graph:

1. If $A_i^u \rightarrow A_j^u$, $A_j^u \rightarrow A_i^u$, and A_i^u surely contributes then A_j^u does not contribute (Incompatibility rule).

2. If $A_i^u \rightarrow A_l^u$, $A_l^u \rightarrow A_j^u$, and A_l^u surely contributes then $A_i^u \rightarrow A_j^u$ (Transitive closure through contributor).

3. If $A_l^u \Rightarrow A_i^u$, $A_l^u \rightarrow A_j^u$, and A_l^u surely contributes then $A_i^u \rightarrow A_j^u$ (Next-edge closure on the left).

4. If $A_j^u \Rightarrow A_l^u$, $A_i^u \rightarrow A_l^u$, and A_l^u surely contributes then $A_i^u \rightarrow A_j^u$ (Next-edge closure on the right).

5. If for all A_l^u either $A_l^u \rightarrow A_i^u$ or $A_j^u \rightarrow A_l^u$ then $A_i^u \Rightarrow A_j^u$ (Next-edge finding).

New edges are added on the precedence graph G_u by the scheduling constraints (precedence and resource constraints) and by the route optimization constraint (whenever a variable $next_i$ is bound a new next-edge is added). Besides computing the incremental closure, the precedence graph also incrementally maintains the set of activities that are possibly next to a given activity A_i^u given the current topology of G_u. As such it allows to effectively reduce the domain of the variables $next_i$ and $prev_i$. Furthermore, the precedence graph constraint propagates the current set of precedence relations expressed on G_u on the start and end variables of activities.

22.5 Heuristic Search

The general principles around search in CP apply to both the planning and scheduling domain:

- Since for complexity reasons constraint propagation cannot remove all impossible values from the domains of variables, heuristic search is required to generate a solution to the problem instance under consideration.

- Once a solution with a given cost is found, this heuristic search can be either continued or restarted with an additional constraint stating that only solutions with a lower cost are searched for. In the case of multiple criteria, this additional constraint can be replaced by a set of constraints authorizing the solution to deteriorate for some criteria if it improves for others.

- Some variables are more constrained than others, depending on the problem instance: some activities lie on a critical path of the precedence graph, some resources are more heavily loaded than others, etc. Focusing on the more constrained variables first is more likely to quickly lead to a solution.

However, the significance of temporal and resource constraints makes it possible to use these principles in domain-specific manners. Let us first consider the case of the pure Job Shop Scheduling Problem [33]. The variables of the problem are basically just the start and end times of activities and the *criterion* variable representing the makespan ($C_{\max}$) Temporal constraints relating these variables are propagated in a perfect manner, *i.e.*, the earliest and latest start and end times resulting from constraint propagation guarantee that the temporal constraints are satisfied. The only remaining constraints are the resource constraints. As there are only unary resources, no two activities A_i and A_j requiring the same resource can overlap in time, *i.e.*, either A_i precedes A_j or A_j precedes A_i (see Section 22.3.1). Following this basic observation, rather than attempting to instantiate the start and end variables, an appealing and often much more efficient strategy consists in deciding in which order activities shall execute, *i.e.*, whether A_i shall execute before A_j or A_j before A_i.

Although it is less immediate, the same type of branching strategy can also be considered for cumulative resources. Indeed, whenever n non-preemptible activities are such that the sum of the capacities required exceeds the available capacity (for a given resource), at least two of these activities cannot overlap in time, and hence must be ordered. An alternative but equivalent view consists in considering a cumulative resource R of capacity $cap(R)$ as a set of $cap(R)$ "lines" of capacity 1, on which activities cannot overlap. Hence, if the activities can be organized along at most c sequences such that (i) an activity A_i requiring capacity $cap(A_i)$ appears in $cap(A_i)$ sequences and (ii) activities in each sequence are totally ordered by temporal constraints, then the satisfaction of the temporal constraints guarantees the satisfaction of the resource constraint.

In practice, the right branching strategy also depends on the optimization criterion (or multiple criteria) to optimize:

- An optimization criterion to minimize is called "regular" if it increases with the end times of the activities. In other terms, a solution S cannot be strictly better than another solution S' if no activity A_i finishes earlier in S than in S'. Examples of regular criteria include the makespan, the average completion time of the activities, the maximal or weighted tardiness of activities, the weighted number of late activities. When the optimization criterion is regular, it is particularly appropriate to solve the resource constraints by ordering activities: on any given branch of the search tree, the value of the criterion obtained by replacing each end time variable by its lower bound is a lower bound for the optimization function. In addition, if at a given node the earliest start and end times satisfy all the constraints of the problem (which is the case for resource constraints if they have been replaced by appropriate temporal constraints and these temporal constraints have been propagated), then these earliest start and end times provide the best solution attainable from this node. "Dominance properties" can also be applied to prune some nodes: whenever it can be shown that for any schedule attainable from a node, an equivalent or better schedule is attainable from another node, the first node can be discarded. For example, if a partial schedule contains a hole on a resource (an interval of time over which it can be shown that no activity requiring the resource can execute), and an activity is scheduled after the hole for no good reason, then the node can be discarded since another branch will lead to a schedule in which this activity (or another) occupies the hole [48].

- An optimization criterion is called "sequence-dependent" if it depends only on the relative order in which activities are executed. Typical example are of course the sum of setup times and the sum of setup costs. When optimizing sequence-dependent criteria, it is once again particularly appropriate to solve the resource constraints by ordering activities: once activities are sequenced, the earliest start and end times that result from constraint propagation can be used as a solution. Note however that the dominance properties that exist for regular criteria cannot be applied to sequence-dependent criteria: for example, it might be worth leaving a hole in a schedule by executing a specific activity later if it enables to save a costly setup.

- Other optimization criteria are more difficult to optimize. For example, work in process time, *i.e.*, the average difference between the end time of the last activity composing a given job and the start time of the first activity of the job, is an irregular criterion which is difficult to optimize as the first activity of each job shall be executed as late as possible while the last activity of each job shall be executed as early as possible. Storage costs, in particular the cost of storing intermediate products, are difficult to optimize for the same reason. In such cases, it is not sufficient to sequence the activities. It is however often the case that once the resource constraints have been solved by sequencing activities, a linear program can be used to determine the optimal solution for the chosen sequences. Hybrid algorithms based on both CP and Mixed Integer Programming (MIP) [64] can be used for this purpose [2].

22.5.1 The Use of Local Search

Even when search can be simplified by looking for good sequences and using dominance properties, search spaces for planning or scheduling problems tend to be very large. In practice, it is often impossible to explore a search space completely and guarantee the delivery of an optimal solution. For an industrial planning or scheduling application it however generally suffices to provide "good" solutions within reasonable time. It is for such applications more important to be robust with respect to variations in the problem instances like variations in problem size, variations in numerical characteristics, and addition of side constraints. This is often achieved by mixing constraint-based tree search with Local Search (LS) or by actually implementing LS with constraints. Local search is taken as an alternative way to explore the search space. Explored neighborhoods vary a lot from an application to another, so it is difficult to establish a general taxonomy of the approaches reported in the literature. We will use two examples to convey the basic ideas.

Caseau and Laburthe [13] describe an algorithm for the Job Shop Scheduling Problem which combines CP and LS. The overall algorithm finds an approximate solution to start with, makes local changes and repairs on it to quickly decrease the makespan and, finally, performs an exhaustive search for decreasing makespans. Given a schedule, a critical path is defined as a sequence of activities where i) for each activity A_i that appears before activity A_j in the sequence A_i indeed precedes A_j in the schedule and ii) the sum of the processing times of the activities in the sequence equals the makespan of the schedule. Two types of local moves are considered:

- "Repair" moves swap two activities scheduled on the same machine to shrink or reduce the number of critical paths.

- "Shuffle" moves [1] keep part of the solution and search through the rest of the solution space to complete it. Each shuffle move is implemented as a constraint-based search algorithm with a limited number of backtracks (typically 10, progressively increased to 100 or 1000), under the constraint that the makespan of the solution must be improved (with a given improvement step, typically 1% of the makespan, progressively decreased to one time unit).

Excellent computational results have been obtained with this approach [13, 14] as well as with other constraint-based implementations of shuffle moves, as reported in [4, 55].

In the same spirit, the best algorithm used by Le Pape and Baptiste [46] for the Preemptive Job Shop Scheduling Problem relies on the combination of:

- a strong constraint propagation algorithm (edge-finding);

- a local optimization operator called "Jackson derivation";

- limited discrepancy search [38] around the best schedule found so far.

Limited discrepancy search is an alternative to depth-first search, which relies on the assumption that a heuristic makes few mistakes throughout the search. Thus, considering the path from the root node of the tree to the first solution found by a depth-first search algorithm, there should be few "wrong turns" (*i.e.*, few nodes which were not immediately selected by the heuristic). The basic idea is to restrict the search to paths that do not diverge more than w times from the choices recommended by the heuristic. Each time this limited search fails to improve on the best current schedule, w is incremented and the process is iterated, until either a better solution is found or it is proven that there is no better solution. It is easy to prove that when w gets large enough, limited discrepancy search is complete. Yet it can be seen as a form of LS around the recommendation of the heuristic. On ten well-known problem instances, each with 100 activities, experimental results show that each of the three techniques mentioned above brings improvements in efficiency, the average deviation to optimal solutions after 10 minutes of CPU time falling from 13.72% when none of these techniques is used to 0.23% when they are all employed.

Globally, the integration of LS and CP is promising whenever LS operators provide a good basis for the exploration of the search space and either side constraints or effective constraint propagation algorithms can be used to prune the search space. The examples presented in the literature represent a significant step toward the understanding of the possible combinations of LS and CP. Yet the definition of a general approach and methodology for integrating LS and CP remains an important area of research.

22.5.2 The Use of Mixed Integer Programming

In industrial applications, scheduling issues are often mixed with resource allocation, capacity planning, or inventory management issues for which MIP is a method of choice.

Several examples have been reported where a hybrid combination of CP and MIP was shown to be more efficient than pure CP or MIP models (cf., for example, [60, 61, 63, 2, 19, 43]). As in the case of local search, there are many ways to combine CP and MIP, and we will just focus on two particular examples.

A dynamic scheduling problem is solved in [63]. In this example, the linear solver includes only temporal constraints (some of which have been added to the initial problem in order to ensure the satisfaction of resource constraints) and the definition of the optimization criterion as the total deviation of start times of activities from the start times of the same activities in a reference schedule. An interesting characteristic of this model is that the optimal continuous solution of the linear sub-problem is guaranteed to be integral; hence, either this solution satisfies all the resource constraints and it is optimal, or it violates some resource constraint which can be used to branch on the order of two conflicting activities. CP is used to limit and select the explored branches.

[19] and [43] consider the case in which it is not certain that an activity will use a given resource, either because there are alternative resources, or because the activity can be left unperformed against a certain cost (see Section 22.1.4). We recall that an unperformed activity will not require capacity, but will obey potential temporal constraints, etc., and will also obey the calendar of the chosen resource. [19, 43] do not consider resource calendars, so an unperformed activity requires its normal processing time to be completed. Note that to our knowledge no MIP approach exists that handles resource calendars.

Also without resource calendars this problem is already challenging for any optimization technique. MIP is a good candidate for representing the cost function, but no good MIP model is known to state that a resource can only perform one activity at a time. CP usually deals well with precedence and resource constraints, but adding an upper bound on the optimization criterion does in general not result in effective constraint propagation. LS operators based on permuting activities are easy to design, but the impact of a permutation on the total cost is hard to estimate. In [19], several cooperative optimization algorithms centered on a MIP model have been proposed and compared with a pre-existing combination of CP and LS:

- The MIP algorithm relies on the default search strategy of CPLEX 9.0 [39].

- The IS+MIP algorithm consists in using CP to construct an initial solution to the problem. This solution is then used as a starting point for CPLEX.

- The IS+MIP+RINS algorithm is similar to IS+MIP but activates the relaxation induced neighborhood search option of CPLEX [20]. Relaxation induced neighborhood search is a form of LS which relies on the continuous relaxation to define a neighborhood of the current solution: the integer variables that have the same values in the solution of the continuous relaxation and in the best solution known so far are fixed to these values and a sub-MIP on the remaining variables is solved (with a limit on the number of nodes explored).

- The IS+MIP+RINS+GD algorithm adds the guided dives option of CPLEX [20] to the IS+MIP+RINS algorithm. When a variable is selected for branching, the "guided dives" strategy will explore first the node in which this variable is fixed to the value that it takes in the best solution known so far.

- The IS+MIP+RINS+GD+MCORE algorithm adds to the IS+MIP+RINS+GD algorithm another form of LS which defines a neighborhood by heuristically reducing the values of "big-M" coefficients of the MIP model.

These algorithms have been tested on 22 job shop instances from the Manufacturing Scheduling Library (MaScLib) [58], with up to 260 activities. The results have shown the interest of all the components that have been added to the initial MIP algorithm. They also show that on pure problems, hybrid algorithms based on MIP can compete with state-of-the-art techniques.

The generalization of these examples into a principled approach is an important research issue for the forthcoming years. In particular, MIP models are often difficult to extend to the representation of additional constraints such as setup times and costs, calendars, etc.

22.6 Conclusions

In the introduction of this chapter we have seen that one of the key factors of the success of Constraint-Based Scheduling lies in the fact that a powerful combination was found of the research fields of Operations Research (OR) and Artificial Intelligence (AI). From OR its efficient algorithms and its culture for searching for efficient algorithms were used. From AI the general modeling and problem-solving paradigm of CP and its culture for searching for natural ways of modeling a problem in the needed real-life detail were used.

In this way Constraint-Based Scheduling preserves the general modeling and problem-solving paradigm of CP while the integration of efficient propagation algorithms improves the overall performance of the approach. Efficient OR algorithms integrated in a CP approach allow the user to benefit from the efficiency of OR techniques in a flexible framework. Although the use of CP in planning is, due to the problem complexity, less mature than its use in scheduling, Constraint-Based Planning follows the same pattern as Constraint-Based Scheduling where CP is used as a framework for integrating efficient special purpose algorithms into a flexible and expressive paradigm. As in several other areas of application, an important way to integrate efficient algorithms in CP for scheduling and planning was found by incorporating them inside global constraints. Sections 22.3 and 22.4 pay attention to such constraint propagation.

Besides the powerful propagation, another strength was identified namely the capacity to in a natural and flexible way model the scheduling or planning problem at hand in the required real-life detail. We want to stress that this capacity is becoming more and more important. Indeed through the widespread adoption of ERP (Enterprise Resource Planning) systems, more and more companies have access to the data that allows them to capture the reality in the detail they need. One of the reasons Advanced Planning and Scheduling systems (APS's) are not as widely adopted as one would think following this observation, is that these offerings often fail to model reality in sufficient detail. This leads to the aforementioned classical drawbacks of one being forced to discard degrees of freedom and side constraints. It's especially on the side constraints that APS's tend to be weak, thus leading to the system solving an oversimplified problem resulting in producing impractical solutions for the original problem. It is here that we believe Constraint-Based Planning and Scheduling have a great, largely unused, potential.

Two other strengths identified in this chapter are i) a natural fit of expressing scheduling specific heuristics using CP tree search, and ii) a proven good potential of combining the CP approach with solution techniques as Local Search, Large Neighborhood Search, and Mixed Integer Programming. We have seen several examples of this in Section 22.5. These strengths are thus about having the flexibility in the approach to adapt the search such that the needed performance to solve the problems is obtained. Although this has indeed been a strength over the years, we want to stress that we believe the field should pay increased attention to providing good default search, *i.e.*, a search procedure that works "out-of-the-box" at least for a certain class of problems. This is much like a lot of the work done in the area of Mixed Integer Programming. That latter work has led to a broadening of the audience that can use Mixed Integer Programming to solve their problems. A similar effect should be obtained for CP in general and Constraint-Based Planning and Scheduling in particular. This, combined with the natural way of modeling problems present in CP, should open up CP for a much broader use than today.

Another main research challenge is on doing planning and scheduling under uncertainty. Uncertainty is inherent to planning and scheduling environments and correctly dealing with it is of invaluable practical importance. Two basic ways for dealing with uncertainty, together with different combination of them, have been studied: reactive (rescheduling) and proactive (robust scheduling). Lots of research has been done starting many years ago but surprisingly few approaches have been applied in practice. We feel the field is ripe to adopt rescheduling and robust scheduling more broadly and believe CP can play an important role there.

Further, more detailed, research challenges link back to the strengths already mentioned. It remains a challenge to study industrial properties in detail. Studies around breakable activities, productivity profiles, continuous production and consumption, unperformed activities, etc., are rare while there is a great need in practice to correctly handle such properties.

In Section 22.4 constraint propagation methods related to the minimization of the weighted number of late activities and to the minimization of setup times and setup costs have been presented. They drastically improve the behavior on problems involving these criteria. However, there are many other interesting optimization criteria. In particular, total tardiness is widely used in industry but until now poor results are obtained on this problem. Constraint propagation on such specific optimization criteria constitutes a very interesting research area. Following the observation that users of planning and scheduling applications often want to define their own criteria, a possibly even more interesting research challenge is to design generic lower-bounding techniques and constraint propagation algorithms that could work for any criterion.

Finally, a research challenge in Constraint-Based Planning is to still better exploit the combination of AI and OR, *i.e.*, to continue to follow the same pattern as Constraint-Based Scheduling where CP is used as a framework for integrating efficient special purpose algorithms into a flexible and expressive paradigm. This will bring all the strengths of Constraint-Based Scheduling mentioned in this chapter to Constraint-Based Planning.

Bibliography

[1] D. Applegate and W. Cook. A computational study of the job-shop scheduling problem. *ORSA Journal on Computing*, 3(2):149–156, 1991.

[2] Ph. Baptiste and S. Demassey. Tight LP bounds for resource constrained project scheduling. *OR Spektrum*, 26:251–262, 2004.

[3] Ph. Baptiste and C. Le Pape. Edge-finding constraint propagation algorithms for disjunctive and cumulative scheduling. In *Proc. 15th Workshop of the U.K. Planning Special Interest Group*, 1996.

[4] Ph. Baptiste, C. Le Pape, and W. Nuijten. Incorporating efficient operations research algorithms in constraint-based scheduling. In *Proc. 1st International Joint Workshop on Artificial Intelligence and Operations Research*, 1995.

[5] Ph. Baptiste, C. Le Pape, and W. Nuijten. *Constraint-Based Scheduling: Applying Constraint Programming to Scheduling Problems*. Kluwer Academic Publishers, 2001.

[6] A. Blum and M. Furst. Fast Planning Through Planning Graph Analysis. *Artificial Intelligence*, 90(1-2):281–300, 1997.

[7] P. Brucker and O. Thiele. A branch and bound method for the general shop problem with sequence dependent setup-times. *OR Spektrum*, 18:145–161, 1996.

[8] J. Carlier. *Problèmes d'Ordonnancement à Contraintes de Ressources : Algorithmes et Complexité*. Thèse de doctorat d'Etat, Université Paris VI, 1984. In French.

[9] J. Carlier and E. Pinson. An algorithm for solving the job-shop problem. *Management Science*, 35(2):164–176, 1989.

[10] J. Carlier and E. Pinson. A practical use of Jackson's preemptive schedule for solving the job shop problem. *Annals of Operations Research*, 26:269–287, 1990.

[11] J. Carlier and E. Pinson. Adjustment of heads and tails for the job-shop problem. *European Journal of Operational Research*, 78:146–161, 1994.

[12] Y. Caseau and F. Laburthe. Improved CLP scheduling with task intervals. In *Proc. 11th International Conference on Logic Programming*, 1994.

[13] Y. Caseau and F. Laburthe. Disjunctive scheduling with task intervals. Technical report, Ecole Normale Superieure, 1995.

[14] Y. Caseau, F. Laburthe, C. Le Pape, and B. Rottembourg. Combining local and global search in a constraint programming environment. *Knowledge Engineering Review* 16:41–68, 2001.

[15] A. Cesta and A. Oddi. Gaining efficiency and flexibility in the simple temporal problem. In *Third International Conference on Temporal Representation and Reasoning (TIME-96)*, 1996.

[16] A. Cesta and C. Stella. A time and resource problem for planning architectures. In *ECP-97*, 1997.

[17] D. Chapman. Planning for Conjunctive Goals. *Artificial Intelligence*, 33:333–377, 1987.

[18] S. Chien, G. Rabideau, R. Knight, R. Sherwood, B. Engelhardt, D. Mutz, T. Estlin, B. Smith, F. Fisher, T. Barrett, G. Stebbins, and D. Tran. ASPEN - Automating Space Mission Operations using Automated Planning and Scheduling. In *Proc. SpaceOps 2000*, 2000.

[19] E. Danna. *Intégration des techniques de recherche locale à la programmation linéaire en nombres entiers*. PhD thesis, Université d'Avignon et des Pays de Vaucluse, 2004.

In French.

[20] E. Danna, E. Rothberg, and C. Le Pape. Exploring relaxation induced neighborhoods to improve MIP solutions. *Mathematical Programming*, 102:71–90, 2005.

[21] R. Dechter, I. Meiri, and J. Pearl. Temporal constraint networks. *Artificial Intelligence*, 49(1-3):61–96, 1991.

[22] M. Dell'Amico and S. Martello. Linear assignment. In *Annotated Bibliographies in Combinatorial Optimization*. John Wiley and Sons, 1997.

[23] M.B. Do and S. Kambhampati. Planning as constraint satisfaction: Solving the planning graph by compiling it into CSP. *Artificial Intelligence*, 132(2):151–182, 2001.

[24] J. Erschler. *Analyse sous contraintes et aide à la décision pour certains problèmes d'ordonnancement*. Thèse de doctorat d'etat, Université Paul Sabatier, 1976.

[25] J. Erschler, P. Lopez, and C. Thuriot. Raisonnement temporel sous contraintes de ressource et problèmes d'ordonnacement. *Revue d'Intelligence Artificielle*, 5:7–32, 1991. In French.

[26] R. Fikes and N. Nilsson. STRIPS: a new approach to the application of theorem proving to problem solving. *Artificial Intelligence*, 2:189–208, 1971.

[27] R. W. Floyd. Algorithm 97: Shortest path. *Communications of the ACM*, 5(6):345, 1962.

[28] F. Focacci. *Solving Combinatorial Optimization Problems in Constraint Programming*. PhD thesis, Università di Ferrara, 2001.

[29] F. Focacci and W. Nuijten. A constraint propagation algorithm for scheduling with sequence dependent setup times. In *Proc. CPAIOR '00*, 2000.

[30] F. Focacci, P. Laborie, and W. Nuijten. Solving scheduling problems with setup times and alternative resources. In *Proc. Fifth International Conference on Artificial Intelligence Planning and Scheduling, AIPS'00*, pages 92–101. AAAI Press, 2000.

[31] M.S. Fox. Constraint-guided scheduling: A short history. *Computers in Industry*, 14: 79–88, 1990.

[32] J. Frank and A. Jónsson. Constraint-Based Attribute and Interval Planning. *Constraints*, 8(4):339–364, 2003.

[33] S. French. *Sequencing and Scheduling: An Introduction to the Mathematics of the Job-Shop*. Wiley & Sons, 1982.

[34] S. Martello G. Carpaneto and P. Toth. Algorithms and code for the assignment problem. *Annals of Operations Research*, 13:193–223, 1988.

[35] M. Ghallab and H. Laruelle. Representation and control in IxTeT, a temporal planner. In *Proc. AIPS-94*, pages 61–67, 1994.

[36] M. Ghallab, D. Nau, and P. Traverso. *Automated Planning: Theory and Practice*. Morgan Kaufmann, 2004.

[37] M. Gondran and M. Minoux. *Graphs and Algorithms*. John Wiley and Sons, 1984.

[38] W. Harvey and M. Ginsberg. Limited discrepancy search. In *Proc. 14th International Joint Conference on Artificial Intelligence*, 1995.

[39] ILOG CPLEX. *ILOG CPLEX 9.0 User's Manual and Reference Manual*. ILOG, S.A., Gentilly, France, 2003.

[40] A. Jonsson, P. Morris, N. Muscettola, K. Rajan, and B. Smith. Planning in Interplanetary Space: Theory and Practice. In *Proc. AIPS-00*, 2000.

[41] P. Laborie. Algorithms for propagation resource constraints in AI planning and scheduling: Existing approaches and new results. *Artificial Intelligence*, 143:151–188, 2003.

[42] P. Laborie and M. Ghallab. Planning with sharable resource constraints. In *Proc. IJCAI-95*, pages 1643–1649, 1995.

[43] C. Le Pape. Experiments with cooperative optimization algorithms for production scheduling. In *Proc. Oberwolfach Workshop on Mathematics in the Supply Chain* 2004.

[44] C. Le Pape. *Des systèmes d'ordonnancement flexibles et opportunistes*. PhD thesis, University Paris XI, 1988. In French.

[45] C. Le Pape. Implementation of resource constraints in ILOG Schedule: A library for the development of constraint-based scheduling systems. *Intelligent Systems Engineering*, 3(2):55–66, 1994.

[46] C. Le Pape and Ph. Baptiste. Heuristic control of a constraint-based algorithm for the preemptive job-shop scheduling problem. *Journal of Heuristics*, 5:305–325, 1999.

[47] C. Le Pape and S. F. Smith. Management of Temporal Constraints for Factory Scheduling. In F. Bodart C. Roland and M. Léonard, editors, *Temporal Aspects in Information Systems*. North-Holland, 1988.

[48] C. Le Pape, P. Couronné, D. Vergamini, and V. Gosselin. Time-versus-capacity compromises in project scheduling. *AISB Quarterly*, 91:19–31, 1995.

[49] O. Lhomme. Consistency techniques for numeric CSPs. In *Proc. 13th International Joint Conference on Artificial Intelligence*, 1993.

[50] H. C. R. Lock. An implementation of the cumulative constraint. Working Paper, University of Karlsruhe, 1996.

[51] A. Lopez and F. Bacchus. Generalizing GraphPlan by Formulating Planning as a CSP. In *Proc. IJCAI-03*, pages 954–960, 2004.

[52] P.D. Martin and D.B. Shmoys. A new approach to computing optimal schedules for the job shop scheduling problem. In S.T. McCormick W.H. Curnigham and M. Queyranne, editors, *Proc. Fifth International IPCO conference, Vancouver, Canada*, pages 389–403. LNCS 1084, 1996.

[53] D. McAllester and D. Rosenblitt. Systematic Nonlinear Planning. In *Proc. AAAI-91* pages 634–639, 1991.

[54] W. Nuijten. *Time and Resource Constrained Scheduling: A Constraint Satisfaction Approach*. PhD thesis, Eindhoven University of Technology, 1994.

[55] W. Nuijten and C. Le Pape. Constraint-based job shop scheduling with ILOG Scheduler. *Journal of Heuristics*, 3:271–286, 1998.

[56] W.P.M. Nuijten, E.H.L. Aarts, D.A.A. van Erp Taalman Kip, and K.M. van Hee. Job shop scheduling by constraint satisfaction. Computing Science Note 93/39, Eindhoven University of Technology, 1993.

[57] W. Nuijten and F. Sourd. New time-bound adjustment techniques for shop scheduling. In *Proc. PMS 2000*, pages 224–226, 2000.

[58] W. Nuijten, T. Bousonville, F. Focacci, D. Godard, and C. Le Pape. Towards an industrial manufacturing scheduling problem and test bed. In *Proc. 9th International Conference on Project Management and Scheduling*, pages 162–165, 2004.

[59] L. Peridy. *Le problème de job-shop : arbitrage et ajustements*. PhD thesis, Universit de Technologie de Compiègne, 1996. In French.

[60] R. Rodosek and M. Wallace. A generic model and hybrid algorithm for hoist scheduling problems. In *Proc. 4th International Conference on Principles and Practice of Constraint Programming*, 1998.

[61] R. Rodosek, M. Wallace, and M. T. Hajian. A new approach to integrating mixed inte-

ger programming and constraint logic programming. *Annals of Operations Research*, 86:63–87, 1999.

[62] E.D. Sacerdoti. A Structure for Plans and Behaviours. Technical Note 109, SRI, 1975.

[63] H. El Sakkout and M. Wallace. Probe backtrack search for minimal perturbation in dynamic scheduling. *Constraints*, 5:359–388, 2000.

[64] A. Schrijver. *Combinatorial Optimization*. Springer-Verlag, 2003.

[65] C. Schwindt. *Resource Allocation in Project Management*. Springer-Verlag, 2005.

[66] D.E. Smith, J. Frank, and A.K. Jonsson. Bridging the gap between planning and scheduling. *Knowledge Engineering Review*, 15(1), 2000.

[67] S. F. Smith. OPIS: A Methodology and Architecture for Reactive Scheduling. *Intelligent Scheduling*, 1994. M. Zweben and M. Fox (editors). Morgan Kaufmann.

[68] S.F. Smith and C.-C. Cheng. Slack-based heuristics for constraint satisfaction. In *Proc. 11th National Conference on Artificial Intelligence*, 1993.

[69] F. Sourd and W. Nuijten. Multiple-machine lower bounds for shop scheduling problems. *INFORMS Journal on Computing*, 12(4):341–352, 2000.

[70] G.L. Steele, Jr. *The Definition and Implementation of a Computer Programming Language Based on Constraints*. PhD thesis, Massachusetts Institute of Technology, 1980.

[71] Ph. Torres and P. Lopez. On not-first/not-last conditions in disjunctive scheduling. *European Journal of Operational Research*, 127:332–343, 2000.

[72] E. Tsang. *Foundations of Constraint Satisfaction*. Academic Press, 1993.

[73] P. van Beek and X. Chen. A constraint programming approach to planning. In *Proc. AAAI-99*, pages 585–590, 1999.

[74] C. Varnier, P. Baptiste, and B. Legeard. Le traitement des contraintes disjonctives dans un problème d'ordonnancement : exemple du hoist scheduling problem. In *Actes 2èmes journées francophones de programmation logique*, 1993.

[75] V. Vidal and H. Geffner. Branching and Pruning: An Optimal Temporal POCL Planner based on Constraint Programming. *Artificial Intelligence*, 2005. To appear.

[76] M. Vilain and H. Kautz. Constraint propagation algorithms for temporal reasoning. In *Proceedings of Fifth National Conference on Artificial Intelligence*, pages 377–382, 1986.

[77] P. Vilim. $O(n \log n)$ filtering algorithms for unary resource constraint. In *Proc. CPAIOR '04*, pages 319–334, 2004.

[78] P. Vilim, R. Bartak, and O. Cepek. Unary resource constraint with optional activities. In *Proc. CP 2004*, pages 62–76, 2004.

Handbook of Constraint Programming   801
Edited by F. Rossi, P. van Beek and T. Walsh
© 2006 Elsevier B.V. All rights reserved

Chapter 23

Vehicle Routing

Philip Kilby and Paul Shaw

This chapter looks a the use of Constraint Programming on an important industrial problem: that of constructing routes for vehicles to visit a set of customers at minimum cost, such as depicted in Figure 23.1. The methods are particularly aimed at the movement of people and goods by road.

This is a very important problem. In the USA in 2001, large trucking (6 or more tyres) logged more than two billion miles. Intercity trucking accounted for more than 1 trillion ton-miles of freight moved – 28% of the total freight ton-miles for the USA [15]. The costs of such movements are huge, so even small fractions of a percent in savings can have a substantial impact at a national level. Supply Chain Optimisation has become a key area for improvement by companies across the world, and vehicle operations will often play a key role in such a system.

The importance of the topic is reflected in the research interest. The literature on the

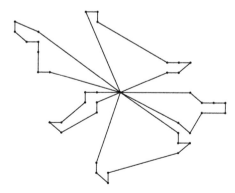

Figure 23.1: A Vehicle Routing Problem with 40 customers, 5 vehicles, and maximum 8 customers per vehicle.

topic is now very extensive – the variety of problems and solution methods explored is indicated in the surveys [111, 13, 14, 76, 35, 73].

An important factor in these problems is that no two companies will operate exactly alike – each has its own operational methods, and each brings their own constraints – like defined areas for drivers, vehicle/customer incompatibilities, and delivery time preferences. While traditional approaches capture the essence of the problem, a software system that is to deliver finished routes must be able to incorporate these myriad individual constraints.

Constraint Programming offers a valuable tool for specifying and solving these dirty, real-world problems. The ability to specify and add new constraints easily is very important.

We will begin by defining and formulating the VRP, and looking at some related problems. We then look at some of the methods employed to solve this problem – methods from the Operations Research literature, and those using a Constraint Programming formulation.

23.1   The Vehicle Routing Problem

The simplest Vehicle Routing Problem (VRP, also called the Capacitated Vehicle Routing Problem, CVRP) is defined formally as follows. The symbols defined here are summarised in Table 23.1 in Section 23.2.1.

A set of n customers is to be served by m vehicles. Each customer must be visited by exactly one vehicle. Customer i has demand r_i, and the sum of demands of customers assigned to vehicle k must be less than the vehicle capacity Q. All vehicles begin and end their route at a single depot.

The objective is to minimise the sum of travel costs, where the generalised cost of travelling from i to j is c_{ij}. Symmetric ($c_{ij} = c_{ji}$) and asymmetric variants exist. For brevity the models presented in this chapter assume symmetric costs, but are easily extended to the asymmetric case.

A number of extensions to the problem have been studied. In the VRP with heterogeneous fleet, vehicle capacities and cost of use differ. Multiple resource problems allow demands to be expressed in terms of a number of different resources l (r_i^l), and each vehicle has capacities specified in terms of each resource (Q_k^l). For example, both load and volume may be restricted in a vehicle, so must be accounted separately. A maximum dimension (for example length) may also be enforced.

The VRP with Time Windows (VRPTW) is often studied [13, 14]. A time window $[a_i, b_i]$ when delivery may commence is specified for each customer i, or multiple time windows may be specified. A vehicle arriving early is usually allowed to wait at the customer's location for the start of the time window. The addition of time constraints makes the problem much more difficult – even finding a feasible (let alone optimal) solution is $\mathcal{NP}$-hard [102].

An "open" version of the problem does not require the vehicle to return to the depot after the last customer. And finally, the multiple depot VRP allows vehicles to be housed at different depots. Usually the number of vehicles at each depot is given, although this may be a decision variable.

23.1.1 Side Constraints

A key feature of vehicle routing problems, as faced in industry, is the variety of constraints that can be added for individual companies. Examples include

- Particular vehicles may be physically constrained from visiting particular customers.

- Customers may have preferences for particular drivers.

- Drivers may have established but fuzzy delivery areas.

- A maximum time or length may be imposed on a route.

- A maximum time or distance between customers may be imposed.

- There may be a requirement to visit one customer before or after another.

- There may be incompatibilities between customers – for example their orders may not be safely carried on the same vehicle.

- Customer orders may be able to be "split", and carried on separate vehicles.

- A particular type of customer must appear on each route – for example each vehicle may be required to pick up a co-driver within the first hour, but the co-drivers are not assigned to specific vehicles *a-priori*.

- Customers may be able to be skipped at a cost.

23.1.2 Related Problems

A number of problems related to the vehicle routing problem have been studied.

The Travelling Salesman Problem (TSP) is the problem of finding the shortest path that visits a set of customers and returns to the first. It is a very well studied problem – see for example the recent book [56] or the reviews [78, 72, 64]. Given an assignment of customers to vehicles, the problem of routing the customers of a single vehicle is a TSP. The TSP with Time Windows ([39, 17]) is the analogous problem for the VRPTW – the VRPTW with a single vehicle. Many heuristics for the VRP and VRPTW work by allocating customers to vehicles, and then solving the resulting TSP or TSPTW problems.

Another related problem class is *Pickup and Delivery* (PDP) problems [83, 38]. Here, rather than goods being delivered from a depot, the goods are picked up en-route, and delivered later. *Dial-a-Ride* problems [29] are pickup and delivery problems where the cargo is people rather than goods. PDP problems have a rich set of constraints: time windows are usually present and precedence constraints ensure that goods are picked up before being delivered. In Dial-a-Ride problems, there may be constraints on maximum length of travel for a passenger, the maximum deviation, and/or the maximum number of intervening stops. The VRP with back-hauls [37] is another pickup-and-delivery type problem with the extra condition that all pickups occur after deliveries are complete. It models a situation where the vehicle is used to make a set of deliveries, and then picks up some items on the way back to the depot.

23.1.3 Reformulation

The VRP also has strong connections to classical scheduling. Several formulations for the VRP have been suggested which cast it as a Job Shop Scheduling Problem with transition times [8] or as an Open Shop Scheduling Problem [7]. Similarly, scheduling problems can be cast as Vehicle Routing Problems with precedence constraints.

However, the reformulation does not seem to offer any advantages on pure problems. Perhaps not surprisingly, scheduling software performs better on pure scheduling problems than VRP software on reformulated problems. Similarly VRP software is able to solve pure VRP instances better than scheduling software.

Beck *et al.*[7] offer some insights into why this is so. They identify five characteristics that distinguish the two problems: alternative resources, temporal constraints, ratio of operation duration to transition time, optimisation criterion, and temporal slack. They demonstrate that converted problems are atypical in each of these five areas. For example, under alternative resources, the authors note that in the VRP there are typically many vehicles capable of making a delivering; whereas in pure job-shop scheduling (JSP) there is exactly one feasible machine for each job. Other scheduling variants also limit the number of feasible machines for a job. When such a scheduling problem is converted to a routing problem, it has a structure not usually found in routing problems. Briefly, the other characteristics, in order, point to the following differences:

- In the VRP time windows on visits are usually independent, whereas time windows on the JSP are interdependent, making long chains.

- In the VRP a visit has small duration compared to the transit time. In the JSP, the reverse is true.

- In the VRP the usual optimisation criteria is first minimise vehicles, then to minimise travel. In the JSP the number of "vehicles" is fixed. The usual JSP criteria – minimise makespan, which equates to minimising the length of the longest route – is not usually studied in connection with the VRP.

- In the JSP the important temporal data is the operation's duration, while in the VRPTW it is the time window applied to the operation.

Constraint programming toolkits [61, 62] were applied to reformulated problems that fall between pure VRP and pure JSP. The study identified the problem impurities that affected the solving technologies, and in particular the impurities that could lead to technology failure. The study also demonstrated that under certain conditions pre-treating impure VRP with JSP technology (and vice versa, pre-treating impure JSP with VRP technology) could significantly improve performance.

23.2 Operations Research Approaches

The vehicle routing problem and its variants have been widely studied. Recent surveys are [111] on the VRP, and [13, 14] for the VRPTW. It is beyond the scope of this chapter to fully review these solution methods.

Constraint Programming approaches make extensive use of methods from the Operations Research literature. It is useful therefore to begin with a brief review of some of the methods that have been proposed by the Operations Research community to solve these problems.

A variety of Constraint Programming approaches have also been developed – many of which use algorithms from the OR literature as building-blocks. These methods are reviewed in more detail in Section 23.3.

We begin by formulating the VRP and VRPTW more formally, using integer linear programming (ILP).

23.2.1 ILP Formulation

The standard VRP and VRPTW problems can be formulated as an ILP in a number of ways. A study of formulations is given in [80]. We use the following "3-index" formulation (from [67]).

Let the set of customers be $C = \{1 \dots n\}$, and vehicles $M = \{1 \dots m\}$. Use 0 to index the depot at route start, and $n+1$ to index the depot at route end. Define $N = C \cup \{0, n+1\}$.

The decision variables are x_{ijk} for $i, j \in N, k \in M$ where x_{ijk} is 1 if vehicle k travels directly from customer i to customer j, 0 otherwise. The constants used in the formulation are given in Table 23.1.

c_{ij}	The cost of travelling from i to j, $i, j \in N$
τ_{ij}	The time to travel from i to j, $i, j \in N$, incorporating the service time at customer i
δ_{ij}	The distance from i to j, $i, j \in N$
r_i	The demand at customer $i \in N$
Q_k	The capacity of vehicle $k \in M$
a_i	The earliest time service can start at customer $i \in N$
b_i	The latest time service can start at customer $i \in N$
K	A large integer

Table 23.1: Problem constants

For convenience, define $r_0 = 0, r_{n+1} = 0, a_0 = 0, a_{n+1} = 0, b_0 = K, b_{n+1} = K$. For time-window constrained problems, b_{n+1} can instead be set to a maximum route time if required.

Problem **VRP** =

$$\text{minimise} \ \ z_{\text{VRP}} = \sum_{k \in M} \sum_{i \in N} \sum_{j \in N} c_{ij} x_{ijk} \tag{23.1}$$

subject to

$$\sum_{k \in M} \sum_{j \in N} x_{ijk} \quad = 1 \qquad \forall i \in C \tag{23.2}$$

$$\sum_{i \in C} r_i \sum_{j \in N} x_{ijk} \quad \leq Q_k \qquad \forall k \in M \tag{23.3}$$

$$\sum_{j \in N} x_{0jk} \quad = 1 \qquad \forall k \in M \tag{23.4}$$

$$\sum_{i \in N} x_{ihk} - \sum_{j \in N} x_{hjk} \quad = 0 \qquad \forall h \in C, \ \forall k \in M \tag{23.5}$$

$$\sum_{i \in N} x_{i(n+1)k} \quad = 1 \qquad \forall k \in M \tag{23.6}$$

$$\sum_{i,j \in S} x_{ijk} \quad \leq |S| - 1 \quad \forall S \subseteq C \tag{23.7}$$

$$x_{ijk} \in \{0, 1\} \qquad\qquad \forall i, j \in N, \ \forall k \in M \tag{23.8}$$

The objective 23.1 is to minimise the sum of the costs of used arcs. Constraints 23.2 ensures that each customer is visited exactly once. Constraints 23.3 enforce the capacity constraints (assuming a heterogeneous fleet). Constraints 23.4 to 23.6 together enforce the flow of vehicles from the start depot, through 0 or more customers to the end depot. Constraints 23.7 are required to ensure there are no subtours (cycles that do not include the depot). Unfortunately, this expands to an exponetial number of constraints, making formulation of this type impractical for real problems.

The VRPTW can be formulated using an extra decision variable t_{ik}, the time vehicle $k \in M$ begins service at customer $i \in N$.

Problem **VRPTW** = minimise z_{VRP} subject to constraints 23.2 to 23.6 and 23.8, plus

$$t_{ik} + \tau_{ij} - K(1 - x_{ijk}) \ \leq t_{jk} \quad \forall i, j \in N, \ \forall k \in M \tag{23.9}$$

$$a_i \leq t_{ik} \leq b_i \qquad \forall i \in N, \ \forall k \in M \tag{23.10}$$

Constraints 23.9 define the arrival times at each customer, and constraints 23.10 enforce the time windows. Constraints 23.7 are no longer required, as the time constraints will ensure there are no subtours.

23.2.2   Methods from the OR Literature

Since the VRP and its variants are $\mathcal{NP}$-hard, the focus has been very strongly on heuristic solution methods. We will describe the usual heuristic approach – initial route construction, improvement through local search, and meta-heuristic methods to escape local optima. We will also indicate the exact methods that have been described.

23.2.3   Construction Methods

Construction methods are used to create an initial solution. Many reported methods are based on an insertion procedure where a customer is selected, then inserted in a route in such a way as to minimise an incremental cost function. A number of constraints can be enforced during construction. It is particularly easy to check within-route constraints (i.e. constraints that only deal with a single route), including time, precedence and capacity constraints. Methods vary in a number of ways.

Parallel versus sequential Sequential procedures focus on a single route, adding customers until no more will fit (e.g. [63]). Parallel methods build a set of routes simultaneously (e.g. [93]). Examples of both can be found in [107]

Seed customers The most successful parallel methods (such as Solomon's *I1* method [107]) use seed customers as the sole customer on a chosen number of routes. These customers act to guide the emerging routes.

Insertion order The order in which customers are inserted can be crucial. Some methods use a scoring system based proximity and other measures ([107, 63]. Some use *regret* (difference in cost between best and next-best insertion points) [36].

Insert position The objective function used to determine insert position may simply try to minimise the additional travel required to visit a customer. Others attempt to take time and other constraints into account, guiding the selection process to maximise the spare time or resources in resulting routes. (The same function may be used for both choosing the customer to insert and the insert position.)

Perhaps the most famous VRP construction method is the "Savings" method of Clarke and Wright [25]. The method starts with each customer on their own route. The "savings" obtained by combining two routes is $S_{ij} = c_{i0} + c_{0j} - c_{ij}$. The method selects the maximum S_{ij} for which the combined route is feasible, and iterates.

Other approaches to route construction include the "sweep" heuristic of Gillet and Miller [51]. Here, a ray centred at the depot is swept in a clockwise direction. Each customer it touches is added to the route until no more will fit. A new route is then begun.

23.2.4 Local Search Methods

Local search looks at the neighbourhood of the current solution to find improved solutions. The neighbourhood is defined in terms of one or more *move operators*: The neighbourhood of a solution is those solutions which can be generated by applying the move operator. The size of the neighbourhood is a key factor: the larger the neighbourhood, the more likely it is to contain good solutions. However, larger neighbourhoods are also more expensive to search.

Several of the operators used in solving routing problems are described below.

2-opt [81] Choose nodes i and j from the same tour, with $i + 1 < j$. Delete arcs $i \rightarrow i+1$ and $j \rightarrow j + 1$. Replace with $i \rightarrow j$ and $i + 1 \rightarrow j + 1$. This reverses the order of nodes from $i + 1$ to j. Neighbourhood size is $O(n^2)$

3-opt [81] Analogous to *3-opt*, 3 arcs are deleted and re-attached in such as way that intermediate sections are not re-ordered. Neighbourhood size is $O(n^3)$. k-opts for $k > 3$ are also possible, but the cost is prohibitive.

Or-opt [86] Choose a parameter K, the maximum length considered. Remove each sequence of customers of length $k = K, \ldots$ down to 1 customers. Test re-inserting them in forwards and backwards orientation between each remaining pair of customers. Re-insert in the cheapest position. Neighbourhood size is $O(Kn^2)$.

Relocate [103] Subset of *Or-opt* moves – move a single customer from one route to the best position in another. Neighbourhood size is $O(n^2)$.

Exchange [103] Choose two customers in different routes, and swap their positions.

Cross [103] Extension of *Exchange*: Choose a sequence of customers $i_1 \ldots j_1$ of length at most K in one route, and $i_2 \ldots j_2$ of length at most K in another, and exchange the two sections. Neighbourhood size is $O(K^2n^2)$.

λ-exchange [87] As for cross except that the routes are re-optimised after the customers are exchanged. Neighbourhood size depends on re-optimisation method, but is at least $O(K^3n^3)$.

GENI exchange [50] An extension of the relocate that allows the receiving route to be minimally re-ordered to accommodate the new customer. It allows i to be inserted into the new route between non-consecutive nodes j and k by reinserting the segment $j + 1 \ldots k - 1$ to a different position.

Ejection chains [54] A sequence of customers is selected and inserted into another route. This may cause some sequence of customers to be "ejected" in order to accommodate the new ones. The procedure forms a chain of such ejections until no customers are left unassigned. This has proved to be a very powerful operator [96, 104, 21, 108]. Neighbourhood size depends on the restrictions imposed on the chain length, but is potentially very large.

Guided Local Search and Limited Discrepancy Search [106, 59] are methods introduced in the context of constraint programming and are discussed in Section 23.4.2.

Local search typically looks at a subset of these operators. The neighbourhood of the current solution will be examined to find cost-reducing moves. Either the first found, or the best found will then be executed. This leads the procedure to a local minimum within the specified neighbourhood.

23.2.5 Meta-Heuristics

Meta-heuristics are used to escape local minima. They do this in one of two ways – either the controlled acceptance of cost-increasing moves, or by neighbourhood expansion.

Many meta-heuristics have been applied to the VRP and related problems. Again, we can only give a brief indication of the variety.

Simulated Annealing [1] Acceptance of cost-increasing moves is controlled by a system parameter called *temperature* by analogy with a crystal annealing process. An increase in cost δ is accepted with probability proportional to $e^{-\delta/T}$. An updating procedure increases T as the process continues so that solutions converges to a (hopefully better) local minimum. Any combination of the local search operators just described can be used to form a search neighbourhood [10, 113, 23].

Tabu Search [52, 53] Tabu search allows a cost-increasing move, and then places the reversal on a "tabu list" so that the move cannot be "undone". This allows the neighbourhood of the new solution can be properly explored. A large number of methods have been suggested using Tabu search for vehicle routing problems – Bräysy and Gendreau [14] highlight fourteen notable applications. A few of the most successful are [26, 110, 24, 112].

Genetic [55] Genetic (also *Memetic* and *Evolutionary*) algorithms use an Darwinian evolution analogy. In the basic form, a population of solutions is created. Individuals are "crossed" to form a new solution with characteristics from both parents. Mutation operators (similar to the local search operators above) can also be applied. Implementations differ in initialisation, mutation and crossing methods. Again, many genetic methods have been suggested – Bräysy and Gendreau select seventeen for comparison. A few of the more successful are [60, 11, 79].

Variable Neighbourhood Search [58] This method considers a sequence of neighbourhoods of increasing size around the current solution. It exhausts one neighbourhood before moving on to the next largest, and will return to the smallest if a significant change has been made. This allows the solution to be improved as much as possible from low-cost, small neighbourhoods before investing the time to examine the larger neighbourhoods. Examples include [92, 12, 28]

23.2.6   Exact Methods

While much emphasis has been placed on heuristic solution, several optimal methods have been developed. Two such approaches are Column Generation and Lagrangian Relaxation. These methods are examined more closely in Section 23.5, where we look at using CP as a subproblem solver.

Other approaches are based on exploiting polyhedral properties of ILP formulations of the VRP. These have benefited from work done in the context of the TSP (e.g. [88]). Naddef and Rinaldi [85] review the branch and cut approach to solving the VRP. The Branch and Cut approach is based on an mixed-integer linear programming formulation of the problem. The linear relaxation of the problem is first solved. If the solution is not integer, *cuts* are then applied. These take the form of new constraints which remove fractional solutions without affecting the optimum. If an integer solution has not been found but no more effective cuts can be generated, a typical branch-and-bound search is employed. New cuts are applied at each branch. The process repeats until an integer solution is found and proved optimal in the usual way.

Cuts of various kinds have been explored [49, 84, 3, 2, 6, 27, 18, 75, 74].

23.3   Constraint Programming Approaches

The Constraint Programming approach to many problem types is to incrementally build a solution, backtracking when an infeasibility is detected, until a solution is found or the problem is proven to have no solution.

This method can be applied to the VRP, but it is usually too inefficient to even consider. In the vast majority of real-world cases, the existence of a solution is never in doubt. The real question is about the quality of the solution found.

In common with all applications of CP to optimisation problems, the search is over a large number of feasible solutions to find the best or near-best, rather than searching a large number of infeasible solutions to find the feasible one.

This change in emphasis is reflected in the way search is conducted. Local search and repair methods have been developed which are able to take advantage of a Constraint Programming framework.

These search methods are discussed in Section 23.5. We begin by presenting two effective constraint-based formulations of the VRP.

23.3.1 Formulating Routing Problems with Constraints

This section details a constraint programming formulation of the VRP with time and quantity of goods constraints maintained along each route. This model can be used as a basis for the capacitated vehicle routing problem, the vehicle routing problem with time windows, the pickup and delivery problem, and other vehicle routing problem variants. The main virtue of constraint programming is versatility, i.e. it allows the modeller to add different complications and extensions without adjustment to the basic model.

The constraint programming model described here is an extension of those described in [19, 90, 31], and also [94], one of the earliest references on the use of Constraints in routing problems. These works all use essentially the same method to model for the routing aspects: path constraints. The multi-vehicle aspects come from [31, 69]. The propagation rules that we describe in this section are implemented in the model described by [90]. They are also used by ILOG Solver [62] sand ILOG Dispatcher [61], which are C++ toolkits for general constraint programming and constraint-based vehicle routing respectively.

As previously, we have n customers orders and a fleet of m vehicles. The term *visit* will be used for each time a vehicle makes a stop. There is one visit per customer and two special visits per vehicle. These two additional visits per vehicle model the starting and stopping places for the vehicle. Let $C = \{1 \ldots n\}$ form the customers, $M = \{1 \ldots m\}$ form the vehicles and $V = \{1 \ldots n + 2m\}$ form the visits. For the special first and last visits of each vehicle k we introduce the notations f_k and l_k. Visit $n + k$ is the first visit of vehicle k ($f_k = n + k$), while l_k is the last visit of vehicle k ($l_k = n + m + k$). The sets $F = \{n + 1 \ldots n + m\}$ and $L = \{n + m + 1 \ldots n + 2m\}$ indicate the set of first and last visits respectively.

To model routes, the integer variable p_i, $i \in V$ with domain $\{1 \ldots n + 2m\}$ models the direct predecessor of each visit i. By convention, each "first" visit of a vehicle has as predecessor the vehicle's "last" visit ($\forall_{k \in M} \ p_{f_k} = l_k$). The predecessor variables form a permutation of V and are subject to the difference constraints:

$$p_i \neq p_j \quad \forall i, j \in V \wedge i < j \tag{23.11}$$

This is equivalent to stating (in the ILP model) that the in-degree and out-degree of each node must be equal to one. A difference constraint propagates according to the rule below. Following [90], we represent the current domain of variable x by $\{\!\{x\}\!\}$

$$x \neq y \ : \ \{\!\{x\}\!\} = \{a\} \rightarrow y \neq a \tag{23.12}$$

where x and y are constrained integer variables, and a is an integer. Propagation rules here will be written as LHS $\rightarrow$ RHS where LHS is a logical combination of conditions on the variable domains whose truth can be easily checked. RHS is a unary constraint or conjunction thereof which can be enforced by simple domain filtering. The above rule only fires when the domain of x is reduced to the single value a. The RHS is enforced by removing the value a from the domain of y.

For each visit i, s_i models its direct successor. The successor variables are kept "coherent" (consistent) with the predecessor variables via the following constrained *element expressions*:

$$s_{p_i} = i \quad \forall i \in V - F \qquad\qquad p_{s_i} = i \quad \forall i \in V - L \qquad\qquad (23.13)$$

The element constraint takes two integer variables y and z and a vector of integers or, in this case, integer variables x. The constraint specifies that z must be equivalent to the yth element of x. This type of constraint is nearly ubiquitous in constraint programming models, and, to the authors' knowledge, supported by all well-known constraint programming engines. It propagates as shown below.

$$z = x[y]$$

$$
\begin{aligned}
\{\!\{y\}\!\} = \{a\} \wedge \exists b \notin \{\!\{z\}\!\} &\rightarrow x[a] \neq b \\
\exists a \, \{\!\{x[a]\}\!\} \cap \{\!\{z\}\!\} = \emptyset &\rightarrow y \neq a \\
\exists b (\forall a \in \{\!\{y\}\!\} \, b \notin \{\!\{x[a]\}\!\}) &\rightarrow z \neq b
\end{aligned}
\qquad\qquad (23.14)
$$

The coherence constraints 23.13 can then be implemented as follows (we show only one of the two forms):

$$s_{p_i} = i \;:\; z = s[p_i] \wedge z = i \qquad\qquad (23.15)$$

Note that the use of the predecessor and successor variables creates a symmetric model which will be reflected in the constraints that will now be introduced. Strictly speaking, the VRP solution space could be specified using only one of the variable sets (predecessor or successor) without changing the set of solutions of the problem. However, by adding both (redundant modelling), additional inferences can be made which can significantly prune the search space.

To model multiple vehicles, a "vehicle variable" v_i of domain $\{1 \ldots m\}$ is introduced for each visit i which represents the vehicle which performs visit i. Naturally, for the first and last visits, the constraints $\forall k \in M \; v_{f_k} = v_{l_k} = k$ are imposed. Along a route, all visits are performed by the same vehicle. This is maintained by constraints of the following form:

$$v_i = v_{p_i} \quad \forall i \in V - F \qquad\qquad v_i = v_{s_i} \quad \forall i \in V - L \qquad\qquad (23.16)$$

These constraints form what is termed a *path constraint* as they maintain information along a path. The above is the simplest form of path constraint; more complex ones will be used to maintain the time and quantity of goods along a path. The above path constraint can be implemented using only element constraints.

Alternatively, less stringent form of consistency can be maintained, called "bounds consistency". This only requires the bounds – lowest and highest legal values – to be maintained. This is much cheaper to store and to use, but can be less powerful. In particular cases, however, it can be sufficient. We will write the bounds as as $\underline{x} := e$, meaning that all values $i < e$ are removed from the domain of x; and $\bar{x} := e$, meaning that all values $i > e$ are removed from the domain of x.

The quantity of goods on the vehicle is one such variable for where the size of the domain and the mode of use means it is more efficient to maintain only bounds consistency. It is modelled by the introduction of a real or integer valued variable at each visit. Let $q_i \geq 0$ be a constrained variable representing the quantity of goods on the vehicle after performing visit i. Let $r_i \neq 0$ be the quantity of goods to be picked up at visit i, if this quantity is negative, it represents a drop off of goods. Then, the following path constraints maintain the load on the vehicles at each point in their route.

$$q_i = q_{p_i} + r_i \quad \forall i \in V - F \qquad\qquad q_i = q_{s_i} - r_{s_i} \quad \forall i \in V - L \qquad (23.17)$$

As the q variables typically have large domains, only bounds consistency is maintained for efficiency. Propagation rules to maintain the above constraints are as follows:

$$
\begin{aligned}
&q_i = q_{p_i} + r_i \\
&\text{Let } P = \{k \mid k \in \{\!\{p_i\}\!\} \wedge \\
&\qquad\qquad \min\{\!\{q_k\}\!\} + r_i \leq \max\{\!\{q_i\}\!\} \wedge \\
&\qquad\qquad \max\{\!\{q_k\}\!\} + r_i \geq \min\{\!\{q_i\}\!\}\} \\
&\text{Then} \\
&\qquad \exists k \in \{\!\{p_i\}\!\}\ k \notin P \rightarrow p_i \neq k \\
&\qquad \exists k \in P\ \forall l \in P\ \min\{\!\{q_k\}\!\} \leq \min\{\!\{q_l\}\!\} \rightarrow q_i \geq \min\{\!\{q_k\}\!\} + r_i \\
&\qquad \exists k \in P\ \forall l \in P\ \max\{\!\{q_k\}\!\} \geq \max\{\!\{q_l\}\!\} \rightarrow q_i \leq \max\{\!\{q_k\}\!\} + r_i
\end{aligned}
\qquad (23.18)
$$

$$
\begin{aligned}
&q_i = q_{s_i} - r_{s_i} \\
&\text{Let } S = \{k \mid k \in \{\!\{s_i\}\!\} \wedge \\
&\qquad\qquad \min\{\!\{q_k\}\!\} - r_k \leq \max\{\!\{q_i\}\!\} \wedge \\
&\qquad\qquad \max\{\!\{q_k\}\!\} - r_k \geq \min\{\!\{q_i\}\!\}\} \\
&\text{Then} \\
&\qquad \exists k \in \{\!\{s_i\}\!\}\ k \notin S \rightarrow s_i \neq k \\
&\qquad \exists k \in S\ \forall l \in S\ \min\{\!\{q_k\}\!\} \leq \min\{\!\{q_l\}\!\} \rightarrow q_i \geq \min\{\!\{q_k\}\!\} - r_k \\
&\qquad \exists k \in S\ \forall l \in S\ \max\{\!\{q_k\}\!\} \geq \max\{\!\{q_l\}\!\} \rightarrow q_i \leq \max\{\!\{q_k\}\!\} - r_i
\end{aligned}
\qquad (23.19)
$$

Vehicles have limited capacity. To model this, element constraints are used to determine limits for the q variables: simple inequalities then restrict the a variables. Assume that the goods capacity of vehicle k is Q_k. The following constraints are then imposed:

$$q_i \leq Q_{v_i} \quad \forall i \in V \qquad (23.20)$$

This formulation models heterogeneous fleets where each vehicle may have different capacity. Note that no constraints of the form $\forall i \in F\ q_i = 0$ are added, which would require that vehicles begin empty. By leaving these quantities otherwise unconstrained, different problems can be modelled. These include mixed pickup and drop off, where the vehicle can begin (partially) full and end (partially) full, and *en route* pickup and delivery problems (see next section).

Time is maintained roughly in the same manner as vehicle load except that waiting is normally allowed and so that path constraint maintains an inequality rather than an equality. Let $t_i \geq 0$ be a constrained variable which represents the time at which service for visit begins.

The following constraints maintain time along vehicle routes:

$$t_i \geq t_{p_i} + \tau_{p_i,i} \quad \forall i \in V - F \qquad \qquad t_i \leq t_{s_i} - \tau_{i,s_i} \quad \forall i \in V - L \qquad (23.21)$$

The propagation methods are omitted as the correspond closely to those already presented for propagating load (23.18, 23.19), the only difference being a cumulative inequality rather than a cumulative equality is maintained to allow waiting time.

Time windows on customers are specified by adding constraints on the t variables. For example, the constraint $a \leq t_i \leq b$ states that customer i must be visited between times a and b. Multiple time windows [90] can also be modelled; for example, the two constraints $a \leq t_i \leq d$ and $t_i \leq b \vee t_i \geq c$ indicates that customer i must be visited either between times a and b, or between times c and d ($a \leq b \leq c \leq d$).[1]

Different vehicles can have different availability windows; Suppose that O_k is the earliest starting time, or origin, of vehicle k and H_k is its latest finishing time, or horizon. Limits on the availability of vehicles are then expressed (again using element constraints and inequalities) as:

$$O_{v_i} \leq t_i \leq H_{v_i} \quad \forall i \in V \qquad (23.22)$$

To avoid cycles of visits which do not involve a first and last visit (subtour elimination), a specialised constraint is described in section 23.3.3. However, one other simple way which propagates less, but has the advantage of not requiring custom constraints, is to make sure that each vehicle has a finite horizon, and that time for service for each visit is strictly positive.

Finally the cost function, which is normally the total distance travelled d, but can more generally involve other components, such as the number of vehicles used, is constrained as follows:

$$d = \sum_{i \in V - F} \delta_{p_i,i} \qquad \qquad d = \sum_{i \in V - L} \delta_{i,s_i} \qquad (23.23)$$

where $\delta_{i,j}$ is the travel distance from visit i to j. Note the use of *both* the predecessor and successor variables to constrain the cost, which is nearly always more effective during search than using one single set. Each term in the sums is maintained by an element constraint, and the total sum by a summation constraint, whose propagation details will be skipped here, except to say that again, only bounds on variables are maintained in the sum.

When the cost-per-kilometer varies according to the vehicle used, the cost function can be generalised. Let C_k be the cost per unit distance of vehicle k. The cost function is then specified as:

$$d = \sum_{i \in V - F} C_{v_i} \delta_{p_i,i} \qquad \qquad d = \sum_{i \in V - L} C_{v_i} \delta_{i,s_i} \qquad (23.24)$$

These costs are maintained as those above, except that there is an additional multiplication constraint per term. This second cost function will not be considered further here.

---

[1] There are various ways of handling constraint disjunction in constraint programming systems. ILOG Solver takes a simple approach to propagating the constraint $c_1 \vee c_2$—when one of the disjuncts becomes violated, the other disjunct is added as a hard constraint in the system. Implication can also be implemented this way by rewriting $c_1 \Rightarrow c_2$ as $\neg c_1 \vee c_2$).

23.3.2   Extensions of the Model

The constraint programming model of the vehicle routing problem described encompasses various standard OR models, such as the vehicle routing problem with capacity constraints (CVRP), the vehicle routing problem with (multiple) time windows (VRPTW), the multi-depot vehicle routing problem (MDVRP), the open vehicle routing problem (OVRP), and the site-dependent vehicle routing problem (SDVRP). (See [98] for a full description of these classifications.) Moreover, any a problem with a mix of features of these basic problems types can be easily accommodated.

By adding additional constraints the model can also be used on pickup-and-delivery problems (PDP), including problems with back-hauls. PDP problems are modelled with negative values of r_i for a delivery, and positive r_i for a pickup.

Assume that each pickup and deliver order o has a pickup visit o_p and a delivery visit o_d. For each order o, the following constraints are imposed, which state the the pickup and delivery visits must be carried out by the same vehicle and that the pickup must be performed before the delivery.

$$v_{o_p} = v_{o_d} \qquad\qquad\qquad t_{o_p} < t_{o_d} \qquad\qquad (23.25)$$

For a back-haul problem, interleaving of pickup and delivery visits is excluded via the following unary constraints on successor and predecessor variables:

$$s_i \neq j \quad \forall i \in P \, \forall j \in D \quad \text{where } P = \{i \,|\, r_i > 0\} \text{ and } D = \{i \,|\, r_i < 0\} \qquad (23.26)$$

which state that no direct link from pickup to delivery is allowed.

23.3.3   Increased Propagation

The model already detailed is a valid and general model for various flavours of vehicle routing problem. The basic model can also be further enriched to solve more complex real-world problems (see section 23.6). However, the constraint propagation of this model can be significantly improved by considering the problem structure as a whole rather than individual constraints. This section deals with such additional propagation algorithms.

Eliminating cycles

This constraint was introduced in [19, 90] and is a very efficient way of avoiding cycles in constraint programming vehicle routing models. The essence is simple: for any chain of customers, it is forbidden to go from the end of a chain to its start. This idea is illustrated in figure 23.2 adapted very slightly from the one shown in [90].

To maintain consistency of this constraint, first assume that a notification is sent to any interested parties whenever a variable is changed (as proposed in [114]). In particular, the NOCYCLE constraint need only be informed when a p variable is bound to a particular value.

Two values b_i, e_i are associated with each visit $i \in V - F$ which represent respectively, the visits which begin and end the chain involving i. The value of b_i is only valid if i is at the end of a chain. Likewise, the value of e_i if only valid if i is at the beginning of a chain. With these variables, the NOCYCLE constraint can be propagated in $O(1)$ time each time a p variable is bound to a value. The method is as follows:

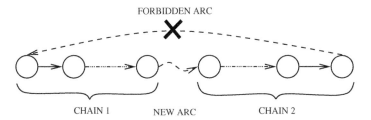

Figure 23.2: Operation of the NoCycle constraint

INITIALISE
forall i **in** $V - F$, $b_i = e_i = i$
forall i **in** $V - F$
  if HASVALUE(p_i)
    SENDEVENT(BOUND(p_i))   { see below }

when BOUND(p_i)
  $\pi = \text{value}(p_i)$ { $\pi \to i$ is new arc }
  $B = b_\pi$ { B is first visit of new chain }
  $E = e_i$ { E is the last visit of new chain }
  $e_B := E$ { := is reversible assignment }
  $b_E := B$ { := is reversible assignment }
  $p_B \neq E$ { disallow the chain looping }

Where "reversible assignment" is noted, this means that the assignment is undone on backtracking, so that the chains maintain their integrity after returning from a dead end.

Connectivity

Caseau and Laburthe [19] propose to go further than subtour eliminations for the TSP by performing a strong connection check to see if all nodes can be reached from the start node. This can be generalised to the model described here by performing a connection check to find the set of visits that can be reached by each vehicle. Let R_k^F be the set of visits reachable from visit f_k (including f_k) in a *forwards* direction—that is, following directed arcs $i \to j$ where $i \in V - L \wedge j \in \{\!\{s_i\}\!\} \wedge k \in v_i \wedge k \in v_j$. This set can be computed by a marking algorithm of complexity linear in the number of arcs considered. Likewise, let R_k^B be the set of visits reachable from visit l_k (including l_k) in a *backwards* direction. Let the set of reachable visits of vehicle k be $R_k = R_k^F \cap R_k^B$. There are two situations where search has reached a dead end and can backtrack. First, if $f_k \notin R_k$, then it means that their is no route from the first visit of vehicle k to its last visit. Second, if $\cup_{k \in M} R_k \neq V$, then there are some visits which cannot be visited by any vehicle. In fact, the second condition subsumes the first, but we highlight the first condition as it can be more efficient to test.

  Caseau and Laburthe [19] also propose that this pruning rule can be transformed into a propagation rule, fixing any arcs which are *necessary* to a connection (that it, without the arc, the already outlined algorithm would detect a dead end). Such an arc $i \to j$ would then be fixed by setting $s_i = j$.

Unfortunately the authors reported that the reduction in search space realized was very small, and did not compensate the large computational cost – detecting such arcs with their algorithm has complexity $O(|V|a)$, where a is the number of arcs considered. However, it is interesting to note here as an indication of the type of search space reduction that can be investigated.

Permutation of predecessor variables

Constraints 23.11 state that all p variables must be different. The well known global *all-diff* constraint of Régin [95] can be used to efficiently maintain generalised arc consistency for a set of variables that must all take different values. See Chapter 6 "Global Constraints" for more information.

23.3.4   An Alternative Formulation

In the formulation presented here, the solution requires a single value for successor and predecessor of a visit to be identified. Pesant *et al.*[90] present an alternative formulation in the context of the TSP that requires the set of *all* successors and predecessors of the visit to be identified.

Two set variables, B_i and A_i, are maintained for each visit that determine *all* visits which must come before (respectively after) visit i. In a TSP, any visit j other than must either come before or after i. In a VRP, this is not the case, and we identify three possibilities (a) i before j on the same vehicle route ($i \in B_j \wedge j \in A_i$) (b) j before on the same vehicle route ($j \in B_i \wedge i \in A_j$) (c) i and j served by different vehicles ($i \notin B_j \cup A_j \wedge j \notin B_i \cup A_i$). The A and B sets are maintained by examination of the time constraints between pairs of visits. This leads to the following constraints for all visits $i \in V$:

$$
\begin{array}{lll}
\text{(a) } B_i \cap A_i = \emptyset & \text{(b) } j \in A_i \Leftrightarrow i \in B_j & \\
\text{(c) } s_i = j \Leftrightarrow A_i = A_j \cup \{j\} & \text{(d) } j \in A_i \wedge l \in A_j \Rightarrow l \in A_i & \\
\text{(e) } v_i \neq v_j \vee j \in B_i \vee j \in A_i & \text{(f) } A_i \cap B_j \neq 0 \Rightarrow s_i \neq j & (23.27) \\
\text{(g) } j \in A_i \Rightarrow t_j \geq t_i + \tau_{i,j}^{\star} & \text{(h) } j \in B_i \Rightarrow t_j \leq t_i - \tau_{j,i}^{\star} &
\end{array}
$$

Here $\tau_{i,j}^{\star}$ is the shortest path (in terms of time) between the start of service of i and the start of service of j. This can be found using a shortest path algorithm, but any lower bound is legal to use, including $\tau_{i,j}$ (making the reasonable assumption that the triangle inequality holds on travel times). In fact in [90] $\tau_{i,j}^{\star} = \tau_{i,j}$.

In the above, constraint (a) says that no visit can be both before and after another visit; constraint (b) states that if i is before j, then j is after i; constraint (c) links the direct successors with the complete successors; constraint (d) enforces the transitive closure which states that if i is before j and j is before l, then i is before l; constraint (e) says that if and j are served by the same vehicle, they must be ordered; constraint (f) says that when at least one visit occurs between two other visits, those two visits cannot be directly linked; finally constraint (h) requires that when visits i and j are ordered in a certain sense, there must be a minimal time gap between them.

These constraints result in more powerful propagations eliminating certain arcs from consideration, or enforcing that two visits must be performed by different vehicles, for example. The before and after sets can also be used to tighten time bounds on visits to strengthen the method proposed in [90]. The following constraints are valid for any customer visit $i \in C$.

$$
\begin{aligned}
d_B &= \sum_{j \in B_i} t_{j,s_j} \quad \{\text{Total duration before } i\} \\
d_A &= \sum_{j \in A_i} t_{p_j,j} \quad \{\text{Total duration after } i\} \\
t_i &\geq t_{f_{v_i}} + d_B \qquad\qquad\qquad\qquad t_i \leq t_{l_{v_i}} - d_A
\end{aligned}
\tag{23.28}
$$

That is, the earliest time that visit i can be started is the start time of the vehicle on which i will be serviced, plus the travel for all visits up to i. A symmetrical constraint limits the latest time that visit i can be completed.

23.3.5 Lower Bounds and Cost-Based Propagation

The cost can be used to limit search through a global constraint. The basic constraint programming model described in Section 23.3.1 will perform propagation through constraints 23.23. Consider in particular, the first of the constraints: CST: $d = \sum_{i \in V-F} \delta_{p_i,i}$. Suppose further that a goal cost G has been identified, so that we require $d \leq G$. (Such a cost is usually provided by finding a solution to the VRP with some cost $G + \epsilon$, resulting in the new tighter cost bound G.) Constraint CST will maintain lower and upper bounds on d computed from a sum of terms, each term of which is the distance from each node's predecessor to the node. During search, not all p_i variables will be bound to a single value, and *bounds* on the contribution of each term will be computed by propagation of the element constraints which constitute each term. Assume that T_i is the term in CST corresponding to visit i. Then:

$$
\underline{T_i} := \min_{j \in p_i} \delta_{j,i} \qquad\qquad\qquad \overline{T_i} := \max_{j \in p_i} \delta_{j,i}
\tag{23.29}
$$

The summation will then maintain bounds on d, the total distance travelled, notably the lower bound:

$$
d_{LB} = \sum_{i \in V-F} \underline{T_i}
\tag{23.30}
$$

The propagation rule $\underline{d} := LB$, ensures that this lower bound is enforced.

Of course, whenever $\sum_{i \in V-F} \underline{T_i} > G$, the domain of d will become empty and force the search to backtrack. However, what happens more often is that propagation will occur, removing arcs which would, if they appeared in the final solution, exceed the cost bound G. Consider the lower bounds on the cost when one visit i has as predecessor a visit h other than its closest predecessor. The new lower bound $d_{LB}^{i,h}$ would then be:

$$
d_{LB}^{i,h} = \sum_{j \in V-F \setminus i} \underline{T_i} + \delta_{h,i}
\tag{23.31}
$$

The following propagation rule then applies:

$$
\exists h \in p_i \; d_{LB}^{i,h} > G \rightarrow p_i \neq h \quad \forall i \in V - F
\tag{23.32}
$$

This logic can also be symmetrically applied to the successor variables.

Although the above method performs cost-based propagation, the lower bound d_{LB} is poor as it does not consider any routing aspects, such as the fact that all predecessor (or successor) variables must take different values. This has the effect of significantly weakening the propagation. Accordingly, better bounds have been proposed in the context of constraint programming, as well as a cost-based propagation methods based on reduced costs.

Better lower bounds

Several better lower bounds have been introduced in the literature which have different complexity/strength trade offs. A simple, strong bound was introduced by Caseau and Laburthe [19] for the TSP, based on a *regret* concept. In general terms, the regret R_x of a variable x is the difference in the cost to assign the variable its best value compared to the cost to assign it to its *second* best. Maximum regret is often used as a variable ordering heuristic.

Although the bound was introduced for the TSP, it can be used for the VRP without any significant change. First, let each visit i have associated its closest allowable visit $\kappa_i = argmin_{j \in p_i} \delta_{j,i}$. Also for each visit $i \in V - F$ where $|\{\{p_i\}\}| > 1$ the second closest visit can be defined as: $\kappa_i^2 = argmin_{j \in p_i \setminus \kappa_i} \delta_{j,i}$. Then the regret R_i of a visit i as $R_i = \delta_{\kappa_i^2, i} - \delta_{\kappa_i, i}$.

The regret-based bound recognises that if i is the closest direct predecessor to both visit j and visit l, then in any solution at least one of j and l cannot be directly followed by i. In this case, an extra distance can be added to d_{LB} equal to the minimum *regret* of j and l.

In the general case, suppose that for any visit $i \in V - L$, i is the closest allowable direct predecessor of a set of visits K_i. Then the regret based lower bound d_{LBR} is given by:

$$d_{LBR} = d_{LB} + \sum_{i \in V - L} R(i, K_i) \tag{23.33}$$

where $R(\emptyset) = 0$ and $R(X) = \sum_{j \in X} R_j - max_{j \in X} R_j$ otherwise.

This bound adds the smallest $|K_i|$ regrets to the basic bound d_{LB} for each contested visit (the visit with the largest regret in the set is assume to link to its closest visit). The bound works very well in practice, as it significantly strengthens the basic bound and is efficient to maintain. A symmetric bound can be computed using the successor variables in place of the predecessor variables, and both can be used for pruning.

Other bounds (for the TSP) have also been introduced based either on minimum spanning trees (MST) and minimum spanning aboresences (MSA). For instance Pesant et al.[90] maintain a minimum spanning tree via an incremental version of Kruskal's algorithm [4] which adjusts the MST when required. Again for the TSP, [19] proposes computing the MSA rooted at a single node. The latter goes further, proposing that a bound based on Lagrangian relaxation of the MSA problem can provide very good bound – very often within 1% of the optimum solution. However, the authors emphasise that because of the cost of computing the lower bounds, these methods should be used when appropriate and with care. For instance, such bounds become much weaker when side constraints such as time windows (especially tight ones) are added. In this case, the high investment does not pay off.

Cost-based propagation

Focacci, Lodi and Milano [46, 47, 45] propose a more effective global constraint allowing cost-based propagation for the TSP and TSP with time windows which can also be applied to the VRP. The idea is that the assignment problem relaxation of the TSP is used (where the subtour constraint is relaxed) to provide a lower bound on the objective. The Hungarian algorithm [71], or an incremental version of it, provides this lower bound d_H (which is a minimum cost matching of visits to visits according to the domains of the predecessor or successor variables).

However, the Hungarian algorithm also produces a *reduced cost* $\bar{c}_{i,j}$ for each possible arc i, j. This reduced cost is a lower bound on the increase in d_H if j was used as the successor of visit for i, instead of the one proposed in the solution to the assignment problem.

A new propagation rule based on the cost goal G and reduced costs can then be used:

$$\exists i \in V - L \, \exists j \in \{\!\{s_i\}\!\} \; d_H + \bar{c}_{i,j} > G \rightarrow s_i \neq j \tag{23.34}$$

This method is covered in detail in Chapter 6 "Global Constraints", or see [46] for a description in the context of the TSPTW.

23.4 Constraint Programming in Search

We have seen that Constraint Programming can offer many advantages when solving routing problems, due to the increased pruning achieved through propagation. We have also seen, in Section 23.2.4, that local search methods have been effective in solving the problems.

However, a difficulty arises when one attempts to put these two methods together in a naïve way. In local search, we may move a customer from one route to another, assigning a new successor $s_i = j$. Later, we may decide to move node j, so that s_i receives a new value. However, this contradicts a basic operating principle in classic Constraint Programming: so called "chronological backtracking". Under chronological backtracking, decisions must be undone in the reverse of the order they were made. So in order to undo the decision $s_i = j$, we would have to undo all operations performed since that time. This would undo all the progress made by local search, and hence is unacceptable.

Two ways around this problem seem to have been identified so far.

The first is to allow a heuristic or meta-heuristic to control search. In this case, the constraint system is used simply as a rule checker. The second way is to insulate the Constraint Programming system from the changes being made at the lower level, by wrapping up local search changes within an *operator*, which is then used within the constraint system. The use of these sorts of operators also allows the user to identify parts of the search that can be handled using traditional backtrack search. These methods are discussed in more detail below.

A third way of using CP is as a subproblem solver. Here, an independent search process generates a sequence of subproblems – usually closely related to the original routing problem – which are solved by CP. This sort of use has more of the flavour of the second class identified above, as the CP system is being used as more than just a rule checker; a full CP framework is being used repeatedly. We will look at some of these methods in Section 23.5.

See also Chapter 5 "Local Search" for methods for doing local search. Focacci *et al.*[48] also look at the use of local search within a constraint framework.

23.4.1   Constraint Programming as a Rule-Checker

Perhaps the easiest way to use a constraint programming framework in solving the Vehicle Routing Problem is to simply use CP-based methods as a rule checker to be applied to individual routes, or collections of routes. The main advantage over other possible methods is that CP is very expressive, and a wide variety of side constraints can be specified and checked efficiently. In addition, a CP-based solver that can handle the core VRP constraints can often be used without algorithmic modification to handle a problem with additional side constraints ([31, 106]).

Using CP as a rule-checker means that the search procedure is handled outside the constraint system. The constraint system is simply called each time a new route (or partial route) is to be tested. However, the CP system is still able to perform the usual propagations, limiting the scope of decision variable and potentially identifying infeasible partial solutions.

De Backer *et al.*[31] discuss in detail the use of CP within a non-chronological framework. They use two representations of the solution – an *active* representation within a constraint programming system that is only instantiated when a constraint check is required, and an *passive* representation used by the local search routines. Within this framework, a full test of all constraints through the whole (partial) solution can be very expensive. They therefore describe a number of methods for improving the efficiency of the CP system. We site three examples – details can be found in the reference.

First, many local search operators operate using a particular criterion – for example identifying the node that can be moved at least cost or maximum regret. A large gain in efficiency can be made by simply testing that criterion first, before performing any constraint checks. So rather than seeing whether it is legal to perform a particular move, the system should first see whether the cost of the move is less that the best found so far. If not, then the constraint checks can be skipped altogether.

Another possibility for improving efficiency is to have specialised propagators for the core constraints. For example, each "move operator" within a local search method may have its own propagator which examines the values produced during the path variable propagation. Illegal moves can then be identified very quickly. Even though they concentrate on the core constraints, since any side constraints will also be potentially affecting the path constraints, these propagators make good use of information from *all* constraints.

Finally it is important to observe that many move operators affect only a subset of the routes in a solution. Most constraint checking can therefore be limited to just those routes that have changed.

De Backer *et al.*[31] describe the use a CP framework for implementing several of the local search and meta-heuristic methods described in Section 23.2.4. The methods proved to be effective – several new "best known" solutions where produced.

23.4.2   Local Search within a Constraint framework

As noted above, *operators* can be defined within a Constraint Programming framework to insulate the Constraint System from non-chronological backtrack. This allows more of the search to take place within a Constraint framework, and hence allows more scope for propagations and other techniques to prune the search space.

Many of the operators used within this type of framework are based on serial insertion and block deletion. These types of modification are well suited to use within a Constraint Programming framework, as they allow the propagations described in Section 23.3.1 to be used in full – both narrowing the potential sites for insertion, and quickly identifying partial solutions that cannot lead to a feasible solution. The formulation is also able to cope with arbitrary side constraints easily. Within-route constraints (like capacity) – which usually form the bulk of constraints – can be checked during insertion.

One such insertion-based technique, developed specifically for use in constraint programming environment, is Large Neighbourhood Search [106]. In this method, a group of "related" customers is removed, and then re-inserted into the existing runs with optimal cost. The customers are related geographically, temporally, or by use of a particular resource. For example, a simple relatedness function is $\mathcal{R}(i,j) = \frac{1}{c_{ij}+V_{ij}}$ where c_{ij} is the cost of travel from i to j, and V_{ij} is $K > 0$ if i and j are on the same vehicle, 0 otherwise. K is chosen to be comparable to the c_{ij}s.

The number of visits removed starts at one, and increases if no improvements have been found, up to some maximum (30 is used in the cited reference). Re-insertion uses exact branch-and-bound procedure with constraint propagation, which can find the minimum insertion cost rapidly.

The method has proved particularly successful on Vehicle Routing Problems, and has since been used in Constraint-based methods for other problems, including crew scheduling [105] and maximal satisfaction problems [82].

The strength of propagations from insertion-style local search is further exploited in a technique proposed by Caseau *et al.*[21]. Three meta-heuristics that involve repeated insertion – Large Neighbourhood Search, Limited Discrepancy Search, and Ejection Chains – are combined. The paper uses these three methods as building-blocks in a system designed to discover new heuristics based on automated "learning". Depending on the data presented, the methods produces heuristics, made up of calls to these building blocks, that are able to produce good solutions. The CP system is acting as a rule checker here, but in addition, traditional CP techniques are used to solve small TSPs with side constraints as described in [19] that appear as subproblems.

Another general-purpose search procedure that has been developed within the constraint literature is Limited Discrepancy Search (LDS) [59, 20, 21]. Many problem-solving methods involve a sequence of steps, a set of actions that can be taken at each step, and a heuristic for ordering the preference for those actions. Following the first preference at each step gives a solution to the problem. LDS systematically looks at the solutions that differ from the heuristic solution by making a different choice at a number of points. So for instance a 1-discrepancy would follow the heuristic at all but one step. At that step it would take the *second-best* choice according to the heuristic. Going against the heuristic at stage one (then following it for the rest of the procedure) gives a 1-discrepancy solution. Going against the heuristic at stage two gives another such solution, etc. So if there were n steps in the solution, n different 1-discrepancy solutions can be generated. A 2-discrepancy solution either twice uses the heuristic's second-best choice during construction, or once uses the third-best choice. In the context of the VRP, LDS can be used during construction. For example, in choosing the next customer to insert, or the insert position.

The Constraint framework is exploited in a method described by Pesant and Gendreau [89] to implicitly search large neighbourhoods. As mentioned previously, large neighbourhoods are more likely to contain good solutions, or allow good solutions to be discovered in fewer steps. However, such neighbourhoods can be expensive to search. Pesant and Gendreau describe a method that allows these larger neighbourhoods to be searched efficiently using branch and bound.

They characterise a neighbourhood $\mathcal{N}$ of a particular solution by a set of finite-domain variables $V = \{v_1, \ldots, v_n\}$, so that each feasible combination of values $\bar{v} = v1 \times \ldots \times v_n$ maps to exactly one neighbour of the current solution, and vice-versa. A systematic, branch and bound exploration of feasible values of $\bar{v}$ then implicitly explores the neighbourhood efficiently. Using lower-bounding functions allows non-productive areas of the neighbourhood to be identified and eliminated.

For example, in the TSP with time windows, an effective neighbourhood is the orientation-preserving 3-opt neighbourhood described in Section 23.2.4. This can be characterised using 3 indices – I, J and K – defining the break points, with the constraint $I \prec J \prec K$ (where $I \prec J$ means "I precedes J in the current tour"). Each feasible I, J, K combination represents one possible 3-opt exchange (and all 3-opt exchanges are represented by an I, J, K combination). Peasant and Gendreau describe how this I, J, K space can be explored using a branch and bound tree of depth three, using two bounding procedures to prune the search.

Bounding, propagation and pruning are being used to implicitly eliminate subsets of neighbours. This allows the more complex and larger neighbourhood structures (e.g. [109]) to be explored effectively.

Rousseau *et al.*[99] describe an approach, based strongly on the ideas presented in [89]. In this hybrid CP/OR approach, methods such as (Large Neighbourhood Search, GENI exchange, Ejection Chains) are embedded as operators within a constraint programming framework. Again, the building blocks chosen are based on serial insertion and deletion – precisely the operators able to benefit most strongly from propagation.

Basic operators are defined which remove and insert customers in a route. New operators can then be defined – for instance the following code implements a simple ejection chain:

$$NEC(c) :\text{-} Insert(c, R) \vee (Remove(C,R) \wedge Insert\ (c,R) \wedge NEC(C)\ )$$

where R and C are variables representing any route or customer. The code attempts to insert c in a feasible route or, if no such route can be found, removes another customer from a route, inserts c in that route, and recurses to find a new home for C. Obviously this method must be modified to prevent cycling etc, but the flavour of CP-based programming is evident.

In the method described, the construction phase, a local search phase and a post-optimisation improvement phase are all defined in terms of the operators. They follow the ideas of [89], exploring the neighbourhoods defined by each operator using branch-and-bound search within a CP framework. As with the previous method, propagation and pruning are working to reduce the number of solutions actually visited.

23.5 Using Constraint Programming as a Subproblem Solver

We focus here on methods that involve solving a sequence of constrained subproblems. These subproblems often share many of the constraints of the original problem, and hence Constraint Programming may be a useful technique to employ.

An example is the method described by Caseau and Laburthe [20] for the VRP. This is an insertion-based technique that interleaves insertion with local search. It uses CP to check the feasibility of insertions and of the neighbourhood moves used in local search. However, it also uses a constraint-based framework to solve the TSPTW sub-problems exactly, using the method described in [19]. Because the whole system is set up within a constraint-based framework, it is easy to implement Limited Discrepancy Search [59] as a solution improvement technique.

Shaw [106] uses a CP-based solver to find exact solutions to the TSPTW subproblems arising in the context of the Large Neighbourhood Search procedure (see Section 23.2.4).

Easton *et al.*[40] use a branch-and-price algorithm to solve the Tavelling Tournament Problem – which is related to the routing problems we examine here. In this approach, integer programming is used to solve the master problem, while constraint programming is used to solve the pricing problem. This approach is discussed in more detail in [66]. The branch-and-price approach is also used in [30] to solve the Vehicle Routing Problem with Time Windows.

Other examples of CP subproblem solvers are given in the next two sections.

23.5.1 Set Covering or Set Partitioning with Column Generation

Set Covering/Partitioning with Column Generation is a linear programming technique used commonly in the Operations Research literature to solve a variety of routing, scheduling and related problems [34, 97, 22, 5, 16, 32, 116]. Column Generation is also the subject of a recent book [33].

In the VRP context, indicator variables are used to specify potential routes: $a_{ik} = 1$ if customer i is visited by route k, 0 otherwise. Columns therefore represent a potential route, indicating which customers are covered, but not the order. The order and the cost c_k of route k can be calculated when the column is constructed, and stored separately.

The approach is to generate a large set K of potential routes (columns), then solve a set partitioning or set covering problem to choose the set of routes which covers all customers at minimum cost. The decision variable is y_k, $y_k = 1$ if route k is used in the solution, 0 otherwise.

$$\textbf{SP: minimise} \sum_{k \in K} c_k y_k \tag{23.35}$$

subject to

$$\sum_{k \in K} y_k a_{ik} = 1 \quad \forall i \in N \tag{23.36}$$

$$y_k \in \{0, 1\} \quad \forall k \in K \tag{23.37}$$

The formulation above is the Set Partitioning formulation, requiring each customer to be covered exactly once. **SP** has the advantage that special structure within the constraint matrix can allow the problem to have integer properties [101]. However, the Set Covering formulation, which allows customers to be visited more than once, is generally somewhat easier to solve. The formulation (**SC**) is obtained by replacing "=" by "$\geq$" in equation 23.36. Repeat visits can usually be handled by simply deleting one. In the following all comments regarding formulation **SP** apply equally to **SC**

Due to the number of potential columns, it is not practical to include all possible routes in K. However, the method of Column Generation allows us to converge to the optimum solution. After solving **SP**, reduced costs for each customer can be obtained using the dual variable associated with each equation 23.36. The Column Generation subproblem can then be solved, where columns are generated by finding paths with negative reduced cost – i.e. sets of customers where the cost of travel is exceeded by the sum of customer reduced costs. This is a type of prize-collecting TSP [42]. An optimal solution to the relaxed form of **SP** is obtained when no more negative reduced-cost paths can be generated.

Constraint programming can be used both in initial column construction phase, and again in the column generation phase. One of the main advantages of the method is that any within-route constraints can be enforced by the column construction procedure, independent of the Set-Partitioning solution mechanism. The method can therefore handle classical VRP, and VRPTW problems, as well as a variety of side constraints. Previously, Dynamic Programming was used [34], but this does not have the flexibility of CP which allows, for example, multiple time windows to be added without fuss [91].

Solving the prize-collecting TSP subproblem in the column generation phase has to obey the same constraints as the original route-construction method (including any side constraints) – it simply has a modified objective. The same constraint-based formulation can therefore be used to solve the prize collection sub-problem.

This approach has been described by Rouseau *et al.*[100] in the context of the TSPTW, but most of the discussion applies to the VRPTW as well. They describe arc elimination and search strategies which speed up solving the prize-collection subproblem.

Junker *et al.*[65] discuss a framework for embedding efficient algorithms into a constraint framework for solving problems that arise in column generation methods. These methods are developed further in [41].

23.5.2 Lagrangian Relaxation

Lagrangian Relaxation is also a standard Operations Research technique, and descriptions can be found in many Operations Research texts (e.g. [70, 115]). The technique is applied to linear programming formulations of a problem where an "easy" problem is being complicated by some additional constraints. The idea is to move the complicating constraints into the objective with a penalty (Lagrangian) multiplier, leaving a much simpler subproblem. Using duality theory, optimal multipliers can then be found by solving a series of subproblems, yielding optimal solutions to the original problem.

There are various ways to apply this technique to the VRP, or VRPTW, depending on the relaxed constraints. Fisher [43, 44] used Lagrangian Relaxation to solve the VRP and VRPTW problems. The relaxation used there leaves a "minimum K-tree" subproblem. More recently, Lagrangian relaxation has been applied to the VRPTW [67]. In the approach described there, the constraints which ensure that each customer is visited exactly once are relaxed – these are constraints 23.2 in the formulation in Section 23.2.1. This gives the Lagrangian objective

$$\text{minimise} \quad z_{\text{LR}}(\lambda) = \sum_{i \in N} \sum_{j \in N} \sum_{k \in M} c_{ij} x_{ijk} - \sum_{i \in N} \lambda_i \left(\sum_{j \in N} \sum_{k \in M} x_{ijk} - 1 \right) \quad (23.38)$$

We wish to find the optimal set of multipliers λ_i, and must therefore solve Problem **LR** = maximize$_{\lambda \in \mathbb{R}^n}$ $z_{\text{LR}}(\lambda)$ subject to constraints 23.3 to 23.10 (without the redundant subtour constraints 23.7).

LR divides into m independent (difficult) problems – one for each vehicle. As with the Column Generation method described above, the subproblem is a sort of prize-collecting TSP, with the Lagrange multiplier λ_i associated with each customer quantifying the "prize" for a vehicle to visit. (At termination, λ_i therefore gives an indication of the "cost" of visiting each customer.) For the strict definition of VRPTW, [67] develop a dynamic programming-based method to solve the elementary shortest path with time windows and capacity constraints subproblem. However, a constraint-based approach could be used which would allow arbitrary side constraints to be applied.

The Lagrangian Relaxation method is an iterative procedure. At iteration t, the current solution is x_{ijk}^t The Lagrangian problem is then solved to find the optimal multiplier λ_i^t for $i \in N$. Unfortunately, in the case of the VRPTW, this optimization is also a difficult problem. [67] describe a cutting plane algorithm using trust regions to solve the Lagrangian dual problem for the pure VRPTW. Given these multipliers, a new x_{ijk}^{t+1} is calculated using the subproblem solver – CP or Dynamic Programming.

Traditionally Lagrangian Relaxation methods have suffered from being tied to a specific formulation of the problem. Constraint Programming allows the possibility to solve subproblems in the presence of a wide variety of side constraints, making the method more widely applicable. However, an exact solution to the subproblem is usually required in order to guarantee convergence of the method.

Benoist *et al.*[9] used Lagrange Relaxation within a constraint programming framework to solve a related routing problem - the "Travelling Tournament Problem" faced in constructing round-robin sports schedules. The method allows for a variety of constraints in composing a draw while minimising the travel time for players. This work is also interesting for the collaborative architecture described that allows CP and Lagrangian Relaxation to work effectively together.

23.6 CP-VRP in the Real World

23.6.1 Real-World Constraints

Up to this point, we have discussed the Vehicle Routing Problem and its variants as they are studied in academia. Starting from the very pure statement of the VRP originally proposed, new constraints and variants reflecting real-world practice have been studied over time.

However, the main difference between VRP in academe and routing practice in the real world remains the almost incredible variety of constraints and objective functions that are seen in day-to-day use – many of which have never been examined in the academic literature.

To bring this into focus, we present a number of examples of operating practice that have been seen by staff at a leading supplier of software for Vehicle Routing.

- Minimising vehicles is seldom an optimisation criteria in day-to-day scheduling. The fleet size is determined periodically, but in between times, drivers are typically on contract, and so are paid for some minimum time whether they drive or not. As a result of this, there is often a constraint that route time exceeds the paid minimum, while being less than the contracted maximum time.

- Meal and rest breaks, within a certain time of starting, and importantly, within a certain time relative to one another, must be inserted into the route automatically

- Subcontracting is common, whereby a shipment is sent using another carrier. The constraint that all visits are completed is therefore often dropped in favour of a cost term in the objective that will automatically drop uneconomic visits.

- A situation has been seen whereby the company only pays for travel to and from the first and last visits of the route, not for the distance on the route itself. There is a constraint which forces the route to be linear, rather than petal-shaped, which in effect forces the last visit to be one of the most distant from the first. In fact the constraint is that the total length of the route is no more than 30% greater than the distance from the first to the last stop.

- In some workplaces, some drivers have secured a strong negotiation position which allows them to choose which stops they wish to perform. Others are able to choose some of their route.

- Cross-docking is another very common practice. For example, a major supermarket has a regional distribution centre. This centre receives goods from suppliers, and distributes goods to stores. To avoid double handling and storage costs, where-ever possible the deliveries are "cross-docked": the goods are taken straight across the dock from a suppliers vehicle to the distribution vehicle. If the supermarket is using its own vehicles to pick up from the supplier, then this constraint is a movable time-window linking two or more routes.

- A similar inter-tour constraint occurs when one vehicle delivers to a scheduled service, such as a ferry or train, and another picks up from the other end. There may be a choice of many scheduled services to use, but two routes must coordinate on the same service. Note that the receiving vehicle is not necessarily identified, but one of a number of vehicles must be tasked to meet the scheduled service.

- In (telecommunications) technician dispatching there can be a requirement to have two technicians at different locations at the same time, so that they can perform end-to-end tests of communications hardware. A constraint is required to force these two visits into different vehicles and for the two visits to occur in the same time window.

- Some long-haul companies use trailer change-over. Here, one vehicle (perhaps while making other deliveries) carries a trailer. At some location and time (decision variables) it meets another vehicle and the trailer is moved to the second vehicle for onward travel. This may be repeated a number of times. Each such change-over represents an inter-tour constraint. Again the vehicles involved are variable.

- The resources at a site may be limited. For instance there may be a limited number of docks or forklifts. The number of vehicles visiting at any one time must therefore be limited. This will be a consideration for example in a supermarket where multiple vehicles are sent to replenish stocks.

- Overtime rates must be taken into account in the objective, but are often expressed in a complicated fashion, including discontinuities, and penalty payments. E.g. $x up to the first half hour, $y for each subsequent half hour, plus $z meal allowance (plus 30 minutes break) if working more than 2 hours.

- In technician dispatching, the truck inventory must be maintained. The inventory of up to 300 types of parts may have to be tracked, and only technicians with sufficient supplies assigned. The technician must return to base to restock when appropriate, or may be able to be resupplied en-route by either meeting another technician and swapping parts, or by a special delivery from base.

- Lots of little, but still important, preferences have been seen, for example shipments to a particular customer in a week must be done by the same driver; or a husband and wife must/may not work together as a team.

Note that while many of the situations listed can be addressed using the models discussed here, some require more elaborate models, and some can only be approximately modelled. In addition, some would require bespoke techniques to find good solutions.

23.6.2 Dynamic Operation

Another important aspect of solving vehicle routing problems in the real world is the dynamic nature of the problems: the problem is shifting even as it is being solved.

The dynamism may be small - where some visits may be added or deleted without changing the general structure of the route, or the entire routing process may be driven by the stops being added, such as in taxi or parcel delivery operations.

Other dynamic aspects of operations include

- A company may have a list of clients it visits, but not all clients will require visiting each day. The stops to be performed may only be finalised as close to dispatch time – or even after.

- Traffic incidents and road works can alter the time taken to drive between two stops.

- It may be difficult to calculate *a-priori* how long a visit will require. If visits take longer than expected, parts of a planned route may have to be re-scheduled.

- Vehicles may break down, requiring visits to be re-scheduled

Algorithms to address these dynamic features of the problem are just beginning to be addressed in the literature [68, 77].

23.6.3   Vehicle Routing Software

The importance of vehicle routing to companies' operations is reflected in the use of vehicle routing software packages. The journal *OR/MS Today* conducts a regular survey of routing software. In their most recent survey [57], twenty routing software systems were analysed. The companies involved reported a total of more than 8,000 systems sold. We refer the reader to a survey such as this for details of available systems.

It should be remembered that the routing aspects are only small part of a routing system. Other features required of software include

- The ability to *geo-code* addresses - that is turn an address into a map location.

- The ability to calculate travel distances and times from one map point to another.

- A graphical user interface for displaying routes.

- The ability to change routes manually, preferably using a graphical interface.

- A method of easily specifying and entering constraints.

- Interfacing with other systems, such as billing and invoice systems.

23.7   Conclusions

We have seen how Constraint Programming can be applied to an important industrial problem. The Constraint Programming approaches have used, and advanced, the substantial body of research on the problem from the Operations Research community. Methods from the OR literature form the basis for many successful CP approaches.

Before the advent of Constraint Programming, the usual approach to solving these problems was to formulate the problem at hand in such a way that the main objectives and core constraints could be handled efficiently. If any side constraints were present, these were often handled in an "ad-hoc" manner. Unfortunately this leads to a wide variety of formulations, each of which is often specific to a fairly narrow class of problems.

The advantage Constraint Programming brings is a much more general method of handling the core and side constraints of routing problems. The formulation presented here is able to model a very wide variety of problems classes seen in the literature and in the real world with the *same set* of variables and core constraints. This formulation can handle capacity, time and incompatibility constraints, and various types of pickup and delivery problem.

In addition, a very wide variety of side constraints can be modelled without affecting the core model. We have already mentioned many different types of side constraints, but there are a large number of others in used in companies around the world. Many of these can be incorporated into the model with very low cost. We have shown how the expressive nature of the model allows constraints to be specified and checked efficiently.

Routing problems of the sort examined here are all $\mathcal{NP}$-hard. Efficiency in exploring a chosen search space is therefore paramount. We have shown how a combination of propagators for generic constraints, along with bespoke propagations, can substantially reduce the number of search nodes actually visited, without affecting the solution quality.

We have shown how performing local search within a Constraint Programming framework can benefit from the pruning of the search space.

Constraint Programming systems allow flexibility in how a new type of constraint, seen for the first time in a particular company, is handled. First, the new constraint can usually be incorporated relatively simply into the model described. As soon as this is done, automatic methods within the Constraint system are usually able to immediately use the constraint to prune search trees. In addition, if the constraint is seen as being core to solving the problem, bespoke propagators can be fashioned which increase the degree to which the search tree is pruned.

We have also seen how Constraint Programming systems offer advantages when used as subproblem solvers. In methods such as Column Generation and Lagrangian Optimisation, subproblems are often generated with an eclectic mix of constraints. Some of these are common to other routing systems, and others are particular to the subproblem environment. Constraint Programming allows the methods developed to solve the routing aspects to be leveraged to solve the related subproblem.

In the future, it would appear that there is still much to be done in terms of hybrid OR and CP methods. This is a very active area of research, and some very interesting methods using advanced techniques from both disciplines are already being seen. It is clear that techniques from Constraint Programming will continue influence developments in this area.

Acknowledgements

The authors wish to acknowledge the immense contribution of Patrick Prosser to their understanding of constraint techniques, particularly as applied to the Vehicle Routing Problem. Thanks Pat.

Philip Kilby is supported by the Australian Research Council and National ICT Australia (NICTA). NICTA is funded through the Australian Government's *Backing Australia's Ability* initiative, in part through the Australian Research Council.

Bibliography

[1]   E. Aarts, J. H. M. Korst, and P. J. M. Van Laarhoven. Simulated annealing. In E. Aarts and J. Lenstra, editors, *Local Search in Combinatorial Optimization*, pages 91–120. John Wiley & Sons, Chichester, 1997.

[2]   N. R. Achuthan, L. Caccetta, and S. P. Hill. A new subtour elimination constraint for the vehicle routing problem. *European Journal of Operational Research*, 91(3): 573–586, 1996.

[3]   N. R. Achuthan, L. Caccetta, and S. P. Hill. An improved branch-and-cut algorithm for the capacitated vehicle routing problem. *Transportation Science*, 37(2):153–169, 2003.

[4]   A. V. Aho, J. E. Hopcroft, and J. D. Ullman. *Data Structures and Algorithms*. Addison-Wesley, 1983.

[5]   R. Anbil, J. J. Forrest, and W. R. Pulleyblank. Column generation and the airline crew pairing problem. *Documenta Mathematica Journal*, Extra Volume ICM III: 677–686, 1998.

[6]   J. Araque, G. Kudva, T. Morin, and J. Pekny. A branch-and-cut algorithm for vehicle routing problems. *Annals of Operations Research*, 50:37, 1994.

[7]   J. Beck, P. Prosser, and E. Selensky. Vehicle routing and job shop scheduling: What's the difference? In M. Kaufmann, editor, *13th International Conference on Automated Planning and Scheduling ICAPS'03*, 2003.

[8]   J. C. Beck, P. Prosser, and E. Selensky. On the reformulation of vehicle routing problems and scheduling problems. In *Proceedings of SARA 2002, Symposium on Abstraction, Reformulation and Approximation*, volume 2371 of *Lecture Notes in Computer Science*, pages 282–289, Berlin, 2002. Springer-Verlag.

[9]   T. Benoist, F. C. Laburthe, and B. Rottembourg. Lagrange relaxation and constraint programming collaborative schemes for traveling tournament problems. In *Proceedings CP-AI-OR'01, Ashford 2001*, 2001.

[10] R. Bent and P. Van Hentenryck. A two-stage hybrid local search for the vehicle routing problem with time windows. *Transportation Science*, 38(4):515, 2004.

[11] J. Berger, M. Barkaoui, and O. Bräysy. A route-directed hybrid genetic approach for the vehicle routing problem with time windows. *INFOR*, 41:179–194, 2003.

[12] O. Bräysy. A reactive variable neighborhood search for the vehicle-routing problem with time windows. *INFORMS Journal on Computing*, 15(4):347 – 368, 2003.

[13] O. Bräysy and M. Gendreau. Vehicle routing problem with time windows, part I: Route construction and local search algorithms. *Transportation Science*, 39(1): 104–118, 2005.

[14] O. Bräysy and M. Gendreau. Vehicle routing problem with time windows, part II: Metaheuristics. *Transportation Science*, 39(1):119, 2005.

[15] Bureau of Transportation Statistics. *National Transportation Statistics (NTS) 2004* Bureau of Transportation Statistics, 2005.

[16] S. Butt and D. Ryan. An optimal solution procedure for the multiple tour maximum collection problem using column generation. *Computers and Operation Research* 26(4):427–441, 1999.

[17] R. W. Calvo. A new heuristic for the traveling salesman problem with time windows. *Transportation Science*, 34(1):113–124, 2000.

[18] V. Campos, A. Corberán, and E. Mota. Polyhedral results for a vehicle routing problem. *European Journal of Operations Research*, 52:75, 1991.

[19] Y. Caseau and F. Laburthe. Solving small TSPs with constraints. In *Proceedings of the 14th International Conference on Logic Programming*, pages 316–330. The MIT Press, 1997.

[20] Y. Caseau and F. C. Laburthe. Heuristics for large constrained vehicle routing problems. *Journal of Heuristics*, 5(3):281–303, 1999.

[21] Y. Caseau, F. C. Laburthe, and G. Silverstein. A meta-heuristic factory for vehicle routing problems. In J. Jaffar, editor, *Proceedings, Principles and Practice of Constraint Programming – CP'99. Alexandria, VA, USA, October 11-14, 1999.*, volume 1713 of *Lecture Notes in Computer Science*, pages 144–159, Heidelberg, 2004. Springer.

[22] D. G. Cattrysse, M. Salomon, and L. N. Van Wassenhove. A set partitioning heuristic for the generalised assignment problem. *Europenal Journal of Operational Research*, 72:167–174, 1994.

[23] W. Chiang and R. Russell. Simulated annealing metaheuristics to vehicle routing problems with time windows. *Annals of Operations Research*, 63:3–27, 1996.

[24] W.-C. Chiang and R. A. Russel. A reactive tabu search metaheuristic for the vehicle routing problem with time windows. *INFORMS Journal on Computing*, 9(4):417–430, 1997.

[25] G. Clarke and J. Wright. Scheduling of vehicles from a central depot to a number of delivery points. *Operations Research*, 12:568–581, 1964.

[26] J.-F. Cordeau, G. Laporte, and A. Mercier. A unified tabu search heuristic for vehicle routing problems with time windows. *Journal of the Operational Research Society*, 52(8):928–936, 2001.

[27] G. Cornuéjols and F. Harche. Polyhedral study of the capacitated vehicle routing problem. *Mathematical Programming*, 60:21, 1993.

[28] P. I. Cowling and R. Keuthen. Embedded local search approaches for routing optimization. *Computers & Operations Research*, 32(3):465–490, 2005.

[29] T. G. Crainic, F. Malucelli, M. Nonato, and F. C. Guertin. Meta-heuristics for a class of demand-responsive transit systems. *INFORMS Journal on Computing*, 17 (1):10–24, 2005.

[30] E. Danna and C. Le Pape. Accelerating branch-and-price with local search: A case study on the vehicle routing problem with time windows. In G. Desaulniers, J. Desrosiers, and M. M. Solomon, editors, *Column Generation*, pages 99–130. Kluwer Academic Publishers, 2005.

[31] B. De Backer, V. Furnon, P. Prosser, P. Kilby, and P. Shaw. Solving vehicle routing problems using constraint programming and metaheuristics. *Journal of Heuristics*, 6(4):501–523, 2000.

[32] G. Desaulniers, J. Lavigne, and F. Soumis. Multi-depot vehicle scheduling problems with time windows and waiting costs. *European Journal of Operational Research*, 111:479–494, 1998.

[33] G. Desaulniers, J. Desrosiers, and M. M. Solomon, editors. *Column Generation*. Springer, 2005.

[34] M. Desrochers, J. Desrosiers, and M. Solomon. A new optimization algorithm for the vehicle routing problem with time windows. *Operations Research*, 40(2):342–354, March 1992.

[35] J. Desrosiers, Y. Dumas, M. M. Solomon, and F. C. Soumis. Time constrained routing and scheduling. In M. O. Ball, T. L. Magnanti, C. L. Monma, and G. L. Nemhauser, editors, *Network Routing*, volume 8 of *Handbooks in Operations Research and Management Science*, chapter 2, pages 35–139. North-Holland, Amsterdam, 1995.

[36] M. Diana and M. M. Dessouky. A new regret insertion heuristic for solving large-scale dial-a-ride problems with time windows. *Transportation Research Part B: Methodological*, 38(6):539–557, 2004.

[37] C. Duhamel, J.-Y. Potvin, and J.-M. Rousseau. A tabu search heuristic for the vehicle routing problem with backhauls and time windows. *Transportation Science*, 31 (1):49–59, Feb 1997.

[38] Y. Dumas, J. Desrosiers, and F. Soumis. The pickup and delivery problem with time windows. *European Journal of Operational Research*, 54(1):7–22, 1991.

[39] Y. Dumas, J. Desrosiers, E. Gelinas, and M. M. Solomon. An optimal algorithm for the traveling salesman problem with time windows. *Operations Research*, 43(2): 367–371, 1995.

[40] K. Easton, G. Nemhauser, and M. Trick. Solving the travelling tournament problem:

A combined integer programming and constraint programming approach. In *Practice and Theory of AutomatedTimetabling IV*, pages 100 – 109. Springer-Verlag, Heidelberg, 2003.

[41]   T. Fahle, U. Junker, S. E. Karisch, N. Kohl, M. Sellmann, and B. Vaaben. Constraint programming based column generation for crew assignment. *Journal of Heuristics* 8(1):59–81, 2002.

[42]   D. Feillet, P. Dejax, and M. Gendreau. Traveling salesman problems with profits. *Transportation Science*, 39(2):188, 2005.

[43]   M. L. Fisher. Optimal solution of vehicle routing problems using minimum K-trees. *Operations Research*, 42(4):626–642, 1994.

[44]   M. L. Fisher and K. O. Jörnsten. Vehicle routing with time windows: Two optimization algorithms. *Operations Research*, 45(3):488–492, 1997.

[45]   F. Focacci, A. Lodi, and M. Milano. Solving TSP with time windows with constraints. In D. De Schreye, editor, *Logic Programming – Proceedings of the 1999 International Conference on Logic Programming*, pages 515–529, Cambridge, MA., 1999. MIT Press.

[46]   F. Focacci, A. Lodi, and M. Milano. Embedding relaxations in global constraints for solving TSP and TSPTW. *Annals of Mathematics and Artificial Intelligence*, 34: 291–311, 2002.

[47]   F. Focacci, A. Lodi, and M. Milano. A hybrid exact algorithm for the TSPTW. *INFORMS Journal on Computing*, 14(4):403–417, 2002.

[48]   F. Focacci, F. Laburthe, and A. Lodi. Local search and constraint programming. In F. Glover and G. Kochenberger, editors, *Handbook of Metaheuristics*, pages 369–403. Kluwer Academic Publishers, 2003.

[49]   R. Fukasawa, J. Lysgaard, M. P. de Aragao, M. Reis, E. Uchoa, and R. Werneck. Robust branch-and-cut-and-price for the capacitated vehicle routing problem. In D. Bienstock and G. Nemhauser, editors, *Integer Programming and Combinatorial Optimization - IPCO 2004*, volume 3064, pages 1–15, Berlin, 2004. Springer-Verlag.

[50]   M. Gendreau, A. Hertz, and G. Laporte. New insertion and postoptimization procedures for the traveling salesman problem. *Operations Research*, 40(6):1086–1094, 1992.

[51]   B. Gillet and L. R. Miller. A heuristic algorithm for the vehicle dispatch problem. *Operations Research*, 22:340–349, 1974.

[52]   F. Glover. Tabu search, part I. *ORSA Journal on Computing*, 1(3):190–206, 1989.

[53]   F. Glover. Tabu search, part II. *ORSA Journal on Computing*, 2(1):4–32, 1990.

[54]   F. Glover. Ejection chains, reference structures and alternating path methods for traveling salesman problems. *Discrete Applied Mathematics*, 65(1-3):223–253, 1996.

[55]   D. E. Goldberg. *Genetic Algorithms in Search, Optimization and Machine Learning* Addison Wesley, Reading, 1989.

[56]   G. Gutin and A. Punnen, editors. *The Traveling Salesman Problems and its Variations*. Kluwer Academic Publishers, Dordrecht, 2002.

[57]   R. Hall. Vehicle routing software survey. *OR/MS Today*, 31(3), 2004.

[58]   P. Hansen and N. Mladenovic. Variable neighborhood search: Principles and applications. *European Journal of Operational Research*, 130(3):449–467, 2001.

[59]   W. D. Harvey and M. L. Ginsberg. Limited discrepancy search. In C. S. Mellish,

editor, *Proceedings of the Fourteenth International Joint Conference on Artificial Intelligence (IJCAI-95)*, volume 1, pages 607–615, Montréal, Québec, Canada, 1995. Morgan Kaufmann.

[60] J. Homberger and H. Gehring. A two-phase hybrid metaheuristic for the vehicle routing problem with time windows. *European Journal of Operational Research*, 162(1):220–238, 2005.

[61] ILOG S.A. *ILOG Dispatcher 4.0 User's Manual*. ILOG S.A., 9 Rue de Verdun, 94253 Gentilly Cedex, France, .

[62] ILOG S.A. *ILOG Solver 6.0 User's Manual*. ILOG S.A., 9 Rue de Verdun, 94253 Gentilly Cedex, France, .

[63] G. Ioannou, M. Kritikos, and G. Prastacos. A greedy look-ahead heuristic for the vehicle routing problem with time windows. *Journal of the Operational Research Society*, 52(5):523–537, 2001.

[64] M. Junger, G. Reinelt, and G. Rinaldi. The traveling salesman problem. In M. Dell'Amico, F. Maffioli, and S. Martello, editors, *Annotated Bibliographies in Combinatorial Optimization*, Wiley Interscience Series in Discrete Mathematics. John Wiley & Sons, 1997.

[65] U. Junker, S. E. Karisch, N. Kohl, B. Vaaben, T. Fahle, and M. Sellmann. A framework for constraint programming based column generation. In J. Jaffar, editor, *5th International Conference of Principles and Practice of Constraint Programming – CP'99*, volume 1713 of *Lecture Notes in Computer Science*, pages 261–275. Springer, 2004.

[66] G. N. K. Easton and M. Trick. CP based branch and price. In M. Milano, editor, *Constraint and Integer Programming: Toward a Unified Methodology*, chapter 7. Springer, 2004.

[67] B. Kallehauge, J. Larsen, and O. B. Madsen. Lagrangean duality applied on vehicle routing with time windows. Technical Report IMM-TR-2001-9, IMM, Technical University of Denmark, DK-2800 Kgs. Lyngby - Denmark, 2001.

[68] P. Kilby, P. Prosser, and P. Shaw. Dynamic VRPs: A study of scenarios. APES Technical Report APES-06-1998, Department of Computer Science, Strathclyde University, Glasgow, Scotland, September 1998.

[69] P. Kilby, P. Prosser, and P. Shaw. A comparison of traditional and constraint-based heuristic methods on vehicle routing problems with side constraints. *Constraints*, 5 (4):389–414, 2000.

[70] B. Korte and J. Vygen. *Combinatorial Optimization: Theory and Algorithms*, volume 21 of *Algorithms and Combinatorics*. Springer, Berlin, 2nd edition, 2002.

[71] H. W. Kuhn. The hungarian method for the assignment problem. *Naval Research Logistics Quarterly*, 2:83–97, 1955.

[72] G. Laporte. The traveling salesman problem: an overview of exact and approximate algorithms. *European Journal of Operational Research*, 59:231–247, 1992.

[73] G. Laporte. The routing problem: An overview of exact and approximate algorithms. *European Journal of Operations Research*, 59:345–358, 1992.

[74] G. Laporte and Y. Nobert. Comb inequalities for the vehicle routing problem. *Methods of Operations Research*, 51:271, 1984.

[75] G. Laporte, Y. Nobert, and M. Desrouchers. Optimal routing with capacity and distance restrictions. *Operations Research*, 33:1050, 1985.

[76] G. Laporte, M. Gendreau, J.-Y. Potvin, and F. Semet. Classical and modern heuris-

tics for the vehicle routing problem. *International Transactions in Operational Research*, 7(4-5):285–300, 2000.

[77] A. Larsen, O. B. G. Madsen, and M. M. Solomon. The a priori dynamic traveling salesman problem with time windows. *Transportation Science*, 38(4):459, 2004.

[78] E. L. Lawler, J. K. Lenstra, A. H. G. R. Kan, and D. B. Shmoys. *The Traveling Salesman Problem: A Guided Tour of Combinatorial Optimization*. John Wiley and Sons, Chichester, 1985.

[79] A. Le Bouthillier and T. G. Crainic. A cooperative parallel meta-heuristic for the vehicle routing problem with time windows. *Computers & Operations Research*, 32 (7):1685–1708, 2005.

[80] A. N. Letchford and J.-J. Salazar-González. Projection results for vehicle routing. *Mathematical Programming*, 105(2):251–274, 2006.

[81] S. Lin. Computer solutions of the traveling salesman problem. *Bell Systems Technical Journal*, 44:2245–2269, 1965.

[82] L. Lobjois, M. Lemaître, and G. Verfaillie. Large neighbourhood search using constraint propagation and greedy reconstruction for valued CSP resolution. In *ECAI Workshop on "Modelling and Solving Problems with Constraints" (14th European Conference on Artificial Intelligence, ECAI 2000), Berlin, Germany, 20 - 25 August 2000*. ECAI, 2000.

[83] Q. Lu and M. Dessouky. An exact algorithm for the multiple vehicle pickup and delivery problem. *Transportation Science*, 38(4):503, 2004.

[84] J. Lysgaard, A. N. Letchford, and R. W. Eglese. A new branch-and-cut algorithm for the capacitated vehicle routing problem. *Mathematical Programming*, 100(2): 423–445, 2004.

[85] D. Naddef and G. Rinaldi. Branch and cut. In P. Toth and D. Vigo, editors, *Vehicle Routing*, volume 9 of *SIAM Monographs on Discrete Mathematics and Applications* SIAM, 2000.

[86] I. Or. *Travelling Salesman-Type Combinatorial Problems and Their Relation to the Logistics of Blood-Banking*. PhD thesis, Department of Industrial Engineering and Management Sciences, Northwest University, Evanston, IL., 1976.

[87] I. H. Osman. Metastrategy simulated annealing and tabu search algorithms for the vehicle routing problem. *Annals of Operations Research*, 41:421–451, 1993.

[88] M. Padberg and G. Rinaldi. A branch-and-cut algorithm for the resolution of large-scale symmetric traveling salesman problems. *SIAM Review*, 33:60, 1991.

[89] G. Pesant and M. Gendreau. A view of local search in constraint programming. In E. C. Freuder, editor, *Principles and Practice of Constraint Programming - CP96* volume 1118 of *Lecture Notes in Computer Science*, pages 353–366. Springer, 1996.

[90] G. Pesant, M. Gendreau, J. Potvin, and J. Rousseau. An exact constraint logic programming algorithm for the travelling salesman with time windows. *Transportation Science*, 32(1), 1998.

[91] G. Pesant, M. Gendreau, J.-Y. Potvin, and J.-M. Rousseau. On the flexibility of constraint programming models: From single to multiple time windows for the traveling salesman problem. *European Journal of Operational Research*, 117(2):253–263, 1999.

[92] M. Polacek, R. F. Hartl, K. Doerner, and M. Reimann. A variable neighborhood search for the multi depot vehicle routing problem with time windows. *Journal of Heuristics*, 10(6):613–627, 2004.

[93] J.-Y. Potvin and J.-M. Rousseau. A parallel route building algorithm for the vehicle routing and scheduling problem with time windows. *European Journal of Operations Research*, 66:331–340, 1993.

[94] J.-F. Puget. Object oriented constraint programming for transportation problems. In *Proceedings of Advanced Software Technology in Air Transport ASTAIR'92*, London, 1992. Royal Aeronautical Society.

[95] J.-C. Regin. A filtering algorithm for constraints of difference in CSPs. In *Proceedings of the Twelfth National Conference on Artificial Intelligence (AAAI-94)*, *Volume 1*, pages 362–367. AAAI, 1994.

[96] C. Rego and C. Roucairol. Parallel tabu search heuristic based on ejection chains for the vehicle routing problem. In I. Osman and J. Kelly, editors, *Metaheuristics: Theory and Applications*. Kluwer Academic Publishers, 1996.

[97] C. C. Ribeiro and F. Soumis. A column generation approach to the multiple-depot vehicle scheduling problem. *Operations research*, 42(1):41–52, 1994.

[98] S. Ropke and D. Pisinger. A unified heuristic for vehicle routing problems with backhauls. *European Journal of Operational Research*. To appear.

[99] L.-M. Rousseau, M. Gendreau, and G. Pesant. Using constraint-based operators to solve the vehicle routing problem with time windows. *Journal of Heuristics*, 8(1): 43–58, 2002.

[100] L.-M. Rousseau, M. Gendreau, G. Pesant, and F. Focacci. Solving VRPTWs with constraint programming based column generation. *Annals of Operations Research*, 130:199–216, 2004.

[101] D. M. Ryan and J. C. Falkner. On the integer properties of scheduling set partitioning models. *European Journal of Operational Research*, 35(3):442–456, 1988.

[102] M. Savelsbergh. Local search in routing problems with time windows. *Annals of Operations Research*, 4(285-305), 1985.

[103] M. W. P. Savelsbergh. The vehicle routing problem with time windows: Minimizing route duration. *ORSA Journal on Computing*, 4(2):146–154, 1992.

[104] J. Schulze and T. Fahle. A parallel algorithm for the vehicle routing problem with time window constraints. *Annals of Operations Research*, 86:585–607, 1999.

[105] M. Sellmann, K. Zervoudakis, P. Stamatopoulos, and T. Fahle. Crew assignment via constraint programming: Integrating column generation and heuristic tree search. *Annals of Operations Research*, 115(1):207–225, 2002.

[106] P. Shaw. Using constraint programming and local search methods to solve vehicle routing problems. In M. Maher and J.-F. Puget, editors, *Fourth International Conference on Principles and Practice of Constraint Programming (CP '98)*. Springer-Verlag, 1998.

[107] M. Solomon. Algorithms for the vehicle routing and scheduling problem with time window constraints. *Operations Research*, 35(254-265), 1987.

[108] H. Sontrop, P. van der Horn, and M. Uetz. Fast ejection chain algorithms for vehicle routing with time windows. In M. J. Blesa, C. Blum, A. Roli, and M. Sampels, editors, *Hybrid Metaheuristics*, volume 3636 of *Lecture Notes in Computer Science*, pages 78–89. Springer-Verlag, Berlin, 2005.

[109] E. Taillard, P. Badeau, M. Gendreau, F. Guertain, and J.-Y. Potvin. A new neighbourhood structure for the vehicle routing problem with time windows. Technical Report CRT-95-66, Centre de Recherche sur les Transports, University of Montreal, 1995.

[110] É. D. Taillard, P. Badeau, M. Gendreau, F. Guertin, and J. Potvin. A tabu search heuristic for the vehicle routing problem with soft time windows. *Transportation Science*, 31:170–186, 1997.

[111] P. Toth and D. Vigo, editors. *The Vehicle Routing Problem*, volume 9 of *SIAM Monographs on Discrete Mathematics and Applications*. SIAM, 2002.

[112] P. Toth and D. Vigo. The granular tabu search and its application to the vehicle-routing problem. *INFORMS Journal on Computing*, 15(4):333–346, 2003.

[113] A. Van Breedam. Improvement heuristics for the vehicle routing problem based on simulated annealing. *European Journal of Operational Research*, 86(3):480–490, 1995.

[114] P. Van Hentenryck, Y. Deville, and C. Teng. A generic arc consistency algorithm and its specializations. *Artificial Intelligence*, 57:291–321, 1992.

[115] L. A. Wolsey and G. L. Nemhauser. *Integer and Combinatorial Optimization*. Wiley-Interscience Series in Discrete Mathematics and Optimization. Wiley-Interscience, New York, 1999.

[116] H. Xu, Z. Chen, S. Rajagopal, and S. Arunapuram. Solving a practical pickup and delivery problem. *Transportation Science*, 37(3):347–364, 2003.

Handbook of Constraint Programming
Edited by F. Rossi, P. van Beek and T. Walsh

Chapter 24

Configuration

Ulrich Junker

Configuration is the task of composing a customized system out of generic components. This task is of concern to everybody as component-based systems are omnipresent in modern industry. Prominent examples of component-based systems are computers, home cinemas, cars, and trucks. Classic examples are kitchen and furniture that can be assembled from a given catalog of components. As the need for customization is growing, more and more products follow the pattern of a component system. New examples are service packs such as telecommunication offers, loans and insurance products, but also travel packages and other examples from the service industry. Finally, we should not forget component-based software systems.

Components are generic in nature and can be produced in mass, but are destined to support customized solutions. The available components for a given type of system are usually described in the form of a catalog. Each catalog item is a product type and describes the functional and technical characteristics of the component. For example, take a printer component. The function is printing. The functional characteristics include printing quality and support of colors. The technical characteristics include printing type (laser, jet) and printing speed.

Whereas the catalog describes the generic knowledge of components, a customer usually has specific requirements for the desired component-based system. For example, the customer wants to set up a home movie studio that allows the filming, editing, and showing of movies and optionally the printing of snapshots and insertion of photos. To match the specific customer requirements, a configuration of the components needs to be determined. A configuration is a set of instances of the available component types that are customized and combined to meet the requirements. A configuration for the home movie studio consists of a video camera with analog output, a video recorder with analog input, and a TV screen. Another configuration consists of a video camera with digital output, a computer with a card for digital video capture, software for video editing, a DVD reader/writer, a printer, and a scanner.

The task of finding a suitable configuration encounters several difficulties. Firstly, there can be a huge number of configurations responding to the customer requirements. The number of alternatives may be large even if a single component needs to be chosen. The customer usually is not satisfied with an arbitrary choice, but has preferences on multiple criteria of the catalog items such as the color or seat material of a desired car. Hence, a configuration problem may correspond to a multicriteria decision-making problem. Normally, a configuration does not consist of a single component, but multiple components. Car configuration problems allow the choice of multiple options that are subject to technical constraints. For example, the choices of a roof rack and of a cabriolet are incompatible. In this case, the configuration problem is a combinatorial problem. In more complex examples such as the configuration of instrumentation and control systems, the number of required components is initially unknown. The problem space of the configuration task then contains a possibly infinite number of candidate configurations. Universally quantified constraints can be used to represent knowledge about unknown parts and we obtain a satisfiability problem in a (decidable) fragment of first-order logic. Finally, a configuration problem can be large in size and involve huge numbers of product types and constraints.

Complex configuration problems are, for example, encountered in the engineering and manufacturing departments of the computer and automotive industries, which need to complete customized sales orders by choosing suitable parts from huge catalogs. This situation has led to the development of configurators that do this completion automatically while respecting difficult technical constraints. However, configurators can also support the sales process and assist the user in choosing options while guaranteeing their compatibility.

Although the first configurators were based on production rules, Constraint Programming (CP) nowadays appears to be the method of choice for solving diverse forms of configuration problems. CP addresses the complete space of possible configurations, no more and no less. End users can formulate arbitrary requirements without taking the risk that their favorite configurations are forgotten. CP handles the combinatorial aspects of configuration problems. CP is able to discover unforeseen interactions between different components and constraints thanks to propagation, search, and learning algorithms. CP can also profit from existing expertise in solving configuration problems by using it for guiding the search.

However, classic CP methods lacked appropriate techniques to represent complex configuration knowledge, to reason about an unknown number of components, to handle user preferences, or to provide explanations when interactive solving ran into failure. Specific research on constraint-based configurators has addressed those points by incorporating techniques from fields such as knowledge representation, theorem proving, and preference handling. This handbook chapter gives a survey of the main techniques.

Section 24.1 explains the diversity of configuration problems and extracts specific challenges for CP. Section 24.2 distinguishes different kinds of knowledge used in configuration problems, which can be used to build rather different constraint models as explained in section 24.3. Section 24.4 presents the problem-solving tasks occurring in configuration.

24.1   What Is Configuration?

24.1.1   A Whole Spectrum of Problems

Configuration has been an outgrowth of research on rule-based expert systems. John McDermott [41] used the term configuration for a specific form of a design task [9], where a system was assembled out of predefined components that are connected in predefined

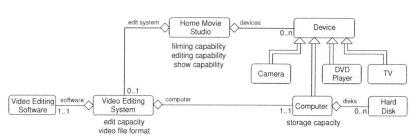

Figure 24.1: Component types of a home movie studio.

ways. Whereas more innovative design tasks often require a suitable modeling of the physical behavior of components [64], work on rule-based configurators focused on the functional aspects of components. Frayman and Mittal summarized those approaches by a general definition of the configuration task [44] and thus provided a foundation of the field of configuration similar to Reiter's for the fault diagnosis in technical systems [49]. The essence of this definition is as follows: A configuration problem is characterized by two constituents:

1. A catalog which describes the generic components in terms of their functional and technical properties and the relationship between both.

2. User requirements and user preferences about the functional characteristics of the desired configuration.

The configuration task consists of finding the following answer:

1. One or more configurations that satisfy all requirements and that optimize the preferences if those requirements are consistent.

2. An explanation of failure in the other case.

A configuration is a set of customized components together with a description of their connections. A component itself is defined by its type, its attributes, and its subcomponents. Attributes may express functional properties such as filming capability or edit capacity in terms of filmed hours (see Figure 24.1). However, attributes may also express technical properties that describe how a given functional property is achieved. For example, the video file format (AVI, MPEG2) used for editing and the storage capacity are technical characteristics. If a given functional property is fulfilled by a single component, then this component is primitive and has no subcomponents. In the movie studio example, a video camera directly realizes the filming functionality. However, a function may also be fulfilled by a combination of components. The combination can be achieved by a composite component that has subcomponents. For example, the storage capacity of a movie studio system may be supplied by a computer as well as the external disks of the computer, which thus all together achieve the required edit capacity. The combination can also be achieved by an architecture that defines how components need to be combined to fulfill the function. For example, the home movie studio may have a video editing system, which consists of a computer, editing software, and other components such as a video capture card and a video recording facility. This video editing system is not a component that can be chosen from a catalog, but a 'functional unit' that describes how other components need to be combined for the purpose of video editing.

The general description of the configuration task covers a large spectrum of concrete configuration problems and can be simplified depending on the application domain and the purpose of the configurator. As explained in [28, 51], it is useful to distinguish configuration for sales and configuration for manufacturing and engineering. Sales configurators address the needs of laymen in business-to-customer applications (B2C) or buyers in business-to-business applications (B2B). Components are described in terms of sales categories and correspond to items that customers can order. Their level of detail is much smaller than that of the parts that can be manufactured. The result of the sales configuration can be used as input for a technical configurator that checks whether the ordered system can be produced. The configurator uses existing product models in the form of bill-of-materials and compatibility tables and chooses a structure and the parts of the product. Whereas sales configurators are highly interactive and user-driven, manufacturing requires configurators that automatically complete given requirements.

The structure of a configured system depends on the application domain. A car configuration usually consists of a small number of features. A configured computer is typically described by a small hierarchy of parts. A custom kitchen may have an unbounded number of parts. An instrumentation-and-control system may additionally require that an unbounded number of parts is packed into an unknown number of racks and boards.

This difference in structure explains why so many different techniques have been applied to configuration problems. A first survey of configuration techniques given by [51] distinguishes rule-based reasoning [41], model-based reasoning [44], and case-based reasoning for configuration. The model-based branch covers approaches based on description logic [42], constraint programming [43, 59], and resource models [31]. The survey now needs to be completed by approaches based on SAT [55], binary decision diagrams [29], integer programming [62], and also answer-set programming [54]. Furthermore, there have been various attempts to combine several techniques in order to enhance the modeling and solving capabilities of a configurator. The diversity of techniques is confirmed by other surveys [27, 58].

Independent of the problem and the approach, a configurator needs to address the following requirements concerning problem solving:

1. Generation of components to carry out the functional requirements.

2. Reasoning about the interactions of multiple components.

3. Detection of cases where the desired functionality cannot be implemented.

A further requirement concerns modeling. The configurator needs to provide a high-level modeling language that allows the configuration expert to model complex systems and to maintain these models.

Rule-based approaches represent functional requirements in terms of assertions in the working memory and map them to components through rules. A rule for selecting a component is fired if there is a requirement needing this component. When executed, a rule can generate new components, customize existing components, or add subcomponents. Depending on the context, the same function may be achieved differently, meaning that we obtain multiple rules of the form:

if function and context 1 and constraints okay then component 1

...

if function and context m and constraints okay then component n

The rule conditions need to check possible interactions with other components and may become very complex. If compatibility constraints between components are changing, then they need to be incorporated into the conditions of multiple rules. This lack of modularity caused a severe maintenance problem in the R1/XCON configurator of DEC computers [41, 4]. Furthermore, rule-based systems usually do not have the capability of detecting cases that cannot be achieved by the given catalog. Nevertheless, rule-based systems may be useful for very simple configuration problems requiring a small number of choices only.

Model-based reasoning addresses the deficiencies of rule-based reasoning. Firstly, it separates the problem description from the solving algorithm, thus allowing an analysis of the problem independent of the chosen approach. Secondly, it requires that the problem description is based on a model of the system to be configured. This model consists of decomposable entities and the interactions between these elements. Modularity or composability is thus well-addressed since components can easily be added or removed without changing the whole model. Thirdly, it requires that this problem description is complete and defines a closed space of possible configurations. If no element of this space satisfies the given requirements, then the problem has no solution.

Description logic (DL) is well-suited to describe component types and their relations. It organizes components types in a taxonomy. Description logic allows us to define complex types out of primitive types. It is able to detect specialization relations between complex types and to test the consistency of types by a process called classification. Classification can be used to solve configuration problems if the configuration knowledge can be completely expressed in the description logic. In most cases, the expressiveness of the description logic is not sufficient and a rule-based or constraint-based engine is used in addition to deal with complex compatibility and numerical constraints. Such a hybrid approach has, for example, been pursued in the CLASSICS-project [42] and in the PLAKON-project [10]. DL-based configurators have been applied to the configuration of telecommunication equipment [42], elevators [61], passenger cabins in aircrafts [27], and many other systems that have a complex structure. They also address the problem of generating a hierarchy of parts and can exploit this hierarchy for problem decomposition [39].

Resource-based approaches [31] are dedicated to complex equipment configuration problems where components provide and consume given resources. For example, the storage devices of a computer system provide storage capacity, but they consume power and slots. The slots are provided by the racks of the computer system. The purpose of the resource-based configuration process is to bring produced and consumed resources in balance, meaning that the consumed resource does not exceed the produced resource. The process starts from initial resource requirements such as a minimal storage capacity, which are consumed from outside and which need to be produced by generating and customizing suitable parts. The resource-based approach is necessary for many configuration problems, but is not sufficient on its own. As such, it is best integrated with other approaches.

Constraint satisfaction problems (CSP) are well-suited to defining a closed space of configurations. They use variables with domains. If the number of variables is fixed, then the space is obtained as the Cartesian product of the domains. Constraints also handle the interaction of multiple components. Compatibility constraints specify which components can be combined. Aggregation constraints (such as sums) are able to deduce global properties such as the produced or consumed amount of a resource. Variables express the possible choices for fulfilling a functional requirement. Since the choice should only be made if the requirement is present, we obtain a conditional disjunction of the form:

    if function then component 1 or ... or component n

The disjunction is encoded by a variable x having as domain the components that can be chosen. However, this variable should only be introduced if the function is indeed required and this may depend on other choices. Hence, new variables and constraints may be activated or generated during the problem solving. A rule-based constraint engine can add new constraints when executing rules and retract them during search thanks to a truth maintenance system (TMS) [15, 12]. For example, the configurator in [28] is based on a TMS. However, the dynamic nature of configuration problems provides a particular challenge for Constraint Programming approaches that maintain local consistency during search. Mittal and Falkenhainer therefore introduced Dynamic CSPs (now called Conditional CSPs) which have optional variables and constraints. Local consistency algorithms for Conditional CSPs have been elaborated in [43, 52]. Stumptner and Haselböck [60, 59, 17] introduced resource-based reasoning into CP and Mailharro [40] extended it with cardinality-based reasoning. The CP approach has successfully been applied to the configuration of cars, computers [18], instrumentation and control systems [40], web services [3].

SAT approaches can be seen as a special case of CP. They mainly handle requirement and compatibility constraints, but no numerical constraints such as resource constraints. They have successfully been applied to car configuration [55]. Answer-set programming [54] formulates configuration knowledge through form of default rules, while ensuring functionally well-justified configurations through groundedness conditions [56]. This approach has been applied to software configuration [65].

Interactive sales configurators are simultaneously solving the configuration problems of multiple customers and require rapid response times. As these problems differ only in the requirements, but not in the catalog, preprocessing techniques can be used to compute configurations in advance. For problems involving a fixed number of parts with small finite domains, it may be possible to represent the whole configuration space compactly by a binary decision diagram [29], an automaton [2], or the decomposable negation normal form [11]. Other knowledge-compilation techniques include synthesis trees [63] and clustertrees [14, 46]. All these techniques are compatible with respect to a CP approach. Knowledge compilation has successfully been applied to car configuration problems [29, 46].

CP is well-suited to define a clear configuration space. It ensures composability by treating interactions between arbitrary components and by deriving global properties of sets of components. It also offers a high freedom in modeling and the modeling is completely declarative. Thus, CP meets the requirement for an expressive and maintainable modeling capability that has been stated above. All these advantages made it the method of choice for configuration. However, configuration problems posed several challenges to CP which are summarized in the next sections.

24.1.2 Modeling Challenges for CP

Most applications of Constraint Programming (CP) concern real-world systems that are modeled in an object-oriented way. CP addresses the combinatorial aspect of the application to be solved. It is often possible to isolate this aspect by generating a constraint model from the given object model. For example, a production plan in a scheduling application is translated into a set of start- and end-time variables and precedence constraints. The object model can be completely ignored when solving the scheduling problem. However, this complete separation of object model and constraint model is not possible for configuration problems, which poses new challenges for the modeling and the modeling language:

Product catalogs: Configurators need to be deeply embedded in business processes and reuse existing product models in order to facilitate modeling and maintenance. Existing product catalogs in the form of database tables need to be mapped to constraint models. Since they strongly influences the structure of the constraint model, they cannot be ignored when discussing constraint models for configuration.

Knowledge representation: Knowledge of the component structure is usually represented in the form of a taxonomy of component types. More specific types add attributes, domain restrictions, and subcomponents. Whereas object-oriented programming assumes that the type of an object is static, it is represented as a variable in constraint-based configuration. Constraint reasoning can specialize the component by reducing the domain of the type variable. The component then inherits the properties of the more specialized types during the solving process, which leads to the activation of new variables and constraints. The constraint engine has to support this inheritance process.

Resource constraints: The number of parts of a configuration may not be bounded, but depends on global resource requirements. Hence, the set of components is not given in this case, but has to be determined as a result of the configuration task. In order to express constraints on those unknown parts, universally quantified constraints are necessary. Furthermore, variables representing the choice of an unknown part will have an open domain that is extended during constraint solving. Constraints on variables with open domains such as resource constraints need to deal with this situation.

Preference models: A further challenge is obtained by the potentially huge set of solutions. Since these solutions differ much in their characteristics, user preferences need to be taken into account when solving the configuration problem.

24.1.3 Problem Solving Challenges for CP

The solving process faces additional challenges that depend on the type of the configuration problem. Configurators for manufacturing and engineering need to handle the following issues in addition to normal solving strategies for CP:

Top-down refinement: a search strategy for finding a configuration cannot make decisions in an arbitrary order, but needs to implement top-down refinement that configures components before their subcomponents and that specializes the type variable before instantiating inherited attributes.

Component generation: resource requirements may require the generation of an unbounded number of parts. Generation steps need to be incorporated into the solving strategy. A careful control of the generation is needed in order to avoid cyclic reproduction of the same state and to avoid the inclusion of parts that do not fulfill any function.

Although interactive sales configurators are treating much simpler problems, they are facing challenges as well:

User Scalability: web-based configurators need to solve many similar problems and this within short response times. It is therefore reasonable to share information between different threads (e.g. learning of strategies, conflicts, and solutions) or to preprocess the catalog by knowledge-compilation techniques.

Explanations: interactive configurators let the user make the choices. As the user may easily encounter over-constrained problems, an explanation of failure in the form of conflicting requirements is needed. An explanation facility is a critical feature for an interactive configurator.

Preference elicitation: interaction cycles can be shortened if the configurator remembers or acquires user preferences. The configurator can thus offer a preferred solution and automatically reactivate preferred choices when the user takes back options that are in conflict with those choices.

24.2   Configuration Knowledge

This section introduces the knowledge that exists about components, namely component catalogs in sub-section 24.2.1, component structure in sub-section 24.2.2, and component constraints in sub-section 24.2.2. It introduces the different ingredients of a component such as functions (features), attributes, subcomponents and connections, and resources and provides the basic vocabulary for formulating constraint models.

24.2.1   Configuration Catalog

The literature distinguishes a large variety of configuration problems. In spite of this diversity, all those problems are based on the notion of a primitive component that does not contain subcomponents and that directly fulfills a required function.

Each primitive component has a concrete type and a set of attributes describing the functional and technical characteristics of the component. Functional characteristics are either capabilities which are described by boolean attributes (such as printing) or capacities which are described by numerical attributes (such as storage capacity). A concrete type is a product type that can be ordered by the customer (in the case of a sales configurator) or that can be produced (in the case of a configurator for manufacturing). The technical characteristics are represented by further attributes that are either uniquely specified for the concrete type or that have multiple options. A primitive component is thus characterized by its type and the values of its attributes.

Knowledge about the available primitive components is available in the form of product catalogs. The product catalogs are an integral part of enterprise resource planning (ERP) systems that support engineering and manufacturing. As it is important to embed configurators into those business processes, configurators need to reuse existing product models to facilitate modeling and maintenance. The product catalogs are available in the form of database tables. Each table describes a technical (component) type. There may be a table for hard disks, another one for video cameras, and another one for DVD players. A technical type defines the functional and technical attributes of a component, but does not specify the values for those characteristics. A technical component can be realized by multiple concrete (component) types. A concrete type specifies a concrete value for each attribute or gives the set of possible attribute values. For example, a concrete screen type may have a fixed size or a small set of possible sizes. The set of possible values can be expressed by an enumeration of values or by a range of two numerical bounds. The domain

Table 24.1: Catalog (video camera).

Type	Output	Input	price
cam1	analog	none	200
cam2	AVI	none	300
cam3	anal.+AVI.	AVI	400
cam4	AVI	AVI	500

of an attribute for a concrete type can thus be a singleton, an interval, or an enumeration of values. Whereas a single database column is sufficient for singleton domains, two columns are needed to represent interval domains. Attributes with enumerated domains may be represented by further tables. As a consequence, a product catalog in the form of a database does not directly reflect the product model. Annotations of the database are needed to interpret them in terms of a product model and to transform them into the following form:

Definition 24.1 (Catalog knowledge). *A configuration catalog is described by a set T of technical types, a set L of concrete types (the leaf types), and a set A of attributes that are all mutually disjoint. Each technical type t in T has a set* attrs$(t) \subseteq A$ *of attributes and a (non-empty) set* subtypes$(t) \subseteq L$ *of concrete types. The set of leaf types of two different technical types are mutually disjoint. Each technical type t has a table which defines a domain $D(a, t')$ for each attribute $a \in$ attrs(t) and each product type $t' \in$ subtypes(t).*

Table 24.1 describes the catalog of video cameras. The first column describes the camera type. The other columns specify the values for the input and output formats and the price.

This catalog is important when setting up a constraint model. Firstly, it provides the domains for the variables that are introduced for attributes. Secondly, it defines a constraint between the concrete type of a component and its attributes. We call this the catalog constraint. This constraint expresses a relationship between functional requirements and the technical characteristics of a primitive component, including its type. Given a user requirement on a functional property (e.g. a maximal price of 300), local consistency methods will remove all concrete types that are unable to provide this property (such as the camera types cam3 and cam4). As a consequence, the remaining types are able to meet this functional requirement. Thus, existing product models yield an important part of a constraint-based configuration model. Catalog constraints are particularly important since they are able to classify a component by reducing the domain of its type variable.

24.2.2 Partonomies and Taxonomies

Whereas sales configurators often deal only with primitive components, manufacturing and engineering needs to refine those components by suitable parts. The part-of-structure of components is therefore of central importance for configuration.

A composite component has a concrete type, a set of attributes, and a set of subcomponents (or parts), which may be primitive or composite components. Following [16, 39], it makes sense to stipulate that components own their subcomponents. Hence, a subcomponent cannot be a part of two different components. Furthermore, the part-of-relation between components must neither contain cycles, nor infinite descending chains. A (sub)-

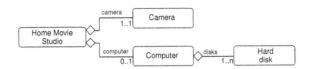

Figure 24.2: A partonomy of functional and technical types.

component may also have a set of connections to other (sub)-components of the configuration. There are no restrictions concerning connections. Subcomponents as well as connected components can be grouped together into subsets of components, which are called ports in [44]. A port contains components that are functionally equivalent for the given problem. We distinguish partonomic ports that contain subcomponents and connection-ports that contain connected components. Partonomic ports own their elements and are mutually disjoint.

The structure of a composite component is defined by a structural product model. The partonomy describes the possible decompositions of components of a given type. Figure 24.2 shows the partonomy of a simple home movie studio. It consists of a camera and an optional computer which can have several hard disks. Such a partonomy can be complemented by a 'topology', which defines the connections between components and which consists of arbitrary relations between the types of a partonomy.

Product models in ERP systems contain information about the partonomy. The bill-of-material (BoM) describes how many subcomponents of which type are needed to assemble or to manufacture a component. A BoM is represented by a graph. The nodes are component types. The edges represent has-Part-relations and are labeled with a cardinality. An edge from type t_1 to type t_2 with label k means that a component of type t_1 contains k subcomponents of type t_2. It can be assumed that a bill-of-material of configurable products is a directed acyclic graph. A BoM can easily be translated into a partonomy. Each node in the BoM corresponds to a technical type and each edge from type t_1 to type t_2 with label k in the BoM is translated into a $1 : k$-relation from t_1 to t_2.

Concrete types specify or restrict the attribute values of a component. They may also specify the number of parts of a component (e.g. the number of wheels of a car). Technical types define the functional and technical attributes and the component structure. They regroup together multiple concrete types. However, it makes sense to further regroup technical types according to their functional characteristics. For example, the device for storing an edited movie can be a hard disk, a DVD writer, or a video recorder, or the camera itself. It therefore makes sense to regroup these technical types under a functional type called storage device. This functional type defines functional attributes such as a writing capability and the storage capacity.

We thus obtain a taxonomy of types that consists of three layers: 1. A hierarchy of functional types. 2. A layer of technical types. 3. The leaf layer of concrete types. It is then possible to create an instance of a functional type, such as a storage device, and to configure it by specializing its type. This process will add new attributes to the component and refine its structure incrementally. A taxonomy thus describes alternative ways to map functional requirements to structure and to refine structural skeletons. Partonomies with taxonomies correspond to bill-of-materials with alternatives. Figure 24.3 shows the partonomy of the

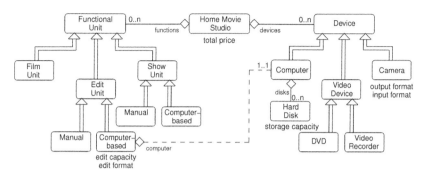

Figure 24.3: A partonomy with taxonomy.

home movie studio which consists of functional units and devices. The functional units describe how the filming, editing, showing functions are realized. The edit and show unit can be manual or computer-based. Depending on these choices, different kind of devices need to be added. There is also a connection port indicated by a dashed line. A partonomy with a taxonomy can be represented in the form of a UML-diagram [16] or by a description logic. We define the structure of a component independent of a formal language:

Definition 24.2 (Structural knowledge). *A structural configuration model consists of a set $\hat{T}$ of functional types, a set T of technical types, a set $\hat{A}$ of attributes, a set $\hat{P}$ of partonomic ports, and a set of $\hat{Q}$ of connection ports, all mutually disjoint:*

1. *Each functional type $t \in \hat{T}$ has a (possibly empty) set* subtypes$(t) \subseteq \hat{T} \cup T$ *of direct subtypes. The set of direct subtypes of two types are mutually disjoint meaning that each type has at most one direct supertype.*

2. *Each functional or technical type t in $\hat{T} \cup T$ has a set* attrs$(t) \subseteq \hat{A}$ *of attributes and a set* ports$(t) \subseteq \hat{P} \cup \hat{Q}$ *of partonomic and connection ports. Each port p has a destination type* type$(t, p) \in \hat{T} \cup T$, *a minimal cardinality* min(t, p), *and a maximal cardinality* max(t, p).

3. *There is no sequence $t_1, \ldots, t_n$ of types in $\hat{T} \cup T$ such that $t_1 = t_n$ and t_i is a subtype of t_{i-1} or the destination type of a partonomic port of t_{i-1}.*

A structural configuration model can be extended by a configuration catalog if both coincide in their technical types as well as in the attributes attrs(t) *of each technical type.*

A configuration can be obtained from a structural model by instantiating a component type. Table 24.2 shows the instance ourStudio of the Home Movie Studio which inherits the attributes and ports of this type. The attributes are assigned to values from the attribute domain and the ports are filled by part lists. For each part, a type is chosen and the part inherits the attributes and ports of this type, meaning that this process is repeated recursively. Hence, a structural configuration model generates a nested data structure when being instantiated. This data structure is central for the modeling and solving of configuration problems. In the remainder of this chapter, we need to refer to different elements of this data structure. Firstly, we will define a view on all the parts of the

Table 24.2: A configuration.

ourStudio: a Home Movie Studio	
. *total price:* 2000 $	(an attribute)
. *functional units:*	(a partonomic port)
. . unit(ourStudio,1): a Film Unit	(a part)
. . unit(ourStudio,2): a Computerized Video Edit Unit	(a part)
. . . *edit capacity:* 20 hours	
. . . *edit format:* AVI	
. . . *computer:* device(ourStudio,2)	(a connection port)
. *devices:*	(a partonomic port)
. . device(ourStudio,1): a Cam4 Camera	(a catalog part)
. . . *output format:* AVI	
. . . *input format:* AVI	
. . device(ourStudio,2): a Computer	(a catalog part)
. . . *external hard disks*	(a partonomic port)
. . . . disk(device(ourStudio,2),1): a Hard Disk	(a catalog part)
. . . . . *storage capacity:* 120 GB	
. . . . disk(device(ourStudio,2),2): a Hard Disk	(a catalog part)
. . . . . *storage capacity:* 160 GB	

component. This view includes also the indirect parts, i.e. the parts of the parts of the component and so on. In the example, the part view contains ourStudio, unit(ourStudio,1), unit(ourStudio,2), device(ourStudio,1), device(ourStudio,2), disk(device(ourStudio,2),1), disk(device(ourStudio,2),2). The part view contains all parts that are generated for a configuration. This information will be needed when we model connection ports as these ports are filled with the generated parts. Secondly, we define a view on all ports of a component. This includes the direct ports of a component, but also the ports of all components that are contained in a given port. As a port describes a set of parts that play the same role in a configuration, most configuration constraints are formulated with the help of ports. For example, if we want to sum the storage capacities of all the hard disks of the home movie studio, we need an indirect port that contains all the hard disks of the studio. Thirdly, we introduce a view on the properties of a direct or indirect port. An example is the storage capacities of our indirect hard disk port. In addition to the attributes, we include other properties, namely the types and the port cardinalities. All these properties can be subject to constraints. The property view is thus essential for the formulation of constraint models. All three views need to have counterparts in an expressive modeling language.

We will define all the three views for an anonymous instance of a component type t Not only does this instance inherit attributes and ports from the direct supertype $super(t$ of t, but also from the indirect supertypes $super^*(t) := \bigcup_{i=0}^{\infty} super^i(t)$. As the anonymous component can be specialized to any subtype of t, we take also attributes and parts of all the subtypes of t into account when defining the views. The direct and indirect subtypes are contained in $subtypes^*(t) := \{t' \in \hat{T} \cup T \cup L \mid t \in super^*(t')\}$. As components need to be specialized to leaf types, we also define the set of leaf types $leaves(t) := subtypes^*(t) \cap L$ where $\hat{L}$ includes the types from $\hat{T}$, T, and L that have no subtype.

Now we formally define the part view. The set $parts(x : t)$ of direct parts of a component x of type t is the smallest set which satisfies the following properties:

1. If p is a single-valued partonomic port of a type in $super^*(t)$ or $subtypes^*(t)$ then the port has a unique part $p(x)$ in $parts(x : t)$ which is an instance of the port's destination type.

2. If p is a multi-valued partonomic port of a type in $super^*(t)$ or $subtypes^*(t)$ then the port has multiple parts $p(x, 1), p(x, 2), p(x, 3), \ldots$ in $parts(x : t)$, which are all instances of the port's destination type.

If a set X of components is given, then their parts are determined by the element-wise application of the *parts*-function and we obtain the set of all direct and indirect parts of x by taking the reflexive and transitive closure:

$$parts(X) := \bigcup_{x:t \in X} parts(x : t) \quad \text{and} \quad parts^*(x : t) := \bigcup_{i=0}^{\infty} parts^i(\{x : t\}) \quad (24.1)$$

The infinite set $parts^*(x : t)$ contains all potential parts for a component x. A configuration of the component x consists of a finite subset of this part universe.

Next we define the port view. The set of ports $ports(x : t)$ of a component x of type t is the set of all ports $p(x)$ such that p is a (partonomic or connection) port of a type in $super^*(t)$. The set of ports of multiple components is obtained by the element-wise application of this operator. The reflexive and transitive closure defines the port view of x:

$$ports(X) := \bigcup_{x:t \in X} ports(x : t) \quad \text{and} \quad ports^*(x : t) := \bigcup_{i=0}^{\infty} ports^i(\{x : t\}) \quad (24.2)$$

Each element $p_1(p_2(\ldots p_k(x)))$ of $ports^*(x : t)$ has a minimal cardinality that is obtained by multiplying the minimal cardinalities of all the p_i's and a maximal cardinality that is obtained by multiplying the maximal cardinalities of all the p_i's. If the maximal cardinality is strictly greater than 1 then the port is called multi-valued. If the maximal cardinality is equal to 1 then it is called single-valued. If the minimal cardinality of a single-valued port is 0 then this port is called optional.

Finally, we define the property view. The set $props(x : t)$ of properties of a component of type t is the smallest set that has the following properties:

1. The leaf type $type(x)$ of component x is in $props(x : t)$.

2. If a is an attribute of a type in $super^*(t)$ then the attribute $a(x)$ of x is in $props(x : t)$.

3. If p is a multi-valued port of a type in $super^*(t)$ then the cardinality $\#p(x)$ of the port $p(x)$ is in $props(x : t)$

The set of properties of multiple components is obtained by the element-wise application of this operator:

$$props(X) := \bigcup_{x:t \in X} props(x : t) \quad (24.3)$$

Given this, we introduce the properties $props(ports^*(x : t))$ of the component and of all its direct and indirect ports. A property of a single-valued port is called single-valued, that of a multi-valued port is called multi-valued, and that of an optional port is called optional.

The constraint model needs to take into account the knowledge of the component structure. If an instance of a functional type is configured, then its type variable has all leaf types of the functional type as possible values. When constraint propagation reduces the domain of this variable, it automatically classifies the component, meaning that the component now belongs to a more specialized type. It then needs to inherit the properties of the specialized type. These properties can require further choices, meaning that new variables and their constraints need to be included in the constraint model. Constraint models that model this inheritance reasoning are therefore dynamic or conditional (see section 24.3.4).

Table 24.3: Compatibility of storage device and video format.

Storage device	Video Format
hard-disk	AVI
hard-disk	MPEG2
DVD	MPEG2
VCR	analog
Digital Camera	AVI
Analog camera	analog

24.2.3 Configuration Constraints

If a catalog specifies unique values for all attributes, then functional requirements can simply be fulfilled by choosing a concrete type for each component. However, additional choices are necessary in the general case in order to configure a component. Firstly, a concrete component type may allow different possible values for technical attributes. Secondly, a component type may not have a fixed function, but permit a choice of alternative functions. In both cases, the attributes of the components may have multiple possible values even if the component type has been chosen. Not all the combinations of those values are legal. Configuration constraints describe which combinations correspond to legal product configurations. There are different kinds of configuration constraints, namely compatibility constraints, requirement constraints and resource constraints.

A compatibility constraint specifies which value combinations are legal. It corresponds to a standard constraint in CSPs and has a relation R and a scope. The relation can be specified by a compatibility table which contains the valid value combinations or by an incompatibility table which contains the invalid combinations. These tables can usually be imported from the existing product model of an ERP system. However, the relation can also be specified by a predicate such as equality, inequality, greater-than. The relation is used to restrict the possible values of direct and indirect properties of a component x of a type t. Hence, the scope is an n-ary tuple $a_1(x), \ldots, a_n(x)$ of properties from $props(ports^*(x:t))$. If these properties are all single-valued, then the constraint is satisfied by a configuration of a component x of type t if the configuration satisfies

$$\exists (v_1, \ldots, v_n) \in R : (a_1(x) = v_1 \wedge \ldots \wedge a_n(x) = v_n) \tag{24.4}$$

The configuration satisfies $a_i(x) = v_i$ iff it assigns the value v_i to the property a_i of x Compatibility constraints may, in particular, be used to restrict combinations of the types of subcomponents. For example, figure 24.3 shows a compatibility constraint between the storage device type of the edit unit and the video file format of the edited movie.

A requirement constraint is also specified by a table and a scope of component properties. However, it expresses a requirement relation between two component properties. A tuple (v_1, v_2) in the requirement table means that the value v_1 of the first property requires the value v_2 for the second property. A requirement constraint for type t has a requirement table R and a scope $a_1(x), a_2(x)$ consisting of single-valued properties from $props(ports^*(x:t))$. The constraint is satisfied by a configuration of a component x of type t if the configuration satisfies

$$\forall (v_1, v_2) \in R : (a_1(x) = v_1 \Rightarrow a_2(x) = v_2) \tag{24.5}$$

Table 24.4: Requirements for devices.

Functional unit	Required Device
Film Unit	Camera
Manual Edit Unit	Video Recorder
Computer-based Edit Unit	Computer
Manual Show Unit	TV
Manual Show Unit	DVD Player
Computer-based Show Unit	Computer

Requirement constraints can be used to restrict combinations of the types of subcomponents. Figure 24.4 shows a requirement constraint between types of the functional units of the home movie studio and the types of its devices. For example, if the functional units include a film unit and a manual show unit, then the devices must include a camera, a TV, and a DVD player.

Compatibility constraints can also be applied to multi-valued properties. For example, a computer component may contain a set of peripheries. This set will be subject to multiple compatibility and requirement constraints. However, these constraints are not applied to the components themselves, but to their types. For example, a scanner may require a printer. Two additional difficulties are arising then. Firstly, it is necessary to specify whether the constraint applies to all or to one value as the set of periphery types can contain multiple elements. Secondly, the table entry itself can represent sets of types, namely all the leaf types that specialize the functional or technical type originally listed in the table. The equality tests $a_i(x) = v_i$ are therefore replaced by intersection tests of the form $a_i(x) \cap V_i \neq \emptyset$. This test is satisfied by a configuration of x if the configuration assigns at least one element of the set V_i to the property a_i of the component x. Hence, a compatibility constraint for type t has a compatibility table R and a scope $a_1(x), \ldots, a_n(x)$ over $props(ports^*(x : t))$. The constraint is satisfied by a configuration of a component x of type t if the configuration satisfies

$$\exists (V_1, \ldots V_n) \in R : (a_1(x) \cap V_1 \neq \emptyset \wedge \ldots \wedge a_n(x) \cap V_n \neq \emptyset) \qquad (24.6)$$

A requirement constraint for type t has a requirement table R and a scope $a_1(x), a_2(x)$ over $props(ports^*(x : t))$. The constraint is satisfied by a configuration of a component x of type t if the configuration satisfies

$$\forall (V_1, V_2) \in R : (a_1(x) \cap V_1 \neq \emptyset) \Rightarrow (a_2(x) \cap V_2 \neq \emptyset) \qquad (24.7)$$

Functional properties such as capacities can be seen as a resource that is provided by a system. An example is the storage capacity of a PC that is obtained as the sum of storage capacity of all its disks. The functional requirements usually state that a minimal amount of such a resource should be provided. To meet those requirements, a sufficient number of parts need to be created and configured. Not only can resources be provided by a system, but they can also be consumed by it. An example is the total power consumption of a PC, which is the sum of the power consumption of the PC and of its parts. The functional requirements usually state that the consumption of such a resource should not exceed a maximal amount. It is also possible that intermediate components consume resources that need to be provided by other components. Following [31], resources thus express a balancing task between consumers and producers. Resource constraints [59] ensure that the amount of a produced resource is greater than or equal to the amount of a consumed resource. A resource constraint is applied to all components of a given type t. The consumers and the producers are both represented by subsets of $ports^*(x : t)$. The produced resource is expressed by a numerical attribute that must be defined for all producers. The consumed resource is expressed by a numerical attribute that must be defined for all consumers. Since both attributes can be different, the root component for the resource constraint can play the role of a producer and consumer. Hence, a resource constraint for a component x of type is specified by a tuple $(Producers, Consumers, produced, consumed)$. This constraint is satisfied by a configuration if this configuration satisfies:

$$\sum_{\substack{p(x) \in Producers \\ o \in p(x)}} produced(o) \geq \sum_{\substack{p(x) \in Consumers \\ o \in p(x)}} consumed(o) \qquad (24.8)$$

This model covers also the case where an initial requirement for a minimal amount of a resource (such as storage capacity) needs to be provided by a component. In this case, the producers are the parts of the component (e.g. the storage devices) and the consumer is the component itself, which has a specific consumed-attribute for formulating the requirement (such as required-storage-capacity). Requirements that limit the amount of a consumed resource (e.g. the price) can be formulated as well. In this case, the consumers are the parts of the component and the producer is the component as well, which has a specific produced-attribute corresponding to the maximal amount.

It is important to understand that resource constraints express a constraint between the total amount of the resource (i.e. the result of the sum), the bounds of the produced or consumed attributes defined in the catalog, and the number of components. In order to meet minimal cardinalities of ports, new components may be generated during the configuration process. This generation is limited to partonomic ports.

Resource constraints can involve other aggregation operators than the sum. Alternatives are min, max, average. Resource constraints can also operate on sets and use a set-union as aggregation operator and the super-set-operator as comparison operator. This is needed to establish a domain for connection-ports. The connection-port (e.g. the storage device of an edit-unit) is a consumed resource that is produced by the actual parts (such as the disks of the computer, the DVD writer of the computer, or the camera).

The constraint knowledge for a component x of type t can be summarized as follows:

Definition 24.3 (Constraint knowledge). *Each type $t \in \hat{T} \cup T$ has a set* Compat$(x : t$ *of compatibility constraints, a set* Requires$(x : t)$ *of requirement constraints, and a set* Resources$(x : t)$ *of resource constraints. These sets are possibly empty.*

Component types have thus been enriched with three types of constraints, namely compatibility, requirement, and resource constraints. They are formulated on expressions that are defined by the structural model. The compatibility and requirement constraints additionally refer to database-tables that can be imported from existing ERP-systems.

24.3 Constraint Models for Configuration

A configuration problem is defined by functional requirements and by a configuration model that describes the possible configurations according to the given configuration knowledge. The configuration models in the literature differ quite substantially in the way choices and constraints are represented, although they use the same product models at their origins. It is indeed possible to build different constraint models for the given configuration knowledge. It is even possible to use different constraint models for different component types, meaning that the configuration model is a hybrid one.

We first define configuration problems in a general way. In particular, we explain when a configuration model satisfies the given functional requirements.

Without loss of generality, it can be assumed that all components that need to be configured are direct or indirect parts of a single root component, which represents the system to be configured. This root component is an instance of a suitable component type, which regroups all the principal components of the system and which contains suitable attributes to describe the functional properties of the system. If such a type does not exist in the given configuration knowledge, then it is straightforward to add such a type description.

Given the type t of the system to be configured, we define a functional space for t and a configuration space. The functional space describes the set of complete combinations of functions that can be achieved by an instance of t and the configuration space describes the set of complete configurations for an instance of type t. Such a configuration needs to describe the leaf type t^* of the instance, the values of each attribute of t^* (including those inherited from supertypes), the number of elements in each partonomic port of t^* (including those inherited from supertypes), the configuration of each element of the partonomic port, and the values of each connection port of t^* (including those inherited from supertypes). Hence, a configuration, in its fully expanded form, is a tree of property-value-pairs. Whereas the function space is finite and obtained as Cartesian product of the domains of the functional attributes of the root component, the configuration space is infinite, but contains finite elements.

The function and the configuration spaces usually are not described explicitly, but implicitly by means of a suitable constraint language. Examples for constraint languages are OPL, the CLP(X)-family, or the API's of constraint libraries. All these languages can be understood as fragments of first-order logic (cf. e.g. [25]) over a fixed structure. They provide a set of predicate symbols, which have a fixed interpretation and which are used to represent the relations of constraints. They also provide a set of function symbols, which have a fixed interpretation and which are used to formulate constrained expressions. Hence, a constraint language can be specified by a first-order language and a structure. For the purpose of configuration, the language is enriched by function symbols representing the ports and properties of components. The interpretation of these additional function symbols can be freely chosen when determining a configuration.

A configuration problem for an instance x of type t is then specified by a set of functional requirements $F(x : t)$ and a configuration model $K(x : t)$. The functional requirements are expressed as constraints on the direct functional properties of the root component. The configuration model[1] is expressed by constraints on arbitrary properties and

---

[1]The term 'configuration model' should not be confused with a logical model of the configuration constraints. The logical model indeed corresponds to a configuration that satisfies those constraints.

ports of the root component, including the functional and technical characteristics. The constraints can contain universal quantifiers, logical connectives, numerical operations, equalities, and comparisons. Compared to Solvers for classical CSPs, a configurator needs to handle these kinds of constraints as well as optional variables, partonomic ports, and variables and constraints with open domains.

A configuration problem has a solution iff the union of the functional requirements and the configuration model is satisfiable, i.e. $F(x : t) \cup K(x : t) \not\models \bot$ [23]. As noted in [28], it is important that the resulting configurations are functionally complete. This means that the configuration S contains sufficient information to decide whether it satisfies an arbitrary requirement or whether it does not satisfy it. S is functionally complete iff either $S \models F(x : t)$ or $S \not\models F(x : t)$ holds for all requirements $F(x : t)$. Functional completeness is easy to achieve in a constraint-based approach. It is sufficient to include the functional properties in the configuration. Or more formally: functional completeness is straightforward if the function space is obtained as a projection of the configuration space on the functional properties.

As the configuration model is expressed in first-order logic, it is not evident whether a configuration problem is decidable. However, configuration problems satisfy the finite model property meaning that the (part) universe of a configuration is finite. The solution can thus be found by an enumeration of the universes. Secondly, the particular partonomic structure and constraint structure used in this chapter allows a complete calculus for proving non-satisfiability of an infeasible configuration problem. The proof can thus be found by enumerating all candidate proofs. The configuration problems considered in this chapter are therefore decidable.

In its most general form, a configuration model must be able to describe configurations in its fully extended form where all parts are clearly distinguished and exhaustively described. However, it often is not necessary to distinguish all parts. For example, it may be reasonable to assume that the wheels of a car have the same characteristics. It is then sufficient to represent their number and their product type, which uniquely determines their attribute values. In even simpler problems such as option selection, it is even sufficient to characterize the set of options by a set of types. Hence, the representation of configurations can be simplified and this simplification leads to simpler problems. Simplified configuration problems are also obtained if the given configuration knowledge has a particular form.

In the next sections, we introduce several kinds of configuration problems. We distinguish static problems describing a configuration by a fixed set of properties and dynamic problems that involve optional properties or even an unbounded number of properties. Static problems include option selection, shopping lists, or the configuration of systems with a fixed and deterministic structure (car configuration). Dynamic problems include systems with optional parts (computer configuration) and systems with an unbounded number of parts (such as rack configuration or bin packing).

24.3.1 Boolean Models for Option Selection

A very simple configuration problem is obtained if the configured system consists of a set of parts which are entirely characterized by their concrete types. An example is the selection of optional parts for the home movie studio such as a scanner, a printer, an external hard disk. Each option is described by an option type, which has no particular attributes, and each option type can be chosen once only. The options may be organized in a taxonomy and are subject to requirement and compatibility constraints. The functional properties of the system are simply represented by boolean attributes that are linked with the option types via requirement constraints.

Definition 24.4 (Option selection problem). *The structural model of an option selection problem consists of a type S corresponding to the configured system, a functional type F regrouping all the functions and a functional type O regrouping all the options. The type S has a partonomic port that contains functions from F and a partonomic port that contains the options O. The type F is the root of a function taxonomy and the type O is the root of an option taxonomy, which has concrete types as leaf types. None of the types has attributes. There are requirement constraints between the types of the functions in the function-port and the types of the options in the options-port. There are requirement and compatibility constraints between the types of options in the options-port.*

The configurations of an option selection problem can be described by a boolean constraint model. This model has the following boolean variables:

- A boolean variable f_i for each type in the function taxonomy $subtypes^*(F)$. This variable has the value 1 iff the configured system has a function of this type.

- A boolean variable t_j for each type in the option taxonomy $subtypes^*(O)$. This variable has the value 1 iff the configured system has an option of this type.

An entry (f, t) in a requirement constraint between the types of the functions in the function-port and the types of the options in the option ports is represented by an implication:

$$f \Rightarrow t \tag{24.9}$$

The direct subtypes $t_1, \ldots, t_n$ of t in the options or function-taxonomy are modeled by a disjunction:

$$t \equiv t_1 \lor \ldots \lor t_n \tag{24.10}$$

A compatibility constraint between the types of the options in the option port can be represented by a set of negative clauses supposing that the constraint has a negative table N which contains the forbidden tuples:

$$\neg t_1 \lor \neg t_2 \quad \text{for all} \quad (t_1, t_2) \in N \tag{24.11}$$

User requirements can be represented by constraints involving the boolean variables f for the function. A boolean problem can be solved by a SAT-solver.

Option selection problems are interesting because they can appear as subproblems of more complex problems. This means that the type S is not the root type of a partonomy, but describes the parts of another type. In this case, the boolean variables need to be skolemized since they depend on a component y. The result of the skolemization are terms such as $f_i(y)$ and $t_j(y)$. An alternative is to use set variables [48] to describe the set of types of all elements in a port. For example, a set variable $t(y)$ could describe all the option types that have been chosen.

24.3.2 Cardinality Models for Shopping Lists

A more complex type of configuration problem is obtained if the functional requirements specify how often a certain functionality should be provided. For example, the home movie studio may require a certain storage capacity for videos and multiple hard disks are needed to provide this capacity. We thus obtain a shopping list and it is necessary to choose the number of instances of a product type. However, the instances need not be distinguished for computing the amount of the consumed and the produced resources as long as these resources have unique values for leaf types.

Definition 24.5 (Shopping list problem). *The structural model of a shopping list problem consists of a type S corresponding to the configured system (the shopping basket), a functional type F regrouping all the functions, and a functional type I regrouping all the items. The type S has a partonomic port that contains functions from F and a partonomic port that contains the items from I. The type F is the root of a function taxonomy and the type is the root of an item taxonomy, which has concrete types as leaf types. The types can have attributes, but the values of an attribute a need to be uniquely specified by the leaf types t in the form of a value $\text{value}(t, a)$. There are binary requirement constraints between a type of a function in the functions-port and the type of an item in the items-port. There are binary requirement and compatibility constraints between the types of the items in the items-port. Furthermore, there are resource constraints between the function-port and the items-port. The consumed resource is an attribute of F and the produced resource is an attribute of I.*

The configurations of a shopping-list problem can be described by a cardinality model. This model has the following integer variables:

- A positive integer variable $\#f_i$ for each type in the function taxonomy $subtypes^*(F)$ This variable indicates how many times the configured system provides a function of this type.

- A positive integer variable $\#t_j$ for each type in the item taxonomy $subtypes^*(I)$ This variable indicates the number of items of this type in the configured system.

An entry (f, t) in a requirement constraint between the types in the function-port and the types in the items-ports is represented by an implication:

$$(\#f \geq 1) \Rightarrow (\#t \geq 1) \tag{24.12}$$

The direct subtypes $t_1, \ldots, t_n$ of t in the item taxonomy or the function taxonomy are modeled by a sum. This is possible since two different subtypes have no leaf type in common:

$$\#t = \#t_1 + \ldots + \#t_n \tag{24.13}$$

A compatibility constraint between the types of the items in the item-port can be encoded by negative clauses if it is specified by an incompatibility table N:

$$\#t_1 = 0 \vee \#t_2 = 0 \quad \text{for all} \quad (t_1, t_2) \in N \tag{24.14}$$

A resource constraint between a resource c that is consumed by the functions in the function port and a resource p that is produced by the items in the item-port can be modeled by a linear constraint:

$$\sum_{t \in leaves(F)} value(t, c) \cdot \#t \leq \sum_{t \in leaves(I)} value(t, p) \cdot \#t \qquad (24.15)$$

User requirements can be represented by constraints involving the integer variables $\#f$ for functions. A shopping-list problem can be solved by an Integer Programming approach similar to that in [62].

Shopping list problems can also appear as subproblems of more complex problems. Similar to option selection problems, a single multi-valued variable can be introduced to describe the number of types in a function port or the number of types in an item port. In the case of shopping-lists, the multi-valued variable is a multi-set or bag variable.

24.3.3 CSP-Models for Customizing Flat Components

The configuration model needs to distinguish individual components if the attribute values of the components are not fully determined by the concrete product type. In this case, additional choices are needed to characterize the components and it is necessary to introduce variables for the attributes. For example, the video edit facility requires the customization of several technical components such as the computer, the editing software, the printer, and the scanner. Each of those components has several attributes which are naturally encoded by variables. Those variables are subject to constraints and we obtain a standard constraint satisfaction problem for this flat configuration problem.

Definition 24.6 (Flat Customization Problem). *The structural model of a flat customization problem consists of a type S corresponding to the configured system, technical types $T_1, \ldots, T_n$ representing the principal components. The types need not be all different. The type S has a partonomic port p_i that contains exactly one instance of type T_i. The type T_i is a technical type that has concrete types as subtypes. The types S and the types T_i have multiple attributes containing functional and technical characteristics. The attributes can have a boolean domain, an enumerated domain, or an interval of integer values. There are arbitrary requirement and compatibility constraints between the direct and indirect attributes of the configured system. There are resource constraints between direct attributes of the configured systems and the attributes of the components.*

The configurations of a flat customization problem can be described by a constraint satisfaction problem. The model has the root component o_0 of type S, the components o_i which are equal to the ports $p_i(o_0)$, and the following variables:

- A variable $a_j(o_0)$ for each attribute a_j of the configured system o_0.

- A variable $a_j(o_i)$ for each attribute a_j of the component o_i.

- A type variable $type(o_i)$ for the type of the component o_i. The domain of this variable are the subtypes of T_i.

The catalog is translated into an element constraint for each attribute a_j and each component o_i where $i = 1, \ldots, n$. If subtype t of type T_i restricts the domain of attribute a_j to $D(t, a_j)$ then the element constraint is as follows:

$$\forall t \in leaves(T_i) : type(o_i) = t \Rightarrow a_j(o_i) \in D(t, a_j) \qquad (24.16)$$

Compatibility constraints can be applied to arbitrary direct and indirect attributes of the configured system, which are represented as variables $a_{j_1}(o_{i_1})$, $a_{j_2}(o_{i_2})$ where i_1, i_2 are in $\{0, \ldots, n\}$. Hence, the compatibility constraint is expressed as a standard constraint:

$$\exists (v_1, v_2) \in R : (a_{j_1}(o_{i_1}) = v_1 \wedge a_{j_2}(o_{i_2}) = v_2) \tag{24.17}$$

Requirement constraints are expressed similarly in their natural form:

$$\forall (v_1, v_2) \in R : (a_{j_1}(o_{i_1}) = v_1 \Rightarrow a_{j_2}(o_{i_2}) = v_2) \tag{24.18}$$

Finally, resource constraints can sum up a produced resource a_j of multiple components in $P \subseteq ports^*(o_0 : S)$ and a consumed resource $a_{j'}$ of multiple components in $C \subseteq ports^*(o_0 : S)$. As the set $ports^*(o_0 : S)$ is equal to the set of components $o_0, o_1, \ldots, o_n$ the resource constraint is expressed in terms of a numerical constraint:

$$\sum_{o_i \in P} a_j(o_i) \geq \sum_{o_i \in C} a_{j'}(o_i) \tag{24.19}$$

The functional requirements for flat component properties can be expressed in terms of any functional attribute, whether it is a direct attribute of the configured system or an attribute of one of its components.

A flat customization problem can be solved by a constraint solver. If the constraint graph is not dense, appropriate decomposition [13, 26] and clustering techniques can be applied [14] to solve it efficiently.

24.3.4 Conditional CSPs for Taxonomic Reasoning

The same functionality can often be realized by components differing greatly in their technical characteristics. As described in section 24.2.2, technical types fulfilling the same functionality are therefore organized in a taxonomy. Subtypes add further attributes, which means that the set of attributes of a component depend on its precise type. We thus obtain taxonomic customization problems. Formulating this problem as a standard CSP would require including a variable for each possible attribute that can be inherited and ensuring that its value is not meaningful in case it is not inherited. As an alternative, Mittal and Falkenhainer [43] introduced dynamic CSPs with optional variables that are activated under certain conditions. As the term dynamic CSP was later used for CSPs able to support constraint addition and retraction, it was proposed to rename the approach into Conditional CSPs [52]. As observed by Bowen and Bahler [7], it is also possible to directly use first-order logic to model taxonomic customization problems. A further proposal is that of composite CSPs [50], where the variable domains may contain sub-CSPs which are activated when this value is chosen. We model taxonomic customization as a Conditional CSP model, since dedicated algorithms have been elaborated for this approach [52, 24].

Definition 24.7 (Taxonomic Customization Problem)**.** *The structural model of a taxonomic customization problem consists of a type S corresponding to the configured system, functional types $T_1, \ldots, T_n$ representing the principal components. The types are not necessarily different to each other. The type S has a partonomic port that contains exactly one instance of T_i. The type T_i is the root of a taxonomy, which has concrete types as leaf types. The types S, the types T_i, and the subtypes of the T_i's have multiple attributes*

containing functional and technical characteristics. The attributes can have a boolean do-
main, an enumerated domain, or an interval of integer values. A constraint on a type t of
the taxonomies can involve any property of type t.

There are different possibilities to represent the type variables of the components. It is
not only necessary to model that components are instances of concrete product types, but
also that they are instances of functional or technical types, such as the technical DVD-type
in the following example: if the video edit device is a DVD, then it requires an MPEG2
format. A possibility is to represent type variables as hierarchical variables [38]. An
alternative is to use the same representation as for flat problems and to express an instance-
of-constraint by a constraint that is satisfied if the value of the type variable is an element
of the set of leaves of the type t. This approach has an efficient implementation [40] and is
conceptually simpler. For example, the element-constraint representing the catalogs need
not be extended to range over functional and technical types. The element-constraint from
section 24.3.3 is therefore valid for taxonomic customization problems.

Attributes are represented by variables, which can be optional. If type t has an attribute
a_j and o_i is an instance of a supertype of t then the variable $a_j(o_i)$ is activated if o_i is
an instance of t. The activation is denoted by $active : a_j(o_i)$, which is a (non-optional!)
boolean variable attached to the attribute:

$$type(o_i) \in leaves(t) \Leftrightarrow active : a_j(o_i) \tag{24.20}$$

The solution of a Conditional CSP just contains the variables for which the active-condition
is true. It is convenient to represent such a solution by a set of attribute-value pairs. Compatibility constraints for type t are only activated if the component is an instance of t:

$$\exists (v_1, \ldots, v_k) \in R : \begin{array}{l} (active : a_{j_1}(o_i) \Rightarrow a_{j_1}(o_i) = v_1) \\ \wedge \ldots \\ \wedge (active : a_{j_k}(o_i) \Rightarrow a_{j_k}(o_i) = v_k) \end{array} \tag{24.21}$$

Requirement constraints can, however, activate variables:

$$\forall (v_1, v_2) \in R : \begin{array}{l} (active : a_{j_1}(o_i) \wedge a_{j_1}(o_i) = v_1) \\ \Rightarrow (active : a_{j_2}(o_i) \wedge a_{j_2}(o_i) = v_2) \end{array} \tag{24.22}$$

The activation of attributes has also an impact on resource constraints. A resource of
type t is provided (or consumed) by a component only if this component is an instance of
t. Hence, a resource constraint can only take active resources into account. It may activate
produced resources and deactivate consumed resources:

$$\sum_{\substack{o \in P \\ active:a_j(o)}} a_j(o) \geq \sum_{\substack{o \in C \\ active:a_{j'}(o)}} a_{j'}(o) \tag{24.23}$$

Although Conditional CSPs handle the inheritance of attributes, they require that all
optional variables and their constraints are created explicitly. The use of universally quantified constraints avoids the creation of optional variables and their constraints if they are
not needed. If a component o is an instance of type t, then instances of the constraints of
t will be created. For this purpose, the quantified variable of the constraint will be substituted by the component o. It is important to note that a quantified constraint of type

t will only be applied to instances of type t. To achieve this, a set variable $instances(t$ is introduced to represent the instances of type t. It is linked to the type-variables via an inverse-constraint:

$$\forall i \in \{0, \ldots, n\} \forall t \in subtypes^*(T_i) : type(o_i) \in leaves(t) \Leftrightarrow o_i \in instances(t) \quad (24.24)$$

The type variable is needed for the catalog constraints, whereas the instance-set variable is used to replace the active-variable. By definition, $x \in instances(t)$ is equivalent to $active : a_j(x)$ and we can reformulate a compatibility constraint as a universally quantified constraint of type t:

$$\forall x \in instances(t) : C(a_{i_1}(x), \ldots, a_{i_k}(x)) \quad (24.25)$$

If o is an element of $instances(t)$, the forall-constraint adds the variables $a_{i_1}(o), \ldots, a_{i_k}(o$ and the constraint $C(a_{i_1}(o), \ldots, a_{i_k}(o))$ to the current CSP. Resource constraints can be adapted by sums that range only over the instances of the types for which the resource is defined.

24.3.5   Conditional CSPs for Simple Partonomic Reasoning

Configurable systems such as computers usually consist of a partonomic hierarchy that has more than two levels. The first level corresponds to the system to be configured and the second level contains the principal components of this system. These principal components may themselves have subcomponents some of which may be optional and some of which depend on the type of the principal component. Furthermore, the subcomponents may be connected to each other. An example is a PC, which has a central unit, which has a processor, which has an optional co-processor. Another example is car configuration with options [43]. We thus obtain a partonomic customization problem which requires the recursive configuration of possibly optional subcomponents and the choice of connections. The problem can again be modeled by a Conditional CSP or by first-order logic.

Definition 24.8 (Simple Partonomic Customization Problem). *The structural model of a simple partonomic customization problem consists of a type S corresponding to the configured system. S is the root of a partonomy with a taxonomy and a topology such that all partonomic and connection ports contain at most one component. The types in the partonomy can have multiple attributes describing functional and technical characteristics. The attributes can have a boolean domain, an enumerated domain, or an interval of integer values. A constraint on a type t of the partonomy can involve any property of type t.*

Special attention needs to be paid naming the properties of subcomponents. Independent of the formalisms, the terms as introduced in section 24.2.2 appear to be the appropriate way. We use the single-valued ports in $ports^*(x : t)$ and the single-valued properties in $props(ports^*(x : t))$ for this purpose.

Not only can a component have optional attributes, it can also have optional subcomponents and optional connections, which become active if the component is an instance of the corresponding type. However, there may also be subcomponents and connections that are optional in the sense that the corresponding relation has a minimal cardinality of 0 and a maximal cardinality of 1. If the subcomponent or connected component does not exist, then they are considered inactive as well. If a component is not active then none of its properties and of its ports are active. Therefore, only a subset of $ports^*(x : t)$ and $props(ports^*(x : t))$ are active in a solution. A solution consists of a set of value-assignments to the active properties and to the active connections.

The activation of ports can be well addressed by a Conditional CSP or a first-order approach if the properties and ports are modeled as follows:

1. The partonomic ports are treated as variables that are assigned to themselves.

2. The properties of partonomic ports are modeled by variables as before.

3. A connection-port p of a component o of type t is treated as a variable $p(o)$. The domain of $p(o)$ contains the possible instances of the destination type $t' := type(t, p)$ from the set of all parts $parts^*(o_0 : S)$ of the root type S. A constraint ensures that the value of $p(o)$ has the type t':

$$\forall o' \in parts^*(o_0 : S) : p(o) = o' \Rightarrow type(o') = t' \qquad (24.26)$$

4. The properties and ports $\xi(p(o))$ of connection-ports are equal to the properties and ports of the component that is assigned to this connection-port. An element-constraint is needed to express this correspondence:

$$\forall o' \in parts^*(o_0 : S) : p(o) = o' \Rightarrow \xi(p(o)) = \xi(o') \qquad (24.27)$$

Hence, single-valued partonomic ports can be handled in a straightforward way. Connection ports, however, are variables that require a special domain management.

24.3.6 Generative CSPs for Complex Partonomic Reasoning

The general case of a configuration problem is obtained when partonomic ports and connection ports can contain an arbitrary number of components. Typical examples occur in equipment configuration where given resource requirements (e.g. on storage capacity) need to be covered by an unknown number of components. Conditional CSPs are no longer appropriate to treat these unbounded configuration problems, since they require the precreation of an infinite number of possible parts. Generative CSPs [60, 59, 17] have been elaborated to handle these complex customization problems. The essence of the generative approach can be described in terms of a first-order formulation.

Definition 24.9 (Complex Partonomic Customization Problem). *The structural model of a complex partonomic customization problem consists of a type S corresponding to the configured system. S is the root of a partonomy with a taxonomy and a topology. The partonomic and connection ports can contain an arbitrary number of components. The types in the partonomy can have multiple attributes describing functional and technical characteristics. The attributes can have a boolean domain, an enumerated domain, or an interval of integer values. A constraint on a type t of the partonomy can involve any property of type t.*

The ports of complex partonomic customization are arbitrary elements of $ports^*(x : t)$ and the properties are arbitrary elements of $props(ports^*(x : t))$. Constraints can thus be formulated on the properties of multi-valued ports. In contrast to an optional port, a multi-valued port is active even if it has no element. Hence, there is not need to dynamically activate multi-valued ports. However, it is necessary to dynamically generate new components to meet cardinality constraints on ports. It is sufficient to generate parts for direct ports $p(x) \in ports(x : t)$ of a component x. This is achieved by a generative constraint that creates the parts when the lower bound of the cardinality is increased and that adds them to the instance-set of t. This instance-set needs to be represented by a set variable [48] with an open domain [40]:

$$\forall i \in \{1, 2, 3, \ldots\} : \#p(o) \geq i \Rightarrow p(o, i) \in instances(t) \qquad (24.28)$$

If a configuration assigns the value k to the cardinality of a direct partonomic port p of a component x, then the configuration will contain the parts $p(x, 1), \ldots, p(x, k)$, but not any other part $p(x, k')$ with $k' > k$. Since the partonomy is acyclic, each configuration can only contain a finite number of parts.

The generative constraint thus generates components on a by-need-basis. It also imposes an important constraint on the port cardinality. If the configuration of the k-th part fails, then it cannot belong to the instance-set meaning that the cardinality of the port is strictly smaller than k. Hence, infinite chains for generating parts are broken as soon as a part cannot be configured. However, infinite ascending chains could be obtained by a search procedure that successively increases the lower bound for the cardinality $\#p(o)$ in a search branch. It is nevertheless possible to impose an upper bound on the cardinality based on the following argument. Since components are generated to meet requirement and resource constraints, we determine how many components each such constraint may generate for the port $p(o)$ and use the sum of those upper bounds as an upper bound of the cardinality. We can compute the upper bound for a resource constraint as soon as the total resource consumption has been established. We suppose that the produced resource of each component in the port is greater than a strictly positive lower bound. We can then calculate the upper bound of the number of components by dividing the total amount of the resource by this lower bound. It is important to note that this upper bound on the cardinality imposes an additional constraint on the configuration space. It eliminates configurations with a large number of parts that don't have any function.

Ports of multi-valued partonomic ports can be modeled by recursive constraints. Let be a single-valued port of the destination type of the partonomic port p. The port $\xi(p(x))$ is then multi-valued. We introduce auxiliary set variables $\xi(p(o), i)$ for the subset that is contributed by the parts $p(o, i + 1), p(o, i + 2), \ldots, p(o, k)$, where k is the cardinality:

$$\xi(p(o)) := \xi(p(o), 0)$$
$$\xi(p(o), i) = \begin{cases} \{\xi(p(o, i + 1))\} \cup \xi(p(o), i + 1) & \text{if } \#p(o) \geq i + 1 \\ \emptyset & \text{otherwise} \end{cases} \qquad (24.29)$$

Multi-valued ports ξ are handled by a similar recursive constraint that directly uses the port $\xi(p(o, i + 1))$ of the $i + 1$st component in the union-operation instead of $\{\xi(p(o, i + 1))\}$. Properties of partonomic ports are calculated in a similar way except that they are formulated on multi-set (or bag) variables instead of the set variables.

If r is a resource of the destination type of a partonomic port, then the resource of the port can be modeled in a recursive way as well. Auxiliary variables $r(p(o), i)$ denote the contribution of the parts $p(o, i + 1), p(o, i + 2), \ldots, p(o, k)$, where k is the cardinality:

$$r(p(o)) := r(p(o), 0)$$
$$r(p(o), i) = \begin{cases} r(p(o, i + 1)) + r(p(o), i + 1) & \text{if } \#p(o) \geq i + 1 \\ \emptyset & \text{otherwise} \end{cases} \qquad (24.30)$$

A connection port of type t is modeled by an open set variable that is a subset of *instances*(t). As the elements of connection ports are not ordered, specific union- and sum-over-set-constraints have been introduced in the generative CSP-approaches [40]. The sum-over-set constraint maintains a local consistency among the lower and upper bounds on the port cardinality, the lower and upper bounds on the sum, the set of required elements in the set variable, and the lower and upper bounds of the resources provided by the required elements.

24.3.7 Complex Cases

Complex configuration models can be obtained by combinations of the previously defined models. In particular, components at the leaf level of the partonomy often do not need to be distinguished, thus allowing the use of a boolean or cardinality model.

Complex problems are also obtained by more sophisticated representations of the functional properties. Functions can be composed of sub-functions meaning that they are represented by a function partonomy. Functions are then assigned to components and sub-functions need to be assigned to their subcomponents. The sub-functions fulfilled by the subcomponents of a component need to be equal to the sub-functions of the function that is fulfilled by the component. This homomorphism can be expressed by an equality of two union-over-set-constraints. The refinement of function occurs, for example, in the configuration of instrumentation-and-control systems [40] and electrical wiring systems [1]. Complex connection reasoning leads to similar problems if connections between principal components are refined by connections between subcomponents.

24.4 Problem Solving for Configuration

Whereas Constraint Programming is used to find a solution or an optimal solution of a CSP, configuration brings in new problem-solving tasks, such as the maintenance of global consistency in interactive configuration, the computation of an explanation if a given set of requirements cannot be satisfied, or the computation of a relaxation of those requirements. The automatic computation of configurations also has particularities. Solution search should produce functionally well-justified configurations instead of an arbitrary configuration. If optimal configurations are required, then the user preferences are rarely specified in terms of a single criterion, but typically involve multiple criteria.

24.4.1 Interactive Configuration

Sales configurators are usually interactive as the functional requirements evolve during the decision-making process. An interactive configurator shows the functional characteristics of the configured system in the form of a web page or a GUI. Each functional attribute is characterized by its possible values. The user can express bounds on these attributes, eliminate possible values, or choose a value. The configurator typically reacts to those user inputs by propagating their logical effects. If a value is no longer possible for an attribute, then the configurator can eliminate it. Interactive configuration has, for example, been studied in [2] and in the CAWICOMS-project [3].

Definition 24.10 (Interactive configuration task). *Given a configuration model $K(x : t)$ user requirement $F(x : t)$, and a set of variables Y representing the functional character-istics, the task consists in finding the set $D(y)$ of legal values for each variable $y \in Y$. A value v is legal for y iff there exists a configuration that satisfies $K(x : t) \cup F(x : t)$ and that assigns v to y.*

This task is solved by maintaining global consistency [19] for the functional require-ments. A domain $D(y)$ of a variable is globally consistent iff each value v in $D(y)$ is legal for y. An initial domain $D_{init}(y)$ taken from the configuration model $K(x : t)$ can be reduced to a maximally global consistent domain $D^*(y)$ by inspecting each value v of $D_{init}(y)$ and by checking whether $F(x : t) \cup K(x : t) \cup \{y = v\}$ is consistent. If this problem is inconsistent, then v will be removed from y's domain. In the other case, the value v for y is supported by a configuration of $F(x : t) \cup K(x : t)$.

The exhaustive application of a procedure for maintaining global consistency requires $n \cdot d$ consistency checks in the worst case, where n is the number of attributes and d is the initial domain size. If a check has been positive and produced a solution, then this solution will support a value for each functional attribute. Strategies for computing diversified solutions can thus significantly reduce the number of checks. Furthermore, the procedure need not be applied to exhaustion, but may compute a lower bound for $D^*(y)$ that contains only supported values and an upper bound that only excludes illegal values.

Local consistency methods such as arc consistency [37] can be used to compute the upper bound. In certain cases, when the constraint network is acyclic, then arc consistency coincides with global consistency [20], meaning that the task has a polynomial cost only. For example, this condition is met if only catalog constraints are given.

Configuration problems that additionally contain compatibility constraints on variables of the same catalog constraint are not acyclic and arc consistency does not remove all illegal values. Preprocessing techniques can then be used to find all solutions of $K(x : t)$. Cluster techniques limit this preprocessing to the clusters of a cluster-tree [14, 46]. An alternative is to use decision diagrams to store the set of precomputed solutions in a factorized way [2, 29]. However, it is also possible to use suitable strategies for the consistency checks performed by the global consistency procedure. Cutset decomposition [13] and learning of strategies (detection of critical variables [36]) are good candidates for performance increases. Further speed-ups can be obtained by algorithms such as LazyAC [53] or PrefAC [5].

It should also be noted that an interactive configurator solves many configuration prob-lems that share the same configuration model $K(x : t)$ and that differ only in the functional requirements. Preprocessing and learning techniques can therefore pay off significantly.

24.4.2 Explanations and Relaxations

The functional requirement $F(x : t)$ is typically a conjunction of user requirements and can alternatively be represented by a set of requirements, which will be supposed in this sub-section. If $F(x : t) \cup K(x : t)$ has no solution, then the configuration problem is overconstrained and some requirements need to be relaxed. In this case, the requirements no longer express hard constraints, but desiderata that are satisfied whenever possible. There are two scenarios where such a situation can arise:

1. The user enters one requirement after the other and the interactive configurator reduces the domains of functional attributes after each entry. As the propagation might not eliminate all illegal values, the propagation can reach a dead-end. To recover from the failure, the user needs to find a minimal set of requirements for which propagation is failing, to choose a culprit from this set, and to remove it. This procedure is iterated until the set of the non-relaxed requirements is consistent.

2. The user enters multiple requirements at once, possibly augmented with a preference order. This set of requirements may be inconsistent, meaning that the configurator will compute a relaxation by removing some requirements. Removed requirements are (globally) inconsistent with respect to the selected requirements. The user needs to understand which requirements are causing the failure of a removed requirement. This explanation will allow the user to change the preferences if the removal of a requirement was not acceptable.

Hence, overconstrained problems lead to a relaxation and an explanation task.

Definition 24.11 (Relaxation task). *Given a set of requirements $F(x : t)$, find a maximal relaxation, i.e. a subset that is consistent with respect to the configuration model $K(x : t)$. If additionally a strict partial order on $F(x : t)$ is given, then find a preferred solution in the sense of [8, 33]. It is obtained by choosing a complete ranking of the requirements and by doing a lexicographic maximization based on this ranking.*

Definition 24.12 (Explanation task). *Given an overconstrained set of requirements $F(x : t)$, find a minimal conflict, i.e. subset that is inconsistent with respect to the configuration model $K(x : t)$. If additionally a strict partial order on $F(x : t)$ is given, then find a preferred conflict in the sense of [33]. It is obtained by choosing a complete ranking of the requirements and by doing an anti-lexicographic minimization based on this ranking.*

Relaxations are usually computed by adding one requirement after the other in the chosen order and by testing the consistency of the current selection after each step. If a solution has been found, then the requirement is kept. Otherwise, it is removed.

Conflicts have traditionally been computed by truth maintenance system (TMS) [15] and several attempts have been made to integrate a TMS into a constraint solver [35, 57]. However, the computed explanations can be far from minimal, in particular if resource constraints are involved (see [33] for an example).

A method for computing minimal and preferred conflicts is presented in [33]. The algorithm called QuickXplain solves the explanation problem by successively removing requirements and by checking the consistency of the remaining requirements. If the remaining requirements are inconsistent, the problem has been reduced in size. If not, then some of the removed requirements do necessarily belong to the conflict. QuickXplain is recursively dividing the explanation problem into subproblems of the same size. For example, the initial set $F(x : t)$ will be split into two subsets C_1 and C_2. It first seeks for conflict elements in C_2 while keeping C_1 in the background (i.e, all constraints of C_1 are active, but they will not be removed while solving the second problem). The first step then consists in removing all elements of C_2 and testing the consistency of $K(x : t) \cup C_1$. If this fails, the empty set is a minimal conflict of the second problem, meaning that the problem has been reduced to C_1. If the test succeeds, then at least one requirement in the second problem is needed for the failure. If the second problem is a singleton, then its element is added to the conflict. If the second problem has multiple elements, it is again split into two parts and the procedure is applied recursively. When the second subproblem has been successfully solved, its minimal conflict is added to the background and the first subproblem is removed from the background. Then the first subproblem is solved. A minimal conflict for the complete problem is then obtained by merging the minimal conflicts of the first and second subproblems.

Evolutions of QuickXplain have been proposed to explain the values chosen in a solution [22] and to find the parts of an overconstrained problem that need to be repaired when restoring the consistency [45].

24.4.3   Searching Solutions

Whereas interactive configurators mainly support propagation and explanation, the automatic search of solutions if an important features of configurators in manufacturing. We discuss the search of solutions for the most general form of configuration problem, which corresponds to a generative CSP. A search procedure for a generative CSP does not only need to choose a value for the different variables of the initial problem. It also needs to take into account variables that are added by inheritance or by the generation of subcomponents. These variables are added when the search procedure is making decisions about a component type or about the cardinality of a partonomic port. It is important to note that decisions about newly generated variables cannot precede the decisions that lead to their generation. As a consequence, the sequence of search decisions that produces a solution needs to respect this order. By doing this, the search configures a component by top-down refinement.

The dynamic nature of complex configuration problems also contradicts some basic postulates of constraint programming that state that it is better to eliminate inconsistent choices a priori by a propagation procedure than doing this a posteriori by analyzing and learning a conflict. Configurators need to make wrong decisions in order to discover that they are wrong. For example, it is possible that a given computer type t is incompatible with respect to the given requirements. However, it may be necessary to generate all the variables and constraints that are inherited from this type in order to discover the incompatibility. This is only possible if the computer has been specialized to the type t. The conflict between the type assignment and the functional requirements that is discovered in this way provides useful information for the ongoing configuration process. Therefore, it is recommended to keep those conflicts [47].

Another issue is obtained by search decisions that choose the number of parts or that choose the functionality of the part. The search should avoid under-charged components and over-fulfilled functions. An example of under-charged components is obtained if two servers are provided for 10 users, although a single one is sufficient. Over-fulfilled functions are obtained if there is a single demand for a printing capability, but two printers are provided. Whereas over-fulfilled functions can be avoided by a suitable constraint model, under-charged components cannot be avoided by constraints. If the search procedure chooses the number of components before configuring them, it can easily end up with under-charged components. Furthermore, it can produce under-charged components if it chooses more components than necessary or if it chooses less functionality than possible.

These problems can be avoided if configurations are produced by decision sequences that respect certain properties. When a component is configured, then the following kinds of decisions should be taken in the following order:

1. First, the values for the functional attributes of the root type of the component are chosen. The functions of the component can be maximized by applying the following preferences. The presence of a capability is preferred to its absence, meaning that the value true is preferred to the value false for boolean attributes. For numerical capacities, higher values are preferred. The search procedure should then assign the best value to each functional attribute. However, trade-off considerations between multiple functional attributes allow the procedure to abandon a best value for an attribute $a_1(o)$ if this allows an improvement for a later attribute $a_2(o)$. The procedure can avoid a high penalization of $a_2(o)$ by auxiliary decisions $a_2(o) \geq v$ that are made before assigning a value to $a_1(o)$. As shown in [32], any Pareto-optimal combination of the attribute values can be found in this way.

2. Once the functional characteristics are chosen, the type variable is specialized by decisions of the form *type* $\in$ *leaves*(t). Multiple specialization decisions can occur for the same type variable. Inherited properties and ports can be configured as soon as they are generated by such a decision. There is no predefined order among the inherited properties and ports, meaning that technical attributes, cardinalities, and connections can be configured in any order if not otherwise specified.

3. The values of the technical attributes are chosen by standard value assignments. There are no predefined preferences between these values.

4. The cardinalities of partonomic ports are chosen by decisions of the form $\#p(o) \leq k$ and smaller values for the bound k are preferred. If such a decision fails, then its negation $\#p(o) > k$ is added to the constraints. This generates a new subcomponent $p(o, k+1)$ that needs to be configured before the next cardinality decision $\#p(o) \leq k+1$ is tried out. The component $p(o, k+1)$ is configured by applying the whole configuration process recursively.

5. Connection ports are configured by membership decisions of the form $o' \in p(o)$. There are no predefined preferences.

The task for searching a functionally well-justified solution can be expressed as follows:

Definition 24.13 (Solution search task). *Find a configuration that satisfies the given functional requirements and the given configuration model by a sequence of search decisions that have the form discussed above and that respect the preferences between values and variables as discussed above.*

Preference programming [34] proposes a language for expressing decisions and preferences for configuration problems. In addition to the structural preferences, specific preferences among the attributes of a component can be expressed as well. Whereas preference programming defines a strategy for producing a solution, other strategies may be needed to recover from a failure. Blind strategies such as min-domain-first ignore the specific structure of a configuration problem and do not appear to be well-adapted for this case. Strategies that move up the failure [36], cutset decomposition [13], or dependency-directed backtracking [15] are better candidates. Learning methods may also be a good way in order to identify critical variables for proving the infeasibility of a subproblem.

Difficult configuration problems can also profit from symmetry-breaking methods [21]. However, the most important issue is to avoid the introduction of symmetries by the configuration model. The partonomic model presented in section 24.2.2 avoids symmetries between parts. The elements of a partonomic port are ordered and the individual elements cannot be referenced inside constraints. They are indistinguishable before being configured. A sequence of search decisions that is inconsistent for one part, will also be inconsistent for the next part. Hence, the configuration of the $k + 1$-st part can start where the configuration of the k-th part has stopped.

24.4.4   Satisfying User Preferences

An advanced issue in configuration is the satisfaction of user preferences. As the layman user does not know the configuration model, she or he will often run into underconstrained or overconstrained situations when specifying the requirements through the form of constraints. Underconstrained situations leave a large set of choices and there is a high risk that users miss their favorite choice. Overconstrained situations are obtained if the users choose their preferred value for each attribute. In the first case, users will not feel very confident about the obtained configuration since they have not explored the limits. In the second case, the users need to toggle through an inconsistent set of requirements and manage the preferences on their own. The need for preference handling for configuration problems has for example been expressed in [28].

Preference-based configurators offer a simple way to specify preferences in an intuitive and qualitative way. CP-nets are a successful formalism for ordering the values of an attribute dependent on the values of parent attributes [6]. Symbolic preference programming permits the user to order the requirements and to specify an order for numerical or qualitative attributes [34]. Given such preferences on multiple attributes (also called criteria), a multi-criteria optimization problem has to be solved. Although any Pareto-optimal solution of this problem may be interesting, it is often more appropriate to guide the user through the set of possible compromises by generating multiple extreme solutions (lexicographic-optimal for different rankings) and balanced solutions [32]. This approach thus generates a small set of preferred solutions of a good diversity. Diversity is ensured by changing the importance of criteria. Diversity can also be enforced by global constraints [30].

Future work on preference-based configurators is needed to develop the full potential of this feature. This includes work on algorithms, on the preference language, and on the preference elicitation methods. Explanations of failure provide a good opportunity to ask for preferences between the possible relaxations. Hence, explanations can play a key role in making preference elicitation more interactive and more efficient.

24.5   Conclusion

This chapter has given an overview on constraint-based configuration while stressing the particularities of configuration. Configuration is not a classical application of Constraint

Programming. The constraint networks are not static, but evolve during problem solving. As such, the formalism of constraint networks is not sufficient to specify a configuration problem and it is necessary to go up to a higher modeling level, which describes the configuration knowledge independent of a problem-solving formalism. Configuration knowledge covers product data as found in the databases of an ERP system, structural models that can be formulated within UML or within a description logic, and the configuration constraints. The structural model includes a description of the functional characteristics and of the alternative ways to map them to a structure.

Depending on the characteristics of the configured system, this knowledge can be compiled into various kinds of constraint models including boolean models, cardinality models, static and dynamic CSP models, and generative CSP models. The latter ones support dynamic activation or generation of variables and constraints and thus create new issues for the search process. The search process has to take dynamically generated variables into account and needs to respect the generation order. The search process is function-driven and should make choices only when they contribute to given functional requirements.

Searching for solutions is not the only problem-solving task that occurs in configuration. Interactive configurators often support a form of (strong) propagation and let the user make the decisions. The user thus has the freedom to try out all of her or his preferred choices with the risk of running into overconstrained problems. Explanation facilities then allow the user to identify conflicting requirements, but still leave them the burden of choice. An alternative is the emerging idea of a preference-based configurator where users enter preferences among the possible values instead of making categoric choices. Preferences are heavily used in recommender systems and the lessons learned in this area may be beneficial for configuration. However, interactive configurators and their explanation facilities can also lead to new possibilities for preference elicitation, meaning that there is a potential for a cross-fertilization between both fields.

Bibliography

[1] Michel Aldanondo, Jacques Lamothe, and Khaled Hadj Hamou. Configurator and CAD: gathering the best of two worlds. In *IJCAI-01 Workshop on Configuration*, pages 1–14, 2001.

[2] Jérôme Amilhastre, Hélène Fargier, and Pierre Marquis. Consistency restoration and explanations in dynamic CSPs application to configuration. *Artificial Intelligence*, 135(1-2):199–234, 2002.

[3] Liliana Ardissono, Alexander Felfernig, Gerhard Friedrich, Anna Goy, Dietmar Jannach, Giovanna Petrone, Ralph Schäfer, and Markus Zanker. A framework for the development of personalized, distributed web-based configuration systems. *AI Magazine*, 24(3):93–110, 2003.

[4] Virginia E. Barker, Dennis E. O'Connor, Judith Bachant, and Elliot Soloway. Expert systems for configuration at Digital: XCON and beyond. *Commununications of the ACM*, 32(3):298–318, 1989.

[5] Christian Bessière, Anaïs. Fabre, and Ulrich Junker. Propagate the right thing: how preferences can speed-up constraint solving. In *Eighteenth International Joint Conference on Artificial Intelligence*, pages 191–196, Acapulco, 2003.

[6] Craig Boutilier, Ronen I. Brafman, Carmel Domshlak, Holger H. Hoos, and David

Poole. Preference-based constrained optimization with CP-nets. *Computational Intelligence*, 20:137–157, 2004.

[7]   James Bowen and Dennis Bahler. Conditional existence of variables in generalised constraint networks. In *Ninth National Conference on Artificial Intelligence (AAAI)* pages 215–220, 1991.

[8]   Gerhard Brewka. Preferred subtheories: An extended logical framework for default reasoning. In *Eleventh International Joint Conference on Artificial Intelligence* pages 1043–1048, 1989.

[9]   David C. Brown and B. Chandrasekaran. *Design problem solving: knowledge structures and control strategies*. Morgan Kaufmann Publishers Inc., San Francisco, CA, USA, 1989.

[10] Roman Cunis, Andreas Günter, Ingo Syska, Heino Peters, and Heiner Bode. Plakon - an approach to domain-independent construction. In *Second International Conference on Industrial and Engineering Applications of Artificial Intelligence and Expert Systems (IAE/AIE)*, pages 866–874, 1989.

[11] Adnan Darwiche. New advances in compiling CNF into decomposable negation normal form. In *Sixteenth European Conference on Artificial Intelligence*, pages 328–332, 2004.

[12] Johan de Kleer. An assumption–based truth maintenance system. *Artificial Intelligence*, 28:127–162, 1986.

[13] Rina Dechter. Enhancement schemes for constraint processing: Backjumping, learning, and cutset decomposition. *Artificial Intelligence*, 41(3):273–312, 1990.

[14] Rina Dechter and Judea Pearl. Tree clustering for constraint networks. *Artificial Intelligence*, 38:353–366, 1989.

[15] Jon Doyle. A truth maintenance system. *Artificial Intelligence*, 12:231–272, 1979.

[16] Alexander Felfernig, Gerhard Friedrich, and Dietmar Jannach. UML as domain specific language for the construction of knowledge-based configurations systems. *International Journal of Software Engineering and Knowledge Engineering*, 10(4):449 – 469, 2000.

[17] Gerhard Fleischanderl, Gerhard Friedrich, Alois Haselböck, Herwig Schreiner, and Markus Stumptner. Configuring large systems using generative constraint satisfaction. *IEEE Intelligent Systems*, 13(4):59–68, 1998.

[18] Felix Frayman and Sanjay Mittal. COSSACK: A constraint-based expert system for configuration. In *Knowledge-Based Expert Systems in Engineering: Planning and Design*, pages 143–166. Computational Mechanics Publications, 1987.

[19] Eugene C. Freuder. Synthesizing constraint expressions. *Communications of the ACM*, 21(11):958–966, 1978.

[20] Eugene C. Freuder. A sufficient condition for backtrack-free search. *Journal of the ACM*, 29(1):24–32, 1982.

[21] Eugene C. Freuder. Eliminating interchangeable values in constraint satisfaction problems. In *Proceedings of the Ninth National Conference on Artificial Intelligence (AAAI)*, pages 227–233, 1991.

[22] Gerhard Friedrich. Elimination of spurious explanations. In *Sixteenth European Conference on Artificial Intelligence*, pages 813–817, 2004.

[23] Gerhard Friedrich and Markus Stumptner. Consistency-based configuration. In *AAAI-99 Workshop on Configuration*, pages 35–40, 1999.

[24] Felix Geller and Michael Veksler. Assumption-based pruning in conditional CSP.

In *Eleventh International Conference on Principles and Practice of Constraint Programming*, pages 241–255, 2005.

[25] Michael R. Genesereth and Nils J. Nilsson. *Logical Foundations of Artificial Intelligence*. Morgan Kaufmann, Palo Alto, CA, 1987.

[26] Georg Gottlob, Nicola Leone, and Francesco Scarcello. A comparison of structural CSP decomposition methods. *Artificial Intelligence*, 124(2):243–282, 2000.

[27] Andreas Günter and Christian Kühn. Knowledge-based configuration: Survey and future directions. In *5th Biannual German Conference on Knowledge-Based Systems*, volume 1570 of *Lecture Notes in Computer Science*, pages 47–66, 1999.

[28] Albert Haag. Sales configuration in business processes. *IEEE Intelligent Systems*, 13(4):78–85, 1998.

[29] Tarik Hadzic, Sathiamoorthy Subbarayan, Rune M. Jensen, Henrik R. Andersen, Jesper Moller, and Henrik Hulgaard. Fast backtrack-free product configuration using a precompiled solution space representation. In *International Conference on Economic, Technical and Organisational aspects of Product Configuration Systems*, pages 131–138, 2004.

[30] Emmanuel Hebrard, Brahim Hnich, Barry O'Sullivan, and Toby Walsh. Finding diverse and similar solutions in constraint programming. In *The Twentieth National Conference on Artificial Intelligence (AAAI)*, pages 372–377, 2005.

[31] Werner E. Juengst and Michael Heinrich. Using resource balancing to configure modular systems. *IEEE Intelligent Systems*, 13(4):50–58, 1998.

[32] Ulrich Junker. Preference-based search and multi-criteria optimization. *Annals of Operations Research*, 130:75–115, 2004.

[33] Ulrich Junker. QUICKXPLAIN: preferred explanations and relaxations for over-constrained problems. In *Nineteenth National Conference on Artificial Intelligence (AAAI)*, pages 167–172, 2004.

[34] Ulrich Junker and Daniel Mailharro. Preference programming: Advanced problem solving for configuration. *Artificial Intelligence for Engineering Design, Analysis and Manufacturing*, 17(1):13–29, 2003.

[35] Narendra Jussien, Romuald Debruyne, and Patrice Boizumault. Maintaining arc-consistency within dynamic backtracking. In *Sixth International Conference on Principles and Practice of Constraint Programming*, pages 249–261, 2000.

[36] Olivier Lhomme. Quick shaving. In *Twentieth National Conference on Artificial Intelligence (AAAI)*, pages 411–415, 2005.

[37] Alan K. Mackworth. Consistency in networks of relations. *Artificial Intelligence*, 8(1):99–118, 1977.

[38] Alan K. Mackworth, Jan A. Mulder, and William S. Havens. Hierarchical arc consistency: exploiting structured domains in constraint satisfaction problems. *Computational Intelligence*, 1:118–126, 1985.

[39] Diego Magro and Pietro Torasso. Decomposition strategies for configuration problems. *Artificial Intelligence for Engineering Design, Analysis and Manufacturing*, 17(1):51–73, 2003.

[40] Daniel Mailharro. A classification and constraint based framework for configuration. *Artificial Intelligence for Engineering Design, Analysis and Manufacturing*, 12(4):383–397, 1998.

[41] John P. McDermott. R1: A rule-based configurer of computer systems. *Artificial Intelligence*, 19:39–88, 1982.

[42] Deborah L. McGuinness and Jon R. Wright. Conceptual modelling for configuration: A description logic-based approach. *Artificial Intelligence for Engineering Design, Analysis and Manufacturing*, 12(4):333–344, 1998.

[43] Sanjay Mittal and Brian Falkenhainer. Dynamic constraint satisfaction problems. In *Eighth National Conference on Artificial Intelligence (AAAI)*, pages 25–32, 1990.

[44] Sanjay Mittal and Felix Frayman. Towards a generic model of configuration tasks. In *Eleventh International Joint Conference on Artificial Intelligence*, pages 1395–1401, 1989.

[45] Barry O'Callaghan, Barry O'Sullivan, and Eugene C. Freuder. Generating corrective explanations for interactive constraint satisfaction. In *Eleventh International Conference on Principles and Practice of Constraint Programming*, pages 445–459, 2005.

[46] Bernard Pargamin. Extending cluster tree compilation with non-boolean variables in product configuration: A tractable approach to preference-based configuration. In *IJCAI-03 Workshop on Configuration*, pages 32–37, Acapulco, Mexico, 2003.

[47] Charles J. Petrie. Constrained decision revision. In *Tenth National Conference on Artificial Intelligence (AAAI)*, pages 393–400, 1992.

[48] Jean-François Puget. PECOS: a high level constraint programming language. In *Proceedings of the 1st Singapore International Conference on Intelligent Systems (SPICIS'92)*, pages 137–142, Singapore, 1992.

[49] Raymond Reiter. A theory of diagnosis from first principles. *Artificial Intelligence* 32:57–952, 1987.

[50] Daniel Sabin and Eugene C. Freuder. Configuration as composite constraint satisfaction. In George F. Luger, editor, *Proceedings of the Artificial Intelligence and Manufacturing Research Planning Workshop*, pages 153–161. AAAI Press, 1996, 1996.

[51] Daniel Sabin and Rainer Weigel. Product configuration frameworks - a survey. *IEEE Intelligent Systems*, 13(4):42–49, 1998.

[52] Mihaela Sabin, Eugene C. Freuder, and Richard J. Wallace. Greater efficiency for conditional constraint satisfaction. In *Ninth International Conference on Principles and Practice of Constraint Programming*, pages 649–663, 2003.

[53] Thomas Schiex, Jean-Charles Régin, Christine Gaspin, and Gérard Verfaillie. Lazy arc consistency. In *Thirteenth National Conference on Artificial Intelligence (AAAI)* pages 216–221, 1996.

[54] Patrik Simons, Ilkka Niemelä, and Timo Soininen. Extending and implementing the stable model semantics. *Artificial Intelligence*, 138(1-2):181–234, 2002.

[55] Carsten Sinz, Andreas Kaiser, and Wolfgang Küchlin. Formal methods for the validation of automotive product configuration data. *Artificial Intelligence for Engineering Design, Analysis and Manufacturing*, 17(1):75–97, 2003.

[56] Timo Soininen, Esther Gelle, and Ilkka Niemelä. A fixpoint definition of dynamic constraint satisfaction. In *Fifth International Conference on Principles and Practice of Constraint Programming*, pages 419–433, 1999.

[57] Mohammed H. Sqalli and Eugene C. Freuder. Inference-based constraint satisfaction supports explanation. In *Thirteenth National Conference on Artificial Intelligence (AAAI)*, pages 318–325, 1996.

[58] Markus Stumptner. An overview of knowledge-based configuration. *AI Communications*, 10(2):111–125, 1997.

[59] Markus Stumptner, Gerhard Friedrich, and Alois Haselböck. Generative constraint-

based configuration of large technical systems. *Artificial Intelligence for Engineering Design, Analysis and Manufacturing*, 12(4):307–320, 1998.

[60] Markus Stumptner and Alois Haselböck. A generative constraint formalism for configuration problems. In *Advances in Artificial Intelligence, Third Congress of the Italian Association for Artificial Intelligence, AI*IA'93*, pages 302–313, 1993.

[61] Gruber T., Olsen G.R, and Runkel J.T. The configuration design ontologies and the VT elevator domain theory. *International Journal of Human-Computer Studies*, 44(4):569–598, 1996.

[62] Erlendur S. Thorsteinsson and Greger Ottosson. Linear relaxations and reduced-cost based propagation of continuous variable subscripts. *Annals of Operations Research*, 115:15–29, 2002.

[63] Rainer Weigel and Boi Faltings. Compiling constraint satisfaction problems. *Artificial Intelligence*, 115(2):257–287, 1999.

[64] Brian C. Williams. Interaction-based invention: Designing novel devices from first principles. In *Proceedings of the Eighth National Conference on Artificial Intelligence (AAAI)*, pages 349–356, 1990.

[65] Katariina Ylinen, Tomi Männistö, and Timo Soininen. Configuring software products with traditional methods - case LINUX family. In *ECAI-02 Workshop on Configuration*, pages 17–22, 2002.

Chapter 25

Constraint Applications in Networks

Helmut Simonis

In this chapter we discuss the use of Constraint Programming (CP) for network applications. Network problems arise in many different domains, we take a rather narrow view in this presentation and concentrate on three areas:

- electrical networks

- water (oil) networks

- data networks

Some of the earliest examples for CLP(R) were for analysing analog circuits, whose behavior can be described by *Ohm's law* for the relation between resistance, voltage and current and *Kirchhoff's laws* which defines how connected circuits behave. This early analysis later was extended to more complex, hybrid networks. One of the most interesting practical problems in this domain is the configuration of electrical power distribution networks (section 25.1), which has been studied with different constraint techniques and for which operational systems exist.

The work on CP models for electrical power distribution networks later led to the study of water distribution networks (section 25.2), which have similar importance in the utilities area. Water networks differ from electrical networks in a number of fundamental ways:

- Water can be stored in the network, reservoirs and water towers are key elements of water distribution systems.

- Water quality can vary. Keeping track of relevant properties is important when mixing water from different sources.

- Many water networks were built in the 19th century. Old pipes may be leaking, losing up to 30 % of the water sent through them. The exact loss rate is typically unknown.

Networks for oil distribution have similar properties, but face additional challenges.

The bulk of constraint applications for networks [60] are in the context of data networks (section 25.3), covering either traditional, connection oriented networks or packet-switched, routed networks like the Internet. We look at a number of different applications in this domain:

- We start with a problem of *application placement* (section 25.3.1) for the Italian Inter banking network, which was one of the first large scale CLP applications in the network domain.

- In many networks, the task of *path placement* (section 25.3.2) is to define the route on which a demand will be sent through the network. This is a fundamental networking problem, for which many competing CP methods have been proposed.

- One possible extension is the use of *multiple paths* (section 25.3.3) for demands, where the secondary path is only active when the primary connection has failed.

- Another possible extension is to add a time dimension, where traffic demands have given start and end times, and demands compete for network bandwidth if they overlap in time. This application is called *Bandwidth on Demand* (section 25.3.4).

- In the previous problems, the network structure and capacity was fixed. The problem of *Network Design* (section 25.3.5) deals with defining connectivity and finding the right link capacity to satisfy a projected set of demands.

- IP (Internet Protocol) networks usually do not use explicit routes for traffic demands. Instead, packets are routed based on a distributed shortest path algorithm. *Metric optimization* (section 25.3.6) deals with choosing metric weights to influence the routing in the network and to optimize the network utilization.

- Many traditional algorithms assume a demand matrix of all communication needs between network nodes. In IP networks this demand matrix is not readily available, *Resilience Analysis* (section 25.3.7) tries to predict network behavior in failure scenarios without explicit knowledge of the demand structure.

- Secondary paths and routing algorithms provide some methods to maintain network communications in case of element failure. The idea of *Bandwidth Protection* (section 25.3.8) offers an alternative, purely local mechanism for improving network resilience.

25.1 Electricity Networks

Electrical networks are controlled by the application of three fundamental relations, Ohm's law and the two Kirchhoff's laws:

Ohm's Law Ohm's Law relates the three fundamental electrical quantities: voltage V current I and resistance Ω, $V = I * \Omega$.

Kirchhoff's Current Law The current flowing into a node or branching point is equal to the sum of the currents leaving the node or branching point.

Kirchhoff's Voltage Law The sum of all the voltages around any closed path in a circuit equals zero.

As an early example for CLP(R), it was shown in [35] (see also [36, 46]), that simple electrical networks can be modeled using linear constraints over continuous domains. The use of constraints allows a very flexible query structure, were given, partial information about voltages, currents and resistance can be used to deduce the missing information. The solver in CLP(R) was restricted to linear constraints only, so that most interesting electrical and electronic circuits can not be modeled. By combining the finite domain and the continuous solver in CHIP, the LOGICIM tool [32] extended the modeling capabilities to hybrid circuits with state. It is perhaps surprising that after the development of non-linear solvers in the nineties (see Chapter 16 "Continuous and Interval Constraints") there has not been a systematic study of the simulation of analog electronic systems with Constraint Programming.

On the other hand there are application problems where the basic laws above are enough to model quite complex electrical circuits. This is the case for electrical power distribution networks, first studied for CLP in [18, 19]. Power distribution networks are formed of high (medium) voltage transmission lines, which link power stations (the producers) to transformer stations (the consumers), which convert the high voltage to lower voltage for actual consumers. The transmission lines form a graph, of which only a subgraph is in active use at any one time. Lines can be enabled and disabled by switches, which can be opened or closed as required. At any time point, the active transmission network forms a forest, with trees rooted in the power stations and consumers at the leaves of the network. Cycles in the network must be avoided, since they will result in malfunctions and equipment damage. The configuration task for a power network consists in controlling the transmission switches in such a way that

- there are no cycles

- all customers are reached

- the capacity of the power stations is not exceeded

- the currents limits of the transmission lines are not exceeded

- loss due to resistance in the transmission lines is minimized

If an element failure occurs in a network, then there is a reconfiguration task to restore supply to all or at least to the most important customers as quickly as possible, while minimizing the number of switch changes. Reaction times in seconds (or faster) is required as a rule.

For maintenance or extension work it is necessary to isolate certain components in the network, so that they are safe to work on. Given a set of such maintenance jobs, we have a planning problem to define the best schedule of operations. This is typically further constrained by release and due dates, resource and manpower limits and other scheduling constraints.

The PlaNets system [18, 19] was developed by the University of Catalonia in Barcelona (UCB) for the Spanish electricity company Enher to tackle these problems. It uses the rational solver of CHIP [25] for the electrical network constraints, and the finite domain solver for the temporal and scheduling aspects of the system.

Recently, other constraints approaches for the reconfiguration problems have been attempted. In [33], the use of a Boolean, BDD [12] based solver is advocated to allow fast reaction times. The use of propositional calculus to represent open or closed switches is natural, but in order to be able to use the Boolean solver also for the electrical constraints, massive simplifications are required. For example, all consumers are assigned the same, unit demand size, and Kirchhoff's current laws are represented with small integers. The system currently is in experimental use at the Danish power company NESA.

25.2   Water (Oil) Networks

The team at UCB working on the PlaNets system cooperated with experts on water distribution systems to form the CLOCWISe consortium to study the use of constraint programming for operational control of water systems [11]. Water distribution system share many aspects with electrical power supply networks. The system forms a network with supply stations (water wells), transmission lines (pipes) and distribution nodes. The flow through nodes follow flow conservation (Kirchhoff's current law), there are capacity limits for wells and pipes, etc. The scheduling scenarios are similar as well, there are configuration and reconfiguration tasks, and more complex planning scenarios. But there are also significant differences:

- Water supply systems use storage facilities, reservoirs and water towers. Levels in these storage nodes evolve over time, producer/consumer models [61] can be used to describe these constraints.

- Pipes can be operated at different flow rates, with significant differences in the energy expended.

- Many pipes are old and therefore leaky, losing water at an unknown, but significant rate. Therefore flow conservation is not preserved, the flow of water entering a pipe is different from the flow leaving the pipe.

- Chemical properties of water from different sources vary, and may be further changed by processing in the network. Mixing laws are quite complex and often non-linear.

The CLOCWISe system deals with these additional constraints using the rational solver of CHIP and its finite domain solver, especially global constraints for scheduling. A quality estimator for water mixing scenarios uses the linear solver, dealing with non-linear constraints by piece-wise linear approximation.

Pipeline transport for petro-chemical products is closely related. The FORWARD C system of Technip [58] contains a module for pipeline transport between a tank farm at a deep water harbor and the tank farm associated with the refinery. The transmission plan can be seen as a sequencing operation in a schedule. Crude oil mixing plays an important role, as it can be used to optimize the throughput of the refinery by mixing crudes with different properties to more closely match the design specification of the refinery.

Studies to schedule more general oil distribution networks with Constraint Programming were largely unsuccessful. There are many non-linear, continuous constraints, the pipes can be used bi-directionally, requiring a detailed view of the contents of the pipe at any given time. When sending two different products, one after the other, through the pipe, the products partially mix at the interface, requiring down-grading of the product, or even producing scrap that needs to be reworked at a refinery. An exception was the pipeline scheduling tool developed by PrologIA for AirLiquide, which was designed to handle parts of their European pipeline system.

25.3 Data Networks

We now consider data network applications, which form the core of this chapter.

25.3.1 Application Placement

The system described in [16] was one of the first constraint applications dealing with networks. It was developed for the Italian Inter-banking network and deals with the placement of applications on servers in the network.

The problem is to place a set of applications **K** on different servers in a network, so that they can run over-night batch jobs with data transmitted by users on nodes in the network. Each server j has limited CPU capacity, denoted $\mathtt{cpu}(j)$, while many nodes of the network can not host any applications. Each user request states that a user on node i needs $\mathtt{dem}(i, k)$ CPU units for application k. If we run application k on a server j, we have to pay a cost $\mathtt{lic}(j, k)$, typically license fees. Transmitting data from user i to server j creates a transport cost $\mathtt{dist}(i, j)$ per unit transported.

We introduce $\{0, 1\}$ decision variables $A_{j,k}$ to indicate if application k is running on server j, and decision variables U_{ij}^k to indicate that the demand of user i for application k is satisfied by server j. We can then express the model in this form

$$\min_{\{A_{jk}, U_{ij}^k\}} \quad \sum_{k \in \mathbf{K}} \sum_{j \in \mathbf{N}} \mathtt{lic}(j, k) A_{jk} + \sum_{k \in \mathbf{K}} \sum_{i \in \mathbf{N}} \sum_{j \in \mathbf{N}} \mathtt{dist}(i, j) \mathtt{dem}(i, k) U_{ij}^k \qquad (25.1)$$

st.

$$\forall j \in \mathbf{N}: \quad \sum_{k \in \mathbf{K}} \sum_{i \in \mathbf{N}} \mathtt{dem}(i, k) U_{ij}^k \leq \mathtt{cpu}(j) \qquad (25.2)$$

$$\forall k \in \mathbf{K}, \forall i \in \mathbf{N}: \quad \sum_{j \in \mathbf{N}} U_{ij}^k = 1 \qquad (25.3)$$

$$\forall k \in \mathbf{K}, \forall i \in \mathbf{N}, \forall j \in \mathbf{N}: \quad U_{ij}^k \implies A_{jk} \qquad (25.4)$$

$$A_{jk} \in \{0, 1\}$$

$$U_{ij}^k \in \{0, 1\}$$

The objective function (25.1) is to minimize the total cost of the system which consists of the license costs and the transportation cost over the network. Each server can handle only jobs up the the limit of its CPU, this is controlled by equation (25.2). Equation (25.3) states that each customer job must be handled by exactly one server. The last constraint (25.4) states that if a customer application is assigned to a server, then the corresponding application must be provided on the server.

Looking at the constraints we see that this model is an extended version of the capacitated warehouse location problem [48]. This is related to the (simpler) uncapacitated warehouse location problem described in [66], one of the first models developed with finite domain constraint programming. Not surprisingly, the problem in [16] was also expressed using the finite domain solver of CHIP [25]. It is doubtful whether for this problem the approach is competitive with state of the art local search methods [47].

Note that the network view of this model is quite simplistic. We only have to pay a transmission cost which depends on the choice of source and sink for each demand. We do not consider if there is enough network capacity to transport the traffic over the network, or which routes should be used. For the application placement model, network capacity is infinite. We will see in the following section how a more detailed view of the network could be used to add more constraints to the problem.

25.3.2   Path Placement

In many data networks we can decide which path is used for a demand, and a central control algorithm is responsible for assigning paths to demands under the capacity constraints of the network. There are three main alternative models for solving this problem, they are called

link-based For each demand we have one decision variable per link which states if the link is used for this demand or not.

path-based For every demand we have one decision variable per possible path between source and destination. We can choose one path per demand.

node-based For every demand we have a decision variable for every node in the network. If its value is 0, then the node is not used by the demand, if it is non-zero, then it gives the successor node. The variables for each demand form a cycle in the graph.

We also present two variants of the path placement problem in this section.

- In the *demand acceptance problem*, we are given a set of demands and have to decide which demands we can accept without exceeding the capacity limits of the network. We are interested in finding a solution which maximizes the value of the accepted demands.

- The *traffic placement problem* uses a fixed set of demands, which all have to be placed. We search for a solution which minimizes the maximal utilization over all network links.

The base-line comparison for these problems is the *CSPF (Constrained Shortest Path First)* algorithm [24], which applies a simple greedy heuristic to place the demands in order of decreasing demand size. For each demand we attempt to place it on the network using a shortest path algorithm in a residual graph, where only edges with more than the required bandwidth are considered. If the demand can be placed, it is accepted, and the free capacity in the network is reduced by its demand size.

We now discuss the different models in more detail, using the following conventions. The network consists of a set of nodes $\mathbf{N}$ and a set of directed edges $\mathbf{E}$. The set $\mathbf{OUT}(n)$ consists of all edges leaving node n, the set $\mathbf{IN}(n)$ of all edges leading to node n. The capacity of an edge is given by $\mathtt{cap}(e)$. The source of an edge is denoted as $\mathtt{source}(e)$, the sink as $\mathtt{sink}(e)$. For every demand in the set $\mathbf{D}$, we have a source ($\mathtt{orig}(d)$) and a destination ($\mathtt{dest}(d)$), a bandwidth requirement $\mathtt{bw}(d)$ and a value $\mathtt{val}(d)$ which indicates the benefit of accepting demand d.

Link-based model

We start with the *demand acceptance problem* in a link-based model, where we use one decision variable for every demand and link of the network. The $\{0, 1\}$ variable X_{de} denotes whether demand d is routed over edge e of the network. For every demand d we also have one $\{0, 1\}$ decision variable Z_d which indicates if the demand is accepted or not. The following model gives a MILP formulation.

$$\max_{\{Z_d, X_{de}\}} \quad \sum_{d \in \mathbf{D}} \mathtt{val}(d) Z_d \tag{25.5}$$

st.

$$\forall d \in \mathbf{D}, \forall n \in \mathbf{N} : \quad \sum_{e \in \mathbf{OUT}(n)} X_{de} - \sum_{e \in \mathbf{IN}(n)} X_{de} = \begin{cases} -Z_d & n = \mathtt{dest}(d) \\ Z_d & n = \mathtt{orig}(d) \\ 0 & \text{otherwise} \end{cases} \tag{25.6}$$

$$\forall e \in \mathbf{E} : \quad \sum_{d \in \mathbf{D}} \mathtt{bw}(d) X_{de} \leq \mathtt{cap}(e) \tag{25.7}$$

$$Z_d \in \{0, 1\}$$
$$X_{de} \in \{0, 1\}$$

The *path constraint* (25.6) states that there is a single path for each accepted demand, linking the Z_d and X_{de} variables. Equation (25.7) states the *capacity constraint*, that for each link the amount of traffic routed over it must be smaller than the link capacity. The objective (25.5) is to maximize the value of the accepted demands.

We often also have *quality of service* constraints attached to the demands. For each demand d we have a quality requirement $\mathtt{req}(d)$ which should not be exceeded in our solution. The quality of the assigned path is calculated as the sum of constants $\mathtt{del}(e)$ for all edges which are used by the path. A typical quality indicator is delay (also called *latency*), which is calculated as the sum of the propagation delays of the links on the selected path. This delay must be smaller than the latency requirement expressed for the demand. The constraints take the form given in equation (25.8). If the required latency is too small, then we may not be able to find any path which satisfies the demand.

$$\forall d \in \mathbf{D} : \quad \sum_{e \in \mathbf{E}} \mathtt{del}(e) X_{de} \leq \mathtt{req}(d) \tag{25.8}$$

The *traffic placement problem* is expressed in a similar form. Here all demands must be accepted, we therefore no longer need Z_d variables. The only variables in the model are $\{0, 1\}$ variables X_{de} which indicate whether demand d is routed over edge e. We still have the *path constraint* (equation 25.10) and an objective function (25.9) which is to minimize the maximal relative utilization of any edge in the network. For this we divide the amount of traffic routed over the edge by the capacity of the edge. A solution with a cost of less than 1 means that the traffic routed over all edges stays within the link capacity, if the cost is greater than 1, then some links exceed their capacity.

$$\min_{\{X_{de}\}} \max_{e \in \mathbf{E}} \frac{1}{\mathrm{cap}(e)} \sum_{d \in \mathbf{D}} \mathrm{bw}(d) X_{de} \qquad (25.9)$$

st.

$$\forall d \in \mathbf{D}, \forall n \in \mathbf{N}: \quad \sum_{e \in \mathbf{OUT}(n)} X_{de} - \sum_{e \in \mathbf{IN}(n)} X_{de} = \begin{cases} -1 & n = \mathrm{dest}(d) \\ 1 & n = \mathrm{orig}(d) \\ 0 & \mathrm{otherwise} \end{cases} \quad (25.10)$$

$$X_{de} \in \{0, 1\}$$

In this model the capacity constraints (25.7) are folded into the objective function, they will appear as linear constraints in a MILP representation. Unfortunately, there seems to be no consensus about the objective function. There are at least two other versions proposed in different papers. One is to minimise the overall network utilization

$$\min_{\{X_{de}\}} \sum_{e \in \mathbf{E}} \sum_{d \in \mathbf{D}} \mathrm{bw}(d) X_{de} \qquad (25.11)$$

while imposing the capacity constraints (25.7). This objective function is closely related to the formulation of the *Integer Multi-Commodity Flow Problem* [3]. The other alternative is proposed in [51] as a compromise which is supposed to return better overall solutions. It minimizes the average link utilization.

$$\min_{\{X_{de}\}} \sum_{e \in \mathbf{E}} \sum_{d \in \mathbf{D}} \frac{\mathrm{bw}(d)}{\mathrm{cap}(e)} X_{de} \qquad (25.12)$$

Overall, demand acceptance and these versions of traffic placement are closely related, but their objectives are different enough to make a direct comparison between results difficult. In later section, we will only describe the demand acceptance problem, the traffic placement variant can be derived in a similar way.

We now discuss a number of proposed algorithms that use the link based model.

Lagrangian relaxation/CP hybrid - path decomposition   A hybrid method for traffic placement is proposed in [51, 52]. It combines *Lagrangian Relaxation (LR)* (see Chapter 15, "Operations Research Methods in Constraint Programming") with constraint programming. Both models are set up in parallel and exchange information during a depth-first search. In the Lagrangian subproblem we dualize the capacity constraints (25.7) into the cost function and keep the path constraints (25.6).

The constraint model uses finite domain $\{0, 1\} X_{de}$ variables and finite domain versions of the path constraints, strengthened by some redundant inequality constraints to remove cycles. In a preprocessing step, some capacity constraints based on s-t cuts are added. The LR model starts with an initial heuristic, possibly infeasible assignment obtained with a CSPF variant.

At each node of the search tree, a limited number of subgradient steps [3] are performed in the LR model. This involves solving $|\mathbf{D}|$ shortest path problems with an LP solver. The results are used to generate new constraints for the FD model, which, through propagation, may lead to further assignments, which are then returned to the LR model. When the LR model is stopped, the current Lagrangian solution is used to decide on the next branching choice, assigning some undecided X_{de} variable. Nodes in the search can be pruned either because the LR model becomes infeasible or because constraint propagation detects a failure.

The results obtained in [51, 52] can not be directly compared with other methods, since the model uses a different cost function (25.12). But [53, 21] describe experiments with a modified version of this decomposition where the more commonly accepted cost function (25.11) is used.

Lagrangian relaxation/CP hybrid - knapsack decomposition   As an alternative Lagrangian Relaxation [53] proposes to relax the path constraints (25.6) while keeping the capacity constraints (25.7). This means that at each subgradient step, we have to solve $|\mathbf{E}|$ independent knapsack ILP problems.

Both [51] and [53] use cost-based filtering [29] from the reduced cost of the X variables of the LP relaxation solved at each subgradient step to fix some values to either 0 or 1. This idea is extended in [22, 23], which adds three more filtering rules. Comparative experiments show that this produces stronger pruning, which improves the quality of the solutions, reduces the number of nodes in the search tree significantly and can lead to overall savings in computation time.

Probe backtracking   *Probe Backtracking Search (PBT)* [27] is used in [43] to solve the traffic placement problem with a link-based model. The idea behind PBT is to split the constraints into two groups, considered "easy" and "hard". The hard constraints and the optimization are handled by a branch&bound backtracking scheme. In each node, one of the hard constraints is replaced by a disjunction of easy constraints, which form the basis of the branching decisions. The system starts with a tentative assignment based on a heuristic. In each node the current set of easy constraints is used to solve a subproblem called *prober* which either detects infeasibility or returns a new tentative, partial assignment. Violations of the hard constraints are resolved by branching on the introduction of additional simple constraints.

For the traffic placement problem the prober finds a cycle-free path for one demand which respects the delay constraint (25.8) and any imposed forbidden and required links. The prober is implemented as an incremental ILP which adds no-good cuts until a valid solution is returned. The search component checks for violations of the capacity constraints; if there are none, a solution has been found. Otherwise, it heuristically selects a link with a capacity violation and a demand routed over it, and calls the prober again, branching on either forbidding or enforcing the selected link for the selected demand.

The probe backtracking scheme can be used with a variety of probing methods, [37] considers the combination with local search, and [38] applies this combination to demand acceptance. The local probe consists of a simulated annealing local search routine which tries to find paths for a set of demands. One of the challenges for the implementation lies in how to incorporate forced links into the neighborhood operator.

Path-based model

The second type of formulation for the path placement problem is the path-based model. In this model we consider for each demand the paths on which it can be routed. Assume that there are $\mathrm{path}(d)$ possible paths for demand d. We introduce a $\{0, 1\}$ decision variable Y_{id} for each possible path for each demand d. The constants h^e_{id} indicate whether path for demand d is routed over edge e. The $\{0, 1\}$ variables Z_d again state whether demand is accepted or not.

$$\max_{\{Z_d, Y_{id}\}} \quad \sum_{d \in \mathbf{D}} \mathrm{val}(d) Z_d \tag{25.13}$$

st.

$$\forall d \in \mathbf{D}: \quad \sum_{1 \leq i \leq \mathrm{path}(d)} Y_{id} = Z_d \tag{25.14}$$

$$\forall e \in \mathbf{E}: \quad \sum_{d \in \mathbf{D}} \mathrm{bw}(d) \sum_{1 \leq i \leq \mathrm{path}(d)} h^e_{id} Y_{id} \leq \mathrm{cap}(e) \tag{25.15}$$

$$Z_d \in \{0, 1\}$$
$$Y_{id} \in \{0, 1\}$$

The objective function (25.13) is the same as for the link based model (25.5). Equation (25.14) links the Z_d and the Y_{id} variables and states that at most one path may be selected for each demand. Equation (25.15) is a modified capacity constraint, stating that the bandwidth required for all selected paths routed over an edge must be smaller than the edge capacity.

Column generation   The direct implementation of a path based model will be difficult due to the very large number of possible paths even in a small graph. This model therefore is a natural candidate for techniques like column generation, where only a limited subset of all possible paths are considered and the objective function can drive the search for finding new paths which improve overall solution quality.

We will discuss this approach used for example in [14] in more detail in section 25.3.5.

Blocking islands   A different, more CSP oriented view of a path-based model is given in [30]. It considers the traffic placement problem without objective function, i.e. all demands must be placed, but we only require a feasible solution. This can be modelled as a CSP where each demand is a variable which ranges over all possible paths. The main idea of this paper is that it is not necessary to describe the domains of the variables explicitly, it is sufficient if we can check whether there still is a possible path for each demand at each step. This corresponds to a forward-checking based constraint propagation, which can be used inside a search routine that assigns paths to demands. Heuristics like dynamic variable and value selection can also be applied, making this a nice example of an implied constraint model.

Key to the implementation of this implied model is the concept of a *blocking island* For a given demand size d, we can partition the nodes in the network into equivalence classes, called d blocking islands. All nodes inside one blocking island can reach each other with paths of at least size d. We know that a demand of size d can be satisfied if both source and sink are in the same d island, and can not be satisfied if they are in different d islands. The blocking islands for different capacity values form a tree, where the root is one island connecting all nodes with capacity 0.

When a path is assigned to a demand, we can update the blocking island tree effectively, and can check if there still is a path for every demand in the new tree. If not, the node in the search tree can be pruned, and we backtrack to a previous choice. The experiments in [30] showed that it can be worthwhile to replace chronological backtracking with a form of conflict-driven backjumping.

The approach can be easily extended to handle the objective function for traffic placement, but it is unclear how to adapt this technique to the demand acceptance problem.

Local search/CP hybrid Another hybrid solver for the demand acceptance problem is described in [41, 42]. It combines local search with finite domain constraint programming in a multi-step procedure, and also combines elements of a path based and a link based model. It starts with a heuristic, CSPF based initial selection of paths to be chosen. In a second step, it tries to add additional demands one by one, at each step calling a local search based repair method to remove any capacity bottlenecks. This repair works by replacing an existing path with a new one. As a third step it uses a hybrid branch&bound routine combining finite domains with local search. The finite domain model initially only consists of the acceptance variables Z_d, the X_{de} variables are only lazily generated on demand. The system finds necessary links for a demand, and imposes capacity constraints on them. It also considers certain cut sets and creates X_{de} variables for each of those links. It then adds a constraint stating that their sum must be equal to the demand variable Z_d as well as the link capacity constraints over all demands on that link.

The local search routine identifies capacity violations and builds a neighborhood by selecting demands currently routed through a violation, and choosing a new shortest path for each demand, using the capacity violation as link metric. The neighborhood is evaluated based on the improvement of the capacity violations, and a move selected using a randomized choice which allows some decrease in quality for some moves. A restart method was incorporated to go back to a previous state if no improvement had been achieved within a given number of steps.

A comparison of this method with a variant of [43] for demand acceptance showed that both were complementary, each method was more successful on some problem instances, while both clearly outperformed CSPF.

Node-based model

In the node-based model the decision variables define successor relations between network nodes, defining paths through a network via the nodes that are traversed. This model is due to [56], which describe this model in terms of a *Bandwidth on Demand* application (see section 25.3.4). For each demand d and each node k in the network, we introduce an integer decision variable S_{kd} with the following domain:

$$S_{kd} :: \begin{cases} \{\texttt{sink}(e)|e \in \mathbf{OUT}(k)\} & k = \texttt{orig}(d) \\ \texttt{orig}(d) & k = \texttt{dest}(d) \\ \{0\} \cup \{\texttt{sink}(e)|e \in \mathbf{OUT}(k)\} & \text{otherwise} \end{cases} \tag{25.16}$$

For each demand the domain for a node contains all possible successors and the value 0, which indicates that the node is not used to route the demand. We add a back-link from the destination of the demand to the source, which does not correspond to an edge in the graph. We now require that for every demand d the set

$$\{< k, S_{kd} > |S_{kd} \neq 0\} \tag{25.17}$$

forms a cycle in the graph (augmented with the back link). In [56], this condition is expressed with the *cycle* constraint [7, 10] of CHIP. This constraint does not allow conditional nodes, the model therefore needs dummy nodes and edges to connect all unused nodes in a second cycle.

The capacity constraint for each node can be expressed with a cumulative constraint [2], which uses two arguments, a set of tasks given by *start, duration* and *resource use* and a resource profile, given as a set of tuples *time point* and *resource limit*.

$$\texttt{cumulative}(\{< S_{id}, 1, \texttt{bw}(d) > |d \in \mathbf{D}\},$$

$$\{< l, m > |0 \leq l \leq n, m = \begin{cases} \infty & l = 0 \\ \texttt{cap}(e) & \exists e \in \mathbf{E} st.\texttt{source}(e) = i, \texttt{sink}(e) = j \\ 0 & \text{otherwise} \end{cases}$$

$$\tag{25.18}$$

In this model we need $|\mathbf{D}|$ cycle constraints and $|\mathbf{N}|$ cumulative constraints to express the conditions of the routing problem, we then have to define a search routine and a $\texttt{min\_max}$ [55] optimization routine to find the optimal solution. Additional conditions like quality of service constraints can be handled by using extra arguments of the cycle constraints.

The cycle constraint probably is not the best choice for this application, the need for dummy nodes and edges in the model destroys much of its propagation potential.

25.3.3 Multiple Paths

In the models of section 25.3.2 we have looked for a single path for each demand. This path is used to transmit the traffic between the source and the destination of the demand. What happens if one of the elements on the path fails? There are three possible scenarios:

- The transmission for the demand is interrupted until the element failure is repaired. This may lead to an outage of several hours and is normally not acceptable.

- We dynamically search for a new path in the modified network and set up the path for transmission. The outage will be much shorter, and is limited by the time required to find a new path.

- We have pre-computed an alternative path, which is *link disjoint* to the original path, so that the element failure does not affect this additional, secondary path. We can immediately switch to the alternative, minimizing the outage.

We will now look at the problem of finding multiple (primary and secondary) paths for demands, where the primary path is used in normal operation, and the secondary is only active when some link on the primary path has failed. We present a link-based, demand acceptance model for this problem, which is an extension of the model in section 25.3.2. In addition to the $\{0, 1\}$ variables Z_d for demand acceptance, and X_{de} for the primary path, we need additional decision variables W_{de}, which indicate whether edge e is used for the secondary path of demand d.

$$\max_{\{Z_d, X_{de}, W_{de}\}} \sum_{d \in \mathbf{D}} \text{val}(d) Z_d \qquad (25.19)$$

st.

$$\forall d \in \mathbf{D}, \forall n \in \mathbf{N}: \quad \sum_{e \in \mathbf{OUT}(n)} X_{de} - \sum_{e \in \mathbf{IN}(n)} X_{de} = \begin{cases} -Z_d & n = \text{dest}(d) \\ Z_d & n = \text{orig}(d) \\ 0 & \text{otherwise} \end{cases}$$

$$(25.20)$$

$$\forall e \in \mathbf{E}: \quad \sum_{d \in \mathbf{D}} \text{bw}(d) * X_{de} \leq \text{cap}(e) \qquad (25.21)$$

$$\forall d \in \mathbf{D}, \forall n \in \mathbf{N}: \quad \sum_{e \in \mathbf{OUT}(n)} W_{de} - \sum_{e \in \mathbf{IN}(n)} W_{de} = \begin{cases} -Z_d & n = \text{dest}(d) \\ Z_d & n = \text{orig}(d) \\ 0 & \text{otherwise} \end{cases}$$

$$(25.22)$$

$$\forall e \in \mathbf{E}, \forall e' \in \mathbf{E} \setminus e: \quad \sum_{d \in \mathbf{D}} \text{bw}(d) * (X_{de} - X_{de'} * X_{de} + X_{de'} * W_{de}) \leq \text{cap}(e)$$

$$(25.23)$$

$$\forall d \in \mathbf{D}, \forall e \in \mathbf{E}: \quad X_{de} + W_{de} \leq 1 \qquad (25.24)$$

$$Z_d \in \{0, 1\}$$

$$X_{de} \in \{0, 1\}$$

$$W_{de} \in \{0, 1\}$$

The model is quite similar to the model in section 25.3.2. The objective function (25.19) is the same, and we also find the path constraint (25.20) and the capacity constraints (25.21) for the primary path. To this we add a path constraint for the secondary path (equation 25.22) and the link-disjoint constraint (25.24) which states that primary and secondary paths for a demand can not share a link. The only complicated, additional constraint is the capacity constraint for the secondary paths (equation 25.23). This expresses the capacity for link e in the case of failure of link e'. The traffic we have to consider is the sum of all primary paths through link e, except for those that were also routed through link e'. In addition we need to consider all secondary paths routed through e, where the primary was routed through the failed link e'. We therefore need a capacity constraint for each link under each failure scenario. This dramatically increases the number of constraints that are required.

The link disjoint constraint is only one way of keeping the primary and secondary paths apart. We can also consider two stronger alternatives, the paths may be *node disjoint* or *SRLG disjoint*.

For *node disjoint* primary and secondary paths we enforce that, except for the source and destination nodes, the paths do not cross the same nodes. This protects the connection even in case of a node failure. We can express this constraint by the equations

$$\forall d \in \mathbf{D}, n \in \mathbf{N} \setminus \{\texttt{orig}(d), \texttt{dest}(d)\} : \sum_{e \in \mathbf{IN}(n)} X_{de} + W_{de} \leq 1 \qquad (25.25)$$

$$\forall d \in \mathbf{D}, n \in \mathbf{N} \setminus \{\texttt{orig}(d), \texttt{dest}(d)\} : \sum_{e \in \mathbf{OUT}(n)} X_{de} + W_{de} \leq 1 \qquad (25.26)$$

Using either (25.25) or (25.26) together with the path constraint is enough to ensure the condition.

The *SRLG disjoint* constraint is a generalization to arbitrary sets of links. A *shared risk link group (SRLG)* is a set of links that we consider might fail together. This can happen for example if several (physical) links are run through the same cable duct, or if multiple logical (layer-3) connections are mapped to the same physical (layer-1) connections, for example multiple carriers using the same sea-cable for a intercontinental connection. To express this constraint, we assume we are given a set **S** of SRLG sets. For each SRLG **SRLG** and each demand d, we express the constraint that primary and secondary path can not share any links in the set.

$$\forall d \in \mathbf{D}, \forall \mathbf{SRLG} \in \mathbf{S} : \sum_{e \in \mathbf{SRLG}} X_{de} + W_{de} \leq 1 \qquad (25.27)$$

The model above is the basis for the solver described in [68]. A linearization of the non-linear constraints (25.23) adds a many new variables and linear constraints. To handle this very large number of capacity constraints required for the failure cases the authors suggested the following decomposition. Initially, the problem is set up without constraints (25.23) and solved with a MILP solver. For the optimal solution the secondary path capacity constraints are checked and, if violated, added (linearized) to the constraint set. The process iterates until no secondary path capacity constraints are violated, in which case an optimal solution to the whole problem is found. This can be seen as a form of *Benders decomposition* (see Chapter 15, "Operations Research Methods in Constraint Programming"), where the secondary path capacity constraints form the sub problems, and all other constraints form the master problem. The *Benders cuts* that are generated take the form of the linearized capacity constraints. This approach allowed a significant speed-up over a standard MILP formulation of the problem.

25.3.4   Bandwidth on Demand

So far, the traffic demands we encountered were all for a single snapshot in time, i.e. all demands were simultaneous. We now consider the *Bandwidth on Demand* scenario where each demand has a fixed start $\texttt{start}(d)$ and end $\texttt{end}(d)$ time, and demands only interact if they overlap in time. The problem is to accept demands so that at no time point the capacity of the network is exceeded. Instead of looking at every time point between the earliest start and the latest end of any demand, we can restrict ourselves to time points when new demands are starting. The set of time points **T** to consider is then given by

$$\mathbf{T} = \{\texttt{start}(d)|d \in \mathbf{D}\} \tag{25.28}$$

We can now formulate the demand acceptance problem for Bandwidth on Demand with the following MILP, which uses the Z_d and X_{de} $\{0, 1\}$ decision variables already familiar from section 25.3.2.

$$\max_{\{Z_d, X_{de}\}} \sum_{d \in \mathbf{D}} \texttt{val}(d) Z_d \tag{25.29}$$

st.

$$\forall d \in \mathbf{D}, \forall n \in \mathbf{N}: \quad \sum_{e \in \mathbf{OUT}(n)} X_{de} - \sum_{e \in \mathbf{IN}(n)} X_{de} = \begin{cases} -Z_d & n = \texttt{dest}(d) \\ Z_d & n = \texttt{orig}(d) \\ 0 & \text{otherwise} \end{cases} \tag{25.30}$$

$$\forall t \in \mathbf{T}, \forall e \in \mathbf{E}: \quad \sum_{\substack{d \in \mathbf{D} \\ \texttt{start}(d) \leq t \\ t < \texttt{end}(d)}} \texttt{bw}(d) X_{de} \leq \texttt{cap}(e) \tag{25.31}$$

$$Z_d \in \{0, 1\}$$
$$X_{de} \in \{0, 1\}$$

We find the objective function (25.29), the path constraint for each demand (25.30) and a modified capacity constraint (equation 25.31). This capacity constraint is now quite similar to the global cumulative constraint [2]. For every time point and every link, the sum of the accepted traffic routed over the link may not exceed the link capacity.

There are many ways to extend the basic Bandwidth on Demand model. Simple modifications are changes of the link capacity over time or general topology changes at fixed time points. We may also consider that demands may be moved from one path to another during their life-time, in order to accommodate changes in the demand structure.

Another natural extension is some form of on-line algorithm, where new demands for future time periods are added from time to time. Previous commitments must be respected, i.e. demands that were accepted at an earlier time point can not be rejected later on. This is easily handled by forcing some of the Z_d variables to be 1.

A much more challenging extension is to relax the fixed start and end times. If demands can be moved in time, we obtain a very difficult combination of the path placement and a cumulative scheduling problem.

France Telecom The problem first described in [39], and then reconsidered in [44] is an on-line version of the Bandwidth on demand problems for ATM networks. When a new demand is entered, we have to check if it can be accepted, possibly by rerouting previously accepted demands. There is a time limit of one minute to decide on acceptance. But once a demand has been accepted, it can not be rejected at a later point in time.

The model of [39] uses a constraint based conflict resolution mechanism which is called when a demand can not be placed on top of the existing set of connections. It selects short paths for the new demands and finds all existing connections which would be in conflict when accepting the new demand on one of the routes. It then creates a constraint model which tries to repair the solution by moving one of the existing connections to a new path. The resulting capacity checks are quite complex, since they have to be performed for every time point between the start and the end of the task considered. A specialized calendar data structure is used to minimize the overhead.

The constraint model for the path constraint takes an unusual form in this model. It is based on an assignment from a n-th hop variable to the links of the network. Therefore, the length of each path must be bounded a priori, and a dummy value for "not used" must be introduced.

The procedure is compared to the on-line CSPF algorithm, which does not consider rerouting of existing connections, and achieves some improvement in the percentage of accepted demands.

The approach in [44] uses the same basic problem formulation, but uses *Valued CSP (VCSP)* (see Chapter 9, "Soft Constraints") as the conflict resolution mechanism. The VCSP is solved by a combination of finite domain, local search and limited discrepancy search [34].

Schlumberger dexa.net   The Bandwidth on demand system for Schlumberger's dexa.net [64] decomposes the problem on a temporal basis. For each time point, a specialized solver for the demand acceptance problem is run, its results form new constraints for the next time point.

This technique is expanded in [17], which proposes three alternative models. In the first one, all orders starting at the same time are processed together, with different events being treated sequentially. In the second model, the overall planning horizon is split into intervals, and all tasks starting in that interval are planned together. In the last model, a Benders decomposition is used to link subproblems for each interval together in the master problem. Tasks which extend over several intervals cause inter-dependency between the sub problems, the generated Benders cuts guide the procedure to the optimal solution. The first two methods are incomplete, the third one is complete. Experiments and the comparison with a MILP formulation show that the temporal decomposition is much faster than, but can not reach the quality of, the Benders decomposition, which in turn is similar to the MILP solution in quality, while requiring significantly less computational effort.

Global constraint model   As described in section 25.3.2, the approach of [56] uses a node-based model. To handle the time dimension of the Bandwidth on Demand problem, the authors replace the cumulative constraints (25.18) with a four dimensional diffn constraint [7].

25.3.5 Network Design and Capacity Planning

The problems in sections 25.3.2 to 25.3.4 were all considering a fixed network structure. The topology of the network and the link capacities were given, the variables were introduced by demands and the overall utilization of the network. When planning to build a network, a different question arises: How should I connect the nodes in my network, and which capacity should I use for each link? A similar problem is considered in capacity planning. Given the current network and set of projected demands, how should I extend the network to cope with future demands. We now consider this problem, following the problem specification in [40]. For every potential edge in the network, we have a set of $\mathtt{alt}(e)$ possible design alternatives with bandwidth $\mathtt{cap}(i,e)$ and cost $\mathtt{cost}(i,e)$. One of these alternatives might be not to use that link. This alternative may have non-zero cost in the case of capacity planning, when the link already exists and we have to pay a decommissioning cost in order to remove it. In our model we have two types of variables, the X_{de} $\{0,1\}$ variables which indicate whether a link is used by a demand, and W_{ie} decision variables which indicate if design alternative i for edge e is chosen.

$$\min_{\{X_{de},W_{ie}\}} \sum_{e\in \mathbf{E}} \sum_{1\leq i\leq \mathtt{alt}(e)} \mathtt{cost}(i,e)W_{ie} \qquad (25.32)$$

st.

$$\forall d \in \mathbf{D}, \forall n \in \mathbf{N}: \quad \sum_{e\in \mathbf{OUT}(n)} X_{de} - \sum_{e\in \mathbf{IN}(n)} X_{de} = \begin{cases} -1 & n = \mathtt{dest}(d) \\ 1 & n = \mathtt{orig}(d) \\ 0 & \text{otherwise} \end{cases} \quad (25.33)$$

$$\forall e \in \mathbf{E}: \quad \sum_{d\in \mathbf{D}} \mathtt{bw}(d)X_{de} \leq \sum_{1\leq i\leq \mathtt{alt}(e)} \mathtt{cap}(i,e)W_{ie} \qquad (25.34)$$

$$\forall e \in \mathbf{E}: \quad \sum_{1\leq i\leq \mathtt{alt}(e)} W_{ie} = 1 \qquad (25.35)$$

$$W_{ie} \in \{0,1\}$$
$$X_{de} \in \{0,1\}$$

The objective function (25.32) is to minimize the total cost of the design. Equation (25.33) states the usual path constraint for each demand. The design choice constraints (25.35) state that for each edge we have to choose one alternative (which might be not to use the link). The capacity constraint (25.34) compares the traffic volume routed over the link with the capacity provided by the chosen design alternative.

ROCOCO benchmarks   Reference [40] provides an evaluation of five alternative solution methods for a set of benchmark problems from France Telecom, and also introduces combinations of additional constraints for this problem to create a broader set of test cases. It looks at a CP, a MILP and a column generation alternative in an attempt to improve first results, and further develops the constraint model into a hybrid with local search and parallel execution on multiple processors. An initial heuristic solution is created with CP, a local search module then tries to improve the solution found, and finally a tree search is started with the best current solution as an upper bound.

The problem sizes range from very small (4-10 nodes) to medium size (15-25 nodes), and a timeout of 10 minutes is imposed. For a design problem that is a very small execution time, this might be explained by the large number of problem variations being tested. Over the implemented variants, the CP+local search routine is the most effective, but unfortunately details of the different models are quite sparse.

The model used by [14] is path based, using column generation in a branch and price and cut framework. The paper describes various cutting planes, which strengthen the basic branch and price framework, which alone is not competitive. But even with the cuts added, the system does not find solutions within the timeout using the default search method. A custom search routine based on limited discrepancy search [34] was used to find solutions, results indicated that is was performing better than [40].

Design for multicast   In [20, 21] a variant of the design problem is studied. Instead of designing a network for point to point demands, the authors consider multi-cast traffic demands. In multi-cast, a traffic source injects traffic to the network which must be delivered to a number of subscribers. The traffic is routed over a tree rooted in the traffic source, with consumers located on the leaf nodes. Multi-cast traffic on IP networks is becoming more and more significant, as it is a much cheaper form of content distribution for applications like video-on-demand, broadcasting, or large scale software updates. The two papers differ in the method used, [20] describes a hybrid of Lagrangian relaxation with constraint programming, while [21] considers a hybrid of a branch-and-price column generation with a finite domain constraint component.

SONET network design   Although also a network design problem, the problem studied in [63] bears little relation to the model shown above. [63] shows results for using Constraint Programming on a design problem of a SONET/SDH optical network. Instead of point-to-point links, SONET networks use fiber rings to which a number of users can be connected via hardware devices. The ring capacity can be filled with traffic between users on the same ring. The objective is to choose the minimal number of rings and of hardware interfaces to satisfy all communication demands.

25.3.6   IGP Metric Optimization

The problems considered in sections 25.3.2 to 25.3.4 were all about explicit traffic placement, i.e. a central control algorithm computed single paths for demands which together satisfied the global capacity constraints. In marked contrast stand networks that use routing and packet switching. Here each packet is forwarded locally not by following a fixed connection between source and destination, but by local routing decisions which control at each node where the packet is sent next. A distributed routing algorithm is used so that each router makes its forwarding decisions only based on local knowledge, and control messages are sent between the nodes to inform them about the overall topology and changes to the connectivity. The routing protocols are designed to converge to a consistent routing after each change within a limited time period, the *re-convergence time* Routing inside the network is controlled by the *Interior Gateway Protocol (IGP)*, routing to destinations outside the current network is controlled by the *Border Gateway Protocol (BGP)* [54]. There are many variants of IGP routing protocols (like RIP, OSPF [49], IS-

IS, EIGRP) [45], which mainly differ in the way the distributed network nodes exchange information and what global view of the network is maintained in each node.

From the outside, IGP routing in a steady state can be seen as an application of shortest path finding. Each link in the network is assigned an edge weight, the *routing metric*, and traffic through the network follows a shortest path between source and destination. By changing the routing metric we can (indirectly) control which paths are chosen and how much traffic can be placed on the network.

An important question is what happens if multiple shortest paths exist between two nodes. Depending on the protocol and its configuration, the system may

- select one of the paths at random

- split traffic between multiple alternatives in a balanced way

- split traffic between multiple alternatives in arbitrary fashion

There typically is also a hardware-based limit on how many (typically 8 or 16) shortest path alternatives can be handled in each node.

All this makes it very hard to predict where traffic will be placed when multiple shortest paths exist. Some of the systems for IGP metric optimization therefore enforce a constraint that only a single shortest path can exist between any two nodes in the network.

We now present an example of a path-based model for IGP metric optimization, which enforces the single shortest path rule. The model uses positive integer (not $\{0, 1\}$) variables W_e for the edge weights. We have $\{0, 1\}$ variables Y_{id} for each demand d and each of the $\texttt{path}(d)$ possible paths for the demand, which indicate whether this path is used. We also introduce continuous variables P_{id} which describe the total weight of the path i for demand d as the sum of the weights of the edges traversed. The $\{0, 1\}$ constants h_{id}^e indicate whether path i for demand d traverses edge e.

$$\min_{\{Y_{id}, W_e\}} \max_{e \in \mathbf{E}} \frac{1}{\text{cap}(e)} \sum_{d \in \mathbf{D}} \text{bw}(d) \sum_{1 \leq i \leq \texttt{path}(d)} h_{id}^e Y_{id} \tag{25.36}$$

st.

$$\forall d \in \mathbf{D} : \sum_{1 \leq i \leq \texttt{path}(d)} Y_{id} = 1 \tag{25.37}$$

$$\forall d \in \mathbf{D}, 1 \leq i \leq \texttt{path}(d) : \quad P_{id} = \sum_{e \in \mathbf{E}} h_{id}^e W_e \tag{25.38}$$

$$\forall d \in \mathbf{D}, 1 \leq i, j \leq \texttt{path}(d) : \quad P_{id} = P_{jd} \implies Y_{id} = Y_{jd} = 0 \tag{25.39}$$

$$\forall d \in \mathbf{D}, 1 \leq i, j \leq \texttt{path}(d) : \quad P_{id} < P_{jd} \implies Y_{jd} = 0 \tag{25.40}$$

$$Y_{id} \in \{0, 1\}$$

$$\text{integer} \quad W_e \geq 1$$

$$P_{id} \geq 0$$

The objective function (25.36) is to minimize the maximal relative utilization of any link in the network. Constraint (25.37) enforces that there is a single, selected shortest path. The weight of each path is controlled by equation (25.38) as the sum of the weights of the traversed edges. Constraint (25.39) states that paths for one demand with the same weight must have identical Y_{id} values, which must be zero, as only one shortest path is allowed. Equation (25.40) states that a path will not be selected if a shorter one exists. Note that this is not intended as an effective model to generate weights, but serves as a declarative problem specification. We now discuss a number of solution approaches to this problem:

Branch and price   A complete method for the unique path weight setting problem is given in [4]. It is based on a path-based model using column generation in a branch and price framework using a hybrid with finite domain constraints. Paths for demands are created lazily using the pricing information from the master problem as a guide.

Preliminary experimental results indicate that the hybrid outperforms more straightforward MILP models, but has difficulty scaling to larger problem instances. One problem is the lack of a good initial solution which can be used as a starting point for the tree search.

Tabu search   A combination of a tabu based local search and a MILP is presented in [5]. It is based on the observation that if a weight setting with fractional values achieves unique paths, then it can be easily converted into a weight setting using integer weights. So a tabu-based local search is first used to derive fractional weight settings, with the MILP converting the result into (small) integer weights. To come up with unique paths in the local search, an ingenious weight assignment is used which assigns weights 2^{-i} to the edges with a different exponent i for each edge. Therefore each path in the network has a unique weight, and the search consists in finding a permutation of the edge assignments which minimizes the traffic load.

This algorithms scales well, although care must be taken not to cause rounding errors in the shortest path calculations due to the extreme range of weight values. Experimental results indicate that in the second part of the algorithm the weights can be re-assigned to integer values ranging from 1 to 200.

Set constraint solver   A more generic problem is solved in [28]. The set based (see Chapter 17, "Beyond Finite Domains") model presented in the paper allows to impose limits on the splitting of flows in each router. This can be used to express the condition mentioned above that the router hardware limits branching in a node to no more than m alternatives.

The model is a combination of set-valued variables describing the paths, continuous variables describing the flow volumes on each edge directed towards a node and integer variables for the edge weights and distance values. It is a good example for the use of different domain types within one model.

Experimental results show that feasible solutions which satisfy the branching limits are obtained easily, but that their quality is not close to the lower bound.

25.3.7   Flow Analysis and Resilience Analysis

So far we have assumed that as part of our problem definition we have a well-defined set of demands: We know who wants to use the network for connections between specific points and how much bandwidth they require. For IP based networks this assumption is not valid. In an operational network there is no (simple) way of collecting data about end-to-end traffic flows, we don't know who is talking to whom and how much bandwidth they use. The only information we can collect is the overall traffic on each edge on the network $\texttt{traf}(e)$ and the external traffic entering $\texttt{ext}^{in}(i)$ and leaving $\texttt{ext}^{out}(j)$ at each node of the network. We can try to reconstruct a demand matrix from these measurements, this is an active research area called *traffic flow analysis*.

A model for this problem is shown below. We use non-negative flow variables F_{ij} to denote the traffic flow from node i to node j in the network. The $[0, 1]$ constants r_{ij}^e define the routing in the network, they indicate what fraction of the flow between nodes i and j is routed over edge e.

$$\forall i, j \in \mathbf{N}: \quad \min_{\{F_{ij}\}} / \max_{\{F_{ij}\}} \quad F_{ij} \tag{25.41}$$

st.

$$\forall e \in \mathbf{E}: \quad \sum_{i,j \in \mathbf{N}} r_{ij}^e F_{ij} = \texttt{traf}(e) \tag{25.42}$$

$$\forall i \in \mathbf{N}: \quad \sum_{j \in \mathbf{N}} F_{ij} = \texttt{ext}^{in}(i) \tag{25.43}$$

$$\forall j \in \mathbf{N}: \quad \sum_{i \in \mathbf{N}} F_{ij} = \texttt{ext}^{out}(j) \tag{25.44}$$

$$F_{ij} \geq 0$$

For every flow, we try to find a lower and an upper bound as the result of an optimization run with the objective (25.41). We know that the sum of all flows routed over an edge is equal to the observed traffic on the edge (25.42), and that the sum of all flows starting (25.43) or ending (25.44) in a node must be equal to the observed external traffic.

The fundamental problem with this approach is that it is very under-constrained. We have $|\mathbf{N}|^2$ flow variables F_{ij}, but only $|\mathbf{E}| + 2|\mathbf{N}|$ constraints. Results in [59] show that the values for the flows can vary in a very wide interval, with no clear preference for any particular value. It is therefore unclear how to use the results for answering further questions about the network, for example how the traffic will change in case of an element failure.

The idea behind *resilience analysis* is to avoid the generation of the intermediate demand matrix, and to pose questions about the network behavior directly in the initial model. For example, we may be interested in understanding the traffic in the network under an element failure and resulting re-routing. The routing in the normal network operation is denoted with r_{ij}^e, the routing after the element failure is given by $r_{ij}^{\bar{e}}$. The model for resilience analysis below uses the flow variables F_{ij} only internally, without trying to deduce particular values.

$$\forall e \in \mathbf{E}: \quad \min_{\{F_{ij}\}} / \max_{\{F_{ij}\}} \quad \sum_{i,j \in \mathbf{N}} r_{ij}^{\bar{e}} F_{ij} \tag{25.45}$$

st.

$$\forall e \in \mathbf{E}: \quad \sum_{i,j \in \mathbf{N}} r^e_{ij} F_{ij} = \texttt{traf}(e) \tag{25.46}$$

$$\forall i \in \mathbf{N}: \quad \sum_{j \in \mathbf{N}} F_{ij} = \texttt{ext}^{in}(i) \tag{25.47}$$

$$\forall j \in \mathbf{N}: \quad \sum_{i \in \mathbf{N}} F_{ij} = \texttt{ext}^{out}(j) \tag{25.48}$$

$$F_{ij} \geq 0$$

The objective function (25.45) now tries to find a value for each edge in the network under the failure scenario, and finds bounds by running minimization and maximization optimization queries. The constraints (25.46, 25.47 and 25.48) are the same as for the traffic flow analysis.

Results in [59] indicate that the bounds on the link traffic in failure scenarios are much tighter, and are close enough for most practical purposes.

In the discussion above, we have oversimplified the use of the actual traffic measurements. The models above only work if a consistent snapshot of all values can be collected. In practice, this poses significant problems. If the data are not collected for exactly the same time periods, then inconsistencies may occur. There are further problems caused by queues in the routers and bugs in implementing data collection facilities in devices of multiple vendors. The data collection process itself uses unreliable communications (UDP) so that some measurements may be lost due to dropped packets. One approach to overcoming these issues is the use of a separate error correction model, which tries to correct values before feeding them into the models above. Another, shown in [71, 70, 72] deals with the problem by integrating incomplete and inconsistent data into the constraint solving process.

25.3.8   Bandwidth Protection

It is very important that a network functions not only when all its elements are working, but that it continues to provide its services when some network elements fail. So far, we have seen two methods of dealing with that issue. In section 25.3.3, we looked at the provisioning of primary and secondary paths in the network, where the secondary path is used when an element on the primary path fails. Depending on the constraint used, this will protect against single link failures, node failures or SRLG failures. In section 25.3.7 we have studied the problem of resilience analysis which considers a routed network without an explicit traffic matrix. The resilience analysis provides bounds on the link utilization in a failure event; if the upper bounds are below a given capacity limit, then the service is guaranteed not to be affected after the re-convergence of the routing protocol.

In this section we discuss a different method for bandwidth protection, first described in [69]. We consider node failures in a network, and try to provide local detours for the traffic around each failed element.

To explain the basic idea, we look at the small example in figure 25.1 taken from [67]. In this network we consider the failure of node j, which is currently used to forward traffic from node c to nodes e and f. A set of possible detours will be to use the paths c, k, l, e and

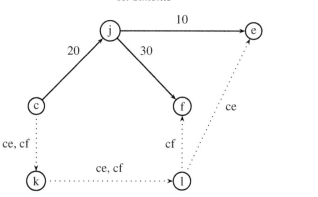

Figure 25.1: Bandwidth Protection Problem

c, k, l, f. But how much capacity do we need to allocate on each link of these detours? We don't know the actual values for the flows between c and e or f, but we can come up with bounds on these values from the bandwidth of the links cj, jf and je. The flow between c and f must be less than 20, and the flow between c and e less than 10. But reserving $20 + 10 = 30$ on the detour links ck and kl is wasteful, the combined value of the flows must be below 20, since they both pass through link cj in the normal state of the network. For the link lf we have to allocate 20, and for the link le 10 units of capacity. Indeed, for every link on the detours we have to allocate the maximal amount that could flow through this link, no matter how the flows through node j are allocated. This leads to the nested optimization problem in (25.49).

$$
\min_{\{X_{fe}\}} \sum_{f \in \mathbf{F}} \sum_{e \in \mathbf{E}} X_{fe}
$$

$$
st. \begin{cases} \forall f \in \mathbf{F}: \begin{cases} \forall n \in \mathbf{N} \setminus \{\text{orig}(f), \text{dest}(f)\}: & \sum_{e \in \mathbf{IN}(n)} X_{fe} = \sum_{e \in \mathbf{OUT}(n)} X_{fe} \\ n = \text{orig}(f): & \sum_{e \in \mathbf{OUT}(n)} X_{fe} = 1 \\ n = \text{dest}(f): & \sum_{e \in \mathbf{IN}(n)} X_{fe} = 1 \end{cases} \\[2em] \forall e \in \mathbf{E}: \quad \text{cap}(e) \geq \begin{cases} \max_{\{Q_{fe}\}} \sum_{f \in \mathbf{F}} X_{fe} Q_{fe} \\ st. \begin{cases} \forall o \in \text{orig}(\mathbf{F}): & \text{ocap}(o) \geq \sum_{f:\text{orig}(f)=o} Q_{fe} \\ \forall d \in \text{dest}(\mathbf{F}): & \text{dcap}(o) \geq \sum_{f:\text{dest}(f)=d} Q_{fe} \end{cases} \end{cases} \\[2em] X_{fe} \in \{0,1\} \\ \text{quan}(f) \geq Q_{fe} \geq 0 \end{cases}
$$

(25.49)

We consider the set $\mathbf{F}$ of all local flows f through the failed element. For each of these flows, we want to provide a single detour around the failure via a link based model from the origin of the flow $\text{orig}(f)$ to its destination $\text{dest}(f)$. For this we introduce $\{0,1\}$

variables X_{fe} which state whether edge e is used in the detour for flow f. We also use continuous variables Q_{fe} to describe the flow volume for flow f that we need to consider for edge e. These flow quantities are constrained by the capacity of the network around the failed element. For every edge, we have to solve a maximization problem, which finds the flow volume that could be forced through that link in the failure case. A feasible solution consists in a choice of the X_{fe} variables which forms a path from source to destination of flow f and which ensures that on each edge the required capacity is below the edge capacity $\texttt{cap}(e)$.

We have to solve this problem for every failure we want to consider, and then need a mechanism which remembers and activates the detours when a failure occurs. The big advantage of this approach is that it is independent of the traffic pattern at the time of failure. Indeed, we don't need any information about traffic flows, or even the routing method used.

How can we actually solve this type of nested optimization problem? In [69], two methods are proposed. The first is a transformation into a MILP, using the Karush-Kuhn-Tucker condition [50] and introducing a set of new variables. This method does not scale well, and can not solve most of the data sets considered in [69].

The second alternative is to decompose the problem into an integer multi-commodity flow problem [3] as the master problem and capacity optimization problems for each edge as subproblems. The master problem generates tentative assignments for the detours, which are checked by the capacity problems. If the capacity of the edge is exceeded, then a cut is generated which is passed back to the master problem and which will change the path assignment. When no capacity constraints are violated, then a solution is found and the procedure stops. The simplest form of cut that can be generated is a no-good which excludes the current solution, but more effective cuts are possible and are described in [69].

Experimental results in [69, 67] show that while the decomposition method works for some large problem instances, it can be beaten by a different transformation of the embedded optimization problem into MILP model. Scalability of the algorithms is still an issue, as the number of flows to be considered increases with increased connectivity in the graph, which also has an impact on the number of possible detours to be considered.

25.4 Conclusion

Before we try to summarize the results in this chapter, we want to mention some related problems where constraint programming has been applied. The problem of frequency assignment in radio networks [1] has been studied quite successfully with different soft constraint methods, this is discussed in some detail in Chapter 9, "Soft Constraints". Constraint programming has also been used for a study of the location of wireless base stations [31]. An emerging domain with interesting challenges for constraint programming is the area of ad-hoc networks [57].

In this chapter we have looked at applications for different network problems, considering electrical, water and especially data networks. The applications for data networks cover a wide range of problems, from design, to risk analysis and operational control. Classical finite domain constraint programming currently seems to be rather limited for these problems, this clearly is a field where hybrid systems are achieving much better results. As an explanation we can see two main contributing factors: one is the important role of cost optimization, the other the large scale of the problems together with the fine granularity of the decisions. LP relaxations and Lagrangian Relaxation (see Chapter 15, "Operations Research Methods in Constraint Programming") seem to provide a much better reasoning on cost bounds than we achieve from individual finite domain or set constraints. At the same time, we often find it easier to construct some feasible solutions and changing them with a restricted neighborhood operator, rather than building very large domain representations from the start.

Limiting factors for the use of hybrid systems are the complexity of designing and evaluating the schemes and the implementation effort required to build a working application. A flexible constraint toolkit like ECLiPSe [15] can help to speed up development, but at the moment building hybrid systems remains still very much a task for specialists.

Is there a way to encapsulate the structure of the problem in some global constraints (see Chapter 6, "Global Constraints"), which hide the algorithmic complexity and provide more high-level abstractions for application developers? Global constraints for graph based problems have been around for some time [7, 10, 9] and have been very useful for rapid application development in other domains [10, 58, 62]. As we have seen in section 25.3.2, they are probably not the right abstraction for the applications discussed here. But there are a number of proposals for new global constraints [8, 13, 26] which may help to solve some of these problems in a more declarative way. Much will depend on how well these constraints will integrate cost reasoning, and which problem size can be handled effectively.

Bibliography

[1] K. Aardal, S. P. M. van Hoesel, A. M. C. A. Koster, C. Mannino, and A. Sassano. Models and solution techniques for frequency assignment problems. *4OR*, 1(4):261–317, 2003.

[2] A. Aggoun and N. Beldiceanu. Extending CHIP in order to solve complex scheduling and placement problems. *Mathematical and Computer Modelling*, pages 57–73, 1993.

[3] R. Ahuja, T. Magnanti, and J. Orlin. *Network Flows*. Prentice Hall, 1993.

[4] F. Ajili, R. Rodosek, and A. Eremin. A branch-price-and-propagate approach for optimising IGP weight setting subject to unique shortest paths. In *Proceedings of the 20th Annual ACM Symposium on Applied Computing (ACM SAC '05)*, Santa Fe, New Mexico, March 2005.

[5] F. Ajili, R. Rodosek, and A. Eremin. A scalable tabu search algorithm for optimising IGP routing. In *2nd International Network Optimization Conference (INOC '05)*, pages 348–354, March 2005.

[6] R. Barták and M. Milano, editors. *Integration of AI and OR Techniques in Constraint Programming for Combinatorial Optimization Problems, Second International Conference, CPAIOR 2005, Prague, Czech Republic, May 30 - June 1, 2005, Proceedings*, volume 3524 of *Lecture Notes in Computer Science*, 2005. Springer. ISBN 3-540-26152-4.

[7] N. Beldiceanu and E. Contejean. Introducing global constraints in CHIP. *Mathematical and Computer Modelling*, 12:97–123, 1994.

[8]   N. Beldiceanu, P. Flener, and X. Lorca. The tree constraint. In Barták and Milano [6], pages 64–78. ISBN 3-540-26152-4.

[9]   A. Bockmayr, N. Pisaruk, and A. Aggoun. Network flow problems in constraint programming. In *Principles and Practice of Constraint Programing - CP 2001*, Paphos, Cyprus, November 2001.

[10] E. Bourreau. *Traitement de Contraintes sur les Graphes en Programmation par Contraintes*. PhD thesis, L'Universite de Paris 13 - Institut Galilee Laboratoire d'Informatique de Paris Nord (L.I.P.N.), March 1999.

[11] M. Brdys, T. Creemers, H. Goosens, J. Riera, A. Heinsbroek, and Z. Lisiak. CLOC-WiSe: Constraint logic for operational constrol of water systems. Technical report, UPC, 2003.

[12] R. E. Bryant. Graph-based algorithms for boolean function manipulation. *IEEE Trans. Computers*, 35(8):677–691, 1986.

[13] H. Cambazard and E. Bourreau. Conception d'une contrainte global de chemin. In *JNPC'04*, 2004.

[14] A. Chabrier. Heuristic branch-and-price-and-cut to solve a network design problem. In *Integration of AI and OR Techniques in Constraint Programming for Combinatorial Optimization Problems CP-AI-OR 03*, Montreal, Canada, May 2003.

[15] A. M. Cheadle, W. Harvey, A. J. Sadler, J. Schimpf, K. Shen, and M. G. Wallace. ECLiPSe: An introduction. Technical Report IC-Parc-03-1, IC-Parc, Imperial College London, 2003.

[16] C. Chiopris and M. Fabris. Optimal management of a large computer network with CHIP. In *2nd Conf Practical Applications of Prolog*, London, UK, April 1994.

[17] Y. Chu and Q. Xia. Bandwidth-on-demand problem and temporal decomposition. In *2nd International Network Optimization Conference (INOC '05)*, pages 542–550, Lisbon, Portugal, March 2005.

[18] T. Creemers, L. R. Giralt, J. Riera, C. Ferrarons, J. Rocca, and X. Corbella. Constrained-based maintenance scheduling on an electric power-distribution network. In *3rd Conference on Practical Applications of Prolog (PAP95)*, Paris, France, April 1995.

[19] T. Creemers, L. Ros, J. Riera, C. Ferrarons, and J. Roca. Smart schedules streamline distribution maintenance. *IEEE Computer Applications in Power*, July 1998.

[20] W. Cronholm and F. Ajili. Strong cost-based filtering for Lagrange decomposition applied to network design. In M. Wallace, editor, *10th International Conference on Principles and Practice of Constraint Programming (CP 2004)*, pages 726–730, Toronto, Canada, 2004. Springer-Verlag.

[21] W. Cronholm and F. Ajili. Hybrid branch-and-price for multicast network design. In *2nd International Network Optimization Conference (INOC '05)*, pages 796–802, Lisbon, Portugal, March 2005.

[22] W. Cronholm, W. Ouaja, and F. Ajili. Strengthening optimality reasoning for a network routing application. In *4th International Workshop on Cooperative Solvers in Constraint Programming (CoSolv '04)*, Toronto, Canada, September 2004.

[23] W. Cronholm, W. Ouaja, and F. Ajili. Strong reduced cost fixing in network routing. In *2nd International Network Optimization Conference (INOC '05)*, pages 688–694, Lisbon, Portugal, March 2005.

[24] B. Davie and Y. Rekhter. *MPLS: Technology and Applications*. Morgan Kauffmann Publishers, 2000.

[25] M. Dincbas, P. Van Hentenryck, H. Simonis, A. Aggoun, T. Graf, and F. Berthier. The constraint logic programming language CHIP. In *FGCS*, pages 693–702, 1988.

[26] G. Dooms, Y. Deville, and P. Dupont. CP(Graph): Introducing a graph computation domain in constraint programming. In van Beek [65], pages 211–225. ISBN 3-540-29238-1.

[27] H. El Sakkout and M. Wallace. Probe backtrack search for minimal perturbation in dynamic scheduling. *Constraints*, 5(4):359–388, 2000.

[28] A. Eremin, F. Ajili, and R. Rodosek. A set-based approach to the optimal IGP weight setting problem. In *2nd International Network Optimization Conference (INOC '05)*, pages 386–392, Lisbon, Portugal, March 2005.

[29] F. Focacci, A. Lodi, and M. Milano. Cost-based domain filtering. In *Principles and Practice of Constraint Programing - CP 1999*, Alexandria, Virginia, October 1999.

[30] C. Frei and B. Faltings. Resource allocation in networks using abstraction and constraint satisfaction techniques. In *Principles and Practice of Constraint Programing - CP 1999*, Alexandria, Virginia, October 1999.

[31] T. Fruehwirth and P. Brisset. Optimal placement of base stations in wireless indoor telecommunication. In *Principles and Practice of Constraint Programing - CP 1998*, Pisa, Italy, October 1998.

[32] T. Graf, P. Van Hentenryck, C. Pradelles, and L. Zimmer. Simulation of hybrid circuits in constraint logic programming. In *IJCAI-89: Proceedings 11th International Joint Conference on Artificial Intelligence*, pages 72–77, Detroit, 1989.

[33] T. Hadzic and H. Andersen. Interactive reconfiguration in power supply restoration. In van Beek [65], pages 767–771. ISBN 3-540-29238-1.

[34] W. D. Harvey and M. L. Ginsberg. Limited discrepancy search. In *IJCAI (1)*, pages 607–615, 1995.

[35] N. Heintze, S. Michaylov, and P. Stuckey. CLP(R) and some electrical engineering problems. In J.-L. Lassez, editor, *Logic Programming: Proceedings of 4th International Conference*, pages 675–703, Melbourne, Australia, September 1987. MIT Press.

[36] J. Jaffar and M. J. Maher. Constraint logic programming: A survey. *Journal of Logic Programming*, 19/20:503–581, 1994.

[37] O. Kamarainen. *Local Probing - A New Framework for Combining Local Search with Backtrack Search*. PhD thesis, IC-Parc, Imperial College London, University of London, December 2003.

[38] O. Kamarainen and H. El Sakkout. Local probing applied to network routing. In *Integration of AI and OR Techniques in Constraint Programming for Combinatorial Optimization Problems CP-AI-OR 04*, Nice, France, April 2004.

[39] M. Lauvergne, P. David, and P. Bauzimault. Connections reservation with rerouting for ATM networks: A hybrid approach with constraints. In P. Van Hentenryck, editor, *Principles and Practice of Constraint Programing - CP 2002*, Cornell University, Ithaca, N.Y., September 2002.

[40] C. Le Pape, L. Perron, J. Regin, and P. Shaw. Robust and parallel solving of a network design problem. In P. Van Hentenryck, editor, *Principles and Practice of Constraint Programing - CP 2002*, Cornell University, Ithaca, N.Y., September 2002.

[41] J. Lever. A local search/constraint propagation hybrid for a network routing problem. In *The 17th International FLAIRS Conference (FLAIRS-2004)*, Miami Beach, Florida, May 2004.

[42] J. Lever. A local search/constraint propagation hybrid for a network routing problem. *International Journal on Artificial Intelligence Tools*, 14(1-2):43–60, 2005.

[43] V. Liatsos, S. Novello, and H. El Sakkout. A probe backtrack search algorithm for network routing. In *Proceedings of the Third International Workshop on Cooperative Solvers in Constraint Programming, CoSolv'03*, Kinsale, Ireland, September 2003.

[44] S. Loudni, P. David, and P. Boizumault. On-line resource allocation for ATM networks with rerouting. In *Integration of AI and OR Techniques in Constraint Programming for Combinatorial Optimization Problems CP-AI-OR 03*, Montreal, Canada, May 2003.

[45] R. Malhotra. *IP Routing*. O'Reilly, Sebastopol, CA, 2002.

[46] K. Marriott and P. Stuckey. *Programming with Constraints: an Introduction*. MIT Press, 1998.

[47] L. Michel and P. Van Hentenryck. A simple tabu search for warehouse location. *European Journal on Operations Research*, pages 576–591, 2004.

[48] P. Mirchandani and R. Francis. *Discrete Location Theory*. Wiley, New York, 1990.

[49] J. T. Moy. *OSPF : Anatomy of an Internet Routing Protocol*. Addison-Wesley, Boston, Ma, 1998.

[50] G. Nemhauser and L. Wolsey. *Integer and Combinatorial Optimization*. Wiley, New York, NY, 1988.

[51] W. Ouaja and B. Richards. A hybrid solver for optimal routing of bandwidth-guaranteed traffic. In *INOC2003*, pages 441–447, 2003.

[52] W. Ouaja and B. Richards. A hybrid multicommodity routing algorithm for traffic engineering. *Networks*, 43(3):125–140, 2004.

[53] W. Ouaja and E. B. Richards. Hybrid Lagrangian relaxation for bandwidth-constrained routing: Knapsack decomposition. In *20th Annual ACM Symposium on Applied Computing (ACM SAC '05)*, pages 383–387, Santa Fe, New Mexico, March 2005.

[54] L. L. Peterson and B. Davie. *Computer Networks*. Morgan Kaufmann, San Francisco, CA, second edition, 2000.

[55] S. Prestwich. Three CLP implementations of branch-and-bound optimization. In *Parallelism and Implementation of Logic and Constraint Logic Programming*, volume 2. Nova Science Publishers, Inc, 1999.

[56] L. Ros, T. Creemers, E. Tourouta, and J. Riera. A global constraint model for integrated routeing and scheduling on a transmission network. In *7th International Conference on Information Networks, Systems and Technologies*, Minsk, October 2001.

[57] Y. Shang, M. P. Fromherz, Y. Zhang, and L. S. Crawford. Constraint-based routing for ad-hoc networks. In *IEEE Int. Conf. on Information Technology: Research and Education (ITRE 2003)*, pages 306–310, Newark, NJ, USA, August 2003.

[58] H. Simonis. Building industrial applications with constraint programming. In H. Comon, C. Marché, and R. Treinen, editors, *CCL*, volume 2002 of *Lecture Notes in Computer Science*, pages 271–309. Springer, 1999. ISBN 3-540-41950-0.

[59] H. Simonis. Resilience analysis in MPLS networks. Technical report, Parc Technologies Ltd, 2003.

[60] H. Simonis. Challenges for constraint programming in networking. In M. Wallace, editor, *Principles and Practice of Constraint Programming - CP 2004. 10th International Conference*, volume 3258 of *LNCS*, Toronto, Canada, September/October

2004. Springer Verlag.

[61] H. Simonis and T. Cornelissens. Modelling producer/consumer constraints. In U. Montanari and F. Rossi, editors, *CP*, volume 976 of *Lecture Notes in Computer Science*, pages 449–462. Springer, 1995. ISBN 3-540-60299-2.

[62] H. Simonis, P. Charlier, and P. Kay. Constraint handling in an integrated transportation problem. *IEEE Intelligent Systems and their applications*, 15(1):26–32, Jan/Feb 2000.

[63] B. M. Smith. Symmetry and search in a network design problem. In Barták and Milano [6], pages 336–350. ISBN 3-540-26152-4.

[64] J. Symes. Bandwidth-on-demand services using MPLS-TE. In *MPLS World Congress 2004*, Paris, France, February 2004.

[65] P. van Beek, editor. *Principles and Practice of Constraint Programming - CP 2005, 11th International Conference, CP 2005, Sitges, Spain, October 1-5, 2005, Proceedings*, volume 3709 of *Lecture Notes in Computer Science*, 2005. Springer. ISBN 3-540-29238-1.

[66] P. Van Hentenryck and J. Carillon. Generality versus specificity: An experience with AI and OR techniques. In *AAAI*, pages 660–664, 1988.

[67] Q. Xia. Traffic diversion problem: Reformulation and new solutions. In *2nd International Network Optimization Conference (INOC '05)*, pages 235–241, Lisbon, Portugal, March 2005.

[68] Q. Xia and H. Simonis. Primary/secondary path generation problem: Reformulation, solutions and comparisons. In *4th International Conference on Networking*, Reunion Island, France, 2005. Springer Verlag.

[69] Q. Xia, A. Eremin, and M. Wallace. Problem decomposition for traffic diversions. In *Integration of AI and OR Techniques in Constraint Programming for Combinatorial Optimization Problems CP-AI-OR 2004*, pages 348–363, Nice, France, April 2004.

[70] N. Yorke-Smith. *Reliable Constraint Reasoning with Uncertain Data*. PhD thesis, IC-Parc, Imperial College London, University of London, June 2004.

[71] N. Yorke-Smith and C. Gervet. On constraint problems with incomplete or erroneuos data. In P. Van Hentenryck, editor, *Principles and Practice of Constraint Programing - CP 2002*, Cornell University, Ithaca, N.Y., September 2002.

[72] N. Yorke-Smith and C. Gervet. Tight and tractable reformulations for uncertain CSPs. In *CP '04 Workshop on Modelling and Reformulating Constraint Satisfaction Problems*, Toronto, Canada, September 2004.

Chapter 26

Bioinformatics and Constraints

Rolf Backofen and David Gilbert

In this chapter we aim to introduce the topic of bioinformatics to an audience of computer scientists, highlight an illustrative selection of those areas in bioinformatics to which constraint techniques have been applied, and suggest where they may be applicable. Bioinformatics is an exciting and rapidly developing field, and we hope that we haven't predicted all the developments in the next few years – indeed we hope that readers of this chapter will contribute to future applicatiions of constraints in bioinformatics!

One of the first issues that needs to be addressed is the what is meant by "bioinformatics" – it is already almost a colloquial word in the scientific community, but its interpretation varies widely. The word bioinformatics has two obvious components – "bio-" and "informatics"; we deal with each of these in turn.

At present the widely accepted interpretation of the "bio" part is *molecular biology*, i.e. the study of the structure and activity of macromolecules essential to life. However are other areas within biology which can be considered to be within the remit of bioinformatics, for example the study of evolution, and genetics.

Informatics is a word which has only recently entered the English language, following the French, German and Russian traditions which broadly agree that its meaning coincides with "computer science". Thus one definition of informatics is "the science of systematic processing of information, using modeling and abstraction of the concrete realization".

Thus, when considering both parts of the word, we consider the proper meaning to be solving problems arising from biology using methodology from computer science, applied mathematics and statistics. We have decided to focus our contribution on work in bioinformatics that involves either the design of a variant of an existing algorithm from the domain of computer science, or the design of a new algorithm.

An alternative term, more or less coinciding with bioinformatics is *computational biology*, used more in North America than in Europe. Waterman[107] considers that there are three interpretations, all of which are valid:

> One, that it is a subset of biology proper and any required mathematics and computer science can be made up on demand; two, that it is a subset of

the mathematical sciences and that biology remains a remote but motivating presence; three: that there are genuine interdisciplinary components, with the original motivation from biology suggesting mathematical problems, which suggest biological experiments.

A good overall introduction to Bioinformatics for computer scientists is [22]. Books that concentrate more on the required mathematical/algorithmic basis of bioinformatics are e.g. [107, 21, 59].

The amount and variety of biological data now available, together with techniques developed so far have enabled research in Bioinformatics to move beyond the study of individual biological components (genes, proteins etc) albeit in a genome-wide context to attempt to study how individual parts cooperate in their operation [60]. Bioinformatics as a scientific activity has now moved closer to the area of Systems Biology [65] which seeks to integrate biological data as an attempt to understand how biological systems function. By studying the relationships and interactions between various parts of a biological system it is hoped that an understandable model of the whole system can be developed. For example the determination that some interaction, and its strength, exists between two entities is a first step to determining network structure and is a crucial step in the modelling and analysis of networks such as gene regulation networks, metabolic pathways and signalling networks. The advent of the new high-throughput technologies (for example gene expression arrays, mass spectrometry) has meant more challenges for computer scientists in terms of the type and quantity of data available for analysis.

There are other fields which broadly apply principles from biology to derive novel approaches in computer science, for example biocomputing, neural computing, genetic algorithms, and evolutionary computing. These are not directly part of Bioinformatics, other than being some of the techniques from computer science which can be applied to biological data.

Since it is rare to find researchers who are both computer scientists and biologists, it is generally the case that effective research in bioinformatics requires the joint effort from scientists in both fields. An important corollary is that in order to achieve such cooperation all parties must use a common language and be prepared to learn about issues from the other side. In fact many researchers from the biological and physical sciences working in bioinformatics have acquired significant computing skills, and may have greater specialist knowledge in mathematics and statistics than do many computer scientists. An illustration of this is the heavy use of Hidden Markov Models in bioinformatics, a topic about which most computer scientists know very little. It is the computer scientist's task to apply the approach of problem abstraction together with efficient algorithm design to the problems from the biological domain.

A challenge for computer scientists who are involved in research in bioinformatics is to achieve results that make a contribution to computer science. Of course this is not the main motivation for biologists; moreover there are some exciting projects in bioinformatics which in the short to medium term are unlikely to contribute to computer science.

26.1 What Biologists Want from Bioinformatics

The great aim of research in bioinformatics is to understand the functioning of living organisms in order to "improve the quality of life". This improvement will be achieved by many means including drug design, identification of genetic risk factors, gene therapy, genetic modification of food crops and animals, etc. Some of these, especially the last, are proving to be controversial.

26.2   The Central Dogma

The study of proteins, how they interact with each other, and how genes are regulated is central to the understanding of the basic principles of the functioning of living organisms.

Proteins comprise approximately 60% of the dry mass of a living cell, and are linear heteropolymers that are constructed from a chain or sequence of monomers called amino acids, of which twenty different types are involved in the composition of proteins. It is widely accepted that the function of proteins (and RNA) is determined by their structure, and it is known that in the majority of cases structure is uniquely determined by the sequence of amino acids, or nucleotides in the case of RNA. The case of *prions* is one example of exception to the latter rule where misfolding causes prion disease [56]. More generally, protein folding can be assisted by molecular chaperones and folding catalysts . Folding catalysts accelerate specific steps in folding, whereas the main function of the molecular chaperones seems to be in preventing off-pathway reactions that lead to protein aggregation and possibly misfolding. [52]

The central dogma of information flow in biology essentially states that the sequence of amino acids making up a protein and hence its structure (folded state) and thus its function, is determined by a two-stage process. The first stage is *transcription* – the process of copying DNA to RNA by an enzyme called RNA polymerase, and the second is that of *translation* – where messenger RNA is decoded to produce polypeptide chains according to the rules specified by the genetic code. This code enables the 20 amino-acids which form proteins to be coded by triples (codons) of the 4 bases of RNA.

> The central dogma states that once 'information' has passed into a protein it cannot get out again. The transfer of information from nucleic acid to nucleic acid, or from nucleic acid to protein, may be possible, but transfer from protein to protein, or from protein to nucleic acid, is impossible. Information here means the precise determination of sequence, either of bases in the nucleic acid or of amino acid residues in the protein.
>
> Francis Crick [25]

Although some proteins, for example transposases, can modify genetic material by inserting DNA sequences, it is not the case that the amino-acid sequences of those proteins is reverse-coded to make sequences of nucleotides.

Thus bioinformatics is concerned in a major way with the elicitation of DNA sequences from genetic material, the annotation of delimited segments (e.g. with information about their function), the control of gene expression (i.e. under what circumstances proteins are transcribed from DNA), and the relationship between the amino acid sequence of proteins and their structure. At present, the only physical methods to determine protein structure are X-ray crystallography and NMR (nucleo-magnetic resonance), both of which are not only very time-consuming, but cannot be applied to all classes of proteins. One of the holy grails of bioinformatics is to develop computational methods to determine protein structure from amino-acid sequence.

26.3   A Classification of Problem Areas

The problem areas in Bioinformatics can be broadly divided into three classes:

Problems specifically related to the Central Dogma: This includes both those related to a specific level of information (i.e., sequence, structure or function), and those that encompass more than one level.

Problems related to data in general: With the exponential growth of knowledge in (molecular) biology, there are rapidly growing problems such as storage, retrieval, and analysis of the data. Hence there are issues of database design for biological resources, representation and visualization of biological knowledge, and the application of data analysis methods such as data mining. A key underlying technique is that of *abstraction* of the data; it is of course imperative that the operations over the abstract data preserve the biological meaning of the operations on the original form of the data.

Simulation of biological processes: This means the prediction of dynamic behavior of a biological system on the basis of its components. Examples include the simulation of protein folding (molecular dynamics) or of metabolic pathways.

In the following we concentrate on the first class of problems, i.e. sequence, structure and function, and select a subset of illustratory examples.

26.4   Sequence Related Problems

26.4.1   Physical Map

In this problem, one has a collection of short, known substrings of the DNA called *probes* with the property that they occur *exactly once* in the DNA, and a set of fragments of the DNA (called *clones*), which (ideally) cover a specific region of interest on the DNA. For both the clones and the probes, the exact location on the DNA and the ordering of the locations are unknown. The goal is to find the ordering of the probes and/or clones in the DNA.

The first step is to check for every probe P_i and every clone C_j, whether C_j contains the substring denoted by P_i. This is done by performing hybridization experiments. Hybridization is the process of forming a (possibly imperfect) double helix out of two DNA or RNA molecules. This can be used to determine which probes occurs in which clones. The result is a matrix $A = (a_{ij})$, where a_{ij} is 1 if probe P_i is hybridizes with clone C_j otherwise 0. Now if there were no errors in the hybridization experiments, then the ordering of the probes could be found be reordering the rows and columns of the matrix such that the resulting matrix has the *consecutive ones* property. But since the experiments are faulty, the problem of finding the ordering minimizing the errors is NP-complete (see e.g., [48, 20])

The ordering of the probes (denoted by a permutation π on the set of probe indices), usually together with a good bound on the distance between to successive probes, constitutes a physical map, which can be used for different purposes. One is to use this map when sequencing the genome. The reason is that sequencing is done by splitting DNA into fragments, which are sequenced in the sequel. The remaining problem is to generate the original DNA-sequence out of sequenced fragments. This is usually done by searching for overlapping fragments. The problem is that DNA contains so-called *repeats*. This are long fragments of DNA which are repeated several times on the DNA. Clearly, such repeats may not be used for the process of generating the original DNA sequence out of overlapping fragments. One way to check this is to use a physical map.

In practical applications, the major problem is the occurrence of errors in the hybridization experiments. *False positives* are entries $a_{ij} = 1$ although probe P_i is not contained in clone C_j. Vice versa, *false negatives* are entries $a_{ij} = 0$, where P_i is contained in clone C_j. In [20], Christof et al. considered a variant of the problem that uses additional information stemming from *end-probes*. These are probes where it is known that they are stemming from the end of the clones (but we do not know which is the left or right end). Let P_i and P_k be the end probes for C_r, and let P_j be another probe different from P_i and P_k that hybridizes with C_r (i.e., $a_{jr} = 1$). Then we know that in the correct ordering π, the value π_j must be between π_i and π_k (i.e., either $\pi_i < \pi_j < \pi_k$ is true, or $\pi_j < \pi_j < \pi_i$), which gives rise to additional *betweenness* constraints. They presented an integer linear programming approach for the above described problem, where a maximum likelihood model is used as an objective function to model the errors in the matrix A. The idea behind the maximum likelihood model is to search for the corrected matrix B that maximizes the likelihood $P[A|B]$, given probabilities for producing false positive and false negative entries in A.

26.4.2 Comparison and Alignment

Overview

The goal of this activity is to compare two sequences, and in addition to return an alignment, i.e. some information regarding those parts which are very similar. When comparing the sequences, additional information e.g. stemming from known structures may be used. In general, sequence alignment is fast, whereas alignment involving structure is slow due to its high complexity.

One of the first fields in bioinformatics was DNA sequence alignment. The reason for the interest in sequence alignment stems from the fact that there are many different proteins which have common ancestors, and that these *homologous* (i.e., related by evolution) proteins have a similar structure and function. In addition, homologous proteins often have similar sequences. Using a reverse reasoning, sequence similarity is used to detect the homology of protein structures.

Clearly, the quality of this approach depends on the similarity measure used, which is determined by a model of evolution. The usual approaches use a model with substitution, deletion or insertion of a single amino-acid (see e.g. [107] for an overview). In this case, sequence alignment can be performed in polynomial time using a dynamic programming approach. There are also new approaches which deal with more complex models of evolution such as [10], who considers in addition duplication of substrings (tandem repeats). A more complex problem is that of multiple sequence alignment [63], which is known to be NP-complete.

On the level of structure comparison, there are many different problems that have been considered. Protein threading extends sequence alignment by incorporating structural information. In this approach an alignment is made between two sequences, one with an unknown structure and the other with a known structure, taking into account the known structure [69]. Again, this problem has been shown to be NP-hard.

Another problem is to compare two different structures by superposing elements using translation and rotation to minimize the atomic coordinate Root Mean Square Deviation (RMSD) [34]. Structures can also be compared at a higher level of abstraction than atomic coordinates by using a topological approach based on secondary structure elements [47] (see Section 26.5.4; this can be performed over topology graphs by detecting maximal cliques [66] or by pattern discovery and structural alignment [44]).

Pairwise sequence alignment

Pairwise sequence alignment is the problem of determining the similarity of two sequences. An alignment of two sequences $a, b \in \Sigma^*$ consists of two sequences u, v of the same length that are generated from a, b via the insertion of gaps. Alignments are evaluated according to scoring functions, which evaluates the number of inserted gaps, and the similarity of different letters u_i and v_i at the same position in the alignment (called substitutions). Multiple sequence alignment is the generalization of the problem to several sequences.

There are different possibilities for constraint-based formalizations of sequence alignment. We will start with a formalization that is commonly used in standard approaches to sequence alignment. We will start with the formal definition of an alignment.

Definition 26.1 (Alignment and Alignment Distance). *Let Σ be an alphabet with $- \notin \Sigma$ For every $u \in (\Sigma \cup \{-\})^*$ we define $u|_\Sigma$ to be the restriction of u to Σ (by deleting all occurrences of $-$ in u). An* alignment *is a pair $(a^\diamond, b^\diamond)$ with $a^\diamond, b^\diamond \in (\Sigma \cup \{-\})^*$ such that $|a^\diamond| = |b^\diamond|$ and there is no position i such that $a_i^\diamond = - = b_i^\diamond$. An* alignment $(a^\diamond, b^\diamond)$ *is an* alignment of (a, b) with $a, b \in \Sigma^*$ if

1. $a^\diamond|_\Sigma = a$, and

2. $b^\diamond|_\Sigma = b$.

Given a cost function w, we define the cost of an alignment by

$$w(a^\diamond, b^\diamond) = \sum_{i=1}^{|a^\diamond|} w(a_i^\diamond, b_i^\diamond).$$

The alignment distance *of a, b is*

$$D(a, b) \;=\; \min\{w(a^\diamond, b^\diamond) \mid (a^\diamond, b^\diamond) \text{ alignment of } (a, b)\}.$$

The alignment $(a^\diamond, b^\diamond)$ is optimal if $D(a, b) = w(a^\diamond, b^\diamond)$.

Instead of using distance-based scoring function, one can also use a similarity measurement for evaluating alignments. Then, one searches for an alignment that maximizes the similarity between the two sequences. As [93] have shown, one can transform each distance-based (global) scoring scheme into a similarity-based, without changing the optimal alignment. Hence, we will consider only the distance-based scoring scheme in the following.

The standard approach to solve the pairwise sequence alignment problem for two sequences a, b is to use to define a dynamic programming matrix $(D_{i,j})$, which stores the cost of the best alignment between the prefixes $a_1 \ldots a_i$ and $b_1 \ldots b_j$. I.e., $D_{i,j} = D(a_1 \ldots a_i, b_1 \ldots b_j)$. This matrix can then be calculated using the following recursion equation:

$$D_{0,0} = 0,$$

$$D_{0,j} = \sum_{k=1}^{j} w(-, b_k),$$

$$D_{i,0} = \sum_{k=1}^{i} w(a_k, -),$$

$$\forall i, j > 0 : D_{i,j} = \min \left\{ \begin{array}{c} D_{i,j-1} + w(-, b_j), \\ D_{i-1,j-1} + w(a_i, b_j), \\ D_{i-1,j} + w(a_i, -) \end{array} \right\}. \tag{26.1}$$

Thus, the standard sequence alignment problem can be solved in quadratic time and space. This changes if one considers different extensions of the original problem. One extension is to consider *parametric sequence alignment*, where the cost parameter for deletion $\delta = w(\sigma, -)$ and substitution $\mu = w(\sigma, \sigma')$ are variable. The reason for considering this parametric version is that it is hard to determine these parameter (especially the cost for deletion). Hence, one is interested in checking whether a given alignment is the same for a complete range of parameters. Yap [110] considered a constraint-based approach for this problem, where he directly encodes the entries of the dynamic programming table $D_{i,j}$ as variables, and the recursion equations as constraints. He considered then different possibilities of pruning in the case that δ and μ are not known (i.e., are not ground).

Other variants extend sequence alignment by considering additional conditions that stem from information on the secondary or ternary structure of the associated molecule. By and large one can say that the difference to sequence alignment is that the scoring function evaluates not single positions in the alignment, but pairs of positions that are related (or close) in the structure. This is especially useful when comparing two RNA-sequences, where it is known that the structure is more conserved than the sequence. Both global [86, 23, 73, 57, 55] and local [5] versions of the RNA sequence/structure alignment have been considered. The multiple RNA sequence/structure alignment problem is even harder than the multiple sequence alignment problem, since successful heuristic approaches like progressive alignment can only be applied either in special cases (like the PMMulti system [55]), or via the combination of sequence/structure and sequence alignment (like the MARNA-system [92]).

There many are other problems that extend sequence alignment (or related problems) using additional information. Examples are the alignment methods used for the detection of alternative spliceforms of proteins [41, 49, 54, 39], or the design of similar protein sequence whose mRNA form a specific RNA-structure [8]. Currently, most of these problems are solved via special dynamic programming approaches. A first approach to apply a general technique for sequence alignment under additional constraints has been presented in [109], where cluster tree elimination was used to efficiently solve pairwise sequence alignment problems with additional constraints.

Multiple sequence alignment

The problem of multiple sequence alignment is to align not only two different sequences, but any number of sequence. This is required to detect biologically important motifs. Formally, a *multiple alignment* for n sequences $S_1, \ldots, S_n$ is given by a character matrix

$$A = (A_{ij})_{1 \leq i \leq n, 1 \leq j \leq K}$$

over the alphabet $\bar{\Sigma} = \Sigma \cup \{-\}$ with the property that S_i can be obtained from $A_{i1} \ldots A_{iK}$ by removing the gaps. In the general formalization, the jth column $A_{1j}, \ldots, A_{nj}$ of the alignment is evaluated using an n-ary function $w(A_{1j}, \ldots, A_{nj})$, and the distance $D(A$ of an alignment A is given by

$$D(A) = \sum_{1 \leq j \leq K} w(A_{1j}, \ldots, A_{nj}).$$

There is a special formalization of the scoring function that is used in most practical applications, namely the sum-of-pairs score. The basic idea of this score is to evaluate an alignment by the sum of all pairwise alignments, which was introduced by Carrillo and Lipman [17]. Here, the distance of an alignment $D(A)$ is given by given by

$$D(A) = \sum_{i < i'} \sum_{1 \leq j \leq K} w_p(A_{ij}, A_{i'j}),$$

where $w_p : \Sigma' \times \Sigma' \to \mathbb{R}$ is a usual pairwise cost function. Of course, this is equivalent to

$$D(A) = \sum_{1 \leq j \leq K} \sum_{i < i'} w_p(A_{ij}, A_{i'j}),$$

and is hence a special case of the general multiple sequence alignment problem, where the cost for a column is given by

$$w(a_1, \ldots, a_n) = \sum_{i < i'} w_p(A_{ij}, A_{i'j})$$

Kececioglu [64, 63] introduced a graph-based formalization of multiple sequence alignment with sum-of-pairs cost function, the *complete maximum-weight trace (CMWT)* formalization. An ILP (integer linear programming) solution for this problem was presented in [84, 62]. In CMWT, the letters of the strings $S_i = s_{i1} \ldots s_{in_i}$ are considered to be the set of vertices $V = V_1 \uplus \ldots \uplus V_n{}^1$ of a complete n-partite graph $G = (V, E)$ (i.e., G satisfies that for every $s_{ij} \in V_i$ and $s_{i'j'} \in V_{i'}$, we have $e = (s_{ij}, s_{i'j'}) \in E$ if and only if $i \neq i'$). G is called the *complete alignment graph* for the sequences $S_1, \ldots, S_n$. An *alignment graph* G' is a subgraph of the complete alignment graph. Alignment graphs can be used to restrict the search for a multiple sequence alignment to a subset of all possible alignments to reduce the search space. For example, let S_1 be AACG and S_2 be AGG. Then the complete alignment graph for AACG and AGG is the 2-partite graph

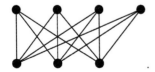

---

[1]Where $\uplus$ is the disjoint union, and V_i is $\{s_{i1}, \ldots, s_{in_i}\}$.

With every edge $e \in E$, there is a positive weight $w(e)$ associated. An alignment A for the sequences $S_1, \ldots, S_n$ *realizes* an edge $e = (s_{ij}, s_{i'j'}) \in E$ of an alignment graph $G = (V, E)$ for the sequences $S_1, \ldots, S_n$ if the jth character of S_i and the j'th character of $S_{i'}$ are aligned in A. For example, consider the alignment

```
A   A   C   G
A   -   G   G   .
```

Then this alignment realizes three edges, indicated by straight lines:

Given an alignment A, the set of all edges realized by A is called the *trace* of A. A set $T \subset E$ of edges is called a *trace* if it is the trace of some alignment A. Given the weight function w, the *weight* of a trace T is $\sum_{e \in T} w(e)$.

Definition 26.2 ((Complete) Maximum-Weight Trace). *Let $S_1, \ldots, S_n$ be sequences, let $G = (V, E)$ be the complete alignment graph for $S_1, \ldots, S_n$, and let w be a weight function. The* complete maximum-weight trace problem *is to find a trace $T \subset E$ that has maximal weight (under w). The* maximum-weight trace problem *is defined analogously for an alignment graph $G = (V, E)$ for $S_1, \ldots, S_n$.*

A remaining problem is that not any subset of edges is a trace (i.e., not every subset of E corresponds to a real alignment). Consider again the two sequences AACG and AGG, and consider the following subset of edges indicated by straight lines:

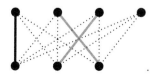

By the definition of a realized edge, this set of edges would correspond to the alignment

```
A   C   A   G
A   G   G   -   ,
```

which is an alignment for the sequences ACAG and AGG instead of AACG and AGG. Hence, this subset of edges is not a trace. The problem are the two crossing edges indicated in grey above.

An ILP-formalization for the pairwise alignment characterizing traces was given in [73][2], which is a follows. Let $G = (V, E)$ be an alignment graph, and let $e_1, \ldots, e_n$ be an enumeration of all alignment edges in E. We say that e_k is *in conflict with* e_l iff e_k and e_l are crossing edges, i.e., $e_k = (s_{1i}, s_{2j})$, $e_l = (s_{1i'}, s_{2j'})$ with neither $i < i' \wedge j < j'$ nor $i' < i \wedge j' < j$. Then one introduces for every edge e_i a boolean variable x_i, where $x_j = 1$

---

[2]In this work, structural condition where formulated in addition to the pure sequence alignment problem

implies that e_i is contained in the trace. Furthermore, let $w_i = w(e_i)$. Then the constraint problem is

$$\text{maximize} \quad \sum_{e_i \in E} w_i \cdot x_i$$

subject to the following constraints:

$$x_i \in \{0, 1\} \tag{26.2}$$

$$x_k + x_l \leq 1 \qquad \forall e_k, e_l \in E \text{ s.t. } e_k \text{ is in conflict with } e_l \tag{26.3}$$

For the multiple sequence alignment step, the condition of non-crossing edges is not so simple. Whether a pair of edges is conflicting might depend on other edges contained in the trace. Consider the following two set of edges for three sequences ABC, ABD and $ABCD$:

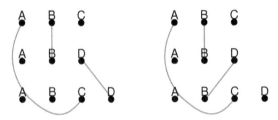

The the first represents for example the following valid alignment:

```
 -   -   A   -   B   C   -
 -   -   -   A   B   -   D   .
 A   B   C   -   -   -   D
```

The second one does not represent a valid alignment, but we cannot identify pairs of conflicting edges.

Hence, we have to extend the definition for the multiple case. For the pairwise case, a trace is nothing else than a set of edges which are strictly ordered *in both components* I.e., a trace is an ordered set of edges $e_1 = (s_{1i_1}, s_{2j_1}), \ldots, e_m = (s_{1i_m}, s_{2j_m})$ with the property that $\forall 1 \leq k < m : i_k < i_{k+1} \wedge j_k < j_{k+1}$. The corresponding definition for the multiple alignment case is as follows.

Given sequences $S_1, \ldots, S_n$ with $S_i = s_{i1} \ldots s_{in_i}$, one defines the *extended alignment graph* $G = (V, E, \prec)$ for $S_1, \ldots, S_n$ to be a triple such that (V, E) is an alignment graph for $S_1, \ldots, S_n$, and $\prec$ is defined by

$$\prec = \{(s_{ij}, s_{ij+1}) \mid 1 \leq i \leq n \wedge 1 \leq j < n_i\}.$$

With $\prec^*$, we denote the transitive closure of $\prec$. Note that $\prec^*$ is a strict partial order of V

Using the extended alignment graph, one can characterize traces. A *connected component* of a graph $G = (V, E)$ is a $\subseteq$-maximal set $V' \subseteq V$ such that for all vertices $v, v' \in V$ there is a path of edges in E connecting v and v'. For any two subsets $X, Y \subseteq V$, we define

$$X \triangleleft Y \text{ if and only if} \quad \exists v \in X \,\exists v' \in Y : v \prec v'.$$

We define $\lhd^*$ to be the transitive closure of $\lhd$. For the sequences AACG and AGG the extended complete alignment graph is

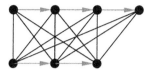

where we have indicated the edges for $\prec$ by arrows.

Theorem 26.3. *Let $S_1, \ldots, S_n$ be sequences, and let $G = (V, E, \prec)$ be the extended alignment graph for $S_1, \ldots, S_n$. Then a subset $T \subseteq E$ is a trace if and only if it does not contain two edges sharing the same node, and $\lhd^*$ is a strict partial order on the connected components of $G' = (V, T)$.*

The question is of course how to enforce the above stated condition in a constraint-based or ILP formalization. For the pairwise case, this is achieved by excluding all conflicting edges with the constraint given in (26.3), thus forcing a strict partial order on the edges. Following [62], then every pair of conflicting edges for the pairwise case corresponds in the extended alignment graph to a *mixed cycle*. This is a cycle in the extended alignment graph that uses at least one alignment edge and at least one edge from the $\prec$-order. Such a mixed cycle is called *critical* if in every sequence, all the nodes used by the cycle occur consecutively in the sequence. Then condition (26.3) is replaced in [62] by excluding all critical mixed cycles, which then gives an ILP-formalization for multiple alignment.

The main problem with the above formulation is that in general, one has to add exponentially many cycle constraints. For this reason, Prestwich et al. proposed in [83] an alternative ILP model, which is transformed to linear pseudo-Boolean (PB, a generalization of SAT which significantly improves expressiveness) form. The model is of polynomial size, and therefore better suited to a generic SAT solver.

Pairwise alignment with conditions: example protein threading

The previous formalization is based on a graph based model of sequence alignment, where one has Boolean variables for every possible alignment edge. The major drawback of this approach is that it uses a huge number of variables. E.g., for pairwise sequence alignment, this model requires quadratically many variables.

Another possible formalization for pairwise sequence alignment that requires less variables has one variable X_i for each position $1 \leq i \leq |S_1|$ of the first sequence S_1. The domain of each variable is the set $\{1, \ldots, |S_2|\}$ of positions in the second sequence. In principle, $X_i = j$ is interpreted as "*position i of the first sequence is aligned with position j of the second one*".

The next step is to encode gaps. An unaligned position j in the second sequence, which correspond to a gap in the first one, are already encoded by the fact that there is no i with $X_i = j$. In addition, one has to encode that a position i in the first sequence is aligned with a gap in the second sequence. One possible way to encode this is by allowing $X_{i-1} = X_i$, which is then interpreted as position i is aligned with a gap. On the other hand, position i is matched (i.e., aligned with some position j in the second sequence) if and only if $X_i =$ and $X_i > X_{i-1}$. Note that this kind of encoding was considered in [109].

In the following, we will consider a special instance of pairwise sequence alignment with additional conditions using a formalization similar to the one described above, namely protein threading. The additional conditions stem from information about the structure of one sequence. For protein threading, we have a sequence s with known structure, and we want to determine the structure of a sequence s' that is homologous (i.e. related via evolution) to s via an appropriate pairwise alignment. The idea is to use the known structure of s to guide structure prediction for s' by simultaneously aligning s' with s and with the known structure of s.

The basic approach for protein threading is to identify first parts of the structure of s that are more likely to be conserved. This is called a *core model for s*, and consists usually of secondary structure elements. The *secondary structure* of a sequence consist of structural elements of high local order. There are two main elements considered for protein threading, namely α-helices (a helical structure) and β-sheets (two or more strands of the protein sequence that are regularly connected). It is assumed that the core models are highly conserved in their length as well as in their interactions. The stretches between two core elements are called *loops*, and the lengths of these loops can vary in the homologous sequence s'. This is captured by the definition of a core model.

Definition 26.4 (Core Model). *Let s be a sequence. A core model for s is a tuple $(m, \vec{c}$ $\vec{\lambda}, \vec{l}_{\min})$, where $\vec{c} = (c_1, \ldots, c_m)$ is the sequence of lengths for the core elements in s, and $\vec{\lambda} = (\lambda_0, \ldots, \lambda_m)$ is the sequence of lengths for the loops between the core elements such that*

$$|s| = \lambda_0 + \sum_{1 \leq i \leq m} (c_i + \lambda_i).$$

The sequence $\vec{l}_{\min} = (l_0^{\min}, \ldots, l_m^{\min})$, consists of the minimal length required to connect the corresponding ends of the core elements (i.e., the minimal length of the loop regions) with $\forall 1 \leq i \leq m : l_i^{\min} \leq \lambda_i$.

Note that the value λ_0 is the length of the initial loop (i.e., the N-terminal loop), while λ_m is the length of the final loop (i.e., the C-terminal loop).

Given a core model $(m, \vec{c}, \vec{\lambda}, \vec{l}_{\min})$ for s, we define the ith *core region* of s to be the set of positions

$$C_i = \left\{ \lambda_0 + \sum_{1 \leq j < i} (c_j + \lambda_j) + k \,\middle|\, 1 \leq k \leq c_i \right\}.$$

The jth position of the ith core is denoted by $C_{i,j}$. Figure 26.1 illustrates a core model with 4 core regions, where the lengths of the core regions is given by the vector $(4, 3, 4, 3)$

In the following, we will define a threading of sequence s' through the core model for s to be a mapping of the core positions to consecutive positions of s'. Since we are using consecutive regions, a threading is uniquely determined by the mapping of the first position of every core region. Furthermore, this implies that there are no gaps allowed in core regions. All gaps in the alignment must occur in the loop regions. In inserting and deleting positions in the loop regions, one must obey the length restrictions imposed by

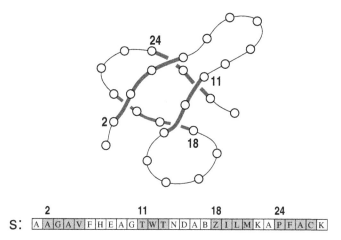

Figure 26.1: Core model. It is supposed that the grey parts of the given structure are the conserved regions. The define the core of the structure. This leads to the definition of 4 core elements.

the core model. Recall here that $l_i^{\min}$ is the minimal length needed to connect C_i and C_{i+1} according to stereochemical restrictions (depending, e.g., on the distance between the last position in C_i and the first position of C_{i+1} in the structural model of s).

Definition 26.5 (Threading). *Let* $\mathbb{M}_C = (m, \vec{c}, \vec{\lambda}, \vec{l}_{\min})$ *be a core model for a sequence* s. *Let* s' *be a sequence. A threading of* s' *through the core model* $\mathbb{M}_C$ *for* s *is a vector*

$$\vec{t} = (t_1, \ldots, t_m) \in \mathbb{N}^m$$

such that

$$1 + l_0^{\min} \leq t_1 \tag{26.4}$$

$$\forall 1 \leq i < m : (t_i + c_i + l_i^{\min}) \leq t_{i+1} \tag{26.5}$$

and

$$t_m + c_m + l_m^{\min} \leq |s'| + 1 \tag{26.6}$$

In the following, we set $c_0 = 0$ for convenience. The conditions (26.4)–(26.6) are called *ordering constraints.* These constraints imply so-called *spacing constraints*, which constitute a domain for the ith value of an arbitrary threading

$$\forall 1 \leq i \leq m : \left[1 + \sum_{j<i} (c_j + l_j^{\min}) \leq t_i \leq |s'| + 1 - \sum_{j \geq i} (c_j + l_j^{\min}) \right] \tag{26.7}$$

The next part is to score the threading. The first step is to define the interactions that are determined by the given structure. Thus, the *interaction graph* describes which core regions contain core positions that are 'neighbors' in some biochemical sense, i.e. that are core positions that interact in the folded structure. Albeit the interactions have to be defined on the level of amino acids, one usually combines all interactions between two core regions into one single interaction. How this complex interaction is evaluated is then hidden in the scoring function.

Definition 26.6 (Interaction Graph). *Let s be a sequence with a core model $\mathbb{M}_C = (m, \vec{c}, \vec{\lambda}, \vec{l}_{\min})$. An interaction graph $\mathbb{I}$ for $\mathbb{M}_C$ is a graph (V, E), where $E \subseteq V^2$ and V is the set of all core regions, i.e.*

$$V = \{C_i \mid 1 \le i \le m\}.$$

Definition 26.7 (Scoring Function). *Let s be a sequence with core model $\mathbb{M}_C = (m, \vec{c}, \vec{\lambda}, \vec{l}_{\min})$ and interaction graph $\mathbb{I}$. A scoring function g for s, $\mathbb{M}_C$, and $\mathbb{I}$ consists of two functions $g_1 \in \mathbb{N}^2$ and $g_2 \in \mathbb{N}^4$ with the property that*

$$g_2(i, j, k, l) \neq 0 \Leftrightarrow (C_i, C_j) \in \mathbb{I}. \tag{26.8}$$

Given a threading $\vec{t}$ of s' to s under the core model $\mathbb{M}_C$, the score of $f(\vec{t})$ of $\vec{t}$ is defined by

$$f(\vec{t}) = \sum_{i=1}^{m} g_1(i, t_i) + \sum_{i=1}^{m} \sum_{j>i}^{m} g_2(i, j, t_i, t_j).$$

This is the form of scoring function that is most often used in protein threading, where only pairwise interactions are considered. But in general, higher-order interactions could be admitted. To include these, one must extend the definition of interaction graph to that of an interaction hypergraph. Furthermore, one must introduce $2n$-ary functions g_n in order to implement n-ary interactions. If the core model has m regions, then $n \le m$. Hence, the fully general form of scoring function is

$$\begin{aligned} f(\vec{t}) &= \sum_{i_1} g_1(i_1, t_{i_1}) + \sum_{i_1} \sum_{i_2 > i_1} g_2(i_1, i_2, t_{i_1}, t_{i_2}) + \dots \\ &+ \sum_{i_1} \sum_{i_2 > i_1} \dots \sum_{i_{m-1} > i_m} g_m(i_1, i_2, \dots, i_m, t_{i_1}, t_{i_2}, \dots, t_{i_m}). \end{aligned}$$

Lathrop and Smith [69] solved the threading problem using a branch-and-bound approach, working on sets of possible threadings $\mathbb{T}$, which are described by finite domains for the t_i's. Reformulating the scoring function slightly, we get the following tight bound using the scoring function itself:

$$\mathrm{lb}(\mathbb{T}) = \min_{\vec{t} \in \mathbb{T}} \sum_{i=1}^{m} \left[g_1(i, t_i) + g_2(i - 1, i, t_{i-1}, t_i) + \sum_{|i-j|>1}^{m} \frac{1}{2} g_2(i, j, t_i, t_j) \right].$$

Of course, it is NP-hard to calculate $\mathrm{lb}(\mathbb{T})$. For that reason, they introduced the following following relaxed scoring function for a set of threadings $\mathbb{T}$:

$$\mathrm{lb}_{\mathrm{poly}}(\mathbb{T}) = \min_{\vec{t} \in \mathbb{T}} \sum_{i=1}^{m} \left[\begin{array}{l} g_1(i, t_i) \\ + \ g_2(i-1, i, t_{i-1}, t_i) \\ + \ \min_{\substack{\vec{u} \in \mathbb{T} \\ u_i = t_i}} \sum_{|i-j|>1} \frac{1}{2} g_2(i, j, t_i, u_j) \end{array} \right],$$

The relaxation is given by the fact that for the calculation of g_2, for every i a different threading $\bar{u}$ can be used. Thus, there is no dependencies anymore for the calculation of the g_2 terms (with the exceptions of the terms $g_2(i-1, i, t_{i-1}, t_i)$), which implies that the bound can be calculated in polynomial time using dynamic programming.

26.4.3 Search and Pattern Discovery

In both sequences (DNA and RNA) and structure (RNA and protein), there are functionally significant regions that are repeated in different entities; these regions can be often described by patterns. A need has arisen to be able to search through genome or protein databases (which may be very large), and identify entries which match the pattern. Obviously, this has a parallel in formal language theory, see for example Searls' excellent discussion in [87]. In reality, biological data is noisy, and in the case of string languages, stochastic approaches have been developed using for example Hidden Markov Models [33] and stochastic context-free grammars [71]. It is of interest to note here that although Dynamic Bayesian Networks [43] can represent Hidden Markov Models, the use of DBNs in bioinformatics for sequence analysis remains an under-exploited area.

Although patterns can be constructed by hand, its preferable to use a mechanized (machine learning) approach, i.e., *pattern discovery* [15, 85]. Finding gene expression sites in DNA may require context sensitive patterns.

One active research field is to design appropriate pattern languages and associated discovery mechanisms which are able to express significant properties of structures as opposed to strings [47, 58].

Pattern discovery can also be performed over protein structures [45] and metabolic pathways.

Sequence pattern matching

The basic biochemical properties of DNA and RNA permit some constraints to be exploited in pattern matching over nucleotide sequences:

- The first property is that of the total ordering of the nucleotides in a sequence, by convention from the $5'$ to the $3'$ end, which can be exploited in pattern matching algorithms.

- The second property is the name associated with a nucleotide. A DNA nucleotide consists of a base – adenine, cytosine guanine, or thymine — plus a molecule of sugar and one of phosphoric acid; such nucleotides are often known by the initial letter of the base that they contain, a, c, g or t. In the case of RNA, thymine is replaced with uracil (u). Thus the names of nucleotides are drawn from a restricted alphabet of size 4: a, c, g, t in the case of DNA, and a, c, g, u in the case of RNA, and patterns can be defined with characters drawn from (a subset of) the alphabet.

- Thirdly, two nucleotides can interact due to the Watson-Crick base pairs: in the case of DNA, a-t and c-g, with both pairs being of roughly equal strength. RNA pairs are a-u, c-g, as well as the weaker g-u, and some other even weaker pairs. This base paring can cause nucleotide sequences to adopt particular conformations due to long-range interactions. This pairing can be exploited both in formal models of the conformations, and also associated techniques to compute over these models.

Sequential Patterns

Tandem repeat	$\alpha\alpha$	<u>acg</u> <u>acg</u>
Simple repeat	$\alpha\beta\alpha$	<u>acg</u> <u>aaa</u> <u>acg</u>
Multiple repeat	$\alpha\beta\alpha\beta_1\alpha$	<u>acg</u> <u>aa</u> <u>acg</u> <u>uu</u> <u>acg</u>

Structural Patterns

Stem loop	$\alpha\beta\alpha^{rc}$	<u>acg</u> <u>aa</u> <u>cgu</u>
Attenuator	$\alpha\beta\alpha^{rc}\beta_1\alpha$	<u>acg</u> <u>aa</u> <u>cgu</u> <u>au</u> <u>acg</u>
Palindrome, even	$\alpha\alpha^r$	<u>acg</u> <u>gca</u>
Palindrome, odd	$\alpha x\alpha^r$	<u>acgagca</u>
Pseudoknot	$\alpha_1\beta\alpha_2\beta_1\ \alpha_1^{rc}\beta_2\alpha_2^{rc}$	<u>acg</u> <u>aa</u> <u>ucu</u> <u>gc</u> <u>cgu</u> <u>aua</u> <u>aga</u>

Table 26.1: Patterns in nucleotide sequences, from [35]

Protein sequences comprise amino-acids which have properties corresponding to the first two above: firstly that they are totally ordered (in this case from the N terminus to the C terminus), and secondly that there are 20 amino acids, i.e. the names are drawn from an alphabet of 20 names (or corresponding letters).

Eidhammer et al. [35] have defined patterns in sequences as consisting of a logical expression on components, where a component is a description of a string of symbols, and a set of constraints. An input string S matches a pattern P if every component in P is matched by some substring of S, such that all the constraints are satisfied and the logical expression evaluates to *True*.

Sequential patterns can be defined using the following constraints:

(1) *length* of a substring to match a specific component;

(2) *distance* in the input string between substrings to match the different components of a pattern;

(3) *contents* of a substring to match a component;

(4) *positions* on the input string where a particular component can match;

The patterns in the PROSITE data base [9] are examples of the sequential class; thus *[AC]-x(2,3)-D* describes a pattern comprising three components, the first being an *A* or a *C*, the second of length 2 or 3 and the last being a *D*.

Structural patterns have in addition at least one *correlation constraint*, between two substrings matching different components, e.g. the substrings should be identical, or the reverse of each other. Examples are repetitions or palindromes, and can correspond to conformations that the sequence can adopt.

Example patterns in nucleotide sequences identified from the literature by Eidhammer et al [35] are given in Table 26.1 below. Pattern components (strings) are indicated by letters from the Greek alphabet: $\alpha, \beta, \ldots$ (with or without indices) and x is a wildcard. The reverse of a component α is indicated by α^r, and α^c is the complement of α. These annotations can be combined: α^{rc} is the reverse complement of α. Strings corresponding to pattern components are underlined.

The CLP version of the Eidhammer et al. system is now no longer available for general use. from the paper describing it. A related but more sophisticated, and faster approach by Thebault e al. is described in [100]. They use a CSP approach, representing structured RNA motifs which interact with other molecules. These motifs occur on more than one sequence and which are related together by possible hybridization. Together with pattern matching algorithms, constraint satisfaction techniques have been implemented in a prototype software system called "MilPat" (http://carlit.toulouse.inra.fr/MilPaT/MilPat.pl) and can be applied to search for tRNA and snoRNA genes on genomic sequences.

Another related approach using CSP is by Morgante et al [82]; the software system SMaRTFinder can be downloaded from http://bioinf.dimi.uniud.it/software/smartfinder. The algorithm locates structured models which are sequences of simple motifs and distance constraints. It combines standard pattern matching procedures with a constraint satisfaction solver, and can search for partial matches. A significant feature of their approach is that the (potentially) exponentially many solutions are represented in compact form as a graph. The time and space necessary to build the graph are linear in the number of occurrences of the component patterns.

Staden's program [97] is an early system which permits search for structural patterns in sequences. A pattern comprises elements, called motifs. There are nine classes of motifs, the simplest of which is just a string of characters. Two other classes include structures: inverted repeat or stem-loop and (direct) repeat. Logical operators AND, OR and NOT can be used to specify whether each motif must be present, is an alternative to another, or must be absent. Constraints can be specified on the length of a motif, the distance between two motifs and the contents of a motif; for the structure classes, constraints can be given on an individual part of the structure, e.g. on the loop of a stem-loop. Percentage match and scoring matrices can be used in searching. In Staden's system there is no possibility to define *general* correlations or relations between parts.

An example of a pattern which can be decribed in Staden's language is

$$tata(\langle(at \text{ OR } cg), -5, -2\rangle \text{ AND } \langle tt(\langle\neg ga, -3, 3\rangle), 2, 6\rangle)$$

which describes a pattern whose 'root' motif is the string $tata$, with two further required motifs. The first of these is between 5 and 2 bases upstream of the $tata$ motif, and can be either at or cg. The second is a tt motif located between 2 and 6 bases downstream of the $tata$ motif, and there must not be a ga motif within 3 bases upstream or downstream of the tt.

As can be seen, the language permits motifs to be overlaid on each other. Although this may seem counter-intuitive when describing biochemical sequences, there are situations when such overlays occur during processing of nucleotides, for example 'cassette genes' [50].

Other languages and associated systems are: *SCRUTINEER* [90], *RNAmot* [40], *RNAMotif* [75] (http://www.scripps.edu/mb/case/casegr-sh-3.5.html), *OVERSEER* [91], *Palingol* [12], *PatScan* [32] (http://www-unix.mcs.anl.gov/compbio/PatScan/HTML/patscan.html), and *PALM* [53]. However *GENLANG* (Searls [89, 88]) is the most general system which has been implemented for searching for structural patterns in nucleotide sequences. It uses an indexed language which has an expressive power between context-free and context-sensitive languages. *String variables* are used to define structures and constraints on the length and contents of the string variables can be specified.

Eidhammer et al. [35] have defined a constraint-based structure description language for biosequences, and give an algorithm plus associated program to solve the structure searching problem as a CSP as well as an implementation in the constraint logic programming language clp(FD) [27]. The language is able to describe two-dimensional structure of biosequences, such as tandem repeats, stem loops, palindromes and pseudo-knots.

26.4.4   Phylogenetic Trees

If we have any set of species that are related, then the relationship between these species (resp. entities) is called a *phylogeny*. When constructing a phylogenetic tree, the task is to set up a tree to show how the different species have evolved from a common ancestor. In addition, the trees generated are often labelled. The labels indicate the time when the species evolved from a common ancestor, or any other measure of the distance between the different species. Note that the construction phylogenetic trees is not necessarily applied to species, but to any kind of entities where we can set up some sort of distance information (e.g., phylogenetic trees can be constructed for languages). In this case the tree constructed may not be rooted.

The problem of constructing phylogenetic trees can be formulated in different ways. The first one is to have a finite set of species or entities $S = \{e_1, \ldots, e_n\}$, and a distance matrix $(d_{ij})_{i,j \in [1..n]}$ containing the pairwise distances between the entities. The problem is to construct a tree, where the edge are labelled by distances and the nodes are labelled entities (using new entities for the inner nodes). The tree is correct if for each two entities e_j, e_k from S, the distance in the tree (by summing up the edges distances along the path connecting them) out of the ordinal set in the tree is $d_j k$. Trees can be constructed from pairwise distances by variety of methods, including UPGMA (unweighted pair group method using arithmetic averages) [96].

Another formulation of the phylogenetic tree construction problem is *parsimony* [38]. Here, one has a set S of sequences (DNA or protein), and a method for calculating costs for relating any two sequences (not restricted to S). The task is then to find a tree, where the leafs are labelled by elements of S and the inner nodes are labelled by other sequences. Furthermore, the tree should have minimal costs according to the given method (i.e., the sum of distances between any two sequences that are directly connected in the tree should be minimal).

Since one, or in the case of parsimony several, optimal trees can be generated by tree building algorithms, an approach such as the bootstrap method [37] is commonly used to assess the significance of some phylogenetic feature and thus give some measure of confidence for the tree.

Although the concept of 'constraints' is widely used in the phylogentic literature, for example in the application to parsimony and maximum likelihood in terms of constraints over edge parameters between substitution sites, [98], almost no work has been done by the computational constraint community. However, related work certainly exists, for example the work by Gent et al [42] on the application of constraint programming to supertrees.

26.5   Structure Related Problems

26.5.1   Structure Prediction

Here one is concerned about the relation between sequence and structure. The sequence can either be from a protein, in which case the problem is sometimes referred as the *protein folding problem*; a more simple variant is that of RNA folding.

Now for natural protein sequences, the protein folds into one stable structure (which is believed to be a structure where the free energy has a global minima), which is completely determined by its amino acids sequence. This native structure determines the function of a protein. Since it is very easy to determine the sequence of a protein, the structure prediction problem consists of determining the structure from a given sequence. This is one of the holy grail of bioinformatics, since protein structure prediction is a very important but notoriously hard problem. It is subject of many ongoing attempts to solved this problem by a variety of methods (see for example the CASP competitions [18] [99]) Note that for artificial sequences, the sequence usually does not determine the structure (i.e., the artificially designed protein will not fold to a stable structure in general).

Proteins have a high level of local organisation (called secondary structure), which consist of α-helices, β-strands and turns). For that reason, there are approaches for predicting secondary structure first, before the overall tertiary structure is determined, as well as approaches with try to predict tertiary structure directly. It is presently believed that protein structure prediction cannot be done purely on the level of secondary structure alone.

A problem related to the protein folding problem is the *inverse protein folding*, which consists of the following. Given a three-dimensional structure, generate a sequence that will fold uniquely into the given structure. Naively, this can be solved using structure prediction (generate a sequence, then predict the structure, and compare the result with the given structure). Clearly, this problem is of interest for drug design, although inverse protein folding is not used in drug design yet. The reason simply that the problem is unsolved (see e.g. [51], where this problem is treatment for lattice proteins).

For RNA, secondary structure is usually related to base pair bonding, and structure prediction is possible on this level (under some restrictions) taken into account thermodynamical energies [113].

26.5.2 Structure-Prediction for Lattice Models of Proteins

Introduction

To tackle protein structure prediction and related problems simplified protein models have been introduced. These simplified models have been successfully used by several groups in the international contest on automated structure prediction. The most important class of simplified models are the so-called lattice models. The simplifications commonly used in this class of models are: 1.) monomers (or residues) are represented using a unified size 2.) bond length is unified 3.) the positions of the monomers are restricted to lattice positions, and 4.) a simplified energy function.

Apart from their use in structure prediction, they have became a major tool for investigating general properties of protein folding. They constitute a genotype (protein sequence) versus phenotype (protein conformation) mapping that can be dealt with using computational methods. Thus, they can be used to investigate evolutionary processes. An example is [14], where so-called neutral networks have been investigated. The edges of the network are pairs of sequences which differ only in one sequence positions, but have the same minimal energy conformation. Thus, a neutral network represents all protein sequences encoding the same protein conformation. The question is whether one can switch between two different neutral networks using only a small number of amino-acid substitutions. If this is the case, then this suggest a way evolution could have produced the diversity of protein conformations found in nature.

The simplest model is the HP-model, which is an important representative of lattice models. It has been introduced by Lau and Dill in [70]. In this model, the 20 letter al-

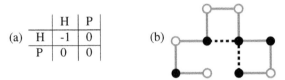

Figure 26.2: Energy matrix and sample conformation for the HP-model

phabet of amino acids is reduced to a two letter alphabet, namely H and P. H represents *hydrophobic* amino acids, whereas P represent *polar* or hydrophilic amino acids. In natural proteins, the hydrophobic amino-acids tend to be in the middle of the protein (forming a compact hydrophobic core), whereas the hydrophilic ones tend to be on the surface of the protein, thus interacting with the surrounding water. This is modeled in the energy function for the HP-model, which is given by the matrix as shown in Figure 26.2(a). It simply states that the energy contribution of a contact between two monomers is -1 if both are H-monomers, and 0 otherwise. Two monomers form a *contact* in some specific conformation if they are not connected via a bond, and the euclidian distance of the positions is 1. A conformation with *minimal energy* (also called *optimal conformation*) is just a conformation with the maximal number of contacts between H-monomers. Just recently, the structure prediction problem has been shown to be NP-complete even for the HP-model [11, 24].

A sample conformation for the sequence PHPHPPHHPH in the two-dimensional lattice with energy -2 is shown in Figure 26.2(b). The white beads represent P, the black ones H monomers. The two contacts are indicated via dashed lines.

So far, most of the existing approaches are heuristic methods like the hydrophobic zipper [28], the genetic algorithm by Unger and Moult [103], the chain growth algorithm by Bornberg-Bauer [13], or monte-carlo approaches with simulating annealing like [7], which is a monte-carlo method applicable for any regular lattice. There are only two approaches available that are able to prove optimality of the found conformations, namely the constraint-hydrophobic core construction (CHCC) [112], and the constraint-based protein folding method [4], which we will describe here in more detail. It is the first methods that is applicable to two different lattices (the cubic lattice, and the face-centered-cubic lattice), and to different energy functions (namely the HP-model and its extension HPNX, which also encodes charged amino acids). Using this constraint-based approach, we were able to find minimal energy conformations (and prove their optimality) for sequences up to length 300. In contrast, the CHCC method, which is not based on constraint programming, was only applied to sequences up to length 86. In the following, we will handle only the cubic lattice, albeit the face-centered-cubic lattice (FCC) is more suited for modeling protein conformations, but is also more complex.

A simple constraint-based formalization

A sequence is an element in $\{H, P\}^*$. With s_i we denote the ith element of a sequence s We say that a monomer with number i in s is even (resp. odd) if i is even (resp. odd). A conformation c of a sequence s is a function

$$c : [1..|s|] \rightarrow \mathbb{Z}^d$$

(where $d = 2$ or $d = 3$ depending on whether we consider a 2-dimensional or a 3-dimensional lattice) such that

1. $\forall 1 \leq i < |s| : ||c(i) - c(i+1)|| = 1$ (where $|| \cdot ||$ is the euclidian norm on $\mathbb{Z}^d$)

2. and $\forall i \neq j : c(i) \neq c(j)$.

The first condition is imposed by the lattice constraint and implies that the distance vector between two successive elements must be a unit-vector (or a negative unit-vector) in every admissible conformation. The second condition is the constraint that the conformation must be self-avoiding.

Given a conformation c of a sequence s, the number of contacts $Contact_s(c)$ in c is defined as the number of pairs (i, j) with $i + 1 < j$ such that

$$s_i = H \wedge s_j = H \wedge ||c(i) - c(j)|| = 1$$

(in other words, the number of pairs of H-monomers that have distance 1 in the conformation c, but are not successive in the sequence s). The energy of c is just $-Contact_s(c)$. With $\vec{e}_x, \vec{e}_y$ and $\vec{e}_z$ we denote the unit vectors $(1, 0, 0)$, $(0, 1, 0)$ or $(0, 0, 1)$, respectively. We say that two points $\vec{p}, \vec{p'} \in \mathbb{Z}^3$ are *neighbors* if $||\vec{p} - \vec{p'}|| = 1$. This is equivalent to the proposition that $\vec{p} = \vec{p'} \pm \vec{e}$ with $\vec{e} \in \{\vec{e}_x, \vec{e}_y, \vec{e}_z\}$.

This can now be directly encoded as a constraint problem. Our constraint problem consists of finite domain variables. We use also Boolean constraint and reified constraints. With *reified constraints* we mean a constraint $x =: (\phi)$, where ϕ is a finite domain constraint. x is a Boolean variable which is 1 if and only if ϕ holds. Technically, this can be achieved via setting x to 1 if the constraint store entails ϕ, and to 0 if the constraint store disentails ϕ. A constraint store *entails* a constraint ϕ if every valuation that makes the constraint store valid also makes ϕ valid. We use also entailment constraints of the form $\phi \rightarrow \psi$, which are interpreted as follows. If a constraint store entails ϕ, then ψ is added to the constraint store. We have implemented the problem using the language Oz [94], which supports finite domain variables, Boolean constraints, reified constraints, entailment constraints and a programmable search module.

Now we can encode the space of all possible conformations for a given sequence as a constraint problem as follows. We introduce for every monomer i new variables X_i, Y_i and Z_i, which denote the x-, y-, and z-coordinate of $c(i)$. Since we are using a cubic lattice, we know that these coordinates are all integers. But we can even restrict the possible values of these variables to the finite domain $[1..2n]$.[3] This is expressed by introducing the constraints

$$X_i \in [1..(2 \cdot length(s)] \wedge Y_i \in [1..(2 \cdot length(s)] \wedge Z_i \in [1..(2 \cdot length(s)]$$

for every $1 \leq i \leq n$. The self-avoidingness is just $(X_i, Y_i, Z_i) \neq (X_j, Y_j, Z_j)$ for $i \neq j$.[4]

For expressing that the distance between two successive monomers is 1, we introduce for every monomer i with $1 \leq i < length(s)$ three variables $Xdiff_i$, $Ydiff_i$ and $Zdiff_i$.

---

[3]We even could have used $[1..n]$. But the domain $[1..2n]$ is more flexible since we can assign an arbitrary monomer the vector (n, n, n), and still have the possibility to represent all possible conformations.

[4]This cannot be directly encoded in Oz [94], but we reduce these constraints to difference constraints on integers.

The value range of these variables is $[0..1]$. Then we can express the unit-vector distance constraint by

$$\text{Xdiff}_i \;=:\; |X_i - X_{i+1}| \qquad \text{Zdiff}_i \;=:\; |Z_i - Z_{i+1}|$$
$$\text{Ydiff}_i \;=:\; |Y_i - Y_{i+1}| \qquad 1 \;=:\; \text{Xdiff}_i + \text{Ydiff}_i + \text{Zdiff}_i.$$

The constraints described above span the space of all possible conformations. I.e., every valuation of X_i, Y_i, Z_i satisfying the constraints introduced above is an *admissible* conformation for the sequence s, i.e. a self-avoiding walk of s. Given partial information about X_i, Y_i, Z_i (expressed by additional constraints as introduced by the search algorithm), we call a conformation c *compatible* with these constraints on X_i, Y_i, Z_i if c is admissible and c satisfies the additional constraints.

The most simplest way to search for conformations with maximal number of contacts would be to add constraints for counting the number of contacts. Then one can directly enumerate the variables X_i, Y_i and Z_i. For HP-type models, we have to count contacts which are always generated between two neighboring H-monomers. For this purpose, one introduces a variable $Contact_{i,j}$ that is 1 if i and j have a contact in every conformation which is compatible with the valuations of X_i, Y_i, Z_i, and 0 otherwise. Then

$$\text{Xdiff}_{i,j} \;=\; |X_i - X_j| \qquad \text{Zdiff}_{i,j} \;=\; |Z_i - Z_j|$$
$$\text{Ydiff}_{i,j} \;=\; |Y_i - Y_j| \qquad Contact_{i,j} \;\in\; \{0,1\}$$
$$(Contact_{i,j} = 1) \;\leftrightarrow\; (\text{Xdiff}_i + \text{Ydiff}_i + \text{Zdiff}_i = 1) \tag{26.9}$$

where $\text{Xdiff}_{i,j}$, $\text{Xdiff}_{i,j}$ and $\text{Zdiff}_{i,j}$ are new variables. The variable $HHContacts$ counts the number of contacts between H-monomers, and is defined by

$$HHContacts = \sum_{\substack{i+1<j\,\wedge \\ s(i)=H\wedge s(j)=H}} Contact_{i,j}. \tag{26.10}$$

Now we could start to apply constraint-based enumeration on X_i, Y_i, Z_i searching for a conformation with maximal number of contacts.

The main problem using this approach alone is that it is very difficult to define good bounds and to find a search heuristic for enumerating low-energy conformation first. Nevertheless, this formulation is in part required for lattice models with an extended alphabet like the HPNX-model [6], which models also electrostatic contacts in addition to hydrophobicity.

Dal Palù et al. [80] considered an extension of the above problem for a much more sophisticated energy function. Since it is not possible to solve the problem optimally or near-optimally in the case of extended energy functions, they integrated additional biological knowledge to achieve good predictions. Starting from a formulation of the protein folding problem for the face-centered cubic lattice similar to the one described in Eq (26.9), they integrated secondary structure information in the prediction process. In a later work, Dal Palù et al. [79] extended the simple formulation Eq (26.9) by introducing variable that have three-dimensional domains (called *Box-domains*) associated, and described a constraint system and propagation techniques for this kind of variables. A similar approach of using variables with three-dimensional domains was successfully used in the PSICO-system [67] for the prediction of protein structure from Nucleic-Magnetic-Resonance (NMR) data. NMR is an experimental technique for determining protein structure. The result is a set of *distance constraint* that give an estimate of the pairwise distances between the atoms of the proteins. Here, the task is to find a structure minimizing an energy function that is compatible with the distance constraints (or to be more precise, that minimizes the violation of distance constraints).

A more sophisticated approach

To overcome the problem of finding good bounds and search heuristics, the set of all conformations was restricted in [4] to a subset of conformations that contains provably all minimal energy conformations. For this purpose, the hydrophobic core, which consists of the the positions occupied by H-monomers, is calculated first. Then, in a second step, a conformation of the HP-sequence is searched that has exactly the hydrophobic core calculated before. Since this problem is a strongly constrained, conformation can be found in relatively short time. Of course, all possible maximal compact hydrophobic cores have to be considered.[5] Formally, a *hydrophobic core* $\mathbb{C}$ is just a set of positions. The number of contacts in a hydrophobic core $\mathbb{C}$ is defined by

$$Contact(\mathbb{C}) = \frac{1}{2}|\{(\vec{p}, \vec{p'}) \mid \vec{p}, \vec{p'} \in \mathbb{C} \wedge \vec{p} \text{ and } \vec{p'} \text{ are neighbors}\}|$$

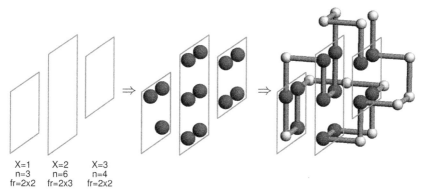

$$
\begin{array}{ccc}
X{=}1 & X{=}2 & X{=}3 \\
n{=}3 & n{=}6 & n{=}4 \\
fr{=}2x2 & fr{=}2x3 & fr{=}2x2
\end{array}
$$

Figure 26.3: The overall approach

Finding all maximally compact hydrophobic cores is an optimization problem itself, which was solved in [4] again in a two-level step. First, the distribution of H-monomers to layers of the form $X = i$ is calculated. Such a distribution is called a frame sequence, and consists of the number of H-monomer in each layer, as well as the minimal rectangle around these monomers. As we will see later, this information can be used to calculate an upper bound on the number of contacts for a specific frame sequence, which allows one to

---

[5]If there is no conformation found for the maximally compact core, then sub-optimal cores have to be considered as well, which is not very often the case.

discard many frame sequences. Then, for a given frame sequence, all possible maximally compact hydrophobic cores having the corresponding frame sequence are generated. Thus, we have the overall 3-level approach depicted in Figure 26.3.

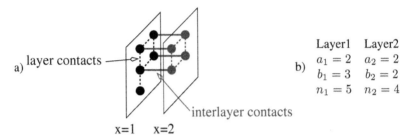

Figure 26.4: a) Layer and Interlayer Contacts   b) Corresponding Frame Sequence

Enumeration of frame sequences   The basic idea for the upper bound on the number of contacts is to classify the contacts into contacts between positions in the same layer (called *layer contacts*), and contacts between positions in successive layers (called *interlayer contacts*). To give an upper bound for a specific frame sequence, one gives separate bounds for the number of layer *and* interlayer contacts for hydrophobic cores have this frame sequence. In Figure 26.4a), a the hydrophobic core for the cubic lattice is shown together with the layer and interlayer contacts. The corresponding frame sequence is given in Figure 26.4b).

For the layer contacts, consider a frame of size $a \times b$ with n H-monomers. For finding the maximal number of layer contacts that any hydrophobic core with this frame can have, Yue and Dill [111] observed that it is much simpler to calculate the surface instead of the number of layer contacts. The *layer surface* of an hydrophobic core $\mathbb{C}$ in layer $x = k$ is the number of positions $\vec{p}$ in layer $x = k$ that are not in $\mathbb{C}$, but neighbors of some position $\vec{p}' \in \mathbb{C}$ ($\vec{p}$ is called a *surface point*). Since every position in the core has 4 neighbors, which are filled by another member of the core or by a surface point, it is clear that surface and contacts are related via the equation

$$4n = 2Contact + 2a + 2b.$$

Hence, minimizing the surface maximizes the number of contacts.

Now whenever we have a layer where a surface point is buried between two position from the core, this core cannot be maximal. We can achieve a more compact one by resorting the core positions in this layer in a way that the gap generated by this surface point is closed (recall that a hydrophobic core is just a set of positions, with no other conditions imposed on them). Under the condition of a maximal compact layer core, this implies that every horizontal and vertical line that goes through the core in some layer must generate 2 surface points. Hence, a frame of size $a \times b$ must generate at least $2a + 2b$ surface points. Furthermore, one can conclude that an optimal frame for n points must minimize $a + b$, which is the case for a nearly quadratic frame. I.e., the best possible adaption of a quadratic frame with $a = \lceil \sqrt{n} \rceil$ and $b = \lceil \frac{n}{a} \rceil$ will have minimal surface, which used as a bound when enumerating number sequences.

For the interlayer contacts in the cubic lattice, one simply observes that every monomer in one layer can have at most one contact in the following layer. Thus, the maximal number of interlayer contacts for two successive layers $X = i$ and $X = i + 1$ having n_i and n_{i+1} monomers is $\min(n_i, n_{i+1})$. Using this upper bounds for layer and interlayer contacts, one can calculate the optimal frame sequence using a dynamic programming approach.

For the face-centered cubic lattice, the calculation of the bound is more complicated. Albeit one can uses also a splitting of the core into successive layers and apply the same bound for layer contacts, the bound for the interlayer contacts is more difficult. The reason is that every H-monomer in one layer can have up to 4 contact in the successive layer. For details the reader is referred to [2].

Construction of hydrophobic cores   Once we have a frame sequence a_k, b_k, n_k for $k = 1 \ldots m$, one has to enumerate the possible hydrophobic cores for this frame sequence. The first step is to fix the frame positions in each layer. That is, we have finite domain variables sy_k and sz_k for the lower left corner of the frame in layer $x = k$. We can choose $sy_1 = sz_1 = 0$ for the first frame. For the remaining frames, we have to enumerate in principle all possible starting positions. But again, we can use bounds to discard combination of values for sy_k, sz_k that may not result in a maximal compact hydrophobic core.

An example of such a bound is the following. A combination is unfavorable if a frame does not completely overlap with the previous frame. Then only the part of the two frames that do overlap can generate interlayer contacts. Hence, we can use the bounds on the interlayer contacts described in the last section to calculate the number of interlayer contacts for the overlapping sub-frames.

Once we have fixed the frames (via determining their lower left corners), we start be enumerating the positions that are actually contained in the core. This can be done by inserting for every position a Boolean variable $c_{\vec{p}}$ for every position $\vec{p}$ that is in one of the fixed frames. Then

$$c_{\vec{p}} = 1 \quad \text{iff} \quad \vec{p} \text{ is in the core.}$$

Clearly, we have

$$\left(\sum_{\vec{p} \text{ is in Layer } x = k} c_{\vec{p}} \right) = n_k.$$

Since a frame is usually tightly filled, this constraint provides good propagation. Finally, we have to encode contacts by using a Boolean variable $Contact_{\vec{p}, \vec{p}'}$ for each pair of neighbors $\vec{p}, \vec{p}'$. Then

$$Contact_{\vec{p}, \vec{p}'} = 1 \Leftrightarrow (c_{\vec{p}} = 1 \wedge c_{\vec{p}'} = 1).$$

Counting $Contact_{\vec{p}, \vec{p}'}$ will gives us the total number of contacts for the core.

We can improve propagation by the following consideration. Usually, hydrophobic cores do not have too many caveats. A *caveat* is a P-monomer which is part of the hydrophobic core and thus buried by H-monomers. This usually produces a non-optimal

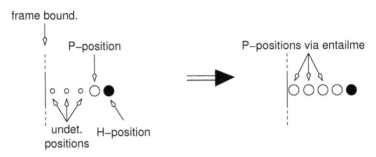

Figure 26.5: Example of the caveat-freeness constraint

core, but must be considered in the case that the optimal cores do not correspond to a valid sequence conformation. If a frame does not contain any caveat, then we know that for any line through the frame, the H-monomers must be consecutive on this line. Now suppose we have two positions $\vec{p}$ and $\vec{p'}$ in the same frame with the property that $\vec{p}$ is the left neighbor of $\vec{p'}$, $c_{\vec{p}} = 0$ (P-position) and $c_{\vec{p}} = 1$ (H-position). Then all positions to the left of $\vec{p}$ on the line through $\vec{p}, \vec{p'}$ must be P-positions as well (see Figure 26.5). For a given pair of left neighbors $\vec{p} = (k, s, t)$ and $\vec{p'} = (k, s+1, t)$, this can be simply expressed by the following entailment constraint:

$$c_{\vec{p}} = 0 \wedge c_{\vec{p'}} = 1 \implies \bigwedge_{\substack{\vec{p''} = (k, s, t) \\ \text{in frame} \\ \text{with } r < s}} c_{\vec{p''}} = 0$$

Of course, we have to introduce such a constraint for every pair of left, right or vertical neighbors. For more details, the reader is referred to [1] and [108]. If caveats are allowed, then one can enumerate them explicitly and add the constraint for the remaining positions.

26.5.3   Protein Docking and Ligand Binding

Protein docking attempts to find the most stable mode of association between two protein molecules, starting from the atomic coordinates of the two isolated components. It can be likened to a 'lock and key' mechanism , where both lock and key are plastic, and distort according to mutual interactions. The protein-protein interfaces are closely packed, similar to protein cores. The aim of any docking algorithm is to optimise the surface area and attractive forces and to minimise the loss of energy due to interaction with the solvent. This is a difficult area of research, but there are general rules. Optimisation must be performed on many degrees of freedom, since this is an example of 6-D problem of rigid body movement - 3 translations and 3 rotations, all of which must be searched. The approaches to rigid surfaces are broadly

1. Given the information of a pair of proteins crystallised together, to *reconstruct* the docking

2. Given the individual proteins separately crystallised, to *predict* their docking. requires trying all combinations of degrees of freedom note that *ligand binding* - small ligands tend to bind in big pockets; ligands are more flexible than proteins

26.5.4 Structure Motif Matching

Protein structures can be described at various levels of detail, ranging from atomic coordinates, through vector approximations to secondary structures elements (SSEs), to 'topological' models. These latter abstractions typically consider a sequence of SSEs, i.e. helices or strands, together with relationships like spatial adjacency within the fold and approximate orientation, neglecting details like lengths and structures of loops, and the lengths of the secondary structure elements themselves. This level of abstraction can be useful to permit very fast algorithms for structure motif matching, discovery and structure comparison. Further, by neglecting many of the details which typically vary between related structures, like lengths and structures of loops, and exact lengths, spatial positions and orientations of SSEs, it has the potential to detect more distant structural relationships than could be found by methods based on more geometrical descriptions. On the other hand, its disadvantages are that there may be structures which, although related at the topological level, are very different from a geometric point of view, and have no meaningful biological relationship.

A TOPS *structure* is a triple (E, H, C) where $E = S_1, \ldots, S_k$ is a sequence of length k of secondary structure elements (SSEs) and H and C are relations over the SSEs, called respectively H-bonds and chiralities. In this description an H-bond constraint refers to a ladder of individual hydrogen bonds between adjacent strands in a sheet. An SSE S is a character from the alphabet $\{\alpha, \beta\}$ standing for helix and strand respectively. Since each SSE in a TOPS structure is associated with a direction *up* or *down* we associate a direction symbol, $+$ or $-$, with each letter of this alphabet. Both H-bonds and chiralities are symmetric relations (non-directed arcs in the graph). An H-bond constrains the types of the two SSE's involved to be strands, and each bond is associated with a relative direction $\delta \in \{P, A\}$, indicating whether the bond is between parallel or anti-parallel strands. Chiralities are associated with handedness $\chi \in \{L, R\}$ (left and right respectively), and only occur between pairs of SSEs of the same type. We denote the H-bond relationship between two SSEs S_i and S_j by (S_i, δ, S_j) and a chirality relationship by (S_i, χ, S_j).

Definition 26.8 (TOPS structure). *Given* $\Sigma = \{\alpha_+, \alpha_-, \beta_+, \beta_-\}$, *then a TOPS structure D is defined by the triple* (S, H_d, C_d), *where*
$S = (S_1, \ldots, S_k), S_i \in \Sigma$
$H_d = \{(S_i, \delta, S_j) | S_i, S_j \in \{\beta_+, \beta_-\}, \delta = P \leftrightarrow S_i = S_j, \delta = A \leftrightarrow S_i \neq S_j\}$
$C_d = \{(S_i, \chi, S_j) | S_i, S_j \in \Sigma, \chi \in \{R, L, \}\}$

As an example, in Figure 26.6 we give a TOPS structure for the protein structure "2bop" (Protein Databank code) both in a form with '2-D' layout as well as in a linear form form. The textual form of the TOPS description for 2bop is:

2bop = (E, H, C), where
$E = (\beta_{+1}, \alpha_{-2}, \alpha_{-3}, \beta_{+4}, \beta_{+5}, \beta_{-6}, \alpha_{+7}, \beta_{-8})$
$H = \{(\beta_{+1}, A, \beta_{-6}), (\beta_{+1}, A, \beta_{-8}), (\beta_{+4}, A, \beta_{-6}), (\beta_{+5}, A, \beta_{-6})\}$
$C = \{(\beta_{+1}, R, \beta_{+4}), (\beta_{-6}, R, \beta_{-8})\}$

A TOPS *pattern*, or *motif*, is similar to a TOPS structure, but is a generalisation which can describe several structures conforming to some common topological characteristics.

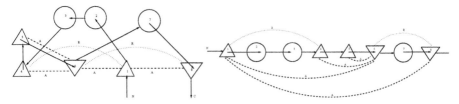

Figure 26.6: TOPS structure for 2bop. Circles represent α-helical secondary structure elements, triangles represent β-strand secondary structure elements, arrows represent loop regions, heavy dotted lines represent hydrogen-bond relationships ('A' – anti-parallel), light dotted lines represent chiralities ('R' — right-handed)

This generalisation is achieved by permitting 'gaps', standing for the insertion of SSEs (and any associated H-bond and chiralities), in the sequence of secondary structure elements; indeed a structure is just a pattern where no inserts are permitted. A gap is described by a pair (n, m) where n stands for the minimum and m for the maximum number of SSEs which can be inserted at that position. The range of n and m is from zero to the largest number of SSE's in any TOPS structures (approximately 60).

In principle, just as for TOPS structures, each SSE in a TOPS pattern is associated with a direction *up* or *down* ($+$ or $-$ respectively) relative to the X-axis, and is a character from the alphabet $\{\alpha, \beta\}$.

However, since any TOPS description of pattern (or a structure) can be flipped about the X-axis without loss of meaning, in order to facilitate pattern matching we associate a *direction variable*, $\oplus$ or $\ominus$ with each SSE in a pattern P s.t. they satisfy the constraint

$$\forall \oplus, \ominus \in P : opp(\oplus, \ominus) \leftrightarrow (\oplus = + \wedge \ominus = -) \vee (\oplus = - \wedge \ominus = +)$$

Note that it is possible, but redundant if we are to perform pattern matching, to associate a similar constraint with each SSE in a structure description.

Definition 26.9 (TOPS pattern). *Given* $\Sigma = \{\alpha_\oplus, \alpha_\ominus, \beta_\oplus, \beta_\ominus\}$ *then a TOPS pattern* $P = (T, H_p, C_p)$, $\forall \oplus, \ominus \in P : opp(\oplus, \ominus)$, *where* $T = (n_0, m_0) - V_1 - (n_1, m_1) - V_2 - \ldots - (n_{k-1}, m_{k-1}) - V_k - (n_k, m_k)$, $V_j \in \Sigma$, $n_j \leq m_j$
$H_p = \{(S_i, \delta, S_j) | S_i, S_j \in \{\beta_\oplus, \beta_\ominus\}, \; \delta = P \leftrightarrow S_i = S_j, \; \delta = A \leftrightarrow S_i \neq S_j\}$
$C_p = \{(S_i, \chi, S_j) | \chi \in \{R, L, \}, \; S_i, S_j \in \Sigma\}$

For example a TOPS pattern which describes plaits (2bop is an instance of a plait) is illustrated in Figure 26.7; arrows between SSEs in the sequence have been annotated with pairs of integers standing for (n_i, m_j), in this case $(0, N)$.

Definition 26.10 (Size of a TOPS structure (resp pattern)). *The size of a TOPS structure* $D = (S, H, C)$ *(resp. pattern) is* $|S|$, *the number of SSEs in the structure (pattern).*

Gilbert et al [47] have defined a simple backtracking algorithm which is guaranteed to find all the ways in which a TOPS pattern matches a TOPS structure; for each match it

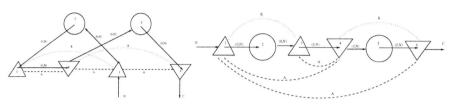

Figure 26.7: TOPS plait motif

returns the set of pairs of corresponding SSEs between the pattern and the structure, and the set of corresponding insert sizes in the pattern.

Finite domain constraints over integers are used in the algorithm in order to prune the search space. A correspondence is established between the SSE numbers in a structure size j and the SSE numbers in a pattern size k $Corr := (d_1, d_2, \ldots, d_k)$, where d_i ($i \in 1 \ldots k$) is a constraint variable representing the number of the SSE in the structure matching SSE i in the pattern. In addition $Ins := (I_1, I_2, \ldots, I_{k-1})$ is the sequence of insert sizes, where I_i ($i \in 1 \ldots k-1$) is a constraint variable representing the number of inserts between SSEs i and $i+1$ in the pattern, The matching algorithm *imposes constraints* on the SSEs in the pattern by setting up constraints for $i \in 1..k$, C1: $1 \leq d_i \leq j$
C2: $n_i \leq I_i \leq m_i$,
C3: $d_i + I_i + 1 = d_{i+1}$
Constraint C1 gives the range of d_i (a pattern cannot have more SSEs than a matching structure); C2 sets up a constraint variable for each insert in the pattern, and C3 ensures that the insert sizes are respected in the matching.

The simple algorithm then proceeds by matching the H-bonds (respecting the parallel/antiparallel labels), the chiralities (respecting the right/left-hand labels) and the SSEs (respecting the type and orientation) between the pattern and the structure.

In fact, matching of TOPS motifs to TOPS structures is an instance of the subgraph isomorphism problem which remains NP-complete for such vertex ordered graphs. There are several non-polynomial algorithms for subgraph isomorphism problem, the most popular being by Ullmann [102] and McGregor [76]. Although these are not straightforwardly adaptable to vertex ordered graphs, the vertex ordering seems to be the property that could considerably improve the algorithm efficiency.

Viksna et al. [106] give a fast matching algorithm for TOPS structures, which is a variant of a method based on constraint satisfaction [76]. The algorithm tries to match edges in the increasing order of edge positions and backtracks if for some edge match can not be found. Since the graphs are ordered, the positions in the target graph to which a given edge may be mapped and which have to be checked can only increase. Two additional ideas are used to make this process more efficient. Firstly, a number of additional labels are assigned to vertices and edges; they comprise the numbers of incoming and outgoing edges of all possible types for a given vertex, whilst for an edge they describes how many "shorter" or "longer" other edges are connected to the endpoints of a given edge. describes how many shorter or longer other edges are connected to the endpoints of a given edge Secondly, if an edge e can not be mapped according to the existing mapping for previous edges, then the next place where this edge can be mapped according to the labels is found, and the minimal match positions of previous edges are advanced in order to be compatible with the minimal position of e. The full algorithm is given in [106].

26.5.5   Structure Motif Discovery

Pattern discovery for sequences is a well-established technique [15] which could be applied to TOPS structures as follows. The first, "pattern driven" (PD) is based on enumerating candidate patterns in a given solution space and picking out the ones with high fitness; the second, "structure driven" (SD) comprises algorithms that try to find patterns by comparing given diagrams and looking for local similarities between them. In SD an algorithm may be based on constructing a local multiple alignment of given sequences and then extracting the patterns from the alignment by combining the segments common to most of the sequences.

Essentially the difference between pattern discovery for sequences and TOPS structures is that techniques for the former assume that the grammar of the former is regular whilst that of the latter is context–sensitive. Thus in a naive version of a PD approach for TOPS diagrams not only would we have to enumerate an exponentially large number of patterns comprising not only all the possible combinations of the SSEs (and their orientations) in a pattern of length k, but also all the possible H-bond and chirality connections over them.

Viksna et al [106] find maximal common subgraphs for a set of TOPS graphs by an exhaustive search comprising repeated extension of an initial subgraph and checking for subgraph isomorphisms in the target set of graphs. In doing so, they exploit the speed of their specialised subgraph isomorphism algorithm for TOPS graphs. Starting with a simple (one vertex) pattern graph, subgraph isomorphism is used to check against all graphs in a given set and in the case of success attempt to extend the already matched pattern graph in all possible ways. Some restrictions on the number of different types of edges and vertices can be deduced from the given set of target graphs and are used by the algorithm. Apart from that, the previous successful match may be used to deduce information about extensions which are more likely to be successful in the next match. In general this does not prune the search space but may help to discover large common subgraphs earlier. The advantage of this approach is that the algorithm has time complexity that is linear with respect to the number of graphs in the given input set.

Gilbert et al. [45] report an heuristic algorithm which discovers patterns of H-bonds (and chiralities) based on the properties of sheets for TOPS diagrams; they also derive patterns on the associated sequences of SSEs and insert sizes. Briefly, the algorithm attempts to discover a new sheet by finding, common to all the target set of diagrams, a (fresh) pair of strands, sharing an H-bond with a particular direction. Then it attempts to extend the sheet by repeatedly inserting a fresh strand which is H-bonded to one of the existing strands in the (current) sheet. The algorithm then finds all further H-bonds between all the members of the current sheet. The entire process is repeated until no more sheets can be discovered; any chirality arcs between the H-bonds in the pattern are then discovered by a similar process. The numbers of inserts between each strand in the pattern are then computed for all the patterns in the learning set, and the minimum and maximum size of the gaps in the corresponding insert positions in the pattern are thus found, and combined with the SSE sequence to give the T-pattern. The result is the least general common TOPS pattern characterising the target set of protein descriptions.

Other methods that are known mostly correspond to the SD approach outlined above, for example as described by Koch et al. [66]. These may be more efficient for sets containing a small number (basically just two) of graphs, but in general cannot be used to find the exact answer to the problem for larger sets.

The goodness of a pattern can be stated in several ways, including the *size* of the pattern, its discriminative performance against a set of positive and negative examples, and its *compression* value. In [46] Gilbert et al describe how to compute the compression of a TOPS pattern with respect to a set of graphs of structures using a general data compression measure applied to the size of the pattern graph and the total size of the components of the structures which are not included in the pattern. This value can be normalised to the range 1 (best) to 0 (worst).

Definition 26.11 (Raw compression). *The raw compression of a pattern length k w.r.t. a set of n structures of lengths $l_1, \ldots, l_n$ is*

$$\Sigma_{i=1}^{n} l_i - (n-1) * k$$

Definition 26.12 (Normalised compression). *The normalised compression of a pattern length k w.r.t. a set of n structures of lengths $l_1, \ldots, l_n$ is*

$$\frac{(n-1)*k}{\Sigma_{i=1}^{n} l_i - min_{i=1}^{n}(l_i)}$$

These definitions can be extended in a natural way to include complete structural definitions (H-bonds and chiralities). When there are only two structures in the set, the compression measure can be used as a measure of structure comparison, as ultilised in the online TOPS system reported by Torrance et al [101] which operates over the TOPS database [77].

26.6 Function Related Problems

26.6.1 Metabolic Pathways

Living organisms function by a complex set of interactions at the molecular level which occur in a highly organised manner. They involve metabolic reactions which transform some compounds (*substrates*) into others (*products*). In general a reaction $S \rightarrow P$ can be described by a transition $S \rightarrow S' \rightarrow P$, transforming the set of substrates S into the set of products P via a transition state S' in which the substrate molecules are distorted into some electronic conformation which more readily converts to the products. In order to occur, $S \rightarrow P$ has a negative free energy, i.e. the free energy of S is greater than that of P; however $S \rightarrow S'$ has a *positive* free energy change, termed the energy of activation. This energy is a barrier preventing $S \rightarrow P$ occurring spontaneously, without which all reactions would occur in an uncontrolled way. Most reactions are catalysed by special proteins called *enzymes* which control the reaction by lowering the energy barrier (i.e. increasing the rate of flow). They do this by binding substrates at combining sites within active sites, positioning substrate molecules in the most favourable orientations for reactions to occur, as well as distorting them in order to favour transition state formation. During this process the enzyme may change shape in order to induce a fit with the substrate, rather than just rely on a rigid 'lock and key' mechanism. In general, reactions can be chained together into paths so that the products of one reaction become the substrates of another [36].

26.6.2 Regulatory Networks

Metabolic reactions can be regulated in two ways. The first is by the direct activation or inhibition of activity of enzymes by small molecules. This method is relatively fast in action, since it directly affects the chain of reactions. Another method of regulation is that of transcriptional regulation, in which the production of the enzyme itself is controlled by a transcription factor (a protein which activates the capacity of a gene to produce another protein). This method is relatively slow, since it indirectly affects the reaction path.

Reactions can be self-regulated using either the direct or transcriptional method, since it is common that products of an immediate or eventual reaction act have a direct or transcriptional effect on enzymes involved earlier in the chain of reactions. These regulatory relationships can be quite complex in that products from one path can regulate enzymes involved in another path.

26.6.3 Querying and Analysing Networks of Cellular Function

In [105] van Helden et al. give a data model for representing and analysing networks of cellular function (metabolic and regulatory pathways). This has been extended by Deville et al. [26] to the general case including signalling pathways. Often the information is stored in a database, with the associated the database model permitting simple analysis to be directly be performed on through a database query language which are often unsuitable for algorithmic use. Specific algorithms with their own data structures are required for more sophisticated analyses. Often graphs are used as representational data structures – these can be compound, reaction, bipartite and hyper-graphs. Object-oriented models can be seen as a generalization of bipartite graphs, where the nodes are typed, permiting detailed descriptions, and the use of inheritance to structure data.

Current computational systems often path navigation routines in addition to simple data retrieval. A simple query is to get all the reactions catalysed by a gene product More complex queries require the application of specialised algorithms, often involving the use of graph analysis. These are for example (adapted from [105])

- find all metabolic pathways that convert compound A into compound B in less than X steps

- find all genes whose expression is directly or indirectly affected by a given compound.

- find all compounds that can be synthesised from a given precursor in less than X steps

- in the complete set of metabolic reactions, find all feedback loops including a given compound, or, in a defined biochemical pathway, find all feedback loops.

Another type of complex queries involve sub-graph extraction. Here the user specifies a set of seed nodes in the network the system is required to extract the portions of the network or sub-graphs that interconnect each pair of seed nodes via the smallest number of individual links. The user can specify the maximum number of individual links, or graph arcs, that can be inserted between any two seed nodes. The resulting sub-graph can then be displayed and analysed. Algorithms for sub graph extraction and maximal path enumeration used in this context have been described in van Helden et al [104]. Examples of major databases and computational systems for storing and analysing biochemical pathway and network data include KEGG (Kyoto Encyclopedia of Genes and Genomes) [61], BioCyc [68], and Amaze [72].

In recent work Dooms et al have described an approach using constraint programming to solve constrained path finding problems in metabolic networks [29] [30], and have applied it to discover pathways from a set of their reactions. [78]. This approach builds on earlier work by the same authors [31] in which they defined a graph computation domain for constraint programming in order to provide a high level modeling language with the data and results are graphs.

26.7 Microarrays

DNA microarrays ("DNA chips") are made by the deposition of DNA spots on a solid support, often a coated glass surface. For an in-depth review, see e.g. [19]. Two main procedures have been used to produce these: photolithography (e.g. by as developed and marketed by Affymetrix Inc. [74], and mechanical gridding [16]. Photolithography is a technique used in the computer microchip industry. There is, however, an inherent length restriction with this *in situ* synthesis technology limiting the probes to about 25 nucleotides in length. This is offset by the use of high-density arrays which allow the use of multiple probes per gene. The arrayed probes can be oligonucleotides (photolithography and gridding) or cDNAs (gridding).

Arrays of thousands of DNA sequences representing part of all of the genome of an organism can be constructed. Such arrays can then be used to compare the relative abundance of the transcriptional products of each of these gene sequences in two DNA or RNA samples, for example from two different cell populations, or from one population exposed to two different stimuli. In the spotting techniques the two samples are first labelled using different fluorescent dyes and are then mixed and hybridized with the arrayed DNA spots. After hybridization, fluorescence measurements are made for each DNA spot, and recording the fluorescence for each dye separately. These measurements are used to determine the ratio, and in turn the relative abundance, of the sequence of each specific gene in the two mRNA or DNA samples. (Adapted from [16]).

The computational challenges can be broadly divided into two major categories:
(1) Normalisation and background correction of microarray data,
(2) Modelling and analysis of the networks that are represented by the sets of genes in the samples.

We briefly overview the second challenge. Network or pathway reconstruction from microarray data is based on observations of the expression of a set of genes under varying conditions such as time-series, targeted mutation or exposure to different evnironmental conditions (stress, starvation etc) [81]. These data are usually taken as steady-state. The goal is to identify which genes control (the expression of) other genes, and the results if these controls. The analysis often involves the clustering of genes by expression data and the analysis of promoter elements within the same clusters. Machine learning techniques are commonly used for reconstgruction of gene networks, for example Soinov et al [95]

A potential application of constraint programming in this area is proposed by Dooms et al [78] is the explanation of DNA microarray experiments using a CSP able to solve pathway discovery problems. However, this area is ripe for the application of constraint computation techniques, both in the processing of low-level (primary) data, as well as in the analysis and interpretation of results, for example cross-referencing into biochemical pathway data.

Bibliography

[1]   R. Backofen. Using constraint programming for lattice protein folding. In Russ B. Altman, A. Keith Dunker, Lawrence Hunter, and Teri E. Klein, editors, *Proceedings of the Pacific Symposium on Biocomputing (PSB'98)*, volume 3, pages 387–398, 1998.

[2]   R. Backofen. A polynomial time upper bound for the number of contacts in the hp-model on the face-centered-cubic lattice (fcc). *Journal of Discrete Algorithms*, 2 (2):161–206, 2004.

[3]   R. Backofen and S. Will. Optimally compact finite sphere packings — hydrophobic cores in the FCC. In *Proc. of the 12th Annual Symposium on Combinatorial Pattern Matching (CPM2001)*, volume 2089 of *Lecture Notes in Computer Science*, pages 257–272, Berlin, 2001. Springer–Verlag.

[4]   R. Backofen and S. Will. A constraint-based approach to structure prediction for simplified protein models that outperforms other existing methods. In *Proceedings of the 19th International Conference on Logic Programming (ICLP 2003)*, pages 49–71, 2003.

[5]   R. Backofen and S. Will. Local sequence-structure motifs in RNA. *Journal of Bioinformatics and Computational Biology (JBCB)*, 2(4):681–698, 2004.

[6]   R. Backofen, S. Will, and E. Bornberg-Bauer. Application of constraint programming techniques for structure prediction of lattice proteins with extended alphabets. *Bioinformatics*, 15(3):234–242, 1999.

[7]   R. Backofen, S. Will, and P. Clote. Algorithmic approach to quantifying the hydrophobic force contribution in protein folding. In Russ B. Altman, A. Keith Dunker, Lawrence Hunter, and Teri E. Klein, editors, *Proceedings of the Pacific Symposium on Biocomputing (PSB 2000)*, volume 5, pages 92–103, 2000.

[8]   R. Backofen, N. Narayanaswamy, and F. Swidan. On the complexity of protein similarity search under mrna structure constraints. In H. Alt and A. Ferreira, editors, *Proc. of 19th International Symposium on Theoretical Aspects of Computer Science (STACS2002)*,, volume 2285 of *Lecture Notes in Computer Science*, pages 274–286, Berlin, 2002. Springer Verlag.

[9]   A. Bairoch, P. Bucher, and K. Hofman. The PROSITE database, its status in 1995. *Nucleic Acids Research*, 24(1):189–196, 1996.

[10] G. Benson. Sequence alignment with tandem repeats. In *Proc. of the First Annual International Conferences on Compututational Molecular Biology (RECOMB97)* pages 27–36, 1997.

[11] B. Berger and T. Leighton. Protein folding in the hydrophobic-hydrophilic (HP) modell is NP-complete. In *Proc. of the Second Annual International Conferences on Compututational Molecular Biology (RECOMB98)*, pages 30–39, New York, 1998.

[12] B. Billoud, M. Kontic, and A. Viari. Palingol: a declarative programming language

to describe nucleic acids' secondary structures and to scan sequence databases. *Nucleic Acids Research*, 24(8):1395–1403, 1996.

[13] E. Bornberg-Bauer. Chain growth algorithms for HP-type lattice proteins. In *Proc. of the 1st Annual International Conference on Computational Molecular Biology (RECOMB)*, pages 47 – 55. ACM Press, 1997.

[14] E. Bornberg-Bauer and H. S. Chan. Modeling evolutionary landscapes: mutational stability, topology, and superfunnels in sequence space. *Proc. Natl. Acad. Sci. USA*, 96(19):10689–94, 1999.

[15] A. Brazma, I. Jonassen, I. Eidhammer, and D. R. Gilbert. Approaches to the automatic discovery of patterns in biosequences. *Journal of Computational Biology*, 5 (2):277–303, 1998.

[16] P. O. Brown and D. Botstein. Exploring the new world of the genome with dna microarrays. *Nature Genetics*, 21:33 – 37, 1999.

[17] H. Carrillo and D. Lipman. The multiple sequence alignment problem in biology. *SIAM Journal of Applied Mathematics*, 48:1073–1082, 1988.

[18] CASP3. http://predictioncenter.llnl.gov/casp3/casp3.html. Third Community Wide Experiment on the Critical Assessment of Techniques for Protein Structure Prediction,, Dec 1998.

[19] J. E. Celis, M. Kruhoffer, I. Gromova, C. Frederiksen, M. Ostergaard, T. Thykjaer, P. Gromov, J. Yu, H. Palsdottir, N. Magnusson, and T. F. Orntoft. Gene expression profiling: monitoring transcription and translation products using dna microarrays and proteomics. *FEBS Letters: Functional Genomics*, 480(1):2–16, 2005.

[20] T. Christof, M. Jünger, J. Kececioglu, P. Mutzel, and G. Reinelt. A branch-and-cut approach to physical mapping with end-probes. In *Proc. of the First Annual International Conferences on Compututational Molecular Biology (RECOMB97)*, pages 84–92. ACM Press, 1997.

[21] P. Clote and R. Backofen. *Computational Molecular Biology: An Introduction*. Mathematical and Computational Biology. Jon Wiley & Sons, Chichester, August 2000. series editor S. Levin. 290 pages.

[22] J. Cohen. Bioinformatics—an introduction for computer scientists. *ACM Computing Surveys*, 36(2):122–158, June 2004.

[23] F. Corpet and B. Michot. RNAlign program: alignment of RNA sequences using both primary and secondary structures. *Comput Appl Biosci*, 10(4):389–99, 1994.

[24] P. Crescenzi, D. Goldman, C. Papadimitrou, A. Piccolboni, , and M. Yannakakis. On the complexity of protein folding. In *Proceedings of STOC 1998*, pages 597–603, 1998.

[25] F. H. C. Crick. On protein synthesis. *Symposium of the Society of Experimental Biology*, 12:138–167, 1958.

[26] Y. Deville, D. Gilbert, J. van Helden, and S. Wodak. An overview of data models for the analysis of biochemical pathways. *Briefings in Bioinformatics*, 4(3):246–259, 2003.

[27] D. Diaz and P. Codognet. A Minimal Extension of the WAM for clp(FD). In D. S. Warren, editor, *Proceedings of the Tenth International Conference on Logic Programming*, pages 774–790, Budapest, Hungary, 1993. The MIT Press.

[28] K. A. Dill, K. M. Fiebig, and H. S. Chan. Cooperativity in protein-folding kinetics. *Proc. Natl. Acad. Sci. USA*, 90:1942 – 1946, 1993.

[29] G. Dooms, Y. Deville, and P. Dupont. Constrained path finding in biochemical

networks. In *Proceedings of JOBIM 2004*, 2004.

[30] G. Dooms, Y. Deville, and P. Dupont. A mozart implementation of CP(bionet). In *Proceedings of the second International Mozart/Oz Conference*, pages 237–250. Springer-Verlag LNAI 3389, 2004.

[31] G. Dooms, Y. Deville, and P. Dupont. CP(graph): Introducing a graph computation domain in constraint programming. In *Proceedings of the Eleventh International Conference on Principles and Practice of Constraint Programming*, pages 211–225, 2005.

[32] M. Dsouza, N. Larsen, and R. Overbeek. Searching for patterns in genomic data. *Trends in Genetics*, 13(12):497–498, 1997.

[33] R. Durbin, S. Eddy, A. Krough, and G. Mitchison. *Biological Sequence and Analysis*. CUP, 1998.

[34] I. Eidhammer, I. Jonassen, and W. R. Taylor. Structure Comparison and Structure Patterns. Technical Report 174, Department of Informatics, University of Bergen, Bergen, Norway, Jul 1999.

[35] I. Eidhammer, D. Gilbert, I. Jonassen, M. Ratnayake, and S. H. Grindhaug. A constraint based structure description language for biosequences. *Constraints*, 6 (2–3):141–156, 2001.

[36] W. H. Elliott and D. C. Elliott. *Biochemistry and Molecular Biology*. OUP, 1997.

[37] J. Feldenstein. Confidence limits on phylogenies: an approach using the bootstrap. *Evolution*, 39:783–791, 1985.

[38] W. M. Fitch. Toward defining the course of evolution: minimum change for a specified tree topology. *Systematic Zoology*, 20:406–416, 1971.

[39] S. Foissac and T. Schiex. Integrating alternative splicing detection into gene prediction. *BMC Bioinformatics*, 6(1):25, 2005.

[40] D. Gautheret, F. Major, and R. Cedergren. Pattern searching/alignment with RNA primary and secondary structures: an effective descriptor for tRNA. *Computer Applications in the Biosciences*, 6:325–331, 1990.

[41] M. S. Gelfand, A. A. Mironov, and P. A. Pevzner. Gene recognition via spliced sequence alignment. *Proc. Natl. Acad. Sci. USA*, 93(17):9061–6, 1996.

[42] I. P. Gent, P. Prosser, B. M. Smith, and W. Wei. Supertree construction with constraint programming. In *ICCP: International Conference on Constraint Programming (CP), LNCS*, pages 837–841, 2003.

[43] Z. Ghahramani. Learning dynamic Bayesian networks. In C. Lee Giles and Marco Gori, editors, *Adaptive Processing of Sequences and Data Structures*, number 1387 in Lecture Notes in Artificial Intelligence, LNAI, pages 168–197. Springer-Verlag, 1998.

[44] D. Gilbert, D. Westhead, J. Thornton, and J. Viksna. Tops cartoons: formalisation, searching and comparison. *RECOMB99 (poster)*, 1999.

[45] D. Gilbert, D. Westhead, J. Viksna, and J. Thornton. Topology-based protein structure comparison using a pattern discovery technique. *Journal of Computers and Chemistry*, 26(1):23–30, 2001.

[46] D. Gilbert, D. Westhead, and J. Viksna. Techniques for comparison, pattern matching and pattern discovery: From sequences to protein topology. In *Artificial Intelligence and Heuristic Methods in Bioinformatics*, pages 128–147. IOS Press, 2003.

[47] D. R. Gilbert, D. R. Westhead, N. Nagano, and J. M. Thornton. Motif–based searching in tops protein topology databases. *Bioinformatics*, 15(4):317–326, 1999.

[48] D. S. Greenberg and S. Istrail. Physical mapping by sts-hybradisation: Algorithmic strategies and the challenge of software evaluation. *Journal of Computational Biology*, 2(2):219–273, 1995.

[49] B. J. Haas, A. L. Delcher, S. M. Mount, J. R. Wortman, R. K. J. Smith, L. I. Hannick, R. Maiti, C. M. Ronning, D. B. Rusch, C. D. Town, S. L. Salzberg, and O. White. Improving the Arabidopsis genome annotation using maximal transcript alignment assemblies. *Nucleic Acids Research*, 31(19):5654–66, 2003.

[50] R. M. Hall and C. M. Collis. Mobile gene cassettes and integrons: capture and spread of genes by site-specific recombination. *Mol Microbiol*, 15(4):593–600, 1995.

[51] W. E. Hart. On the computational complexity of sequence design problems. In *Proc. of the First Annual International Conferences on Compututational Molecular Biology (RECOMB97)*, pages 128–136, Santa Fe, New Mexico, 1997.

[52] F. U. Hartl and J. Martin. Molecular chaperones in cellular protein folding. *Current Opinion in Structural Biology*, 5(92):92–102, 1995.

[53] C. Helgesen and P. Sibbald. PALM - a pattern language for molecular biology. In L. Hunter, D. Searls, and J. Shavlik, editors, *Proceedings First International Conference on Intelligent Systems for Molecular Biology*, pages 172–180. AAAI Press, 1993.

[54] M. Hiller, K. Huse, M. Platzer, and R. Backofen. Creation and disruption of protein features by alternative splicing – a novel mechanism to modulate function. *Genome Biol*, 6(7):R58, 2005.

[55] I. L. Hofacker, S. H. Bernhart, and P. F. Stadler. Alignment of RNA base pairing probability matrices. *Bioinformatics*, 2004.

[56] A. Horwich and J. Weissman. Deadly conformations: Protein misfolding in prion disease. *Cell*, 89:499–510, 1997.

[57] T. Jiang, G. Lin, B. Ma, and K. Zhang. A general edit distance between RNA structures. *Journal of Computational Biology*, 9(2):371–88, 2002.

[58] I. Jonassen, I. Eidhammer, and W. R. Taylor. Discovery of local packing motifs in protein structures. *Proteins*, 34(2):206–219, 1999.

[59] N. C. Jones and P. A. Pevzner. *An Introduction to Bioinformatics Algorithms (Computational Molecular Biology)*. The MIT Press, 2004.

[60] M. Kanehisa. Grand challenges in bioinformatics. *Bioinformatics*, 14(4):309, 1998.

[61] M. Kanehisa and S. Goto. KEGG: Kyoto Encyclopedia of Genes and Genomes. *Nucleic Acids Res.*, 28:27–30, 2000.

[62] J. Kececioglu, H.-P. Lenhof, K. Mehlhorn, P. Mutzel, K. Reinert, and M. Vingron. A polyhedral approach to sequence alignment problems. *Discrete Applied Mathematics*, 104(1-3):143–186, 2000.

[63] J. D. Kececioglu. The maximum weight trace problem in multiple sequence alignment. In Alberto Apostolico, Maxime Crochemore, Zvi Galil, and Udi Manber, editors, *Proc. 4th Symp. Combinatorical Pattern Matching*, pages 106–119, 1993.

[64] J. D. Kececioglu. *Exact and Approximation Algorithms for DNA Sequence Reconstruction*. PhD thesis, University of Arizona, 1991.

[65] H. Kitano. Looking beyond the details: a rise in system-oriented approaches in genetics and molecular biology. *Current Genetics*, 41(1):1–10, 2002.

[66] I. Koch, T. Lengauer, and E. Wanke. An algorithm for finding maximal common subtopologies in a set of protein structures. *Journal of Computational Biology*, 3(2):

289–306, 1996.

[67] L. Krippahl and P. Barahona. Psico: Solving protein structures with constraint programming and optimization. *Constraints*, 7(4-3):317–331, 2002.

[68] M. Krummenacker, S. Paley, L. Mueller, T. Yan, and P. D. Karp. Querying and
computing with BioCyc databases. *Bioinformatics*, 21(16):3454–3455, 2005.

[69] R. H. Lathrop and T. F. Smith. Global optimum protein threading with gapped
alignment and empirical pair score functions. *Journal of Molecular Biology*, 255:
641–665, 1996.

[70] K. F. Lau and K. A. Dill. A lattice statistical mechanics model of the conformational
and sequence spaces of proteins. *Macromolecules*, 22:3986 – 3997, 1989.

[71] F. Lefebvre. A grammar-based unification of several alignment and folding algorithms. In David J. States, Pamkaj Agarwal, Terry Gaasterland, Lawrence Hunter,
and Randall Smith, editors, *Proceedings of the Fourth International Conference on
Intelligent Systems for Molecular Biology*, pages 143–154, Menlo Park, June 12–15
1996. AAAI Press.

[72] C. Lemer, E. Antezana, F. Couche, F. Fays, X. Santolaria, R. Janky, Y. Deville,
J. Richelle, and S. Wodak. The aMAZE LightBench: a web interface to a relational
database of cellular processes. *Nucleic Acids Res.*, 32:D443–D448, 2004.

[73] H. P. Lenhof, K. Reinert, and M. Vingron. A polyhedral approach to RNA sequence
structure alignment. *Journal of Computational Biology*, 5(3):517–30, 1998.

[74] R. J. Lipshutz, S. P. Fodor, T. R. Gingeras, and D. J. Lockhart. High density synthetic
oligonucleotide arrays. *Nature Genetics*, 21:20 – 24, 1999.

[75] T. Macke, D. Ecker, R. Gutell, D. Gautheret, D. Case, and R. Sampath. RNAMotif, an RNA secondary structure definition and search algorithm. *Nucleic Acids
Research*, 29(22):4724–4735, 2001.

[76] J. J. McGregor. Relational consistency algorithms and their application in finding
subgraph and graph isomorphisms. *Information Sciences*, 19:229–250, 1979.

[77] I. Michalopoulos, G. M. Torrance, D. R. Gilbert, and D. R. Westhead. Tops: an
enhanced database of protein structural topology. *Nucleic Acids Research, Database
issue*, 32:D251–D254, 2003.

[78] Y. Deville P. D. G. Dooms. Constrained metabolic network analysis: discovering
pathways using CP(Graph). In *Workshop on Constraint Based Methods for Bioinformatics*, pages 29–35, 2005.

[79] A. D. Palù, A. Dovier, and E. Pontelli. A new constraint solver for 3d lattices
and its application to the protein folding problem. In Geoff Sutcliffe and Andrei
Voronkov, editors, *Logic for Programming, Artificial Intelligence, and Reasoning,
12th International Conference, LPAR 2005, Montego Bay, Jamaica, December 2-
6, 2005, Proceedings*, volume 3835 of *Lecture Notes in Computer Science*, pages
48–63. Springer, 2005.

[80] A. Dal Palu, A. Dovier, and F. Fogolari. Constraint Logic Programming approach
to protein structure prediction. *BMC Bioinformatics*, 5(1):186, 2004.

[81] D. Pe'er, A. Regev, G. Elidan, and N. Friedman. Inferring subnetworks from perturbed expression profiles. *Bioinformatics*, 17(Suppl 1):S215–224, 2001.

[82] A. Policriti, N. Vitacolonna, M. Morgante, and A. Zuccolo. Structured motifs
search. *Journal of Computational Biology*, 12(8):1065–1082, 2005.

[83] S. D. Prestwich, D. G. Higgins, and O. O'Sullivan. A sat-based approach to multiple sequence alignment. In Francesca Rossi, editor, *Principles and Practice of*

Constraint Programming - CP 2003, 9th International Conference, CP 2003, Kinsale, Ireland, September 29 - October 3, 2003, Proceedings, volume 2833 of *Lecture Notes in Computer Science*, pages 940–944. Springer, 2003.

[84] K. Reinert, H.-P. Lenhof, P.Mutzel, K. Melhorn, and J. Kececioglu. A branch-and-cut algorithm for multiple sequence alignment. In *Proc. of the First Annual International Conferences on Compututational Molecular Biology (RECOMB97)*, pages 241–249, Santa Fe, New Mexico, 1997.

[85] I. Rigoutsos and A. Floratos. Combinatorial pattern discovery in biological sequences. *Bioinformatics*, 14(1):55–67, 1998.

[86] D. Sankoff. Simultaneous solution of the RNA folding, alignment and protosequence problems. *SIAM J. Appl. Math.*, 45(5):810–825, 1985.

[87] D. Searls. The computational linguistics of biological sequences. In Lawrence Hunter, editor, *Artificial Intelligence and Molecular Biology*, chapter 2, pages 47–120. AAAI/MIT Press, 1993.

[88] D. Searls. String variable grammar: A logic grammar formalism for the bioligical language of DNA. *Journal of Logic Programming*, 24(1–2):73–102, July/August 1995.

[89] D. Searls and S. Dong. A syntactic pattern recognition system for DNA sequences. In C. R. Cantor H. A. Lim, J. Fickett and R. J. Robbins, editors, *Proceedings Second International Conference on Bioinformatics, Supercomputing, and Complex Genome Analysis*, pages 89–101. World Scientific, 1993.

[90] P. R. Sibbald and P. Argos. Scrutineer: a computer program that flexibly seeks and describes motifs and profiles in protein sequences databases. *Computer Applications in the Biosciences*, 6(3):279–288, 1990.

[91] P. R. Sibbald, H. Sommerfeldt, and P. Argos. Overseer: a nucleotide sequence searching tool. *Computer Applications in the Biosciences*, 8(1):45–48, 1992.

[92] S. Siebert and R. Backofen. MARNA: multiple alignment and consensus structure prediction of RNAs based on sequence structure comparisons. *Bioinformatics*, 21 (16):3352–9, 2005.

[93] T. Smith and M. Waterman. Comparison of biosequences. *Adv. appl. Math.*, 2: 482–489, 1981.

[94] G. Smolka. The Oz programming model. In Jan van Leeuwen, editor, *Computer Science Today*, Lecture Notes in Computer Science, vol. 1000, pages 324–343. Springer-Verlag, Berlin, 1995.

[95] L. Soinov, M. Krestyaninova, and A. Brazma. Towards reconstruction of gene networks from expression data by supervised learning. *Genome Biology*, 4(1):R6, 2003.

[96] R. R. Sokal and C. D. Michener. A statistical method for evaluating systematic relationships. *University of Kansas Scientific Bulletin*, 28:1409–1438, 1958.

[97] R. Staden. Searching for Patterns in Protein and Nucleic Acid Sequences. In R. F. Doolittle, editor, *Methods in Enzymology, Vol. 183*, pages 193–211. Academic Press, 1990.

[98] M. Steel2 and D. Penny. Parsimony, likelihood, and the role of models in molecular phylogenetics. *Molecular Biology and Evolution*, 17:839–850, 2000.

[99] M. J. Sternberg, P. A. Bates, L. A. Kelley, and R. M. MacCallum. Progress in protein structure prediction: assessment of CASP3. *Curr Opin Struct Biol*, 9(3):368–373, 1999.

[100] P. Thebault, S. de Givry, T. Schiex, and C. Gaspin. Combining constraint processing and pattern matching to describe and locate structured motifs in genomic sequences. In Christian Bessiere, Brahim Hnich, Toby Walsh, and Zeynep Kiziltan, editors, *The Fifth Workshop on Modelling and Solving Problems with Constraints*, pages 53–60, 2005.

[101] G. M. Torrance, D. R. Gilbert, I. Michalopoulos, and D. R. Westhead. Protein structure topological comparison, discovery and matching service. *Bioinformatics* 21(10):2537–2538, 2005.

[102] J. R. Ullmann. An algorithm for subgraph isomorphism. *Journal of the ACM*, 23 (1):31–42, January 1976.

[103] R. Unger and J. Moult. Genetic algorithms for protein folding simulations. *Journal of Molecular Biology*, 231:75–81, 1993.

[104] J. van Helden, D. Gilbert, L. Wernisch, M. Schroeder, and S. Wodak. Application of regulatory sequence analysis and metabolic network analysis to the interpretation of gene expression data. In *Computational Biology, LNCS 2006*, pages 147 – 163. LNCS, 2000.

[105] J. van Helden, A. Naim, R. Mancuso, M. Eldridge, L. Wernisch, D. Gilbert, , and S. J. Wodak. Representing and analysing molecular and cellular function in the computer. *Journal of Biological Chemistry*, 381(9–10):921–935, 2000.

[106] J. Viksna and D. Gilbert. Pattern matching and pattern discovery algorithms for protein topologies. In *WABI: International Workshop on Algorithms in Bioinformatics, WABI, LNCS 2149*, pages 98–111, 2001.

[107] M. Waterman. *Introduction to Computational Biology*. Chapman & Hall, London, 1995.

[108] S. Will. Constraint-based hydrophobic core construction for protein structure prediction in the face-centered-cubic lattice. In Russ B. Altman, A. Keith Dunker, Lawrence Hunter, and Teri E. Klein, editors, *Proceedings of the Pacific Symposium on Biocomputing 2002 (PSB 2002)*, pages 661–672, Singapore, 2002. World Scientific Publishing Co. Pte. Ltd.

[109] S. Will, A. Busch, and R. Backofen. Efficient constraint-based sequence alignment by cluster tree elimination. In *Proceedings of the Workshop on Constraint Based Methods in Bioinformatics (WCB05)*, pages 66–74, 2005.

[110] R. H. C. Yap. Parametric sequence alignment with constraints. *Constraints*, 6(2/3): 157–172, 2001.

[111] K. Yue and K. A. Dill. Sequence-structure relationships in proteins and copolymers. *Physical Review E*, 48(3):2267–2278, September 1993.

[112] K. Yue and K. A. Dill. Forces of tertiary structural organization in globular proteins. *Proc. Natl. Acad. Sci. USA*, 92:146 – 150, 1995.

[113] M. Zuker. On Finding All Foldings of an RNA Molecule. *Science*, 244:48–52, 1989.

Index

Printed and bound by CPI Group (UK) Ltd, Croydon, CR0 4YY

03/10/2024

01040428-0018